Lecture Notes in Computer Scien

Commenced Publication in 1973
Founding and Former Series Editors:
Gerhard Goos, Juris Hartmanis, and Jan van Leeuwen

Hugo Krawczyk (Ed.)

Public-Key Cryptography – PKC 2014

17th International Conference
on Practice and Theory in Public-Key Cryptography
Buenos Aires, Argentina, March 26-28, 2014
Proceedings

 Springer

Volume Editor

Hugo Krawczyk
IBM T.J.Watson Research Center
1101 Kitchawan Road, Yorktown Heights, NY 10598, USA
E-mail: hugokraw@us.ibm.com

ISSN 0302-9743   e-ISSN 1611-3349
ISBN 978-3-642-54630-3   e-ISBN 978-3-642-54631-0
DOI 10.1007/978-3-642-54631-0
Springer Heidelberg New York Dordrecht London

Library of Congress Control Number: 2014932835

LNCS Sublibrary: SL 4 – Security and Cryptology

Typesetting: Camera-ready by author, data conversion by Scientific Publishing Services, Chennai, India

Printed on acid-free paper

Springer is part of Springer Science+Business Media (www.springer.com)

Preface

PKC 2014, the 17th Annual IACR International Conference on Practice and Theory of Public-Key Cryptography, was held in Buenos Aires, Argentina, during March 26–28, 2014. The conference, sponsored by the International Association for Cryptologic Research (IACR), focuses on all technical aspects of public-key cryptography - including theory, design, analysis, cryptanalysis, implementation and applications. This was the first PKC to be held in South America.

These proceedings contain 38 papers selected by the Program Committee from a total of 145 submissions - the second highest number in the conference's history. The many high-quality submissions made it easy to build a good program but also required rejecting good papers. Each submission was judged by at least three reviewers, or four in the case of submissions by Program Committee members. The selection process included five weeks of focused independent review followed by five weeks of lengthy discussions. At the end of the 10-week review period the reports and discussions produced over 38,000 lines of text, a testament to the dedication and thoroughness of the Program Committee members. This wonderful work would have been impossible without the collaboration of 150 members of our community that served as external reviewers. To them and all the members of the Program Committee I am truly grateful. My sincere gratitude goes also to the hundreds of authors that submitted their excellent work - without them there wouldn't be a conference.

The program also featured two excellent invited lectures: "Post-Snowden Cryptography" by Adi Shamir and "Multilinear Maps and Obfuscation" by Shai Halevi. On behalf of the Program Committee, I would like to thank Adi and Shai for kindly accepting our invitation.

The work of a program chair and a successful conference depend on many people that deserve special thanks. Ariel Waissbein and Juan Garay, the conference general chairs, did a wonderful job organizing the event and managing its many complexities. Shai Halevi's excellent submission and review software was pivotal for the smooth management of the review process, and he was kind enough to patiently answer my many questions. A special mention goes to the PKC steering committee for their organization of the PKC conferences for so many years and for giving us the opportunity to bring cryptography to this part of the planet. Finally, I want to thank our sponsors: Argentina's Ministry of Science, Technology and Productive Innovation, Fundación Sadosky, IBM Research, and Microsoft Research.

February 2014   Hugo Krawczyk

PKC 2014
The 17th IACR International Conference on Practice and Theory of Public-Key Cryptography

Buenos Aires, Argentina

March 26–28, 2014

Sponsored by the
International Association of Cryptologic Research

General Chair

Ariel Waissbein

General Co-chair

Juan A. Garay   Yahoo Labs, USA

Program Chair

Hugo Krawczyk   IBM T.J. Watson Research Center, USA

Program Committee

Michel Abdalla	École Normale Supérieure and CNRS, France
Masayuki Abe	NTT, Japan
Paulo Barreto	University of São Paulo, Brazil
Alexandra Boldyreva	Georgia Institute of Technology, USA
Colin Boyd	NTNU, Norway and QUT, Australia
David Cash	Rutgers University, USA
Jung Hee Cheon	Seoul National University, Korea
Nelly Fazio	City College of CUNY, USA
Sanjam Garg	IBM Research, USA
Dov Gordon	Applied Communication Sciences, USA
Jens Groth	University College London, UK

External Reviewers

PKC Steering Committee

Moti Yung (Secretary)   Google Inc., and Columbia University, USA
Yuliang Zheng (Chair)   University of North Carolina at Charlotte, USA

Sponsoring Institutions

Fundación Sadosky, Argentina
IBM Research, USA
Microsoft Research, USA
Ministry of Science, Technology and Productive Innovation, Argentina

Table of Contents

Chosen Ciphertext Security

Re-encryption

Verifiable Outsourcing

Cryptanalysis I

Identity- and Attribute-Based Encryption

Enhanced Encryption

Signature Schemes

Cryptanalysis II

Related-Key Security

Functional Authentication

Quantum Impossibility

Privacy

Protocols

Simple Chosen-Ciphertext Security
from Low-Noise LPN

Eike Kiltz[1],[*], Daniel Masny[1], and Krzysztof Pietrzak[2],[**]

[1] Horst-Görtz Institute for IT Security and Faculty of Mathematics,
Ruhr-Universität Bochum
[2] IST Austria

Abstract. Recently, Döttling et al. (ASIACRYPT 2012) proposed the first chosen-ciphertext (IND-CCA) secure public-key encryption scheme from the learning parity with noise (LPN) assumption. In this work we give an alternative scheme which is conceptually simpler and more efficient. At the core of our construction is a trapdoor technique originally proposed for lattices by Micciancio and Peikert (EUROCRYPT 2012), which we adapt to the LPN setting. The main technical tool is a new double-trapdoor mechanism, together with a trapdoor switching lemma based on a computational variant of the leftover hash lemma.

1   Introduction

The Learning Parity with Noise (LPN) problem has found a wide range of applications in symmetric cryptography, including encryption [1] and authentication [2,3,4]. Public-key primitives seem considerably harder to achieve. In particular, it is still an open problem to construct a public-key encryption scheme from the (standard) LPN problem. The LPN problem is very attractive, because of its similarity to the well-studied syndrome decoding problem and its assumed hardness in a post-quantum world. Further, many LPN based schemes are very efficient, such that they can be used even in low-cost RFID devices.

The first step towards a public-key encryption (PKE) scheme from LPN was made by Alekhnovich [5] who proposed a chosen-plaintext (IND-CPA) secure PKE based on a low-noise variant of LPN (low-noise LPN). A straightforward variant of Alekhnovich's PKE scheme can be seen as the LPN analog of Regev's encryption scheme from the learning with errors (LWE) problem. The LPN problem states that the distribution $\mathcal{D}_{\text{LPN}_{n,m,p}} = \{(\mathbf{A}, \mathbf{As} + \mathbf{e}) \mid \mathbf{A} \xleftarrow{\$} \mathbb{Z}_2^{m \times n}, \mathbf{e} \xleftarrow{\$} \mathcal{B}_p^m, \mathbf{s} \xleftarrow{\$} \mathbb{Z}_2^n\}$ is indistinguishable from uniform, where $\mathcal{B}_p$ is the the Bernoulli distribution with parameter p, i.e., $\Pr[x = 1 : x \leftarrow \mathcal{B}_p] = p$. Whereas in standard LPN the Bernoulli parameter p is constant ($p = 0.1$ is a typical choice), in low-noise LPN we have $p = \Theta(1/\sqrt{n})$, where n is the dimension of the LPN

[*] Supported by a Sofja Kovalevskaja Award of the Alexander von Humboldt Foundation and the German Federal Ministry for Education and Research.
[**] Supported by the European Research Council, ERC Starting Grant (259668-PSPC).

H. Krawczyk (Ed.): PKC 2014, LNCS 8383, pp. 1–18, 2014.

secret. When we decrease the Bernoulli parameter p, the LPN problem can only become easier. Indeed, while the best known algorithm for solving standard LPN runs in time $2^{O(n/\log n)}$ [6], low-noise LPN can be solved in time $2^{O(\sqrt{n})}$. Hence, for low-noise LPN, the dimension of the LPN secret has to be increased accordingly, which results in less efficient schemes. See also [7] for concrete efficiency considerations.

CCA-SECURE ENCRYPTION FROM LOW-NOISE LPN. Recently, Döttling, Müller-Quade and Nascimento [8] showed how to extend Alekhnovich's IND-CPA secure scheme in order to get a chosen-ciphertext (IND-CCA) secure scheme. Like for Alekhnovich's scheme, their security proof is in the standard model (in particular, no random oracles), and relies on the low noise LPN assumption. During decryption only a certain part of the secret key is known and a q-ary erasure code is used to reconstruct the missing parts. Due to the additional overhead of the erasure code, the scheme has to add matrices $\mathbf{B}_1, \ldots, \mathbf{B}_q$ to the public-key, where the parameter q is estimated in [8] to be at least 400.[1] Hence the complexity of the scheme is estimated to be a couple of hundred times worse than Alekhnovich's scheme.

CCA-SECURE ENCRYPTION FROM LWE. In a work predating [8], Micciancio and Peikert [9] extended Regev's LWE-based encryption scheme into a simple and efficient IND-CCA secure encryption scheme. Both schemes are randomness-recovering, but unlike [8], the scheme from [9] does not use erasure codes which results in considerably more compact (public and secret) keys.

This raises the question, whether it's possible to shorten the keys in the LPN setting by using the techniques from [9]. Unfortunately, it turns out that a straight forward application of their techniques will not work. Informally, using the leftover hash lemma as in [9] in the (binary) LPN setting results in an error that cannot be corrected using error correcting codes.

1.1   Our Contributions

In this work, we propose a simple and efficient IND-CCA secure PKE scheme from low-noise LPN. Compared to the IND-CPA secure scheme by Alekhnovich, we only loose roughly a factor two in efficiency.[2]

At a technical level, we design a new (tag-based) *double trapdoor function* which has two independent trapdoors. Each of these trapdoors depends on a hidden tag. If the function is evaluated with respect to a hidden tag, the corresponding trapdoor disappears and the function is hard to invert. For all other tags, the function can be inverted efficiently using one of the trapdoors. Our *switching lemma* (Lemma 4) shows that, under the LPN assumption, the hidden tags contained in the trapdoors can be switched without being noticed by any efficient adversary. The main difference to [9] is that we replace the leftover hash

---

[1] Stating a more exact value for q is difficult as in [8] no upper bound is given and the analysis is only sketched.

[2] Interestingly, the factor two between IND-CPA and IND-CCA security is also observed in the Diffie-Hellman world [10,11] and in the lattice world [12].

lemma by a computational variant based on the LPN problem with low noise. We use this double-trapdoor function to construct a tag-based encryption (TBE) scheme. (The latter can be efficiently transformed into a CCA-secure encryption scheme [13].) During the security reduction from low-noise LPN, we replace the first hidden tag with the challenge tag. Since this step is only *computationally indistinguishable* we have to give a security reduction in which the simulator has no access to the trapdoor being switched to the challenge tag. Here the second trapdoor is used to answer decryption queries correctly. Once both hidden tags are switched to the challenge tag, the simulator is not able to decrypt a message related to this challenge tag which allows us to argue about indistinguishability of the PKE scheme. We remark that previous LPN or LWE-based switching techniques (e.g., [9]) relied on purely statistical arguments such that a second trapdoor was not needed for simulating the decryption queries.

EFFICIENCY. This tag-based encryption scheme directly implies a CCA-secure PKE scheme [13]. Compared to [8], this results in much smaller key sizes and comparable ciphertext size. Concretely, our scheme only has to add two matrices $\mathbf{B}_0, \mathbf{B}_1$ to the public-key and hence we expect the keys of our scheme be to a couple of hundred times smaller than that of [8]. We remark that our techniques can be extended to the case of LWE, but the resulting scheme is worse than the one from [9]. While for LPN replacing the leftover hash lemma is *necessary* to decrease the weight of the error, replacing the leftover hash lemma in the LWE setting actually has the opposite effect.

1.2 Open Problems

Designing an IND-CPA secure PKE from LPN with constant noise remains an open problem. Already a construction with any noise level $\omega(1/\sqrt{n})$ would be interesting to achieve.

2 Preliminaries

We use bold lower-case letters like $\mathbf{a} \in \mathbb{Z}_2^n$ to denote vectors and bold upper-case letters like $\mathbf{A} \in \mathbb{Z}_2^{n \times n}$ for matrices. With $|\mathbf{a}|$ we denote the Hamming weight (i.e., the number of 1's) of $\mathbf{a}$. We denote by $x \xleftarrow{\$} X$ that x is sampled according to the distribution X. If X is a set, then this denotes that x is sampled uniformly at random from X. Instead of using $\oplus$ for addition modulo 2, we use $+$ and $-$ to get a more generic construction, which adapts more easily to larger fields (for which addition and subtraction is not the same) as used in the LWE assumption.

2.1 The Bernoulli Distribution

$\mathcal{B}_p$ denotes the Bernoulli distribution with parameter $0 \le p \le 1/2$, i.e., $x \xleftarrow{\$} \mathcal{B}_p$ is the random variable over $\{0, 1\}$ with $\Pr[x = 1] = p$. To bound the tail of the sum of independent Bernoulli random variabels, we will use the following Chernoff bounds.

Chernoff bound: For $\mathbf{d} \xleftarrow{\$} \mathcal{B}_p^m$ and $\delta > 0$:

$$\Pr_{\mathbf{d}}[|\mathbf{d}| > (1+\delta)pm] < e^{-\frac{\min(\delta, \delta^2)}{3}pm} \qquad (1)$$

in particular, for $\delta = 1$ $\qquad \Pr_{\mathbf{d}}[|\mathbf{d}| > 2pm] < e^{-pm/3} \qquad (2)$

2.2   Learning Parity with Noise

Let $n \in \mathbb{N}$ be the size of the secret solution vector, $m > n$ the number of the given samples and $0 \le p \le 1/2$ the Bernoulli parameter of the noise distribution.

THE $\text{LPN}_{n,m,p}$ PROBLEM. The $\text{LPN}_{n,m,p}$ problem is the problem of solving a set of linear equations perturbed by some noise. To define the decision version of LPN we consider the distribution

$$\mathcal{D}_{\text{LPN}_{n,m,p}} = ((\mathbf{A}, \mathbf{As} + \mathbf{e}) \mid \mathbf{A} \xleftarrow{\$} \mathbb{Z}_2^{m \times n}, \mathbf{e} \xleftarrow{\$} \mathcal{B}_p^m, \mathbf{s} \xleftarrow{\$} \mathbb{Z}_2^n).$$

The challenge is to distinguish $\mathcal{D}_{\text{LPN}_{n,m,p}}$ from uniform $(\mathbf{A}, \mathbf{b}) \in \mathbb{Z}_2^{m \times n} \times \mathbb{Z}_2^m$. The advantage of an algorithm A in breaking the $\text{LPN}_{n,m,p}$ assumption is

$$\mathbf{Adv}_{\text{LPN}_{n,m,p}}(\mathsf{A}) = |\Pr[\mathsf{A}(\mathbf{A}, \mathbf{b}) = 1] - \Pr[\mathsf{A}(\mathbf{A}', \mathbf{b}') = 1]|,$$

where $(\mathbf{A}, \mathbf{b}) \xleftarrow{\$} \mathcal{D}_{\text{LPN}_{n,m,p}}$ and $(\mathbf{A}', \mathbf{b}') \xleftarrow{\$} \mathbb{Z}_2^{m \times n} \times \mathbb{Z}_2^m$.

The hardness of $\text{LPN}_{n,m,p}$ depends on the choice of the secret size n, the amount of samples m and the error distribution $\mathcal{B}_p$. Whereas in the standard LPN assumption the Bernoulli parameter p is constant, we use the "low-noise" version with $p \approx 1/\sqrt{n}$.

Below we introduce two variants of $\text{LPN}_{n,m,p}$ which we'll use in our construction, both variants are basically equivalent to the standard $\text{LPN}_{n,m,p}$ assumption.

KNAPSACK LPN. The knapsack LPN distribution [14] is

$$\mathcal{D}_{\text{KLPN}_{n,m,p}^m} = ((\mathbf{A}, \mathbf{EA}) \mid \mathbf{A} \xleftarrow{\$} \mathbb{Z}_2^{m \times (m-n)}, \mathbf{E} \xleftarrow{\$} \mathcal{B}_p^{m \times m}).$$

and the advantage of an A is defined as

$$\mathbf{Adv}_{\text{KLPN}_{n,m,p}^m}(\mathsf{A}) = |\Pr[\mathsf{A}(\mathbf{A}, \mathbf{EA}) = 1] - \Pr[\mathsf{A}(\mathbf{A}, \mathbf{B}') = 1]|,$$

where $(\mathbf{A}, \mathbf{EA}) \xleftarrow{\$} \mathcal{D}_{\text{KLPN}_{n,m,p}^m}$ and $\mathbf{B}' \xleftarrow{\$} \mathbb{Z}_2^{m \times (m-n)}$.

Knapsack LPN is as hard as LPN, the reduction stated below loses a factor of m due to a standard hybrid argument because we directly defined the m-fold knapsack LPN distribution (i.e., $\mathbf{E}$ contains m vectors, not just one).

Lemma 1. *For all algorithms* B *there exists an algorithm* A *that runs in roughly the same time as* A *and* $\mathbf{Adv}_{\text{LPN}_{n,m,p}}(\mathsf{A}) \ge \frac{1}{m}\mathbf{Adv}_{\text{KLPN}_{n,m,p}^m}(\mathsf{B})$.

EXTENDED KNAPSACK LPN. The Knapsack LPN problem remains hard in the presence of additional leakage $\mathbf{Ez}$ about $\mathbf{E}$. The extended knapsack EKLPN distribution is defined as

$$\mathcal{D}_{\mathrm{EKLPN}^m_{n,m,p}} = ((\mathbf{A}, \mathbf{EA}, \mathbf{z}, \mathbf{Ez}) \mid \mathbf{A} \xleftarrow{\$} \mathbb{Z}_2^{m \times (m-n)}, \mathbf{E} \xleftarrow{\$} \mathcal{B}_p^{m \times m}, \mathbf{z} \xleftarrow{\$} \mathcal{B}_p^m)$$

and A's advantage is

$$\mathbf{Adv}_{\mathrm{EKLPN}^m_{n,m,p}}(\mathsf{A}) = |\Pr[\mathsf{A}(\mathbf{A}, \mathbf{EA}, \mathbf{z}, \mathbf{Ez}) = 1] - \Pr[\mathsf{A}(\mathbf{A}, \mathbf{B}, \mathbf{z}, \mathbf{b}) = 1]|,$$

where $(\mathbf{A}, \mathbf{EA}, \mathbf{z}, \mathbf{Ez}) \xleftarrow{\$} \mathcal{D}_{\mathrm{EKLPN}^m_{n,m,p}}$, $\mathbf{B} \xleftarrow{\$} \mathbb{Z}_2^{m \times (m-n)}$, and $\mathbf{b} \xleftarrow{\$} \mathbb{Z}_2^m$.

The following lemma is a special case of [15, Theorem 3.1], who use a more general notion of the ELWE problem based on LWE and the leakage vector $\mathbf{z}$ is sampled from an arbitrary distribution (not just $\mathcal{B}_p^m$).

Lemma 2. *For all algorithms* B *there exists an algorithm* A *that runs in roughly the same time as* A *and* $\mathbf{Adv}_{\mathrm{LPN}_{n,m,p}}(\mathsf{A}) \geq \frac{1}{2m}\mathbf{Adv}_{\mathrm{EKLPN}^m_{n,m,p}}(\mathsf{B})$.

2.3 Asymptotically Good Codes

In order to state the security of our scheme in asymptotic terms we need asymptotically good linear codes, these are $[m, Rm, \delta m]$ codes with a constant rate R, constant relative distance δ and arbitrary large block length m. Moreover, we want the code to be efficiently constructible in order to get a uniform construction, and of course encoding and decoding need to be efficient to get an efficient scheme. Such codes exist:

Lemma 3 ([16]). *For any rate* $0 < R < 1$, *there exists a binary linear error-correcting code family which is polynomial time constructible, encodable and decodable and can decode from up to* $\lfloor \frac{\delta n}{2} \rfloor$ *errors where* $\delta \approx \frac{1}{2}(1 - R)$.

We emphasis, that for concrete instantiations of the scheme, an arbitrary, suitable error correction code can be used and the asymptotic behavior is not important.

2.4 Game-Based Proofs

We use game-based proofs [17]. A game G consists of an Initialize and a Finalize procedure, and possibly other procedures. An adversary A is executed in the game by first calling Initialize. Next, he can make arbitrary calls to the other procedures, some multiple times, some only once, depending on the specification of G. Finally, A makes one single call to Finalize which ends the game. The output of the game, denoted as G^A, is defined as the output of Finalize.

2.5 Tag-Based Encryption

A tag-based encryption scheme with tag-space $\mathcal{T}$ and message-space $\mathcal{M}$ consist of the following three PPT algorithms TBE = (Gen, Enc, Dec).

- Gen(1^k) outputs a secret key sk and a public key pk.
- Enc(pk, τ, M) outputs a ciphertext c of $M \in \mathcal{M}$ with respect to tag $\tau \in \mathcal{T}$.
- Dec(sk, τ, C) outputs the decrypted message M of ciphertext C with respect to tag $\tau \in \mathcal{T}$, or $\perp$.

We require the standard correctness condition Dec($sk, \tau,$ Enc(pk, τ, M)) $= M$ for all τ, M and all (sk, pk) in the range of Gen($\cdot$). To define security, let the advantage of an adversary A in the selective-tag weak CCA game [18] be

$$\mathbf{Adv}_{\mathrm{TBE}}(\mathsf{A}) = \left| \Pr[\mathrm{G}_{\mathrm{TBE}}^{\mathsf{A}} = 1] - \frac{1}{2} \right|,$$

where the games defining $\mathrm{G}_{\mathrm{TBE}}$ are defined in Figure 1. Here the term *selective* models the fact that A has to commit to the challenge tag τ^* in the beginning, before seeing the public-key.

Initialize(τ^*)

$(sk, pk) \leftarrow$ Gen(1^k)

Return pk

Finalize(d)

Return ($b_M = d$)

Challenge(M_0, M_1) //one time

$b_M \overset{\$}{\leftarrow} \{0, 1\}$;

Return Enc(pk, τ^*, M_{b_M})

queryDec(τ, C)//many times

If $\tau \neq \tau^*$ return Dec(sk, τ, C)

Else return $\perp$

Fig. 1. Games constituting $\mathrm{G}_{\mathrm{TBE}}$

To construct an IND-CCA secure PKE, it is sufficient to construct a secure TBE (in the above sense) with tag-space $\mathcal{T}$ exponential in n [18]. The overhead of this transformation is small. It essentially consists of a one-time signature or a message-authentication code plus a commitment.

3   Tag-Based Encryption

3.1   Double Trapdoor Generator

We use a matrix representation $\mathbf{H}_\tau \in \mathbb{Z}_2^{n \times n}$ for finite field elements $\tau \in \mathbb{F}_{2^n}$ [19,12]. The structure of a finite field implies certain properties: $\mathbf{H}_\tau + \mathbf{H}_{\tau'} = \mathbf{H}_{\tau + \tau'}$ and $\mathbf{0} = \mathbf{H}_0$ for the zero element of the field. In particular all matrices $\mathbf{H}_\tau - \mathbf{H}_{\tau'} = \mathbf{H}_{\tau - \tau'} \neq \mathbf{H}_0$ for $\tau \neq \tau'$ are invertible.

Let n and m be two parameters and let $\mathbf{G} \in \mathbb{Z}_2^{m \times n}$ be a generator matrix for an efficiently decodable code. (This was called gadget matrix in [9].) The trapdoor generator is the following PPT algorithm which takes as input two tags $\tau_0, \tau_1 \in \mathbb{F}_{2^n}$:

$\underline{\mathsf{Gen}_{\mathrm{td}}(1^n, \tau_0, \tau_1) \to (\mathbf{T}_0, \mathbf{T}_1, ek).}$ Sample $\mathbf{T}_0, \mathbf{T}_1 \xleftarrow{\$} \mathcal{B}_p^{m \times m}$ and $\mathbf{A} \xleftarrow{\$} \mathbb{Z}_2^{m \times n}$

Let $\mathbf{B}_0 := \mathbf{T}_0 \mathbf{A} - \mathbf{GH}_{\tau_0}$, $\mathbf{B}_1 := \mathbf{T}_1 \mathbf{A} - \mathbf{GH}_{\tau_1}$ and $ek = (\mathbf{A}, \mathbf{B}_0, \mathbf{B}_1)$

$\underline{\text{Initialize}(t, \tau_0, \tau_1, \tau') // \mathrm{G}_{\mathrm{real}}}$
$(\mathbf{T}_0, \mathbf{T}_1, ek) \leftarrow \mathsf{Gen}_{\mathrm{td}}(1^n, \tau_0, \tau_1)$
$\mathbf{z} \xleftarrow{\$} \mathcal{B}_p^m$; $\mathbf{T} \xleftarrow{\$} \mathcal{B}_p^{m \times m}$;
Return $(\mathbf{T}_t, ek, \mathbf{z}, \mathbf{Tz})$

$\underline{\text{Initialize}(t, \tau_0, \tau_1, \tau') // \mathrm{G}_{\mathrm{uniform}}}$
$(\mathbf{T}_0, \mathbf{T}_1, ek) \leftarrow \mathsf{Gen}_{\mathrm{td}}(1^n, \tau_0, \tau_1)$;
Parse $ek = (\mathbf{A}, \mathbf{B}_0, \mathbf{B}_1)$
$\mathbf{B}'_t := \mathbf{B}_t$; $\mathbf{B}'_{\bar{t}} \xleftarrow{\$} \mathbb{Z}_2^{m \times n}$;
$ek' := (\mathbf{A}, \mathbf{B}'_0, \mathbf{B}'_1)$;
$\mathbf{z} \xleftarrow{\$} \mathcal{B}_p^m$; $\mathbf{T} := \mathbf{T}_{\bar{t}}$;
Return $(\mathbf{T}_t, ek', \mathbf{z}, \mathbf{Tz})$

$\underline{\text{Initialize}(t, \tau_0, \tau_1, \tau') // \mathrm{G}_{\mathrm{corr}}}$
$\tau'_t := \tau_t$; $\tau'_{\bar{t}} := \tau'$;
$(\mathbf{T}_0, \mathbf{T}_1, ek) \leftarrow \mathsf{Gen}_{\mathrm{td}}(1^n, \tau'_0, \tau'_1)$;
$\mathbf{z} \xleftarrow{\$} \mathcal{B}_p^m$; $\mathbf{T} := \mathbf{T}_{\bar{t}}$;
Return $(\mathbf{T}_t, ek, \mathbf{z}, \mathbf{Tz})$

$\underline{\text{Finalize}(d)} \quad // \mathrm{G}_{\mathrm{real, uniform, corr}}$
Return d

Fig. 2. Procedures defining games $\mathrm{G}_{\mathrm{real}}, \mathrm{G}_{\mathrm{uniform}}, \mathrm{G}_{\mathrm{corr}}$. Here $ek := (\mathbf{A}, \mathbf{B}_0, \mathbf{B}_1) = (\mathbf{A}, \mathbf{T}_0 \mathbf{A} - \mathbf{GH}_{\tau_0}, \mathbf{T}_1 \mathbf{A} - \mathbf{GH}_{\tau_1})$ as defined in Section 3.1.

Looking ahead, a trapdoor $\mathbf{T}_i$ ($i \in \{0, 1\}$) output by $\mathsf{Gen}_{\mathrm{td}}(1^n, \tau_0, \tau_1)$ can be used to invert the tag-based trapdoor function

$$f^\tau(\mathbf{s}, \mathbf{e}, \mathbf{e}'_0, \mathbf{e}'_1) = (\mathbf{As} + \mathbf{e}, (\mathbf{GH}_\tau + \mathbf{B}_0)\mathbf{s} + \mathbf{e}'_0, (\mathbf{GH}_\tau + \mathbf{B}_1)\mathbf{s} + \mathbf{e}'_1).$$

whenever $\tau \neq \tau_i$ (for one $i \in \{0, 1\}$) and the error $\mathbf{T}_i \mathbf{e} + \mathbf{e}'_i$ is small enough, so it can be corrected (using the code given by $\mathbf{G}$) as follows: given $(\mathbf{c}, \mathbf{c}_0, \mathbf{c}_1)$ $(= f^\tau(\mathbf{s}, \mathbf{e}, \mathbf{e}'_0, \mathbf{e}'_1))$, compute $(\mathbf{T}_i \; \mathbf{I}) \cdot (-\mathbf{c} \; \mathbf{c}_i)^\mathsf{T} = \mathbf{GH}_{\tau - \tau_i} \mathbf{s} - \mathbf{T}_i \mathbf{e} + \mathbf{e}'_i$, use error correction to decode $\mathbf{H}_{\tau - \tau_i} \mathbf{s}$, and then the invertability of $\mathbf{H}_{\tau - \tau_i}$ (recall that we assume $\tau \neq \tau_i$) to reconstruct $\mathbf{s}$ The remaining inputs $\mathbf{e}, \mathbf{e}'_0, \mathbf{e}'_1$ can now easily be computed.

The "switching lemma" below states that under the LPN assumption, the output of the trapdoor generator computationally hides the tags τ_0, τ_1, even if there is some additional information about the trapdoor leaked. This lemma will allow us to switch either τ_0 or τ_1 to an arbitrary tag $\tau' \in \mathbb{Z}_2^n$. During the switching procedure, we still have access to the other trapdoor. This allows us to answer decryption queries during a CCA security proof.

Lemma 4. *For every PPT algorithm* A *there exists a PPT algorithm* B *such that:*

$$|\Pr[\mathrm{G}_{\mathrm{real}}^{\mathsf{A}} = 1] - \Pr[\mathrm{G}_{\mathrm{corr}}^{\mathsf{A}} = 1]| \leq 3m \cdot \mathbf{Adv}_{\mathrm{LPN}_{m-n, m, p}}(\mathsf{B}).$$

where games $\mathrm{G}_{\mathrm{real}}$ *and* $\mathrm{G}_{\mathrm{corr}}$ *are defined in Figure 2.*

Proof. The proof follows by the following two equations combined with Lemma 1 and 2

$$|\Pr[G_{\text{real}}^{\mathsf{A}} = 1] - \Pr[G_{\text{uniform}}^{\mathsf{A}} = 1]| \leq \mathbf{Adv}_{\text{KLPN}_{n,m,p}^m}(\mathsf{B}) \tag{3}$$

$$|\Pr[G_{\text{corr}}^{\mathsf{A}} = 1] - \Pr[G_{\text{uniform}}^{\mathsf{A}} = 1]| \leq \mathbf{Adv}_{\text{EKLPN}_{n,m,p}^m}(\mathsf{B}), \tag{4}$$

where game G_{uniform} is also defined in Figure 2.

To prove (3) we construct an algorithm B which on input a $\mathcal{D}_{\text{KLPN}_{n,m,p}^m}$ or a random sample, simulates $G_{\text{real}}^{\mathsf{A}}$ or $G_{\text{uniform}}^{\mathsf{A}}$, respectively. $\mathsf{B}(\mathbf{A}, \mathbf{B})$ simulates A's view as follows.

Initialize(t, τ_0, τ_1, τ')

$\mathbf{z} \xleftarrow{\$} \mathcal{B}_p^m; \quad \mathbf{T}, \mathbf{T}_t \xleftarrow{\$} \mathcal{B}_p^{m \times m};$

$\mathbf{B}_t := \mathbf{T}_t \mathbf{A} - \mathbf{G} \mathbf{H}_{\tau_t}; \quad \mathbf{B}_{\bar{t}} := \mathbf{B} - \mathbf{G} \mathbf{H}_{\tau_{\bar{t}}};$

$ek := (\mathbf{A}, \mathbf{B}_0, \mathbf{B}_1);$

Return $(\mathbf{T}_t, ek, \mathbf{z}, \mathbf{T}\mathbf{z})$

Finalize(d)

Return d

We now analyse $\mathsf{B}(\mathbf{A}, \mathbf{B})$'s simulation. $\mathbf{A}$ is always uniform, $\mathbf{z}$ and $\mathbf{T}\mathbf{z}$ are distributed as in the real and random game. B generates $\tau_{\bar{t}}$, $\mathbf{T}_t$ and $\mathbf{B}_t$ exactly as Gen_{td}.

KLPN Case: $\mathbf{B} = \mathbf{T}_{\bar{t}}\mathbf{A}$ implies that $\mathbf{B}_{\bar{t}} = \mathbf{T}_{\bar{t}}\mathbf{A} - \mathbf{G}\mathbf{H}_{\tau_{\bar{t}}}$ has the same distribution as in G_{real}. Hence B simulates G_{real} and $\Pr[G_{\text{real}}^{\mathsf{A}} = 1] = \Pr[\mathsf{B}(\mathbf{A}, \mathbf{B}) = 1 \mid (\mathbf{A}, \mathbf{B}) \xleftarrow{\$} \mathcal{D}_{\text{KLPN}_{n,m,p}^m}]$.

Uniform Case: $\mathbf{B}$ is uniform and this implies that $\mathbf{B}_{\bar{t}}$ is uniform, too. Since $\mathbf{B}_{\bar{t}}$ is independent of $\mathbf{T}_{\bar{t}}$, $\mathbf{T}\mathbf{z}$ has the correct distribution. Hence B simulates G_{uniform} and $\Pr[G_{\text{uniform}}^{\mathsf{A}} = 1] = \Pr[\mathsf{B}(\mathbf{A}, \mathbf{B}) = 1 \mid (\mathbf{A}, \mathbf{B}) \text{ uniform}]$.

This concludes the proof of (3).

To prove (4) we use the $\text{EKLPN}_{m-n,m,p}^m$ assumption. We reuse B, now with input $\mathsf{B}(\mathbf{A}, \mathbf{z}, \mathbf{B}, \mathbf{b})$ and change it slightly by setting $\mathbf{B}_{\bar{t}} := \mathbf{B} - \mathbf{G}\mathbf{H}_{\tau'}$ and replacing $\mathbf{T}\mathbf{z}$ by $\mathbf{b} = \mathbf{T}_{\bar{t}}\mathbf{z}$ during the Initialize procedure. With almost the same argument B simulates in the uniform case G_{uniform} and in the LPN case G_{corr} correctly.

3.2 Description of the Scheme

Our scheme uses the following parameters whose concrete choices will be justified later.

- The dimension n of the LPN secret (with $n = \Theta(k^2)$) and $m \geq 2n$ controlling the security of the scheme. (See Theorem 2.)
- A constant $0 < c < 1/4$ defining:

- The Bernoulli parameter $p = \sqrt{c/m}$.
- The bounding parameter $\beta = 2\sqrt{cm}$ to check consistency during decryption.
- A binary linear error-correcting code $\mathbf{G} : Z_2^n \to Z_2^m$ which corrects up to αm errors for some α with $4c < \alpha < 1$.

– Further, we use an efficient error correcting code with generator matrix $\mathbf{G}_2 :$ $\mathcal{M} \to \mathbb{Z}_2^\ell$ where the parameter $\ell \geq m$ is chosen such that the encoding scheme is able to correct at least $2\ell\sqrt{c}/\sqrt{m} = 2\ell p$ errors (note that $\mathbf{G}$ must correct a constant fraction of errors, whereas $\mathbf{G}_2$ only needs to correct a square root fraction).

The following three algorithms describe our $\mathsf{TBE} = (\mathsf{Gen}, \mathsf{Enc}, \mathsf{Dec})$ based on LPN with tag space $\mathcal{T} = \mathbb{F}_{2^n} \setminus \{0\}$:

$\underline{\mathsf{Gen}(1^k) \to (sk, pk)}$. The algorithm calls the trapdoor generator $\mathsf{Gen}_{\mathsf{td}}(1^n, 0, 0) \to$ $(\mathbf{T}_0, \mathbf{T}_1, (\mathbf{A}, \mathbf{B}_0, \mathbf{B}_1))$ and picks $\mathbf{C} \xleftarrow{\$} \mathbb{Z}_2^{\ell \times n}$. The private and public key is defined as

$$sk := (0, \mathbf{T}_0) \in \mathbb{Z}_2^n \times \mathbb{Z}_2^{m \times m}, \quad pk := (\mathbf{A}, \mathbf{B}_0, \mathbf{B}_1, \mathbf{C}) \in (\mathbb{Z}_2^{m \times n})^3 \times \mathbb{Z}_2^{\ell \times n}.$$

(Recall that $\mathbf{B}_i = \mathbf{T}_i \mathbf{A}$.)
$\underline{\mathsf{Enc}(pk, \tau, M) \to C = (\mathbf{c}, \mathbf{c}_0, \mathbf{c}_1, \mathbf{c}_2)}$. The algorithm picks

$$\mathbf{e}_1 \xleftarrow{\$} \mathcal{B}_p^m; \quad \mathbf{e}_2 \xleftarrow{\$} \mathcal{B}_p^\ell; \quad \mathbf{T}_0', \mathbf{T}_1' \xleftarrow{\$} \mathcal{B}_p^{m \times m} \text{ and } \mathbf{s} \xleftarrow{\$} \mathbb{Z}_2^n$$

and defines

$$
\begin{aligned}
\mathbf{c} &:= \mathbf{As} + \mathbf{e}_1 & \in \mathbb{Z}_2^m \\
\mathbf{c}_0 &:= (\mathbf{GH}_\tau + \mathbf{B}_0)\mathbf{s} + \mathbf{T}_0'\mathbf{e}_1 & \in \mathbb{Z}_2^m \\
\mathbf{c}_1 &:= (\mathbf{GH}_\tau + \mathbf{B}_1)\mathbf{s} + \mathbf{T}_1'\mathbf{e}_1 & \in \mathbb{Z}_2^m \\
\mathbf{c}_2 &:= \mathbf{Cs} + \mathbf{e}_2 + \mathbf{G}_2(M). & \in \mathbb{Z}_2^\ell
\end{aligned}
$$

$\underline{\mathsf{Dec}(sk, \tau, C) \to (M \text{ or } \perp)}$. The algorithm parses $sk = (\tau_0, \mathbf{T}_0)$ and computes

$$\tilde{\mathbf{c}}_0 := (\mathbf{T}_0 \ \mathbf{I}) \cdot \begin{pmatrix} -\mathbf{c} \\ \mathbf{c}_0 \end{pmatrix} \quad (= \mathbf{GH}_{\tau - \tau_0}\mathbf{s} + (\mathbf{T}_0' - \mathbf{T}_0)\mathbf{e}_1).$$

Then it uses the error correction property of $\mathbf{G}$ to reconstruct $\mathbf{H}_{\tau - \tau_0}\mathbf{s}$ (from the error $(\mathbf{T}_0' - \mathbf{T}_0)\mathbf{e}_1$), and further computes $\mathbf{s} = \mathbf{H}_{\tau - \tau_0}^{-1} \mathbf{H}_{\tau - \tau_0}\mathbf{s}$. If

$$\underbrace{|\mathbf{c} - \mathbf{As}|}_{\mathbf{e}_1} \leq \beta \ \wedge \ \underbrace{|\mathbf{c}_0 - (\mathbf{GH}_\tau + \mathbf{B}_0)\mathbf{s}|}_{\mathbf{T}_0'\mathbf{e}_1} < \frac{\alpha m}{2} \ \wedge \ \underbrace{|\mathbf{c}_1 - (\mathbf{GH}_\tau + \mathbf{B}_1)\mathbf{s}|}_{\mathbf{T}_1'\mathbf{e}_1} \leq \frac{\alpha m}{2}$$

$$(5)$$

is true, compute $\mathbf{c}_2 - \mathbf{Cs} = \mathbf{G}_2(M) + \mathbf{e}_2$ and reconstruct (using the error correction property of $\mathbf{G}_2$) M and output it, otherwise output $\perp$.

The scheme has a couple of straightforward simplifications which we did not apply in order to facilitate the proof. First, $\tau_0 = 0$ can be omitted from sk and the description of the scheme. Second, the matrix $\mathbf{B}_1$ can be chosen uniformly. (The latter is shown implicitly in the proof.)

We also remark that that scheme is randomness-recovering and can therefore also be seen as an adaptive tag-based trapdoor function [13], where the domain consists of sampling $(\mathbf{s}, \mathbf{e}_1, \mathbf{T}_0' \mathbf{e}_1, \mathbf{T}_1' \mathbf{e}_1, \mathbf{e}_2)$ as in Enc.

A discussion how to transform the TBE scheme into a IND-CCA secure encryption scheme is done in Appendix A.

3.3   Correctness and Equivalence of the Trapdoors

Theorem 1 (Corectness). *Let* $\mathbf{G}$, $\mathbf{G}_2$ *be the codes given above. Then with overwhelming probability over the choice of the public and secret keys and for all* $\tau \in \mathcal{T}$, $M \in \mathcal{M}$, $\mathsf{Dec}(sk, \tau, C)$ *outputs* M *with overwhelming probability over* $C \leftarrow \mathsf{Enc}(pk, \tau, M)$.

Proof. We start with showing why the chosen $\beta = 2\sqrt{cm}$, $p = \sqrt{c/m}$ are suitable for our application. The Chernoff bound 2 yields:

$$\Pr_{\mathbf{e} \xleftarrow{\$} \mathcal{B}_p^m} [\, |\mathbf{e}| > \underbrace{\beta}_{=2pm} \,] < e^{-pm/3} = 2^{-\Theta(\sqrt{m})} \tag{6}$$

The analysis of our choice of the constants $4c < \alpha < 1$ is a bit more involved. We start by upper bounding the probability p' that the inner product $\mathbf{t}^T \mathbf{e}$ of $\mathbf{e}$ with a vector $\mathbf{t} \xleftarrow{\$} \mathcal{B}_p^m$ is 1, assuming the Hamming weight of $\mathbf{e}$ is at most β. Note that a necessary condition for $\mathbf{t}^T \mathbf{e} = 1$ is that $\mathbf{t}[i] = 1$ for at least one of the i's where $\mathbf{e}[i] = 1$. We use this in the second step below, the third step follows by the union bound

$$p' = \Pr_{\mathbf{t}}[\mathbf{t}^T \mathbf{e} = 1 \mid |\mathbf{e}| \leq \beta] \leq \Pr_{\mathbf{t}}[\exists i : (\mathbf{e}[i] = 1) \wedge (\mathbf{t}[i] = 1) \mid |\mathbf{e}| \leq \beta] \leq \beta p = 2c$$

Let $\mathbf{T} \xleftarrow{\$} \mathcal{B}_p^{m \times m}$. By the Chernoff bound (1) we have with $\delta = \alpha/(2p') - 1$ (note that $p' \leq 2c < \alpha/2$)

$$\Pr_{\mathbf{T}} \left[|\mathbf{Te}| > \frac{\alpha}{2} m \mid |\mathbf{e}| \leq \beta \right] = \Pr_{\mathbf{T}} [|\mathbf{Te}| > (1 + \delta) p' m \mid |\mathbf{e}| \leq \beta] < e^{-\frac{\min(\delta, \delta^2)}{3} p' m}. \tag{7}$$

Now $\delta p' = \alpha/2 - p' \geq \alpha/2 - 2c > 0$ and $\delta = \alpha/(2p') - 1 \geq \alpha/(4c) - 1 > 0$ are lower bounded by constants and therefore

$$\Pr_{\mathbf{T}} \left[|\mathbf{Te}| > \frac{\alpha}{2} m \mid |\mathbf{e}| \leq \beta \right] < e^{-\frac{\min(\delta, \delta^2)}{3} p' m} = 2^{-\Theta(m)}. \tag{8}$$

As C is a properly generated ciphertext

$$|\mathbf{e}_1| \leq \beta \ \wedge \ |\mathbf{T}_0 \mathbf{e}_1| \leq \frac{\alpha m}{2} \ \wedge \ |\mathbf{T}_1 \mathbf{e}_1| \leq \frac{\alpha m}{2}$$

holds with overwhelming probability $1 - 2^{-\Theta(\sqrt{m})}$ by (6) and (8), assume this is the case. Then by the error correction property of the code $\mathbf{G}$ we decode the correct $\mathbf{s}$ from $\tilde{\mathbf{c}}_0 := \mathbf{GH}_{\tau - \tau_0}\mathbf{s} + (\mathbf{T}_0' - \mathbf{T}_0)\mathbf{e}_1$ since the error term satisfies $|(\mathbf{T}_0' - \mathbf{T}_0)\mathbf{e}_1| \leq \alpha m$. Moreover, the consistency check 5 will pass.

It remains to show that the correct message M is reconstructed. We use $\mathbf{G}_2$ to derive M from $\mathbf{c}_2 - \mathbf{Cs} = \mathbf{e}_2 + \mathbf{G}_2(M)$, which gives the correct M if the Hamming weight of $\mathbf{e}_2 \xleftarrow{\$} \mathcal{B}_p^\ell$ lies within the $2\ell\sqrt{c}/\sqrt{m} = 2\ell p$ bits error correction capacity of $\mathbf{G}_2$. Using the Chernoff bound 2 we can upper bound the probability of this not being the case (the last step uses $\ell \geq m$, which we assumed is the case)

$$\Pr_{\mathbf{e}_2}[|\mathbf{e}_2| > 2\ell p] < e^{-\ell p/3} = e^{-\ell\sqrt{c}/3\sqrt{m}} = 2^{-\Omega(\sqrt{m})}$$

The next lemma will be central in our security proof. It states that the output distribution of a decryption oracle is basically independent of which of two possible secret keys the oracle uses to decrypt.

Lemma 5. *Let* $\mathsf{Dec0} = \mathsf{Dec}$ *and let* $\mathsf{Dec1}$ *be defined like* Dec, *except that* $\mathbf{c}_1$ *instead of* $\mathbf{c}_0$ *is used to reconstruct* $\mathbf{s}$. *Then, with overwhelming probability over the choice of the public and secret keys,* $\mathsf{Dec0}$ *and* $\mathsf{Dec1}$ *have the same output distribution: Let* $(\mathbf{T}_0, \mathbf{T}_1, (\mathbf{A}, \mathbf{B}_0, \mathbf{B}_1)) \leftarrow \mathsf{Gen}_{\mathsf{td}}(1^n, \tau_0, \tau_1)$, $sk_0 = (\tau_0, \mathbf{T}_0)$, $sk_1 = (\tau_1, \mathbf{T}_1)$ *and* $pk := (\mathbf{A}, \mathbf{B}_0, \mathbf{B}_1, \mathbf{C})$ *with* $\mathbf{C} \xleftarrow{\$} \mathbb{Z}_2^{\ell \times n}$. *Then*

$$\Pr_{pk, sk_0, sk_1}[\forall \tau_0, \tau_1, \tau \notin \{\tau_0, \tau_1\}, \mathbf{C} : (\mathsf{Dec0}(sk_0, \tau, C) = \mathsf{Dec1}(sk_1, \tau, C)] \geq 1 - 2^{-\Theta(m)}$$

Proof. If $M = \mathsf{Dec0}(sk_0, \tau, C = (\mathbf{c}, \mathbf{c}_0, \mathbf{c}_1, \mathbf{c}_2))$, then by the consistency check (5) of $\mathsf{Dec} = \mathsf{Dec0}$ we reconstruct some $\mathbf{s}$ where

$$\mathbf{e} := \mathbf{c} - \mathbf{As} \text{ with } |\mathbf{e}| \leq \beta$$
$$\wedge \quad \mathbf{t}_0 := \mathbf{c}_0 - (\mathbf{GH}_\tau + \mathbf{B}_0)\mathbf{s} \text{ with } |\mathbf{t}_0| \leq \alpha m/2$$
$$\wedge \quad \mathbf{t}_1 := \mathbf{c}_1 - (\mathbf{GH}_\tau + \mathbf{B}_1)\mathbf{s} \text{ with } |\mathbf{t}_1| \leq \alpha m/2$$

Using the above notation, the computation of $\mathsf{Dec1}(sk_1, \tau, C)$ can be expressed as

$$\tilde{\mathbf{c}}_1 := \mathbf{c}_1 - \mathbf{T}_1\mathbf{c} = (\mathbf{GH}_\tau + \mathbf{B}_1)\mathbf{s} + \mathbf{t}_1 - \mathbf{T}_1\mathbf{As} - \mathbf{T}_1\mathbf{e} = \mathbf{GH}_{\tau - \tau_1}\mathbf{s} + \mathbf{t}_1 - \mathbf{T}_1\mathbf{e}.$$

$\mathsf{Dec1}(sk_1, \tau, C)$ reconstructs the same $\mathbf{s}$ if the error term $|\mathbf{t}_1 - \mathbf{T}_1\mathbf{e}|$ is at most $\leq \alpha m$. We already know that $|\mathbf{t}_1| \leq \alpha m/2$. Thus, by the triangle inequality it is sufficient to show $|\mathbf{T}_1\mathbf{e}| \leq \alpha m/2$ to guarantee the correct decoding of $\mathbf{s}$. By (8), the probability that this is the case when we chose some $\mathbf{e}$ satisfying $|\mathbf{e}| = \beta'$ (for any $\beta' \leq \beta$) at *random*, is

$$\Pr_{\mathbf{e}, |\mathbf{e}| = \beta', \mathbf{T}_1}[|\mathbf{T}_1\mathbf{e}| \leq \alpha m/2] \geq 1 - 2^{-\Theta(m)},$$

We need the above to hold fore every small $\mathbf{e}$, not just a randomly chosen one. Taking the union bound over all $2^{\log(m)O(\sqrt{m})}$ possible $\mathbf{e} \in \mathbb{Z}_2^m$ satisfying $|\mathbf{e}| \leq \beta = 2\sqrt{cm} = \Theta(\sqrt{m})$ we further get

$$\Pr_{\mathbf{T}_1}[\forall \mathbf{e}, |\mathbf{e}| \leq \beta : |\mathbf{T}_1\mathbf{e}| \leq \alpha m/2] \geq 1 - 2^{-\Theta(m) + \log(m)O(\sqrt{m})} = 1 - 2^{-\Theta(m)}$$

This shows that with overwhelming probability over the choice of $\mathbf{T}_1$ the same $\mathbf{s}$, and thus also the same message M is computed by $\mathsf{Dec1}(sk_1, \tau, C)$. The proof that whenever $\mathsf{Dec1}$ outputs some $M \neq \perp$, then $\mathsf{Dec0}$ must output the same M (with overwhelming probability over the choice of $\mathbf{T}_0$) is symmetric.

3.4 Proof of Security

Theorem 2 (CCA Security). *If the* LPN *assumption holds,* TBE *from Section 3.2 is secure against* selective-tag weak CCA *adversaries. In particular, for every PPT algorithm* A *there exist PPT algorithms* B *and* C *with roughly the same running time, such that:*

$$\mathbf{Adv}_{\mathrm{TBE}}(\mathsf{A}) \leq 6m \cdot \mathbf{Adv}_{\mathrm{LPN}_{m-n,m,p}}(\mathsf{B}) + \mathbf{Adv}_{\mathrm{LPN}_{n,m+\ell,p}}(\mathsf{C}) + \mathrm{negl}(n).$$

Proof. Let A be an adversary attacking TBE. The games used in the proof are given in Figure 3, where G_1 is the same as the original TBE security game from Figure 1.

Initialize(τ^*)   //G_1
$\overline{(\mathbf{T}_0, \mathbf{T}_1, ek)} \leftarrow \mathsf{Gen}_{\mathrm{td}}(1^n, 0, 0);$
$\mathbf{e}^* \xleftarrow{\$} \mathcal{B}_p^m; \quad \mathbf{s}^* \xleftarrow{\$} \mathbb{Z}_2^n \quad \mathbf{C} \xleftarrow{\$} \mathbb{Z}_2^{\ell \times n};$
$\mathbf{c}^* := \mathbf{As}^* + \mathbf{e}^*;$
$\mathbf{T}_0^* \xleftarrow{\$} \mathcal{B}_p^{m \times m}; \quad \mathbf{c}_0^* := (\mathbf{GH}_{\tau^*} + \mathbf{B}_0)\mathbf{s}^* + \mathbf{T}_0^* \mathbf{e}^*$
$\mathbf{T}_1^* \xleftarrow{\$} \mathcal{B}_p^{m \times m}; \quad \mathbf{c}_1^* := (\mathbf{GH}_{\tau^*} + \mathbf{B}_1)\mathbf{s}^* + \mathbf{T}_1^* \mathbf{e}^*$
$sk = (0, \mathbf{T}_0);$
Return $pk := (ek, \mathbf{C})$

Initialize(τ^*)   //$G_{2,3}$
$\overline{(\mathbf{T}_0, \mathbf{T}_1, ek)} \leftarrow \mathsf{Gen}_{\mathrm{td}}(1^n, 0, \tau^*);$
$\mathbf{e}^* \xleftarrow{\$} \mathcal{B}_p^m; \quad \mathbf{s}^* \xleftarrow{\$} \mathbb{Z}_2^n \quad \mathbf{C} \xleftarrow{\$} \mathbb{Z}_2^{\ell \times n}$
$\mathbf{c}^* := \mathbf{As}^* + \mathbf{e}^*;$
$\mathbf{T}_0^* \xleftarrow{\$} \mathcal{B}_p^{m \times m}; \quad \mathbf{c}_0^* := (\mathbf{GH}_{\tau^*} + \mathbf{B}_0)\mathbf{s}^* + \mathbf{T}_0^* \mathbf{e}^*$
$\mathbf{T}_1^* := \mathbf{T}_1; \quad \mathbf{c}_1^* = \mathbf{T}_1^* \mathbf{c}^*;$
$sk = (0, \mathbf{T}_0); \quad //G_2$
$sk = (\tau^*, \mathbf{T}_1); \quad //G_3$
Return $pk := (ek, \mathbf{C})$

Initialize(τ^*)   //$G_{4,5}$
$\overline{(\mathbf{T}_0, \mathbf{T}_1, ek)} \leftarrow \mathsf{Gen}_{\mathrm{td}}(1^n, \tau^*, \tau^*)$
$\mathbf{e}^* \xleftarrow{\$} \mathcal{B}_p^m; \quad \mathbf{s}^* \xleftarrow{\$} \mathbb{Z}_2^n; \quad \mathbf{C} \xleftarrow{\$} \mathbb{Z}_2^{\ell \times n}$
$\mathbf{c}^* := \mathbf{As}^* + \mathbf{e}^*; \quad //G_4$
$\mathbf{c}^* \xleftarrow{\$} \mathbb{Z}_2^m; \quad //G_5$
$\mathbf{T}_0^* := \mathbf{T}_0; \quad \mathbf{c}_0^* = \mathbf{T}_0^* \mathbf{c}^*$
$\mathbf{T}_1^* := \mathbf{T}_1; \quad \mathbf{c}_1^* = \mathbf{T}_1^* \mathbf{c}^*$
$sk = (\tau^*, \mathbf{T}_1)$
Return $pk := (ek, \mathbf{C})$

queryDec(τ, C)   //G_{1-5}
If $(\tau = \tau^*)$ Return $\perp$
Return $\mathsf{Dec}(sk, \tau, C)$

Finalize(d)   //G_{1-5}
Return $(b_M = d)$

Challenge(M_0, M_1)   //G_{1-4}
$b_M \xleftarrow{\$} \{0,1\};$
$\mathbf{e}_2^* \xleftarrow{\$} \mathcal{B}_p^\ell;$
$\mathbf{c}_2^* := \mathbf{Cs}^* + \mathbf{e}_2^* + \mathbf{G}_2(M_{b_M})$
Return $C^* = (\mathbf{c}^*, \mathbf{c}_0^*, \mathbf{c}_1^*, \mathbf{c}_2^*)$

Challenge(M_0, M_1)   //G_5
$\mathbf{c}_2^* \xleftarrow{\$} \mathbb{Z}_2^\ell$
Return C^*

Fig. 3. The different procedures of the games 1 to 5. G_1 is exactly the same as G_{TBE}, where the message-independent part of a Challenge query is already pre-computed in Initialize.

From G_1 to G_2 we switch the hidden trapdoor tag of trapdoor $\mathbf{T}_1$ from 0 to τ^*.

Lemma 6. *There exists a PPT algorithm* B *such that*

$$| \Pr[G_1^{\mathsf{A}} = 1] - \Pr[G_2^{\mathsf{A}} = 1] | \leq | \Pr[G_{\mathrm{real}}^{\mathsf{B}} = 1] - \Pr[G_{\mathrm{corr}}^{\mathsf{B}} = 1] |$$
$$\leq 3m \cdot \mathbf{Adv}_{\mathrm{LPN}_{m-n,m,p}}(\mathsf{B}),$$

where games G_{real} *and* G_{corr} *are defined in Figure 2.*

Proof. We describe algorithm B who simulates G_1 in G_{real} or G_2 in G_{corr}.

Initialize(τ^*)
$(ek, \mathbf{T}_0, \mathbf{e}^*, \mathbf{T}_1^* \mathbf{e}^*) \leftarrow$ Initialize$(0, 0, 0, \tau^*)$;
$\mathbf{C} \xleftarrow{\$} \mathbb{Z}_2^{\ell \times n}$; $\mathbf{s}^* \xleftarrow{\$} \mathbb{Z}_2^n$;
$\mathbf{c}^* := \mathbf{A}\mathbf{s}^* + \mathbf{e}^*$;
$\mathbf{T}_0^* \xleftarrow{\$} \mathcal{B}_p^{m \times m}$;
$\mathbf{c}_0^* := (\mathbf{G}\mathbf{H}_{\tau^*} + \mathbf{B}_0)\mathbf{s}^* + \mathbf{T}_0^* \mathbf{e}^*$;
$\mathbf{c}_1^* := (\mathbf{G}\mathbf{H}_{\tau^*} + \mathbf{B}_1)\mathbf{s}^* + \mathbf{T}_1^* \mathbf{e}^*$;
Return $pk := (ek, \mathbf{C})$

Challenge(M_0, M_1)
$b_M \xleftarrow{\$} \{0, 1\}$;
$\mathbf{e}_2^* \xleftarrow{\$} \mathcal{B}_p^\ell$;
$\mathbf{c}_2^* := \mathbf{C}\mathbf{s}^* + \mathbf{e}_2^* + \mathbf{G}_2(M_{b_M})$
Return C^*

queryDec(τ, C)
If ($\tau = \tau^*$) Return $\perp$
Return Dec($sk = (0, \mathbf{T}_0), \tau, C$)

Finalize(d)
Finalize($b_M = d$)

The definition of G_{real} and G_{corr} imply the correctness of the output of Initialize. $\mathbf{e}^*$ and $\mathbf{T}_1^* \mathbf{e}^*$ have the correct distribution, too. Hence B simulates G_1 in G_{real} or G_2 in G_{corr}. The Lemma follows using Lemma 4.

In a next lemma we show that the adversary isn't able to distinguish whether the simulator uses the trapdoor $\mathbf{T}_0$ or $\mathbf{T}_1$ to answer decryption queries. To show this lemma, we use equivalence of the trapdoors shown in Lemma 5.

Lemma 7. $|\Pr[G_2^A = 1] - \Pr[G_3^A = 1]| \leq \text{negl}(n)$.

Proof. We have to prove that an adversary can't figure out which trapdoor is used to answer decryption queries. Otherwise he is able to distinguish G_2 from G_3. Lemma 5 already shows that Dec has the same output for two different trapdoors with overwhelming probability, if the tags related to the trapdoors are not queried. In our case, τ_0 and τ_1 are either 0 or τ^*. The adversary is not allowed to query $0 \notin \mathcal{T}$ and τ^*. Hence he has only a negligible chance to distinguish G_2 and G_3

From G_3 to G_4 we switch the hidden trapdoor tag of trapdoor $\mathbf{T}_0$ from 0 to τ^*. Its proof is analogue to the one of Lemma 6 and therefore omitted.

Lemma 8. *There exists a PPT algorithm* B *such that*

$$|\Pr[G_3^A = 1] - \Pr[G_4^A = 1]| \leq |\Pr[G_{real}^B = 1] - \Pr[G_{corr}^B = 1]|$$
$$\leq 3m \cdot \mathbf{Adv}_{\text{LPN}_{m-n,m,p}}(B),$$

where games G_{real} *and* G_{corr} *are defined in Figure 2.*

In game G_5, the last game, we make the challenge ciphertext independent of the plaintexts M_0 and M_1.

Lemma 9. *There exists a PPT algorithm* C *such that*

$$|\Pr[\mathsf{G}_4^\mathsf{A} = 1] - \Pr[\mathsf{G}_5^\mathsf{A} = 1]| \leq \mathbf{Adv}_{\mathrm{LPN}_{n,m+\ell,p}}(\mathsf{C}).$$

Proof. We give a description of C and show, that he simulates G_4 and G_5 correctly. C receives a LPN challenge $(\mathbf{A}, \mathbf{C}), (\mathbf{b_A}, \mathbf{b_C})$ where $(\mathbf{b_A}, \mathbf{b_C}) = (\mathbf{As} + \mathbf{e}_1, \mathbf{Cs} + \mathbf{e}_2)$ or uniform.

Initialize(τ^*)
___
$\mathbf{T}_0, \mathbf{T}_1 \xleftarrow{\$} \mathcal{B}_p^{m \times m}$;
$\mathbf{B}_0 := \mathbf{T}_0 \mathbf{A} - \mathbf{GH}_{\tau^*}$;
$\mathbf{B}_1 := \mathbf{T}_1 \mathbf{A} - \mathbf{GH}_{\tau^*}$;
$\mathbf{c}^* := \mathbf{b_A}$;
$\mathbf{T}_0^* := \mathbf{T}_0$; $\mathbf{c}_0^* := \mathbf{T}_0^* \mathbf{b_A}$;
$\mathbf{T}_1^* := \mathbf{T}_1$; $\mathbf{c}_1^* := \mathbf{T}_1^* \mathbf{b_A}$;
Return $pk := (\mathbf{A}, \mathbf{B}_0, \mathbf{B}_1, \mathbf{C})$

queryDec(τ, C)
___
If $(\tau = \tau^*)$ Return $\bot$
Return Dec$((\tau^*, \mathbf{T}_1), \tau, C)$

Challenge(M_0, M_1)
___
$b_M \xleftarrow{\$} \{0, 1\}$;
$\mathbf{c}_2 := \mathbf{b_C} + \mathbf{G}_2(M_{b_M})$
Return C^*

Finalize(d)
___
Finalize($b_M = d$)

Now we analyse if C simulates correctly. First note that $\mathbf{A}$ and $\mathbf{C}$ are uniformly distributed, as required.

LPN Case: $\mathbf{b_A} = \mathbf{As} + \mathbf{e}_1$ and $\mathbf{b_C} = \mathbf{Cs} + \mathbf{e}_2$. To show that G_4 is simulated correctly, we have to show, that the distribution of c^* is correct. We implicitly set $\mathbf{s}^* = \mathbf{s}$, $\mathbf{e}_1^* = \mathbf{e}_1$ and $\mathbf{e}_2^* = \mathbf{e}_2$.

$$\mathbf{c}^* := \mathbf{b_A} = \mathbf{As}^* + \mathbf{e}_1^*$$
$$\mathbf{c}_0^* := \mathbf{T}_0^* \mathbf{b_A} = (\mathbf{GH}_{\tau^*} - \mathbf{GH}_{\tau^*} + \mathbf{T}_0^* \mathbf{A})\mathbf{s}^* + \mathbf{T}_0^* \mathbf{e}_1^* = (\mathbf{GH}_{\tau^*} + \mathbf{B}_0)\mathbf{s}^* + \mathbf{T}_0^* \mathbf{e}_1^*$$
$$\mathbf{c}_1^* := \mathbf{T}_1^* \mathbf{b_A} = (\mathbf{GH}_{\tau^*} + \mathbf{B}_1)\mathbf{s}^* + \mathbf{T}_1^* \mathbf{e}_1^*$$
$$\mathbf{c}_2^* := \mathbf{b_C} + \mathbf{G}_2(M_{b_M}) = \mathbf{Cs}^* + \mathbf{e}_2^* + \mathbf{G}_2(M_{b_M}).$$

Uniform Case: $\mathbf{c}_2^*$ is independent of M_{b_M} since $\mathbf{b_C}$ is uniformly distributed and hence $\mathbf{b_C} + \mathbf{G}_2(M_{b_M})$ is uniform, too. In this case, C simulates G_5.

In G_5, the challenge ciphertext is independent of the message and hence from the challenge bit b_M. The best, an adversary can do now, is to guess b_M and output the guess.

Lemma 10. $\Pr[\mathsf{G}_5^\mathsf{A} = 1] = \Pr[\mathsf{G}_5^\mathsf{A} = 0] = \frac{1}{2}$.

Combining the Lemmas 6–10 concludes the theorem:

$$\mathbf{Adv}_{\mathrm{TBE}}(A)$$

$$= \left| \Pr[G^A_{\mathrm{TBE}} = 1] - \frac{1}{2} \right|$$

$$\leq \left| \Pr[G^A_2 = 1] + 3m \cdot \mathbf{Adv}_{\mathrm{LPN}_{m-n,m,p}}(B) - \frac{1}{2} \right|$$

$$\leq \left| \Pr[G^A_3 = 1] + \mathrm{negl}(n) + 3m \cdot \mathbf{Adv}_{\mathrm{LPN}_{m-n,m,p}}(B) - \frac{1}{2} \right|$$

$$\leq \left| \Pr[G^A_4 = 1] + \mathrm{negl}(n) + 6m \cdot \mathbf{Adv}_{\mathrm{LPN}_{m-n,m,p}}(B) - \frac{1}{2} \right|$$

$$\leq \left| \Pr[G^A_5 = 1] + \mathbf{Adv}_{\mathrm{LPN}_{n,m+\ell,p}}(C) + \mathrm{negl}(n) + 6m \cdot \mathbf{Adv}_{\mathrm{LPN}_{m-n,m,p}}(B) - \frac{1}{2} \right|$$

$$\leq 6m \cdot \mathbf{Adv}_{\mathrm{LPN}_{m-n,m,p}}(B) + \mathbf{Adv}_{\mathrm{LPN}_{n,m+\ell,p}}(C) + \mathrm{negl}(n).$$

References

1. Gilbert, H., Robshaw, M., Seurin, Y.: How to encrypt with the LPN problem. In: Aceto, L., Damgård, I., Goldberg, L.A., Halldórsson, M.M., Ingólfsdóttir, A., Walukiewicz, I. (eds.) ICALP 2008, Part II. LNCS, vol. 5126, pp. 679–690. Springer, Heidelberg (2008) 1
2. Hopper, N.J., Blum, M.: Secure human identification protocols. In: Boyd, C. (ed.) ASIACRYPT 2001. LNCS, vol. 2248, pp. 52–66. Springer, Heidelberg (2001) 1
3. Katz, J., Shin, J.S., Smith, A.: Parallel and concurrent security of the HB and HB+ protocols. Journal of Cryptology 23(3), 402–421 (2010) 1
4. Kiltz, E., Pietrzak, K., Cash, D., Jain, A., Venturi, D.: Efficient authentication from hard learning problems. In: Paterson, K.G. (ed.) EUROCRYPT 2011. LNCS, vol. 6632, pp. 7–26. Springer, Heidelberg (2011) 1
5. Alekhnovich, M.: More on average case vs approximation complexity. In: 44th Annual Symposium on Foundations of Computer Science, pp. 298–307. IEEE Computer Society Press (October 2003) 1
6. Blum, A., Kalai, A., Wasserman, H.: Noise-tolerant learning, the parity problem, and the statistical query model. In: 32nd ACM STOC Annual ACM Symposium on Theory of Computing, pp. 435–440. ACM Press (May 2000) 2
7. Damgård, I., Park, S.: Is public-key encryption based on lpn practical? Cryptology ePrint Archive, Report 2012/699 (2012), http://eprint.iacr.org/ 2
8. Döttling, N., Müller-Quade, J., Nascimento, A.C.A.: Ind-cca secure cryptography based on a variant of the lpn problem. In: Wang, X., Sako, K. (eds.) ASIACRYPT 2012. LNCS, vol. 7658, pp. 485–503. Springer, Heidelberg (2012) 2, 3, 16
9. Micciancio, D., Peikert, C.: Trapdoors for lattices: Simpler, tighter, faster, smaller. In: Pointcheval, D., Johansson, T. (eds.) EUROCRYPT 2012. LNCS, vol. 7237, pp. 700–718. Springer, Heidelberg (2012) 2, 3, 6
10. Kurosawa, K., Desmedt, Y.G.: A new paradigm of hybrid encryption scheme. In: Franklin, M. (ed.) CRYPTO 2004. LNCS, vol. 3152, pp. 426–442. Springer, Heidelberg (2004) 2

11. Hofheinz, D., Kiltz, E.: Secure hybrid encryption from weakened key encapsulation. In: Menezes, A. (ed.) CRYPTO 2007. LNCS, vol. 4622, pp. 553–571. Springer, Heidelberg (2007) 2

12. Agrawal, S., Boneh, D., Boyen, X.: Efficient lattice (H)IBE in the standard model. In: Gilbert, H. (ed.) EUROCRYPT 2010. LNCS, vol. 6110, pp. 553–572. Springer, Heidelberg (2010) 2, 6

13. Kiltz, E., Mohassel, P., O'Neill, A.: Adaptive trapdoor functions and chosen-ciphertext security. In: Gilbert, H. (ed.) EUROCRYPT 2010. LNCS, vol. 6110, pp. 673–692. Springer, Heidelberg (2010) 3, 10

14. Micciancio, D., Mol, P.: Pseudorandom knapsacks and the sample complexity of LWE search-to-decision reductions. In: Rogaway, P. (ed.) CRYPTO 2011. LNCS, vol. 6841, pp. 465–484. Springer, Heidelberg (2011) 4

15. Alperin-Sheriff, J., Peikert, C.: Circular and KDM security for identity-based encryption. In: Fischlin, M., Buchmann, J., Manulis, M. (eds.) PKC 2012. LNCS, vol. 7293, pp. 334–352. Springer, Heidelberg (2012) 5

16. Justesen, J.: Class of constructive asymptotically good algebraic codes. IEEE Transactions on Information Theory 18(5), 652–656 (1972) 5

17. Bellare, M., Rogaway, P.: The security of triple encryption and a framework for code-based game-playing proofs. In: Vaudenay, S. (ed.) EUROCRYPT 2006. LNCS, vol. 4004, pp. 409–426. Springer, Heidelberg (2006) 5

18. Kiltz, E.: Chosen-ciphertext security from tag-based encryption. In: Halevi, S., Rabin, T. (eds.) TCC 2006. LNCS, vol. 3876, pp. 581–600. Springer, Heidelberg (2006) 6

19. Cramer, R., Damgård, I.: On the amortized complexity of zero-knowledge protocols. In: Halevi, S. (ed.) CRYPTO 2009. LNCS, vol. 5677, pp. 177–191. Springer, Heidelberg (2009) 6

20. Boneh, D., Canetti, R., Halevi, S., Katz, J.: Chosen-ciphertext security from identity-based encryption. SIAM Journal on Computing 36(5), 1301–1328 (2007) 16

21. Boneh, D., Katz, J.: Improved efficiency for CCA-secure cryptosystems built using identity-based encryption. In: Menezes, A. (ed.) CT-RSA 2005. LNCS, vol. 3376, pp. 87–103. Springer, Heidelberg (2005) 16, 17

22. Dodis, Y., Kiltz, E., Pietrzak, K., Wichs, D.: Message authentication, revisited. In: Pointcheval, D., Johansson, T. (eds.) EUROCRYPT 2012. LNCS, vol. 7237, pp. 355–374. Springer, Heidelberg (2012) 17

23. Jain, A., Krenn, S., Pietrzak, K., Tentes, A.: Commitments and efficient zero-knowledge proofs from learning parity with noise. In: Wang, X., Sako, K. (eds.) ASIACRYPT 2012. LNCS, vol. 7658, pp. 663–680. Springer, Heidelberg (2012) 17

A IND-CCA Secure Encryption

There are generic constructions to transform a TBE to an IND-CCA PKE. [20] is based on one-time signatures (OTS). The other one is based on a message authentication code (MAC) and a commitment scheme [21].

To transform a TBE to an IND-CCA secure encryption, we do not use a OTS based on LPN like in [8], since this transformation would be too expensive. This would cause a large tag, since the the verification key of the OTS is the tag. Further, the size of the ciphertext grows with a bigger tag and the ciphertext will be signed with the OTS. In order to use this approach a collision resistant hash function is necessary to shrink the ciphertext to the message size signed by the signature.

More efficient is the technique based on a commitment scheme and a MAC [21]. LPN-based euf MACs have a large secret to which we have to commit [22]. This commitment is used as the tag for the TBE. A large secret key will cause again a large commitment, large tag and even larger ciphertext. The MAC is used to create a tag for the ciphertext of a TBE. The advantage of this transformation is, that we do not need a collision resistant hash function.

In the commitment and MAC-based transformation, the MAC has to be existential unforgeable given one tag query for an arbitrary message. A pairwise independent function fulfils this task in a less complex way and with a smaller secret compared to LPN-based MACs. But now we have to shrink the size of the ciphertext to the domain of the pairwise independent function. A collision resistant hash function leads to an efficient transformation of a TBE to an IND-CCA PKE. As alternative to a collision resistant hash function, we could also use an almost pairwise independent hash function instead of the pairwise independent hash function. As commitment scheme, we use the simple and efficient construction of [23]. Their commitment scheme is perfectly binding and computationally hiding.

B   An IND-CPA Secure Public Key Encryption Scheme

The following three algorithms describe an IND-CPA-PKE = (Gen, Enc, Dec). The scheme is a simplified version of the TBE to achieve just IND-CPA security. An IND-CPA adversary plays the G_{TBE} without having access to qeryDec. This makes the proof and hence the scheme much easier, since there is no need for having access to a trapdoor to answer decryption queries. Further an efficient error correction code $\mathbf{G}$ is required to reconstruct the message. This code corrects up to αm errors with $4c < \alpha < 1$ for Bernoulli parameter $p = \sqrt{c/m}$, and maps the message space $\mathcal{M}$ into $\mathbb{Z}_2^\ell$. The dimensions n, $m-n$ of the LPN secrets (with $n = \Theta(k^2)$) controll the security of the scheme.

$\underline{\text{Gen}(1^k) \to (sk, pk)}$. The algorithm picks $\mathbf{A} \xleftarrow{\$} \mathbb{Z}_2^{m \times n}$, $\mathbf{T} \xleftarrow{\$} \mathcal{B}_p^{\ell \times m}$ and sets $\mathbf{C} = \mathbf{TA}$. The private key is $\mathbf{T}$ and the public key $pk := (\mathbf{A}, \mathbf{C})$.

$\underline{\text{Enc}(pk, M) \to C = (\mathbf{c}, \mathbf{c}_2)}$. Sample $\mathbf{e}_1 \xleftarrow{\$} \mathcal{B}_p^m$; $\mathbf{e}_2 \xleftarrow{\$} \mathcal{B}_p^\ell$ and $\mathbf{s} \xleftarrow{\$} \mathbb{Z}_2^n$ and set

$$\mathbf{c} := \mathbf{As} + \mathbf{e}_1 \quad \text{and} \quad \mathbf{c}_2 := \mathbf{Cs} + \mathbf{e}_2 + \mathbf{G}(M).$$

$\underline{\text{Dec}(sk, C) \to (M \text{ or } \bot)}$. The algorithm computes

$$\tilde{\mathbf{c}} := (\mathbf{T} \ \mathbf{I}) \cdot \begin{pmatrix} -\mathbf{c} \\ \mathbf{c}_2 \end{pmatrix} \quad (= \mathbf{G}(M) - \mathbf{Te}_1 + \mathbf{e}_2).$$

Output M, which is reconstructed from $\tilde{\mathbf{c}}$ by using $\mathbf{G}$.

A SIMPLE TRAPDOOR FUNCTION. By changing the construction a little bit, one obtains a simple trapdoor function. A trapdoor $\mathbf{T} \in \mathbb{Z}_2^{m \times n}$ output by $\mathsf{Gen}(1^n)$ can be used to invert the trapdoor function

$$f^\tau(\mathbf{s}, \mathbf{e}_1, \mathbf{e}_2) = (\mathbf{As} + \mathbf{e}_1, (\mathbf{C} + \mathbf{G})\mathbf{s} + \mathbf{e}_2).$$

$\mathbf{s}$ is reconstructed by using the error correction of code $\mathbf{G}$. Details can be seen in the correctness of the PKE. When $\mathbf{s}$ is reconstructed, $\mathbf{e}_1$ and $\mathbf{e}_2$ are easily obtained by subtracting $\mathbf{As}$ and $(\mathbf{C} + \mathbf{G})\mathbf{s}$ from the output of the function.

CORRECTNESS. The encoding scheme has to correct an error $\mathbf{e}_2 - \mathbf{Te}_1$, for $\mathbf{e}_1, \mathbf{e}_2 \xleftarrow{\$} \mathcal{B}_p^m$ with overwhelming probability. The correctness follows from the correctness of the proposed TBE. To give an example, for message space $\mathbb{Z}_2^n$ and $\ell = m$, the generator matrix $\mathbf{G}$ of the TBE can be used. This encoding scheme is stronger than necessary, since it corrects even an error $\mathbf{T}_2\mathbf{e}_2 - \mathbf{T}_1\mathbf{e}_1$ for $\mathbf{e}_1, \mathbf{e}_2 \xleftarrow{\$} \mathcal{B}_p^m$, $\mathbf{T}_1, \mathbf{T}_2 \xleftarrow{\$} \mathcal{B}_p^{m \times m}$ with overwhelming probability.

SECURITY.

Theorem 3. *If the* LPN *assumption holds,* PKE *is secure against* IND-CPA *adversaries. In particular, for every PPT algorithm* A *there exist PPT algorithms* B *and* C *with roughly the same running time, such that:*

$$\mathbf{Adv}_{\mathrm{TBE}}(\mathsf{A}) \leq \ell \cdot \mathbf{Adv}_{\mathrm{LPN}_{m-n,m,p}}(\mathsf{B}) + \mathbf{Adv}_{\mathrm{LPN}_{n,m+\ell,p}}(\mathsf{C}) + \mathrm{negl}(n).$$

PROOF SKETCH. First we switch $\mathbf{C} = \mathbf{TA}$ to a uniform $\mathbf{C}$. If an adversary has less advantage in the uniform setting, we will break the $\mathrm{KLPN}_{m-n,m,p}^\ell$ assumption. Then we switch $\mathbf{c}^*, \mathbf{c}_2^*$ to uniform by using a $\mathrm{LPN}_{n,m+\ell,p}$ instance $\mathbf{A}, \mathbf{C}, \mathbf{b}_\mathbf{A}, \mathbf{b}_\mathbf{C}$ and setting $\mathbf{c}^* = \mathbf{b}_\mathbf{A}$, $\mathbf{c}_2^* = \mathbf{b}_\mathbf{B} + \mathbf{G}(M)$. Now the ciphertext is uniform and the advantage of an adversary is negligible.

Leakage-Flexible CCA-secure Public-Key Encryption: Simple Construction and Free of Pairing

Baodong Qin[1,2] and Shengli Liu[1,*]

[1] Department of Computer Science and Engineering, Shanghai Jiao Tong University, Shanghai 200240, China
[2] College of Computer Science and Technology, Southwest University of Science and Technology, Mianyang 621010, China
{qinbaodong,slliu}@sjtu.edu.cn

Abstract. In AsiaCrypt 2013, Qin and Liu proposed a new approach to CCA-security of Public-Key Encryption (PKE) in the presence of bounded key-leakage, from any universal hash proof system (due to Cramer and Shoup) and any one-time lossy filter (a simplified version of lossy algebraic filters, due to Hofheinz). They presented two instantiations under the DDH and DCR assumptions, which result in leakage rate (defined as the ratio of leakage amount to the secret-key length) of $1/2 - o(1)$. In this paper, we extend their work to broader assumptions and to flexible leakage rate, more specifically to leakage rate of $1 - o(1)$.

- We introduce the Refined Subgroup Indistinguishability (RSI) assumption, which is a subclass of subgroup indistinguishability assumptions, including many standard number-theoretical assumptions, like the quadratic residuosity assumption, the decisional composite residuosity assumption and the subgroup decision assumption over a group of known order defined by Boneh et al.
- We show that universal hash proof (UHP) system and one-time lossy filter (OT-LF) can be simply and efficiently constructed from the RSI assumption. Applying Qin and Liu's paradigm gives simple and efficient PKE schemes under the RSI assumption.
- With the RSI assumption over a specific group (free of pairing), public parameters of UHP and OT-LF can be chosen in a flexible way, resulting in a leakage-flexible CCA-secure PKE scheme. More specifically, we get the first CCA-secure PKE with leakage rate of $1 - o(1)$ without pairing.

Keywords: Public-key encryption, leakage flexibility, chosen-ciphertext security.

* Supported by the National Natural Science Foundation of China (Grant No. 61170229, 61133014 and 61373153), the Specialized Research Fund for the Doctoral Program of Higher Education (Grant No. 20110073110016), and the Scientific innovation projects of Shanghai Education Committee (Grant No. 12ZZ021).

H. Krawczyk (Ed.): PKC 2014, LNCS 8383, pp. 19–36, 2014.

1   Introduction

Traditional security models (e.g., semantic security [17]) of cryptographic schemes assume that the secret key or the internal secret state involved in a cryptosystem is completely unknown to adversaries. However, in the real world, an adversary may obtain partial knowledge of the secret information via a side channel attack [18]. Side channel attacks gain (secret) information from physical attributions (e.g., timing, power consumption, etc.) revealed by a computing device. Inspired by side channel attacks, many cryptographic researchers have contributed their work to design of cryptosystems that remain secure even if an adversary obtains some information on the secret keys, including symmetric-key encryption [11,13,30], public-key encryption [1,27,2,4,5,31], digital signatures [21,14], identity-based encryption [7,15,24].

To model security against side channel attacks, it is natural to consider an adversary that only learns a limited amount of information on the secret key. Otherwise, the security of the system will be compromised completely. A simple yet general model of key-leakage is the bounded-leakage model [1]. It is formalized by allowing an adversary to adaptively and repeatedly choose functions of the secret key and gain the outputs of the functions as long as the total amount of leaked information on the secret key is bounded by some parameter λ (called the leakage amount). Clearly, from this perspective, the leakage amount must be strictly smaller than the secret-key length $|sk|$. We call the ratio $\lambda/|sk|$ the relative leakage or the leakage rate of a cryptosystem. An obvious goal of designing a leakage-resilient cryptosystem is to make its leakage rate as close to 1 as possible. There are also other security models for leakage-resilience that consider more complicated scenarios of key leakage, e.g., auxiliary input model [11], continual-leakage model [5,9] and continual auxiliary input model [33]. Nevertheless, many works from those complicated models rely on the results from the bounded-leakage model as basic building blocks [19]. In this paper, we consider the bounded-leakage model in the setting of public-key encryption.

Prior Constructions and Limitations. Inspired by Halderman et al.'s "cool boot" attacks [18], Akavia et al. [1] formalized the notion of leakage-resilient chosen-plaintext security (LR-CPA) in the bounded-leakage model. Since then, many encryption schemes [32,16,3,27,19] have been proved secure in this model. In particular, Naor and Segev presented a generic construction of LR-CPA secure PKE schemes from any hash proof system (HPS) [8]. Moreover, they gave some efficient instantiations based on the DDH and k-linear assumptions, where the relative leakage is flexibly ranging over $[0, 1)$. We also call such PKE *leakage-flexible*. In [27], Naor and Segev also extended the framework of key leakage to the setting of chosen-ciphertext attacks, i.e., leakage-resilient chosen-ciphertext security (LR-CCA). They showed how to achieve LR-CCA secure PKE schemes by relying on the Naor-Yung paradigm which results in (impractical) leakage flexible PKE schemes or the hash proof systems which result in an efficient variant of the Cramer-Shoup cryptosystem with leakage-rate 1/6. Later, some new variants of the Cramer and Shoup cryptosystem [25,26] are showed to be

LR-CCA secure but with a leakage-rate smaller than $1/4$. Very recently, Qin and Liu [31] proposed a novel approach to achieve LR-CCA security by replacing the universal$_2$ hash proof system in Naor and Segev's HPS-based framework with a new primitive called one-time lossy filter. This results in efficient constructions of LR-CCA secure PKE schemes based on the DDH and DCR assumptions with leakage rate $1/2 - o(1)$.

The open problem of constructing a practical LR-CCA secure PKE scheme with flexible leakage was solved by Dodis et al. [10]. They showed that Naor and Segev's generic construction in the Naor-Yung paradigm can be made efficient under the Symmetric External Diffie-Hellman (SXDH) and Decisional Linear (DLIN) assumptions related to bilinear pairing on elliptic curves. Another leakage-flexible CCA-secure PKE scheme was due to Galindo et al. [15]. Their construction is obtained by applying the CHK transform [6] to their identity-based encryption scheme with master-key leakage flexibility (without rigorous proof) under the DLIN assumption on pairing-friendly groups. We observe that all existing leakage-flexible CCA-secure PKE schemes rely on assumptions over pairing-friendly groups. Moreover, even though they are practical, the constructions are complicated and computations inevitably involve pairings.

Our Contributions. In this paper, we define a class of assumptions called *Refined Subgroup Indistinguishability (RSI)* assumptions which are similar to the *Subgroup Indistinguishability (SI)* assumptions (due to Brakerski and Goldwasser [4]) except for the restriction to cyclic groups. Specifically, a subgroup indistinguishability problem is defined by a finite commutative multiplicative group $\mathbb{G}$, which is a direct product of two groups $\mathbb{G} = G_{\tau_1} \times G_{\tau_2}$ of order τ_1, τ_2 respectively. It requires that $\gcd(\tau_1, \tau_2) = 1$ and G_{τ_2} is a cyclic group. The subgroup indistinguishability assumption states that a random element of $\mathbb{G}$ is computationally indistinguishable from a random element in G_{τ_1}. Brakerski and Goldwasser [4] showed that the DCR and QR assumptions are two special cases of the subgroup indistinguishability assumptions. In the Refined Subgroup Indistinguishability (RSI) problem, we further require that the subgroup G_{τ_1} is also cyclic. Nevertheless, all known instances of SI problems can be modified to RSI problems. Moreover, the instantiations of RSI assumption under the DCR and QR assumptions are operated over groups of unknown order. We can also instantiate the RSI assumption over a specific group of known order (without pairing).

We further show that the RSI assumption implies efficient construction of leakage-resilient CCA-secure PKE schemes by presenting simple and efficient constructions of universal hash proof systems and one-time lossy filters under the RSI assumption. Here we follow Qin and Liu's paradigm [31](details in Section 4.1) of constructing leakage-resilient CCA-secure PKE from universal HPS and OT-LF, but we extend their work to the RSI assumption.

When instantiating over a specific group of known order (without pairing), we obtain a simple and efficient CCA-secure PKE scheme with leakage-rate of $1 - o(1)$. This is the first leakage-resilient CCA-secure PKE with leakage rate $1 - o(1)$, but free of pairing.

Organization. The rest of this paper is organized as follows. Basic notations and definitions are introduced in Section 2. The definition of refined subgroup indistinguishability assumptions and instantiations are presented in Section 3. Our leakage-resilient CCA-secure PKE schemes from the refined subgroup indistinguishability assumptions are given in Section 4. Finally, we summarize this paper in Section 5.

2   Preliminary

Notations. Let $\kappa \in \mathbb{N}$ denote a security parameter and 1^κ denote the string of κ ones. We say that a function $\epsilon(\kappa)$ is negligible in κ if for all polynomial ploy and sufficiently large κ, $\epsilon(\kappa) \leq 1/\text{ploy}(\kappa)$. For $n \in \mathbb{N}$, we write $[n]$ for the set $\{1, \ldots, n\}$. We denote by $|s|$ the length of a bitstring s and by $|S|$ the size of a set S. Moreover, $s \leftarrow_R S$ denotes the operation of sampling an element s from S uniformly at random. We denote $y \leftarrow A(x)$ the operation of running A with input x, and assigning y as the result. We write $\log s$ for logarithms over the reals with base 2.

Statistical Distance. The *statistical distance* between two random variables X and Y over a finite set Ω is defined as $\Delta(X, Y) = \frac{1}{2} \sum_{\omega \in \Omega} |\Pr[X = \omega] - \Pr[Y = \omega]|$. A random variable X is called ϵ-uniform over Ω, if $\Delta(X, Y) \leq \epsilon$, where Y is a uniform distribution. Let X and Y be two families of random variables indexed by a security parameter κ. We say that X and Y are statistically indistinguishable and write $X \approx_s Y$ if for all polynomial ploy and sufficiently large κ, $\Delta(X, Y) \leq 1/\text{ploy}(\kappa)$. If for any PPT algorithm $\mathcal{A}$, its advantage in distinguishing between X and Y defined as $|\Pr[\mathcal{A}(X) = 1] - \Pr[\mathcal{A}(Y) = 1]|$ is negligible in κ, we say that X and Y are computationally indistinguishable and write $X \approx_c Y$.

Min-Entropy and Average Min-Entropy. The *min-entropy* of a random variable X is $H_\infty(X) = -\log(\max_x \Pr[X = x])$. The average min-entropy X conditioned on a random variable Y is formally defined by Dodis et al. [12] as $\widetilde{H}_\infty(X|Y) = -\log\left(E_{y \leftarrow Y}[2^{-H_\infty(X|Y=y)}]\right)$.

Definition 1 (Universal hash). *A family of functions $\mathcal{H} = \{h : X \to Y\}$ is called universal if, for all distinct $x, x' \in X$, $\Pr_{h \leftarrow_R \mathcal{H}}[h(x) = h(x')] = 1/|Y|$.*

The following lemma shows that a universal hash function can be used as a randomness extractor.

Lemma 1 ([12]). *Let X and Y be random variables such that $X \in \{0,1\}^n$ and $\widetilde{H}_\infty(X|Y) \geq v$. Let $\mathcal{H} = \{h : \{0,1\}^n \to \{0,1\}^m\}$ be a family of universal hash functions. If $m \leq v - 2\log(1/\epsilon)$, then for $h \leftarrow_R \mathcal{H}$ it holds that $\Delta((Y, h, h(X)), (Y, h, U_m)) \leq \epsilon$, where U_m is uniform over $\{0,1\}^m$.*

Public-Key Encryption. A public-key encryption scheme PKE with message space $\mathcal{M}$ consists of three PPT algorithms (Kg, Enc, Dec). For a security parameter 1^κ, the randomized key generation algorithm $\text{Kg}(1^\kappa)$ produces a public/secret key pair (PK, SK). For a public key PK, the randomized encryption algorithm $\mathsf{Enc}(PK, M)$ creates a ciphertext C of the message $M \in \mathcal{M}$. For a secret key SK and a ciphertext C, the decryption algorithm $\mathsf{Dec}(SK, C)$ returns a message $M \in \mathcal{M}$ or a special rejection symbol $\perp$. For consistency, we require that $\mathsf{Dec}(SK, \mathsf{Enc}(PK, M)) = M$ always holds, for all $\kappa \in \mathbb{N}$, all $(PK, SK) \leftarrow \mathsf{Kg}(1^\kappa)$ and all $M \in \mathcal{M}$.

For security, we consider the standard notion of leakage-resilient chosen-ciphertext (LR-CCA) security in the bounded leakage model [27]. In this model, the adversary is allowed to query a decryption oracle $\mathcal{D}_{sk}(\cdot)$ which returns $\mathsf{Dec}(sk, C)$ for a query C, and a leakage oracle $\mathcal{O}_{sk}^\lambda(\cdot)$ which returns $f_i(sk)$ for a leakage function $f_i : \{0,1\}^* \rightarrow \{0,1\}^{\lambda_i}$. The adversary can adaptively query either of these two oracles polynomial times, with the following restrictions: (1) the total amount of information leaked is bounded by $\sum_i \lambda_i \leq \lambda$; (2) after seeing the challenge ciphertext, the adversary is not allowed to query the decryption oracle with the challenge ciphertext and query the leakage oracle at all.

Definition 2 (Leakage-resilient CCA-secure PKE). *We say that a PKE scheme* $\mathsf{PKE} = (\mathsf{Kg}, \mathsf{Enc}, \mathsf{Dec})$ *is* λ-*LR-CCA secure if, for any PPT adversary, the following function* $\mathsf{Adv}_{\mathsf{PKE}, \mathcal{A}}^{\lambda\text{-lr-cca}}(\kappa)$ *is negligible in* κ:

$$
\mathsf{Adv}_{\mathsf{PKE}, \mathcal{A}}^{\lambda\text{-lr-cca}}(\kappa) :=
$$
$$
\left| \Pr \left[\gamma' = \gamma : \begin{array}{l} (PK, SK) \leftarrow \mathsf{Kg}(1^\kappa), \gamma \leftarrow_R \{0,1\}, \\ (M_0, M_1, St) \leftarrow \mathcal{A}^{\mathcal{D}_{sk}(\cdot), \mathcal{O}_{sk}^\lambda(\cdot)}(PK) \text{ s.t. } |M_0| = |M_1|, \\ C^* \leftarrow \mathsf{Enc}(PK, M_\gamma), \gamma' \leftarrow \mathcal{A}^{\mathcal{D}_{sk}(\cdot)}(St, C^*). \end{array} \right] - \tfrac{1}{2} \right|.
$$

The *leakage rate* of a λ-LR-CCA secure PKE scheme is defined as $\lambda/|SK|$, where $|SK|$ denotes the secret-key length. If $\lambda/|SK|$ can be made arbitrarily close to 1 by properly choosing the parameter of the scheme, we call such scheme *leakage-flexible*.

One-Time Lossy Filters. One-time lossy filter (OT-LF), a simplified lossy algebraic filter [20], is a special collection of one-way functions. It can be operated in either an "injective mode", in which the function is injective (not requiring efficiently invertible), or a "lossy mode", in which the function is non-injective.

Definition 3. *A collection of* $(\mathsf{Dom}, \ell_{\mathsf{LF}})$-*one-time lossy filter consists of three PPT algorithms* $(\mathsf{FGen}, \mathsf{FEval}, \mathsf{FTag})$. *The key generation algorithm* $\mathsf{FGen}(1^\kappa)$, *on input* 1^κ, *generates an evaluation key* ek *and a trapdoor* td *(that allows for efficiently sampling a lossy tag). The evaluation key* ek *defines a tag space* $\mathcal{T} = \{0,1\}^* \times \mathcal{T}_c$ *that contains the disjoint sets of lossy tags* $\mathcal{T}_{loss} \subseteq \mathcal{T}$ *and injective tags* $\mathcal{T}_{inj} \subseteq \mathcal{T}$. *For an evaluation key* ek *and a tag* $t \in \mathcal{T}$, *the evaluation algorithm* $\mathsf{FEval}(ek, t, x)$ *maps* $x \in \mathsf{Dom}$ *to a unique image* $y = f_{ek,t}(x)$. *For a trapdoor* td *and an auxiliary part* $t_a \in \{0, 1\}^*$, *the lossy tag generation algorithm* $\mathsf{FTag}(td, t_a)$ *computes a core tag* $t_c \in \mathcal{T}_c$ *such that* $(t_a, t_c) \in \mathcal{T}_{loss}$. *We require that OT-LF has the following properties.*

Lossiness. *If* t *is injective, then so is the function* $f_{ek,t}(x)$. *If* t *is lossy, then* $f_{ek,t}(x)$ *computes a lossy function, which has only* $2^{\ell_{\mathsf{LF}}}$ *possible outputs.*

Additionally, it is possible to set the evaluation key so that the parameter ℓ_{LF} is constant even for larger domain.

Indistinguishability. *A lossy tag and a random tag are computationally indistinguishable for any PPT adversary $\mathcal{A}$, i.e.,*

$$\mathsf{Adv}_{\mathsf{LF},\mathcal{A}}^{\mathsf{ind}}(\kappa) := |\Pr[\mathcal{A}(ek,(t_a,t_c)) = 1] - \Pr[\mathcal{A}(ek,(t_a,t_c')) = 1]|$$

is negligible in κ, where $(ek,td) \leftarrow \mathsf{FGen}(1^\kappa)$, $t_a \leftarrow \mathcal{A}(ek)$, $t_c \leftarrow \mathsf{FTag}(td,t_a)$ and $t_c' \leftarrow_R \mathcal{T}_c$.

Evasiveness. *It is hard to generate a fresh non-injective tag for any PPT adversary $\mathcal{A}$ even given a lossy tag, i.e.,*

$$\mathsf{Adv}_{\mathsf{LF},\mathcal{A}}^{\mathsf{eva}}(\kappa) := \Pr\left[\begin{array}{cc} (t_a',t_c') \neq (t_a,t_c) \,\wedge & (ek,td) \leftarrow \mathsf{FGen}(1^\kappa), \\ (t_a',t_c') \in \mathcal{T} \setminus \mathcal{T}_{inj} & : t_a \leftarrow \mathcal{A}(ek), t_c \leftarrow \mathsf{FTag}(td,t_a), \\ & (t_a',t_c') \leftarrow \mathcal{A}(ek,(t_a,t_c)). \end{array}\right]$$

is negligible in κ.

Hash Proof System. Hash proof system (HPS) was introduced by Cramer and Shoup [8]. For simplicity, we describe it as a key-encapsulation mechanism, as did in [22].

Let $\mathcal{PK}$, $\mathcal{SK}$ and $\mathcal{K}$ be the sets of public keys, secret keys and encapsulated keys. Let $\mathcal{C}$ be the set of (all possible) ciphertexts and $\mathcal{V} \subset \mathcal{C}$ be the set of all *valid* ciphertexts. Let $\mathcal{W}$ be a set and let χ be an injective map from $\mathcal{W}$ to $\mathcal{V}$. If for any ciphertext $c \in \mathcal{V}$, there exists a $w \in \mathcal{W}$ such that $\chi(w) = c$, we say that $(\mathcal{C}, \mathcal{V}, \mathcal{W}, \chi)$ is a subset membership problem and w is a witness of c. We require that there are efficient algorithms for sampling $sk \in \mathcal{SK}$, $c \in \mathcal{V}$ together with a witness $w \in \mathcal{W}$ and $c \in \mathcal{C} \setminus \mathcal{V}$ uniformly at random.

Let $\Lambda_{sk} : \mathcal{C} \to \mathcal{K}$ be a family of hash functions indexed by $sk \in \mathcal{SK}$. We say that Λ_{sk} is projective if there exists a projection $\mu : \mathcal{SK} \to \mathcal{PK}$ such that $\mu(sk)$ defines the action of Λ_{sk} over the subset $\mathcal{V}$. In contrast, nothing is guaranteed for $c \in \mathcal{C} \setminus \mathcal{V}$. In a hash proof system, it should be hard to compute $\Lambda_{sk}(c)$ from $\mu(sk)$ and $c \in \mathcal{C} \setminus \mathcal{V}$, which is guaranteed by the universal property of HPS (defined later in Definition 4). A HPS assumes the hardness of the subset membership problem over $\mathcal{C}$, meaning that for any PPT adversary

$$\mathsf{Adv}_{\mathsf{HPS},\mathcal{A}}^{\mathsf{smp}}(\kappa) = \Pr[\mathcal{A}(\mathcal{C},\mathcal{V},c) = 1 \mid c \leftarrow_R \mathcal{V}] - \Pr[\mathcal{A}(\mathcal{C},\mathcal{V},c) = 1 \mid c \leftarrow_R \mathcal{C} \setminus \mathcal{V}]$$

is negligible in κ.

Definition 4 (Universal hash proof system). *A hash proof system (HPS) consists of a tuple of PPT algorithms $(\mathsf{Param}, \mathsf{Priv}, \mathsf{Pub})$. The parameter generation algorithm $\mathsf{Param}(1^\kappa)$, on input 1^κ, generates an instance of $\mathsf{param} = (\mathsf{group}, \mathcal{C}, \mathcal{V}, \mathcal{PK}, \mathcal{SK}, \mathcal{K}, \mu, \Lambda_{(\cdot)})$, where group may contain additional structural parameters. For $sk \in \mathcal{SK}$ and $c \in \mathcal{C}$, the private evaluation algorithm $\mathsf{Priv}(sk,c)$ computes $\mathsf{Priv}(sk,c) = \Lambda_{sk}(c)$. For $pk = \mu(sk)$ and a witness w indicating that $c \in \mathcal{V}$, the public evaluation algorithm $\mathsf{Pub}(pk,c,w)$ computes $\mathsf{Pub}(pk,c,w) = \Lambda_{sk}(c)$.*

We say that a hash proof system is ϵ-universal, if for all $pk = \mu(sk)$, all $c \in \mathcal{C} \setminus \mathcal{V}$ and all $K \in \mathcal{K}$, it holds that $\Pr[\mathsf{Priv}(sk, c) = K \mid \mu(sk) = pk] \leq \epsilon$, where the probability space is defined by choosing $sk \in \mathcal{SK}$ uniformly at random. We sometimes call the above value ϵ as the error rate of HPS.

Chameleon Hash Function. A chameleon hash function [23] CH is essentially a keyed and randomized hash function, which consists of three PPT algorithms $(\mathsf{HGen}, \mathsf{HEval}, \mathsf{HEquiv})$. The key generation algorithm $\mathsf{HGen}(1^\kappa)$, on input a security parameter 1^κ, returns a key pair (ek_{ch}, td_{ch}). Given a preimage $x \in \{0,1\}^*$ and a randomness $r \in \mathcal{R}$, $\mathsf{HEval}(ek_{ch}, x; r)$ computes a hash value y. If r is uniformly distributed over $\mathcal{R}$, so is y over its range. We require that CH is collision-resistant, meaning that for any PPT adversary $\mathcal{A}$, the following probability

$$\mathsf{Adv}^{cr}_{\mathsf{CH}, \mathcal{A}}(1^\kappa) :=$$
$$\Pr\left[\begin{matrix} (x', r') \neq (x, r) \wedge \\ \mathsf{HEval}(ek_{ch}, x'; r') = \mathsf{HEval}(ek_{ch}, x; r) \end{matrix} : \begin{matrix} (ek_{ch}, td_{ch}) \leftarrow \mathsf{HGen}(1^\kappa) \\ (x', r', x, r) \leftarrow \mathcal{A}(ek_{ch}) \end{matrix} \right]$$

is negligible in κ. We further require that given x, r, x' and the trapdoor td_{ch}, $\mathsf{HEquiv}(td_{ch}, x, r, x')$ computes r' such that $\mathsf{HEval}(ek_{ch}, x'; r') = \mathsf{HEval}(ek_{ch}, x; r)$ and the distribution r' is uniform over $\mathcal{R}$ given only ek_{ch} and x.

3 Refined Subgroup Indistinguishability Assumption

In this section, we present the formal definition of Refined Subgroup Indistinguishability (RSI) assumption and instantiate it under two number-theoretical assumptions.

Let $\mathsf{Gen}(1^\kappa)$ be a group generation algorithm that, on input a security parameter 1^κ, outputs a description of a finite commutative multiplicative group $\mathcal{G} = (\mathbb{G}, T, g, h)$, where $\mathbb{G}$ is a direct product of two groups: $\mathbb{G} = G_{\tau_1} \times G_{\tau_2}$, such that each group G_{τ_i} is a cyclic group of order τ_i, and g, h are generators of G_{τ_1}, G_{τ_2} respectively. We require that: (1) elements in $\mathbb{G}$ are efficiently checkable; (2) $\gcd(\tau_1, \tau_2) = 1$. This implies that $\mathbb{G}$ is also a cyclic group with order $\tau_1 \tau_2$; (3) an upper bound $T \geq \tau_1 \cdot \tau_2$ is given in the group description, such that for $x \leftarrow_R \mathbb{Z}_T$, $x \bmod \tau_1 \tau_2$ is ϵ-uniform over $\mathbb{Z}_{\tau_1 \tau_2}$, where $\epsilon = \epsilon(\kappa)$ is negligible in κ. This implies that for $x \leftarrow_R \mathbb{Z}_T$, g^x (resp. h^x) is ϵ-uniform over G_{τ_1} (resp. G_{τ_2}).

Definition 5. *Let* $\mathcal{G} = (\mathbb{G}, T, g, h) \leftarrow \mathsf{Gen}(1^\kappa)$. *The refined subgroup indistinguishability (RSI) assumption in group* $\mathbb{G}$ *states that for any PPT adversary* $\mathcal{A}$, *the advantage*

$$\mathsf{Adv}^{rsi}_{\mathcal{G}, \mathcal{A}}(\kappa) := |\Pr[\mathcal{A}(\mathcal{G}, \tau) = 1 \mid \tau \leftarrow_R G_{\tau_1}] - \Pr[\mathcal{A}(\mathcal{G}, \tau) = 1 \mid \tau \leftarrow_R \mathbb{G}]|$$

is negligible in κ.

From the above refined subgroup indistinguishability assumption, it is not hard to derive the following lemma.

Lemma 2. *Let* $\mathcal{G} = (\mathbb{G}, T, g, h) \leftarrow \mathsf{Gen}(1^\kappa)$. *If the refined subgroup indistinguishability assumption in group* $\mathbb{G}$ *holds, then for any PPT adversary* $\mathcal{B}$

$$|\Pr[\mathcal{B}(\mathcal{G}, x) = 1 \mid x \leftarrow_R G_{\tau_1}] - \Pr[\mathcal{B}(\mathcal{G}, x) = 1 \mid x \leftarrow_R \mathbb{G} \setminus G_{\tau_1}]| \leq 2\mathsf{Adv}^{\mathrm{rsi}}_{\mathcal{G}, \mathcal{A}}(\kappa) \quad (1)$$

$$|\Pr[\mathcal{B}(\mathcal{G}, x) = 1 \mid x \leftarrow_R G_{\tau_1}] - \Pr[\mathcal{B}(\mathcal{G}, x \cdot h) = 1 \mid x \leftarrow_R G_{\tau_1}]| \leq 2\mathsf{Adv}^{\mathrm{rsi}}_{\mathcal{G}, \mathcal{A}}(\kappa) \quad (2)$$

Finally, we present two instantiations of the refined subgroup indistinguishability assumptions: one is over groups of unknown order and the other is over groups of known order.

Example 1 (Instantiation under the QR assumption). Let p, q, p', q' be distinct primes with $p = 2p' + 1$ and $q = 2q' + 1$. For security parameter κ, p' and q' are both at least κ bits in length. Let $N = pq$ and $N' = p'q'$. From [8], $\mathbb{Z}_N^*$ has a unique subgroup $\mathbb{J}_N$ which is the set of elements in $\mathbb{Z}_N^*$ with Jacobi symbol 1. Let $\mathbb{QR}_N$ be the set of the quadratic residues modulo N and $G_2 = \{\pm 1\}$. Then, $\mathbb{J}_N = \mathbb{QR}_N \times G_2$ and $\gcd(2, N') = 1$. Additionally, $h = -1$ generates G_2, and for a random $x \leftarrow_R \mathbb{Z}_N^*$, with overwhelming probability $g = x^2 \bmod N$ generates group $\mathbb{QR}_N$. Set $T = (N - 1)/4$. Then, for $x \leftarrow_R \mathbb{Z}_T$, $x \bmod 2N'$ is $O(2^{-\kappa})$-uniform in $\mathbb{Z}_{2N'}$. The quadratic residuosity (QR) assumption states that it is hard to distinguish a random element in $\mathbb{J}_N$ from a random element in $\mathbb{QR}_N$. So, the QR assumption is an instantiation of the RSI assumption if we set $(\mathbb{G}, T, g, h) \leftarrow \mathsf{Gen}(1^\kappa)$, where $\mathbb{G} = \mathbb{J}_N$, $G_{\tau_1} = \mathbb{QR}_N$ (with $\tau_1 = N'$), $G_{\tau_2} = \{\pm 1\}$ (with $\tau_2 = 2$), $T = (N - 1)/4$, $g = x^2 \bmod N$ (for $x \leftarrow_R \mathbb{Z}_N^*$) and $h = -1$.

Example 2 (Instantiation over a group of known order). Let $\mathbf{p}, p, q$ be distinct primes with $\mathbf{p} = 2pq + 1$. For security parameter κ, p and q are both at least κ bits in length. Clearly, $\mathbb{Z}_\mathbf{p}^*$ has a unique subgroup of order $N = pq$, denoted by $\mathbb{QR}_\mathbf{p}$, which is the set of the quadratic residues modulo $\mathbf{p}$. Moreover, $\gcd(p, q) = 1$ and $\mathbb{QR}_\mathbf{p}$ can be uniquely decomposed as a direct product $\mathbb{QR}_\mathbf{p} = G_p \times G_q$, where G_p, G_q are cyclic groups of prime orders p, q respectively. For $x, y \leftarrow_R \mathbb{Z}_\mathbf{p}^*$, with overwhelming probability $g = x^q \bmod \mathbf{p}$ generates G_p and $h = y^p \bmod \mathbf{p}$ generates G_q. The refined subgroup indistinguishability assumption over group $\mathbb{QR}_\mathbf{p}$ is conjectured to hold if integer factorization of N is hard [28]. So, we obtain an instantiation of RSI assumption by setting $(\mathbb{G}, T, g, h) \leftarrow \mathsf{Gen}(1^\kappa)$, where $\mathbb{G} = \mathbb{QR}_\mathbf{p}$, $G_{\tau_1} = G_p$ (with $\tau_1 = p$), $G_{\tau_2} = G_q$ (with $\tau_2 = q$), $T = pq$, $g = x^q \bmod \mathbf{p}$ (for $x \leftarrow_R \mathbb{Z}_\mathbf{p}^*$) and $h = y^p$ (for $y \leftarrow_R \mathbb{Z}_\mathbf{p}^*$).

4   Leakage-Resilient CCA-secure PKE under the RSI Assumption

Following Qin and Liu's generic construction of leakage-resilient CCA-secure PKE schemes from any universal hash proof systems and any one-time lossy filters [31], we present an efficient instantiation under the refined subgroup indistinguishability assumption in this section.

The rest of this section is organized as follows. In Section 4.1, we give an overview of Qin and Liu's approach to leakage-resilient CCA-security. In section 4.2 and Section 4.3, we present efficient constructions of universal hash proof system and one-time lossy filter from any RSI assumption respectively. Finally, in Section 4.4, we show how to construct a leakage-flexible (with leakage rate of $[0,1)$) PKE scheme under a specific RSI assumption.

4.1 Review of Qin and Liu's Approach to LR-CCA Security

Recently, Qin and Liu [31] proved that a universal hash proof (UHP) system, combined with a one-time lossy filter (OT-LF), yields a public-key encryption (PKE) scheme that is secure against key-leakage chosen-ciphertext attacks. This approach results in a simple and efficient CCA-secure PKE scheme with a higher leakage rate than those constructions solely from UHPs [27,25].

More precisely, they applied a UHP system as a basic (CPA-secure) encryption scheme to hide the plaintext and then applied an OT-LF as a message authentication code (MAC) to verify the well-formedness of the ciphertext. In fact, the HPS is used as a key encapsulation mechanism and the encapsulated key is exactly the hash value $\Lambda_{sk}(c)$, which functions in two ways: (1) it is used as an input of a random extractor to distill a random string for hiding a plaintext; (2) it is used as a MAC key to authenticate one-time lossy filter's tag. By the hardness of the underlying subset membership problem and the universality property of HPS, $\Lambda_{sk}(c)$ is computationally indistinguishable from a random variable that has at least $\log(1/\epsilon)$ min-entropy if HPS is ϵ-universal. While in the security proof, the challenge ciphertext uses a lossy LF tag which results in a MAC that only reveals a constant amount of information on $\Lambda_{sk}(c)$. Thus, the PKE scheme can withstand almost $\log(1/\epsilon)$-bit leakage of the secret key. Suppose that (Param, Priv, Pub) is an ϵ-universal HPS, (FGen, FEval, FTag) is a $(\mathcal{K}, \ell_{\mathsf{LF}})$-one-time lossy filter, $\mathcal{H}$ is a family of universal hash functions from $\mathcal{K}$ to $\{0,1\}^m$. Then, the PKE scheme (Kg, Enc, Dec) with message space $\{0,1\}^m$ from [31] works as follows.

- $(PK, SK) \leftarrow \mathsf{Kg}(1^\kappa)$. Run $\mathsf{Param}(1^\kappa)$ to produce a HPS instance: param $=$ (group, $\mathcal{C}, \mathcal{V}, \mathcal{PK}, \mathcal{SK}, \mathcal{K}, \mu, \Lambda_{(\cdot)}$). Pick $sk \leftarrow_R \mathcal{SK}$ and set $pk = \mu(sk)$. Run $(ek, td) \leftarrow \mathsf{FGen}(1^\kappa)$. Return $PK = (pk, ek)$ and $SK = sk$.
- $C \leftarrow \mathsf{Enc}(PK, M)$. For $M \in \{0,1\}^m$, it samples a random $c \in \mathcal{V}$ together with its witness w, and then computes $K = \mathsf{Pub}(pk, c, w)$. Next, it samples $h \leftarrow_R \mathcal{H}$ and $t_c \leftarrow_R \mathcal{T}_c$. Finally, it returns

$$C = (c, h, h(K) \oplus M, \mathsf{FEval}(ek, t, K), t_c)$$

where $t = (t_a, t_c)$ and $t_a = (c, h, h(K) \oplus M)$.
- $M/\perp \leftarrow \mathsf{Dec}(SK, C)$: For $C = (c, h, \psi, v, t_c)$, it computes $K' = \mathsf{Priv}(sk, c)$, and then checks whether $\mathsf{FEval}(ek, t, K') = v$ where $t = ((c, h, \psi), t_c)$. If not, it returns $\perp$, else returns $M = h(K') \oplus \psi$.

From [31], the security of the above scheme is established by the following theorem.

Theorem 1. *If there exists an ϵ-universal HPS and a $(\mathcal{K}, \ell_{\mathsf{LF}})$-one-time lossy filter, then there exists a CCA-secure PKE scheme with any leakage of λ bits,* *as long as $\lambda \leq \log(1/\epsilon) - m - \ell_{\mathsf{LF}} - \omega(\log \kappa)$, where m is the plaintext length. Additionally, by reducing the error rate ϵ of HPS, the leakage rate in the above scheme can be arbitrarily close to $\log(1/\epsilon)/|sk|$.*

4.2 Universal Hash Proof System from the RSI Assumption

Let $\mathcal{G} = (\mathbb{G}, T, g, h)$, where $\mathbb{G} = G_{\tau_1} \times G_{\tau_2}$, be a group description returned by $\mathsf{Gen}(1^\kappa)$. We can build a subset membership problem by setting $\mathcal{C} = \mathbb{G}$ and $\mathcal{V} = G_{\tau_1}$ (with witness set $\mathcal{W} = \mathbb{Z}_T$). From Lemma 2, this subset membership problem is hard under the refined subgroup indistinguishability assumption. Next, we build a universal hash proof system for $(\mathcal{C}, \mathcal{V})$.

Construction 1 (UHP). *The hash proof system* $(\mathsf{Param}, \mathsf{Priv}, \mathsf{Pub})$ *is defined as follows:*

- $\mathsf{Param}(1^\kappa)$: *run* $\mathcal{G} = (\mathbb{G}, T, g, h) \leftarrow \mathsf{Gen}(1^\kappa)$, *where* $\mathbb{G} = G_{\tau_1} \times G_{\tau_2}$. *Define*

$$\mathcal{C} = \mathbb{G}, \quad \mathcal{V} = G_{\tau_1}, \quad \mathcal{W} = \mathbb{Z}_T, \quad \mathcal{PK} = \mathbb{G}, \quad \mathcal{SK} = \mathbb{Z}_T, \quad \mathcal{K} = \mathbb{G}.$$

Clearly, for $c \in \mathcal{V}$, *there exists a witness* $w \in \mathcal{W}$ *such that* $c = g^w$. *For* $sk = x \in \mathcal{SK}$ *and* $c \in \mathcal{C}$, *we define*

$$\mu(sk) = g^x \in \mathbb{G}, \quad \Lambda_{sk}(c) = c^x \in \mathbb{G}$$

Finally, $\mathsf{Param}(1^\kappa)$ *outputs* $\mathsf{param} = (\mathcal{G}, \mathcal{C}, \mathcal{V}, \mathcal{PK}, \mathcal{SK}, \mathcal{K}, \mu, \Lambda_{(\cdot)})$.
- $\mathsf{Priv}(sk, c)$: *for* $sk \in \mathcal{SK}$ *and* $c \in \mathcal{C}$, *compute* $K = \Lambda_{sk}(c) = c^x$, *where* $sk = x$.
- $\mathsf{Pub}(pk, c, w)$: *for* $pk = \mu(sk) = g^x \in \mathbb{G}$ *and a witness* $w \in \mathcal{W}$ *such that* $c = g^w \in \mathbb{G}$, *compute* $K = pk^w$ *which equals* $\Lambda_{sk}(c) = c^x$.

Theorem 2. *Suppose that* $\tilde{q} \geq 2$ *is the smallest prime factor of* τ_2. *Then, construction 1 gives a* $1/\tilde{q}$-*universal hash proof system.*

Proof. Clearly, correctness follows from the definitions of the projection μ and the projective hash function $\Lambda_{sk}(\cdot)$, and the hardness of the subset membership follows from the RSI assumption and Lemma 2. It remains to prove its universality. To do so, it suffices to show that for all $pk = \mu(sk) \in \mathcal{PK}$, all $c \in \mathcal{C} \setminus \mathcal{V}$ and all $K \in \mathcal{K}$, it holds that $\Pr[\Lambda_{sk}(c) = K \mid \mu(sk) = pk] \leq 1/\tilde{q}$. Recall that g has order τ_1. So, $pk = g^{sk} = g^{sk \bmod \tau_1}$ is determined only by the value $sk \bmod \tau_1$. If sk is uniform in $\mathbb{Z}_{\tau_1 \tau_2}$ and $\gcd(\tau_1, \tau_2) = 1$, by the Chinese Remainder Theorem, it holds that $sk \bmod \tau_2$ is still uniform over $\mathbb{Z}_{\tau_2}$ even for a fixed pk. Moreover, for any element $c \in \mathcal{C} \setminus \mathcal{V}$, it has a non-trivial component of order (at least) $\tilde{q}$ and thus c^{sk} has at least $\tilde{q}$ possible values uniformly distributed over its support. This means that $\Pr[\Lambda_{sk}(c) = K \mid \mu(sk) = pk] \leq 1/\tilde{q}$. □

REDUCING THE ERROR RATE. As introduced in [8], we can reduce the error rate of a universal hash proof system from ϵ to ϵ^n by a trivial "n-fold parallelization".

4.3 One-Time Lossy Filter from the RSI Assumption

In this section, we first propose a variant of one-time lossy filters, namely all-but-one (ABO) lossy functions. Then, we show how to construct an ABO lossy function under the refined subgroup indistinguishability assumption. Finally, we show how to derive a one-time lossy filter from an ABO lossy function with large tag space, whose size is determined by κ.

ALL-BUT-ONE LOSSY FUNCTIONS. ABO lossy functions are a family of functions parameterized with a tag. All tags are injective, leading to injective functions, except for one lossy tag, leading to a lossy function. ABO lossy functions are conceptionally simpler than one-time lossy filters. For one-time lossy filters, a tag consists of an auxiliary and a core tag part; lossy tags are produced via a trapdoor for any auxiliary tags. For ABO lossy functions, it simply uses arbitrary bit strings as tags. There is only one lossy tag which can be predetermined.

Definition 6 (ABO lossy functions). *A collection of* (Dom, ℓ)-*ABO lossy functions with tag space* B *consists of two PPT algorithms* $(\mathsf{ABOGen}, \mathsf{ABOEval})$. *The key generation algorithm* $\mathsf{ABOGen}(1^\kappa, b^*)$ *takes as input a security parameter* 1^κ *and any* $b^* \in B$, *and samples an evaluation key* ek. *The evaluation algorithm* $\mathsf{ABOEval}(ek, b, x)$, *for* $b \in B$ *and* $x \in \mathsf{Dom}$, *computes* $f_{ek,b}(x)$. *We require the following properties.*

Lossiness. *For injective tags (i.e.,* $b \neq b^*$), $\mathsf{ABOEval}(ek, b, x)$ *computes an injective function* $f_{ek,b}(x)$. *For the lossy tag* b^*, $\mathsf{ABOEval}(ek, b^*, x)$ *computes a lossy function* $f_{ek,b^*}(x)$ *which only reveals at most* ℓ-*bit information of* x. *We require that by setting the parameter of evaluation key* ek, *the size of domain* Dom *is flexible even for constant* ℓ.

Hidden lossy tag. *For any PPT adversary* $\mathcal{A}$ *and for any* $b_0^*, b_1^* \in B$, *the following advantage*

$$\mathsf{Adv}_{\mathsf{ABO},\mathcal{A}}(\kappa) := |\Pr[\mathcal{A}(1^\kappa, ek_0) = 1] - \Pr[\mathcal{A}(1^\kappa, ek_1) = 1]|$$

is negligible in κ, *where* $ek_0 \leftarrow \mathsf{ABOGen}(1^\kappa, b_0^*)$ *and* $ek_1 \leftarrow \mathsf{ABOGen}(1^\kappa, b_1^*)$.

The conception of ABO lossy functions is very similar to ABO lossy *trapdoor* functions introduced by Peikert and Waters [29]. However, we do not require efficient inversion. Instead, we require that the lossy function reveals only a constant amount of information on its input even for flexibly large domain. The following construction from an ABO lossy function $(\mathsf{ABOGen}, \mathsf{ABOEval})$ with a tag space B (even for $B = \{0, 1\}$) results in a new one $(\widetilde{\mathsf{ABOGen}}, \widetilde{\mathsf{ABOEval}})$ with tag space $B^{\tilde{n}}$ for any positive integer $\tilde{n}$ (the analogous construction for ABO lossy trapdoor functions are shown in [29]).

Construction 2. *Let* $(\mathsf{ABOGen}, \mathsf{ABOEval})$ *be a collection of* (Dom, ℓ)-*ABO lossy functions with tag space* B. *We define* $(\widetilde{\mathsf{ABOGen}}, \widetilde{\mathsf{ABOEval}})$ *as follows.*

- $\widetilde{\mathsf{ABOGen}}(1^\kappa, \widetilde{b}^*)$: *for* $\widetilde{b}^* = (b_1^*, \cdots, b_{\widetilde{n}}^*) \in B^{\widetilde{n}}$, *it runs* $ek_i \leftarrow \mathsf{ABOGen}(1^\kappa, b_i^*)$, $i = 1, \ldots, \widetilde{n}$, *and returns* $\widetilde{ek} = (ek_1, \ldots, ek_{\widetilde{n}})$.
- $\widetilde{\mathsf{ABOEval}}(\widetilde{ek}, \widetilde{b}, x)$: *for* $\widetilde{b} = (b_1, \cdots, b_{\widetilde{n}}) \in B^{\widetilde{n}}$ *and* $x \in \mathsf{Dom}$, *it computes*

$$f_{\widetilde{ek},\widetilde{b}}(x) = (f_{ek_1,b_1}(x), \ldots, f_{ek_{\widetilde{n}},b_{\widetilde{n}}}(x)).$$

Lemma 3. *Construction 2 gives a collection of* $(\mathsf{Dom}, \widetilde{n}\ell)$*-ABO lossy functions with tag space* $B^{\widetilde{n}}$.

Proof. The proof is nearly straightforward. First, for a lossy tag $\widetilde{b}^*$, all $f_{ek_i,b_i^*}(x)$s work in lossy mode and thus reveal at most $\widetilde{n}\ell$-bit information of their common input x. Secondly, for an injective tag $\widetilde{b} \neq \widetilde{b}^*$, there must exist an index $i \in [\widetilde{n}]$ such that $b_i \neq b_i^*$. That is, $f_{ek_i,b_i}(x)$ computes an injective function and so does $f_{\widetilde{ek},\widetilde{b}}(x)$. $\square$

FROM RSI ASSUMPTION TO ABO LOSSY FUNCTIONS. We start from a RSI instance to derive a collection of ABO lossy functions with tag space $\{0,1\}$.

Construction 3. *Let* $\mathcal{G} = (\mathbb{G}, T, g, h)$ *and* $\mathbb{G} = G_{\tau_1} \times G_{\tau_2}$ *be defined as in Section 3. Let* $I = (I_{i,j}) \in G_{\tau_2}^{n \times n}$ *be an* $n \times n$ *matrix over group* G_{τ_2}, *where* $I_{i,j} = 1$ *if* $i \neq j$ *and* $I_{i,i} = h$ *for all* $i, j \in [n]$. *Set* $B = \{0,1\}$ *and* $\mathsf{Dom} = \mathbb{Z}_{\tau_2}^n$. *We define* $(\mathsf{ABOGen}, \mathsf{ABOEval})$ *as follows.*

- $\mathsf{ABOGen}(1^\kappa, b^*)$: *for* $b^* \in B$, *it picks* $r_1, \ldots, r_n, s_1, \ldots, s_n \leftarrow_R \mathbb{Z}_T$ *and sets*

$$R = \begin{pmatrix} g^{r_1} \\ g^{r_2} \\ \vdots \\ g^{r_n} \end{pmatrix} \quad S = \begin{pmatrix} g^{r_1 s_1} h^{b^*} & g^{r_1 s_2} & \cdots & g^{r_1 s_n} \\ g^{r_2 s_1} & g^{r_2 s_2} h^{b^*} & \cdots & g^{r_2 s_n} \\ \vdots & \vdots & \ddots & \vdots \\ g^{r_n s_1} & g^{r_n s_2} & \cdots & g^{r_n s_n} h^{b^*} \end{pmatrix}$$

Finally, $\mathsf{ABOGen}(1^\kappa, b^*)$ *returns* $ek = (R, S) \in \mathbb{G}^n \times \mathbb{G}^{n \times n}$.
- $\mathsf{ABOEval}(ek, b, x)$: *for* $ek = (R, S)$, $b \in B$ *and* $x = (x_1, \ldots, x_n) \in \mathbb{Z}_{\tau_2}^n$, *it computes*

$$f_{ek,b}(x) := \left(x \cdot R, x \cdot (S \otimes I^{-b})\right) = \left(g^{\sum_{i=1}^n x_i r_i}, \left(g^{s_j \cdot \sum_i^n x_i r_i} \cdot h^{(b^*-b)x_j}\right)_{j=1}^n\right)$$

where $\otimes$ *denotes the component-wise product of matrices over* $\mathbb{G}$.

Lemma 4. *Construction 3 forms a collection of* $(\mathbb{Z}_{\tau_2}^n, \log \tau_1)$*-ABO lossy functions with tag space* $B = \{0,1\}$.

Proof. It is a straightforward calculation to verify that: (1) for $b = b^*$, $f_{ek,b^*}(x)$ is completely determined by $g^{\sum_{i=1}^n x_i r_i}$ which has only τ_1 possible values; (2) for $b \neq b^*$, $f_{ek,b}(x)$ completely determines the vector $(h^{(b^*-b)x_1}, \ldots, h^{(b^*-b)x_n})$, hence $(x_1, \ldots, x_n)$. So it is an injective map. The remainder is to show its hidden lossy tag property. Let $S[j, k]$ denote the entry of matrix S, located by row j and column k. For any $b_0^*, b_1^* \in B$, let $\mathcal{EK}_i = (R_i, S_i)$, $0 \leq i \leq n$, be the distribution on the function evaluation key, where $R_i = R$ and S_i is almost the same as S except that the first i diagonal elements of S_i are now $(S_i[j,j] = g^{r_j s_j} h^{b_1^*})_{1 \leq j \leq i}$ while the last $n - i$ diagonal elements of S_i are $(S_i[j,j] = g^{r_j s_j} h^{b_0^*})_{i+1 \leq j \leq n}$. Clearly, $\mathcal{EK}_0$ is the distribution output by $\mathsf{ABOGen}(1^\kappa, b_0^*)$ and $\mathcal{EK}_n$ is the distribution output by $\mathsf{ABOGen}(1^\kappa, b_1^*)$. It suffices to show that for any $1 \leq i \leq n$, $\mathcal{EK}_{i-1}$ and $\mathcal{EK}_i$ are computationally indistinguishable under the RSI assumption. To do so, we again define two distributions $\mathcal{EK}'_{i-1} = (R'_{i-1}, S'_{i-1})$ and $\mathcal{EK}'_i = (R'_i, S'_i)$, where $\mathcal{EK}'_{i-1}$ is almost the same as $\mathcal{EK}_{i-1}$ except for the value of $R'_{i-1}[i]$ and $(S'_{i-1}[i,k])_{k \in [n]}$. Now $R'_{i-1}[i] := g^{r_i} h$ while $R_{i-1}[i] = g^{r_i}$, and $(S'_{i-1}[i,k])_{k \in [n]} = ((g^{r_i} h)^{s_k} h^{b_0^*})_{k \in [n]}$ while $(S_{i-1}[i,k])_{k \in [n]} = (g^{r_i s_k} h^{b_0^*})_{k \in [n]}$. Similarly, $\mathcal{EK}'_i$ is almost the same as $\mathcal{EK}_i$ except for the value of $R'_i[i]$ and $(S'_i[i,k])_{k \in [n]}$. Now $R'_i[i] := g^{r_i} h$ while $R_i[i] = g^{r_i}$, and $(S'_i[i,k])_{k \in [n]} = ((g^{r_i} h)^{s_k} h^{b_1^*})_{k \in [n]}$ while $(S_i[i,k])_{k \in [n]} = (g^{r_i s_k} h^{b_1^*})_{k \in [n]}$. It is a straightforward reduction to show that if there exists a PPT algorithm $\mathcal{A}$ that can distinguish $\mathcal{EK}_{i-1}$ and $\mathcal{EK}'_{i-1}$, we can construct a PPT algorithm $\mathcal{D}$ to distinguish the distributions defined in the left side of Eq. (2). This also applies to $\mathcal{EK}_i$ and $\mathcal{EK}'_i$. From Lemma 2, it follows that

$$\Pr[\mathcal{A}(ek) = 1 \mid ek \leftarrow_R \mathcal{EK}_{i-1}] - \Pr[\mathcal{A}(ek) = 1 \mid ek \leftarrow_R \mathcal{EK}'_{i-1}] \leq 2\mathsf{Adv}^{\mathsf{rsi}}_{\mathcal{G},\mathcal{D}}(\kappa) \quad (3)$$

$$\Pr[\mathcal{A}(ek) = 1 \mid ek \leftarrow_R \mathcal{EK}_i] - \Pr[\mathcal{A}(ek) = 1 \mid ek \leftarrow_R \mathcal{EK}'_i] \leq 2\mathsf{Adv}^{\mathsf{rsi}}_{\mathcal{G},\mathcal{D}}(\kappa) \quad (4)$$

Additionally, given $r_1, \ldots, r_n, s_1, \ldots, s_n \leftarrow_R \mathbb{Z}_T$, (R'_{i-1}, S'_{i-1}) take exactly the same values as (R'_i, S'_i) except that $S'_{i-1}[i,i] = (g^{r_i} h)^{s_i} h^{b_0^*}$ but $S'_i[i,i] = (g^{r_i} h)^{s_i} h^{b_1^*}$. Next we will show that $S'_{i-1}[i,i]$ is statistically indistinguishable to $S'_i[i,i]$, given the value of $r_1, \ldots, r_n, s_1, \ldots, s_n$.

Observe that the information of s_i is characterized by g^{s_i} in both (R'_{i-1}, S'_{i-1}) and (R'_i, S'_i). If s_i is chosen from $\mathbb{Z}_{\tau_1 \tau_2}$ uniformly at random, $s_i \bmod \tau_2$ is uniform over $\mathbb{Z}_{\tau_2}$ even conditioned on the value of $s_i \bmod \tau_1$, according to Chinese Remainder Theorem. Now that s_i is ϵ-uniform over $\mathbb{Z}_{\tau_1 \tau_2}$, so $s_i \bmod \tau_2$ is also ϵ-uniform over $\mathbb{Z}_{\tau_2}$, even conditioned on the value of $g^{s_i} = g^{s_i \bmod \tau_1}$. Consequently,

$$S'_{i-1}[i,i] =$$
$$(g^{r_i} h)^{s_i} h^{b_0^*} = g^{r_i s_i} h^{s_i \bmod \tau_2 + b_0^*} \approx_s g^{r_i s_i} h^{s_i \bmod \tau_2 + b_1^*} = (g^{r_i} h)^{s_i} h^{b_1^*} = S'_i[i,i].$$

So, $\mathcal{EK}'_{i-1} \approx_s \mathcal{EK}'_i$. Combined with Eq. (3) and Eq. (4), we have that $\mathcal{EK}_{i-1} \approx_c \mathcal{EK}_i$ holds for all i. This completes the proof of Lemma 4. $\qquad \square$

Applying the method of Construction 2, we can amplify the tag space $\{0,1\}$ in Construction 3 to space $\{0,1\}^{\tilde{n}}$ for any positive integer $\tilde{n}$, resulting in a $(\mathbb{Z}^n_{\tau_2}, \tilde{n} \log \tau_1)$-ABO lossy function. However, the information revealed by the lossy function increases linearly with the extension factor (i.e., $\tilde{n}$) of the tag space via this method. To solve this problem, we can set R as a global parameter. That is, each function evaluation key ek_i has the same R but different S_i. As we proved earlier, for a lossy tag b_i^*, $f_{ek_i, b^*}(x)$ is completely determined by the value $x \cdot R = g^{\sum_{i=1}^{n} x_i r_i}$ which has τ_1 possible values. Thus, the $\tilde{n}$ concatenation

$f_{ek_1, b_1^*}(x) || \cdots || f_{ek_{\tilde{n}}, b_{\tilde{n}}^*}(x)$ in Construction 2 still has τ_1 possible values. In this way, we have a $(\mathbb{Z}_{\tau_2}^n, \log \tau_1)$-ABO lossy function with large tag space $B = \{0,1\}^{\tilde{n}}$ for any positive integer $\tilde{n}$.

Next, we show that if the order τ_2 of G_{τ_2} is large enough, it is possible to obtain ABO lossy function with large tag space directly. For a security parameter κ, let $\theta = \omega(\log \kappa)$ be a suitable tag length. We assume that $\theta \leq \lfloor \log \tau_2 \rfloor - 1$. Set $\tau_2' = \lfloor \tau_2/(2^\theta - 1) \rfloor$ and thus $\tau_2' \geq 2$. We introduce two variants of Construction 3.

Variant I. This variant is the same as Construction 3, except for the tag space and the domain. In this case, we set $B = \{0,1\}^\theta$ and $\mathsf{Dom} = \mathbb{Z}_{\tau_2'}^n$. Clearly, for an injective tag b and an input $x = (x_1, \ldots, x_n) \in \mathbb{Z}_{\tau_2'}^n$, $|(b^* - b)x_i| \leq \tau_2$ for all i. Since h has order τ_2, x_i is completely determined by the group element $h^{(b^* - b)x_i}$ and the value $(b^* - b)$, i.e., $x_i = (\log_h h^{(b^* - b)x_i})/(b^* - b)$. Thus, $f_{ek, b}(x)$ computes an injective function. While for the lossy tag b^*, $f_{ek, b^*}(x)$ reveals at most $\log \tau_1$ bits information of its input x. In this case, Construction 3 now becomes a collection of $(\mathbb{Z}_{\tau_2'}^n, \log \tau_1)$-ABO lossy functions with tag space $B = \{0,1\}^\theta$. Additionally, we can amplify the domain size with large n without increasing the parameter $\log \tau_1$. Construction 3 is in fact the special case of $\theta = 1$.

Variant II. If τ_2 is a prime or the smallest prime factor of τ_2 is larger than $2^\theta - 1$, we can set $B = \{0,1\}^\theta$ and $\mathsf{Dom} = \mathbb{Z}_{\tau_2}^n$. In this case, $\gcd(b^* - b, \tau_2) = 1$, hence $(b^* - b)^{-1} \mod \tau_2$ always exists. It is not hard to see that Construction 3 now becomes a collection of $(\mathbb{Z}_{\tau_2}^n, \log \tau_1)$-ABO lossy functions with tag space $B = \{0,1\}^\theta$.

If τ_1 is a prime, we further choose $n = 1$ and $\mathsf{Dom} = \mathbb{Z}_{\tau_1 \tau_2}$ (note that the domain is now further enlarged to $\mathbb{Z}_{\tau_1 \tau_2}$), and reduce the evaluation key ek to one group element $g^{r_1 s_1} h^{b^*}$. Then, for $x \in \mathbb{Z}_{\tau_1 \tau_2}$ and $b \neq b^*$, $f_{ek, b}(x) = g^{r_1 s_1 x} h^{(b^* - b)x}$ is injective, and gives a collection of $(\mathbb{Z}_{\tau_1 \tau_2}, \log \tau_1)$-ABO lossy functions, which is just the case used later in Section 4.4.

FROM ABO LOSSY FUNCTIONS TO ONE-TIME LOSSY FILTERS. We start from a collection of ABO lossy functions with a large tag space determined by security parameter κ and a family of chameleon hash functions, to derive a collection of one-time lossy filters.

Construction 4. *Let* $(\mathsf{ABOGen}, \mathsf{ABOEval})$ *be a collection of* (Dom, ℓ)-*ABO lossy functions with tag space* B *and let* $(\mathsf{HGen}, \mathsf{HEval}, \mathsf{HEquiv})$ *be a chameleon hash function from* $\{0,1\}^* \times \mathcal{R}$ *to* B. *We define* $\mathsf{LF} = (\mathsf{FGen}, \mathsf{FEval}, \mathsf{FTag})$ *as follows.*

- *$\mathsf{FGen}(1^\kappa)$: for a security parameter 1^κ, it first runs $(ek_{ch}, td_{ch}) \leftarrow \mathsf{HGen}(1^\kappa)$. Then, $\mathsf{FGen}(1^\kappa)$ selects $t_a^* \in \{0,1\}^*$ and $t_c^* \in \mathcal{R}$ uniformly at random, and computes $b^* = \mathsf{HEval}(ek_{ch}, t_a^*; t_c^*)$; Next, it runs $ek' \leftarrow \mathsf{ABOGen}(1^\kappa, b^*)$. Finally, it returns $ek = (ek_{ch}, ek')$ and $td = (td_{ch}, t_a^*, t_c^*)$. Set $\mathcal{T} = \{0,1\}^* \times \mathcal{R}$ and $\mathcal{T}_{loss} = \{(t_a, t_c) : \mathsf{HEval}(ek_{ch}, t_a; t_c) = b^*\}$.*
- *$\mathsf{FEval}(ek, t, x)$: for $t = (t_a, t_c) \in \mathcal{T}$ and $x \in \mathsf{Dom}$, it computes*

$$b = \mathsf{HEval}(ek_{ch}, t_a; t_c) \text{ and } f_{ek, t}(x) = f_{ek', b}(x).$$

– $\mathsf{FTag}(td, t_a)$: *for* $td = (td_{ch}, t_a^*, t_c^*)$ *and* $t_a \in \{0, 1\}^*$, *it computes*

$$t_c = \mathsf{HEquiv}(td_{ch}, t_a^*, t_c^*, t_a).$$

Theorem 3. *Construction 4 gives a collection of* (Dom, ℓ)-*one-time lossy filters.*

Proof. The proof is very similar to the concrete DCR-based construction in [31]. Due to space limitation, we give it in the full version of this paper. □

4.4 An Efficient Leakage-Flexible CCA-secure PKE

In the previous two subsections, we presented the generic constructions of universal hash proof systems and one-time lossy filters from the refined subgroup indistinguishability assumptions. According to Theorem 1, we immediately obtain the following theorem.

Theorem 4. *Let* $\mathcal{G} = (\mathbb{G}, g, h, T) \leftarrow \mathsf{Gen}(1^\kappa)$, *where* $\mathbb{G} = G_{\tau_1} \times G_{\tau_2}$. *Suppose that the smallest prime factor of* τ_2 *is* $\widetilde{q} \geq 2$. *If the refined subgroup indistinguishability assumption holds over group* $\mathbb{G}$, *then we can construct a* λ-*LR-CCA secure PKE scheme with message space* $\{0, 1\}^m$, *where the amount of leakage is bounded by* $\lambda \leq \mathfrak{n} \log \widetilde{q} - \log \tau_1 - m - \omega(\log \kappa)$ *and* $\mathfrak{n}$ *is a positive integer. In particular, the leakage rate can be made to approach* $\log \widetilde{q} / \log T$.

Next, we instantiate our generic construction under the RSI assumption introduced in Example 2 and obtain a leakage-flexible CCA-secure PKE scheme without pairing. (However, in our QR-based instantiation both the leakage-rate and the parameter are rather poor. The main reason is that the universality of the underlying hash proof system and the lossiness of the underlying one-time lossy filter are not good. For details, see the full version of this paper.)

Parameters. Recall that in Example 2, $\mathbf{p} = 2pq + 1$ is a prime and p, q both are primes too. So, $\mathbb{G} = \mathbb{QR}_{\mathbf{p}}$ can be decomposed as a direct product of two prime-order groups: $\mathbb{QR}_{\mathbf{p}} = G_p \times G_q$. If we choose $\mathfrak{n} = 1$, then by Theorem 2, we may obtain a $1/q$-universal hash proof system with secret key space $\mathcal{SK} = \mathbb{Z}_{pq}$ and encapsulated key space $\mathcal{K} = \mathbb{QR}_{\mathbf{p}}$. While by Theorem 3 for **Variant II**, we can obtain a $(\mathbb{Z}_{pq}, \log p)$-one-time lossy filter. Observe that, every element $K \in \mathbb{QR}_{\mathbf{p}}$ can be efficiently encoded as an element $K' \in \mathbb{Z}_{pq}$ by setting $K' := K - 1$ if $1 \leq K \leq pq$ and $K' := \mathbf{p} - K - 1$ if $pq + 1 \leq K \leq \mathbf{p} - 1$. So, by Theorem 4, we obtain a PKE scheme with leakage $\lambda \leq \log q - \log p - m - \omega(\log \kappa)$. Particularly, the ciphertext only contains two group elements in $\mathbb{Z}_{\mathbf{p}}^*$ (ignoring the other length fixed elements, e.g., the description of a universal hash function and an auxiliary tag). For a 80-bit security level, we choose $m = 80$, $\omega(\log \kappa) = 160$, $|p| = 512$ and $|q| \geq 512$. It suffices to guarantee that pq is hard to factor and thus the refined subgroup indistinguishability assumption in group $\mathbb{QR}_{\mathbf{p}}$ holds. In this case, $\lambda \leq \log q - 752$ and $|SK| \leq \log q + 512$. Therefore, the leakage rate $\frac{\lambda}{|SK|} = \frac{\log q - 752}{\log q + 512} = 1 - \frac{1264}{\log q + 512}$ is arbitrarily close to 1 if we choose a sufficiently large q.

Finally, we give a parameter comparison (for 80-bit security level) of this scheme with known leakage-flexible schemes [10,15] in Table 1 where $1 - \alpha$ denotes the leakage rate, "SXDH" denotes the symmetric external Diffie-Hellman assumption, "DLIN" denotes the decisional linear assumption and "RSI" denotes the refined subgroup indistinguishability assumption. Assume that elements in a group of order q can be encoded as bit strings of length $|q|$. From Table 1, we can see that the ciphertext size (in bits) in our scheme grows slightly faster than the other three schemes. Nevertheless, our scheme has some interesting properties that do not exist in other schemes: simple construction, constant number of group elements in ciphertext and free of pairing.

Table 1. Parameters of leakage-flexible CCA-secure PKE schemes

Scheme	Group Type	Assumption	Group Size # bits	Ciphertext Size # $\mathbb{G}$	Pairing
DHLW10 [10]	Prime	SXDH	160	$\lceil (2/\alpha)(2 + 1/2) \rceil + 16$	Yes
DHLW10 [10]	Prime	DLIN	160	$\lceil (3/\alpha)(3 + 1/2) \rceil + 35$	Yes
GHV12 [15]	Prime	DLIN	160	$2\lceil 4/\alpha \rceil + 6$	Yes
Ours	Composite	RSI	$\lceil 1264/\alpha \rceil$	2	**No**

5   Conclusion

We proposed a simple and efficient construction of LR-CCA secure PKE scheme based on the Refined Subgroup Indistinguishability (RSI) assumption, which is a more general group of assumptions and can be instantiated under many number-theoretical assumptions. Our construction follows a recently proposed approach for leakage-resilient chosen-ciphertext security [31]. However, the known results in [31] has only a small leakage rate of $1/2 - o(1)$. Our construction further improved the leakage rate to $1 - o(1)$ under the RSI assumption over a pairing-free group of known order. As far as we know, this is the first pairing-free LR-CCA secure PKE with leakage rate of $1 - o(1)$.

References

1. Akavia, A., Goldwasser, S., Vaikuntanathan, V.: Simultaneous hardcore bits and cryptography against memory attacks. In: Reingold, O. (ed.) TCC 2009. LNCS, vol. 5444, pp. 474–495. Springer, Heidelberg (2009)
2. Alwen, J., Dodis, Y., Naor, M., Segev, G., Walfish, S., Wichs, D.: Public-key encryption in the bounded-retrieval model. In: Gilbert, H. (ed.) EUROCRYPT 2010. LNCS, vol. 6110, pp. 113–134. Springer, Heidelberg (2010)
3. Boneh, D., Halevi, S., Hamburg, M., Ostrovsky, R.: Circular-secure encryption from decision Diffie-Hellman. In: Wagner, D. (ed.) CRYPTO 2008. LNCS, vol. 5157, pp. 108–125. Springer, Heidelberg (2008)
4. Brakerski, Z., Goldwasser, S.: Circular and leakage resilient public-key encryption under subgroup indistinguishability. In: Rabin, T. (ed.) CRYPTO 2010. LNCS, vol. 6223, pp. 1–20. Springer, Heidelberg (2010)

5. Brakerski, Z., Kalai, Y.T., Katz, J., Vaikuntanathan, V.: Overcoming the hole in the bucket: Public-key cryptography resilient to continual memory leakage. In: FOCS 2010, pp. 501–510. IEEE Computer Society (2010)
6. Canetti, R., Halevi, S., Katz, J.: Chosen-ciphertext security from identity-based encryption. In: Cachin, C., Camenisch, J. (eds.) EUROCRYPT 2004. LNCS, vol. 3027, pp. 207–222. Springer, Heidelberg (2004)
7. Chow, S.S.M., Dodis, Y., Rouselakis, Y., Waters, B.: Practical leakage-resilient identity-based encryption from simple assumptions. In: Al-Shaer, E., Keromytis, A.D., Shmatikov, V. (eds.) CCS 2010, pp. 152–161. ACM (2010)
8. Cramer, R., Shoup, V.: Universal hash proofs and a paradigm for adaptive chosen ciphertext secure public-key encryption. In: Knudsen, L.R. (ed.) EUROCRYPT 2002. LNCS, vol. 2332, pp. 45–64. Springer, Heidelberg (2002)
9. Dodis, Y., Haralambiev, K., López-Alt, A., Wichs, D.: Cryptography against continuous memory attacks. In: FOCS 2010, pp. 511–520. IEEE Computer Society (2010)
10. Dodis, Y., Haralambiev, K., López-Alt, A., Wichs, D.: Efficient public-key cryptography in the presence of key leakage. In: Abe, M. (ed.) ASIACRYPT 2010. LNCS, vol. 6477, pp. 613–631. Springer, Heidelberg (2010)
11. Dodis, Y., Kalai, Y.T., Lovett, S.: On cryptography with auxiliary input. In: Mitzenmacher, M. (ed.) STOC 2009, pp. 621–630. ACM (2009)
12. Dodis, Y., Ostrovsky, R., Reyzin, L., Smith, A.: Fuzzy extractors: How to generate strong keys from biometrics and other noisy data. SIAM J. Comput. 38(1), 97–139 (2008)
13. Dziembowski, S., Pietrzak, K.: Leakage-resilient cryptography. In: FOCS 2008, pp. 293–302. IEEE Computer Society (2008)
14. Faust, S., Kiltz, E., Pietrzak, K., Rothblum, G.N.: Leakage-resilient signatures. In: Micciancio, D. (ed.) TCC 2010. LNCS, vol. 5978, pp. 343–360. Springer, Heidelberg (2010)
15. Galindo, D., Herranz, J., Villar, J.L.: Identity-based encryption with master key-dependent message security and leakage-resilience. In: Foresti, S., Yung, M., Martinelli, F. (eds.) ESORICS 2012. LNCS, vol. 7459, pp. 627–642. Springer, Heidelberg (2012)
16. Gentry, C., Peikert, C., Vaikuntanathan, V.: Trapdoors for hard lattices and new cryptographic constructions. In: Dwork, C. (ed.) STOC 2008, pp. 197–206. ACM (2008)
17. Goldwasser, S., Micali, S.: Probabilistic encryption. J. Comput. Syst. Sci. 28(2), 270–299 (1984)
18. Halderman, J.A., Schoen, S.D., Heninger, N., Clarkson, W., Paul, W., Calandrino, J.A., Feldman, A.J., Appelbaum, J., Felten, E.W.: Lest we remember: Cold boot attacks on encryption keys. In: van Oorschot, P.C. (ed.) USENIX Security Symposium 2008, pp. 45–60. USENIX Association (2008)
19. Hazay, C., López-Alt, A., Wee, H., Wichs, D.: Leakage-resilient cryptography from minimal assumptions. In: Johansson, T., Nguyen, P.Q. (eds.) EUROCRYPT 2013. LNCS, vol. 7881, pp. 160–176. Springer, Heidelberg (2013)
20. Hofheinz, D.: Circular chosen-ciphertext security with compact ciphertexts. In: Johansson, T., Nguyen, P.Q. (eds.) EUROCRYPT 2013. LNCS, vol. 7881, pp. 520–536. Springer, Heidelberg (2013)
21. Katz, J., Vaikuntanathan, V.: Signature schemes with bounded leakage resilience. In: Matsui, M. (ed.) ASIACRYPT 2009. LNCS, vol. 5912, pp. 703–720. Springer, Heidelberg (2009)

22. Kiltz, E., Pietrzak, K., Stam, M., Yung, M.: A new randomness extraction paradigm for hybrid encryption. In: Joux, A. (ed.) EUROCRYPT 2009. LNCS, vol. 5479, pp. 590–609. Springer, Heidelberg (2009)
23. Krawczyk, H., Rabin, T.: Chameleon signatures. In: NDSS 2000. The Internet Society (2000)
24. Lewko, A.B., Rouselakis, Y., Waters, B.: Achieving leakage resilience through dual system encryption. In: Ishai, Y. (ed.) TCC 2011. LNCS, vol. 6597, pp. 70–88. Springer, Heidelberg (2011)
25. Li, S., Zhang, F., Sun, Y., Shen, L.: A new variant of the Cramer-Shoup leakage-resilient public key encryption. In: Xhafa, F., Barolli, L., Pop, F., Chen, X., Cristea, V. (eds.) INCoS 2012, pp. 342–346. IEEE (2012)
26. Liu, S., Weng, J., Zhao, Y.: Efficient public key cryptosystem resilient to key leakage chosen ciphertext attacks. In: Dawson, E. (ed.) CT-RSA 2013. LNCS, vol. 7779, pp. 84–100. Springer, Heidelberg (2013)
27. Naor, M., Segev, G.: Public-key cryptosystems resilient to key leakage. In: Halevi, S. (ed.) CRYPTO 2009. LNCS, vol. 5677, pp. 18–35. Springer, Heidelberg (2009)
28. González Nieto, J.M., Boyd, C., Dawson, E.: A public key cryptosystem based on the subgroup membership problem. In: Qing, S., Okamoto, T., Zhou, J. (eds.) ICICS 2001. LNCS, vol. 2229, pp. 352–363. Springer, Heidelberg (2001)
29. Peikert, C., Waters, B.: Lossy trapdoor functions and their applications. In: Dwork, C. (ed.) STOC 2008, pp. 187–196. ACM (2008)
30. Pietrzak, K.: A leakage-resilient mode of operation. In: Joux, A. (ed.) EUROCRYPT 2009. LNCS, vol. 5479, pp. 462–482. Springer, Heidelberg (2009)
31. Qin, B., Liu, S.: Leakage-resilient chosen-ciphertext secure public-key encryption from hash proof system and one-time lossy filter. In: Sako, K., Sarkar, P. (eds.) ASIACRYPT 2013, Part II. LNCS, vol. 8270, pp. 381–400. Springer, Heidelberg (2013)
32. Regev, O.: On lattices, learning with errors, random linear codes, and cryptography. In: Gabow, H.N., Fagin, R. (eds.) STOC 2005, pp. 84–93. ACM (2005)
33. Yuen, T.H., Chow, S.S.M., Zhang, Y., Yiu, S.M.: Identity-based encryption resilient to continual auxiliary leakage. In: Pointcheval, D., Johansson, T. (eds.) EUROCRYPT 2012. LNCS, vol. 7237, pp. 117–134. Springer, Heidelberg (2012)

A Black-Box Construction of a **CCA2** Encryption Scheme from a Plaintext Aware (**sPA1**) Encryption Scheme

Dana Dachman-Soled

University of Maryland
danadach@ece.umd.edu

Abstract. We present a construction of a CCA2-secure encryption scheme from a plaintext aware (sPA1), weakly simulatable public key encryption scheme. The notion of plaintext aware, weakly simulatable public key encryption has been considered previously by Myers, Sergi and shelat (SCN, 2012) and natural encryption schemes such as the Damgård Elgamal Scheme (Damgård, Crypto, 1991) and the Cramer-Shoup Lite Scheme (Cramer and Shoup, SIAM J. Comput., 2003) were shown to satisfy these properties.

Recently, Myers, Sergi and shelat (SCN, 2012) defined an extension of non-malleable CCA1 security, called cNM-CCA1, and showed how to construct a cNM-CCA1-secure encryption scheme from a plaintext aware and weakly simulatable public key encryption scheme. Our work extends and improves on this result by showing that a full CCA2-secure encryption scheme can be constructed from the same assumptions.

Keywords: CCA2-secure encryption, plaintext aware encryption, weakly simulatable public key encryption, black-box.

1 Introduction

The basic security requirement for public key encryption schemes is Chosen Plaintext Attack (CPA) security [17] (also known as semantic security), which ensures security against a *passive*, eavesdropping adversary. A stronger security requirement for public key encryption schemes, which ensures that they remain secure even in the face of an *active* adversary, is known as Adaptive Chosen Ciphertext Attack (CCA2) security. More specifically, a CCA2-secure encryption scheme is guaranteed to be secure even against an adversary who has access to a decryption oracle and may use it to decrypt any ciphertext of its choice except for the challenge ciphertext itself. This captures real-life scenarios where the adversary has control over network traffic which allows the adversary, in effect, to decrypt all ciphertexts of its choice.

There is a significant body of work on constructing CCA2-secure encryption schemes from specific computational hardness assumptions (c.f. [10,19,8,20]), as well as from various lower level primitives (c.f. [14,7,23,29,31,24,32]). Nevertheless, the central question in this area remains open: To determine the relationship

H. Krawczyk (Ed.): PKC 2014, LNCS 8383, pp. 37–55, 2014.

between CCA2 and CPA-secure encryption—whether a CCA2-secure encryption scheme can be constructed assuming only the existence of a CPA-secure encryption scheme, or whether CCA2-security requires stronger assumptions. Although a partial answer was given in [16], the larger question remains open for both black-box and non-black-box constructions. Moreover, several important variants of the question such as whether a CCA2 secure encryption scheme can be constructed from a CCA1-secure encryption scheme[1] remain open.

In this paper, we consider a strong type of CPA-secure public key encryption scheme which is also *plaintext aware* (sPA1), *weakly simulatable*, and enjoys *perfect correctness*[2] and show how to construct full CCA2-secure public key encryption schemes from such a CPA-secure encryption scheme. Moreover, the CCA2 construction presented is black-box in the underlying CPA-secure scheme, although our security reduction is *non black-box*.

Although the required assumptions are strong—we discuss and provide more details on the assumptions of plaintext awareness and weak simulatability below—we view our new construction of CCA2 encryption from plaintext aware, weakly simulatable PKE as meaningful progress since our underlying assumption is an assumption which was not previously known to imply CCA2 security. Moreover, to the best of our knowledge, this is the first construction of a CCA2 scheme from encryption schemes with seemingly weaker or incomparable security to CCA2 and requiring no additional assumptions. Finally, we present new proof techniques for proving CCA2 security, which may be useful for constructing CCA2 secure encryption from other lower-level primitives.

1.1   Our Assumptions

Our work relies on a strong assumption on the underlying CPA-secure encryption scheme called *plaintext awareness*. The notion of a plaintext aware encryption scheme was first introduced in the seminal paper of Bellare and Rogaway [5] and the notion was further studied by Bellare et al. [2]. Both of these works dealt with the notion of plaintext awareness in the Random Oracle model. Subsequently, Bellare and Palacio [4] considered extending the notion of plaintext awareness to the plain model[3]. In this work, we are also interested in the notion of plaintext awareness in the plain model without random oracles. Informally, an encryption scheme is plaintext aware (called sPA1 in [4]) if for every efficient ciphertext creator, C, there exists an efficient plaintext extractor, C^*, that outputs the same value as the decryption algorithm on ciphertexts outputted by C.

---

[1] A CCA1-encryption scheme is one where the adversary has oracle access to the decryption oracle up to the point that it receives the challenge ciphertext.

[2] We can remove the requirement of perfect correctness by using the transformation of [15] to transform a public key encryption scheme with decryption error to a public key encryption scheme with perfect correctness. Note that each transformation in the sequence of transformations given in the proof of Theorem 3 of [15] preserves both simulatability and plaintext awareness of the underlying encryption scheme.

[3] We note that prior to the work of [4], Herzog et al. [21] considered a notion of plaintext awareness in the key registration model.

This type of assumption is known as a knowledge assumption (other examples of knowledge assumptions include the knowledge of exponent assumption [18,3] and extractable collision resistant hash functions [6]) and is thus a non-falsifiable assumption. Despite the strength of the assumption, the notion of plaintext awareness is meant to capture an intuitive property of certain encryption schemes that an efficient adversary cannot create a valid ciphertext without "knowing" the corresponding plaintext.

It is not hard to see that any plaintext aware encryption scheme is itself also CCA1-secure, since the plaintext extractor can be used to simulate the decryption oracle in the CCA1 experiment. However, plaintext aware encryption *does not* directly imply CCA2-secure encryption since the plaintext extractor is not guaranteed to work correctly when the ciphertext creator receives a valid encryption as input. Thus, when the adversary queries the CCA2 decryption oracle after receiving the challenge ciphertext CT^* in the CCA2 experiment, the extractor may not be able to simulate the decryption oracle. In fact, since we are given no guarantees on the output of the plaintext extractor when the ciphertext creator receives CT^* as input, it would seem that constructing CCA2-secure encryption from plaintext aware encryption is just as hard as constructing CCA2-secure encryption from CCA1-secure encryption; we have the extra guarantee of a plaintext extractor, but the extractor seems useless for queries made after the challenge ciphertext is received.

Recently, a fascinating result by Myers, Sergi and shelat [26], showed that by adding an additional assumption that the plaintext aware public key encryption scheme is also weakly simulatable, the above problem can be partially overcome. Essentially, they present a new construction and show that the plaintext extractor can still be useful for simulating the decryption oracle for a *constant* number of parallel queries made after the adversary receives the challenge ciphertext when the underlying plaintext aware public key encryption scheme is also *weakly simulatable*.

The notion of *simulatable* public key encryption was first introduced by Damgård and Nielsen [12] in the context of non-committing encryption. Loosely speaking, [12] define a simulatable public key encryption scheme to be an encryption scheme with special algorithms for obliviously sampling public keys and random ciphertexts without learning the corresponding secret keys and plaintexts; in addition, both of these oblivious sampling algorithms should be efficiently invertible. An incomparable notion of *simulatable* public key encryption was introduced by [13] and was shown to imply CCA2-secure encryption. Here, the public key encryption scheme has an invertible algorithm f for obliviously sampling random ciphertexts (but not public keys) and in addition, $f(r)$, where r is a random string, and C, where C is an honestly generated ciphertext are indistinguishable, *even when given access to a decryption oracle*. The weakly simulatable encryption schemes used in this work are strictly weaker than both of the above notions. They are weaker than the [12] notion since only the *ciphertext* and not the public key has an invertible oblivious sampling algorithm and they are weaker than the [13] notion since the attacker is not given access to the decryption oracle.

In their work, [26] defined an extension of non-malleable CCA1 security, called cNM-CCA1, where an adversary can make c adaptive parallel decryption queries after seeing the challenge ciphertext. Then, [26] showed how to construct cNM-CCA1 encryption from plaintext aware and weakly simulatable public key encryption for any constant c. Similar assumptions of plaintext aware and weakly simulatable public key encryption were previously made by [13]. Moreover, as shown by Myers, Sergi and shelat [26] natural encryption schemes such as the Dåmgard Elgamal encryption scheme (DEG) and the lite version of Cramer-Shoup encryption scheme (CS-lite) satisfy both of these properties under the DDH assumption and a suitable extension of the Diffie-Hellman Knowledge (DHK) assumption (see [4] for discussion of the DHK assumption).

Following the work of [26], it is interesting to explore how far we can take the assumption of the existence of a plaintext aware and weakly simulatable public key encryption scheme and what the power of this assumption is relative to the assumption of the existence of a CCA2-secure encryption scheme.

1.2 Our Results

Informally, we show the following:

Theorem 1 (Informal). *There is a black-box construction of CCA2-secure encryption from plaintext aware and weakly simulatable public key encryption with perfect correctness.*

Our result extends the work of [26] by showing that plaintext aware and weakly simulatable public key encryption can, in fact, be used to achieve full CCA2 security.

Finally, the assumption of a plaintext aware encryption scheme can be viewed as an assumption that allows us to use strong non-black-box techniques on the *adversary* in the security reduction. More specifically, we leverage the code of the adversary by using it to extract crucial information that the adversary must "know." This raises the intriguing question of whether we can present a construction of CCA2 from CPA where the security proof uses non-black-box access to the adversary. Such reductions are known to be more powerful than black-box reductions in the setting of multiparty computation as first shown in the seminal work of Barak [1]. But it has not been clear how to leverage these techniques in the non-interactive setting of public key encryption.

1.3 Technical Overview

We adapt and combine many of the techniques of [22], [26] and, in addition, we introduce new techniques as discussed in detail below.

The construction. On security parameter k, the scheme will consist of a one-time signature as well as both inner and outer ciphertexts, with corresponding public keys. More specifically, two inner ciphertexts will be encrypted under public keys pk_{in_0}, pk_{in_1}, and k outer ciphertexts will be encrypted using k public keys chosen out of k pairs of public keys $(pk_1^0, pk_1^1), \ldots, (pk_k^0, pk_k^1)$. The selection of the k public keys $pk_1^{b_1}, \ldots, pk_k^{b_k}$ will depend on bits of the verification key, vksig, chosen for the one-time signature (as in [14,26]).

In particular, a ciphertext will consist of the following:

Verification key: A verification key, vksig, for the one-time signature scheme, generated by GenSig.

Inner ciphertexts: Two ciphertexts $CT_{in_0} = \text{Enc}(pk_{in_0}, \tilde{s}_0)$, $CT_{in_1} = \text{Enc}(pk_{in_1}, \tilde{s}_1)$ where $\tilde{s}_0, \tilde{s}_1$ are additive secret shares of $m||r$, m is the message to be encrypted, r is the randomness used to encrypt the outer ciphertexts (as described below), and $||$ denotes concatenation.

Outer ciphertexts: k ciphertexts $CT_1, \ldots, CT_k$ computed the following way: $r_1||\cdots||r_k \leftarrow \text{prg}(r)$, where prg is a pseudorandom generator. Each $CT_i = \text{Enc}(pk_i^{\text{vksig}_i}, CT_{in_0}||CT_{in_1}; r_i)$.

Signature: A signature $\sigma = \text{Sign}(\text{sksig}, CT_1||\cdots||CT_k)$.

The security reduction. We consider a modified CCA2 experiment where the decryption oracle is replaced with the plaintext extractor guaranteed by the plaintext awareness property of the underlying encryption scheme. Note that once the adversary receives the challenge ciphertext in the CCA2 experiment, we have no guarantees on whether the plaintext extractor returns messages that are consistent with the answers of the decryption oracle. Therefore, we define a *bad extraction event* as the event that the plaintext extractor and decryption oracle disagree on a query submitted by the adversary A to the decryption oracle. We consider a sequence of hybrids and show that (1) In the first hybrid, the probability of bad extraction event ocurring is negligible (due to the security guarantees of the plaintext aware, weakly simulatable encryption scheme) and (2) In consecutive hybrids the probability of bad extraction event occurring differs by a negligible amount (since the occurrence of a bad extraction event can be detected in each hybrid). Put together, these imply that the decryption oracle and plaintext extractor agree (even for queries after the challenge ciphertext is received) in the original experiment with all but negligible probability. Furthermore, this implies that the CCA2 experiment can be simulated without knowing the secret key of the inner encryption scheme (by using the plaintext extractor to decrypt oracle queries), which immediately implies the CCA2 security of the scheme. To show (1), we use techniques similar to those of [26]. To show (2), we build upon the sequence of hybrids used by [22].

The main new technical challenge in this work is showing that property (2) holds for each pair of consecutive hybrids. More specifically, in the final two hybrids, which we denote here by $\tilde{H}_0, \tilde{H}_1$, we run the CCA2 experiment with the CCA2 adversary, but use the plaintext extractor to decrypt the inner ciphertexts CT_{in_0}, CT_{in_1}. Additionally, in $\tilde{H}_0$, the value $\tilde{s}_0 \oplus \tilde{s}_1$ is set to a random string, while in $\tilde{H}_1$, value $\tilde{s}_0 \oplus \tilde{s}_1$ is set honestly to $(r||m_\beta)$. Note that if a bad extraction event does not occur, then the view of the adversary in $\tilde{H}_1$ is identical to its view in the original CCA2 experiment. By previous arguments, we have that the probability of a bad extraction event is negligible in $\tilde{H}_0$. To argue that the probability of bad extraction event occurring differs by a negligible amount in these final two hybrids, we must reduce to the semantic security of the inner encryption scheme. However, a bad extraction event—in which the plaintext extractor disagrees with the decryption oracle—cannot be detected unless the adversary has the secret keys corresponding to the inner encryptions and if this is the case, it seems that we cannot hope to reduce to semantic security.

Thus, we consider a modified experiment where at the beginning of the experiment we fix a bit $b \leftarrow_\$ \{0,1\}$ and a *modified bad extraction event* defined as the event that the plaintext extractor and decryption oracle disagree specifically on the decryption of CT_{in_b} for a query submitted by the adversary A. Since $b \leftarrow_\$ \{0,1\}$ is chosen uniformly at random, independent of all other variables, we show that the probability that the *first* bad extraction event occurs on CT_{in_b} is exactly half the probability that the first bad extraction event occurs on either CT_{in_0} or CT_{in_1}. Now, a semantic security adversary will choose $b \leftarrow_\$ \{0,1\}$ at the outset and will embed its challenge public key and ciphertext in place of $pk_{in_{1-b}}$ and $CT^*_{in_{1-b}}$, respectively. Moreover, the semantic security adversary will embed an honestly generated public key and ciphertext in place of pk_{in_b} and $CT^*_{in_b}$, respectively. This means that the semantic security adversary can decrypt ciphertexts encrypted under pk_{in_b} and thus can successfully detect the occurence of modified bad extraction event.

1.4   Related Work

In their seminal work, Dolev et al. [14] presented the first construction of CCA2-encryption from the lower-level primitive of enhanced trapdoor permutations. However, the [14] construction is not black-box and requires the use of generic non-interactive zero knowledge proofs. Subsequently, Pass et al. [28] presented a new definition of non-malleability and presented a construction from CPA to non-malleable CPA requiring non-black box use of the underlying encryption scheme. Choi et al. [9] gave a black-box version of this result thereafter. Myers and shelat [27] showed how to construct many-bit CCA2-encryption from single-bit cca2-encryption and Hohenberg et al. [22] extended their result and showed how to build CCA2-encryption from any detectable chosen ciphertext (DCCA) secure encryption scheme. As discussed previously, [26] show how to construct a cNM-CCA1-secure encryption scheme from a plaintext aware, weakly simulatable public key encryption scheme.

A different line of work introduced new low-level primitives and showed how to construct CCA2 encryption from these low-level primtives. Examples are constructions of CCA2-secure encryption from the primitives of identity-based encryption [7], tag-based encryption [23], lossy trapdoor functions [29], correlated products [31], adaptive trapdoor functions [24], and extractable hash proofs [32].

Finally, several works [10,19,8,20] construct CCA2-encryption directly from various number-theoretic assumptions.

2 Preliminaries

2.1 CCA2 Security

Definition 1 (CCA2 Security). *Let $\mathcal{E} = (\mathsf{Gen}, \mathsf{Enc}, \mathsf{Dec})$ be an encryption scheme and let the random variable $\mathsf{CCA2\text{-}Exp}_\beta(\mathcal{E}, A, k)$ where $\beta \in \{0, 1\}$, $A = (A_1, A_2)$ are ppt algorithms and $k \in \mathsf{N}$, denote the result of the following probabilistic experiment:*

$\mathsf{CCA2\text{-}Exp}_\beta(\mathcal{E}, A, k)$

- $(pk, sk) \leftarrow_\$ \mathsf{Gen}(1^k)$
- $(m_0, m_1, state_A) \leftarrow_\$ A_1^{\mathsf{Dec}(sk, \cdot)}(pk)$
- $y \leftarrow_\$ \mathsf{Enc}(pk, m_\beta)$
- $D \leftarrow_\$ A_2^{\mathsf{Dec}(sk, \cdot)}(y, state_A)$

We require that the output of A_1 satisfies $|m_0| = |m_1|$ and that A_2 does not query y to its oracle.

$(\mathsf{Gen}, \mathsf{Enc}, \mathsf{Dec})$ is CCA2-secure if for any ppt algorithms $A = (A_1, A_2)$ the following two ensembles are computationally indistinguishable:

$$\{\mathsf{CCA2\text{-}Exp}_0(\mathcal{E}, A, k)\}_{k \in \mathsf{N}} \overset{c}{\approx} \{\mathsf{CCA2\text{-}Exp}_1(\mathcal{E}, A, k)\}_{k \in \mathsf{N}}.$$

2.2 Plaintext Awareness for Multiple Key Setup

We follow [26] for the following definition.

$\mathsf{sPA1}_\ell(E, C, C^*, k)$:

- Let $R[C]$, $R[C^*]$ be randomly chosen bit strings for C and C^*.
- $((pk_i, sk_i))_{i \in [\ell(k)]} \leftarrow_\$ \mathsf{Gen}(1^k)$
- $st \leftarrow ((pk_i)_{i \in [\ell(k)]}, R[C])$
- $C^{C^*(st, \cdot)}\left((pk_i)_{i \in [\ell(k)]}\right)$
- Let $Q = \{(q_i = (pk_{j_i}, c_i), m_i)\}$ be the set of queries C made to C^* until it halted and C^*'s responses to them. Return $\bigwedge_{i=1}^{|Q|}(m_i = \mathsf{Dec}_{sk_{j_i}}(c_i))$.

In the above experiment, C is a ciphertext creator, and C^* is a stateful ppt algorithm called the *extractor* that takes as input the state information st and a ciphertext given by the ciphertext creator C, and will return the decryption of that ciphertext and the updated state st. The state information is initially set to the public key pk and the adversary C's random coins. It gets updated by C^* as C^* answers each query that the adversary C submits. The above experiment returns 1 if all the extractor's answers to queries are the true decryption of those queries under sk. Otherwise, the experiment returns 0.

Definition 2 (sPA1$_\ell$). *Let ℓ be a polynomial. Let $\mathcal{E} = (\mathsf{Gen}, \mathsf{Enc}, \mathsf{Dec})$ be an asymmetric encryption scheme. Let the ciphertext-creator adversary C and the extractor C^* be ppt algorithms. For $k \in \mathsf{N}$, the sPA1-advantage of C relative to C^* is defined as:*

$$Adv^{\mathsf{sPA1}_\ell}(\mathcal{E}, C, C^*) = \Pr[\mathsf{sPA1}(\mathcal{E}, C, C^*, k) = 0]$$

The extractor C^* is a successful sPA1$_\ell$-extractor for the ciphertext-creator adversary C if for all $k \in \mathsf{N}$, the function $Adv^{\mathsf{sPA1}_\ell}(\mathcal{E}, C, C^*)$ is negligible. The encryption scheme $\mathcal{E}$ is called sPA1$_\ell$ multi-key secure if for any ppt ciphertext creator there exists a successful sPA1$_\ell$-extractor.

As shown by [26], both the Damgard Elgamal encryption scheme (DEG) and the lite version of Cramer-Shoup encryption scheme (CS-lite) are sPA1$_\ell$ secure under a suitable generalization of the DHK1 assumption.

2.3   Weakly Simulatable Encryption Scheme

As in [26], we consider a notion of simulatability similar to the one of Dent [13], but where the attacker is not given access to the decryption oracle. If an encryption scheme satisfies this weaker notion of simulatability, we say it is weakly simulatable.

Definition 3 (Weakly Simulatable Encryption Scheme). *An asymmetric encryption scheme $(\mathsf{Gen}, \mathsf{Enc}, \mathsf{Dec})$ is weakly simulatable if there exist two poly-time algorithms (f, f^{-1}) where f is deterministic and f^{-1} is probabilistic, such that for all $k \in \mathsf{N}$ there exists the polynomial function $p(\cdot)$ where $l = p(k)$, we have the following correctness properties:*

- *f on inputs of public key pk (in the range of Gen) and a random string $r \in \{0,1\}^l$, returns elements in $\mathcal{C}$, where $\mathcal{C}$ is the set of all possible "ciphertext"-strings that can be submitted to the decryption oracle (notice that $C \in \mathcal{C}$ might not be a valid ciphertext).*
- *f^{-1} on input of a public key pk (in the range of Gen) and an element $C \in \mathcal{C}$ outputs elements of $\{0,1\}^l$.*
- *$f(pk, f^{-1}(pk, C)) = C$ for all $C \in \mathcal{C}$.*

And the following security properties. No polynomial time attacker A has probability better than $1/2 + \mu(k)$ of winning the following experiment, where μ is some negligible function.

- *The challenger generates a random key pair $(pk, sk) \leftarrow_\$ \mathsf{Gen}(1^k)$, and chooses randomly $b \in \{0,1\}$.*
- *The attacker A executes on the input 1^k and the public key pk outputs $m \in \mathcal{M}$. The challenger sends A the pair $(f^{-1}(pk, c = \mathsf{Enc}(pk, m)), c)$ if $b = 0$, or $(r, f(pk, r))$ for some randomly generated element $r \in \{0,1\}^l$ if $b = 1$. The attacker A terminates by outputting a guess b' for b. A wins if $b = b'$ and its advantage is defined in the usual way.*

Lemma 1. *If $\mathcal{E}$ is a weakly simulatable encryption scheme, then $\mathcal{E}$ is CPA-secure.*

[26] show that DEG and CS-lite schemes can both be weakly simulatable when instantiated in proper groups.

2.4   PA1⁺–An Extension of Plaintext Awareness

[26] additionally consider an augmented notion of plaintext awareness in which the ciphertext creator has access to an oracle that produces random bits, PA1⁺. The extractor receives the answers to any queries generated by the creator, but only at the time these queries are issued. This oracle is meant to model the fact that the plaintext extractor might not receive all of the random coins used by the ciphertext creator *at the beginning* of the experiment. By introducing this oracle, we require the extractor to work even when it receives the random coins at the same time as the ciphertext creator. This modification has implications when the notion of plaintext awareness is computational. However, in our case, as in [26], we require statistical plaintext awareness, and as argued by [26], allowing access to such an oracle does not affect the sPA1$_\ell$ security.

Any encryption scheme that is sPA1$_\ell$ secure is also sPA1$_\ell^+$ secure.

Definition 4. *Define the sPA1$_\ell^+$ experiment in a similar way to the sPA1$_\ell$ experiment. The only difference between the two is that during the sPA1$_\ell^+$ experiment, the ciphertext creator has access to a random oracle $\mathcal{O}$ that takes no input, but returns independent uniform random strings upon each access. Any time the creator accesses the oracle, the oracle's response is forwarded to both the creator and the extractor.*

If an encryption scheme would be deemed sPA1$_\ell$ secure, when we replace the sPA1$_\ell$ experiment in the definition with the modified sPA1$_\ell^+$ experiment, then the encryption scheme is said to be sPA1$_\ell^+$ secure.

Lemma 2 (Appeared in [26].). *If an encryption scheme $\mathcal{E}$ is sPA1$_\ell$ secure, then it is sPA1$_\ell^+$ secure.*

2.5   Strong One-Time Signature Scheme

We follow here the definition of [9]. Informally, a strong one-time signature scheme (GenSig, Sign, Ver) is an existentially unforgeable signature scheme, with the restriction that the signer signs at most one message with any key. This means that an efficient adversary, upon seeing a signature on a message m of his choice, cannot generate a valid signature on a different message, or a different valid signature on the same message m. Such schemes can be constructed in a black-box way from one-way functions [25,30], and thus from any semantically-secure encryption scheme (Gen, Enc, Dec).

3 The Scheme

We present a CCA2-secure encryption scheme $\mathcal{E}_{\mathsf{cca}} = (\mathsf{Gen}_{\mathsf{cca}}, \mathsf{Enc}_{\mathsf{cca}}, \mathsf{Dec}_{\mathsf{cca}})$ from any scheme $\mathcal{E}_{\mathsf{pa-cpa}} = (\mathsf{Gen}_{\mathsf{pa-cpa}}, \mathsf{Enc}_{\mathsf{pa-cpa}}, \mathsf{Dec}_{\mathsf{pa-cpa}})$ which is a plaintext aware, weakly simulatable public key encryption scheme with perfect correctness and any scheme $(\mathsf{GenSig}, \mathsf{Sign}, \mathsf{Ver})$, which is a strong one-time signature scheme and any pseudorandom generator prg. See Figure 1.

Encryption Scheme $\mathcal{E}_{\mathsf{cca}} = (\mathsf{Gen}_{\mathsf{cca}}, \mathsf{Enc}_{\mathsf{cca}}, \mathsf{Dec}_{\mathsf{cca}})$

Key Generation $\mathsf{Gen}_{\mathsf{cca}}(1^k)$:
- $[pk_{in_b}, sk_{in_b}]_{b \in \{0,1\}} \leftarrow_\$ \mathsf{Gen}_{\mathsf{pa-cpa}}(1^k)$;
- $[pk_i^b, sk_i^b]_{b \in \{0,1\}, i \in [k]} \leftarrow_\$ \mathsf{Gen}_{\mathsf{pa-cpa}}(1^k)$;
- $pk \leftarrow ([pk_{in_b}]_{b \in \{0,1\}}, [pk_i^b]_{b \in \{0,1\}, i \in [k]})$;
- $sk \leftarrow ([sk_{in_b}]_{b \in \{0,1\}}, [sk_i^b]_{b \in \{0,1\}, i \in [k]})$
- Return (pk, sk)

Encryption $\mathsf{Enc}_{\mathsf{cca}}(pk, m)$:
- $(\mathsf{vksig}, \mathsf{sksig}) \leftarrow_\$ \mathsf{GenSig}(1^k)$
- $r \leftarrow_\$ \{0,1\}^k$
- $\tilde{s}_0 \leftarrow_\$ \{0,1\}^\ell$, where $\ell = k + |m|$; $\tilde{s}_1 \leftarrow (r\|m) \oplus \tilde{s}_0$
- $CT_{in_0} \leftarrow_\$ \mathsf{Enc}_{\mathsf{pa-cpa}}(pk_{in_0}, \tilde{s}_0)$; $CT_{in_1} \leftarrow_\$ \mathsf{Enc}_{\mathsf{pa-cpa}}(pk_{in_1}, \tilde{s}_1)$
- $r_1\|\cdots\|r_k = \mathsf{prg}(r)$
- For $1 \leq i \leq k$, $CT_i \leftarrow \mathsf{Enc}_{\mathsf{pa-cpa}}(pk_i^{\mathsf{vksig}_i}, CT_{in_0}\|CT_{in_1}; r_i)$
- Return $CT = (CT_1\|\cdots\|CT_k, \mathsf{vksig}, \sigma = \mathsf{Sign}(\mathsf{sksig}, CT_1\|\cdots\|CT_k))$

Decryption $\mathsf{Dec}_{\mathsf{cca}}(sk, (CT = CT_1\|\cdots\|CT_n, \mathsf{vksig}, \sigma))$
- If $\mathsf{Ver}(\mathsf{vksig}, CT, \sigma) = \bot$, output $\bot$.
- Otherwise, $CT_{in_0}\|CT_{in_1} \leftarrow \mathsf{Dec}_{\mathsf{pa-cpa}}(sk_1^{\mathsf{vksig}_1}, CT_1)$
- $\tilde{s}_0 \leftarrow \mathsf{Dec}_{\mathsf{pa-cpa}}(sk_{in_0}, CT_{in_0})$
- $\tilde{s}_1 \leftarrow \mathsf{Dec}_{\mathsf{pa-cpa}}(sk_{in_1}, CT_{in_1})$
- $(r\|m) \leftarrow \tilde{s}_0 \oplus \tilde{s}_1$
- $(r_1\|\cdots\|r_k) \leftarrow \mathsf{prg}(r)$
- If for all i, $CT_i = \mathsf{Enc}_{\mathsf{pa-cpa}}(pk_i^{\mathsf{vksig}_i}, CT_{in_0}\|CT_{in_1}; r_i)$ return m
- Else return $\bot$.

Fig. 1. The CCA2-Secure Encryption Scheme $\mathcal{E}_{\mathsf{cca}}$

Theorem 2. *Encryption scheme $\mathcal{E}_{\mathsf{cca}}$, presented in Figure 1, is CCA2-secure under the assumptions that $\mathcal{E}_{\mathsf{pa-cpa}} = (\mathsf{Gen}_{\mathsf{pa-cpa}}, \mathsf{Enc}_{\mathsf{pa-cpa}}, \mathsf{Dec}_{\mathsf{pa-cpa}})$ is a plaintext aware, weakly simulatable public key encryption scheme with perfect correctness, the scheme $(\mathsf{GenSig}, \mathsf{Sign}, \mathsf{Ver})$ is a strong one-time signature scheme and prg is a pseudorandom generator.*

Note that the Damgard Elgamal encryption scheme (DEG) and the lite version of Cramer-Shoup encryption scheme (CS-lite) are plaintext aware, weakly simulatable and have perfect correctness.

Since strong one-time signature schemes and pseudorandom generators can be constructed in a black-box manner from CPA-secure public key encryption we have the following corollary:

Corollary 1. *There is a black-box construction of a* CCA2*-secure public key encryption scheme from any plaintext aware, weakly simulatable public key encryption scheme with perfect correctness.*

4 Security Analysis

We begin by defining an experiment which is different than the regular CCA2 experiment, but will be useful in our analsysis of $\mathcal{E}_{cca}$:

NESTED INDISTINGUISHABILITY EXPERIMENT FOR SCHEME $\mathcal{E}_{cca}$:

We define the expriment N-Exp(β, z) for $\beta, z \in \{0,1\}$.

For every adversary $A = (A_1, A_2)$ participating in a CCA2 experiment, we consider a corresponding ciphertext creator C_A (described below) and ciphertext extractor C^* (as guaranteed by the security of the encryption scheme $\mathcal{E}_{pa\text{-}cpa}$), interacting with an oracle $\mathcal{O}$ (described below). Let the random variable N-Exp$_{\beta,z}(\mathcal{E}_{cca}, A, k)$, where $\beta, z \in \{0,1\}$ and $k \in \mathsf{N}$, denote the result of the following probabilistic experiment:

N-Exp$_{\beta,z}(\mathcal{E}_{cca}, A, k)$:

- C_A receives public keys $[pk_{in_b}]_{b\in\{0,1\}}, \{pk_i^b\}_{b\in\{0,1\}, i\in[k]}$ from the sPA1$_{2k+2}^+$ experiment
- C_A chooses $(\mathsf{sksig}^*, \mathsf{vksig}^*) \leftarrow_\$ \mathsf{GenSig}(1^k; r_{\mathsf{sksig}})$, where r_{sksig} consists of the first k bits of C_A's random tape.
- C_A sets $pk = [pk_{in_b}]_{b\in\{0,1\}}, \{pk_i^b\}_{b\in\{0,1\}, i\in[k]}$.
- C_A chooses a random tape for A and begins an emulation of A_1 on input pk.
- Whenever C_A receives query $CT = (CT_1||\cdots||CT_k, \mathsf{vksig}, \sigma)$ from A, C_A checks $\mathsf{Ver}(\mathsf{vksig}, CT_1||\cdots||CT_k, \sigma) = 1$. If not, C_A returns $\bot$. If so, C_A submits CT_i, where i is the first index s.t. $\mathsf{vksig}_i^* \neq \mathsf{vksig}$, to the extractor to obtain $(CT_{in_0}||CT_{in_1})$. If there is no such index, C_A returns $\bot$ and halts. Otherwise, C_A submits CT_{in_0} and CT_{in_1} to the extractor to obtain $\tilde{s}_0, \tilde{s}_1$. C_A computes $r||m = \tilde{s}_0 \oplus \tilde{s}_1$ and checks that $CT_1, \ldots, CT_n$ were computed correctly. If not, C_A returns $\bot$. If so, C_A returns m. Eventually A_1 returns (m_0, m_1, st) and halts. C_A outputs (m_0, m_1).
- C_A queries its oracle $\mathcal{O}$ and $\mathcal{O}$ returns $r_1, \ldots, r_k$ where $r_1 = f^{-1}(pk_1^{\mathsf{vksig}_1^*}, CT_1^*), \ldots, r_k = f^{-1}(pk_1^{\mathsf{vksig}_k^*}, CT_k^*)$ and where $CT_1^*, \ldots, CT_k^*$ are computed in the following way:

1. $r \leftarrow_\$ \{0,1\}^k, r_1, \ldots, r_n \leftarrow \mathsf{prg}(r)$.
2. $\tilde{s}_0 \leftarrow_\$ \{0,1\}^\ell$
3. If $z = 0$ then $\tilde{s}_1 \leftarrow_\$ \{0,1\}^\ell$.
4. Else if $z = 1$ then $\tilde{s}_1 \leftarrow (r\|m_\beta) \oplus \tilde{s}_0$.
5. $CT^*_{in_0} \leftarrow_\$ \mathsf{Enc}_{\mathsf{pa\text{-}cpa}}(pk_{in_0}, \tilde{s}_0); CT^*_{in_1} \leftarrow_\$ \mathsf{Enc}_{\mathsf{pa\text{-}cpa}}(pk_{in_1}, \tilde{s}_1)$
6. For $1 \le i \le k$, $CT^*_i \leftarrow \mathsf{Enc}_{\mathsf{pa\text{-}cpa}}(pk_i^{\mathsf{vksig}^*_i}, CT^*_{in_0}\|CT^*_{in_1}; r_i)$

- C_A computes $CT^*_i = f(r_i)$ for each i and the signature σ^*. C_A returns $CT^* = (CT^*_1\|\cdots\|CT^*_k, \mathsf{vksig}^*, \sigma^*)$ to A
- Whenever C_A receives query $CT = (CT_1\|\cdots\|CT_k, \mathsf{vksig}, \sigma)$ from A, C_A checks $\mathsf{Ver}(\mathsf{vksig}, CT_1\| \cdots \|CT_k, \sigma) = 1$. If not, C_A returns $\perp$. If so, C_A submits CT_i, where i is the first index s.t. $\mathsf{vksig}_i \ne \mathsf{vksig}^*_i$, to the extractor to obtain $(CT_{in_0}\|CT_{in_1})$. If there is no such index, C_A returns $\perp$ and halts. Otherwise, C_A submits CT_{in_0} and CT_{in_1} to the extractor to obtain $\tilde{s}_0, \tilde{s}_1$. C_A computes $r\|m = \tilde{s}_0 \oplus \tilde{s}_1$ and checks that $CT_1, \ldots, CT_n$ were computed correctly. If not, C_A returns $\perp$. If so, C_A returns m. Eventually A_2 outputs D and halts.

We require that the output of A_1 satisfies $|m_0| = |m_1|$ and that A_2 does not query CT^* to its oracle.

Definition 5 (Nested Indistinguishability). *We say that* $\mathcal{E}_{\mathsf{cca}} = (\mathsf{Gen}_{\mathsf{cca}}, \mathsf{Enc}_{\mathsf{cca}}, \mathsf{Dec}_{\mathsf{cca}})$ *is* nested-indistinguishable *if for any ppt algorithms* $A = (A_1, A_2)$ *and for* $\beta \in \{0,1\}$ *the following two ensembles are computationally indistinguishable:*

$$\left\{ \mathsf{N\text{-}Exp}_{\beta,0}(\mathcal{E}_{\mathsf{cca}}, A, k) \right\}_{k\in\mathbb{N}} \overset{c}{\approx} \left\{ \mathsf{N\text{-}Exp}_{\beta,1}(\mathcal{E}_{\mathsf{cca}}, A, k) \right\}_{k\in\mathbb{N}}.$$

Consider the following event:

Definition 6 (The Bad Extraction Event). *We say that a* bad extraction event *has occurred during an execution of the nested indistinguishability experiment if at some point* A *submits a decryption query* $CT = (CT_1\|\cdots\|CT_n, \mathsf{vksig}, \sigma)$ *such that one of the following occurs:*

- $C^*(st, CT_i) \ne \mathsf{Dec}_{\mathsf{pa\text{-}cpa}}(sk_i^{\mathsf{vksig}_i}, CT_i)$ *where* i *is the first index such that* $\mathsf{vksig}^*_i \ne \mathsf{vksig}_i$.
- $C^*(st, CT_{in_0}) \ne \mathsf{Dec}_{\mathsf{pa\text{-}cpa}}(sk_{in_0}, CT_{in_0})$
- $C^*(st, CT_{in_1}) \ne \mathsf{Dec}_{\mathsf{pa\text{-}cpa}}(sk_{in_1}, CT_{in_1})$

Definition 7 (The Forging Signature Event). *We say that a* forging signature event *has occurred during an execution of the nested indistinguishability experiment if at some point* A *submits a decryption query* $(CT = (CT_1\|\cdots\|CT_n, \mathsf{vksig}, \sigma))$ *such that* $\mathsf{vksig} = \mathsf{vksig}^*$ *and* $\mathsf{Ver}(\mathsf{vksig}, CT, \sigma) = 1$.

Our main theorem, Theorem 2, is immediately implied by the following two lemmas:

Lemma 3. *Assume that the scheme $\mathcal{E}_{\mathsf{pa\text{-}cpa}} = (\mathsf{Gen}_{\mathsf{pa\text{-}cpa}}, \mathsf{Enc}_{\mathsf{pa\text{-}cpa}}, \mathsf{Dec}_{\mathsf{pa\text{-}cpa}})$ is a plaintext aware, weakly simulatable public key encryption scheme with perfect correctness. Then encryption scheme $\mathcal{E}_{\mathsf{cca}}$ is nested-indistinguishable.*

Lemma 4. *Assume that the scheme $\mathcal{E}_{\mathsf{pa\text{-}cpa}} = (\mathsf{Gen}_{\mathsf{pa\text{-}cpa}}, \mathsf{Enc}_{\mathsf{pa\text{-}cpa}}, \mathsf{Dec}_{\mathsf{pa\text{-}cpa}})$ is a plaintext aware, weakly simulatable public key encryption scheme with perfect correctness, the scheme $(\mathsf{GenSig}, \mathsf{Sign}, \mathsf{Ver})$ is a strong one-time signature scheme and prg is a pseudorandom generator. Then for $\beta \in \{0,1\}$ and for every ppt adversary A:*

$$\{\mathsf{N\text{-}Exp}_{\beta,1}(\mathcal{E}_{\mathsf{cca}}, A, k)\}_{k \in \mathbb{N}} \overset{s}{\approx} \{\mathsf{CCA2\text{-}Exp}_{\beta}(\mathcal{E}_{\mathsf{cca}}, A, k)\}_{k \in \mathbb{N}}$$

Lemma 3 follows by a straightforward reduction to semantic security of $\mathcal{E}_{\mathsf{pa\text{-}cpa}}$. Lemma 4 follows in a straightforward manner from the fact that Bad Extraction Event and Forging Signature Event occur with at most negligible probability when $z = 1$ along with the perfect correctness of $\mathcal{E}_{\mathsf{pa\text{-}cpa}}$.

In what follows, we focus our attention on proving that Bad Extraction Event occurs with at most negligible probability when $z = 1$. The proof that Forging Signature Event occurs with negligible probability is straightforward and can be found in the full version [11]. To show this we proceed in the following way:

- In Section 4.1 we prove that Bad Extraction Event occurs with negligible probability in the Nested Indistinguishability Experiment when $z = 0$.
- In Section 4.2 we use the fact that Bad Extraction Event occurs with negligible probability in the Nested Indistinguishability Experiment when $z = 0$ to prove that Bad Extraction Event also occurs with negligible probability in the Nested Indistinguishability Experiment when $z = 1$.

4.1 Bad Extraction Event When $z = 0$

In this section we prove the following lemma:

Lemma 5. *Bad Extraction Event occurs with negligible probability when $z = 0$.*

We proceed by considering a sequence of hybrids:

Hybrid H_0: Proceeds exactly as the nested indistinguishability game for $z = 0$.

Hybrid H_1: Proceeds exactly like H_0 except that fresh randomness r_i is used to encrypt each $CT_i^* = \mathsf{Enc}_{\mathsf{pa\text{-}cpa}}(pk_i^{\mathsf{vksig}_i}, CT_{in_0}^*||CT_{in_1}^*; r_i)$, instead of the prg.

Claim. The probability of a Bad Extraction Event in H_1 and H_0 differs by a negligible amount.

This follows in a straightforward manner from the security of the prg.

Hybrid H_2: Proceeds exactly like H_1 except the oracle $\mathcal{O}$ returns uniformly random $r_1, \ldots, r_k$.

Claim. The probability of Bad Extraction Event in H_2 is negligible.

The claim follows due to the fact that the view of C_A in the nested indistinguishability experiment in Hybrid H_2 is identical to the view of C_A in the $\mathsf{sPA1}^+_{2k+2}$ experiment (since in H_2 the oracle $\mathcal{O}$ simply returns uniformly random coins $r_1, \ldots, r_k$, as does the oracle in the $\mathsf{sPA1}^*_{2k+2}$ experiment). Thus, by the $\mathsf{sPA1}^+_{2k+2}$-secuirty of $\mathcal{E}_{\mathsf{pa\text{-}cpa}}$, C^* is guaranteed to return the same value as $\mathsf{Dec}_{\mathsf{pa\text{-}cpa}}$ on all ciphertexts submitted by C_A with all but negligible probability.

Claim. The probability of a Bad Extraction Event in H_1 and H_2 differs by a negligible amount.

Proof. Assume towards contradiction that there exists a ppt adversary A such that a Bad Extraction Event in H_1 and H_2 differs by a non-negligible amount $p = p(k)$ when interacting with A, C_A, C^*. We present a ppt adversary B breaking the weak simulatability of $\mathcal{E}_{\mathsf{pa\text{-}cpa}}$.

B participates in an external experiment where B plays the security game of the weakly simulatable encryption scheme $\mathcal{E}_{\mathsf{pa\text{-}cpa}}$ while internally interacting with the adversary A and the corresponding ciphertext creator C_A and extractor C^* in the following way:

- B receives $\hat{pk}_1, \ldots, \hat{pk}_k$ from the external simulatability security experiment.
- B chooses a random tape r_{C_A} for the ciphertext creator C_A.
- B computes $(\mathsf{sksig}^*, \mathsf{vksig}^*) \leftarrow_{\$} \mathsf{GenSig}(1^k; r_{\mathsf{sksig}})$, where r_{sksig} consists of the first k bits of r_{C_A}.
- B generates public key, secret key pairs $[pk_{in_b}, sk_{in_b}]_{b \in \{0,1\}}, \{pk_i^{1-\mathsf{vksig}^*_i}, sk_i^{1-\mathsf{vksig}^*_i}\}_{i \in [k]}$ and for $i \in [k]$ sets $pk_i^{\mathsf{vksig}^*_i} = \hat{pk}_i$.
- B instantiates C_A with random tape r_{C_A} on input $[pk_{in_b}]_{b \in \{0,1\}}, \{pk_i^b\}_{b \in \{0,1\}, i \in [k]}$.
- Eventually C_A outputs (m_0, m_1). At this point, B plays the part of the oracle $\mathcal{O}$ and does the following:
  1. Choose $\tilde{s}_0, \tilde{s}_1 \leftarrow_{\$} \{0,1\}^\ell$ and compute $CT^*_{in_0} \leftarrow_{\$} \mathsf{Enc}_{\mathsf{pa\text{-}cpa}}(pk_{in_0}, \tilde{s}_0)$; $CT^*_{in_1} \leftarrow_{\$} \mathsf{Enc}_{\mathsf{pa\text{-}cpa}}(pk_{in_1}, \tilde{s}_1)$
  2. Submit $CT^*_{in_0} || CT^*_{in_1}$ to its external challenger.
  3. Receives $(r_1, CT^*_1), \ldots, (r_k, CT^*_k)$ from its external challenger, where for each i, $r_i = f^{-1}(pk_i, c = \mathsf{Enc}_{\mathsf{pa\text{-}cpa}}(pk_i, CT^*_{in_0} || CT^*_{in_1}))$ if $b = 0$ or $(r_i, f(pk_i, r_i))$ for randomly generated r_i if $b = 1$.

  B forwards $r_1, \ldots, r_k$ to C_A on behalf of oracle $\mathcal{O}$ and continues the emulation of C_A.
- If at any point during the emulation, Bad Extraction Event occurs (which B can check by decrypting using $[sk_{in_b}]_{b \in \{0,1\}}, \{sk_i^{1-\mathsf{vksig}^*_i}\}_{i \in [k]}$), B aborts and outputs 1.
- Otherwise, B outputs 0.

Note that for $\beta \in \{0,1\}$, B perfectly simulates C_A's view in Hybrid H_1 when $b = 0$ and perfectly simulates C_A's view in Hybrid H_2. Thus, B outputs 1 in the case that $b = 0$ in the external experiment with probability p_1 and B outputs

1 in the case that $b = 1$ in the external experiment with probability p_2 where $p_1 - p_2 > p$. Since by hypothesis, p is non-negligible, we have that B breaks the security of the weakly simulatable encryption scheme $\mathcal{E}_{\text{pa-cpa}}$.

Lemma 5 follows immediately from Claims 4.1, 4.1 and 4.1.

4.2   Bad Extraction Event When $z = 1$

In this section we prove the following lemma:

Lemma 6. *Bad Extraction Event occurs with negligible probability when $z = 1$.*

To aid in our analysis, we define a second experiment "Modified Nested Indistinguishability" and a second Bad Extraction Event, "Modified Bad Extraction Event". The Modified Nested Indistinguishability experiment is *identical* to the Nested Indistinguishability experiment except that an additional random variable $b \leftarrow_{\$} \{0, 1\}$ is chosen at the very beginning of the experiment. The Modified Bad Extraction Event will then depend on the value of b chosen during the experiment. Details follow.

Definition 8 (The Modified Bad Extraction Event). *We say that a modified bad extraction event has occurred during an execution of the nested indistinguishability experiment if at some point A submits a decryption query $CT = (CT_1\|\cdots\|CT_n, \text{vksig}, \sigma)$ such that one of the following occurs:*

- $C^*(st, CT_i) \neq \text{Dec}_{\text{pa-cpa}}(\text{sk}_i^{\text{vksig}_i}, CT_i)$ *where i is the first index such that* $\text{vksig}_i^* \neq \text{vksig}_i$.
- $C^*(st, CT_{in_b}) \neq \text{Dec}_{\text{pa-cpa}}(sk_{in_b}, CT_{in_b})$

Claim. For every ppt adversary $A = (A_1, A_2)$ and for $\beta \in \{0, 1\}$, Modified Bad Extraction Event occurs in $\text{M-N-Exp}_{\beta, z}(\mathcal{E}_{\text{cca}}, A, k)$ with negligible probability when $z = 0$.

This follows immediately from the fact that for every ppt adversary $A = (A_1, A_2)$, Bad Extraction event occurs in $\text{N-Exp}_{\beta, z}(\mathcal{E}_{\text{cca}}, A, k)$ with negligible probability when $z = 0$.

Claim. If for some ppt adversary $A = (A_1, A_2)$ we have that Bad Extraction Event occurs with probability p_1 in $\text{N-Exp}_{\beta, z}(\mathcal{E}_{\text{cca}}, A, k)$ when $z = 1$ then Modified Bad Extraction Event occurs with probability at least $p_1/2$ in $\text{M-N-Exp}_{\beta, z}(\mathcal{E}_{\text{cca}}, A, k)$ when $z = 1$.

Proof. Let A be a ppt adversary such that Bad Extraction Event occurs with probability p_1 in the experiment $\text{N-Exp}_{\beta, 1}(\mathcal{E}_{\text{cca}}, A, k)$. Let event E be the event that for some query, $CT = (CT_1\|\cdots\|CT_k, \text{vksig}, \sigma)$, one of the following occurs.

$$C^*(st, CT_i) \neq \text{Dec}_{\text{pa-cpa}}(\text{sk}_i^{\text{vksig}_i}, CT_i) \tag{1}$$

where i is the first index such that $\text{vksig}_i^* \neq \text{vksig}_i$.

OR
$$C^*(st, CT_{in_0}) \neq \mathsf{Dec}_{\mathsf{pa\text{-}cpa}}(sk_{in_0}, CT_{in_0}) \tag{2}$$

OR
$$C^*(st, CT_{in_1}) \neq \mathsf{Dec}_{\mathsf{pa\text{-}cpa}}(sk_{in_1}, CT_{in_1}) \tag{3}$$

and this is the *first such query* made by A during the experiment. Note that the probability that event E occurs in $\mathsf{N\text{-}Exp}_{\beta,1}(\mathcal{E}_{\mathsf{cca}}, A, k)$ and the probability that E occurs in $\mathsf{M\text{-}N\text{-}Exp}_{\beta,1}(\mathcal{E}_{\mathsf{cca}}, A, k)$ is p_1.

We consider an experiment, $\mathsf{M\text{-}N\text{-}Exp}'_{beta,z}(\mathcal{E}_{\mathsf{cca}}, A, k)$, identical to the Modified Nested Indistinguishability experiment except the value of b is chosen "on the fly" at the first point when event E occurs. It is straightforward to see that the probability of event E in $\mathsf{M\text{-}N\text{-}Exp}'_{\beta,1}(\mathcal{E}_{\mathsf{cca}}, A, k)$ is also p_1 (the same as the probability of E in the experiment $\mathsf{M\text{-}N\text{-}Exp}_{\beta,1}(\mathcal{E}_{\mathsf{cca}}, A, k)$).

Now, if event E was triggered by a query $CT = (CT_1\|\cdots\|CT_k, \mathsf{vksig}, \sigma)$ in $\mathsf{M\text{-}N\text{-}Exp}'_{beta,1}(\mathcal{E}_{\mathsf{cca}}, A, k)$ such that (1) occurs, then modified bad extraction event also occurs. Alternatively, if event E was triggered by a query $CT = (CT_1\|\cdots\|CT_k, \mathsf{vksig}, \sigma)$ in $\mathsf{M\text{-}N\text{-}Exp}'_{beta,1}(\mathcal{E}_{\mathsf{cca}}, A, k)$ such that (2) or (3) occurs, then modified bad extraction event occurs with probability exactly $1/2$. Thus, modified bad extraction event occurs in $\mathsf{M\text{-}N\text{-}Exp}'_{beta,1}(\mathcal{E}_{\mathsf{cca}}, A, k)$ with probability at least $p_1/2$. Since the view of C_A is identical in $\mathsf{M\text{-}N\text{-}Exp}'_{beta,1}(\mathcal{E}_{\mathsf{cca}}, A, k)$ and in $\mathsf{M\text{-}N\text{-}Exp}_{beta,1}(\mathcal{E}_{\mathsf{cca}}, A, k)$ we have that modified bad extraction event occurs in $\mathsf{M\text{-}N\text{-}Exp}_{\beta,1}(\mathcal{E}_{\mathsf{cca}}, A, k)$ with probability at least $p_1/2$.

Claim. The probability of a Modified Bad Extraction Event when $z = 0$ and $z = 1$ differs by a negligible amount.

Proof. Assume towards contradiction that there is a ppt adversary A such that the probability of a Modified Bad Extraction Event in $\mathsf{M\text{-}N\text{-}Exp}_{beta,0}(\mathcal{E}_{\mathsf{cca}}, A, k)$ is $p_0 = p_0(k)$, the probability of a Modified Bad Extraction Event in $\mathsf{M\text{-}N\text{-}Exp}_{beta,1}(\mathcal{E}_{\mathsf{cca}}, A, k)$ is $p_1 = p_1(k)$ and $p(k) = p_1(k) - p_0(k)$ is non-negligible. We present a ppt adversary B that uses A to break the semantic security of $\mathcal{E}_{\mathsf{pa\text{-}cpa}}$.

B participates in an external semantic security experiment for encryption scheme $\mathcal{E}_{\mathsf{pa\text{-}cpa}}$ while internally emulating a run of $\mathsf{M\text{-}N\text{-}Exp}$ with C_A, A and playing the part of the oracle $\mathcal{O}$. More specifically, B receives a public key $pk_{\mathsf{pa\text{-}cpa}}$ from the semantic security experiment for the encryption scheme $\mathcal{E}_{\mathsf{pa\text{-}cpa}}$ and does the following:

- B chooses $b \leftarrow_\$ \{0, 1\}$. and sets $pk_{in_{1-b}} = pk_{\mathsf{pa\text{-}cpa}}$
- B chooses $(pk_{in_b}, sk_{in_b}) \leftarrow_\$ \mathsf{Gen}_{\mathsf{pa\text{-}cpa}}(1^k)$ and $[pk_i^b, sk_i^b]_{b\in\{0,1\}, i\in[k]} \leftarrow_\$ \mathsf{Gen}_{\mathsf{pa\text{-}cpa}}(1^k)$.
- B chooses a random tape r_{C_A} for C_A and begins an emulation of C_A with input $([pk_{in_b}]_{b\in\{0,1\}}, [pk_i^b]_{b\in\{0,1\}, i\in[k]})$.
- At some point C_A outputs m_0, m_1. At this point, B, playing the part of the oracle $\mathcal{O}$, returns $r_1, \ldots, r_k$ where $(r_1, CT_1^*) = f^{-1}(pk_1^{\mathsf{vksig}_1^*}, CT_1^*), \ldots, (r_k, CT_k^*) = f^{-1}(pk_1^{\mathsf{vksig}_k^*}, CT_k^*)$ and $CT_1^*, \ldots, CT_k^*$ are computed in the following way:

- $r \leftarrow_\$ \{0,1\}^k, r_1, \ldots, r_n \leftarrow \mathsf{prg}(r)$.
- $(\mathsf{sksig}, \mathsf{vksig}) \leftarrow_\$ \mathsf{GenSig}(1^k)$
- Choose $\tilde{s}_b \leftarrow_\$ \{0,1\}^\ell$, $\tilde{s}_{1-b}^0 \leftarrow_\$ \{0,1\}^\ell$ and set $\tilde{s}_{1-b}^1 \leftarrow (r\|m_\beta) \oplus \tilde{s}_b$.
- B returns $M_0 = \tilde{s}_{1-b}^0, M_1 = \tilde{s}_{1-b}^1$ to its external challenger and receives ciphertext $CT_{\mathsf{pa\text{-}cpa}}$ in return.
- B sets $CT_{in_b}^* \leftarrow_\$ \mathsf{Enc}_{\mathsf{pa\text{-}cpa}}(pk_{in_0}, \tilde{s}_b)$ and sets $CT_{in_{1-b}}^* = CT_{\mathsf{pa\text{-}cpa}}$.
- For $1 \leq i \leq k$, $CT_i^* \leftarrow \mathsf{Enc}_{\mathsf{pa\text{-}cpa}}(pk_i^{\mathsf{vksig}}, CT_{in_0}^* \| CT_{in_1}^* ; r_i)$

- B continues the emulation of C_A, A.
- If the event Modified Bad Extraction Event occurs, B aborts and outputs 1.
- Otherwise, B outputs 0.

Note that for $\beta \in \{0,1\}$, B perfectly simulates C_A's view in the experiment M-N-Exp$(\beta, 0)$. Thus, B outputs 1 in the case that it receives an encryption of M_1 with probability p_1 and B outputs 1 in the case that it receives an encryption of M_0 with probability p_2 where $p_1 - p_2 > p$. Since by hypothesis, p is non-negligible, we have that B breaks the semantic security of $\mathcal{E}_{\mathsf{pa\text{-}cpa}}$.

Together, Claims 4.2, 4.2 and 4.2 immediately imply Lemma 6.

References

1. Barak, B.: How to go beyond the black-box simulation barrier. In: FOCS, pp. 106–115 (2001)
2. Bellare, M., Desai, A., Pointcheval, D., Rogaway, P.: Relations among notions of security for public-key encryption schemes. In: Krawczyk, H. (ed.) CRYPTO 1998. LNCS, vol. 1462, pp. 26–45. Springer, Heidelberg (1998)
3. Bellare, M., Palacio, A.: The knowledge-of-exponent assumptions and 3-round zero-knowledge protocols. In: Franklin, M. (ed.) CRYPTO 2004. LNCS, vol. 3152, pp. 273–289. Springer, Heidelberg (2004)
4. Bellare, M., Palacio, A.: Towards plaintext-aware public-key encryption without random oracles. In: Lee, P.J. (ed.) ASIACRYPT 2004. LNCS, vol. 3329, pp. 48–62. Springer, Heidelberg (2004)
5. Bellare, M., Rogaway, P.: Optimal asymmetric encryption. In: De Santis, A. (ed.) EUROCRYPT 1994. LNCS, vol. 950, pp. 92–111. Springer, Heidelberg (1995)
6. Bitansky, N., Canetti, R., Chiesa, A., Tromer, E.: From extractable collision resistance to succinct non-interactive arguments of knowledge, and back again. In: ITCS, pp. 326–349 (2012)
7. Canetti, R., Halevi, S., Katz, J.: Chosen-ciphertext security from identity-based encryption. In: Cachin, C., Camenisch, J.L. (eds.) EUROCRYPT 2004. LNCS, vol. 3027, pp. 207–222. Springer, Heidelberg (2004)
8. Cash, D., Kiltz, E., Shoup, V.: The twin diffie-hellman problem and applications. J. Cryptology 22(4), 470–504 (2009)
9. Choi, S.G., Dachman-Soled, D., Malkin, T., Wee, H.M.: Black-box construction of a non-malleable encryption scheme from any semantically secure one. In: Canetti, R. (ed.) TCC 2008. LNCS, vol. 4948, pp. 427–444. Springer, Heidelberg (2008)
10. Cramer, R., Shoup, V.: Universal hash proofs and a paradigm for adaptive chosen ciphertext secure public-key encryption. In: Knudsen, L.R. (ed.) EUROCRYPT 2002. LNCS, vol. 2332, pp. 45–64. Springer, Heidelberg (2002)

11. Dachman-Soled, D.: A black-box construction of a cca2 encryption scheme from a plaintext aware encryption scheme. IACR Cryptology ePrint Archive 2013, 680 (2013)
12. Damgård, I.B., Nielsen, J.B.: Improved non-committing encryption schemes based on a general complexity assumption. In: Bellare, M. (ed.) CRYPTO 2000. LNCS, vol. 1880, pp. 432–450. Springer, Heidelberg (2000)
13. Dent, A.W.: The cramer-shoup encryption scheme is plaintext aware in the standard model. In: Vaudenay, S. (ed.) EUROCRYPT 2006. LNCS, vol. 4004, pp. 289–307. Springer, Heidelberg (2006)
14. Dolev, D., Dwork, C., Naor, M.: Nonmalleable cryptography. SIAM J. Comput. 30(2), 391–437 (2000)
15. Dwork, C., Naor, M., Reingold, O.: Immunizing encryption schemes from decryption errors. In: Cachin, C., Camenisch, J.L. (eds.) EUROCRYPT 2004. LNCS, vol. 3027, pp. 342–360. Springer, Heidelberg (2004)
16. Gertner, Y., Malkin, T., Myers, S.: Towards a separation of semantic and CCA security for public key encryption. In: Vadhan, S.P. (ed.) TCC 2007. LNCS, vol. 4392, pp. 434–455. Springer, Heidelberg (2007)
17. Goldwasser, S., Micali, S.: Probabilistic encryption. J. Comput. Syst. Sci. 28(2), 270–299 (1984)
18. Hada, S., Tanaka, T.: On the existence of 3-round zero-knowledge protocols. In: Krawczyk, H. (ed.) CRYPTO 1998. LNCS, vol. 1462, pp. 408–423. Springer, Heidelberg (1998)
19. Hanaoka, G., Kurosawa, K.: Efficient chosen ciphertext secure public key encryption under the computational diffie-hellman assumption. In: Pieprzyk, J. (ed.) ASIACRYPT 2008. LNCS, vol. 5350, pp. 308–325. Springer, Heidelberg (2008)
20. Haralambiev, K., Jager, T., Kiltz, E., Shoup, V.: Simple and efficient public-key encryption from computational diffie-hellman in the standard model. In: Nguyen, P.Q., Pointcheval, D. (eds.) PKC 2010. LNCS, vol. 6056, pp. 1–18. Springer, Heidelberg (2010)
21. Herzog, J.C., Liskov, M., Micali, S.: Plaintext awareness via key registration. In: Boneh, D. (ed.) CRYPTO 2003. LNCS, vol. 2729, pp. 548–564. Springer, Heidelberg (2003)
22. Hohenberger, S., Lewko, A., Waters, B.: Detecting dangerous queries: A new approach for chosen ciphertext security. In: Pointcheval, D., Johansson, T. (eds.) EUROCRYPT 2012. LNCS, vol. 7237, pp. 663–681. Springer, Heidelberg (2012)
23. Kiltz, E.: Chosen-ciphertext security from tag-based encryption. In: Halevi, S., Rabin, T. (eds.) TCC 2006. LNCS, vol. 3876, pp. 581–600. Springer, Heidelberg (2006)
24. Kiltz, E., Mohassel, P., O'Neill, A.: Adaptive trapdoor functions and chosen-ciphertext security. In: Gilbert, H. (ed.) EUROCRYPT 2010. LNCS, vol. 6110, pp. 673–692. Springer, Heidelberg (2010)
25. Lamport, L.: Constructing digital signatures from a one-way function. Technical Report SRI-CSL-98, SRI International Computer Science Laboratory (1979)
26. Myers, S., Sergi, M., Shelat, A.: Blackbox construction of a more than non-malleable CCA1 encryption scheme from plaintext awareness. In: Visconti, I., De Prisco, R. (eds.) SCN 2012. LNCS, vol. 7485, pp. 149–165. Springer, Heidelberg (2012)
27. Myers, S., Shelat, A.: Bit encryption is complete. In: FOCS, pp. 607–616 (2009)

28. Pass, R., Shelat, A., Vaikuntanathan, V.: Construction of a non-malleable encryption scheme from any semantically secure one. In: Dwork, C. (ed.) CRYPTO 2006. LNCS, vol. 4117, pp. 271–289. Springer, Heidelberg (2006)
29. Peikert, C., Waters, B.: Lossy trapdoor functions and their applications. SIAM J. Comput. 40(6), 1803–1844 (2011)
30. Rompel, J.: One-way functions are necessary and sufficient for secure signatures. In: STOC, pp. 387–394 (1990)
31. Rosen, A., Segev, G.: Chosen-ciphertext security via correlated products. SIAM J. Comput. 39(7), 3058–3088 (2010)
32. Wee, H.: Efficient chosen-ciphertext security via extractable hash proofs. In: Rabin, T. (ed.) CRYPTO 2010. LNCS, vol. 6223, pp. 314–332. Springer, Heidelberg (2010)

Chosen Ciphertext Security via UCE

Takahiro Matsuda and Goichiro Hanaoka

Research Institute for Secure Systems (RISEC),
National Institute of Advanced Industrial Science and Technology (AIST), Japan
{t-matsuda,hanaoka-goichiro}@aist.go.jp

Abstract. Bellare, Hoang, and Keelveedhi (CRYPTO'13) introduced a security notion for a family of (hash) functions called *universal computational extractor* (UCE), and showed how it can be used to realize various kinds of cryptographic primitives in the standard model whose (efficient) constructions were only known in the random oracle model. Although the results of Bellare et al. have shown that UCEs are quite powerful and useful, the notion of UCE is new, and its potential power and limitation do not seem to have been clarified well. To further widen and deepen our understanding of UCE, in this paper we study the construction of chosen ciphertext secure (CCA secure) public key encryption (PKE), one of the most important primitives in the area of cryptography to which (in)applicability of UCEs was not covered by the work of Bellare et al.

We concretely consider the setting in which other than a UCE, we only use chosen plaintext secure (CPA secure) PKE as an additional building block, and obtain several negative and positive results. As our negative results, we show difficulties of instantiating the random oracle in the Fujisaki-Okamoto (FO) construction (PKC'99) with a UCE, by exhibiting pairs of CPA secure PKE and a UCE for which the FO construction instantiated with these pairs becomes insecure (assuming that CPA secure PKE and a UCE exist at all). Then, as our main positive result, we show how to construct a CCA secure PKE scheme using only CPA secure PKE and a UCE as building blocks. Furthermore, we also show how to extend this result to a CCA secure deterministic PKE scheme for block sources (with some constraint on the running time of the sources). Our positive results employ the ideas and techniques from the Dolev-Dwork-Naor (DDN) construction (STOC'91), and for convenience we abstract and formalize the "core" structure of the DDN construction as a stand-alone primitive that we call *puncturable tag-based encryption*, which might be of independent interest.

1 Introduction

Background and Motivation. For the constructions of cryptographic primitives in which we use a hash function as a building block, if we can view the hash function as a random oracle [8], then in most cases we can obtain simple and practical constructions. Moreover, there are some cryptographic primitives whose (efficient) constructions are known only if we use a random oracle. However, random oracles do not exist in the real world, and there are several problems for security proofs in the random oracle model (e.g. [13,23,31]). Therefore, it is in general desirable to consider the constructions of cryptographic primitives without using random oracles.

H. Krawczyk (Ed.): PKC 2014, LNCS 8383, pp. 56–76, 2014.

In CRYPTO 2013, Bellare, Hoang, and Keelveedhi [4] introduced a new security notion for a family of (hash) functions called *universal computational extractor* (UCE), whose main purpose is to "instantiate" and "replace" random oracles used in a wide class of the constructions of cryptographic primitives with UCEs. The UCE security is intended to capture the security satisfied by a hash function that "behaves like a random oracle" as close as possible, and roughly guarantees that outputs of a hash function (in the family) look random, as long as the inputs to the hash function are hard-to-find even given the related information (called *leakage*) of the inputs, and as long as the inputs are independent of a function index that specifies the function from the family.[1] Bellare et al. [4] showed how UCEs can be used to realize various kinds of cryptographic primitives in the standard model whose (efficient) constructions were only known in the random oracle model (such as deterministic public key encryption [3] and message-locked encryption [7]).

Although the results of Bellare et al. have shown that a UCE is quite powerful and useful, the notion of UCE is new, and its potential power and limitation do not seem to have been clarified well. To further widen and deepen our understanding of UCE, in this paper we study the construction of chosen ciphertext secure (CCA secure) public key encryption (PKE) [33,36,19], one of the most important primitives in the area of cryptography for which we have witnessed the great success in the literature (e.g. [9,20,21,1,34]) and yet to which (in)applicability of UCE was not covered by the work of Bellare et al. (In fact, Bellare et al. showed the instantiability of the random oracle in the OAEP scheme [9], but they only showed the chosen plaintext (CPA) security.) As a first step towards clarifying the usefulness of UCEs in the context of constructing CCA secure PKE, in this paper we concretely consider the setting where, other than a UCE, we only use CPA secure PKE as an additional (and seemingly minimal) building block, and obtain several negative and positive results.

Our Contributions. In this paper, we investigate the usefulness and (in)applicability of UCEs in the context of constructing CCA secure PKE. As mentioned above, we concretely study the setting in which other than a UCE, we only use CPA secure PKE as an additional building block, and obtain several negative and positive results.

Our starting point is the Fujisaki-Okamoto (FO) construction [20] which constructs CCA secure PKE from a random oracle and a CPA secure PKE scheme (satisfying some property on cardinality of ciphertexts). As our negative results, in Section 3, we show the difficulties of instantiating the random oracle in the FO construction with a UCE if we simply put a function index of a UCE into a public key. Specifically, we first show that (assuming that CPA secure PKE and a UCE exist) there exists a pair of CPA secure PKE and a UCE for which the FO construction instantiated with this pair is *not* even CPA secure. This result is shown by designing a pair of a CPA secure PKE

---

[1] Actually, "UCE" is not a single security notion, but a family of security notions for a function family, from which a particular notion is specified when we specify what class of "sources" we will consider. For more details, see the explanation and the formal definition in Section 2.1. For convenience, in the introduction, when we just write "UCE" (resp. "UCE security"), we mean a function family that satisfies some version of UCE security notions (resp. one of UCE security notions), and exactly which notion is used will be specified in the formal statements given in Sections 3 and 5.

scheme having a "weak randomness" and a UCE having a function-index-dependent "weak input" so that when this pair is used as building blocks in the FO construction, the resulting PKE scheme has a public-key-dependent "weak plaintext," which is weak in the sense that a ciphertext leaks the information of whether or not this weak plaintext is encrypted. We then further investigate whether the FO construction can be secure for "public-key-independent" messages, which could be still useful for example in the setting where the FO construction is used as a key encapsulation mechanism (KEM) by encrypting a random message and using it as a session-key (for SKE). We show another negative result for this case by exhibiting yet another pair of CPA secure PKE and a UCE such that when used as building blocks, the FO construction is *not* CCA1 secure even if we restrict an adversary to choose two uniformly random (and hence public-key-independent) plaintexts as its challenge plaintexts and allow the adversary to make only one decryption query. This result is obtained by designing a pair of CPA secure PKE and a UCE which have a public-key-dependent "critical ciphertext" whose decryption result reveals the (essential part of) secret key. For more details, see Section 3.

Given the above negative results, we depart from the original FO construction [20]. By employing the ideas and techniques from the classical Dolev-Dwork-Naor (DDN) construction [19] together with a UCE, we obtain several positive results. Specifically, in Section 5, as our main positive result we show how to construct a CCA secure PKE scheme using only a CPA secure PKE scheme and a UCE. We actually construct a CCA secure key encapsulation mechanism (KEM), but by combining it with a CCA secure SKE scheme, we obtain a full-fledged CCA secure PKE scheme [17]. Furthermore, we show how this KEM can be extended to obtain a deterministic PKE (DPKE) scheme that is CCA secure for block sources (with some additional constraint on the running time of the sources), using the same building blocks as above. To the best of our knowledge, our DPKE scheme is the first scheme which achieves CCA security for block sources in the standard model without using lossy trapdoor functions (TDFs) [35] or related primitives (though we have some non-standard restriction on the running time of sources). By noting that a CCA secure DPKE scheme (for block sources with bounded running time) is as it is an injective TDF which satisfies adaptively one-wayness [26], this result immediately yields an adaptively one-way TDF as well. We also show how to weaken the assumption on the UCE security if the underlying PKE scheme is additionally a lossy encryption scheme [6]. The ideas and techniques for our proposed constructions are explained in more details in "*Overview of Techniques*" paragraph below.

Our positive results clarify not only a new and important primitive for which UCEs are useful, but also insights for the "gap" between CPA and CCA security for PKE. Specifically, our results imply that if there exists a CPA secure PKE scheme and a UCE, then there exist a CCA secure PKE scheme and a CCA secure DPKE for block sources (with some constraint on the running time). This could be contrasted with the current state-of-the-art attempts for constructing PKE schemes that satisfy security which is as close as CCA security, using only a CPA secure PKE scheme as a building block. The current best security is bounded CCA security [16] (more precisely, non-malleability under bounded-CCA [15] and its slightly stronger variant [30]). Therefore, our results serve as a concrete evidence that a UCE is quite a strong primitive, and has the power to "jump" the currently known gap between CPA and CCA security for PKE schemes.

As explained in details below, in our proposed constructions, we employ the ideas and techniques from the DDN construction [19]. For ease of notation and reducing the description complexity, we abstract the "core" structure of the DDN construction as tag-based encryption (TBE) [28,25] with some special property, and formalize it as a stand-alone primitive which we call *puncturable TBE* (PTBE). This formalization may be useful for understanding the security proof of the DDN construction, and future works that use the ideas and the techniques of the DDN construction in a similar way to ours, and may be of independent interest. For more details, see Section 4.

Due to space limitation, most of the proofs of the theorems and lemmas in this paper are omitted and will be given in the full version, and we only give proof sketches or intuitive explanations.

Overview of Techniques. Our proposed CCA secure KEM is based on the DDN construction [19], which originally constructs a CCA secure PKE scheme using a CPA secure PKE scheme, a non-interactive zero-knowledge (NIZK) proof, and a one-time signature scheme. In the original DDN construction, the NIZK proof roughly ensures that each "component"-ciphertext from the underlying CPA secure PKE scheme is in a valid form, i.e. it is in the range of the encryption algorithm and encrypts the same value. Here, if there is another mechanism that ensures the "validity" of component-ciphertexts, then we can remove the NIZK proof from this construction. This is the place where a UCE comes into play. Specifically, by relying on the power of UCE, for the DDN construction we realize the mechanism of the "randomness-recovering decryption" (also called "witness-recovering decryption") [20,21,35,10,37,32,24,29], where (a part of) randomness used to generate a ciphertext is recovered in the decryption process, and this recovered randomness is used to check the validity of the component-ciphertexts by re-encryption. This "decrypt-then-re-encrypt"-style validity check works as an alternative of the NIZK proof in the original DDN construction. Actually, such a mechanism of recovering randomness in the decryption process usually causes a circularity between a plaintext and a randomness (used to generate the ciphertext itself), but in our construction this circularity can be overcome by the security of a UCE.

Then, our proposed CCA secure KEM is obtained by applying one more enhancement to this "DDN without NIZK" construction. Specifically, we implement the mechanism of preventing the "re-use" of component-ciphertexts in the DDN construction, which is originally realized by a one-time signature (i.e. the technique of using a verification key of the one-time signature as a kind of "non-reusable tag" in each ciphertext), with a commitment scheme. This change not only leads to smaller ciphertexts, but also (by appropriately combining it with a UCE) to a scheme with "full randomness-recovering," namely, in the decryption process an entire randomness is recovered. Hence, with a similar observation in [10], we also obtain a CCA secure DPKE scheme for block sources. (However, we need to put some additional constraint on the sources, due to the requirement on UCE security notions that we use.) For more details about our constructions, see Section 5.

Related Work. The notion of CCA security for PKE was formalized by Naor and Yung [33] and Rackoff and Simon [36]. Since the introduction of the notion, CCA secure PKE schemes have been studied in a number of papers, and thus we only briefly review constructions from general cryptographic assumptions. Dolev, Dwork, and Naor [19] showed the first construction of a CCA secure PKE scheme, from a CPA secure scheme and a NIZK proof system, based on the construction by Naor and Yung [33] that achieves weaker non-adaptive CCA (CCA1) security. Canetti, Halevi, and Katz [14] showed how to transform an identity-based encryption scheme into a CCA secure PKE scheme. Kiltz [25] showed that the transform of [14] is applicable to a weaker primitive of tag-based encryption (TBE). Peikert and Waters [35] showed how to construct a CCA secure PKE scheme from a *lossy* trapdoor function (TDF). Subsequent works showed that TDFs with weaker security/functionality properties are sufficient for obtaining CCA secure PKE schemes [37,26,39]. Myers and Shelat [32] showed that a CCA secure PKE scheme for 1-bit plaintexts can be turned into one for arbitrarily long plaintexts. Hohenberger, Lewko, and Waters [24] showed that CCA secure PKE can be constructed from a PKE scheme with a weaker security notion called detectable CCA security. Lin and Tessaro [27] showed how to amplify weak CCA security into strong (ordinary) CCA secure one. Recently, Sahai and Waters [38] showed how (among other primitives) CCA secure PKE can be constructed using indistinguishability obfuscation [2,22]. Very recently, Matsuda and Hanaoka [29] showed how to construct CCA secure PKE using obfuscation for point functions (with multi-bit output), and Dachman-Soled [18] showed a construction from PKE satisfying (the standard model) plaintext-awareness as well as some additional "simulatability" property. We note that our proposed constructions and these two constructions [29,18] have the properties that they all rely on the ideas and techniques of the DDN construction [19].

2   Preliminaries

In this section, we review the basic notation and the definitions of primitives.

Basic Notation. $\mathbb{N}$ denotes the set of all natural numbers. For $m, n \in \mathbb{N}$, we define $[n] := \{1, \ldots, n\}$, and "$\mathsf{Func}_{m \to n}$" denotes the set of all functions F of the form $F : \{0,1\}^m \to \{0,1\}^n$. "$x \leftarrow y$" denotes that x is chosen uniformly at random from y if y is a finite set, x is output from y if y is a function or an algorithm, or y is assigned to x otherwise. If x and y are strings, then "$|x|$" denotes the bit-length of x, "$x\|y$" denotes the concatenation x and y, and "$(x \overset{?}{=} y)$" is defined to be 1 if $x = y$ and 0 otherwise. "(P)PTA" stands for a *(probabilistic) polynomial time algorithm*. For a finite set S, "$|S|$" denotes its size. If $\mathcal{A}$ is a probabilistic algorithm, then "$y \leftarrow \mathcal{A}(x; r)$" denotes that $\mathcal{A}$ computes y as output by taking x as input and using r as randomness. $\mathcal{A}^{\mathcal{O}}$ denotes an algorithm $\mathcal{A}$ with oracle access to $\mathcal{O}$. A function $\epsilon(k) : \mathbb{N} \to [0, 1]$ is said to be *negligible* if for all positive polynomials $p(k)$ and all sufficiently large $k \in \mathbb{N}$, we have $\epsilon(k) < 1/p(k)$. Throughout the paper, we use the character "k" for the security parameter. For an algorithm M, we denote by $\mathsf{t_M} = \mathsf{t_M}(k)$ the maximum (worst-case) running time of M when M is run with security parameter k.

2.1   Universal Computational Extractor (UCE)

Here, we recall the definition of UCE (universal computational extractor) [4], which is a family of security notions for a (hash) function family. We first recall the syntax of a function family, and then the definitions of UCE security. We also introduce a property that we call *smoothness* which is used in our negative results in Section 3.

Syntax. Let $m, n : \mathbb{N} \to \mathbb{N}$ be functions of k. A family of functions (function family) $\mathcal{F}$ with input length m and output length n consists of the following two deterministic PTAs (FKG, F): FKG is the key generation algorithm which takes 1^k as input, and outputs a function index κ.; F is the evaluation algorithm that takes a function index κ and a string $x \in \{0, 1\}^m$ as input, and outputs a string $y \in \{0, 1\}^n$. For notational convenience, we write $\mathsf{F}_\kappa(\cdot)$ to mean $\mathsf{F}(\kappa, \cdot)$.

UCE Security. Before giving the formal definitions, we give some overview. As mentioned earlier, the UCE security is a family of security notions, from which a particular notion is specified when we specify a class S of "sources" $\mathcal{S}$. A source is a part of an adversary's algorithm that is responsible for computing the inputs to the function $\mathsf{F}_\kappa(\cdot)$ (that are chosen independently of the function index κ) together with some relevant information called *leakage L*, where the independence of the inputs from κ is captured by allowing $\mathcal{S}$ only oracle access to the function. The UCE security for the class S (UCE[S] security, for short), states that for any PPTA adversary, called *distinguisher*, who receives the function index κ and the leakage L, cannot tell whether L is computed by a source $\mathcal{S} \in$ S using the function $\mathsf{F}_\kappa(\cdot)$ or using a random function, better than a random guess. How strong/weak, and how useful UCE[S] security is depends on what restrictions we put on the class S of sources. The wider the class S is, the stronger UCE[S] security becomes. In other words, for classes S and S' of sources, if S $\subseteq$ S', then UCE[S'] security implies UCE[S] security.

In the proceedings version [4], Bellare et al. considered a class of computationally unpredictable sources (which we denote by $\mathsf{S}^{\mathrm{cup}}$), which roughly requires that given a leakage L computed by a source $\mathcal{S}$ in the class under the situation $\mathcal{S}$ has oracle access to a random function, it is hard to find any query to the oracle made by $\mathcal{S}$. Bellare et al. used UCE[$\mathsf{S}^{\mathrm{cup}}$] secure function families to achieve a number of positive results. Unfortunately, however, Brzuska, Farshim, and Mittelbach [12] later showed that if indistinguishability obfuscation [2,22] is possible, then UCE[$\mathsf{S}^{\mathrm{cup}}$] security is unachievable (see also [5]). Since Garg et al. [22] recently showed a candidate construction of it, as mentioned in [5], currently it seems more likely that indistinguishability obfuscation is possible than UCE[$\mathsf{S}^{\mathrm{cup}}$] secure function families exist. To avoid the attack by Brzuska et al. [12], Bellare et al. [5] suggested several approaches for weakening the UCE[$\mathsf{S}^{\mathrm{cup}}$] security by putting several restrictions on the sources so that the indistinguishability obfuscation-based attack is not possible (and they re-achieved their results of [4] by using appropriately weakened versions of UCE security notions). In this paper, we adopt the two approaches suggested in [5] for weakening UCE[$\mathsf{S}^{\mathrm{cup}}$] security: to consider statistical unpredictability, and to put the restrictions on the running time and the number of queries of sources.

Now we proceed to the formal definitions. Let $\mathcal{F} = (\mathsf{FKG}, \mathsf{F})$ be a function family with input length $m = m(k)$ and output length $n = n(k)$. A *source* $\mathcal{S}$ (for $\mathcal{F}$) is an oracle PPTA that takes 1^k as input, expects to have access to an oracle $\mathcal{O} \in \mathsf{Func}_{m \to n}$, and outputs some value $L \in \{0, 1\}^*$ (called *leakage*). For a pair of a source $\mathcal{S}$ and an adversary $\mathcal{A}$ (called "distinguisher"), consider the UCE experiment $\mathrm{Expt}^{\mathrm{UCE}}_{\mathcal{F}, (\mathcal{S}, \mathcal{A})}(k)$ that is defined as in Fig. 1 (leftmost).

$$\begin{array}{l|l|l|l}
\mathsf{Expt}^{\mathsf{UCE}}_{\mathcal{F},(\mathcal{S},\mathcal{A})}(k): & \mathsf{Expt}^{\mathsf{UNP}}_{\mathcal{S},\mathcal{P}}(k): & \mathsf{Expt}^{\mathsf{CPA}}_{\Pi,\mathcal{A}}(k): & \mathsf{Expt}^{\mathsf{CCA}}_{\Gamma,\mathcal{A}}(k): \\
\kappa \leftarrow \mathsf{FKG}(1^k) & \mathcal{O}(\cdot) \leftarrow \mathsf{Func}_{m \to n} & (pk, sk) \leftarrow \mathsf{PKG}(1^k) & (pk, sk) \leftarrow \mathsf{KKG}(1^k) \\
\mathcal{O}_1(\cdot) \leftarrow \mathsf{F}_\kappa(\cdot) & L \leftarrow \mathcal{S}^{\mathcal{O}}(1^k) & (m_0, m_1, \mathsf{st}) & (c^*, K_1^*) \\
\mathcal{O}_0(\cdot) \leftarrow \mathsf{Func}_{m \to n} & \text{Let } Q \text{ be } \mathcal{S}\text{'s queries} & \qquad \leftarrow \mathcal{A}_1(pk) & \qquad \leftarrow \mathsf{Encap}(pk) \\
b \leftarrow \{0,1\} & \quad \text{submitted to } \mathcal{O}. & b \leftarrow \{0,1\} & K_0^* \leftarrow \{0,1\}^k \\
L \leftarrow \mathcal{S}^{\mathcal{O}_b}(1^k) & x' \leftarrow \mathcal{P}(1^k, L) & c^* \leftarrow \mathsf{Enc}(pk, m_b) & b \leftarrow \{0,1\} \\
b' \leftarrow \mathcal{A}(1^k, \kappa, L) & \text{Return 1 iff } x' \in Q. & b' \leftarrow \mathcal{A}_2(\mathsf{st}, c^*) & b' \leftarrow \mathcal{A}^{\mathcal{O}}(pk, c^*, K_b^*) \\
\text{Return } (b' \overset{?}{=} b). & & \text{Return } (b' \overset{?}{=} b). & \text{Return } (b' \overset{?}{=} b).
\end{array}$$

Fig. 1. The experiments for defining security. The UCE experiment for a function family $\mathcal{F}$ (left-most), the UNP experiment for a source $\mathcal{S}$ (second-left), the CPA security experiment for a PKE scheme Π (second-right), and the CCA security experiment for a KEM Γ (rightmost).

Definition 1. *We say that a function family $\mathcal{F}$ is UCE[S]-secure if for all sources $\mathcal{S} \in$ S and for all PPTAs $\mathcal{A}$, $\mathsf{Adv}^{\mathsf{UCE}}_{\mathcal{F},(\mathcal{S},\mathcal{A})}(k) := 2 \cdot |\Pr[\mathsf{Expt}^{\mathsf{UCE}}_{\mathcal{F},(\mathcal{S},\mathcal{A})}(k) = 1] - 1/2|$ is negligible.*

We next define the classes of the sources that we treat in this paper. For a source $\mathcal{S}$ and a PPTA $\mathcal{P}$ (called "predictor"), consider the *unpredictability* experiment $\mathsf{Expt}^{\mathsf{UNP}}_{\mathcal{S},\mathcal{P}}(k)$ defined as in Fig. 1 (second-left).[2]

Definition 2. *For polynomials $t, q > 0$, we say that a source $\mathcal{S}$ is (t, q)-computationally (resp. statistically) unpredictable, denoted by $\mathcal{S} \in \mathsf{S}^{\mathsf{cup}}_{t,q}$ (resp. $\mathcal{S} \in \mathsf{S}^{\mathsf{sup}}_{t,q}$), if (1) $\mathcal{S}$'s running time is at most t and $\mathcal{S}$ makes at most q queries, and (2) for all PPTAs (resp. all computationally unbounded algorithms) $\mathcal{P}$, $\mathsf{Adv}^{\mathsf{UNP}}_{\mathcal{S},\mathcal{P}}(k) := \Pr[\mathsf{Expt}^{\mathsf{UNP}}_{\mathcal{S},\mathcal{P}}(k) = 1]$ is negligible. Furthermore, we just say that a source $\mathcal{S}$ is computationally (resp. statistically) unpredictable, denoted by $\mathcal{S} \in \mathsf{S}^{\mathsf{cup}}$ (resp. $\mathcal{S} \in \mathsf{S}^{\mathsf{sup}}$), if $\mathcal{S}$ is (t, q)-computationally (resp. statistically) unpredictable for some positive polynomials t, q.*

We remark that our definition of (t, q)-computationally/statistically unpredictable source is simpler than the "parallel sources" introduced in [5], which also considers some restrictions on the running time, the number of queries (and the output length), and additionally on how the source is run "parallelly." We choose not to use the definition of the parallel sources in [5] as it is, because in this paper we do not need to consider the "parallel run" of the sources, in which case we believe our definitions are more straight-forward and simpler. We note that any (t, q)-computationally/statistically unpredictable sources that we defined above can always be cast as computationally/statistically unpredictable parallel sources of [5] with appropriate parameters.[3]

We also remark that we could also consider the restriction on the output length of the sources (i.e. the length of leakage). In this paper we choose not to do so for simplicity. However, we note that in each of our results for which we use a UCE security notion as an assumption, the output length of the sources used in the security proofs will be clear.

---

[2] Bellare et al. [4] introduced two kinds of definitions for unpredictability, (ordinary) *"unpredictability"* and *"simple unpredictability,"* and showed their equivalence. The unpredictability in our paper is the simple unpredictability in [4], which is simpler and easier to work with.

[3] More precisely, our definition of the class $\mathsf{S}^{\mathsf{cup}}_{t,q}$ (resp. $\mathsf{S}^{\mathsf{sup}}_{t,q}$) is strictly contained by the class $\mathcal{S}^{\mathsf{cup}} \cap \mathcal{S}^{\mathsf{prl}}_{t,0,q}$ (resp. $\mathcal{S}^{\mathsf{sup}} \cap \mathcal{S}^{\mathsf{prl}}_{t,0,q}$) in [5].

Smoothness. To show our negative results in Section 3, it is useful to introduce the following property of a function family.

Definition 3. *Let* $\mathcal{F} = (\mathsf{FKG}, \mathsf{F})$ *be a function family with input length* $m = m(k)$ *and output length* $n = n(k)$. *We define the* smoothness *of* $\mathcal{F}$, *denoted by* $\mathsf{Smth}_{\mathcal{F}}(k)$, *as* $\mathsf{Smth}_{\mathcal{F}}(k) := \mathbf{E}_{\kappa \leftarrow \mathsf{FKG}(1^k)} \left[\max_{y \in \{0,1\}^n} \Pr_{x \leftarrow \{0,1\}^m} [\mathsf{F}_\kappa(x) = y] \right]$.

The following lemma states a simple fact that a function family satisfying a very weak form of UCE security has negligible smoothness.

Lemma 1. *Let* $\mathcal{F}$ *be a function family with input length* $m = m(k)$ *and output length* $n = n(k)$ *satisfying* $m, n \in \omega(\log k)$. *If* $\mathcal{F}$ *is* $\mathsf{UCE}[\mathsf{S}^{\mathsf{sup}}_{O(m+n+k),1}]$ *secure, then* $\mathsf{Smth}_{\mathcal{F}}(k)$ *is negligible.*

2.2 Basic Primitives

Public Key Encryption. A public key encryption (PKE) scheme Π consists of the three PPTAs (PKG, Enc, Dec) with the following interface:

Key Generation:	Encryption:	Decryption:
$(pk, sk) \leftarrow \mathsf{PKG}(1^k)$	$c \leftarrow \mathsf{Enc}(pk, m)$	$m \text{ (or } \perp) \leftarrow \mathsf{Dec}(sk, c)$

where Dec is a deterministic algorithm, (pk, sk) is a public/secret key pair, and c is a ciphertext of a plaintext m under pk. We require for all $k \in \mathbb{N}$, all (pk, sk) output by $\mathsf{PKG}(1^k)$, and all m, it holds that $\mathsf{Dec}(sk, \mathsf{Enc}(pk, m)) = m$.

For $\mathsf{ATK} \in \{\mathsf{CPA}, \mathsf{CCA1}\}$, we say that a PKE scheme Π is ATK secure if for all PPTAs $\mathcal{A} = (\mathcal{A}_1, \mathcal{A}_2)$, $\mathsf{Adv}^{\mathsf{ATK}}_{\Pi, \mathcal{A}}(k) := 2 \cdot |\Pr[\mathsf{Expt}^{\mathsf{ATK}}_{\Pi, \mathcal{A}}(k) = 1] - 1/2|$ is negligible, where the experiment $\mathsf{Expt}^{\mathsf{CPA}}_{\Pi, \mathcal{A}}(k)$ is defined as in Fig. 1 (second-right), and the experiment $\mathsf{Expt}^{\mathsf{CCA1}}_{\Pi, \mathcal{A}}(k)$ is defined as in $\mathsf{Expt}^{\mathsf{CPA}}_{\Pi, \mathcal{A}}(k)$, except that $\mathcal{A}_1$ has access to the decryption oracle $\mathsf{Dec}(sk, \cdot)$. In both of the experiments, it is required that $|m_0| = |m_1|$.

Here, we recall one of the requirements for the building block PKE scheme for the original FO construction [20]. We say that a PKE scheme $\Pi = (\mathsf{PKG}, \mathsf{Enc}, \mathsf{Dec})$ has the *large ciphertext cardinality* property if for all pk output by $\mathsf{PKG}(1^k)$, it holds that $\min_m |\{\mathsf{Enc}(pk, m; r) | r \in \{0,1\}^*\}| \le k^{\omega(1)}$. (Not all PKE schemes have this property, but any CPA secure PKE scheme can be turned into one satisfying it [20].)

Key Encapsulation Mechanism. A key encapsulation mechanism (KEM) Γ consists of the three PPTAs (KKG, Encap, Decap) with the following interface:

Key Generation:	Encapsulation:	Decapsulation:
$(pk, sk) \leftarrow \mathsf{KKG}(1^k)$	$(c, K) \leftarrow \mathsf{Encap}(pk)$	$K \text{ (or } \perp) \leftarrow \mathsf{Decap}(sk, c)$

where Decap is a deterministic algorithm, (pk, sk) is a public/secret key pair, and c is a ciphertext of a session-key $K \in \{0,1\}^k$ under pk. We require for all $k \in \mathbb{N}$, all (pk, sk) output by $\mathsf{KKG}(1^k)$, and all (c, K) output by $\mathsf{Encap}(pk)$, it holds that $\mathsf{Decap}(sk, c) = K$.

We say that a KEM Γ is CCA secure if for all PPTAs $\mathcal{A}$, $\mathsf{Adv}^{\mathsf{CCA}}_{\Gamma, \mathcal{A}}(k) := 2 \cdot |\Pr[\mathsf{Expt}^{\mathsf{CCA}}_{\Gamma, \mathcal{A}}(k) = 1] - 1/2|$ is negligible, where the experiment $\mathsf{Expt}^{\mathsf{CCA}}_{\Gamma, \mathcal{A}}(k)$ is defined as in Fig. 1 (rightmost). In the experiment, the oracle $\mathcal{O}$ is the decapsulation oracle $\mathsf{Decap}(sk, \cdot)$, and $\mathcal{A}$ is not allowed to query c^*.

Commitment Scheme. (We only define a non-interactive commitment scheme that has a setup procedure, which is sufficient for our purpose.) A commitment scheme $\mathcal{C}$ consists of the following two PPTAs (CKG, Com): CKG takes 1^k as input, and outputs a commitment key ck.; Com takes ck and a message m, and outputs a commitment c.

For security of a commitment scheme, we require the standard *hiding* and *binding* properties. We in fact need weaker properties for both: hiding for messages chosen independently of a commitment key, and binding in which one of the messages needs to be chosen before a commitment key is given, which we call *target-binding*. (The difference between (ordinary) binding and target-binding is similar to the difference between collision resistance and target collision resistance of a hash function.) Due to space limitation, we omit the formal definitions. See the full version for them.

We also require the size of a commitment to be k when generated using a commitment key ck output by $\mathsf{CKG}(1^k)$. This is not a strong requirement if we only consider computational security notions. In particular, a commitment scheme satisfying the above functionality/security requirements can be constructed from any CPA secure PKE.

3 Uninstantiability of the Fujisaki-Okamoto Construction

In this section, we show our negative results: uninstantiability of the random oracle in the Fujisaki-Okamoto (FO) construction [20] with a UCE secure function family.

This section is organized as follows: In Section 3.1, we review the FO construction [20] in which the random oracle is replaced with a function family. In Section 3.2, we show a pair of a CPA secure PKE scheme (with large ciphertext cardinality) and a UCE[S] secure function family (for some class S of sources) which, when used as building blocks, makes the FO construction CPA *insecure*. This attack is demonstrated by using a public-key-dependent plaintext. Then in Section 3.3, we show a pair of a CPA secure PKE scheme (with large ciphertext cardinality) a UCE[S'] secure function family (for another class S' of sources) which, when used as building blocks, makes the FO construction CCA1 *insecure*. This attack is possible even if an adversary has to use public-key-independent plaintexts as its challenge plaintexts, and is allowed to make only one decryption query.

Important Remarks. We would like to emphasize that our results are *not* showing that the FO construction is in general insecure in the standard model. Rather, we show that there are particular pairs of a CPA secure PKE scheme and a function family satisfying some UCE security notions that make the FO construction insecure. Furthermore, our result is only about the FO construction [20] in which we instantiate the random oracle by putting a function index of the used function family into a public key. It would be interesting and worth clarifying the (im)possibility of instantiating the random oracle in [20] in a way different from ours, and the random oracles in the "hybrid-encryption"-style FO construction [21], with UCE secure function families.

$\mathsf{PKG_{FO}}(1^k)$:	$\mathsf{Enc_{FO}}(PK_{FO}, m; r)$:	$\mathsf{Dec_{FO}}(SK_{FO}, C_{FO})$:
$(pk, sk) \leftarrow \mathsf{PKG}(1^k)$	$(pk, \kappa) \leftarrow PK_{FO}$	$(sk, pk, \kappa) \leftarrow SK_{FO}$
$\kappa \leftarrow \mathsf{FKG}(1^k)$	$\alpha \leftarrow (r\|m)$	$\alpha \leftarrow \mathsf{Dec}(sk, C_{FO})$
$PK_{FO} \leftarrow (pk, \kappa)$	$R \leftarrow \mathsf{F}_\kappa(\alpha)$	If $\alpha = \perp$ then return $\perp$.
$SK_{FO} \leftarrow (sk, pk, \kappa)$	$C_{FO} \leftarrow \mathsf{Enc}(pk, \alpha; R)$	$R \leftarrow \mathsf{F}_\kappa(\alpha)$
Return (PK_{FO}, SK_{FO}).	Return C_{FO}.	Parse α as $(r, m) \in \{0,1\}^{k+k}$.
		If $\mathsf{Enc}(pk, \alpha; R) = C_{FO}$
		then return m else return $\perp$.

Fig. 2. The FO construction $\Pi_{FO}[\Pi, \mathcal{F}]$ based on a PKE scheme Π and a function family $\mathcal{F}$

3.1 The Fujisaki-Okamoto Construction Using a Function Family

Firstly, for ease of notation, we introduce the following conditions for a pair of a PKE scheme and a function family that can be used as building blocks of the FO construction.

Definition 4. *Let $\Pi = (\mathsf{PKG}, \mathsf{Enc}, \mathsf{Dec})$ be a PKE scheme and $\mathcal{F}$ be a function family. We say that the pair $(\Pi, \mathcal{F})$ is FO-compatible if (1) the plaintext space of Π is $\{0,1\}^{2k}$, (2) the randomness space of Enc is $\{0,1\}^k$, (3) Π has the large ciphertext cardinality property[4], and (4) the input length and output length of $\mathcal{F}$ are $2k$ and k, respectively.*

Now, using a FO-compatible pair $(\Pi, \mathcal{F})$ as building blocks, we define the PKE scheme $\Pi_{FO}[\Pi, \mathcal{F}] = (\mathsf{PKG_{FO}}, \mathsf{Enc_{FO}}, \mathsf{Dec_{FO}})$ (with plaintext space $\{0,1\}^k$), which we call the *FO construction*, as in Fig. 2.

As mentioned earlier, this PKE scheme can be seen as the original FO construction [20] in which the random oracle is instantiated with the function family $\mathcal{F}$ by putting a function index for $\mathcal{F}$ into a public key. There would be several other ways for instantiating the random oracle with a function family. However, since the original FO construction [20] uses just one random oracle, we believe that the construction in Fig. 2 is the most natural and straightforward instantiation of the random oracle for the original FO construction [20].

3.2 Counterexample for Public-Key-Dependent Plaintexts

This subsection is devoted to proving the following result.

Theorem 1. *Assume that there exists a FO-compatible pair of a CPA secure PKE scheme and a UCE[S] secure function family with $\mathsf{S}^{sup}_{O(k),1} \subseteq \mathsf{S} \subseteq \mathsf{S}^{cup}$. Then, there exists a FO-compatible pair of a CPA secure PKE scheme $\widetilde{\Pi}$ and a UCE[S] secure function family $\widetilde{\mathcal{F}}$ such that the FO construction $\Pi_{FO}[\widetilde{\Pi}, \widetilde{\mathcal{F}}]$ is not CPA secure.*

Proof of Theorem 1. Let $(\Pi = (\mathsf{PKG}, \mathsf{Enc}, \mathsf{Dec}), \mathcal{F} = (\mathsf{FKG}, \mathsf{F}))$ be a FO-compatible pair of a CPA secure PKE scheme Π and a UCE[S] secure function family guaranteed to exist by the assumption of the theorem. Then, we construct another PKE scheme $\widetilde{\Pi} = (\widetilde{\mathsf{PKG}}, \widetilde{\mathsf{Enc}}, \widetilde{\mathsf{Dec}})$ based on Π, and another function family $\widetilde{\mathcal{F}} = (\widetilde{\mathsf{FKG}}, \widetilde{\mathsf{F}})$ based on $\mathcal{F}$, as in Fig. 3 (left-top and left-bottom, respectively). It is straightforward to see

---

[4] This is the property required for the building PKE scheme in the original FO construction [20]. We recall the definition of this property in Section 2.2.

$\mathsf{PKG}(1^k):$	$\widehat{\mathsf{PKG}}(1^k):$	$\widehat{\mathsf{Enc}}(PK,m;r):$
Return $(pk,sk) \leftarrow \mathsf{PKG}(1^k).$	$r^\star \leftarrow \{0,1\}^k$	$(pk,pk',\kappa',c^\star) \leftarrow PK$

$\widetilde{\mathsf{Enc}}(pk,m;r):$

$\gamma \leftarrow (r \stackrel{?}{=} 0^k)$

$c \leftarrow \mathsf{Enc}(pk,m;r)$

Return $C \leftarrow (\gamma,c).$

$\widetilde{\mathsf{Dec}}(sk,C):$

$(\gamma,c) \leftarrow C$

Return $m \leftarrow \mathsf{Dec}(sk,c).$

$\widehat{\mathsf{PKG}}(1^k):$

$r^\star \leftarrow \{0,1\}^k$

$(pk,sk) \leftarrow \mathsf{PKG}(1^k;r^\star)$

$(pk',sk') \leftarrow \mathsf{PKG}'(1^k)$

$\kappa' \leftarrow \mathsf{FKG}'(1^k)$

$r' \leftarrow \mathsf{F}'_{\kappa'}(r^\star)$

$c^\star \leftarrow \mathsf{Enc}'(pk',r^\star;r')$

$PK \leftarrow (pk,pk',\kappa',c^\star)$

$SK \leftarrow (sk,sk')$

Return $(PK,SK).$

$\widehat{\mathsf{Enc}}(PK,m;r):$

$(pk,pk',\kappa',c^\star) \leftarrow PK$

If $r = 0^k$ then

Parse m as (m_1,m_2)

$\qquad \in \{0,1\}^{k+k}.$

$r'' \leftarrow \mathsf{F}'_{\kappa'}(m_2)$

$c_2 \leftarrow \mathsf{Enc}'(pk',m_2;r'')$

Return $C \leftarrow (1\|m_1\|c_2).$

Else

$c \leftarrow \mathsf{Enc}(pk,m;r)$

Return $C \leftarrow (0\|c).$

End if

$\mathsf{FKG}(1^k):$

$\kappa \leftarrow \mathsf{FKG}(1^k); \quad v^\star \leftarrow \{0,1\}^k$

Return $\widetilde{\kappa} \leftarrow (\kappa,v^\star).$

$\mathsf{F}_{\widetilde{\kappa}}(x):$

$(\kappa,v^\star) \leftarrow \widetilde{\kappa}$

Parse x as $(x_1,x_2) \in \{0,1\}^{k+k}.$

$y \leftarrow \begin{cases} 0^k & \text{if } v^\star \in \{x_1,x_2\} \\ \mathsf{F}_\kappa(x) & \text{otherwise} \end{cases}$

Return $y.$

$\widehat{\mathsf{Dec}}(SK,C):$

$(sk,sk') \leftarrow SK$

Parse C as (γ,c) s.t. $|\gamma| = 1.$

If $\gamma = 0$ then return $m \leftarrow \mathsf{Dec}(sk,c).$

Parse c as $(m_1,c_2) \in \{0,1\}^k \times \{0,1\}^\star.$

$m_2 \leftarrow \mathsf{Dec}'(sk',c_2)$

Return $m \leftarrow (m_1\|m_2).$

Fig. 3. The building blocks for the FO construction used for showing the uninstantiability: The PKE scheme $\widetilde{\Pi}$ (left-top), the PKE scheme $\widehat{\Pi}$ (right), and the function family $\widetilde{\mathcal{F}}$ (left-bottom)

that the pair $(\widehat{\Pi}, \widetilde{\mathcal{F}})$ is FO-compatible if so is the pair $(\Pi, \mathcal{F})$. In particular, $\widetilde{\Pi}$ satisfies correctness, and preserves the large ciphertext cardinality property of Π.

Note that $\widetilde{\Pi}$ is designed to have a "weak randomness" $r = 0^k$, and $\widetilde{\mathcal{F}}$ is designed to have a "weak input" $v^\star$ which appears in the function index. We can exploit these "weaknesses" from each building block for attacking the CPA security of $\Pi_{\mathsf{FO}}[\widetilde{\Pi}, \widetilde{\mathcal{F}}]$.

The following lemmas, together with Lemma 1, imply Theorem 1.

Lemma 2. *If the PKE scheme Π is* CPA *secure, then so is the PKE scheme $\widetilde{\Pi}$ constructed as in Fig. 3 (left-top).*

Lemma 3. *For any* S *such that* $\mathsf{S} \subseteq \mathsf{S}^{\mathsf{cup}}$, *if the function family $\mathcal{F}$ is* UCE[S] *secure, then so is the function family $\widetilde{\mathcal{F}}$ constructed as in Fig. 3 (left-bottom).*

Lemma 4. *If* $\mathsf{Smth}_{\widetilde{\mathcal{F}}}(k)$ *is negligible, then the FO construction $\Pi_{\mathsf{FO}}[\widetilde{\Pi}, \widetilde{\mathcal{F}}]$ is not* CPA *secure.*

Lemma 2 is trivial to see, because in the CPA experiment, the probability that the "weak randomness" $r = 0^k$ is chosen is exponentially small. A high level intuition for the proof of Lemma 3 is that the "weak input" $v^\star$ is only in a function index $\widetilde{\kappa}$, chosen uniformly at random and hidden information-theoretically from a source in the unpredictability experiment, and thus it does not do any harm to the UCE[S] security of the underlying function family $\mathcal{F}$.

Finally, we provide a sketch for the proof of Lemma 4. Recall that a public key PK_{FO} of the FO construction $\Pi_{\mathsf{FO}}[\widetilde{\Pi}, \widetilde{\mathcal{F}}]$ is of the form $PK_{\mathsf{FO}} = (pk, \widetilde{\kappa} = (\kappa, v^\star)),$

where $v^\star$ is the "weak input" of $\widetilde{\mathcal{F}}$. Now, let us observe what happens when we encrypt the "weak input" $v^\star$ by $\mathsf{Enc}_{\mathsf{FO}}(PK_{\mathsf{FO}}, \cdot)$. By the design of $\widetilde{\Pi}$, $\widetilde{\mathcal{F}}$, and $\Pi_{\mathsf{FO}}[\widetilde{\Pi}, \widetilde{\mathcal{F}}]$, for any randomness $r \in \{0, 1\}^k$ used in $\mathsf{Enc}_{\mathsf{FO}}(PK_{\mathsf{FO}}, \cdot)$, we have

$$\mathsf{Enc}_{\mathsf{FO}}(PK_{\mathsf{FO}}, v^\star; r) = \widetilde{\mathsf{Enc}}(pk, (r\|v^\star); \mathsf{F}_{\widetilde{\kappa}}(r\|v^\star)) = \widetilde{\mathsf{Enc}}(pk, (r\|v^\star); 0^k) = (1\|c'),$$

where $c' = \mathsf{Enc}(pk, (r\|v^\star); 0^k)$, and hence the first bit of $\mathsf{Enc}_{\mathsf{FO}}(PK_{\mathsf{FO}}, v^\star)$ is always 1. On the other hand, if we encrypt a random plaintext m, then by the smoothness of $\widetilde{\mathcal{F}}$ (which is guaranteed to be negligible by the UCE[S] security of $\widetilde{\mathcal{F}}$, which is in turn based on the UCE[$\mathsf{S}^{\mathsf{sup}}_{O(k),1}$] security of $\mathcal{F}$ and Lemmas 1 and 3), the probability that the first bit of $\mathsf{Enc}_{\mathsf{FO}}(PK_{\mathsf{FO}}, m)$ becomes 1 is negligible. This difference can be used to break the CPA security of $\Pi_{\mathsf{FO}}[\widetilde{\Pi}, \widetilde{\mathcal{F}}]$. $\square$

3.3 Counterexample for Public-Key-Independent Plaintexts

Here, we consider whether the FO construction can provide security for public-key-independent plaintexts (such as uniform random values). If this is possible, then the FO construction may be still used as a secure KEM by encrypting a random message and using it as a session-key. Unfortunately, however, we show that this is not the case. Specifically, this subsection is devoted to proving the following theorem.

Theorem 2. *Assume that there exists a FO-compatible pair of a* CPA *secure PKE scheme* (PKG, Enc, Dec) *and a* UCE[S] *secure function family with* $\mathsf{S}^{\mathsf{cup}}_{O(t_{\mathsf{PKG}}+t_{\mathsf{Enc}}),1} \subseteq \mathsf{S} \subseteq \mathsf{S}^{\mathsf{cup}}$. *Then, there exists a FO-compatible pair of a* CPA *secure PKE scheme* $\widehat{\Pi}$ *and a* UCE[S] *secure function family* $\widehat{\mathcal{F}}$ *such that the FO construction* $\Pi_{\mathsf{FO}}[\widehat{\Pi}, \widehat{\mathcal{F}}]$ *is not* CCA1 *secure. Furthermore, the* CCA1 *attack for* $\Pi_{\mathsf{FO}}[\widehat{\Pi}, \widehat{\mathcal{F}}]$ *succeeds even if an adversary uses two uniformly random plaintexts as its challenge plaintexts and makes only one decryption query.*

Proof of Theorem 2. Let $(\Pi = (\mathsf{PKG}, \mathsf{Enc}, \mathsf{Dec}), \mathcal{F} = (\mathsf{FKG}, \mathsf{F}))$ be a FO-compatible pair as before. Without loss of generality, we assume that the randomness space of PKG in Π is $\{0, 1\}^k$. (This can be freely adjusted by using an appropriate pseudorandom generator.) To simplify the notation, let us write $\Pi' = (\mathsf{PKG}', \mathsf{Enc}', \mathsf{Dec}')$ to mean Π in which the plaintext space is restricted to $\{0, 1\}^k$ (say, by defining $\mathsf{Enc}'(pk, m; r) := \mathsf{Enc}(pk, (m\|0^k); r)$). Similarly, let us write $\mathcal{F}' = (\mathsf{FKG}', \mathsf{F}')$ to mean $\mathcal{F}$ in which the input length is restricted to k-bit (say, as above, by defining[5] $\mathsf{F}'_\kappa(x) := \mathsf{F}_\kappa(x\|0^k)$).

Using Π, Π', and $\mathcal{F}'$ as building blocks, we construct the PKE scheme $\widehat{\Pi} = (\widehat{\mathsf{PKG}}, \widehat{\mathsf{Enc}}, \widehat{\mathsf{Dec}})$ as in Fig. 3 (right). Furthermore, we will again use $\widetilde{\mathcal{F}}$ (constructed based on $\mathcal{F}$ as in Fig. 3 (left-bottom)) as the function family $\widehat{\mathcal{F}}$ for the proof of this theorem. It is not hard to see that the pair $(\widehat{\Pi}, \widetilde{\mathcal{F}})$ is FO-compatible if so is the pair $(\Pi, \mathcal{F})$. In particular, $\widehat{\Pi}$ satisfies correctness, and preserves the large ciphertext cardinality property of Π.

---

[5] Padding inputs by some default value does not destroy the UCE[S] security for S considered here. Namely, if $\mathcal{F}$ is UCE[S] secure, then so is $\mathcal{F}'$.

The following lemmas, together with Lemmas 1 and 3, imply Theorem 2.

Lemma 5. *Assume that the PKE schemes Π and Π' are CPA secure, and the function family $\mathcal{F}'$ is $\mathsf{UCE}[\mathsf{S}^{\mathrm{cup}}_{O(t_{\mathsf{PKG}}+t_{\mathsf{Enc}}),1}]$ secure. Then the PKE scheme $\widehat{\Pi}$ constructed as in Fig. 3 (right) is CPA secure.*

Lemma 6. *If $\mathsf{Smth}_{\widetilde{\mathcal{F}}}(k)$ is negligible, then the FO construction $\Pi_{\mathsf{FO}}[\widehat{\Pi}, \widetilde{\mathcal{F}}]$ is not CCA1 secure. Furthermore, the CCA1 attack succeeds even if an adversary uses two uniformly random plaintexts as its challenge plaintexts and makes only one decryption query.*

We give intuitive explanations for the proofs of the above lemmas. Regarding Lemma 5, note that in the PKE scheme $\widehat{\Pi}$, an encryption $c^\star$ of the randomness $r^\star$ used to generate the "main" public key pk is publicized as part of a public key of $\widehat{\Pi}$. Furthermore, the randomness r' for generating $c^\star$ is computed also from $r^\star$ by using the function family $\mathcal{F}'$. However, the correlation among $r^\star$, pk, and $c^\star$ is dealt with by the $\mathsf{UCE}[\mathsf{S}^{\mathrm{cup}}_{O(t_{\mathsf{PKG}}+t_{\mathsf{Enc}}),1}]$ security of the function family $\mathcal{F}'$ and the CPA security of Π', and then the CPA security of $\widehat{\Pi}$ follows from the CPA security of Π.

Regarding Lemma 6, recall that a public key PK_{FO} of the FO construction $\Pi_{\mathsf{FO}}[\widehat{\Pi}, \widetilde{\mathcal{F}}]$ is of the form $PK_{\mathsf{FO}} = (PK = (pk, pk', \kappa', c^\star), \widetilde{\kappa} = (\kappa, v^\star))$. Here, observe that if we decrypt the following "critical ciphertext" $C^\star_{\mathsf{FO}} = (1\|v^\star\|c^\star)$ which can be constructed once PK_{FO} is given, then the decryption result is $r^\star$ (which is the last k-bit of $\widehat{\mathsf{Dec}}(SK, C^\star_{\mathsf{FO}})$ and is the randomness used to generate sk). This follows from the properties of $\widehat{\Pi}$, $\widetilde{\mathcal{F}}$, and $\Pi_{\mathsf{FO}}[\widehat{\Pi}, \widetilde{\mathcal{F}}]$ such that

(1) $\widehat{\mathsf{Dec}}(SK, C^\star_{\mathsf{FO}}) = \widehat{\mathsf{Dec}}(SK, (1\|v^\star\|c^\star)) = (v^\star\|\mathsf{Dec}'(sk', c^\star)) = (v^\star\|r^\star)$,

(2) $\mathsf{F}_{\widetilde{\kappa}}(v^\star\|r^\star) = 0^k$, and

(3) $\widehat{\mathsf{Enc}}(PK, (v^\star\|r^\star); \mathsf{F}_{\widetilde{\kappa}}(v^\star\|r^\star)) = \widehat{\mathsf{Enc}}(PK, (v^\star\|r^\star); 0^k)$
$= (1\|v^\star\|\mathsf{Enc}'(pk', r^\star; \mathsf{F}'_{\kappa'}(r^\star))) = (1\|v^\star\|c^\star) = C^\star_{\mathsf{FO}}$.

Then, from $r^\star$ we can recover sk, which is the "main" secret key. This means that a CCA1 adversary can submit the "critical ciphertext" $C^\star_{\mathsf{FO}}$ as its decryption query, and obtain sk. Since with overwhelming probability the challenge ciphertext $C^\star_{\mathsf{FO}}$ is of the form $C^\star_{\mathsf{FO}} = (0\|\mathsf{Enc}(pk, (r^*\|m_b); \mathsf{F}_\kappa(r^*\|m_b)))$ due to the negligible smoothness of $\widetilde{\mathcal{F}}$, knowing sk allows the adversary to decrypt and tell the challenge bit, no matter what plaintexts are used (and thus even if they are public-key-independent). $\qquad\square$

4   Puncturable Tag-Based Encryption

In our proposed constructions in Section 5, we will use the "core" structure that appears in the DDN construction [19]. To ease the notation and reduce the description complexity of our proposed constructions, here we introduce and formalize an abstraction of the structure in the DDN construction as a special type of TBE [28,25], which we call *puncturable tag-based encryption* (PTBE).[6] We remark that there would be several possible

---

[6] The name "puncturable" is borrowed from the name of the primitive "puncturable" pseudorandom function [38].

ways to formalize the "core" structure of the DDN construction, and our formalization here is one which is convenient for our purpose.

Intuitively, a PTBE scheme is a TBE scheme that has two modes for decryption: The normal mode and the punctured mode. The normal mode is just the normal decryption process of a TBE scheme. In the punctured mode, we can generate a "punctured" secret key $\widehat{sk}_{tag^*}$ which can be used to decrypt all ciphertexts that are generated under tags tag that are different from tag*, while the information of plaintexts does not leak from ciphertexts that are generated under the "punctured point" tag tag*, even given the punctured secret key $\widehat{sk}_{tag^*}$. (This is as if we can "puncture" the tag space, and hence the name of the primitive.)

More formally, a PTBE scheme consists of the five PPTAs $(\mathsf{TKG}, \mathsf{TEnc}, \mathsf{TDec}, \mathsf{Punc}, \widehat{\mathsf{TDec}})$ among which the latter three algorithms are deterministic, with the following interface:

Key Generation: **Encryption:**   **Decryption:**

$(pk, sk) \leftarrow \mathsf{TKG}(1^k)$ $c \leftarrow \mathsf{TEnc}(pk, \mathsf{tag}, m)$ $m \text{ (or } \bot) \leftarrow \mathsf{TDec}(sk, \mathsf{tag}, c)$

Puncturing: **Punctured Decryption:**

$\widehat{sk}_{tag^*} \leftarrow \mathsf{Punc}(sk, tag^*)$ $m \text{ (or } \bot) \leftarrow \widehat{\mathsf{TDec}}(\widehat{sk}_{tag^*}, \mathsf{tag}, c)$

where (pk, sk) is a public/secret key pair, c is a ciphertext of a plaintext m under pk and a tag $\mathsf{tag} \in \{0,1\}^k$, and $\widehat{sk}_{tag^*}$ is a "punctured" secret key corresponding to a tag $tag^* \in \{0,1\}^k$.

Correctness. We require for all $k \in \mathbb{N}$, all tags $tag^*, \mathsf{tag} \in \{0,1\}^k$ such that $tag^* \neq \mathsf{tag}$, all (pk, sk) output by $\mathsf{TKG}(1^k)$, all m, and all c output by $\mathsf{TEnc}(pk, \mathsf{tag}, m)$, it holds that $\mathsf{TDec}(sk, \mathsf{tag}, c) = \widehat{\mathsf{TDec}}(\mathsf{Punc}(sk, tag^*), \mathsf{tag}, c) = m$.

We stress that the above correctness is only guaranteed for the case in which a ciphertext c is generated from $\mathsf{TEnc}(pk, \mathsf{tag}, \cdot)$ and $\mathsf{tag} \neq tag^*$. We do not specify anything when these conditions are not guaranteed.

Extended CPA Security: CPA Security in the Presence of a Punctured Secret Key. As a security requirement for a PTBE scheme, we define *extended CPA security* (eCPA security, for short) which requires that CPA security hold even in the presence of a punctured secret key.

Definition 5. *We say that a PTBE scheme $\mathcal{T}$ is eCPA secure if for all PPTAs $\mathcal{A} = (\mathcal{A}_0, \mathcal{A}_1, \mathcal{A}_2)$, $\mathsf{Adv}_{\mathcal{T},\mathcal{A}}^{\mathsf{eCPA}}(k) := 2 \cdot |\Pr[\mathsf{Expt}_{\mathcal{T},\mathcal{A}}^{\mathsf{eCPA}}(k) = 1] - 1/2|$ is negligible, where the experiment $\mathsf{Expt}_{\mathcal{T},\mathcal{A}}^{\mathsf{eCPA}}(k)$ is defined as follows:*

$\mathsf{Expt}_{\mathcal{T},\mathcal{A}}^{\mathsf{eCPA}}(k) : [\, (\mathsf{tag}^*, \mathsf{st}) \leftarrow \mathcal{A}_0(1^k); \; (pk, sk) \leftarrow \mathsf{TKG}(1^k);$

$\widehat{sk}_{tag^*} \leftarrow \mathsf{Punc}(sk, tag^*); \; (m_0, m_1, \mathsf{st}') \leftarrow \mathcal{A}_1(\mathsf{st}, pk, \widehat{sk}_{tag^*}); \; b \leftarrow \{0,1\};$

$c^* \leftarrow \mathsf{TEnc}(pk, \mathsf{tag}^*, m_b); \; b' \leftarrow \mathcal{A}_2(\mathsf{st}', c^*); \; \text{Return } (b' \stackrel{?}{=} b). \,],$

where in the experiment it is required that $|m_0| = |m_1|$.

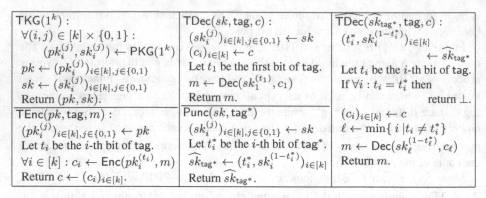

Fig. 4. A concrete instantiation of a PTBE scheme $\mathcal{T}$ based on a CPA secure PKE Π

Concrete Instantiation of PTBE. Since PTBE is intended to abstract the structure that appears in the DDN construction [19], the concrete instantiation of PTBE is exactly one that is used in [19], which is constructed from any CPA secure PKE scheme. Specifically, given a CPA secure PKE scheme $\Pi = (\mathsf{PKG}, \mathsf{Enc}, \mathsf{Dec})$, we construct a PTBE scheme $\mathcal{T} = (\mathsf{TKG}, \mathsf{TEnc}, \mathsf{TDec}, \mathsf{Punc}, \widehat{\mathsf{TDec}})$ as in Fig. 4. In the full version of our paper, we will give the proof for the eCPA security of $\mathcal{T}$.

One of the merits of considering PTBE as a stand-alone primitive would be that it can be instantiated from other primitives, such as broadcast encryption and a multi-user PKE scheme/KEM. A potential advantage of instantiations with these alternative building blocks is that the public key and/or ciphertext size could be much shorter than the simplest construction from a CPA secure PKE scheme. For example, if we use a broadcast encryption scheme by Boneh, Gentry, and Waters [11] to instantiate a PTBE scheme, then a ciphertext consists of a constant number of group elements (in bilinear groups), regardless of the security parameter k.

5 Chosen Ciphertext Security via UCE

In this section, we show our positive results: Specifically, in Section 5.1, we show the proposed CCA secure KEM based on a PTBE scheme, a commitment scheme, and a UCE secure function family (for which we will specify the class of sources shortly). Since the first two building blocks can be constructed from CPA secure PKE, our KEM can be constructed only from CPA secure PKE and a UCE secure function family.

Due to space limitations, our result on a DPKE scheme is not included in this proceedings version, and we refer the reader to the full version. In Section 5.2, we instead give brief overview of the result, as well as several extensions of our positive results.

5.1 CCA Secure KEM

Let $\mathcal{T} = (\mathsf{TKG}, \mathsf{TEnc}, \mathsf{TDec}, \mathsf{Punc}, \widehat{\mathsf{TDec}})$ be a PTBE scheme and $\mathcal{C} = (\mathsf{CKG}, \mathsf{Com})$ be a commitment scheme. We assume the plaintext/message space of both $\mathcal{T}$ and $\mathcal{C}$ to be $\{0,1\}^k$, and the randomness space of TEnc in $\mathcal{T}$ and Com in $\mathcal{C}$ to be $\{0,1\}^\ell$ and

KKG(1^k) :	Encap(PK) :	Decap(SK, C) :
$(pk, sk) \leftarrow$ TKG(1^k)	$(pk, ck, \kappa) \leftarrow PK$	$(sk, PK) \leftarrow SK$; $(pk, ck, \kappa) \leftarrow PK$
$ck \leftarrow$ CKG(1^k)	$\alpha \leftarrow \{0,1\}^k$	$(\mathsf{tag}, c) \leftarrow C$
$\kappa \leftarrow$ FKG(1^k)	$\beta \leftarrow \mathsf{F}_\kappa(\alpha)$	$\alpha \leftarrow$ TDec(sk, tag, c)
$PK \leftarrow (pk, ck, \kappa)$	Parse β as (r, r', K)	If $\alpha = \bot$ then return $\bot$.
$SK \leftarrow (sk, PK)$	$\quad \in \{0,1\}^{\ell + \ell' + k}$.	$\beta \leftarrow \mathsf{F}_\kappa(\alpha)$
Return (PK, SK).	$\mathsf{tag} \leftarrow$ Com($ck, \alpha; r'$)	Parse β as $(r, r', K) \in \{0,1\}^{\ell + \ell' + k}$.
	$c \leftarrow$ TEnc($pk, \mathsf{tag}, \alpha; r$)	If TEnc($pk, \mathsf{tag}, \alpha; r$) $= c$
	$C \leftarrow (\mathsf{tag}, c)$	and Com($ck, \alpha; r'$) = tag
	Return (C, K).	$\quad$ then return K else return $\bot$.

Fig. 5. The proposed CCA secure KEM Γ

$\{0,1\}^{\ell'}$, respectively, for some positive polynomials $\ell = \ell(k)$ and $\ell' = \ell'(k)$. Let $\mathcal{F} =$ (FKG, F) be a function family with input length k and output length $\ell(k) + \ell'(k) + k$. Then, our proposed KEM $\Gamma =$ (KKG, Encap, Decap) is constructed as in Fig. 5.

Alternative Decapsulation Algorithm. To show the CCA security of the proposed KEM Γ, it is useful to consider the following alternative decapsulation algorithm AltDecap. For a k-bit string tag* $\in \{0,1\}^k$ and a key pair (PK, SK) output by KKG(1^k), where $PK = (pk, ck, \kappa)$ and $SK = (sk, PK)$, we define an "alternative" secret key $\widehat{SK}_{\mathsf{tag}^*}$ associated with tag* $\in \{0,1\}^k$ by $\widehat{SK}_{\mathsf{tag}^*} = (\mathsf{tag}^*, \widehat{sk}_{\mathsf{tag}^*}, PK)$, where $\widehat{sk}_{\mathsf{tag}^*} =$ Punc(sk, tag^*). AltDecap takes an "alternative" secret key $\widehat{SK}_{\mathsf{tag}^*}$ defined as above and a ciphertext $C = (\mathsf{tag}, c)$ as input, and runs as follows:

AltDecap($\widehat{SK}_{\mathsf{tag}^*}, C$): If tag* $=$ tag, then return $\bot$. Otherwise, run in exactly the same way as Decap(SK, C), except that "$\alpha \leftarrow \widehat{\mathsf{TDec}}(\widehat{sk}_{\mathsf{tag}^*}, \mathsf{tag}, c)$" is executed instead of "$\alpha \leftarrow$ TDec(sk, tag, c)."

The following lemma is easy to see due to the correctness of the underlying PTBE scheme $\mathcal{T}$ and the validity check of c by re-encryption performed at the last step.

Lemma 7. *Let* tag* $\in \{0,1\}^k$ *be a string and let* (PK, SK) *be a key pair output by* KKG(1^k). *Furthermore, let* $\widehat{SK}_{\mathsf{tag}^*}$ *be an alternative secret key as defined above. Then, for any ciphertext* $C = (\mathsf{tag}, c)$ *(which could be outside the range of* Encap(PK)*) satisfying* tag $\neq$ tag*, *it holds that* Decap(SK, C) = AltDecap($\widehat{SK}_{\mathsf{tag}^*}, C$).

Security of Γ. The security of Γ is guaranteed by the following theorem.

Theorem 3. *Assume that the PTBE scheme $\mathcal{T}$ is* eCPA *secure, the commitment scheme C is hiding and target-binding, and the function family $\mathcal{F}$ is* UCE[$\mathsf{S}_{t,1}^{\mathsf{cup}}$] *secure with* $t = O(t_{\mathsf{TKG}} + t_{\mathsf{TEnc}} + t_{\mathsf{Punc}} + t_{\mathsf{CKG}} + t_{\mathsf{Com}})$. *Then, the KEM Γ constructed as in Fig. 5 is* CCA *secure.*

Proof Sketch of Theorem 3. Let $\mathcal{A}$ be any PPTA adversary that attacks the KEM Γ in the sense of CCA security. Consider the following sequence of games: (Here, the values with asterisk (*) represent those related to the challenge ciphertext for $\mathcal{A}$.)

Game 1: This is the experiment $\text{Expt}_{\Gamma,\mathcal{A}}^{\text{CCA}}(k)$ itself.

Game 2: Same as Game 1, except that all decapsulation queries $C = (\text{tag}, c)$ satisfying $\text{tag} = \text{tag}^*$ are answered with $\bot$.

Game 3: Same as Game 2, except that all decapsulation queries C are answered with $\text{AltDecap}(\widehat{SK}_{\text{tag}^*}, C)$, where $\widehat{SK}_{\text{tag}^*}$ is the alternative secret key corresponding to (PK, SK) and tag^*.

Game 4: Same as Game 3, except that r^*, r'^*, K_1^* are picked uniformly at random, independently of $\beta^* = F_\kappa(\alpha^*)$. That is, the steps "$\beta^* \leftarrow F_\kappa(\alpha^*)$; Parse β^* as $(r^*, r'^*, K_1^*) \in \{0,1\}^{\ell+\ell'+k}$" in Game 3 are replaced with the step "$(r^*, r'^*, K_1^*) \leftarrow \{0,1\}^{\ell+\ell'+k}$," and we do not compute β^* anymore.

For $i \in [4]$, let S_i denote the event that $\mathcal{A}$ succeeds in guessing the challenge bit (i.e. $b' = b$ occurs) in Game i. Note that $\text{Adv}_{\Gamma,\mathcal{A}}^{\text{CCA}}(k) = 2 \cdot |\Pr[\mathsf{S}_1] - 1/2| \leq 2 \cdot \sum_{i\in[3]} |\Pr[\mathsf{S}_i] - \Pr[\mathsf{S}_{i+1}]| + 2 \cdot |\Pr[\mathsf{S}_4] - 1/2|$. We will show that $|\Pr[\mathsf{S}_i] - \Pr[\mathsf{S}_{i+1}]|$ is negligible for each $i \in [3]$ and that $\Pr[\mathsf{S}_4] = 1/2$, which proves the theorem.

Firstly, notice that $|\Pr[\mathsf{S}_1] - \Pr[\mathsf{S}_2]|$ can be upperbounded by the probability of $\mathcal{A}$ making a decapsulation query $C = (\text{tag}, c)$ satisfying $\text{tag} = \text{tag}^*$, $c \neq c^*$, and $\text{Decap}(SK, C) \neq \bot$. In the full proof, we will show that such a query can be used to break the target-binding property of the commitment scheme $\mathcal{C}$, and hence $\mathcal{A}$ will submit a query of this type only with negligible probability, due to the target-binding property of the commitment scheme $\mathcal{C}$.

It is easy to see that $\Pr[\mathsf{S}_2] = \Pr[\mathsf{S}_3]$ holds, because the behavior of the oracle in Game 2 and that in Game 3 are identical due to Lemma 7.

To show the upperbound of $|\Pr[\mathsf{S}_3] - \Pr[\mathsf{S}_4]|$, we need to use the $\text{UCE}[\mathsf{S}_{t,1}^{\text{cup}}]$ security of the function family $\mathcal{F}$. Define the source $\mathcal{S}$ that takes 1^k as input, expects to have access to an oracle $\mathcal{O} \in \text{Func}_{k \to (\ell+\ell'+k)}$, and computes an output (leakage) $L = (pk, ck, \text{tag}^*, \widehat{sk}_{\text{tag}^*}, c^*, K^*)$ in the following way:

$$\mathcal{S}^{\mathcal{O}}(1^k) : [\ (pk, sk) \leftarrow \text{TKG}(1^k); \ ck \leftarrow \text{CKG}(1^k); \ \alpha^* \leftarrow \{0,1\}^k; \ \beta^* \leftarrow \mathcal{O}(\alpha^*);$$

$$\text{Parse } \beta^* \text{ as } (r^*, r'^*, K^*).; \ \text{tag}^* \leftarrow \text{Com}(ck, \alpha^*; r'^*); \ \widehat{sk}_{\text{tag}^*} \leftarrow \text{Punc}(sk, \text{tag}^*);$$

$$c^* \leftarrow \text{TEnc}(pk, \text{tag}^*, \alpha^*; r^*); \ \text{Return } L \leftarrow (pk, ck, \text{tag}^*, \widehat{sk}_{\text{tag}^*}, c^*, K^*). \ ].$$

Defined as above, it is obvious that $\mathcal{S}$ satisfies the restrictions on the running time and the number of queries. Furthermore, due to the hiding property of the commitment scheme $\mathcal{C}$ and the eCPA security of the PTBE scheme $\mathcal{T}$, it is straightforward to see that $\mathcal{S}$ is computationally unpredictable, and thus it holds that $\mathcal{S} \in \mathsf{S}_{t,1}^{\text{cup}}$. Then, in the full proof, we will show that there exists a PPTA $\mathcal{B}_{\text{u}}$ that takes as input a function index κ, a leakage $L = (pk, ck, \text{tag}^*, \widehat{sk}_{\text{tag}^*}, c^*, K^*) \leftarrow \mathcal{S}^{\mathcal{O}}(1^k)$, where $\mathcal{O} \in \text{Func}_{k \to (\ell+\ell'+k)}$ is either $F_\kappa(\cdot)$ or a random function, simulates Game 3 or Game 4 perfectly for $\mathcal{A}$ depending on $\mathcal{B}_{\text{u}}$'s challenge bit, and has the UCE advantage $\text{Adv}_{\mathcal{F},(\mathcal{S},\mathcal{B}_{\text{u}})}^{\text{UCE}}(k) = |\Pr[\mathsf{S}_3] - \Pr[\mathsf{S}_4]|$. Hence, $|\Pr[\mathsf{S}_3] - \Pr[\mathsf{S}_4]|$ is negligible by the $\text{UCE}[\mathsf{S}_{t,1}^{\text{cup}}]$ security of $\mathcal{F}$.

Finally, in Game 4, the "real" session-key K_1^* is independent of the challenge ciphertext C^* and is a uniformly random value, and thus the challenge bit b is information-theoretically hidden from $\mathcal{A}$'s view. This implies $\Pr[\mathsf{S}_4] = 1/2$. $\quad\square$

5.2 Further Results and Extensions

CCA *Secure DPKE for Block Sources with Bounded Running Time.* Note that our proposed KEM has the property that a randomness used to generate a ciphertext is entirely recovered in the decryption process. Here, by deriving the randomness r and r' (used for generating c and tag) from a plaintext m (instead of deriving them from the "seed" α picked randomly) by the UCE secure function family $\mathcal{F}$, we obtain a DPKE scheme. We can show that this DPKE scheme is CCA secure for block sources [10] (i.e. each plaintext sampled from the source has high min-entropy, even conditioned on all the previous plaintexts), as long as the sources satisfy an additional constraint that their running time is bounded by some predetermined polynomial $t' = t'(k)$ (we call such a block source t'-*bounded block source*). This additional constraint on the running time of the sources is due to our security proof in which the source for a UCE secure function family has to execute a t'-bounded block source for DPKE (that chooses the challenge plaintexts), and thus we have to rely on $\text{UCE}[\mathsf{S}_{t,1}^{\mathrm{cup}}]$ security where t must be large enough to allow the execution of the t'-bounded block source for DPKE (and other algorithms that need to be run for the security proof).

Although CCA security for block sources with bounded running time is clearly weaker than that for ordinary block sources, the constraint on the running time of the sources would not be a severe limitation in practice, because in most cases messages that are going to be encrypted will be chosen by honest parties and we do not expect picking messages to be computationally expensive.[7] We stress that we do not put any restriction on the running time of the "main" adversary who may perform decryption queries and any computationally heavy operations, as long as it runs in polynomial time.

Function Families with Short Output Length. For our proposed KEM, we use a function family $\mathcal{F}$ with output length $\ell + \ell' + k$, which could be long (the actual length depends on how the PTBE scheme is instantiated). However, by employing a pseudorandom generator $\mathsf{G} : \{0,1\}^k \to \{0,1\}^{\ell+\ell'+k}$, we can replace $\mathcal{F}$ with a function family with output length k. This extension is however at the cost of using slightly stronger UCE security. Specifically, now we have to rely on the $\text{UCE}[\mathsf{S}_{t',1}^{\mathrm{cup}}]$ security where $t' = t + t_{\mathsf{G}}$ and t is as stated in Theorem 3. This extension is also applicable to our DPKE scheme.

Weakening the UCE Assumption Using Lossy Encryption. We notice that in the security proof of our proposed KEM, if the underlying PTBE scheme is instantiated using a *lossy encryption* scheme [6] and the underlying commitment scheme is statistically hiding (which can be constructed from any lossy encryption scheme), then the source $\mathcal{S}$ used in the proof of Theorem 3 can be modified to show that it is statistically unpredictable. Specifically, this can be shown by considering an additional game between Game 3 and Game 4 in which we use lossy public keys for public keys corresponding to tag* when generating a challenge ciphertext. (For this, in the full version of our paper we will also introduce a lossy-encryption-analogue of PTBE.)

Therefore, at the cost of employing a stronger assumption on the underlying PKE scheme, we can weaken the assumption on $\mathcal{F}$ to be $\text{UCE}[\mathsf{S}_{t',1}^{\mathrm{sup}}]$ security where t' is

---

[7] This observation is due to one of the anonymous reviewers.

dependent on the underlying lossy encryption scheme (and other building blocks). (We will specify t' in the full version.)

We note that similar tradeoffs about the assumptions among building blocks for constructing CCA secure PKE/KEM were shown in [29].

Acknowledgement. The authors would like to thank Pooya Farshim for giving us a detailed overview of their attack [12] on UCE security using indistinguishability obfuscation. The authors would also like to thank Jacob Schuldt, the members of the study group "Shin-Akarui-Angou-Benkyou-Kai," and the anonymous reviewers of PKC 2014 for their helpful comments and suggestions. In particular, the authors are grateful to one of the reviewers for pointing out some issue in the security proof of our DPKE scheme, and for suggesting considering CCA security of DPKE for block sources with bounded running time.

References

1. Abdalla, M., Bellare, M., Rogaway, P.: The oracle Diffie-Hellman assumptions and an analysis of DHIES. In: Naccache, D. (ed.) CT-RSA 2001. LNCS, vol. 2020, pp. 143–158. Springer, Heidelberg (2001)
2. Barak, B., Goldreich, O., Impagliazzo, R., Rudich, S., Sahai, A., Vadhan, S.P., Yang, K.: On the (im)possibility of obfuscating programs. In: Kilian, J. (ed.) CRYPTO 2001. LNCS, vol. 2139, pp. 1–18. Springer, Heidelberg (2001)
3. Bellare, M., Boldyreva, A., O'Neill, A.: Deterministic and efficiently searchable encryption. In: Menezes, A. (ed.) CRYPTO 2007. LNCS, vol. 4622, pp. 535–552. Springer, Heidelberg (2007)
4. Bellare, M., Hoang, V.T., Keelveedhi, S.: Instantiating random oracles via UCEs. In: Canetti, R., Garay, J.A. (eds.) CRYPTO 2013, Part II. LNCS, vol. 8043, pp. 398–415. Springer, Heidelberg (2013)
5. Bellare, M., Hoang, V.T., Keelveedhi, S.: Instantiating random oracles via UCEs. Updated full version of [4] (2013), http://eprint.iacr.org/2013/424
6. Bellare, M., Hofheinz, D., Yilek, S.: Possibility and impossibility results for encryption and commitment secure under selective opening. In: Joux, A. (ed.) EUROCRYPT 2009. LNCS, vol. 5479, pp. 1–35. Springer, Heidelberg (2009)
7. Bellare, M., Keelveedhi, S., Ristenpart, T.: Message-locked encryption and secure deduplication. In: Johansson, T., Nguyen, P.Q. (eds.) EUROCRYPT 2013. LNCS, vol. 7881, pp. 296–312. Springer, Heidelberg (2013)
8. Bellare, M., Rogaway, P.: Random oracles are practical: A paradigm for designing efficient protocols. In: CCS 1993, pp. 62–73 (1993)
9. Bellare, M., Rogaway, P.: Optimal asymmetric encryption. In: De Santis, A. (ed.) EUROCRYPT 1994. LNCS, vol. 950, pp. 92–111. Springer, Heidelberg (1995)
10. Boldyreva, A., Fehr, S., O'Neill, A.: On notions of security for deterministic encryption, and efficient constructions without random oracles. In: Wagner, D. (ed.) CRYPTO 2008. LNCS, vol. 5157, pp. 335–359. Springer, Heidelberg (2008)
11. Boneh, D., Gentry, C., Waters, B.: Collusion resistant broadcast encryption with short ciphertexts and private keys. In: Shoup, V. (ed.) CRYPTO 2005. LNCS, vol. 3621, pp. 258–275. Springer, Heidelberg (2005)
12. Brzuska, C., Farshim, P., Mittelbach, A.: Personal communication (December 2013)

13. Canetti, R., Goldreich, O., Halevi, S.: The random oracle methodology, revisited. In: STOC 1998, pp. 209–218 (1998)
14. Canetti, R., Halevi, S., Katz, J.: Chosen-ciphertext security from identity-based encryption. In: Cachin, C., Camenisch, J.L. (eds.) EUROCRYPT 2004. LNCS, vol. 3027, pp. 207–222. Springer, Heidelberg (2004)
15. Choi, S.G., Dachman-Soled, D., Malkin, T., Wee, H.: Black-box construction of a non-malleable encryption scheme from any semantically secure one. In: Canetti, R. (ed.) TCC 2008. LNCS, vol. 4948, pp. 427–444. Springer, Heidelberg (2008)
16. Cramer, R., Hanaoka, G., Hofheinz, D., Imai, H., Kiltz, E., Pass, R., Shelat, A., Vaikun-tanathan, V.: Bounded CCA2-secure encryption. In: Kurosawa, K. (ed.) ASIACRYPT 2007. LNCS, vol. 4833, pp. 502–518. Springer, Heidelberg (2007)
17. Cramer, R., Shoup, V.: Design and analysis of practical public-key encryption schemes secure against adaptive chosen ciphertext attack. SIAM J. Computing 33(1), 167–226 (2003)
18. Dachman-Soled, D.: A black-box construction of a CCA2 encryption scheme from a plaintext aware (sPA1) encryption scheme. In: Krawczyk, H. (ed.) PKC 2014. LNCS, vol. 8383, pp. 37–55. Springer, Heidelberg (2014), http://eprint.iacr.org/2013/680
19. Dolev, D., Dwork, C., Naor, M.: Non-malleable cryptography. In: STOC 1991, pp. 542–552 (1991)
20. Fujisaki, E., Okamoto, T.: How to enhance the security of public-key encryption at minimum cost. In: Imai, H., Zheng, Y. (eds.) PKC 1999. LNCS, vol. 1560, pp. 53–68. Springer, Heidelberg (1999)
21. Fujisaki, E., Okamoto, T.: Secure integration of asymmetric and symmetric encryption schemes. In: Wiener, M. (ed.) CRYPTO 1999. LNCS, vol. 1666, pp. 537–554. Springer, Heidelberg (1999)
22. Garg, S., Gentry, C., Halevi, S., Raykova, M., Sahai, A., Waters, B.: Candidate indistin-guishability obfuscation and functional encryption for all curcuits. In: FOCS 2013, pp. 40–49 (2013)
23. Goldwasser, S., Kalai, Y.T.: On the (in)security of the Fiat-Shamir paradigm. In: FOCS 2003, pp. 102–113 (2003)
24. Hohenberger, S., Lewko, A., Waters, B.: Detecting dangerous queries: A new approach for chosen ciphertext security. In: Pointcheval, D., Johansson, T. (eds.) EUROCRYPT 2012. LNCS, vol. 7237, pp. 663–681. Springer, Heidelberg (2012)
25. Kiltz, E.: Chosen-ciphertext security from tag-based encryption. In: Halevi, S., Rabin, T. (eds.) TCC 2006. LNCS, vol. 3876, pp. 581–600. Springer, Heidelberg (2006)
26. Kiltz, E., Mohassel, P., O'Neill, A.: Adaptive trapdoor functions and chosen-ciphertext security. In: Gilbert, H. (ed.) EUROCRYPT 2010. LNCS, vol. 6110, pp. 673–692. Springer, Heidelberg (2010)
27. Lin, H., Tessaro, S.: Amplification of chosen-ciphertext security. In: Johansson, T., Nguyen, P.Q. (eds.) EUROCRYPT 2013. LNCS, vol. 7881, pp. 503–519. Springer, Heidelberg (2013)
28. MacKenzie, P.D., Reiter, M.K., Yang, K.: Alternatives to non-malleability: Definitions, constructions, and applications. In: Naor, M. (ed.) TCC 2004. LNCS, vol. 2951, pp. 171–190. Springer, Heidelberg (2004)
29. Matsuda, T., Hanaoka, G.: Chosen ciphertext security via point obfuscation. In: Lindell, Y. (ed.) TCC 2014. LNCS, vol. 8349, pp. 95–120. Springer, Heidelberg (2014)
30. Matsuda, T., Matsuura, K.: Parallel decryption queries in bounded chosen ciphertext attacks. In: Catalano, D., Fazio, N., Gennaro, R., Nicolosi, A. (eds.) PKC 2011. LNCS, vol. 6571, pp. 246–264. Springer, Heidelberg (2011)
31. Maurer, U.M., Renner, R.S., Holenstein, C.: Indifferentiability, impossibility results on reductions, and applications to the random oracle methodology. In: Naor, M. (ed.) TCC 2004. LNCS, vol. 2951, pp. 21–39. Springer, Heidelberg (2004)

32. Myers, S., Shelat, A.: Bit encryption is complete. In: FOCS 2009, pp. 607–616 (2009)
33. Naor, M., Yung, M.: Public-key cryptosystems provably secure against chosen ciphertext attacks. In: STOC 1990, pp. 427–437 (1990)
34. Okamoto, T., Pointcheval, D.: REACT: Rapid enhanced-security asymmetric cryptosystem transform. In: Naccache, D. (ed.) CT-RSA 2001. LNCS, vol. 2020, pp. 159–174. Springer, Heidelberg (2001)
35. Peikert, C., Waters, B.: Lossy trapdoor functions and their applications. In: STOC 2008, pp. 187–196 (2008)
36. Rackoff, C., Simon, D.R.: Non-interactive zero-knowledge proof of knowledge and chosen ciphertext attack. In: Feigenbaum, J. (ed.) CRYPTO 1991. LNCS, vol. 576, pp. 433–444. Springer, Heidelberg (1992)
37. Rosen, A., Segev, G.: Chosen-ciphertext security via correlated products. In: Reingold, O. (ed.) TCC 2009. LNCS, vol. 5444, pp. 419–436. Springer, Heidelberg (2009)
38. Sahai, A., Waters, B.: How to use indistinguishability obfuscation: Deniable encryption, and more (2013), http://eprint.iacr.org/2013/454
39. Wee, H.: Efficient chosen-ciphertext security via extractable hash proofs. In: Rabin, T. (ed.) CRYPTO 2010. LNCS, vol. 6223, pp. 314–332. Springer, Heidelberg (2010)

Proxy Re-encryption from Lattices

Elena Kirshanova

Horst Görtz Institute for IT-Security
Faculty of Mathematics
Ruhr University Bochum, Germany
`elena.kirshanova@rub.de`

Abstract. We propose a new unidirectional proxy re-encryption scheme based on the hardness of the LWE problem. Our construction is collusion-safe and does not require any trusted authority for the re-encryption key generation. We extend a recent trapdoor definition for a lattice of Micciancio and Peikert. Our proxy re-encryption scheme is provably CCA-1 secure in the selective model under the LWE assumption.

Keywords: Proxy re-encryption, lattices, learning with errors.

1 Introduction

There are a number of applications (distributed file system of [3], email forwarding) which require that some data encrypted for Alice has to be re-encrypted to Bob. A naive way Alice can accomplish this task is to decrypt the data with her secret key and then encrypt the resulting plaintext under Bob's public key. But this approach requires Alice to actively participate to perform the procedures. Moreover, she needs to repeat the encryption for any further user she wants to resend the message to. In a proxy re-encryption (PRE) scheme, a proxy is given a special information (a re-encryption key) that allows it to translate a ciphertext intended for Alice into a ciphertext of the same message encrypted under Bob's key. In this setting we will call Alice the delegator and Bob the delegatee. The proxy cannot, however, learn either the underlying plaintext or the secret key of either Alice or Bob.

In 1998, Blaze *et al.* ([6]) proposed the first proxy re-encryption scheme. Their construction is based on the ElGamal encryption scheme ([8]): for a group $\mathbb{G}$ of prime order p and g a generator of the group, Alice and Bob choose their key pair (a, g^a) and (b, g^b), $a, b \leftarrow \mathbb{Z}_p^*$. The encryption of a message m intended for Alice then has the form $c = (c_1, c_2) = (mg^r, (g^a)^r)$ for a randomly chosen $r \leftarrow \mathbb{Z}_p^*$. The re-encryption key from Alice to Bob is $\mathsf{rk}_{(Alice \to Bob)} = b/a$, and the proxy translates the ciphertext c to Bob by computing $c' = (c_1, c_2^{b/a}) = (mg^r, (g^b)^r)$. The scheme is CPA secure under the Decisional Diffie-Hellman assumption in $\mathbb{G}$. From the re-encryption key the proxy can easily compute a/b, that allows it to convert the ciphertexts in the inverse direction. Such PRE schemes are called *bidirectional*. More desirable in practice are *unidirectional* schemes, in which a re-encryption key works only in one direction.

H. Krawczyk (Ed.): PKC 2014, LNCS 8383, pp. 77–94, 2014.

In the above PRE scheme if the proxy and one of the parties collude, they can recover the secret key of another party. The second issue is that a proxy knowing $rk_{A \to B} = b/a$ and $rk_{B \to C} = c/b$ can compute $rk_{A \to C} = c/a$. Ateniese *et al.* in [3] listed desired properties for PRE schemes; among them are:

- *Non-interactivity*: $rk_{(Alice \to Bob)}$ can be generated by Alice alone using Bob's public key; no trusted authority is needed.
- *Proxy transparency*: neither the delegator nor the delegatees are aware of the presence of a proxy, i.e. a recipient of a ciphertext cannot distinguish whether the ciphertext is the original encryption or whether it was re-encrypted. The property is achieved in [6].
- *Key optimality*: the size of Bob's secret key remains constant, regardless of how many delegations he accepts.
- *Collusion resilience* (also called *master key security* in [3] and [4]): it is hard for the coalition of the proxy and Bob to compute Alice's secret key.
- *Non-transitivity*: it should be hard for the proxy to re-delegate the decryption right, namely to compute $rk_{A \to C}$ from $rk_{A \to B}$, $rk_{B \to C}$.

1.1 Related Work

Bidirectional proxy re-enryption scheme was proposed by Blaze *et al.* in [6], while a unidirectional construction firstly appeared as a building block of a secure distributed file system in [3], [4]. The formal definition of CCA security for PRE with a bidirectional scheme is present in [7]. CCA security is achieved for the unidirectional setting in [12]. Both schemes use bilinear pairings.

The possibility of using lattice-based assumptions for PRE constructions was shown by Xagawa in [18], but the scheme lacks a complete security analysis. Like Blaze *et al.* the scheme modifies the ElGamal encryption scheme adding the re-encryption key of the form $rk_{A \to B} = b/a$, where a and b are discrete logarithms of the public keys of Alice and Bob, the scheme of Xagawa and Tanaka is an analogous modification of Regev's encryption scheme ([16]). And, as its ElGamal counterpart, it is bidirectional, it does not provide collusion safeness, neither it is non-interactive: a trusted party is needed to generate the re-encryption keys.

1.2 Our Contribution

The main contribution of this paper is a *unidirectional* single-hop proxy re-encryption scheme based on the hardness of lattice-based problems. Prior to [10] there was no known construction that is both unidirectional and multi-hop. But even in [10] this combination comes at the cost of allowing the ciphertext to grow linearly with respect to the number of re-encryptions. Although Gentry in [9] mentions that a fully-homomorphic scheme can achieve multi-use and unidirectionality simultaneously, the constructions of FHE are far from practical. We achieve *CCA-1 security* in the selective model ([4]). Our scheme is the first lattice-based construction that achieves *collusion resilience* and *non-interactivity*. We apply the trapdoor delegation technique proposed in [15]. However, we have to extend the definition of a lattice trapdoor of [15]. The generalization might prove useful for functionalities other than proxy re-encryption as well.

2   Definitions

This section recalls the definition of *unidirectional* proxy re-encryption and the game-based definition of security, where we follow the selective model of Ateniese *et al.* ([3]), but in the chosen-ciphertext security setting, which was formalized in [7]. We are interested in the unidirectional case (i.e. a re-encryption key from pk to pk′ should not provide the ability to re-encrypt from pk′ to pk).

Definition 1 (Unidirectional PRE). *A unidirectional, proxy re-encryption scheme is a tuple of algorithms* (KeyGen, ReKeyGen, Enc, ReEnc, Dec)*:*

- $(\mathsf{pk}, \mathsf{sk}) \leftarrow \mathsf{KeyGen}(1^n)$. *On input the security parameter* 1^n, *the key genera-tion algorithm* KeyGen *outputs a key pair* $(\mathsf{pk}, \mathsf{sk})$.
- $\mathsf{rk}_{\mathsf{pk} \to \mathsf{pk}'} \leftarrow \mathsf{ReKeyGen}(\mathsf{pk}, \mathsf{sk}, \mathsf{pk}')$. *On input a private key* sk *of a delegator and a public key of a delegatee* pk′, *algorithm* ReKeyGen *outputs a unidirec-tional re-encryption key* $\mathsf{rk}_{\mathsf{pk} \to \mathsf{pk}'}$.
- $c \leftarrow \mathsf{Enc}(\mathsf{pk}, m)$. *On input a public key* pk *and a message* m, *algorithm* Enc *outputs a ciphertext* c.
- $c' \leftarrow \mathsf{ReEnc}(\mathsf{rk}_{\mathsf{pk} \to \mathsf{pk}'}, c)$. *On input a re-encryption key* $\mathsf{rk}_{\mathsf{pk} \to \mathsf{pk}'}$ *and a cipher-text* c', *algorithm* ReEnc *outputs a ciphertext* c' *decryptable under the secret key* sk′.
- $m \leftarrow \mathsf{Dec}(\mathsf{sk}, \mathsf{pk}, c)$. *On input a secret key* sk, *a public key* pk *and a ciphertext* c', *algorithm* Dec *outputs a message* m *or the error symbol* $\perp$.

Definition 2 (Multi/Single-hop PRE). *A proxy re-encryption scheme is called multi-hop if a proxy can apply further re-encryptions to already re-encryp-ted ciphertext. In a single-hop setting a ciphertext can be re-encrypted only once.*

The requirements for correctness of decryption depend on whether the scheme is multi-hop or single-hop. Informally, the decryption algorithm should output the correct plaintext, no matter whether the ciphertext is "freshly" encrypted or re-encrypted.

Definition 3 (Single-hop PRE Correctness). *A proxy re-encryption scheme* (KeyGen, KeyGen, ReKeyGen, Enc, ReEnc, Dec) *correctly decrypts for the plaintext space* $\mathcal{M}$ *if:*

- *For all* $(\mathsf{pk}, \mathsf{sk})$ *output by* KeyGen *and for all* $m \in \mathcal{M}$, *it holds that* $\mathsf{Dec}(\mathsf{sk}, \mathsf{Enc}(\mathsf{pk}, m)) = m$.
- *For any re-encryption key* $\mathsf{rk}_{\mathsf{pk} \to \mathsf{pk}'}$ *output by* ReKeyGen(sk, pk, pk′) *and any* $c = \mathsf{Enc}(\mathsf{pk}, m)$ *it holds that* $\mathsf{Dec} = (\mathsf{sk}', \mathsf{ReEnc}(rk_{\mathsf{pk} \to \mathsf{pk}'} c)) = m$.

We give the game-based definition of security for PRE schemes. A discussion follows the definition.

Definition 4 (Unidirectional PRE-CCA1 Game). *Let* 1^n *be the security parameter,* $\mathcal{A}$ *be any ppt adversary. Consider the following experiment for a PRE scheme* $\Pi = $ (KeyGen, ReKeyGen, Enc, ReEnc, Dec) *with a plaintext space* $\mathcal{M}$, *a key space* $\mathcal{K}$ *and a ciphertext space* $\mathcal{C}$ *(the arrows represent interac-tion between the adversary and the scheme* Π *):*

$PRE_{A,\Pi}^{CCA1}(n)$		$\mathcal{A}$
1.$(pk^*, sk^*) \leftarrow KeyGen(1^n)$		
Add (pk^*, sk^*) to $\mathcal{H}$	$\xrightarrow{\quad 1^n, pk^* \quad}$	
2.$(pk_H, sk_H) \leftarrow KeyGen(1^n)$	$\xleftarrow{\text{Add an honest user}}$	
$(pk_H, sk_H) \in \mathcal{H}$	$\xrightarrow{\quad pk_H \quad}$	
3.$(pk_C, sk_C) \leftarrow KeyGen(1^n)$	$\xleftarrow{\text{Add a corrupted user}}$	
$(pk_C, sk_C) \in \mathcal{C}$	$\xrightarrow{\quad (pk_C, sk_C) \quad}$	
4. If $(pk, sk) \in \mathcal{H}$	$\xleftarrow{\quad c, pk \quad}$	$c \in \mathscr{C}$
$m = Dec(c, sk)$	$\xrightarrow{\quad m \quad}$	
5. If $pk, pk' \in \mathcal{H}$ or $pk, pk' \in \mathcal{C}$	$\xleftarrow{\quad (pk, pk') \quad}$	$(pk, pk') \in \mathcal{K} \times \mathcal{K}$
$rk_{pk \rightarrow pk'} = ReKeyGen(pk, pk')$	$\xrightarrow{\quad rk_{pk \rightarrow pk'} \quad}$	
	$\cdots$	
	Repeat steps 2-5 $poly(n)$ times	
	$\cdots$	
	$\xleftarrow{\quad m_0, m_1 \quad}$	$m_0, m_1 \in \mathcal{M}$
6. $b \rightarrow \{0, 1\}$		
$c^* = Enc(pk^*, m_b)$	$\xrightarrow{\quad c^* \quad}$	
	$\cdots$	
	Repeat steps 2,3,5 $poly(n)$ times	
If $b = b'$ output 1	$\xrightarrow{\quad b' \quad}$	$b' \in \{0, 1\}$
else output 0		

An adversary $\mathcal{A}$ wins the game with advantage ϵ if the probability, taken over the random choices of $\mathcal{A}$ and of the oracles, that the experiment $PRE_{A,\Pi}^{CCA1}(n)$ outputs 1, is at least $1/2 + \epsilon$.

To describe the security model we first classify all of the users into *honest* ($\mathcal{H}$) and *corrupted* ($\mathcal{C}$). In the honest case an adversary knows only a public key, whereas for a corrupted user the adversary has both secret and public keys.

We start by choosing a target user (pk^*, sk^*) and label it as honest. While an adversary queries for the keys, we disallow any adaptive corruption: the adversary cannot be given a decryption key for any user from $\mathcal{H}$ during the game. The adversary can ask for a decryption of a ciphertext c for any user. The adversary is given access to a re-encryption key from pk to pk' forbidding the case when $pk \in \mathcal{H}$ and $pk' \in \mathcal{C}$, which is equivalent to an adaptive corruption of pk. Note that the generation of a re-encryption key from a corrupted to a honest party can be accomplished by the adversary himself, since he knows the secret key of a delegator. As long as he can query for the re-encryption key, the adversary can also perform a re-enryption at any time.

After the challenge ciphertext c^* has been produced, we still allow the adversary to query for the re-encryption keys, so he can also re-encrypt c^*.

Definition 5 (PRE-CCA1 Security). *A unidirectional proxy re-encryption scheme is CCA-1 secure, if any ppt adversary wins the Unidirectional PRE-CCA1 Game only with negligible advantage.*

3 Lattices

We denote column-vectors by lower-case bold letters, so row-vectors are represented via transposition (e.g., $\mathbf{b}^t$). Matrices are denoted by upper-case bold letters, an additive subgroup of $m \times n$ matrices over $\mathbb{R}$ is denoted by $M_{m,n}$. For any $\mathbf{B} \in M_{m,n}$ we denote $\sigma_i(\mathbf{B})$ as decreasingly ordered sequence of singular values of $\mathbf{B}$. A symmetric matrix $\boldsymbol{\Sigma} \in M_{n,n}$ is *semidefinite*, if $\mathbf{x}^t \boldsymbol{\Sigma} \mathbf{x} \geq 0$ for all nonzero $\mathbf{x} \in \mathbb{R}^n$. For any $\mathbf{B} \in M_{n,n}$, the unique matrix $\mathbf{B}^+$ is the Moore-Penrose pseudoinverse, if $\mathbf{BB}^+\mathbf{B} = \mathbf{B}, \mathbf{B}^+\mathbf{BB}^+ = \mathbf{B}^+$ and $\mathbf{BB}^+, \mathbf{B}^+\mathbf{B}$ are symmetric. For any matrix $\mathbf{B}$ the symmetric matrix $\boldsymbol{\Sigma} = \mathbf{BB}^t$ is positive definite. We denote then $\mathbf{B} = \sqrt{\boldsymbol{\Sigma}}$. A function $f : \mathbb{N} \to \mathbb{R}$ is called *negligible*, denoted $f(n) = \mathsf{negl}(n)$, if for every $c \in \mathbb{N}$ there is an integer n_c such that $f(n) \leq n^c, \forall n \geq n_c$. Throughout the paper the parameter $r = w(\sqrt{\log n})$ represents a fixed function $r \approx \sqrt{\ln(2/\epsilon)/\pi}$ that arises from the randomized-rounding operation from $\mathbb{R}$ to $\mathbb{Z}$ and corresponds to the so-called *smoothing parameter* for $\mathbb{Z}^n$ (the definition of the smoothing parameter follows).

3.1 Lattice Definition

Let $\mathbf{B} = \{\mathbf{b}_1, \ldots, \mathbf{b}_n\} \subset \mathbb{R}^m$ be a set of n linearly independent vectors. The *lattice* Λ of *rank* n generated by the basis $\mathbf{B}$ is the set of vectors

$$\Lambda = \mathcal{L}(\mathbf{B}) = \{\mathbf{Bc} : \mathbf{c} \in \mathbb{Z}^n\}.$$

We will work with *full-rank* integer lattices, i.e. $\Lambda \subset \mathbb{Z}^m$ with $m = n$. The *dual* lattice Λ^* is the set is the set of all vectors $\mathbf{y} \in \mathbb{R}^m$ satisfying $\langle \mathbf{x}, \mathbf{y} \rangle \in \mathbb{Z}$ for all vectors $\mathbf{x} \in \Lambda$. If $\mathbf{B}$ is a basis of an arbitrary lattice Λ, then $\mathbf{B}^* = \mathbf{B}(\mathbf{B}^t\mathbf{B})^{-1}$ is a basis for Λ^*. For a full-rank lattice, $\mathbf{B}^* = \mathbf{B}^{-t}$. We refer to $\tilde{\mathbf{B}}$ as a Gram-Schmidt orthogonalization of $\mathbf{B}$.

So-called *q-ary integer lattices* are of particular interest in cryptography. These lattices satisfy the relation $q\mathbb{Z}^m \subseteq \Lambda \subseteq \mathbb{Z}^m$ for some integer q. For a matrix $\mathbf{A} \in \mathbb{Z}_q^{n \times m}$, integers q, m, n, we define two full-rank m-dimensional q-ary lattices:

$$\Lambda(\mathbf{A}^t) = \{\mathbf{y} \in \mathbb{Z}^m : \exists \mathbf{s} \in \mathbb{Z}_q^n \text{ s.t. } \mathbf{y} \equiv \mathbf{A}^t\mathbf{s} \mod q\}$$

$$\Lambda^\perp(\mathbf{A}) = \{\mathbf{y} \in \mathbb{Z}^m : \mathbf{Ay} \equiv 0 \mod q\}.$$

3.2 Gaussians on Lattices

We define the n-dimensional Gaussian function on $\mathbb{R}^n$ centered at 0:

$$\rho(\mathbf{x}) = \exp(-\pi \cdot \|\mathbf{x}\|^2).$$

For any matrix $\mathbf{B}$ we define a density function of a Gaussian distribution for $\mathbf{x} \in \mathrm{span}(\mathbf{B})$ and for $\boldsymbol{\Sigma} = \mathbf{BB}^t \geq 0$:

$$\rho_{\sqrt{\boldsymbol{\Sigma}}} = \rho(\mathbf{B}^+\mathbf{x}) = \exp(-\pi \cdot \mathbf{x}^t \boldsymbol{\Sigma}^+ \mathbf{c}).$$

Normalizing the above expression by its total measure over span($\boldsymbol{\Sigma}$), we obtain a probability density function of the continuous Gaussian distribution $D_{\sqrt{\boldsymbol{\Sigma}}}$. The covariance matrix of this distribution is $\frac{\boldsymbol{\Sigma}}{2\pi}$, we ignore the $\frac{1}{2\pi}$ factor and refer to $\boldsymbol{\Sigma}$ as the covariance matrix of $D_{\sqrt{\boldsymbol{\Sigma}}}$.

The continuous Gaussian distribution $D_{\sqrt{\boldsymbol{\Sigma}}}$ can be discretized to a lattice (or to the "shift" of the lattice) as follows: for $\Lambda \subset \mathbb{R}^n, \mathbf{c} \in \mathbb{R}^n$ and positive semidefinite $\boldsymbol{\Sigma} > \mathbf{0}$ such that $(\Lambda + \mathbf{c}) \cap$ span($\boldsymbol{\Sigma}$) is nonempty, the *discrete Gaussian distribution* is

$$D_{\Lambda+\mathbf{c},\sqrt{\boldsymbol{\Sigma}}} = \frac{\rho_{\sqrt{\boldsymbol{\Sigma}}}(\mathbf{x})}{\rho_{\sqrt{\boldsymbol{\Sigma}}}(\Lambda+\mathbf{x})}, \forall \mathbf{x} \in \Lambda + \mathbf{c},$$

where the denominator is merely a normalization factor.

In the definition of the so-called *smoothing parameter* η_ϵ (originally defined in [13]) we follow the notion of [15].

Definition 6. *For a positive semidefinite matrix $\boldsymbol{\Sigma}$ and a lattice $\Lambda \subset$ span($\boldsymbol{\Sigma}$), we say that $\sqrt{\boldsymbol{\Sigma}} > \eta_\epsilon(\Lambda)$ if $\rho_{\sqrt{\boldsymbol{\Sigma}^+}}(\Lambda^*) \leq 1 + \epsilon$.*

We will also use the following tail bound on discrete Gaussians.

Lemma 7 ([5], Lemma 1.5). *Let $\Lambda \subset \mathbb{R}^n$ be a lattice and $r \leq \eta_\epsilon(\Lambda)$ for some $\epsilon \in (0,1)$. For any $\mathbf{c} \in$ span(Λ), we have*

$$\Pr[\|D_{\Lambda+\mathbf{c},r}\| \geq r\sqrt{n}] \leq 2^{-n} \cdot \frac{1+\epsilon}{1-\epsilon}.$$

If $\mathbf{c} = 0$ then the inequality holds for any $r > 0$, with $\epsilon = 0$.

3.3 Useful Tools

Here we recall some useful facts about subgaussian random variable and the singular value of a matrix. A detailed overview on subgaussian probability distribution is given in [17]. As the name suggests, subgaussian random variable generalizes the notion of Gaussian random variable in the sense that it has the property of a super-exponential tail decay.

Definition 8. *A random variable X is subgaussian with parameter s, if $\exists C$ such that $\forall t \geq 0$*

$$\Pr[|X| > t] \leq C \exp(-\pi t^2/s^2).$$

In [17] it is proved that the above definition is equivalent to the inequality for the moment-generating function: $\mathbb{E}[\exp(tX)] \leq \exp(\frac{1}{2}Cs^2t^2)$, $\forall t \in \mathbb{R}$. Since we deal with discrete Gaussians, we will use a more loose definition of the so-called δ-subgaussian variable due to [15]:

Definition 9. *For $\delta > 0$ a random variable X is δ-**subgaussian** with parameter $s > 0$ if for all $t \in \mathbb{R}$, the (scaled) moment-generating function satisfies*

$$\mathbb{E}[2\pi t X] \leq \exp(\delta) \cdot \exp(\pi s^2 t^2).$$

Other than the Gaussian distribution itself, Bernoulli distributed and any bounded random variable are classical examples for subgaussians. Note that if we concatenate independent δ_i-subgaussian random variable with common parameter s into a vector, we obtain a $(\Sigma\delta_i)$ subgaussian vector with parameter s. It is easy to see that for a finite number of independent Gaussian random variables X_i with zero mean, their sum $\Sigma_i X_i$ is a Gaussian random variable with parameter $s = \sqrt{\Sigma_i s_i^2}$. This property is called *rotation invariance* in [17] and also transfers to the subgaussians. In the security proof of our proxy re-encryption scheme we will use the following fact.

Fact 10. *Let $X_1, X_2, \ldots, X_n$ be independent, zero-mean subgaussian random variables with parameter s and $a = (a_1, a_2, \ldots, a_n) \in \mathbb{R}^n$. Then $\Sigma_k(a_k X_k)$ is a subgaussian random variable with parameter $s\|a\|$.*

One can view the addition and subtraction of the subgaussians as the inner product of a subgaussian vector and a $\{0, -1, 1\}$-vector. In our security proof we use this fact to show that the result of a product of a δ-subgaussian matrix (treated as a concatenation of δ-subgaussian columns) by a matrix with $\{0, -1, 1\}$ entries is a δ-subgaussian matrix with a slightly larger parameter s.

Here we recall two facts about the singular values of a random matrix. The first lemma from [17] shows an upper bound on the singular value of the matrix with Gaussian entries adapted to the 0-subgaussian case. The second result ([11]) bounds the singular value of the product of two matrices.

Lemma 11. *Let $A \in \mathbb{R}^{n \times m}$ be a δ-subgaussian random matrix with parameter s. There exist a universal constant $C > 0$ such that for any $t \geq 0$ we have $\sigma_1(A) \leq C \cdot s \cdot (\sqrt{m} + \sqrt{n} + t)$ except with probability at most $2\exp(\delta)\exp(-\pi t^2)$.*

Lemma 12 (Theorem 3.3.16 in [11]). *Let $A \in M_{m,n}, B \in M_{n,m}$ and $\ell = \min\{m, n\}$. The following inequalities hold for the decreasingly ordered singular values of AB:*

$$\sigma_i(AB) \leq \sigma_i(A)\sigma_1(B) \quad \text{for } i = 1, \ldots, \ell.$$

3.4   Hard Problems

There are two lattice-based one-way functions associated with matrix $\mathbf{A} \in \mathbb{Z}_q^{n \times m}$ for $m = poly(n)$:

- $f_\mathbf{A}(\mathbf{x}) = \mathbf{A}\mathbf{x} \mod q, \mathbf{x} \in \mathbb{Z}^m$;
- $g_\mathbf{A}(\mathbf{e}, \mathbf{s}) = \mathbf{s}^t \mathbf{A} + \mathbf{e}^t \mod q$ for $\mathbf{s} \in \mathbb{Z}_q^n$ and a Gaussian $\mathbf{e} \in \mathbb{Z}^m$.

Given a vector $\mathbf{u}$, finding a short preimage $\mathbf{x}'$ such that $f_\mathbf{A}(\mathbf{x}') = \mathbf{u}$ is an instantiation of the SIS problem, which is at least as hard as solving the of Shortest Independent Vector Problem (SIVP) on n-dimensional lattices ([1], [13]). The problem to invert $g_\mathbf{A}(\mathbf{e}, \mathbf{s})$, where $\mathbf{e} \leftarrow D_{\alpha q}$, is known as LWE$_{q,\alpha}$ problem and is as hard as quantumly solving SIVP on n-dimensional lattices ([16]). The decisional-LWE problem asks to distinguish the output of $g_\mathbf{A}$ from uniform.

4   G-trapdoor and Algorithms

In this section we briefly describe the main results of [15]: the definition of a so-called **G**-trapdoor and the algorithms $\mathsf{Invert}^{\mathcal{O}}$ and $\mathsf{Sample}^{\mathcal{O}}$ for the LWE and SIS problems.

4.1   Trapdoor Generation

In short, a **G**-trapdoor is a transformation (represented by a matrix **R**) from a public matrix **A** to a special matrix **G**. **G** has such a structured form that solving SIS and LWE problems for this matrix (i.e. inverting $g_\mathbf{G}$ and $f_\mathbf{G}$) can be done efficiently, while for a uniform **A** these problems are believed to be hard. As an example of a matrix **G** Micciancio and Peikert in [15] consider $\mathbf{G} = \mathbf{I}_n \otimes \mathbf{g}^t \in \mathbb{Z}_q^{n \times nk}$, where

$$\mathbf{g}^t = [1 \quad 2 \quad 4 \ldots 2^{k-1}] \in \mathbb{Z}_q^{1 \times k}, \quad q = 2^k.$$

They also give efficient algorithms for inverting $g_\mathbf{g}(s, \mathbf{e}) = s \cdot \mathbf{g}^t + \mathbf{e}^t \mod q$ and Gaussian sampling from preimages of $f_\mathbf{g}(\mathbf{x}) = \langle \mathbf{g}, \mathbf{x} \rangle \mod q$. By executing these algorithms n times, one solves the same problems for **G**.

In order to embed this structured matrix into a (uniformly looking) matrix **A** together with a transformation **R**, one should start with a uniform matrix $\mathbf{A}_0$ and a matrix **R** and construct $\mathbf{A} = [\mathbf{A}_0| - \mathbf{A}_0\mathbf{R} + \mathbf{G}]$. For an appropriate choice of dimensions $(\mathbf{A}, \mathbf{AR})$ is $\mathsf{negl}(n)$-far from uniform by the Leftover Hash Lemma. Using **R** one can transform:

$$[\mathbf{A}_0| - \mathbf{A}_0\mathbf{R} + \mathbf{G}]\begin{bmatrix} \mathbf{R} \\ \mathbf{I} \end{bmatrix} = \mathbf{G}$$

and, therefore, invert one-way functions $g_\mathbf{A}, f_\mathbf{A}$.

In [15] an invertible matrix **H** is used as: $\mathbf{A} = [\mathbf{A}_0| - \mathbf{A}_0\mathbf{R} + \mathbf{HG}]$ to construct a CCA-secure encryption scheme. In this case the knowledge of both **R** and **H** is needed to perform the transformation. Note, that if **H** is a zero-matrix, then $[\mathbf{A}_0| - \mathbf{A}_0\mathbf{R}]\begin{bmatrix} \mathbf{R} \\ \mathbf{I} \end{bmatrix} = \mathbf{0}$, and solving LWE (or SIS) for **A** does not longer reduce to solving the same problems for **G**. This fact is used to construct a challenge ciphertext.

To achieve CCA-security for *re-encryption*, we need to have a pair of transformations $(\mathbf{R}_1, \mathbf{R}_2)$ for **A**: $\mathbf{R}_1$ to generate re-encryption keys (i.e. to solve SIS) and $\mathbf{R}_2$ to decrypt (i.e. to solve LWE). Let us define the generalized definition of a **G**-trapdoor:

Definition 13. *Let* $\mathbf{A} = [\mathbf{A}_0|\mathbf{A}_1|\ldots|\mathbf{A}_{k-1}] \in \mathbb{Z}_q^{n \times m}$ *for* $k \geq 2$, *and* $\mathbf{A}_0 \in \mathbb{Z}_q^{n \times \bar{m}}$, $\mathbf{A}_1, \ldots, \mathbf{A}_{k-1} \in \mathbb{Z}_q^{n \times w}$ *with* $\bar{m} \geq w \geq n$ *and* $m = \bar{m} + (k - 1) \cdot w$ *(typically,* $w = n\lceil \log q \rceil$ *). A* **G**-*trapdoor for* $\mathbf{A}$ *is a sequence of matrices* $\mathbf{R} = [\mathbf{R}_1|\mathbf{R}_2|\ldots|\mathbf{R}_{k-1}] \in \mathbb{Z}^{\bar{m} \times (k-1)w}$ *such that:*

$$[\mathbf{A}_0|\mathbf{A}_1|\ldots|\mathbf{A}_{k-1}] \begin{bmatrix} \mathbf{R}_1 & \mathbf{R}_2 & \cdots & \mathbf{R}_{k-1} \\ \mathbf{I} & \mathbf{0} & \cdots & \mathbf{0} \\ \vdots & \vdots & \ddots & \vdots \\ \mathbf{0} & \mathbf{0} & \cdots & \mathbf{I} \end{bmatrix} = [\mathbf{H}_1\mathbf{G}|\mathbf{H}_2\mathbf{G}|\cdots|\mathbf{H}_{k-1}\mathbf{G}]$$

for invertible matrices $\mathbf{H}_i \in \mathbb{Z}_q^{n \times n}$ *and a fixed* $\mathbf{G} \in \mathbb{Z}_q^{n \times w}$.

To generate a pseudorandom matrix $\mathbf{A} \in \mathbb{Z}_q^{n \times m}$ with a $\mathbf{G}$-trapdoor $\mathbf{R} \in \mathbb{Z}_q^{\bar{m} \times (k-1)w}$ one should iteratively execute the algorithm $\mathsf{GenTrap}^{\mathcal{D}}$ of [15] but for $k-1$ invertible $\mathbf{H}_i$'s and for Gaussian $\mathbf{R}_i \leftarrow D_s^{\bar{m} \times w}$ for some $s \geq \eta_\epsilon(\mathbb{Z})$.

4.2 Algorithms

Here we show how to use a generalized trapdoor for the inversion of the function $g_{\mathbf{A}}(\mathbf{s}, \mathbf{e}) = \mathbf{s}^t \mathbf{A} + \mathbf{e}^t \bmod q$ and preimage sampling for $f_{\mathbf{A}}(\mathbf{x}) = \mathbf{A}\mathbf{x} \bmod q$, where $\mathbf{A} \in \mathbb{Z}_q^{n \times m}$ has a trapdoor $\mathbf{R} \in \mathbb{Z}^{(m-w) \times w}$ that satisfies Def. 13. The algorithms below generalize the algorithms $\mathsf{Invert}^{\mathcal{O}}$ and $\mathsf{Sample}^{\mathcal{O}}$ of [15].

LWE Inversion. We start by showing how to use the extended notion of a $\mathbf{G}$-trapdoor to invert an LWE sample $\mathbf{b}^t = \mathbf{s}^t \mathbf{A} + \mathbf{e}^t \bmod q$. We refer to this procedure as $\mathsf{Invert}^{\mathcal{O}}(\mathbf{R}, \mathbf{A}, \mathbf{b}, \mathbf{H}_i)$ and emphasize in the input that $\mathbf{H}_i$ is an invertible matrix, while the other $\mathbf{H}_j, j \neq i$ can be zero. So for $\mathbf{A} = [\mathbf{A}_0|\mathbf{H}_1\mathbf{G} - \mathbf{R}_1\mathbf{A}_0|\ldots|\mathbf{H}_i\mathbf{G} - \mathbf{R}_i\mathbf{A}_0|\ldots]$:

1. Compute $\widehat{\mathbf{b}}^t = \mathbf{b} \begin{bmatrix} \mathbf{R}_1 & \mathbf{R}_2 & \cdots & \mathbf{R}_{k-1} \\ \mathbf{I} & \mathbf{0} & \cdots & \mathbf{0} \\ \vdots & \vdots & \ddots & \vdots \\ \mathbf{0} & \mathbf{0} & \cdots & \mathbf{I} \end{bmatrix} = [\mathbf{H}_1\mathbf{G}|\ldots|\mathbf{H}_i\mathbf{G}|\ldots\mathbf{H}_{k-1}\mathbf{G}] \in \mathbb{Z}_q^{(k-1)w}$;

2. Set $\widehat{\mathbf{b}}_1^t = \widehat{\mathbf{b}}^t[w \cdot (i-1)\ldots w \cdot i]$;
3. Obtain $(\dot{\mathbf{s}}, \dot{\mathbf{e}})$ by inverting $\widehat{\mathbf{b}}_1^t$ for $\mathbf{G}$. So $(\dot{\mathbf{s}}, \dot{\mathbf{e}})$ satisfies $\widehat{\mathbf{b}}_1^t = \dot{\mathbf{s}}\mathbf{G} + \dot{\mathbf{e}} \bmod q$.
4. Compute $\mathbf{s} = \mathbf{H}_i^{-t}\dot{\mathbf{s}} \in \mathbb{Z}_q^n$ and $\mathbf{e} = \mathbf{b} - \mathbf{A}^t\mathbf{s} \in \mathbb{Z}_q^m$. Output $(\mathbf{s}, \mathbf{e})$.

The algorithm produces a correct output, if the error vector $\mathbf{e}$ is "short enough": $\|\mathbf{e}\| < q/(2\|\mathbf{B}\|s)$ where $\mathbf{B}$ is a basis for $\Lambda^\perp(\mathbf{G})$ and $s = \sqrt{\sigma_1(\mathbf{R}_i)^2 + 1}$. For the detailed proof of correctness see theorem 5.4 in [15].

Gaussian Sampling. We show below how to sample a Gaussian vector $\mathbf{x} \in \mathbb{Z}_q^m$ for a matrix $\mathbf{A} = [\mathbf{A}_0|\ldots|\mathbf{A}_{k-1}] \in \mathbb{Z}_q^{n \times m}$ with the generalized trapdoor $\mathbf{R} \in \mathbb{Z}_q^{\bar{m} \times (k-1)w}$ and $k-1$ invertible $\mathbf{H}_i$'s given a coset $\mathbf{u} \in \mathbb{Z}_q^n$.

The intuition behind the algorithm $\mathsf{Sample}^{\mathcal{O}}$ of [15] is the following: for two distributions X and Y with covariance matrices $\mathbf{\Sigma}_X$ and $\mathbf{\Sigma}_Y$, the covariance of their sum is $\mathbf{\Sigma}_X + \mathbf{\Sigma}_Y$. A spherical Gaussian distribution with a standard deviation s has covariance matrix $s^2\mathbf{I}$. Therefore, having $\mathbf{\Sigma}_X$ and a parameter s as inputs, we can "adjust" $\mathbf{\Sigma}_Y$ such that $X + Y$ is a spherical Gaussian with standard deviation s.

So having as input a coset $\mathbf{u}$, a matrix $\mathbf{A}$ with a trapdoor $\mathbf{R}$, an invertible $\mathbf{H}$ and a parameter for the output distribution s, we first sample a vector $\mathbf{z}$ for the matrix $\mathbf{G}$ with fixed parameter $r\sqrt{\Sigma_{\mathbf{G}}}$ (for the construction from section 4.1 $\sqrt{\Sigma_{\mathbf{G}}} = 2$). Then we multiply $\mathbf{x}' = \begin{bmatrix} \mathbf{R} \\ \mathbf{I} \end{bmatrix} \mathbf{z}$. The resulting vector $\mathbf{x}'$ satisfies $\mathbf{A}\mathbf{x}' = \mathbf{u}$, but has covariance matrix $\Sigma_{\mathbf{x}'} = [\mathbf{R}|\mathbf{I}]^T(r\Sigma_{\mathbf{G}})[\mathbf{R}^t|\mathbf{I}]$. In order to output a vector $\mathbf{x}$ as spherical Gaussian with parameter s we add a vector $\mathbf{p}$ with covariance $\Sigma_{\mathbf{p}} = s^2\mathbf{I} - [\mathbf{R}|\mathbf{I}]^T(r\Sigma_{\mathbf{G}})[\mathbf{R}^t|\mathbf{I}]$.

1. Choose $\mathbf{p} \leftarrow D_{\mathbb{Z}^m, r\sqrt{\Sigma_{\mathbf{p}}}}$. View it as $\mathbf{p}^t = [\mathbf{p}_1|\mathbf{p}_2|\dots|\mathbf{p}_k]$, where $\mathbf{p}_1 \in \mathbb{Z}^{\bar{m}}$, $\mathbf{p}_2, \dots, \mathbf{p}_k \in \mathbb{Z}^w$.
2. Compute $\overline{\mathbf{w}}_1 = \mathbf{A}_0(\mathbf{p}_1 - \mathbf{R}_1\mathbf{p}_2)$, $\overline{\mathbf{w}}_i = -\mathbf{A}_0\mathbf{R}_i\mathbf{p}_{i+1}$ for $i = 2, \dots, (k-1)$;
3. Compute $\mathbf{w}_i = \mathbf{G}\mathbf{p}_{i+1}$ for $i = 1, \dots, (k-1)$;
4. Let $\mathbf{v}_1 = \mathbf{H}_1^{-1}(\mathbf{u} - \overline{\mathbf{w}}_1) - \mathbf{w}_1$, $\mathbf{v}_i = -\mathbf{H}_i^{-1}\overline{\mathbf{w}}_i - \mathbf{w}_i$ for $i = 2, \dots, (k-1)$;
5. For each $i = 1, \dots, (k-1)$ choose $\mathbf{z}_i \leftarrow D_{\Lambda_{\mathbf{v}_i}^{\perp}(\mathbf{G}), r\sqrt{\Sigma_{\mathbf{G}}}}$. Concatenate the obtained vectors to get $\mathbf{z}^t = [\mathbf{z}_1|\dots|\mathbf{z}_{k-1}] \in \mathbb{Z}^{(k-1)w}$;
6. Output $\mathbf{x} = \mathbf{p} + \begin{bmatrix} \mathbf{R}_1 & \mathbf{R}_2 & \cdots & \mathbf{R}_{k-1} \\ \mathbf{I} & \mathbf{0} & \cdots & \mathbf{0} \\ \vdots & \vdots & \ddots & \vdots \\ \mathbf{0} & \mathbf{0} & \cdots & \mathbf{I} \end{bmatrix} \cdot \mathbf{z} \in \mathbb{Z}^m$.

5   Chosen Ciphertext Secure Proxy Re-encryption

In this section we present our main result: the proxy re-encryption scheme that employs a $\mathbf{G}$-trapdoor with the associated algorithms from the previous section. Before giving the formal description of the scheme we provide an intuition behind the generation of the re-encryption keys. The ability to sample short vectors for any coset can be extended to performing the sampling algorithm for any $n \times m$ matrix in a column-wise fashion, that is for each column (coset) we can output a Gaussian column-vector and after m samplings concatenate the result into a matrix. This idea was used in a trapdoor delegation algorithm in [15]. If the input matrix is some public key matrix $\mathbf{A}'$, then the result of sampling (a matrix $\mathbf{X}$) is a transformation $\mathbf{A} \cdot \mathbf{X} = \mathbf{A}'$ between two public keys.

In order to accomplish both tasks: re-encryption key generation and decryption, we propose to use the generalized definition of a $\mathbf{G}$-trapdoor (Def. 13). Thus, we achieve a re-encryption functionality: we sample small matrices with one $\mathbf{G}$-trapdoor ($\mathbf{R}_1$), and at the same time we perform the decryption operation using another $\mathbf{G}$-trapdoor ($\mathbf{R}_2$).

5.1   Construction of the Single-Hop PRE

Let 1^n be the security parameter and let r refer to a fixed function $w(\sqrt{\log n})$.

– The modulus q is defined as a large enough prime power $q = p^e = poly(n)$ and $k = O(\log q) = O(\log n)$. We define $\bar{m} = O(nk)$ and the total dimension of the public key as $m = \bar{m} + 2nk$.

- $\mathbf{G} \in \mathbb{Z}_q^{n \times nk}$ is a matrix of a special structure (see section 4.2 for an example), so there are efficient algorithms to invert $g_{\mathbf{G}}$ and to sample for $f_{\mathbf{G}}$.
- the trapdoors $\mathbf{R}_i$'s are sampled from the Gaussian $\mathcal{D} = D_{\mathbb{Z}, w(\sqrt{\log n})}^{\bar{m} \times nk}$, so that $(\mathbf{A}_0, \mathbf{A}_0 \mathbf{R}_1, \mathbf{A}_0 \mathbf{R}_2)$ is negl(n)-far from uniformly chosen matrices $(\mathbf{U}_1, \mathbf{U}_2, \mathbf{U}_3) \in \mathbb{Z}_q^{n \times \bar{m}} \times \mathbb{Z}_q^{n \times nk} \times \mathbb{Z}_q^{n \times nk}$ for $\mathbf{A}_0 \leftarrow \mathbb{Z}_q^{n \times \bar{m}}$ and for any $\mathbf{R}_1, \mathbf{R}_2 \leftarrow \mathcal{D}$.
- All the invertible matrices $\mathbf{H} \in \mathbb{Z}_q^{n \times n}$ that are used in the scheme, are chosen from a set with the "unit differences" property (see [15] for an example): for any two $\mathbf{H}', \mathbf{H}''$ their difference $\mathbf{H}' - \mathbf{H}''$ is also invertible.
- the LWE error rate α for single-hop PRE should satisfy $1/\alpha = O((nk)^3) \cdot r^3$.

We encode the message space $\{0,1\}^{nk}$ to the cosets of $\Lambda/2\Lambda$ for the lattice $\Lambda = \Lambda(\mathbf{G}^t)$ using any basis $\mathbf{B} \in \mathbb{Z}^{nk}$ of Λ, namely for a message $\mathbf{m} \in \{0,1\}^{nk}$ we define the encoding function as $\mathsf{enc}(\mathbf{m}) = \mathbf{Bm} \in \mathbb{Z}^{nk}$. Notice that this mapping can be efficiently inverted.

- KeyGen(1^n): choose $\mathbf{A}_0 \leftarrow \mathbb{Z}_q^{n \times \bar{m}}$, $\mathbf{R}_1, \mathbf{R}_2 \leftarrow \mathcal{D}$ and an invertible matrix $\mathbf{H} \leftarrow \mathbb{Z}_q^{nk \times nk}$. Compose the matrix $\mathbf{A} = [\mathbf{A}_0 | \mathbf{A}_1 | \mathbf{A}_2] = [\mathbf{A}_0| - \mathbf{A}_0 \mathbf{R}_1| - \mathbf{A}_0 \mathbf{R}_2] \in \mathbb{Z}_q^{n \times m}$ and set the public key as $\mathsf{pk} = (\mathbf{A}, \mathbf{H})$. The secret key is the matrix $sk = [\mathbf{R}_1 | \mathbf{R}_2] \in \mathbb{Z}^{\bar{m} \times 2nk}$ with small entries. Notice that

$$[\mathbf{A}_0 | \mathbf{A}_1 | \mathbf{A}_2] \begin{bmatrix} \mathbf{R}_1 & \mathbf{R}_2 \\ \mathbf{I} & \mathbf{0} \\ \mathbf{0} & \mathbf{I} \end{bmatrix} = [\mathbf{0}|\mathbf{0}] \in \mathbb{Z}_q^{n \times 2nk}.$$

- Enc($\mathsf{pk} = ([\mathbf{A}_0 | \mathbf{A}_1 | \mathbf{A}_2],\ \mathbf{H}), \mathbf{m} \in \{0,1\}^{nk}$): choose a non-zero invertible matrix $\mathbf{H}_u$, and a vector $\mathbf{s} \leftarrow \mathbb{Z}_q^n$. Set $\mathbf{A}_u = [\mathbf{A}_0 | \mathbf{A}_1 + \mathbf{HG} | \mathbf{A}_2 + \mathbf{H}_u \mathbf{G}]$. Sample three error vectors $\mathbf{e}_0 \leftarrow D_{\mathbb{Z}, \alpha q}^{\bar{m}}$, $\mathbf{e}_1, \mathbf{e}_2 \leftarrow D_{\mathbb{Z}, s}^{nk}$, where $s^2 = (\|\mathbf{e}_0\|^2 + \bar{m}(\alpha q)^2) \cdot r^2$. The composed error vector is a concatenation of the chosen vectors $\mathbf{e} = (\mathbf{e}_0, \mathbf{e}_1, \mathbf{e}_2) \in \mathbb{Z}^m$. Compute

$$\mathbf{b}^t = 2(\mathbf{s}^t[\mathbf{A}_0 | \mathbf{A}_1 + \mathbf{HG} | \mathbf{A}_2 + \mathbf{H}_u \mathbf{G}] \bmod q) + \mathbf{e}^t + (\mathbf{0}, \mathbf{0}, \mathsf{enc}(\mathbf{m}))^t \bmod 2q,$$

where the first zero vector has dimension $\bar{m}$, the second has dimension nk. Output the ciphertext $c = (\mathbf{H}_u, \mathbf{b}) \in \mathbb{Z}_q^{n \times n} \times \mathbb{Z}_{2q}^m$.
- Dec($\mathsf{pk} = ([\mathbf{A}_0 | \mathbf{A}_1 | \mathbf{A}_2],\ \mathbf{H}), sk = [\mathbf{R}_1 | \mathbf{R}_2], c = (\mathbf{H}_u, \mathbf{b})$): Using matrix $\mathbf{H}_u$ compute $\mathbf{A}_u = [\mathbf{A}_0 | \mathbf{A}_1 + \mathbf{HG} | \mathbf{A}_2 + \mathbf{H}_u \mathbf{G}]$.
  1. If c has invalid form or $\mathbf{H}_u = \mathbf{0}$, output $\bot$.
  2. With the secret key call an algorithm $\mathsf{Invert}^{\mathcal{O}}([\mathbf{R}_1 | \mathbf{R}_2],\ \mathbf{A}_u, \mathbf{b}, \mathbf{H}_u)$. On this input the algorithm (section 4.2) computes the product:

$$[\mathbf{A}_0 | \mathbf{A}_1 + \mathbf{HG}| - \mathbf{A}_2 + \mathbf{H}_u \mathbf{G}] \begin{bmatrix} \mathbf{R}_1 & \mathbf{R}_2 \\ \mathbf{I} & \mathbf{0} \\ \mathbf{0} & \mathbf{I} \end{bmatrix} = [\mathbf{HG}|\mathbf{H}_u \mathbf{G}] \in \mathbb{Z}_q^{n \times 2nk}.$$

As output we receive two vectors $\mathbf{z} \in \mathbb{Z}_q^n$ and $\mathbf{e} = (\mathbf{e}_0, \mathbf{e}_1, \mathbf{e}_2) \in \mathbb{Z}_q^{\bar{m}} \times \mathbb{Z}_q^{nk} \times \mathbb{Z}_q^{nk}$ that satisfy $\mathbf{b}^t = \mathbf{z}^t \mathbf{A}_u + \mathbf{e}^t \bmod q$.

3. Check the lengths of the obtained vectors, namely, if $\|\mathbf{e}_0\| \geq \alpha q \sqrt{\bar{m}}$ or $\|\mathbf{e}_j\| \geq \alpha q \sqrt{2\bar{m}nk} \cdot w(\sqrt{\log n})$ for $j = 1, 2$, output $\perp$.

4. Parse $\mathbf{v} = \mathbf{b} - \mathbf{e} \bmod 2q$ as $\mathbf{v} = (\mathbf{v}_0, \mathbf{v}_1, \mathbf{v}_2) \in \mathbb{Z}_{2q}^{\bar{m}} \times \mathbb{Z}_{2q}^{nk} \times \mathbb{Z}_{2q}^{nk}$. If $\mathbf{v}_0 \notin 2\Lambda(\mathbf{A}_0^t)$, output $\perp$. Otherwise, compute

$$\mathbf{v}^t \begin{bmatrix} \mathbf{R}_1 \ \mathbf{R}_2 \\ \mathbf{I} \quad \mathbf{0} \\ \mathbf{0} \quad \mathbf{I} \end{bmatrix} \bmod 2q \in \mathbb{Z}_{2q}^{nk}$$

and apply enc^{-1} to the last nk coordinates.

- ReKeyGen($\mathsf{pk} = ([\mathbf{A}_0|\mathbf{A}_1|\mathbf{A}_2], \ \mathbf{H}), \mathsf{sk} = [\mathbf{R}_1|\mathbf{R}_2], \mathsf{pk}' = ([\mathbf{A}_0'|\mathbf{A}_1'|\mathbf{A}_2'], \ \mathbf{H}')$):

1. Using the first part of a secret key - the Gaussian matrix $\mathbf{R}_1$ - and the invertible $\mathbf{H} \in \mathbb{Z}_q^{n \times n}$ from the public key, execute $\mathsf{Sample}^{\mathcal{O}}$ (section 4.2) to sample from the cosets of the $\mathbf{A}_0'$. Specifically, we sample column-wise so that for each column of the $\mathbf{A}_0'$ we obtain an $\bar{m} + nk$-dimensional column of the re-encryption key. After sampling $\bar{m}$ times we receive an $(\bar{m} + nk) \times \bar{m}$ matrix and parse it as two matrices $\mathbf{X}_{00} \in \mathbb{Z}^{\bar{m} \times \bar{m}}$ and $\mathbf{X}_{10} \in \mathbb{Z}^{nk \times \bar{m}}$ matrices with Gaussian entries of parameter s.

$$[\mathbf{A}_0| - \mathbf{A}_0\mathbf{R}_1 + \mathbf{H}\mathbf{G}] \begin{bmatrix} \mathbf{X}_{00} \\ \mathbf{X}_{10} \end{bmatrix} = [\mathbf{A}_0'].$$

2. Continue sampling for the cosets obtained from the columns of the matrix $[\mathbf{A}_1' + \mathbf{H}'\mathbf{G}]$ of pk'. But this time we increase (as explained in the Gaussian sampling algorithms in section 4.2), the Gaussian parameter of the resulting sampled matrix up to $s\sqrt{\bar{m}/2}$

$$[\mathbf{A}_0| - \mathbf{A}_0\mathbf{R}_1 + \mathbf{H}\mathbf{G}] \begin{bmatrix} \mathbf{X}_{01} \\ \mathbf{X}_{11} \end{bmatrix} = [\mathbf{A}_1' + \mathbf{H}'\mathbf{G}].$$

To achieve a correct re-encryption for the last sampling change the cosets by adding $-\mathbf{A}_2 = \mathbf{A}_0\mathbf{R}_2$:

$$[\mathbf{A}_0| - \mathbf{A}_0\mathbf{R}_1 + \mathbf{H}\mathbf{G}] \begin{bmatrix} \mathbf{X}_{02} \\ \mathbf{X}_{12} \end{bmatrix} = [\mathbf{A}_2' + \mathbf{A}_0\mathbf{R}_2],$$

where $\mathbf{X}_{01}, \mathbf{X}_{02} \in \mathbb{Z}^{\bar{m} \times nk}$, $\mathbf{X}_{11}, \mathbf{X}_{12} \in \mathbb{Z}^{nk \times nk}$ with entries distributed as Gaussian with parameter $s\sqrt{\bar{m}}$.

3. The re-encryption key is a matrix with Gaussian entries:

$$\mathsf{rk} = \begin{bmatrix} \mathbf{X}_{00} \ \mathbf{X}_{01} \ \mathbf{X}_{02} \\ \mathbf{X}_{10} \ \mathbf{X}_{11} \ \mathbf{X}_{12} \\ \mathbf{0} \quad \mathbf{0} \quad \mathbf{I} \end{bmatrix} \in \mathbb{Z}^{m \times m}.$$

For any matrix $\mathbf{B} \in \mathbb{Z}^{n \times nk}$ the re-encryption key satisfies:

$$[\mathbf{A}_0|\mathbf{A}_1 + \mathbf{H}\mathbf{G}|\mathbf{A}_2 + \mathbf{B}] \cdot \begin{bmatrix} \mathbf{X}_{00} \ \mathbf{X}_{01} \ \mathbf{X}_{02} \\ \mathbf{X}_{10} \ \mathbf{X}_{11} \ \mathbf{X}_{12} \\ \mathbf{0} \quad \mathbf{0} \quad \mathbf{I} \end{bmatrix} = [\mathbf{A}_0'|\mathbf{A}_1' + \mathbf{H}'\mathbf{G}|\mathbf{A}_2' + \mathbf{B}] \quad (1)$$

– ReEnc(rk, $c = (\mathbf{H}_u, \mathbf{b})$): to change the underlying public key in the ciphertext component $\mathbf{b}$ compute $\mathbf{b}'^t =$

$$\mathbf{b}^t \cdot \mathsf{rk} = \mathbf{s}^t[\mathbf{A}_0'|\mathbf{A}_1' + \mathbf{H}'\mathbf{G}|\mathbf{A}_2' + \mathbf{H}_u\mathbf{G}] + \widetilde{\mathbf{e}}^t + (0, 0, \mathsf{enc}(\mathbf{m}))^t \bmod 2q, \quad (2)$$

where $\widetilde{\mathbf{e}} = (\widetilde{\mathbf{e}}_0, \widetilde{\mathbf{e}}_1, \widetilde{\mathbf{e}}_2)$ and $\widetilde{\mathbf{e}}_0 = \mathbf{e}_0\mathbf{X}_{00} + \mathbf{e}_1\mathbf{X}_{10}, \widetilde{\mathbf{e}}_1 = \mathbf{e}_0\mathbf{X}_{01} + \mathbf{e}_1\mathbf{X}_{11}, \widetilde{\mathbf{e}}_2 = \mathbf{e}_0\mathbf{X}_{02} + \mathbf{e}_1\mathbf{X}_{12} + \mathbf{e}_2$. Finally, output $c' = (\mathbf{H}_u, \mathbf{b}')$.

Remark 14. *Instead of mapping a message $\mathbf{m} \in \{0,1\}^{nk}$ to the lattice cosets, one can use a more common encoding for lattice-based schemes: $\mathsf{enc}(\mathbf{m}) = \mathbf{m}\lfloor\frac{q}{2}\rfloor$. In this case one should add an extra syndrome $\mathbf{A}_3 \in \mathbb{Z}_q^{n \times nk}$ to the public key and sample one more error vector $\mathbf{e}_3 \in\leftarrow D_{\mathbb{Z},\alpha q}^m$ for the encryption, so a ciphertext is of the form $\mathbf{b}^t = \mathbf{s}^t[\mathbf{A}_0|\mathbf{A}_1 + \mathbf{HG}|\mathbf{A}_2 + \mathbf{H}_u\mathbf{G}|\mathbf{A}_3] + (\mathbf{e}_0, \mathbf{e}_1, \mathbf{e}_2, \mathbf{e}_3)^t + (0, 0, 0, \mathsf{enc}(\mathbf{m}))^t \bmod q$. For the re-encryption key generation one more sampling is needed: $[\mathbf{A}_0| - \mathbf{A}_0\mathbf{R}_1 + \mathbf{HG}]\begin{bmatrix}\mathbf{X}_{03} \\ \mathbf{X}_{13}\end{bmatrix} = [\mathbf{A}_3' - \mathbf{A}_3]$, which results in an extended (columns $\begin{bmatrix}\mathbf{X}_{03} \\ \mathbf{X}_{13}\end{bmatrix}$ are added) re-encryption key. All the arguments below on correctness and security can be easily adapted for this case.*

5.2 Correctness

In the re-encrypted ciphertext the error terms are larger than in the original ciphertext (that is the ones that have not been re-encrypted). In the following lemma we show that with the appropriate choice of the LWE parameters α and q the decryption algorithm can tolerate the noise growth.

Lemma 15. *Our PRE scheme with message space $\mathcal{M} = \{0,1\}^{nk}$ decrypts correctly.*

Proof. Recall that by Definition 3 we have to show that the decryption algorithm outputs a correct plaintext both for the original and for the re-encrypted ciphertext. So first of all we describe an original encryption under a public key pk and then proceed with its re-encryption to another public key pk′.

Let $\mathsf{pk} = ([\mathbf{A}_0|\mathbf{A}_1|\mathbf{A}_2], \mathbf{H})$, $\mathsf{pk}' = ([\mathbf{A}_0'|\mathbf{A}_1'|\mathbf{A}_2'], \mathbf{H}')$ be the public keys output by KeyGen(1^n) together with two trapdoors $\mathsf{sk} = [\mathbf{R}_1|\mathbf{R}_2]$, $\mathsf{sk}' = [\mathbf{R}_1'|\mathbf{R}_2']$, so the first pair (pk, sk) will be the delegator's keys, the second (pk′, sk′) will be for the delegatee. We run the ReKeyGen(pk, sk, pk′) algorithm to obtain

$$\mathsf{rk}_{\mathsf{pk}\to\mathsf{pk}'} = \begin{bmatrix} \mathbf{X}_{00} & \mathbf{X}_{01} & \mathbf{X}_{02} \\ \mathbf{X}_{10} & \mathbf{X}_{11} & \mathbf{X}_{12} \\ 0 & 0 & \mathbf{I} \end{bmatrix}.$$

As we apply this re-encryption key to a ciphertext $\mathbf{b}$ that encrypts a message $\mathbf{m} \in \{0,1\}^{nk}$ under the delegator's public key $\mathsf{pk} = [\mathbf{A}_0|\mathbf{A}_1|\mathbf{A}_2], \mathbf{H}$ with the invertible matrix $\mathbf{H}_u$ and $\mathbf{e} = (\mathbf{e}_0, \mathbf{e}_1, \mathbf{e}_2)$, we have $\mathbf{b}^t \cdot \mathsf{rk}_{\mathsf{pk}\to\mathsf{pk}'} =$

$$(2\mathbf{s}^t[\mathbf{A}_0|\mathbf{A}_1 + \mathbf{HG}|\mathbf{A}_2 + \mathbf{H}_u\mathbf{G}] + \mathbf{e}^t + (0, 0, \mathsf{enc}(\mathbf{m})^t) \cdot \mathsf{rk}_{\mathsf{pk}\to\mathsf{pk}'}$$

$$= s^t[\mathbf{A}_0\mathbf{X}_{00} + (\mathbf{A}_1 + \mathbf{HG})\mathbf{X}_{10}|\mathbf{A}_0\mathbf{X}_{01} + \mathbf{A}_1\mathbf{X}_{11}|\mathbf{A}_0\mathbf{X}_{02} + \mathbf{A}_1\mathbf{X}_{12} + \mathbf{A}_2 + \mathbf{H}_u\mathbf{G}]+$$

$$(\mathbf{e}_0\mathbf{X}_{00} + \mathbf{e}_1\mathbf{X}_{10}, \mathbf{e}_0\mathbf{X}_{02} + \mathbf{e}_1\mathbf{X}_{11}, \mathbf{e}_0\mathbf{X}_{02} + \mathbf{e}_1\mathbf{X}_{12} + \mathbf{e}_2)^t + (\mathbf{0}, \mathbf{0}, \mathrm{enc}(\mathbf{m}))^t =$$

$$= s^t[\mathbf{A}_0'|\mathbf{A}_1'\mathbf{H}'\mathbf{G}|\mathbf{A}_2' + \mathbf{H}_u\mathbf{G}] + (\widetilde{\mathbf{e}}_0, \widetilde{\mathbf{e}}_1, \widetilde{\mathbf{e}}_2)^t + (\mathbf{0}, \mathbf{0}, \mathrm{enc}(\mathbf{m}))^t,$$

where the last equation follows from Eq.(1) of the re-encryption key $\mathrm{rk}_{pk \to pk'}$.

Now we estimate how the re-encryption algorithm affects the noise and justify the correctness of the decryption for a re-encrypted ciphertext. The arguments for the original ciphertexts are essentially the same as in [Lemma 6.2] of [15].

In the decryption procedure we multiply a (re-encrypted) ciphertext (and thus its error term) by $\mathsf{sk}' = [\mathbf{R}_1'|\mathbf{R}_2']$ padded with the identity matrix. So in order to obtain a correct output, we require that in the Eq.(2) both terms $\widetilde{\mathbf{e}}_0\mathbf{R}_1' + \widetilde{\mathbf{e}}_1$ and $\widetilde{\mathbf{e}}_0\mathbf{R}_2' + \widetilde{\mathbf{e}}_2$ satisfy the length condition of the decryption algorithm: $\widetilde{\mathbf{e}}_0\mathbf{R}_1' + \widetilde{\mathbf{e}}_1$, $\widetilde{\mathbf{e}}_0\mathbf{R}_2' + \widetilde{\mathbf{e}}_2 \in \mathcal{P}_{1/2}(q \cdot \mathbf{B}^{-t})$. The terms expand under the multiplication as

$$\widetilde{\mathbf{e}}_0\mathbf{R}_1' + \widetilde{\mathbf{e}}_1 = \mathbf{e}_0\mathbf{X}_{00}\mathbf{R}_1' + \mathbf{e}_1\mathbf{X}_{10}\mathbf{R}_1' + \mathbf{e}_0\mathbf{X}_{01} + \mathbf{e}_1\mathbf{X}_{11}, \tag{3a}$$

$$\widetilde{\mathbf{e}}_0\mathbf{R}_2' + \widetilde{\mathbf{e}}_2 = \mathbf{e}_0\mathbf{X}_{00}\mathbf{R}_2' + \mathbf{e}_1\mathbf{X}_{10}\mathbf{R}_2' + \mathbf{e}_0\mathbf{X}_{02} + \mathbf{e}_1\mathbf{X}_{12} + \mathbf{e}_2, \tag{3b}$$

where $(\mathbf{e}_0, \mathbf{e}_1, \mathbf{e}_2) \in \mathbb{Z}^m$ is the error vector of the original ciphertext $\mathbf{b}$.

Since we are interested in upper bounds for the length of (3a) and (3b), we should estimate how the length of the Gaussian vectors $\mathbf{e}_0, \mathbf{e}_1, \mathbf{e}_2$ is affected by the matrix multiplication. We analyze each term of Eq.(3b) separately (the same arguments hold for the terms of (3a)).

According to the sampling algorithm, the parameter s for each column of the $\mathbf{X}_{00}$ (and of $\mathbf{X}_{10}$) is as small as $\sqrt{\sigma_1(\mathbf{R}_1)^2 + 1} \cdot \sqrt{\sigma_1(\Sigma_\mathbf{G}) + 2} \cdot r$, where $\mathbf{R}_1$ is the trapdoor that was used in the re-encryption key generation. Combining Lemmas 11 and 12 and the fact that for the $\mathbf{G}$ matrix $\sigma_1(\Sigma_\mathbf{G}) = 4$, we obtain

$$\sigma_1(\mathbf{X}_{00}\mathbf{R}_2') \le \sigma_1(\mathbf{X}_{00}) \cdot \sigma_1(\mathbf{R}_2') \le C \cdot 4\sqrt{6}\bar{m} \cdot \sqrt{\sigma_1(\mathbf{R}_1)^2 + 1} \cdot r^2,$$

where $C \approx 1/2\pi$. By Lemma 7, we have $\|\mathbf{e}_0\| < \alpha q \sqrt{\bar{m}}$ and therefore

$$\|\mathbf{e}_0\mathbf{X}_{00}\mathbf{R}_2'\| < \alpha q \frac{2\sqrt{6}}{\pi} \bar{m}^{3/2} \sqrt{\sigma_1(\mathbf{R}_1)^2 + 1} \cdot r.$$

Both $\mathbf{e}_1, \mathbf{e}_2$ are sampled from the Gaussian distribution with parameter s, where $s^2 = (\|\mathbf{e}_0\|^2 + \bar{m}(\alpha q)^2) \cdot r^2$, so their lengths are bounded as $\|\mathbf{e}_1\|, \|\mathbf{e}_2\| < \alpha q \sqrt{2\bar{m}nk} \cdot r$. Hence, for the second term of Eq. (3b) it holds that

$$\|\mathbf{e}_1\mathbf{X}_{10}\mathbf{R}_2'\| < \alpha q \frac{3\sqrt{6}}{\pi} \bar{m}\sqrt{2\bar{m}nk} \cdot \sqrt{\sigma_1(\mathbf{R}_1)^2 + 1} \cdot r^3.$$

Now we analyze the singular value for matrix $\mathbf{X}_{02}$ that was sampled with parameter $s\sqrt{\bar{m}/2}$ (the same holds for $\mathbf{X}_{01}, \mathbf{X}_{12}, \mathbf{X}_{11}$):

$$\sigma_1(\mathbf{X}_{02}) \le 2\sqrt{3}\bar{m} \cdot \sqrt{\sigma_1(\mathbf{R}_1)^2 + 1} \cdot r,$$

which implies $\|\mathbf{e}_0\,\mathbf{X}_{02}\| \leq 2\sqrt{3}\alpha q\bar{m} \cdot \sqrt{\sigma_1(\mathbf{R}_1)^2 + 1} \cdot r$ and $\|\mathbf{e}_1\mathbf{X}_{12}\| \leq \sqrt{2}\alpha q\bar{m} \cdot \sqrt{2\bar{m}nk} \cdot \sqrt{\sigma_1(\mathbf{R}_1)^2 + 1} \cdot r^2$. By inspecting the remaining term and taking into account the fact that $\bar{m} = O(nk)$ and $\sigma_1(\mathbf{R}_1) \leq O(\sqrt{nk}) \cdot r$, finally we have

$$\|\widetilde{\mathbf{e}}_0\mathbf{R}_2' + \widetilde{\mathbf{e}}_2\| < \alpha q \cdot O(nk)^3 \cdot r^3.$$

By taking $1/\alpha = O(nk)^3 \cdot r^3$ we have the desired property for both error terms, $\widetilde{\mathbf{e}}_0\mathbf{R}_1' + \widetilde{\mathbf{e}}_1$, $\widetilde{\mathbf{e}}_0\mathbf{R}_2' + \widetilde{\mathbf{e}}_2 \in \mathcal{P}_{1/2}(q \cdot \mathbf{B}^{-t})$.

The security proof for our PRE scheme is essentially an adapted version of [15] [Theorem 6.3] to the proxy re-encryption model with a generalized $\mathbf{G}$-trapdoor. As discussed in section 4.2, in order to solve LWE for any matrix $\mathbf{A}$ it is necessary to know both a transformation $\mathbf{R}$ and at least one invertible $\mathbf{H}$ embedded into $\mathbf{A}$. So we construct a simulator in a way that as long as there is a nonzero matrix $\mathbf{H}$ in a ciphertext, we are able to transform it to a $\mathbf{G}$-matrix and decrypt, but once $\mathbf{H}$ equals to the zero matrix, no $\mathbf{R}$-transformation can be applied to a ciphertext to reduce it to a $\mathbf{G}$-matrix and recover a message. So when no invertible $\mathbf{H}$ is involved, we embed our LWE samples into a ciphertext and hence, decryption of the challenge helps us in deciding LWE.

Theorem 16. *The above scheme is PRE-CCA1-secure assuming the hardness of decision-LWE$_{q,\alpha'}$ for $\alpha' = \alpha/3 \geq 2\sqrt{n}/q$.*

Proof. First, by [[14], Theorem 3.1] we transform the samples from LWE distribution $A_{\mathbf{s},\alpha'}$ of the form $(\mathbf{a}, b = \langle \mathbf{s}, \mathbf{a} \rangle/q + e \mod 1) \in \mathbb{Z}_q^n \times \mathbb{T}$ to the form $(\mathbf{a}, 2(\langle \mathbf{s}, \mathbf{a} \rangle \mod q) + e' \mod 2q)$ with $e' \to D_{\mathbb{Z},\alpha q}$ via mapping $b \mapsto 2qb + D_{\mathbb{Z}-2qb,s}$, where $s^2 = (\alpha q)^2 - (2\alpha' q)^2 \geq 4n \geq \eta_\epsilon(\mathbb{Z})^2$. The transformation maps the uniform distribution over $\mathbb{Z}_q^n \times \mathbb{T}$ to the discretized uniform distribution over $\mathbb{Z}_q^n \times \mathbb{Z}_{2q}$.

Once the LWE samples are of the desired form, we construct column-wise a matrix $\mathbf{A}_0^*$ out of these samples and a vector $\mathbf{b}^*$ out of the corresponding components b's. A target's user public key is generated as follows: choose two invertible matrices $\mathbf{H}_1^*, \mathbf{H}_2^* \in \mathbb{Z}_q^{n \times n}$, the secret $\mathbf{R}_1^*, \mathbf{R}_2^* \leftarrow \mathcal{D}$ and output $\mathsf{pk}^* = ([\mathbf{A}_0^*| - \mathbf{A}_0^*\mathbf{R}_1^* - \mathbf{H}_1^*\mathbf{G}| - \mathbf{A}_0^*\mathbf{R}_2^* - \mathbf{H}_2^*\mathbf{G}], \mathbf{H}_1^*)$. Since the target user belongs to the set of honest users (we do not reveal his secret key), the matrix $\mathbf{H}_2^*$ remains statistically hidden from the adversary.

To generate the public key of an honest user we choose two matrices $\mathbf{X}_{00} \in \mathbb{Z}_q^{\bar{m} \times \bar{m}}$, $\mathbf{X}_{01} \in \mathbb{Z}_q^{nk \times \bar{m}}$ from a Gaussian distribution with parameter s and set

$$\mathbf{A}_0' = [\mathbf{A}_0^*| - \mathbf{A}^*\mathbf{R}_1^*] \begin{bmatrix} \mathbf{X}_{00} \\ \mathbf{X}_{10} \end{bmatrix}.$$

Next, we choose $\mathbf{R}_1', \mathbf{R}_2' \in \mathbb{Z}_q^{\bar{m} \times nk}$ from a distribution $\mathcal{B}$ defined over $\mathbb{Z}$, that outputs 0 with probability $1/2$ and ± 1 with probability $1/4$ each. We calculate the rest of the public key as

$$\mathbf{A}_0'\mathbf{R}_1' = [\mathbf{A}_0^*| - \mathbf{A}^*\mathbf{R}_1^*] \begin{bmatrix} \mathbf{X}_{00} \\ \mathbf{X}_{10} \end{bmatrix} \cdot \mathbf{R}_1', \quad \mathbf{A}_0'\mathbf{R}_2' = [\mathbf{A}_0^*| - \mathbf{A}^*\mathbf{R}_1^*] \begin{bmatrix} \mathbf{X}_{00} \\ \mathbf{X}_{10} \end{bmatrix} \cdot \mathbf{R}_2'.$$

So the whole public key of a honest user is $\mathsf{pk}' = ([\mathbf{A}'_0| - \mathbf{A}'_0\mathbf{R}'_1| - \mathbf{A}'_0\mathbf{R}'_2 - \mathbf{H}^*_2\mathbf{G}],\ \mathbf{H}')$ for some randomly chosen invertible $\mathbf{H}' \in \mathbb{Z}^{n \times n}_q$. We add $-\mathbf{H}^*_2\mathbf{G}$ to each honest key. If we choose $\bar{m} \geq n \lg q + 2\frac{nk}{\delta}$ for a small δ, then by ([2]), $\mathbf{A}'_0\mathbf{R}'_1$ is $\mathsf{negl}(n)$-far from uniform, then again $-\mathbf{H}^*_2$ is hidden from the adversary. We denote $\begin{bmatrix} \mathbf{X}_{01} \\ \mathbf{X}_{11} \end{bmatrix} = \begin{bmatrix} \mathbf{X}_{00} \\ \mathbf{X}_{10} \end{bmatrix} \cdot \mathbf{R}'_1$ and $\begin{bmatrix} \mathbf{X}_{02} \\ \mathbf{X}_{12} \end{bmatrix} = \begin{bmatrix} \mathbf{X}_{00} \\ \mathbf{X}_{10} \end{bmatrix} \cdot \mathbf{R}'_2$. Each entry of the resulting matrices $\mathbf{X}_{01}, \mathbf{X}_{11}, \mathbf{X}_{02}, \mathbf{X}_{12}$ is the inner product of a Gaussian $\bar{m}$-dimensional row-vector (of either $\mathbf{X}_{00}$ or $\mathbf{X}_{10}$) and a $\{0, -1, 1\}$-vector with half of the coordinates equal zero, which is equivalent to $\bar{m}/2$ additions of Gaussians with parameter s. Since in the scheme we sample $\begin{bmatrix} \mathbf{X}_{01} \\ \mathbf{X}_{11} \end{bmatrix}, \begin{bmatrix} \mathbf{X}_{02} \\ \mathbf{X}_{12} \end{bmatrix}$ with parameter $s\sqrt{\bar{m}/2}$, the simulated re-encryption key

$$\mathsf{rk}_{\mathsf{pk}^* \to \mathsf{pk}'} = \begin{bmatrix} \mathbf{X}_{00} & \mathbf{X}_{01} & \mathbf{X}_{02} \\ \mathbf{X}_{10} & \mathbf{X}_{11} & \mathbf{X}_{12} \\ \mathbf{0} & \mathbf{0} & \mathbf{I} \end{bmatrix} \tag{4}$$

has the same distribution as a re-encryption key in the scheme. We generate the public keys and secret keys for corrupted users in the same way as in the scheme.

To generate a re-encryption key $\mathsf{rk}_{\mathsf{pk}' \to \mathsf{pk}''}$ for any two $\mathsf{pk}' \neq \mathsf{pk}^*, \mathsf{pk}''$ with invertible matrices $\mathbf{H}', \mathbf{H}''$ as corresponding second components, where either both public keys are corrupted or honest, we sample with $\mathbf{H}'$ a matrix $\begin{bmatrix} \mathbf{X}'_{00} \\ \mathbf{X}'_{10} \end{bmatrix}$ for a fixed parameter s and $\begin{bmatrix} \mathbf{X}'_{01} \\ \mathbf{X}'_{11} \end{bmatrix}, \begin{bmatrix} \mathbf{X}'_{02} \\ \mathbf{X}'_{12} \end{bmatrix}$ with fixed $s\sqrt{\bar{m}/2}$ as in the scheme. Note that by fixing the output standard deviation we achieve the same distribution of the re-encryption keys between two honest and two corrupted users, while the trapdoor matrices in these two cases have different parameters: r for a Gaussian $\mathbf{R}$ in the corrupted case, and $\sqrt{2\pi}$ for $\mathcal{B}$-distributed $\mathbf{R}$ of an honest user.

To answer the decryption queries for a ciphertext $c = (\mathbf{b}^t, \mathbf{H}_u)$, where

$$\mathbf{b}^t = \mathbf{s}^t[\mathbf{A}'_0| - \mathbf{A}'_0\mathbf{R}'_1 + \mathbf{H}'\mathbf{G}| - \mathbf{A}'_0\mathbf{R}'_2 - (\mathbf{H}^*_2 - \mathbf{H}_u)\mathbf{G}] + \mathbf{e}^t + (\mathbf{0}, \mathbf{0}, \mathsf{enc}(\mathbf{m}))^t$$

under the honest public key $\mathsf{pk}' = [\mathbf{A}'_0| - \mathbf{A}'_0\mathbf{R}'_1| - \mathbf{A}'_0\mathbf{R}'_2 - \mathbf{H}^*_2\mathbf{G}],\ \mathbf{H}')$ we first check that $\mathbf{H}_u$ is invertible. Then we use the fact that $\mathbf{H}^*_2 - \mathbf{H}_u \in \mathbb{Z}^{n \times n}_q$ is an invertible matrix. So for the second step of our decryption algorithm we call $\mathsf{Invert}^{\mathcal{O}}$ on inputs $([\mathbf{R}'_1|\mathbf{R}'_2], \mathbf{A}_u = [\mathbf{A}'_0| - \mathbf{A}'_0\mathbf{R}'_1 + \mathbf{H}'\mathbf{G}| - \mathbf{A}'_0\mathbf{R}'_2 - (\mathbf{H}^*_2 - \mathbf{H}_u)\mathbf{G}], \mathbf{b}^t, (\mathbf{H}^*_2 - \mathbf{H}_u))$ and receive $\mathbf{z} \in \mathbb{Z}^n_q$ and $\mathbf{e} \in \mathbb{Z}^m_q$ such that $\mathbf{b}^t = \mathbf{z}^t\mathbf{A}_u + \mathbf{e}^t$ mod q. If the length of $\mathbf{e}$ is short enough (step 3) and for $\mathbf{v} = \mathbf{b} - \mathbf{e} = (\mathbf{v}_0, \mathbf{v}_1, \mathbf{v}_2)$ it holds that $\mathbf{v}_0 \in \mathbb{Z}^{\bar{m}}_q$ and $\mathbf{v}_0 \in 2\Lambda(\mathbf{A}^t_0)$ (step 4), then $\mathbf{v}$ can be expressed as

$$\mathbf{v}^t = 2(\mathbf{s}^t\mathbf{A}_u \mod q) + (\mathbf{0}, \mathbf{0}, \mathsf{enc}(\mathbf{m})^t \mod 2q.$$

To proceed with the decryption we multiply

$$\mathbf{v}^t \begin{bmatrix} \mathbf{R}_1 & \mathbf{R}_2 \\ \mathbf{I} & \mathbf{0} \\ \mathbf{0} & \mathbf{I} \end{bmatrix} = 2(\mathbf{s}^t[\mathbf{H}'\mathbf{G}|(\mathbf{H}^*_2 - \mathbf{H}_u)\mathbf{G}] \mod q) + (\mathbf{0}, \mathsf{enc}(\mathbf{m})) \mod 2q.$$

Applying enc^{-1} to the last nk coordinates we are able to decrypt with the message $\mathbf{m}$. To answer the re-encryption query from $\mathsf{pk}' = [\mathbf{A}_0'| - \mathbf{A}_0'\mathbf{R}_1'| - \mathbf{A}_0'\mathbf{R}_2' - \mathbf{H}_2^*\mathbf{G}]$ with $\mathbf{H}' \in \mathbb{Z}_q^{n \times n}$ to $\mathsf{pk}'' = [\mathbf{A}_0''| - \mathbf{A}_0''\mathbf{R}_1''| - \mathbf{A}_0''\mathbf{R}_2'' - \mathbf{H}_2^*\mathbf{G}]$ with
$\mathbf{H}'' \in \mathbb{Z}_q^{n \times n}$ we apply $\mathsf{rk}_{\mathsf{pk}' \to \mathsf{pk}''} = \begin{bmatrix} \mathbf{X}_{00}' & \mathbf{X}_{01}' & \mathbf{X}_{02}' \\ \mathbf{X}_{10}' & \mathbf{X}_{11}' & \mathbf{X}_{12}' \\ \mathbf{0} & \mathbf{0} & \mathbf{I} \end{bmatrix}$ generated as in the original.

The re-encryption transforms

$$\mathbf{b}^t = \mathbf{s}^t[\mathbf{A}_0'| - \mathbf{A}_0'\mathbf{R}_1' + \mathbf{H}'\mathbf{G}| - \mathbf{A}_0'\mathbf{R}_2' - (\mathbf{H}_2^* - \mathbf{H}_u)\mathbf{G}] + \mathbf{e}^t + (\mathbf{0}, \mathbf{0}, \mathsf{enc}(\mathbf{m}))^t$$

to $\mathbf{b}'^t = \mathbf{s}^t[\mathbf{A}_0''| - \mathbf{A}_0''\mathbf{R}_1'' + \mathbf{H}''\mathbf{G}| - \mathbf{A}_0''\mathbf{R}_2'' - (\mathbf{H}_2^* - \mathbf{H}_u)\mathbf{G}] + \widetilde{\mathbf{e}}^t + (\mathbf{0}, \mathbf{0}, \mathsf{enc}(\mathbf{m}))^t$,
decryptable under $\mathsf{sk}'' = [\mathbf{R}_1''|\mathbf{R}_2'']$.

To answer the decryption query we proceed in the same way as for any honest user; note that in this case the ciphertext is of the form $\mathbf{b}^t =$

$$2(\mathbf{s}^t[\mathbf{A}_0^*| - \mathbf{A}_0^*\mathbf{R}_1^*| - \mathbf{A}_0^*\mathbf{R}_2^* - (\mathbf{H}_2^* - \mathbf{H}_u)\mathbf{G}] \bmod q) + \mathbf{e}^t + (\mathbf{0}, \mathbf{0}, \mathsf{enc}(\mathbf{m}))^t \bmod 2q.$$

To summarize, we can answer the decryption queries of a ciphertext $c = (\mathbf{b}^t, \mathbf{H}_u)$ for any honest user as long as $\mathbf{H}_u \neq \mathbf{H}_2^*$, which is the case with overwhelming probability. If $\mathbf{H}_u = \mathbf{H}_2^*$ we answer the decryption query with $\perp$.

Finally, for the challenge ciphertext that encrypts the message $\mathbf{m} \in \{0, 1\}^{nk}$ under pk^*, we choose $\mathbf{H}_u = \mathbf{H}_2^*$, in which case the encryption is of the form

$$\mathbf{b}^t = 2(\mathbf{s}^t[\mathbf{A}_0^*| - \mathbf{A}_0^*\mathbf{R}_1^*| - \mathbf{A}_0^*\mathbf{R}_2^*] \bmod q) + \mathbf{e}^t + (\mathbf{0}, \mathbf{0}, \mathsf{enc}(\mathbf{m}))^t \bmod 2q$$

for some $\mathbf{s} \in \mathbb{Z}_q^n$ and small $\mathbf{e}$. But instead of calculating this vector $\mathbf{b}$, we take the vector $\mathbf{b}^*$ prepared at the beginning of the game. Notice that if the simulator receives the LWE distribution, then $\mathbf{b}^{*t} = 2(\mathbf{s}^t\mathbf{A}_0^* \bmod q) + \widehat{\mathbf{e}}_0^t \bmod q$, where $\mathbf{s} \leftarrow \mathbb{Z}_q^n, \widehat{\mathbf{e}}_0 \leftarrow D_{\mathbb{Z}, \alpha q}$. We set the first nk coordinates of $\mathbf{b}^t$ to $\mathbf{b}^{*t}$. We set the last $2nk$ coordinates of $\mathbf{b}$ to

$$\mathbf{b}_1^t = \mathbf{b}_0^t\mathbf{R}_1^* + \widehat{\mathbf{e}}_1^t \bmod 2q \in \mathbb{Z}_{2q}^{nk}, \tag{5}$$

$$\mathbf{b}_2^t = \mathbf{b}_0^t\mathbf{R}_2^* + \widehat{\mathbf{e}}_2^t + \mathsf{enc}(\mathbf{m}) \bmod 2q \in \mathbb{Z}_{2q}^{nk}, \tag{6}$$

where $\widehat{\mathbf{e}}_1, \widehat{\mathbf{e}}_2 \leftarrow D_{\alpha q \sqrt{m} \cdot r}^{nk}$. Then the challenge ciphertext is $(\mathbf{b} = (\mathbf{b}_0^t, \mathbf{b}_1^t, \mathbf{b}_2^t), \mathbf{H}_2^*)$, which has the same distribution as any ciphertext in the scheme, since $\widehat{\mathbf{e}}_0^t\mathbf{R}_1 + \widehat{\mathbf{e}}_1^t$ – the resulting noise terms in $\mathbf{b}_1^t$ – is according to [[16] Corollary 3.10] within $\mathsf{negl}(n)$-distance from $D_{\mathbb{Z}, s}$, where $s^2 = (\|\widehat{\mathbf{e}}_0\|^2 + \bar{m}(\alpha q)^2) \cdot r^2$ – the parameter for vectors $\mathbf{e}_1, \mathbf{e}_2$ in the scheme. The same applies for the noise terms in $\mathbf{b}_2^t$.

Note that $(\mathbf{A}_0^*, \mathbf{b}^*, \mathbf{A}_0^*\mathbf{R}_1^*, \mathbf{A}_0^*\mathbf{R}_2^*, -\mathbf{b}^*\mathbf{R}_1^*, -\mathbf{b}^*\mathbf{R}_2^*)$ is $\mathsf{negl}(n)$-uniform for $\mathbf{R}_1^* \leftarrow \mathcal{D}, \mathbf{R}_2^* \leftarrow \mathcal{D}$ by the leftover hash lemma. So the simulated challenge ciphertext has the same distribution as any encrypted message.

6   Conclusions

We presented a unidirectional proxy re-encryption scheme based on hard problems on lattices. It can be seen from the security proof that our generalized $\mathbf{G}$-trapdoor definition leads to a CCA-1 secure construction, but we cannot achieve

CCA-2 security. Another limitation of our construction is that its security is proved in the selective model only. We leave it as an open problem to construct a CCA-2 secure lattice-based construction in the adaptive setting.

Acknowledgements. I thank Alex May for careful reading and valuable comments, Chris Peikert for fruitful discussions and S. Aleshnikov for suggesting the topic.

References

1. Ajtai, M.: Generating hard instances of lattice problems. In: Proceedings of STOC, pp. 99–108 (1996)
2. Alwen, J., Peikert, C.: Generating shorter bases for hard random lattices. Theory of Computing Systems 48(3), 535–553 (2011)
3. Ateniese, G., Fu, K., Green, M., Hohenberger, S.: Improved proxy re-encryption schemes with applications to secure distributed storage. In: NDSS, pp. 29–43 (2005)
4. Ateniese, G., Fu, K., Green, M., Hohenberger, S.: Improved proxy re-encryption schemes with applications to secure distributed storage. In: ACM TISSEC, pp. 29–43 (2006)
5. Banaszczyk, W.: New bounds in some transference theorems in the geometry of numbers. Mathematische Annalen 296(1), 625–635 (1993)
6. Blaze, M., Bleumer, G., Strauss, M.J.: Divertible protocols and atomic proxy cryptography. In: Nyberg, K. (ed.) EUROCRYPT 1998. LNCS, vol. 1403, pp. 127–144. Springer, Heidelberg (1998)
7. Canetti, R., Hohenberger, S.: Chosen-ciphertext secure proxy re-encryption. In: Proc. of ACM-CCS 2007, pp. 185–194. ACM Press (2007)
8. El Gamal, T.: A public key cryptosystem and a signature scheme based on discrete logarithms. In: Blakely, G.R., Chaum, D. (eds.) CRYPTO 1984. LNCS, vol. 196, pp. 10–18. Springer, Heidelberg (1985)
9. Gentry, C.: A fully homomorphic encryption scheme. PhD thesis, Stanford University (2009)
10. Green, M., Ateniese, G.: Identity-based proxy re-encryption. In: Katz, J., Yung, M. (eds.) ACNS 2007. LNCS, vol. 4521, pp. 288–306. Springer, Heidelberg (2007)
11. Horn, R.A., Johnson, C.R.: Topics in Matrix Analysis. Cambridge University Press (1994)
12. Libert, B., Vergnaud, D.: Unidirectional chosen-ciphertext secure proxy re-encryption. In: Cramer, R. (ed.) PKC 2008. LNCS, vol. 4939, pp. 360–379. Springer, Heidelberg (2008)
13. Micciancio, D., Regev, O.: Worst-case to average-case reductions based on gaussian measures. In: SIAM J. on Computing, pp. 372–381 (2004)
14. Peikert, C.: An efficient and parallel gaussian sampler for lattices. In: Rabin, T. (ed.) CRYPTO 2010. LNCS, vol. 6223, pp. 80–97. Springer, Heidelberg (2010)
15. Micciancio, D., Peikert, C.: Trapdoors for lattices: Simpler, tighter, faster, smaller. In: Pointcheval, D., Johansson, T. (eds.) EUROCRYPT 2012. LNCS, vol. 7237, pp. 700–718. Springer, Heidelberg (2012)
16. Regev, O.: On lattices, learning with errors, random linear codes, and cryptography. In: STOC, pp. 84–93. ACM Press (2005)
17. Vershynin, R.: Introduction to the non-asymptotic analysis of random matrices (2011), http://www-personal.umich.edu/~romanv/papers/non-asymptotic-rmt-plain.pdf
18. Xagawa, K.: Cryptography with Lattices. PhD thesis, Tokyo Institute of Technology (2010), http://xagawa.net/pdf/2010Thesis.pdf

Re-encryption, Functional Re-encryption, and Multi-hop Re-encryption: A Framework for Achieving Obfuscation-Based Security and Instantiations from Lattices

Nishanth Chandran[1], Melissa Chase[1], Feng-Hao Liu[2,*],
Ryo Nishimaki[3], and Keita Xagawa[3]

[1] Microsoft Research
{nichandr,melissac}@microsoft.com
[2] University of Maryland
fenghao@cs.umd.edu
[3] NTT Secure Platform Laboratories
{nishimaki.ryo,xagawa.keita}@lab.ntt.co.jp

Abstract. In this work we define multiple relaxations to the definition of correctness in secure obfuscation. While still remaining meaningful, these relaxations provide ways to obfuscate many primitives in a more direct and efficient way. In particular, we first show how to construct a secure obfuscator for the re-encryption primitive from the Decisional Learning with Errors (DLWE) assumption, without going through fully homomorphic encryption. This can be viewed as a meaningful way to trade correctness for efficiency. Next, we show how our tools can be used to construct secure obfuscators for the functional re-encryption and multi-hop unidirectional re-encryption primitives. In the former case, we improve upon the efficiency of the only previously known construction that satisfies the stronger notion of collusion-resistant obfuscation (due to Chandran *et al.* - TCC 2012) and obtain a construction with input ciphertexts of *constant* length. In the latter case, we provide the first known obfuscation-based definition and construction; additionally, our scheme is the first scheme where the size of the ciphertexts does not grow with every hop.

1 Introduction

Program obfuscation. Informally, an obfuscator [6] is an algorithm that converts a program into another program that has the same behavior but is "completely unintelligible", in that it reveals no information besides what can be learned from observing the input/output behavior. Most previous works have focused on impossibility results or constructions for extremely simple programs. In one of the first works on obfuscating more complex cryptographic functionalities, Hohenberger *et al.* [25] showed how to securely obfuscate the re-encryption functionality. The re-encryption functionality (introduced by [7] and more formally defined in [5]) is parameterized by two public keys

---

* This work was done while the author was an intern at Microsoft Research.

H. Krawczyk (Ed.): PKC 2014, LNCS 8383, pp. 95–112, 2014.
© International Association for Cryptologic Research 2014

for an encryption scheme. It takes as input a ciphertext of message m under the first public key, and outputs a ciphertext of the same message m under the second public key. Re-encryption has many applications, ranging from secure distributed file servers, to outsourced filtering of encrypted spam, to the iTunes DRM system.

Why secure obfuscation for re-encryption? The use of obfuscation-based definitions for re-encryption is particularly appealing for many reasons. First, secure obfuscation results in a definition of security for re-encryption that is much stronger than several previous definitions. It simultaneously captures many game-based properties defined in earlier formalizations of re-encryption and guarantees that the proxy cannot learn *anything* beyond what is revealed by the input-output behavior of the re-encryption functionality (which it must inherently learn). Second, note that if we have a protocol that is secure when making use of an "ideal" re-encryption functionality, then the security of the system will be preserved when the untrusted proxy is given a program that is a secure obfuscation of the same functionality. Finally, the secure obfuscation definition for re-encryption is clean and easy to use, which is particularly relevant for a primitive such as re-encryption for which multiple variants of security definitions have been studied. Additionally, it also makes it easier to define security for the more complex functionalities that we consider, such as multi-hop and functional re-encryption. In light of these advantages, and given the widespread applications of proxy re-encryption, obtaining efficient constructions that satisfy the definition of secure obfuscation is very important from both a theoretical and a practical perspective.

Why re-encryption? Beyond the direct applications mentioned above, studying re-encryption may help advance the more general study of obfuscation. One of the few areas in obfuscation which has seen positive results is the case where the output of the program is encrypted [22, 13]. Since re-encryption is one of the simplest such functionalities, it makes a good starting place for further study.

Constructing re-encryption schemes. Hohenberger *et al.* [25] (and also independently Hofheinz *et al.* [24]) introduced the notion of *average-case secure obfuscation*, which has been the standard definition of obfuscation in these works; it captures the idea that the obfuscated program reveals nothing to an adversary when the associated encryption key is chosen at random and unknown to the adversary. The work of Hohenberger *et al.* [25] showed how to securely obfuscate the re-encryption functionality under this definition assuming a bilinear pairing. In the interest of basing primitives on a variety of assumptions, it is natural to ask: *can we construct a secure obfuscator for the re-encryption functionality based on other types of assumptions?* In addition, their scheme has the limitation that the input and output encryption schemes are different, in other words, the program takes as input ciphertexts under one encryption scheme and outputs ciphertexts under not just a different key but a different scheme. While this may be alright in certain scenarios, many applications (e.g. multi-hop re-encryption) require input and output schemes to have the same structure to allow for cascading, i.e. taking a re-encrypted ciphertext and re-encrypting it again.

As noted in [15] the re-encryption functionality can be securely realized given any fully homomorphic encryption (FHE) scheme [28, 15]; the re-encryption key is simply $K_{\mathsf{pk} \to \widehat{\mathsf{pk}}} = \mathsf{Enc}_{\widehat{\mathsf{pk}}}(\mathsf{sk})$ and the re-encryption program, on input $c = \mathsf{Enc}_{\mathsf{pk}}(m)$, computes $\mathsf{Enc}_{\widehat{\mathsf{pk}}}(c)$ and then $\mathsf{Eval}_{\mathsf{evk}}(f, c, K_{\mathsf{pk} \to \widehat{\mathsf{pk}}})$, where f is the decryption circuit, to obtain $\text{Enc}_{\widehat{\text{pk}}}(m)$. (This can be generalized to achieve essentially any functionality with encrypted output.) We know constructions of FHE based on a variety of lattice-based assumptions [15, 16, 11, 10, 17, 9, 8], so this might give lattice-based constructions for re-encryption.

There are however two issues with this approach: First, FHE is a very strong primitive, and despite significant progress, it is still very expensive; ideally constructing a simple functionality like re-encryption should not require such heavyweight tools. More importantly, by the definition of correctness of program obfuscation, a secure obfuscator for the re-encryption functionality must output ciphertexts that have a distribution that is statistically close to the distribution output by the ideal re-encryption circuit *for all inputs*. In particular, this statistical closeness must hold even for invalid ciphertexts. The only way we know to achieve such a distribution is through bootstrapping [15], which is the most computationally expensive part of the FHE constructions (and not included the more efficient somewhat homomorphic encryption (SHE) schemes).

Challenges in lattice based constructions. Thus one might ask, *what about simpler lattice-based constructions?* More concretely, can we achieve an obfuscation-based notion of re-encryption without bootstrapping? Under previous obfuscation definitions, this seems very challenging, and, interestingly, the challenge arises not from the security requirements (VBB obfuscation), but from the correctness property (referred to as *preserving functionality*). Intuitively, the issue is as follows: a well-formed ciphertext is formed by encoding the message and then adding a small amount of random noise; this is what would be produced by the unobfuscated program, and an obfuscation which preserves functionality would have to produce ciphertexts that are similarly distributed. This means that no matter what ciphertext the adversary chooses as input (even an invalid ciphertext formed by adding a lot of noise), the obfuscated program must either recognize that the ciphertext is invalid, or output ciphertexts with small, independently generated noise. The only way we know to do this is to use bootstrapping, which essentially runs the decryption algorithm under a layer of encryption and thus can detect poorly formed ciphertexts or remove the noise from the input ciphertext and produce an output ciphertext with fresh small noise. However, as mentioned above, bootstrapping is very expensive, thus we would like to consider meaningful notions that can be achieved with simpler techniques.

Our contributions. Definitionally, our first contribution is to examine different weaker notions of correctness. We propose two new definitions, which are relaxations of the standard notion of preserving functionality. We then evaluate the implications of these definitions, focusing for concreteness on re-encryption primitives. Next, we consider how to construct schemes satisfying these weaker definitions. We define two tools, which we call blurring and key-switching, essentially formalizing a number of techniques that were used in various FHE constructions. While these techniques are not new, we provide general definitions, independent of any specific instantiation, thus allowing them to be used abstractly as tools in general constructions. Finally, we consider two additional re-encryption primitives, functional re-encryption and multi-hop re-encryption, and use our new tools and definitions to solve several previously open problems.

1.1   Our Results and Techniques

Relaxing correctness in secure obfuscation. We define two relaxations of correctness for the definition of secure obfuscation that allow more efficient constructions of re-encryption (and other) schemes. The first relaxation, informally, guarantees only that the output distribution of the obfuscated program and the ideal functionality are statistically close on so called "well-formed" inputs (i.e. a subset of all the inputs to the functionality). The security property (average case VBB) is still the standard notion (and is guaranteed on all inputs); such a relaxation of the correctness can be viewed as a form of "correctness in the semi-honest setting", in that correctness is guaranteed whenever the adversary selects inputs to the obfuscated program honestly. The next relaxation guarantees that the output of the obfuscator on well-formed inputs is correct with respect to some algorithm. (For example, they might both decrypt to the same value in case of a decryption algorithm.) Finally, we consider a correctness guarantee that says that the output distribution of the obfuscated program is computationally indistinguishable from that of the ideal functionality. (We might for example consider an obfuscator which satisfies this computational correctness over all inputs, and additionally satisfies one of the above notions on the set of well formed inputs.) We view these three relaxations to correctness of the secure obfuscation definition as important contributions of this work and believe they maybe applicable to other functionalties beyond re-encryption. Finally, we emphasize that these are relaxations only to the *correctness* of the scheme. We still maintain the guarantee that the obfuscated program reveals no more than what can be computed given black box access to the functionality.

Abstractions for two lattice-based techniques. Our next contribution is to abstract out two mechanisms that we need for re-encryption from the previous works of [15, 10], and implement these mechanisms with several instantiations. In particular, we provide abstractions for (1) key-switching and (2) blurring. These two mechanisms are designed to be used together: the key-switching mechanism is used to transform a ciphertext $\mathsf{Enc}_{\mathsf{pk}}(m)$ into another ciphertext $\mathsf{Enc}_{\widehat{\mathsf{pk}}}(m)$. However the output distribution of this mechanism might be different from a fresh ciphertext of message m under public key $\widehat{\mathsf{pk}}$; the blurring mechanism is used to smooth out this difference. We define two variants: a strong blurring and a weak blurring mechanism. At a high level, using strong blurring helps us achieve the first relaxation of correctness; weak blurring enables us to achieve the second and third relaxations.

We then proceed to show how to implement the key switching mechanism as well as the strong and weak blurring mechanisms using: a) Regev's encryption scheme [27], and b) the dual Regev encryption scheme [19].

We remark here that while the notions of key switching and blurring are not new, we provide a formal definition of the properties that we require from these two notions. To the best of our knowledge, this is the first such definition of these notions and we hope it will help these techniques to find other applications.

Contribution to lattice-based schemes and secure obfuscation. The problems we encounter in satisfying the obfuscation-based definitions of security seem to be fundamental to most lattice-based schemes; we hope that our relaxations will also help lead to lattice-based obfuscations for other functionalities.

1.2 Applications of Our Results

We apply our tools to construct schemes for re-encryption and two useful variants: functional re-encryption, and multi-hop unidirectional re-encryption.

Re-encryption. We first show that using any fully homomorphic encryption scheme with a strong blurring mechanism, one can obtain a secure obfuscation of a re-encryption scheme that satisfies the standard definition of correctness (i.e., the output is statistically close to the ideal functionality on *all* inputs).

Given that FHE is overkill, we provide direct, more efficient, constructions based on the Decisional Learning with Errors (DLWE) assumption [27] via the realizations of key switching and blurring mentioned above. With strong blurring, the correctness of this scheme is guaranteed on all well-formed inputs (i.e., the output of our re-encryption program is statistically close to $\mathsf{Enc}_{\widehat{\mathsf{pk}}}(m)$ for all honestly generated ciphertexts $c = \mathsf{Enc}_{\mathsf{pk}}(m)$). With weak blurring, we obtain a secure obfuscation whose output distribution (on *all* ciphertexts) is computationally indistinguishable from that of the re-encryption functionality. (Moreover, re-encryptions of honestly generated ciphertexts still decrypt correctly.)

All the above constructions provide a tradeoff between using (less efficient but powerful) FHE to achieve the strongest definition of correctness and using efficient specific lattice-based schemes to achieve slightly weaker notions of correctness. Again, all these constructions satisfy a strong obfuscation-based notion of security (average case VBB [25] and collusion resistance [13]).

Functional re-encryption and collusion-resistant obfuscation. Once we construct the basic re-encryption schemes, we turn our attention towards a more complex primitive, known as functional re-encryption, which incorporates access control into the re-encryption functionality. The work of Chandran, Chase, and Vaikuntanathan [13] introduced this primitive and showed an obfuscation-based result. Informally, a program implementing functional re-encryption is parameterized by an input public key pk, n output public keys $\widehat{\mathsf{pk}}_1, \cdots, \widehat{\mathsf{pk}}_n$, and an access policy $F : [D] \to [n]$. The program takes as input a ciphertext of message m with tag $i \in [D]$ under input public key pk and outputs a ciphertext of the same message m under $\widehat{\mathsf{pk}}_{F(i)}$. Functional re-encryption can be used to implement a server that forwards a user Alice's email to other recipients, depending on the tag (or the content) of the email, but at the same time hides the message and the access policy from the server. Chandran *et al.* also introduced the notion of collusion-resistant obfuscation in the context of functional re-encryption, which, informally, guarantees that the obfuscated program remains secure even when the server can collude with some of the recipients. They gave a pairing-based construction of functional re-encryption (for access policies with poly-size domain) satisfying collusion-resistant obfuscation.

Using our framework, we obtain constructions with varied levels of correctness and efficiency, similar to the tradeoffs in our constructions of the basic re-encryption primitive. All of our constructions satisfy the strong security definition of the collusion-resistant obfuscation. We remark that in our schemes the size of the input ciphertext is constant (as opposed to the construction of [13], in which the size of the input ciphertext is $\mathcal{O}(D)$). Our output ciphertext, on the other hand is of size $\mathcal{O}(n)$ (as opposed to constant in [13]); however, each of the n recipients still only needs to receive a constant size block of that ciphertext.

Multi-hop unidirectional proxy re-encryption. Traditionally, most re-encryption schemes are single-hop, in the sense that the ciphertext produced by the re-encryption process is of a different form and cannot be re-encrypted again. The exception are a few schemes beginning with [7] which are multi-hop, but bi-directional, which means that any re-encryption key which allows re-encryption from Alice to Bob also allows re-encryption from Bob to Alice (and thus both secret keys are necessary to generate the re-encryption key). In many settings however, this is not desirable - intuitively, Bob should not need to trust Alice in order for Alice to be able to forward her mail to Bob. Thus, it seems desirable to have a scheme which allows the output of the re-encryption process to be re-encrypted again, but which does not require this kind of trust. That is the problem we consider here (referred to from here on as multi-hop re-encryption).

In this work, we present the first obfuscation based definitions and constructions for multi-hop unidirectional proxy re-encryption schemes. We remark that the problem of constructing multi-hop re-encryption schemes was first posed in [5]; a major drawback of previous schemes [21, 14] is that the ciphertext size grows linearly with the number of re-encryptions. Here we construct L-hop re-encryption schemes (where a ciphertexts can be re-encrypted up to L times) in which ciphertexts do not grow with re-encryption.[1]

Our results also translate to the ideal lattice setting based on the ring-LWE assumption [26]. For simplicity, we focus here on the general lattice setting.

2   Definitions for Obfuscation

In this section, we present our relaxed definitions of correctness in average-case secure obfuscation. We first recall the definition of average-case secure obfuscation with collusion as defined by Chandran *et al.* [13] and present the relaxed definitions of correctness with respect to this definition. As the Chandran et al definition is a generalization of the average case obfuscation definition by Hohenberger et al [25], similar relaxations can also be applied in that setting.

Informally, average-case obfuscation guarantees that obfuscation hides the program as long as it is chosen at random from a given family; resistance against collusion addresses the case where we would like these obfuscation guarantees to hold even when some types of information about the program being obfuscated may be available to the adversary. (This for example captures the case where the adversary in a re-encryption scheme holds both the obfuscated re-encryption program and some of the decryption keys.)

More formally, we consider families $\{C_\lambda\}$ that have the following form. Any $C_{\mathcal{K}} \in C_\lambda$ is parameterized by a set of "secret" keys $\mathcal{K} = \{k_1, k_2, \cdots, k_\ell\}$ (potentially in addition to any other parameters) that are chosen at random from some specified distribution. Now, define a (non-adaptively chosen) subset of keys represented through a

---

[1] L-hop *re*-encryption does not follow from i-hop encryption [18]: the latter allow users to evaluate multiple functions sequentially and homomorphically only under *one* public key.

set of indices $\mathcal{T} \subseteq [\ell]$, where $[\ell]$ denotes the set $\{1, 2, \cdots, \ell\}$. We would like to construct an obfuscation of the circuit, denoted by $\mathsf{Obf}(C_\mathcal{K})$, so that $\mathsf{Obf}(C_\mathcal{K})$ is a "secure obfuscation" of $C_\mathcal{K}$ (in the sense of [25]) even against an adversary that knows the set of keys $\{k_i\}_{i \in \mathcal{T}}$. More precisely, in addition to their usual inputs and oracles, [13] give both the adversary and the simulator access to a (non-adaptively chosen) subset $\{k_i\}_{i \in \mathcal{T}} \subseteq \mathcal{K}$ of the keys. This can be seen as auxiliary information about the circuit $C_\mathcal{K} \leftarrow C_\lambda$.

Finally, we modify the definition to allow some parts of the circuit to be hidden in a worst case sense. This was addressed in [13] for the case of functional re-encryption by adding an additional definition saying that an obfuscation is secure with respect to a class of functions $\mathbb{F}$ if there exists a simulator Sim which satisfies the collusion resistant average-case black box property for all $f \in \mathbb{F}$. It seems more natural and more general to incorporate this directly into the definition of secure obfuscation, so that is the approach we will take here. The formal definition of collusion-resistant secure obfuscation is as follows.

Definition 2.1 (Average-case Obfuscation with Collusion). *Let $\{C_\lambda\}$ be a family of circuits $C_{\mathcal{K}, w}$ indexed by values from the sets $\mathbb{K}(\lambda)$ and $\mathbb{W}(\lambda)$, where each $\mathcal{K} \in \mathbb{K}$ is of the form $(k_1, \ldots, k_\ell)$. A PPT algorithm Obf that takes as input a (probabilistic) circuit and outputs a new (probabilistic) circuit is a collusion-resistant secure obfuscator for the family $\{C_\lambda\}$ in the average-case over $\mathbb{K}$ and in the worst case over $\mathbb{W}$, if it satisfies the following properties:*

Preserving functionality: *There exists a negligible function $\mathsf{ngl}(\cdot)$ such that for any input length λ and any $C \in C_\lambda$:*
$$\Pr[\exists x \in \{0, 1\}^\lambda : C' \leftarrow \mathsf{Obf}(C); \Delta(C'(x), C(x)) \geq \mathsf{ngl}(\lambda)] < \mathsf{ngl}(\lambda),$$
where $\Delta(\cdot, \cdot)$ denotes statistical distance, and the probability is taken over the random coins of Obf.

Polynomial slowdown: *There exists a polynomial $p(\lambda)$ such that for sufficiently large λ, for any $C \in C_\lambda$, $|\mathsf{Obf}(C)| \leq p(|C|)$.*

Average case virtual black-boxness (ACVBB) against collusion with worst-case hiding over $\mathbb{W}$: *For any $w \in \mathbb{W}(\lambda)$, let $C_{\lambda, w}$ be the set of circuits $C_{\mathcal{K}, w} \in C_\lambda$. (When w is fixed, we specify a circuit in $C_{\lambda, w}$ by $C_\mathcal{K}$.) There exists a PPT simulator Sim and a negligible function $\mathsf{ngl}(\cdot)$ such that for all PPT distinguishers D, all sufficiently long input lengths λ, all $w \in \mathbb{W}(\lambda)$, and all subsets $\mathcal{T} \in [\ell]$:*
$$\left| \begin{array}{l} \Pr[C_\mathcal{K} \leftarrow C_{\lambda, w} : D^{C_\mathcal{K}}(\mathsf{Obf}(C_\mathcal{K}), \{k_i\}_{i \in \mathcal{T}}) = 1] \\ -\Pr[C_\mathcal{K} \leftarrow C_{\lambda, w} : D^{C_\mathcal{K}}(\mathsf{Sim}^{C_\mathcal{K}}(1^\lambda, \{k_i\}_{i \in \mathcal{T}}), \{k_i\}_{i \in \mathcal{T}}) = 1] \end{array} \right| < \mathsf{ngl}(\lambda).$$

The probability is over the selection of a random circuit of $C_\mathcal{K}$ from $C_{\lambda, w}$, and the coins of the distinguisher, the simulator, the oracle and the obfuscator.

Note that in the case where we do not wish to consider collusion-resistance, one can simply use the same definition as above where $\mathcal{T}$ is the empty set and $\ell = 1$. Our relaxations of correctness in secure obfuscation, which we will discuss below, apply to the non-collusion case as well.

Relaxed correctness in secure obfuscation. We next proceed to show how we can relax the "preserving functionality" notion defined above. This will enable us to obtain more

efficient constructions for various functionalities related to re-encryption. We shall relax this notion in three different ways: the first relaxation informally guarantees that
the output distribution of the obfuscated program and the ideal functionality are statistically close only on a subset of all the inputs to the functionality; the second relaxation
informally guarantees that on a subset of all the inputs to the functionality, and for some
algorithm Dec (this algorithm would typically be a decryption algorithm), the output of
Dec applied to the output of the program and the output of Dec applied to the output
of the ideal functionality results in the same value; the third relaxation informally guarantees that the output of the program and the output of the functionality, on a subset of
all the inputs, are computationally indistinguishable to all PPT adversaries (typically,
this subset is parameterized by the set of corrupted parties in the system and this captures the idea that on inputs where the ideal functionality produces encryptions under
honest parties' keys, the adversary shouldn't be able to distinguish the output of the
obfuscated program from the ideal program). Note that, in most cases, this third property only makes sense in combination with one of previous two relaxations, because
we do want some guarantee that the obfuscated program works as expected; in our re-
encryption case, for example, we can combine this with the second relaxed correctness,
to ensure that the program's output is indistinguishable from random encryptions, and
at the same time honestly generated and re-encrypted ciphertexts decrypt correctly.

Definition 2.2 (Relaxed Average-Case Obfuscation with Collusion). *For an obfuscation algorithm* Obf *which satisfies the polynomial slowdown and average-case collusion resistant virtual black-boxness properties as in Definition 2.1, we define the
following relaxations of the correctness property:*

Preserving functionality with respect to Π: *Let* Π *be a set of pairs* $(\mathcal{K}, x)$ *where* $\mathcal{K}$
is an index for the circuit and x *is an input. The obfuscated circuit is guaranteed to
agree with the original circuit only on input pairs in the subset* Π. *That is, there exists a
negligible function* $\mathsf{ngl}(\cdot)$ *such that for any input length* λ *and any* $C_{\mathcal{K}} \in \mathcal{C}_{\lambda}$, *and every
x such that* $(\mathcal{K}, x) \in \Pi$: $\Pr[C'_{\mathcal{K}} \leftarrow \mathsf{Obf}(C_{\mathcal{K}}); \Delta(C'_{\mathcal{K}}(x), C_{\mathcal{K}}(x)) \geq \mathsf{ngl}(\lambda)] < \mathsf{ngl}(\lambda)$,
where the probability is over the random coins of Obf. *For inputs outside* Π, *there is
no guarantee for the output of* $C'_{\mathcal{K}}(x)$. *When* Π *is the set of all possible inputs, this
corresponds to the standard notion of "preserving functionality" (Definition 2.1).*

Preserving Dec *correctness with respect to* Π: *Let* Π *be a set of pairs* $(\mathcal{K}, x)$ *where
$\mathcal{K}$ is an index for the circuit and* x *is an input, and* $\mathcal{D}ec(\cdot, \cdot)$ *be some algorithm. The
obfuscated circuit is guaranteed to agree with the original circuit only on input pairs
in the subset* Π, *under the algorithm* Dec. *That is, for all* $(\mathcal{K}, x) \in \Pi$, *for all* $C'_{\mathcal{K}} \leftarrow$
$\mathsf{Obf}(C_{\mathcal{K}})$, *we require that* $\Pr[y \leftarrow C_{\mathcal{K}}(x), y' \leftarrow C'_{\mathcal{K}}(x) : \mathcal{D}ec(\mathcal{K}, y) = \mathcal{D}ec(\mathcal{K}, y')] =
1 - \mathsf{ngl}(\lambda)$ *for some negligible* ngl.

Computationally preserving functionality with respect to $\Pi_{\bar{\mathcal{T}}}$: *Let* $\bar{\mathcal{T}}$ *be a set in* $[\ell]$
(usually the set $\mathcal{T} = [\ell] \setminus \bar{\mathcal{T}}$*), and let* $\Pi_{\bar{\mathcal{T}}}$ *be a subset (potentially dependent on* $\mathcal{T}$*) of
pairs* $(\mathcal{K}, x)$ *where* $\mathcal{K} = (k_1, \ldots, k_\ell)$ *is an index for circuit and* x *is an input. For any
pair of circuits* C, C', *denote by* $O_{\mathcal{K}, C, C'}(\cdot)$ *the program that on input* x, *outputs* $C'(x)$
if $(\mathcal{K}, x) \in \Pi_{\bar{\mathcal{T}}}$ *and* $C(x)$ *otherwise. Then for all PPT adversaries* A, *we require that:*

$$
\left| \begin{array}{l} \Pr\left[C_{\mathcal{K}} \leftarrow C_{\lambda}, C'_{\mathcal{K}} \leftarrow \mathsf{Obf}(C_{\mathcal{K}}) : A^{O_{\mathcal{K}, C_{\mathcal{K}}, C'_{\mathcal{K}}}(\cdot)}(\{k_i\}_{i \in \mathcal{T}}) = 1\right] \\ \quad - \Pr\left[C_{\mathcal{K}} \leftarrow C_{\lambda} : A^{C_{\mathcal{K}}(\cdot)}(\{k_i\}_{i \in \mathcal{T}}) = 1\right] \end{array} \right| < \mathsf{ngl}(\lambda).
$$

3 Our Framework and Instantiations

In this section, we define and construct several new tools which will be useful for our applications. First we present two abstract properties, and argue that we can implement them trivially with FHE. Then we show they can be achieved much more efficiently for the Regev [27] and dual Regev [19] encryption schemes.

3.1 Notions of Key-Switching and Blurring

Key switching. Let $\Sigma = (\mathsf{Gen}, \mathsf{Enc}, \mathsf{Dec})$ be a semantically secure encryption scheme. The first property we consider is the existence of a key-switching mechanism. Here we formalize a property based on an idea from Brakerski and Vaikuntanathan [10]: briefly, a key-switching mechanism allows one to directly convert ciphertexts encrypted under one public key to ciphertexts encrypted under a second public key. More formally our definition is as follows:

Definition 3.1 (Key-Switching Mechanism). *A key-switching mechanism for an encryption scheme* $\Sigma = (\mathsf{Gen}, \mathsf{Enc}, \mathsf{Dec})$ *consists of two algorithms:*

$-\mathsf{SwGen}(\mathsf{pk}, \mathsf{sk}, \widehat{\mathsf{pk}})$: *Let* $(\mathsf{pk}, \mathsf{sk})$ *be a pair of "source" keys output by* Gen, *and* $\widehat{\mathsf{pk}}$ *be a "target" public key* $((\widehat{\mathsf{pk}}, \cdot)$ *is output by* $\mathsf{Gen})$. *The algorithm takes* $(\mathsf{pk}, \mathsf{sk}, \widehat{\mathsf{pk}})$ *as input, and outputs a switch-key* $K_{\mathsf{pk} \to \widehat{\mathsf{pk}}}$ *that can transform ciphertexts encrypted under* pk *to ciphertexts encrypted under* $\widehat{\mathsf{pk}}$.

$-\mathsf{Sw}(K_{\mathsf{pk} \to \widehat{\mathsf{pk}}}, c)$: *The algorithm takes a switch-key* $K_{\mathsf{pk} \to \widehat{\mathsf{pk}}}$ *and a ciphertext c as input, and outputs a ciphertext* $\hat{c}$.

The key-switching mechanism is correct *if for all* $(\mathsf{pk}, \mathsf{sk}), (\widehat{\mathsf{pk}}, \widehat{\mathsf{sk}}) \leftarrow \mathsf{Gen}(1^\lambda)$, *for all* $K_{\mathsf{pk} \to \widehat{\mathsf{pk}}} \leftarrow \mathsf{SwGen}(\mathsf{pk}, \mathsf{sk}, \widehat{\mathsf{pk}})$, *for all* $m \in \{0, 1\}$ *and for all* $c \leftarrow \mathsf{Enc}_{\mathsf{pk}}(m)$, $c' \leftarrow \mathsf{Sw}(K_{\mathsf{pk} \to \widehat{\mathsf{pk}}}, c)$, *it holds that* $\mathsf{Dec}_{\widehat{\mathsf{sk}}}(c') = m$. *More generally, the key-switching mechanism is* correct on set $\Pi = \{(\mathsf{pk}, \mathsf{sk}, c)\}$ *if for all* $(\widehat{\mathsf{pk}}, \widehat{\mathsf{sk}}) \leftarrow \mathsf{Gen}(1^\lambda)$, *for all* $K_{\mathsf{pk} \to \widehat{\mathsf{pk}}} \leftarrow \mathsf{SwGen}(\mathsf{pk}, \mathsf{sk}, \widehat{\mathsf{pk}})$, *and for all* $c' \leftarrow \mathsf{Sw}(K_{\mathsf{pk} \to \widehat{\mathsf{pk}}}, c)$, *it holds that* $\mathsf{Dec}_{\widehat{\mathsf{sk}}}(c') = \mathsf{Dec}_{\mathsf{sk}}(c)$.

Remark 3.2. The idea of a key-switching mechanism was introduced by Brakerski and Vaikuntanathan [10] to construct fully homomorphic encryption schemes. They used an approach where the SwGen algorithm is given pk, sk and then samples $\widehat{\mathsf{pk}}, \widehat{\mathsf{sk}}$ on its own, and outputs a switch-key that allows one to transform ciphertexts under pk to $\widehat{\mathsf{pk}}$. This suffices for the construction of fully homomorphic encryption. However, for our applications we require the switch-key generation algorithm to take the source keys and the target public key as input, and to output the switch-key without knowing the secret key $\widehat{\mathsf{sk}}$.

To make key-switching an interesting notion, we need some property guaranteeing at the very least that the switch-key does not allow the holder to decrypt messages. We require something stronger, essentially that the switch-key reveals nothing at all about the input public key to anyone who does not hold either of the secret keys. We capture this with a simulation based definition:

Definition 3.3 (Security of Key-Switching Mechanism). *We say the Key-Switching Mechanism is secure if there exists a simulated key generation algorithm* $\mathsf{SimSwGen}(\widehat{\mathsf{pk}})$ *that only takes as input the target public key (and not the source keys) and can output a switch-key such that for any PPT adversary the following two distributions are indistinguishable:*

$$\{(\mathsf{pk}, \mathsf{sk}), (\widehat{\mathsf{pk}}, \widehat{\mathsf{sk}}) \leftarrow \mathsf{Gen}(1^\lambda); K_{\mathsf{pk} \to \widehat{\mathsf{pk}}} \leftarrow \mathsf{SwGen}(\mathsf{pk}, \mathsf{sk}, \widehat{\mathsf{pk}}) :$$
$$(\mathsf{pk}, \widehat{\mathsf{pk}}, K_{\mathsf{pk} \to \widehat{\mathsf{pk}}})\}$$
$$\{(\mathsf{pk}, \mathsf{sk}), (\widehat{\mathsf{pk}}, \widehat{\mathsf{sk}}) \leftarrow \mathsf{Gen}(1^\lambda); K_{\mathsf{pk} \to \widehat{\mathsf{pk}}} \leftarrow \mathsf{SimSwGen}(\widehat{\mathsf{pk}}) :$$
$$(\mathsf{pk}, \widehat{\mathsf{pk}}, K_{\mathsf{pk} \to \widehat{\mathsf{pk}}})\}$$

Blurring. The second property that we consider is what we call a blurring mechanism. At a high level, the goal is to take a ciphertext and produce a new unrelated-looking ciphertext that encrypts the same message. This kind of re-randomization is hard to achieve in lattice-based constructions, so we relax this restriction somewhat and consider definitions in which guarantees only hold for a restricted set of ciphertexts, or against computationally bounded adversaries.

Informally, weak blurring says that if we take any string c and blur it, then this is indistinguishable from the string produced by taking a new ciphertext of some (perhaps different) message and blurring it, even given the ciphertext c (but not the secret key). This is true for all strings c and not just "well-formed" (or honestly generated) ciphertexts. Furthermore, the blurred ciphertext and c will still decrypt to the same message for the "well-formed" ciphertexts c. Strong blurring, on the other hand, additionally says that if we take a "well-formed" ciphertext c and blur it, then this is indistinguishable from the string produced by taking a new ciphertext of the same message and blurring it, even given the secret key sk and the ciphertext c. (This follows from statistical closeness of the two distributions). More formally, we define these properties as follows:

Definition 3.4 (Blurring). *Given an encryption scheme* $\Sigma = (\mathsf{Gen}, \mathsf{Enc}, \mathsf{Dec})$, *we consider the following two blurring properties: Let* Π *be a set of public-key, secret-key, ciphertext tuples, i.e.* $(\mathsf{pk}, \mathsf{sk}, c)$. *Let* $\mathsf{Blur}(\mathsf{pk}, c)$ *be an algorithm which takes as input a public key and a ciphertext and produces a new ciphertext* $\tilde{c}$. *Then we can consider the following two properties:*

Weak Blurring: *We say* Blur *is a weak blurring mechanism where the correctness holds for* Π *if the following two properties hold.*

(1) Hiding: for any PPT adversary A, the following are indistinguishable.
Experiment 0: $\mathsf{pk} \leftarrow \mathsf{Gen}(1^\lambda), c \leftarrow A(\mathsf{pk}),$ *output* $(\mathsf{pk}, c, \mathsf{Blur}(\mathsf{pk}, c))$.
Experiment 1: $\mathsf{pk} \leftarrow \mathsf{Gen}(1^\lambda), c \leftarrow A(\mathsf{pk}),$ *output* $(\mathsf{pk}, c, \mathsf{Enc}_{\mathsf{pk}}(0))$.

(2) Correctness: There exists negligible ngl *such that, for all* $(\mathsf{pk}, \mathsf{sk}, c) \in \Pi$,
$$\Pr[\hat{c} \leftarrow \mathsf{Blur}(\mathsf{pk}, c) : \mathsf{Dec}_{\mathsf{sk}}(\hat{c}) = \mathsf{Dec}_{\mathsf{sk}}(c)] = 1 - \mathsf{ngl}(\lambda).$$

Strong Blurring: *We say* Blur *is a strong blurring mechanism with respect to* Π *if it is a weak blurring mechanism where correctness holds for* Π *with the following additional property: For every* $(\mathsf{pk}, \mathsf{sk}, c) \in \Pi$, *let* $m = \mathsf{Dec}_{\mathsf{sk}}(c)$; *then we require that* $\Delta((c, \mathsf{Blur}(\mathsf{pk}, c)), (c, \mathsf{Blur}(\mathsf{pk}, \mathsf{Enc}_{\mathsf{pk}}(m)))) < \mathsf{ngl}(\lambda).$

We note that many existing works consider similar definitions of re-randomization[2]. Strong blurring where Π is the set of all ciphertexts and valid key pairs would be equivalent to the definition in [23]. Weak blurring where Π is the set of all ciphertexts and valid key pairs is very similar in spirit to the definition of semantic security for universal re-encryption presented in [20].

One direct application of such a blurring mechanism is to achieve function privacy for any fully homomorphic encryption (FHE) scheme for which we can blur the ciphertexts produced by the evaluation algorithm. (See the full version.)

Implementations Using Function Private FHE. We note that both of these properties can be achieved easily given an appropriate FHE scheme. Given a   key private and function private FHE, we can construct a key-switching mechanism by evaluating the decryption circuit as discussed in the introduction. We can build strong blurring with respect to *all inputs* similarly. (See the full version.)

As a consequence, we can use the lattice-based FHE by Brakerski [8] (based on Regev's encryption) and our blurring mechanism for Regev-based schemes (see the next section) to implement an encryption scheme that has: (1) key switching, (2) strong blurring with respect to *all inputs*, and, (3) key privacy. In our constructions of functional re-encryption and multi-hop re-encryption, this approach gives the strongest obfuscation results, at the cost of efficiency.

3.2 Implementations Using Regev's Encryption Scheme

Recall that Regev's encryption scheme has the following structure: $\mathsf{pk} = (A, b)$ where $A \in \mathbb{Z}_q^{N \times n}$, $b \in \mathbb{Z}_q^N$, and $\mathsf{sk} = s \in \mathbb{Z}_q^n$ where $b = A \cdot s + e$ for some noise vector e, sampled from some distribution χ^N where χ is B-bounded. The encryption has the following structure: $c = (c_1, c_2) = r^\top \cdot (A, b) + (0^n, m \cdot \lceil q/2 \rceil)$ where r is a random vector in $\{0,1\}^N$. For details, see [27]. In what follows, let $\Sigma = (\mathsf{Gen}, \mathsf{Enc}, \mathsf{Dec})$ be Regev's encryption scheme.

Key-switching mechanism. As discussed in Remark 3.2, the requirements on key-switching in the context of re-encryption are slightly different from those in the FHE application. Thus, the construction from [10] does not work directly. We now show how we can modify that scheme to obtain a key-switching algorithm which does satisfy our requirements. Consider the following algorithms:

$\mathsf{SwGen}(\mathsf{pk}, \mathsf{sk}, \widehat{\mathsf{pk}})$: Parse $\mathsf{sk} = s \in \mathbb{Z}_q^n$. For $i \in [n], \tau \in [\lceil \log q \rceil]$, compute $K_{i,\tau} \leftarrow \mathsf{Enc}_{\widehat{\mathsf{pk}}}(0) + (0^n, s_i \cdot 2^\tau)$, where s_i denotes the i-th component of the vector s. Output $K_{\mathsf{pk} \rightarrow \widehat{\mathsf{pk}}} = \{K_{i,\tau}\}_{i \in [n], \tau \in [\lceil \log q \rceil]}$.

$\mathsf{SimSwGen}(\widehat{\mathsf{pk}})$: Let n, q be the parameters from $\widehat{\mathsf{pk}}$. For $i \in [n], \tau \in [\lceil \log q \rceil]$, compute $K_{i,\tau} \leftarrow \mathsf{Enc}_{\widehat{\mathsf{pk}}}(0)$, and output $K_{\mathsf{pk} \rightarrow \widehat{\mathsf{pk}}} = \{K_{i,\tau}\}_{i \in [n], \tau \in [\lceil \log q \rceil]}$.

$\mathsf{Sw}(K_{\mathsf{pk} \rightarrow \widehat{\mathsf{pk}}}, c)$: first parse $c = (c_1, c_2) \in \mathbb{Z}_q^n \times \mathbb{Z}_q$, and $K_{\mathsf{pk} \rightarrow \widehat{\mathsf{pk}}} = \{K_{i,\tau}\}_{i \in [n], \tau \in [\lceil \log q \rceil]}$. Denote by $c_{1,i}$ the i-th component of c_1, and denote the bit-

---

[2] We remark here, that our blurring technique is similar in spirit to the smudging technique proposed by Asharov *et al.* [4]. However, we abstract out the technique and formally define "blurring," independent of any specific encryption construction.

decomposition of $c_{1,i}$ as $\{c_{1,i,\tau}\}_{\tau \in [[\log q]]}$, i.e. $c_{1,i} = \sum_{\tau \in [[\log q]]} c_{1,i,\tau} 2^\tau$, where each $c_{1,i,\tau} \in \{0, 1\}$. Then output $\hat{c} = (0^n, c_2) + \sum_{i,\tau} c_{1,i,\tau} \cdot K_{i,\tau}$

The above construction has the same structure as the one in [10], so the correctness and security follow from the DLWE assumption. (See the full version.)

Blurring mechanism. Consider the following two blurring algorithms:

SBlur(pk, c; E), where $E \in \mathbb{Z}$ is a parameter hardcoded into the algorithm defining an appropriate error distribution (we will consider SBlur with different values for E): Parse pk $= (A, b) \in \mathbb{Z}_q^{N \times n} \times \mathbb{Z}_q^N$, sample $f \leftarrow [-E, E] \cap \mathbb{Z}$, and output $c + \text{Enc}_{\text{pk}}(0) + (0^n, f)$.

WBlur(pk, c): Output $c + \text{Enc}_{\text{pk}}(0)$.

Our idea for weak blurring is simple. We just add an encryption of 0 to the ciphertext. Since the distribution of $\text{Enc}_{\text{pk}}(0)$ is pseudo-random for Regev's encryption scheme, doing this computationally blurs the output. Also, Regev's encryption scheme is additively homomorphic (with a small blow up of noise), so this preserves the correctness of decryption.

For strong blurring, our idea is to blur the randomness as well. We recall that the ciphertext c has the form $(u, u^\top \cdot s) + (0^n, m \cdot [q/2]) + (0^n, z)$ where $z = r^\top \cdot e$ is the error term and $u = r^\top \cdot A$. Adding an encryption of 0 will blur our the first term $(u, u^\top \cdot s)$ (by a leftover hash lemma argument). The additional error e will blur out the last term z. For $E \cdot \lambda^{\omega(1)} < q/4$, decryption will still be correct. This idea also allows us to blur a subset sum of polynomially many ciphertexts. Thus, we can blur the ciphertexts after the key switching algorithm above. For a detailed analysis of weak and strong blurring see the full version.

3.3 Implementations Using the Dual Regev Encryption Scheme

In this section, we present another implementation of these mechanisms using the dual Regev encryption scheme. We remark that the dual Regev scheme appeared in [19], but we make a slight modification to the ciphertext and secret key that allows us to implement a key-switching mechanism.

The dual Regev encryption scheme we use here has the following structure: pk $= (A, u)$ where $A \in \mathbb{Z}_q^{n \times N}$ and $u \in \mathbb{Z}_q^n$ are uniformly random, and sk $= S \in \mathbb{Z}_q^{N \times N}$ such that S is a short basis of $\Lambda^\perp(A)$. The encryption has the following structure: $c = (c_1, c_2) = s^\top \cdot (A, u) + e^\top + (0^N, m \cdot [q/2])$ where $s \leftarrow \chi^n, e \leftarrow \chi^{N+1}$ are noise vectors, sampled (independently) from some B-bounded distribution χ. For details see the full version. In what follows, let $\Sigma = (\text{Gen}, \text{Enc}, \text{Dec})$ be the dual Regev encryption scheme.

Key-switching mechanism. Consider the following algorithms:

SwGen(pk, sk, $\widehat{\text{pk}}$): Parse pk $= (A, u_A) \in \mathbb{Z}_q^{n \times N} \times \mathbb{Z}_q^n$, $\widehat{\text{pk}} = (B, u_B) \in \mathbb{Z}_q^{n' \times N'} \times \mathbb{Z}_q^{n'}$, and sk $= S \in \mathbb{Z}_q^{N \times N}$. First sample short noise matrices $V \leftarrow \chi^{n' \times n'}, X \leftarrow \chi^{n' \times (N'+1)}$. Let $(\tilde{B}, \tilde{u}_B) = V \cdot (B, u_B) + X$. Then sample some short $Z \in \mathbb{Z}_q^{N \times N'}, z \in \mathbb{Z}_q^N$ such that $A \cdot (Z, z) = (\tilde{B}, \tilde{u}_B - u_A)$. This can be done by using the sampling algorithm SampleD($S, A, \cdot, \sigma_z$) at each column of the matrix $(\tilde{B}, \tilde{u}_B - u_A)$, together with the secret key S, and parameter $\sigma_z = \omega(\sqrt{n \log n \log q})$. Finally output $K_{\mathsf{pk} \to \widehat{\mathsf{pk}}} = (Z, z)$.

$\mathsf{SimSwGen}(\widehat{\mathsf{pk}})$: Let n, q be the parameters from $\widehat{\mathsf{pk}}$ and $\sigma_z = \omega(\sqrt{n \log n \log q})$ be an additional parameter of the encryption. Output (Z, z) chosen by taking $N' + 1$ independent samples from $D_{\mathbb{Z}^N, \sigma_z}$ (a discrete Gaussian on $\mathbb{Z}^N$ with parameter σ_z).

$\mathsf{Sw}(K_{\mathsf{pk} \to \widehat{\mathsf{pk}}}, c)$: first parse $c = (c_1, c_2) \in \mathbb{Z}_q^N \times \mathbb{Z}_q$, and $K_{\mathsf{pk} \to \widehat{\mathsf{pk}}} = (Z, z) \in \mathbb{Z}_q^{N \times N'} \times \mathbb{Z}_q^N$. Output $\hat{c} = (c_1, c_2) \cdot \left(\begin{smallmatrix} Z & z \\ 0 & 1 \end{smallmatrix} \right)$.

The correctness of the construction follows by a direct examination. Take an encryption of 0 for example: let $c = \mathsf{Enc}(0) = s^\top (A, u_A) + e^\top$. If we apply the switch key algorithm, we get a transformed ciphertext:

$$s^\top (A \cdot Z, A \cdot z + u_A) + e^\top = s^\top (\tilde{B}, \tilde{u}_B) + e^\top = s^\top V \cdot (B, u_B) + s^\top \cdot X + e^\top$$

Since V, X and s are short, we can view $s^\top V$ as another short $s'^\top$, and $s^\top \cdot X + e^\top$ as a slightly larger error $e'^\top$. Thus, this transformed ciphertext can be decrypted correctly.

The security argument is slightly trickier. First we observe that the matrix $(\tilde{B}, \tilde{u}_B)$ is computationally indistinguishable from a uniformly random matrix. This is because the security of DLWE holds even if the secret is sampled from the noise distribution $\chi^{n'}$ as shown by Applebaum et al. [3]. Thus, the distribution (Z, z) such that $A \cdot (Z, z) = (\tilde{B}, \tilde{u}_B)$ is computationally indistinguishable from the distribution (Z', z') such that $A \cdot (Z', z') = (U, u)$ where (U, u) is a uniformly random matrix. As shown by Gentry et al. [19], (Z, z) can be sampled (up to a negligible statistical distance) by the $\mathsf{SampleD}(A, S, \cdot, \sigma_z)$ as above, and (Z', z') is just the discrete Gaussian on $\mathbb{Z}^N$ with parameter σ_z. Thus, the security holds. For formal statements and proofs see the full version.

Blurring mechanism. Consider the following two blurring algorithms:

$\mathsf{SBlur}(\mathsf{pk}, c; E)$, where $E \in \mathbb{Z}$ is a parameter hardcoded into the algorithm: First parse $\mathsf{pk} = (A, u) \in \mathbb{Z}_q^{n \times N} \times \mathbb{Z}_q^n$. Then sample $p \leftarrow (E \cdot \chi)^n$, and $e \leftarrow (E \cdot \chi)^{N+1}$, and output $c + p^\top \cdot (A, u) + e^\top$.

$\mathsf{WBlur}(\mathsf{pk}, c)$: Output $c + \mathsf{Enc}_{\mathsf{pk}}(0)$.

Our idea for weak blurring is simple. We just add an encryption of 0. Since $\mathsf{Enc}_{\mathsf{pk}}(0)$ is pseudo-random, it will computationally blur the output. Also, the dual Regev encryption scheme is additively homomorphic (with a small blow up of noise), so it won't hurt the correctness.

For strong blurring, we need to blur the randomness as well. Recall that the ciphertext is of the form $s^\top \cdot (A, u) + e^\top$ for $s \leftarrow \chi^n, e \leftarrow \chi^{N+1}$ where χ is a B-bounded distribution. Suppose the distribution has the following property: $(E \cdot \chi)^N$ is statistically close to $y + (E \cdot \chi)^N$ for any $y \in \mathbb{Z}_q^N$ such that $\|y\|_\infty \leq B$. Then we can simply use $E \cdot \chi$ to blur the randomness. In fact, if χ is the Gaussian distribution (as it is in our setting) and the parameters satisfy $E \geq B \cdot \lambda^{\omega(1)}$, then this property can be achieved. See the full version for details.

Remark 3.5. We also propose an alternative implementation for key-switching in the dual Regev encryption scheme. The key observation is that the key-switching mechanism in Regev's encryption scheme as described in Section 3.2 can be easily adapted to the dual Regev scheme. Since the dual Regev scheme has the same structure for the decryption algorithm, (i.e. it computes the inner product of a ciphertext and a secret key, as Regev's scheme does for its decryption algorithm), a key-switching mechanism can be obtained in the same way. On the other hand, we will keep the same the blurring mechanism as above.

Remark 3.6. The dual Regev encryption scheme can be extended to a variety of identity-based encryption (IBE) and hierarchical identity-based encryption (HIBE) schemes as shown in [19, 12, 1, 2]. We further observe that our constructions of key switching and blurring in the dual Regev scheme can be naturally extended to these dual Regev based (H)IBE schemes.

4 Applications of Our Tools

In this section, we sketch how we can use the tools developed in the previous section to construct secure obfuscators for various re-encryption based primitives. More detailed descriptions appear in the full version. For each primitive we first define an ideal circuit family whose obfuscation would give a solution to the problem, and then we show how to obfuscate it.

4.1 Obfuscating Re-encryption

We first construct a simple re-encryption scheme. In re-encryption a user Alice with public key pk wants to allow an untrusted server to translate ciphertexts encrypted under her public key into ciphertexts encrypting the same message under the public key $\widehat{\mathsf{pk}}$ of another user Bob. She generates a re-encryption program, which the server can use to perform the translation without decrypting.

The ideal re-encryption circuit family. Each circuit $C_{\mathsf{pk},\mathsf{sk},\widehat{\mathsf{pk}}}$ is parameterized by a source key pair $(\mathsf{pk}, \mathsf{sk})$, and a target public key $\widehat{\mathsf{pk}}$. On input ciphertext c, it decrypts using sk, encrypts the result under $\widehat{\mathsf{pk}}$, and outputs the resulting $\hat{c}$.

Obfuscating re-encryption. Intuitively, if Alice could obfuscate the above circuit, then she could give the resulting program to the server. The program would have the same functionality, so it would allow the server to correctly translate ciphertexts from pk to $\widehat{\mathsf{pk}}$. At the same time it would reveal no more information than if the server had access to a trusted party who would compute re-encryption for it; in particular, this means the program would not help the server at all in decrypting messages as long as it doesn't know Bob's secret key. (If Bob and the server collude, they can of course decrypt any messages encrypted for Alice, but this is inherent in the functionality of re-encryption.)

We build on an encryption scheme with a key-switching mechanism and a blurring mechanism. To obfuscate $C_{\mathsf{pk},\mathsf{sk},\widehat{\mathsf{pk}}}$, Obf (1) computes the re-encryption key as $K_{\mathsf{pk}\to\widehat{\mathsf{pk}}} \leftarrow \mathsf{SwGen}(\mathsf{pk}, \mathsf{sk}, \widehat{\mathsf{pk}})$, and (2) generates the description of a re-encryption program that has the re-encryption key $K_{\mathsf{pk}\to\widehat{\mathsf{pk}}}$ hardcoded and on input ciphertext c computes and outputs $\hat{c} \leftarrow \mathsf{Blur}(\widehat{\mathsf{pk}}, \mathsf{Sw}(K_{\mathsf{pk}\to\widehat{\mathsf{pk}}}, c))$.

Theorem (informal). The above scheme satisfies ACVBB for the re-encryption functionality. With weak or strong blurring (resp.), it preserves functionality with respect to Π, or computationally preserves functionality and preserves Dec-correctness for Π, where Π is the set of honestly generated ciphertexts.

Interpreting the correctness guarantees. First, we note that in many scenarios, a scheme which satisfies Dec-correctness on the set Π of honestly-generated ciphertexts may be sufficient. Essentially, this says that whenever the server applies the re-encryption program to an honest ciphertext, the result will be another ciphertext which will decrypt to the correct message.

A scheme which computationally preserves functionality with respect to the set of all ciphertexts essentially guarantees that for any party without Bob's secret key, the output of the re-encryption program looks like a fresh random encryption. In particular, any party who eavesdrops on ciphertexts sent to the server and on the resulting ciphertexts sent to Bob will not be able to link each re-encrypted ciphertext to the original ciphertext from which it was formed.

Statistically preserving functionality with respect to the set Π of honestly-generated ciphertexts means that when the re-encryption program is applied to an honest ciphertext, *even Bob* can't distinguish the result from a freshly generated encryption. For example, if the server collects a set of ciphertexts, shuffles them, and then sends them all to Bob, even if Bob saw the original ciphertexts as they were sent to the server, he won't be able to link them to the ciphertexts he receives. This might be useful in privacy applications, e.g. if we want to guarantee that Bob can't tell who uploaded a particular message.

Finally, the standard definition of preserving functionality guarantees that the recipient Bob can't distinguish the output of the re-encryption from a fresh encryption, even if the initial ciphertext was not well formed.

4.2 Obfuscating Functional Re-encryption

Functional re-encryption, introduced by [13], extends the re-encryption to allow Alice to include an access policy when forming the re-encryption key, after which the server (without learning the access policy), can convert any ciphertext encrypted under Alice's public key into a ciphertext encrypted for the appropriate recipient (depending on the message and the access policy).

As in [13], we consider a message space in which each message consists of a short tag and a potentially longer message, and specify the policy function by defining a function F which maps tags to the appropriate recipients. For now, we consider the simple case where each tag is mapped to a different recipient. (The general case results in a larger re-encryption key; see the full version.)

The ideal circuit family. Each circuit $C_{\mathsf{pk},\mathsf{sk},\widehat{\mathsf{pk}}_1,\ldots\widehat{\mathsf{pk}}_n,F}$ is parameterized by an input key pair, a list of n output public keys, and the function F. On input ciphertext c, it decrypts c to obtain tag i and message m, then for each recipient j, if $F(i) = j$ it encrypts m under $\widehat{\mathsf{pk}}_j$, and otherwise it encrypts $\perp$ under $\widehat{\mathsf{pk}}_j$. It outputs the resulting list of ciphertexts. In our application above, the server could then forward each ciphertext to the appropriate recipient, but only the one for which $F(i) = j$ will decrypt to anything meaningful. (This circuit is somewhat different from the one in [13]; for a discussion, see the full version.)

Obfuscating functional re-encryption. Again, if we could obfuscate this functionality, we would obtain a program that Alice could safely give the server that would allow it to perform the re-encryption without learning anything about the messages. Furthermore, if we guarantee that our obfuscation worst-case hides the class of policy functions F then we know that the server will learn nothing about Alice's access policy; if the obfuscation is collusion resistant then these guarantees hold even if the server colludes with some subset of the recipients.

We build on a key-private encryption scheme with key-switching and blurring mechanisms. Roughly, Alice's public key consists of a public key pk_i for every possible i, and encryption of (m, i) for Alice computes $\Sigma.\mathsf{Enc}_{\mathsf{pk}_i}(m)$. The recipients use Σ directly. To obfuscate $C_{\mathsf{pk},\mathsf{sk},\widehat{\mathsf{pk}}_1,\ldots,\widehat{\mathsf{pk}}_n,F}$, Obf (1) computes a switch-key $K_{i \to F(i)} \leftarrow \mathsf{SwGen}(\mathsf{pk}_i, \widehat{\mathsf{pk}}_{F(i)})$ for each i (all these keys together, sorted based on $F(i)$, make up the re-encryption key rk_F), and (2) generates the description of a re-encryption program that has this rk_F hardcoded and, on input ciphertext c, computes $\hat{c}_j \leftarrow \mathsf{Blur}(\widehat{\mathsf{pk}}_j, \mathsf{Sw}(K_{F^{-1}(j) \to j}, c))$ for each $j \in [n]$ and outputs the list of ciphertexts $\hat{c}_1, \ldots, \hat{c}_n$.

Theorem (informal). This scheme satisfies collusion-resistant ACVBB with worst-case case hiding for F, and correctness depending on the blurring used.

4.3   Obfuscating Multi-hop Re-encryption

In multi-hop re-encryption, there are n users, each with his own key pair. Any of these users can choose to allow their messages to be re-encrypted to other users. We describe these choices with a directed graph, where each vertex corresponds to a user, and an edge from i to j in G means user i wants to allow re-encryption from ciphertexts under his public key (pk_i) to ciphertexts under pk_j. L-hop re-encryption allows each ciphertext to be re-encrypted L times. (Formally, we also assume each ciphertext reveals how many times it has been re-encrypted. We omit this below for simplicity; see the full version for details.)

The ideal circuit family for G. Each circuit $C_{\mathsf{pk}_1,\mathsf{sk}_1,\ldots,\mathsf{pk}_n,\mathsf{sk}_n}$ is parameterized by n key pairs $(\mathsf{pk}_i, \mathsf{sk}_i)$. On input i, j and a ciphertext c, if $(i, j) \in G$ it decrypts c using sk_i, then encrypts the result under pk_j, and outputs the resulting $\hat{c}$; otherwise it outputs an encryption of $\perp$ under pk_j.

The Obfuscation. If we could design many separate re-encryption programs which together form an obfuscation of the above functionality, we would obtain programs that each user could safely give the server that would allow it to perform the re-encryption without learning anything about the messages. Moreover, since this circuit distinguishes between an edge from i to j and an edge from j to i (G is a directed graph), the obfuscation would give a unidirectional re-encryption scheme.

We build on a key private encryption scheme with a key-switching mechanism and a blurring mechanism. To form a program using $(\mathsf{pk}_i, \mathsf{sk}_i)$, pk_j (for $(i, j) \in G$), user i will (1) compute a re-encryption key $K_{\mathsf{pk}_i \to \mathsf{pk}_j} \leftarrow \mathsf{SwGen}(\mathsf{pk}_i, \mathsf{sk}_i, \mathsf{pk}_j)$, and

(2) generate the description of a re-encryption program that has the re-encryption key $K_{\text{pk}_i \to \text{pk}_j}$ hardcoded and on input ciphertext c computes and outputs $\hat{c} \leftarrow \text{Blur}(\text{pk}_j, \text{Sw}(K_{\text{pk}_i \to \text{pk}_j}, c))$.

Theorem (informal). The combined programs satisfy collusion-resistant ACVBB, where correctness depends on the blurring algorithm used.

References

[1] Agrawal, S., Boneh, D., Boyen, X.: Efficient lattice (H)IBE in the standard model. In: Gilbert, H. (ed.) EUROCRYPT 2010. LNCS, vol. 6110, pp. 553–572. Springer, Heidelberg (2010)

[2] Agrawal, S., Boneh, D., Boyen, X.: Lattice basis delegation in fixed dimension and shorter-ciphertext hierarchical IBE. In: Rabin, T. (ed.) CRYPTO 2010. LNCS, vol. 6223, pp. 98–115. Springer, Heidelberg (2010)

[3] Applebaum, B., Cash, D., Peikert, C., Sahai, A.: Fast cryptographic primitives and circular-secure encryption based on hard learning problems. In: Halevi, S. (ed.) CRYPTO 2009. LNCS, vol. 5677, pp. 595–618. Springer, Heidelberg (2009)

[4] Asharov, G., Jain, A., López-Alt, A., Tromer, E., Vaikuntanathan, V., Wichs, D.: Multiparty computation with low communication, computation and interaction via threshold FHE. In: Pointcheval, D., Johansson, T. (eds.) EUROCRYPT 2012. LNCS, vol. 7237, pp. 483–501. Springer, Heidelberg (2012)

[5] Ateniese, G., Fu, K., Green, M., Hohenberger, S.: Improved proxy re-encryption schemes with applications to secure distributed storage. In: NDSS. The Internet Society (2005)

[6] Barak, B., Goldreich, O., Impagliazzo, R., Rudich, S., Sahai, A., Vadhan, S.P., Yang, K.: On the (im)possibility of obfuscating programs. In: Kilian, J. (ed.) CRYPTO 2001. LNCS, vol. 2139, pp. 1–18. Springer, Heidelberg (2001)

[7] Blaze, M., Bleumer, G., Strauss, M.: Divertible protocols and atomic proxy cryptography. In: Nyberg, K. (ed.) EUROCRYPT 1998. LNCS, vol. 1403, pp. 127–144. Springer, Heidelberg (1998)

[8] Brakerski, Z.: Fully homomorphic encryption without modulus switching from classical GapSVP. In: Safavi-Naini, R., Canetti, R. (eds.) CRYPTO 2012. LNCS, vol. 7417, pp. 868–886. Springer, Heidelberg (2012)

[9] Brakerski, Z., Gentry, C., Vaikuntanathan, V.: (Leveled) fully homomorphic encryption without bootstrapping. In: Goldwasser, S. (ed.) ITCS, pp. 309–325. ACM (2012)

[10] Brakerski, Z., Vaikuntanathan, V.: Efficient fully homomorphic encryption from (standard) LWE. In: Ostrovsky, R. (ed.) FOCS, pp. 97–106. IEEE (2011)

[11] Brakerski, Z., Vaikuntanathan, V.: Fully homomorphic encryption from ring-lwe and security for key dependent messages. In: Rogaway, P. (ed.) CRYPTO 2011. LNCS, vol. 6841, pp. 505–524. Springer, Heidelberg (2011)

[12] Cash, D., Hofheinz, D., Kiltz, E., Peikert, C.: Bonsai trees, or how to delegate a lattice basis. Journal of Cryptology 25(4), 601–639 (2012)

[13] Chandran, N., Chase, M., Vaikuntanathan, V.: Functional re-encryption and collusion-resistant obfuscation. In: Cramer, R. (ed.) TCC 2012. LNCS, vol. 7194, pp. 404–421. Springer, Heidelberg (2012)

[14] Chu, C.-K., Tzeng, W.-G.: Identity-based proxy re-encryption without random oracles. In: Garay, J.A., Lenstra, A.K., Mambo, M., Peralta, R. (eds.) ISC 2007. LNCS, vol. 4779, pp. 189–202. Springer, Heidelberg (2007)

[15] Gentry, C.: Fully homomorphic encryption using ideal lattices. In: Mitzenmacher, M. (ed.) STOC, pp. 169–178. ACM (2009)

[16] Gentry, C.: Toward basing fully homomorphic encryption on worst-case hardness. In: Rabin, T. (ed.) CRYPTO 2010. LNCS, vol. 6223, pp. 116–137. Springer, Heidelberg (2010)

[17] Gentry, C., Halevi, S.: Fully homomorphic encryption without squashing using depth-3 arithmetic circuits. In: Ostrovsky, R. (ed.) FOCS, pp. 107–109. IEEE (2011)

[18] Gentry, C., Halevi, S., Vaikuntanathan, V.: i-hop homomorphic encryption and rerandomizable yao circuits. In: Rabin, T. (ed.) CRYPTO 2010. LNCS, vol. 6223, pp. 155–172. Springer, Heidelberg (2010)

[19] Gentry, C., Peikert, C., Vaikuntanathan, V.: Trapdoors for hard lattices and new cryptographic constructions. In: Dwork, C. (ed.) STOC, pp. 197–206. ACM (2008)

[20] Golle, P., Jakobsson, M., Juels, A., Syverson, P.F.: Universal re-encryption for mixnets. In: Okamoto, T. (ed.) CT-RSA 2004. LNCS, vol. 2964, pp. 163–178. Springer, Heidelberg (2004)

[21] Green, M., Ateniese, G.: Identity-based proxy re-encryption. In: Katz, J., Yung, M. (eds.) ACNS 2007. LNCS, vol. 4521, pp. 288–306. Springer, Heidelberg (2007)

[22] Hada, S.: Secure obfuscation for encrypted signatures. In: Gilbert, H. (ed.) EUROCRYPT 2010. LNCS, vol. 6110, pp. 92–112. Springer, Heidelberg (2010)

[23] Hemenway, B., Libert, B., Ostrovsky, R., Vergnaud, D.: Lossy encryption: Constructions from general assumptions and efficient selective opening chosen ciphertext security. In: Lee, D.H., Wang, X. (eds.) ASIACRYPT 2011. LNCS, vol. 7073, pp. 70–88. Springer, Heidelberg (2011)

[24] Hofheinz, D., Malone-Lee, J., Stam, M.: Obfuscation for cryptographic purposes. In: Vadhan, S.P. (ed.) TCC 2007. LNCS, vol. 4392, pp. 214–232. Springer, Heidelberg (2007)

[25] Hohenberger, S., Rothblum, G.N., Shelat, A., Vaikuntanathan, V.: Securely obfuscating re-encryption. In: Vadhan, S.P. (ed.) TCC 2007. LNCS, vol. 4392, pp. 233–252. Springer, Heidelberg (2007)

[26] Lyubashevsky, V., Peikert, C., Regev, O.: On ideal lattices and learning with errors over rings. In: Gilbert, H. (ed.) EUROCRYPT 2010. LNCS, vol. 6110, pp. 1–23. Springer, Heidelberg (2010)

[27] Regev, O.: On lattices, learning with errors, random linear codes, and cryptography. Journal of the ACM 56, Article 34, 6 (2009), A preliminary version appeared in STOC 2005 (2005)

[28] Rivest, R., Adleman, L., Dertouzos, M.: On data banks and privacy homomorphisms. In: Foundations of Secure Computation, pp. 169–177. Academic Press (1978)

Verifiable Set Operations over Outsourced Databases[*]

Ran Canetti[1,2], Omer Paneth[1], Dimitrios Papadopoulos[1],
and Nikos Triandopoulos[3,1]

[1] Dept. of Computer Science, Boston University, USA
[2] Dept. of Computer Science, Tel Aviv University, Israel
[3] RSA Laboratories, Cambridge MA, USA

Abstract. We study the problem of verifiable delegation of computation over outsourced data, whereby a powerful worker maintains a large data structure for a weak client in a verifiable way. Compared to the well-studied problem of verifiable computation, this setting imposes additional difficulties since the verifier also needs to check the consistency of updates succinctly and without maintaining large state. We present a scheme for verifiable evaluation of *hierarchical set operations* (unions, intersections and set-differences) applied to a collection of *dynamically changing sets of elements* from a given domain. The verification cost incurred is proportional only to the size of the final outcome set and to the size of the query, and is *independent of the cardinalities of the involved sets*. The cost of updates is *optimal* (involving $O(1)$ modular operations per update). Our construction extends that of [Papamanthou et al., CRYPTO 2011] and relies on a modified version of the *extractable collision-resistant hash function* (ECRH) construction, introduced in [Bitansky et al., ITCS 2012] that can be used to succinctly hash univariate polynomials.

1 Introduction

Outsourcing of storage and computation to the cloud has become a common practice for both enterprises and individuals. In this setting, typically, a client with bounded computational and storage capabilities wishes to outsource its database to a cloud provider and, over time, issue queries over the database that are answered by powerful servers.

We consider a client that outsources a dataset D to a server. The client can then issue to the server *informational* queries that are answered according to D, or it can issue *update* queries that change D, for example by inserting or removing elements. This model captures a variety of real-world applications such as outsourced relational databases, streaming datasets and outsourced file systems. We also consider the more general setting where multiple other clients can issue informational queries to D, while only one designated source client can issue update queries. For example, consider a company that outsources its data to a cloud service provider that will also be responsible for accommodating queries from the company's multiple customers.

---

[*] Research supported in part by the Check Point Institute for Information Security, an NSF EAGER grant, an NSF Algorithmic foundations grant 1218461, the Simons award for graduate students in theoretical computer science, and NSF grants CNS-1012798 and CNS-1012910.

H. Krawczyk (Ed.): PKC 2014, LNCS 8383, pp. 113–130, 2014.

In such outsourcing scenarios, clients may want to verify the integrity of the outsourced operations over the dataset D to protect themselves against servers that provide wrong results because they are themselves malicious or have been compromised by an external attacker, or simply provide false results (e.g., inaccurate or inconsistent data) due to bugs. Specifically, when answering a client's query, the server will also compute a *proof* of the integrity of the data used to compute the answer as well as the integrity of the computation, i.e., that the correct function was computed. For this purpose, we allow the source client to perform some preprocessing on D before outsourcing it to the server, and to save a small *verification state* that allows it to verify the server's proofs. Analogously, when issuing an update query, the source client will also update its verification state. If the verification state can be made public we say that the server's proofs are *publicly verifiable*, which is particularly important in the multi-client setting.

Several different measures of efficiency can be considered in this setting. First, the time it takes for the client to verify a proof should be short, ideally some fixed polynomial in the security parameter that is independent of the size of server's computation cost and the size of D. Second, the server's computational overhead in computing proofs should be kept minimal. Additional efficiency properties include small proof sizes, efficient update queries as well as non-interactive solutions where the client sends a query and receives back an answer and a proof in one round of interaction.

Set Operations over Outsourced Databases. This work focuses on the problem of verifying *general set operations* in the above outsourcing setting. That is, we consider a dataset D that consists of m sets $S_1, ..., S_m$, where the clients' queries are arbitrary set operations over D represented as formulas of union, intersection, and set-difference gates over some of the inputs $S_1, ..., S_m$. A particularly interesting case is when the sets appearing at intermediate steps of the computation are much larger than the final answer (e.g., consider a number of unions, followed by an intersection resulting in the empty set). The motivation for set operations comes from their great expressiveness and the range of computations that can be mapped by them. Real-world applications of general set operations include a wide class of SQL database queries, keyword search with elaborate queries, access control management and similarity measurement, hence a practical protocol for verifiable general set operations would be of great importance.

Verifiable Computation - The Generic Approach. The settings considered here are closely related to the setting of verifiable computation that has been extensively studied in recent years. In verifiable computation the client outsources a computation to the server and receives an answer that can be quickly verified. The main difference is that in verifiable computation it is usually assumed that the input to the computation is short and known to both parties, while in our settings the server's answers are computed over the outsourced dataset that must also be authenticated. This problem was addressed in the work of [15] on *memory delegation* with a construction based on Micali's CS proofs. One possible approach for designing a *practical* protocol is based on the memory delegation solution where Micali's CS proofs are replaced by a *succinct non-interactive argument-of-knowledge* (SNARK). Good candidates for more practical constructions of such a SNARK are provided in the recent works of [4, 6, 27].

However, one major obstacle for implementing the generic approach described above (discussed already in [27]) is that it only considers computations that are represented as boolean or arithmetic circuits. For example, in the context of set operations the transformation from formulas of set operations to circuits can be extremely wasteful as the number of sets participating in every query and the set sizes may vary dramatically between queries. Here, another source of inefficiency is that the generic approach considers a universal circuit that gets the query, in the form of the set-operation formula, as input which introduces additional overheads. Overall, while asymptotically the computational overhead of the server can be made poly-logarithmic, in practice the large constants involved can be an obstacle for using the generic solution for set operations.

Our Result. In this work we propose a new practical scheme for publicly verifiable secure delegation of general set operations. The verification state is of constant size and the proof verification time is $O(t + \delta)$ where t is the size of the query formula and δ is the answer set size. That is, a main advantage of our scheme is that the verification time and the proof length do not grow with the sizes of all other sets involved in the computation. For instance, the intersection of two unions, each defined over a constant number of sets each having a large cardinality, may result in intermediate results of size $O(|D|)$ but only produce the empty set as output; in this extreme case, our scheme provides optimal, constant-time verification. The dependence on the answer size is inherent since the client must receive the answer set from the server. Another advantage of our scheme over the generic approach is that is does not involve translating the problem to an arithmetic or boolean circuit. In particular, the server will need to perform only $4N$ exponentiations in a group with a symmetric bilinear pairing, where N is the sum of the sizes of all the intermediate sets in the evaluation of the set formula.

For updates, the source client maintains an update state of length $O(m)$, where m is the number of sets in the dataset, and it can add or remove a single element for every set in constant time. The source then updates the server and all other clients with a new verification state. We note that our definitions and construction can be extended to support also *server-assisted updates*, where the source client updates a given set in D to a new set defined as the output of a set operation performed by the server, thus updating a large number of elements at once—details are deferred to the full version [13].

Overview of Techniques. The starting point for our construction is the scheme of Papamanthou, Tamassia and Triandopoulos [26] that supports verification of a single set operation, one union or intersection, over t sets in time $O(t + \delta)$, where δ is the answer size. The "naive" way to extend that scheme to support general set-operation formulas is to have the server provide a separate proof for each intermediate set produced in the evaluation of the formula. However, proving the security of such an extended scheme is problematic. The problem is that in the scheme of [26] the proofs do not necessarily compose. In particular, it might be easy for a malicious server to come up with a false proof corresponding to an incorrect answer set without "knowing" what this incorrect answer is (if the malicious server would be able to also find the answer set, the scheme of [26] would not have been secure). Therefore, to make the security proof of the naive scheme go though, the server would also have to prove to the client that it "knows" all the intermediate sets produced in the evaluation of the query formula. One way for the server to prove knowledge of these sets is to send them to the client, however, this will result in a proof that is as long as the entire server computation.

To solve this problem we need to further understand the structure of the proofs in [26] which is based on the notion of a bilinear accumulator [24]. We can think of a bilinear accumulator as a succinct hash of a large set that makes use of a representation of a set by its *characteristic polynomial* (i.e., a polynomial that has as roots the set elements). The main idea in our work is to use a different type of accumulator, a *knowledge accumulator*, that has "knowledge" properties, i.e., the only way for an algorithm to produce a valid accumulation value is to "know" the set that corresponds to this value. This knowledge property of our accumulator together with the soundness of the proof for every single operation allows us to prove the soundness of the composed scheme. Our construction of knowledge accumulators is very similar to the previous constructions of knowledge commitments in [6, 20], which are based on the q-PKE assumption, a variant of the knowledge-of-exponent assumption [16]. We capture the knowledge properties of our accumulator by using the notion of an *extractable collision-resistant hash function* (ECRH), originally introduced in [6]. However, we follow the weaker definition of ECRH with respect to auxiliary input, for which the recent negative evidence presented in [7] does not apply and the auxiliary-input distributions we consider here are not captured by the negative result of [11] either.

We also need to change the way a single set operation is proven. Specifically, in [26], a proof for a single union of sets requires one accumulation value for every element in the union. This will again result in a proof that is as long as the entire server computation. Instead our scheme involves proofs that are independent of the set sizes.

Moreover, in order to verify a proof in our scheme, the client only needs to know the accumulation values for the sets that participate in a computation. Instead of storing the accumulation values of all sets in the dataset, the client only stores a constant-size verification state that contains a special hash of these accumulation values. We compute this special hash using an *accumulation tree*, introduced in [25]. This primitive can be thought of as a special "tree hash" that makes use of the algebraic structure of accumulators to provide authentication paths of constant length.

Finally we note that our definition of security follows the popular framework of *authenticated data structures* introduced in [29].

Related Work. The very recent work of [3] also considers a practical secure database delegation scheme supporting a restricted class of queries, namely functions expressed by arithmetic circuits of degree up to 2. This scheme is based on homomorphic MACs and appears practical while also having a security proof that is based on standard hardness assumptions. However, their solution is only privately verifiable and it does not support deletions from the dataset. In a sense, the work of [3] is complementary to ours, as arithmetic and set operations are two desirable classes of computations for a database outsourcing scheme.

With respect to set operations, previous works focused mostly on the aspect of privacy and less on the aspect of integrity [2, 10, 18, 21]. There exists a number of works from the database community that address this problem [22, 30], but to the best of our knowledge, this is the first work that directly addresses the case of nested operations.

Characteristic polynomials for set representation have been used before in the cryptography literature (see for example [24, 26]) and this directly relates our work with a line of publications coming from the *cryptographic accumulators* literature [12, 24].

Indeed our ECRH construction, viewed as a mathematical object, is identical to a pair of bilinear accumulators (introduced in [24]) with related secret key values. Our ECRH can be viewed as an extractable extension to the bilinear accumulator that allows an adversarial party to prove knowledge of a subset to an accumulated set (without explicitly providing said subset). It also allows us to use the notion of *accumulation trees* which was originally defined for bilinear accumulators.

The *authenticated data structure* (ADS) paradigm, originally introduced in [29], appears extensively both in the cryptography and databases literature (see for example [1, 19, 22, 23, 26, 31, 32]). A wide range of functionalities has been authenticated in this context including range queries and basic SQL joins.

2 Tools and Definitions

We denote with l the security parameter and with $\nu(l)$ a negligible function. We say that an event can occur with negligible probability if its occurrence probability is upper bounded by a negligible function. Respectively, an event takes place with overwhelming probability if its complement takes place with negligible probability. In our technical exposition we adopt the *access complexity* model: Used mainly in the memory checking literature [8, 17], this model allows us to measure complexity expressed in the number of primitive cryptographic operations made by an algorithm without considering the related security parameter.

Bilinear Pairings. Let $\mathbb{G}$ be a cyclic multiplicative group of prime order p, generated by g. Let also $\mathbb{G}_T$ be a cyclic multiplicative group with the same order p and $e : \mathbb{G} \times \mathbb{G} \to \mathbb{G}_T$ be a bilinear pairing with the following properties: (1) Bilinearity: $e(P^a, Q^b) = e(P, Q)^{ab}$ for all $P, Q \in \mathbb{G}$ and $a, b \in \mathbb{Z}_p$; (2) Non-degeneracy: $e(g, g) \neq 1$; (3) Computability: There is an efficient algorithm to compute $e(P, Q)$ for all $P, Q \in \mathbb{G}$. We denote with $pub := (p, \mathbb{G}, \mathbb{G}_T, e, g)$ the bilinear pairings parameters, output by a randomized polynomial-time algorithm GenBilinear on input 1^l.

For cleaner presentation, in what follows we assume a symmetric (Type 1) pairing e. In [13] we discuss the modifications needed to implement our construction in the (more efficient) asymmetric pairing case (see [14] for a general discussion of pairings).

Our security analysis makes use of the following two assumptions :

Assumption 1 (q-**Strong Bilinear Diffie-Hellman** [9]). *For any poly-size adversary $\mathcal{A}$ and for q being a parameter of size $poly(l)$, the following holds:*

$$\Pr\left[\begin{array}{c} pub \leftarrow \mathsf{GenBilinear}(1^l); s \leftarrow_R \mathbb{Z}_p^*; \\ (z, \gamma) \in \mathbb{Z}_p^* \times \mathbb{G}_T \leftarrow \mathcal{A}(pub, (g, g^s, ..., g^{s^q})) \ s.t. \ \gamma = e(g, g)^{1/(z+s)} \end{array} \right] \leq \nu(l)] .$$

Assumption 2 (q-**Power Knowledge of Exponent** [20]). *For any poly-size adversary $\mathcal{A}$, there exists a poly-size extractor $\mathcal{E}$ such that:*

$$\Pr\left[\begin{array}{c} pub \leftarrow \mathsf{GenBilinear}(1^l); a, s \leftarrow_R \mathbb{Z}_p^*; \sigma = (g, g^s, ..., g^{s^q}, g^a, g^{as}, ..., g^{as^q}) \\ (c, \tilde{c}) \leftarrow \mathcal{A}(pub, \sigma); (a_0, ..., a_n) \leftarrow \mathcal{E}(pub, \sigma) \\ s.t. \ e(\tilde{c}, g) = e(c, g^a) \ \wedge \ c \neq \prod_{i=0}^{n} g^{a_i s^i} for \ n \leq q \end{array} \right] \leq \nu(l) .$$

Extractable Collision-Resistant Hash Functions. These functions (or ECRH for short) were introduced in [6] as a strengthening of the notion of collision-resistant hash functions. The key property implied by an ECRH is the hardness of oblivious sampling from the image space. Informally, for a function f, sampled from an ECRH function ensemble, any adversary producing a hash value h must have knowledge of a value $x \in Dom(f)$ s.t. $f(x) = h$. Formally, an ECRH function is defined as follows:

Definition 1 (ECRH [6]). *A function ensemble $\mathcal{H} = \{\mathcal{H}_l\}_l$ from $\{0,1\}^{t(l)}$ to $\{0,1\}^l$ is an ECRH if:*

Collision-Resistance. *For any poly-size adversary $\mathcal{A}$:*

$$\Pr_{h \leftarrow \mathcal{H}_l} \left[x, x' \leftarrow \mathcal{A}(1^l, h) \text{ s.t. } h(x) = h(x') \wedge x \neq x' \right] \leq \nu(l) .$$

Extractability. *For any poly-size adversary $\mathcal{A}$, there exists poly-size extractor $\mathcal{E}$ s.t.:*

$$\Pr_{h \leftarrow \mathcal{H}_l} \left[\begin{array}{c} y \leftarrow \mathcal{A}(1^l, h); x' \leftarrow \mathcal{E}(1^l, h) \\ \text{s.t. } \exists x : h(x) = y \wedge h(x') \neq y \end{array} \right] \leq \nu(l) .$$

An ECRH Construction from q-PKE. We next provide an ECRH construction from the q-PKE assumption defined above. In [6] the authors suggest that an ECRH can be constructed directly from q-PKE (without explicitly providing the construction). Here we present the detailed construction and a proof of the required properties with respect to q-PKE for extractability and q-SBDH for collision-resistance.

- To sample from $\mathcal{H}_l$, choose $q \in O(poly(l))$, run algorithm GenBilinear(1^l) to generate bilinear pairing parameters $pub = (p, \mathbb{G}, \mathbb{G}_T, e, g)$ and sample $a, s \leftarrow_R \mathbb{Z}_p^* \times \mathbb{Z}_p^*$ s.t. $a \neq s$. Output public key $pk = (pub, g^s, ..., g^{s^q}, g^a, g^{as}, ..., g^{as^q})$ and trapdoor information $sk = (s, a)$. It should be noted that the pk fully describes the chosen function h. Trapdoor sk can be used for a more efficient computation of hash values, by the party initializing the ECRH .
- To compute a hash value on $\mathbf{x} = (x_1, ..., x_q)$, output $h(\mathbf{x}) = \left(\prod_{i \in [q]} g^{x_i s^i}, \prod_{i \in [q]} g^{a x_i s^i} \right)$.

Lemma 1. *If the q-SBDH and q-PKE assumptions hold, the above is a $(q \cdot l, 4l)$-compressing ECRH.*

Proof. Extractability follows directly from the q-PKE assumption. To argue about collision-resistance, assume there exists adversary $\mathcal{A}$ outputting with probability ϵ, $(\mathbf{x}, \mathbf{y})$ such that there exists $i \in [q]$ with $x_i \neq y_i$ and $h(\mathbf{x}) = h(\mathbf{y})$. We denote with $P(r)$ the q-degree polynomial from $\mathbb{Z}_p[r]$, $\sum_{i \in [q]} (x_i - y_i) r^i$. From the above, it follows that $\sum_{i \in [q]} x_i s^i = \sum_{i \in [q]} y_i s^i$. Hence, while $P(r)$ is not the 0-polynomial, the evaluation of $P(r)$ at point s is $P(s) = 0$ and s is a root of $P(r)$. By applying a randomized polynomial factorization algorithm as in [5], one can extract the (up to q) roots of $P(r)$ with overwhelming probability, thus computing s. By choosing a to compute the second part of the public key to run $\mathcal{A}$ and then randomly selecting $c \in \mathbb{Z}_p^*$ and computing $\beta = g^{1/(c+s)}$ one can output $(c, e(g, \beta))$, breaking the q-SBDH with probability $\epsilon(1 - \epsilon')$ where ϵ' is the negligible probability of error in the polynomial factoring algorithm. Therefore any poly-size $\mathcal{A}$ can find a collision only with negligible probability. The $4l$ factor follows from the representation cost of elliptic curve points as a pair of p-bit coefficients. □

One natural application for the above ECRH construction would be the compact computational representation of polynomials from $\mathbb{Z}_p[r]$ of degree $\leq q$. A polynomial $P(r)$ with coefficients $p_1, ..., p_q$ can be succinctly represented by the hash value $h(P) = (f, f') = \left(\prod_{i \in [q]} g^{p_i s^i}, \prod_{i \in [q]} g^{ap_i s^i} \right)$.

Authenticated Data Structure Scheme. Such schemes, originally defined in [26], model verifiable computations over outsourced data structures. Let D be any data structure supporting queries and updates. We denote with $auth(D)$ some authenticated information on D and with d the digest of D, i.e., a succinct secure computational description of D. An authenticated data structure scheme ADS is a collection of six algorithms shown in Figure 1. Let $\{accept, reject\} = check(q, a(q), D_h)$ be a method that decides whether $a(q)$ is a correct answer for query q on data structure D_h (this method is not part of the scheme but only introduced for ease of notation.) Then an authenticated data structure scheme ADS should satisfy the following:

1. $\{sk, pk\} \leftarrow \mathbf{genkey}(1^k)$. Outputs secret and public keys, given the security parameter l.
2. $\{auth(D_0), d_0\} \leftarrow \mathbf{setup}(D_0, sk, pk)$: Computes the authenticated data structure $auth(D_0)$ and its respective digest, d_0, given data structure D_0, the secret key sk and the public key pk.
3. $\{auth(D_{h+1}), d_{h+1}, upd\} \leftarrow \mathbf{update}(u, auth(D_h), d_h, sk, pk)$: On input update u on data structure D_h, the authenticated data structure $auth(D_h)$ and the digest d_h, it outputs the updated data structure D_{h+1} along with $auth(D_{h+1})$, the updated digest d_{h+1} and some relative information upd. It requires the secret key for execution.
4. $\{D_{h+1}, auth(D_{h+1}), d_{h+1}\} \leftarrow \mathbf{refresh}(u, D_h, auth(D_h), d_h, upd, pk)$: On input update u on data structure D_h, the authenticated data structure $auth(D_h)$, the digest d_h and relative information upd output by $\mathbf{update}$, it outputs the updated data structure D_{h+1} along with $auth(D_{h+1})$ and the updated digest d_{h+1}, without access to sk.
5. $\{a(q), \Pi(q)\} \leftarrow \mathbf{query}(q, D_h, auth(D_h), pk)$: On input query q on data structure D_h and $auth(D_h)$ it returns the answer to the query $a(q)$, along with a proof $\Pi(q)$.
6. $\{accept, reject\} \leftarrow \mathbf{verify}(q, a(q), \Pi(q), d_h, pk)$: On input query q, an answer $a(q)$, a proof $\Pi(q)$, a digest d_h and pk, it outputs either "accept" or "reject".

Fig. 1. Authenticated data structure

Correctness. We say that ADS is *correct* if, for all $l \in \mathbb{N}$, for all (sk, pk) output by algorithm **genkey**, for all $(D_h, auth(D_h), d_h)$ output by one invocation of **setup** followed by polynomially-many invocations of **refresh**, where $h \geq 0$, for all queries q and for all $a(q), \Pi(q)$ output by $query(q, D_h, auth(D_h), pk)$, with all but negligible probability, whenever $check(q, a(q), D_h)$ accepts, so does **verify**$(q, a(q), \Pi(q), d_h, pk)$.

Security. Let $l \in \mathbb{N}$ be a security parameter and $(sk, pk) \leftarrow genkey(1^l)$ and $\mathcal{A}$ be a poly-size adversary that is only given pk and has oracle access to all algorithms of the ADS. The adversary picks an initial state of the data structure D_0 and computes $D_0, auth(D_0), d_0$ through oracle access to algorithm **setup**. Then, for $i = 0, ..., h = poly(l)$, $\mathcal{A}$ issues an update u_i for the data structure D_i and outputs $D_{i+1}, auth(D_{i+1})$ and d_{i+1} through oracle access to algorithm **update**. At any point during these update queries, he can make polynomially many oracle calls to algorithms **prove** and **verify**. Finally the adversary picks an index $0 \leq t \leq h + 1$, a query q, an answer $a(q)$ and a proof $\Pi(q)$. We say that an ADS is *secure* if for all large enough $k \in \mathbb{N}$, for all poly-size adversaries $\mathcal{A}$ it holds that:

$$\Pr\left[\begin{array}{c} (q, a(q), \Pi(q), t) \leftarrow \mathcal{A} \text{ s.t} \\ \text{accept} \leftarrow \mathbf{verify}(q, a(q), \Pi(q), d_t, pk) \wedge \text{reject} \leftarrow check(q, a(q), D_t) \end{array} \right] \leq \nu(l)$$

where the probability is taken over the randomness of **genkey** and the coins of $\mathcal{A}$. The above security definition maps the mode of operation of an outsourced computation protocol where the database used is originally "finger-printed" by a trusted party that is also solely responsible for dynamically changing it. Clients can trust that the answers they get are "as-good-as" computed by the trusted party.

Set Representation with Polynomials. Sets can be represented with polynomials, using the notion of characteristic polynomial, e.g., as introduced in [18, 24, 26]. Given a set $X = \{x_1, .., x_m\}$, the polynomial $\mathcal{C}_X(r) = \prod_{i=1}^{m}(x_i + r)$ from $\mathbb{Z}_p[r]$, where r is a formal variable, is called the *characteristic polynomial* of X (when possible we will denote this polynomial simply by $\mathcal{C}_X$). Characteristic polynomials constitute representations of sets by polynomials that have the additive inverses of their set elements as roots. What is of particular importance to us is that characteristic polynomials enjoy a number of homomorphic properties w.r.t. set operations. For example, given sets A, B with $A \subseteq B$, it must hold that $\mathcal{C}_B | \mathcal{C}_A$ and given sets X, Y with $I = X \cap Y$, $\mathcal{C}_I = gcd(\mathcal{C}_X, \mathcal{C}_Y)$.

The following lemma characterizes the efficiency of computing the characteristic polynomial of a set.

Lemma 2 ([28]). *Given set $X = x_1, ..., x_n$ with elements from $\mathbb{Z}_p$, characteristic polynomial $\mathcal{C}_X(r) := \sum_{i=0}^{n} c_i r^i \in \mathbb{Z}_p[r]$ can be computed with $O(n \log n)$ operations with FFT interpolation.*

Note that, while the notion of a unique characteristic polynomial for a given set is well-defined, from elementary algebra it is known that there exist many distinct polynomials having as roots the additive inverses of the elements in this set. For instance, recall that multiplication of a polynomial in $\mathbb{Z}_p[r]$ with an invertible unit in $\mathbb{Z}_p^*$ leaves the roots of the resulting polynomial unaltered. We define the following:

Definition 2. *Given polynomials $P(r), Q(r) \in \mathbb{Z}_p[r]$ with degree n, we say that they are* associate *(denoted as $P(r) \approx_a Q(r)$) iff $P(r)|Q(r)$ and $Q(r)|P(r)$.*

Thus, associativity can be equivalently expressed by requesting that $P(r) = \lambda Q(r)$ for some $\lambda \in \mathbb{Z}_p^*$.

Note that although polynomial-based set representation provides a way to verify the correctness of set operations by employing corresponding properties of the characteristic polynomials, it does not provide any computational speedup for this verification process. Intuitively, verifying operations over sets of cardinality n, involves dealing with polynomials of degree n with associated cost that is proportional to performing operations directly over the sets themselves. We overcome this obstacle, by applying our ECRH construction (which can be naturally defined over univariate polynomials with coefficients in $\mathbb{Z}_p$, as already discussed) to the characteristic polynomial $\mathcal{C}_X$: Set X will be succinctly represented by hash value $h(\mathcal{C}_X) = \left(g^{\mathcal{C}_X(s)}, g^{a\mathcal{C}_X(s)}\right)$ (parameter q is an upper bound on the cardinality of sets that can hashed), and a operation of sets X and Y will be optimally verified by computing only on hash values $h(\mathcal{C}_X)$ and $h(\mathcal{C}_Y)$.

Observe that, while every set has a uniquely defined characteristic polynomial, not every polynomial is a characteristic polynomial of some set. Hence extractability of sets from hash values is not guaranteed. For our ADS construction, we will combine the use of the ECRH construction for sets, with an authentication mechanism deployed by the source in a pre-processing phase over the hash values of the original m sets.

3   Setup and Update Algorithms

An *authenticated data structure* (ADS) is a protocol for secure data outsourcing involving the owner of a dataset (referred to as *source*), an untrusted server and multiple clients that issue computational queries over the dataset. The protocol consists of a pre-processing phase where the source uses a secret key to compute some authentication information over the dataset D, outsources D along with this information to the server and publishes some public digest d related to the current state of D. Subsequently, the source can issue update queries for D (which depend on the data type of D), in which case, the source updates the digest and both the source and the server update the authentication information to correspond consistently with the updated dataset state. Moreover, multiple clients (including the source itself), issue computational queries q addressed to the server, which responds with appropriate answer α and proof of correctness Π. Responses can be verified both for *integrity of computation* of q and *integrity of data* used (i.e., that the correct query was run on the correct dataset D) with access only to public key and digest d.

Here we present an ADS supporting hierarchical set operations. We assume a data structure D consisting of m sorted sets $S_1, ..., S_m$, consisting of elements from $\mathbb{Z}_p$,[1] where sets can change under element insertions and deletions; here, p is a l-bit prime number and l is a security parameter. If $M = \sum_{i=1}^{m} |S_i|$, then the total space complexity needed to store D is $O(m + M)$. The supported class of queries is any set-operation formula over a subset of the sets S_i, consisting of unions and intersections.

In this section we present the scheme algorithms for original setup and updates. The basic idea is to use the ECRH construction from Section 2 to represent sets S_i by the hash values $h(\mathcal{C}_{S_i})$ of their characteristic polynomials. For the rest of the paper, we will refer to value $h(\mathcal{C}_{S_i})$ as h_i, implying the hash value of the characteristic polynomial of

---

[1] Actually elements must come from $\mathbb{Z} \setminus \{s, 1, ..., m\}$, because s is the secret key in our construction and the m smallest integers modulo p will be used for numbering the sets.

the i-th set of D or the i-th set involved in a query, when obvious from the context. Recall that a hash value h consists of two group elements, $h = (f, f')$. We will refer to the first element of h_i as f_i, i.e., for a set $S_i = (x_1, ..., x_n)$, $f_i = g^{\prod_{j=1}^{n}(x_j+s)}$ and likewise for f_i'.

During the setup phase, the source computes the m hash values $h(C_{S_i})$ of sets S_i and then deploys an authentication mechanism over them, that will provide proofs of integrity for these values under some public digest that corresponds to the current state of D. This mechanism should be able to provide proofs for statements of the form "h_i is hash of the i-th set of the current version of D."

While there exist multiple such mechanisms in the literature (e.g., digital signatures, Merkle trees), here we will be using *accumulation trees*, introduced in [25] (and specifically in the bilinear group setting in [26]) as an alternative to Merkle trees that yields constant time updates and constant size proofs. In our construction, we use the accumulation tree to verify the correctness of hash values for the sets involved in a particular query. On a high level, the public tree digest guarantees the integrity of the hash values and in turn the hash values validate the elements of the sets.

An accumulation tree AT is a tree with $\lceil 1/\epsilon \rceil$ levels, where $0 < \epsilon < 1$ is a parameter chosen upon setup, and m leaves. Each internal node of T has degree $O(m^{\epsilon})$ and T has constant height for a fixed ϵ. Intuitively, it can be seen as a "flat" version of Merkle trees. Each leaf node contains the (first half of the) hash value of a set S_i and each internal node contains the (first half of the) hash of the values of its children. Since, under our ECRH construction, hash values are elements in $\mathbb{G}$ we will need to map these bilinear group elements to values in $\mathbb{Z}_p^*$ at each level of the tree before they can be used as inputs for the computation of hash values of higher level nodes. This can be achieved by a function ϕ that outputs a bit level description of hash values under some canonical representation of $\mathbb{G}$ (see below). The setup and update algorithms of our ADS construction can be seen in Figure 2:

The runtime of setup is $O(m + M)$ as computation of the hash values using the secret key takes $O(M)$ and the tree construction has access complexity $O(m)$ for post-order traversal of the tree as it has constant height and it has m leaves. Similarly, update and refresh have access complexity of $O(1)$.

Remark 1. Observe that the only algorithms that make explicit use of the trapdoor s are **update** and **setup** when updating hash value efficiently. Both algorithm can be executed without s (given only the public key) in time $\tilde{O}(D)$.

4 Query Responding and Verification

As mentioned before, we wish to achieve two verification properties: *integrity-of-data* and *integrity-of-computation*. We begin with our algorithms for achieving the first property, and then present two protocols for achieving the second one, i.e., for validating the correctness of a single set operation (union or intersection). These algorithms will be used as subroutines by our final query responding and verification processes.

Algorithm $\{sk, pk\} \leftarrow$**genkey**(1^l). The owner of D runs the sampling algorithm for our ECRH, chooses an injective[2] function $\phi : \mathbb{G} \setminus \{1_{\mathbb{G}}\} \rightarrow \mathbb{Z}_p^*$, and outputs $\{\phi, pk, sk\}$.

Algorithm $\{auth(D_0), d_0\} \leftarrow$ **setup**(D_0, sk, pk). The owner of D computes values $f_i = g^{\prod_{x \in S_i}(x_i + s)}$ for sets S_i. Following that, he constructs an accumulation tree AT over values f_i. A parameter $0 < \epsilon < 1$ is chosen. For each node v of the tree, its value $d(v)$ is computed as follows. If v is a leaf corresponding to f_i then $d(v) = f_i^{(i+s)}$ where the number i is used to denote that this is the i-th set in D (recall that, by definition, sets S_i contain elements in $[m + 1, ..., p - 1]$). Otherwise, if $N(v)$ is the set of children of v, then $d(v) = g^{\prod_{u \in N(v)}(\phi(d(u)) + s)}$ (note that the exponent is the characteristic polynomial of the set containing the elements $\phi(d(u))$ for all $u \in N(v)$). Finally, the owner outputs $\{auth(D_0) = f_1, ..., f_t, d(v) \; \forall v \in AT, d_0 = d(r)\}$ where r is the root of AT.

Algorithm$\{auth(D_{h+1}), d_{h+1}, upd\} \leftarrow$ **update**$(u, auth(D_h), d_h, sk, pk)$. For the case of insertion of element x in the i-th set, the owner computes $x + s$ and $\eta = f_i^{x+s}$. For deletion of element x from S_i, the owner computes $(x + s)^{-1}$ and $\eta = f_i^{(x+s)^{-1}}$. Let v_0 be the leaf of AT that corresponds to the i-th set and $v_1, ..., v_{\lceil 1/\epsilon \rceil}$ the node path from v_0 to r. Then, the owner sets $d'(v_0) = \eta$ and for $j = 1, ..., \lceil 1/\epsilon \rceil$ he sets $d'(v_j) = d(v_j)^{(\phi(d'(v_{j-1})) + s)(\phi(d(v_{j-1})) + s)^{-1}}$. He replaces node values in $auth(D_h)$ with the corresponding computed ones to produce $auth(D_{h+1})$. He then sets $upd = d(v_0), ..., d(r), x, i, b$ where b is a bit denoting the type of operation and sends upd to server. Finally, he publishes updated digest $d_{h+1} = d'(r)$.

Algorithm $\{D_{h+1}, auth(D_{h+1}), d_{h+1}\} \leftarrow$ **refresh**$(u, D_h, auth(D_h), d_h, upd, pk)$. The server replaces values in $auth(D_h)$ with the corresponding ones in upd, d_h with d_{h+1} and updates set S_i accordingly.

Fig. 2. Setup and update operations

Authenticity of Hash Values. We present two algorithms that make use of the accumulation tree deployed over the hash values of S_i in order to prove and verify that the sets used for answering are the ones specified by the query description.

Algorithm $\pi \leftarrow QueryTree(pk, d, i, auth(D))$ The algorithm computes proof of membership for value x_i validating that it is the i-th leaf of the accumulation tree. Let v_0 be the i-th node of the tree an $v_1, ..., v_{\lceil 1/\epsilon \rceil}$ be the node path from v_0 to the root r. For $j = 1, ..., \lceil 1/\epsilon \rceil$ let $\gamma_j = g^{\prod_{u \in N(v_j) \setminus \{v_{j-1}\}}(\phi(d(u)) + s)}$ (note that the exponent is the characteristic polynomial of the set containing the elements $\phi(d(u))$ for all $u \in N(v)$ except for node v_{j-1}). The algorithm outputs $\pi := (d(v_0), \gamma_1), ..., (d(v_{\lceil 1/\epsilon \rceil - 1}), \gamma_{\lceil 1/\epsilon \rceil})$.

Algorithm $\{0, 1\} \leftarrow VerifyTree(pk, d, i, x, \pi)$. The algorithm verifies membership of x as the i-th leaf of the tree by checking the equalities: (i) $e(d(v_1), g) = e(x, g^i g^s)$; (ii) for $j = 1, ..., \lceil 1/\epsilon \rceil - 1$, $e(d(v_j), g) = e(\gamma_j, g^{\phi(d(v_{j-1}))} g^s)$; (iii) $e(d, g) = e(\gamma_{\lceil 1/\epsilon \rceil}, g^{\phi(d(v_{\lceil 1/\epsilon \rceil - 1}))} g^s)$. If none of them fails, it outputs accept.

The above algorithms make use of the property that for any two polynomials $A(r), B(r)$ with $C(r) := A(r) \cdot B(r)$, for our ECRH construction it must be that $e(f(C), g) = e(f(A), f(B))$. In particular for sets, this allows the construction of a

---

[2] The restriction that ϕ is injective is in fact too strong; it suffices that it is collision-resistant. A good candidate for ϕ is a CRHF that hash the bit-level description of an element of $\mathbb{G}$ to $\mathbb{Z}_p^*$.

single-element proof for set membership (or subset more generally). For example, for element $x_1 \in X = \{x_1, ..., x_n\}$ this witness is the value $g^{\prod_{i=2}^{n}(x_i+s)}$. Intuitively, for the integrity of a hash value, the proof consists of such set membership proofs starting from the desired hash value all the way to the root of the tree, using the sets of children of each node. The following lemma (stated in [26], for an accumulation tree based on bilinear accumulators; it extends naturally to our ECRH) holds for these algorithms:

Lemma 3 ([26]). *Under the q-SBDH assumption, for any adversarially chosen proof π with (j, x^*, π) s.t. VerifyTree$(pk, d, j, x^*, \pi) \to 1$, it must be that x^* is the j-th element of the tree except for negligible probability. Algorithm QueryTree has access complexity $O(m^\epsilon \log m)$ and outputs a proof of $O(1)$ group elements and algorithm VerifyTree has access complexity $O(1)$.*

Algorithms for the Single Operation Case. The algorithms presented here are used to verify that a set operation was performed correctly, by checking a number of relations between the hash values of the input and output hash values, that are related to the type of set operation. The authenticity of these hash values is not necessarily established. Since these algorithms will be called as sub-routines by the general proof construction and verification algorithms, this property should be handled at that level.

Intersection. Let $I = S_1 \cap ... \cap S_t$ be the wanted operation. Set I is uniquely identified by the following two properties: **(Subset)** $I \subseteq S_i$ for all S_i and **(Complement Disjointness)** $\cap_{i=1}^{t}(S_i \setminus I) = \emptyset$. The first captures that all elements of I appear in all of S_i and the second that no elements are left out.

Regarding the subset property, we argue as follows. Let X, S be sets s.t. $S \subseteq X$ and $|X| = n$. Observe that $\mathcal{C}_S | \mathcal{C}_X$, i.e. $\mathcal{C}_X$ can be written as $\mathcal{C}_X = \mathcal{C}_S(r)Q(r)$ where $Q(r) \in \mathbb{Z}_p[r]$ is $\mathcal{C}_{X \setminus S}$. The above can be verified by checking the equality: $e(f_S, W) = e(f_X, g)$ where $W = g^{Q(s)}$. If we denote with W_i the values $g^{\mathcal{C}_{S_i \setminus I}(s)}$, the subset property can be verified by checking the above relation for I w.r.t each of S_i.

For the second property, we make use of the fact that $\mathcal{C}_{S_i \setminus I}(r)$ are disjoint for $i = 1, ..., t$ if and only if there exist polynomials $q_i(r)$ s.t. $\sum_{i=1}^{t} \mathcal{C}_{S_i \setminus I}(r)q_i(r) = 1$, i.e. the gcd of the characteristic polynomials of the the complements of I w.r.t S_i should be 1. Based on the above, we propose the algorithms in Figure 3 for the case of a single intersection:

Algorithm$\{\Pi, f_I\} \leftarrow$ *proveIntersection*$(S_1, ..., S_t, I, h_1, ..., h_t, h_I, pk)$.
1. Compute values $W_i = g^{\mathcal{C}_{S_i \setminus I}(s)}$.
2. Compute polynomials $q_i(r)$ s.t. $\sum_{i=1}^{t} \mathcal{C}_{S_i \setminus I}(r)q_i(r) = 1$ and values $F_i = g^{q_i(s)}$.
3. Let $\Pi = \{(W_1, F_1), ..., (W_t, F_t)\}$ and output $\{\Pi, f_I\}$.

Algorithm$\{$accept,reject$\} \leftarrow$ *verifyIntersection*$(f_1, ..., f_t, \Pi, f_I, pk)$.
1. Check the following equalities. If any of them fails output reject, otherwise accept:
   - $e(f_I, W_i) = e(f_i, g)$ $\forall i = 1, ..., t$
   - $\prod_{i=1}^{t} e(W_i, F_i) = e(g, g)$.

Fig. 3. Intersection proof construction and verification

Union. Now we want to provide a similar method for proving the validity of a union operation of some sets. Again we denote set $U = S_1 \cup ... \cup S_t$ and let h_i be the corresponding hash values as above. The union set U is uniquely characterized by the following two properties: **(Superset)** $S_i \subseteq U$ for all S_i and **(Membership)** For each element $x_i \in U$, $\exists j \in [t]$ s.t. $x_i \in S_j$. These properties can be verified, with values W_i, w_j for $i = 1, ...t$ and $j = 1, ..., |U|$ defined as above checking the following equalities (assuming h_U is the hash value of U):

$$e(f_i, W_i) = e(f_U, g) \qquad \forall i = 1, ..., t$$
$$e(g^{x_j} g^s, w_j) = e(f_U, g) \qquad \forall j = 1, ..., |U| \ .$$

The problem with this approach is that the number of equalities to be checked for the union case is linear to the number of elements in the output set. Such an approach would lead to an inefficient scheme for general operations (each intermediate union operation the verification procedure would be at least as costly as computing that intermediate result). Therefore, we are interested in restricting the number of necessary checks. In the following we provide a union argument that achieves this.

Our approach stems from the fundamental inclusion-exclusion principle of set theory. Namely for set $U = A \cup B$ it holds that $U = (A + B) \setminus (A \cap B)$ where $A + B$ is a simple concatenation of elements from sets A, B (allowing for multisets), or equivalently, $A + B = U \cup (A \cap B)$. Given the hash values h_A, h_B the above can be checked by the bilinear equality $e(f_A, f_B) = e(f_U, f_{A \cap B})$. Thus one can verify the correctness of h_U by checking a number of equalities independent of the size of U by checking that the above equality holds. In practice, our protocol for the union of two sets, consists of a proof for their intersection, followed by a check for this relation. Due to the extractability property of our ECRH, the fact that h_I is included in the proof acts as a proof-of-knowledge by the prover for the set I, hence we can remove the necessity to explicitly include I in the answer.

There is another issue to be dealt with. Namely that this approach does not scale well with the number of input sets for the union operation. To this end we will recursively apply our construction for two sets in pairs of sets until finally we have a single union output. Let us describe the semantics of a set union operation over t sets. For the rest of the section, without loss of generality, we assume $\exists k \in \mathbb{N}$ s.t. $2^k = t$, i.e., t is a power of 2. Let us define as $U_1^{(1)}, ..., U_{t/2}^{(1)}$ the sets $(S_1 \cup S_2), ..., (S_{t-1} \cup S_t)$. For set U it holds that $U = U_1 \cup ... \cup U_{t/2}$ due to the commutativity of the union operation.

All intermediate results $U_i^{(j)}$ will be represented by their hash values $h_{U_i^{(j)}}$ yielding a proof that is of size independent of their cardinality. One can use the intuition explained above, based on the inclusion-exclusion principle, in order to prove the correctness of (candidate) hash values $h_{U_i^{(1)}}$ corresponding to sets U_i and, following that, apply repeatedly pairwise union operations and provide corresponding arguments, until set U is reached. Semantically this corresponds to a binary tree $\mathcal{T}$ of height k with the original sets S_i at the t leaves (level 0), sets $U_i^{(1)}$ as defined above at level 1, and so on, with set U at the root at level k. Each internal node of the tree corresponds to a set resulting from the union operation over the sets of its two children nodes. In general we denote by $U_1^{(j)}, ..., U_{t/2^j}^{(j)}$ the sets appearing at level j. We propose the algorithms in Figure 4 for proof construction and verification for a single union.

We denote by A, B the two sets corresponding to the children nodes of each non-leaf node of $\mathcal{T}$, by U, I their union and intersection respectively and by F the final union output.

Algorithm$\{\Pi, f_F\} \leftarrow proveUnion(S_1, ..., S_t, U, h_1, ..., h_t, h_U, pk)$.

1. Initialize $\Pi = \emptyset$.
2. For each $U_i^{(j)}$ of level $j = 1, ..., k$, corresponding to sets U, I as defined above, compute U, I and values h_U, h_I. Append values h_U, h_I to Π.
3. For each $U_i^{(j)}$ of level $j = 1, ..., k$, run algorithm $proveIntersection(A, B, h_A, h_B, pk)$ to receive (Π_I, f_I) and append Π_I to Π. Observe that sets A, B and their hash values have been computed in the previous step.
4. Output $\{\Pi, f_F\}$. (h_F has already been computed at step (2) but is provided explicitly for ease of notation).

Algorithm$\{accept, reject\} \leftarrow verifyUnion(f_1, ..., f_t, \Pi, f_F, pk)$.

1. For each intersection argument $\{\Pi_I, f_I\} \in \Pi$ run $verifyIntersection(f_A, f_B, \Pi_I, f_I, pk)$. If for any of them it outputs reject, output reject.
2. For each node of $\mathcal{T}$ check the equality $e(f_A, f_B) = e(f_U, f_I)$. If any check fails, reject.
3. For each hash value $h_U \in \Pi$ check $e(f_U, g^a) = e(f_U', g)$ and likewise for values h_I. If any check fails output reject, otherwise accept.

Fig. 4. Union proof construction and verification

Analysis of the Algorithms. Let $N = \sum_{i=1}^{t} |S_i|$ and $\delta = |I|$ or $|F|$ respectively, depending on the type of operations. For both cases, the runtimes of the algorithms are $O(N \log^2 N \log \log N \log t)$ for proof construction and $O(t + \delta)$ for verification and the proofs contain $O(t)$ bilinear group elements. A proof of the complexity analysis for these algorithms can be found in the full version of our paper [13].

It can be shown that these algorithms, along with appropriately selected proofs-of-validity for their input hash values can be used to form a complete ADS scheme for the case of a single set operation. Here however, these algorithms will be executed as subroutines of the general proof construction and verification process for our ADS construction for more general queries, presented in the next section. In [13], we present similar algorithms for the set difference operation.

Hierarchical Set-Operation Queries. We now use the algorithms we presented in the previous subsection to define appropriate algorithms **query**, **verify** for our ADS scheme. A hierarchical set-operations computation can be abstracted as a tree, the nodes of which contain sets of elements. For a query q over t sets $S_1, ..., S_t$, corresponding to such a computation, each leaf of the tree $\mathcal{T}$ contains an input set for q and each internal node is related to a set operation (union or intersection) and contains the set that results to applying this set operation on its children nodes. Finally the root of the tree contains the output set of q. In order to maintain the semantics of a tree, we assume that each input is treated as a distinct set, i.e., t is not the number of different sets that appear in q, but the total number of involved sets counting multiples. Another way to see the above, would be to interpret t as the length of the set-operations formula corresponding to q.[3]

Without loss of generality, assume q is defined over the t first sets of D. For reasons of simplicity we describe the mode of operation of our algorithms for the case where all sets S_i are at the same level of the computation, i.e., all leafs of $\mathcal{T}$ are at the same level. The necessary modifications in order to explicitly cover the case where original sets occur higher in $\mathcal{T}$, are implied in a straight-forward manner from the following analysis, since any set S_i encountered at an advanced stage of the process can be treated in the exact same manner as the sets residing at the tree leafs. The algorithms for query processing and verification of our ADS scheme are described in Figure 5.

Each answer from the server is accompanied by a proof that includes a number of hash values for all sets computed during answer computation, the exact structure of which depends on the type of operations. The verification process is essentially split in two parts. First, the client verifies the validity of the hash values of the sets used as input (i.e., the validity of sets specified in q) and subsequently, that the hash values included in the proof respect the relations corresponding to the operations in q, all the way from the input hash values to the hash value of the returned answer α.

Intuitively, with the algorithms from the previous section a verifier can, by checking a small number of bilinear equations, gain trust on the hash value of a set computed by a single set operation. The proof for q is constructed by putting together smaller proofs for all the internal nodes in $\mathcal{T}$. Let Π be a concatenation of single union and single intersection proofs that respect q, i.e., each node in $\mathcal{T}$ corresponds to an appropriate type of proof in Π. The hash value of each intermediate result will also be included in the proof and these values at level i will serve as inputs for the verification process at level $i+1$. The reason the above strategy will yield a secure scheme is that the presence of the hash values serves as proof by a cheating adversary that he has "knowledge" of the sets corresponding to these partial results. If one of these sets is not honestly computed, the extractability property allows an adversary to either attack the collision-resistance of the ECRH or break the q-SBDH assumption directly, depending on the format of the polynomial used to cheat.

Observe that the size of the proof Π is $O(t + \delta)$. This follows from the fact that the t proofs π_i consist of a constant number of group elements and Π is of size $O(t)$ since each of the $O(|T|) = O(t)$ nodes participates in a single operation. Also, there are δ coefficients b_i therefore the total size of Π is $O(t + \delta)$. The runtime of the verification algorithm is $O(t + \delta)$ as steps 2,3 takes $O(t)$ operations and steps 4,5 take $O(\delta)$. A proof of the complexity analysis for these algorithms can be found in the full version of our paper. We can now state the following theorem that is our main result (full proof in [13]).

Theorem 1. *The scheme $\mathcal{AHSO} = \{$**genkey**, **setup**, **query**, **verify**, **update**, **refresh**$\}$ is a dynamic $\mathcal{ADS}$ scheme for queries q from the class of hierarchical set-operations formulas involving unions, intersections and set difference operations. Assuming a data structure D consisting of m sets $S_1, ..., S_m$, and a hierarchical set-operations query q involving t of them, computable with asymptotic complexity $O(N)$ with answer size*

---

[3] More generally q can be seen as a DAG. Here, for simplicity of presentation we assume that all sets S_i participate only once in q hence it corresponds to a tree.

D is the most recent version of the data structure and let $auth(D), d$ be the corresponding authenticated values and public digest. Let q be a set-operation formula with nested unions and intersections and $\mathcal{T}$ be the corresponding semantics tree. For each internal node $v \in \mathcal{T}$ let $R_1, ..., R_{t_v}$ denote the sets corresponding to its children nodes and O be the set that is produced by executing the operation in v (union or intersection) over R_i. Finally, denote by $\alpha = x_1, ..., x_\delta$ the output set of the root of $\mathcal{T}$.

Algorithm $\{\alpha, \Pi\} \leftarrow$ **query**$(q, D, auth(D), pk)$.

1. Initialize $\Pi = \emptyset$.
2. Compute proof-of-membership π_i for value f_i by running *Query-Tree*$(pk, d, i, auth(D))$ for $i \in [t]$ and append π_i, f_i to Π.
3. For each internal node $v \in \mathcal{T}$ (as parsed with a DFS traversal):
   - Compute set O and its hash value $h_O = h(\mathcal{C}_O)$.
   - If v corresponds to a set intersection, obtain Π_v by running *proveIntersection*$(R_1, ..., R_t, h_1, ..., h_t, O, h_O, pk)$. For each subset witness $W_i \in \Pi$ corresponding to polynomial $\mathcal{C}_{R_i \setminus O}$, compute values $\tilde{W}_i = g^{a\mathcal{C}_{R_i \setminus O}(s)}$. Let $\mathcal{W}_v = \{W_1, ..., W_{t_v}\}$. Append $\Pi_v, \mathcal{W}_v, h_O$ to Π.
   - If v corresponds to a set union, obtain Π_v by running *proveUnion*$(R_1, ..., R_t, h_1, ..., h_t, O, h_O, pk)$. Append Π_v, h_O to Π.
4. Append to Π the coefficients $(c_0, ..., c_\delta)$ of the polynomial $\mathcal{C}_\alpha$ (already computed at step 3) and output $\{\alpha, \Pi\}$.

Algorithm $\{$accept,reject$\} \leftarrow$ **verify**(q, α, Π, d, pk). For internal node $v \in \mathcal{T}$, let $\eta_1, ..., \eta_{t_v}$ denote the hash values of its children node sets $\in \Pi$ (for internal nodes at level 1, the values η_i are the values f_i).

1. Parse each hash value $h \in \Pi$ as $h = (f, f')$.
2. Verify the validity of values f_i. For each value $f_i \in \Pi$ run *VerifyTree*(pk, d, i, f_i, π_i). If it outputs reject for any of them, output reject and halt.
3. For each internal node $v \in \mathcal{T}$ (as parsed with a DFS traversal):
   - Check the equality $e(f_O, g^a) = e(g, f'_O)$. If it does not hold, reject and halt.
   - If v corresponds to a set intersection:
     (a) Run *verifyIntersection*$(\eta_1, ..., \eta_{t_v}, \Pi_v, f_O, pk)$, If it rejects, reject and halt.
     (b) For each pair $W_i, \tilde{W}_i \in \Pi_v$, check the equality $e(W_i, g^a) = e(\tilde{W}_i, g)$. If any of the checks fails, output reject and halt.
   - If v corresponds to a set union, run *verifyUnion*$(\eta_1, ..., \eta_{t_v}, \Pi_v, f_O, pk)$. If it outputs reject, output reject and halt.
4. Validate the correctness of coefficients **c**. Choose $z \leftarrow_R \mathbb{Z}_p^*$ and compare the values $\sum_{i=0}^{\delta} c_i z^i$ and $\prod_{i=1}^{\delta} (x_i + z)$. If they are not equivalent, output reject and halt.
5. Check the equality $e(\prod_{i=0}^{\delta} g^{c_i s^i}, g) = e(f_\alpha, g)$. If it holds output accept, otherwise reject.

Fig. 5. General set-operations proof construction and verification

δ, $\mathcal{AHSO}$ *has the following properties: (i)* correct *and* secure *under the q-SBDH and the q-PKE assumptions; (ii) the complexity of algorithm* **genkey** *is $O(|D|)$; (iii) that of* **setup** *is $O(m + |D|)$ (iv) that of* **query** *is $O(N \log^2 N \log \log N \log t + tm^\epsilon \log m)$ for $0 < \epsilon \leq 1$ and it yields proofs of $O(t + \delta)$ group elements; (v) that of* **verify** *is $O(t + \delta)$;*

(vi) and those of **update** *and* **refresh** *are* $O(1)$; *(vii) the authenticated data structure consists of* $O(m)$ *group elements; (viii) the public digest* d *is a single group element.*

Corollary 1. *If the server maintains a list of* m *fresh proofs* $\pi_1, ..., \pi_m$ *for the validity of values* f_i, **refresh** *has complexity* $O(m^{2\epsilon} \log m)$, *in order to update the* m^ϵ *proofs* π_i *affected by an update, and* **query** *has complexity* $O(N \log^2 N \log \log N \log t + t)$.

Corollary 2. *In a two-party setting, where only the source issues queries, proofs consist of* $O(t)$ *elements.*

Proof Sketch. Due to the interactive nature of the security game, extracting directly from a successful cheating adversary $\mathcal{A}$ is not possible. Recall however, that all algorithms of $\mathcal{AHSO}$ can be efficiently run with access to pk only. Hence the existence of $\mathcal{A}$ implies the existence of (non-interactive) $\mathcal{A}'$ that upon input pk, runs $\mathcal{A}$ internally providing perfect simulation of the security game and finally outputs the cheating tuple of $\mathcal{A}$. The proof accompanying this cheating answer consists of polynomially many hash values of our ECRH, therefore there exists corresponding extractor $\mathcal{E}'$ that upon the same input outputs the correct pre-image polynomials with overwhelming probability. We then proceed to show that each of these polynomials must be an associate of the characteristic polynomial of the correctly computed set at that point of the computation (or the q-SBDH can be broken). From this, it immediately follows that this holds also for set α^* hence, if it is not the correctly computed set corresponding to query q, the characteristic polynomial of the correctly computed set α and the characteristic polynomial of α^* form a collision for the ECRH. $\qquad\square$

References

[1] Atallah, M.J., Cho, Y., Kundu, A.: Efficient data authentication in an environment of untrusted third-party distributors. In: ICDE, pp. 696–704 (2008)

[2] Ateniese, G., De Cristofaro, E., Tsudik, G.: (If) size matters: Size-hiding private set intersection. In: Catalano, D., Fazio, N., Gennaro, R., Nicolosi, A. (eds.) PKC 2011. LNCS, vol. 6571, pp. 156–173. Springer, Heidelberg (2011)

[3] Backes, M., Fiore, D., Reischuk, R.M.: Verifiable delegation of computation on outsourced data. Cryptology ePrint Archive. Report 2013/469 (2013)

[4] Ben-Sasson, E., Chiesa, A., Genkin, D., Tromer, E., Virza, M.: Snarks for c: Verifying program executions succinctly and in zero knowledge. In: Canetti, R., Garay, J.A. (eds.) CRYPTO 2013, Part II. LNCS, vol. 8043, pp. 90–108. Springer, Heidelberg (2013)

[5] Berlekamp, E.R.: Factoring polynomials over large finite fields*. In: Proceedings of the Second ACM Symposium on Symbolic and Algebraic Manipulation, SYMSAC 1971, p. 223. ACM, New York (1971)

[6] Bitansky, N., Canetti, R., Chiesa, A., Tromer, E.: From extractable collision resistance to succinct non-interactive arguments of knowledge, and back again. In: ITCS, pp. 326–349 (2012)

[7] Bitansky, N., Canetti, R., Paneth, O., Rosen, A.: Indistinguishability obfuscation vs. auxiliary-input extractable functions: One must fall. Cryptology ePrint Archive, Report 2013/641 (2013)

[8] Blum, M., Evans, W.S., Gemmell, P., Kannan, S., Naor, M.: Checking the correctness of memories. Algorithmica 12(2/3), 225–244 (1994)

[9] Boneh, D., Boyen, X.: Short signatures without random oracles. In: Cachin, C., Camenisch, J.L. (eds.) EUROCRYPT 2004. LNCS, vol. 3027, pp. 56–73. Springer, Heidelberg (2004)

[10] Boneh, D., Waters, B.: Conjunctive, subset, and range queries on encrypted data. In: Vadhan, S.P. (ed.) TCC 2007. LNCS, vol. 4392, pp. 535–554. Springer, Heidelberg (2007)

[11] Boyle, E., Pass, R.: Limits of extractability assumptions with distributional auxiliary input. Cryptology ePrint Archive. Report 2013/703 (2013)

[12] Camenisch, J.L., Lysyanskaya, A.: Dynamic accumulators and application to efficient revocation of anonymous credentials. In: Yung, M. (ed.) CRYPTO 2002. LNCS, vol. 2442, pp. 61–76. Springer, Heidelberg (2002)

[13] Canetti, R., Paneth, O., Papadopoulos, D., Triandopoulos, N.: Verifiable set operations over outsourced databases. Cryptology ePrint Archive. Report 2013/724 (2013)

[14] Chatterjee, S., Menezes, A.: On cryptographic protocols employing asymmetric pairings - the role of psi revisited. Discrete Applied Mathematics 159(13), 1311–1322 (2011)

[15] Chung, K.-M., Kalai, Y.T., Liu, F.-H., Raz, R.: Memory delegation. In: Rogaway, P. (ed.) CRYPTO 2011. LNCS, vol. 6841, pp. 151–168. Springer, Heidelberg (2011)

[16] Damgård, I.B.: Towards practical public key systems secure against chosen ciphertext attacks. In: Feigenbaum, J. (ed.) CRYPTO 1991. LNCS, vol. 576, pp. 445–456. Springer, Heidelberg (1992)

[17] Dwork, C., Naor, M., Rothblum, G.N., Vaikuntanathan, V.: How efficient can memory checking be? In: Reingold, O. (ed.) TCC 2009. LNCS, vol. 5444, pp. 503–520. Springer, Heidelberg (2009)

[18] Freedman, M.J., Nissim, K., Pinkas, B.: Efficient private matching and set intersection. In: Cachin, C., Camenisch, J.L. (eds.) EUROCRYPT 2004. LNCS, vol. 3027, pp. 1–19. Springer, Heidelberg (2004)

[19] Goodrich, M.T., Tamassia, R., Triandopoulos, N.: Efficient authenticated data structures for graph connectivity and geometric search problems. Algorithmica 60(3), 505–552 (2011)

[20] Groth, J.: Short pairing-based non-interactive zero-knowledge arguments. In: Abe, M. (ed.) ASIACRYPT 2010. LNCS, vol. 6477, pp. 321–340. Springer, Heidelberg (2010)

[21] Kissner, L., Song, D.: Privacy-preserving set operations. In: Shoup, V. (ed.) CRYPTO 2005. LNCS, vol. 3621, pp. 241–257. Springer, Heidelberg (2005)

[22] Martel, C.U., Nuckolls, G., Devanbu, P.T., Gertz, M., Kwong, A., Stubblebine, S.G.: A general model for authenticated data structures. Algorithmica 39(1), 21–41 (2004)

[23] Naor, M., Nissim, K.: Certificate revocation and certificate update. IEEE Journal on Selected Areas in Communications 18(4), 561–570 (2000)

[24] Nguyen, L.: Accumulators from bilinear pairings and applications. In: Menezes, A. (ed.) CT-RSA 2005. LNCS, vol. 3376, pp. 275–292. Springer, Heidelberg (2005)

[25] Papamanthou, C., Tamassia, R., Triandopoulos, N.: Authenticated hash tables. In: ACM CCS, pp. 437–448 (2008)

[26] Papamanthou, C., Tamassia, R., Triandopoulos, N.: Optimal verification of operations on dynamic sets. In: Rogaway, P. (ed.) CRYPTO 2011. LNCS, vol. 6841, pp. 91–110. Springer, Heidelberg (2011)

[27] Parno, B., Howell, J., Gentry, C., Raykova, M.: Pinocchio: Nearly practical verifiable computation. In: IEEE SP Symposium, pp. 238–252 (2013)

[28] Preparata, F., Sarwate, D., I. U. A. U.-C. C. S. LAB: Computational Complexity of Fourier Transforms Over Finite Fields. DTIC (1976)

[29] Tamassia, R.: Authenticated data structures. In: Di Battista, G., Zwick, U. (eds.) ESA 2003. LNCS, vol. 2832, pp. 2–5. Springer, Heidelberg (2003)

[30] Yang, Y., Papadias, D., Papadopoulos, S., Kalnis, P.: Authenticated join processing in outsourced databases. In: SIGMOD Conference, pp. 5–18 (2009)

[31] Yiu, M.L., Lin, Y., Mouratidis, K.: Efficient verification of shortest path search via authenticated hints. In: ICDE, pp. 237–248 (2010)

[32] Zheng, Q., Xu, S., Ateniese, G.: Efficient query integrity for outsourced dynamic databases. IACR Cryptology ePrint Archive, 2012:493 (2012)

Verifiable Oblivious Storage

Daniel Apon, Jonathan Katz, Elaine Shi, and Aishwarya Thiruvengadam

University of Maryland, College Park, MD 20742, USA
{dapon,jkatz,elaine,aish}@cs.umd.edu

Abstract. We formalize the notion of *Verifiable Oblivious Storage* (VOS),
where a client outsources the storage of data to a server while ensuring
data confidentiality, access pattern privacy, and integrity and freshness
of data accesses. VOS generalizes the notion of Oblivious RAM (ORAM)
in that it allows the server to perform computation, and also explicitly
considers data integrity and freshness.

We show that allowing server-side computation enables us to construct
asymptotically more efficient VOS schemes whose bandwidth overhead
cannot be matched by any ORAM scheme, due to a known lower bound
by Goldreich and Ostrovsky. Specifically, for large block sizes we can construct a VOS scheme with constant bandwidth per query; further, answering queries requires only poly-logarithmic server computation. We
describe applications of VOS to Dynamic Proofs of Retrievability, and
RAM-model secure multi-party computation.

1 Introduction

Oblivious RAM (ORAM) is a notion first proposed by Goldreich and Ostrovsky [20] in the context of protecting software from piracy. They consider an
application in which a trusted CPU wishes to hide its memory-access patterns
from an attacker who can view (and possibly modify) the entire contents of
memory. Recently, as cloud computing has gained in popularity, ORAM has
been recast as a means to securely outsource storage to an untrusted server,
while hiding access patterns from the server.

In this paper, we propose Verifiable Oblivious Storage (VOS), which generalizes the notion of ORAM by allowing the storage medium to perform computation. In addition, it also explicitly incorporates notions of integrity and freshness.
We will refer to integrity and freshness as verifiability in this paper.

Formally Defining VOS. Our first contribution is to formally define VOS,
and to differentiate the notion of VOS from ORAM. While we are the first to
formalize the VOS notion, VOS has implicitly been used by other researchers
earlier, often being referred to as ORAM. For example, Williams and Sion [35]
recently proposed a scheme that improves round-complexity to $O(1)$ — since
their scheme leverages server-side computation, it is implicitly a VOS scheme.

An important difference between VOS and ORAM schemes is that VOS
schemes can be constructed to achieve asymptotically better bandwidth overhead than what can be achieved by any ORAM scheme. This is because all

H. Krawczyk (Ed.): PKC 2014, LNCS 8383, pp. 131–148, 2014.

ORAM schemes are subject to a well-known lower bound result by Goldreich and Ostrovsky [20]. This result, however, does not apply to VOS.

Several applications where ORAM was previously employed can immediately achieve asymptotic bandwidth savings if we simply replace the ORAM with a VOS construction. For example, we know from prior work that RAM-model secure multi-party computation [24] and Dynamic Proofs of Retrievability [9] can be built using ORAM as a building block. In both these applications, the party storing data (or a share of the data) can perform computation. By replacing the underlying ORAM with a VOS in these constructions [9,24], we can immediately obtain asymptotic bandwidth savings as illustrated in Section 5.

Asymptotically Efficient VOS Construction. We show that, by allowing server-side computation, VOS schemes can be constructed that beat the known logarithmic lower bound on the bandwidth cost for any ORAM scheme [20]. Specifically, we show that there exists a VOS scheme with block size $\beta = \hat{\Omega}(\lambda)$ (where λ is the security parameter) having $O(\beta)$ bandwidth cost for reading or writing a block; this scheme has $O(\beta)$ client-side storage, and uses only $O(1)$ roundtrips and requires only $O(\beta \cdot \text{poly} \log n) \cdot \text{poly}(\lambda)$ server-side computation per data access. This is asymptotically better than what any ORAM scheme can hope to achieve since, due to the lower bound by Goldreich and Ostrovsky, any ORAM scheme must have bandwidth cost $\Omega(\beta \log n)$ to read or write a block of β bits. *Note that this lower bound holds regardless of the block size β.*

1.1 Technical Highlight

Generic ORAM-to-VOS Compiler in the Semi-honest Model. To construct efficient VOS schemes, we rely on fully homomorphic encryption (FHE) to encrypt and outsource the entire ORAM memory, as well as the ORAM client's secret state. The server can now perform computation on behalf of the client, without learning any secrets. The only occasion when the server needs to contact the client is to seek the client's help to decrypt the next physical address or sequence of physical addresses to read or write. The use of FHE or PIR to outsource the ORAM client's computation has been mentioned in earlier works [16,26]. The main challenge, however, is *how to ensure security when the server is malicious, and may arbitrarily deviate from the prescribed computation.*

Generic ORAM-to-VOS Compiler in the Malicious Model. Achieving security against a malicious server is much trickier in the VOS setting than in ORAM. While ORAM achieves integrity and freshness in a straightforward way by employing standard storage integrity techniques such as message authentication codes and Merkle hash trees, in VOS, we need to worry about a server that can arbitrarily deviate from the prescribed computation.

Naive applications of well-known techniques such as SNARKS [3,4,15] result in server computation that is linear in the size of the dataset. Instead, we leverage efficient Verifiable RAM computation (VC-RAM) to enforce honest server behavior. This allows us to achieve sublinear server computation. In VC-RAM, a client outsources a large memory array to a server in a preprocessing step. Afterwards in an online stage, the client specifies a sequence of inputs, and asks the server to compute a RAM program over the outsourced memory array and the inputs. Each query made by the client can result in updates to the server's memory array. VC-RAM allows a client to verify the result of these RAM computations, and meanwhile, the server's computation overhead is sublinear (in the data size) for sublinear-time queries.

Although VC-RAM has been informally mentioned in earlier works [2,4,7], we make the contribution of explicitly formalizing *stateful* VC-RAM (for repeated queries) and its security. We also present an efficient VC-RAM scheme with constant proof size and prover computation that is comparable to the run-time of the RAM program (as opposed to the dataset size).

Non-generic Optimizations for Specific Schemes. We then apply these techniques to two existing ORAM schemes, the Path ORAM [33] and the Hierarchical ORAM by Goodrich and Mitzenmacher [21] that was later improved by Kushilevitz et al. [25]. The resulting VOS schemes are referred to as Path VOS and Hierarchical VOS respectively.

Applying Verifiable RAM Computation (VC-RAM) straight out-of-the-box is not sufficient to achieve the claimed asymptotic bounds for the Path VOS. We show how to tailor our VC-RAM techniques for the Path VOS to shave a $O(\log n)$ factor off the server computation. Similarly, for the hierarchical VOS, we propose rebalancing techniques that can shave poly log log n to log n factors from the bandwidth cost, at increased (but still sublinear) server computation.

While the Path VOS is asymptotically better than the hierarchical VOS, the hierarchical VOS is necessary for our dynamic PoR application, since the Path VOS does not satisfy the next-read pattern hiding property [9].

1.2 Related Work

Oblivious RAM (ORAM) was first proposed by Goldreich and Ostrovsky [20], and later improved in a series of works [13, 14, 16, 19, 21–23, 25, 27–30, 32–36]. Recently, ORAM has been used in outsourcing storage [21,34,36], and in secure two-party computation to achieve sublinear amortized cost [16,24].

ORAM with implicit server computation has appeared in several works [16, 35], while still being referred to as ORAM. Williams and Sion rely on server-side computation to achieve a single-round ORAM scheme [35]. Their scheme ensures privacy against a malicious server but not integrity and freshness and has an asymptotic bandwidth cost of $\tilde{O}(\beta \log^2 n)$. In comparison, our VOS scheme is asymptotically more efficient, and ensures both privacy and integrity/freshness against a malicious server. Gentry et al. [16] proposed using homomorphic encryption to improve ORAM bandwidth cost. However, their scheme is only secure in the semi-honest model, and is also asymptotically more expensive in bandwidth than our construction. Mayberry et al. also proposed to leverage PIR techniques in combination with ORAM [26]. They too are implicitly using VOS; their scheme is not secure in the malicious model, and is asymptotically less efficient than our construction.

Private Information Retrieval (PIR) [6, 11, 12, 18] allows a client to access a dataset on the server obliviously. Single-server PIR techniques can achieve $O(\beta)$ bandwidth cost per query using FHE techniques [6] for large enough block sizes β. However, single-server PIR requires server computation that is linear in the size of the dataset. Also, PIR works for public datasets; in VOS, we consider a private dataset owned by the client, which is not exposed to the server.

2   Definitions of Verifiable Oblivious Storage

We use $((c\_out, c\_state), (s\_out, s\_state)) \leftarrow \mathsf{protocol}((c\_in, c\_state), (s\_in, s\_state))$ to denote a (stateful) protocol between a client and server, where c_in and c_out are the client's input and output; s_in and s_out are the server's input and output; and c_state and s_state are the client and server's states before and after the protocol.

We define the notion of *Verifiable Oblivious Storage* (VOS), in which a client outsources the storage of data to a server while ensuring privacy of the data and verifiability and obliviousness of access to that data.

Definition 1 (Verifiable Oblivious Storage). *A Verifiable Oblivious Storage (VOS) scheme consists of the following interactive protocols between a client and a server.*

- $((\bot, z), (\bot, Z)) \leftarrow \mathsf{Setup}(1^\lambda, (D, \bot), (\bot, \bot))$: An interactive protocol where the client's input is a memory array $D[1..n]$ where each memory *block* has bit-length β; and the server's input is $\bot$. At the end of the Setup protocol, the client has secret state z, and server's state is Z (which typically encodes the memory array D).
- $((\mathsf{data}, z'), (\bot, Z')) \leftarrow \mathsf{Access}((\mathsf{op}, z), (\bot, Z))$: To access data, the client starts in state z, with an input op where $\mathsf{op} := (\mathsf{read}, ind)$ or $\mathsf{op} := (\mathsf{write}, ind, \mathsf{data})$; the server starts in state Z, and has no input. In a correct execution of the protocol, the client's output data is the current value of the memory D at location ind (for writes, the output is the old value of $D[ind]$ before the write takes place). The client and server also update their states to z' and Z' respectively. The client outputs $\mathsf{data} := \bot$ if the protocol execution aborted.

We say that a VOS scheme is correct, if for any initial memory $D \in \{0, 1\}^{\beta n}$, for any operation sequence $\mathsf{op}_1, \mathsf{op}_2, \ldots, \mathsf{op}_m$ where $m = \mathrm{poly}(\lambda)$, an $\mathsf{op} := (\mathsf{read}, ind)$ operation would always return the last value written to the logical location ind (except with negligible probability).

2.1   Security Definition

We adopt a standard simulation-based definition of secure computation [8], requiring that a real-world execution "simulate" an ideal-world (reactive) functionality $\mathcal{F}$. At an intuitive level, our definition captures the privacy and verifiability requirements for an honest client, in the presence of a malicious server.

Ideal World. We define an ideal functionality $\mathcal{F}$ that maintains an up-to-date version of the data D on behalf of the client, and answers the client's access queries.

- *Setup.* An environment $\mathcal{Z}$ gives an initial database D to the client. The client sends D to an ideal functionality $\mathcal{F}$. $\mathcal{F}$ notifies the ideal-world adversary $\mathcal{S}$ (of the setup operation, but not of the data contents D). The ideal-world adversary $\mathcal{S}$ says ok or abort to $\mathcal{F}$. $\mathcal{F}$ then says ok or $\perp$ to the client accordingly.
- *Access.* In each time step, the environment $\mathcal{Z}$ specifies an operation op := (read, ind) or op := (write, ind, data) as the client's input. The client sends op to $\mathcal{F}$. $\mathcal{F}$ notifies the ideal-world adversary $\mathcal{S}$ (without revealing to $\mathcal{S}$ the operation op). If $\mathcal{S}$ says ok to $\mathcal{F}$, $\mathcal{F}$ sends $D[ind]$ to the client, and updates $D[ind] :=$ data accordingly if this is a write operation. The client then forwards $D[ind]$ to the environment $\mathcal{Z}$. If $\mathcal{S}$ says abort to $\mathcal{F}$, $\mathcal{F}$ sends $\perp$ to the client.

Real World. In the real world, an environment $\mathcal{Z}$ gives an honest client a database D. The honest client runs the Setup protocol with the server $\mathcal{A}$. Then at each time step, $\mathcal{Z}$ specifies an input op := (read, ind) or op := (write, ind, data) to the client. The client then runs the Access protocol with the server. The environment $\mathcal{Z}$ gets the view of the adversary $\mathcal{A}$ after every operation. The client outputs to the environment the data fetched or $\perp$ (indicating abort).

Definition 2 (Simulation-based security: privacy + verifiability). *We say that a protocol $\Pi_{\mathcal{F}}$ securely computes the ideal functionality $\mathcal{F}$ if for any probabilistic polynomial-time real-world adversary (i.e., server) $\mathcal{A}$, there exists an ideal-world adversary $\mathcal{S}$, such that for all non-uniform, polynomial-time environment $\mathcal{Z}$, there exists a negligible function* negl *such that*

$$|\Pr[\text{REAL}_{\Pi_{\mathcal{F}},\mathcal{A},\mathcal{Z}}(\lambda) = 1] - \Pr[\text{IDEAL}_{\mathcal{F},\mathcal{S},\mathcal{Z}}(\lambda) = 1]| \leq \text{negl}(\lambda)$$

This definition is simulation-based [8] where the client is honest, and the server is corrupted. (The client is never malicious in our setting.) The definition also simultaneously captures *privacy* and *verifiability*. Intuitively, privacy ensures that the server cannot observe the data contents or the access pattern. Verifiability ensures that the client is guaranteed to read the correct data from the server — if the server happens to cheat, the client can detect it and abort the protocol.

3 ORAM to VOS: Generic Compilation Techniques

In this section, we describe how to generically transform any given ORAM scheme to an efficient VOS scheme. In Section 4, we give two specific VOS schemes - Path VOS and Hierarchical VOS. These are derived from the two classes of ORAM schemes, the hierarchical construction [20] and its variants [21, 23, 25, 29, 34–36], and the binary-tree scheme [30] and its variants [13, 16, 33].

3.1 Preliminary: Oblivious RAM

In this paper, we use a slightly different formalization of ORAM from that of Goldreich-Ostrovsky [20] to make notation simpler for our generic compiler.

An ORAM can be defined by a pair of algorithms ORAM := (Init, Next):

- $(D_o, st) \leftarrow \text{Init}(1^\lambda, D)$: Takes in storage array D containing n blocks each of bit length β, produces storage array D_o, and initial ORAM client state st.
- $(\text{out}, \{\text{raddr}\}, \{\text{waddr}\}, \{\text{data}\}, st) \leftarrow \text{Next}(\text{op}, st, \{\text{fetched}\})$: Each ORAM operation $\text{op} := (\text{read}, ind)$ or $\text{op} := (\text{write}, ind, \text{data})$ will proceed in *multiple rounds*. Each round will invoke the ORAM.Next algorithm with the following inputs: 1) current read/write operation op; 2) the (secret) ORAM client state st; and 3) a set of blocks $\{\text{fetched}\}$ fetched from the last round. If this is the first round for an operation op, this fetched set is empty by convention. The ORAM.Next function in turn outputs a set of addresses to read in the next round denoted $\{\text{raddr}\}$; a set of addresses $\{\text{waddr}\}$ and data $\{\text{data}\}$ to write in the next round; updates the client state st; and if this is the last round, ORAM.Next also outputs the block read out.

The Next algorithm performs one round of the ORAM client computation.

Our notation is explained in the table below:

st	secret ORAM client state	‖	$\{\text{raddr}\}$	physical addr to read from
ind	logical index of a block	‖	$\{\text{waddr}\}$	physical addr to write to
$\text{op} := (\text{read}, ind)$ or $\text{op} := (\text{write}, ind, \text{data})$	a read/write operation	‖	$\{\text{fetched}\}$	data blocks fetched from storage
out	the last logical block read	‖	$\{\text{data}\}$	data blocks to be written

Security is defined in terms of the inability of any PPT adversary to distinguish the access patterns generated by an honest execution of the ORAM client, from those output by a simulator that does not see the sequence of logical operations.

Definition 3 (ORAM security). *We say that an ORAM scheme is secure, if there exists a stateful simulator* Sim, *such that for any PPT adversary* $\mathcal{A}$,

$$\left| \Pr\left[\mathcal{A}^{O[st](\cdot)}(1^\lambda) = 1 \right] - \Pr\left[\mathcal{A}^{\text{Sim}(1^\lambda, m)}(1^\lambda) = 1 \right] \right| \leq \text{negl}(\lambda) \tag{1}$$

where m is the number of oracle queries made by the adversary $\mathcal{A}$; and $O[st](\cdot)$ denotes a stateful oracle O, with secret state st. The oracle O takes in an operation op *and outputs a sequence of read and write physical addresses. Formally,*

Oracle O:

Initialization. On input D containing n blocks each of β bits, initialize a storage array D_o containing n_o blocks each of size β_o. Initialize the set $\{\mathsf{fetched}\}$ to be an empty set. Run $st := \mathsf{ORAM.Init}(1^\lambda, n, \beta)$.

Data Access. On the j-th input op_j, $j \in \mathbb{N}$, perform the following:
- First, initialize the output array $\Gamma := \emptyset$.
- For rnd $= 1$ to R_j where R_j is the total number of rounds for the j-th operation[a]:
    - Run $(\mathsf{out}, \{\mathsf{raddr}\}, \{\mathsf{waddr}\}, \{\mathsf{data}\}, st) \leftarrow \mathsf{ORAM.Next}(\mathsf{op}, st, \{\mathsf{fetched}\})$
    - Let $D_o[\{\mathsf{waddr}\}] := \{\mathsf{data}\}$, and let $\{\mathsf{fetched}\} := D_o[\{\mathsf{raddr}\}]$.
    - Append $\{\mathsf{raddr}\}$ and $\{\mathsf{waddr}\}$ to the output set Γ.
- Finally, output Γ.

---

[a] In all known ORAM constructions, due to the obliviousness requirement, R_j is a public value determined by the ORAM scheme description itself, and does not depend on the input sequence.

We use $D_o[\{\mathsf{waddr}\}] := \{\mathsf{data}\}$ and $\{\mathsf{fetched}\} := D_o[\{\mathsf{raddr}\}]$ to denote writing $\{\mathsf{data}\}$ to a set of write addresses $\{\mathsf{waddr}\}$, and reading from a set of read addresses $\{\mathsf{raddr}\}$ respectively. We assume that $\{\mathsf{waddr}\}$ and $\{\mathsf{data}\}$ are ordered sets, and we simply write each block data into each waddr in the specified order.

Deterministic vs. Randomized ORAM. In general, the ORAM client algorithms Init and Next can be randomized. However, the Next algorithm can be made deterministic by choosing a PRF key k at random and including it in the client state st. Whenever Next requires random bits, this can be generated pseudorandomly from key k. If the randomized ORAM is secure, then the resulting ORAM with a deterministic Next algorithm is also secure due to the security of the PRF. Therefore, without loss of generality, in our generic ORAM-to-VOS compiler, we will assume an ORAM scheme with a deterministic Next algorithm.

3.2 Compilation in the Semi-honest Model

Intuition. The intuition is to have the client outsource the ORAM memory encrypted under an FHE scheme to the server. The client can then outsource all its computation to the server as well, since the server can homomorphically operate over the encrypted data. In this manner, the server only contacts the client whenever it is necessary for interaction during the computation.

ORAM-to-VOS Compiler in the Semi-honest Model. Figure 1 describes how to transform an ORAM scheme to a VOS scheme that is secure under a semi-honest server.

Theorem 1. *Let* $\mathsf{FHE} = (\mathsf{KeyGen}, \mathsf{Enc}, \mathsf{Dec}, \mathsf{Eval})$ *be a semantically secure FHE scheme and let* $\mathsf{ORAM} = (\mathsf{Init}, \mathsf{Next})$ *be a secure ORAM scheme. Then, the generic compiler in Figure 1 gives a Verifiable Oblivious Storage (VOS) construction secure under a semi-honest server.*

- Setup: Client runs $(pk, sk) \leftarrow$ FHE.KeyGen(1^λ). Client runs $(D_o, st) \leftarrow$ ORAM.Init$(1^\lambda, D)$.

  For $i = 1$ to $|D_o|$, the client computes $\overline{D_o}[i] :=$ FHE.Enc$_{pk}(D_o[i])$. The client also computes $\overline{st} :=$ FHE.Enc$_{pk}(st)$. Finally, the client sends $\left(pk, \{\overline{D_o}[i]\}_{i \in |D_o|}, \overline{st}\right)$ to the server.

- Access: For the j-th operation op, let R_j denote the number of ORAM rounds necessary for the j-th operation.

  First, the client encrypts $\overline{op} :=$ FHE$_{pk}(op)$ and sends it to the server.

  For rnd $= 1$ to R_j:

  - If this is not the first round, i.e., if rnd $\neq 1$, the server performs memory reads and writes: $\overline{D_o}[\{waddr\}] := \{\overline{data}\}$, and $\{\overline{fetched}\} := \overline{D_o}[\{raddr\}]$, where $\{raddr\}$ and $\{waddr\}$ are the read and write addresses returned by the client in the previous round, and data is the part of the FHE evaluation outcome in the previous round.
  - The server homomorphically evaluates the ORAM.Next circuit once[a]: $(\overline{out}, \{\overline{raddr}\}, \{\overline{waddr}\}, \{\overline{data}\}, \overline{st}) \leftarrow$ FHE.Eval(ORAM.Next$(\overline{op}, \overline{st}, \{\overline{fetched}\}))$
  - Server sends client $\{\overline{raddr}\}, \{\overline{waddr}\}$. The client decrypts them using sk, and sends the clear-text $\{raddr\}, \{waddr\}$ to the server.

  Finally, server sends $\overline{out}$ to the client, and the client decrypts it.

---

[a] The first round of the first operation does not depend on $\{\overline{fetched}\}$. Therefore $\{\overline{fetched}\}$ need not be provided as an input.

Fig. 1. ORAM-to-VOS generic compiler: semi-honest model

The proof of Theorem 1 reduces to the security of the encryption scheme and the ORAM scheme in a straightforward manner. We refer the reader to our online technical report [1] for a detailed proof.

Optimization: Handling Addresses Independent of Secret Information. In the construction above, the server performs as much computation as possible and only seeks the client's help when it needs to decrypt the next set of physical addresses to read from or write to. In many ORAM schemes, there are read/write operations whose physical addresses do not depend on secret client state, memory contents, or the logical addresses accessed. Examples are the reshuffling operations of the hierarchical ORAM scheme [20] and its variants [21–23, 25, 34, 36] and the eviction operations of the binary-tree based ORAM [30] and its variants [33]. To achieve better efficiency, such reshuffling and eviction operations, can be performed by the server (on its own) homomorphically, without seeking the client's help to decrypt the physical addresses.

3.3 Handling Malicious Servers

One way to handle a malicious server is to rely on a Succinct Non-Interactive Argument of Knowledge (SNARK). However, if done naively, the circuit for the SNARK will have size that is at least linear in n, i .e., the size of the outsourced memory D. This requires the server to perform a linear amount of computation to produce a proof of correctness.

Instead, we rely on efficient Verifiable RAM Computation (VC-RAM) to enforce honest server behavior. Verifiable RAM computation has been informally introduced in the literature by Ben-Sasson et al. [2] and Bitansky et al. [4]. We, however, need a stateful version of verifiable RAM computation. Braun et al. also informally proposed and implemented verifiable RAM computation [7].

We define a *stateful* version of verifiable RAM compute, where each query can result in updates to the outsourced dataset. Below, we explicitly formalize this notion of stateful, multi-query VC-RAM. Relying on the same ideas as Ben-Sasson et al. [2] and Bitansky et al. [4], we show that verifying RAM computation can be done efficiently, resulting in server computation that is comparable to the run-time of the RAM program (as opposed to the size of the memory); succinct proofs of size $O(\lambda)$; and efficient client verification time that is not too much worse than simply reading the input and output.

Verifiable RAM Computation. Consider a scenario where a client outsources a memory array D to a server. Let f denote a RAM program agreed upon by the client and the server. At each time step t, the client supplies a small input x_i, and the server computes the RAM program f over x_i and the current state of memory D. The RAM program produces an answer which is sent to the client. It may also update the memory contents outsourced to the server – hence our notion of VC-RAM is stateful. Verifiability requires that the client be able to check that the RAM computation results returned by the server are correct.

Definition 4 (Verifiable RAM Computation). *A (non-interactive) Verifiable RAM Computation (VC-RAM) scheme consists of the following algorithms:*

$(z, Z) \leftarrow$ Setup$(1^\lambda, D, f)$: Given an initial memory arrary $D[1..n]$ where each memory word has bit-length ℓ, a RAM program description f, output initial server state Z (which typically encodes D), and the initial client state z.

$(\overline{y}, Z') \leftarrow$ Compute(x, Z): Given a small input x to the RAM program f, the server's current state Z, output an encoded answer $\overline{y}$, and updated server state Z'. [1]

$(y, b, z') \leftarrow$ Verify$(x, \overline{y}, z)$: Given the input x, the client's current state z, an encoded answer $\overline{y}$, output a decoded answer y, a bit b indicating whether to accept this answer, and updated client state z'.

Correctness is defined as usual. We require that for any parameters n and ℓ, for any initial memory array $D \in \{0,1\}^{\ell n}$, for any polynomial-sized RAM program f which terminates in polynomial time, for any query sequence $x_1, x_2, \ldots, x_m$ where $m = \text{poly}(\lambda)$,

$$\Pr\left[\exists i : \begin{array}{l} (y_i \neq f(D, x_1, x_2, \ldots, x_i)) \\ \vee (b_i = 0) \end{array} \middle| \begin{array}{l} (z, Z_0) \leftarrow \text{Setup}(1^\lambda, D, f) \\ \forall i \in \{1, 2, \ldots, m\} : \\ \quad (y_i, Z_i) \leftarrow \text{Compute}(x_i, Z_{i-1}) \\ \quad (y_i, b_i, z) \leftarrow \text{Verify}(x_i, \overline{y}_i, z) \end{array} \right] \leq \text{negl}(\lambda)$$

---

[1] In the specific VC-RAM construction we describe, the encoded answer $\overline{y}$ includes the answer itself y, a proof vouching for its correctness, and an updated digest of the outsourced memory.

In particular, we use the notation $y_i := f(D, x_1, x_2, \ldots, x_i)$ to denote the outcome of the i-th query, starting with an initial memory array of D, and after computing the RAM program f on queries $x_1, x_2, \ldots, x_i$. Note that each query is stateful, i.e., may result in updates to the memory array D.

Definition 5 (Verifiability of VC-RAM). *We say that a VC-RAM scheme is verifiable, if for any polynomial time (stateful) adversary $\mathcal{A}$ the following holds.*

$$
\Pr \left[
\begin{array}{l}
\exists i : (b_i = 1) \wedge \\
(y_i \neq f(D, x_1, x_2, \ldots, x_i))
\end{array}
\middle|
\begin{array}{l}
(D, f) \leftarrow \mathcal{A}(1^\lambda) \\
(z, Z) \leftarrow \mathsf{Setup}(1^\lambda, D, f) \\
(x_1, \overline{y}_1) \leftarrow \mathcal{A}(Z) \\
\forall i \in \{1, 2, \ldots, m\} : \\
\quad (y_i, b_i, z) \leftarrow \mathsf{Verify}(x_i, \overline{y}_i, z) \\
\quad (x_{i+1}, \overline{y}_{i+1}) \leftarrow \mathcal{A}(y_i, b_i)
\end{array}
\right] \leq \mathsf{negl}(\lambda)
$$

Note again that the adversary $\mathcal{A}$ is stateful, and we do not write its state explicitly for simplicity.

Theorem 2. *There exists a non-interactive VC-RAM scheme such that for each query: the server runs in time $\tilde{O}(\tau \log n)\mathrm{poly}(\lambda)$ where τ is the run-time of the RAM program in the unauthenticated setting; the verifier runs in time $O((|x| + |y|)\lambda)$; and the client-server bandwidth cost is $|x| + |y| + O(\lambda)$.*

Note that the client-server bandwidth cost has to be at least $|x| + |y|$, i.e., the number of bits necessary to transmit the query x and the answer y. Therefore, the only additional cost is $O(\lambda)$ for transmitting an updated digest of the outsourced memory and a proof vouching for the correctness of the result.

We explain the intuition for the VC-RAM construction. The full construction can be found in our online technical report [1]. The high level idea is to build a Merkle tree over all outsourced memory, such that the client keeps the up-to-date root digest. To verify a RAM computation, we build a "verifier circuit" which takes in a trace of the computation, including 1) the CPU states before and after every computation step; 2) the memory contents fetched in every computation step; and 3) the Merkle-tree digest before and after each computation step. This verifier circuit checks the trace of the computation: 1) it checks that every memory read and write is correct using memory checking; and 2) it checks that every CPU computation step is correct. The server then constructs a SNARK for this "verifier circuit". Since this verifier circuit has size that is roughly the time of the RAM computation, we can achieve prover efficiency, i.e., the prover time is roughly the time of the RAM computation rather than the size of the entire dataset.

Relying on VC-RAM to Enforce Honest Server Behavior. In our semi-honest VOS construction described in Section 3.2, the client essentially outsources all of its ORAM memory (encrypted under FHE) to the server, as well as the ORAM's secret client state (also encrypted under FHE).

During each data access operation, in every round of interaction, the server performs some RAM computation on behalf of the client, and sends a message to the client to seek its help decrypting certain physical addresses. Using VC-RAM, the server can attach a succinct proof along with every message sent to the client, vouching for the correctness of the message. If the message sent to the client deviates from correct message, the client will surely detect it (except with negligible probability).

Due to space limits, we state the theorem below, and give the formal presentation of the malicious-model ORAM-to-VOS compiler in our online technical report [1].

Theorem 3. *Assuming existence of SNARKs, collision resistant hash functions, and a semantically secure FHE scheme, the aforementioned VOS construction (described in detail in our online technical report [1]) is secure against a malicious server.*

Proof. (sketch.) Due to the proof of the semi-honest model compiler (Theorem 1), it suffices to show that a malicious server cannot deviate from the protocol without being detected — this is ensured by the security of the VC-RAM scheme.

4 Optimizations for Specific ORAM Schemes

4.1 Background on Path ORAM

Stefanov et al. recently proposed the Path ORAM [33]. They formally prove that to achieve $n^{-\alpha(n)}$ failure probability, the (recursive) Path ORAM construction achieves $O(\alpha(n)\beta \log^2 n/\log \chi)$ client-side storage, and $O(\beta \log^2 n/\log \chi)$ bandwidth cost — χ is a term related to the block size where the block size $\beta = \chi \log n$ bits. Specifically, to make the failure probability negligible, we can use any $\alpha(n) := \omega(1)$.

Of particular interest is the case when the block size is $\Omega(\lambda)$ — in practical storage outsourcing applications, this is typically the case. Since $n = \text{poly}(\lambda)$, the number of recursions would be $O(1)$.

Lemma 1 (Path ORAM [33]). *For reasonably large block sizes $\beta = \Omega(\lambda)$, Path ORAM achieves bandwidth cost of $O(\beta \log n)$, a client-side storage of $O(\alpha(n)\beta \log n)$, and $O(1)$ rounds, with a failure probability of $n^{-\alpha(n)}$. Specifically, to achieve negligible failure probability, it suffices to use any $\alpha(n) := \omega(1)$.*

We briefly introduce the Path ORAM algorithm below.

Server Data Layout. The blocks on the server are organized into a binary tree of height roughly $\log n$. Each node in the tree is a bucket of $O(1)$ capacity. We use the notation $\mathcal{P}(x)$ to denote the path from the leaf node x to the root node, containing all buckets on the path. Additionally, $\mathcal{P}(x, \ell)$ denotes the bucket in $\mathcal{P}(x)$ at level ℓ in the tree.

Access(op):

Let op := (read, ind) or op := (write, ind, data) denote the current operation.

1. Set x := pos[ind]. Pick a fresh new leaf x_n. Store pos[ind] = x_n.
2. Request all blocks in the path $\mathcal{P}(x)$ from the server.
3. Set stash := stash $\cup\, \mathcal{P}(x)$.
4. Let data* be the current block in stash with index ind.
   If op is a write operation, set stash := (stash $-\{(ind, x, \text{data}^*)\})\cup\{(ind, x_n, \text{data})\}$.
   Else let stash := (stash $- \{(ind, x, \text{data})\}) \cup \{(ind, x_n, \text{data})\}$.
5. For $\ell = L$ to 0 (where L is the leaf level, and 0 is the root), do:
   Let S be the set of all $\{(ind', x', \text{data}')\} \in$ stash such that $\mathcal{P}(x, \ell) = \mathcal{P}(x', \ell)$.
   S := Select min($|S|$, bucketsize) blocks from S.
   Set stash := stash $- S$.
   If $|S| <$ bucketsize, pad S with dummy blocks to bucketsize.
   Client sends S to the server to write in bucket $\mathcal{P}(x, \ell)$.

The output to the client is data*, plus the updated position map pos.

Fig. 2. Access protocol for Path ORAM (non-recursive)

Client Data Layout. The client holds a position map where pos[ind] records the up-to-date designated leaf node for block ind. A block ind's designated leaf node is x implies that the block resides somewhere along the path $\mathcal{P}(x)$.

The client also holds a small stash of size $O(\alpha(n) \log n)$ for overflowing blocks, where any $\alpha(n) := \omega(1)$ allows us to achieve negligible failure probability.

Data Access. To perform any data access operation op, where op := (read, ind) or op := (write, ind, data), the client runs the Access protocol described in Figure 2. At Step 1, the block being read or written to is randomly remapped to a new leaf. At Step 2, the client requests a path of data blocks from the server. At Step 3, the local is merged with the data received from the server. At Step 4, the read/write operation is performed. At Step 5, the stash is written back into the tree, greedily pushing data blocks as close to the leaves as possible.

Recursive Path ORAM. The Path ORAM construction above requires the client to store a position map of $O(n \log n)$ bits. However, the client can store the position map on the server in a smaller ORAM. This is called the recursive Path ORAM. Particularly, if the block size $\beta := \Omega(\lambda)$, and $n = \text{poly}(\lambda)$, then the depth of the recursion is constant.

4.2 Path VOS

We can use the generic compilation techniques described in Section 3 to compile Path ORAM to a VOS scheme — henceforth referred to as the Path VOS algorithm.

Path VOS (non-recursive, semi-honest model)

Setup. Given a memory array D, client lays out D into an initial ORAM-tree as in the Path ORAM algorithm, and creates an initial position map accordingly. The client encrypts the initial ORAM-tree under FHE, and an empty stash, and outsources both the FHE-encrypted ORAM-tree and stash to the server. The client keeps the position map locally.

Access. Let op := (read, ind) or op := (write, ind, data) denote the current operation.

- *Client:* Looks up its local position map $x := \mathsf{pos}[ind]$. Pick a fresh random new leaf x'. Compute $\overline{\mathsf{op}} := \mathsf{FHE.Enc(op)}$, $\overline{x}' := \mathsf{FHE.Enc}(x')$. Send $(\overline{\mathsf{op}}, x, \overline{x}')$ to the server.
- *Server:* Let $\mathsf{WritePath}(\mathcal{P}, \mathsf{stash}, \mathsf{op}, x')$ denote the circuit (Steps 3 to 5 in Figure 2) that on inputting a path $\mathcal{P}$, a stash stash, and the current operation op, returns the current value of the requested block ind, overwrites the block ind's designated leaf tag to x', overwrites the block ind with new data if this is a write operation, and write back blocks in $\mathcal{P} \cup \mathsf{stash}$ to the path $\mathcal{P}$, greedily packing them as close to the leaf as possible. The server homomorphically computes $(\overline{\mathsf{out}}, \overline{\mathcal{P}(x)}, \overline{\mathsf{stash}}) \leftarrow \mathsf{FHE.Eval}(\mathsf{WritePath}(\overline{\mathcal{P}(x)}, \overline{\mathsf{stash}}, \overline{\mathsf{op}}, \overline{x}'))$. The server sends to the client the FHE-encrypted result of the read $\overline{\mathsf{out}}$.

Fig. 3. Path VOS (non-recursive, semi-honest model)

The semi-honest version of the Path VOS protocol is described in Figure 3. We can use the VC-RAM techniques described in Section 3.3 to compile the semi-honest protocol to one that is secure against a malicious server.

Recursive Path VOS. In the above (non-recursive) Path VOS protocol, the client needs to store a position map of size $O(n \log n)$ bits. This client-side storage may be avoided by recursively outsourcing the position map to the server in a smaller VOS scheme. When the block size is $\beta = \Omega(\lambda)$, the depth of recursion is $O(1)$. The resulting recursive Path VOS scheme will therefore have $O(1)$ roundtrips for each data access.

Tailored VC-RAM Techniques for Path ORAM. Based on the semi-honest protocol described above, and the VC-RAM techniques described in Section 3.3, we immediately obtain a Path VOS protocol with $\tilde{O}(\beta \log^2 n) \mathsf{poly}(\lambda)$ server computation per data access[2], for block sizes $\beta = \tilde{\Omega}(\lambda)$. (The small increase in block size is due to FHE.)

We observe that by overlaying the Path ORAM tree structure on top of the Merkle tree, we can shave a logarithmic factor off the server computation. Recall that in our VC-RAM construction, the client maintains a Merkle-hash tree digest of the ORAM-memory outsourced to the server. To prove that any RAM computation is correct, the server computes a SNARK for a "verifier circuit" which verifies 1) that every memory access is correct (through the Merkle tree); and 2) every step of CPU computation is correct. In particular, the extra $\log n$ factor comes from the cost.

---

[2] Throughout this paper, the notation $\tilde{O}(f(n))$ hides $\log(f(n))$ factors.

In the case of Path ORAM, since Path ORAM itself is a tree structure, we can overlay the Merkle tree on top of Path ORAM's tree structure. In this way, when Path ORAM accesses a path from the root to a leaf, the underlying memory checking scheme can vouch for the correctness of the entire path with $O(\log n)$ hashes. This can allow us to shave a $O(\log n)$ factor off the server computation for Path VOS.

Theorem 4 (Path VOS). *Assume collision resistant hash functions, the ring LWE assumption with suitable parametrization [5, 17], and the q-PDH and q-PKE assumptions [15]. Let $\alpha(n)$ denote any function such that $\alpha(n) := \omega(1)$.*

There exists a secure VOS scheme for reasonably large block size $\beta = \tilde{\Omega}(\lambda)$, with $O(\beta)$ bandwidth cost, $\tilde{O}(\alpha(n) \cdot \beta \log n)\mathrm{poly}(\lambda)$ server computation per data access, $O(\beta n)$ server-side storage, $O(\beta)$ client-side storage, and $O(\beta + \lambda^2)$ client computation per data access. Furthermore, the failure probability is $n^{-\alpha(n)}$, i.e., negligible in n for any $\alpha(n) := \omega(1)$.

Proof of security follows in a similar manner as the security proof for the generic compiler in the malicious model (Theorem 3).

4.3   The Hierarchical VOS

We propose a hierarchical VOS construction based on the Goodrich-Mitzenmacher ORAM (GM-ORAM) scheme [21] and its variants [25]. Although this hierarchical VOS construction achieves worse asymptotics than the Path VOS mentioned in the previous section, it is necessary later for our dynamic proofs of retrievability scheme — since the Path VOS scheme does not satisfy the next-read pattern hiding property (NRPH) proposed by Cash et al. [9]. (All of our VOS compilers are NRPH-preserving since they do not alter the sequence of accesses as dictated by the underlying ORAM.)

Although the basic idea is similar as before, to use FHE to outsource computation to the server, and use SNARK to enforce honest server behavior, we propose a "read/write (un)balancing" trick that allows us to reduce the bandwidth cost. The idea is that if we apply the generic ORAM-to-VOS compiler on the GM-ORAM scheme, reads will require more bandwidth than writes, since write is basically a homomorphic shuffling operation which the server can perform all on its own without interacting with the client. Therefore, we adjust the scheme to penalize writes while reducing the cost of reads. Note that in the traditional ORAM setting, writes cost more bandwidth, and that is why Kushilevitz et al. [25] propose a read/write balancing trick where they penalize reads to save on writes — our trick is the opposite of theirs since the read/write cost comparison is reverse in the VOS setting. Due to space constraints, we only give our main theorem for the Hierarchical VOS below, and defer the detailed construction to our online technical report [1].

Theorem 5. *Let $g(n)$ denote some function on n. Assume collision resistant hash functions, the ring LWE assumption with suitable parametrization [5, 17], and the q-PDH and q-PKE assumptions [15]. Then, there exists a VOS scheme* *for a reasonably large block size $\beta = \tilde{\Omega}(\lambda)$, with $O(\beta \log n / \log g(n))$ bandwidth cost, and $\tilde{O}(\beta g(n) \log^3 n / \log g(n))\text{poly}(\lambda)$ server computation (per data access), where n is the total number of blocks and λ is the security parameter.*

The following table shows some interesting special cases of Theorem 5.

$g(n)$	server computation	bandwidth overhead
n^ϵ for constant $\epsilon < 1$	$\tilde{O}(\beta n^\epsilon \log^2 n)\text{poly}(\lambda)$	$O(\beta)$
$\log n$	$\tilde{O}(\beta \log^4 n / \log \log n)\text{poly}(\lambda)$	$O(\beta \log n / \log \log n)$
constant $c > 1$	$\tilde{O}(\beta \log^3 n)\text{poly}(\lambda)$	$O(\beta \log n)$

5   Applications: Efficient Dynamic Proofs of Retrievability

For applications such as Dynamic Proofs of Retrievability, and RAM-model secure multi-party computation where the party storing the data (or a share of the data) can perform computation, often, just directly replacing the ORAM scheme with a VOS scheme can reduce the asymptotic communication overhead.

We show how VOS can be useful in Dynamic Proofs of Retrievability, based on the results of Cash et al. [9]. We note that two recent results have yielded more practical dynamic PoR schemes [10, 31]. Our dynamic PoR description helps demonstrate why distinguishing between VOS and ORAM can aid theoretical understanding. For a practical implementation, the recent schemes by Shi et al. [31] and Chandran et al. [10] are recommended.

Recently Cash et al. [9] show how to leverage a blackbox ORAM scheme to construct a dynamic proof of retrievability (PoR) scheme with $O(\beta \lambda \log^2 n)$ cost (both in terms of bandwidth and server computation) per data access. They require the underlying ORAM to have a special property which they call *"next-read pattern hiding"* (NRPH).

In the dynamic PoR scheme by Cash et al., they assume a passive server which does not perform any active computation. We observe that if we replaced the ORAM scheme in their construction with a VOS scheme (which also needs to satisfy the NRPH property), we would be able to obtain a dynamic PoR scheme (with server computation), which achieves smaller asymptotic bandwidth cost than Cash et al. [9].

The Path ORAM algorithm (and hence Path VOS too), however, does not satisfy the NRPH property, as pointed out by Cash et al. [9]. However, they showed that the GM-ORAM scheme and its variants indeed satisfy the NRPH property. Therefore, we rely on the hierarchical VOS described in Section 4.3 to build our dynamic PoR scheme.

Theorem 6. *Let $g(n)$ denote some function on n. Assume collision resistant hash functions, the ring LWE assumption with suitable parametrization [5, 17], and the q-PDH and q-PKE assumptions [15]. Then, there exists a dynamic proof of retrievability scheme for reasonably large block size $\beta = \tilde{\Omega}(\lambda)$, with*

$O(\beta \log n / \log g(n))$ *bandwidth cost and* $O(\beta g(n) \log^3 n / \log g(n)) \text{poly}(\lambda)$ *server computation for each read operation;* $O(\beta \lambda \log n / \log g(n))$ *bandwidth cost and* $O(\beta \lambda g(n) \log^3 n / \log g(n)) \text{poly}(\lambda)$ *server computation for each write or audit operation; with* $O(\beta)$ *client-storage and* $O(\beta n)$ *server storage. In the above,* n *is the total number of blocks and* λ *is the security parameter.*

Below are some interesting special cases of the above theorem. "R:" stands for read cost, and "W/A:" stands for write/audit cost.

$g(n)$	server computation	bandwidth overhead
n^ϵ for constant $\epsilon < 1$	R: $\tilde{O}(\beta n^\epsilon \log^2 n) \text{poly}(\lambda)$	R: $O(\beta)$
	W/A: $\tilde{O}(\beta \lambda n^\epsilon \log^2 n) \text{poly}(\lambda)$	W/A: $O(\beta \lambda)$
$\log n$	R: $\tilde{O}(\beta \log^4 n / \log \log n) \text{poly}(\lambda)$	R: $O(\beta \log n / \log \log n)$
	W/A: $\tilde{O}(\beta \lambda \log^4 n / \log \log n) \text{poly}(\lambda)$	W/A: $O(\beta \lambda \log n / \log \log n)$
constant $c > 1$	R: $\tilde{O}(\beta \log^3 n) \text{poly}(\lambda)$	R: $O(\beta \log n)$
	W/A: $\tilde{O}(\beta \lambda \log^3 n) \text{poly}(\lambda)$	W/A: $O(\beta \lambda \log n)$

In comparison to Cash et al. [9], using Verifiable Oblivious Storage (VOS), we can reduce the bandwidth cost to $O(\beta \log n / \text{poly} \log \log n)$ for reads, and $O(\beta \lambda \log n / \text{poly} \log \log n)$ for writes, with poly-logarithmic server computation. Furthermore, we can reduce the bandwidth cost to $O(\beta)$ for reads, and $O(\beta \lambda)$ for writes, with $O(\beta n^\epsilon) \text{poly}(\lambda)$ amount of server computation for a constant $\epsilon < 1$.

Other Applications. Gordon et al. recently proposed to use ORAM to achieve amortized sublinear-time secure two-party computation [24]. In their setting, Alice's input is a large database, and Bob repeatedly makes queries over the database. Alice wishes to protect the privacy of her database, while Bob wishes to protect the privacy of his query. Using ORAM, Gordon et al. show that the cost of securely querying the database can be sublinear when amortizing the ORAM setup cost over all future queries. Since both parties (each storing a share of the data) perform computation in this setting, we can simply replace the ORAM with VOS, and asymptotically, this gives savings in terms of bandwidth overhead.

6   Conclusion and Open Problems

This paper separates VOS from ORAM, and shows that VOS need not be subject to ORAM's lower bounds, since it is a different model where server computation is allowed. The constructions proposed in this paper use general primitives such as FHE and SNARKs. An interesting open question is to see how to construct a practically efficient VOS scheme (potentially without FHE or SNARKs) that outperforms the best known ORAM in terms of bandwidth overhead. It would also be interesting to consider how to construct VOS schemes that are asymptotically more bandwidth efficient than ORAM from weaker assumptions, e.g., without SNARKs or non-falsifiable assumptions.

Acknowledgments. This research was funded by NSF under grant number CNS-1314857, by a Google Faculty Research Award, and by the US Army Research Laboratory and the UK Ministry of Defence under Agreement Number W911NF-06-3-0001. The views and conclusions contained herein are those of the authors and should not be interpreted as representing the official policies, either expressed or implied, of the US Army Research Laboratory, the U.S. Government, the UK Ministry of Defense, or the UK Government. The US and UK Governments are authorized to reproduce and distribute reprints for Government purposes notwithstanding any copyright notation hereon.

We thank Hubert Chan, Charalampos Papamanthou, Emil Stefanov, and Hong-Sheng Zhou for helpful discussions, and the anonymous reviewers for their insightful comments.

References

1. Apon, D., Katz, J., Shi, E., Thiruvengadam, A.: Verifiable oblivious storage. Online technical report version of this paper (2013),
   http://www.cs.umd.edu/~elaine/docs/vos.pdf
2. Ben-Sasson, E., Chiesa, A., Genkin, D., Tromer, E.: Fast reductions from rams to delegatable succinct constraint satisfaction problems: extended abstract. In: ITCS (2013)
3. Bitansky, N., Canetti, R., Chiesa, A., Tromer, E.: From extractable collision resistance to succinct non-interactive arguments of knowledge, and back again. In: ITCS (2012)
4. Bitansky, N., Canetti, R., Chiesa, A., Tromer, E.: Recursive composition and bootstrapping for snarks and proof-carrying data. In: STOC (2013)
5. Brakerski, Z., Gentry, C., Vaikuntanathan, V.: (Leveled) fully homomorphic encryption without bootstrapping. In: ITCS (2012)
6. Brakerski, Z., Vaikuntanathan, V.: Efficient fully homomorphic encryption from (standard) LWE. In: FOCS (2011)
7. Braun, B., Feldman, A.J., Ren, Z., Setty, S., Blumberg, A.J., Walfish, M.: Verifying computations with state. In: SOSP (2013)
8. Canetti, R.: Security and composition of multiparty cryptographic protocols. Journal of Cryptology 13(1), 143–202 (2000)
9. Cash, D., Küpçü, A., Wichs, D.: Dynamic proofs of retrievability via oblivious RAM. In: Johansson, T., Nguyen, P.Q. (eds.) EUROCRYPT 2013. LNCS, vol. 7881, pp. 279–295. Springer, Heidelberg (2013)
10. Chandran, N., Kanukurthi, B., Ostrovsky, R.: Locally updatable and locally decodable codes. In: Lindell, Y. (ed.) TCC 2014. LNCS, vol. 8349, pp. 489–514. Springer, Heidelberg (2014)
11. Chor, B., Gilboa, N.: Computationally private information retrieval (extended abstract). In: STOC (1997)
12. Chor, B., Goldreich, O., Kushilevitz, E., Sudan, M.: Private information retrieval. In: IEEE Symposium on Foundations of Computer Science (FOCS), pp. 41–50 (1995)
13. Chung, K.-M., Pass, R.: A simple oram (2013),
   https://eprint.iacr.org/2013/243.pdf
14. Damgård, I., Meldgaard, S., Nielsen, J.B.: Perfectly secure oblivious RAM without random oracles. In: Ishai, Y. (ed.) TCC 2011. LNCS, vol. 6597, pp. 144–163. Springer, Heidelberg (2011)

15. Gennaro, R., Gentry, C., Parno, B., Raykova, M.: Quadratic span programs and succinct NIZKs without PCPs. In: Johansson, T., Nguyen, P.Q. (eds.) EURO-CRYPT 2013. LNCS, vol. 7881, pp. 626–645. Springer, Heidelberg (2013)

16. Gentry, C., Goldman, K.A., Halevi, S., Julta, C., Raykova, M., Wichs, D.: Optimizing ORAM and using it efficiently for secure computation. In: De Cristofaro, E., Wright, M. (eds.) PETS 2013. LNCS, vol. 7981, pp. 1–18. Springer, Heidelberg (2013)

17. Gentry, C., Halevi, S., Smart, N.P.: Fully homomorphic encryption with polylog overhead. In: Pointcheval, D., Johansson, T. (eds.) EUROCRYPT 2012. LNCS, vol. 7237, pp. 465–482. Springer, Heidelberg (2012)

18. Gentry, C., Ramzan, Z.: Single-database private information retrieval with constant communication rate. In: Caires, L., Italiano, G.F., Monteiro, L., Palamidessi, C., Yung, M. (eds.) ICALP 2005. LNCS, vol. 3580, pp. 803–815. Springer, Heidelberg (2005)

19. Goldreich, O.: Towards a theory of software protection and simulation by oblivious RAMs. In: STOC (1987)

20. Goldreich, O., Ostrovsky, R.: Software protection and simulation on oblivious RAMs. J. ACM (1996)

21. Goodrich, M.T., Mitzenmacher, M.: Privacy-preserving access of outsourced data via oblivious RAM simulation. In: Aceto, L., Henzinger, M., Sgall, J. (eds.) ICALP 2011, Part II. LNCS, vol. 6756, pp. 576–587. Springer, Heidelberg (2011)

22. Goodrich, M.T., Mitzenmacher, M., Ohrimenko, O., Tamassia, R.: Oblivious RAM simulation with efficient worst-case access overhead. In: CCSW (2011)

23. Goodrich, M.T., Mitzenmacher, M., Ohrimenko, O., Tamassia, R.: Privacy-preserving group data access via stateless oblivious RAM simulation. In: SODA (2012)

24. Gordon, S.D., Katz, J., Kolesnikov, V., Krell, F., Malkin, T., Raykova, M., Vahlis, Y.: Secure two-party computation in sublinear (amortized) time. In: ACM CCS (2012)

25. Kushilevitz, E., Lu, S., Ostrovsky, R.: On the (in)security of hash-based oblivious RAM and a new balancing scheme. In: SODA (2012)

26. Mayberry, T., Blass, E.-O., Chan, A.: Efficient private file retrieval by combining oram and pir (2013), http://eprint.iacr.org/2013/086

27. Ostrovsky, R.: Efficient computation on oblivious RAMs. In: STOC (1990)

28. Ostrovsky, R., Shoup, V.: Private information storage (extended abstract). In: STOC (1997)

29. Pinkas, B., Reinman, T.: Oblivious RAM revisited. In: Rabin, T. (ed.) CRYPTO 2010. LNCS, vol. 6223, pp. 502–519. Springer, Heidelberg (2010)

30. Shi, E., Chan, T.-H.H., Stefanov, E., Li, M.: Oblivious RAM with $O\left((logN)^3\right)$ worst-case cost. In: Lee, D.H., Wang, X. (eds.) ASIACRYPT 2011. LNCS, vol. 7073, pp. 197–214. Springer, Heidelberg (2011)

31. Shi, E., Stefanov, E., Papamanthou, C.: Practical dynamic proofs of retrievability. In: ACM CCS (2013)

32. Stefanov, E., Shi, E., Song, D.: Towards practical oblivious RAM. In: NDSS (2012)

33. Stefanov, E., van Dijk, M., Shi, E., Fletcher, C., Ren, L., Yu, X., Devadas, S.: Path oram: An extremely simple oblivious ram protocol. In: ACM CCS (2013)

34. Williams, P., Sion, R.: Usable PIR. In: NDSS (2008)

35. Williams, P., Sion, R.: Single round access privacy on outsourced storage. In: CCS (2012)

36. Williams, P., Sion, R., Carbunar, B.: Building castles out of mud: practical access pattern privacy and correctness on untrusted storage. In: ACM CCS (2008)

Achieving Privacy in Verifiable Computation with Multiple Servers – Without FHE and without Pre-processing*

Prabhanjan Ananth[1], Nishanth Chandran[2],
Vipul Goyal[2], Bhavana Kanukurthi[1], and Rafail Ostrovsky[3]

[1] Department of Computer Science, UCLA
prabhanjan@cs.ucla.edu, bhavanak@cs.bu.edu
[2] Microsoft Research India
{nichandr,vipul}@microsoft.com
[3] Departments of Computer Science and Mathematics, UCLA
rafail@cs.ucla.edu

Abstract. Cloud services provide a powerful resource to which weak clients may outsource their computation. While tremendously useful, they come with their own security challenges. One of the fundamental issues in cloud computation is: how does a client efficiently verify the correctness of computation performed on an untrusted server? Furthermore, how can the client be assured that the server learns nothing about its private inputs? In recent years, a number of proposals have been made for constructing verifiable computation protocols. Unfortunately, solutions that guarantee privacy of inputs (in addition to the correctness of computation) rely on the use of fully homomorphic encryption (FHE). An unfortunate consequence of this dependence on FHE, is that all hope of making verifiable computation implementable in practice hinges on the challenge of making FHE deployable in practice. This brings us to the following question: do we need fully homomorphic encryption to obtain privacy in verifiable computation protocol which achieves input privacy?

Another drawback of existing protocols is that they require the client to run a pre-processing stage, in which the work done by the client is proportional to the function being outsourced and hence the outsourcing benefit is obtained only in an amortized sense. This brings us to our next question: can we build verifiable computation protocols that allow

---

* The first, fourth and fifth authors were supported in part by NSF grants CNS-0830803; CCF-0916574; IIS-1065276; CCF-1016540; CNS-1118126; CNS-1136174; and in part by the Defense Advanced Research Projects Agency through the U.S. Office of Naval Research under Contract N00014-11-1-0392. The fifth author was also supported US-Israel BSF grant 2008411, OKAWA Foundation Research Award, IBM Faculty Research Award, Xerox Faculty Research Award, B. John Garrick Foundation Award, Teradata Research Award, and Lockheed-Martin Corporation Research Award. This material is also based upon work supported by the Defense Advanced Research Projects Agency through the U.S. Office of Naval Research under Contract N00014-11-1-0392. The views expressed are those of the author and do not reflect the official policy or position of the Department of Defense or the U.S. Government.

H. Krawczyk (Ed.): PKC 2014, LNCS 8383, pp. 149–166, 2014.

the client to efficiently outsource even a computation that it wishes to execute just once?

In this paper, we consider a model in which the client outsources his computation to multiple (say $n \geq 2$) servers. In this model, we construct verifiable computation protocols that do not make use of FHE and that do not have a pre-processing stage. In the two-server setting, we present an extremely practical protocol based only on one-way functions. We also present a solution, based on the DDH assumption, for the multi-server model for any arbitrary n. All these protocols are secure as long as at least one server is honest. Finally, even in the n-server model, we present a solution based solely on one-way functions. This protocol tolerates up to a constant fraction of corrupted servers.

Keywords: Verifiable computation, delegatable computation, input/output privacy, garbled circuits.

1   Introduction

Recently, there have been a number of proposals for non-interactive verifiable computation protocols (also called delegation of computation) (c.f., [AIK10, GGP10, CKV10]). In this scenario, we have a computationally weak client talking to a powerful (but un-trusted) server. The client wishes to get the outcome of a desired computation (say a function $\mathcal{F}$ evaluated on an input x) with the help of the server. If the server is malicious, one could ask that the correctness of the output **and** the privacy of the input (and possibly output) of the client still be preserved. Of course, it is also imperative that the work done by the client in verifying the correctness of the output be much lesser than the work done in computing $\mathcal{F}(x)$ on his own.

Unfortunately, to the best of our knowledge, all proposed solutions that meet this security requirement, have the following two drawbacks: they rely on the assumption of fully homomorphic encryption (FHE) and they work in a pre-processing model which requires the weak client to perform work proportional to $\mathcal{F}$ during an initial pre-processing phase and only guarantees that the work done in the online phase is low. First, we see the reliance on fully homomorphic encryption as a drawback for two reasons: a) the verifiable computation protocols so obtained, are inefficient in practice since they require the client to perform FHE encryption (which, typically, is less efficient than regular encryption and have enormous public keys) as well as require the server to perform expensive computation on encrypted data; b) from a theoretical perspective, it would be interesting to base protocols for verifiable computation on weaker or (relatively more) well-studied cryptographic hardness assumptions[1]. Hence, an interesting

---

[1] The recent result of [BV13] constructs a *leveled* FHE scheme under the LWE assumption that matches the best-known assumption for lattice-based PKE. However, all standard FHE (i.e., non-leveled) schemes additionally require a much stronger circular security assumption.

question to ask is: *do we need fully homomorphic encryption to obtain privacy in non-interactive verifiable computation protocols?*

The second drawback of existing solutions is that they require the client to perform work proportional to $\mathcal{F}$ during an initial pre-processing phase. In addition to being a strong assumption, it is also meaningful only in settings where the client wishes to compute the same function many times. This brings us to the next question: *can we build verifiable computation protocols that allow the client to efficiently outsource computations (even ones that it wishes to execute just once)?*

In this work, we are interested in addressing the above questions. Before we do so, we first present some intuition on the challenge of avoiding FHE. First, note that in a non-interactive verifiable computation protocol, the client sends a single message to the server (that can be viewed as an "encryption" of x), and the server responds back with a single message from which the client can recover $\mathcal{F}(x)$ (hence this message must look like an encryption of $\mathcal{F}(x)$). If we require the client's computational complexity to be independent of $\mathcal{F}$, then inherently, every verifiable computation protocol seems to have an FHE scheme embedded in it[2]. In fact, even if we allow interaction between the client and the server, to the best of our knowledge we do not know verifiable computation protocols that achieve *privacy* without FHE.

1.1   Multi-server Model for Verifiable Computation

In light of the challenge in removing FHE in the single-server model, we turn to a model of verifiable computation in which a single client outsources its computation to multiple (say n) servers. Note that if, all n servers are un-trusted (and colluding), then this is equivalent to outsourcing computation to a single server, and again it seems that we require FHE to obtain secure protocols. Hence, we consider a model in which a single client, holding an input x, wishes to outsource the computation of some function $\mathcal{F}$, to a set of servers $\mathcal{S}_1, \cdots, \mathcal{S}_n$, such that client performs very little computation (independent of $\mathcal{F}$) *throughout the protocol* and yet has a guarantee that none of the servers learn x, nor can they force the client to accept any other output, other than the right value of $\mathcal{F}(x)$, even if up to $n - 1$ of the servers are malicious and colluding. (Note that in the multi-server model, this is the strongest security one can achieve.)

Communication Model. Since client efficiency is our primary concern, we work in a model where the client sends and receives a single message, similar to the single-server non-interactive communication model. In particular, consider any (arbitrary) ordering of the servers. In our communication model, the client prepares a message and sends it (only) to the first server. Each intermediate server (except the first and the last server) receives a message from the previous server,

---

[2] This is not entirely true if the client is allowed to work in time proportional to $\mathcal{F}$ in the pre-processing stage, but it does seem like the only way we know how to obtain privacy in such protocols.

performs some computation, and, sends the outgoing message to the next server. The last server, upon doing its computation, sends the resulting message back to the client. After receiving this message, the client either accepts or rejects.

1.2   Our Results and Techniques

We provide general positive results in the above model for any PPT computable function without relying on FHE and without requiring a pre-processing stage. Our constructions guarantee both: privacy for the input (and output) of the client, as well as the correctness of the output (in case client outputs accept). We now state the various results that we obtain in this work:

- We first consider the 2-server case. In this setting, we present a protocol that can be obtained from any non-private verifiable computation protocol[3] and any collision-resistant hash function. This protocol is secure (i.e, guarantees privacy and soundness) as long as at least one of the two servers is not corrupted.
- Furthermore, in the 2-server case, if we allow each server to send a message to the other (i.e., we add one new message from the second server to the first), we are able to achieve a highly practical protocol solely based on one-way functions. In fact, in this protocol, the client only needs to send $2\kappa(\lambda_x + \lambda_y)$ random bits, where λ_x and λ_y are the input and output lengths respectively and κ is the security parameter, (and then additionally perform a lookup), while the two servers only need to generate and evaluate a garbled circuit each (the work done by the two servers can be run in parallel further minimizing the time of the protocol execution).
- Next, we consider the n-server case. That is a client outsources the computation to n servers. Here, we construct a protocol based solely on the Decisional Diffie-Hellman (DDH) assumption that is secure as long as at least one of the n servers is not corrupted. The computational complexity of the client throughout the protocol is independent of $\mathcal{F}$, the function being outsourced; in particular it is $\mathcal{O}(\kappa \cdot \lambda_x)$. Since there is no preprocessing, there are no restrictions on which functions the servers might evaluate for the client. The function to be evaluated may even be different in different protocols executions (as long as there is a mechanism for the servers to get the function description without affecting the computational complexity of the client). The primary tool this construction relies on is the notion of rerandomizable Yao's garbled circuits due to Gentry, Halevi, and, Vaikuntanathan [GHV10] which we carefully put together along with a specific proxy re-encryption scheme [BBS98].
- Finally, we also show how to obtain a secure protocol in the n-server case that is based solely on one-way functions. This protocol is secure as long as a constant fraction of the n servers are not corrupted.

---

[3] That is, a verifiable computation protocol that does not necessarily guarantee any privacy.

An added feature of all our protocols is that by using universal circuits, we can hide not just the input (x), but also the function $(\mathcal{F})$ being outsourced. This would be particularly useful in the case when the function description is short but the computational complexity of evaluating $\mathcal{F}$ is high. Finally, we note that our solutions do not suffer from the "rejection-bit" problem (that most earlier solutions suffer from) as we do not employ a pre-processing stage.

Remarks. We stress that we *do not* assume that the multiple malicious servers do not collude. Similar to standard secure multi-party computation protocols, all of our protocols are secure even when $n-1$ out of the n servers are malicious and colluding with each other. We remark that one could potentially reduce the communication between servers by making use of a fully homomorphic encryption (FHE) scheme; however, our goal is to not rely on FHE due to its inefficiency. Furthermore, it would seem unlikely for us to obtain an n-server protocol where server communication is independent of the function without relying on FHE as this would lead to a secure multi-party computation protocol with constant communication complexity (without relying on FHE). We stress that the lack of **any** positive results in getting privacy for outsourcing computation without FHE, makes it important to consider models such as ours.

We stress that, similar to standard MPC, in our protocol also, $n-1$ malicious servers could jointly collude and send their entire state to the honest server; this would mean that the honest server could learn the client's input. However, we do not view this as a serious limitation as this issue exists even in any MPC protocol that tolerates t corruptions. However, we stress that this problem does not arise in our setting as long as at most $n-2$ servers are corrupted. Even if $n-2$ servers send their state to one other server, it learns nothing as the protocol tolerates $n-1$ corruptions.

We finally remark that while one can obtain a private protocol for outsourcing computation in the multi-server model by simply secret sharing the clients input to the n servers and running a standard MPC protocol, our work shows that one can obtain significant efficiency gains when dealing with the specific problem of outsourcing computation (namely by leveraging the fact that the client is honest). In the 2-server setting, our protocol is even faster than standard *semi-honest* secure 2PC as we do not need to make use of oblivious transfer protocols (or zero-knowledge proofs/cut-and-choose techniques to obtain malicious security). We believe that our work can be a stepping stone towards obtaining faster protocols even in the multi-server setting.

Related work and open questions. As mentioned earlier, the works of Gennaro et al. [GGP10], Chung et al. [CKV10], Applebaum et al. [AIK10] were the firsts to consider non-interactive verifiable computation (with privacy) in the single server model. All the above protocols rely on fully homomorphic encryption to obtain privacy of the client's input. The works of [GKR08, KR09, GLR11, BCCT12, DFH12], and [GGPR13], all consider the problem of delegating computation, but without privacy (and obtain protocols for various classes of functions and under different assumptions). The works of [BGV11, FG12] consider outsourcing the computation of polynomials (but not the inputs), while the work of [PRV12] considers (non-private) outsourcing of specific class of functions without FHE. Of course, one could additionally make these protocols private, by "enveloping them" under an FHE scheme; however, this is what we wish to avoid. Note that one could obtain a private verifiable computation protocol from an attribute-based encryption scheme that has the property of attribute-hiding (using the construction of [PRV12]); however, we remark that while recent work has constructed attribute-based encryption for all polynomial time functions [GVW13, GGH⁺13], these works do not obtain attribute hiding. Furthermore, even then, using this transform, we will only get a verifiable computation protocol in the pre-processing model. Finally, the work of Goldwasser *et al.* [GKP⁺13] shows how to construct reusable garbled circuits and from this show how to obtain a private scheme for delegating computation; however their construction makes use of a FHE scheme.

The works of Canetti *et al.* [CRR11, CRR12] were the first to consider verifiable computation in the multi-server setting. While they do not consider privacy of the client's inputs, they provide an unconditional guarantee of the client receiving the correct output (as long as at least one server is honest). The servers do not communicate in their model, however their protocol works only for a restricted class of functions (logspace uniform NC circuits). They also have a result based on computational assumptions that work for arbitrary polynomial sized circuits.

Kamara and Raykova [KR11] consider the problem of outsourcing computation in the "multi-tenant" setting, in which there any mutually untrusting tenants (clients) running computations on the same trusted server (*physical machine*). Our solutions can be extended to this setting and achieve an improvement in efficiency (e.g., the protocol in Section 4.1) compared to the solutions of [KR11].

In our work, we obtain protocols in which the client sends a single message to the first server and receives a single message from the last server, but each of the servers send and receive one message each. A very interesting open problem would be to obtain a private protocol, in which the client sends a single message to each of the servers and receives a single message from each of the servers, and can obtain the correct result from this (i.e., a model in which the servers do not communicate with each other at all).

Organization of the paper. We begin, in Section 2, by defining our security and communication model for multi-server verifiable computation. In Section 3, we give an overview of the main tools, that we use in constructing our protocols. We present our main n-server protocol based on the DDH assumption in Section 4.2. We describe an improvement of this protocol in which the client works in time independent of n in the full version [ACG⁺14]. We refer the reader to the full version for details of our two 2-server protocols and the n-server protocol based on one-way functions (that tolerates a constant fraction of corrupt servers). We also refer the reader to the full version for more details of the constructions and for all the proofs.

2   Verifiable Computation in the Multi-server Setting

Let $\mathcal{VC}_{\text{multiserv}} = (\mathcal{C}, \mathcal{S}_1, \ldots, \mathcal{S}_n)$ be a multi-server delegation scheme where $\mathcal{C}$ denotes the client and $\mathcal{S}_1, \ldots, \mathcal{S}_n$ denote the servers. The scheme basically consists of two stages - the first is the (one-time) setup stage and the second is the online stage. In the setup stage, denoted by $\mathsf{Setup}_{\mathcal{VC}_{\text{multiserv}}}$, some computation is performed by the clients and the servers. The output of the setup stage consists of information public to everyone, as well as some secret information for the client as well as the servers. We stress that this stage is different from the standard pre-processing stage in literature as the work done in this stage is independent of the function $\mathcal{F}$ or the input x^4.

The second stage is the online stage when the client delegates the job of evaluating $\mathcal{F}$ on an input x to the set of servers. In this stage, the client runs in time independent of the complexity of the function $\mathcal{F}$.

A note on the setup stage. In all our constructions, the setup stage is independent of the function $\mathcal{F}$. As a result, the computational complexity of this stage is independent of the complexity of function $\mathcal{F}$. This is a much stronger condition than the proposed single-server delegation protocol [GGP10, CKV10] where the setup stage was allowed to run in time proportional to the complexity of $\mathcal{F}$. Another important advantage of the setup stage being independent of the function being delegated is that the client can execute this setup stage once (irrespective of the function being delegated) and store the secret state, which can then be reused for delegating *any* function, making our protocol efficient if the client wishes to delegate a number of different functions.

A multi-server delegation scheme should satisfy the properties of correctness, soundness and privacy. We refer the reader to the full version for the definitions.

3   Building Blocks

3.1   A Variant of Garbled Circuits

Yao in his seminal paper [Yao82] introduced the notion of garbled circuits to construct a secure two-party computation protocol. For this work, as we will explain later, we will consider a variant of the garbled circuit construction, denoted by YaoGarbledCkt, – namely, one in which the output wires are fixed. In this variant, the output wire keys are given externally to YaoGarbledCkt which in turn generates a garbled circuit with these fixed output wire keys. Though this violates the one-time soundness property of the garbled circuits, we will show, that this still ensures the privacy of the inputs which suffices for our construction. We formally show the proof of this claim in the full version.

---

[4] This requirement of having the setup stage to be independent of the function of the client makes our model significantly stronger than the ones considered in prior works.

In more detail, YaoGarbledCkt is a probabilistic polynomial time algorithm that takes as input a circuit $\mathcal{F}^5$, randomness R_1, R_2, and fixed output wire keys. Let the keys for the output wire be denoted by $\mathbf{w}_{out} = \{((w_{out,1}^0, w_{out,1}^1), \ldots, (w_{out,\mu}^0, w_{out,\mu}^1))\}$. It generates a garbled circuit according to Yao [Yao82]. R_1 is the randomness used to generate the input wire keys. R_2 is the randomness used to generate the wire keys for the rest of the circuit along with the four ciphertexts associated with every gate of the circuit. We will denote the collection of garbled gates by GC. Given the input wires corresponding to an input x, one can "evaluate" the garbled circuit and finally decode the output wires in order to obtain $\mathcal{F}(x)$.

To aid the construction we give later, we define another functionality, namely YaoGarbledCkt$_{in}$, that does the following. YaoGarbledCkt$_{in}$ takes as input randomness R_1, and outputs just the input wires corresponding to GC which is the output of YaoGarbledCkt$(\mathcal{F}; (R_1, R_2))$. As we will see later, the client will use this algorithm to compute just the input wire keys for his input x, corresponding to the garbled circuit GC, without generating the entire garbled circuit (GC) itself. The procedure YaoGarbledCkt$_{in}$ can be derived from YaoGarbledCkt such that the computational complexity of YaoGarbledCkt$_{in}$ depends only on the size of the input to the function and not on the size of the garbled circuit itself. For more details, refer to the full version.

Re-randomizable Garbled circuits. In [GHV10], Gentry *et al.* gave an alternate construction of garbled circuits whose security was shown, based on the Decisional Diffie Hellman (DDH) assumption. The advantage of their construction was that the garbled circuits that were obtained from their approach could be rerandomized. We say that a garbled circuit produced by YaoGarbledCkt is rerandomizable when there exists an algorithm reRand which on input a garbled circuit produces a different garbled circuit such that no computationally bounded adversary can distinguish whether a given garbled circuit is obtained as a result of rerandomization or was computed from YaoGarbledCkt, even when given the original garbled circuit. To explain this in more detail, we first define reRand. reRand takes as input a garbled circuit GC_1 (constructed from $\mathcal{F}$ and with fixed output wires $\mathbf{w}_{out}$) and outputs another garbled circuit GC_2 (whose output wires are also fixed to $\mathbf{w}_{out}$) such that the distribution of GC_1 is computationally indistinguishable from that of GC_2 even if the distinguisher is given access to $\mathcal{F}$ and the randomness used to compute GC_1. In addition to GC_1, reRand takes as input randomness (R_1, R_2) (and is denoted reRand$(GC_1, (R_1, R_2))$). R_1 is used to re-randomize the input wires while R_2 is used to re-randomize the rest of circuit. Note that the procedure reRand re-randomizes only the garbled circuit and not the output wires. So it does not need to take as input $\mathbf{w}_{out}$. Gentry *et al.* construct re-randomizable garbled circuits whose output wires are also randomized; as mentioned earlier, we require a variant of garbled circuits whose output wires remain the same, even after re-randomizing. We will show that the

---

[5] We use the same symbol to denote the function as well as the circuit computing the function.

construction of Gentry *et al.* can be used even for our purposes and the security of the construction holds. For more details, we refer the reader to the full version.

We now define another functionality, namely $\mathsf{reRand_{in}}$, on the lines of $\mathsf{YaoGarbledCkt_{in}}$ as follows. $\mathsf{reRand_{in}}$ takes as input randomness R_1 and $\mathbf{w}_{\mathsf{GC}_1,\mathsf{in}}$, which are the input wire keys of a garbled circuit GC_1, and outputs $\mathbf{w}_{\mathsf{GC}_2,\mathsf{in}}$ which are the input wire keys corresponding to GC_2 where GC_2 is the output of $\mathsf{reRand}(\mathsf{GC}_1; (R_1, R_2))$. Like in the case of $\mathsf{YaoGarbledCkt_{in}}$, the $\mathsf{reRand_{in}}$ algorithm can be easily derived from reRand such that the computational complexity of $\mathsf{reRand_{in}}$ depends only on the size of the input to the function and not the size of the garbled circuit itself.

3.2 Re-encryption Scheme

Informally, a re-encryption scheme allows a third party, who possesses a re-encryption key, to transform ciphertexts encrypted under one public key pk_1 into ciphertexts of the same message under a different public key pk_2, without learning anything about the contents of the message m. Various constructions of re-encryption schemes are known; we require a re-encryption scheme that is also additively homomorphic. We show such a scheme and provide more details about it in the full version.

4 Constructions of Verifiable Computation Protocols

In this section, we shall present our protocols for verifiable computation in the multi-server model. We shall first begin by describing a protocol in the 2-server case that can be built from any non-private verifiable computation protocol coupled with any collision-resistant hash function family. We will then build our n-server protocol that is based on the Decisional Diffie-Hellman assumption. Our n-server protocol based on one-way functions (but handling only a constant fraction of corrupt servers) is given in the full version.

4.1 The Two-Server Case

We wish to construct a verifiable computation protocol that allows a client $\mathcal{C}$ to outsource the computation of $\mathcal{F}$ on input x to two servers $\mathcal{S}_1$ and $\mathcal{S}_2$ with a guarantee on both privacy and soundness when at least one server is honest. We present two protocols for this purpose.

Solution 1: The high level idea for the first protocol is as follows. $\mathcal{C}$ will pick a seed to pseudo-random function (PRF) family and send the seed to $\mathcal{S}_1$. The client will also generate the output wires of a garbled circuit for function $\mathcal{F}$ (as described in Section 3.1 using $\mathsf{YaoGarbledCkt_{in}}$) and send them to $\mathcal{S}_1$. Finally, the client also picks a key to a collision-resistant hash function (call the description of this function H) and sends H to $\mathcal{S}_1$ and $\mathcal{S}_2$. Upon receiving input x, $\mathcal{C}$ picks the corresponding input wires in the garbled circuit for x and sends them to $\mathcal{S}_2$.

$\mathcal{S}_1$ generates a garbled circuit for $\mathcal{F}$ using randomness produced by the PRF seed and the output wires given by $\mathcal{C}$. $\mathcal{S}_1$ then computes a hash of this garbled circuit using H and sends the result of this hash to $\mathcal{C}$ along with a proof that the computation was performed honestly (we use the non-private verifiable computation protocol in order to do this). $\mathcal{S}_1$ will send the garbled circuit produced to $\mathcal{S}_2$. $\mathcal{S}_2$ will compute a hash of the garbled circuit received from $\mathcal{S}_1$ and send that to $\mathcal{C}$. $\mathcal{S}_2$ will also evaluate the garbled circuit using the input wires received from $\mathcal{C}$ and send the resulting output wire to $\mathcal{C}$.

The client finally checks three things: a) The non-private verifiable computation with $\mathcal{S}_1$ succeeded, b) the hash output values received from both servers were the same and c) the output wire received from $\mathcal{S}_2$ was indeed a valid output wire. If all three checks succeed, then the client decodes the output from the received output wire and learns $\mathcal{F}(x)$. For more details, we refer the reader to the full version.

Solution 2: We next present a highly practical two-server protocol based solely on one-way functions. For this protocol alone, we will have each server send a message to the other server.

The protocol works as follows. The client sends each server $\mathcal{S}_i$ (for $i \in \{1, 2\}$), a seed to a pseudo-random function K_i. Each $\mathcal{S}_i$ uses K_i and generates the garbled circuit (GC_i) for the function $\mathcal{F}$[6]. Additionally, the client also sends input wires of GC_1 (resp. GC_2), corresponding to his input, to $\mathcal{S}_2$ (resp. $\mathcal{S}_1$). Each server evaluates the garbled circuit it receives from the other server using the input wires it receives from the client and sends the output wires to the client. $\mathcal{C}$ checks the output wires it receives from both servers to make sure they are valid. If they are both valid, it decodes them to obtain the output values contained in them. If both these values are the same, it accepts the output value and rejects otherwise[7]. For more details of this protocol, we refer the reader to the full version.

While the communication between servers cannot be reduced in this protocol, we feel the practical efficiency of this protocol outweighs any overhead caused due to that extra message from $\mathcal{S}_2$ to $\mathcal{S}_1$. Indeed, the only work done by the client is to generate short randomness and finally do a look-up to obtain the output. The only work done by the servers is to generate (and evaluate) a single garbled circuit each (that can also be done in parallel by both the servers). We stress that while 2-PC protocols can be used to obtain a similar result, we need the underlying 2-PC protocol used to be secure against malicious adversaries. Such a 2-PC protocol would need to use either the cut-and-choose approach or zero-knowledge proofs, both of which are inefficient.

---

[6] Actually $\mathcal{C}$ needs to only give the servers the randomness for generating the input and output wires. The servers can pick their own randomness to generate the garbled circuit (consistent with these input and output wires). Security of our protocol holds even in this case – since we have that at least one server is honest, at least one garbled circuit is generated honestly. This is sufficient to guarantee security.

[7] Note that the above protocol can be modified trivially so that the client sends just one message to $\mathcal{S}_1$ and receives just one message from $\mathcal{S}_2$.

This protocol for verifiable computation is similar in spirit to a protocol by Mohassel and Franklin [MF06] to achieve efficient, malicious, 2-PC in a model where the malicious party may get some information-leakage. Our protocol, used in the context of verifiable computation, is fully secure. It, of course, avoids the use of oblivious transfer protocols and, can additionally allow the servers to run in parallel, thereby achieving better efficiency. One drawback of this solution is that its security is guaranteed only when the servers do not learn whether or not the client accepted the response. We stress that none of our other solutions suffer from this drawback.

4.2 The n-Server Case

In this section, we present our n-server verifiable computation protocol based on the DDH assumption. The high level idea behind constructing such a protocol for functionality $\mathcal{F}(x)$ works as follows: the client generates the input and output wires corresponding to GC_1 (where GC_1 is the garbled circuit for evaluating $\mathcal{F}$). $\mathcal{S}_1$ generates GC_1 (and all the wires corresponding to it). Each server $\mathcal{S}_i$ (for $1 \leq i \leq n-1$), then re-randomizes GC_i and sends it $\mathcal{S}_{i+1}$. The client re-randomizes his input wires ($n-1$ times) to obtain the wires corresponding to input x (according to the re-randomized garbled circuit GC_{n-1}). $\mathcal{S}_n$ obtains the re-randomized input wires corresponding to input x. (NIZK proofs need to be used to ensure that the re-randomizations are done correctly; likewise signature and encryption schemes need to be used to ensure that messages are sent via secure authenticated channels – we omit those details for now.[8]) $\mathcal{S}_n$ then evaluates the final garbled circuit and returns the output to the client. The client re-randomizes his output wires $n-1$ times to obtain the output wires corresponding to GC_{n-1}. Using the work of Gennaro et al. [GGP10], one can then show that if $\mathcal{S}_n$ returned a "correct" output wire, then he must have obtained it by evaluating the "honestly" re-randomized garbled circuit on the right input wires – therefore the protocol guarantees soundness. One can then show the privacy of this protocol from the fact that even if one of the servers does the re-randomization honestly, the re-randomized input and output wires will reveal no information to the dishonest servers (i.e., the adversary) about x and $\mathcal{F}(x)$.

Remark. Recently, the work of [BHR12] built adaptively secure garbled circuits which remain secure even if the input is chosen after seeing the garbled circuit. Such security is needed in verifiable computation protocols where the garbled circuit is generated in the pre-processing stage. In our protocol, the garbled circuits are always generated in the online stage. So standard garbled circuits as proven secure in the work of [LP09], suffice for our purposes.

---

[8] Alternatively, one can use techniques of cut-and-choose in order to make sure that the servers honestly create (or re-randomize) the garbled circuits; we leave the details of this construction to the full version of the paper.

While this, along with a few other ideas, forms the underlying intuition for our result, the main limitation of the above approach is that the client works proportional to n.

To this end, observe that the client works proportional to n because he needs to re-randomize both the input wires as well as the output wires. For the sake of simplicity, for now, we only discuss how to avoid the client's re-randomization of the output wires. One idea to accomplish this is to fix all the output wires (of all garbled circuits) to some specific value. However, this results in two issues. The first issue is that it is not immediately clear that this protocol guarantees privacy. However, we show that Yao's garbled circuit and it's re-randomization remains private even when using fixed output wires. We will use this to show that our protocol guarantees privacy. We refer the reader to the full version for the details.

The next, and more important, issue with this change, is that it no longer guarantees soundness. (Since the servers know the fixed output wires, $\mathcal{S}_n$ could just send a correct output wire without evaluating the garbled circuit GC_{n-1}.) We fix this by using an idea from the work of Applebaum et al. [AIK10]. We use a message authentication scheme MAC = (MACtag, MACverify) and modify the functionality $\mathcal{F}$ to $\mathcal{G}$: instead of computing just $\mathcal{F}(x)$, $\mathcal{G}$, takes as additional inputs K_1, K_2. $\mathcal{G}(x, K_1, K_2)$ executes $\mathcal{F}$ on input x to obtain y. It then computes $y \oplus K_1$ and then produces $y_{MAC} = \text{MACtag}(K_2, y \oplus K_1)$. Now, one can show that the soundness of the protocol comes from security of the message authentication code. This is an overview of our main construction which we describe below. In this construction, the client still works proportional to n but he no longer re-randomizes the output wires.

In our full version, we describe how to avoid the client's re-randomization of the input wires, thereby making the client's running time independent of n.

Our n−Server Construction

Setup stage. During the Key Generation stage, each server $\mathcal{S}_i$ generates the secret key-public key $(\text{sk}_i, \text{pk}_i)$ pairs for an encryption scheme $(\text{KeyGen}_{\text{Enc}}, \text{Enc}, \text{Dec})$ that is CCA2 secure. Further, the client generates (SK, VK) for the signature scheme $(\text{KeyGen}_{\text{Sign}}, \text{Sign}, \text{Ver})$ that is existentially unforgeable under chosen message attack. The servers $\mathcal{S}_1, \ldots, \mathcal{S}_{n-1}$ generate $(\text{SK}_1, \text{VK}_1), \ldots, (\text{SK}_{n-1}, \text{VK}_{n-1})$ respectively for the signature scheme $(\text{KeyGen}_{\text{Sign}}, \text{Sign}, \text{Ver})$. Let MAC = (MACtag, MACverify) be a message authentication scheme which is existentially unforgeable against chosen message attack. MACtag on input a MAC key K and a message m produces a message authentication code m_{MAC} for m. MACverify on input key K, message m and a tag m'_{MAC}, outputs 1 if m'_{MAC} is a valid message authentication code for m under the key K else it outputs 0. Let $\text{Comm}(m)$ denote the commitment to a message m (that is at least computationally hiding and binding). We let $\text{Open}(c)$ denote the opening of a commitment c. Further, the servers use a non-interactive zero knowledge proof (NIZK) system (in the CRS model) $(\text{Prover}_{\text{Rel}}, \text{Verifier}_{\text{Rel}})$ defined for a relation Rel in NP that satisfies the standard notions of correctness, soundness, and zero-knowledge. The zero knowledge simulator for this proof system is denoted by $\mathsf{Sim_{Rel}}$. We also use the following pseudo-random function families:

1. $\mathsf{PRF_{gc}}(\cdot, \cdot)$ is used by $\mathcal{S}_1$ to output the randomness for generating all the wires of GC_1 with the exception of the input and output wires alone. Without loss of generality, assume that the output length of the PRF is sufficiently long enough to garble the circuit $\mathcal{G}$ [9] which is defined with respect to the delegated function $\mathcal{F}$ as follows. $\mathcal{G}$ on input (x, K_1, K_2) outputs $\mathsf{MACtag}(K_2, \mathcal{F}(x) \bigoplus K_1)$.

2. For $2 \leq i \leq n-1$, $\mathsf{PRF_{re}}(\cdot, \cdot)$ is used by $\mathcal{S}_i$ to re-randomize the entire circuit GC_{i-1} except the input wire keys. As before, assume that the output of PRF is sufficiently long enough to rerandomize the garbled circuit of $\mathcal{G}$ (which is defined above).

3. $\mathsf{PRF_{in}}(\cdot, \cdot)$ is used by $\mathcal{S}_1$ to generate the keys for the input wires corresponding to GC_1. Additionally it will be used by the client to generate the keys for the input wires (without having to generate all of GC_1). Further $\mathcal{S}_i$ (for $2 \leq i \leq n-1$) uses $\mathsf{PRF_{in}}(\cdot, \cdot)$ to rerandomize the input wire keys of GC_i.

We now describe our protocol $\mathcal{P}$.

1. Client on input x does the following:
   (a) $\mathcal{C}$ picks a key α_1 for $\mathsf{PRF_{gc}}(\cdot, \cdot)$ and $n-2$ keys $\{\alpha_2, \ldots, \alpha_{n-1}\}$ for the pseudorandom function $\mathsf{PRF_{re}}(\cdot, \cdot)$ uniformly at random. In addition he also picks keys $\beta_1, \ldots, \beta_{n-1}$ to be used by $\mathcal{S}_i$ to evaluate $\mathsf{PRF_{in}}(\cdot, \cdot)$ uniformly at random.
   (b) $\mathcal{C}$ computes commitments to each of these PRF keys. Let $\mathbf{c}^\alpha = \{c_1^\alpha, \ldots, c_{n-1}^\alpha\} \stackrel{\text{def}}{=} \{\mathsf{Comm}(\alpha_1), \ldots, \mathsf{Comm}(\alpha_{n-1})\}$ and $\mathbf{c}^\beta = \{c_1^\beta, \ldots, c_{n-1}^\beta\} \stackrel{\text{def}}{=} \{\mathsf{Comm}(\beta_1), \ldots, \mathsf{Comm}(\beta_{n-1})\}$.
   (c) $\mathcal{C}$ sets $d_i^\alpha = \mathsf{Open}(c_i^\alpha)$ and $d_i^\beta = \mathsf{Open}(c_i^\beta)$ for all $1 \leq i \leq n-1$. Let $\mathbf{d}^\alpha = \{d_1^\alpha, \ldots, d_{n-1}^\alpha\}$ and $\mathbf{d}^\beta = \{d_1^\beta, \ldots, d_{n-1}^\beta\}$.
   (d) Let the client's input be $x = x_1 \cdots x_{\lambda_x}$, where each x_i is a bit. The client picks K_1 uniformly at random (where K_1 is of the same length as $\mathcal{F}(x)$) and also picks a MAC key K_2. Let K_2 be of length λ_{K_2}. λ is such that $\lambda = \lambda_x + \lambda_{K_1} + \lambda_{K_2}$.
   (e) $\mathcal{C}$ picks an execution id, id[10], and obtains the keys for the input wires of the garbled circuit GC_1 (to be defined later) by

---

[9] This assumption requires the knowledge of the size of the circuit being delegated by the client before the PRF keys are generated. This in turn makes the key generation stage dependent on the function being delegated. This dependency can be eliminated as follows. Instead of using just one output of PRF to garble the circuit, use multiple PRF outputs to garble the circuit. Using sufficiently many PRF outputs the entire circuit can be garbled. For convenience sake, in our protocol description the garbling of the entire circuit is done using just one output of the PRF.

[10] This id needs to be unique for each execution. This can be achieved by the client, either by maintaining state and ensuring that ids do not repeat, or by the client picking the id at random from a sufficiently large domain (and one can then argue that except with negligible probability, the id will be unique).

evaluating $\mathsf{YaoGarbledCkt_{in}}(\mathcal{F}, \mathsf{PRF_{in}}(\beta_1, \mathsf{id}))$. Let the keys (corresponding to 0 and 1) for the input wires be denoted by $\mathbf{w}_{\mathsf{GC}_1,\mathsf{in}} = \{(w^0_{\mathsf{GC}_1,\mathsf{in},1}, w^1_{\mathsf{GC}_1,\mathsf{in},1}), \ldots, (w^0_{\mathsf{GC}_1,\mathsf{in},\lambda}, w^1_{\mathsf{GC}_1,\mathsf{in},\lambda})\}$ where $w^0_{\mathsf{GC}_1,\mathsf{in},i}$ denotes the key for the ith input wire representing bit 0 while $w^1_{\mathsf{GC}_1,\mathsf{in},i}$ denotes the ith wire representing the bit 1 in the garbled circuit GC_1.

(f) The client $\mathcal{C}$ then does the following. It computes $\mathsf{reRand_{in}}\Big(\mathsf{reRand_{in}}$

$\Big(\cdots(\mathsf{reRand_{in}}(\mathbf{w}_{\mathsf{GC}_1,\mathsf{in}}; \mathsf{PRF_{in}}(\beta_2, \mathsf{id}))); \cdots\Big); \mathsf{PRF_{in}}(\beta_{n-1}, \mathsf{id})\Big)$ to obtain $\mathbf{w}_{\mathsf{GC}_{n-1},\mathsf{in}} = ((w^0_{\mathsf{GC}_{n-1},\mathsf{in},1}, w^1_{\mathsf{GC}_{n-1},\mathsf{in},1}), \cdots, (w^0_{\mathsf{GC}_{n-1},\mathsf{in},\lambda}, w^1_{\mathsf{GC}_{n-1},\mathsf{in},\lambda}))$. Let $\mathbf{w}^X_{\mathsf{GC}_{n-1},\mathsf{in}} = (w^{X_0}_{\mathsf{GC}_{n-1},\mathsf{in},1}, \ldots, w^{X_\lambda}_{\mathsf{GC}_{n-1},\mathsf{in},\lambda})$ denote the input wire keys corresponding to the input $X = (x, K_1, K_2)$ for the garbled circuit GC_{n-1}.

(g) Client $\mathcal{C}$ picks the output wire keys $w_{\mathsf{out}} = \{(w^0_{\mathsf{out},1}, w^1_{\mathsf{out},1}), \ldots, (w^0_{\mathsf{out},\mu}, w^1_{\mathsf{out},\mu})\}$. For simplicity we assume that these are chosen uniformly at random, even though we won't rely on that property in any of our proofs.

(h) Client $\mathcal{C}$ picks random strings $\mathsf{CRS}_1, \ldots, \mathsf{CRS}_{n-1}$ to be used as common reference string for the NIZK proofs.

(i) For $1 \leq i \leq n-1$, $\mathcal{C}$ sets $\mathsf{msg}_i = (\mathsf{id}, d^\alpha_i, d^\beta_i, \mathbf{c}^\alpha, \mathbf{c}^\beta, \mathsf{CRS}_1, \ldots, \mathsf{CRS}_i, \mathbf{w}_{\mathsf{out}})$. Further, $\mathcal{C}$ sets $\mathsf{msg}_n = (\mathsf{id}, \mathbf{c}^\alpha, \mathbf{c}^\beta, \mathbf{w}^X_{\mathsf{GC}_{n-1},\mathsf{in}}, \mathsf{CRS}_1, \ldots, \mathsf{CRS}_{n-1}, \mathbf{w}_{\mathsf{out}})$.

(j) Let $\sigma^{\mathsf{msg}_i}_i$ be the signature of $\mathsf{Enc}_{\mathsf{pk}_i}(\mathsf{msg}_i)$ using signing key SK for all $1 \leq i \leq n$.

(k) $\mathcal{C}$ sends $\mathsf{Enc}_{\mathsf{pk}_1}(\mathsf{msg}_1), \ldots, \mathsf{Enc}_{\mathsf{pk}_n}(\mathsf{msg}_n)$ along with $\sigma^{\mathsf{msg}_1}_1, \ldots, \sigma^{\mathsf{msg}_n}_n$ to $\mathcal{S}_1$.

2. Server $\mathcal{S}_1$ on input $\mathcal{F}$ and upon receiving $(\mathsf{Enc}_{\mathsf{pk}_1}(\mathsf{msg}_1), \ldots, \mathsf{Enc}_{\mathsf{pk}_n}(\mathsf{msg}_n), \sigma^{\mathsf{msg}_1}_1, \ldots, \sigma^{\mathsf{msg}_n}_n)$ from the client does the following:

(a) Compute the modified functionality $\mathcal{G}$ which does the following. $\mathcal{G}$ on input (x, K_1, K_2) executes $\mathcal{F}$ on input x to obtain y. It then computes $y \oplus K_1$ and then produces $y_{\mathsf{MAC}} = \mathsf{MACtag}(K_2, y \oplus K_1)$. It outputs (y, y_{MAC}).

(b) $\mathcal{S}_1$ verifies signature $\sigma^{\mathsf{msg}_1}_1$ on the input message $\mathsf{Enc}_{pk_1}(\mathsf{msg}_1)$ by executing $\mathsf{Ver}(\mathsf{VK}, \mathsf{Enc}_{pk_1}(\mathsf{msg}_1), \sigma^{\mathsf{msg}_1}_1)$. If Ver outputs reject then it aborts.

(c) $\mathcal{S}_1$ decrypts $\mathsf{Enc}_{\mathsf{pk}_1}(\mathsf{msg}_1)$ using sk_1 to obtain msg_1 which is parsed as $(\mathsf{id}, d^\alpha_1, d^\beta_1, \mathbf{c}^\alpha, \mathbf{c}^\beta, \mathsf{CRS}_1, \mathbf{w}_{\mathsf{out}})$.

(d) $\mathcal{S}_1$ evaluates $\mathsf{PRF_{gc}}(\alpha_1, \mathsf{id})$ and $\mathsf{PRF_{in}}(\beta_1, \mathsf{id})$ and uses the randomness output by the two PRFs to compute $\mathsf{YaoGarbledCkt}$ on input $\mathcal{G}$, to obtain GC_1. In other words, $\mathsf{YaoGarbledCkt}(\mathcal{F}, \mathbf{w}_{\mathsf{out}}; (\mathsf{PRF_{in}}(\beta_1, \mathsf{id}), \mathsf{PRF_{gc}}(\alpha_1, \mathsf{id})))$ outputs GC_1 as well as the input wires corresponding to GC_1.

(e) $\mathcal{S}_1$ then computes a proof π_1 using CRS_1 as the CRS for the statement: "There exists witness d^α_1, d^β_1 such that

    i. $d^\alpha_1 = \mathsf{Open}(c^\alpha_1)$ and $d^\beta_1 = \mathsf{Open}(c^\beta_1)$;
    ii. GC_1 is the garbled circuit output by $\mathsf{YaoGarbledCkt}(\mathcal{G}; (\mathsf{PRF_{in}}(\beta_1, \mathsf{id}), \mathsf{PRF_{gc}}(\alpha_1, \mathsf{id})))$."

More formally, the proof is generated as follows. Consider the following relation:

$$\mathsf{Rel}_1 = \Big\{ \big((c_1^\alpha, c_1^\beta, \mathsf{GC}_1), (d_1^\alpha, d_1^\beta)\big) \ :$$

$$d_1^\alpha = \mathsf{Open}(c_1^\alpha), d_1^\beta = \mathsf{Open}(c_1^\beta), d_1^\alpha = (\alpha_1, R_1^\alpha), \ d_1^\beta = (\beta_1, R_1^\beta),$$

$$\mathsf{GC}_1 = \mathsf{YaoGarbledCkt}((\mathcal{G}, \mathbf{w}_{\mathsf{out}}); (\mathsf{PRF}_{\mathsf{in}}(\beta_1, \mathsf{id}), \mathsf{PRF}_{\mathsf{gc}}(\alpha_1, \mathsf{id}))) \Big\}$$

Execute $\mathsf{Prover}_{\mathsf{Rel}_1}((c_1^\alpha, c_1^\beta, \mathsf{GC}_1), (d_1^\alpha, d_1^\beta))$ to obtain the proof π_1.

(f) Generate signature $\sigma_{\mathcal{S}_1}$ for the message (GC_1, π_1).

(g) $\mathcal{S}_1$ lets $\pi = \{\pi_1\}$, and gives $(\mathsf{GC}_1, \pi, \mathsf{Enc}_{pk_2}(\mathsf{msg}_2), \ldots, \mathsf{Enc}_{pk_n}(\mathsf{msg}_n),$
$\sigma_{\mathcal{S}_1}, \sigma_2^{\mathsf{msg}_2}, \ldots, \sigma_n^{\mathsf{msg}_n})$ to $\mathcal{S}_2$.

3. Server $\mathcal{S}_i$ $(2 \le i \le n-1)$ upon receiving $\mathcal{F}$ and $(\mathsf{GC}_1, \ldots, \mathsf{GC}_{i-1}, \pi,$
$\mathsf{Enc}_{pk_i}(\mathsf{msg}_i), \ldots, \mathsf{Enc}_{pk_n}(\mathsf{msg}_n), \sigma_{\mathcal{S}_1}, \ldots, \sigma_{\mathcal{S}_{i-1}}, \sigma_i^{\mathsf{msg}_i}, \ldots, \sigma_n^{\mathsf{msg}_n})$ from $\mathcal{S}_{i-1}$
does the following:

(a) $\mathcal{S}_i$ verifies signature $\sigma_i^{\mathsf{msg}_i}$ on the input message $\mathsf{Enc}_{pk_i}(\mathsf{msg}_i)$ by executing $\mathsf{Ver}(\mathsf{VK}, \mathsf{Enc}_{pk_i}(\mathsf{msg}_i), \sigma_i^{\mathsf{msg}_i})$. If Ver outputs reject then it aborts.

(b) $\mathcal{S}_i$ parses π as $\pi_1, \ldots, \pi_{i-1}$. It then verifies signatures $\sigma_{\mathcal{S}_1}, \ldots, \sigma_{\mathcal{S}_{i-1}}$ on the messages $(\mathsf{GC}_1, \pi_1), \ldots, (\mathsf{GC}_{i-1}, \pi_{i-1})$ using the verification keys $\mathsf{VK}_1, \ldots, \mathsf{VK}_{i-1}$ respectively.

(c) $\mathcal{S}_i$ then decrypts $\mathsf{Enc}_{pk_i}(\mathsf{msg}_i)$ using secret key sk_i to obtain msg_i which is parsed as $(\mathsf{id}, d_i^\alpha, d_i^\beta, \mathbf{c}^\alpha, \mathbf{c}^\beta, \mathsf{CRS}_1, \ldots, \mathsf{CRS}_i, \mathbf{w}_{\mathsf{out}})$.

(d) $\mathcal{S}_i$ verifies all the NIZK proofs in π as follows. It first parses π as $\pi_1, \ldots, \pi_{i-1}$. It then executes $\mathsf{Verifier}_1((c_1^\alpha, c_1^\beta, \mathsf{GC}_1), \mathsf{CRS}_1, \pi_1)$ and $\mathsf{Verifier}_j((c_j^\alpha, c_j^\beta, \mathsf{GC}_j, \mathsf{GC}_{j-1}), \mathsf{CRS}_j, \pi_j)$ for all $2 \le j \le i-1$. $\mathcal{S}_i$ aborts if any of the verifiers $\mathsf{Verifier}_j$, for $1 \le j \le i-1$, aborts.

(e) $\mathcal{S}_i$ evaluates $\mathsf{PRF}_{\mathsf{re}}(\alpha_i, \mathsf{id})$ and $\mathsf{PRF}_{\mathsf{in}}(\beta_i, \mathsf{id})$ and uses the randomness output by the 2 PRFs to rerandomize the garbled circuit GC_{i-1}. More formally, it computes $\mathsf{reRand}(\mathsf{GC}_{i-1}; (\mathsf{PRF}_{\mathsf{in}}(\beta_i, \mathsf{id}), \mathsf{PRF}_{\mathsf{re}}(\alpha_i, \mathsf{id})))$ to obtain GC_i.

(f) $\mathcal{S}_i$ computes a proof π_i with respect to CRS_i for the statement:
"There exists witness d_i^α and d_i^β such that
  i. $d_i^\alpha = \mathsf{Open}(c_i^\alpha)$ and $d_i^\beta = \mathsf{Open}(c_i^\beta)$;
  ii. GC_i is the garbled circuit output by $\mathsf{reRand}(\mathsf{GC}_{i-1}; (\mathsf{PRF}_{\mathsf{in}}(\beta_i, \mathsf{id}), \mathsf{PRF}_{\mathsf{re}}(\alpha_i, \mathsf{id})))$."
More formally, consider the following relation:

$$\mathsf{Rel}_1 = \Big\{ \big((c_i^\alpha, c_i^\beta, \mathsf{GC}_i, \mathsf{GC}_{i-1}), (d_i^\alpha, d_i^\beta)\big) \ :$$

$$d_i^\alpha = \mathsf{Open}(c_i^\alpha), d_i^\beta = \mathsf{Open}(c_i^\beta), d_i^\alpha = (\alpha_i, R_i^\alpha), \ d_i^\beta = (\beta_i, R_i^\beta),$$

$$\mathsf{GC}_i = \mathsf{reRand}(\mathsf{GC}_{i-1}; (\mathsf{PRF}_{\mathsf{in}}(\beta_i, \mathsf{id}), \mathsf{PRF}_{\mathsf{re}}(\alpha_i, \mathsf{id}))) \Big\}$$

Execute $\mathsf{Prover}_{\mathsf{Rel}_i}((c_i^\alpha, c_i^\beta, \mathsf{GC}_i), (d_i^\alpha, d_i^\beta))$ to obtain the proof π_i.

(g) Generate signature $\sigma_{\mathcal{S}_i}$ for the message (GC_i, π_i).

(h) $\mathcal{S}_i$ lets $\pi = \pi \cup \{\pi_i\}$, and sends $(\mathsf{GC}_1, \ldots, \mathsf{GC}_i, \mathsf{Enc}_{pk_{i+1}}(\mathsf{msg}_{i+1}), \ldots,$
$\mathsf{Enc}_{pk_n}(\mathsf{msg}_n), \sigma_{\mathcal{S}_1}, \ldots, \sigma_{\mathcal{S}_i}, \sigma_{i+1}^{\mathsf{msg}_{i+1}}, \ldots, \sigma_n^{\mathsf{msg}_n})$ to $\mathcal{S}_{i+1}$.

4. Server $\mathcal{S}_n$ does the following upon receiving $\mathcal{F}$ and $(\mathsf{GC}_1, \ldots, \mathsf{GC}_{n-1}, \pi,$ $\mathsf{Enc}_{pk_n}(\mathsf{msg}_n), \sigma_{\mathcal{S}_1}, \ldots, \sigma_{\mathcal{S}_{n-1}}, \sigma_n^{\mathsf{msg}_n})$:

   (a) $\mathcal{S}_n$ verifies signature $\sigma_n^{\mathsf{msg}_n}$ on the input message $\mathsf{Enc}_{pk_n}(\mathsf{msg}_n)$ by executing $\mathsf{Ver}(\mathsf{VK}, \mathsf{Enc}_{pk_n}(\mathsf{msg}_n), \sigma_n^{\mathsf{msg}_n})$. If Ver outputs reject then it aborts.

   (b) $\mathcal{S}_i$ parses π as $\pi_1, \ldots, \pi_{n-1}$. It then verifies signatures $\sigma_{\mathcal{S}_1}, \ldots, \sigma_{\mathcal{S}_{n-1}}$ on the messages $(\mathsf{GC}_1, \pi_1), \ldots, (\mathsf{GC}_{n-1}, \pi_{n-1})$ using the verification keys $\mathsf{VK}_1, \ldots, \mathsf{VK}_{n-1}$ respectively.

   (c) $\mathcal{S}_n$ then decrypts $\mathsf{Enc}_{pk_n}(\mathsf{msg}_n)$ using secret key sk_i to obtain msg_i which is parsed as $(\mathsf{id}, \mathbf{c}^\alpha, \mathbf{c}^\beta, \mathbf{w}^X_{\mathsf{GC}_{n-1}, \mathsf{in}}, \mathsf{CRS}_1, \ldots, \mathsf{CRS}_{n-1}, \mathbf{w}_{\mathsf{out}})$. Further, $\mathbf{w}^X_{\mathsf{GC}_{n-1}, \mathsf{in}}$ is parsed as $(w^{X_1}_{\mathsf{GC}_{n-1}, \mathsf{in}, 1}, \ldots, w^{X_\lambda}_{\mathsf{GC}_{n-1}, \mathsf{in}, \lambda})$.

   (d) $\mathcal{S}_n$ verifies all the NIZK proofs in π as follows. It first parses π as $\pi_1, \ldots, \pi_{n-1}$. It then executes $\mathsf{Verifier}_1((c_1^\alpha, c_1^\beta, \mathsf{GC}_1), \mathsf{CRS}, \pi_1)$ and $\mathsf{Verifier}_j((c_j^\alpha, c_j^\beta, \mathsf{GC}_j, \mathsf{GC}_{j-1}), \mathsf{CRS}, \pi_j)$ for all $2 \leq j \leq n-1$. $\mathcal{S}_n$ aborts if any of the verifiers $\mathsf{Verifier}_j$, for $1 \leq j \leq n-1$, aborts.

   (e) If $\mathcal{S}_n$ accepts all the NIZK proofs and signatures, it uses $\mathbf{w}^X_{\mathsf{GC}_{n-1}}$ to evaluate the garbled circuit GC_{n-1} to obtain the wire keys $\mathbf{w}^z_{\mathsf{out}}$. It then determines $\mathbf{z} = z_1 \cdots z_{|\mathcal{G}_{\mathsf{out}}|}$ [11] such that the set of wire keys $\{w_{\mathsf{out}, 1}, \ldots, w_{\mathsf{out}, |\mathcal{G}_{\mathsf{out}}|}\}$ represents $\mathbf{w}^z_{\mathsf{out}}$. $\mathcal{S}_n$ sends $\mathbf{z}$ to the client $\mathcal{C}$.

5. Client on receiving $\mathbf{z}$ from $\mathcal{S}_n$ does the following:

   (a) $\mathcal{C}$ parses $\mathbf{z}$ as (y, y_{MAC}).

   (b) $\mathcal{C}$ executes $\mathsf{MACverify}_{K_2}(y, y_{\mathsf{MAC}})$. If the output of $\mathsf{MACverify}$ is 0 then it outputs Reject. Else, it computes y' where $y' = y \oplus K_1$ and then it outputs Accept.

It is easy to see that correctness follows from the correctness of Yao and other underlying primitives. We defer the proof of privacy and soundness to the full version.

References

[ACG+14] Ananth, P., Chandran, N., Goyal, V., Kanukurthi, B., Ostrovsky, R.: Achieving privacy in verifiable computation with multiple servers – without fhe and without pre-processing. IACR Cryptology ePrint Archive (2014)

[AIK10] Applebaum, B., Ishai, Y., Kushilevitz, E.: From secrecy to soundness: Efficient verification via secure computation. In: Abramsky, S., Gavoille, C., Kirchner, C., Meyer auf der Heide, F., Spirakis, P.G. (eds.) ICALP 2010, Part I. LNCS, vol. 6198, pp. 152–163. Springer, Heidelberg (2010)

[BBS98] Blaze, M., Bleumer, G., Strauss, M.J.: Divertible protocols and atomic proxy cryptography. In: Nyberg, K. (ed.) EUROCRYPT 1998. LNCS, vol. 1403, pp. 127–144. Springer, Heidelberg (1998)

[BCCT12] Bitansky, N., Canetti, R., Chiesa, A., Tromer, E.: From extractable collision resistance to succinct non-interactive arguments of knowledge, and back again. In: Proceedings of the 3rd Innovations in Theoretical Computer Science Conference, ITCS 2012, pp. 326–349. ACM, New York (2012)

---

[11] $|\mathcal{G}_{\mathsf{out}}|$ denotes the length of the output of the function $\mathcal{G}$.

[BGV11]   Benabbas, S., Gennaro, R., Vahlis, Y.: Verifiable delegation of computation
           over large datasets. In: Rogaway, P. (ed.) CRYPTO 2011. LNCS, vol. 6841,
           pp. 111–131. Springer, Heidelberg (2011)
[BHR12]   Bellare, M., Hoang, V.T., Rogaway, P.: Adaptively secure garbling with
           applications to one-time programs and secure outsourcing. In: Wang, X.,
           Sako, K. (eds.) ASIACRYPT 2012. LNCS, vol. 7658, pp. 134–153. Springer,
           Heidelberg (2012)
[BV13]   Brakerski, Z., Vaikuntanathan, V.: Lattice-based fhe as secure as pke.
           Cryptology ePrint Archive, Report 2013/541 (2013),
           http://eprint.iacr.org/
[CKV10]   Chung, K.-M., Kalai, Y., Vadhan, S.: Improved delegation of computation
           using fully homomorphic encryption. In: Rabin, T. (ed.) CRYPTO 2010.
           LNCS, vol. 6223, pp. 483–501. Springer, Heidelberg (2010)
[Cra12]   Cramer, R. (ed.): TCC 2012. LNCS, vol. 7194. Springer, Heidelberg (2012)
[CRR11]   Canetti, R., Riva, B., Rothblum, G.N.: Practical delegation of compu-
           tation using multiple servers. In: Chen, Y., Danezis, G., Shmatikov,
           V. (eds.) ACM Conference on Computer and Communications Security,
           pp. 445–454. ACM (2011)
[CRR12]   Canetti, R., Riva, B., Rothblum, G.N.: Two protocols for delegation of
           computation. In: Smith, A. (ed.) ICITS 2012. LNCS, vol. 7412, pp. 37–61.
           Springer, Heidelberg (2012)
[DFH12]   Damgård, I., Faust, S., Hazay, C.: Secure two-party computation with
           low communication. In: Cramer, R. (ed.) TCC 2012. LNCS, vol. 7194,
           pp. 54–74. Springer, Heidelberg (2012)
[FG12]   Fiore, D., Gennaro, R.: Publicly verifiable delegation of large polynomi-
           als and matrix computations, with applications. In: ACM Conference on
           Computer and Communications Security, pp. 501–512 (2012)
[GGH+13]   Garg, S., Gentry, C., Halevi, S., Sahai, A., Waters, B.: Attribute based
           encryption for circuits from multilinear maps. In: Canetti, R., Garay, J.A.
           (eds.) CRYPTO 2013, Part II. LNCS, vol. 8043, pp. 479–499. Springer,
           Heidelberg (2013)
[GGP10]   Gennaro, R., Gentry, C., Parno, B.: Non-interactive verifiable comput-
           ing: Outsourcing computation to untrusted workers. In: Rabin, T. (ed.)
           CRYPTO 2010. LNCS, vol. 6223, pp. 465–482. Springer, Heidelberg (2010)
[GGPR13]   Gennaro, R., Gentry, C., Parno, B., Raykova, M.: Quadratic span programs
           and succinct nizks without pcps. In: Johansson, T., Nguyen, P.Q. (eds.)
           EUROCRYPT 2013. LNCS, vol. 7881, pp. 626–645. Springer, Heidelberg
           (2013)
[GHV10]   Gentry, C., Halevi, S., Vaikuntanathan, V.: i-hop homomorphic encryption
           and rerandomizable yao circuits. In: Rabin, T. (ed.) CRYPTO 2010. LNCS,
           vol. 6223, pp. 155–172. Springer, Heidelberg (2010)
[GKP+13]   Goldwasser, S., Kalai, Y.T., Popa, R.A., Vaikuntanathan, V., Zeldovich,
           N.: Overcoming the worst-case curse for cryptographic constructions. In:
           CRYPTO (2013)
[GKR08]   Goldwasser, S., Kalai, Y.T., Rothblum, G.N.: Delegating computation: in-
           teractive proofs for muggles. In: Dwork, C. (ed.) STOC, pp. 113–122. ACM
           (2008)
[GLR11]   Goldwasser, S., Lin, H., Rubinstein, A.: Delegation of computation with-
           out rejection problem from designated verifier cs-proofs. IACR Cryptology
           ePrint Archive 2011, 456 (2011)

[GVW13]   Gorbunov, S., Vaikuntanathan, V., Wee, H.: Attribute-based encryption
for circuits. In: STOC (2013)

[KR09]   Kalai, Y.T., Raz, R.: Probabilistically checkable arguments. In: Halevi, S.
(ed.) CRYPTO 2009. LNCS, vol. 5677, pp. 143–159. Springer, Heidelberg
(2009)

[KR11]   Kama, S., Raykova, M.: Secure outsourced computation in a multi-tenant
cloud. In: Workshop on Cryptography and Security in the Clouds (2011)

[LP09]   Lindell, Y., Pinkas, B.: A proof of security of yao's protocol for two-party
computation. J. Cryptology 22(2), 161–188 (2009)

[MF06]   Mohassel, P., Franklin, M.K.: Efficiency tradeoffs for malicious two-party
computation. In: Yung, M., Dodis, Y., Kiayias, A., Malkin, T. (eds.) PKC
2006. LNCS, vol. 3958, pp. 458–473. Springer, Heidelberg (2006)

[PRV12]   Parno, B., Raykova, M., Vaikuntanathan, V.: How to delegate and verify in public: Verifiable computation from attribute-based encryption. In:
Cramer, R. (ed.) TCC 2012. LNCS, vol. 7194, pp. 422–439. Springer, Heidelberg (2012)

[Yao82]   Yao, A.C.-C.: Protocols for secure computations (extended abstract). In:
23rd Annual Symposium on Foundations of Computer Science (FOCS),
Chicago, Illinois, USA, November 3-5, pp. 160–164 (1982)

Efficient Delegation of Zero-Knowledge Proofs of Knowledge in a Pairing-Friendly Setting

Sébastien Canard[1], David Pointcheval[2], and Olivier Sanders[1,2]

[1] Orange Labs, Applied Crypto Group, Caen, France
[2] École normale supérieure, CNRS & INRIA, Paris, France

Abstract. Since their introduction in 1985, by Goldwasser, Micali and Rackoff, followed by Feige, Fiat and Shamir, zero-knowledge proofs have played a significant role in modern cryptography: they allow a party to convince another party of the validity of a statement (proof of membership) or of its knowledge of a secret (proof of knowledge). Cryptographers frequently use them as building blocks in complex protocols since they offer quite useful soundness features, which exclude cheating players. In most of modern telecommunication services, the execution of these protocols involves a prover on a portable device, with limited capacities, and namely distinct trusted part and more powerful part. The former thus has to delegate some computations to the latter. However, since the latter is not fully trusted, it should not learn any secret information.

This paper focuses on proofs of knowledge of discrete logarithm relations sets (DLRS), and the delegation of some prover's computations, without leaking any critical information to the delegatee. We will achieve various efficient improvements ensuring perfect zero-knowledge against the verifier and partial zero-knowledge, but still reasonable in many contexts, against the delegatee.

1   Introduction

Zero-Knowledge Proofs of Knowledge. The past three decades have witnessed the emergence of several new cryptographic notions. In 1985, Goldwasser, Micali and Rackoff [16] introduced the concept of zero-knowledge interactive proofs that enable an entity, called the *prover*, to convince another entity, called the *verifier*, of the validity of a statement without revealing anything else beyond the assertion of this statement. In other words, one wants to prove that a statement is in the set of the valid statements, hence the notion of *zero-knowledge proof of membership*. They were followed by Feige, Fiat and Shamir [12] with the notion of *zero-knowledge proof of knowledge* (ZKPK) in which the prover convinces the verifier not only of the validity of a statement but also that it possesses a witness for this fact.

Since these seminal papers, many ZKPK have been introduced, such as the Schnorr's protocol [25], that provide efficient ways of proving knowledge of a discrete logarithm in finite groups with known order, and even with unknown order [14,15]. In modern cryptography, these proofs of knowledge are heavily used

H. Krawczyk (Ed.): PKC 2014, LNCS 8383, pp. 167–184, 2014.

for authentication but also as building blocks in more complex protocols, such as group signature schemes [1,11,4,21] or Direct Anonymous Attestation (DAA) schemes [5,3]. Indeed, such protocols usually require to prove that some public elements, relying on private values, are well-formed. For anonymous authentications, one classically wants to prove one's knowledge of a secret key related to a public key certified by a given authority, without revealing the secret key, the public key, nor the certificate itself. They can be efficiently addressed by using Schnorr-like interactive ZKPK. Moreover, these interactive proofs can be turned into non-interactive proofs or signatures using the Fiat-Shamir paradigm [13,24], in the random oracle model [2].

Discrete-Logarithm Relation Sets. More complex protocols, such as group signature schemes or DAA schemes, involve several proofs of knowledge of discrete logarithms or of representations in a fixed or variable basis: they deal with a *Discrete-Logarithm Relation Set* (or DLRS, as defined by Kiayias, Tsiounis and Yung [20]), *i.e* a set of relations involving objects and free variables. Extensions of the Schnorr's protocol can be applied to this setting, but they require the prover to compute many exponentiations for the first round of the protocol (the commitments).

Pairing-Friendly Settings. Elliptic curves with or without pairing-friendly groups have been widely used for the past few years, since they offer many new features and provide communication-wise efficient protocols. They allow to prove complex relations with still reasonable efficiency, namely when compared with the RSA setting. Indeed, most of the recent group signature schemes [11,17,4,21] or DAA schemes [6,10,3] are based on groups ($\mathbb{G}_1$, $\mathbb{G}_2$ and $\mathbb{G}_T$) of prime order with a bilinear map ($e : \mathbb{G}_1 \times \mathbb{G}_2 \to \mathbb{G}_T$).

The main interesting feature is definitely the possibility of non-interactive zero-knowledge proofs in the standard model, using the so-called Groth-Sahai methodology [18]. Unfortunately, while reducing the number of interactions is quite useful, this leads to quite costly protocols, for both the prover and the verifier. They are currently totally impractical on constrained devices.

Delegation of Computation. However, most of these complex cryptographic primitives, such as anonymous authentications and DAAs, achieve their ultimate impact when implemented on portable and mobile devices. This increases the contrast between the important needs to embed these protocols in such lightweight devices and their practical limitations when performing many exponentiations or pairing evaluations. A common way to overcome this problem is to delegate (when possible) some computations to a more powerful, but not fully trusted, delegatee as in [5,7,3,8]. Since the latter entity cannot have access to secret values, most of the computations on the prover's side have to be performed by the constrained device, which reduces the benefits of server-aided cryptography. Moreover, if the DLRS involved in the protocol contains several relations or variables, the overall computational cost may remain prohibitive. One may argue that exponentiations in the first flow of Schnorr's protocol are precomputable. This is true if the basis is fixed, but when the proof is used as a building block in a more complex construction, the basis is not always fixed or known in advance (as *e.g.* in DAA schemes [5,3]). The lack of way to efficiently delegate the prover's side of the proof of knowledge may then prevent portable devices to get access to all features of modern cryptography.

Although the delegatee might not be fully trusted, it may have access to some additional information. For example, let us consider the following setting: a SIM-card in a smartphone. This is probably the best illustration of a lightweight but fully trusted device (the SIM-card with embedded secrets) within a more powerful but partially trusted device (the smartphone with more and more powerful processors, and even co-processors). In case of group signature or anonymous authentication to a server, only the SIM-card knows the secret key to perform authentication, and no information about the identity of the actual user should leak to the server. However, while not trusted enough to learn the secret key, since it can potentially be corrupted by a virus, the smartphone anyway already knows its owner. As a consequence, the anonymity has to be enforced with respect to the server but not to the smartphone (it has other means to learn owner's identity). However, the secret key should not be leaked to neither the server nor the smartphone.

Such a SIM-card together with a smartphone issuing anonymous authentication illustrates well the relaxation on the security model that seems reasonable in practice: during delegation of computation, some additional information can be leaked to the helper until it does not help it to impersonate the real prover. We will thus provide several security models in which the delegatee might be given access to some extra knowledge. We however stress that the delegatee should remain unable to recover the secrets or to impersonate the prover, but still being able to handle a significant part of the prover's computations.

Achievements. In this paper, we provide an efficient way to delegate the prover's side of zero-knowledge proofs of knowledge for any DLRS in a group $\mathbb{G}_1$. Our method enables a delegator to use the computational power of a delegatee to prove knowledge of witnesses for any DLRS with significantly fewer computations than with the classical Schnorr's based protocol. While lifting the verification relation into $\mathbb{G}_T$, and thus involving pairing computations on the verifier's side, no pairing computations have to be performed on the prover's side (for both the delegator and the delegatee). Moreover, the computations that remain to be done by the delegator do not rely on the objects involved in the DLRS, but on a fixed basis only, they can thus all be precomputed.

By decreasing the computational cost for the constrained devices (the delegator), our work improves on the efficiency of protocols using zero-knowledge proofs of knowledge and thus enables engineers to embed complex primitives on such devices.

More precisely, we provide two constructions in which the delegator essentially computes as many exponentiations of a fixed basis as the number of secret discrete logarithms involved in the relations, whatever the number of relations is. We illustrate the effective gain on concrete examples.

2   Preliminaries

In this section, we provide a basic review of the tools that will be used throughout this paper. Namely, we recall the notations of bilinear maps and zero-knowledge proofs of knowledge together with the concept of Discrete-Logarithm Relations Sets (DLRS) and the Schnorr's protocol for such relations.

2.1   Pairing-Friendly Groups

Let $\mathbb{G}_1, \mathbb{G}_2, \mathbb{G}_T$ be three groups of prime order p. In the following, we will use additive notations for $\mathbb{G}_1$ and $\mathbb{G}_2$, but multiplicative notations for $\mathbb{G}_T$. Elements of $\mathbb{G}_1$ will be written in uppercase $(G, X, T, \ldots)$ and elements of $\mathbb{G}_2$ will be written $(\widetilde{G}, \widetilde{X}, \widetilde{T}, \ldots)$. Pairing-friendly settings are defined by $\mathbb{G}_1, \mathbb{G}_2, \mathbb{G}_T$ along with a bilinear map $e : \mathbb{G}_1 \times \mathbb{G}_2 \to \mathbb{G}_T$ with the following properties:

1. for all $X \in \mathbb{G}_1, \widetilde{X} \in \mathbb{G}_2$ and $a, b \in \mathbb{Z}_p$ we have $e([a]X, [b]\widetilde{X}) = e(X, \widetilde{X})^{ab}$;
2. for $X \neq 0$ and $\widetilde{X} \neq 0$, $e(X, \widetilde{X}) \neq 1$;
3. e is efficiently computable.

We emphasize that our protocols will work in any pairing-friendly setting: in both the symmetric (*i.e.*, $\mathbb{G}_1 = \mathbb{G}_2$) and asymmetric (*i.e.*, $\mathbb{G}_1 \neq \mathbb{G}_2$) cases. In the following, the setting $(p, \mathbb{G}_1, \mathbb{G}_2, \mathbb{G}_T, G, \widetilde{G}, e)$ defines the bilinear environment, with $\mathbb{G}_1 = \langle G \rangle$, $\mathbb{G}_2 = \langle \widetilde{G} \rangle$, and $\mathbb{G}_T = \langle e(G, \widetilde{G}) \rangle$. All the three groups being of the same prime order p.

2.2   Zero-Knowledge Proofs of Knowledge

Interactive zero-knowledge proofs of knowledge have been introduced by Goldwasser, Micali and Rackoff [16] and formalized by Feige, Fiat and Shamir [12]. We recall here the informal definition.

Definition 1. *An interactive protocol between a prover $\mathcal{P}$ and a verifier $\mathcal{V}$ is a zero-knowledge proof of knowledge of a private witness w for $\mathcal{P}$ that a public information Y satisfies a relation R if the three following properties are satisfied.*

– **Completeness:** *for an honest prover $\mathcal{P}$ with correct witness w and an honest verifier $\mathcal{V}$, the protocol succeeds with overwhelming probability.*
– **Soundness:** *for any prover $\widetilde{\mathcal{P}}$ that is accepted by a verifier $\mathcal{V}$ with non negligible probability, it is possible to construct a probabilistic polynomial time Turing machine $\mathcal{E}$ (called extractor) that can extract a valid witness w by interacting with $\widetilde{\mathcal{P}}$.*
– **Zero-knowledge:** *for every verifier $\mathcal{V}$, there exists a probabilistic polynomial-time Turing machine $\mathcal{S}$ (called simulator) that just takes Y as input and outputs a string that is indistinguishable from the transcript of the communications between an honest prover $\mathcal{P}$ with a valid witness w and $\mathcal{V}$.*

The soundness property models the fact that in order to be accepted, the prover must actually know a valid witness, while the zero-knowledge property shows that the real protocol with the prover that uses the witness w does not leak more information than a simulation that does not know the witness.

$$\mathcal{P} \qquad\qquad\qquad\qquad\qquad\qquad\qquad\qquad\qquad\qquad\qquad \mathcal{V}$$

$$\forall j \in \{1, ..., m\}, k_j \xleftarrow{\$} \mathbb{Z}_p$$

$$\forall i \in \{1, ..., r\}, K_i \leftarrow \sum_{j \in \mathcal{J}_i} [k_j] A_{v_{i,j}} \quad \xrightarrow{\{K_i\}_i}$$

$$\xleftarrow{\quad c \quad} \qquad\qquad\qquad c \xleftarrow{\$} \{0,1\}^\ell$$

$$\forall j \in \{1, ..., m\}, s_j \leftarrow k_j + c\alpha_j \bmod p \quad \xrightarrow{\{s_j\}_j} \quad \forall i \in \{1, ..., r\},$$
$$K_i + [c]V_i \stackrel{?}{=} \sum_{j \in \mathcal{J}_i} [s_j] A_{v_{i,j}}$$

Setting: A group $\mathbb{G}$ of prime order p and a DLRS $\mathcal{R}$ in $\mathbb{G}$: for $A_1, ..., A_w, V_1, ..., V_r \in \mathbb{G}$, and $\mathcal{J}_1, ..., \mathcal{J}_r \subseteq \{1, ..., w\}$, the prover $\mathcal{P}$ knows variables $\alpha_1, ..., \alpha_m \in \mathbb{Z}_p$ such that $V_i = \sum_{j \in \mathcal{J}_i} [\alpha_j] A_{v_{i,j}}$, for $i = 1, ..., r$.

Fig. 1. The Extended Schnorr's Protocol for any DLRS $\mathcal{R}$

2.3 Discrete-Logarithm Relations Set

Discrete-logarithm relations sets (DLRSs) were introduced by Kiayias et al. [20] to describe sets of relations involving secret variables that correspond to discrete logarithms. Many cryptographic protocols [22,10,3] require some entity to prove that some public elements (a ciphertext, a certificate, ...) relying on several secret values, are well-formed and based on a DLRS. They thus require a proof of knowledge for a DLRS. More formally, a DLRS can be defined as follows:

Definition 2. *A DLRS $\mathcal{R}$ on the group $\mathbb{G}$ (of prime order p) with r relations over m variables and $w + r$ objects in $\mathbb{G}$ is a set of relations $R_1, ..., R_r$ defined over objects $A_1, ..., A_w, V_1, ..., V_r \in \mathbb{G}$ and the free variables $\alpha_1, ..., \alpha_m \in \mathbb{Z}_p$ where R_i, for $i = 1, ..., r$, is to be interpreted as: $V_i = \sum_{j \in \mathcal{J}_i} [\alpha_j] A_{v_{i,j}}$, where $\mathcal{J}_i \subseteq \{1, ..., m\}$ and $v_{i,j} \in \{1, ..., w\}$ for $i = 1, ..., r$ and $j \in \mathcal{J}_i$. We will write $\mathcal{R}(\alpha_1, ..., \alpha_m)$ to denote the conjunction of all the relations R_i on the variables $\alpha_1, ..., \alpha_m$.*

Remark 3. The above definition is given in a group $\mathbb{G}$, but it could be in any group. In our practical applications, as we will work in pairing-friendly settings, relations could be all in $\mathbb{G}_1$ but also all in $\mathbb{G}_2$ or in both $\mathbb{G}_1$ and $\mathbb{G}_2$. In the following, we will describe our results in the group $\mathbb{G}_1$, with companion values in $\mathbb{G}_2$, and we will give evidences that it can also work in the general case.

Using these notations, a prover that knows witnesses $\alpha_1, ..., \alpha_m$ such that $\mathcal{R}(\alpha_1, ..., \alpha_m) = 1$ will generally use the 3-flow zero-knowledge proof of knowledge described in Figure 1 (which is easily derived from the Schnorr's protocol [25] for groups of known order). This protocol then corresponds to a proof of knowledge for a DLRS. The completeness comes from the fact that for valid witnesses $\alpha_1, ..., \alpha_m$ that satisfy, for all i, $V_i = \sum_{j \in \mathcal{J}_i} [\alpha_j] A_{v_{i,j}}$, then for all $i \in \{1, ..., r\}$,

$$\sum_{j \in \mathcal{J}_i} [s_j] A_{v_{i,j}} = \sum_{j \in \mathcal{J}_i} [k_j + c\alpha_j] A_{v_{i,j}} = \sum_{j \in \mathcal{J}_i} [k_j] A_{v_{i,j}} + [c] \sum_{j \in \mathcal{J}_i} [\alpha_j] A_{v_{i,j}} = K_i + [c]V_i.$$

The complexity for the prover is: $\sum_{i=1}^{r} \#\mathcal{J}_i$ multiplications by scalars in $\mathbb{G}$ and $\sum_{i=1}^{r}(\#\mathcal{J}_i - 1)$ additions in $\mathbb{G}$ to get the commitments K_i for $i \in \{1,...,r\}$.

For complex DLRSs, it can represent too many computations. In the next section, we explain how to delegate such proofs of knowledge of DLRSs, where the constrained device has to compute m scalar multiplications in $\mathbb{G}_2$ to prove knowledge of $\alpha_1, \ldots, \alpha_m$ satisfying a DLRS $\mathcal{R}$ in $\mathbb{G}_1$, no matter how many relations R_i are involved in $\mathcal{R}$.

3   Delegating Proofs of Knowledge

As in [5,7,3], we will split the prover into a trusted device which has a limited computational power and a more powerful, but untrusted, machine. As in DAA [5] schemes, the trusted device will be called the TPM (Trusted Platform Module) and the untrusted machine will be called the host.

3.1   Our First Protocol

We consider the following situation: the TPM knows witnesses $(\alpha_1, \ldots, \alpha_m)$ for the DLRS $\mathcal{R}$, such that $\mathcal{R}(\alpha_1, \ldots, \alpha_m) = 1$, and wants to use the computational power of the host to prove knowledge of these witnesses. Since the host is not trusted, we do not want to give $(\alpha_1, \ldots, \alpha_m)$ to it (else it would be able to impersonate the TPM). However, we allow it to get access to more information than a standard verifier (see Theorem 5). This is a common requirement in DAA schemes and, more generally, in server-aided cryptography (see *e.g.* [8]).

Intuition. Informally, we do not want the TPM to have to compute $[k_j]A_{v_{i,j}}$ for all the pairs (i, j), as in the extended Schnorr's protocol, then we essentially lift them to $\mathbb{G}_T$, by applying pairing with $\widetilde{G}$, and then the K_i's become

$$e\left(K_i, \widetilde{G}\right) = e\left(\sum_{j \in \mathcal{J}_i} [k_j]A_{v_{i,j}}, \widetilde{G}\right) = \prod_{j \in \mathcal{J}_i} e\left(A_{v_{i,j}}, [k_j]\widetilde{G}\right) = \prod_{j \in \mathcal{J}_i} e\left(A_{v_{i,j}}, \widetilde{Z}_j\right).$$

The verification $K_i \overset{?}{=} \sum_{j \in \mathcal{J}_i} [s_j]A_{v_{i,j}} - [c]V_i$ would then become

$$\prod_{j \in \mathcal{J}_i} e\left(A_{v_{i,j}}, \widetilde{Z}_j\right) \overset{?}{=} e\left(\sum_{j \in \mathcal{J}_i} [s_j]A_{v_{i,j}} - [c]V_i, \widetilde{G}\right).$$

This is the reason why the TPM can just compute $\widetilde{Z}_j = [k_j]\widetilde{G}$, for $k = 1, \ldots, m$.

A First Note. However, it cannot directly send these values to the verifier. Otherwise, the zero-knowledge property obtained by our protocol would not be equivalent to the one of the initial Extended Schnorr's protocol, from the

TPM	Host	Verifier
$\forall j \in \{1,\ldots,m\},$	$\forall i \in \{1,\ldots,r\},$	
$k_j \xleftarrow{\$} \mathbb{Z}_p, \widetilde{Z}_j \leftarrow [k_j]\widetilde{G}$	$(b_{i,j})_j \xleftarrow{\$} (\mathbb{Z}_p^*)^m, (t_{i,j})_j \xleftarrow{\$} (\mathbb{Z}_p)^m$	
	such that $\sum_{k \in \mathcal{J}_i} t_{i,k} = 0 \bmod p$	

$$\xrightarrow{\{\widetilde{Z}_j\}_j} \forall i \in \{1,\ldots,r\}, \forall j \in \mathcal{J}_i,$$
$$Z_{i,j} \leftarrow [b_{i,j}^{-1}]A_{v_{i,j}}$$
$$\widetilde{B}_{i,j} \leftarrow [b_{i,j}](\widetilde{Z}_j + [t_{i,j}]\widetilde{A}_{i,j})$$
$$\xrightarrow{\{Z_{i,j}, \widetilde{B}_{i,j}\}_{i,j}}$$

$$\forall j \in \{1,\ldots,m\}, \xleftarrow{\quad c \quad} \qquad\qquad \xleftarrow{\quad c \quad} \quad c \xleftarrow{\$} \{0,1\}^\ell$$
$$s_j \leftarrow k_j + c\alpha_j \bmod p$$
$$\xrightarrow{\{s_j\}_j} \qquad\qquad \xrightarrow{\{s_j\}_j} \forall i \in \{1,\ldots,r\}$$
$$e\left(\sum_{j \in \mathcal{J}_i} [s_j]A_{v_{i,j}} - [c]V_i, \widetilde{G}\right) \stackrel{?}{=} \prod_{j \in \mathcal{J}_i} e(Z_{i,j}, \widetilde{B}_{i,j})$$

Setting: A pairing-friendly setting $(p, \mathbb{G}_1, \mathbb{G}_2, \mathbb{G}_T, G, \widetilde{G}, e)$ and a DLRS $\mathcal{R}$ in $\mathbb{G}_1$: for $A_1, \ldots, A_w, V_1, \ldots, V_r \in \mathbb{G}_1$, and $\mathcal{J}_1, \ldots, \mathcal{J}_r \subseteq \{1, \ldots, w\}$, the TPM knows variables $\alpha_1, \ldots, \alpha_m \in \mathbb{Z}_p$ such that $V_i = \sum_{j \in \mathcal{J}_i} [\alpha_j]A_{v_{i,j}}$, for $i = 1, \ldots, r$.
Notations: For $i = 1, \ldots, w$, we denote $a_i \in \mathbb{Z}_p$ the discrete logarithms such that $A_i = [a_i]G$, and, for $i = 1, \ldots, r$ and $j \in \mathcal{J}_i$, one computes $\widetilde{A}_{i,j} = \left[\frac{1}{a_{v_{i,j}}} \prod_{k \in \mathcal{J}_i} a_{v_{i,k}}\right] \widetilde{G}$ that are added to the public parameters (see Section 3.2 for details).
Players' inputs: The public input contains $G, \widetilde{G}, \{V_i\}_i, \{\mathcal{J}_i\}_i, \{A_j\}_j$ and the $\{\widetilde{A}_{i,j}\}_{i,j}$; The TPM additionally knows $\{\alpha_i\}_i$.

Fig. 2. Delegation of Proof of Knowledge of Witnesses for a DLRS

verifier's view: from $\widetilde{Z}_j = [k_i]\widetilde{G}$ and $s_j = k_j - c\alpha_j \bmod p$, one would be able to compute $[c^{-1}]\left(\widetilde{Z}_j - [s_j]\widetilde{G}\right) = [c^{-1}][c\alpha_j]\widetilde{G} = [\alpha_j]\widetilde{G}$. This might be too much information about α_j. These values are thus just sent to the host who will compute blinded versions $Z_{i,j} \leftarrow [b_{i,j}^{-1}]A_{v_{i,j}}$ and $\widetilde{B}_{i,j} \leftarrow [b_{i,j}](\widetilde{Z}_j + [t_{i,j}]\widetilde{A}_{i,j})$, with random scalars $(b_{i,j})_{i,j}$ and $(t_{i,j})_{i,j}$ and additional elements $(\widetilde{A}_{i,j})_{i,j}$ (defined in Figure 2), so that for any i,

$$\prod_{j \in \mathcal{J}_i} e\left(A_{v_{i,j}}, \widetilde{Z}_j\right) = \prod_{j \in \mathcal{J}_i} e\left(Z_{i,j}, \widetilde{B}_{i,j}\right) / \prod_{j \in \mathcal{J}_i} e\left(A_{v_{i,j}}, [t_{i,j}]\widetilde{A}_{i,j}\right)$$

where the latter denominator is equal to, with $c_i = \prod_{k \in \mathcal{J}_i} a_{v_{i,k}}$,

$$\prod_{j \in \mathcal{J}_i} e\left([a_{v_{i,j}}]G, [t_{i,j}/a_{v_{i,j}}] \prod_{k \in \mathcal{J}_i} [a_{v_{i,k}}]\widetilde{G}\right) = e\left(G, \left[\left(\sum_{j \in \mathcal{J}_i} t_{i,j}\right) c_i\right]\widetilde{G}\right)$$

By choosing $(t_{i,j})_{i,j}$ such that $\sum_{j \in \mathcal{J}_i} t_{i,j} = 0 \bmod p$, it is equal to $1_{\mathbb{G}_T}$.

A Second Note. If one just uses the factors $(b_{i,j})_{i,j}$, but not $(t_{i,j})_{i,j}$, the values $(Z_{i,j})_{i,j}$ and $(\widetilde{B}_{i,j})_{i,j}$ would reveal to much information too. Let us consider any pair (i,j) such that $j \in \mathcal{J}_i$ and $k = v_{i,j}$: $e(Z_{i,j}, \widetilde{B}_{i,j}) = e(A_k, \widetilde{Z}_j)$, and thus

$$\left(e(Z_{i,j}, \widetilde{B}_{i,j})/e(A_k, [s_j]\widetilde{G}) \right)^{1/c} = e\left(A_k, [c^{-1}]\left(\widetilde{Z}_j - [s_j]\widetilde{G} \right) \right) = e\left(A_k, \alpha_j \widetilde{G} \right).$$

Then, $e(A_k, \widetilde{G})^{\alpha_j}$ would leak, which is again too much information about α_j.

In the case of a singleton $\mathcal{J}_i = \{j\}$, $V_i = [\alpha_j]A_k$ indeed leaks this information too, but in case of larger sets, such information does not leak, and thus should not leak from the proof either.

Description. These blinding factors $(b_{i,j})_{i,j}$ and $(t_{i,j})_{i,j}$ will make the protocol zero-knowledge from the verifier's view (as formally proven in Section 4). This leads to the 3-flow protocol described on Figure 2, that enables the TPM to prove knowledge of $(\alpha_1, \ldots, \alpha_m)$ with fewer computations than in the extended Schnorr's protocol (see Figure 1).

Example I. Let us consider the following example:

$$V_1 = [\alpha_1]A_1 \qquad \ldots \qquad V_q = [\alpha_1]A_q$$
$$V_{q+1} = [\alpha_2]A_{q+1} \qquad \ldots \qquad V_{q+s} = [\alpha_2]A_{q+s}$$
$$V_{q+s+1} = [\alpha_1]A_{q+s+1} + [\alpha_2]A_{q+s+n+1} \quad \ldots \quad V_{q+s+n} = [\alpha_1]A_{q+s+n} + [\alpha_2]A_{q+s+2n}$$

Using the extended Schnorr's protocol described on Figure 1, one would require $q+s+2n$ multiplications by scalars in $\mathbb{G}_1$ (group exponentiations) and n additions in $\mathbb{G}_1$ from the TPM. With our protocol (see Figure 2), the TPM has to compute only 2 multiplications by scalars in $\mathbb{G}_2$ (group exponentiations).

3.2 Additional Computations

One might have noted that the public parameters must now contain several $\widetilde{A}_{i,j}$ that may not be known in practice. However, in most cases, there is no need of additional values. First, when $\mathcal{J}_i = \{j\}$ is a singleton, $\widetilde{A}_{i,j} = \widetilde{G}$. Second, when $\mathcal{J}_i = \{\alpha, \beta\}$ is a pair, and $v_{i,\alpha} = u$ and $v_{i,\beta} = v$, then $\widetilde{A}_{i,\alpha} = [a_v]\widetilde{G}$ and $\widetilde{A}_{i,\beta} = [a_u]\widetilde{G}$. Thus, $\widetilde{A}_{i,\alpha} = A_v$ and $\widetilde{A}_{i,\beta} = A_u$ in the case of symmetric pairing (*i.e.*, $\mathbb{G}_1 = \mathbb{G}_2$). Our above Example I involves singletons and pairs only, and thus the $\widetilde{A}_{i,j}$ can be easily publicly computed. However, in Section 5, we provide another delegation protocol that does not present these limitations, and can thus be used in more situations.

3.3 Computational Cost

Since the TPM is considered to be far less powerful than the host and the verifier, we want to decrease its computational load even if it involves a slight increase of work for the host and for the verifier. Let us evaluate the computational cost for each party (see Table 1):

Table 1. Complexity Comparisons

		Prover	Verifier
	TPM	Host	
Ext. Schnorr		$JM + (J-r)A$	$JM + (J-r)A$
Example I		$(q+s+2n)M + nA$	$(q+s+2n)M + nA$
Example II		$7M + 2A$	$7M + 2A$
Example III		$9M + 3A$	$9M + 3A$
Figure 2	mM_2	$J(M_1 + 2M_2 + A_2)$	$J(M_1 + A_1 + P + M_T)$ $+r(M_1 + P - M_T)$
Example I	$2M_2$	$(q+s+2n)(M_1 + 2M_2 + A_2)$	$(2q+2s+3n)(M_1 + P)$ $+(q+s+2n)A_1 + nM_T$
Example II	$2M_2$	$7(M_1 + 2M_2 + A_2)$	$12(M_1 + P) + 7A_1 + 2M_T$
Example III	$6M_2$	$9(M_1 + 2M_2 + A_2)$	$15(M_1 + P) + 9A_1 + 3M_T$
Figure 3	mM_2	$J(2M_1 + 2M_2 + A_2 + A_1)$ $-rA_1$	$(J+r)(M_1 + A_1 + P)$ $+(J-r)M_T$
Example I	$2M_2$	$(q+s+2n)(2M1 + 2M_2 + A_2)$ $+nA_1$	$(2q+2s+3n)(M_1 + A_1 + P)$ $+nM_T$
Example II	$2M_2$	$7(2M_1 + 2M_2 + A_2) + 2A_1$	$12(M_1 + A_1 + P) + 2M_T$
Example III	$6M_2$	$9(2M_1 + 2M_2 + A_2) + 3A_1$	$15(M_1 + A_1 + P) + 3M_T$

Generic DLRS: m secret scalars, r relations each involving J_i elements respectively for $i = 1, \ldots, r$, and thus globally $J = \sum J_i$.

For the extended Schnorr, all computations have to be done by the TPM itself. A, A_1, A_2 denote point additions in $\mathbb{G}, \mathbb{G}_1, \mathbb{G}_2$ respectively; M, M_1, M_2 denote point multiplications by a scalar in $\mathbb{G}, \mathbb{G}_1, \mathbb{G}_2$ respectively; M_T denotes multiplication in $\mathbb{G}_T$; P denotes a pairing.

- the TPM has to compute m multiplications by a scalar in $\mathbb{G}_2$ (one *per* variable α_i), which are moreover all precomputable. Its computational cost is thus independent of the number of relations, which can be very useful when a variable is involved in many relations (as in our above Example I);
- the host has to compute $\sum_{i=1}^{r} \#\mathcal{J}_i$ multiplications by a scalar in $\mathbb{G}_1$ and at most the same number of additions in $\mathbb{G}_2$ and twice as many multiplications by a scalar in $\mathbb{G}_2$;
- the verifier has to compute $\sum_{i=1}^{r} \#\mathcal{J}_i$ additions in $\mathbb{G}_1$, $r + \sum_{i=1}^{r} \#\mathcal{J}_i$ multiplications by a scalar in $\mathbb{G}_1$, $r + \sum_{i=1}^{r} \#\mathcal{J}_i$ pairings, and some multiplications in $\mathbb{G}_T$.

3.4   More Examples

We now provide some concrete examples, with comparisons of the complexity computations on Table 1: Extended Schnorr is the natural 3-round protocol between a prover and a verifier, while the two other protocols are the delagated protocols proposed above (in Section 3) and below (in Section 5). One can note that our protocols with delagation drastically reduce the computational cost for the TPM with respect to the Prover in the basic protocol. To this aim, one can indeed use $\mathbb{G}_2$ as the efficient group and $\mathbb{G}_1$ as the less efficient group in the pairing-friendly setting.

Example II. In 2007, Shacham [26] described an encryption scheme based on the DLIN assumption. This is a Cramer-Shoup variant of the linear encryption, where the first triple is a linear tuple used for masking the plaintext in the fourth element, while the last element helps to verify validity with a hash proof system (see also [19]). With the public parameters $(G_1, G_2, G_3) \in \mathbb{G}_1^3$ and the public key $(H_1, H_2, C_1, C_2, D_1, D_2) \in \mathbb{G}_1^6$ and a collision-resistant hash function $\mathcal{H}$, to encrypt a message $M \in \mathbb{G}_1$, one computes, for random scalars $\alpha_1, \alpha_2 \in \mathbb{Z}_p$:

$$\left(\begin{array}{ll} U_1 = [\alpha_1]G_1, \quad U_2 = [\alpha_2]G_2, \quad U_3 = [\alpha_1 + \alpha_2]G_3, \\ E = M + [\alpha_1]H_1 + [\alpha_2]H_2, \qquad V = [\alpha_1](C_1 + [u]D_1) + [\alpha_2](C_2 + [u]D_2) \end{array} \right)$$

where $u = \mathcal{H}(U_1, U_2, U_3, E) \in \mathbb{Z}_p$. We may need to prove, as in [9], that (U_1, U_2, U_3, E, V) is a valid ciphertext. Since 2 secret variables (α_1 and α_2) are involved in the 4 relations to be checked for ciphertext validity (on U_1, U_2, U_3, and V), our protocol only requires 2 multiplications by a scalar from the TPM.

Example III. In [23], the authors provided a group signature with message-dependent opening (GS-DMO) scheme secure in the random oracle model. With the public parameters $(U, V, G, H) \in \mathbb{G}_1^4$, to issue a signature σ, one has to prove knowledge of $\alpha, \beta, x, \delta_1, \delta_2, \delta_3 \in \mathbb{Z}_p$ such that:

$$\left(\begin{array}{lll} T_1 = [\alpha]U, & T_2 = [\beta]V, & T_3 = [\alpha + \beta]H, \\ 0 = [x]T_1 - [\delta_1]U, & 0 = [x]T_2 - [\delta_2]V, & 0 = [x]T_5 - [\delta_3]G \end{array} \right)$$

where $T_1, T_2, T_3, T_5 \in \mathbb{G}_1$ are part of the signature σ. Since 6 secret variables are involved in these relations, our protocol only requires 6 multiplications by a scalar from the TPM.

3.5   Security Properties

The protocol described on Figure 2 may actually be divided in two parts: a proof of knowledge between $\mathcal{P}$ (TPM + host) and $\mathcal{V}$ (verifier) and a proof of knowledge between $\mathcal{P}$ (TPM) and $\mathcal{V}$ (host). We consider the security of each part in the following theorems, which proofs are provided in Section 4.

Theorem 4. *The protocol described on Figure 2 is a 3-move zero-knowledge proof of knowledge of the witnesses $\alpha_1, ..., \alpha_m$ between $\mathcal{P}$ (TPM + host) and $\mathcal{V}$ (verifier), where the description of $\mathcal{R}$ is the unique auxiliary input.*

The first theorem essentially shows that this proof of knowledge does not leak any information outside the host. But one may wonder if the host learns a lot of information. This is the goal of the second theorem below that says that the host just learns $\{[\alpha_i]\widetilde{G}\}_i$, which is not enough to impersonate the TPM later.

Theorem 5. *The protocol described on Figure 2 is a 3-move zero-knowledge proof of knowledge of the witnesses $\alpha_1, ..., \alpha_m$ between $\mathcal{P}$ (TPM) and $\mathcal{V}$ (host), where the auxiliary input contains the description of $\mathcal{R}$ and the additional values $\{[\alpha_i]\widetilde{G}\}_i$.*

3.6 Discussions

Honest Verifier Zero-Knowledge. As usual, this protocol is actually a zero-knowledge proof of knowledge if the challenge c is selected from $\{0, 1\}^\ell$ and the proof is repeated k times with ℓ logarithmically bounded in the security parameter and $2^{k\ell}$ super-polynomial. If one wants the soundness in one execution only, which implies 2^ℓ to be super-polynomial, then the protocol is no longer zero-knowledge but *honest-verifier zero-knowledge* only.

Precomputation. As already noticed, if computations of a party are independent of external values, they can be prepared and stored in advance. This is the case of the elements $\widetilde{Z}_j$ computed by the TPM.

For example let us consider the Sign protocol of the DAA scheme from [3, page 32]. The TPM has to prove knowledge of its secret key s involved in two relations (namely $K = [s]J$ and $W = [s]S$). Since the authors use the standard Schnorr's protocol, this leads to 2 multiplications by a scalar for the TPM, one of which (the one involving J) has to be computed *online* because J is determined by the *basename* submitted by the verifier. Using our protocol, the TPM only has to compute one multiplication by a scalar, and it can even be precomputed, since the basis $\widetilde{G}$ is a public parameter.

We even emphasize that these precomputations (the group elements $\widetilde{Z}_j$) can even be sent to the host. The TPM just has to store the scalars k_j, or even a seed (and some index), as off-line pre-computed coupons [15].

Extra Inputs. In the Theorem 5, we allow the host to learn the elements $[\alpha_j]\widetilde{G}$ for all $j \in \{1, ..., m\}$. In the DAA scheme considered above, this means that the host can learn $[s]\widetilde{G}$, which does not endanger the security properties.

Indeed, the non-frameability property of their scheme is based on the fact that the adversary does not know s. However, recovering s from both $[s]G$ and $[s]\widetilde{G}$ is not known to be much easier than recovering s from $[s]G$ alone. As a consequence, the non-frameability still holds.

However, one could argue that this additional information helps to break the anonymity property. But as already remarked, one does not require to enforce anonymity of the TPM with respect to the host, since the latter already knows which TPM is inserted (or even sees the signature which is sent outside). And as explained in [7], in DAA schemes and in server-aided version of group signatures, the host is not adversarially-controlled in the anonymity experiment, but just for the impersonation or frameability.

More General Relations. The protocol described on Figure 2 only considers relations in $\mathbb{G}_1$. But as already said, our protocol would work the same way if all relations were in $\mathbb{G}_2$, by simply swapping the role of $\mathbb{G}_1$ and $\mathbb{G}_2$ in our protocol described in Figure 2.

However, one could have to prove knowledge of variables involved in relations in both $\mathbb{G}_1$ and $\mathbb{G}_2$. In such a case the host would need to know a commitment in $\mathbb{G}_2$ (to compute the proof for relations in $\mathbb{G}_1$) and one in $\mathbb{G}_1$ (for the relations in $\mathbb{G}_2$). The computational cost for the TPM would then depend on the type of the pairing. For pairings of Type 1 or Type 2, the computational cost will remain the same because of the isomorphism. For pairings of Type 3 (without any efficient isomorphism), the TPM would have to compute the values in both groups, and thus with a multiplication by a scalar in $\mathbb{G}_1$ and a multiplication by a scalar in $\mathbb{G}_2$ for each variable involved in both $\mathbb{G}_1$ and $\mathbb{G}_2$. In any case, the computational cost remains independent of the number of relations.

4   Security Proofs

We now formally prove the two above theorems. Completeness and soundness will be similar for both, but the zero-knowledge property will involve two different simulators.

4.1   Completeness

It follows from the construction explained in Section 3.1: The verifier checks whether

$$e\left(\sum_{j\in\mathcal{J}_i}[s_j]A_{v_{i,j}} - [c]V_i, \widetilde{G}\right) \stackrel{?}{=} \prod_{j\in\mathcal{J}_i} e(Z_{i,j}, \widetilde{B}_{i,j}).$$

Since, for all $i \in \{1,\ldots,r\}$, $V_i = \sum_{j\in\mathcal{J}_i}[\alpha_j]A_{v_{i,j}}$ and for all $j \in \{1,\ldots,m\}$, $s_j = k_j + c\alpha_j \bmod p$, then $\sum_{j\in\mathcal{J}_i}[s_j]A_{v_{i,j}} = \sum_{j\in\mathcal{J}_i}[k_j + c\alpha_j]A_{v_{i,j}} = \sum_{j\in\mathcal{J}_i}[k_j]A_{v_{i,j}} + [c]V_i$, and one easily verifies that both sides are equal to $e\left(\sum_{j\in\mathcal{J}_i}[k_j]A_{v_{i,j}}, \widetilde{G}\right)$, which proves the completeness.

4.2   Soundness

Let $\{Z_{i,j}, \widetilde{B}_{i,j}\}_{i,j}$ be the values sent to the verifier at the first flow. If the adversary (trying to impersonate $\mathcal{P}$ (TPM + host)) can answer successfully with probability significantly greater than $1/2^\ell$, then it can send $\{s_j\}_j$ and $\{s'_j\}_j$ for two different challenges c and c': $\forall i \in \{1,\ldots,r\}$,

$$e\left(\sum_{j\in\mathcal{J}_i}[s_j]A_{v_{i,j}} - [c]V_i, \widetilde{G}\right) = \prod_{j\in\mathcal{J}_i} e(Z_{i,j}, \widetilde{B}_{i,j}) = e\left(\sum_{j\in\mathcal{J}_i}[s'_j]A_{v_{i,j}} - [c']V_i, \widetilde{G}\right),$$

which leads to $e\left(\sum_{j\in\mathcal{J}_i}[s_j - s'_j]A_{v_{i,j}} - [c - c']V_i, \widetilde{G}\right) = 1_{\mathbb{G}_T}$ and thus, from the non-degeneracy of the pairing, $\sum_{j\in\mathcal{J}_i}[s_j - s'_j]A_{v_{i,j}} - [c - c']V_i = 0_{\mathbb{G}_1}$. As a consequence, $\alpha_j = (s_j - s_j')/(c - c')$ for $j = 1, \ldots, m$, we have $V_i = \sum_{j \in \mathcal{J}_i} [\alpha_j] A_{v_{i,j}}$ for $i = 1, \ldots, r$. This is thus a solution to the DLRS $\mathcal{R}$.

4.3 Zero-Knowledge w.r.t. the Host

For Theorem 5, we assume the host already knows (or can learn, as explained above) $T_j = [\alpha_j]\widetilde{G}$, $\forall j \in \{1, \ldots, m\}$. The simulator operates as follows:

- it first selects $c \stackrel{\$}{\leftarrow} \{0,1\}^\ell$ and $\{s_j\}_j \stackrel{\$}{\leftarrow} \mathbb{Z}_p$;
- it computes: $\widetilde{Z}_j \leftarrow [s_j]\widetilde{G} - [c]T_j$, for all $j \in \{1, \ldots, m\}$;
- it then outputs $\{\widetilde{Z}_j\}_j$, and waits for the challenge and rewinds in case of incorrect guess of c;
- it eventually answers $\{s_j\}_j$.

This is statistically indistinguishable from transcripts generated during a real protocol between the TPM and the host. Since the initial guess for c is perfectly hidden in $\{\widetilde{Z}_j\}_j$, the probability of successful simulation is $1/2^\ell$, which is non-negligible for a logarithmic value ℓ. For a larger ℓ, it remains honest-verifier zero-knowledge.

4.4 Zero-Knowledge w.r.t. the Verifier

For Theorem 4, the verifier just knows the public parameters: $G, \widetilde{G}, \{A_j\}_j, \{V_i\}$. The simulator operates as follows:

- it first selects $c \stackrel{\$}{\leftarrow} \{0,1\}^\ell$ and $\{s_j\}_j \stackrel{\$}{\leftarrow} \mathbb{Z}_p$;
- it computes $K_i \leftarrow \sum_{j \in \mathcal{J}_i}[s_j]A_{v_{i,j}} - [c]V_i$, for all $i \in \{1, \ldots, r\}$;
- it additionally selects, for $i \in \{1, \ldots, r\}$ and $j \in \mathcal{J}_i$, $u_{i,j} \stackrel{\$}{\leftarrow} \mathbb{Z}_p^*$ and $U_{i,j} \stackrel{\$}{\leftarrow} \mathbb{G}_1 \setminus \{0_{\mathbb{G}_1}\}$, such that $\sum_{j \in \mathcal{J}_i} U_{i,j} = K_i$ (which conditions the last $U_{i,j}$);
- it then computes, for $i \in \{1, \ldots, r\}$ and $j \in \mathcal{J}_i$, $Z_{i,j} = [u_{i,j}^{-1}]U_{i,j}$ and $\widetilde{B}_{i,j} = [u_{i,j}]\widetilde{G}$;
- it then outputs $\{Z_{i,j}, \widetilde{B}_{i,j}\}_{i,j}$, and waits for the challenge and rewinds in case of incorrect guess of c;
- it eventually answers $\{s_j\}_j$.

A problem can occur with the above simulation if some elements get zero while it is not allowed. But the large order of the groups makes this problem to happen with negligible probability only. We exclude these bad cases in the following.

In order to prove the zero-knowledge property, we need to show that our simulated tuples are indistinguishable from the tuples generated during a real protocol, for the verifier. In a real protocol, the verifier sees: $[Z_{i,j}, \widetilde{B}_{i,j}], c, \{s_j\}_j$, where $Z_{i,j} = [b_{i,j}^{-1}]A_{v_{i,j}} = [a_{v_{i,j}}/b_{i,j}]G$ for random non-zero scalars $b_{i,j}$, and $\widetilde{B}_{i,j} = [b_{i,j}](\widetilde{Z}_j + [t_{i,j}]\widetilde{A}_{i,j}) = [b_{i,j}/a_{v_{i,j}} \cdot (k_j a_{v_{i,j}} + t_{i,j} \prod_{k \in \mathcal{J}_i} a_{v_{i,k}})]\widetilde{G}$ for random scalars $t_{i,j}$, such that $\sum_{j \in \mathcal{J}_i} t_{i,j} = 0 \bmod p$.

Let us denote $u'_{i,j} = (b_{i,j}/a_{v_{i,j}}) \cdot (k_j a_{v_{i,j}} + t_{i,j} \prod_{k \in \mathcal{J}_i} a_{v_{i,k}})$, for $i = 1, \ldots, r$ and $j \in \mathcal{J}_i$. Then $\widetilde{B}_{i,j} = [u'_{i,j}]\widetilde{G}$. Since the $b_{i,j}$'s are independent random scalars, the $u'_{i,j}$'s are also independent random scalars, and thus follow the same distribution as the $u_{i,j}$'s.

With such a notation and $d_i = \prod_{k \in \mathcal{J}_i} a_{v_{i,k}}$, we have $Z_{i,j} = [(u'_{i,j})^{-1}(k_j a_{v_{i,j}} + t_{i,j} d_i)]G$. Let us denote $U'_{i,j} = [k_j a_{v_{i,j}} + t_{i,j} d_i]G$. Since the $t_{i,j}$ are random scalars with the unique constraint that $\sum_{j \in \mathcal{J}_i} t_{i,j} = 0 \bmod p$, for $i = 1, \ldots, r$, then the $U'_{i,j}$'s are random elements in $\mathbb{G}_1$ with the constraint that, for $i = 1, \ldots, r$,

$$\sum_{j \in \mathcal{J}_i} U'_{i,j} = \left[\sum_{j \in \mathcal{J}_i} k_j a_{v_{i,j}}\right]G = \sum_{j \in \mathcal{J}_i} [s_j - c\alpha_j]A_{v_{i,j}} = \sum_{j \in \mathcal{J}_i} [s_j]A_{v_{i,j}} - [c]V_i = K_i.$$

As a consequence, in the real protocol execution, for $i \in \{1, \ldots, r\}$ and $j \in \mathcal{J}_i$, $Z_{i,j} = [(u'_{i,j})^{-1}]U'_{i,j}$ and $\widetilde{B}_{i,j} = [u'_{i,j}]\widetilde{G}$, where the $u'_{i,j}$'s and $U'_{i,j}$'s follow the same distributions as the $u_{i,j}$'s and $U_{i,j}$'s generated by our simulator.

5 Delegating with Weaker Assumptions

5.1 Description

As said in Section 3.2, our first protocol required the knowledge of the elements $\widetilde{A}_{i,j}$. In many applications, such as our first example, this is not a strong requirement. However, in some other cases, this can be a problem. We thus now provide another protocol for the same delegation from the TPM to the host, with just a slight increase of the computations for the host, but without any additional information. The main difference with our first protocol is that the Host now needs to additionally compute the H_i's which permit to blind the $\widetilde{A}_{i,j}$'s. This protocol is described on Figure 3 and the obtained efficiency is given in Table 1.

5.2 Security Results

Theorem 6. *The protocol described on Figure 3 is a 3-move zero-knowledge proof of knowledge of the witnesses $\alpha_1, \ldots, \alpha_m$ between $\mathcal{P}$ (TPM + host) and $\mathcal{V}$ (verifier), where the description of $\mathcal{R}$ is the unique auxiliary input.*

As for Theorems 4 and 5, the first theorem essentially shows that this proof does not leak any information outside the host, and the next one says that the host just learns $\{[\alpha_i]\widetilde{G}\}_i$, which is not enough to impersonate the TPM later.

Theorem 7. *The protocol in Figure 3 is a 3-move zero-knowledge proof of knowledge of the witnesses $\alpha_1, \ldots, \alpha_m$ between $\mathcal{P}$ (TPM) and $\mathcal{V}$ (host), where the auxiliary input contains the description of $\mathcal{R}$ and the additional values $\{[\alpha_i]\widetilde{G}\}_i$.*

TPM	Host	Verifier
$\forall j \in \{1,\ldots,m\}$,	$\forall i \in \{1,\ldots,r\}$,	
$k_j \xleftarrow{\$} \mathbb{Z}_p, \widetilde{Z}_j \leftarrow [k_j]\widetilde{G}$	$(b_{i,j})_j \xleftarrow{\$} (\mathbb{Z}_p^*)^m, (t_{i,j})_j \xleftarrow{\$} (\mathbb{Z}_p)^m$	
	$H_i \leftarrow \sum_{j \in \mathcal{J}_i}[t_{i,j}]A_{v_{i,j}}$	

$$\xrightarrow{\quad \{\widetilde{Z}_j\}_j \quad}$$

$$\forall i \in \{1,\ldots,r\}, \forall j \in \mathcal{J}_i,$$
$$Z_{i,j} \leftarrow [b_{i,j}^{-1}]A_{v_{i,j}}$$
$$\widetilde{B}_{i,j} \leftarrow [b_{i,j}](\widetilde{Z}_j + [t_{i,j}]\widetilde{G})$$

$$\xrightarrow{\quad \{H_i\}_i, \{Z_{i,j}, \widetilde{B}_{i,j}\}_{i,j} \quad}$$

$$\xleftarrow{\quad c \quad} \qquad\qquad \xleftarrow{\quad c \quad} \quad c \xleftarrow{\$} \{0,1\}^\ell$$

$\forall j \in \{1,\ldots,m\}$,
$s_j \leftarrow k_j + c\alpha_j \bmod p$

$$\xrightarrow{\quad \{s_j\}_j \quad} \qquad\qquad \xrightarrow{\quad \{s_j\}_j \quad} \quad \forall i \in \{1,\ldots,r\}$$

$$e\left(H_i + \sum_{j \in \mathcal{J}_i}[s_j]A_{v_{i,j}} - [c]V_i, \widetilde{G}\right) \overset{?}{=} \prod_{j \in \mathcal{J}_i} e(Z_{i,j}, \widetilde{B}_{i,j})$$

Setting: A pairing-friendly setting $(p, \mathbb{G}_1, \mathbb{G}_2, \mathbb{G}_T, G, \widetilde{G}, e)$ and a DLRS $\mathcal{R}$ in $\mathbb{G}_1$: for $A_1, \ldots, A_w, V_1, \ldots, V_r \in \mathbb{G}_1$, and $\mathcal{J}_1, \ldots, \mathcal{J}_r \subseteq \{1,\ldots,w\}$, the TPM knows variables $\alpha_1, \ldots, \alpha_m \in \mathbb{Z}_p$ such that $V_i = \sum_{j \in \mathcal{J}_i}[\alpha_j]A_{v_{i,j}}$, for $i = 1,\ldots,r$.

Players' inputs: The public input contains $G, \widetilde{G}, \{V_i\}_i, \{\mathcal{J}_i\}_i, \{A_j\}_j$; The TPM knows $\{\alpha_i\}_i$.

Fig. 3. Delegation of Proof of Knowledge of Witnesses for a DLRS (without additional information)

5.3 Proofs of the Theorems

Completeness. The verifier checks, for $i = 1,\ldots,r$, $e(H_i + \sum_{j \in \mathcal{J}_i}[s_j]A_{v_{i,j}} - [c]V_i, \widetilde{G}) = \prod_{j \in \mathcal{J}_i} e(Z_{i,j}, \widetilde{B}_{i,j})$, where

$$e\left(H_i + \sum_{j \in \mathcal{J}_i}[s_j]A_{v_{i,j}} - [c]V_i, \widetilde{G}\right) = e\left(H_i + \sum_{j \in \mathcal{J}_i}[k_j]A_{v_{i,j}}, \widetilde{G}\right)$$

and

$$\prod_{j \in \mathcal{J}_i} e(Z_{i,j}, \widetilde{B}_{i,j}) = \prod_{j \in \mathcal{J}_i} e(A_{v_{i,j}}, \widetilde{Z}_j + [t_{i,j}]\widetilde{G}) = \prod_{j \in \mathcal{J}_i} e(A_{v_{i,j}}, [k_j + t_{i,j}]\widetilde{G})$$

$$= e\left(\sum_{j \in \mathcal{J}_i}[t_{i,j}]A_{v_{i,j}} + \sum_{j \in \mathcal{J}_i}[k_j]A_{v_{i,j}}, \widetilde{G}\right) = e\left(H_i + \sum_{j \in \mathcal{J}_i}[k_j]A_{v_{i,j}}, \widetilde{G}\right).$$

Soundness. The proof is similar to the one in Section 4 since everything was on the left-hand side of the verification equation, that remains the same plus a constant H_i.

5.4   Zero-Knowledge w.r.t. the Host

The protocol between the TPM and the host is the same as the first protocol, and thus the security analysis is the same as in Section 4.

5.5   Zero-Knowledge w.r.t. the Verifier

As in Section 4, the verifier just knows the public parameters: $G, \widetilde{G}, \{A_j\}_j, \{V_i\}$. The simulator operates as follows:

- it first selects $c \xleftarrow{\$} \{0,1\}^\ell$ and $\{s_j\}_j \xleftarrow{\$} \mathbb{Z}_p$;
- it computes $K_i \leftarrow \sum_{j \in \mathcal{J}_i} [s_j] A_{v_{i,j}} - [c] V_i$, for all $i \in \{1, \dots, r\}$;
- it additionally selects, for $i \in \{1, \dots, r\}$ and $j \in \mathcal{J}_i$, $u_{i,j} \xleftarrow{\$} \mathbb{Z}_p^*$ and $U_{i,j} \xleftarrow{\$} \mathbb{G}_1 \backslash \{0_{\mathbb{G}_1}\}$, with no constraint;
- it then computes, for $i \in \{1, \dots, r\}$, $H_i = \sum_{j \in \mathcal{J}_i} U_{i,j} - K_i$ and for $j \in \mathcal{J}_i$, $Z_{i,j} = [u_{i,j}^{-1}] U_{i,j}$ and $\widetilde{B}_{i,j} = [u_{i,j}] \widetilde{G}$;
- it then outputs $\{H_i\}_i, \{Z_{i,j}, \widetilde{B}_{i,j}\}_{i,j}$, and waits for the challenge and rewinds in case of incorrect guess of c;
- it eventually answers $\{s_j\}_j$.

As in Section 4, a problem can occur with the above simulation if some elements gets zero while it is not allowed. But the large order of the groups makes this problem to happen with negligible probability only. We exclude these bad cases in the following analysis.

In a real protocol, the verifier sees: $\{H_i\}_i, \{Z_{i,j}, \widetilde{B}_{i,j}\}, c, \{s_j\}_j$, where $H_i = \sum_{j \in \mathcal{J}_i} [t_{i,j}] A_{v_{i,j}} = \sum_{j \in \mathcal{J}_i} [t_{i,j} a_{v_{i,j}}] G$, for random scalars $t_{i,j}$, $Z_{i,j} = [b_{i,j}^{-1}] A_{v_{i,j}} = [a_{v_{i,j}}/b_{i,j}] G$ for random non-zero scalars $b_{i,j}$, and $\widetilde{B}_{i,j} = [b_{i,j}](\widetilde{Z}_j + [t_{i,j}] \widetilde{A}_{i,j}) = [b_{i,j}/a_{v_{i,j}} \cdot (k_j a_{v_{i,j}} + t_{i,j} \prod_{k \in \mathcal{J}_i} a_{v_{i,k}})] \widetilde{G}$.

Let us denote $u_{i,j}' = (b_{i,j}/a_{v_{i,j}}) \cdot (k_j a_{v_{i,j}} + t_{i,j} \prod_{k \in \mathcal{J}_i} a_{v_{i,k}})$, for $i = 1, \dots, r$ and $j \in \mathcal{J}_i$. Then $\widetilde{B}_{i,j} = [u_{i,j}'] \widetilde{G}$. Since the $b_{i,j}$'s are independent random scalars, the $u_{i,j}'$'s are also independent random scalars, and thus follow the same distribution as the $u_{i,j}$'s.

With such a notation and $d_i = \prod_{k \in \mathcal{J}_i} a_{v_{i,k}}$, we have $Z_{i,j} = [(u_{i,j}')^{-1}(k_j a_{v_{i,j}} + t_{i,j} d_i)] G$. Let us denote $U_{i,j}' = [k_j a_{v_{i,j}} + t_{i,j} d_i] G$. Since the $t_{i,j}$ are random scalars, then the $U_{i,j}'$'s are random elements in $\mathbb{G}_1$. Eventually,

$$\sum_{j \in \mathcal{J}_i} U_{i,j}' = [\sum_{j \in \mathcal{J}_i} k_j a_{v_{i,j}} + t_{i,j} d_i] G = K_i + \sum_{j \in \mathcal{J}_i} [t_{i,j}] A_{v_{i,j}} = K_i + H_i.$$

As a consequence, in the real protocol execution, for $i \in \{1, \dots, r\}$, $H_i = \sum_{j \in \mathcal{J}_i} U_{i,j} - K_i$, and for $j \in \mathcal{J}_i$, $Z_{i,j} = [(u_{i,j}')^{-1}] U_{i,j}'$ and $\widetilde{B}_{i,j} = [u_{i,j}'] \widetilde{G}$, where the $u_{i,j}'$'s and $U_{i,j}'$'s follow the same distributions as the $u_{i,j}$'s and $U_{i,j}$'s generated by our simulator.

Acknowledgments. This work was supported in part by the French ANR-12-INSE-0014 SIMPATIC Project.

References

1. Bellare, M., Micciancio, D., Warinschi, B.: Foundations of group signatures: Formal definitions, simplified requirements, and a construction based on general assumptions. In: Biham, E. (ed.) EUROCRYPT 2003. LNCS, vol. 2656, pp. 614–629. Springer, Heidelberg (2003)
2. Bellare, M., Rogaway, P.: Random oracles are practical: A paradigm for designing efficient protocols. In: Ashby, V. (ed.) ACM CCS 1993: 1st Conference on Computer and Communications Security, pp. 62–73. ACM Press (November 1993)
3. Bernhard, D., Fuchsbauer, G., Ghadafi, E., Smart, N.P., Warinschi, B.: Anonymous attestation with user-controlled linkability. Int. J. Inf. Sec. 12(3), 219–249 (2013)
4. Bichsel, P., Camenisch, J., Neven, G., Smart, N.P., Warinschi, B.: Get shorty via group signatures without encryption. In: Garay, J.A., De Prisco, R. (eds.) SCN 2010. LNCS, vol. 6280, pp. 381–398. Springer, Heidelberg (2010)
5. Brickell, E.F., Camenisch, J., Chen, L.: Direct anonymous attestation. In: Atluri, V., Pfitzmann, B., McDaniel, P. (eds.) ACM CCS 2004: 11th Conference on Computer and Communications Security, pp. 132–145. ACM Press (October 2004)
6. Brickell, E., Chen, L., Li, J.: Simplified security notions of direct anonymous attestation and a concrete scheme from pairings. Int. J. Inf. Sec. 8(5), 315–330 (2009)
7. Canard, S., Coisel, I., De Meulenaer, G., Pereira, O.: Group signatures are suitable for constrained devices. In: Rhee, K.-H., Nyang, D. (eds.) ICISC 2010. LNCS, vol. 6829, pp. 133–150. Springer, Heidelberg (2011)
8. Canard, S., Coisel, I., Devigne, J., Gallais, C., Peters, T., Sanders, O.: Toward generic method for server-aided cryptography. In: Qing, S., Zhou, J., Liu, D. (eds.) ICICS 2013. LNCS, vol. 8233, pp. 373–392. Springer, Heidelberg (2013)
9. Cathalo, J., Libert, B., Yung, M.: Group encryption: Non-interactive realization in the standard model. In: Matsui, M. (ed.) ASIACRYPT 2009. LNCS, vol. 5912, pp. 179–196. Springer, Heidelberg (2009)
10. Chen, L., Page, D., Smart, N.P.: On the design and implementation of an efficient daa scheme. In: Gollmann, D., Lanet, J.-L., Iguchi-Cartigny, J. (eds.) CARDIS 2010. LNCS, vol. 6035, pp. 223–237. Springer, Heidelberg (2010)
11. Delerablée, C., Pointcheval, D.: Dynamic fully anonymous short group signatures. In: Nguyên, P.Q. (ed.) VIETCRYPT 2006. LNCS, vol. 4341, pp. 193–210. Springer, Heidelberg (2006)
12. Feige, U., Fiat, A., Shamir, A.: Zero knowledge proofs of identity. In: Aho, A.V. (ed.) STOC, pp. 210–217. ACM (1987)
13. Fiat, A., Shamir, A.: How to prove yourself: Practical solutions to identification and signature problems. In: Odlyzko, A.M. (ed.) CRYPTO 1986. LNCS, vol. 263, pp. 186–194. Springer, Heidelberg (1987)
14. Girault, M.: An identity-based identification scheme based on discrete logarithms modulo a composite number (rump session). In: Damgård, I.B. (ed.) EUROCRYPT 1990. LNCS, vol. 473, pp. 481–486. Springer, Heidelberg (1991)
15. Girault, M., Poupard, G., Stern, J.: On the fly authentication and signature schemes based on groups of unknown order. Journal of Cryptology 19(4), 463–487 (2006)
16. Goldwasser, S., Micali, S., Rackoff, C.: The knowledge complexity of interactive proof-systems (extended abstract). In: Sedgewick, R. (ed.) STOC, pp. 291–304. ACM (1985)
17. Groth, J.: Fully anonymous group signatures without random oracles. In: Kurosawa, K. (ed.) ASIACRYPT 2007. LNCS, vol. 4833, pp. 164–180. Springer, Heidelberg (2007)

18. Groth, J., Sahai, A.: Efficient non-interactive proof systems for bilinear groups. In: Smart, N.P. (ed.) EUROCRYPT 2008. LNCS, vol. 4965, pp. 415–432. Springer, Heidelberg (2008)
19. Hofheinz, D., Kiltz, E.: Secure hybrid encryption from weakened key encapsulation. In: Menezes, A. (ed.) CRYPTO 2007. LNCS, vol. 4622, pp. 553–571. Springer, Heidelberg (2007)
20. Kiayias, A., Tsiounis, Y., Yung, M.: Traceable signatures. In: Cachin, C., Camenisch, J.L. (eds.) EUROCRYPT 2004. LNCS, vol. 3027, pp. 571–589. Springer, Heidelberg (2004)
21. Libert, B., Peters, T., Yung, M.: Group signatures with almost-for-free revocation. In: Safavi-Naini, R., Canetti, R. (eds.) CRYPTO 2012. LNCS, vol. 7417, pp. 571–589. Springer, Heidelberg (2012)
22. Nakanishi, T., Fujii, H., Hira, Y., Funabiki, N.: Revocable group signature schemes with constant costs for signing and verifying. In: Jarecki, S., Tsudik, G. (eds.) PKC 2009. LNCS, vol. 5443, pp. 463–480. Springer, Heidelberg (2009)
23. Ohara, K., Sakai, Y., Emura, K., Hanaoka, G.: A group signature scheme with unbounded message-dependent opening. In: Kefei, C., Qi, X., Weidong, Q., Ninghui, L., Wen-Guey, T. (eds.) ASIACCS, pp. 517–522. ACM (2013)
24. Pointcheval, D., Stern, J.: Security arguments for digital signatures and blind signatures. Journal of Cryptology 13(3), 361–396 (2000)
25. Schnorr, C.-P.: Efficient identification and signatures for smart cards. In: Brassard, G. (ed.) CRYPTO 1989. LNCS, vol. 435, pp. 239–252. Springer, Heidelberg (1990)
26. Shacham, H.: A cramer-shoup encryption scheme from the linear assumption and from progressively weaker linear variants. IACR Cryptology ePrint Archive 2007:74 (2007)

Rounding and Chaining LLL: Finding Faster Small Roots of Univariate Polynomial Congruences[*]

Jingguo Bi[1], Jean-Sébastien Coron[2], Jean-Charles Faugère[3,4,5],
Phong Q. Nguyen[6,1], Guénaël Renault[4,3,5], and Rina Zeitoun[7,4,3,5]

[1] Tsinghua University, Institute for Advanced Study, Beijing 100084, China
jingguobi@mail.tsinghua.edu.cn
[2] University of Luxembourg
jean-sebastien.coron@uni.lu
[3] INRIA, POLSYS, Centre Paris-Rocquencourt, F-78153, Le Chesnay, France
[4] Sorbonne Universités, UPMC Univ Paris 06, Équipe POLSYS, LIP6 UPMC, F-75005,
Paris, France
[5] CNRS, UMR 7606, LIP6 UPMC, F-75005, Paris, France
jean-charles.faugere@inria.fr,
guenael.renault@lip6.fr
[6] INRIA, France
http://www.di.ens.fr/~pnguyen
[7] Oberthur Technologies, 420 rue d'Estienne d'Orves, CS 40008, 92705 Colombes, France
r.zeitoun@oberthur.com

Abstract. In a seminal work at EUROCRYPT '96, Coppersmith showed how to find all small roots of a univariate polynomial congruence in polynomial time: this has found many applications in public-key cryptanalysis and in a few security proofs. However, the running time of the algorithm is a high-degree polynomial, which limits experiments: the bottleneck is an LLL reduction of a high-dimensional matrix with extra-large coefficients. We present in this paper the first significant speedups over Coppersmith's algorithm. The first speedup is based on a special property of the matrices used by Coppersmith's algorithm, which allows us to provably speed up the LLL reduction by rounding, and which can also be used to improve the complexity analysis of Coppersmith's original algorithm. The exact speedup depends on the LLL algorithm used: for instance, the speedup is asymptotically quadratic in the bit-size of the small-root bound if one uses the Nguyen-Stehlé L^2 algorithm. The second speedup is heuristic and applies whenever one wants to enlarge the root size of Coppersmith's algorithm by exhaustive search. Instead of performing several LLL reductions independently, we exploit hidden relationships between these matrices so that the LLL reductions can be somewhat chained to decrease the global running time. When both speedups are combined, the new algorithm is in practice hundreds of times faster for typical parameters.

Keywords: Coppersmith's Algorithm, Small Roots of Polynomial Equations, LLL, Complexity, Speedup, RSA.

---

[*] During the preparation of this paper, J. Bi and P. Q. Nguyen were supported in part by NSFC's Key Project Grant 61133013, China's 973 Program, Grant 2013CB834205, and J. Bi was also supported by NSFC Grant 61272035 and China Postdoctoral Science Foundation Grant 2013M542417. Part of this work was also supported by the HPAC grant (ANR-11-BS02-013) and by the EXACTA grant (ANR-09-BLAN-0371-01) of the French National Research Agency.

H. Krawczyk (Ed.): PKC 2014, LNCS 8383, pp. 185–202, 2014.

1 Introduction

At EUROCRYPT '96, Coppersmith [7,6,8] showed how to find efficiently all small roots of polynomial equations (modulo an integer, or over the integers). The simplest (and perhaps most popular) result is the following: Given an integer N of unknown factorization and a monic polynomial $f(x) \in \mathbb{Z}[x]$ of degree δ, Coppersmith's lattice-based algorithm finds all integers $x_0 \in \mathbb{Z}$ such that $f(x_0) \equiv 0 \pmod{N}$ and $|x_0| \leq N^{1/\delta}$ in time polynomial in $\log N$ and δ. This has many applications in public-key cryptanalysis (*e.g.* attacking special cases of RSA and factoring with a hint), but also in a few security proofs (such as in RSA-OAEP [22]). Accordingly, Coppersmith's seminal work has been followed up by dozens of articles (see May's survey [14] for references), which introduced new variants, generalizations, simplifications and applications.

All these small-root algorithms are based on the same idea of finding new polynomial equations using lattice basis reduction: it reduces the problem of finding small roots to finding LLL-short vectors in a lattice. This can theoretically be done in polynomial time using the LLL algorithm [13], but is by no means trivial in practice: the asymptotic running time is a high-degree polynomial, because the lattice is huge. More precisely, May's recent survey [14] gives for Coppersmith's lattice-based algorithm the complexity upper bound $O(\delta^5 \log^9 N)$ using the Nguyen-Stehlé L^2 algorithm [18] as the reduction algorithm. A careful look gives a slightly better upper bound: asymptotically, one may take a matrix of dimension $O(\log N)$, and bit-size $O((\log^2 N)/\delta)$, resulting in a complexity upper bound $O((\log^9 N)/\delta^2)$ using L^2. In typical applications, δ is small ≤ 9 but $\log N$ is the bit-size of an RSA modulus, *i.e.* at least 1024 bits, which makes the theoretical running time daunting: $\log^9 N$ is already at least 2^{90}. For more powerful variants of Coppersmith's algorithm, the running time is even worse, because the lattice dimension and/or the bit-size increase: for instance, Coron [9] gives the upper bound $O(\log^{11} W)$ for finding small roots over bivariate equations over the integers (W plays a role similar to N in the univariate congruence case), using L^2.

The bottleneck of all Coppersmith-type small-root algorithms is the LLL reduction. Despite considerable attention, no significant improvement on the running time has been found, except that LLL algorithms have improved since [8], with the appearance of L^2 [18] and $\tilde{L}^1$ [20]. And this issue is reflected in experiments (see [10]): in practice, one settles for sub-optimal parameters, which means that one can only find small roots up to a bound lower than the asymptotic bound. To illustrate this point, the celebrated Boneh-Durfee attack [1] on RSA with short secret exponent has the theoretical bound $d \leq N^{1-1/\sqrt{2}} \approx N^{0.292}$, but the largest d in the Boneh-Durfee experiments is only $d \approx N^{0.280}$ with a 1000-bit N, and much less for larger N, *e.g.* $d \approx N^{0.265}$ for 4000-bit N.

OUR RESULTS. We present two speedups over Coppersmith's algorithm for finding small roots of univariate polynomial congruences, which can be combined in practice.

The first speedup is provable and depends on the LLL algorithm used: if one uses L^2 [18], the total bit-complexity is upper bounded by $O(\log^7 N)$, which gives a speedup $\Theta((\log^2 N)/\delta^2)$ quadratic in the bit-size of the small-root bound $N^{1/\delta}$; and if one uses $\tilde{L}^1$, the total complexity is upper bounded by $O(\log^{6+\varepsilon} N)$ for any $\varepsilon > 0$ using fast integer arithmetic, which gives a speedup $O((\log N)/\delta)$ linear in the bit-size of the small-root bound $N^{1/\delta}$. This speedup comes from combining LLL reduction with rounding:

instead of LLL-reducing directly a matrix with huge entries, we suitably round the coefficients before LLL reduction to make them much smaller, and show that the LLL output allows to derive sufficiently short vectors in the original lattice. In practice, this means that for any instantiation of Coppersmith's algorithm achieving a small-root bound X, we can drastically reduce the size of the coefficients of the matrix to be LLL-reduced and achieve essentially the same small-root bound: asymptotically, the bit-size is reduced by a factor $(\log N)/\delta$, which implies that the speedup is quadratic when using the popular L^2 algorithm, or quasi-linear using the more theoretical $\tilde{L}^1$ algorithm. This rounding strategy is very natural, but it is folklore that it fails in the worst case: when an arbitrary non-singular matrix is rounded, it may even become singular, and the situation is worse for LLL reduction. However, we show that a well-chosen rounding strategy surprisingly works for the special matrices used by Coppersmith's algorithm: this is because the matrices to be reduced are triangular matrices whose diagonal entries are reasonably balanced, which can be exploited. Interestingly, this peculiar property can also be used to improve the complexity upper bound of Coppersmith's original algorithm, without changing the algorithm: if one uses $\tilde{L}^1$ [20], one can obtain the same complexity upper bound as in our rounding-based algorithm, up to constants.

Our second speedup is heuristic and applies whenever one wants to enlarge the root size X of Coppersmith's algorithm by exhaustive search: it is well-known that any root size X can be extended to mX by applying m times the algorithm on "shifted" polynomials. This enlargement is necessary when one wants to go beyond Coppersmith's bound $N^{1/\delta}$, but it is also useful to optimize the running time below $N^{1/\delta}$: beyond a certain root size below $N^{1/\delta}$, it is folklore that it is faster to use exhaustive search than Coppersmith's algorithm with larger parameters. In this setting, one applies Coppersmith's algorithm with the same modulus N but different polynomials which are all "shifts" of the initial polynomial $f(x)$: $f_t(x) = f(X \cdot t + x)$ for varying t, where $0 \leqslant t < N^{1/\delta}/X$. We show that this creates hidden relationships between the matrices to be LLL reduced, which can be exploited in practice: instead of performing LLL reductions independently of say, matrices B_1 and B_2, we chain the LLL reductions. More precisely, after LLL reducing B_1 into a reduced basis C_1, we reduce a matrix of the form $C_1 \times P$ for some well-chosen matrix P, instead of the matrix B_2. And this process can be iterated to drastically reduce the global running time.

When both speedups are combined, the new algorithm is in practice hundreds of times faster for typical parameters. Finally, our work helps to clarify the asymptotic complexity of Coppersmith's algorithm for univariate polynomial congruences. Despite the importance of the algorithm, it seems that the dependence on the polynomial degree δ was not well-understood: as previously mentioned, May's survey [14] gave an upper bound including a factor δ^5, and Coppersmith's journal article [8] gave an upper bound growing exponentially in δ. Our final complexity upper bound is independent of δ: it only depends on the bit-size of the modulus N.

Surprisingly, our improvements only apply for now to Coppersmith's algorithm for finding all small roots of univariate polynomial equations, and not to more sophisticated variants such as the gcd generalization used for factoring with a hint. This seems to be the first significant difference between Coppersmith's algorithm and its gcd generalization. It is an interesting open problem to obtain significant speedup for other small-root algorithms.

RELATED WORK. Our first speedup is based on rounding. Rounding has been used in lattice reduction before: for instance, Buchmann [2] used rounding to rigorously estimate when a computation with real lattices can be alternatively performed using integer bases; and the $\tilde{L}^1$ [20] algorithm is also based on rounding. However, it seems that none of the previous work identified the special structure of matrices which we exploit. Our second speedup is based on chaining. Chaining has also been used in lattice reduction before, e.g. in the MIMO context [15], but our technique and analysis seem to be a bit different. Thus, both rounding and chaining are folklore strategies, but our work seems to be their first application to Coppersmith's algorithm.

ROADMAP. In Sect. 2, we recall background on lattices and Coppersmith's small-root algorithm. In Sect. 3, we present and analyze our first speedup of Coppersmith's algorithm: rounding LLL. In Sect. 4, we present and analyze our second speedup of Coppersmith's algorithm: chaining LLL. In Sect. 5, we present experimental results with both speedups. Finally, we discuss the case of other small-root algorithms in Sect. 6.

We refer the reader to the full Eprint version of this paper for further details, especially for all missing proofs.

2 Background and Notation

We use row representation for matrices: vectors are row vectors denoted by bold lower-case letters, matrices are denoted by uppercase letters, and their coefficients are denoted by lowercase letters. All logarithms are in base 2. Let $\| \|$ and $\langle , \rangle$ be the Euclidean norm and inner product of $\mathbb{R}^n$. The Euclidean norm is naturally extended to polynomials as follows: if $f(x) = \sum_{i=0}^{n} f_i x^i \in \mathbb{R}[x]$, then $\|f\| = (\sum_{0 \le i \le n} f_i^2)^{1/2}$. We use the following matrix norms: if $M = (m_{i,j})$ is an $n \times m$ matrix, then $\|M\|_2 = \max_{\|\mathbf{x}\| \neq 0} \frac{\|\mathbf{x}M\|}{\|\mathbf{x}\|}$, and $\|M\|_\infty = \max_{1 \le j \le m} \sum_{i=1}^{n} |m_{i,j}|$. Then: $\|M\|_2 \le \sqrt{n}\|M\|_\infty$. If $x \in \mathbb{R}$, we denote by $\lceil x \rfloor$ a closest integer to x.

2.1 Lattices

LATTICES. A lattice L is a discrete subgroup of $\mathbb{R}^m$: there exist $n(\le m)$ linearly independent vectors $\mathbf{b}_1, \ldots, \mathbf{b}_n \in \mathbb{R}^m$ s.t. L is the set $\mathscr{L}(\mathbf{b}_1, \ldots, \mathbf{b}_n)$ of all integral linear combinations of the $\mathbf{b}_i$'s. Here, we mostly consider full-rank lattices, i.e. $n = m$. The (co-)volume of L is $\mathrm{vol}(L) = \sqrt{\det(BB^t)}$ for any basis B of L, where B^t denotes B's transpose. If B is square, then $\mathrm{vol}(L) = |\det B|$, and if B is further triangular, then $\mathrm{vol}(L)$ is simply the product of the diagonal entries of B in absolute value.

GRAM-SCHMIDT ORTHOGONALIZATION. Let $\mathbf{b}_1, \cdots, \mathbf{b}_n \in \mathbb{R}^m$ be linearly independent vectors. The Gram-Schmidt orthogonalization is the family $(\mathbf{b}_1^\star, \ldots, \mathbf{b}_n^\star)$ defined recursively as: $\mathbf{b}_1^\star = \mathbf{b}_1$ and for $i \ge 2$, $\mathbf{b}_i^\star$ is the component of the vector $\mathbf{b}_i$ which is orthogonal to the linear span of $\mathbf{b}_1, \cdots, \mathbf{b}_{i-1}$. Then $\mathbf{b}_i^\star = \mathbf{b}_i - \sum_{j=1}^{i-1} \mu_{i,j} \mathbf{b}_j^\star$, where $\mu_{i,j} = \langle \mathbf{b}_i, \mathbf{b}_j^\star \rangle / \|\mathbf{b}_j^\star\|^2$ for $1 \le j < i \le n$.

SIZE-REDUCTION. A basis $B = (\mathbf{b}_1, \cdots, \mathbf{b}_n)$ is *size-reduced* if its Gram-Schmidt orthogonalization satisfies $|\mu_{i,j}| \leq 1/2$, for all $1 \leq j < i \leq n$. There is a classical (elementary) algorithm which size-reduces a basis $(\mathbf{b}_1, \ldots, \mathbf{b}_n)$ of an integer lattice $L \subseteq \mathbb{Z}^m$, in polynomial time, without ever modifying the Gram-Schmidt vectors $\mathbf{b}_i^\star$: this algorithm is included in the original LLL algorithm [13] (e.g. it is the sub-algorithm RED in the description of LLL in [4]). In the special case that the input basis is (square) lower-triangular, the running-time of this size-reduction algorithm is $O(n^3 b^2)$ without fast integer arithmetic, and $n^3 \tilde{O}(b)$ using fast-integer arithmetic, where $b = \max_{1 \leq i \leq n} \log \|\mathbf{b}_i\|$.

LLL AND SHORT LATTICE VECTORS. Coppersmith's small-root method requires the ability to efficiently find reasonably short vectors in a lattice. This can be achieved by the celebrated LLL algorithm [13] which outputs a non-zero $\mathbf{v} \in L$ s.t. $\|\mathbf{v}\| \leq 2^{\frac{n-1}{4}} \mathrm{vol}(L)^{1/n}$. Nguyen and Stehlé [18] introduced the L^2 algorithm, a faster variant of LLL which can output similarly short vectors in time $O(n^4 m(n+b)b)$ without fast integer arithmetic. The recent $\tilde{L}^1$ algorithm by Novocin *et al.* [20] can output similarly short vectors for a full-rank lattice in time $O(n^{5+\varepsilon}b + n^{\omega+1+\varepsilon}b^{1+\varepsilon})$ for any $\varepsilon > 0$ using fast integer arithmetic, where $\omega \leq 2.376$ is the matrix multiplication complexity constant. However, this algorithm is considered to be mostly of theoretical interest for now: $\tilde{L}^1$ is currently not implemented anywhere, as opposed to L^2. When assessing the complexity of LLL reduction, it is therefore meaningful to mention two complexities: one (closer to the real world) using L^2 without fast integer arithmetic, and another using $\tilde{L}^1$ using fast integer arithmetic and fast linear algebra.

The complexity upper bound of LLL reduction can sometimes be decreased by some polynomial factor. In particular, when the Gram-Schmidt norms of the input basis are balanced, the LLL algorithm requires fewer loop iterations than in the worst case. More precisely, [11, Th. 1.1] showed that the classical upper bound $O(n^2 b)$ on the number of iterations can be replaced by $O\left(n^2 \log \frac{max\|\mathbf{b}_i^\star\|}{min\|\mathbf{b}_i^\star\|}\right)$.

2.2 Coppersmith's Method for Finding Small Roots

At EUROCRYPT '96, Coppersmith [7,6,8] showed how to find efficiently all small roots of polynomial equations (modulo an integer, or multivariate over the integers), which is surveyed in [14,16]. We now review the simplest result, following the classical Howgrave-Graham approach [12]: In Sect. 6, we will discuss the main variants of this result.

Theorem 1 (Coppersmith [7,8]). *There is an algorithm which, given as input an integer N of unknown factorization and a monic polynomial $f(x) \in \mathbb{Z}[x]$ of degree δ and coefficients in $\{0, \ldots, N-1\}$, outputs all integers $x_0 \in \mathbb{Z}$ such that $f(x_0) \equiv 0 \pmod{N}$ and $|x_0| \leq N^{1/\delta}$ in time polynomial in $\log N$ and δ.*

In all the paper, we consider polynomials verifying $2 < \delta + 1 < (\log N)/2$ since other cases are trivial. Furthermore, Coppersmith's algorithm does not directly achieve the bound $N^{1/\delta}$: indeed, it finds efficiently all roots up to some bound X ($< N^{1/\delta}$) depending on an integer parameter $h \geq 2$, chosen asymptotically to be $h = O((\log N)/\delta)$. When h is sufficiently large, then X becomes sufficiently close to $N^{1/\delta}$ so that one can find all roots up to $N^{1/\delta}$. However, it is well-known that the bound $X = N^{1/\delta}$ should not be reached by taking such a large h. Instead, it is faster to use a smaller h, and perform exhaustive search on the most significant bits of the solutions (see Section 4 for more details).

We now explain Coppersmith's algorithm. The core idea consists in reducing the problem to solving univariate polynomial equations over the integers, by transforming modular roots into integral roots. More precisely, it constructs a polynomial $g(x) \in \mathbb{Z}[x]$ such that: if $x_0 \in \mathbb{Z}$ is such that $f(x_0) \equiv 0 \pmod{N}$ and $|x_0| \leq X$, then $g(x_0) = 0$ and can be solved easily over $\mathbb{Z}$. To do so, it uses the following elementary criterion:

Lemma 1 (Howgrave-Graham [12]). *Let $g(x) \in \mathbb{Z}[x]$ be a polynomial with at most n non-zero coefficients. Let M be an integer ≥ 1. Assume that $\|g(xX)\| < \frac{M}{\sqrt{n}}$ for some $X \in \mathbb{R}$. If $x_0 \in \mathbb{Z}$ is such that $g(x_0) \equiv 0 \pmod{M}$ and $|x_0| \leq X$, then $g(x_0) = 0$.*

Lemma 1 will be used with $M = N^{h-1}$ and $g(x)$ found by lattice reduction. Let $h \geq 2$ be an integer and define the following family of $n = h\delta$ polynomials:

$$g_{i,j}(x) = (x)^j N^{h-1-i} f^i(x) \quad 0 \leq i < h, 0 \leq j < \delta \tag{1}$$

These n polynomials satisfy: if $f(x_0) \equiv 0 \pmod{N}$ for some $x_0 \in \mathbb{Z}$, then $g_{i,j}(x_0) \equiv 0 \pmod{N^{h-1}}$. In order to apply Lemma 1 for a bound $X \geq 1$ to be determined later, Coppersmith's algorithm constructs the n-dimensional lattice L spanned by the rows of the $n \times n$ matrix B formed by the n coefficient vectors of $g_{i,j}(xX)$, where the polynomials are ordered by increasing degree (*e.g.* in the order $(i,j) = (0,0),(0,1),\cdots,(0,\delta-1),(1,0),\cdots(h-1,\delta-1)$) and the coefficients are ordered by increasing monomial degree: the first coefficient is thus the constant term of the polynomial. The matrix B is lower triangular, and its n diagonal entries are:

$$\left(N^{h-1}, N^{h-1}X, \ldots, N^{h-1}X^{\delta-1}, \ldots, N^0 X^{\delta h-\delta}, \ldots, N^0 X^{\delta h-2}, N^0 X^{\delta h-1} \right), \tag{2}$$

because $f(x)$ is monic. In other words, the exponent of X increases by one at each row, while the exponent of N decreases by one every δ rows. It follows that $\mathrm{vol}(L) = \det(B) = N^{\frac{1}{2}n(h-1)}X^{\frac{1}{2}n(n-1)}$. The LLL algorithm is applied to the matrix B, which provides a non-zero polynomial $v(x) \in \mathbb{Z}[x]$ such that $\|v(xX)\| \leq 2^{\frac{n-1}{4}} \mathrm{vol}(L)^{\frac{1}{n}} = 2^{\frac{n-1}{4}} N^{\frac{h-1}{2}} X^{\frac{n-1}{2}}$. It follows that the polynomial $v(x)$ satisfies Lemma 1 with $M = N^{h-1}$ and $g(x) = v(x)$ if $X \leq \frac{1}{\sqrt{2}} N^{\frac{h-1}{n-1}} (n+1)^{-\frac{1}{n-1}}$. The dimension of B is $n = h\delta$, and the entries of the matrix B have bit-size $O(h \log N)$, therefore the running time of L^2 without fast integer arithmetic is $O(\delta^6 h^7 \log N + \delta^5 h^7 \log^2 N)$, which is $O(\delta^5 h^7 \log^2 N)$ because $\delta + 1 < (\log N)/2$, and the running time of $\tilde{L}^1$ is $O(h^{6+\varepsilon}\delta^{5+\varepsilon}\log N + h^{\omega+2+2\varepsilon}\delta^{\omega+1+\varepsilon}\log^{1+\varepsilon} N)$ for any $\varepsilon > 0$ using fast integer arithmetic and $\tilde{L}^1$, where $\omega \leq 2.376$ is the matrix multiplication complexity constant. We obtain the following concrete version of Th. 1:

Corollary 2. *Coppersmith's algorithm of Th. 1 with $h = \lfloor \log N/\delta \rfloor$ and $X = \lfloor 2^{-1/2} N^{\frac{h-1}{n-1}} (n+1)^{-\frac{1}{n-1}} \rfloor$ runs in time $O((\log^9 N)/\delta^2)$ without fast integer arithmetic using L^2, or $O((\log^{7+\varepsilon} N)/\delta)$ for any $\varepsilon > 0$ using fast integer arithmetic and $\tilde{L}^1$.*

Sketch of Proof: One can show that the cost of the root computation step performed at the end of Coppersmith's algorithm is less than the one of the LLL reduction. Moreover the number of loop iterations performed by Coppersmith's algorithm to find all solutions smaller than $N^{1/\delta}$ by exhaustive search is at most $O(N^{1/\delta}/X)$ which can be shown to be $O(1)$. Thus, from the analysis preceding Cor. 2, the asymptotic complexity of Coppersmith's algorithm is the one of one call to LLL (L^2 or $\tilde{L}^1$), with $h = \lfloor \log N/\delta \rfloor$. $\square$

We will later see that the complexity upper bounds of Cor. 2 with L^2 and $\tilde{L}^1$ can actually be decreased. Indeed, we will uncover a special property of Coppersmith's matrix (see Lemma 2), which implies that $O\left(\frac{max\|\mathbf{b}_i^*\|}{min\|\mathbf{b}_i^*\|}\right) = O(N)$, so that the number of loop iterations $O\left(n^2 \log \frac{max\|\mathbf{b}_i^*\|}{min\|\mathbf{b}_i^*\|}\right)$ on the input basis used by Coppersmith's algorithm is $O(n^2 \log N)$ instead of the all-purpose bound $O(n^2 h \log N)$ [11]. By taking this observation into account, the upper bounds $O((\log^8 N)/\delta)$ and $O(\log^{6+\varepsilon} N)$ are respectively achieved for the L^2 and $\tilde{L}^1$ algorithms. In the sequel, we present another method improving Cor. 2, based on the same special property of Coppersmith's matrix, and which can be easily implemented.

3 Speeding Up Coppersmith's Algorithm by Rounding

Our first main result is the following speedup over Coppersmith's algorithm:

Theorem 3. *There is an algorithm (namely, Alg. 1) which, given as input an integer N of unknown factorization and a monic polynomial $f(x) \in \mathbb{Z}[x]$ of degree δ and coefficients in $\{0, \ldots, N-1\}$, outputs all integers $x_0 \in \mathbb{Z}$ such that $f(x_0) \equiv 0 \pmod{N}$ and $|x_0| \leq N^{1/\delta}$ in time $O(\log^7 N)$ without fast integer arithmetic using the L^2 algorithm [18], or $O(\log^{6+\varepsilon} N)$ for any $\varepsilon > 0$ using fast integer arithmetic and the $\tilde{L}^1$ algorithm [20] in Step 7.*

3.1 Rounding for Coppersmith's Algorithm

The bottleneck of Coppersmith's algorithm is the LLL reduction of the matrix B, whose dimension is $n = h\delta$, and whose entries have bit-size $O(h \log N)$. Asymptotically, we have $h = O(\log N/\delta)$ so the dimension is $O(\log N)$ and the bit-size is $O((\log^2 N)/\delta)$. We will modify Coppersmith's algorithm in such a way that we only need to LLL-reduce a matrix of the same dimension but with much smaller entries, namely bit-length $O(\log N)$.

To explain the intuition behind our method, let us first take a closer look at the matrix B and uncover some of its special properties:

Lemma 2. *Let $X \leq N^{1/\delta}$. The maximal diagonal coefficient of Coppersmith's matrix B is $N^{h-1}X^{\delta-1} < N^h$, the minimal diagonal coefficient is $X^{h\delta-\delta} \leq N^{h-1}$, and $\frac{N^{h-1}X^{\delta-1}}{X^{h\delta-\delta}} \geq N^{1-1/\delta}$ if $h \geq 2$. Furthermore, if $X \geq \Omega(N^{\frac{h-1}{n-1}})$, $h \geq 2$ and $h\delta = O(\log N)$ then $X^{h\delta-\delta} \geq N^{h-O(1)}$.*

Proof. The ratio $\frac{N^{h-1}X^{\delta-1}}{X^{h\delta-\delta}}$ is exactly $N^{h-1}/X^{h\delta-2\delta+1}$ which is clearly $\geq N^{1-1/\delta}$ if $X \leq N^{1/\delta}$ and $h \geq 2$. Now, let $X_0 = N^{\frac{h-1}{n-1}}$ so that $X = \Omega(X_0)$. We have $N^{1/\delta}/N^{\frac{h-1}{n-1}} \leq N^{1/(h\delta-1)}$, therefore $X_0 \geq N^{1/\delta - 1/(h\delta - 1)} = N^{(h\delta - 1 - \delta)/(\delta(h\delta - 1))}$. Hence $X_0^\delta \geq N^{(h\delta - 1 - \delta)/(h\delta - 1)} = N^{1 - \delta/(h\delta - 1)}$ and thus $X_0^{h\delta - \delta} > N^{h-2}$. Since $X = \Omega(X_0)$ and $h\delta = O(\log N)$, we obtain $X^{h\delta - \delta} \geq N^{h - O(1)}$. □

This implies that the diagonal coefficients of B are somewhat balanced: the matrix B is not far from being reduced. In fact, the first row of B has norm N^{h-1} which is extremely close to the bound $N^{h-1}/\sqrt{n}$ required by Lemma 1: intuitively, this means that it should not be too difficult to find a lattice vector shorter than $N^{h-1}/\sqrt{n}$.

To take advantage of the structure of B, we first size-reduce B to make sure that the subdiagonal coefficients are smaller than the diagonal coefficients. Then we round the entries of B so that the smallest diagonal coefficient becomes $\lfloor c \rfloor$ where $c > 1$ is a parameter. More precisely, we create a new $n \times n$ triangular matrix $\tilde{B} = (\tilde{b}_{i,j})$ defined by:

$$\tilde{B} = \left\lfloor cB / X^{h\delta - \delta} \right\rceil \tag{3}$$

By Lemma 2, we have: $b_{i,i} \geq X^{h\delta - \delta}$ and $\tilde{b}_{i,i} \geq \lfloor c \rfloor$. We LLL-reduce the rounded matrix $\tilde{B}$ instead of B: let $\tilde{\mathbf{v}} = \mathbf{x}\tilde{B}$ be the first vector of the reduced basis obtained. If we applied to B the unimodular transformation that LLL-reduces $\tilde{B}$, we may not even obtain an LLL-reduced basis in general. However, because of the special structure of B, it turns out that $\mathbf{v} = \mathbf{x}B$ is still a short non-zero vector of L, as shown below:

Lemma 3. *Let $B = (b_{i,j})$ be an $n \times n$ lower-triangular matrix over $\mathbb{Z}$ with strictly positive diagonal. Let $c > 1$. If $\tilde{B} = \lfloor cB / \min_{i=1}^{n} b_{i,i} \rceil$ and $\mathbf{x}\tilde{B}$ is the first vector of an LLL-reduced basis of $\tilde{B}$, then $0 < \|\mathbf{x}B\| < \left(n \|\tilde{B}^{-1}\|_2 + 1\right) 2^{\frac{n-1}{4}} \det(B)^{\frac{1}{n}}$.*

Proof. Let $\alpha = \min_{i=1}^{n} b_{i,i}/c$, so that $\tilde{B} = \lfloor B/\alpha \rceil$. Define the matrix $\bar{B} = \alpha \tilde{B}$ whose entries are $\bar{b}_{i,j} = \alpha \tilde{b}_{i,j}$. Then $0 \leq b_{i,j} - \bar{b}_{i,j} < \alpha$, therefore $\|B - \bar{B}\|_2 < n\alpha$. We have:

$$\|\mathbf{x}B\| \leq \|\mathbf{x}(B - \bar{B})\| + \|\mathbf{x}\bar{B}\| \leq \|\mathbf{x}\| \times \|B - \bar{B}\|_2 + \alpha \|\mathbf{x}\tilde{B}\| < n\|\mathbf{x}\|\alpha + \alpha\|\mathbf{x}\tilde{B}\|.$$

Let $\tilde{\mathbf{v}} = \mathbf{x}\tilde{B}$. Then $\|\mathbf{x}\| \leq \|\tilde{\mathbf{v}}\| \|\tilde{B}^{-1}\|_2$, and we obtain $\|\mathbf{x}B\| < \left(n\|\tilde{B}^{-1}\|_2 + 1\right) \alpha \|\tilde{\mathbf{v}}\|$. The matrix $\tilde{B}$ is lower-triangular with all diagonal coefficients strictly positive because $c > 1$. Since $\tilde{\mathbf{v}} = \mathbf{x}\tilde{B}$ is the first vector of an LLL-reduced basis of $\tilde{B}$, and $\tilde{B}$ is non-singular, $\mathbf{x}B \neq 0$ and we have:

$$\alpha \|\tilde{\mathbf{v}}\| \leq \alpha 2^{\frac{n-1}{4}} \det(\tilde{B})^{\frac{1}{n}} = 2^{\frac{n-1}{4}} \det(\bar{B})^{\frac{1}{n}} \leq 2^{\frac{n-1}{4}} \det(B)^{\frac{1}{n}},$$

where we used the fact that matrices $\tilde{B}$, $\bar{B}$ and B are lower-triangular. The result follows by combining both inequalities. □

If $\mathbf{x}B$ is sufficiently short, then it corresponds to a polynomial of the form $v(xX)$ for some $v(x) \in \mathbb{Z}[x]$ satisfying Lemma 1, and the rest proceeds as in Coppersmith's algorithm. The whole rounding algorithm is given in Alg. 1, which will be shown to admit a lower complexity upper-bound than Coppersmith's algorithm to compute all roots up to $N^{1/\delta}$.

Algorithm 1. Coppersmith's Method with Rounding

Input: Two integers $N \geq 1$ and $h \geq 2$, a univariate degree-δ monic polynomial $f(x) \in \mathbb{Z}[x]$ with coefficients in $\{0,\ldots,N-1\}$ and $2 < \delta + 1 < (\log N)/2$.

Output: All $x_0 \in \mathbb{Z}$ s.t. $|x_0| \leq N^{1/\delta}$ and $f(x_0) \equiv 0 \mod N$.

1: Let $n = h\delta$, X the bound given in Th. 4, $c = (3/2)^n$ and $t = 0$.
2: **while** $Xt < N^{1/\delta}$ **do**
3:     $f_t(x) = f(Xt + x) \in \mathbb{Z}[x]$.
4:     Build the $n \times n$ matrix B whose rows are the $g_{i,j}(xX)$'s defined by (1).
5:     Size-reduce B without modifying its diagonal coefficients.
6:     Compute the matrix $\tilde{B} = \lfloor cB/X^{h\delta-\delta} \rceil$ obtained by rounding B.
7:     Run the L^2 algorithm [18] on the matrix $\tilde{B}$.
8:     Let $\tilde{\mathbf{v}} = \mathbf{x}\tilde{B}$ be the first vector of the reduced basis obtained.
9:     The vector $\mathbf{v} = \mathbf{x}B$ corresponds to a polynomial of the form $v(xX)$ for some $v(x) \in \mathbb{Z}[x]$.
10:    Compute all the roots x_0' of the polynomial $v(x) \in \mathbb{Z}[x]$ over $\mathbb{Z}$.
11:    Output $x_0 = x_0' + Xt$ for each root x_0' which satisfies $f_t(x_0') \equiv 0 \pmod{N}$ and $|x_0'| \leq X$.
12:    $t \leftarrow t + 1$.
13: **end while**

We now justify the bound X given in Alg. 1. In order for Lemma 3 to be useful, we need to exhibit an upper bound for $\|\tilde{B}^{-1}\|_2$:

Lemma 4. *Let $B = (b_{i,j})$ be an $n \times n$ size-reduced lower-triangular matrix over $\mathbb{Z}$ with strictly positive diagonal. Let $c > 1$. If $\tilde{B} = \lfloor cB/\min_{i=1}^{n} b_{i,i} \rceil$, then $\|\tilde{B}^{-1}\|_2 \leq \sqrt{n} \left(\frac{3c-2}{2c-2}\right)^{n-1}/\lfloor c \rceil$.*

By combining Lemmas 3 and 4, we obtain the following small-root bound X for Alg. 1:

Theorem 4. *Given as input two integers $N \geq 1$ and $h \geq 2$, a rational $c > 1$, and a univariate degree-δ monic polynomial $f(x) \in \mathbb{Z}[x]$ with coefficients in $\{0,\ldots,N-1\}$, one loop of Alg. 1, corresponding to $t < N^{1/\delta}/X$, outputs all $x_0 = Xt + x_0' \in \mathbb{Z}$ s.t. $|x_0'| \leq X$ and $f(x_0) = 0 \mod N$, where $n = h\delta$ and*

$$X = \left\lfloor \frac{N^{\frac{h-1}{n-1}}\kappa_1^{-2/(n-1)}}{\sqrt{2}\,n^{1/(n-1)}} \right\rfloor \quad \text{with} \quad \kappa_1 = n^{3/2}\left(\frac{3c-2}{2c-2}\right)^{n-1}\lfloor c \rceil^{-1} + 1.$$

Proof. Combining Lemma 4 with Lemma 3 where $\det(B)^{1/n} = N^{\frac{h-1}{2}}X^{\frac{n-1}{2}}$, we get $0 < \|\mathbf{x}B\| < \kappa_1 2^{\frac{n-1}{4}}N^{\frac{h-1}{2}}X^{\frac{n-1}{2}}$. It follows that Lemma 1 is satisfied with $M = N^{h-1}$ and $v(xX)$ corresponding to $\mathbf{x}B$ if $\|\mathbf{x}B\| \leq N^{h-1}/\sqrt{n}$. This gives the following condition on the bound X: $X \leq N^{(h-1)/(n-1)}2^{-1/2}n^{-1/(n-1)}\kappa_1^{-2/(n-1)}$. $\square$

The bound X of Th. 4 is never larger than that of Cor. 2. However, if one selects $c \geq (3/2)^n$, then the two bounds are asymptotically equivalent. This is why Alg. 1 uses $c = (3/2)^n$.

3.2 Running Time: Proof of Theorem 3

The original matrix B had entries whose bit-size was $O(h \log N)$. Let $\beta = \frac{N^h X^{\delta-1}}{X^{h\delta-\delta}}$ be the ratio between the maximal diagonal coefficient and the minimal diagonal coefficient of $\tilde{B}$. If B is size-reduced, the entries of the new matrix $\tilde{B} = \lfloor cB/X^{h\delta-\delta} \rfloor$ are upper bounded by $c\beta$.

By Lemma 2, we know that if $h \geq 2$, then $\beta \geq N^{1-1/\delta}$, and if further $X \geq \Omega(N^{\frac{h-1}{n-1}})$ and $h\delta = O(\log N)$, then $\beta = N^{O(1)}$. Hence, the bit-size of $\tilde{B}$'s entries is $\leq \log c + O(\log N)$. And the dimension of $\tilde{B}$ is the same as B, *i.e.* $h\delta$. It follows that the running time of L^2 in Step 7 is $O(\delta^6 h^6 (\log c + \log N) + \delta^5 h^5 (\log c + \log N)^2)$ without fast integer arithmetic, which is $O(\delta^5 h^5 (\log c + \log N)^2$ because $\delta < (\log N)/2 - 1$, and is $O((h\delta)^{5+\varepsilon} (\log c + \log N) + (h\delta)^{\omega+1+\varepsilon} (\log c + \log N)^{1+\varepsilon})$ for any $\varepsilon > 0$ using fast integer arithmetic and $\tilde{L}^1$ in Step. 7, where $\omega \leq 2.376$ is the matrix multiplication complexity constant.

This leads to our main result (Th. 3), a variant of Coppersmith's algorithm with improved complexity upper bound. More precisely, as in Coppersmith's algorithm, one can easily prove that the number of loops performed in Alg. 1 is at most constant. Indeed, when $c = (3/2)^n$, then $\kappa_1^{\frac{-2}{n-1}}$ converges to 1. This means that the bound X achieved by Th. 4 is asymptotically equivalent to the one achieved by Cor. 2, which completes the proof of Th. 3, because $\log c = O(\log N)$ when $c = (3/2)^n$.

Remark: Surprisingly, Lemma 2 also allows to prove that the $\tilde{L}^1$ algorithm, when carefully analyzed using the balancedness of the Gram-Schmidt norms, already achieves the complexity bound $O(\log^{6+\varepsilon} N)$ given in Th. 3. Indeed, using Th. 6 from [20] which gives the $\tilde{L}^1$ complexity upper bound $O(n^{3+\varepsilon} \tau) = O(\log^{3+\varepsilon} N\tau)$ where τ is the total number of iterations, and combining it with [11] applied to Coppersmith's matrix (Lemma 2), which gives $\tau = O(n^2 \log N) = O(\log^3 N)$, allows to retrieve the above complexity $O(\log^{6+\varepsilon} N)$. However, we propose in this paper a direct improvement of Coppersmith's method based on elementary tools and which can therefore be easily implemented on usual computer algebra systems (*e.g.* Sage, Magma, NTL) with immediate practical impact on cryptanalyses. Furthermore, we are not aware of any implementation of the $\tilde{L}^1$ algorithm for the time being, which makes a practical comparison tricky.

In the sequel, we present a method that allows to speed up the exhaustive search which is performed to reach Coppersmith's bound $N^{1/\delta}$.

4   Chaining LLL

As recalled in Section 2.2, in order to find all solutions which are close to the bound $N^{1/\delta}$, one should not use a very large dimension (*i.e.* $n = O(\log N)$). Instead, it is better to use a lattice of reasonable dimension and to perform exhaustive search on the most significant bits of x until finding all solutions. Namely, we consider polynomials $f_t(x) = f(X \cdot t + x)$ where $0 \leqslant t < \frac{N^{1/\delta}}{X}$ and $X = \lfloor 2^{\frac{-1}{2}} N^{\frac{h-1}{n-1}} (n+1)^{-\frac{1}{n-1}} \rfloor$. Thus, an initial solution x_0 that can be written $x_0 = X \cdot t_0 + x_0'$ is obtained by finding the solution x_0' of the polynomial f_{t_0}. In this case, this solution satisfies $|x_0'| < X$ and it has a correct size for LLL to find it using a lattice of dimension n. For each polynomial f_t, one runs LLL on a certain matrix (Step 4 of Alg. 1). In Section 4.1, we describe a method that allows to take advantage of the LLL performed for the case $t = i$ to reduce (in practice) the complexity of the LLL performed for the case $t = i + 1$. Thereafter, in Section 4.2 we combine this improvement with the rounding approach described in Section 3. The proofs of the results presented in this section can be found in the full version of this paper.

4.1 Exploiting Relations between Consecutive Lattices

The following proposition discloses a surprising connection between the lattice used for the case $t = i$ and the next lattice used for $t = i + 1$. This connection is based on the well-known *Pascal matrix* $P = (p_{s,t})$ defined as the $n \times n$ lower-triangular matrix whose non-zero coefficients are the binomials: $p_{s,t} = \binom{s}{t}$ for $0 \le t \le s \le n - 1$.

Proposition 1. *Let B be a basis of the n-dimensional lattice used by Coppersmith's algorithm to find all small roots of the polynomial* $f_i(x) = f(X \cdot i + x)$, *where X is the small-root bound. Then $B \cdot P$ is a basis of the "next" lattice used for the polynomial* $f_{i+1}(x)$.

Proof. Because all lattice bases are related by some unimodular matrix, it suffices to prove the statement for a special basis B. We thus only consider the special basis $B = B_i$ formed by the n shifted polynomials constructed from $f_i(x)$ and written in the basis $\mathscr{B} = (1, xX^{-1}, (xX^{-1})^2, \ldots, (xX^{-1})^{n-1})$. For the case $t = i + 1$, one tries to solve the polynomial

$$f_{i+1}(x) = f(X \cdot (i+1) + x) = f(X \cdot i + x + X) = f_i(x + X).$$

Therefore, the shifted polynomials constructed from f_{i+1} are the same as for the case $t = i$, but written in the different basis $\mathscr{B}' = (1, xX^{-1} + 1, (xX^{-1} + 1)^2, \ldots, (xX^{-1} + 1)^{n-1})$. Yet, we need to return to the original representation of the polynomials, *i.e.* in the basis $\mathscr{B}$. To this end, we use the following property regarding the lower triangular Pascal matrix P: $\mathscr{B}'^T = P \cdot \mathscr{B}^T$. As a consequence, left-multiplying each side of this equality by the matrix B_i proves that the matrix $B_i \cdot P$ is a basis of the lattice used for finding small roots of the polynomial $f_{i+1}(x)$. $\square$

The proposition allows us to use different matrices to tackle the polynomial $f_{i+1}(x)$ than the one initially used by Coppersmith's method. In particular, we can use a matrix of the form $B^R \cdot P$ where B^R is an LLL-reduced basis of the previous lattice used to solve $f_i(x)$: intuitively, it might be faster to LLL-reduce such matrices than the initial Coppersmith's matrix. Although we are unable to prove this, we can show that the vectors of such a matrix are not much longer than that of B:

Corollary 5. *Let B_i^R be the LLL-reduced matrix used for solving f_t for $t = i$ and P be the Pascal matrix. The matrix $B_{i+1} = B_i^R \cdot P$ spans the same lattice used for solving the case $t = i + 1$. This matrix consists of vectors $\mathbf{b}_{i+1,j}$ whose norms are close to vector norms of the LLL-reduced matrix B_i^R. Namely, for all $1 \le j \le n$ we have:* $\|\mathbf{b}_{i+1,j}\| < \sqrt{n} \cdot 2^{n-1} \cdot \|\mathbf{b}_{i,j}^R\|$. *In particular, for the case $i = t_0$ the first vector of B_{i+1} has a norm bounded by* $2^{n-1} \cdot N^{h-1}$.

Cor. 5 shows us that vectors of B_{i+1} are relatively close to the ones in the LLL-reduced matrix B_i^R. Thus, we intuitively expect the LLL-reduction of B_{i+1} to be less costly than the one of the original Coppersmith's matrix. However, our bounds are too weak to rigorously prove this. Yet, one can use this property iteratively to elaborate a new method which *chains* all LLL reductions as follows. First, one LLL-reduces B_0 for the case $t = 0$. This gives a reduced matrix B_0^R. Then, one iterates this process by performing LLL reduction on $B_{i+1} = B_i^R \cdot P$ (for $i \geq 0$) to obtain B_{i+1}^R and so forth until all solutions are found (each time by solving the polynomial corresponding to the first vector of B_i^R).

In the sequel, we study this *chaining method* by performing similar roundings as in Section 3 before each call of LLL reduction.

4.2   Rounding and Chaining LLL

During the exhaustive search described in Section 4.1, we perform the LLL algorithm on the matrix $B_{i+1} = B_i^R \cdot P$ for $0 \leqslant i < N^{1/\delta}/X$, where B_i^R is LLL-reduced. It is worth noticing that the structure of B_i^R and thereby of B_{i+1}, is different from the original Coppersmith's matrix B_0 (in particular, it is not triangular anymore). Yet, we are able to show that under certain conditions on B_{i+1} verified experimentally, one can combine the rounding technique of Section 3 with the chaining technique of Section 4.1. Indeed, we show that during the chaining loop, one can size-reduce B_{i+1} and then round its elements for all $i \geq 0$ as follows:

$$\tilde{B}_{i+1} = \left\lfloor cB_{i+1} / \min_{1 \leq i \leq n} \|\mathbf{b}_i^\star\| \right\rceil , \tag{4}$$

where $\mathbf{b}_i^\star$ are Gram-Schmidt vectors of B_{i+1} and c is a rational that will be determined later. Then, one applies LLL on the rounded matrix $\tilde{B}_{i+1}$ as performed in Section 3. We obtain an LLL-reduced matrix $\tilde{B}_{i+1}^R$ and a unimodular matrix $\tilde{U}_{i+1}$ such that $\tilde{U}_{i+1} \cdot \tilde{B}_{i+1} = \tilde{B}_{i+1}^R$. Then one shows that by applying $\tilde{U}_{i+1}$ on B_{i+1}, the first vector of this matrix $\tilde{U}_{i+1} \cdot B_{i+1}$ is a short vector that allows to find the solutions provided that they are smaller than a bound X that will be determined latter. For the sake of clarity, in the sequel we denote by B the matrix B_{i+1}, and by $\mathbf{x}B$, the first vector of matrix $\tilde{U}_{i+1} \cdot B_{i+1}$. We would like to exhibit an upper-bound on $\|\mathbf{x}B\|$. To this end, we will need, as in Section 3, to upper-bound the value $\|\tilde{B}^{-1}\|_2$. This is done in the following lemma:

Lemma 5. *Let $B = (b_{i,j})$ be an $n \times n$ non-singular integral matrix and $\alpha \geq 1$ such that $n\alpha\|B^{-1}\|_2 < 1$. Then the matrix $\tilde{B} = \lfloor B/\alpha \rfloor$ is invertible with $\|\tilde{B}^{-1}\|_2 \leq \alpha\|B^{-1}\|_2(1 - n\alpha\|B^{-1}\|_2)^{-1}$.*

As one can see, this value depends on $\|B^{-1}\|_2$ which is given in Lemma 6.

Lemma 6. *Let B be an $n \times n$ non-singular size-reduced matrix, with Gram-Schmidt vectors $\mathbf{b}_i^\star$. Then $\|B^{-1}\|_2 \leq \sqrt{n}(3/2)^{n-1}/\min_{1 \leq i \leq n}\|\mathbf{b}_i^\star\|$.*

One can now give an upper-bound on $\|\mathbf{x}B\|$:

Corollary 6. *Let $B = (b_{i,j})$ be an $n \times n$ size-reduced non-singular matrix over $\mathbb{Z}$. Let $\alpha \geq 1$ such that $n^2\alpha\|B^{-1}\|_2 < 1$. Then $\tilde{B} = \lfloor cB/\min_{1\leq i\leq n}\|\mathbf{b}_i^\star\|\rfloor = \lfloor B/\alpha\rfloor$ is non-singular. And if $\mathbf{x}\tilde{B}$ is the first vector of an LLL-reduced basis of $\tilde{B}$, then: $0 < \|\mathbf{x}B\| <$*

$$\frac{c^{\frac{n+1}{n}}}{(c-n^{3/2}(3/2)^{n-1})(c-n^{5/2}(3/2)^{n-1})^{1/n}} \; 2^{\frac{n-1}{4}} \; \det(B)^{\frac{1}{n}}.$$

Again, if $\|\mathbf{x}B\|$ is sufficiently short, then it corresponds to a polynomial of the form $v(xX)$ for some $v(x) \in \mathbb{Z}[x]$ satisfying Lemma 1. In particular, for the case $t = t_0$, solving this polynomial equation would allow to retrieve the solution x_0. Note that the condition $n^2\alpha\|B^{-1}\|_2 < 1$ specified in Cor. 6 gives a condition on the rational c. Indeed, since $\alpha = \min_{1\leq i\leq n}\|\mathbf{b}_i^\star\|/c$ and using Lemma 6, one gets:

$$n^2\alpha\|B^{-1}\|_2 \leqslant n^2 \frac{\min_{1\leq i\leq n}\|\mathbf{b}_i^\star\|}{c} \frac{\sqrt{n}(3/2)^{n-1}}{\min_{1\leq i\leq n}\|\mathbf{b}_i^\star\|} \leqslant \frac{n^{5/2}(3/2)^{n-1}}{c} < 1 \text{ that is } c \text{ should be such}$$

that $c > n^{5/2}(3/2)^{n-1}$. The whole chaining and rounding algorithm is depicted in Algorithm 2. Note that in practice, we do not need to perform Step 8 of Alg. 2 and that $\min_{1\leq i\leq n}\|\mathbf{b}_{t+1\,i}^\star\|$ can be estimated instead of being computed in Step 9 (see Section 4.3 for more details).

Algorithm 2. Coppersmith's Method with Chaining and Rounding

Input: Two integers $N \geq 1$ and $h \geq 2$, a univariate degree-δ monic polynomial $f(x) \in \mathbb{Z}[x]$ with coefficients in $\{0,\ldots,N-1\}$ and $2 < \delta+1 < (\log N)/2$.

Output: All $x_0 \in \mathbb{Z}$ s.t. $|x_0| \leq N^{1/\delta}$ and $f(x_0) \equiv 0 \mod N$.

1: Perform Step 1 and Steps 3 to 7 of Alg. 1. Step 7 returns $\tilde{B}_0^R$ and $\tilde{U}_0$ such that $\tilde{U}_0 \cdot \tilde{B}_0 = \tilde{B}_0^R$.

2: Let $n = h\delta$, X the bound given in Th. 7, $c = n^{\frac{5}{2}}(\frac{3}{2})^n$, $t = 0$, P is the $n \times n$ lower triangular Pascal matrix.

3: Compute the matrix $\tilde{U}_0 \cdot B_0$, where B_0 is the matrix computed in Step 5 of Alg. 1.

4: The first vector of $\tilde{U}_0 \cdot B_0$ corresponds to a polynomial of the form $v(xX)$ for some $v(x) \in \mathbb{Z}[x]$.

5: Compute and output all roots $x_0 \in \mathbb{Z}$ of $v(x)$ satisfying $f(x_0) \equiv 0 \pmod{N}$ and $|x_0| \leq X$.

6: **while** $Xt < N^{1/\delta}$ **do**

7:     Compute the matrix $B_{t+1} = \tilde{U}_t \cdot B_t \cdot P$.

8:     Size-reduce B_{t+1}.

9:     Compute the matrix $\tilde{B}_{t+1} = \lfloor cB_{t+1}/\min_{1\leq i\leq n}\|\mathbf{b}_{t+1\,i}^\star\|\rfloor$ obtained by rounding B_{t+1}.

10:     Run L^2 algorithm on matrix $\tilde{B}_{t+1}$ which returns $\tilde{B}_{t+1}^R$ and $\tilde{U}_{t+1}$ s.t. $\tilde{U}_{t+1} \cdot \tilde{B}_{t+1} = \tilde{B}_{t+1}^R$.

11:     Compute the matrix $\tilde{U}_{t+1} \cdot B_{t+1}$.

12:     The first vector of $\tilde{U}_{t+1} \cdot B_{t+1}$ corresponds to a polynomial of the form $v(xX)$.

13:     Compute all the roots x_0' of the polynomial $v(x) \in \mathbb{Z}[x]$ over $\mathbb{Z}$.

14:     Output $x_0 = x_0' + Xt$ for each root x_0' which satisfies $f(x_0' + Xt) \equiv 0 \pmod{N}$ and $|x_0'| \leq X$.

15:     $t \leftarrow t+1$.

16: **end while**

In the following, we give a small-root bound X on the solution x_0' sufficient to guarantee success:

Theorem 7. *Given as input two integers $N \geq 1$ and $h \geq 2$, a rational $c > n^{5/2}(3/2)^{n-1}$, and a univariate degree-δ monic polynomial $f(x) \in \mathbb{Z}[x]$ with coefficients in $\{0, \dots, N-1\}$, one loop of Alg. 2, corresponding to $t < N^{1/\delta}/X$, outputs all $x_0 = Xt + x_0' \in \mathbb{Z}$ s.t. $|x_0'| \leq X$ and $f(x_0) = 0 \mod N$, and $n = h\delta$, where*

$$X = \left\lfloor \frac{N^{\frac{h-1}{n-1}} \kappa_2^{\frac{-2}{n-1}}}{\sqrt{2} n^{1/(n-1)}} \right\rfloor \quad and \quad \kappa_2 = \frac{c^{\frac{n+1}{n}}}{(c - n^{3/2}(3/2)^{n-1})(c - n^{5/2}(3/2)^{n-1})^{1/n}}.$$

The bound X of Th. 7 is never larger than that of Cor. 2. However, if one selects $c > n^{5/2}(3/2)^{n-1}$, then the two bounds are asymptotically equivalent. This is why Alg. 2 uses $c = n^{5/2}(3/2)^n$.

4.3   Complexity Analysis: A Heuristic Approach

The complexity of Alg. 2 relies on the complexity of the LLL-reduction performed in Step 10. The cost of this reduction depends on the size of coefficients in matrix $B = \tilde{B}_{t+1}$, which itself depends on the value $\min_{1 \leq i \leq n} \|\mathbf{b}_i^\star\|$. The exact knowledge of this value does not seem straightforward to obtain without computing the Gram-Schmidt matrix explicitly. However, experiments show that the Gram-Schmidt curve is roughly decreasing, *i.e.* $\min_{1 \leq i \leq n} \|\mathbf{b}_i^\star\| \approx \|\mathbf{b}_n^\star\|$ and is roughly symmetric: *i.e.* $\log \|\mathbf{b}_i^\star\| - \log \|\mathbf{b}_{n/2}^\star\| \approx \log \|\mathbf{b}_{n/2}^\star\| - \log \|\mathbf{b}_{n-i+1}^\star\|$. If we assume these two experimental facts, we deduce that $\|\mathbf{b}_{n/2}^\star\| \approx |\det(B)|^{1/n}$. By duality, this means that $\|\mathbf{b}_n^\star\| \approx |\det(B)|^{2/n}/\|\mathbf{b}_1^\star\|$. Furthermore, from the definition of the Gram-Schmidt orthogonalization, we know that $\|\mathbf{b}_1^\star\| = \|\mathbf{b}_1\|$, where $\mathbf{b}_1$ is the first vector of matrix B. Therefore we have:

$$\min_{1 \leq i \leq n} \|\mathbf{b}_i^\star\| \approx \|\mathbf{b}_n^\star\| \approx |\det(B)|^{2/n} \|\mathbf{b}_1^\star\|^{-1} = N^{h-1} X^{n-1} \|\mathbf{b}_1\|^{-1}, \tag{5}$$

Thus, we need an estimation on $\|\mathbf{b}_1\|$. Since in practice matrix $B = B_{t+1} = \tilde{U}_i \cdot B_i \cdot P$ is already nearly size-reduced, one can skip Step 8 of Alg. 2. Therefore, vector $\mathbf{b}_1$ is the first vector of matrix $\tilde{U}_i \cdot B_i \cdot P$. Using Cor. 6, one deduces that the first vector of matrix $\tilde{U}_i \cdot B_i$ is roughly as short as the first vector of an LLL-reduced matrix. From the well-known experimental behavior of LLL [17], we can model the first vector of the LLL-reduced basis as a "random" vector of norm $\approx 1.02^n |\det(B)|^{1/n}$. Since the Pascal matrix P has a norm smaller than 2^{n-1}, one gets the bound $\|\mathbf{b}_1\| \leqslant \sqrt{n} 2^{n-1} 1.02^n |\det(B)|^{1/n}$. Therefore, we deduce that: $\min_{1 \leq i \leq n} \|\mathbf{b}_i^\star\| \approx |\det(B)|^{1/n}/(\sqrt{n} 2^{n-1} 1.02^n)$. In practice, we conjecture that $\min_{1 \leq i \leq n} \|\mathbf{b}_i^\star\| > |\det(B)|^{1/n}/\beta^n$, where $\beta < 2$ (see Fig. 5 in Sec. 5).

This discussion leads to the following heuristic approach regarding the method: firstly, one should rather use the estimation (5) in Step 9 of Alg. 2, instead of explicitly computing the Gram-Schmidt matrix; secondly, one can skip Step 8 of Alg. 2. This heuristic version of Algorithm 2 is the one we used during our experiments, all these assumptions were always verified.

To conclude our analysis, it suffices to reduce a rounded matrix such that $\max_{1 \leq i \leq n} \|\tilde{\mathbf{b}}_i^\star\| \leq c \max_{1 \leq i \leq n} \|\mathbf{b}_i^\star\| / \min_{1 \leq i \leq n} \|\mathbf{b}_i^\star\| \leqslant c\beta^{2n}$, instead of being such that $\max_{1 \leq i \leq n} \|\tilde{\mathbf{b}}_i^\star\| \leq \beta^n |\det(B)|^{1/n}$. This means that we are trading entries of size $O(n)$.

Therefore, by considering $n = O(\log N)$, we obtain the same complexity as in Theorem 3 but in a heuristic way. However, even if both asymptotic complexities are identical, in practice for reasonable dimensions the speed-up brought by using Alg. 2 rather than Alg. 1 is considerable (see Section 5). Indeed, the LLL-reduction of matrix $\tilde{U}_i \cdot B_i \cdot P$ (Step 10 of Alg. 2) performs surprisingly faster than expected. This comes from the fact that for reasonable dimensions, the Gram-Schmidt curve of this matrix remains quite close to the one of matrix $\tilde{U}_i \cdot B_i$, where $\tilde{U}_i \cdot B_i$ turns out to be LLL-reduced (or nearly). Besides, the overall running-time of Alg. 2 is approximately the time spent to perform one LLL-reduction, multiplied by the number of executed loops, $i.e.$ by $N^{1/\delta}/X$.

5 Experiments

We implemented Coppersmith's algorithm and our improvements (Algs. 1 and 2) using Shoup's NTL library [21]. However, for the LLL reduction, we used the fplll implementation [3] by Cadé $et\ al.$, which includes the L^2 algorithm [18]: fplll is much faster than NTL for Coppersmith's matrices. It should be stressed that fplll is a wrapper which actually implements several variants of LLL, together with several heuristics: L^2 is only used as a last resort when heuristic variants fail. This means that there might be a discrepancy between the practical running time and the theoretical complexity upper bound of LLL routines. Our test machine is a 2.93-GHz Intel Core 2 Duo processor E7500 running on Fedora. Running times are given in seconds. Like in [10], we used the case $\delta = 3$, and N an RSA-type modulus: the exact polynomial congruence is derived from RSA encryption with public exponent δ. Then, one loop of Coppersmith's algorithm , with $n = 3h$, can find all roots x_0 as long as $|x_0'| \le X = \lfloor 2^{-1/2} N^{\frac{h-1}{n-1}} n^{-\frac{1}{n-1}} \rfloor$. For a fixed h, the rounding strategy (Alg. 1) gives a worse bound than X, but the difference can be made arbitrarily small by increasing the parameter c: in our experiments, we therefore chose the smallest value of c such that $\kappa_1^{\frac{-2}{n-1}}$ and $\kappa_2^{\frac{-2}{n-1}}$ are larger than 0.90, so that the new bound is never less than the old bound X by more than 10%, which is essentially the same. However, we note that the value c can be taken smaller in practice.

Furthermore, it is worth noticing that since the value α is not significant in itself, in order to increase the efficiency, one can round matrices at negligible cost by taking $\alpha := 2^{\lfloor \log_2(\alpha) \rfloor}$ and performing shifts of $\lfloor \log_2(\alpha) \rfloor$ bits. In the same vein, one can increment t by 2 instead of 1 in Coppersmith's algorithm or in Step 12 of Alg. 1, and one can multiply the matrix $\tilde{U}_i \cdot B_i$ by P^2 instead of P in Step 7 of Alg. 2. This comes from the fact that if $0 < x_0' < X$ (resp. $-X < x_0' < 0$), then $x_0' - X$ (resp. $x_0' + X$) is also a valid solution. This refinement allows to divide by 2 the global timing of Coppersmith's algorithm and Alg. 1. However, it seems to be much less relevant when applied to Alg. 2.

Figures 1 and 2 summary our limited experiments respectively comparing one loop of Coppersmith's algorithm with Alg. 1 and Alg. 2 in practice. They provide the bit-length of X and the corresponding running times of the lattice reduction only, because the cost of solving a univariate equation over $\mathbb{Z}$ turns out to be much less in practice. Running times are given as averages over 5 samples. For a typical case where $\lceil \log N \rceil = 2048$, the whole Coppersmith's algorithm would perform in $((\lfloor 2048/3 - 666 \rfloor)/2) \times 6431.2 \approx 6.7$ years and the new Alg. 2 would perform in $(\lfloor 2048/3 - 666 \rfloor) \times 15.52 \approx 11.8$ days, which is about 207 times faster (see Fig. 2 and 6).

Size of N	Data type	Parameter h				
		10	15	20	25	30
1024	Size of X	318	324	328	331	332
	$T_{original}$	2.54	30.48	216.3	793.4	3720.8
	$T_{rounded}$	0.68	4.49	18.22	48.17	175.9
	Speed-up	3.74	6.79	11.87	16.47	21.16
2048	Size of X	634	650	658	663	666
	$T_{original}$	13.47	150.7	865.7	3078	10146.7
	$T_{rounding}$	3.14	17.79	63.3	166.4	379.8
	Speed-up	4.29	8.40	13.67	18.50	26.72
4096	Size of X	1270	1302	1318	1327	1333
	$T_{original}$	41.45	582.6	3162	11968	42053
	$T_{rounded}$	7.07	43.25	157.5	449.8	1301.5
	Speed-up	5.86	13.47	20.07	26.61	32.31

Fig. 1. Bounds and running time of rounding method for cubic congruences

Size of N	Data type	Parameter h				
		10	15	20	25	30
1024	Size of X	316	323	327	330	332
	$T_{original}$	2.14	23.55	161.55	646.37	1955.1
	T_{rc}	0.04	0.42	1.71	5.56	12.71
	$Speed-up_{rc}$	53.5	56.07	94.47	116.25	153.83
2048	Size of X	633	649	657	663	666
	$T_{original}$	8.21	95.12	641.22	2299.5	6431.2
	T_{rc}	0.07	0.55	2.39	7.75	15.52
	$Speed-up_{rc}$	117.28	172.95	268.29	296.71	414.38
4096	Size of X	1270	1302	1318	1327	1333
	$T_{original}$	27.64	378.62	2226	8303.2	25813
	T_{rc}	0.11	0.87	3.73	11.72	29.65
	$Speed-up_{rc}$	251.27	435.19	596.78	708.46	870.6

Fig. 2. Bounds and running time of rounding plus chaining method for cubic congruences

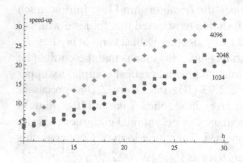

Fig. 3. Speed-up of rounding method

Fig. 4. Speed-up of rounding plus chaining method

From Figure 3, we see that we already get significant speedups (say, larger than 10) even for small values of h and typical sizes of N, by using the rounding method (Alg. 1). The speedup grows when $\log N$ or h grows: for fixed N, the speedup grows roughly a bit less than quadratically in h, whereas the theoretical analysis gives a speedup linear in h. From Figure 4, we see that we can obtain more speedups as the sizes of N or h increase, by using the rounding and chaining method (Alg. 2). Hence, our improvement is practical and allows to get much closer to the asymptotic small-root bound. Furthermore, we verify the assumption on value $\min_{1 \leq i \leq n} \|b_i^\star\|$ for matrix B. Let $\max_{1 \leq i \leq n} \|\mathbf{b}_i^\star\| \approx \beta_1^n \mathrm{vol}(L)^{1/n}$ and $\min_{1 \leq i \leq n} \|\mathbf{b}_i^\star\| \approx \beta_2^n \mathrm{vol}(L)^{1/n}$. In this paper, we have assumed that $\beta_1 = 1/\beta_2$. We summary the results of our experiments for $\lceil \log N \rceil = 512$ with dimensions $30, 60, 90, 120, 150$ in Table 5. We can see that $\beta_1 \times \beta_2 \approx 1$ and that $\beta_1 \leq 2$. This means our assumptions are reasonable.

6   Other Small-Root Algorithms

Other small-root algorithms (see the surveys [14,16]) are based on the same main ideas where LLL reduction plays a crucial role. Due to the different structure of the matrices in these settings, a direct application of our new approach does not seem to provide

Data	Parameter h				
type	10	20	30	40	50
β_1	1.7582	1.8751	1.9093	1.9218	1.9435
β_2	0.5460	0.5271	0.5155	0.5091	0.5077
product	0.9600	0.9883	0.9842	0.9785	0.9867

Fig. 5. Beta values for $\lceil \log N \rceil = 512$

	$\log N$		
	1024	2048	4096
Original	5.8 days	6.7 years	1757782 years
Alg. 2	1.8 hours	11.8 days	4038 years
Speed-up	77	207	435

Fig. 6. Timings comparisons for the total method

the same speedup. We leave it as an open problem to obtain polynomial (non-constant) speedups for these other small-root algorithms: this might be useful to make practical attacks on certain fully homomorphic encryption schemes (see [5]). See the extended version of this paper for a further discussion on these generalizations.

Acknowledgements. We would like to thank the anonymous reviewers of PKC'14 for their valuable comments.

References

1. Boneh, D., Durfee, G.: Cryptanalysis of RSA with private key d less than $N^{0.292}$. IEEE Transactions on Information Theory 46(4), 1339 (2000)
2. Buchmann, J.: Reducing lattice bases by means of approximations. In: Huang, M.-D.A., Adleman, L.M. (eds.) ANTS 1994. LNCS, vol. 877, pp. 160–168. Springer, Heidelberg (1994)
3. Cadé, D., Pujol, X., Stehlé, D.: FPLLL library, version 3.0 (September 2008), http://perso.ens-lyon.fr/damien.stehle
4. Cohen, H.: A course in computational algebraic number theory. Graduate Texts in Mathematics, vol. 138. Springer, Berlin (1993)
5. Cohn, H., Heninger, N.: Approximate common divisors via lattices. IACR Cryptology ePrint Archive 2011:437 (2011)
6. Coppersmith, D.: Finding a small root of a bivariate integer equation; factoring with high bits known. In: Maurer, U.M. (ed.) EUROCRYPT 1996. LNCS, vol. 1070, pp. 178–189. Springer, Heidelberg (1996)
7. Coppersmith, D.: Finding a small root of a univariate modular equation. In: Maurer, U.M. (ed.) EUROCRYPT 1996. LNCS, vol. 1070, pp. 155–165. Springer, Heidelberg (1996)
8. Coppersmith, D.: Small solutions to polynomial equations, and low exponent RSA vulnerabilities. J. Cryptology 10(4), 233–260 (1997); Journal version [7][6]
9. Coron, J.-S.: Finding small roots of bivariate integer polynomial equations: A direct approach. In: Menezes, A. (ed.) CRYPTO 2007. LNCS, vol. 4622, pp. 379–394. Springer, Heidelberg (2007)
10. Coupé, C., Nguyên, P.Q., Stern, J.: The effectiveness of lattice attacks against low-exponent RSA. In: Imai, H., Zheng, Y. (eds.) PKC 1999. LNCS, vol. 1560, pp. 204–218. Springer, Heidelberg (1999)
11. Daudé, H., Vallée, B.: An upper bound on the average number of iterations of the lll algorithm. Theor. Comput. Sci. 123(1), 95–115 (1994)
12. Howgrave-Graham, N.: Finding small roots of univariate modular equations revisited. In: Darnell, M.J. (ed.) Cryptography and Coding 1997. LNCS, vol. 1355, pp. 131–142. Springer, Heidelberg (1997)

13. Lenstra, A.K., Lenstra Jr., H.W., Lovász, L.: Factoring polynomials with rational coefficients. Mathematische Ann. 261, 513–534 (1982)
14. May, A.: Using LLL-reduction for solving RSA and factorization problems: A survey. In: [19] (2010)
15. Najafi, H., Jafari, M., Damen, M.-O.: On adaptive lattice reduction over correlated fading channels. IEEE Transactions on Communications 59(5), 1224–1227 (2011)
16. Nguyen, P.Q.: Public-key cryptanalysis. In: Luengo, I. (ed.) Recent Trends in Cryptography. Contemporary Mathematics, vol. 477. AMS–RSME (2009)
17. Nguyên, P.Q., Stehlé, D.: LLL on the average. In: Hess, F., Pauli, S., Pohst, M. (eds.) ANTS 2006. LNCS, vol. 4076, pp. 238–256. Springer, Heidelberg (2006)
18. Nguyen, P.Q., Stehlé, D.: An LLL algorithm with quadratic complexity. SIAM J. of Computing 39(3), 874–903 (2009)
19. Nguyen, P.Q., Vallée, B. (eds.): The LLL Algorithm: Survey and Applications. Information Security and Cryptography. Springer (2010)
20. Novocin, A., Stehlé, D., Villard, G.: An LLL-reduction algorithm with quasi-linear time complexity: extended abstract. In: Proc. STOC 2011, pp. 403–412. ACM (2011)
21. Shoup, V.: Number Theory C++ Library (NTL) version 5.4.1, http://www.shoup.net/ntl/
22. Shoup, V.: OAEP reconsidered. J. Cryptology 15(4), 223–249 (2002)

Elliptic and Hyperelliptic Curves: A Practical Security Analysis

Joppe W. Bos[1], Craig Costello[1], and Andrea Miele[2,*]

[1] Microsoft Research, Redmond, WA, USA
[2] LACAL, EPFL, Lausanne, Switzerland

Abstract. Motivated by the advantages of using elliptic curves for discrete logarithm-based public-key cryptography, there is an active research area investigating the potential of using hyperelliptic curves of genus 2. For both types of curves, the best known algorithms to solve the discrete logarithm problem are generic attacks such as Pollard rho, for which it is well-known that the algorithm can be sped up when the target curve comes equipped with an efficiently computable automorphism. In this paper we incorporate all of the known optimizations (including those relating to the automorphism group) in order to perform a systematic security assessment of two elliptic curves and two hyperelliptic curves of genus 2. We use our software framework to give concrete estimates on the number of core years required to solve the discrete logarithm problem on four curves that target the 128-bit security level: on the standardized NIST CurveP-256, on a popular curve from the Barreto-Naehrig family, and on their respective analogues in genus 2.

1 Introduction

In the last couple of decades, the use of elliptic curves, or *genus 1 curves*, has become a popular and standardized choice to instantiate public-key cryptography [25,29]. The security of these cryptographic schemes relies on the difficulty of the elliptic curve discrete logarithm problem (ECDLP). Currently, the best known algorithms to solve this problem are the so-called "generic" attacks, such as the parallelized version [37] of the Pollard rho algorithm [33], which has been used to solve large instances of the ECDLP (cf. [22,12,8,2]). It is well-known that this algorithm can be optimized by a constant factor when the target curve comes equipped with an efficiently computable group automorphism [39,15]. For example, all elliptic curves can efficiently compute the inverse of a point and this negation map can be used to speed up the run-time by at most a factor $\sqrt{2}$. When the cardinality of the automorphism group is larger, such as for the elliptic curves proposed in [18], a higher speedup is expected when solving the ECDLP.

Jacobians of hyperelliptic curves of genus 2 have also been considered for cryptographic applications [26] (also see [5,27]). Just as with their elliptic curve

---

* Most of this work was done while the third author was an intern in the Cryptography Research group at Microsoft Research.

H. Krawczyk (Ed.): PKC 2014, LNCS 8383, pp. 203–220, 2014.

counterpart, the best known algorithms to solve the discrete logarithm in such groups are the generic ones. The practical potential of genus 2 curves in public-key cryptography has recently been highlighted by the fast performance numbers presented in [7]. For cryptographically interesting curves over large prime fields, it is possible to achieve larger automorphism groups in genus 2 (see [15]). This not only aids the cryptographer (e.g. [17,7]), but also the cryptanalyst: one can expect a larger speed-up when computing the (H)ECDLP on curves from these families [15].

In this paper we investigate the *practical* speed-up of Pollard rho when exploiting the automorphism group. We use the methods presented in [9,6] for situations where only the negation map is available, and extend these techniques to curves with a larger group automorphism. As examples in the elliptic case, we use two curves that target the 128-bit security level: the NIST Curve P-256 [36] and a BN-curve [3] – the automorphism groups on these two curves are of size two and six respectively, which are the minimum and maximum possible sizes for genus 1 curves over large prime fields. To mimic these choices in the hyperelliptic case[1], we use two curves from [7], where the automorphism groups are of size two and ten – these are the minimum and maximum possible sizes for cryptographically interesting genus 2 curves over large prime fields. We implemented efficient field and curve arithmetic that was optimized for each of these four curves, and derived the best parameters to make use of the automorphism optimization.

We obtain security estimates for these four curves using parameters and implementations that were devised to minimize the practical inconveniences arising from the group automorphism optimization. When taking the standardized NIST Curve P-256 as a baseline for the 128-bit security level, we show that curves with a larger automorphism group (of cardinality $m > 2$) indeed sacrifice some security. The constant-factor speedup, however, is lower in practice than the often cited $\sqrt{m}$. Nevertheless, using both theoretical and experimental analysis, we provide parameters which push the performance of the Pollard rho algorithm close to what can be achieved in practice.

2   Preliminaries

General Group Elements. We use $\mathcal{J}_C$ to denote the Jacobian group of a curve C over a finite field $\mathbf{F}_q$, where $q > 3$ is prime. For our purposes, C and $\mathcal{J}_C$ can be identified when C is an elliptic curve, where our group elements are all points $(x, y) \in \mathbf{F}_q \times \mathbf{F}_q$ satisfying $C/\mathbf{F}_q : y^2 = x^3 + ax + b$, together with the identity element $\mathcal{O}$. In genus 2, our curves are assumed to be of the form $C/\mathbf{F}_q : y^2 = x^5 + f_3 x^3 + f_2 x^2 + f_1 x + f_0$. In this case we write general elements of the Jacobian group (i.e. weight 2 divisors) in their *Mumford representation* as

---

[1] The fact that the BN curve is *pairing-friendly*, while our chosen genus 2 "analogue" is not, does not make a difference in the context of our ECDLP Pollard rho analysis. We wanted curves with large automorphism groups, and we choose *the* BN curve as one interesting example.

$(u(x), v(x)) = (x^2 + u_1 x + u_0, v_1 x + v_0) \in \mathbf{F}_q[x] \times \mathbf{F}_q[x]$, such that $u(x_1) = u(x_2) = 0$, $v(x_1) = y_1$ and $v(x_2) = y_2$, where (x_1, y_1) and (x_2, y_2) are two (not necessarily distinct) points in the set $C(\overline{\mathbf{F}}_q)$, and where $y_1 \neq -y_2$. The canonical embedding of C into $\mathcal{J}_C$ maps $(x_1, y_1) \in C(\mathbf{F}_q)$ to the divisor with Mumford representation $(x - x_1, y_1)$ – we call such divisors *degenerate*. Since $\#C \approx p$ and $\#\mathcal{J}_C \approx p^2$, the probability of encountering a degenerate divisor randomly from $\mathcal{J}_C$ is $O(\frac{1}{p})$; this is also the probability that the sum of two random elements in $\mathcal{J}_C$ is a degenerate divisor [31, Lemma 1]. Combining these probabilities with standard Pollard rho heuristics allows us to ignore the existence of degenerate divisors in practice – in all of the cases considered in this work, it is straightforward to see that an optimized random walk is more likely to solve the discrete logarithm problem than it is to walk into a degenerate divisor. Note that in the unlikely event one encounters a degenerate divisor, such that our general-case formulas compute divisors which are not on the Jacobian, this can be dealt with at almost no additional cost by performing a sanity check on all active walks, once in a while. Another solution is to perform such a sanity check on the distinguished elements only (see the description of the parallel Pollard rho algorithm below) and to discard such incorrect elements.

The Pollard rho Algorithm. The Pollard rho algorithm [33] can be used to compute discrete logarithms in arbitrary groups, but here we give a description that is specific to our context of Jacobian groups. Suppose we are given $P \in \mathcal{J}_C$ that generates a group of large prime order n: given some $Q \in \langle P \rangle$, the (hyper-) elliptic curve discrete logarithm problem (H)ECDLP is to find $k \in \mathbf{Z}/n\mathbf{Z}$ such that $Q = [k]P$. At the highest level, the idea is to compute pseudo-random elements of the form $P_i = [a_i]P + [b_i]Q$ for known non-zero $a_i, b_i \in \mathbf{Z}/n\mathbf{Z}$, such that if a collision $P_i = P_j$ is found with $b_i \neq b_j$, then taking $k := (a_j - a_i)/(b_i - b_j) \in \mathbf{Z}/n\mathbf{Z}$ is a solution to the (H)ECDLP. The *birthday paradox* implies that we can expect to find such a collision after computing around $\sqrt{\frac{\pi n}{2}}$ group elements P_i, provided they are chosen independently and uniformly at random [23]. In practice we use the so-called r-*adding walk*, which starts with r precomputed group elements $S_j = [c_j]P + [d_j]Q$, for non-zero $c_j, d_j \in \mathbf{Z}/n\mathbf{Z}$ and $0 \leq j < r$. On input of a group element P_i, we use a *partition function* $\ell : \langle P \rangle \rightarrow \{0, 1, \ldots, r-1\}$ to define an *iteration function* $f : \langle P \rangle \rightarrow \langle P \rangle$, which computes the next element as $P_{i+1} = f(P_i) = P_i + S_{\ell(P_i)}$. Put simply, the iteration function chooses one of the r precomputed elements to add to P_i in order to step to P_{i+1}. On top of the minor costs of evaluating ℓ and updating the $a_i, b_i \in \mathbf{Z}/n\mathbf{Z}$, each such step comes at the cost of a single Jacobian group operation. Keeping every group element encountered in the walk imposes exponential (and therefore infeasible) storage requirements, which is why the parallel Pollard rho algorithm [37] stores only a small fraction of the elements we come across: the so-called *distinguished points*. Storage of $O(\log n)$ group elements suffices when roughly $\sqrt{n} \log n$ out of n group elements are distinguished [16, Exercise 14.2.15]. In practice one can use a simple check to determine whether the group element P_i is classed as distinguished, in which case it is reported to a central location, along with the corresponding a_i and b_i. Only these distinguished 'points' need to be cross-checked against one another for collisions; when two walks coincide at a non-distinguished point and this collision goes undetected, the deterministic iteration function guarantees that these walks continue along the same path until they arrive at the same distinguished point.

Affine Additions with Amortized Inversions. As mentioned above, each step of a random walk requires the addition of two distinct Jacobian group elements. In the context of scalar multiplications, additions on the Jacobian are usually performed in projective space, where all inversions are avoided until the very end, at which point the result is normalized via a single inversion. In the context of Pollard rho however, it is preferred to work in affine space for two main reasons. Firstly, we need a way to suitably define and efficiently check a distinguished point criterion on *every* group element that is computed; since there are many distinct tuples of projective coordinates corresponding to a unique affine point, there is currently no known method to do this efficiently when working in projective space. Secondly, optimized versions of Pollard rho run many concurrent random walks to take advantage of Montgomery's simultaneous inversion method [30]. If enough concurrent walks are used, then the amortized cost of each individual field inversion becomes roughly 3 field multiplications – this makes affine Weierstrass coordinates the fastest known coordinate system to work with for cryptanalysis. On elliptic curves, such amortized point additions require 5 $\mathbf{F}_q$ multiplications, 1 $\mathbf{F}_q$ squaring and 6 $\mathbf{F}_q$ additions; on genus 2 curves, these additions cost 20 $\mathbf{F}_q$ multiplications, 4 $\mathbf{F}_q$ squarings and 48 $\mathbf{F}_q$ additions [14] – see Table 1 in Section 4.

Exploiting Automorphisms. The Pollard rho algorithm can be sped up by a constant factor if the presence of automorphisms on C is exploited [39,15]. Let m denote the cardinality of the automorphism group, $\mathrm{Aut}(C)$, which we assume is cyclic[2] with generator ψ; in genus 2, ψ extends in the natural way to $\mathcal{J}_C$ under the canonical embedding described above. For all $R, R' \in \langle P \rangle$, define an equivalence relation $\sim$ on $\langle P \rangle$ by $R \sim R'$ if and only if $R = \psi^i(R')$ for some $0 \leq i < m$. Note that there are around n/m such equivalence classes in $\langle P \rangle$, and that $m \geq 2$ since $\mathrm{Aut}(C)$ contains (at least) the identity map id and the negation/involution map "$-$". We write $\tilde{R}$ for the unique *representative* of the class containing R, i.e. $\tilde{R}_1 = \tilde{R}_2$ if and only if $R_1 \sim R_2$. An efficient way of choosing such representatives is imperative to an optimized implementation of the Pollard rho algorithm, so we give the fine-grained details for each of the curves under consideration in Section 4. The important point is that each time the iteration function computes a new group element P_{i+1} via an addition, it now immediately computes *the* representative element $\tilde{P}_{i+1}$, thereby accounting for m elements at a time. This effectively reduces the size of the set on which we walk by a factor of m, which theoretically reduces the expected time to a collision by a constant factor $\sqrt{m}$. In practice however, computing these representatives incurs an overhead which reduces the actual speedup obtained; one of the contributions

---

[2] This is always the case for curves of cryptographic interest over large prime fields with $g \leq 2$ (see [15]).

of this work is to optimize parameter selection in a variety of scenarios to see how close we can get to this theoretical $\sqrt{m}$ improvement.

3   Handling Fruitless Cycles

It is well known that certain practical issues are encountered when exploiting the automorphism optimization [39,18,15,9,6]. Walks will end up in *fruitless cycles* – endless small loops where many fruitless collisions are found over-and-over again (the collisions are fruitless because they have the same a_i and b_i). At a high level, these collisions occur because the automorphism ψ, which generates Aut(C), has a minimal polynomial of small degree; for all scenarios in this paper, ψ satisfies $\sum_{i=0}^{d} e_i \psi^i = 0$ for $e_i \in \mathbf{Z}$ and where $d \leq 5$. Since each step in a walk involves the addition of an element from a relatively small fixed table, it is possible that the same table element (or a very small subset of them) is added multiple times in succession, and that these contributions to the walk are annihilated by unfortunate linear combinations of powers of ψ (which sum to zero). The most simple and frequently occurring example is when the negation map sends the walk into a fruitless 2-cycle: the partition function will choose the same table element twice in a row (i.e $\ell(P_i) = \ell(P_{i+1}) = \ell(P_i + S_{\ell(P_i)})$) with probability $1/r$, and the representative $\tilde{P}_{i+1}$ of the equivalence class $\{P_{i+1}, -P_{i+1}\}$ will be $\tilde{P}_{i+1} = -P_{i+1} = -(P_i + S_{\ell(P_i)})$ with probability $1/2$, meaning that $\tilde{P}_{i+2} = \tilde{P}_i$ with probability $1/(2r)$. This is analyzed in more detail for different cycle lengths and values of $m = \#\mathrm{Aut}(C)$ in [15].

In this section we summarize the current literature and discuss how to reduce the occurrence of fruitless cycles, how to detect when they occur, and subsequently how to deal with a walk that is stuck in such a cycle.

3.1   Cycle Reduction

In [39], a 'look-ahead' technique is described to reduce the event of 2-cycles. This method starts by computing a candidate point $\hat{P}$ for P_{i+1} as usual, i.e. computing $\hat{P} = P_i + S_{\ell(P_i)}$; if $\ell(\hat{P}) \neq \ell(P_i)$, then we set $P_{i+1} = \hat{P}$ and continue, otherwise we discard the point $\hat{P}$ and compute another candidate point by adding the next lookup table element $S_{\ell(P_i)+1 \bmod r}$ to P_i. Note that the probability that r lookup elements result in invalid candidates is extremely low, i.e. r^{-r}. As analyzed in [9], using this look-ahead technique lowers the probability to enter a 2-cycle from $\frac{1}{2r}$ to $\frac{1}{2r^3} + \mathcal{O}(\frac{1}{r^4})$. This technique can be generalized to longer cycles as well [39,9]. Note that if a point gets discarded, it means that we have computed the group operation but did not take a step forward in our pseudo-random walk. We refer to this event as a *fruitless step due to cycle reduction*. In this work we use a 2-cycle reduction technique that slightly modifies the above approach, as we detail in Section 3.3.

3.2   Escaping Fruitless Cycles

Even if the probability of a fruitless cycle is lowered using the look-ahead strategy in Section 3.1, the walks will still eventually enter a fruitless cycle, which clearly must be dealt with. The first step towards a remedy is to detect that a walk is trapped; the next step is to then escape the fruitless cycle in a deterministic way, such that if any other walk encounters the same cycle, they both end up exiting using the exact same point. The idea described in [18] is to occasionally store a sequence of points and to check for repetitions by comparing new points to these stored points. If a cycle has been detected, then one can escape by applying a modified iteration function to a representative of the cycle – in [18], the point with smallest x- or y-coordinate is proposed to be the representative. In [9] it is observed that many modified iteration functions used to escape the cycle are insufficient, and can result in the walk recurring to the same fruitless cycle soon after it "escapes". As observed in [15,9], one example of how to properly escape cycles is to *double* the representative of the fruitless cycle – our implementations use this approach.

3.3   Handling Fruitless Cycles in Practice

In this subsection we compute a lower-bound on the number of fruitless steps we expect to perform in order to state an upper-bound on the (theoretical) speedup. For this analysis, we measure the cost of the additional (fruitless) computations we have to perform in order to deal with cycles. To analyze this cost, we use a function c which expresses the cost of certain operations in terms of the number of modular multiplications. We summarize which strategy we use in our implementation and outline how we select the various parameters, based on our analysis, to perform cycle reduction and cycle escaping.

In [9], different scenarios and varied parameters for both cycle reduction and cycle escaping techniques are implemented and compared. The recommendations are to use medium sized values of r (since larger values might decrease the performance by introducing cache-misses), to reduce the event of 2-cycles only (not any higher cycles), and to escape cycles by doubling the cycle's representative. This combination of choices was able to achieve a 1.29 times speedup over not using the negation map on architectures supporting the x64 instruction set, while from a theoretical perspective a speedup of 1.38 should be possible (both speedups are slightly below $\sqrt{2}$). A follow-up paper [6] takes a different approach on the single instruction, multiple data (SIMD) Cell processor. Since multiple walks are processed by the same instructions, all of which must follow identical computational steps, the cycle reduction technique is completely omitted. Instead, the walk is modified to occasionally check for fruitless cycles – different cycle lengths are detected at different points in time, but if a cycle is detected, this is resolved by escaping from it by again doubling the cycle's representative.

We now analyze the maximum expected speedup in more detail. Assume we perform $w > 0$ steps, and that at every step we can enter a cycle with probability p, if we are not in a cycle already. Once we enter a cycle at step $0 < i \leq w$, all subsequent $w - i$ steps are fruitless. Hence, after w steps we expect to have computed $W(w, p)$ fruitless steps where

$$W(w, p) = \sum_{i=0}^{w-1} p(1 - p)^i (w - i) = \frac{(1 - p)^{w+1} + p(w + 1) - 1}{p}. \tag{1}$$

Using this simple analysis (which is similar to the analysis from [6]), one can compute the ratio between the number of fruitful steps and the number of total steps. For example, the implementation described in [6] uses $r = 2048$, checks for 2-cycles every 48 iterations, and checks for larger cycles much less frequently. Since 2-cycles occur with probability $\frac{1}{2r}$, the expected number of multiplications due to fruitful steps (per 48 iterations) is $c(f) \cdot (48 - W(48, \frac{1}{2 \cdot 2048}))$, where $c(f)$ is the cost to compute the iteration function expressed in multiplications, which in this setting is $c(f) = 6$. The total number of multiplications computed is then $48 \cdot c(f) + c(D)$, where the latter is the cost for point doubling in order to escape the 2-cycle, which is $c(D) = 7$ in the elliptic curve case. Ignoring the various implementation overheads, this analysis shows that a speedup of at most $0.97\sqrt{2}$ is expected when taking only 2-cycles into account.

In our implementations, we chose to follow an approach closer to that which is described in [9]. The reason is that we *do* want to use the cycle reduction technique to lower the probability for walks to enter 2-cycles (at the price of occasionally computing fruitless cycles due to cycle reduction). We remark that in a SIMD setting, such as that considered in [6], an approach without cycle reduction might be more efficient in practice. We note that using the 2-cycle reduction technique also reduces the event of 3-cycles, which can only occur if $3 \mid \#\mathrm{Aut}(C)$, for which the BN curve is the only such scenario in this paper. As shown in [15], 3-cycles occur only if we add representatives from the same partition three times in a row – this repetition is exactly what we aim to avoid using the 2-cycle reduction technique.

We check for cycles every α steps by recording the β points $\{\alpha, \alpha + 1, \ldots, \alpha + \beta - 1\}$ (or an appropriate subset of these points), and checking if the $(\alpha + \beta)$th point occurs in the list of recorded points. If it does, then we select a fruitless cycle representative and use this point to double out of this fruitless cycle: this heuristically eliminates recurring cycles [9].

We modify the cycle reduction technique from [39,9], as described in Section 3.1. In order to avoid, with probability r^{-r}, the scenario where all of the r lookup table elements give rise to an invalid next point, we simply add a point from another precomputed lookup table $\tilde{f}$ (which also contains r elements), as follows:

$$p_{i+1} = \begin{cases} p_i + f_{\ell(p_i)} & \text{if } \ell(p_i) \neq \ell(p_i + f_{\ell(p_i)}), \\ p_i + \tilde{f}_{\ell(p_i)} & \text{otherwise.} \end{cases}$$

Following the analysis from [9], this reduces the probability to enter a 2-cycle from $(mr)^{-1}$ to approximately $\frac{4}{(mr)^3}$. For practical values of r, this makes 4-cycles the most likely event to occur, with probability approximately $(mr)^{-2}$ (assuming independence of the precomputed values S_i). Due to this cycle reduction technique, we expect that one out of r steps is fruitless (since the probability that $\ell(p_i) = \ell(p_i + f_{\ell(p_i)})$ is $\frac{1}{r}$). Hence, the fraction of all steps that are fruitful is $\frac{r-1}{r}$.

4   Target Curves and Their Automorphism Groups

In this section we discuss our chosen target curves and the associated parameter choices and optimizations in the context of Pollard rho. The computational costs for divisor addition, computing the equivalence class representative, and updating the a_i and b_i values are summarized in the worst and average case in Table 1. The average case costs are used in our analysis, but we include the worst case costs for settings (like parallel architectures) where all the walks must always perform the same (worst-case) computational steps.

We choose to target two curves in genus 1 and two curves in genus 2. All four of these curves have a prime order between 254 and 256 bits. The two elliptic curves have $m = 2$ and $m = 6$, which are the respective minimum and maximum values of $m = \#\mathrm{Aut}(C)$ for cryptographically interesting genus 1 curves over prime fields; likewise, the two hyperelliptic curves have $m = 2$ and $m = 10$, which are the respective minimum and maximum values of $m = \#\mathrm{Aut}(C)$ for genus 2 curves of cryptographic interest over prime fields.

In each case we also outline our parameter choices for handling fruitless cycles. We follow the analysis and notation as outlined in Section 3.3, with a primary goal that less than one percent of the steps we compute are fruitless. We assume that the cost of a modular multiplication and modular squaring are equivalent: if required, the analysis can be trivially adjusted to reflect any other cost ratio. In order to sufficiently reduce the probability of cycles to occur, we always take $r \geq 1024$ (we did not use the idea from [6] to reduce the storage of the r precomputed points). Furthermore, in order to detect much longer (and much less likely) cycles, we take $\beta = 32$, so that we can detect and deal with cycles up to length 32. More precisely, given a probability p to enter a cycle at every step, and a value for α (we check for cycles every α steps), we estimate the fraction of all computation that is *fruitful* using Eq. (1), as

$$\frac{c(f) \cdot (\alpha - W(\alpha, p))}{\alpha \cdot c(f) + c(D)} \cdot \frac{r-1}{r}, \tag{2}$$

where the first fraction is due to the cycle detection and escaping (we assume that we always compute a doubling to escape), and the second fraction incorporates the fruitless steps due to the cycle reduction technique. Although we give the costs of updating the a_i and b_i, we omit these from our analysis – the correct a_i and b_i can be recovered when needed, when each path starts at a random point derived from a random seed, as described in [2].

4.1   Target Curves in Genus 1

NIST CurveP-256. Let $q = 2^{256} - 2^{224} + 2^{192} + 2^{96} - 1$, and define $E/\mathbf{F}_q \colon y^2 = x^3 - 3x + b$, with b=0x5AC635D8AA3A93E7B3EBBD55769886BC651D06B0CC53B0F63BCE3C3E27D2604B.

This curve has a 256-bit prime order n and is defined in NIST's Digital Signature Standard [36]. In this case $\text{Aut}(E) = \{id, -\}$, meaning that $(x, y) \sim (x, -y)$, so we take the representative of each class to be the point with the odd y-coordinate (when $0 \leq y < q$). In the worst case, the cost of computing this representative is a negation in $\mathbf{F}_q$, and updating the corresponding (a_i, b_i) pair costs two negations in $\mathbf{Z}/n\mathbf{Z}$. On average though, these costs are halved, since we have already computed (and detected) the representative half of the time.

In order to derive parameters for the cycle detection, we use $p = (2r)^{-2}$ as the probability to enter a 4-cycle, which (due to the cycle-reduction technique) is higher than the probability to enter a 2-cycle – see Section 3.3. The elliptic curve group operation costs are taken as $c(f) = c(A) = 6$ and $c(D) = 7$. Using the parameters $r = 1024$, $\alpha = 7 \cdot 10^4$ and $\beta = 32$, we expect that around one percent of the computed steps are fruitless: Eq.(2) evaluates to 0.9907.

BN254. Let q be the 254-bit prime obtained when $u = -(2^{62} + 2^{55} + 1)$ is plugged into $q(u) = 36u^4 + 36u^3 + 24u^2 + 6u + 1$. The Barreto-Naehrig (BN) curve [3] $E/\mathbf{F}_q: y^2 = x^3 + 2$ has a 254-bit prime order n, and has been used in several of the "speed-record" papers for pairing computations that target the 128-bit security level (e.g. [1,21]). Since $q \equiv 1 \bmod 3$, there exists $\zeta \neq 1 \in \mathbf{F}_q$ such that $\zeta^3 = 1$, meaning that $E(\mathbf{F}_q)$ has additional automorphisms, e.g. $\phi :$ $E \to E, (x, y) \mapsto (\zeta x, y)$. In fact, $\text{Aut}(E) = \{id, -, \phi, -\phi, \phi^2, -\phi^2\}$, so that the points (x, y), $(x, -y)$, $(\zeta x, y)$, $(\zeta x, -y)$, $(\zeta^2 x, y)$ and $(\zeta^2 x, -y)$ are all equivalent under $\sim$. We take the representative of each equivalence class to be the point whose x-coordinate has least absolute value and whose y-coordinate is odd. In the worst case, computing this representative costs one multiplication, two negations and one addition in $\mathbf{F}_q$, and updating the corresponding (a_i, b_i) pair costs two multiplications in $\mathbf{Z}/n\mathbf{Z}$; we exploit $\zeta^2 x = -(\zeta + 1)x$ to compute the x-coordinate of $\phi^2(P)$ from the x-coordinates of $\phi(P)$ and P without any further multiplications. On average however, we only need the negation to get the odd y-coordinate half of the time; to update the (a_i, b_i), we compute the two $\mathbf{Z}/n\mathbf{Z}$ multiplications two thirds of the time, while in the remaining one third of the cases, we average a single $\mathbf{Z}/n\mathbf{Z}$ addition.

In order to derive parameters for the cycle detection, we use $p = (6r)^{-2}$ as the adjusted probability to enter a 4-cycle (taking the group automorphism into account). In this case the elliptic curve group operation costs are taken as $c(f) = c(A) = 7$ and $c(D) = 8$, where both costs incorporate the additional multiplication to compute the representative. Using $r = 1024$ and $\beta = 32$, we find that a corresponding α value (for which we expect that around one percent of the computed steps is fruitless) as $\alpha = 6 \cdot 10^5$, which is almost an order of magnitude larger than in the NIST CurveP-256 setting: in this case, evaluating Eq. (2) gives 0.9911.

4.2   Target Curves in Genus 2

Generic1271. Let $q = 2^{127} - 1$ and $C/\mathbf{F}_q: y^2 = x^5 + a_3 x^2 + a_2 x^2 + a_1 x +$ a_0 with $a_3 = $ 0x1A237F07B8BB79AEBA5011C3FA697D2D, $a_2 =$0x63D7B6834F8A4F3DBDBD141CE55EA675,

$a_1 = $ 0x44642D7B9E492BE2E3C4F8A36F0C4236, $a_0 = $ 0x504351F67810EFACF06E3A6E5C532F0. This curve was recently used in [7] as a "generic" instance of a (degree 5) genus 2 curve, since it has no special structure and the order of its Jacobian is a 254-bit prime n. Here $\mathrm{Aut}(C) = \{id, -\}$, which extends to $\mathcal{J}_C$ to give that the divisors $(x^2 + u_1 x + u_0, v_1 x + v_0)$ and $(x^2 + u_1 x + u_0, -v_1 x - v_0)$ are equivalent under $\sim$. Thus, we take the representative of each class to be the divisor whose v_0-coordinate is odd. In the worst case, the cost of computing this representative is two negations in $\mathbf{F}_q$, and updating the corresponding (a_i, b_i) pair costs two negations in $\mathbf{Z}/n\mathbf{Z}$. On average these costs are again halved since we already have the correct representative half of the time.

In order to derive parameters for the cycle detection, we use exactly the same parameters as in the NIST CurveP-256 setting, since the automorphism groups are the same, and only the costs of the group operations differ: $c(f) = c(A) = 24$ and $c(D) = 28$ in this case: Eq.(2) evaluates to 0.9907 (when $\alpha = 7 \cdot 10^4$, $\beta = 32$ and $r = 1024$).

4GLV127-BK. Let $q = 2^{64} \cdot (2^{63} - 27443) + 1$. The Buhler-Koblitz [11] curve $C/\mathbf{F}_q : y^2 = x^5 + 17$ gives rise to a Jacobian whose group order is a 254-bit prime n. Since $q \equiv 1 \bmod 5$, there exists $\zeta \neq 1$ in $\mathbf{F}_q$ such that $\zeta^5 = 1$, which gives rise to additional automorphisms on C, e.g. $\phi : C \to C, (x, y) \mapsto (\zeta x, y)$. The map ϕ extends to weight-2 divisors as $\phi : \mathcal{J}_C \to \mathcal{J}_C, (x^2 + u_1 x + u_0, v_1 x + v_0) \mapsto (x^2 + \zeta u_1 x + \zeta^2 u_0, \zeta^4 v_1 x + v_0)$. Here $\mathrm{Aut}(C) = \{id, -, \phi, -\phi, \ldots, \phi^4, -\phi^4\}$, so we take the representative of each class to be the divisor whose u_1-coordinate has least absolute value *and* whose v_0-coordinate is odd. In the worst case, the cost of finding this representative is six multiplications, one squaring, three additions and two negations in $\mathbf{F}_q$; it takes three multiplications, three additions and a negation (this time we use $\zeta^4 = -(\zeta^3 + \zeta^2 + \zeta + 1)$ to save a multiplication) to first determine the minimum value in $\{\zeta^i u_1\}$ for $0 \leq i \leq 4$, another two multiplications to compute the corresponding $\zeta^{2i} u_0$ and $\pm \zeta^{4i} v_1$, and finally one negation for the v_0-coordinate. To comply with the formulas in [14], we must also recompute the two extended coordinates $u_1 u_0$ and u_1^2, which additionally incurs a multiplication and a squaring. Updating the (a_i, b_i) pair costs two multiplications in $\mathbf{Z}/n\mathbf{Z}$. On average though, we only need the three $\mathbf{F}_q$ multiplications and one $\mathbf{F}_q$ squaring for u_0, v_1, $u_1 u_0$ and u_1^2 in eight of the ten cases (one of the ten needs only one $\mathbf{F}_q$ negation, the other case needs no computation), and we only need to negate v_0 in five of the ten cases. For updating (a_i, b_i) on average, we need two $\mathbf{Z}/n\mathbf{Z}$ multiplications in eight of the ten cases, two $\mathbf{Z}/n\mathbf{Z}$ negations in one of them, while the remaining case leaves (a_i, b_i) unchanged.

Taking the size of the automorphism group into account gives $p = (10r)^{-2}$ as the adjusted probability to enter a 4-cycle. Including the average number of additional multiplications to compute the representative of the equivalence class in the iteration function, the costs become $c(f) = 30\frac{1}{5}$ and $c(D) = 34\frac{1}{5}$. An α value for which we expect that around one percent of the computed steps is fruitless is $\alpha = 10^6$: this is over an order of magnitude larger compared to the Generic1271 setting: evaluating Eq.(2) gives 0.9943 in this case (when $\beta = 32$ and $r = 1024$).

Table 1. Cost of the Pollard rho iteration for the selected genus g curves, where $m = \#\text{Aut}$ and q is the prime field characteristic. We denote modular multiplications, modular squarings and modular additions/subtractions with **M**, **S** and **a** respectively. When updating the a_i and b_i values, we compute modulo n instead of modulo q.

curve	g	m	divisor addition	compute representative worst	compute representative average	update a_i, b_i worst	update a_i, b_i average
CurveP-256	1	2	$5M + S + 6a$	$1a$	$\frac{1}{2}a$	$2a_n$	$1a_n$
BN254	1	6	$5M + S + 6a$	$1M + 3a$	$1M + \frac{5}{2}a$	$2M_n$	$\frac{4}{3}M_n + \frac{1}{3}a_n$
Generic1271	2	2	$20M + 4S + 48a$	$2a$	$1a$	$2a_n$	$1a_n$
4GLV127-BK	2	10	$20M + 4S + 48a$	$6M + 1S + 5a$	$\frac{27}{5}M + \frac{4}{5}S + \frac{3}{5}a$	$2M_n$	$\frac{8}{5}M_n + \frac{1}{5}a_n$

4.3 Other Curves of Interest

In this subsection we briefly mention the application of the Pollard rho algorithm to other popular curves that have appeared in the literature and that target the 128-bit security level.

Other Genus 1 Curves. Bernstein's Curve25519 [4] and Hisil's ecfp256e [24] both facilitate fast timings for scalar multiplications without the existence of additional morphisms, so besides the faster modular arithmetic that is possible over these pseudo-Mersenne primes, the application of Pollard rho to these two curves is identical to the case of CurveP-256. There are other j-invariant zero curves (that are not pairing-friendly) which have been put forward for fast ECC using the Gallant-Lambert-Vanstone (GLV) technique [18]: the prime order curve $E/\mathbf{F}_q\colon y^2 = x^3 + 2$ with $q = 2^{256} - 11733$ was used by Longa and Sica [28], while the prime order curve $E/\mathbf{F}_q\colon y^2 = x^3 + 7$ with $q = 2^{256} - 2^{32} - 977$ is proposed in the SEC standard [13] and is subsequently used in Bitcoin [32]. In both of these cases, the automorphism group is the same as that for BN254, so Pollard rho is optimized identically.

There exist numerous families of curves that come equipped with non-trivial morphisms which are useful in the context of scalar multiplications, but which are not useful in the context of Pollard rho. This is often the case for curves that contain efficiently computable endomorphisms which are not automorphisms, like the families of **Q**-curves recently proposed by Smith [34]. On the other hand, Galbraith-Lin-Scott (GLS) curves [17] do facilitate a constant-factor speedup in Pollard rho, since the GLS endomorphism gives rise to small orbits and is typically much faster than a group operation (it usually involves one multiplication by a fixed constant).

Other Genus 2 Curves. The authors of [7] recently used the Kummer surface found by Gaudry and Schost [20] to achieve fast scalar multiplications in genus 2. Interestingly, there is no known way to exploit the fast arithmetic on the Kummer surface in Pollard rho, since only pseudo-additions exist there. Discrete logarithm instances must therefore be mapped back to the full Jacobian group, where, besides the smaller prime subgroup resulting from the imposed cofactor of 16 on

Kummer1271, the optimal application of Pollard rho is identical to the case of Generic1271.

In addition to BK curves of the form $y^2 = x^5 + b$, the performance of 4-dimensional scalar decompositions on curves of the form $C/\mathbf{F}_q : y^2 = x^5 + ax$ was also recently investigated [7]. Similar to the BK curves, the endomorphisms on these curves are very efficient in comparison to a group addition, so they facilitate significant speedups in Pollard rho. Here we have $m = 8$, so it would be interesting to see how close we can get to a $\sqrt{8}$ speedup in this case.

As is the case in the elliptic curve setting, there are several genus 2 families that possess maps which are useful to the cryptographer, but which offer no known benefit to the cryptanalyst – see [19] for some examples of endomorphisms which are not automorphisms. Thus, the application of Pollard rho to these families is identical to the case of Generic1271.

5   Performance Results

In order to systematically compare the security of the genus 1 and genus 2 curves from the previous section, we designed and implemented a software framework for 64-bit platforms supporting the x64 instruction set. This modular design is capable of switching various features on or off: for example, using the automorphism optimization, employing different techniques for handling fruitless cycles, using different finite fields, or using different curve arithmetic. We implemented dedicated modular arithmetic for the special prime fields considered in this work (see Section 4); for each curve, we optimized the modular multiplication by hand in assembly, which resulted in a significant performance speedup compared to compiling our native C-code. All of the experimental results presented in this section have been obtained using an Intel Core i7-3520M (Ivy Bridge), running at 2893.484 MHz, and with the so-called *turbo boost* and *hyper-threading* features disabled.

We do not claim that the performance numbers reported in this section are the best possible. In a real attack, which focuses on a single curve target, the curve arithmetic and the arithmetic in the finite field should be optimized even further in assembly – we spent a moderate amount of time per curve to achieve good performance. We expect however, that the relative timings between the curves would remain roughly invariant under such further optimizations.

5.1   Correctness

In order to make sure that our software framework works correctly and behaves as expected, we searched for curves defined over the same base fields as our target curves (as outlined in Section 4), but with smaller (around 45-bit) prime-order subgroups (we note that ψ stabilizes these prime-order subgroups in all cases). We ran our implementations and enabled all the "statistic-gathering" options: this slows down the cost of a single step, but does not alter the behavior of the algorithm. We computed 10 batches of 10^3 Pollard rho computations for solving

Table 2. Summary of the number of steps required when solving the DLP in a prime order subgroup n $(2^{N-1} < n < 2^N)$ on the four (modified) curves we consider in this work. We computed 10 batches of 10^3 discrete logarithms and we display the minimum and maximum number of average steps out of these 10 batches, as well as the overall average. We used a 32-adding walk and a distinguished point property with $d = 8$, which we expect to occur once every 2^8 steps. The expected estimate is derived using Eq. (4).

curve	N	min	avg	max	expected
NIST CurveP-256	45	6 528 891	6 703 125	6 959 881	6 702 814
BN254	47	12 766 948	13 130 659	13 353 056	13 114 481
Generic1271	45	6 936 215	7 087 854	7 311 815	7 137 587
4GLV127-BK	45	5 339 249	5 489 583	5 668 256	5 489 249

discrete logarithm instances in these subgroups, both with and without the use of the automorphism optimization.

Pollard rho without the Group Automorphism Optimization. Assume we use an r-adding walk without the automorphism optimization (we take $m = 1$, where m is the cardinality of the group automorphism that is used). Experimental results from [35] suggest that using a larger r-value, such as $r \geq 16$, results in practical behavior that is closer to a truly random walk and gives a run-time that is close to the expected $\sqrt{\frac{\pi n}{2}}$. This is in agreement with the heuristic analysis from [2, Appendix B], which refines the arguments from [10], where it is shown that the average number of pseudo-random group elements required to find a collision (and solve the DLP) using an r-adding walk is

$$\sqrt{\frac{\pi n}{2m(1 - \frac{1}{r})}}, \tag{3}$$

where n is the size of the prime order subgroup. We use the parallel (i.e. distinguished point) version of Pollard rho, such that approximately one out of every 2^d points is distinguished. When computing w walks concurrently, Eq. (3) can be adjusted to

$$\sqrt{\frac{\pi n}{2m(1 - \frac{1}{r})}} + w \cdot 2^{d-1}. \tag{4}$$

This is because we need to perform an additional $w \cdot 2^{d-1}$ steps after two walks arrive at the same point: on average, 2^{d-1} steps are required to reach the next distinguished point, where both walks will be sent to the central database and the collision will be detected. For each scenario, Table 2 summarizes the average minimum, average and maximum steps of these 10 batches together with the theoretical number of steps we expect to take to solve the DLP. In all four cases, the average number of steps observed in practice matches the expected number of steps almost exactly: the difference is below one percent.

Pollard rho with the Group Automorphism Optimization. When using the group automorphism with $m = \#\mathrm{Aut}(C)$, we can encounter two types of

Table 3. A comparison of the expected (exp.) and real number of fruitless steps (**FS**) and fruitful steps when computing 10 batches of 10^3 discrete logarithms (as in Table 2) but using the group automorphism optimization. The genus-g curves have $m = \#\mathrm{Aut}(C)$ and we check for cycles up to length β every α steps.

	NIST P-256	BN254	Generic1271	4GLV127-BK
(g, m)	$(1, 2)$	$(1, 6)$	$(2, 2)$	$(2, 10)$
(α, β)	$(7 \cdot 10^4, 32)$	$(6 \cdot 10^5, 32)$	$(7 \cdot 10^4, 32)$	$(10^6, 32)$
exp. # of fruitful steps (Eq.(4))	4 668 485	5 274 669	4 971 221	1 712 170
real # of fruitful steps (s)	4 643 787	5 271 219	5 010 354	1 723 756
exp. # of trapped **FS** (Eq. (5))	38 537	41 671	41 538	8185
real # of trapped **FS**	33 349	28 526	42 122	4835
exp. # of cycle reduction **FS**	4535	5148	4893	1683
real # of cycle reduction **FS**	4582	5173	4911	1687

fruitless steps: those due to the 2-cycle reduction technique and those which are performed when a walk is trapped in fruitless cycles. Due to the cycle reduction technique we use (see Section 3.3), the probability of 2-cycles and 3-cycles (if the latter can occur) have been reduced significantly. In fact, the probability to enter a 4-cycle becomes the most likely event by far, so we use the approximation $p = 1/(mr)^2$ (see Section 3.3) for the probability of entering any cycle. We check for cycles every α steps, where α depends on the curve (see Section 4), and we escape these cycles if necessary. If s is the expected number of steps required to solve the DLP, then the expected number of fruitless steps spent in fruitless cycles is

$$\frac{s}{\alpha} \cdot W(\alpha, (mr)^{-2}), \tag{5}$$

where W is as in Eq. (1).

Table 3 summarizes the results of running Pollard rho with the group automorphism optimization, where it is clear that the number of fruitful steps observed is very close to what we expect. Hence, we can expect to achieve a speedup if the practical cost of the iteration function is not increased too much. We note that the number of fruitless steps due to the 2-cycle reduction technique is also consistent with the prediction.

Interestingly, for the two curves with a larger automorphism group (i.e. with $m > 2$), the number of trapped fruitless cycles is lower than the expected value, which can be explained as follows. Since we expect fruitless cycles to occur much less frequently, the α parameter has been chosen significantly larger than for the curves with $m = 2$. In our benchmark runs, we solve the smaller DLP instances that are outlined in Table 2; if one of the walks gets trapped in a fruitless cycle, then, with overwhelming probability, one of the other concurrent walks will solve the DLP before this trapped walk has computed all of the fruitless $\alpha + \beta$ steps that are required to escape from this fruitless cycle. This behavior is not incorporated in our estimate for the total number of trapped fruitless steps. We ran larger instances of the DLP and, as expected, the total number of trapped fruitless steps increased.

Table 4. The performance of our implementations expressed in the number of cycles per step without (32-adding walk) and with (1024-adding walk) the usage of the group automorphism running 2048 walks concurrently. For each curve, the expected speedup (which takes into account the additional cost of computing the equivalence class representative) and the speedup found in practice are stated together with the expected number of single-core years to solve a discrete logarithm. The security of each curve is given when taking NIST CurveP-256 as the baseline for the 128-bit security level.

curve	performance		speedup		core	sec
	without	with	exp.	real	years	
NIST CurveP-256	1129	1185	$\sqrt{2}$	$0.947\sqrt{2}$	$3.946 \cdot 10^{24}$	128.0
BN254	1030	1296	$\frac{6}{7} \cdot \sqrt{6} \approx 0.857\sqrt{6}$	$0.790\sqrt{6}$	$9.486 \cdot 10^{23}$	125.9
Generic1271	986	1043	$\sqrt{2}$	$0.940\sqrt{2}$	$1.736 \cdot 10^{24}$	126.8
4GLV127-BK	1398	1765	$\frac{120}{151} \cdot \sqrt{10} \approx 0.795\sqrt{10}$	$0.784\sqrt{10}$	$1.309 \cdot 10^{24}$	126.4

5.2 Implementation Results

In order to optimize performance, we conducted several experiments to find the best parameters for instantiating the Pollard rho algorithm in practice: we varied the number of partitions in the adding walks (but restricted to $r \geq 1024$ when using the group automorphism optimization) and the number of concurrent walks. For all four curves, we found that 2048 concurrent walks resulted in low costs for amortized inversions and gave the best performance. Using 2048 concurrent walks contradicts the advice from [9], which might be explained by the fact that our platform has a large cache so that "cache-misses" will only occur for a much larger number of concurrent walks. In regards to the optimal size of the lookup table, our benchmark runs showed that using 32-adding walks are best when the automorphism optimization is not used, and that 1024-adding walks are best when it is.

In Table 4 we state the performance numbers using the parameters above. We save computation by exploiting the fact that one does not need to update the a_i and b_i values [2]: this is especially significant for the curves with $m > 2$. Note that the number of computer cycles per step, when not using the group automorphism optimization, is lower for the BN254 curve compared to CurveP-256. This is surprising since the BN254 curve does not use a special prime. A partial explanation is that the CurveP-256 arithmetic is relatively slow, especially compared to the other NIST curves, and the addition of two residues might result in a carry occupying an additional word, which slows down the computation. On the other hand, the BN254 curve is defined over a 254-bit prime, such that subtraction-less Montgomery multiplication [38] can be used to save a conditional subtraction in every modular multiplication. Furthermore, the addition of two residues does not result in a carry occupying another word, which saves instructions. We suspect, however, that a hand-tweaked assembly implementation of NIST's CurveP-256 can be made slightly more efficient than the subtraction-less Montgomery arithmetic using the x64 instruction set.

Table 4 states the expected speedup of Pollard rho using the automorphism (which takes into account the additional cost of choosing representatives), as well as the speedup we observed. This experimental speedup is consistently five to seven percent lower than the expected one, except for the 4GLV127-BK curve – such differences can be expected, as our analysis did not take extra modular additions, subtractions and negation into account, nor did we consider various overheads due to the usage of additional memory latencies. In the case of the BK curve, these additional factors constitute a much smaller fraction of the factors that were included in the analysis, which is why our experiments results match the expected numbers even closer. For each curve, Table 4 also reports the expected number of single Intel Core i7-3520M core years required to solve a discrete logarithm instance. This estimate assumes that we use the group automorphism optimization and takes into account that we have to perform slightly more steps, increasing the estimate from Eq. (3) such that we take fruitless cycles into account, in line with the analysis from Section 4. Based on this estimate, we also give the security level for each curve using the NIST CurveP-256 as the baseline for 128-bit security. Hence, this security estimate takes into account the different available optimizations for each curve, as well as the varying performance for the base field arithmetic.

6   Conclusions

We analyzed the practical security of elliptic curves and genus 2 hyperelliptic curves over prime fields using the Pollard rho algorithm. We developed a software framework implementing the state-of-the-art techniques to make use of the group automorphism optimization, which is targeted at 64-bit architectures that support the x64 instruction set. We detailed optimized parameter selection when dealing with practical issues, such as reducing, detecting and escaping fruitless cycles; in particular, we analyzed these choices for curves with large automorphism groups, which have not yet received a detailed analysis in the literature.

We studied the performance of the Pollard rho algorithm on two elliptic curves and two genus 2 curves of cryptographic interest, all of which are estimated to provide around 128 bits of security. Our first conclusion is that, reassuringly, the practical security of all four curves considered is almost equivalent. Our second conclusion is that curves having large a large group automorphism of cardinality $m > 2$ can not achieve a speedup of $\sqrt{m}$: one has to pay a penalty for finding the representative of the equivalence class. Nevertheless, a constant-factor improvement is possible when dealing with fruitless cycles, and our analysis shows how to optimize this improvement in practice.

Acknowledgments. We thank Michael Naehrig for pointing out further optimizations and the anonymous reviewers for their insightful comments.

References

1. Aranha, D.F., Karabina, K., Longa, P., Gebotys, C.H., López, J.: Faster explicit formulas for computing pairings over ordinary curves. In: Paterson, K.G. (ed.) EUROCRYPT 2011. LNCS, vol. 6632, pp. 48–68. Springer, Heidelberg (2011)

2. Bailey, D.V., Batina, L., Bernstein, D.J., Birkner, P., Bos, J.W., Chen, H.-C., Cheng, C.-M., van Damme, G., de Meulenaer, G., Perez, L.J.D., Fan, J., Güneysu, T., Gurkaynak, F., Kleinjung, T., Lange, T., Mentens, N., Niederhagen, R., Paar, C., Regazzoni, F., Schwabe, P., Uhsadel, L., Herrewege, A.V., Yang, B.-Y.: Breaking ECC2K-130. Cryptology ePrint Archive, Report 2009/541 (2009), http://eprint.iacr.org/2009/541

3. Barreto, P.S.L.M., Naehrig, M.: Pairing-friendly elliptic curves of prime order. In: Preneel, B., Tavares, S. (eds.) SAC 2005. LNCS, vol. 3897, pp. 319–331. Springer, Heidelberg (2006)

4. Bernstein, D.J.: Curve25519: New Diffie-Hellman speed records. In: Yung, M., Dodis, Y., Kiayias, A., Malkin, T. (eds.) PKC 2006. LNCS, vol. 3958, pp. 207–228. Springer, Heidelberg (2006)

5. Bernstein, D.J.: Elliptic vs. Hyperelliptic, part I. Talk at the ECC (September 2006), slides at http://cr.yp.to/talks/2006.09.20/slides.pdf

6. Bernstein, D.J., Lange, T., Schwabe, P.: On the correct use of the negation map in the Pollard rho method. In: Catalano, D., Fazio, N., Gennaro, R., Nicolosi, A. (eds.) PKC 2011. LNCS, vol. 6571, pp. 128–146. Springer, Heidelberg (2011)

7. Bos, J.W., Costello, C., Hisil, H., Lauter, K.: Fast cryptography in genus 2. In: Johansson, T., Nguyen, P.Q. (eds.) EUROCRYPT 2013. LNCS, vol. 7881, pp. 194–210. Springer, Heidelberg (2013)

8. Bos, J.W., Kaihara, M.E., Kleinjung, T., Lenstra, A.K., Montgomery, P.L.: Solving a 112-bit prime elliptic curve discrete logarithm problem on game consoles using sloppy reduction. International Journal of Applied Cryptography 2(3), 212–228 (2012)

9. Bos, J.W., Kleinjung, T., Lenstra, A.K.: On the use of the negation map in the Pollard rho method. In: Hanrot, G., Morain, F., Thomé, E. (eds.) ANTS-IX. LNCS, vol. 6197, pp. 66–82. Springer, Heidelberg (2010)

10. Brent, R.P., Pollard, J.M.: Factorization of the eighth Fermat number. Mathematics of Computation 36(154), 627–630 (1981)

11. Buhler, J., Koblitz, N.: Lattice basis reduction, Jacobi sums and hyperelliptic cryptosystems. Bull. Australian Math. Soc. 58(1), 147–154 (1998)

12. Certicom. Press release: Certicom announces elliptic curve cryptosystem (ECC) challenge winner (2002), http://www.certicom.com/index.php/2002-press-releases/ 38-2002-press-releases/340-notre-dame-mathematician-solves-eccp -109-encryption-key-problem-issued-in-1997

13. Certicom Research. Standards for efficient cryptography 2: Recommended elliptic curve domain parameters. Standard SEC2, Certicom (2000)

14. Costello, C., Lauter, K.: Group law computations on Jacobians of hyperelliptic curves. In: Miri, A., Vaudenay, S. (eds.) SAC 2011. LNCS, vol. 7118, pp. 92–117. Springer, Heidelberg (2012)

15. Duursma, I.M., Gaudry, P., Morain, F.: Speeding up the discrete log computation on curves with automorphisms. In: Lam, K.-Y., Okamoto, E., Xing, C. (eds.) ASIACRYPT 1999. LNCS, vol. 1716, pp. 103–121. Springer, Heidelberg (1999)

16. Galbraith, S.D.: Mathematics of public key cryptography. Cambridge University Press (2012)

17. Galbraith, S.D., Lin, X., Scott, M.: Endomorphisms for faster elliptic curve cryptography on a large class of curves. J. Cryptology 24(3), 446–469 (2011)

18. Gallant, R.P., Lambert, R.J., Vanstone, S.A.: Faster point multiplication on elliptic curves with efficient endomorphisms. In: Kilian, J. (ed.) CRYPTO 2001. LNCS, vol. 2139, pp. 190–200. Springer, Heidelberg (2001)

19. Gaudry, P., Kohel, D.R., Smith, B.A.: Counting points on genus 2 curves with real multiplication. In: Lee, D.H., Wang, X. (eds.) ASIACRYPT 2011. LNCS, vol. 7073, pp. 504–519. Springer, Heidelberg (2011)

20. Gaudry, P., Schost, É.: Genus 2 point counting over prime fields. J. Symb. Comput. 47(4), 368–400 (2012)

21. Geovandro, C.C.F.P., Simplício Jr., M.A., Naehrig, M., Barreto, P.S.L.M.: A family of implementation-friendly BN elliptic curves. Journal of Systems and Software 84(8), 1319–1326 (2011)

22. Harley, R.: Elliptic curve discrete logarithms project, http://pauillac.inria.fr/~harley/

23. Harris, B.: Probability distributions related to random mappings. The Annals of Mathematical Statistics 31, 1045–1062 (1960)

24. Hisil, H.: Elliptic curves, group law, and efficient computation. PhD thesis (2010)

25. Koblitz, N.: Elliptic curve cryptosystems. Mathematics of Computation 48(177), 203–209 (1987)

26. Koblitz, N.: Hyperelliptic cryptosystems. Journal of Cryptology 1(3), 139–150 (1989)

27. Lange, T.: Elliptic vs. Hyperelliptic, part II. Talk at the ECC (September 2006), slides at http://www.hyperelliptic.org/tanja/vortraege/ECC_06.ps

28. Longa, P., Sica, F.: Four-dimensional Gallant-Lambert-Vanstone scalar multiplication. In: Wang, X., Sako, K. (eds.) ASIACRYPT 2012. LNCS, vol. 7658, pp. 718–739. Springer, Heidelberg (2012)

29. Miller, V.S.: Use of elliptic curves in cryptography. In: Williams, H.C. (ed.) CRYPTO 1985. LNCS, vol. 218, pp. 417–426. Springer, Heidelberg (1986)

30. Montgomery, P.L.: Speeding the Pollard and elliptic curve methods of factorization. Mathematics of Computation 48(177), 243–264 (1987)

31. Nagao, K.: Improving group law algorithms for Jacobians of hyperelliptic curves. In: Bosma, W. (ed.) ANTS-IV. LNCS, vol. 1838, pp. 439–447. Springer, Heidelberg (2000)

32. Nakamoto, S.: Bitcoin: A peer-to-peer electronic cash system (2009), http://bitcoin.org/bitcoin.pdf

33. Pollard, J.M.: Monte Carlo methods for index computation (mod p). Mathematics of Computation 32(143), 918–924 (1978)

34. Smith, B.A.: Families of fast elliptic curves from Q-curves. In: Sako, K., Sarkar, P. (eds.) ASIACRYPT 2013, Part I. LNCS, vol. 8269, pp. 61–78. Springer, Heidelberg (2013)

35. Teske, E.: On random walks for Pollard's rho method. Mathematics of Computation 70(234), 809–825 (2001)

36. U.S. Department of Commerce/National Institute of Standards and Technology. Digital Signature Standard (DSS). FIPS-186-4 (2013), http://nvlpubs.nist.gov/nistpubs/FIPS/NIST.FIPS.186-4.pdf

37. van Oorschot, P.C., Wiener, M.J.: Parallel collision search with cryptanalytic applications. Journal of Cryptology 12(1), 1–28 (1999)

38. Walter, C.D.: Montgomery exponentiation needs no final subtractions. Electronics Letters 35(21), 1831–1832 (1999)

39. Wiener, M.J., Zuccherato, R.J.: Faster attacks on elliptic curve cryptosystems. In: Tavares, S., Meijer, H. (eds.) SAC 1998. LNCS, vol. 1556, pp. 190–200. Springer, Heidelberg (1999)

Discrete Logarithm in $GF(2^{809})$ with FFS

Razvan Barbulescu, Cyril Bouvier, Jérémie Detrey, Pierrick Gaudry,
Hamza Jeljeli, Emmanuel Thomé, Marion Videau, and Paul Zimmermann

CARAMEL project-team, LORIA, INRIA / CNRS / Université de Lorraine,
Campus Scientifique, BP 239, 54506 Vandœuvre-lès-Nancy Cedex, France
`first name.last name@loria.fr`

Abstract. The year 2013 has seen several major complexity advances
for the discrete logarithm problem in multiplicative groups of small-
characteristic finite fields. These outmatch, asymptotically, the Function
Field Sieve (FFS) approach, which was so far the most efficient algorithm
known for this task. Yet, on the practical side, it is not clear whether
the new algorithms are uniformly better than FFS. This article presents
the state of the art with regard to the FFS algorithm, and reports data
from a record-sized discrete logarithm computation in a prime-degree
extension field.

Keywords: Discrete logarithm, Function field sieve, Cryptanalysis,
Number theory.

1 Introduction

The discrete logarithm problem (DLP) is the cornerstone of a large part of public-
key cryptography. Multiplicative groups of finite fields were the first proposed
groups for cryptography, meeting the requirements of fast arithmetic and a hard
discrete logarithm problem. Since almost the beginning though, the discrete
logarithm problem is known to be of subexponential complexity in these groups,
with the most efficient algorithms being those from the Number Field Sieve
family, of complexity $L_{\#G}(1/3, c)$ for computing discrete logarithms in $G = GF(p^n)^{\times}$, where we use the conventional notation

$$L_{\#G}(\alpha, c) = \exp\left((c + o(1))(\log \#G)^{\alpha}(\log\log \#G)^{1-\alpha}\right).$$

To this regard, alternatives to these choices of groups, such as elliptic curve
cryptography, are of course considered. With elliptic curves, a smaller group size
allows for the same security against potential attackers. In spite of the existence
of such alternatives, multiplicative groups of finite fields remain of primary importance for cryptography, because of their widespread use in many protocols
and their implementations, such as the Diffie–Hellman key exchange [12], the
ElGamal encryption system [13] or the Digital Signature Algorithm [27]. Another typical situation where the DLP in multiplicative groups of finite fields is
of crucial importance is the area of pairing-based cryptography.

H. Krawczyk (Ed.): PKC 2014, LNCS 8383, pp. 221–238, 2014.

We focus here on multiplicative groups of finite fields of small characteristic, the archetypal examples of which being the binary fields $GF(2^n)$. These fields offer some implementation advantages for the cryptographer, which make them a natural choice (the most usually chosen fields being prime fields). Invented by Adleman [2] in 1994, the Function Field Sieve has been the most efficient algorithm known to solve the DLP in finite fields of small characteristic for quite a long time. It earned its first successes from 2001 onwards [17,18], the latest record computations being in the fields $GF(2^{613})$ [21] and $GF(2^{619})$ [8].

In 2013, several works have significantly changed the landscape and improved the asymptotic complexity for solving the DLP in small-characteristic finite fields. Successive improvements lowered the complexity from $L(1/3)$ down to $L(1/4 + o(1))$ [19], and later down to quasi-polynomial complexity [9]. A common feature of these improved algorithms is their reliance on an appropriately sized subfield. Hence, the new algorithms perform well for finite fields which readily provide such a subfield. All published DLP records which have used these improved algorithms satisfy this criterion, the culminating computation to date being in the field $GF(2^{6168})=GF((2^{24})^{257})$. On the other hand, finite fields which have no such subfield, such as fields of prime extension degree $GF(2^p)$, are less amenable to the newer approaches. One must first apply the new algorithms to the DLP in an extension $GF(2^{kp})$ for an appropriate k, and only then solve the DLP in $GF(2^p)$ as a by-product. Complexity analysis shows that this approach is asymptotically faster than FFS, despite the large intermediary field $GF(2^{kp})$.

Motivation. In practical terms, though, determining the cut-off point where FFS is surpassed by the new methods is not obvious. No practical data exists as of yet where the $L(1/4+o(1))$ or quasi-polynomial algorithms have been applied to fields of prime extension degree. The FFS approach, on the other hand, is complicated enough so that its runtime is difficult to extrapolate from previous experiments, all the more so given that experimental data with FFS is quite scarce (the computation from [21] is 8 years old, and the report [8], while doing better than the former, involved only a small amount of resources). One of the motivations of the present article is to provide new record computation data for fields of prime extension degree by computing discrete logarithms in $GF(2^{809})$.

Another line of work made important by the recent developments in the computation of discrete logarithms in small characteristic finite fields is the assessment of their reach in the context of pairing-based cryptography, as studied for instance by the preprint [1]. Indeed, the fields of definition of pairings on elliptic curves and Jacobians of genus-2 curves offer almost by construction the required criterion for the new algorithms to apply optimally, or fall close at the very least. Re-assessing the security levels for finite fields which were once thought to offer strong DLP hardness calls again for a serious FFS study, because of its potential use in this context. The new algorithms allow to do the so-called descent step all the way down to tiny elements, much smaller than what any FFS/NFS-DL variant can reach. For best performance, it is perfectly reasonable to organize this descent by combining several algorithms, as proposed in [1]. It is expected that the early steps of the descent are best done with the same techniques as for the FFS algorithm, including in particular the sieving technique.

It is an important feature of our work that all software used is original work freely available for download, the main component being the cado-nfs software suite [6] (although cado-nfs originally focuses on the Number Field Sieve, recent additions cover FFS as well). The development of the present work has led to several preprints and articles providing detailed insights on the improvements of the individual steps of FFS [7,10,11,16]. For brevity, this article does not repeat these details, and the interested reader is referred to these articles for more detail.

Roadmap. This article is organized as follows. Section 2 recalls classical facts about the FFS algorithm. Section 3 gives the details about the different steps involved in the computation of discrete logarithms in (a prime order subgroup of) GF(2^{809})$^\times$. Section 4 discusses ways to optimize the computation cost by balancing the sieving and linear algebra step. Section 5 explores the cost of solving the discrete logarithm problem in a kilobit-sized field, namely GF(2^{1039})$^\times$.

2   A Brief Overview of FFS

The goal of this section is to provide the readers with a primer on FFS, so that they can have a better insight into the various steps of the algorithm along with the computations they involve. However, for brevity purposes, this presentation is in no way complete nor exhaustive. For more details, we refer the interested reader to the extensive literature on this topic, starting from the first theoretical articles [2,3,25] to the algorithmic advances and implementation reports which followed [18,14,15,7,11,10,16].

2.1   Index Calculus

The Function Field Sieve algorithm belongs to the family of so-called *index calculus* methods for computing discrete logarithms in a cyclic group G.

Writing G multiplicatively and assuming that it is generated by an element g of prime order $\ell = \#G$, the core idea is to collect many equalities, or *relations*, of the form

$$\prod_i \alpha_i^{e_i} = 1,$$

where the elements α_i all belong to a predefined subset of G called the *factor base*, and where the exponents e_i all lie in $\mathbb{Z}/\ell\mathbb{Z}$. When taking the discrete logarithm in base g, each relation then yields a linear equation in $\mathbb{Z}/\ell\mathbb{Z}$,

$$\sum_i e_i \log_g(\alpha_i) \equiv 0 \pmod{\ell},$$

whose unknowns are the discrete logarithms of the elements α_i of the factor base. This is known as the *relation collection* step.

Once enough such relations have been found (typically, more than the size of the factor base), one can solve the corresponding system of linear equations and retrieve the logarithms of the factor base elements. This step is usually referred to as the *linear algebra* step. It is often directly preceded by a *filtering* step, whose chief purpose is to prepare the matrix from the collected relations; some simplifications and Gaussian elimination are typically performed at this stage.

Finally, the discrete logarithm of a given element $h \in G$ is computed thanks to the last step, known as the *individual logarithm* step. The idea here is to rewrite h as a product $\prod_i \alpha_i^{f_i}$ of elements of the factor base. The discrete logarithm of h is then

$$\log_g(h) \equiv \sum_i f_i \log_g(\alpha_i) \pmod{\ell}.$$

2.2   FFS-Specific Considerations

In the case of FFS, one can detail further the various steps of the index calculus algorithm, mostly due to the fact that G is the multiplicative subgroup of a finite field $GF(p^n)$, where the characteristic p is a small prime (*e.g.*, $p = 2$ in this work).

Relation Collection. Let us write k to denote the base field $GF(p)$, and let f and g be two monic polynomials in $k[t][x]$ such that their resultant in x contains an irreducible factor $\varphi(t)$ of degree n. The key to collecting relations in FFS is then based on the following commutative diagram, whose maps are ring homomorphisms:

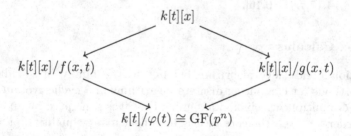

Let us now consider an element of the form $a(t) - b(t)x \in k[t][x]$. Following the maps on the left-hand side of the diagram, we first obtain an element of $k[t][x]/f(x,t)$, which can be viewed as a principal ideal in the ring of integers of the corresponding function field $k(t)[x]/f(x,t)$. As this is a Dedekind domain, there is a unique factorization in prime ideals. The same also applies to the right-hand side of the diagram, corresponding to the function field $k(t)[x]/g(x,t)$, thus yielding two factorizations of the same element $a(t) - b(t)x$. Strictly speaking, there is no reason for $k[t][x]/f(x,t)$ to be the full ring of integers of $k(t)[x]/f(x,t)$, but this technicality can easily be dealt with after a study of the singularities of the curve of equation $f(x, t) = 0$.

When pushing these two factorizations into the finite field $k[t]/\varphi(t) \cong \mathrm{GF}(p^n)$, we then obtain an equality between two products of elements of the finite field. Should all these elements belong to the factor base, we would then have computed a *relation*.

In FFS, there are in fact two factor bases: one for each side of the diagram. Indeed, when considering the principal ideal corresponding to $a(t) - b(t)x$ in $k(t)[x]/f(x, t)$, we will say that it is *smooth* if its factorization involves only prime ideals whose norms have degree less than or equal to a parameter called the *smoothness bound*. Therefore, the factor base on this side will correspond to the prime ideals $\langle q(t), x - r(t)\rangle$ of $k(t)[x]/f(x, t)$ for which $\deg(q)$ is less than or equal to this smoothness bound. In general, by degree of an ideal of the factor base we understand the degree of its norm. The factor base for the g side can be constructed in a similar fashion.

All in all, finding relations in FFS amounts to looking for elements of the form $a(t) - b(t)x$ in $k[t][x]$ whose corresponding images in $k[t][x]/f(x, t)$ and $k[t][x]/g(x, t)$ are both smooth. Whether or not these images factor nicely can be decided by considering the factorizations of the polynomials $\mathrm{Res}_x(a(t) - b(t)x, f(x, t))$ and $\mathrm{Res}_x(a(t) - b(t)x, g(x, t))$. These resultants are commonly referred to as *norms* because of the link to the norm of the ideal generated by $a(t) - b(t)x$ in the two rings.[1]

The relation collection process can be greatly accelerated by using sieving techniques. Another important acceleration can be achieved thanks to the so-called *sieving by special*-q technique. It relies on the fact that one can easily restrict the relation collection to elements $a(t) - b(t)x$ which are divisible by an arbitrary prime ideal q on the (say) f side. This way, when considering $a(t) - b(t)x$ over $k[t][x]/f(x, t)$, one knows that the corresponding principal ideal is divisible by q, thus lowering by $\deg(q)$ the degree of the remaining part and therefore increasing the probability that it is smooth. One can then apply this technique for many special-q's of degree below the smoothness bound in order to achieve a large speed-up.

Polynomial Selection. In order to further increase the probability to find doubly-smooth elements $a(t) - b(t)x$ all the while keeping arithmetic computations to a minimum in the relation collection step, one has to pay extra care to the selection of the polynomials f and $g \in k[t][x]$. Similar to the case of the Number Field Sieve (NFS), several criteria exist in the literature in order to rate polynomials to be used in FFS [7].

A typical choice of polynomials involves a g which is linear in x, but many degrees of freedom remain. Due to the bad impact a poor choice of polynomials can have on the relation collection step, it is deemed important to dedicate some

---

[1] As in the case for the Number Field Sieve, it is possible to generalize the setting somewhat by allowing non-monic polynomials f and g. In that case the norms and the resultants do not coincide exactly. This is not a concern for the present work.

CPU time to carefully select good polynomial pairs. This preliminary step is usually known as the *polynomial selection* step.

Individual Logarithms. In the FFS context, individual logarithms are computed thanks to the *descent* step, which reuses several key aspects of the relation collection step. Indeed, the sieving methods developed for the latter can help us rewrite "large" elements (*i.e.*, of high degree) of $GF(p^n)$ into products of smaller elements. This way, starting from h and recursively working our way down, we end up considering only products of elements of the factor base, all of whose discrete logarithms are known after the linear algebra step. We can then backtrack this descent and reconstruct the discrete logarithms of the larger elements and, ultimately, of h.

3   Discrete Logarithm Computation in $GF(2^{809})$

In this work, we have chosen to attack the discrete logarithm problem in a subgroup which is not $GF(2^{809})^\times$ itself, but rather one of its prime-order subgroups, namely the subgroup of prime order ℓ, where ℓ is the 202-bit prime factor of $2^{809} - 1$ given by

$$\ell = 4148386731260605647525186547488842396461625774241327567978137.$$

The other factor of $2^{809} - 1$ is also prime, and 608 bits long.

The motivation for this choice is related to the cryptographic applications, for which the discrete logarithm problem is to be solved only in a subgroup whose size is large enough to resist Pollard's ρ attack. We recall, as a comparison, that the original DSA (digital signature algorithm) setup recommends a 160-bit prime order subgroup in the multiplicative group of a 1024-bit finite field [27]. Here, the chosen subgroup is rather over-sized than under-sized, given the expected difficulty of Pollard's ρ attack on a 202-bit group.

Extrapolations from the hardness of our discrete logarithm computation to the hardness of the full discrete logarithm computation in the group $GF(2^{809})^\times$ are easy to obtain, as one can get satisfactory estimates by keeping most timings unchanged, and scaling the linear algebra cost by a roughly 4-fold linear factor (the complexity of the linear algebra step being dominated by the cost of multiplying an integer modulo ℓ by a word-size integer).

In the following sub-sections, we discuss the choices of parameters made for this computation, and present benchmarks and estimates for the various steps of the FFS algorithm.

Notations. For the sake of compactness, in the following, we represent a polynomial of $GF(2)[t]$ by the integer obtained when considering the polynomial over $\mathbb{Z}$ then evaluating it at $t = 2$; we write this integer in hexadecimal so that sparseness is still visible. For instance, `0x11` represents $t^4 + 1$, and `0xb00001` is $t^{23} + t^{21} + t^{20} + 1$.

3.1   Polynomial Selection

We used the criteria defined in [7] to select the polynomials. It appears that monic polynomials $f(x,t)$ and $g(x,t)$ of degree 6 and 1 in x, respectively, were the best choice. We therefore computed the α value—a quantity that is similar to the one used when estimating the quality of NFS polynomials [26]—for all the irreducible polynomials of degree 6 in x for which the degree in t of the coefficient of x^i is at most $12 - 2i$. Relying on sieving techniques for acceleration purposes, this computation took about 2,760 hours on one core of an Intel Core i5-2500 CPU running at 3.3 GHz. We see it as a pre-computation since, when associated with different polynomials g, f can be used to compute discrete logarithms in any field GF(2^n) with n ranging roughly from 700 to 900.

With this setting, the degree of the resultant in x of f and g is 6 times the degree in t of the constant coefficient of g. Since we want this resultant to have an irreducible factor of degree 809, this imposes this constant coefficient to have a degree at least 135. According to [7], our choice may be driven by the α value and by the factorization pattern of the resultant. As it turns out, among the few polynomials $f(x,t)$ that were preselected for having an α value around -6, all but one have arithmetic properties that force a small factor of degree 2 in the resultant, independently of the linear polynomial g. For those polynomials, the degree in t of the constant coefficient of g would have to be at least 136 in order to leave enough room for an irreducible factor of degree 809 to exist in the resultant. For this reason, we chose for f the only polynomial that we have found to have a nice α-value and that forces only a factor of degree 1 in the resultant, which is expected to be better [7, §3.3]:

$$f(x,t) = x^6 + \texttt{0x7}x^5 + \texttt{0x6b}x^3 + \texttt{0x1ab}x^2 + \texttt{0x326}x + \texttt{0x19b3}.$$

As far as $g(x,t)$ is concerned, no special care was taken for its selection, as it can be found in a few seconds and it did not make any difference in the subsequent computations. We therefore picked a linear monic polynomial whose constant term (with respect to x) is a sparse polynomial of degree 135 in t:

$$g(x,t) = x + \texttt{0x800000000000000000000000000001e7eaa}.$$

The resultant in x of $f(x,t)$ and $g(x,t)$ is $(t+1)$ times an irreducible factor $\varphi(t)$ of degree 809 that we take as defining polynomial for GF(2^{809}):

$\varphi(t) = \texttt{0x3ffffffffffffffffffffffffffffffffffffe8000000000000000000000000}$
$\texttt{0cc0cfaeb0e000000000000000000000000000000004dffffffffffffffffc}$
$\texttt{3c3ffc3c3c3fce3c2133fffffffffffffe9697fe96804c84c97e0b0000c0}$
$\texttt{0cf9b0f7675354e79f4cf7c97e29.}$

This choice of polynomials was driven solely by the efficiency of the relation collection. The genus of the curve corresponding to $f(x,t) = 0$ is 19, which is not especially low. The class number is 2073600, which is rather large, and there are some singular points. The only ones that we have to take care of for the computation are the ones at $(x,t) = (\omega,\omega)$, where $\omega^2 + \omega + 1 = 0$, which splits into 2 places, and of course its conjugate. All these complications have essentially no influence on the running time but require some care in the implementation.

N.B. Since g was chosen to be linear in x, the corresponding function field $GF(2)(t)[x]/g(x,t)$ is a rational function field. Therefore, to remain consistent with the established terminology, we will refer to the corresponding side (*i.e.*, the right-hand side in the commutative diagram of Section 2.2) as the *rational side*. Conversely, the f side of the diagram will be referred to as the *algebraic side*.

3.2   Relation Collection

The relation collection was performed using the implementation described in [11]. This is a rather classical sieving method using lattice-sieving for various special-$\mathfrak{q}$'s. We actually ran the relation collection step for two different sets of parameters, in order to compare and be able to see how the tuning of this phase influences the filtering and linear algebra steps.

The terminology used in [11] is the classical one, where the *factor base bound* is the limit for the degree of the irreducible polynomials that are sieved, and the *large-prime bound* refers to the limit for the degree of the polynomials allowed in a relation (*i.e.*, the smoothness bound). These notions are very similar to the ones used when sieving relations for factoring integers using NFS (see for instance [23]); irreducible polynomials of a given degree playing the role of prime numbers of a given number of bits, we keep the "large-prime" terminology for convenience. Likewise, the discussion below uses terminology which is heavily borrowed from NFS implementation folklore. In particular, the I and J parameters directly relate to the dimensions of the sieved area in what is customarily called the (i,j)-*plane* in the lattice sieving context. Typically, the number of $a(t) - b(t)x$ polynomials considered for a given special-$\mathfrak{q}$ is given by 2^{I+J}.

For the two parameter sets that we considered, we used a skewness of 2 (the skewness being the degree gap in the coefficients $a(t)$ and $b(t)$ of the functions $a(t) - b(t)x$ considered in the algorithm), and we only considered the special-$\mathfrak{q}$'s on the rational side, since we are in a range where the rational side yields larger norms than the algebraic side. We used a factor base bound of degree 23 (inclusive). The main difference between our two sets of parameters is the large-prime bound.

Case 1: Large-Prime Bound of 27. In that case, we used $I = J = 15$, which were chosen to yield enough relations per special-$\mathfrak{q}$, despite a low large-prime bound. Only $(a(t), b(t))$ pairs for which the norms on both sides (once removed the factors obtained from sieving) have degree at most 81 were actually considered as candidates for a complete factorization attempt. In other words, we allowed for three large primes of maximum degree on each side.

All the special-$\mathfrak{q}$'s of degree 24 to 27 (inclusive) were sieved, producing a bit more than 52 million relations (possibly non-unique). The relevant data is summarized in the following table. The running times are given for a single core of an Intel Core i5-2500 CPU running at 3.3 GHz (Sandy Bridge microarchitecture). In particular, this assumes the presence of the PCLMULQDQ instruction for carry-less multiplication. In practice, most of our computations were done using the idle time of a cluster[2] whose 4-year old processors do not support this instruction, and therefore took twice as much time. On the other hand, we expect faster runtime on Intel's new Haswell processor family that provides a much better implementation of the PCLMULQDQ instruction than the Sandy Bridge and Ivy Bridge microarchitectures.

deg q	number of rels	s/rel	rels/sp-q	accumulated rels	accumulated time
24	6,940,249	1.48	9.93	6,940,249	2,853 h
25	9,926,294	1.91	7.39	16,866,543	8,119 h
26	14,516,775	2.42	5.62	31,383,318	17,877 h
27	20,645,456	3.38	4.15	52,028,774	37,260 h

Case 2: Large-Prime Bound of 28. In that case, we used $I = J = 14$, which was enough to get a decent rate of relations per special-q. The threshold was again set to 3 times the large-prime bound, that is, 84 for both sides. We sieved all the special-q's of degree 24 to 28 (inclusive), and produced more than 117 million relations, distributed as in the following table:

deg q	number of rels	s/rel	rels/sp-q	accumulated rels	accumulated time
24	9,515,069	0.41	13.61	9,515,069	1,083 h
25	13,816,908	0.54	10.29	23,331,977	3,155 h
26	20,538,387	0.65	7.95	43,870,364	6,863 h
27	29,652,781	0.86	5.96	73,523,145	13,946 h
28	43,875,232	1.07	4.57	117,398,377	26,986 h

In both cases, we obtained a number of relations that provided a reasonable excess (the excess is defined as the difference between the number of unique relations collected and the number of ideals involved).

3.3 Filtering

The filtering step is split in three stages:

- duplicate: remove duplicate relations from the relation collection step;
- purge: remove singletons (ideals that appear in only one relation) and remove relations while the excess is positive (*i.e.*, there are still more relations than ideals);
- merge: beginning of Gaussian elimination.

The filtering step was performed using the implementation described in [10]. It was run identically on the two sets of relations produced by the relation collection step.

―――――――――――――――
[2] We acknowledge the support of the Région Lorraine and the CPER MISN TALC project who gave us access to this cluster.

Case 1: Large-Prime Bound of 27. In total, 52,028,774 relations were collected. They produced 30,142,422 unique relations (42 % were duplicates). After the first singleton removal, about 29M relations remained as well as 19M ideals (so the excess was around 10M). At the end of the purge algorithm, there were 9.6M relations and as many ideals. The final matrix (after the merge algorithm) had 3.68M rows and columns (with, in average, 100 non-zero coefficients per row, which is close to optimal for our linear algebra implementation).

Case 2: Large-Prime Bound of 28. In total, 117,398,377 relations were collected. They produced 67,411,816 unique relations (43 % duplicates). After the first singleton removal, about 65M relations remained as well as 37M ideals (so the excess was around 28M). At the end of the purge algorithm, there were 13.6M relations and as many ideals. The final matrix (after the merge algorithm) had 4.85M rows and columns (with, in average, 100 non-zero coefficients per row).

For the actual computation, relations collected with both values of the large-prime bound were considered to produce the matrix. This is of course not "fair", in the sense that if the computation were to be run again, we would have only one of the two relation sets. On the other hand, it was a pity not to use all what we had at hand to reduce the cost of the linear algebra.

In this setting, starting from an input set of 78.8M unique relations, we obtained a matrix with 3,602,667 rows and columns, and an average of 100 non-zero coefficients per row. The matrix contains small values that fit within one processor word. Around 90% of the non-zero coefficients are ± 1.

3.4 Linear Algebra

The linear system to be solved is of the form $Mw = 0$, where M is the sparse matrix produced by the filtering step. We solved the linear system modulo the subgroup of order ℓ, which is a 202-bit prime, using the Wiedemann algorithm as a solver. This algorithm iterates a very large number of sparse-matrix–vector products of the form $v' \leftarrow Mv$, where v and v' are dense vectors. Either for the simple Wiedemann or for its block variant [22], the algorithm returns a vector of the kernel of the matrix. This vector is with high probability non-trivial. In practice, one run of the algorithm is sufficient to find a solution.

The computation was carried out on NVIDIA GPUs. The implementation used Residue Number System (RNS) arithmetic to accelerate arithmetic over $\mathbb{Z}/\ell\mathbb{Z}$, since this representation system offers the opportunity to increase the parallelism between the computational units, and is well suited to the GPU execution framework. This approach is described in details in [16].

This linear algebra step was actually computed twice on two different setups, whose choice was driven by the hardware which was available to us at that time. A CPU implementation was also developed to serve as a reference point.

Dual-GPU Setup. A simple Wiedemann algorithm was run on a single node equipped with two NVIDIA GeForce GTX 680 graphics processors. On this setup, the sparse-matrix–vector product takes 144 ms, including 16 ms for inter-GPU communication. The total computation time sums up to 18 days: 12 days on both GPUs for computing the initial sequence, 35 minutes for computing the minimal polynomial, and 6 days on both GPUs for computing a vector of the kernel.

Eight-GPU Setup. Another option was tried, using a different computing facility[3] equipped with slightly different hardware. We used four distinct nodes, each equipped with two NVIDIA Tesla M2050 graphics processors, and ran the block Wiedemann algorithm with blocking parameters $m = 8$ and $n = 4$. An iteration took 169 ms on each node, with 27 ms for the inter-GPU communication. The initial sequence computation required 2.6 days in parallel on the 4 nodes. The linear generator computation required 2 hours in parallel using 16 jobs on a 4-node cluster with Intel Xeon E5-2609 CPUs at 2.4 GHz connected with Infiniband QDR network. Finally, computing the kernel vector required 1.8 days in parallel on the 4 GPU nodes. All in all, this computation took a total wall-clock time of about 4.5 days.

CPU Implementation. For comparison purposes, we also developed a software implementation of block Wiedemann based on the RNS representation for the arithmetic and using the SSE-4.2 and AVX SIMD instruction sets. We exploited the data-level parallelism in order to multiply the sparse matrix by several vectors in parallel. For instance, using 64-bit RNS moduli, a 128-bit SSE register can hold two RNS residues coming from two distinct vectors, thus allowing us to multiply the matrix by these two vectors in parallel. The SSE implementation offers the advantage of using integer arithmetic while AVX only supports packed floating-point arithmetic.

The experiment was run on a cluster of Intel Core i5-2500 CPU running at 3.3 GHz connected with Infiniband QDR network. Each node of the cluster contains 4 cores. The matrix was split into 4 balanced parts and distributed over 4 threads running on a single node. With the SSE-4.2 implementation, an iteration requires 5 seconds to compute the product of M by two vectors, while the AVX version computes the product with four vectors in 12.1 seconds. The SSE implementation using integer arithmetic ends up being the fastest, despite its lower data parallelism. Even though we did not run the full computation of the linear algebra, our SSE implementation running on 4 nodes with the blocking parameters $m = 16$ and $n = 8$ should take a total of 68.4 days, or 26,267 core-hours (15,120 core-hours for computing the initial sequence, 1,067 core-hours for the linear generators, and 10,080 core-hours for computing a kernel vector).

---

[3] This work was realized with the support of HPC@LR, a Center of Competence in High-Performance Computing from the Languedoc-Roussillon region, funded by the Languedoc-Roussillon region, the European Union and the Université Montpellier 2 Sciences et Techniques. The HPC@LR Center is equipped with an IBM hybrid Supercomputer.

From the non-zero kernel vector coming out of the linear algebra step, we obtained the discrete logarithms of 39,319,911 elements of the factor base, among which 98.6 % of the degree-28 ideals.

3.5 Descent

Once the discrete logarithms of almost all elements up to the large-prime bound have been found, we compute individual logarithms using the classical strategy of descent by special-q.

More precisely, we start by splitting the target element into the quotient of two elements of about half the degree, using an Euclidean algorithm that we stop in the middle. Randomizing the target allows to repeat that step until the two elements are smoother than average. In our case, after a dozen of minutes, we managed to rewrite the target in terms of elements of degree at most 90 (in comparison, straight out of the Euclidean algorithm, we have a numerator and a denominator whose degree is at most 405).

Then we "descended" these elements of degree less than or equal to 90 but above 28, by considering them as special-q's in the relation collection implementation, so that they are rewritten as ideals of smaller degree. Hence a tree is built where the discrete logarithm of a node can be deduced from the discrete logarithms of each of its children, which are of smaller degree. At the end of this process, one of the degree-28 ideals involved in the tree was not known from the linear algebra step, and was therefore "re-descended" to known degree-28 ideals.

The overall cost of the individual logarithm step is less than one hour, and therefore was not thoroughly investigated.

There are cases, however, where the cost of the descent step could become critical. First, we could imagine that if such a finite field is used in real life for securing communications, then the number of individual logarithms to solve becomes very large. Besides this admittedly highly hypothetical scenario, it is important to take into account the new discrete logarithm algorithms where the bottleneck is the descent step. For instance, in [1], the estimates for computing a discrete logarithm in $GF(3^{6 \times 509})$ is around 2^{74} operations, with about half of the time spent in the Euclidean algorithm and classical descent steps which are exactly the same algorithms as in FFS.

As already performed in [1], in order to optimize our descent implementation, it would be necessary to make a careful study of the cost required to descend an element of a given degree down to the large-prime bound. Indeed, once we know the average costs to fully descend elements of degree less than a given integer d, it is possible to deduce an estimate for the cost of a complete descent of a polynomial of degree d. For this, we run a few special-q sievings for random ideals of degree d and, for each relation, we compute the corresponding cost to go down to the large-prime bound. It is then possible to tune the parameters of the sieving for a special-q of degree d in order to optimize the expected total time to fully descend it. Then we can continue with degree $d + 1$, and so on. This approach is for instance implemented in the NFS context in the cado-nfs software package [5].

As for the Euclidean step, it is also possible to optimize it using the sieving strategy explained in [20]. It is presented in the case of the Number Field Sieve, but it applies *mutatis mutandis* to FFS after having replaced integers with polynomials.

3.6 Computation Result

Since it is a generator of the order-ℓ subgroup of GF(2^{809})$^\times$, we considered the element t as the basis for the discrete logarithm computations. Then, the logarithms of the elements of the factor base were readily available after the linear algebra step. For instance,

$$\log_t(t+1) \equiv 1070821051716025354315829874 36 \backslash$$
$$79898652591427309486844885702574 \quad (\text{mod } \ell).$$

As an illustration of the descent step, we computed the discrete logarithm of a "random" element. We decided to step away from the tradition of taking the logarithm of decimals of π, and took as a "random" input the integer RSA-1024 (converted into a polynomial of degree 1023 in t using the same encoding as above). It was reduced modulo $\varphi(t)$ before taking its discrete logarithm. We then obtain

$$\log_t(\text{RSA-1024}) \equiv 29997870719116434854500200834 2 \backslash$$
$$08349771549879083381254164707 96 \quad (\text{mod } \ell).$$

A short Magma script is given in Appendix for verification purposes.

4 Balancing Sieving and Linear Algebra

In retrospect, it is now clear that the strategy of using a large-prime bound of 27 is better than 28: in the same amount of sieving time, one obtains a post-merge matrix that is smaller.

The question of where to stop sieving is not so easy to answer in advance, but with the data that we have collected, we can give some hints for future choices.

With this objective in mind, we ran the filtering step for various numbers of relations (always produced with a large-prime bound of 27), and estimated both the sieving time for getting these relations, along with the linear algebra time for the corresponding matrix. The relations were added in increasing lexicographical order of the special-q's. We estimate the cost of the linear algebra step as the product of the size by the total weight of the matrix, which is theoretically proportional to the running time. With this metric, the linear algebra step described in Section 3.4—using the matrix mentioned at the end of Section 3.3—has a cost of about 1298 and corresponds to 36 days on one GTX 680 GPU (this running time is the same for both the dual- and the eight-GPU setups). Estimates for the CPU running time of the linear algebra step are also reported, based on our software reference implementation.

# rels	matrix size after singleton removal	matrix size after merge	lin. alg. cost	sieve CPU time ($\times 10^3$ h)	linear algebra GPU time ($\times 10^3$ h)	CPU time ($\times 10^3$ h)
27.7M	14.1M × 14.0M	4.99M	2493	15.4	1.65	55.4
31.3M	16.6M × 15.1M	4.46M	1995	17.8	1.32	40.4
33.9M	18.6M × 16.1M	4.28M	1837	20.2	1.22	37.2
36.5M	20.4M × 16.8M	4.15M	1723	22.7	1.14	34.9
39.1M	22.1M × 17.4M	4.04M	1633	25.1	1.08	33.7
41.7M	23.7M × 17.9M	3.94M	1560	27.5	1.03	31.6
44.2M	25.1M × 18.3M	3.87M	1498	29.9	0.99	30.3
46.8M	26.5M × 18.6M	3.80M	1444	32.4	0.96	29.2
49.4M	27.7M × 18.9M	3.73M	1396	34.8	0.92	28.3
52.0M	28.9M × 19.1M	3.68M	1354	37.2	0.90	27.4

One can then use the above estimates to tailor the balance between the sieving and the linear algebra steps to the available CPU and GPU resources. For instance, in a CPU-only context, a minimal running time of $57.4 \cdot 10^3$ core-hours is achieved after sieving around 34M relations, even though most of the other options fall very close. Similarly, if one has 50 CPU cores and 4 GPUs at hand, an optimal wall-clock time of 686 hours is obtained when stopping sieving after only about 31M relations.

5   Towards GF(2^{1039})

After GF(2^{809}), the next natural milestone is to reach a prime-degree extension field of kilobit size. A nice target is GF(2^{1039}), because it echoes the rather recent factorization of $2^{1039} - 1$ which was the first kilobit SNFS integer factorization [4]. In particular, there are subgroups in the multiplicative group that are not amenable to a discrete logarithm computation based on Pollard's ρ, since the two largest prime factors of $2^{1039} - 1$ are 752 and 265 bits long, respectively, and are both far beyond what is feasible with an exponential algorithm.

5.1   Relation Collection

As mentioned in [11], it is a rather easy task to obtain a set of relations that is complete—in the sense that it yields a system with (far) more equations than unknowns—so that we can expect it to be full-rank or close to full-rank. We ran our software with exactly the same parameters as in [11], namely:

- a polynomial $f(x,t)$ of degree 6 in x, which is not as good as the one we used for GF(2^{809}), since its α-value is around -5;
- a large-prime bound of 33 on each side;
- a factor base bound of 25 on each side;
- a threshold value of 99;
- a sieving range with parameters $I = J = 15$.

The relation collection was performed for a large range of special-q's, in the following order: first the rational special-q's of degree 26 to 30, then the algebraic special-q's of degree 28 to 29, and finally, again the rational special-q's of degree 31 and 32. For the rational special-q's of degree 32, we sieved only about half of the range. The computing time for this relation collection step was equivalent to 124 core-years on an Intel i5-2500 at 3.3 GHz as the one used in [11]. On a 768-core cluster of Intel E5-2650 at 2.0 GHz to which we have access, this corresponds to 3 months.

After having computed a bit more than 1.2 billion relations (which corresponds to the start of the rational degree-31 range), we got our first complete system. The corresponding matrix had 110 million rows and columns, with an average weight of 100 non-zero coefficients per row. The rate of duplicates, at this stage, was 32.5 %.

As we sieved more and more special-q's, the time to get a relation increased with the degree of the special-q's, the rate of duplicates increased as well, but on the other hand, the matrix produced by the filtering stage was getting smaller.

After having computed about 2 billion relations, we got a duplicate rate of 37.7 % and a matrix with 67 million rows and columns. In total, we obtained 2.6 billion relations, leading to 1.6 billion unique relations (duplicate rate of 38.5 %). The final matrix had then 60 million rows and columns, with an average row-weight of 100.

We then stopped the relation collection because we had reached a point where the size of the matrix was decreasing very slowly, and we could not really expect to save much more by just sieving larger and larger special-q's. Still, we remark that the estimates in [11] were indeed accurate.

5.2 Linear Algebra

We ran some computer experiments in order to estimate the running time that the linear algebra step would take. For these experiments, we worked in the subgroup whose order is the 265-bit prime factor of $2^{1039} - 1$.

The maximum available memory on our graphics cards is 4 GB, which is far below what is needed to store the matrix and the temporary vectors. However, this fits in the 64 GB of RAM of the CPU host of our cards. Therefore, our timings include the additional cost of on-the-fly data transfers between the CPU and the GPU. The sparse-matrix–vector product on a single GPU then requires 14.3 seconds, which leads to an estimate of 82 GPU-years for the whole linear algebra phase (assuming a simple Wiedemann implementation).

The CPU version of our implementation could run two interleaved sparse-matrix–vector products on a 16-core dual Intel E5-2650 node in 37 seconds, leading to an estimate of 1408 core-years for the whole linear algebra step, or 22 months on a 768-core cluster to which we have access (assuming blocking parameters $n = 96$, $m = 192$). Because of the important memory requirements for this step, we were unable to perform benchmarking experiments on our Intel i5-2500 machines.

Although this computation is clearly feasible, we did not start it for real. The first reason is related to the sensibility of the block Wiedemann algorithm to the blocking parameters m and n. While the cost of the computation of the sequence terms of the form ${}^t x M^i y$ can be estimated with reasonable accuracy, we do not have an equally solid estimation for the cost of the middle step of the block Wiedemann algorithm for such blocking factors: our current software is probably unable to treat the corresponding input, and various optimization and distribution opportunities have to be explored in order to make this computation practical. The second reason for not running the computation for $GF(2^{1039})$ is that, based on our experiments with $GF(2^{809})$, we want to try other parameters than the ones proposed in [11]. For instance, lowering the large-prime bound to 32 would certainly make life easier for the linear algebra; there is still some work to do in order to make our sieving code efficient in that case.

6 Conclusion

With an overall total of 7.6 core-years and 0.1 GPU-years—or 59 bits of security[4,5], approximately—our computation of discrete logarithms in $GF(2^{809})^{\times}$ claimed a running time which is not immense, especially in comparison to large integer factorization records [23]. It brings important data, however, towards the assessment of the feasibility limit of discrete logarithms in $GF(2^p)$ for prime extension degrees p. Given our experimental data and our running time projections, it is apparent that reaching larger sizes is possible using current hardware and software technology, going even to kilobit-sized fields provided one affords the necessary time.

Further experiments of this kind, both for FFS and for the more recent $L(1/4 + o(1))$ and quasi-polynomial algorithms, are indeed necessary in order to establish the actual cut-off points between those different algorithms.

References

1. Adj, G., Menezes, A., Oliveira, T., Rodríguez-Henríquez, F.: Weakness of $\mathbb{F}_{3^{6*509}}$ for discrete logarithm cryptography, preprint, 24 pages (2013), http://eprint.iacr.org/2013/446
2. Adleman, L.M.: The function field sieve. In: Huang, M.-D.A., Adleman, L.M. (eds.) ANTS 1994. LNCS, vol. 877, pp. 108–121. Springer, Heidelberg (1994)
3. Adleman, L.M., Huang, M.D.A.: Function field sieve method for discrete logarithms over finite fields. Inf. Comput. 151(1-2), 5–16 (1999)
4. Aoki, K., Franke, J., Kleinjung, T., Lenstra, A.K., Osvik, D.A.: A kilobit special number field sieve factorization. In: Kurosawa, K. (ed.) ASIACRYPT 2007. LNCS, vol. 4833, pp. 1–12. Springer, Heidelberg (2007)
5. Bai, S., Bouvier, C., Filbois, A., Gaudry, P., Imbert, L., Kruppa, A., Morain, F., Thomé, E., Zimmermann, P.: CADO-NFS, an implementation of the number field sieve algorithm (2013), development version http://cado-nfs.gforge.inria.fr/

---

[4] Estimated using the formula $\log_2$(running-time-in-seconds $\times 3.3 \cdot 10^9$ ops/second).
[5] That is, a mere 0.007 Olympic-size swimming pools brought to a boil [24].

6. Bai, S., Filbois, A., Gaudry, P., Kruppa, A., Morain, F., Thomé, E., Zimmermann, P.: CADO-NFS, Crible Algébrique: Distribution, Optimisation - Number Field Sieve, http://cado-nfs.gforge.inria.fr/

7. Barbulescu, R.: Selecting polynomials for the Function Field Sieve. 23 pages (2013), http://hal.inria.fr/hal-00798386 (preprint)

8. Barbulescu, R., Bouvier, C., Detrey, J., Gaudry, P., Jeljeli, H., Thomé, E., Videau, M., Zimmermann, P.: The relationship between some guy and cryptography, ECC 2012, rump session talk (humoristic) (2012), http://ecc.rump.cr.yp.to/

9. Barbulescu, R., Gaudry, P., Joux, A., Thomé, E.: A quasi-polynomial algorithm for discrete logarithm in finite fields of small characteristic, 8 pages (2013), http://hal.inria.fr/hal-00835446 (preprint)

10. Bouvier, C.: The filtering step of discrete logarithm and integer factorization algorithms, 22 pages (2013), http://hal.inria.fr/hal-00734654 (preprint)

11. Detrey, J., Gaudry, P., Videau, M.: Relation collection for the Function Field Sieve. In: Nannarelli, A., Seidel, P.M., Tang, P.T.P. (eds.) Proceedings of ARITH-21, pp. 201–210. IEEE (2013)

12. Diffie, W., Hellman, M.E.: New directions in cryptography. IEEE Transactions on Information Theory 22(6), 644–654 (1976)

13. ElGamal, T.: A public key cryptosystem and a signature scheme based on discrete logarithms. IEEE Transactions on Information Theory 31(4), 469–472 (1985)

14. Granger, R., Holt, A.J., Page, D.L., Smart, N.P., Vercauteren, F.: Function field sieve in characteristic three. In: Buell, D.A. (ed.) ANTS 2004. LNCS, vol. 3076, pp. 223–234. Springer, Heidelberg (2004)

15. Hayashi, T., Shimoyama, T., Shinohara, N., Takagi, T.: Breaking pairing-based cryptosystems using η_T pairing over $GF(3^{97})$. In: Wang, X., Sako, K. (eds.) ASIACRYPT 2012. LNCS, vol. 7658, pp. 43–60. 7658, Heidelberg (2012)

16. Jeljeli, H.: Accelerating iterative SpMV for Discrete Logarithm Problem using GPUs, 11 pages (2013), http://hal.inria.fr/hal-00734975 (preprint)

17. Joux, A., Lercier, R.: Discrete logarithms in GF(2^n) (521 bits), email to the NMBRTHRY mailing list (September 2001),
    http://listserv.nodak.edu/archives/nmbrthry.html

18. Joux, A., Lercier, R.: The function field sieve is quite special. In: Fieker, C., Kohel, D.R. (eds.) ANTS 2002. LNCS, vol. 2369, pp. 431–445. Springer, Heidelberg (2002)

19. Joux, A.: A new index calculus algorithm with complexity L(1/4 + o(1)) in very small characteristic, To appear in Selected Areas in Cryptography, 12 pages (2013), http://eprint.iacr.org/2013/095 (preprint)

20. Joux, A., Lercier, R.: Improvements to the general number field sieve for discrete logarithms in prime fields. A Comparison with the Gaussian Integer Method 72(242), 953–967 (2003)

21. Joux, A., Lercier, R.: Discrete logarithms in GF(2^{607}) and GF(2^{613}). E-mail to the NMBRTHRY mailing list (September 2005),
    http://listserv.nodak.edu/archives/nmbrthry.html

22. Kaltofen, E.: Analysis of Coppersmith's block Wiedemann algorithm for the parallel solution of sparse linear systems. Mathematics of Computation 64(210), 777–806 (1995)

23. Kleinjung, T., Aoki, K., Franke, J., Lenstra, A.K., Thomé, E., Bos, J.W., Gaudry, P., Kruppa, A., Montgomery, P.L., Osvik, D.A., te Riele, H., Timofeev, A., Zimmermann, P.: Factorization of a 768-bit RSA modulus. In: Rabin, T. (ed.) CRYPTO 2010. LNCS, vol. 6223, pp. 333–350. Springer, Heidelberg (2010)

24. Lenstra, A.K., Kleinjung, T., Thomé, E.: Universal security. In: Fischlin, M., Katzenbeisser, S. (eds.) Buchmann Festschrift. LNCS, vol. 8260, pp. 121–124. Springer, Heidelberg (2013)
25. Matsumoto, R.: Using C_{ab} curves in the function field sieve. IEICE Trans. Fund. E82-A(3), 551–552 (1999)
26. Murphy, B.A.: Polynomial selection for the number field sieve integer factorisation algorithm. Phd thesis, Australian National University (1999)
27. National Institute of Standards and Technology: Digital signature standard, DSS (2013), http://nvlpubs.nist.gov/nistpubs/FIPS/NIST.FIPS.186-4.pdf

Magma Verification Script

```
UP<t> := PolynomialRing(GF(2));
hex2pol := func<x | UP!Intseq(x, 2)>;

phi := hex2pol(0x3ffffffffffffffffffffffffffffffffffffe80000000000000\
    0000000000cc0cfaeb0e00000000000000000000000000000000004dffffffffff\
    ffffc3c3ffc3c3c3fce3c2133fffffffffffffe9697fe96804c84c97e0b0000c\
    00cf9b0f7675354e79f4cf7c97e29);
assert Degree(phi) eq 809 and IsIrreducible(phi);

N    := 2^809-1;
ell  := Factorization(N)[1][1];
h    := N div ell;

rsa1024 := hex2pol(0xc05748bbfb5acd7e5a77dc03d9ec7d8bb957c1b95d9b\
    206090d83fd1b67433ce83ead7376ccfd612c72901f4ce0a2e07e322d438ea4\
    f34647555d62d04140e1084e999bb4cd5f947a76674009e2318549fd102c5f7\
    596edc332a0ddee3a355186b9a046f0f96a279c1448a9151549dc663da8a6e8\
    9cf8f511baed6450da2c1cb);
log1024 :=
    2999787071911643485450020083420834977154987908338125416470796;

Modexp(rsa1024, h, phi) eq Modexp(t, h*log1024, phi);
```

Identity-Based Lossy Trapdoor Functions: New Definitions, Hierarchical Extensions, and Implications

Alex Escala[1], Javier Herranz[2], Benoît Libert[3], and Carla Ràfols[4]

[1] Scytl Secure Electronic Voting, Spain
[2] Universitat Politècnica de Catalunya - BarcelonaTech,
Dept. Matemàtica Aplicada IV, Spain
[3] Technicolor, France
[4] Ruhr-Universität Bochum,
Horst Görtz Institut für IT-Sicherheit, Germany

Abstract. Lossy trapdoor functions, introduced by Peikert and Waters (STOC'08), have received a lot of attention in the last years, because of their wide range of applications. The notion has been recently extended to the identity-based setting by Bellare *et al.* (Eurocrypt'12). An identity-based trapdoor function (IB-TDF) satisfying the lossy property introduced by Bellare *et al.* can be used to construct other cryptographic primitives in the identity-based setting: encryption schemes with semantic security under chosen-plaintext attacks, deterministic encryption schemes, and hedged encryption schemes that maintain some security when messages are encrypted using randomness of poor quality. However, the constructed primitives can be proved secure only against *selective* adversaries who select the target identity upfront.

Our first contribution is an alternative definition for the lossiness of an identity-based trapdoor function. We prove that an IB-TDF satisfying the new property can be used to construct all the aforementioned primitives, in the identity-based setting, with security against *adaptive* adversaries. We further consider the new definition and its implications in the more general scenario of *hierarchical* identity-based cryptography, which has proved very useful both for practical applications and to establish theoretical relations with other cryptographic primitives (including encryption with chosen-ciphertext security or with forward-security).

As a second contribution, we describe a pairing-based hierarchical IB-TDF satisfying the new definition of lossiness against either selective or, for hierarchies of constant depth, adaptive adversaries. This is also the first example of hierarchical trapdoor functions based on traditional (*i.e.*, non-lattice-related) number theoretic assumptions. As a direct consequence of our two contributions, we obtain a hierarchical identity-based (HIB) encryption scheme with chosen-plaintext security, a HIB deterministic encryption scheme and a HIB hedged encryption scheme, all of them with security against adaptive adversaries.

H. Krawczyk (Ed.): PKC 2014, LNCS 8383, pp. 239–256, 2014.

1   Introduction

1.1   (Identity-Based) Lossy Trapdoor Functions

Lossy trapdoor functions, as introduced by Peikert and Waters in [25], have been proved very powerful in theoretical cryptography and received a lot of attention in the recent years (see, e.g., [17,21,10,22,30]). Lossy trapdoor functions are function families that can be instantiated in two different modes. In the injective mode, the function is injective and can be inverted using a trapdoor. In lossy mode, the function is (highly) non-injective since its image size is much smaller than the size of the domain. The key point is that lossy instantiations of the function must be indistinguishable from injective instantiations.

In their seminal paper [25], Peikert and Waters showed that lossy trapdoor functions provide black-box constructions of chosen-ciphertext secure (IND-CCA) public-key encryption schemes as well as universal one-way and collision-resistant hash functions. Later on, other applications of lossy trapdoor functions were discovered: they gave rise to deterministic encryption schemes [2] in the standard model [6], public-key hedged encryption schemes maintaining some security in the absence of reliable encryption coins [3] and even public-key encryption with selective-opening security [4] (*i.e.*, which offer certain security guarantees in case of sender corruption).

Recently, Bellare, Kiltz, Peikert and Waters [5] introduced the notion of identity-based (lossy) trapdoor function (IB-TDF), which is the analogue of lossy trapdoor functions in the setting of identity-based cryptography [28]. In the identity-based scenario, users' public keys are directly derived from their identities, whereas secret keys are delivered by a trusted master entity. In this way, the need for digital certificates, which usually bind public keys to users in traditional public-key cryptography, is drastically reduced. Throughout the last decade, several generalizations of identity-based cryptography were put forth, including hierarchical identity-based encryption [18], attribute-based encryption [26,19] or predicate encryption [8,23]. In the setting of hierarchical identity-based cryptography, identities are organized in a hierarchical way, so that a user who holds the secret key of an identity id can generate, use and distribute valid secret keys for any identity that is a descendant of id in the hierarchy. Hierarchical identity-based encryption (HIBE) is of great interest due to both practical and theoretical reasons. On the practical side, many organizations and systems that may need (identity-based) cryptographic solutions are organized in a hierarchical way. On the theoretical side, generic constructions [11,12] are known to transform a weakly secure HIBE scheme (*i.e.*, IND-CPA security against selective adversaries) into (public-key) encryption schemes with strong security properties, like chosen-ciphertext security [12] or forward-security [1,11], where private keys are updated in such a way that past encryptions remain safe after a key exposure.

Bellare *et al.* [5] proposed instantiations of identity-based lossy trapdoor functions based on bilinear maps and on lattices (as noted in [5], almost all IBE schemes belong to these families). Moreover, they show that their definition of partial-lossiness for identity-based trapdoor functions leads to the same cryptographic results as lossy trapdoor functions, but in the selective identity-based setting only, where the attacker must choose the target identity upfront in the attack game. Namely, in the case of selective adversaries, IB-TDFs satisfying their definition imply identity-based encryption with semantic security, identity-based deterministic encryption and identity-based hedged encryption. In [5], it was left as an open problem to prove that the same results hold in the case of adaptive adversaries.

1.2   Our Two Main Contributions

NEW DEFINITION OF PARTIAL LOSSINESS AND ITS APPLICATIONS. From a theoretical standpoint, we first define a new security property for hierarchical identity-based trapdoor functions (HIB-TDFs). For the particular (non-hierarchical) case of IB-TDFs, the new security property is different to the property of partial lossiness defined by Bellare *et al.* [5]. We show that a HIB-TDF which satisfies this new property can be used to obtain the same kind of results that are derived from standard lossy trapdoor functions [25]. Namely, they lead to standard encryption schemes, to deterministic encryption schemes for block sources, and to non-adaptive hedged encryption schemes (also for block sources), which are secure in the hierarchical identity-based setting, against adaptive-id adversaries. Since IB-TDFs are a particular case of HIB-TDFs, our results for adaptive adversaries solve the above mentioned open problem in [5]. Interestingly, the pairing-based IB-TDF of Bellare *et al.* [5] can be proved to also satisfy the new security property. See the full version of the paper [16] for more details on this. As a consequence, it provides *adaptive*-id secure deterministic and hedged IBE schemes, and not only selectively secure ones as initially believed.

CONSTRUCTION OF A PAIRING-BASED HIERARCHICAL TRAPDOOR FUNCTION. On the constructive side, we focus on pairing-based hierarchical systems and leave possible constructions based on lattices as an open line for future work. Our intuition, however, is that pairing-based HIB-TDFs seem harder to construct than their lattice-based counterpart. Indeed, no hierarchical trapdoor function is currently known to rely on traditional number theoretic assumptions whereas, in the lattice world, constructions have been known since the results of Cash, Hofheinz, Kiltz and Peikert [13].

Using bilinear maps, we build a HIB-TDF and prove that it satisfies our new definition of partial lossiness under mild assumptions in prime order groups. As an intermediate step, we design a hierarchical predicate encryption (HPE) system [27,24] with suitable anonymity properties. Perhaps surprisingly, although this scheme is proved secure only against weak *selective* adversaries (who select their target attribute set before seeing the public parameters), we are able to turn it into a HIB-TDF providing security (namely, our new version of partial lossiness) against *adaptive* adversaries for hierarchies of constant depth. To the best of our knowledge, our HIB-TDF gives rise to the first hierarchy of trapdoor functions which does not rely on lattices: realizing such a hierarchy using number theoretic techniques was identified as an open problem in [13].

Beyond its hierarchical nature, our construction brings out an alternative design principle for (H)IB-TDFs. The idea is to rely on hierarchical predicate encryption (HPE) to deal with hierarchies. Namely, public parameters consist of a matrix of HPE encryptions and, when the function has to be evaluated, the latter matrix is turned into a matrix of (anonymous) HIBE ciphertexts. The homomorphic properties of the underlying HIBE then make it possible to evaluate the function while guaranteeing a sufficient amount of lossiness in lossy mode. It seems possible to abstract away the properties of the underlying HPE system in order to obtain a HIB-TDF via a semi-generic transformation. However, the HPE scheme we describe seems to be the only candidate with the required algebraic structure.

While the pairing-based IB-TDF construction of Bellare *et al.* [5] builds on an adaptively secure anonymous IBE, our HIB-TDF is obtained from a *selective* weakly attribute-hiding HPE system. This result is somewhat incomparable with [5]: on the one hand, we start from a more powerful primitive – because predicate encryption implies anonymous IBE – but, on the other hand, we need a weaker security level to begin with. Both (H)IB-TDF constructions rely on specific algebraic properties in the underlying IBE/HPE and neither is generic.

1.3   Implications

Combining our HIB-TDF with the theoretical implications of our new security property, we obtain: (1) a modular way to build adaptive-id secure HIBE schemes from HIB-LTDFs, (2) the first secure deterministic HIBE scheme for block sources[1], (3) the first HIBE scheme, for block sources, that (non-adaptively) hedges against bad randomness, as advocated by Bellare *et al.* [3]. All these schemes are secure against both selective and adaptive-id adversaries.

In the case of adaptive adversaries, these results only hold for hierarchies of constant depth (said otherwise, we do not provide full security). However, using our definition of partial lossiness or that of Bellare *et al.* [5], this appears very difficult to avoid. The reason is that both definitions seem inherently bound to the partitioning paradigm. Namely, they assume the existence of alternative public parameters, called *lossy parameters*, where the identity space is partitioned into subsets of injective and lossy identities (this is, identities which lead to injective and lossy functions respectively). The definition of [5] intuitively captures that a fraction δ of identities are lossy in the case of lossy parameters. In the hierarchical setting, the analogy with HIBE schemes suggests that all ancestors of a lossy identity be lossy themselves. Hence, unless one can make sure that certain lossy identities only have lossy descendants, the fraction δ seems doomed to exponentially decline with the depth of the hierarchy.

Finally, due to the results of Canetti, Halevi and Katz [11], our construction also implies the first forward-secure deterministic and hedged public-key encryption schemes (note that, as pointed out in [11], selective security suffices to give

---

[1] See [31] for a recent and independent construction, in the (non-hierarchical) IBE case.

forward-secure cryptosystems). Although our scheme is not practical due to large ciphertexts and keys, it provides the first feasibility results in these directions.

2 Background

2.1 Some Complexity Assumptions

We will consider groups $(\mathbb{G}, \hat{\mathbb{G}}, \mathbb{G}_T)$ of prime order p for which an asymmetric bilinear map $e : \mathbb{G} \times \hat{\mathbb{G}} \rightarrow \mathbb{G}_T$ is efficiently computable. We will assume that the DDH assumption holds in both $\mathbb{G}$ and $\hat{\mathbb{G}}$, which implies that no isomorphism is efficiently computable between $\mathbb{G}$ and $\hat{\mathbb{G}}$. The assumptions that we need are sometimes somewhat stronger than DDH. However, they have *constant* size (*i.e.* we de not rely on q-type assumptions) and were previously used in [15].

The Bilinear Diffie Hellman Assumption (BDH): in asymmetric bilinear groups $(\mathbb{G}, \hat{\mathbb{G}}, \mathbb{G}_T)$ of prime order p, no PPT adversary can distinguish the distribution $D_1 = \{(g, \ g^a, \ g^c, \ \hat{g}, \ \hat{g}^a, \ \hat{g}^b, \ e(g,\hat{g})^{abc}) \mid a,b,c \xleftarrow{R} \mathbb{Z}_p\}$, from $D_2 = \{(g, \ g^a, \ g^c, \ \hat{g}, \ \hat{g}^a, \ \hat{g}^b, \ e(g,\hat{g})^z) \mid a,b,c,z \xleftarrow{R} \mathbb{Z}_p\}$.

The $\mathcal{P}$-BDH$_1$ Assumption: in asymmetric bilinear groups $(\mathbb{G}, \hat{\mathbb{G}}, \mathbb{G}_T)$ of prime order p, the distribution $D_1 = \{(g, g^b, g^{ab}, g^c, \hat{g}, \hat{g}^a, \hat{g}^b, g^{abc}) \mid a,b,c \xleftarrow{R} \mathbb{Z}_p\}$ is indistinguishable from $D_2 = \{(g, g^b, g^{ab}, g^c, \hat{g}, \hat{g}^a, \hat{g}^b, g^z) \mid a,b,c,z \xleftarrow{R} \mathbb{Z}_p\}$ for any PPT algorithm.

The DDH$_2$ Assumption: in asymmetric bilinear groups $(\mathbb{G}, \hat{\mathbb{G}}, \mathbb{G}_T)$ of prime order p, the distribution $D_1 = \{(g, \ \hat{g}, \ \hat{g}^a, \ \hat{g}^b, \ \hat{g}^{ab}) \mid a,b \xleftarrow{R} \mathbb{Z}_p\}$ is computationally indistinguishable from $D_2 = \{(g, \ \hat{g}, \ \hat{g}^a, \ \hat{g}^b, \ \hat{g}^z) \mid a,b,z \xleftarrow{R} \mathbb{Z}_p\}$.

2.2 Hierarchical Identity-Based (Lossy) Trapdoor Functions

This section recalls formal definitions of (hierarchical) identity-based lossy trapdoor function.

SYNTAX. A hierarchical identity-based trapdoor function (HIB-TDF) is a tuple of efficient algorithms HF = (HF.Setup, HF.MKg, HF.Kg, HF.Del, HF.Eval, HF.Inv). The setup algorithm HF.Setup takes as input a security parameter $\varrho \in \mathbb{N}$, the (constant) number of levels in the hierarchy $d \in \mathbb{N}$, the length of the identities $\mu \in \text{poly}(\varrho)$ and the length of the function inputs $n \in \text{poly}(\varrho)$, and outputs a set of global public parameters pms, which specifies an input space InpSp, an identity space IdSp and the necessary mathematical objects and hash functions. The master key generation algorithm HF.MKg takes as input pms and outputs a master public key mpk and a master secret key msk. The key generation algorithm HF.Kg takes as input pms, msk and a hierarchical identity $(\text{id}_1, \ldots, \text{id}_\ell) \in \text{IdSp}$, for some $\ell \geq 1$ and outputs a secret key $\mathbf{SK}_{(\text{id}_1, \ldots, \text{id}_\ell)}$. The delegation algorithm HF.Del takes as input pms, mpk, a hierarchical identity $(\text{id}_1, \ldots, \text{id}_\ell)$, a secret key $\mathbf{SK}_{(\text{id}_1, \ldots, \text{id}_\ell)}$ for it, and an additional identity $\text{id}_{\ell+1}$; the output is a secret key $\mathbf{SK}_{(\text{id}_1, \ldots, \text{id}_\ell, \text{id}_{\ell+1})}$ for the hierarchical identity $(\text{id}_1, \ldots, \text{id}_\ell, \text{id}_{\ell+1})$ iff $(\text{id}_1, \ldots, \text{id}_\ell, \text{id}_{\ell+1}) \in \text{IdSp}$. The evaluation algorithm HF.Eval takes as input pms, mpk, an identity id $= (\mathsf{id}_1, \ldots, \mathsf{id}_\ell)$ and a value $X \in \mathsf{InpSp}$; the result of the evaluation is denoted as C. Finally, the inversion algorithm HF.Inv takes as input pms, mpk, a hierarchical identity id $= (\mathsf{id}_1, \ldots, \mathsf{id}_\ell)$, a secret key $\mathbf{SK}_{\mathsf{id}}$ for it and an evaluation C, and outputs a value $\tilde{X} \in \mathsf{InpSp}$.

A HIB-TDF satisfies the property of correctness if we have the equaltity $\mathsf{HF.Inv}\big(\mathsf{pms}, \mathsf{mpk}, \mathsf{id}, \mathbf{SK}_{\mathsf{id}}, \mathsf{HF.Eval}(\mathsf{pms}, \mathsf{mpk}, \mathsf{id} = (\mathsf{id}_1, \ldots, \mathsf{id}_\ell), X)\big) = X$, for any $X \in \mathsf{InpSp}$, any pms, (mpk, msk) generated by HF.Setup and HF.MKg, any hierarchical identity $(\mathsf{id}_1, \ldots, \mathsf{id}_\ell) \in \mathsf{IdSp}$ and any key $\mathbf{SK}_{(\mathsf{id}_1, \ldots, \mathsf{id}_\ell)}$ generated either by running HF.Kg$(\mathsf{pms}, \mathsf{msk}, (\mathsf{id}_1, \ldots, \mathsf{id}_\ell))$ or by applying the delegation algorithm HF.Del to secret keys of shorter hierarchical identities.

Before formalizing the new definition of partial lossiness for a HIB-TDF, let us recall the notion of *lossiness*: if f is a function with domain $\mathrm{Dom}(f)$ and image $\mathrm{Im}(f) = \{f(x) \ : \ x \in \mathrm{Dom}(f)\}$, we say that f is ω-lossy if $\lambda(f) \geq \omega$, where $\lambda(f) = \log \frac{|\mathrm{Dom}(f)|}{|\mathrm{Im}(f)|}$.

To define lossiness for HIB-TDFs, it is useful to consider extended HIB-TDFs, which differ from standard HIB-TDFs in that, in the latter, the algorithm HF.Setup specifies in pms an auxiliary input space AuxSp, and HF.MKg admits an auxiliary input $aux \in \mathsf{AuxSp}$. Given a HIB-TDF HF $=$ (HF.Setup, HF.MKg, HF.Kg, HF.Del, HF.Eval, HF.Inv), a *sibling* for HF is an extended HIB-TDF LHF $=$ (HF.Setup, LHF.MKg, LHF.Kg, HF.Del, HF.Eval, HF.Inv) whose delegation, evaluation and inversion algorithms are those of HF, and where an auxiliary space AuxSp is contained in pms $\leftarrow$ HF.Setup(ϱ), so that IdSp $\subset$ AuxSp.

Looking ahead, we will define, as in [5], two different experiments: one corresponding to the standard setup and one corresponding to the lossy setup, in one of them the experiment will interact with a standard HIB-TDF, in the other one with a sibling in which some identities lead to lossy evaluation functions. The notion of extended HIB-TDF will serve to construct both of these functions as an extended HIB-TDF but with different auxiliary inputs $\boldsymbol{y}^{(0)}, \boldsymbol{y}^{(1)}$.

3   A New Security Definition for (H)IB-TDFs

The basic security property of a trapdoor function is *one-wayness*, which means that the function is hard to invert without the suitable secret key. In the identity-based setting, one-wayness is required to hold even when the adversary has access to secret keys for some identities. *Partial lossiness* for identity-based trapdoor functions was introduced in [5], where it was proved to imply one-wayness. Roughly speaking, partial lossiness requires that the weighted difference of the probability that any adversary outputs 1 in the lossy or in the real experiment is negligible. These weights account for the fact that, in the lossy experiment in the adaptive case, some identities may lead to lossy functions, which can be detected by any adversary $\mathcal{A}$ that queries the secret key for such an identity. As a result, there is an asymmetry when comparing the real and the lossy experiments which is compensated by the weights.

For the selective case, the weights can simply be set to 1 and it can be proved that an IB-TDF satisfying their notion of partial lossiness in the selective scenario can be used to build: (1) identity-based encryption (IBE) schemes with selective IND-CPA security, (2) selectively secure deterministic IBE schemes, (3) selectively secure hedged IBE schemes. However, these results are not known to be true in the adaptive setting. In fact, the definition is not known to imply the IND-ID-CPA security of the resulting IBE scheme in the adaptive-id scenario.

To address this question, we propose an alternative definition for the partial lossiness of (hierarchical) identity-based trapdoor functions — in particular, the definition is also different from the one of Bellare *et al.* when the hierarchy depth is equal to 1, the case considered in [5]. We will show that a HIB-TDF satisfying this new definition gives, in the adaptive-id case, a secure construction of the same primitives we mentioned for the selective-id case.

3.1   The Formal Definition

As in [5], we define two different experiments, a lossy experiment and a real experiment. For any adversary $\mathcal{A}$ against a HIB-TDF, the $\mathsf{REAL}^{\mathcal{A}}_{\mathsf{HF},\mathsf{LHF},\mathcal{P},\omega,\zeta}$ experiment and the $\mathsf{LOSSY}^{\mathcal{A}}_{\mathsf{HF},\mathsf{LHF},\mathcal{P},\omega,\zeta}$ experiment are parameterized by the security parameter ϱ (which is usually omitted in the notation) and some values $\zeta(\varrho), \omega(\varrho)$. The experiment also takes as input the specification of some algorithm $\mathcal{P}$ which takes as input ζ, pms, mpk_1, msk_1, IS, $\mathsf{id}^\star$, and outputs a bit d_2. This algorithm must be efficient for any non-negligible ζ. To simplify notations, we write REAL instead of $\mathsf{REAL}^{\mathcal{A}}_{\mathsf{HF},\mathsf{LHF},\mathcal{P},\omega,\zeta}$ and LOSSY instead of $\mathsf{LOSSY}^{\mathcal{A}}_{\mathsf{HF},\mathsf{LHF},\mathcal{P},\omega,\zeta}$.

We present the two experiments as a single experiment depending on a bit β: the challenger $\mathcal{C}$, who interacts with the adversary $\mathcal{A}$, runs either REAL if $\beta = 0$ or LOSSY if $\beta = 1$. Also, some instructions of both experiments depend on whether *selective* or *adaptive* security is being considered. We say that a hierarchical identity $\mathsf{id} = (\mathsf{id}_1, \ldots, \mathsf{id}_\ell)$ is a *prefix* of another one $\mathsf{id}^\star = (\mathsf{id}_1^\star, \ldots, \mathsf{id}_{\ell^\star}^\star)$ if $\ell \leq \ell^\star$ and $\mathsf{id}_i = \mathsf{id}_i^\star$ for every $i = 1, \ldots, \ell$. We denote this fact by $\mathsf{id} \leq \mathsf{id}^\star$.

0. First, $\mathcal{C}$ chooses global parameters pms by running HF.Setup. The parameters pms are given to the adversary $\mathcal{A}$, who replies by choosing a hierarchical identity $\mathsf{id}^\dagger = (\mathsf{id}_1^\dagger, \ldots, \mathsf{id}_{\ell^\dagger}^\dagger)$, for some $\ell^\dagger \leq d$.
1. The challenger $\mathcal{C}$ runs $(\mathsf{mpk}_0, \mathsf{msk}_0) \leftarrow \mathsf{HF}.\mathsf{MKg}(\mathsf{pms})$ and $(\mathsf{mpk}_1, \mathsf{msk}_1) \leftarrow \mathsf{LHF}.\mathsf{MKg}(\mathsf{pms}, aux = \mathsf{id}^\dagger)$. The adversary $\mathcal{A}$ receives mpk_β and lists $IS \leftarrow \emptyset$, $QS \leftarrow \emptyset$ are initialized.
2. $\mathcal{A}$ can make adaptive queries for hierarchical identities $\mathsf{id} = (\mathsf{id}_1, \ldots, \mathsf{id}_\ell)$.
   - **Create-key**: $\mathcal{A}$ chooses an identity id and $\mathcal{C}$ creates a private key SK_{id}. If $\beta = 0$, SK_{id} is created by running $\mathsf{HF}.\mathsf{Kg}(\mathsf{pms}, \mathsf{msk}_0, \mathsf{id})$. If $\beta = 1$, it is created by running $\mathsf{LHF}.\mathsf{Kg}(\mathsf{pms}, \mathsf{msk}_1, \mathsf{id})$. The list QS is updated as $QS = QS \cup \{\mathsf{id}\}$.
   - **Create-delegated-key**: $\mathcal{A}$ provides a tuple $\mathsf{id} = (\mathsf{id}_1, \ldots, \mathsf{id}_\ell)$ and $\mathsf{id}_{\ell+1}$ such that $\mathsf{id} \in QS$. The challenger $\mathcal{C}$ then computes a delegated key $SK_{\mathsf{id}'}$ for $\mathsf{id}' = (\mathsf{id}_1, \ldots, \mathsf{id}_{\ell+1})$ by running the delegation algorithm $\mathsf{HF}.\mathsf{Del}(\mathsf{pms}, \mathsf{mpk}_\beta, SK_{\mathsf{id}}, \mathsf{id}_{\ell+1})$ before setting $QS = QS \cup \{\mathsf{id}'\}$.

- **Reveal-key**: $\mathcal{A}$ provides id with the restriction that if $\mathcal{A}$ is selective, then id $\not\leq$ id†. $\mathcal{C}$ returns $\perp$ if id $\notin QS$. Otherwise, SK_{id} is returned to $\mathcal{A}$ and the list IS is updated as $IS = IS \cup \{id\}$.

3. $\mathcal{A}$ outputs a hierarchical identity id$^\star = (id_1^\star, \ldots, id_{\ell^\star}^\star)$. If $\mathcal{A}$ is selective, then id$^\star = $ id†. In the adaptive case, no element of IS can be a prefix of id*.

4. The adversary can make adaptive queries such as the ones described in step 2, with the restriction that for **Reveal-key** queries the id provided by $\mathcal{A}$ must satisfy id $\not\leq$ id*.

5. The adversary outputs a bit $d_{\mathcal{A}} \in \{0, 1\}$. Let d_1 be the bit $d_1 := \left(\forall \ id \in IS, \lambda \left(\mathsf{HF.Eval}(\mathsf{pms}, \mathsf{mpk}_1, id, \cdot) \right) = 0 \right) \wedge \left(\lambda \left(\mathsf{HF.Eval}(\mathsf{pms}, \mathsf{mpk}_1, id^\star, \cdot) \right) \geq \omega \right)$.

6. The challenger $\mathcal{C}$ sets d_2 to be the output of the pre-output stage $\mathcal{P}$ with input $\zeta, \mathsf{pms}, \mathsf{mpk}_1, \mathsf{msk}_1, IS, id^\star$.

7. The final output of the experiment consists of the bits $\{d_{\mathcal{A}}, d_{\neg abort}^{\mathcal{A}}\}$, where $d_{\neg abort}^{\mathcal{A}} = d_1 \wedge d_2 \in \{0, 1\}$.

For notational convenience, from now on, let us define $d_{exp}^{\mathcal{A}} = d_{\mathcal{A}} \wedge d_{\neg abort}^{\mathcal{A}}$.

Definition 1. *A HIB-TDF is (ω, δ)-partially lossy if it admits a sibling and an efficient pre-output stage $\mathcal{P}$ such that for all PPT adversaries $\mathcal{A}$ and for all non-negligible ζ, there exist two non-negligible values ϵ_1, ϵ_2 such that $\delta = \epsilon_1 \epsilon_2$ is non-negligible and the following three conditions hold:*

(i) the following advantage function is negligible in the security parameter ϱ:

$$\mathbf{Adv}_{\mathsf{HF,LHF},\mathcal{P},\omega,\zeta}^{lossy}(\mathcal{A}) = |\Pr[d_{exp}^{\mathcal{A}} = 1| \ \mathsf{REAL}] - \Pr[d_{exp}^{\mathcal{A}} = 1| \ \mathsf{LOSSY}]| \quad (1)$$

(ii) $\Pr[d_{\neg abort}^{\mathcal{A}} = 1 \mid \mathsf{REAL}] \geq \epsilon_1$.

(iii) if $\mathcal{A}$ is such that $\Pr[d_{\mathcal{A}} = 1 \mid \mathsf{REAL}] - \frac{1}{2} > \zeta$, then

$$\Pr[d_{\mathcal{A}} = 1 \mid \mathsf{REAL} \wedge d_{\neg abort}^{\mathcal{A}} = 1] - \frac{1}{2} > \epsilon_2 \cdot \zeta, \quad (2)$$

where δ may be a function of q the maximal number of key queries of $\mathcal{A}$.

Some Intuition. As we mentioned, to account for the asymmetry between the real and the lossy experiment, Bellare *et al.* defined the advantage of a distinguisher among the lossy and real experiments as the *weighted* difference of the probability of outputting 1 in the real case minus the same probability in the lossy case. Our solution is different. We always execute in parallel two instances of the master key generation protocol, one in the real and one in the lossy mode (the adversary does not notice this). The experiments output a bit d_1 which is computed in the same way in both the real and lossy settings and which depends on the secret key queries and the challenge identity chosen by the adversary: for example, if a query would force the LOSSY experiment to output $d_1 = 0$ indicating that the adversary queried for a secret key of a lossy identity, then it also forces the REAL experiment to output $d_1 = 0$. For the sake of intuition, let us think of $d^{\mathcal{A}}_{\neg abort}$ as the bit d_1 and temporarily ignore d_2, whose purpose is explained later. By defining the output of the experiment as the logical AND between the output $d_{\mathcal{A}}$ of the adversary and a bit $d^{\mathcal{A}}_{\neg abort}$, we just avoid having to introduce weights in condition (i) in Definition 1. This is a difference with [5] which is crucial to prove that lossy identity-based trapdoor functions imply other primitives in the adaptive-id case.

Condition (i) can be seen as the natural (non-weighted) analogue of the security definition of [5], while the other conditions might look more artificial. We provide some more intuition on why condition (i) alone is not useful to guarantee that security reductions can be done from a scheme Π built from an HIB-TDF to the HIB-TDF itself in the adaptive setting. First, we add condition (ii) to rule out some cases in which the condition (i) would be trivial to satisfy, like the case where the procedure $\mathcal{P}$ aborts with overwhelming probability or the case where the sibling admits only lossy identities: in any of these scenarios, we would have $d^{\mathcal{A}}_{\neg abort} = 1$ with negligible probability, which would render the scheme useless.

A more serious problem, which motivates condition (iii), is that, in the reduction, the output of a potential adversary $\mathcal{A}$ with meaningful advantage ε against Π does not necessarily help to contradict condition (i) because the output of $\mathcal{A}$ needs to be conditioned to $d^{\mathcal{A}}_{\neg abort} = 1$ and the output of $\mathcal{A}$ may not be independent of $d^{\mathcal{A}}_{\neg abort} = 1$. To solve that, the reduction might try to abort after certain events, for example after some secret key queries have been done. However, such events could be related to the underlying HIB-TDF scheme, so the reduction would not be black-box. Condition (iii) guarantees that, if an adversary has some meaningful advantage against the scheme built from the HIB-TDF, it will also have meaningful advantage when $d_{\neg abort} = 1$, this is, when all the secret key queries correspond to injective identities and the challenge identity is lossy. Roughly said, this condition ensures that the probability of aborting is somewhat independent of the behavior of any computationally bounded adversary.

We have not discussed the role of d_2 yet. If $d_{\neg abort}$ was just defined as d_1, condition (iii) would be quite hard to satisfy: intuitively we would not be allowing the security reduction to make extra aborts related to events which depend on the HIB-TDF, which is unnecessarily restrictive. To handle this problem, we allow the experiment to consider an efficient algorithm $\mathcal{P}$, which depends on the HIB-TDF and outputs a bit d_2, and we define $d_{\neg abort} = d_1 \wedge d_2$. Finally, we stress that the incorporation of algorithm $\mathcal{P}$ results in a more general and flexible security definition: although one could define the security of HIB-TDF without taking into account the existence of such an algorithm $\mathcal{P}$, it would make it more difficult for a HIB-TDF to satisfy it. On the other hand, if $\mathcal{P}$ is the trivial algorithm which always outputs $d_2 = 1$, this is equivalent to considering the security definition without the algorithm $\mathcal{P}$, which is enough to prove the security of our HIB-TDF against selective adversaries, indeed. To prove the security of our HIB-TDF against adaptive adversaries, we will define $\mathcal{P}$ as the artificial abort stage in the security proof of Waters' IBE scheme [29].

3.2   Implications of Lossy (H)IB-TDFs: The Example of (H)IBE

Using the same argument as in [5], it is quite easy to prove that a HIB-TDF which enjoys the new version of the partial lossiness property is already one-way, in both the selective and adaptive settings. In this section we prove that a HIB-TDF which satisfies our new security definition can be used to build other primitives in the hierarchical identity-based scenario, with security against adaptive adversaries. We detail the example of hierarchical identity-based encryption (HIBE) with IND-CPA security[2]. The construction is the direct adaptation of the Peikert-Waters construction [25] in the public-key setting.

Let HF be a HIB-TDF with message space $\{0,1\}^n$ and (ω, δ) partial lossiness, and $\mathcal{H}$ a family of pairwise independent hash functions from $\{0,1\}^n$ to $\{0,1\}^l$ where $l \leq \omega - 2\lg(1/\epsilon_{LHL})$ for some negligible ϵ_{LHL}. The HIBE scheme has message space $\{0,1\}^l$. Its setup, key generation and key delegation algorithms are basically the same ones as those for HF, the rest are as follows:

MKGen(pms)	**Enc**(pms, mpk, m, id)	**Dec**(pms, mpk, $\mathbf{SK}_{id}$, C, id)
$(\text{mpk}', \text{msk}) \leftarrow$	$x \leftarrow \{0,1\}^n$	$x = \text{HF.Inv(pms,}$
$\quad$ HF.MKg(1^k)	$c_1 = \text{HF.Eval(pms, mpk}', \text{id}, x)$	$\quad$ mpk$'$, $\mathbf{SK}_{id}$, c_1, id)
$h \leftarrow \mathcal{H}$	$c_2 = h(x) \oplus m$	$m = c_2 \oplus h(x)$
mpk $= (\text{mpk}', h)$	Return $C = (c_1, c_2)$	Return m
Return mpk		

We prove the following theorem.

Theorem 1. *If* HF *is* (ω, δ)-*partially lossy for some non-negligible value of* δ, *then the HIBE scheme* Π *described is IND-ID-CPA secure. In particular, for every IND-ID-CPA adversary* $\mathcal{B}$ *against* Π *there exists a PPT adversary* $\mathcal{A}$ *against* HF *such that* $\mathbf{Adv}_{\mathsf{HF},\mathsf{LHF},\mathcal{P},\omega,\zeta}^{\mathrm{lossy}}(\mathcal{A}) \geq \frac{2}{3} \cdot \delta \cdot \mathbf{Adv}^{\mathrm{ind-id-cpa}}(\mathcal{B}) - \nu(\varrho)$, *for some negligible function* ν. *Both adversaries* $\mathcal{A}$ *and* $\mathcal{B}$ *run in comparable times; whenever* $\mathcal{B}$ *is selective, so is* $\mathcal{A}$ *(for their respective experiments).*

Proof. Let us assume that an adversary $\mathcal{B}$ has advantage at least ζ in breaking the IND-ID-CPA security of the HIBE scheme Π, for some non-negligible ζ. We build an adversary $\mathcal{A}$ that breaks the condition (i) of Definition 1 assuming that conditions (ii) and (iii) are satisfied. Our adversary $\mathcal{A}$, who interacts with a challenger that runs either the experiment REAL or the experiment LOSSY, proceeds to simulate the challenger in the IND-ID-CPA game with $\mathcal{B}$ as follows.

Our adversary $\mathcal{A}$ forwards an identity id† to its challenger, which is an arbitrary identity in the adaptive case or corresponds to the challenge identity chosen by $\mathcal{B}$ in the selective case. When the challenger runs the setup and gives the output to $\mathcal{A}$, $\mathcal{A}$ forwards this information to $\mathcal{B}$ together with a hash function $h \leftarrow \mathcal{H}$. When $\mathcal{B}$ asks for a secret key for a hierarchical identity id, $\mathcal{A}$ forwards the query to the experiment and relays the latter's reply to $\mathcal{B}$. At some point, $\mathcal{B}$ outputs $(m_0, m_1, \text{id}^\star)$, with id† = id* in the selective case. Adversary $\mathcal{A}$ then forwards

---
[2] The cases of deterministic HIBE and hedged HIBE are discussed in the full version of this paper [16].

id* to its challenger, chooses $\gamma \leftarrow \{0,1\}$ at random and encrypts m_γ under the identity id*. After some more secret key queries, $\mathcal{B}$ outputs a guess γ' and $\mathcal{A}$ outputs $d_\mathcal{A} = 1$ if $\gamma = \gamma'$ and $d_\mathcal{A} = 0$ otherwise.

In the REAL setting, we have $\Pr[\gamma' = \gamma|\ \mathsf{REAL}] - \frac{1}{2} = \Pr[d_\mathcal{A} = 1|\ \mathsf{REAL}] - \frac{1}{2} \geq \zeta$, since $\mathcal{A}$ perfectly simulated the IND-ID-CPA game with $\mathcal{B}$. This inequality can be combined with conditions (ii) and (iii) of the definition of (ω, δ)-partial lossiness (which we assume to be satisfied by HF), and we obtain

$$\Pr[d^\mathcal{A}_{\neg abort} = 1\ |\ \mathsf{REAL}] \cdot \left(\Pr[d_\mathcal{A} = 1\ |\ \mathsf{REAL} \wedge d^\mathcal{A}_{\neg abort} = 1] - \frac{1}{2} \right) > \epsilon_1 \epsilon_2 \zeta. \quad (3)$$

On the other hand, in the LOSSY setting when id* is lossy, the advantage of $\mathcal{B}$ in guessing γ is negligible. Indeed, since h is a pairwise independent hash function, the Leftover Hash Lemma [20] (more precisely, its variant proved in [14]) implies that the distribution of c_2 given c_1 is statistically uniform. We thus have $\Pr[d_\mathcal{A} = 1|\ \mathsf{LOSSY} \wedge d^\mathcal{A}_{\neg abort} = 1] \leq 1/2 + \epsilon_{LHL}$, for some negligible function ϵ_{LHL}. Since $d^\mathcal{A}_{exp} = d^\mathcal{A}_{\neg abort} \wedge d_\mathcal{A}$, we can express $\Pr[d^\mathcal{A}_{exp} = 1\ |\ \mathsf{LOSSY}]$ as

$$\Pr[d_\mathcal{A} = 1\ |\ \mathsf{LOSSY} \wedge d^\mathcal{A}_{\neg abort} = 1]\, \Pr[d^\mathcal{A}_{\neg abort} = 1\ |\ \mathsf{LOSSY}]$$

$$\leq (\frac{1}{2} + \epsilon_{LHL}) \cdot \Pr[d^\mathcal{A}_{\neg abort} = 1\ |\ \mathsf{LOSSY}]$$

$$\leq \frac{1}{2} \cdot \left(\Pr[d^\mathcal{A}_{\neg abort} = 1\ |\ \mathsf{REAL}] + \mathbf{Adv}^{lossy}_{\mathsf{HF,LHF},\mathcal{P},\omega,\zeta}(\mathcal{A}) \right) + \nu, \quad (4)$$

for some negligible function $\nu \in \mathsf{negl}(\varrho)$. The last equality follows from the fact that $\Pr[d^\mathcal{A}_{\neg abort} = 1|\ \mathsf{LOSSY}] - \Pr[d^\mathcal{A}_{\neg abort} = 1|\ \mathsf{REAL}] \leq \mathbf{Adv}^{lossy}_{\mathsf{HF,LHF},\mathcal{P},\omega,\zeta}(\mathcal{A})$: otherwise, we can build a distinguisher[3] against condition (i) of the partial lossiness definition. If we plug (4) into the definition of $\mathbf{Adv}^{lossy}_{\mathsf{HF,LHF},\mathcal{P},\omega,\zeta}(\mathcal{A})$, we find

$$\mathbf{Adv}^{lossy}_{\mathsf{HF,LHF},\mathcal{P},\omega,\zeta}(\mathcal{A}) = \left| \Pr[d^\mathcal{A}_{exp} = 1\ |\ \mathsf{REAL}] - \Pr[d^\mathcal{A}_{exp} = 1\ |\ \mathsf{LOSSY}] \right|$$

$$\geq \left| \Pr[d^\mathcal{A}_{\neg abort} = 1\ |\ \mathsf{REAL}] \cdot \left(\Pr[d_\mathcal{A} = 1\ |\ \mathsf{REAL} \wedge d^\mathcal{A}_{\neg abort} = 1] - \frac{1}{2} \right) \right|$$

$$- \frac{1}{2} \cdot \mathbf{Adv}^{lossy}_{\mathsf{HF,LHF},\mathcal{P},\omega,\zeta}(\mathcal{A}) - \nu,$$

so that there exists $\tilde{\nu} \in \mathsf{negl}(\varrho)$ such that $\mathbf{Adv}^{lossy}_{\mathsf{HF,LHF},\mathcal{P},\omega,\zeta}(\mathcal{A})$ is at least

$$\frac{2}{3} \cdot \left| \Pr[d^\mathcal{A}_{\neg abort} = 1\ |\ \mathsf{REAL}] \cdot \left(\Pr[d_\mathcal{A} = 1\ |\ \mathsf{REAL} \wedge d^\mathcal{A}_{\neg abort} = 1] - \frac{1}{2} \right) \right| - \tilde{\nu}.$$

Using (3) and $\delta = \epsilon_1 \epsilon_2$, we have that the right-hand-side member of the above expression is at least $(2/3) \cdot \delta \cdot \zeta - \nu$. This means that $\mathbf{Adv}^{lossy}_{\mathsf{HF,LHF},\mathcal{P},\omega,\zeta}(\mathcal{A})$ is non-negligible, which contradicts condition (i). $\qquad \square$

---

[3] This distinguisher $\mathcal{A}_1$ is obtained from $\mathcal{A}$ by ignoring $d_\mathcal{A} \in \{0,1\}$ and replacing it by a 1, so that $d^\mathcal{A}_{\neg abort} = d^\mathcal{A}_{exp}$.

4 A Hierarchical Identity-Based (Lossy) Trapdoor Function

The design of our new HIB-TDF and its security analysis use as a key ingredient an HPE scheme which is described in the full version of the paper [16]. Let us first provide some intuition on the reason why a HPE scheme simplifies our task.

The pairing-based IB-TDF of Bellare *et al.* [5] uses an anonymous IBE scheme as a building block. To construct a HIB-TDF, a natural idea is thus to use an anonymous HIBE system. One difficulty is that, at least in the world of pairings, anonymous IBE schemes are usually harder to extend to a hierarchy than non-anonymous ones. Indeed, private keys have to contain extra randomization components because, if the randomization material were included in the public parameters, ciphertexts would betray the identity of receivers. Moreover, as already mentioned in [5], anonymity is not sufficient by itself: what we need is a way to propertly embed an auxiliary input in the public parameters without the adversary noticing the difference between two distinct auxiliary inputs. Adapting the Boyen-Waters anonymous HIBE [9] to achieve this is not straightforward. On the other hand, HPE schemes make it possible to naturally embed auxiliary inputs in the attribute vectors of HPE ciphertexts, which are included in the public parameters of the function. When the function has to be evaluated for a specific identity, our construction uses a mechanism to turn HPE ciphertexts into a matrix of HIBE ciphertexts and this is where the interaction between auxiliary inputs and hierarchical identities leads to functions that can be injective or lossy. From the resulting matrix of HIBE ciphertexts, the function evaluation proceeds by computing a matrix-vector product in the exponent, as done in many lossy TDF construcitons (see, e.g., [25,17,21,30]), and takes advantage of homomorphic properties in the underlying HIBE system.

More precisely, our lossy function is obtained by including a $n \times n$ matrix of HPE ciphertexts in the master public parameters. As in the DDH-based function of [25], each row of the matrix is associated with an encryption exponent, which is re-used throughout the entire row. Each column corresponds to a different set of public parameters in the HPE system.

The HIB-TDF that we construct is actually an extended HIB-TDF, and so the master key generation protocol takes an auxiliary input. Depending on the value of this auxiliary input, we obtain the trapdoor (injective) function or a partially lossy function, used in the security proofs. Actually, all HPE ciphertexts in the above-mentioned matrix correspond to different hierarchical vectors $(\mathbf{y}_1, \ldots, \mathbf{y}_d) \in \mathbb{Z}_p^{d \cdot \mu}$, depending on the auxiliary input. The selective weak attribute-hiding property of the HPE scheme guarantees that the two setups are computationally indistinguishable.

In order to evaluate a function for some hierarchical identity $\mathsf{id} = (\mathsf{id}_1, \ldots, \mathsf{id}_\ell)$, the first step of the evaluation algorithm computes a transformation on HPE ciphertexts so as to obtain a matrix of Boneh-Boyen HIBE ciphertexts [7] in their anonymized variant suggested by Ducas [15]. During this transformation, a set of inner products $\{\langle \mathbf{y}_{i_1}, \mathsf{id}_{i_1} \rangle\}_{i_1=1}^{\ell}$ is calculated in the exponent in the diagonal entries of the matrix. The transformation provides a $n \times n$ matrix (7) of anonymous HIBE ciphertexts that are always well-formed in non-diagonal entries. As for diagonal entries, they contain "perturbed" HIBE ciphertexts: at each level, one ciphertext component contains a perturbation factor of the form $\langle \mathbf{y}_{i_1}, \mathsf{id}_{i_1} \rangle$. In this matrix of HIBE ciphertexts, random encryption exponents are again re-used in all positions at each row.

The function evaluation is carried out as in [25], by computing a matrix-vector product in the exponent and taking advantage of homomorphic properties of the HIBE scheme over the randomness space. The function output can be seen as a set of n anonymous HIBE ciphertexts – one for each input bit – which are well-formed ciphertexts if and only if the corresponding input bit is 0 (*i.e.*, if and only if the perturbation factors $\{\langle \mathbf{y}_{i_1}, \mathsf{id}_{i_1} \rangle\}_{i_1=1}^{\ell}$ are left out when computing the matrix-vector product in the exponent). The function is thus inverted by testing the well-formedness of each HIBE ciphertext using the private key.

4.1 Description

HF.Setup(ϱ, d, n, μ): given a security parameter $\varrho \in \mathbb{N}$, the (constant) desired number of levels in the hierarchy $d \in \mathbb{N}$ and integers $\mu, n \in \mathsf{poly}(\varrho)$ specifying the length of identities and that of function inputs, respectively, choose asymmetric bilinear groups $(\mathbb{G}, \hat{\mathbb{G}}, \mathbb{G}_T)$ of prime order $p > 2^{\varrho}$. Define $\mathsf{InpSp} = \{0,1\}^n$, $\Sigma_{\mathsf{ID}} = \{(1, \mathbf{x}) : \mathbf{x} \in \mathbb{Z}_p^{\mu-1}\}$, $\mathsf{IdSp} = \Sigma_{\mathsf{ID}}^{(\leq d)}$ and $\mathsf{AuxSp} = \mathbb{Z}_p^{d \cdot \mu}$. The public parameters are $\mathsf{pms} = \left(p, (\mathbb{G}, \hat{\mathbb{G}}, \mathbb{G}_T), d, n, \mu, \mathsf{InpSp}, \mathsf{IdSp}, \mathsf{AuxSp}\right)$.

Since HF is an extended HIB-TDF, the master key generation algorithm of our HIB-TDF receives an auxiliary input $\mathbf{y} \in \mathsf{AuxSp}$. Here, it is seen as a concatenation of d row vectors $\mathbf{y}_1, \ldots, \mathbf{y}_d \in \mathbb{Z}_p^{\mu}$. Notation $\Delta(i, j)$ is used for the Kronecker's delta function (that is, $\Delta(i, j) = 1$ if $i = j$, and is equal to 0 otherwise).

HF.MKg$(\mathsf{pms}, \mathbf{y})$: parse the auxiliary input as $\mathbf{y} = [\mathbf{y}_1 | \ldots | \mathbf{y}_d] \in \mathbb{Z}_p^{d \cdot \mu}$, and proceed as follows.

1. Choose $\alpha_v \xleftarrow{R} \mathbb{Z}_p^*$, $\boldsymbol{\alpha}_w \xleftarrow{R} (\mathbb{Z}_p^*)^n$, and $\boldsymbol{\alpha}_h \xleftarrow{R} (\mathbb{Z}_p^*)^{d \times (\mu+1) \times n}$. Define $v = g^{\alpha_v}$, $\hat{v} = \hat{g}^{\alpha_v}$, $\mathbf{w} = g^{\boldsymbol{\alpha}_w} \in \mathbb{G}^n$ and $\hat{\mathbf{w}} = \hat{g}^{\boldsymbol{\alpha}_w} \in \hat{\mathbb{G}}^n$. Likewise, set up vectors $\mathbf{h} = g^{\boldsymbol{\alpha}_h} \in \mathbb{G}^{d \times (\mu+1) \times n}$ and $\hat{\mathbf{h}} = \hat{g}^{\boldsymbol{\alpha}_h} \in \hat{\mathbb{G}}^{d \times (\mu+1) \times n}$. Define

$$\mathsf{PP}_{core} := \left(v, \ \{\mathbf{w}[l_1]\}_{l_1=1}^n, \ \{\mathbf{h}[i_1, i_2, l_1]\}_{i_1 \in \{1, \ldots, d\}, i_2 \in \{0, \ldots, \mu\}, \ l_1 \in \{1, \ldots, n\}}\right)$$

2. For $i_1 = 1$ to d, parse $\mathbf{y}_{i_1}$ as $(\mathbf{y}_{i_1}[1], \ldots, \mathbf{y}_{i_1}[\mu]) \in \mathbb{Z}_p^{\mu}$. For $l_2 = 1$ to n, do the following.

   a. Choose $\mathbf{s}[l_2] \xleftarrow{R} \mathbb{Z}_p^*$ and compute $\mathbf{J}[l_2] = v^{\mathbf{s}[l_2]}$ as well as

   $$\mathbf{C}_w[l_2, l_1] = \mathbf{w}[l_1]^{\mathbf{s}[l_2]},$$
   $$\mathbf{C}[i_1, i_2, l_2, l_1] = \left(\mathbf{h}[i_1, 0, l_1]^{\mathbf{y}_{i_1}[i_2] \cdot \Delta(l_2, l_1)} \cdot \mathbf{h}[i_1, i_2, l_1]\right)^{\mathbf{s}[l_2]}$$

   for each $i_1 \in \{1, \ldots, d\}$, $i_2 \in \{1, \ldots, \mu\}$, $l_1 \in \{1, \ldots, n\}$.

b. Define a $n \times n$ matrix $\{\mathbf{CT}[l_2, l_1]\}_{l_2, l_1 \in \{1,...,n\}}$ of HPE ciphertexts

$$\mathbf{CT}[l_2, l_1] = \big(\mathbf{J}[l_2], \mathbf{C}_w[l_2, l_1], \{\mathbf{C}[i_1, i_2, l_2, l_1]\}_{i_1 \in \{1,...,d\},\ i_2 \in \{1,...,\mu\}}\big). \quad (5)$$

The master public key consists of $\mathsf{mpk} := \big(\mathsf{PP}_{core}, \{\mathbf{CT}[l_2, l_1]\}_{l_2, l_1 \in \{1,...,n\}}\big)$ while the master secret key is $\mathsf{msk} := (\hat{v}, \hat{\mathbf{w}}, \hat{\mathbf{h}})$. For each $l_1 \in \{1, \dots, n\}$, it will be convenient to view $(\mathsf{PP}_{core}, \mathsf{msk})$ as a vector of HPE master key pairs $(\mathsf{mpk}[l_1], \mathsf{msk}[l_1])$, with

$$\mathsf{mpk}[l_1] = \big(v, \mathbf{w}[l_1], \{\mathbf{h}[i_1, i_2, l_1]\}_{i_1 \in \{1,...,d\}, i_2 \in \{0,...,\mu\}}\big)$$
$$\mathsf{msk}[l_1] = \big(\hat{v}, \hat{\mathbf{w}}[l_1], \{\hat{\mathbf{h}}[i_1, i_2, l_1]\}_{i_1 \in \{1,...,d\}, i_2 \in \{0,...,\mu\}}\big).$$

HF.Kg$(\mathsf{pms}, \mathsf{msk}, (\mathsf{id}_1, \dots, \mathsf{id}_\ell))$: to generate a key for an identity $(\mathsf{id}_1, \dots, \mathsf{id}_\ell) \in \mathsf{IdSp}$, parse msk as $(\hat{v}, \hat{\mathbf{w}}, \hat{\mathbf{h}})$ and id_{i_1} as $\mathsf{id}_{i_1}[1] \dots \mathsf{id}_{i_1}[\mu]$ for $i_1 = 1$ to ℓ. Choose $\mathbf{r}_w, \mathbf{r}_1, \dots, \mathbf{r}_\ell \xleftarrow{R} (\mathbb{Z}_p^*)^n$, choose $\mathbf{s} \xleftarrow{R} (\mathbb{Z}_p^*)^{d \times \mu \times \ell \times n}$, $\mathbf{s}' \xleftarrow{R} (\mathbb{Z}_p^*)^{d \times n}$, and $\mathbf{s}_w \xleftarrow{R} (\mathbb{Z}_p^*)^{d \times \mu \times n}$. For each $l_1 \in \{1, \dots, n\}$, compute the decryption component $\mathbf{SK}_D = (\mathbf{D}, \mathbf{D}_w, \{\mathbf{D}_{i_1}\}_{i_1=1}^\ell)$ of the key as $\mathbf{D}_{i_1}[l_1] = \hat{v}^{\mathbf{r}_{i_1}[l_1]}$ and

$$\mathbf{D}[l_1] = \prod_{i_1=1}^{\ell} \Big(\prod_{i_2=1}^{\mu} \hat{\mathbf{h}}[i_1, i_2, l_1]^{\mathsf{id}_{i_1}[i_2]}\Big)^{\mathbf{r}_{i_1}[l_1]} \cdot \hat{\mathbf{w}}[l_1]^{\mathbf{r}_w[l_1]}, \quad \mathbf{D}_w[l_1] = \hat{v}^{\mathbf{r}_w[l_1]}, \quad (6)$$

while the delegation component $\mathbf{SK}_{DL}$ consists of

$$\big(\{\mathbf{K}[j, k, l_1]\}_{j,k,l_1},\ \{\mathbf{L}[j, l_1]\}_{j,l_1},\ \{\mathbf{L}[j, k, i_1, l_1]\}_{j,k,i_1,l_1},\ \{\mathbf{L}_w[j, k, l_1]\}_{j,k,l_1}\big),$$

with $j \in \{\ell+1, \dots, d\}$, $k \in \{1, \dots, \mu\}$, $i_1 \in \{1, \dots, \ell\}$ and $l_1 \in \{1, \dots, n\}$, as

$$\mathbf{K}[j, k, l_1] = \prod_{i_1=1}^{\ell} \Big(\prod_{i_2=1}^{\mu} \hat{\mathbf{h}}[i_1, i_2, l_1]^{\mathsf{id}_{i_1}[i_2]}\Big)^{\mathbf{s}[j,k,i_1,l_1]} \cdot \hat{\mathbf{h}}[j, k, l_1]^{\mathbf{s}'[j,l_1]} \cdot \hat{\mathbf{w}}[l_1]^{\mathbf{s}_w[j,k,l_1]},$$

$$\mathbf{L}[j, l_1] = \hat{v}^{\mathbf{s}'[j,l_1]}, \qquad \mathbf{L}[j, k, i_1, l_1] = \hat{v}^{\mathbf{s}[j,k,i_1,l_1]} \quad \text{and} \quad \mathbf{L}_w[j, k, l_1] = \hat{v}^{\mathbf{s}_w[j,k,l_1]}.$$

Output $\mathbf{SK}_{(\mathsf{id}_1,...,\mathsf{id}_\ell)} = (\mathbf{SK}_D, \mathbf{SK}_{DL})$.

HF.Del$(\mathsf{pms}, \mathsf{mpk}, (\mathsf{id}_1, \dots, \mathsf{id}_\ell), \mathbf{SK}_{(\mathsf{id}_1,...,\mathsf{id}_\ell)}, \mathsf{id}_{\ell+1})$: parse $\mathbf{SK}_{(\mathsf{id}_1,...,\mathsf{id}_\ell)}$ as a HF private key of the form $(\mathbf{SK}_D, \mathbf{SK}_{DL})$, and the identifier $\mathsf{id}_{\ell+1}$ as a string $\mathsf{id}_{\ell+1}[1] \dots \mathsf{id}_{\ell+1}[\mu] \in \Sigma_{\mathsf{ID}}$. The idea is to run, for $l_1 = 1$ to n, the key derivation algorithm **Delegate**$(\mathsf{mpk}[l_1], (\mathsf{id}_1, \dots, \mathsf{id}_\ell), \mathbf{SK}_{(\mathsf{id}_1,...,\mathsf{id}_\ell)}[l_1], \mathsf{id}_{\ell+1})$ of the HPE scheme, as specified in the full version of the paper, where $\mathbf{SK}_{(\mathsf{id}_1,...,\mathsf{id}_\ell)}[l_1] = (\mathbf{SK}_D[l_1], \mathbf{SK}_{DL}[l_1])$ is defined by

$$\mathbf{SK}_D[l_1] = (\mathbf{D}[l_1], \mathbf{D}_w[l_1], \{\mathbf{D}_{i_1}[l_1]\}_{i_1=1}^{\ell})$$
$$\mathbf{SK}_{DL}[l_1] = \big(\{\mathbf{K}[j, k, l_1]\}_{j,k},\ \{\mathbf{L}[j, l_1]\}_j,\ \{\mathbf{L}[j, k, i_1, l_1]\}_{j,k,i_1}, \{\mathbf{L}_w[j, k, l_1]\}_{j,k}\big).$$

Specifically, for $l_1 = 1$ to n, do the following.

1. Randomize $\mathbf{SK}_{DL}[l_1]$ by raising all its component to some $z \xleftarrow{R} \mathbb{Z}_p^*$. Call this new key $\widehat{\mathbf{SK}}_{DL}[l_1]$ and write its elements with a hat (e.g., $\widehat{K}[j,k,l_1] = \mathbf{K}[j,k,l_1]^z$).

2. Compute a *partial decryption key*

$$\widetilde{\mathbf{K}}[\ell+1, l_1] = \prod_{k=1}^{\mu} \widehat{\mathbf{K}}[\ell+1,k,l_1]^{\mathrm{id}_{\ell+1}[k]} = \prod_{i_1=1}^{\ell} \Big(\prod_{i_2=1}^{\mu} \widehat{\mathbf{h}}[i_1,i_2,l_1]^{\mathrm{id}_{i_1}[i_2]} \Big)^{\tilde{\mathbf{s}}[\ell+1,i_1,l_1]}$$

$$\cdot \Big(\prod_{k=1}^{\mu} \widehat{\mathbf{h}}[\ell+1,k,l_1]^{\mathrm{id}_{\ell+1}[k]} \Big)^{\mathbf{s}'[\ell+1,l_1]} \cdot \widehat{\mathbf{w}}[l_1]^{\tilde{\mathbf{s}}_w[\ell+1,l_1]},$$

$$\widetilde{\mathbf{L}}[\ell+1,\ell+1,l_1] = \widehat{\mathbf{L}}[\ell+1,l_1],$$

$$\widetilde{\mathbf{L}}[\ell+1,i_1,l_1] = \prod_{k=1}^{\mu} \widehat{\mathbf{L}}[\ell+1,k,i_1,l_1]^{\mathrm{id}_{\ell+1}[k]} = \hat{v}^{\tilde{\mathbf{s}}[\ell+1,i_1,l_1]} \quad \text{for } i_1 \in \{1,\dots,\ell\},$$

$$\widetilde{\mathbf{L}}_w[\ell+1,l_1] = \prod_{k=1}^{\mu} \widehat{L}_w[\ell+1,k,l_1]^{\mathrm{id}_{\ell+1}[k]} = \hat{v}^{\tilde{\mathbf{s}}_w[\ell+1,l_1]}$$

where we define $\tilde{\mathbf{s}}[\ell+1,i_1,l_1] = z \cdot (\sum_{k=1}^{\mu} \mathbf{s}[\ell+1,k,i_1,l_1] \cdot \mathrm{id}_{\ell+1}[k])$, for $i_1 \in \{1,\dots,\ell\}$, and $\tilde{\mathbf{s}}_w[\ell+1,l_1] = z \cdot (\sum_{k=1}^{\mu} \mathbf{s}[\ell+1,k,l_1] \cdot \mathrm{id}_{\ell+1}[k])$.

3. For all $j \in \{\ell+2,\dots,d\}$, $k \in \{1,\dots,\mu\}$, compute re-randomized versions of the partial decryption key by raising the partial decryption key to random powers $\tau_{j,k} \xleftarrow{R} \mathbb{Z}_p^*$.

$$\mathbf{K}[\ell+1,l_1]^{(j,k)} = \widetilde{\mathbf{K}}[\ell+1,l_1]^{\tau_{j,k}}, \qquad \mathbf{L}_w[\ell+1,l_1]^{(j,k)} = \widetilde{\mathbf{L}}_w[\ell+1,l_1]^{\tau_{j,k}},$$

$$\{\mathbf{L}[\ell+1,i_1,l_1]^{(j,k)} = \widetilde{\mathbf{L}}[\ell+1,i_1,l_1]^{\tau_{j,k}}\}_{i_1=1}^{\ell+1}.$$

These values will be used to compute the delegation component of the new key at step 5.

4. Compute a decryption component $\mathbf{SK}'_D[l_1] = (\mathbf{D}'[l_1], \mathbf{D}'_w[l_1], \{\mathbf{D}'_{i_1}[l_1]\}_{i_1=1}^{\ell+1})$ for the delegated key by setting $\mathbf{D}'[l_1] = \mathbf{D}[l_1] \cdot \widetilde{\mathbf{K}}[\ell+1,l_1]$ as well as $\mathbf{D}'_w[l_1] = \mathbf{D}_w[l_1] \cdot \widetilde{\mathbf{L}}_w[\ell+1,l_1]$. Then, define $\mathbf{D}'_{\ell+1}[l_1] = \widetilde{\mathbf{L}}[\ell+1,\ell+1,l_1]$ and, for each $i_1 \in \{1,\dots,\ell\}$, set $\mathbf{D}'_{i_1}[l_1] = \mathbf{D}_{i_1}[l_1] \cdot \widetilde{\mathbf{L}}[\ell+1,i_1,l_1]$.

5. Finally, compute a delegation component for the delegated key. For each $j \in \{\ell+2,\dots,d\}$, set $\mathbf{L}'[j,l_1] = \widehat{\mathbf{L}}[j,l_1]$. Then, for each $k \in \{1,\dots,\mu\}$, $i_1 \in \{1,\dots,\ell+1\}$, set $\mathbf{K}'[j,k,l_1] = \widehat{\mathbf{K}}[j,k,l_1] \cdot \mathbf{K}[\ell+1,l_1]^{(j,k)}$ and

$$\mathbf{L}'_w[j,k,l_1] = \widehat{\mathbf{L}}_w[j,k,l_1] \cdot \mathbf{L}_w[\ell+1,l_1]^{(j,k)}$$

$$\mathbf{L}'[j,k,i_1,l_1] = \widehat{\mathbf{L}}[j,k,i_1,l_1] \cdot \mathbf{L}[\ell+1,i_1,l_1]^{(j,k)},$$

with $\widehat{\mathbf{L}}[j,k,\ell+1,l_1] = 1$ for all j,k. The delegation component $\mathbf{SK}'_{DL}$ is

$$\mathbf{SK}'_{DL}[l_1] = (\{\mathbf{K}'[j,k,l_1]\}_{j,k}, \{\mathbf{L}'[j,l_1]\}_j, \{\mathbf{L}'[j,k,i_1,l_1]\}_{j,k,i_1}, \{\mathbf{L}'_w[j,k,l_1]\}_{j,k}),$$

with $j \in \{\ell+2, \ldots, d\}$, $k \in \{1, \ldots, \mu\}$, $i_1 \in \{1, \ldots, \ell+1\}$. Return the delegated private key $\mathbf{SK}_{(\mathsf{id}_1, \ldots, \mathsf{id}_\ell, \mathsf{id}_{\ell+1})}[l_1] = (\mathbf{SK}'_D[l_1], \mathbf{SK}'_{DL}[l_1])$.

Return $\{\mathbf{SK}_{(\mathsf{id}_1, \ldots, \mathsf{id}_\ell, \mathsf{id}_{\ell+1})}[l_1]\}_{l_1=1}^n$.

HF.Eval$(\mathsf{pms}, \mathsf{mpk}, (\mathsf{id}_1, \ldots, \mathsf{id}_\ell), X)$: Given a n-bit input $X = x_1 \ldots x_n \in \{0,1\}^n$, for $i_1 = 1$ to ℓ, parse id_{i_1} as $\mathsf{id}_{i_1}[1] \ldots \mathsf{id}_{i_1}[\mu]$. For $l_1 = 1$ to n, do the following.

1. Compute modified HPE ciphertexts by defining

$$
\mathbf{C}_{\mathsf{id}}[i_1, l_2, l_1] = \prod_{i_2=1}^{\mu} \mathbf{C}[i_1, i_2, l_2, l_1]^{\mathsf{id}_{i_1}[i_2]}
$$

$$
= \left(\mathbf{h}[i_1, 0, l_1]^{\langle \mathbf{y}_{i_1}, \mathsf{id}_{i_1} \rangle \cdot \Delta(l_2, l_1)} \cdot \prod_{i_2=1}^{\mu} \mathbf{h}[i_1, i_2, l_1]^{\mathsf{id}_{i_1}[i_2]}\right)^{\mathbf{s}[l_2]}
$$

for each $i_1 \in \{1, \ldots, \ell\}$, $l_1, l_2 \in \{1, \ldots, n\}$. The modified ciphertexts are

$$
\mathbf{C}_{\mathsf{id}}[l_2, l_1] = \left(\mathbf{J}[l_2], \{\mathbf{C}_{\mathsf{id}}[i_1, l_2, l_1]\}_{i_1=1}^{\ell}\right) \in \mathbb{G}^{\ell+1}. \tag{7}
$$

The resulting $\{\mathbf{C}_{id}[l_2, l_1]\}_{l_2, l_1 \in \{1, \ldots, n\}}$ thus form a $n \times n$ matrix of anonymous HIBE ciphertexts for the identity $\mathsf{id} = (\mathsf{id}_1, \ldots, \mathsf{id}_\ell)$.

2. Using the vector $X \in \{0,1\}^n$, compute $C_{\mathsf{id},v} = \prod_{l_2=1}^n \mathbf{J}[l_2]^{x_{l_2}} = v^{\langle \mathbf{s}, X \rangle}$, $\mathbf{CT}_{\mathsf{id},w}[l_1] = \prod_{l_2=1}^n \mathbf{C}_w[l_2, l_1]^{x_{l_2}} = \mathbf{w}[l_1]^{\langle \mathbf{s}, X \rangle}$ and

$$
\mathbf{CT}_{\mathsf{id}}[i_1, l_1] = \prod_{l_2=1}^{n} \mathbf{C}_{\mathsf{id}}[i_1, l_2, l_1]^{x_{l_2}} \tag{8}
$$

$$
= \mathbf{h}[i_1, 0, l_1]^{\mathbf{s}[l_1] \cdot x_{l_1} \cdot \langle \mathbf{y}_{i_1}, \mathsf{id}_{i_1} \rangle} \cdot \left(\prod_{i_2=1}^{\mu} \mathbf{h}[i_1, i_2, l_1]^{\mathsf{id}_{i_1}[i_2]}\right)^{\langle \mathbf{s}, X \rangle}
$$

Output

$$
C = \left(C_{\mathsf{id},v}, \{\mathbf{CT}_{\mathsf{id},w}[l_1]\}_{l_1=1}^n, \{\mathbf{CT}_{\mathsf{id}}[i_1, l_1]\}_{i_1 \in \{1, \ldots, \ell\}, l_1 \in \{1, \ldots, n\}}\right)' \in \mathbb{G}^{n+1+n \times \ell}. \tag{9}
$$

HF.Inv$(\mathsf{pms}, \mathsf{mpk}, (\mathsf{id}_1, \ldots, \mathsf{id}_\ell), \mathbf{SK}_{(\mathsf{id}_1, \ldots, \mathsf{id}_\ell)}, C)$: parse the decryption component $\mathbf{SK}_D$ of the private key as a tuple of the form $(\mathbf{D}, \mathbf{D}_w, \mathbf{D}_{\bar{w}}, \{\mathbf{D}_{i_1}\}_{i_1=1}^{\ell})$ and the output C as per (9). Then, for $l_1 = 1$ to n, set $x_{l_1} = 0$ if

$$
e(C_{\mathsf{id},v}, \mathbf{D}[l_1]) \cdot e(\mathbf{CT}_{\mathsf{id},w}[l_1], \mathbf{D}_w[l_1])^{-1} \cdot \prod_{i_1=1}^{\ell} e(\mathbf{CT}_{\mathsf{id}}[i_1, l_1], \mathbf{D}_{i_1}[l_1])^{-1} = 1_{\mathbb{G}_T}.
$$

Otherwise, set $x_{l_1} = 1$. Eventually, return $X = x_1 \ldots x_n \in \{0,1\}^n$. (10)

From (8), we see that, with overwhelming probability, if there exists $i_1 \in \{1, \ldots, d\}$ such that $\langle \mathbf{y}_{i_1}, \mathsf{id}_{i_1} \rangle \neq 0$, relation (10) is satisfied if and only if $x_{l_1} = 0$. Indeed, in this case, the output (9) is distributed as a vector of n Boneh-Boyen anonymous HIBE ciphertexts. These ciphertexts correspond to the same encryption exponent $\langle \mathbf{s}, X \rangle$ and are generated under n distinct master public keys sharing the same component $v \in \mathbb{G}$.

When the function is prepared for the injective mode, the auxiliary input consists of a vector $\mathbf{y}^{(0)} = [(1, 0, \ldots, 0)| \ldots |(1, 0, \ldots, 0)] \in \mathbb{Z}_p^{d \cdot \mu}$. Since $\mathsf{id}_{i_1}[1] = 1$

for each i_1, this implies injectivity since $\langle \mathbf{y}_{i_1}^{(0)}, \mathsf{id}_{i_1} \rangle \neq 0$ for each $i_1 \in \{1, \ldots, \ell\}$. In the partially lossy mode, a suitable choice of $\mathbf{y}^{(1)}$ ensures that $\langle \mathbf{y}_{i_1}, \mathsf{id}_{i_1} \rangle = 0$ for each $i_1 \in \{1, \ldots, \ell\}$ with non-negligible probability, which leads to high non-injectivity: from (8), we see that (9) only consists of valid HIBE ciphertexts, so that the inversion algorithm always outputs 0^n.

In the full version of the paper [16], we prove that, under the $\mathcal{P}$-BDH$_1$ and DDH$_2$ assumptions, the scheme provides selective security and adaptive security (for a constant number of levels) for appropriate choices of the auxiliary input.

References

1. Anderson, R.: Two Remarks on Public Key Cryptology. Invited lecture. In: ACM Conference on Computer and Communications Security (1997)
2. Bellare, M., Boldyreva, A., O'Neill, A.: Deterministic and Efficiently Searchable Encryption. In: Menezes, A. (ed.) CRYPTO 2007. LNCS, vol. 4622, pp. 535–552. Springer, Heidelberg (2007)
3. Bellare, M., Brakerski, Z., Naor, M., Ristenpart, T., Segev, G., Shacham, H., Yilek, S.: Hedged Public-Key Encryption: How to Protect against Bad Randomness. In: Matsui, M. (ed.) ASIACRYPT 2009. LNCS, vol. 5912, pp. 232–249. Springer, Heidelberg (2009)
4. Bellare, M., Hofheinz, D., Yilek, S.: Possibility and Impossibility Results for Encryption and Commitment Secure under Selective Opening. In: Joux, A. (ed.) EUROCRYPT 2009. LNCS, vol. 5479, pp. 1–35. Springer, Heidelberg (2009)
5. Bellare, M., Kiltz, E., Peikert, C., Waters, B.: Identity-Based (Lossy) Trapdoor Functions and Applications. In: Pointcheval, D., Johansson, T. (eds.) EUROCRYPT 2012. LNCS, vol. 7237, pp. 228–245. Springer, Heidelberg (2012)
6. Boldyreva, A., Fehr, S., O'Neill, A.: On Notions of Security for Deterministic Encryption, and Efficient Constructions without Random Oracles. In: Wagner, D. (ed.) CRYPTO 2008. LNCS, vol. 5157, pp. 335–359. Springer, Heidelberg (2008)
7. Boneh, D., Boyen, X.: Efficient Selective-ID Secure Identity-Based Encryption Without Random. In: Cachin, C., Camenisch, J.L. (eds.) EUROCRYPT 2004. LNCS, vol. 3027, pp. 223–238. Springer, Heidelberg (2004)
8. Boneh, D., Waters, B.: Conjunctive, Subset, and Range Queries on Encrypted Data. In: Vadhan, S.P. (ed.) TCC 2007. LNCS, vol. 4392, pp. 535–554. Springer, Heidelberg (2007)
9. Boyen, X., Waters, B.: Anonymous Hierarchical Identity-Based Encryption (Without Random Oracles). In: Dwork, C. (ed.) CRYPTO 2006. LNCS, vol. 4117, pp. 290–307. Springer, Heidelberg (2006)
10. Boyen, X., Waters, B.: Shrinking the Keys of Discrete-Log-Type Lossy Trapdoor Functions. In: Zhou, J., Yung, M. (eds.) ACNS 2010. LNCS, vol. 6123, pp. 35–52. Springer, Heidelberg (2010)
11. Canetti, R., Halevi, S., Katz, J.: A Forward-Secure Public-Key Encryption Scheme. In: Biham, E. (ed.) EUROCRYPT 2003. LNCS, vol. 2656, pp. 255–271. Springer, Heidelberg (2003)
12. Canetti, R., Halevi, S., Katz, J.: Chosen-Ciphertext Security from Identity-Based Encryption. In: Cachin, C., Camenisch, J.L. (eds.) EUROCRYPT 2004. LNCS, vol. 3027, pp. 207–222. Springer, Heidelberg (2004)
13. Cash, D., Hofheinz, D., Kiltz, E., Peikert, C.: Bonsai Trees, or How to Delegate a Lattice Basis. In: Gilbert, H. (ed.) EUROCRYPT 2010. LNCS, vol. 6110, pp. 523–552. Springer, Heidelberg (2010)

14. Dodis, Y., Reyzin, L., Smith, A.: Fuzzy Extractors: How to Generate Strong Keys from Biometrics and Other Noisy Data. In: Cachin, C., Camenisch, J.L. (eds.) EUROCRYPT 2004. LNCS, vol. 3027, pp. 523–540. Springer, Heidelberg (2004)
15. Ducas, L.: Anonymity from Asymmetry: New Constructions for Anonymous HIBE. In: Pieprzyk, J. (ed.) CT-RSA 2010. LNCS, vol. 5985, pp. 148–164. Springer, Heidelberg (2010)
16. Escala, A., Herranz, J., Libert, B., Ràfols, C.: Identity-Based Lossy Trapdoor Functions: New Definitions, Hierarchical Extensions, and Implications. Cryptology ePrint Archive: Report 2012/503 (2012)
17. Freeman, D.M., Goldreich, O., Kiltz, E., Rosen, A., Segev, G.: More Constructions of Lossy and Correlation-Secure Trapdoor Functions. In: Nguyen, P.Q., Pointcheval, D. (eds.) PKC 2010. LNCS, vol. 6056, pp. 279–295. Springer, Heidelberg (2010)
18. Gentry, C., Silverberg, A.: Hierarchical ID-Based Cryptography. In: Zheng, Y. (ed.) ASIACRYPT 2002. LNCS, vol. 2501, pp. 548–566. Springer, Heidelberg (2002)
19. Goyal, V., Pandey, O., Sahai, A., Waters, B.: Attribute-Based Encryption for Fine-Grained Access Control of Encrypted Data. In: ACM CCS 2006 (2006)
20. Håstad, J., Impagliazzo, R., Levin, L., Luby, M.: A Pseudorandom Generator from any One-Way Function. SIAM Journal on Computing 28(4) (1999)
21. Hemenway, B., Ostrovsky, R.: Lossy Trapdoor Functions from Smooth Homomorphic Hash Proof Systems. Electronic Colloquium on Computational Complexity (ECCC) 16, 127 (2009)
22. Hofheinz, D.: All-But-Many Lossy Trapdoor Functions. In: Pointcheval, D., Johansson, T. (eds.) EUROCRYPT 2012. LNCS, vol. 7237, pp. 209–227. Springer, Heidelberg (2012)
23. Katz, J., Sahai, A., Waters, B.: Predicate Encryption Supporting Disjunctions, Polynomial Equations, and Inner Products. In: Smart, N.P. (ed.) EUROCRYPT 2008. LNCS, vol. 4965, pp. 146–162. Springer, Heidelberg (2008)
24. Okamoto, T., Takashima, K.: Hierarchical Predicate Encryption for Inner-Products. In: Matsui, M. (ed.) ASIACRYPT 2009. LNCS, vol. 5912, pp. 214–231. Springer, Heidelberg (2009)
25. Peikert, C., Waters, B.: Lossy Trapdoor Functions and their Applications. In: STOC 2008. ACM Press (2008)
26. Sahai, A., Waters, B.: Fuzzy Identity-Based Encryption. In: Cramer, R. (ed.) EUROCRYPT 2005. LNCS, vol. 3494, pp. 457–473. Springer, Heidelberg (2005)
27. Shi, E., Waters, B.: Delegating Capabilities in Predicate Encryption Systems. In: Aceto, L., Damgård, I., Goldberg, L.A., Halldórsson, M.M., Ingólfsdóttir, A., Walukiewicz, I. (eds.) ICALP 2008, Part II. LNCS, vol. 5126, pp. 560–578. Springer, Heidelberg (2008)
28. Shamir, A.: Identity-Based Cryptosystems and Signature Schemes. In: Blakely, G.R., Chaum, D. (eds.) CRYPTO 1984. LNCS, vol. 196, pp. 47–53. Springer, Heidelberg (1985)
29. Waters, B.: Efficient Identity-Based Encryption Without Random Oracles. In: Cramer, R. (ed.) EUROCRYPT 2005. LNCS, vol. 3494, pp. 114–127. Springer, Heidelberg (2005)
30. Wee, H.: Dual Projective Hashing and Its Applications — Lossy Trapdoor Functions and More. In: Pointcheval, D., Johansson, T. (eds.) EUROCRYPT 2012. LNCS, vol. 7237, pp. 246–262. Springer, Heidelberg (2012)
31. Xie, X., Xue, R., Zhang, R.: Deterministic Public Key Encryption and Identity-Based Encryption from Lattices in the Auxiliary-Input Setting. In: Visconti, I., De Prisco, R. (eds.) SCN 2012. LNCS, vol. 7485, pp. 1–18. Springer, Heidelberg (2012)

Bounded-Collusion Identity-Based Encryption from Semantically-Secure Public-Key Encryption: Generic Constructions with Short Ciphertexts

Stefano Tessaro[1],* and David A. Wilson[2]

[1] University of California, Santa Barbara
[2] MIT

Abstract. To circumvent the lack of generic constructions of identity-based encryption (IBE), Dodis *et al.* (EUROCRYPT '02) introduced the notion of *bounded-collusion IBE* (BC-IBE), where attackers only learn secret keys of an a-priori bounded number t of identities. They provided a *generic* BC-IBE construction from any semantically-secure encryption scheme which, however, suffers from a $\omega(t)$ blow-up in ciphertext size. Goldwasser *et al.* (TCC 2012) recently presented a generic construction with no ciphertext-length blow-up. Their construction requires an underlying public-key scheme with a key homomorphism, as well as a hash-proof-style security definition that is strictly stronger than semantic security. This latter requirement in particular reduces the applicability of their construction to existing schemes.

In this paper, we present the *first* generic constructions of BC-IBE from *semantically-secure* encryption schemes with no ciphertext-length blow-up. Our constructions require different degrees of key-homomorphism and malleability properties that are usually easy to verify. We provide concrete instantiations based on the DDH, QR, NTRU, and LWE assumptions. For all of these assumptions, our schemes present the smallest BC-IBE ciphertext size known to date. Our NTRU-based construction is particularly interesting, due to the lack of NTRU-based IBE constructions as well as the fact that it supports fully-homomorphic evaluation.

Our results also yield new constructions of bounded CCA-secure cryptosystems.

1 Introduction

PUBLIC-KEY ENCRYPTION. One of the classic and best-studied models of secure communication is that of *public-key encryption (PKE)* [12], in which each individual independently generates a *public key / secret key* pair. Anyone possessing the public key can encrypt a message such that only the individual with the associated secret key can decrypt. To date, there are innumerable PKE constructions proven secure based on a wide variety of hardness assumptions.

---

* Research done while the author was with MIT CSAIL.

H. Krawczyk (Ed.): PKC 2014, LNCS 8383, pp. 257–274, 2014.

However, the basic public-key model lacks a well-developed structure for public key verification. One can encrypt messages using a public key, but the model implies a trust that the public key belongs to a specific individual, unless an expensive public-key infrastructure is in place. In order to make explicit these assumptions and avoid potential difficulties with key distribution, cryptographers have explored other models of encryption.

IDENTITY-BASED ENCRYPTION. The identity-based encryption (IBE) model, introduced by Shamir in 1984 [30], attempts to alleviate the above concerns. In this model, a trusted center generates a master secret key and public parameters for the entire system. Anyone can encrypt a message to any user of the system using only these global public parameters and the user's *identity*. To decrypt, a user must obtain the secret key for their identity from the trusted center (who presumably authenticates the user before distributing the key).

The security model for IBE assumes that the adversary can adaptively obtain an arbitrary number of secret keys for users in the system, and requires that messages encrypted to any other user still be indistinguishable to the adversary. This models the idea that an individual's messages are still secure even if an arbitrary number of other users of the system collude against that user.

The first constructions of IBE came in 2001, by Boneh and Franklin [5] and Cocks [9]. Both of these constructions assumed the existence of random oracles; however, subsequent work by Boneh and Boyen [3] and Waters [32] achieved IBE in the standard model. There now exist a number of IBE constructions in both the random oracle and standard models, under hardness assumptions of problems in bilinear groups (e.g. [5,7,3,32]), various forms of the Quadric Residuosity (QR) problem (e.g. [9,6]), and the Learning With Errors problem (e.g. [20,8,1]). Some of these, and in particular all those based on the standard QR problem, additionally require random oracles. *However, no constructions of IBE are known from generic primitives.*

BOUNDED-COLLUSION IBEs. As an attempt to come up with constructions under a wider range of assumptions, cryptographers began looking at a variant of IBE known as *Bounded-Collusion IBE* (BC-IBE). In this model, one only guarantees security against an adversary who obtains secret keys associated with at most t identities, where the size of the parameters of the system are allowed to depend on t. Falling short of achieving full security, the bounded-collusion model can be a realistic assumption in many settings, and is in fact a necessary restriction to achieve the more general notion of functional encryption [24]. Additionally, it has been studied in other settings, notably broadcast encryption and revocation (e.g. [17,18,19,27,29,25,13]).

The first construction of BC-IBE came in the context of key-insulated systems in [15]. This paper gave a general reduction from any semantically secure public-key cryptosystem to a BC-IBE scheme. However, their construction suffers from a large ciphertext-size blowup – the resulting ciphertext length is a factor $\omega(t)$ larger than that of the underlying encryption scheme. To mitigate this, this work was recently followed by that of Goldwasser *et al.* [22]: They provide a new construction that relies on a public-key encryption scheme which exhibits *key-homomorphic* properties, i.e., secret keys and public keys are elements of respective groups (with possibly different operations, which we denote by $+$ and $\cdot$), and there exists a homomorphism μ such that $\mu(\mathsf{sk} + \mathsf{sk}') = \mu(\mathsf{sk}) + \mu(\mathsf{sk}')$, where $\mu(\mathsf{sk})$ and $\mu(\mathsf{sk}')$ are valid public keys for which sk and sk' yield correct decryption, respectively. More concretely, the *GLW construction* generates multiple public-key / secret-key pairs $(\mathsf{pk}_1, \mathsf{sk}_1), \ldots, (\mathsf{pk}_n, \mathsf{sk}_n)$, letting the public parameters and the master secret key of the scheme be $\mathsf{pp} = (\mathsf{pk}_1, \ldots \mathsf{pk}_n)$ and $\mathsf{msk} = (\mathsf{sk}_1, \ldots, \mathsf{sk}_n)$, respectively. Then, an efficient map ϕ associates every identity ID with a vector $[id_1, \ldots, id_n]$, and a message m is encrypted for an identity ID as the ciphertext $c = \mathsf{Enc}(\mathsf{pk}_{\mathrm{ID}}, m)$, where $\mathsf{pk}_{\mathrm{ID}} = \prod_{i=1}^n \mathsf{pk}_i^{id_i}$. By the existence of μ, this ciphertext can be decrypted using $\mathsf{sk}_{\mathrm{ID}} = \sum_{i=1}^n id_i \cdot \mathsf{sk}_i$, since the homomorphism guarantees that $\mathsf{pk}_{\mathrm{ID}} = \mu(\mathsf{sk}_{\mathrm{ID}})$. The map ϕ is subjected to a combinatorial requirement that disallows computing $\mathsf{sk}_{\mathrm{ID}}$ given $\mathsf{sk}_{\mathrm{ID}'}$ for t different $\mathrm{ID}' \neq \mathrm{ID}$. The GLW construction *preserves* the ciphertext size of the underlying encryption, but its security requires the latter to satisfy a property which is *strictly* stronger than semantic security. This property is inspired by the security of hash-proof systems [11], and in particular does not allow the homomorphism μ to be one-to-one. This somewhat hinders the applicability of their framework to existing encryptions schemes not designed with this security goal in mind.

OUR CONTRIBUTIONS. In this paper, we seek for generic constructions of BC-IBE which rely on encryption schemes that solely satisfy the *standard* security notion of semantic security in addition to some syntactical, non-security-related, properties which can be easily verified. Our constructions have the added benefit of conceptual simplicity, and the resulting instantiations from concrete assumptions either outperform or abstract existing BC-IBE constructions along different axes.

In summary, this paper makes three main contributions:

1. As our first contribution, we revisit the GLW approach in the context of *selective* security. The latter security notion only demands security for attackers attempting to break the confidentiality of messages encrypted for an *a-priori specified identity* (in particular, independently of the parameters of the scheme). We prove that the GLW approach is *selectively* secure for every *semantically secure* encryption scheme with key-homomorphic properties whenever ϕ satisfies a slightly stronger property that the one used in [22], namely that of cover-freeness introduced in [16] and used in several other works (e.g. [27,10,14], and others). While being strictly weaker than the notion of full security, selective security is sufficient for some applications, as discussed below.

2. Whenever the underlying semantically-secure scheme satisfies an additional new property – which we call *weak multi-key malleability* – we prove that the GLW construction achieves *full* BC-IBE security, i.e., confidentiality holds even with respect an identity chosen adaptively after learning the parameters of the schemes as well as secret keys for at most t other identities.

Roughly, our malleability property states that given the encryption of $c = \mathsf{Enc}(\mathsf{pk}, m)$ of an *unknown* message m under a known public key pk, and given an additional public-key / secret-key pair $(\mathsf{pk}', \mathsf{sk}')$, we can efficiently produce a ciphertext which is indistinguishable from an encryption of m under $\mathsf{pk} \cdot \mathsf{pk}'$. An example scheme with this property is ElGamal encryption – hence we directly obtain a DDH-based BC-IBE scheme from ElGamal encryption.

3. As our third contribution, we provide a new, alternative construction that relies on a different form of malleability (which we simply call multi-key malleability), and does not require any explicit key-homomorphic structure. Intuitively, our notion requires that given $c = \mathsf{Enc}(\mathsf{pk}, m)$ for an unknown message m, and another public key pk', we can obtain a new ciphertext c which decrypts to m under a combination of the secret keys sk and sk' associated with pk and pk'. We provide an efficient instantiation based on NTRU [26], exploiting it multi-key homomorphic properties recently observed by Lopez-Alt et al. [28]. This is of particular interest due to the fact that no fully-secure NTRU-based IBE scheme is known to date. Moreover, our constructions support homomorphic evaluation of ciphertexts, and this is the only construction of identity-based fully homomorphic encryption beyond the recent result by Gentry, Sahai, and Waters [21].

To conclude, we stress that our instantiation of the GLW approach is somewhat orthogonal to the one by Goldwasser et al.: Our instantiation requires indeed somewhat *larger* public-parameters at the cost of a weaker assumption on the underlying encryption scheme, hence leading to wider applicability and often smaller ciphertexts. Nonetheless, we believe that large ciphertexts are generally a more limiting factor than large parameters, especially in settings where many messages are encrypted with the same parameters.

A summary of our instantiations and their parameters is given in Table 1 comparing them to previously known best constructions. For LWE and NTRU, the best previously known construction was obtained by using the construction of [15]. We also provide a construction based on QR which does not outperform the one of [22], even though we find it conceptually simpler.

FROM IBE TO CCA-SECURITY. A somewhat related problem is that of building bounded-CCA secure public-key encryption [10]: Concretely, for t-bounded CCA security, semantic security must hold also for attackers which can decrypt up to t ciphertexts other than the challenge ciphertext for which we attempt to break confidentiality. We note that by re-interpreting a result of Boneh et al. [4], every construction of a BC-IBE scheme *selectively* secure against t-collusions directly yields a t-bounded CCA secure PKE. Hence, our BC-IBE constructions also directly yield better bounded-CCA-secure constructions, in terms of ciphertext size and/or conceptual simplicity. When applying our framework to ElGamal, for example, we obtain a construction which is equivalent to the one proposed in [10], for which a direct security proof was given. Moreover, our instantiation from NTRU is indeed more efficient than the best fully CCA-secure construction from NTRU given by Steinfeld et al. [31].

Table 1. Comparison with previous works on BC-IBE. Here t is the collusion parameter and $|\mathcal{ID}|$ is the total number of identities in the system. PK and ciphertext size implicitly include the security parameter. The upper section of the table considers generic constructions, whereas the lower section describes existing constructions from concrete assumptions. Note that linear hash proof property implies semantic security, while being strictly stronger than it.

Construction	Assumptions	Ciphertext size	PK size
DKXY02 [15]	Semantically secure PKE	$\Theta(t \log|\mathcal{ID}|)$ PKE ciphertexts	$\Theta(t^2 \log|\mathcal{ID}|)$ PKE PKs
GLW12 [22]	PKE w/linear hash proof and key homomorphism	Same as underlying PKE	$\Theta(t \log|\mathcal{ID}|)$ PKE PKs
This work	Semantic-secure PKE; key homomorphism, weak multi-key malleability	Same as underlying PKE	$\Theta(t^2 \log|\mathcal{ID}|)$ PKE PKs
This work	Semantic-secure PKE; multi-key malleability	Same as underlying PKE	$\Theta(t^2 \log|\mathcal{ID}|)$ PKE PKs
DKXY02 [15]	DDH	3 group elements	$\Theta(t)$ group elements
GLW12 [22]	DDH	3 group elements	$\Theta(t \log|\mathcal{ID}|)$ group elts
This work	DDH	2 group elements	$\Theta(t^2 \log|\mathcal{ID}|)$ group elts
GLW12 [22]	QR	2 RSA group elements	$\Theta(t \log|\mathcal{ID}|)$ group elts
This work	LWE	Same as GPV [20]	$\Theta(t^2 \log|\mathcal{ID}|)$ GPV PKs
This work	NTRU	Same as NTRU-Encrypt [26]	$\Theta(t^2 \log|\mathcal{ID}|)$ NTRU PKs

2 Preliminaries

2.1 Public-Key Encryption

PKE SYNTAX. As usual, a *public-key encryption (PKE) scheme* is a triple of efficient algorithms PKE $=$ (Gen, Enc, Dec) where:

- Gen is the (randomized) *key generation algorithm*: it takes no input (other than the security parameter 1^k , which is implicit and generally omitted), and outputs a public-key / secret-key pair (pk, sk).
- Enc and Dec are the (randomized) *encryption* and the (deterministic) *decryption* algorithms, such that for all valid public-key / secret-key pairs (pk, sk) output by Gen, and all messages m, the probability $\mathsf{P}[\mathsf{Dec}(sk, \mathsf{Enc}(\mathsf{pk}, m)) \neq m]$ is negligible, where the probability is taken over the random coins of the encryption algorithm Enc.

Often, we allow public-key encryption schemes to additionally depend on explicit *public parameters* pp (randomly generated in an initial phase and shared across multiple instances of the PKE scheme) on which all of Gen, Enc, and Dec are allowed to depend. Examples include the description of a group G with its generator g. We will often omit them in the descriptions of generic constructions from PKE schemes.

SECURITY OF PKE. We define *security against chosen-plaintext attacks* (for short, *IND-CPA security*) [23,2] for a PKE scheme PKE = (Gen, Enc, Dec) via a security game involving an adversary $\mathcal{A}$ which is initially given the public key pk, and subsequently outputs a pair of equal-length messages m_0, m_1. The adversary continues after receiving a *challenge ciphertext* $c^* \xleftarrow{\$} \mathsf{Enc}(\mathsf{pk}, m_b)$ for a random secret bit b, and then finally outputs a guess b' for b. We say that PKE is (τ, ε)-*ind-cpa-secure* if all attackers $\mathcal{A}$ with time complexity at most τ guess the right bit (i.e., $b' = b$) with probability at most $\frac{1+\varepsilon}{2}$. Moreover, it is simply *ind-cpa secure* if for all polynomials p, there exists a negligible function ν such that the scheme is $(p(k), \nu(k))$-ind-cpa-secure for all values of the security parameter k. We also consider *security against chosen ciphertext attacks* (for short, *IND-CCA security*), where the adversary is additionally able to decrypt ciphertexts under the constraint that a decryption query for the challenge ciphertext is never asked. We say that PKE is (τ, t, ε)-ind-cca-secure if any attacker with time complexity τ and making at most t decryption queries guesses b with probability at most $\frac{1+\varepsilon}{2}$. The asymptotic notion of *t-ind-cca-secure* is defined accordingly.

2.2   Identity-Based Encryption

Recall that an *identity-based encryption (IBE)* scheme for identity set $\mathcal{ID}$ is a 4-tuple of algorithms IBE = (IBEGen, IBEExtract, IBEEnc, IBEDec) satisfying the following syntactical properties:

- IBEGen is the randomized *parameter generator algorithm* which returns a pair (msk, pp), where msk is the so-called *master secret key*, and pp are the *public parameters*.
- The *extraction algorithm* IBEExtract, on input the master secret-key msk and a valid identity ID $\in \mathcal{ID}$ returns a secret key $\mathsf{sk}_{\mathrm{ID}} \xleftarrow{\$} \mathsf{IBEExtract}(\mathsf{msk}, \mathrm{ID})$ associated with this identity.
- The encryption algorithm IBEEnc takes as inputs the public parameters pp, an identity ID $\in \mathcal{ID}$, and a message m, and returns a ciphertext $c \xleftarrow{\$} \mathsf{IBEEnc}(\mathsf{pp}, \mathrm{ID}, m)$ such that for the associated deterministic algorithm IBEDec, $\mathsf{IBEDec}(\mathsf{sk}_{\mathrm{ID}}, \mathsf{IBEEnc}(\mathsf{pp}, \mathrm{ID}, m)) = m$ with overwhelming probability for each (pp, msk) output by Gen and sk_{ID} output by IBEExtract(msk, ID).

The notion of IND-CPA security is extended to the setting of IBE. The adversary, given the public parameters pp, can obtain keys $\mathsf{sk}_{\mathrm{ID}}$ for identities ID of its choice (via so-called *extraction queries*), and outputs at some point a pair of equal-length challenge messages m_0, m_1, together with a *challenge identity* ID^* for which no extraction query has been issued. It then obtains an encryption of m_b for the challenge identity ID^* and for a random bit b. The adversary is asked to guess b, constrained on not asking a key extraction query for ID^*. We also consider a weaker security notion, called *selective IND-CPA security*:

Here, the adversary is required to choose its challenge identity *beforehand*, and only subsequently learns the public parameters and is given access to the IBEExtract oracle.

In analogy to the case of conventional PKE, we say that IBE is (τ, t, ε)-cpa-secure if all τ-time adversaries $\mathcal{A}$ making t extraction queries output b with probability at most $\frac{1+\varepsilon}{2}$ in the CPA-security game above. Similarly, we define (τ, t, ε)-selective-cpa-secure likewise for the selective-CPA game above, as well as the asymptotic notions of t-cpa and t-selective-cpa security.

3 Revisiting the GLW Construction

In the first part of this paper, we revisit the IBE construction for bounded-collusion security proposed by Goldwasser, Lewko, and Wilson [22] – henceforth, we refer to this construction as the *GLW construction*. We show two generic results, the first one for selective security and the second one for full IBE security. Then, we discuss a new instantiation of this paradigm based on DDH. Two more instantiations based on the LWE and QR assumptions are deferred to the full version for lack of space.

3.1 The GLW Construction

SECRET-KEY TO PUBLIC-KEY HOMOMORPHISMS. Throughout this section, we (tacitly) consider only public-key cryptosystems PKE = (Gen, Enc, Dec) with the property that secret and public keys are elements of groups G and H, respectively. For convenience and ease of distinction, we will denote the group operations on G and H as $+$ and $\cdot$, respectively.

Definition 1 (Secret-key to public-key homomorphism). *We say that* PKE *admits a* secret-key to public-key homomorphism *if there exists a map* $\mu : G \rightarrow H$ *such that:*

(i) μ *is a homomorphism, i.e., for all* sk, sk$' \in G$, *we have* $\mu(\text{sk} + \text{sk}') = \mu(\text{sk}) \cdot \mu(\text{sk}')$;

(ii) *Every output* (sk, pk) *of* Gen *satisfies* pk $= \mu(\text{sk})$.

We stress that we are *not* requiring that every element sk $\in G$ is a valid secret key output by Gen. This will be important in our LWE instantiation below. In this case, we still want to make sure that decryption is correct: In particular, we say below that μ *satisfies n-correctness* if for any $n' \leq n$ valid secret keys sk$_1, \ldots,$ sk$_{n'}$ output by Gen, the probability P[Dec(sk, Enc(μ(sk), m)) $\neq m$] is negligible for all messages m, where the probability is over the coins of Enc and where sk $=$ sk$_1 + \cdots +$ sk$_{n'}$. (This property is implicitly satisfied for all n if all elements of G are valid secret keys.)

Also note that the map μ does *not* need to be efficiently computable for our applications, even though the map is often very efficient. Additionally, we observe that in case the scheme depends on some explicit public parameter (like a generator or a matrix, as will be the case in our examples below), μ is indeed allowed to be parameter-dependent.

THE GLW CONSTRUCTION. Goldwasser, Lewko, and Wilson [22] presented a generic approach to build a bounded-collusion secure IBE from a public-key encryption scheme admitting a secret-key to public-key homomorphism. Specifically, let $\mathsf{PKE} = (\mathsf{Gen}, \mathsf{Enc}, \mathsf{Dec})$ be such a public-key encryption scheme with homomorphism $\mu : G \to H$ satisfying n-correctness, and let $\phi : \mathcal{ID} \to \{0,1\}^n$ be a polynomial-time computable function, called the *identity map*. (With a slight abuse of notation, it will be convenient to consider the output ϕ as a subset of $\{1, \ldots, n\}$, encoded in the canonical way as an n-bit string.) Then, the GLW construction for PKE and ϕ gives rise to the following IBE scheme $\mathsf{IBE} = (\mathsf{IBEGen}, \mathsf{IBEExtract}, \mathsf{IBEEnc}, \mathsf{IBEDec})$ with identities from the set $\mathcal{ID}$ defined as follows (where additionally $\mathsf{IBEDec}(\mathsf{sk}_{\mathrm{ID}}, c) = \mathsf{Dec}(\mathsf{sk}_{\mathrm{ID}}, c)$)

IBEGen:	IBEExtract($\mathbf{sk}$, ID):	IBEEnc($\mathbf{pk}$, ID, m):
$(\mathbf{pk}, \mathbf{sk}) \xleftarrow{\$} \mathsf{Gen}^n$	$\mathsf{sk}_{\mathrm{ID}} = \sum_{i \in \phi(\mathrm{ID})} \mathbf{sk}[i]$	$\mathsf{pk}_{\mathrm{ID}} = \prod_{i \in \phi(\mathrm{ID})} \mathbf{pk}[i]$
$\mathsf{msk} \leftarrow \mathbf{sk}$	Return $\mathsf{sk}_{\mathrm{ID}}$	$c \xleftarrow{\$} \mathsf{Enc}(\mathsf{pk}_{\mathrm{ID}}, m)$
$\mathsf{pp} \leftarrow \mathbf{pk}$		Return c
Return $(\mathsf{msk}, \mathsf{pp})$		

The notation $(\mathbf{pk}, \mathbf{sk}) \xleftarrow{\$} \mathsf{Gen}^n$ denotes running Gen n times, with independent random coins, and $\mathbf{pk}, \mathbf{sk}$ are vectors such that $(\mathbf{pk}[i], \mathbf{sk}[i])$ is the output of the i-th execution of Gen. First note that correctness of IBE follows trivially from the correctness of PKE and the existence of a secret-key to public-key homomorphism μ with n-correctness, since $\mathsf{pk}_{\mathrm{ID}} = \mu(\mathsf{sk}_{\mathrm{ID}})$ holds for all IDs and $\mathsf{sk}_{\mathrm{ID}}$ is the sum of at most n valid secret keys. We stress that a central advantage of the above construction is that IBE ciphertexts are ciphertexts of the underlying encryption scheme PKE. Also, note that if PKE relies on some public parameters, these are generated once and used across all uses of Gen, Enc, and Dec.

INSTANTIATING THE IDENTITY MAP. We still need to discuss how the map ϕ is instantiated. In all constructions of this paper, we rely on constructions based on *cover-free sets*, following previous work on bounded-collusion IBE [15], bounded-CCA security [10], and bounded security for FDH signatures [14]. Concretely, let $2^{[n]}$ be the set of subsets of $[n] := \{1, \ldots, n\}$.

Definition 2 (Cover-free sets). *We say that $\phi : \mathcal{ID} \to 2^{[n]}$ is (t, s)-cover free if $|\phi(x)| = s$ for all $x \in \mathcal{ID}$, and moreover $\phi(x_t) \setminus \bigcup_{i=1}^{t-1} \phi(x_i) \neq \emptyset$ for all $x_1, \ldots, x_t \in \mathcal{ID}$, i.e., the set $\phi(x_t)$ is not covered by the union of $\phi(x_1), \ldots, \phi(x_{t-1})$.*

In general, we will equivalently think of ϕ as a map $\mathcal{ID} \to \{0,1\}^n$, where we output the characteristic vector of the associated set, instead of the set itself. The following gives the currently best-known construction of cover-free sets.

Theorem 1 ([10]). *For all integers $t \geq 1$, there exists a polynomial-time computable (t, s)-cover-free map $\phi : \mathcal{ID} \to \{0,1\}^n$, where $n = 16t^2 \log |\mathcal{ID}|$ and $s = 4t \log |\mathcal{ID}|$.*

We note that Goldwasser, Lewko, and Wilson used a weaker requirement of ϕ that only requires linear independence of the vectors $\phi(x_1), \ldots, \phi(x_t)$. In this case, the output length n can be reduced to $O(t \log |\mathcal{ID}|)$, or even $O(t)$ if we allow both identities as well as components of $\phi(x)$ to be elements of $\mathbb{Z}_p$ for some large prime p. However, the price they pay compared to our results below is that the underlying encryption scheme is required to satisfy a harder to show notion than in our results given below assuming cover-freeness, and this is often reflected in instantiations with larger ciphertexts.

3.2   Selective Security of the GLW Construction

We start with selective security, which will be important to obtain bounded CCA-secure cryptosystems with short ciphertexts, as we explain below in Section 5. In the following, let PKE = (Gen, Enc, Dec) be an arbitrary public-key encryption scheme which admits secret-key to public-key homomorphism, and let IBE be the IBE scheme resulting from the above construction, using an underlying identity map ϕ.

Theorem 2 (Selective ID Security of GLW). *Assume that* PKE *is ind-cpa-secure, and that ϕ is $(t + 1, s)$-cover free. Then, the GLW construction is t-selective-cpa-secure.*

Proof. Let $\mathcal{A}$ be a selective-cpa adversary for IBE which outputs $b' = b$ with probability at least $(1 + n\varepsilon)/2$, and which makes at most t extraction queries. We construct an ind-cpa adversary $\mathcal{B}$ for PKE from $\mathcal{A}$, guessing the bit b with probability $\frac{1+\varepsilon}{2}$. Concretely, the adversary $\mathcal{B}$ first runs $\mathcal{A}$, obtaining the challenge identity ID^*, and chooses an index i^* uniformly at random from the set $S^* = \{i : \mathrm{id}_i^* = 1\}$, where $\phi(\mathrm{ID}^*) = [\mathrm{id}_1^*, \ldots, \mathrm{id}_n^*]$. It then gets a public key pk^* from the underlying CPA game, and computes $(\mathbf{pk}[j], \mathbf{sk}[j]) \xleftarrow{\$} \mathsf{Gen}$ for all $j \in [n] \setminus \{i^*\}$. Finally, it sets $\mathbf{pk}[i^*] = \mathsf{pk}^* \cdot \left(\prod_{j \neq i^*} \mathbf{pk}[j]^{-\mathrm{id}_j^*} \right)$.

The adversary $\mathcal{B}$ then gives $\mathsf{pp} = \mathbf{pk}$ to $\mathcal{A}$ and runs it until it outputs a pair (m_0, m_1). In particular, $\mathcal{A}$'s extraction queries for $\mathrm{ID} \neq \mathrm{ID}^* \in \mathcal{ID}$ are replied by computing $[\mathrm{id}_1, \ldots, \mathrm{id}_n] = \phi(\mathrm{ID})$ and, if $\mathrm{id}_{i^*} = 0$, returning $\mathsf{sk}_{\mathrm{ID}} := \sum_i \mathrm{id}_i \cdot \mathbf{sk}[i]$. Note that if $\mathrm{id}_{i^*} = 1$, then $\mathcal{B}$ cannot answer the extraction query, as it does not know any corresponding $\mathbf{sk}[i^*]$. In this case, it returns $\bot$, and sets a flag bad to true. When the adversary $\mathcal{A}$ outputs a pair (m_0, m_1) of messages of equal length, $\mathcal{B}$ forwards them to the CPA, obtaining a challenge ciphertext c^*, which it then gives back to $\mathcal{A}$, and its simulated execution is continued until it outputs a bit b'. To conclude, $\mathcal{B}$ outputs the bit b' if bad is not set to true, and returns a random bit otherwise. Note that we have $\mathsf{pk}_{\mathrm{ID}^*} = \mathsf{pk}^*$ by our definition.

Since ϕ is $(t + 1, s)$-cover-free, we know that there exists at least one i^* such that $\mathrm{id}_{i^*}^* = 1$, but $\mathrm{id}_{i^*} = 0$ for all vectors $\phi(\mathrm{ID})$ corresponding to the (at most t) extraction queries $\mathrm{ID} \neq \mathrm{ID}^*$. Intuitively, such an index i^* is hence chosen with probability at least $1/|S^*| = 1/s \geq 1/n$, and conditioned on this, the simulation is easily seen to be perfect. Formally, we let $\mathsf{Win}_{\mathsf{PKE}}$ and $\mathsf{Win}_{\mathsf{IBE}}$ be the events that $\mathcal{B}$ and $\mathcal{A}$ guess the bit in the respective security games. Then,

$$
\begin{aligned}
\mathsf{P}\left[\mathsf{Win}_{\mathsf{PKE}}\right] &= \mathsf{P}\left[\mathsf{Win}_{\mathsf{PKE}} \wedge \mathsf{bad} = \mathtt{false}\right] + \mathsf{P}\left[\mathsf{Win}_{\mathsf{PKE}} \wedge \mathsf{bad} = \mathtt{true}\right] \\
&\geq \mathsf{P}\left[\mathsf{bad} = \mathtt{false}\right] \cdot \mathsf{P}\left[\mathsf{Win}_{\mathsf{PKE}} \mid \mathsf{bad} = \mathtt{false}\right] \\
&\quad + \mathsf{P}\left[\mathsf{bad} = \mathtt{true}\right] \cdot \mathsf{P}\left[\mathsf{Win}_{\mathsf{PKE}} \mid \mathsf{bad} = \mathtt{true}\right] .
\end{aligned}
$$

Now, clearly, $\mathsf{P}\left[\mathsf{bad} = \mathtt{true}\right] = 1 - \mathsf{P}\left[\mathsf{bad} = \mathtt{false}\right]$, and $\mathsf{P}\left[\mathsf{Win}_{\mathsf{PKE}} \mid \mathsf{bad} = \mathtt{true}\right] \geq \frac{1}{2}$, since $\mathcal{B}$ outputs a random bit if bad is $\mathtt{true}$. Moreover, one can verify that $\mathsf{P}\left[\mathsf{bad} = \mathtt{false}\right] \geq \frac{1}{n}$, and, as the simulation is perfect, $\mathsf{P}\left[\mathsf{Win}_{\mathsf{PKE}} \mid \mathsf{bad} = \mathtt{false}\right] = \mathsf{P}\left[\mathsf{Win}_{\mathsf{IBE}}\right]$. Formalizing these last two argument actually requires some (standard) extra work, using the fact that all random coins are independent of the choice of i^*, but we dispense with the details in this version. Plugging in terms into the above concludes the proof.   □

3.3   Full Security of GLW

We note that the above proof strategy used in Theorem 2 fails when we do not know the challenge identity ID^* at the point in time when the reduction $\mathcal{B}$ sets the public parameters pp. However, an additional syntactic requirement on the underlying cryptosystem PKE yields full security, as we show below. This requirement is captured by the following definition.

Definition 3 (Weak Multi-Key Malleability). *We say that* PKE *is weakly n-key malleable if there exists an efficient algorithm* $\mathsf{Simulate}$ *such that for all messages m, all $I \subseteq [n]$, and all $i \in I$, the probability distributions D_0 and D_1 are computationally indistinguishable, where with $(\mathbf{pk}, \mathbf{sk}) \xleftarrow{\$} \mathsf{Gen}^n$, D_b consists of $(\mathbf{pk}, \mathbf{sk}[[n] \setminus \{i\}], c_b)$ such that*

(1) $c_0 \xleftarrow{\$} \mathsf{Enc}(\prod_{i \in I} \mathbf{pk}[i], m)$;
(2) $c \xleftarrow{\$} \mathsf{Enc}(\mathbf{pk}[i], m)$, $c_1 \xleftarrow{\$} \mathsf{Simulate}(i, I, c, \mathbf{pk}, \mathbf{sk}[[n] \setminus \{i\}])$.

In other words, given a ciphertext c encrypting with public key $\mathbf{pk}[i]$ (where i is part of some set I) an arbitrary *unknown* message m, we can efficiently generate a ciphertext c' encrypting the same message m under the *product* of the keys $\mathbf{pk}[j]$ for $j \in I$ without knowing the secret key $\mathbf{sk}[i]$, but still possibly using $\mathbf{sk}[j]$ for $j \neq i$. The resulting ciphertext has the right distribution in the eyes of a computationally bounded distinguisher.

The proof of the following theorem follows a similar approach to the one of Theorem 2, and is deferred to the full version.

Theorem 3 (Full Security of GLW). *Assume that* PKE *is ind-cpa-secure and weakly n-key malleable, and that ϕ is $(t+1, s)$-cover free. Then, the GLW construction is t-cpa-secure.*

3.4 Instantiation from DDH

We present a simple instantiation of the above paradigm based on the *Decisional Diffie-Hellman (DDH)* assumption and the ElGamal cryptosystem. The resulting scheme has smaller ciphertexts than earlier BC-IBE schemes [22,15], both requiring *three* group elements.

Concretely, let G be a group with prime order $|G| = q$ and generator g. Recall that the *ElGamal cryptosystem* has secret key $\mathsf{sk} \xleftarrow{\$} \mathbb{Z}_q$ and public key $\mathsf{pk} = g^{sk}$.

For a message $m \in G$, the encryption algorithm is $\mathsf{Enc}(\mathsf{pk}, m) = (g^r, m \cdot \mathsf{pk}^r)$, where $r \xleftarrow{\$} \mathbb{Z}_q$, whereas $\mathsf{Dec}(\mathsf{sk}, (c_1, c_2)) = c_2 \cdot c_1^{-\mathsf{sk}}$. ElGamal is easily shown to be ind-cpa-secure under the DDH assumption. Moreover, we observe the following two properties of the ElGamal cryptosystem:

1. ElGamal admits a secret-key to public-key homomorphism $\mu : \mathbb{Z}_q \to G$ where $\mu(x) = g^x$, and n-correctness is satisfied for any n.
2. Moreover, it satisfies (perfect) weak n-key malleability: Namely, just consider the algorithm that for all $I \subseteq [n]$, $i \in I$, and secret- and public-key vectors **sk** and **pk**, outputs

$$c^* = \mathsf{Simulate}(i, I, \mathbf{pk}, \mathbf{sk}[[n] \setminus \{i\}], (c_1, c_2)) = (c_1, c_2 \cdot c_1^{\sum_{j \neq i} \mathbf{sk}[j]}) . \qquad (1)$$

In particular, the resulting IBE scheme with identities $\mathcal{ID}$ obtained by plugging ElGamal into the GLW construction, for any $(t+1, s)$-cover-free map $\phi : \mathcal{ID} \to \{0,1\}^n$, is as follows, and Theorem 3 implies its t-ibe-cpa security under the DDH assumption. (The decryption algorithm remains the same as in the original ElGamal scheme.)

IBEGen:	IBEExtract(msk = sk, ID):	IBEEnc(pp = $(g, \mathbf{pk})$, ID, m):
$g \xleftarrow{\$} G$	$[\mathrm{id}_1, \dots, \mathrm{id}_n] \leftarrow \phi(\mathrm{ID})$	$[\mathrm{id}_1, \dots, \mathrm{id}_n] \leftarrow \phi(\mathrm{ID})$
$\mathbf{sk} \xleftarrow{\$} \mathbb{Z}_q^n$, $\mathbf{pk}[i] \leftarrow g^{\mathbf{sk}[i]}$	$\mathsf{sk}_{\mathrm{ID}} \leftarrow \sum_{i=1}^{n} \mathrm{id}_i \cdot \mathbf{sk}[i]$	$r \xleftarrow{\$} \mathbb{Z}_q$
$\mathsf{pp} \leftarrow (g, \mathbf{pk})$, $\mathsf{msk} \leftarrow \mathbf{sk}$	Return $\mathsf{sk}_{\mathrm{ID}}$	$c \leftarrow (g^r, m \cdot \prod_{i=1}^{n} \mathbf{pk}[i]^{r \cdot \mathrm{id}_i})$
Return $(\mathsf{pp}, \mathsf{msk})$		Return c

3.5 Instantiations from LWE and QR

We achieve an additional instantiation of the above paradigm starting from the GPV cryptosystem [20]. We thus achieve BC-IBE based on the *learning with errors (LWE)* assumption (with polynomial modulus for selective security and subexponential modulus for full semantic security).

Additionally, we achieve an instantiation under the *quadratic residuosity (QR)* assumption based on a simplified variant of the QR-based PKE scheme from [22]. We defer the details of both of these constructions to the full version.

4   Construction from Multi-key Malleability

4.1   Bounded-IBE Construction

We present a further construction of BC-IBE from PKE schemes which satisfy a different notion of key malleability than the one given above, which we first introduce. Our notion requires that given an encryption of a message under one public key, we are asking for the ability to produce a new ciphertext of the same message which decrypts under a combination of secret keys (e.g., the product) for which we only know the corresponding public keys. Note that we are only asking for decryptability under the combination of the secret keys. In particular, in contrast to the above notion of weak key-malleability, the distribution of the resulting ciphertext may not be a valid encryption under some well-defined combination of the corresponding public keys, and moreover, we require ability to compute this ciphertext without knowledge of any secret keys.

Definition 4 (Multi-Key Malleability). *Let* PKE *be a public-key encryption scheme. We say that* PKE *is* n-key *malleable if there exist algorithms* Modify *and* Combine *such that the following properties hold:*

(i) *For all valid messages* m, *all* $I \subseteq [n]$, *and all* $i \in I$, *the following probability is negligible (taken over the coins of* Enc*):*

$$P\left[\begin{array}{l} (\mathbf{pk}, \mathbf{sk}) \xleftarrow{\$} \mathsf{Gen}^n, c \xleftarrow{\$} \mathsf{Enc}(\mathbf{pk}[i], m), \\ c' \xleftarrow{\$} \mathsf{Modify}(i, I, \mathbf{pk}, c) \end{array} : \mathsf{Dec}(\mathsf{Combine}(I, \mathbf{sk}), c') \neq m \right].$$

(ii) *For all* $I \subseteq [n]$, Combine$(I, \mathbf{sk})$ *does not depend on* $\mathbf{sk}[i]$ *for* $i \notin I$.

(iii) *For all* $I \subseteq [n]$ *and all valid public-key / secret-key vectors* $(\mathbf{pk}, \mathbf{sk})$, *for all* $i, j \in I$, *the values* Modify$(i, I, \mathbf{pk}, \mathsf{Enc}(\mathbf{pk}[i], m))$ *and* Modify$(j, I, \mathbf{pk}, \mathsf{Enc}(\mathbf{pk}[j], m))$ *are equally distributed.*

We note that Property (iii) above is not really necessary (a computational relaxation would suffice), but will make the presentation somewhat simpler and is true in the only instantiation we give below.

THE IBE CONSTRUCTION AND ITS SECURITY. For an identity map $\phi : \mathcal{ID} \rightarrow \{0,1\}^n$, we now propose a construction of an identity-based encryption scheme IBE = (IBEGen, IBEExtract, IBEEnc, IBEDec) from an n-key malleable encryption scheme PKE = (Gen, Enc, Dec). The decryption algorithm is unaltered, i.e., IBEDec = Dec, and moreover the construction consists of the following algorithms. (Note that the choice of i as $\min\{\phi(\mathrm{ID})\}$ below within IBEEnc is purely arbitrary.)

IBEGen:	IBEExtract(msk = $\mathbf{sk}$, ID):	IBEEnc(pp = $\mathbf{pk}$, ID, m):
$(\mathbf{pk}, \mathbf{sk}) \xleftarrow{\$} \mathsf{Gen}^n$	$\mathrm{sk_{ID}} \leftarrow \mathsf{Combine}(\phi(\mathrm{ID}), \mathbf{sk})$	$i \leftarrow \min\{\phi(\mathrm{ID})\}$
msk $\leftarrow \mathbf{sk}$	Return $\mathrm{sk_{ID}}$	$c' \xleftarrow{\$} \mathsf{Enc}(\mathbf{pk}[i], m)$
pp $\leftarrow \mathbf{pk}$		$c \leftarrow \mathsf{Modify}(i, \phi(\mathrm{ID}), \mathbf{pk}, c')$
Return (msk, pp)		Return c

Correctness of the scheme follows by Property **(i)** above. The following theorem establishes security of our new construction. The proof is deferred to the full version.

Theorem 4. *Assume that* PKE *is ind-cpa-secure and n-key malleable, and that ϕ is $(t + 1, s)$-cover free. Then,* IBE *is t-ibe-cpa-secure.*

4.2 NTRU-Based Instantiation and Fully-Homomorphic IBE

We provide an instantiation of the above constructing using the multi-key homomorphic properties of NTRU-based public-key encryption [28], which we first review. For some parameters r, n and q (where q is a prime), consider the ring of polynomials $R = \mathbb{Z}[x]/(x^r + 1)$, and let χ be a B-bounded distribution on R, i.e., with overwhelming probability, χ samples a polynomial from R whose coefficients are all at most B in absolute value. All operations on polynomials are to be understood as over the ring $R_q = R/qR$. The NTRU cryptosystem is such that key generation Gen samples $f, g \xleftarrow{\$} \chi$ subject to the constraint that $f \equiv 1 \pmod 2$, and sets $\mathsf{pk} = 2g/f$ and $\mathsf{sk} = f$. (Possibly, f needs to be resampled until it admits an inverse in R_q, and χ is such that this happens with good probability.) The message $b \in \{0, 1\}$ is encrypted as

$$\mathsf{Enc}(\mathsf{pk}, m) = h \cdot \mathsf{pk} + 2e + b \,,$$

where $h, e \xleftarrow{\$} \chi$. Finally, decryption, given c, outputs $\mathsf{Dec}(\mathsf{sk}, c) = \mathsf{sk} \cdot c \pmod 2$. To see why decryption is correct, note that

$$\mathsf{sk} \cdot c \equiv f \cdot (2h \cdot g/f + 2e + b) \equiv 2h \cdot g + 2e \cdot f + f \cdot b \pmod q \,.$$

If $B \leq \sqrt{q/2}/r$, then all coefficients from $h \cdot g$ and $e \cdot f$ are of size at most $r^2 B^2 < q/2$. Consequently, $2hg$ and $2ef$ only have even coefficients, and are 0 modulo 2. And finally, $f \cdot b$ clearly always equals b modulo 2.

The scheme was proven ind-cpa-secure under a fairly ad-hoc assumption in [28], where it was also shown to have strong homomorphic properties we address below, and which we exploit for our construction.

THE IBE SCHEME. We turn now to building an IBE scheme from the above NTRU-based PKE scheme PKE using the above generic approach. In the following, we assume that r is our security parameter, $q = 2^{n^\varepsilon}$ for some constant $\varepsilon < 1$, $B = \mathsf{poly}(r)$, and $n = \Theta(r^\delta)$ for some constant $\delta < 1$.

We first show ℓ-key malleability exploiting the multi-key homomorphic properties of NTRU shown in [28]. To this end, we define the algorithm Combine which given $I \subseteq [\ell]$ and $\mathbf{sk} \in R_q^\ell$ outputs

$$\mathsf{Combine}(I, \mathbf{sk}) = \prod_{i \in I} \mathbf{sk}[i] \,.$$

Moreover, we also define the (randomized) function Modify, which given $I \subseteq [\ell]$, $i \in I$, $c \in R_q$, and $\mathbf{pk} \in R_q^\ell$, outputs

$$\mathsf{Modify}(i, I, c, \mathbf{pk}) = c + \sum_{j \in I \setminus \{i\}} h_j \cdot \mathbf{pk}[j] \,,$$

where h_j for $j \in I \setminus \{i\}$ are sampled independently from the B-bounded distribution χ as above. Now, Properties (ii) and (iii) in Definition 4 are immediate to verify. Moreover, for Property (i), fix $I \subseteq [\ell]$ and $i \in I$, and $\mathbf{pk}, \mathbf{sk} \in R_q^\ell$, each consisting of ℓ B-bounded polynomials as components, then define c as

$$c = \mathsf{Modify}(i, I, \mathsf{Enc}(\mathbf{pk}[i], b), \mathbf{pk}) = \sum_{j \in I} h_j \cdot \mathbf{pk}[j] + 2e + b ,$$

and observe that

$$\mathsf{Dec}(\mathsf{Combine}(I, \mathbf{sk}), c) = \left(\prod_{i \in I} \mathbf{sk}[i] \right) \cdot \left(\sum_{j \in I} h_j \cdot \mathbf{pk}[j] + 2e + b \right) \pmod 2 .$$

In particular,

$$\left(\prod_{i \in I} \mathbf{sk}[i] \right) \cdot \left(\sum_{j \in I} h_j \cdot \mathbf{pk}[j] + 2e + b \right) \equiv$$

$$\sum_{j \in I} 2 h_j \cdot g_j \cdot \prod_{i \in I \setminus \{j\}} f_\ell + \left(2e \cdot \prod_{i \in I} f_\ell \right) + b \cdot \left(\prod_{i \in I} f_\ell \right) .$$

Note that in the above sum, only products of at most $|I| + 1$ B-bounded polynomials occurs. The coefficients of the resulting products have size at most $r^{|I|} \cdot B^{|I|+1}$, which (given previous parameter choices) is smaller than $q/2$ as long as $|I| = o(n^\varepsilon)$. This yields correct decryption as no wraparound (modulo q) occurs.

THE FINAL SCHEME. Overall, this yields to the following scheme, for any identity mapping $\phi : \mathcal{ID} \to \{0,1\}^\ell$ which is $(s, t+1)$-cover-free for some $s = o(n^\varepsilon)$, which is t-ind-cpa secure by Theorem 4.

IBEGen:	IBEExtract(msk = sk, ID)	IBEEnc(pp = pk, ID, m):
$f_1, \ldots, f_n \xleftarrow{\$} \chi$	$\mathsf{sk}_{\mathrm{ID}} \leftarrow \prod_{i \in \phi(\mathrm{ID})} \mathbf{sk}[i]$	$h_1, \ldots, h_n, e \xleftarrow{\$} \chi$
$(f_i \equiv 1 \pmod 2), f_i \in R_q^*)$	Return $\mathsf{sk}_{\mathrm{ID}}$	$c \leftarrow \sum_{i \in \phi(\mathrm{ID})} \mathbf{pk}[i] \cdot h_i$
$g_1, \ldots, g_n \xleftarrow{\$} \chi$		$\qquad + 2e + m$
$\mathsf{msk} \leftarrow (f_1, \ldots, f_n)$		Return c
$\mathsf{pp} \xleftarrow{\$} (2g_1/f_1, \ldots 2g_n/f_n)$		
Return (msk, pp)		

FULLY-HOMOMORPHIC IBE. The above instantiation has additionally the property of being fully-homomorphic in the following sense:

Given encryptions $\mathsf{IBEEnc}(\mathrm{ID}, m_1), \ldots, \mathsf{IBEEnc}(\mathrm{ID}, m_t)$, and a function $f : \{0,1\}^t \to \{0,1\}$, we can compute a ciphertext which decrypts to $f(m_1, \ldots, m_t)$ under $\mathsf{sk}_{\mathrm{ID}}$ using the homomorphic-evaluation procedures given in [28].

We note that in general one can provide a construction, along the lines given above, from multi-key fully-homomorphic encryption to fully-homomorphic identity-based encryption for bounded collusions. We defer a full discussion to the full version of this paper, noting in passing that the above is the only instantiation of this paradigm we are aware of.

5   Applications: Bounded CCA Security with Short Ciphertexts

In this section, we revisit the generic transform by Boneh, Canetti, Halevi, and Katz [4] in the context of BC-IBE, and use it to obtain constructions of bounded-CCA2 secure encryption schemes with short ciphertexts from any semantically secure scheme with a secret-key to public-key homomorphism.

THE BCHK TRANSFORM . Boneh et al [4] present a construction of an encryption scheme PKE = (Gen, Enc, Dec) from a selectively-secure IBE scheme IBE = (IBEGen, IBEExtract, IBEEnc, IBEDec) and a strong one-time signature scheme SS = (Gen$_{SS}$, Sign, Verify). They then proceed to prove chosen-ciphertext security of the resulting PKE.

Of note is that in their reduction to the selective security of IBE, the reduction makes at most one IBEExtract query for each decryption query it receives from the adversary, and no other parameters change. Thus, their proof carries through exactly in the bounded-collusion case, yielding:

Theorem 5. *If* IBE *is t-selective-ibe-cpa-secure, and if* SS *is strongly one-time secure, then* PKE *is t-CCA secure.*

APPLICATIONS. Using previous results, we directly obtain bounded CCA PKE constructions from DDH, QR, NTRU, and (standard) LWE using the constructions of the previous sections. In particular, note that only standard LWE is required as we only need selective security to instantiate the above paradigm. Moreover, the resulting DDH construction is essentially equivalent to the one presented in [10], and our construction thus provides an abstraction to obtain the same construction.

As an example, we give the t-CCA PKE based on the NTRU assumption that comes from applying Theorem 5 to the BC-IBE of Section 4.2. (Here the parameters q, χ, R_q^* are defined as in that section.)

Gen:	Enc(pk, m):	Dec(sk, (vk, c, σ)):
$f_1, \ldots, f_n \overset{\$}{\leftarrow} \chi$	$(\text{sk}_{SS}, \text{vk}_{SS}) \overset{\$}{\leftarrow} \text{Gen}_{SS}$	If Verify(vk, c, σ) = 0
$\quad (f_i \equiv 1 \pmod 2), f_i \in R_q^*$	$h_1, \ldots, h_n, e \overset{\$}{\leftarrow} \chi$	then
$g_1, \ldots, g_n \overset{\$}{\leftarrow} \chi$	$c \leftarrow$	$\quad m \leftarrow \perp$
sk $\leftarrow (f_1, \ldots, f_n)$	$\quad \sum_{i \in \phi(\text{vk}_{SS})} \mathbf{pk}[i] \cdot h_i + 2e + m$	Else
pk $\leftarrow (2g_1/f_1, \ldots, 2g_n/f_n)$	$\sigma \overset{\$}{\leftarrow} \text{Sign}(\text{sk}_{SS}, c)$	$\quad \text{sk}_{vk} \leftarrow \prod_{i \in \phi(\text{vk})} \mathbf{sk}[i]$
Return (pk, sk).	Return (vk$_{SS}$, c, σ).	$\quad m \leftarrow \text{sk}_{vk} \cdot c \pmod 2$
		Return m

The ciphertext size of the CCA scheme generated by the BCHK transform is the same as the ciphertext size of the IBE scheme (and hence of the NTRU encryption scheme), plus a verification key and signature. Steinfeld *et al.* [31] show a (fully) CCA-secure construction based on NTRU; their ciphertext contains k ciphertexts of the underlying NTRUEncrypt algorithm (where $k = \Theta(1)$ is a parameter that depends on the hardness assumption used, but is at least 4), and additionally a verification key, a signature, and a blinded message. (Since the NTRUEncrypt ciphertexts are polynomials in R_q, they will typically be much larger than the other values.) Thus, we obtain a constant-factor improvement in ciphertext size by moving to the bounded-query model, in addition to the conceptual simplicity of the proof.

Acknowledgments. The authors wish to thank Shafi Goldwasser for insightful feedback and motivating us to write the present paper.

The research of this paper was partially supported by NSF Contract CCF-1018064. Moreover, this material is based on research sponsored by DARPA under agreement numbers FA8750-11-C-0096 and FA8750-11-2-0225. The U.S. Government is authorized to reproduce and distribute reprints for Governmental purposes notwithstanding any copyright notation thereon. The views and conclusions contained herein are those of the authors and should not be interpreted as necessarily representing the official policies or endorsements, either expressed or implied, of DARPA or the U.S. Government.

References

1. Agrawal, S., Boneh, D., Boyen, X.: Lattice basis delegation in fixed dimension and shorter-ciphertext hierarchical IBE. In: Rabin, T. (ed.) CRYPTO 2010. LNCS, vol. 6223, pp. 98–115. Springer, Heidelberg (2010)
2. Bellare, M., Desai, A., Pointcheval, D., Rogaway, P.: Relations among notions of security for public-key encryption schemes. In: Krawczyk, H. (ed.) CRYPTO 1998. LNCS, vol. 1462, pp. 26–45. Springer, Heidelberg (1998)
3. Boneh, D., Boyen, X.: Secure identity based encryption without random oracles. In: Franklin, M. (ed.) CRYPTO 2004. LNCS, vol. 3152, pp. 443–459. Springer, Heidelberg (2004)
4. Boneh, D., Canetti, R., Halevi, S., Katz, J.: Chosen-ciphertext security from identity-based encryption. SIAM Journal on Computing 36(5), 1301–1328 (2007)
5. Boneh, D., Franklin, M.: Identity-based encryption from the weil pairing. In: Kilian, J. (ed.) CRYPTO 2001. LNCS, vol. 2139, pp. 213–229. Springer, Heidelberg (2001)
6. Boneh, D., Gentry, C., Hamburg, M.: Space-efficient identity based encryption without pairings. In: 48th Annual Symposium on Foundations of Computer Science, pp. 647–657. IEEE Computer Society Press (October 2007)
7. Canetti, R., Halevi, S., Katz, J.: A forward-secure public-key encryption scheme. In: Biham, E. (ed.) EUROCRYPT 2003. LNCS, vol. 2656, pp. 255–271. Springer, Heidelberg (2003)
8. Cash, D., Hofheinz, D., Kiltz, E., Peikert, C.: Bonsai trees, or how to delegate a lattice basis. In: Gilbert, H. (ed.) EUROCRYPT 2010. LNCS, vol. 6110, pp. 523–552. Springer, Heidelberg (2010)
9. Cocks, C.: An identity based encryption scheme based on quadratic residues. In: Honary, B. (ed.) Cryptography and Coding 2001. LNCS, vol. 2260, pp. 360–363. Springer, Heidelberg (2001)
10. Cramer, R., Hanaoka, G., Hofheinz, D., Imai, H., Kiltz, E., Pass, R., Shelat, A., Vaikuntanathan, V.: Bounded CCA2-secure encryption. In: Kurosawa, K. (ed.) ASIACRYPT 2007. LNCS, vol. 4833, pp. 502–518. Springer, Heidelberg (2007)

11. Cramer, R., Shoup, V.: Universal hash proofs and a paradigm for adaptive chosen ciphertext secure public-key encryption. In: Knudsen, L.R. (ed.) EUROCRYPT 2002. LNCS, vol. 2332, pp. 45–64. Springer, Heidelberg (2002)
12. Diffie, W., Hellman, M.E.: New directions in cryptography. IEEE Transactions on Information Theory 22(6), 644–654 (1976)
13. Dodis, Y., Fazio, N.: Public key broadcast encryption for stateless receivers. In: Feigenbaum, J. (ed.) DRM 2002. LNCS, vol. 2696, pp. 61–80. Springer, Heidelberg (2003)
14. Dodis, Y., Haitner, I., Tentes, A.: On the instantiability of hash-and-sign RSA signatures. In: Cramer, R. (ed.) TCC 2012. LNCS, vol. 7194, pp. 112–132. Springer, Heidelberg (2012)
15. Dodis, Y., Katz, J., Xu, S., Yung, M.: Key-insulated public key cryptosystems. In: Knudsen, L.R. (ed.) EUROCRYPT 2002. LNCS, vol. 2332, pp. 65–82. Springer, Heidelberg (2002)
16. Erdös, P., Frankel, P., Furedi, Z.: Families of finite sets in which no set is covered by the union of r others. Israeli Journal of Mathematics 51, 79–89 (1985)
17. Fiat, A., Naor, M.: Broadcast encryption. In: Stinson, D.R. (ed.) CRYPTO 1993. LNCS, vol. 773, pp. 480–491. Springer, Heidelberg (1994)
18. Gafni, E., Staddon, J., Yin, Y.L.: Efficient methods for integrating traceability and broadcast encryption. In: Wiener, M. (ed.) CRYPTO 1999. LNCS, vol. 1666, pp. 372–387. Springer, Heidelberg (1999)
19. Garay, J.A., Staddon, J., Wool, A.: Long-lived broadcast encryption. In: Bellare, M. (ed.) CRYPTO 2000. LNCS, vol. 1880, pp. 333–352. Springer, Heidelberg (2000)
20. Gentry, C., Peikert, C., Vaikuntanathan, V.: Trapdoors for hard lattices and new cryptographic constructions. In: Ladner, R.E., Dwork, C. (eds.) 40th ACM STOC Annual ACM Symposium on Theory of Computing, pp. 197–206. ACM Press, New York (May 2008)
21. Gentry, C., Sahai, A., Waters, B.: Homomorphic encryption from learning with errors: Conceptually-simpler, asymptotically-faster, attribute-based. Cryptology ePrint Archive, Report 2013/340 (2013), http://eprint.iacr.org/
22. Goldwasser, S., Lewko, A., Wilson, D.A.: Bounded-collusion IBE from key homomorphism. In: Cramer, R. (ed.) TCC 2012. LNCS, vol. 7194, pp. 564–581. Springer, Heidelberg (2012)
23. Goldwasser, S., Micali, S.: Probabilistic encryption. Journal of Computer and System Sciences 28(2), 270–299 (1984)
24. Gorbunov, S., Vaikuntanathan, V., Wee, H.: Functional encryption with bounded collusions via multi-party computation. In: Safavi-Naini, R., Canetti, R. (eds.) CRYPTO 2012. LNCS, vol. 7417, pp. 162–179. Springer, Heidelberg (2012)
25. Halevy, D., Shamir, A.: The LSD broadcast encryption scheme. In: Yung, M. (ed.) CRYPTO 2002. LNCS, vol. 2442, pp. 47–60. Springer, Heidelberg (2002)
26. Hoffstein, J., Pipher, J., Silverman, J.H.: NTRU: A ring-based public key cryptosystem. In: Buhler, J.P. (ed.) ANTS 1998. LNCS, vol. 1423, pp. 267–288. Springer, Heidelberg (1998)
27. Kumar, R., Rajagopalan, S., Sahai, A.: Coding constructions for blacklisting problems without computational assumptions. In: Wiener, M. (ed.) CRYPTO 1999. LNCS, vol. 1666, pp. 609–623. Springer, Heidelberg (1999)
28. López-Alt, A., Tromer, E., Vaikuntanathan, V.: On-the-fly multiparty computation on the cloud via multikey fully homomorphic encryption. In: Karloff, H.J., Pitassi, T. (eds.) 44th ACM STOC Annual ACM Symposium on Theory of Computing, pp. 1219–1234. ACM Press (May 2012)

29. Naor, D., Naor, M., Lotspiech, J.: Revocation and tracing schemes for stateless receivers. In: Kilian, J. (ed.) CRYPTO 2001. LNCS, vol. 2139, pp. 41–62. Springer, Heidelberg (2001)
30. Shamir, A.: Identity-based cryptosystems and signature schemes. In: Blakely, G.R., Chaum, D. (eds.) CRYPTO 1984. LNCS, vol. 196, pp. 47–53. Springer, Heidelberg (1985)
31. Steinfeld, R., Ling, S., Pieprzyk, J., Tartary, C., Wang, H.: NTRUCCA: How to strengthen NTRUEncrypt to chosen-ciphertext security in the standard model. In: Fischlin, M., Buchmann, J., Manulis, M. (eds.) PKC 2012. LNCS, vol. 7293, pp. 353–371. Springer, Heidelberg (2012)
32. Waters, B.: Efficient identity-based encryption without random oracles. In: Cramer, R. (ed.) EUROCRYPT 2005. LNCS, vol. 3494, pp. 114–127. Springer, Heidelberg (2005)

A Framework and Compact Constructions for Non-monotonic Attribute-Based Encryption

Shota Yamada[1,*], Nuttapong Attrapadung[2],
Goichiro Hanaoka[2], and Noboru Kunihiro[1]

[1] The University of Tokyo
{yamada@it.,kunihiro}@k.u-tokyo.ac.jp
[2] National Institute of Advanced Industrial Science and Technology (AIST)
{n.attrapadung,hanaoka-goichiro}@aist.go.jp

Abstract. In this paper, we propose new non-monotonic attribute-based encryption schemes with compact parameters. The first three schemes are key-policy attribute-based encryption (KP-ABE) and the fourth scheme is ciphertext-policy attribute-based encryption (CP-ABE) scheme.

- Our first scheme achieves the shortest ciphertext overhead in the literature. Compared to the scheme by Attrapadung et al. (PKC2011), which is the best scheme in terms of the ciphertext overhead, our scheme shortens ciphertext overhead by 33%. The scheme also reduces the size of the master public key to about half.
- Our second scheme is proven secure under the decisional bilinear Diffie-Hellman (DBDH) assumption, which is one of the most standard assumptions in bilinear groups. Compared to the non-monotonic KP-ABE scheme from the same assumption by Ostrovsky et al. (ACM-CCS'07), our scheme reduces the size of the master public key and the ciphertext to about half.
- Our third scheme is the first non-monotonic KP-ABE scheme that can deal with unbounded size of set and access policies. That is, there is no restriction on the size of attribute sets and the number of allowed repetition of the same attributes which appear in an access policy. The master public key of our scheme consists of only constant number of group elements.
- Our fourth scheme is the first non-monotonic CP-ABE scheme that can deal with unbounded size of set and access policies. The master public key of the scheme consists of only constant number of group elements.

We construct our KP-ABE schemes in a modular manner. We first introduce special type of predicate encryption that we call two-mode identity based broadcast encryption (TIBBE). Then, we show that any TIBBE scheme that satisfies certain condition can be generically converted into non-monotonic KP-ABE scheme. Finally, we construct efficient TIBBE schemes and apply this conversion to obtain the above new non-monotonic KP-ABE schemes.

Keywords: Attribute-based encryption, non-monotonic access structure, compact parameters.

* The first author is supported by a JSPS Research Fellowship for Young Scientists.

H. Krawczyk (Ed.): PKC 2014, LNCS 8383, pp. 275–292, 2014.

1   Introduction

In many systems, a server monitors access to sensitive data so that only certain users can access it. If the server is not fully trusted, the data must be encrypted. However, a standard public key encryption scheme is not appropriate, because it severely limits the users who can access the contents.

To solve this problem, Sahai and Waters [31] were the first to study attribute-based encryption (ABE). In ABE, one can encrypt data for a set of receivers that satisfy certain condition. In Sahai and Waters' scheme, a ciphertext and a private key are associated with a set of attributes, and the key can decrypt the ciphertext if and only if these sets overlap more than certain threshold. Goyal, Pandey, Sahai, and Waters [16] further extended their result and proposed schemes that support finer-grained access control. In their scheme, a ciphertext is associated with a set of attributes, and a private key is associated with an access structure that is specified by a Boolean formula. Decryption is possible when the set satisfies this Boolean formula. Their schemes are called key-policy ABE (KP-ABE), because the key specifies the access structure. Ciphertext-policy ABE (CP-ABE) is complementary form to KP-ABE in the sense that a ciphertext specifies an access structure while a key is associated with a set of attributes. The first studies of CP-ABE appear in [5,12].

The above schemes can express a wide class of access structures, but they are still limited because they only support a monotonic access structure. In particular, they cannot deal with an access structure that is associated with a Boolean formula that includes the negation of attributes. This is not convenient for real world applications. One possible solution to this problem is to explicitly include attributes that express absence of attributes in the attribute space, as suggested in [16]. For example, in the CP-ABE case, to generate a key for an attribute x_1, one should generate the key for a set that includes x_1 and attributes "Not x_j" for all attribute x_j such that $x_j \neq x_1$, using the underlying monotonic CP-ABE system. Then, a ciphertext for "Not x_2" can be decrypted by the key as desired, because "Not x_2" $\in \{x_1$, "Not x_2", "Not x_3", $\ldots, \}$. This solution works well in the settings where attribute space is small, but does not work if the attribute space is exponentially large.

Ostrovsky, Sahai, and Waters [28] addressed this problem and constructed the first KP-ABE scheme that supports a non-monotonic access structure by using an idea from the Naor-Pinkas revocation scheme [25]. Following their work, several non-monotonic KP/CP-ABE schemes have been proposed [21,26,3,27].

Our Contributions. In this paper, we propose new non-monotonic ABE schemes. Our new schemes either improve efficiency or achieve a new functionality that was previously not possible. We propose the following four schemes. The first three schemes are KP-ABE schemes and the last one is CP-ABE scheme.

- The first scheme has very compact ciphertexts. The ciphertext overhead of our scheme consists of only two group elements, which is even shorter than the currently shortest scheme of [3]. Furthermore, the scheme also reduces the size of master public key to about half while the private key size is slightly larger.

- The second scheme is proven secure under the decisional bilinear Diffie-Hellman (DBDH) assumption, which is one of the weakest number theoretic assumptions in bilinear groups. The public key and the ciphertext size of our scheme are about half the size of the scheme in [28], which is secure under the same assumption. The encryption algorithm of our scheme is at least two times faster than the existing scheme, but our decryption algorithm is somewhat slower.
- The third scheme is the first non-monotonic KP-ABE scheme in the standard model that supports fully unbounded attribute sets and access policies. That is, there is no restriction on the size of the attribute set, or on the number of times the same attributes can appear in an access policy. The master public key of the scheme is very compact: it consists of only constant number of group elements. Such a construction has previously only been possible in the random oracle model [21].
- The fourth scheme is the first non-monotonic CP-ABE scheme that supports fully unbounded size of attribute sets and access policies. The master public key of our scheme consists of only constant number of group elements.

We construct the above KP-ABE schemes in a modular way. First, we define a new predicate encryption that we call two mode identity based broadcast encryption (TIBBE). In TIBBE, a ciphertext is associated with a set of identities. A private key is associated with an identity and certain "type". There are two types of keys in the system. First type keys can decrypt the ciphertext iff the identity is included in the set, while the second type keys can iff the identity is *not* included. The notion of TIBBE is an extension of identity based broadcast encryption (IBBE) and identity based revocation (IBR). We show that any TIBBE scheme with a certain property can be generically converted into a non-monotonic KP-ABE scheme. This can be seen as an extension of the previous result in [3] that converts any IBBE scheme with certain properties into a (monotonic) KP-ABE scheme. Finally, we construct efficient TIBBE schemes. By applying our conversion to these schemes, we obtain our new non-monotonic KP-ABE schemes.

While we construct KP-ABE schemes in a modular way, our construction of the above non-monotonic CP-ABE scheme is more direct. Our construction is based on the (monotonic) CP-ABE scheme recently proposed by [30]. We extend their scheme to support a non-monotonic access structure by applying an idea from the IBR scheme in [21] to the CP-ABE setting.

Finally, we remark that all our schemes are selectively secure. Constructing adaptively secure schemes with similar property is left open for future research.

Other Related Works. After the work of Sahai and Waters [31], many CP/KP-ABE schemes have been proposed [16,15,32,17]. The first adaptively secure ABE schemes were proposed in [20] using composite order groups. Later, schemes on prime order groups were proposed [26,27,19,24]. The settings with multiple-authorities are investigated in several works [10,1,11,22]. To construct a scheme with even more general access structure is an important direction of research. Recently, there are significant progress toward this direction [33,13,14].

2 Preliminaries

2.1 Notation

We will treat a vector as a row vector, unless stated otherwise. For any vector $\mathbf{a} = (a_1, \ldots, a_n) \in \mathbb{Z}_p^n$, $g^{\mathbf{a}} = (g^{a_1}, \ldots, g^{a_n})$. For $\mathbf{a}, \mathbf{z} \in \mathbb{Z}_p^n$, we denote their inner product as $\langle \mathbf{a}, \mathbf{z} \rangle = \mathbf{a} \cdot \mathbf{z}^{\top} = \sum_{i=1}^{n} a_i z_i$. We denote by $\mathbf{e}_i$ the i-th unit vector: its i-th component is one, all others are zero. We also denote by $[n]$ a set $\{1, \ldots, n\}$ for an integer $n > 0$ and $[n_1, \ldots, n_m] = [n_1] \times \cdots \times [n_m]$ for integers $n_1, \ldots, n_m > 0$. For a set U, we define $2^U = \{S | S \subseteq U\}$ and $\binom{U}{<k} = \{S | S \subseteq U, |S| < k\}$ for $k \leq |U|$.

2.2 Definition of Predicate Encryption

Here, we define the syntax of predicate encryption. We emphasize that we do not consider attribute hiding in this paper.[1]

SYNTAX. Let $R = \{R_N : A_N \times B_N \to \{0, 1\} \mid N \in \mathbb{N}^c\}$ be a relation family where A_N and B_N denote "key attribute" and "ciphertext attribute" spaces and c is some fixed constant. The index $N = (n_1, n_2, \ldots, n_c)$ of R_N denotes the numbers of bounds for corresponding parameters. If an index N is not required, we say that R is an unbounded relation. A predicate encryption (PE) scheme for R consists of the following algorithms:

Setup$(\lambda, N) \to (\mathsf{mpk}, \mathsf{msk})$: The setup algorithm takes as input a security parameter λ and a index N of the relation R_N and outputs a master public key mpk and a master secret key msk.

KeyGen$(\mathsf{msk}, \mathsf{mpk}, X) \to \mathsf{sk}_X$: The key generation algorithm takes as input the master secret key msk, the master public key mpk, and a key attribute $X \in A_N$. It outputs a private key sk_X. We assume X is included in sk_X implicitly.

Encrypt$(\mathsf{mpk}, \mathsf{M}, Y) \to C$: The encryption algorithm takes as input a master public key mpk, the message M, and a ciphertext attribute $Y \in B_N$. It will output a ciphertext C.

Decrypt$(\mathsf{mpk}, C, Y, \mathsf{sk}_X) \to \mathsf{M}$ or $\perp$: We assume that the decryption algorithm is deterministic. The decryption algorithm takes as input the public parameters mpk, a ciphertext C, ciphertext attribute $Y \in B_N$ and a private key sk_X. It outputs the message M or $\perp$ which represents that the ciphertext is not in a valid form.

We require correctness of decryption: that is, for all λ, N, all $(\mathsf{mpk}, \mathsf{msk})$ produced by Setup(λ, N), all $X \in A_N, Y \in B_N$ such that $R(X, Y) = 1$, and all sk_X returned by KeyGen$(\mathsf{msk}, \mathsf{mpk}, X)$, Decrypt$(\mathsf{mpk}, \mathsf{Encrypt}(\mathsf{mpk}, \mathsf{M}, Y), Y, \mathsf{sk}_X) = \mathsf{M}$ holds.

SECURITY. We now define the security for an PE scheme Π. This security notion is defined by the following game between a challenger and an attacker $\mathcal{A}$.

At first, the challenger runs the setup algorithm and gives mpk to $\mathcal{A}$. Then $\mathcal{A}$ may adaptively make key-extraction queries. We denote this phase **Phase1**. In this phase, if $\mathcal{A}$ submits X to the challenger, the challenger returns $\mathsf{sk}_X \leftarrow$ KeyGen$(\mathsf{msk}, \mathsf{mpk}, X)$. At some point, $\mathcal{A}$ outputs two equal length messages

---

[1] This is called "public-index" predicate encryption, categorized in [9].

M_0 and M_1 and challenge ciphertext attribute $Y^\star \in B_N$. $Y^\star$ cannot satisfy $R(X, Y^\star) = 1$ for any attribute X such that $\mathcal{A}$ already queried private key for X. Then the challenger flips a random coin $\beta \in \{0, 1\}$, runs $\mathsf{Encrypt}(\mathsf{mpk}, M_\beta, Y^\star) \to C^\star$ and gives challenge ciphertext $C^\star$ to $\mathcal{A}$. In **Phase2**, $\mathcal{A}$ may adaptively make queries as in **Phase1** with following added restriction: $\mathcal{A}$ cannot make a key-extraction query for X such that $R(X, Y^\star) = 1$. At last, $\mathcal{A}$ outputs a guess β' for β. We say that $\mathcal{A}$ succeeds if $\beta' = \beta$ and denote the probability of this event by $\mathrm{Pr}_{\mathcal{A},\Pi}^{PE}$. The advantage of an attacker $\mathcal{A}$ is defined as $\mathsf{Adv}_{\mathcal{A},\Pi}^{PE} = |\mathrm{Pr}_{\mathcal{A},\Pi}^{PE} - \frac{1}{2}|$. We say that Π is fully secure if $\mathsf{Adv}_{\mathcal{A},\Pi}^{PE}$ is negligible for all probabilistic polynomial time (PPT) adversary $\mathcal{A}$.

A weaker notion called selective security can be defined as in the above game with the exception that the adversary $\mathcal{A}$ has to choose the challenge ciphertext index $Y^\star$ before the setup phase but private key queries $X_1, \ldots, X_q$ can still be adaptive. All schemes proposed in this paper are selectively secure.

2.3   Linear Secret Sharing Scheme and Attribute-Based Encryption

Here, we first define linear secret sharing scheme (LSSS) following [4] and then define key/ciphertext-policy atrribute based encryption scheme as an instance of PE.

Definition 1 (Access Structure). *Let $\mathcal{P} = \{\mathcal{P}_1, \ldots, \mathcal{P}_n\}$ be a set of parties. A collection $\mathbb{A} \subset 2^{\mathcal{P}}$ is said to be monotone if, for all B, C, if $B \in \mathbb{A}$ and $B \subset C$, then $C \in \mathbb{A}$ holds. An access structure (resp., monotonic access structure) is a collection (resp., monotone collection) $\mathbb{A} \subset 2^{\mathcal{P}} \setminus \{\emptyset\}$. The sets in $\mathbb{A}$ are called the authorized sets, and the sets not in $\mathbb{A}$ are called the unauthorized sets.*

Definition 2 (Linear Secret Sharing Scheme). *Let $\mathcal{P}$ be a set of parties. Let L be an $\ell \times m$ matrix. Let $\pi : \{1, \ldots, \ell\} \to \mathcal{P}$ be a function that maps a row to a party for labeling. A secret sharing scheme π for access structure $\mathbb{A}$ over a set of parties $\mathcal{P}$ is a linear secret-sharing scheme (LSSS) in $\mathbb{Z}_p$ and is represented by (L, π) if it consists of two efficient algorithms:*

$\mathsf{Share}_{L,\pi}$. *There exists an efficient algorithm which takes as input $s \in \mathbb{Z}_p$ which is to be shared. It chooses $s_2, \ldots, s_m \xleftarrow{s} \mathbb{Z}_p$ and let $\mathbf{s} = (s, s_2, \ldots, s_m)$. It outputs $L \cdot \mathbf{s}$ as the vector of ℓ shares. The share $\lambda_i = \langle \mathbf{L}_i, \mathbf{s} \rangle$ belongs to party $\pi(i)$, where $\mathbf{L}_i$ denotes the i-th row of L.*

$\mathsf{Recon}_{L,\pi}$. *The algorithm takes as input an access set $S \in \mathbb{A}$. Let $I = \{i | \pi(i) \in S\}$. It outputs a set of constants $\{(i, \mu_i)\}_{i \in I}$ which has a linear reconstruction property: $\sum_{i \in I} \mu_i \cdot \lambda_i = s$.*

TERMINOLOGY FOR NON-MONOTONIC ACCESS STRUCTURE. We recall a technique by Ostrovsky Sahai, and Waters [28] to move from monotonic access structures to non-monotonic access structure. They assume a family $\{\Pi_\mathbb{A}\}_{\mathbb{A} \in \mathcal{AS}}$ of linear secret sharing schemes for a set of monotonic access structures $\mathbb{A}$. For each such access structure $\mathbb{A} \in \mathcal{AS}$, the set $\mathcal{P}$ of underlying parties has the following properties: The names of the parties in $\mathcal{P}$ may be of two types: either the name is normal (like x) or it is primed (like x'), and if $x \in \mathcal{P}$ then $x' \in \mathcal{P}$ and vice versa. Conceptually, prime attributes are associated with negation of unprimed attributes.

A family $\mathcal{AS}$ of non-monotone access structures can be defined as follows. For each access structure $\mathbb{A} \in \mathcal{AS}$ over a set of parties $\mathcal{P}$, one defines a possibly non-monotonic access structure $NM(\mathbb{A})$ over the set $\tilde{\mathcal{P}}$ of all unprimed parties in $\mathcal{P}$. For every set $\tilde{S} \subset \tilde{\mathcal{P}}$, $N(\tilde{S})$ is defined as $N(\tilde{S}) = \tilde{S} \cup \{x' | x \in \tilde{\mathcal{P}} \backslash \tilde{S}\}$. Then, $NM(\mathbb{A})$ is defined by saying that $\tilde{S}$ is authorized in $NM(\mathbb{A})$ if and only if $N(\tilde{S})$ is authorized in $\mathbb{A}$. For each access set $X \in NM(\mathbb{A})$, there is a set in $\mathbb{A}$ containing the elements in X and primed elements for each party not in X.

KEY-(CIPHERTEXT) POLICY ATTRIBUTE-BASED ENCRYPION. Let $\mathcal{U} = \{0,1\}^*$ be an attribute space and $N = (n, \varphi)$ specify the corresponding bounds (the maximum numbers) on the size of attribute sets, the number of allowed repetition of same attributes which appear in a policy, respectively. Let $\mathcal{AS}_\varphi$ be a collection of access structures over $\mathcal{U}$ such that every access structure in $\mathcal{AS}_\varphi$ is specified by an access formula in which same attributes do not appear more than φ times. A bounded key (resp. ciphertext)-policy attribute-based encryption for $\mathcal{AS}_\varphi$ is a predicate encryption for $R_{(n,\varphi)}^{\mathsf{KP}} : \mathcal{AS}_\varphi \times \binom{\mathcal{U}}{<n} \to \{0,1\}$ (resp. $R_{(n,\varphi)}^{\mathsf{CP}} : \binom{\mathcal{U}}{<n} \times \mathcal{AS}_\varphi \to \{0,1\}$) defined by $R_{(n,\varphi)}^{\mathsf{KP}}(\mathbb{A}, \omega) = 1$ (resp. $R_{(n,\varphi)}^{\mathsf{CP}}(\omega, \mathbb{A}) = 1$) iff $\omega \in \mathbb{A}$ (for $\omega \subseteq U$ such that $|\omega| < n$ and $\mathbb{A} \in \mathcal{AS}_\varphi$). Let $\mathcal{AS}$ be a collection of access structure over $\mathcal{U}$. An unbounded key (resp., ciphertext)-policy attribute-based encryption scheme is a predicate encryption for $R^{\mathsf{KP}} : \mathcal{AS} \times 2^\mathcal{U} \to \{0,1\}$ (resp., $R^{\mathsf{CP}} : 2^\mathcal{U} \times \mathcal{AS} \to \{0,1\}$) defined by $R^{\mathsf{KP}}(\mathbb{A}, \omega) = 1$ (resp. $R^{\mathsf{CP}}(\omega, \mathbb{A}) = 1$) iff $\omega \in \mathbb{A}$ (for $\omega \subseteq U$ and $\mathbb{A} \in \mathcal{AS}$).

We note that the scheme of [27] (which was called unbounded ABE) can achieve the unbounded attribute set size, but it is still limited to the number of allowed repetition. Currently, only few KP-ABE schemes that are unbounded in full sence are known [21,23,30]. Note that the scheme in [21] uses random oracle model. In the CP-ABE setting, only scheme that is unbounded in full sense is recently proposed [30].

2.4   Number Theoretic Assumptions

We use groups $(\mathbb{G}, \mathbb{G}_T)$ of prime order p with an efficiently computable mapping $e : \mathbb{G} \times \mathbb{G} \to \mathbb{G}_T$ s.t. $e(g^a, h^b) = e(g, h)^{ab}$ for any $(g, h) \in \mathbb{G} \times \mathbb{G}$, $a, b \in \mathbb{Z}$ and $e(g, h) \neq 1_{\mathbb{G}_T}$ whenever $g, h \neq 1_{\mathbb{G}}$.

Decisional Bilinear Diffie-Hellman (DBDH) Assumption. We say that an adversary $\mathcal{A}$ breaks the DBDH assumption on $(\mathbb{G}, \mathbb{G}_T)$ if $\mathcal{A}$ runs in polynomial time and $\frac{1}{2}|\Pr[\mathcal{A}(g, g^a, g^b, g^s, e(g, g)^{abs}) \to 0] - \Pr[\mathcal{A}(g, g^a, g^b, g^s, T) \to 0]|$ is negligible where $g \xleftarrow{\$} \mathbb{G}$, $T \xleftarrow{\$} \mathbb{G}_T$, $a, b, s \xleftarrow{\$} \mathbb{Z}_p$.

n-Decisional Bilinear Diffie-Hellman Exponent (n-DBDHE) Assumption [7]. We say that an adversary $\mathcal{A}$ breaks the n-DBDHE assumption on $(\mathbb{G}, \mathbb{G}_T)$ if $\mathcal{A}$ runs in polynomial time and $\frac{1}{2}|\Pr[\mathcal{A}(g, \{g^{a^i}\}_{i \in [2n]\backslash\{n+1\}}, g^s, e(g, g)^{s \cdot a^{n+1}}) \to 0] - \frac{1}{2}|\Pr[\mathcal{A}(g, \{g^{a^i}\}_{i \in [2n]\backslash\{n+1\}}, g^s, T) \to 0]|$ is negligible where $g \xleftarrow{\$} \mathbb{G}$, $T \xleftarrow{\$} \mathbb{G}_T$, $a, s \xleftarrow{\$} \mathbb{Z}_p$.

3   Linear Two-Mode Identity Based Broadcast Encryption and Conversion to Non-monotonic KP-ABE

In this section, we first introduce the two mode inner product encryption scheme (TIPE) and two mode identity based broadcast encryption schemes (TIBBE) and explain how the latter can be derived from the former. Then, we propose a general transformation that transforms any TIBBE scheme that satisfies a certain condition into a non-monotonic KP-ABE scheme. Our transformation is an extension of the generic transformation proposed in [3], which converts any IBBE scheme with certain conditions into (monotonic) KP-ABE scheme.

3.1   Definition of TIPE and TIBBE

In a TIPE scheme, a ciphertext is associated with a vector $\mathbf{y}$. A private key is associated with type $\in \{\mathsf{ZIPE}, \mathsf{NIPE}\}$ and a vector $\mathbf{x}$. Decryption is possible iff type $= \mathsf{ZIPE}$ and $\langle \mathbf{x}, \mathbf{y} \rangle = 0$, or type $= \mathsf{NIPE}$ and $\langle \mathbf{x}, \mathbf{y} \rangle \neq 0$. In a TIBBE scheme, a ciphertext is associated with a set of identities S. A private key is associated with type $\in \{\mathsf{IBBE}, \mathsf{IBR}\}$ and an identity ID. Decryption is possible iff type $= \mathsf{IBBE}$ and $\mathsf{ID} \in S$, or type $= \mathsf{IBR}$ and $\mathsf{ID} \notin S$.

Here, we formally define TIPE and TIBBE as instances of PE as follows.

TWO-MODE INNER PRODUCT ENCRYPTION SCHEME. TIPE is a predicate encryption for $R_{(n,p)}^{\mathsf{TIPE}} : (\mathbb{Z}_p^n \times \{\mathsf{ZIPE}, \mathsf{NIPE}\}) \times \mathbb{Z}_p^n \to \{0, 1\}$ defined by $R_{(n,p)}^{\mathsf{TIPE}}((\mathbf{x}, \text{type}), \mathbf{y}) = 1$ iff $(\langle \mathbf{x}, \mathbf{y} \rangle = 0 \wedge \text{type} = \mathsf{ZIPE}) \vee (\langle \mathbf{x}, \mathbf{y} \rangle \neq 0 \wedge \text{type} = \mathsf{NIPE})$.

TWO-MODE IDENTITY BASED BROADCAST ENCRYPTION SCHEME. TIBBE is a predicate encryption for $R_n^{\mathsf{TIBBE}} : (\mathcal{I} \times \{\mathsf{IBBE}, \mathsf{IBR}\}) \times \binom{\mathcal{I}}{<n} \to \{0, 1\}$ defined by $R_n^{\mathsf{TIBBE}}((\mathsf{ID}, \text{type}), S) = 1$ iff $(\mathsf{ID} \in S \wedge \text{type} = \mathsf{IBBE}) \vee (\mathsf{ID} \notin S \wedge \text{type} = \mathsf{IBR})$.

In later sections, we construct TIPE schemes instead of TIBBE schemes when it is simpler to describe. TIBBE scheme can be derived from TIPE scheme by the following technique due to [18]. The setup algorithm of the TIBBE scheme is the same as TIPE scheme. To generate a private key for $(\mathsf{ID}, \mathsf{IBBE})$ (resp. $(\mathsf{ID}, \mathsf{IBR})$), one runs key generation algorithm of TIPE scheme to obtain a private key for $(\mathbf{x}, \mathsf{ZIPE})$ (resp. $(\mathbf{x}, \mathsf{NIPE})$) where $\mathbf{x} = (1, \mathsf{ID}, \ldots, \mathsf{ID}^{n-1})$. To encrypt a message M for a set $S = (\mathsf{ID}_1, \ldots, \mathsf{ID}_k)$, one defines $\mathbf{y} = (y_1, \ldots, y_n)$ as a coefficient vector from $P_S[Z] = \sum_{i=1}^{k+1} y_i Z^{i-1} = \prod_{\mathsf{ID}_j \in S} (Z - \mathsf{ID}_j)$ where, if $k + 1 < n$, the coordinates $y_{k+1}, \ldots, y_n$ are all set to 0. Then, one runs encryption algorithm of TIPE scheme to encrypt M for a vector $\mathbf{y}$. To decrypt a ciphertext, one first defines $\mathbf{x}$ and $\mathbf{y}$ as above and runs the decryption algorithm of the TIPE scheme. Since $\mathsf{ID} \in S \Leftrightarrow P_S(\mathsf{ID}) = 0 \Leftrightarrow \langle \mathbf{x}, \mathbf{y} \rangle = 0$, the correctness of the resulting TIBBE scheme follows from the correctness of the underlying TIPE scheme. Furthermore, by the embedding lemma [8], the resulting TIBBE scheme is selectively secure if the underlying TIPE scheme is selectively secure.

3.2   Linear Two-Mode Identity Based Broadcast Encryption Template

We define a template for two-mode IBBE schemes that ensures that they give rise to selective secure non-monotonic KP-ABE schemes. We call this a linear

TIBBE template. Let $\mathbb{G}, \mathbb{G}_T$ be underlying bilinear groups of order p. The identity space of the scheme is $\mathcal{I} = \mathbb{Z}_p$. A linear TIBBE scheme is determined by parameters $n, n_1, n_2, \bar{n}_1, \in \mathbb{N}$, a distribution $\mathcal{G}$ on vectors of functions, and functions $\mathcal{D}^{\mathsf{IBBE}}$, $\mathcal{D}^{\mathsf{IBR}}$. $\mathcal{G}$'s output is tuple of functions $(f_1^{\mathsf{IBBE}}, f_2^{\mathsf{IBBE}}, f_1^{\mathsf{IBR}}, f_2^{\mathsf{IBR}}, F)$ where $f_1^{\mathsf{IBBE}} : \mathcal{I} \to \mathbb{G}, f_2^{\mathsf{IBBE}} : \mathcal{I} \to \mathbb{G}^{n_1}, f_1^{\mathsf{IBR}} : \mathcal{I} \to \mathbb{G}, f_2^{\mathsf{IBR}} : \mathcal{I} \to \mathbb{G}^{\bar{n}_1}, F : (\mathcal{I})^{\leq n-1} \times \mathbb{Z}_p \to \mathbb{G}^{\leq n_2}$. Here, we allow F to be probabilistic whereas all other functions are assumed to be deterministic. $\mathcal{D}^{\mathsf{IBBE}}$ and $\mathcal{D}^{\mathsf{IBR}}$ are functions such that $\mathcal{D}^{\mathsf{IBBE}} : \mathbb{G}^{n_1+1} \times \mathcal{I} \times \mathbb{G}^{n_2} \times \binom{\mathcal{I}}{<n} \to \mathbb{G}_T, \mathcal{D}^{\mathsf{IBR}} : \mathbb{G}^{\bar{n}_1+1} \times \mathcal{I} \times \mathbb{G}^{n_2} \times \binom{\mathcal{I}}{<n} \to \mathbb{G}_T$.

Setup(λ, n) : Given a security parameter $\lambda \in \mathbb{N}$ and a bound $n \in \mathbb{Z}$ on the number of identities per ciphertext, the algorithm selects bilinear groups $(\mathbb{G}, \mathbb{G}_T)$ of prime order $p > 2^\lambda$ and a generator $g \xleftarrow{\$} \mathbb{G}$. It computes $e(g,g)^\alpha$ for a random $\alpha \xleftarrow{\$} \mathbb{Z}_p$ and chooses functions $(f_1^{\mathsf{IBBE}}, f_2^{\mathsf{IBBE}}, f_1^{\mathsf{IBR}}, f_2^{\mathsf{IBR}}, F) \xleftarrow{\$} \mathcal{G}$. The master secret key consists of $\mathsf{msk} = \alpha$ while the master public key is $\mathsf{mpk} = (g, e(g,g)^\alpha, \{f_1^{\mathsf{type}}, f_2^{\mathsf{type}}\}_{\mathsf{type} \in \{\mathsf{IBBE}, \mathsf{IBR}\}}, F, n, n_1, n_2, \bar{n}_1)$.

KeyGen$(\mathsf{msk}, \mathsf{mpk}, (\mathsf{ID}, \mathsf{type}))$: To generate a private key for ID of type $\mathsf{type} \in \{\mathsf{IBBE}, \mathsf{IBR}\}$, it chooses $r \xleftarrow{\$} \mathbb{Z}_p$. Then, it computes the private key as

$$\mathsf{sk}_{(\mathsf{ID}, \mathsf{type})} = (d_1, d_2) = \left(g^\alpha \cdot f_1^{\mathsf{type}}(\mathsf{ID})^r, f_2^{\mathsf{type}}(\mathsf{ID})^r \right).$$

Encrypt$(\mathsf{mpk}, \mathsf{M}, S)$: To encrypt $\mathsf{M} \in \mathbb{G}_T$ for a set of identities $S = (\mathsf{ID}_1, \ldots, \mathsf{ID}_k)$ where $k < n$, it chooses $s \xleftarrow{\$} \mathbb{Z}_p$ and computes the ciphertext as

$$C = (C_0, C_1) = (\mathsf{M} \cdot e(g,g)^{\alpha s}, F(\mathsf{ID}_1, \ldots, \mathsf{ID}_k, s)).$$

Decrypt$(\mathsf{mpk}, C, S, \mathsf{sk}_{(\mathsf{ID}, \mathsf{type})})$: It parses $\mathsf{sk}_{(\mathsf{ID}, \mathsf{type})} = (d_1, d_2)$ and $C = (C_0, C_1)$ then runs

$$\mathcal{D}^{\mathsf{type}}\big((d_1, d_2), \mathsf{ID}, C_1, S\big) \to e(g,g)^{\alpha \cdot s},$$

and obtains $\mathsf{M} = C_0 / e(g,g)^\alpha$.

We also require that for all $(f_1^{\mathsf{IBBE}}, f_2^{\mathsf{IBBE}}, f_1^{\mathsf{IBR}}, f_2^{\mathsf{IBR}}, F) \xleftarrow{\$} \mathcal{G}$, the following property must hold. [2]

Correctness. For all $\alpha, r, s \in \mathbb{Z}_p$, randomness for F, $(\mathsf{ID}, \mathsf{type}) \in \mathcal{I} \times \{\mathsf{IBBE}, \mathsf{IBR}\}$, $S = \{\mathsf{ID}_1, \ldots, \mathsf{ID}_k\} \in \binom{\mathcal{I}}{<n}$ such that $(\mathsf{type} = \mathsf{IBBE} \wedge \mathsf{ID} \in S) \vee (\mathsf{type} = \mathsf{IBR} \wedge \mathsf{ID} \notin S)$ and randomness for F, we have

$$\mathcal{D}^{\mathsf{type}}\left(\big(g^\alpha \cdot f_1^{\mathsf{type}}(\mathsf{ID})^r, f_2^{\mathsf{type}}(\mathsf{ID})^r \big), \mathsf{ID}, F(\mathsf{ID}_1, \ldots, \mathsf{ID}_k, s), S \right) = e(g,g)^{\alpha \cdot s}.$$

3.3 Generic Conversion from Linear TIBBE to Non-monotonic KP-ABE

Let $\Pi_{\mathsf{TIBBE}} = (\mathsf{Setup}', \mathsf{Keygen}', \mathsf{Encrypt}', \mathsf{Decrypt}')$ be a linear TIBBE system. We construct a non-monotonic KP-ABE scheme from Π_{TIBBE} as follows.

Setup(λ, n) : It simply outputs $\mathsf{Setup}'(\lambda, n) \to (\mathsf{mpk}, \mathsf{msk})$.

---

[2] In [3], the authors also assume a property called linearity. However, we do not need this property.

KeyGen(msk, mpk, $\tilde{\mathbb{A}}$) : The input to the algorithm is the master secret key msk, the master public key mpk, and a non-monotonic access structure $\tilde{\mathbb{A}}$ such that we have $\tilde{\mathbb{A}} = NM(\mathbb{A})$ for some monotonic access structure $\mathbb{A}$ over a set $\mathcal{P}$ of attributes and associated with a linear secret sharing scheme (L, π). Let L be an $\ell \times m$ matrix. First, it generates shares of α with (L, π). Namely, it chooses a vector $\mathbf{s} = (s_1, \ldots, s_m)$ such that $s_1 = \alpha$ and $s_2, \ldots, s_m \xleftarrow{\$} \mathbb{Z}_p$ and calculates $\lambda_i = \langle \mathbf{L}_i, \mathbf{s} \rangle$ for each $i = 1, \ldots, \ell$. The party corresponds to share λ_i is $\pi(i) = \breve{x}_i$, where x_i is underlying attribute, and can be primed (i.e., negated) or unprimed (non-negated). Then for each $i = 1, \ldots, \ell$, it picks $r_i \xleftarrow{\$} \mathbb{Z}_p$ and sets D_i for each $i = 1, \ldots, \ell$ as follows.

$$D_i = \begin{cases} \left(d'_{i,1} = g^{\lambda_i} \cdot f_1^{\mathsf{IBBE}}(x_i)^{r_i}, \ d'_{i,2} = f_2^{\mathsf{IBBE}}(x_i)^{r_i} \right) & \text{if } \pi(i) = x_i \\ \left(d'_{i,1} = g^{\lambda_i} \cdot f_1^{\mathsf{IBR}}(x_i)^{r_i}, \ d'_{i,2} = f_2^{\mathsf{IBR}}(x_i)^{r_i} \right) & \text{if } \pi(i) = x'_i. \end{cases}$$

It then outputs the private key as $\mathsf{sk}_{\tilde{\mathbb{A}}} = \{D_i\}_{i=1}^{\ell}$

Encrypt(mpk, M, ω) : It simply outputs Encrypt'(mpk, M, ω).

Decrypt(mpk, C, ω, $\mathsf{sk}_{\tilde{\mathbb{A}}}$) : Assume first that the policy $\tilde{\mathbb{A}}$ is satisfied by the attribute set ω, so that decryption is possible. Since $\tilde{\mathbb{A}} = NM(\mathbb{A})$ for some access structure $\mathbb{A}$ associated with a linear secret sharing scheme (L, π), we have $\omega' = N(\omega) \in \mathbb{A}$ and we let $I = \{i | \pi(i) \in \omega'\}$. Since ω' is authorized in $\mathbb{A}$, the receiver can efficiently compute reconstruction coefficients $\{(i, \mu_i)\}_{i \in I} = \mathsf{Recon}_{L,\pi}(\omega')$ such that $\sum_{i \in I} \mu_i \lambda_i = \alpha$. It parses $C = (C_0, C_1)$, $\mathsf{sk}_{\tilde{\mathbb{A}}} = \{D_i\}_{i=1}^{\ell}$ where $D_i = (d'_{i,1}, d'_{i,2})$ and computes $e(g, g)^{s \cdot \lambda_i}$ for each $i \in I$ as follows. (The correctness is shown later.)

$$\begin{cases} \mathcal{D}^{\mathsf{IBBE}}\left((d'_{i,1}, d'_{i,2}), x_i, C_1, \omega \right) \to e(g, g)^{s \cdot \lambda_i} & \text{if } \pi(i) = x_i \quad (1a) \\ \mathcal{D}^{\mathsf{IBR}}\left((d'_{i,1}, d'_{i,2}), x_i, C_1, \omega \right) \to e(g, g)^{s \cdot \lambda_i} & \text{if } \pi(i) = x'_i. \quad (1b) \end{cases}$$

Finally, it recovers message by $C_0 \cdot \prod_{i \in I} \left(e(g, g)^{s \cdot \lambda_i} \right)^{-\mu_i} = \mathsf{M}$.

CORRECTNESS. We now verify that equations (1a) and (1b) are correct. (1a) and (1b) follow from the correctness of the underlying TIBBE scheme by seeing D_i as a private key for $\left(\mathsf{ID} = x_i, \mathsf{type} \in \{\mathsf{IBBE}, \mathsf{IBR}\} \right)$ that is derived from $\mathsf{msk} = \lambda_i$ using randomness r_i. The security of the resulting scheme is established by the following Theorem. The proof is similar to that of Theorem 1 in [3] and can be found in full version of this paper.

Theorem 1. *If the underlying TIBBE scheme is selectively secure, then the resulting KP-ABE system above is also selectively secure.*

REMARK. We have described the conversion for TIBBE scheme with a restriction that the number of identities per ciphertext is bounded by n. However, the same conversion also applies to a TIBBE scheme without such a restriction. In particular, we can apply the above conversion to our TIBBE scheme in Sec. 6.

4   TIPE Scheme with Compact Ciphertexts

In this section, we propose a TIPE scheme with compact ciphertext size. As we explained in Sec. 3.1, we can obtain a TIBBE scheme from the TIPE scheme. By applying the conversion in Sec. 3 to this TIBBE scheme, we obtain a new non-monotonic KP-ABE scheme with very short ciphertexts. The ciphertext overhead is 33% shorter than the non-monotonic KP-ABE ciphertext in [3] (the shortest in the literature). It also reduces the number of pairing operations in the decryption algorithm from 3 to 2. The public key size of our scheme is about half that of the existing scheme, but the private key of our scheme is slightly longer.

$\mathsf{Setup}(\lambda, n)$: It chooses bilinear groups $(\mathbb{G}, \mathbb{G}_T)$ of prime order $p > 2^\lambda$ with $g \xleftarrow{\$} \mathbb{G}$. It also picks $v, \alpha \xleftarrow{\$} \mathbb{Z}_p$ and $\mathbf{u} = (u_1, \ldots, u_n) \xleftarrow{\$} \mathbb{Z}_p^n$. Then it sets $V = g^v$ and $U = (U_1, \ldots, U_n) = g^{\mathbf{u}}$. It finally outputs the master public key $\mathsf{mpk} = (g, U_1, \ldots, U_n, V, e(g,g)^\alpha)$ and the master secret key $\mathsf{msk} = \alpha$.

$\mathsf{KeyGen}(\mathsf{msk}, \mathsf{mpk}, (\mathbf{x}, \mathsf{type}))$: To generate a private key for $(\mathbf{x} = (x_1 \neq 0, \ldots, x_n) \in \mathbb{Z}_p^* \times \mathbb{Z}_p^{n-1}, \mathsf{type} \in \{\mathsf{ZIPE}, \mathsf{NIPE}\})$, it chooses $r \xleftarrow{\$} \mathbb{Z}_p$ and computes

$$
\begin{cases}
\mathsf{sk}_{(\mathbf{x},\mathsf{ZIPE})} = \begin{pmatrix} D_1 = g^\alpha V^r, & D_2 = g^r, \\ \{K_i = (U_1^{-\frac{x_i}{x_1}} U_i)^r\}_{i=2}^n \end{pmatrix} & \text{if type} = \mathsf{ZIPE} \\[3ex]
\mathsf{sk}_{(\mathbf{x},\mathsf{NIPE})} = \begin{pmatrix} D_1 = g^\alpha U_1^r, & D_2 = g^r, & D_3 = V^r, \\ \{K_i = (U_1^{-\frac{x_i}{x_1}} U_i)^r\}_{i=2}^n \end{pmatrix} & \text{if type} = \mathsf{NIPE}.
\end{cases}
$$

$\mathsf{Encrypt}(\mathsf{mpk}, \mathsf{M}, \mathbf{y})$: To encrypt $\mathsf{M} \in \mathbb{G}_T$ for the vector $\mathbf{y} = (y_1, \ldots, y_n) \in \mathbb{Z}_p^n$, it picks $s \xleftarrow{\$} \mathbb{Z}_p$ and computes the ciphertext as

$$
C = \left(C_0 = \mathsf{M} \cdot e(g,g)^{\alpha s}, C_1 = g^s, C_2 = (V U_1^{y_1} \cdots U_n^{y_n})^{-s} \right).
$$

$\mathsf{Decrypt}(\mathsf{mpk}, C, \mathbf{y}, \mathsf{sk}_{(\mathbf{x},\mathsf{type})})$: It computes

$$
\begin{cases}
e(C_1, D_1 \cdot \prod_{i=2}^n K_i^{y_i}) \cdot e(C_2, D_2) = e(g,g)^{s\alpha} & \text{if type} = \mathsf{ZIPE} \\[3ex]
e(C_1, D_1) \cdot \left(e(C_1, D_3 \prod_{i=2}^n K_i^{y_i}) \cdot e(C_2, D_2) \right)^{\frac{x_1}{\langle \mathbf{x}, \mathbf{y} \rangle}} = e(g,g)^{s\alpha} & \text{if type} = \mathsf{NIPE}
\end{cases}
$$

and recovers the message by $C_0/e(g,g)^{s\alpha} = \mathsf{M}$.

We construct the above scheme by combining the IPE scheme derived from the spatial encryption scheme in [8,2] and a variant of the NIPE scheme proposed in [3] so that they share the master public key and the ciphertext. The non-monotonic KP-ABE scheme derived from the above TIPE scheme has compact parameters, because of this share of parameters. The main technical challenge in the proof of the security of the scheme is to simulate the key generation oracle for two different types (i.e., ZIPE and NIPE) of keys *simultaneously*. To achieve this, we use a significantly different strategy to simulate NIPE keys than the security proof in [3]. The following theorem addresses the security of the scheme.

Theorem 2. *The above TIPE scheme is selectively secure under the n-DBDHE assumption.*

Before proving the theorem, we recall following lemma that is implicit in [8].

Lemma 1. *([8]) Let $\mathbb{G}$ be a multiplicative group with prime order p and g be its generator. Let n, m be some integer bounded by polynomial of λ, $\mathbf{a}$ be $\mathbf{a} = (a, a^2, \ldots, a^n) \in \mathbb{Z}_p^n$, $\tilde{\alpha}, \{w_i\}_{i=0}^m$ be elements in $\mathbb{Z}_p$, $\{\mathbf{z}_i\}_{i=0}^m$ be vectors in $\mathbb{Z}_p^n$. We also assume that $\mathbf{h} = (h_1, \ldots, h_n) \in \mathbb{Z}_p^n$ satisfies $\langle \mathbf{h}, \mathbf{z}_0 \rangle \neq 0$ and $\langle \mathbf{h}, \mathbf{z}_i \rangle = 0$ for $i \in [m]$. Then, there exists an PPT BHSim which takes $(\tilde{\alpha}, \{\mathbf{z}_i\}_{i=0}^m, \{w_i\}_{i=0}^m, \mathbf{h}, \{g^{a^i}\}_{i \in [2n] \setminus \{n+1\}})$ as input and outputs $(g^{a^{n+1} + \tilde{\alpha}} \cdot (g^{\langle \mathbf{z}_0, \mathbf{a} \rangle + w_0})^r, \{(g^{\langle \mathbf{z}_i, \mathbf{a} \rangle + w_i})^r\}_{i=1}^m)$ where $r \xleftarrow{\$} \mathbb{Z}_p$.*

Proof. (of Theorem 2.) We construct $\mathcal{B}$ that decides if $T = e(g, g)^{a^{n+1} s}$ given $(g, \{g^{a^i}\}_{i \in [2n] \setminus \{n+1\}}, g^s, T) \in \mathbb{G}^{2n+1} \times \mathbb{G}_T$ by using the selective adversary $\mathcal{A}$ against our scheme. We denote by $\mathbf{a}$ a vector $(a, a^2, \ldots, a^n)$.

Setup of Master Public Key. At the outset of the game, the adversary $\mathcal{A}$ declares the challenge vector $\mathbf{y}^\star = (y_1^\star, \ldots, y_n^\star) \in \mathbb{Z}_p^n$. $\mathcal{B}$ picks $\tilde{\alpha}, \tilde{v} \xleftarrow{\$} \mathbb{Z}_p$, $\tilde{\mathbf{u}} = (\tilde{u}_1, \ldots, \tilde{u}_n) \xleftarrow{\$} \mathbb{Z}_p^n$ and sets mpk as

$$\mathsf{mpk} = (g = g, e(g, g)^\alpha = e(g^a, g^{a^n}) \cdot e(g, g)^{\tilde{\alpha}}, \mathbf{U} = g^{\mathbf{a}} \cdot g^{\tilde{\mathbf{u}}}, V = g^{-\langle \mathbf{a}, \mathbf{y}^\star \rangle} \cdot g^{\tilde{v}}),$$

and gives it to $\mathcal{A}$. Here, we implicitly set $\alpha = \tilde{\alpha} + a^{n+1}$, $\mathbf{u} = \mathbf{a} + \tilde{\mathbf{u}}$, and $v = -\langle \mathbf{a}, \mathbf{y}^\star \rangle + \tilde{v}$.

Phase1 and 2. When $\mathcal{A}$ queries private key for $(\mathbf{x} = (x_1, \ldots, x_n), \mathsf{type}) \in \mathbb{Z}_p^* \times \mathbb{Z}_p^{n-1} \times \{\mathsf{ZIPE}, \mathsf{NIPE}\}$, $\mathcal{B}$ answers as follows.

– If $\mathsf{type} = \mathsf{ZIPE}$, we have $\langle \mathbf{x}, \mathbf{y}^\star \rangle \neq 0$. In this case, $\mathcal{B}$ first sets $\mathbf{z}_0 = -\mathbf{y}^\star, \mathbf{z}_1 = \mathbf{0}, \mathbf{z}_i = -\frac{x_i}{x_1}\mathbf{e}_1 + \mathbf{e}_i$ for $i = 2, \ldots, n$, $w_0 = \tilde{v}, w_1 = 1$, and $w_i = -\frac{x_i}{x_1}\tilde{u}_1 + \tilde{u}_i$ for $i = 2, \ldots, n$. Then $\mathcal{B}$ runs $\mathsf{BHSim}(\tilde{\alpha}, \{\mathbf{z}_i\}_{i=0}^n, \{w_i\}_{i=0}^n, \mathbf{x}, \{g^{a^i}\}_{i \in [2n] \setminus \{n+1\}}) \to (Z_0, \{Z_i\}_{i=1}^n)$ and returns $(D_1, D_2, \{K_i\}_{i=2}^n) = (Z_0, Z_1, \{Z_i\}_{i=2}^n)$. We claim that $(D_1, D_2, \{K_i\}_{i=2}^n)$ is distributed the same as real private key. At first, we check that the input to BHSim is in a valid form. To see this, it suffices to check that $\langle \mathbf{x}, \mathbf{z}_0 \rangle = \langle \mathbf{x}, -\mathbf{y}^\star \rangle \neq 0$, $\langle \mathbf{x}, \mathbf{z}_1 \rangle = \langle \mathbf{x}, \mathbf{0} \rangle = 0$, and $\langle \mathbf{x}, \mathbf{z}_i \rangle = \langle \mathbf{x}, -\frac{x_i}{x_1}\mathbf{e}_1 + \mathbf{e}_i \rangle = -x_1 \cdot \frac{x_i}{x_1} + x_i = 0$ for $i = 2, \ldots, n$. Since the input to BHSim is in a valid form, $D_1 = Z_0 = g^{\tilde{\alpha} + a^{n+1}}(g^{-\langle \mathbf{a}, \mathbf{y}^\star \rangle} \cdot g^{\tilde{v}})^r = g^\alpha V^r$, $D_2 = Z_1 = (g^{\langle \mathbf{0}, \mathbf{a} \rangle + 1})^r = g^r$, and

$$K_i = Z_i = (g^{\langle -\frac{x_i}{x_1}\mathbf{e}_1 + \mathbf{e}_i, \mathbf{a} \rangle - \frac{x_i}{x_1}\tilde{u}_1 + \tilde{u}_i})^r = (g^{-\frac{x_i}{x_1}(a + \tilde{u}_1)} \cdot g^{a^i + \tilde{u}_i})^r = (U_1^{-\frac{x_i}{x_1}} \cdot U_i)^r$$

for $i \in \{2, \ldots, n\}$ where $r \xleftarrow{\$} \mathbb{Z}_p$ as desired.

If $\mathsf{type} = \mathsf{NIPE}$, we have $\langle \mathbf{x}, \mathbf{y}^\star \rangle = 0$. In this case, $\mathcal{B}$ first sets $\mathbf{z}_0 = \mathbf{e}_1, \mathbf{z}_1 = \mathbf{0}, \mathbf{z}_i = -\frac{x_i}{x_1}\mathbf{e}_1 + \mathbf{e}_i$ for $i = 2, \ldots, n$, $\mathbf{z}_{n+1} = -\mathbf{y}^\star$, $w_0 = \tilde{u}_1, w_1 = 1$, $w_i = -\frac{x_i}{x_1}\tilde{u}_1 + \tilde{u}_i$ for $i = 2, \ldots, n$, and $w_{n+1} = \tilde{v}$. Then $\mathcal{B}$ runs $\mathsf{BHSim}(\tilde{\alpha}, \{\mathbf{z}_i\}_{i=0}^{n+1}, \{w_i\}_{i=0}^{n+1}, \mathbf{x}, \{g^{a^i}\}_{i \in [2n] \setminus \{n+1\}}) \to (Z_0, \{Z_i\}_{i=1}^{n+1})$ and returns $(D_1, D_2, D_3, \{K_i\}_{i=2}^n) = (Z_0, Z_1, Z_{n+1}, \{Z_i\}_{i=2}^n)$. We claim that $(D_1, D_2, D_3, \{K_i\}_{i=2}^n)$ is distributed the same as real private key. At first, we check that the input to BHSim is in a valid form. To see this, it suffices to check that $\langle \mathbf{x}, \mathbf{z}_0 \rangle = \langle \mathbf{x}, \mathbf{e}_1 \rangle = x_1 \neq 0$, $\langle \mathbf{x}, \mathbf{z}_1 \rangle = \langle \mathbf{x}, \mathbf{0} \rangle = 0$, $\langle \mathbf{x}, \mathbf{z}_i \rangle = \langle \mathbf{x}, -\frac{x_i}{x_1}\mathbf{e}_1 + \mathbf{e}_i \rangle = 0$ for $i = 2, \ldots, n$, and $\langle \mathbf{x}, \mathbf{z}_{n+1} \rangle = \langle \mathbf{x}, -\mathbf{y}^* \rangle = 0$. Since the input to BHSim is in a valid form, we have

$$D_1 = Z_0 = g^{\tilde{\alpha} + a^{n+1}} \cdot (g^{\langle \mathbf{a}, \mathbf{e}_1 \rangle} \cdot g^{\tilde{u}_1})^r = g^\alpha \cdot (g^{a + \tilde{u}_1})^r = g^\alpha U_1^r$$

where $r \xleftarrow{\$} \mathbb{Z}_p$. We can also check that $D_2 = g^r$ and $\{K_i\}_{i=2}^n = \{(U_1^{-\frac{x_i}{x_1}} \cdot U_i)^r\}_{i=2}^n$ by exactly the same computation as in the case of type = ZIPE. Finally, we have that $D_3 = Z_{n+1} = (g^{-\langle \mathbf{a}, \mathbf{y}^* \rangle + \tilde{v}})^r = V^r$ as desired.

Challenge. At some point in the game, $\mathcal{A}$ submits a pair of ciphertexts (M_0, M_1) to $\mathcal{B}$. $\mathcal{B}$ flips a random coin $\beta \xleftarrow{\$} \{0, 1\}$ and returns $(C_0, C_1, C_2) = (M_\beta \cdot e(g^s, g^{\tilde{\alpha}}) \cdot T, g^s, (g^s)^{-(\langle \mathbf{y}^*, \tilde{\mathbf{u}} \rangle + \tilde{v})})$ to $\mathcal{A}$. Since

$$(g^s)^{-(\langle \mathbf{y}^*, \tilde{\mathbf{u}} \rangle + \tilde{v})} = (g^{\langle -\mathbf{a}, \mathbf{y}^* \rangle + \tilde{v}} \cdot g^{\langle \mathbf{a} + \tilde{\mathbf{u}}, \mathbf{y}^* \rangle})^{-s} = (V U_1^{y_1^*} \cdots U_n^{y_n^*})^{-s}$$

and $e(g^s, g^{\tilde{\alpha}}) \cdot e(g, g)^{a^{n+1}s} = e(g, g)^{s\alpha}$, the ciphertext is in a valid form if $T = e(g, g)^{a^{n+1}s}$.

Guess. Finally, $\mathcal{A}$ outputs its guess β' for β. If $\beta' = \beta$, $\mathcal{A}$ outputs 1 for its guess. Otherwise, it outputs 0. If $T = e(g, g)^{sa^{n+1}}$, the above simulation is perfect and thus $\mathcal{A}$ has non-negligible advantage. On the other hand, If T is a random element in $\mathbb{G}_T$, $\mathcal{A}$'s advantage is 0. Therefore, if $\mathcal{A}$ breaks our scheme with non-negligible advantage, $\mathcal{B}$ has a non-negligible advantage against the n-DBDHE assumption.

5   TIPE Scheme from the DBDH Assumption

In this section, we propose a TIPE scheme from the DBDH assumption, which is one of the weakest assumptions in bilinear groups. By sequentially applying the conversions from TIPE to TIBBE in Sec. 3.1 and from TIBBE to non-monotonic KP-ABE in Sec. 3 to the scheme, we obtain a new non-monotonic KP-ABE scheme from the DBDH assumption. Compared to the Non-monotonic KP-ABE scheme from the same assumption in [28], the public key and ciphertext size of our scheme are approximately half the size of theirs, and the private key size is comparable.

Setup(λ, n) : It chooses bilinear groups $(\mathbb{G}, \mathbb{G}_T)$ of prime order $p > 2^\lambda$ with $g \xleftarrow{\$} \mathbb{G}$. It also picks $u, \alpha \xleftarrow{\$} \mathbb{Z}_p$ and $\mathbf{v} = (v_1, \ldots, v_n) \xleftarrow{\$} \mathbb{Z}_p^n$. Then it sets $U = g^u$ and $\mathbf{V} = (V_1, \ldots, V_n) = g^{\mathbf{v}}$. It finally outputs the master public key mpk $= (g, U, V_1, \ldots, V_n, e(g, g)^\alpha)$ and the master secret key msk $= \alpha$.

Encrypt$(\text{mpk}, M, \mathbf{y})$: To encrypt $M \in \mathbb{G}_T$ for the vector $\mathbf{y} = (y_1, \ldots, y_n) \in \mathbb{Z}_p^n$, it picks $s \xleftarrow{\$} \mathbb{Z}_p$ and computes the ciphertext as

$$C = \left(C_0 = M \cdot e(g, g)^{\alpha s}, C_1 = g^s, \{E_i = (U^{y_i} V_i)^{-s}\}_{i=1, \ldots n}\right).$$

KeyGen$(\text{msk}, \text{mpk}, (\mathbf{x}, \text{type}))$: To generate a private key for $\left(\mathbf{x} = (x_1, \ldots, x_n) \in \mathbb{Z}_p^n, \text{type} \in \{\text{ZIPE}, \text{NIPE}\}\right)$, it chooses $r \xleftarrow{\$} \mathbb{Z}_p$ and computes

$$\begin{cases} \mathsf{sk}_{(\mathbf{x},\mathsf{ZIPE})} = \left(D_1 = g^\alpha \cdot (V_1^{x_1} \cdots V_n^{x_n})^r, D_2 = g^r \right) & \text{if type} = \mathsf{ZIPE} \\ \mathsf{sk}_{(\mathbf{x},\mathsf{NIPE})} = \left(D_1 = g^\alpha U^r, D_2 = (V_1^{x_1} \cdots V_n^{x_n})^r, D_3 = g^r \right) & \text{if type} = \mathsf{NIPE}. \end{cases}$$

$\mathsf{Decrypt}(\mathsf{mpk}, C, \mathbf{y}, \mathsf{sk}_{(\mathbf{x},\mathsf{type})})$: It computes

$$\begin{cases} e(C_1, D_1) \cdot e(\prod_{i=1}^{n} E_i^{x_i}, D_2) = e(g,g)^{s\alpha} & \text{if type} = \mathsf{ZIPE} \\ e(C_1, D_1) \cdot \left(e(\prod_{i=1}^{n} E_i^{x_i}, D_3) \cdot e(C_1, D_2) \right)^{\frac{1}{\langle \mathbf{x},\mathbf{y} \rangle}} = e(g,g)^{s\alpha} & \text{if type} = \mathsf{NIPE} \end{cases}$$

and recovers the message by $C_0 / e(g,g)^{s\alpha} = \mathsf{M}$.

The following theorem addresses the security of the scheme. The proof will be found in the full version of this paper.

Theorem 3. *The above TIPE scheme is selectively secure under the DBDH assumption.*

6 Unbounded TIBBE Scheme

In the TIBBE schemes derived from the TIPE schemes in Sec. 4 and 5, the number of identities per ciphertext is bounded by a parameter n. In this section, we propose a TIBBE scheme without such a restriction. The structure of the construction can be seen as a combination of the IBBE scheme implicit in KP-ABE scheme in [30] and the IBR scheme in [21]. By applying the conversion in Sec. 3 to the scheme, we obtain the first non-monotonic KP-ABE scheme in the standard model that does not restrict the number of attributes per ciphertext or the number of times the same attribute can be used in an access formula associated with a private key.

$\mathsf{Setup}(\lambda)$: It chooses bilinear groups $(\mathbb{G}, \mathbb{G}_T)$ of prime order $p > 2^\lambda$ with $g \xleftarrow{\$} \mathbb{G}$. It also picks $H, U, V, W \xleftarrow{\$} \mathbb{G}$ and $b, \alpha \xleftarrow{\$} \mathbb{Z}_p$. Then it sets $B = g^b, B' = g^{b^2}, V' = V^b$. It finally outputs the master public key $\mathsf{mpk} = (g, H, U, W, B, B', V, V', e(g,g)^\alpha)$ and the master secret key $\mathsf{msk} = \alpha$.

$\mathsf{Encrypt}(\mathsf{mpk}, \mathsf{M}, S)$: To encrypt $\mathsf{M} \in \mathbb{G}_T$ for the set of identities $S = (\mathsf{ID}_1, \dots, \mathsf{ID}_k) \subset \mathbb{Z}_p$, it chooses $s, t_1, \dots, t_k \xleftarrow{\$} \mathbb{Z}_p$ and random $s_1, \dots, s_k \in \mathbb{Z}_p$ such that $s_1 + \dots + s_k = s$ and computes the ciphertext as $C =$

$$\left(C_0 = \mathsf{M} \cdot e(g,g)^{\alpha s}, C_1 = g^s, \begin{cases} C_{i,1} = W^{-s}(U^{\mathsf{ID}_i}H)^{-t_i}, C_{i,2} = g^{t_i} \\ C'_{i,1} = (B'^{\mathsf{ID}_i}V')^{-s_i}, C'_{i,2} = B^{s_i} \end{cases}_{i \in [k]} \right).$$

$\mathsf{KeyGen}(\mathsf{msk}, \mathsf{mpk}, (\mathsf{ID}, \mathsf{type}))$: To generate a private key for $\mathsf{ID} \in \mathbb{Z}_p$, it chooses $r \xleftarrow{\$} \mathbb{Z}_p$ and computes the private key as

$$\begin{cases} \mathsf{sk}_{(\mathsf{ID},\mathsf{IBBE})} = \left(D_1 = g^\alpha \cdot W^r, D_2 = (U^{\mathsf{ID}}H)^r, D_3 = g^r \right) & \text{if type} = \mathsf{IBBE} \\ \mathsf{sk}_{(\mathsf{ID},\mathsf{IBR})} = \left(D_1 = g^\alpha \cdot (B')^r, D_2 = (B^{\mathsf{ID}}V)^r, D_3 = g^r \right) & \text{if type} = \mathsf{IBR}. \end{cases}$$

Decrypt(mpk, C, S, sk$_{(\text{ID,type})}$): We assume that in the case of type $=$ IBBE, ID is contained in ID $\in S = \{\text{ID}_1, \ldots, \text{ID}_k\}$, so that decryption is possible. Therefore, there is an $\tau \in [k]$ such that ID $=$ ID$_\tau$. It computes

$$\begin{cases} e(C_1, D_1) \cdot e(C_{\tau,1}, D_3) \cdot e(C_{\tau,2}, D_2) = e(g,g)^{s\alpha} & \text{if type} = \text{IBBE} \\ e(C_1, D_1) \cdot \prod_{i=1}^{k} \left(e(C'_{i,1}, D_3) \cdot e(C'_{i,2}, D_2)\right)^{\frac{1}{\overline{\text{(ID}_i - \text{ID)}}}} = e(g,g)^{s\alpha} & \text{if type} = \text{IBR} \end{cases}$$

and recovers the message by $C_0 / e(g,g)^{s\alpha} = \mathsf{M}$.

We can prove selective security of the scheme under the new assumption that we call n-(A) assumption which is secure in the generic group model. The definition of the assumption and the proof will appear in the full version of this paper.

7   Unbounded Non-monotonic CP-ABE Scheme

In this section, we propose the first non-monotonic CP-ABE scheme that does not restrict the size of the attributes set or the number of times the same attribute can be used in an access formula. Our starting point for the construction of the scheme is the unbounded (monotonic) CP-ABE scheme in [30]. To support the non-monotonic access structure, we first construct a suitable revocation mechanism, which can be seen as a ciphertext-policy version of the IBR scheme in [21]. Then, we combine this with the CP-ABE scheme in [30] to obtain our new scheme. Because some parameters are shared between the two schemes, the public key of our scheme is only one group element longer than that of the scheme in [30], while our scheme supports a more general access structure.

Setup(λ) : It chooses bilinear groups $(\mathbb{G}, \mathbb{G}_T)$ of prime order $p > 2^\lambda$ with $g \xleftarrow{\$} \mathbb{G}$. It also picks $b, \alpha \xleftarrow{\$} \mathbb{Z}_p$ and $H, U, V, W \xleftarrow{\$} \mathbb{G}$. Then it sets $V' = U^b$ and outputs the master public key mpk $= (g, H, U, V, V', W, e(g,g)^\alpha)$ and the master secret key msk $= (\alpha, b)$.

KeyGen(msk, mpk, ω) : To generate a private key for a set of attributes $\omega = \{\omega_1, \ldots \omega_k\} \subset \mathbb{Z}_p$, it chooses $r, r_1, \ldots, r_k \xleftarrow{\$} \mathbb{Z}_p$ and random $r'_1, \ldots, r'_k \in \mathbb{Z}_p$ such that $r'_1 + \ldots + r'_k = r$. It then outputs the private key as

$$\mathsf{sk}_\omega = \left(D_1 = g^\alpha W^r, D_2 = g^r, \begin{cases} K_{i,1} = V^{-r}(U^{\omega_i}H)^{r_i}, & K_{i,2} = g^{r_i} \\ K'_{i,1} = (U^{b\omega_i}H^b)^{r'_i}, & K'_{i,2} = g^{br'_i} \end{cases}_{i \in [k]} \right).$$

Encrypt(mpk, $\mathsf{M}, \tilde{\mathbb{A}}$) : The input to the algorithm is the master public key mpk, the message $\mathsf{M} \in \mathbb{G}_T$ and a non-monotonic access structure $\tilde{\mathbb{A}}$ such that we have $\tilde{\mathbb{A}} = NM(\mathbb{A})$ for some monotonic access structure $\mathbb{A}$ over a set $\mathcal{P}$ of attributes and associated with a linear secret sharing scheme (L, π). Let L be an $\ell \times m$ matrix. First, it picks random $\mathbf{s} = (s, s_2, \ldots, s_m) \xleftarrow{\$} \mathbb{Z}_p^m$ and computes share of s for $\pi(i)$ by $\lambda_i = \langle \mathbf{L}_i \cdot \mathbf{s} \rangle$ for $i = 1, \ldots, \ell$. It then computes $C_0 = \mathsf{M} \cdot e(g,g)^{\alpha \cdot s}$, $C_1 = g^s$. It also computes $(C_{i,1}, C_{i,2}, C_{i,3})$ for every $i = 1, \ldots, \ell$ as follows.

$$
\begin{cases}
C_{i,1} = W^{\lambda_i} V^{t_i}, \ C_{i,2} = (U^{x_i} H)^{-t_i}, \ C_{i,3} = g^{t_i} & \text{if } \pi(i) = x_i \\
C_{i,1} = W^{\lambda_i} (V')^{t_i}, \ C_{i,2} = (U^{x_i} H)^{-t_i}, \ C_{i,3} = g^{t_i} & \text{if } \pi(i) = x'_i
\end{cases}
$$

where $t_i \xleftarrow{\$} \mathbb{Z}_p$. The final output is $C = (C_0, C_1, \{C_{i,1}, C_{i,2}, C_{i,3}\}_{i \in [\ell]})$.

$\mathsf{Decrypt}(\mathsf{mpk}, C, \omega, \mathsf{sk}_{\tilde{\mathbb{A}}})$: Assume first that the policy $\tilde{\mathbb{A}}$ is satisfied by the attribute set ω, so that decryption is possible. Since $\tilde{\mathbb{A}} = NM(\mathbb{A})$ for some access structure $\mathbb{A}$ associated with a linear secret sharing scheme (L, π), we have $\omega' = N(\omega) \in \mathbb{A}$ and we let $I = \{i | \pi(i) \in \omega'\}$. Since ω' is authorized in $\mathbb{A}$, the receiver can efficiently compute reconstruction coefficients $\{(i, \mu_i)\}_{i \in I} = \mathsf{Recon}_{L, \pi}(\omega')$ such that $\sum_{i \in I} \mu_i \lambda_i = s$. It parses $C = (C_0, C_1, \{C_{i,1}, C_{i,2}, C_{i,3}\}_{i \in [\ell]})$, $\mathsf{sk}_\omega = (D_1, D_2, \{K_{i,1}, K_{i,2}, K'_{i,1}, K'_{i,2}\}_{i \in [k]})$ and computes $e(g,g)^{r \cdot \lambda_i}$ for each $i \in I$ as

$$
\begin{cases}
e(C_{i,1}, D_2) \cdot e(C_{i,2}, K_{\tau,2}) \cdot e(C_{i,3}, K_{\tau,1}) \to e(g, W)^{r \lambda_i} & \text{if } \pi(i) = x_i \\
e(C_{i,1}, D_2) \cdot \prod_{j \in [k]} \left(e(C_{i,3}, K'_{j,1}) \cdot e(C_{i,2}, K'_{j,2}) \right)^{\frac{1}{x_i - \omega_j}} = e(g, W)^{r \lambda_i} & \text{if } \pi(i) = x'_i
\end{cases}
$$

where τ is the index such that $\omega_\tau = x_i$. Such τ exists if $i \in I$ and $\pi(i)$ is non-negated attribute. Next, it computes $e(C_1, D_1) \cdot \prod_{i \in I} \left(e(g, W)^{r \lambda_i} \right)^{-\mu_i} = e(g^s, g^\alpha) e(g, W)^{sr} e(g, W)^{-r \sum_{i \in I} \mu_i \lambda_i} = e(g,g)^{\alpha \cdot s}$. Finally, it recovers the message by $C_0 / e(g,g)^{s\alpha} = \mathsf{M}$.

We can prove selective security of the scheme under the new assumption that we call n-(B) assumption which is secure in the generic group model. The definition of the assumption and the proof will appear in the full version of this paper.

8 Comparisons

Here, we compare our schemes with existing schemes. In Table 1, we compare non-monotonic KP-ABE schemes with compact ciphertexts. In Table 2, we compare non-monotonic KP-ABE schemes from the DBDH assumption. In Table 3 (resp., 4), we compare the KP (resp., CP)-ABE schemes which allow unbounded size for set of attributes associated with ciphertext (resp., private key). In these tables, $\bar{n} = |\text{attribute set}| = |\omega|$, n is the maximum bound of $\bar{n}$ (i.e., $|\omega| < n$), φ is the number of allowed repetition of the same attributes which appear in a policy, and t_1 and t_2 are the number of non-negated and negated attributes that appear in an access policy. We also let $t = t_1 + t_2$. The terms "reg-exp." and "mult-exp." refer to regular and multi-exponentiation in $\mathbb{G}$ and $\mathbb{G}_T$. The Pippenger algorithm [29] can efficiently compute the latter. The term "pair" refers to pairing computation. The column "unbounded set" in Table 3 (resp., 4) states whether unbounded attribute set size is allowed for ciphertext (resp., for key) or not. The columun "unbounded multi-use" states whether unboudned reuse of the same policy for a key (resp., ciphertext) is allowed or not.

In Table 2, we only highlight the encryption cost. As for the efficiency of the decryption algorithm, our scheme in Sec. 5 is somewhat slower than [28], because of the additional exponentiations. Note that the schemes in [27] achieve adaptive security, whereas all the other schemes achieve only selective security.

Table 1. Comparison of non-monotonic KP-ABE with compact ciphertexts

Schemes	Master public key size $(|\mathbb{G}|, |\mathbb{G}_T|)$	Ciphertext overhead $|\mathbb{G}|$	Private key size $|\mathbb{G}|$	Computational cost for encryption (reg,mult)-exp	decryption (pair,mult-exp)	Assumption
ALP [3]	$(2n+2, 1)$	3	$(n+1)t$	$(2, 2)$	$(3, 3^*)$	n-DBDHE
Ours in Sec. 4.	$(n+2, 1)$	2	$(n+1)t + t_2$	$(2, 1)$	$(2, 2^*)$	n-DBDHE

* These multi-exponentiation is heavier than that needed in the encryption algorithm.

Table 2. Comparison of non-monotonic KP-ABE schemes from the DBDH

Schemes	Master public key size $(|\mathbb{G}|, |\mathbb{G}_T|)$	Ciphertext overhead $|\mathbb{G}|$	Private key size $|\mathbb{G}|$	Encryption cost reg-exp.	mult-exp.
OSW [28]	$(2n+2, 0)$	$2n-1$	$2t_1 + 3t_2$	2	$2n^\ddagger$
Ours in Sec. 5	$(n+2, 1)$	$n+1$	$2t_1 + 3t_2$	2	n

† For simplicity, we compare these schemes in a most basic form. However, we can modify the schemes so that the ciphertext size only depends on $\bar{n}$ instead of n, which might be preferable in many case, by the technique in [28]. As a result, master public key and the private key becomes larger, whereas it makes ciphertext size smaller and encryption/decryption cost lower.

‡ These multi-exponentiations are heavier than that of our scheme in Sec. 5.

Table 3. Comparison of KP-ABE schemes with unbounded attribute set size

Schemes	Access structure	Ciphertext overhead $(|\mathbb{G}|)$	unbounded set	Private key size$(\mathbb{G})$	unbounded multi-use	Assumption
LSW[21]	non-monotone	$3\bar{n}+1$	Yes	$2t + t_2$	Yes	RO+n-MEBDH
OT[27]	non-monotone	$14\bar{n}\varphi + 5$	Yes	$14t + 5$	No	DLIN
RW[30]	monotone	$2\bar{n} + 1$	Yes	$3t_1$	Yes	n-1assumption
LW[23]	monotone	$3\bar{n} + 1$	Yes	$4t_1$	Yes	assumption 1-4
Ours in Sec. 6	non-monotone	$4\bar{n} + 1$	Yes	$3t$	Yes	n-(A) assumption

§ LW scheme [23] is constructed in composite order group.

Table 4. Comparison of CP-ABE schemes with unbounded attribute set size

Schemes	Access structure	Ciphertext overhead $(|\mathbb{G}|)$	unbounded multi-use	Private key size$(\mathbb{G})$	unbounded set	Assumption
OT[27]	non-monotone	$14t + 5$	No	$14\bar{n}\varphi + 5$	Yes	DLIN
RW[30]	monotone	$3t_1 + 1$	Yes	$2\bar{n} + 2$	Yes	n-2 assumption
Ours in Sec. 7	non-monotone	$3t + 1$	Yes	$4\bar{n} + 2$	Yes	n-(B) assumption

Acknowledgement. We thank Yannis Rouselakis, Brent Waters, anonymous reviewers of PKC 2014, and members of Shin-Akarui-Angou-Benkyoukai for their helpful discussions and comments.

References

1. Attrapadung, N., Imai, H.: Conjunctive broadcast and attribute-based encryption. In: Shacham, H., Waters, B. (eds.) Pairing 2009. LNCS, vol. 5671, pp. 248–265. Springer, Heidelberg (2009)
2. Attrapadung, N., Libert, B.: Functional encryption for inner product: Achieving constant-size ciphertexts with adaptive security or support for negation. In: Nguyen, P.Q., Pointcheval, D. (eds.) PKC 2010. LNCS, vol. 6056, pp. 384–402. Springer, Heidelberg (2010)
3. Attrapadung, N., Libert, B., de Panafieu, E.: Expressive key-policy attribute-based encryption with constant-size ciphertexts. In: Catalano, D., Fazio, N., Gennaro, R., Nicolosi, A. (eds.) PKC 2011. LNCS, vol. 6571, pp. 90–108. Springer, Heidelberg (2011)
4. Beimel, A.: Secure Schemes for Secret Sharing and Key Distribution. PhD thesis, Israel Institute of Technology, Technion, Haifa, Israel (1986)
5. Bethencourt, J., Sahai, A., Waters, B.: Ciphertext-policy attribute-based encryption. In: IEEE Symposium on Security and Privacy, pp. 321–334 (2007)
6. Boneh, D., Boyen, X.: Secure identity based encryption without random oracles. In: Franklin, M. (ed.) CRYPTO 2004. LNCS, vol. 3152, pp. 443–459. Springer, Heidelberg (2004)
7. Boneh, D., Gentry, C., Waters, B.: Collusion resistant broadcast encryption with short ciphertexts and private keys. In: Shoup, V. (ed.) CRYPTO 2005. LNCS, vol. 3621, pp. 258–275. Springer, Heidelberg (2005)
8. Boneh, D., Hamburg, M.: Generalized identity based and broadcast encryption schemes. In: Pieprzyk, J. (ed.) ASIACRYPT 2008. LNCS, vol. 5350, pp. 455–470. Springer, Heidelberg (2008)
9. Boneh, D., Sahai, A., Waters, B.: Functional Encryption: Definitions and Challenges. In: Ishai, Y. (ed.) TCC 2011. LNCS, vol. 6597, pp. 253–273. Springer, Heidelberg (2011)
10. Chase, M.: Multi-authority attribute based encryption. In: Vadhan, S.P. (ed.) TCC 2007. LNCS, vol. 4392, pp. 515–534. Springer, Heidelberg (2007)
11. Chase, M., Chow, S.S.M.: Improving privacy and security in multi-authority attribute-based encryption. In: ACM Conference on Computer and Communications Security, pp. 121–130 (2009)
12. Cheung, L., Newport, C.C.: Provably secure ciphertext policy abe. In: ACM Conference on Computer and Communications Security, pp. 456–465 (2007)
13. Garg, S., Gentry, C., Halevi, S., Sahai, A., Waters, B.: Attribute-based encryption for circuits from multilinear maps. In: Canetti, R., Garay, J.A. (eds.) CRYPTO 2013, Part II. LNCS, vol. 8043, pp. 479–499. Springer, Heidelberg (2013)
14. Gorbunov, S., Vaikuntanathan, V., Wee, H.: Attribute-based encryption for circuits. In: STOC, pp. 545–554 (2013)
15. Goyal, V., Jain, A., Pandey, O., Sahai, A.: Bounded ciphertext policy attribute based encryption. In: Aceto, L., Damgård, I., Goldberg, L.A., Halldórsson, M.M., Ingólfsdóttir, A., Walukiewicz, I. (eds.) ICALP 2008, Part II. LNCS, vol. 5126, pp. 579–591. Springer, Heidelberg (2008)
16. Goyal, V., Pandey, O., Sahai, A., Waters, B.: Attribute-based encryption for fine-grained access control of encrypted data. In: ACM Conference on Computer and Communications Security, p. 89 (2006)
17. Hohenberger, S., Waters, B.: Attribute-based encryption with fast decryption. In: Kurosawa, K., Hanaoka, G. (eds.) PKC 2013. LNCS, vol. 7778, pp. 162–179. Springer, Heidelberg (2013)

18. Katz, J., Sahai, A., Waters, B.: Predicate encryption supporting disjunctions, polynomial equations, and inner products. In: Smart, N.P. (ed.) EUROCRYPT 2008. LNCS, vol. 4965, pp. 146–162. Springer, Heidelberg (2008)
19. Lewko, A.: Tools for simulating features of composite order bilinear groups in the prime order setting. In: Pointcheval, D., Johansson, T. (eds.) EUROCRYPT 2012. LNCS, vol. 7237, pp. 318–335. Springer, Heidelberg (2012)
20. Lewko, A., Okamoto, T., Sahai, A., Takashima, K., Waters, B.: Fully secure functional encryption: Attribute-based encryption and (Hierarchical) inner product encryption. In: Gilbert, H. (ed.) EUROCRYPT 2010. LNCS, vol. 6110, pp. 62–91. Springer, Heidelberg (2010)
21. Lewko, A.B., Sahai, A., Waters, B.: Revocation systems with very small private keys. In: IEEE Symposium on Security and Privacy, pp. 273–285 (2010)
22. Lewko, A., Waters, B.: Decentralizing attribute-based encryption. In: Paterson, K.G. (ed.) EUROCRYPT 2011. LNCS, vol. 6632, pp. 568–588. Springer, Heidelberg (2011)
23. Lewko, A., Waters, B.: Unbounded HIBE and attribute-based encryption. In: Paterson, K.G. (ed.) EUROCRYPT 2011. LNCS, vol. 6632, pp. 547–567. Springer, Heidelberg (2011)
24. Lewko, A., Waters, B.: New proof methods for attribute-based encryption: Achieving full security through selective techniques. In: Safavi-Naini, R., Canetti, R. (eds.) CRYPTO 2012. LNCS, vol. 7417, pp. 180–198. Springer, Heidelberg (2012)
25. Naor, M., Pinkas, B.: Efficient trace and revoke schemes. In: Frankel, Y. (ed.) FC 2000. LNCS, vol. 1962, pp. 1–20. Springer, Heidelberg (2001)
26. Okamoto, T., Takashima, K.: Fully secure functional encryption with general relations from the decisional linear assumption. In: Rabin, T. (ed.) CRYPTO 2010. LNCS, vol. 6223, pp. 191–208. Springer, Heidelberg (2010)
27. Okamoto, T., Takashima, K.: Fully secure unbounded inner-product and attribute-based encryption. In: Wang, X., Sako, K. (eds.) ASIACRYPT 2012. LNCS, vol. 7658, pp. 349–366. Springer, Heidelberg (2012)
28. Ostrovsky, R., Sahai, A., Waters, B.: Attribute-based encryption with non-monotonic access structures. In: ACM Conference on Computer and Communications Security, pp. 195–203 (2007)
29. Pippenger, N.: On the evaluation of powers and related problems (preliminary version). In: FOCS, pp. 258–263 (1976)
30. Rouselakis, Y., Waters, B.: Practical constructions and new proof methods for large universe attribute-based encryption. In: ACM Conference on Computer and Communications Security, pp. 463–474 (2013)
31. Sahai, A., Waters, B.: Fuzzy identity-based encryption. In: Cramer, R. (ed.) EUROCRYPT 2005. LNCS, vol. 3494, pp. 457–473. Springer, Heidelberg (2005)
32. Waters, B.: Ciphertext-policy attribute-based encryption: An expressive, efficient, and provably secure realization. In: Catalano, D., Fazio, N., Gennaro, R., Nicolosi, A. (eds.) PKC 2011. LNCS, vol. 6571, pp. 53–70. Springer, Heidelberg (2011)
33. Waters, B.: Functional encryption for regular languages. In: Safavi-Naini, R., Canetti, R. (eds.) CRYPTO 2012. LNCS, vol. 7417, pp. 218–235. Springer, Heidelberg (2012)

Online/Offline Attribute-Based Encryption

Susan Hohenberger and Brent Waters

Johns Hopkins University and University of Texas at Austin

Abstract. Attribute-based encryption (ABE) is a type of public key encryption that allows users to encrypt and decrypt messages based on user attributes. For instance, one can encrypt a message to any user satisfying the boolean formula ("crypto conference attendee" AND "PhD student") OR "IACR member". One drawback is that encryption and key generation computational costs scale with the complexity of the access policy or number of attributes. In practice, this makes encryption and user key generation a possible bottleneck for some applications.

To address this problem, we develop new techniques for ABE that split the computation for these algorithms into two phases: a preparation phase that does the vast majority of the work to encrypt a message or create a secret key *before* it knows the message or the attribute list/access control policy that will be used (or even the size of the list or policy). A second phase can then rapidly assemble an ABE ciphertext or key when the specifics become known. This concept is sometimes called "online/offline" encryption when only the message is unknown during the preparation phase; we note that the addition of unknown attribute lists and access policies makes ABE significantly more challenging.

One motivating application for this technology is mobile devices: the preparation work can be performed while the phone is plugged into a power source, then it can later rapidly perform ABE operations on the move without significantly draining the battery.

1 Introduction

Attribute-Based Encryption (ABE) was introduced by Sahai and Waters [20] as a more expressive form of encryption where one can encrypt according to some policy. For example, in a large corporate setting one might encrypt data to the policy of ("PROCUREMENT" AND "MANAGER") OR "ACCOUNTING". There are two main flavors of ABE. In Key-Policy ABE [10], a key is associated with a boolean formula ϕ and a ciphertext with a set S of attributes. One can decrypt iff the set S satisfies the formula ϕ. Alternatively, in Ciphertext-Policy ABE the roles are flipped; a key is associated with a set of attributes and the ciphertext with an access formula.

One challenge in building systems that use Attribute-Based Encryption is that the added functionality may come with a significant cost compared to standard public key cryptography. Consider a Key-Policy ABE system. Here the encryption time will scale with the number of attributes assigned to the ciphertext and key generation time will scale with the size of the boolean formula ascribed to a

H. Krawczyk (Ed.): PKC 2014, LNCS 8383, pp. 293–310, 2014.

user's private key. These costs could impact several applications. If the encryption algorithm is run on a mobile device, encryption time and battery power are of large importance. In other applications, authority servers that generate users' private keys may become a bottleneck. In both of these scenarios, *an exacerbating factor is that the cost for operations may vary widely between each ciphertext and key; thus forcing a system to provision for a load that matches a worst case scenario.* See [4,18,23] for further ABE performance cost details.

In this work, we aim to mitigate this problem by introducing methods for online/offline encryption and key generation in Attribute-Based Encryption. By moving the majority of the cost of an encryption and key generation into an offline phase, a system will be able to smooth the computational (and power) demand over a longer range of time, and thus only need the resources to handle the average case load.

Applications for this Technology. One motivating application for splitting the work this way is that a mobile device could be programmed to automatically do ABE preparation work whenever it is plugged into a power source, and then when it is unplugged, ABE ciphertexts could be rapidly formed with a significant reduction in battery consumption.

Another potential advantage of splitting work this way is that in some applications the online and offline work can be performed in different devices. One might perform the offline work for several encryptions on a high-end server and store these intermediate ciphertexts on a sensor device such that the small device never needs to perform a full encryption. In other applications, for security reasons a designer might wish to limit the number of outward facing servers that have access to the master secret key (or equivalent). Using online/offline techniques he could have several servers performing offline operations, but relatively fewer required for the final online step to generate a user's private key. While a corrupted offline server (without the master secret) could not break the system, in collusion it could produce outputs that would allow an eventual key holder to do so. Therefore, application of this idea would require further analysis and techniques to mitigate this scenario.

Background on Online/Offline Cryptography. Even, Goldreich and Micali [9] initiated online/offline techniques for signatures and Shamir and Tauman [22] introduced a general method using chameleon hash functions. In the context of signatures, one would like to perform most of the work for signing a message in the offline phase, but without knowing what the message to be signed is. Later in the online phase the signer will learn the message and given the offline work should be able to sign it relatively quickly.

The focus of our investigation is on moving encryption computation offline. In the basic encryption setting, the job is to perform most of the work for encryption offline, before the message is known. This is one of the reasons that stream ciphers, such as RC4, are sometimes preferred over certain block ciphers, because they operate by generating a pseudorandom string (which can be done offline) and then XORing it with the plaintext (in the online phase).

Let's next consider the task of moving encryption computation offline for Identity-Based Encryption (IBE), where neither the message nor the recipient's identity is known during the offline phase. Guo et al. [12] give an offline encryption system for Identity-Based Encryption (and other works [17,16,8,21] proposed different variants). We illustrate the main idea as a KEM[1] variant of the Boneh-Boyen [5] IBE system. In the offline phase, one will create a ciphertext by encrypting to a random identity $x \in \mathbb{Z}_p$ with randomness $s \in \mathbb{Z}_p$. The resulting BB-type ciphertext will have the form $C_1 = g^s, C_2 = (u^x h)^s$ and the encapsulated key will be $e(g,g)^{\alpha s}$, where the bilinear group description $\mathbb{G}$ of order p and $g, u, h, e(g,g)^{\alpha}$ are in the public parameters. The offline algorithm will store these ciphertext components as well as remember x and s; these together will consist of what we call an *intermediate ciphertext*. In the online phase, the encryptor will learn that she wishes to encrypt to a certain identity $\mathcal{I} \in \mathbb{Z}_p$. To do this, she simply adds a small "correction factor" $r \cdot (\mathcal{I} - x) \in \mathbb{Z}_p$ to the ciphertext components C_1, C_2. The computation only takes one multiplication and subtraction in $\mathbb{Z}_p$. A modified decryption algorithm with the correct private key can then extract the required symmetric key. We note that treating the system as a Key Encapsulation Mechanism allows us to separate the issues of learning the identity in the online phase versus learning the message in the online phase.

The Challenge for ABE. From the above description, one can see that the correction techniques critically rely on there being well-known algebraic relationships between the Boneh-Boyen hashes of different identities. Unfortunately, these do not exist in most initial ABE systems [10,6,24] as an attribute for string x would typically be represented as either a random group element h_x in the parameters or as the result of a (random oracle modeled) hash function $H(x)$. A second challenge is that the size and structure of ciphertext descriptors is more complex in ABE systems. For instance, in a KP-ABE system the number of attributes associated with a ciphertext may vary widely between each encryption. If one encrypts to a small number in each offline stage, the intermediate ciphertext may be not useable. If one encrypts to a large or maximum number in each offline phase, it can result in much wasted work. Using offline computation efficiently becomes a challenge in this setting. For ciphertext-policy ABE, finding a good solution is more challenging as the "unknown" is an complex access structure.

Our Contributions. We develop new techniques for online/offline ABE encryption and key generation that tackle these challenges. The first non-trivial task is to identity ABE constructions that have the required algebraic structure to enable online/offline computation. Unfortunately, most existing schemes do not. However, a few do. We first identified the recent "large universe" construction of Lewko and Waters [14] as a candidate base scheme due to its algebraic structure

---

[1] A key encapsulation mechanism, where the public key ciphertext encapsulates a symmetric key which could later be used to symmetrically encrypt the plaintext.

that appears amenable to adding correction factors.[2] We finally decided to use a recent more efficient prime-order variant due to Rouselakis and Waters [19]. (We are not aware of any other ABE schemes that can support a similarly efficient online/offline tradeoff.)

We begin by designing online/offline encryption algorithms for Key-Policy ABE. For our first construction we assume a set number of attributes that will be associated with each ciphertext. In this setting we develop a correction technique for the KP-ABE [19] system. We prove security by directly reducing to the security of [19]. This has the advantage of simplicity in that we do not need to revisit the guts of the prior proof. In addition, we will automatically inherenit any future improvements in the proof for the underlying scheme.

For reasons, discussed above assuming a fixed number of attributes per ciphertext is undesirable. To this end we come up with a method of "pooling" work done offline. In this system an encryptor will continuously create offline ciphertext pieces and add these to a pool. When the encryption algorithm later needs to encrypt to a set S of attributes, it grabs $|S|$ pieces from the pool connecting each one to a single attribute from S. The work per attribute is dominated by one multiplication in $\mathbb{Z}_p$. We describe this as a "connect and correct" approach.

We extend our offline encryption approach to the more complex case of Ciphertext-Policy ABE. The challenge here is that a CP-ABE ciphertext is associated with a Linear Secret Sharing Scheme (LSSS) matrix. Again, we develop a pooling technique. However, in this application for each row of the matrix M given online, we will need to correct each ciphertext component to an LSSS share in the exponent and to the corresponding attribute. Finally, we show how online/offline key generation can be derived from our encryption techniques. We observe a symmetry between CP-ABE encryption and KP-ABE key generation that allows us to develop an online/offline pair of algorithms for the latter.

Combining with Outsourcing for ABE. We make a brief detour here to discuss how the results of this work might be combined with prior ABE results to make a practical overall system.

In 2011, Green, Hohenberger and Waters [11] presented a solution for outsourcing the decryption of ABE ciphertexts. That is, they assumed that ABE ciphertexts might be stored in the cloud. They then showed how a user can provide the cloud with a *single* translation key that allows the cloud to translate *any* ABE ciphertext satisfied by that user's attributes into a very short El Gamal-style ciphertext, without the cloud being able to read any part of the user's messages. These transmitted ciphertexts are short (saving on bandwidth and receiving time), but also quick to decrypt (with roughly one or two exponentiations). Thus, the ability to outsource decryption to the cloud allows a mobile device to quickly decrypt an ABE-encrypted message.

---

[2] Interestingly, [14] aimed for a large universe construction in the standard model and thus our use of the schemes's additional structure is a byproduct of removing the random oracles.

Conversely, the results of this work allow a mobile device to quickly *encrypt* an ABE-encrypted message. These two results could be combined into one system, where a mobile device would be fully ABE operational while drastically reducing the computational costs for both decryption (with the help of the cloud) and encryption (with the help of a preparation phase while the phone charges). We believe that creative solutions of this sort can be implemented transparently, but will provide noticeably better performance for users.

2   Definitions for Online/Offline ABE

We work in the key encapsulation mechanism (KEM) setting, where the attribute-based ciphertext hides a symmetric session key that can then be used to symmetrically encrypt data of arbitrary length. The goal in the online/offline setting is to allow as much precomputation of attribute-based ciphertext as possible *without* knowing the intended access policy (ciphertext-policy) or set of attributes (key-policy). We refer the reader to [13] for a review of access structures, linear secret sharing schemes (LSSS) and related conventions.

Definition 1 (Online/Offline Attribute-Based KEM Specification). *Let S represent a set of attributes and $\mathbb{A}$ an access structure. For generality, we will define (I_{key}, I_{enc}) as the inputs to the extract and online encryption functions respectively. In a KP-ABE scheme $(I_{key}, I_{enc}) := (\mathbb{A}, S)$, while in a CP-ABE scheme, we have $(I_{key}, I_{enc}) := (S, \mathbb{A})$. We define the function f as follows:*

$$f(I_{key}, I_{enc}) := \begin{cases} 1 & \text{if } I_{enc} \in I_{key} \text{ in KP-AB setting} \\ 1 & \text{if } I_{key} \in I_{enc} \text{ in CP-AB setting} \\ 0 & \text{otherwise.} \end{cases}$$

An online/offline KP-AB (resp., CP-AB) key-encapsulation mechanism for access structure space $\mathcal{G}$ is a tuple of the following algorithms:

Setup$(\lambda, U) \rightarrow (\text{PK}, \text{MK})$. *The setup algorithm takes as input a security parameter λ and a universe description U, which defines the set of allowed attributes in the system. It outputs the public parameters PK and the master secret key MK.*

Extract$(\text{MK}, I_{key}) \rightarrow \text{SK}$. *The extract algorithm takes as input the master secret key MK and an access structure (resp., set of attributes) I_{key} and outputs a private key SK associated with the attributes.*

Offline.Encrypt$(\text{PK}) \rightarrow \text{IT}$. *The offline encryption algorithm takes as input the public parameters PK and outputs an intermediate ciphertext IT.*

Online.Encrypt$(\text{PK}, \text{IT}, I_{enc}) \rightarrow (\text{key}, \text{CT})$. *The online encryption algorithm takes as input the public parameters PK, an intermediate ciphertext IT and a set of attributes (resp., access structure) I_{enc} and outputs a session key key and a ciphertext CT.*

Decrypt(SK, CT) → key. *The decryption algorithm takes as input a private key SK for I_{key} and a ciphertext CT associated with I_{enc} and decapsulates ciphertext CT to recover a session key key if S satisfies $\mathbb{A}$ or the error message $\perp$ otherwise.*

For a fixed universe description U and $\lambda \in \mathbb{N}$, the KP-AB correctness property requires that for all (PK, MK) $\in$ Setup(λ, U), *all* $S \subseteq U$, *all* $\mathbb{A} \in \mathcal{G}$, *all* SK $\in$ Extract(MK, $\mathbb{A}$), *if* (key, CT) $\in$ Online.Encrypt(PK, Offline.Encrypt(PK), S) *and if S satisfies $\mathbb{A}$, then* Decrypt(SK, CT) *outputs* key. *CP-AB correctness is defined analogously, with the last inputs to* Extract *and* Online.Encrypt *reversed.*

Security Model for Online/Offline AB-KEM. Let $\Pi = ($Setup, Extract, Offline.Encrypt, Online.Encrypt, Decrypt) be an AB-KEM for access structure space $\mathcal{G}$, and consider the following experiment for an adversary $\mathcal{A}$, parameter λ and attribute universe U:

The Online/Offline AB-KEM experiment OO-ABKEM-Exp$_{\mathcal{A},\Pi}(\lambda, U)$:

Setup. The challenger runs the Setup algorithm and gives the public parameters, PK to the adversary.

Phase 1. The challenger initializes an empty table T, an empty set D and an integer counter $j = 0$. Proceeding adaptively, the adversary can repeatedly make any of the following queries:

  - Create(I_{key}): The challenger sets $j := j + 1$. It runs the key generation algorithm on I_{key} to obtain the private key SK and stores in table T the entry (j, I_{key}, SK).
    Note: Create can be repeatedly queried with the same input.
  - Corrupt(i): If there exists an ith entry in table T, then the challenger obtains the entry (i, I_{key}, SK) and sets $D := D \cup \{I_{key}\}$. It then returns to the adversary the private key SK. If no such entry exists, then it returns $\perp$.
  - Decrypt(i, CT): If there exists an ith entry in table T, then the challenger obtains the entry (i, I_{key}, SK) and returns to the adversary the output of the decryption algorithm on input (SK, CT). If no such entry exists, then it returns $\perp$.

Challenge. The adversary gives a challenge value I_{enc}^* such that for all $I_{key} \in D$, $f(I_{key}, I_{enc}^*) \neq 1$. The challenger runs the algorithm Online.Encrypt(PK, Offline.Encrypt(PK), I_{enc}^*) to obtain (key*, CT*). It then randomly selects a bit b. If $b = 0$, it returns (key*, CT*) to the adversary. If $b = 1$, it selects a random session key R in the session key space and returns (R, CT^*).

Phase 2. Phase 1 is repeated with the restrictions that the adversary cannot

  - trivially obtain a private key for the challenge ciphertext. That is, it cannot issue a Corrupt query that would result in a value I_{key} which satisfies $f(I_{key}, I_{enc}^*) = 1$ being added to D.
  - issue a decryption query on the challenge ciphertext CT*.

Guess. The adversary outputs a guess b' of b. The output of the experiment is 1 if and only if $b = b'$.

Definition 2 (Online/Offline AB-KEM Security). *An online/offline AB-KEM* Π *is CCA-secure (or secure against* chosen-ciphertext attacks*) for attribute universe* U *if for all probabilistic polynomial-time adversaries* $\mathcal{A}$, *there exists a negligible function negl such that:*

$$\Pr[\text{OO-ABKEM-Exp}_{\mathcal{A},\Pi}(\lambda, U) = 1] \leq \frac{1}{2} + negl(\lambda).$$

CPA Security. We say that a system is *CPA*-secure (or secure against *chosen-plaintext attacks*) if we remove the Decrypt oracle in both Phase 1 and 2.

Selective Security. We say that a system is *selectively* secure if we add an Init stage before Start where the adversary outputs the challenge I^*_{enc} (instead of waiting until Challenge).

3   A KP-ABE Scheme with Online/Offline Encryption

We now show how to extend the unbounded KP-ABE scheme of Rouselakis and Waters [19, Appendix C] to be an online/offline system. We will work in a key encapsulation mechanism (KEM) model as specified in Defintion 2, so that we can focus on preparing for an unknown attribute set. Any plaintext can be encrypted in a hybrid manner during the online phase by a symmetric cipher keyed with the encapsulated key. We first show a simple system that assumes a bound P on the maximum number of attributes that can be used to encrypt a ciphertext. We show how to remove this bound in Section 3.2.

Setup(λ, U). The setup algorithm takes in a security parameter λ and a universe U of attributes. chooses a bilinear group $\mathbb{G}$ of prime order $p \in \Theta(2^\lambda)$. It also chooses random generators $g, h, u, w \in \mathbb{G}$ and picks a random exponent $\alpha \in \mathbb{Z}_p$. It then sets the keys as:

$$PK = (\mathbb{G}, p, g, h, u, w, e(g,g)^\alpha), \quad MSK = (PK, \alpha).$$

We assume that the universe of attributes can be encoded as elements in $\mathbb{Z}_p$.

Extract$(MSK, (M, \rho))$. The extract algorithm takes as input the master secret key MSK and an LSSS access structure (M, ρ). Let M be an $\ell \times n$ matrix. The function ρ associates rows of M to attributes. The algorithm initially chooses random values $y_2, \ldots, y_n \in \mathbb{Z}_p$. It then computes ℓ shares of the master secret key as $(\lambda_1, \lambda_2, \ldots, \lambda_\ell) := M \cdot (\alpha, y_2, \ldots, y_n)^T$ (where T denotes the transpose). It then picks ℓ random exponents $t_1, t_2, \ldots, t_\ell \in \mathbb{Z}_p$. For $i = 1$ to ℓ, it computes

$$K_{i,0} := g^{\lambda_i} w^{t_i} \ K_{i,1} := \left(u^{\rho(i)} h\right)^{-t_i} \ K_{i,2} := g^{t_i}.$$

The private key is SK $:= ((M, \rho), \{K_{i,0}, K_{i,1}, K_{i,2}\}_{i \in [1,\ell]})$.

Offline.Encrypt(PK). The offline encryption algorithm takes in the public parameters only. Here we describe the basic system which assumes a maximum bound of P attributes will be associated with any ciphertext. We describe more advanced variations in Section 3.2. The algorithm first picks a random $s \in \mathbb{Z}_p$ and computes

$$\text{key} := e(g,g)^{\alpha s} \quad C_0 := g^s.$$

Next, for $j = 1$ to P, it chooses random $r_j, x_j \in \mathbb{Z}_p$ and computes

$$C_{j,1} := g^{r_j} \quad C_{j,2} := (u^{x_j}h)^{r_j}w^{-s}.$$

One can view this as encrypting for a random attribute x_j, where this will be corrected in the online phase. The work done in the offline phase is roughly equivalent to the work of the regular encryption algorithm in [19, Appendix C].
    The intermediate ciphertext is $\text{IT} := (\text{key}, C_0, \{r_j, x_j, C_{j,1}, C_{j,2}\}_{j \in [1,P]})$.

Online.Encrypt(PK, IT, S). The online encryption KEM algorithm takes as input the public parameters, an intermediate ciphertext IT, and a set of attributes $S = (A_1, A_2, \ldots, A_{k \leq P})$. For $j = 1$ to k, it computes $C_{j,3} := (r_j \cdot (A_j - x_j)) \mod p$. Intuitively, this will correct to the proper attributes. It sets the ciphertext:
$$\text{CT} := (S, C_0, \{C_{j,1}, C_{j,2}, C_{j,3}\}_{j \in [1,k]}).$$
The encapsulated key is key. The dominant cost is one multiplication in $\mathbb{Z}_p$ per attribute in S.

Decrypt(SK, CT). The decryption algorithm in the KEM setting recovers the encapsulated key. It takes as input a ciphertext $\text{CT} = (S, C_0, \{C_{j,1}, C_{j,2}, C_{j,3}\}_{j \in [1,k]})$ for attribute set S and a private key $\text{SK} = ((M, \rho), \{K_{i,0}, K_{i,1}, K_{i,2}\}_{i \in [1,\ell]})$ for access structure (M, ρ). If S does not satisfy this access structure, then the algorithm issues an error message. Otherwise, it sets $I := \{i : \rho(i) \in S\}$ and computes constants $w_i \in \mathbb{Z}_p$ such that $\sum_{i \in I} w_i \cdot M_i = (1, 0, \ldots, 0)$, where M_i is the i-th row of the matrix M. Then it then recovers the encapsulated key by calculating key :=

$$\prod_{i \in I} \left(e(C_0, K_{i,0}) \cdot e(C_{j,1}, K_{i,1}) \cdot e(C_{j,2} \cdot u^{C_{j,3}}, K_{i,2}) \right)^{w_i} = e(g,g)^{\alpha s} \qquad (1)$$

where j is the index of the attribute $\rho(i)$ in S (it depends on i). This does not increase the number of pairing operations over [19, Appendix C], although it adds $|I|$ exponentiations.

Correctness. If the attribute set S of the ciphertext is authorized, we have that $\sum_{i \in I} w_i \lambda_i = \alpha$. Therefore, key:

$$:= \prod_{i \in I} \left(e(C_0, K_{i,0}) \cdot e(C_{j,1}, K_{i,1}) \cdot e(C_{j,2} \cdot u^{C_{j,3}}, K_{i,2}) \right)^{w_i}$$

$$= \prod_{i \in I} (e(g^s, g^{\lambda_i} w^{t_i}) \cdot e(g^{r_j}, (u^{\rho(i)} h)^{-t_i}) \cdot e((u^{x_j} h)^{r_j} w^{-s} \cdot u^{r_j(\rho(i)-x_j)}, g^{t_i}))^{w_i}$$

$$= \prod_{i \in I} (e(g,g)^{s\lambda_i} \cdot e(g,w)^{st_i} \cdot e(g,u)^{-r_j t_i \rho(i)} \cdot$$

$$e(g,h)^{-r_j t_i} \cdot e(g,u)^{\rho(i) r_j t_i} \cdot e(g,h)^{r_j t_i} \cdot e(g,w)^{-st_i})^{w_i}$$

$$= \prod_{i \in I} e(g,g)^{sw_i \lambda_i} = e(g,g)^{s\alpha}.$$

Recall that in the symmetric setting $e(g,u) = e(u,g)$, for all $g, u \in \mathbb{G}$, although this scheme can operate in an asymmetric setting with small alterations.

3.1   Proof of Selective Security

Discussion on Security. We shortly show that the security of our online/offline system can be directly based on the security of the underlying Rouselakis-Waters [19, Appendix C] system. The Rouselakis-Waters system that we reduce security to is selectively secure based on a "q-type" assumption in prime order groups. We remark that our techniques appear to be equally ammenable to transforming the Lewko-Waters [15] system to an online/offline system. The Lewko-Waters system is proven selectively secure from a static assumption in composite order groups. If such a transformation were done (as well as a reduction to their scheme), the new scheme would inherit those assumptions.

In [10, Section 9], Goyal et al. discuss how to combine delegation in their ABE systems with the techniques of Canneti-Halevi-Katz [7] to build a CCA secure ABE scheme from a CPA one. We believe that a similar delegation structure exists in our schemes, so that similar techniques would likely work out (although we do not work out the details here).

Theorem 1. *The above online/offline KP-AB-KEM scheme is selectively CPA-secure with respect to Definition 2 assuming that the scheme of Rouselakis and Waters [19, Appendix C] is a selectively CPA-secure KP-ABE system.*

Proof. To prove the theorem, we will show that any PPT attacker $\mathcal{A}$ with a non-negligible advantage in the OO-ABKEM-Exp experiment against the above scheme, which we will denote $\Pi_{OO} = $ (Setup, Extract, Offline.Encrypt, Online.Encrypt, Decrypt), can be used to break the selective CPA-security of the Rouselakis-Waters scheme, which we will denote $\Pi_{RW} = $ (Setup$_{RW}$, Extract$_{RW}$, Encrypt$_{RW}$, Decrypt$_{RW}$), with a PPT simulator $\mathcal{B}$.

The simulator plays the challenger and interacts with $\mathcal{A}$ in OO-ABKEM-Exp with security parameter λ and the universe of attributes set to $U = \mathbb{Z}_p$.

Initialization. Initially, $\mathcal{B}$ receives an attribute set $S^* = \{A_1^*, A_2^*, \ldots, A_k^*\} \subseteq U$ from $\mathcal{A}$ and gives it to the RW challenger.

Setup. Next, $\mathcal{B}$ receives the public parameters $\text{PK} = (\mathbb{G}, p, g, h, u, w, e(g, g)^\alpha)$ from the RW challenger and passes them to $\mathcal{A}$ unchanged.

Phase 1. The secret keys are the same in both schemes, so any key generation request from $\mathcal{A}$ is passed to the RW challenger to obtain the key.

Challenge. $\mathcal{B}$ chooses two distinct, random messages m_0, m_1 in the RW message space and sends them to its RW challenger, and receives back a challenge cipher-text $\text{CT}_{RW}^* = (S^*, C, C_0, \{C_{j,1}, C_{j,2}\}_{j \in [1,|S^*|]})$. Here C is the encrypted message times $e(g, g)^{\alpha s}$, $C_0 = g^s$ and for each attribute $A_j \in S^*$, we have $C_{j,1} = g^{r_j}$ and $C_{j,2} = (u^{A_j} h)^{r_j} w^{-s}$.

It then selects random values $z_1, \ldots, z_{|S|} \in \mathbb{Z}_p$ and computes the ciphertext CT_{OO}^* as (S^*, C_0) followed by

$$C_{j,1}^* := C_{j,1} = g^{r_j} \quad C_{j,2}^* := C_{j,2} \cdot u^{-z_j} = (u^{A_j} h)^{r_j} w^{-s} u^{-z_j} \quad C_{j,3}^* := z_j.$$

To see why this is a correctly formed ciphertext, one needs to recall the third pairing of equation 1, where one must compute $e(C_{j,2}^* \cdot u^{C_{j,3}^*}, K_{i,2})$, as well as observe that the ciphertext is randomized to have the proper distribution. The z_j blinding will cancel out in this step. Next, $\mathcal{B}$ guess which message was encrypted $\tau_\mathcal{B} \in \{0, 1\}$ and computes $\text{key}_{guess} := C/m_{\tau_\mathcal{B}}$. Finally, $\mathcal{B}$ then sends to $\mathcal{A}$ the tuple $(\text{key}_{guess}, \text{CT}_{OO}^*)$.

Phase 2. $\mathcal{B}$ proceeds as in Phase 1.

Guess. Eventually, $\mathcal{A}$ outputs a bit $\tau_\mathcal{A}$. If $\tau_\mathcal{A} = 0$ (meaning that $\mathcal{A}$ guesses that key_{guess} is the key encapsulated by CT_{OO}^*), then $\mathcal{B}$ outputs $\tau_\mathcal{B}$. If $\tau_\mathcal{A} = 1$ (meaning that $\mathcal{A}$ guesses that key_{guess} is a random key), then $\mathcal{B}$ outputs $1 - \tau_\mathcal{B}$. The distribution for $\mathcal{A}$ is perfect. Thus, if $\mathcal{A}$ has advantage ϵ in the OO-ABKEM-Exp experiment, then $\mathcal{B}$ breaks the RW KP-ABE system with the same probability.

3.2   A More Advanced System: Pooling Attributes for an Unbounded System

Previously, we presented a system that imposed a bound of P attributes associated with any ciphertext. We presented P as if it was a system-wide bound for all ciphertexts, for simplicity. A slightly less naive solution would involve creating a set of intermediate ciphertexts prepared for different sizes of attribute sets, and then pulling the "right-sized IT" off-the-shelf during the online phase (e.g., create one IT for a set of size 1, another for a set of size 2, etc.). However, these approaches could prove wasteful, as certain ITs may be created and stored without being used.

Pooling Construction. Instead, we introduce the idea of "pooling" to eliminate waste during the offline phase. The intermediate ciphertext is now comprised of two logical types of objects: a main module and an attribute module. During the offline phase(s), an arbitrary number of main and attribute modules are independently created. During the online phase for attribute set S, one main module and $|S|$ attribute modules will be consumed. The critical feature of this approach is that any attribute module can be attached to any main module. The online phase uses exactly what it needs, and any modules left in the pool can be used on subsequent ciphertexts.

Specifically, during Offline.Encrypt, a main module is computed as follows. It picks a random $s \in \mathbb{Z}_p$ and sets $\mathrm{IT}_{main} := (\mathsf{key}, C_0, C_w)$, where these values are computed as

$$\mathsf{key} := e(g,g)^{\alpha s} \ C_0 := g^s \ C_w := w^{-s}.$$

During Offline.Encrypt, an attribute module is computed as follows. It picks a random $r, x \in \mathbb{Z}_p$ and sets $\mathrm{IT}_{att} := (r, x, C_1', C_2')$, where these values are computed as

$$C_1' := g^r \ C_2' := (u^x h)^r.$$

During Online.Encrypt for an attribute set S, the algorithm selects any one main module $\mathrm{IT}_{main} := (\mathsf{key}, C_0, C_w)$ and any $|S|$ attribute modules $\mathrm{IT}_{att,j} := (r_j, x_j, C_{j,1}', C_{j,2}')$ available in the pool. Finally, it computes CT as $(S, C_0, \{C_{j,1}, C_{j,2}, C_{j,3}\}_{j \in [1,|S|]})$, where

$$C_{j,1} := C_{j,1}' = g^{r_j} \ C_{j,2} := C_{j,2}' \cdot C_w = (u^{x_j} h)^{r_j} \cdot w^{-s} \ C_{j,3} := r_j \cdot (A_j - x_j).$$

The encapsulated key is key.

Security Discussion. The dominant cost in the online encryption algorithm is 2 modular multiplications per attribute in S. To formally capture the pooling model, the specification and security definition in Section 2 would need to be expanded to have the Offline.Encrypt algorithm keep state (e.g., the pool) between iterations and to pass this state into Online.Encrypt as well. Since pooling does not impact the structure or distribution of the final ciphertexts over Section 3 and the adversary in the security experiment only views final ciphertexts, it is relatively straightforward to prove the selective security of the pooling scheme.

4   A CP-ABE Scheme with Online/Offline Encryption

We now turn our attention to developing online/offline CP-ABE systems. This is intuitively harder than KP-ABE, because the structure of ciphertext is more complex. We must now be able to create an intermediate ciphertext in the offline phase that can be quickly be translated to a ciphertext for a hitherto unknown access structure. To do this, we will use and extend the basic "correction" and pooling concepts introduced for KP-ABE. Our online/offline system is based on the unbounded CP-ABE scheme of Rouselakis and Waters [19, Section 4], where again it takes a special algebraic structure to make this work, which most other CP-ABE systems do not appear to have. As before, we are working in the KEM model. We'll first show a simple system that assumes a bound P on the maximum number of rows in an LSSS access structure that will be used to encrypt. We will subsequently discuss how to remove this bound.

Setup(λ, U). The setup algorithm chooses a bilinear group $\mathbb{G}$ of prime order $p \in \Theta(2^\lambda)$. It also chooses random generators $g, h, u, v, w \in \mathbb{G}$ and picks a random exponent $\alpha \in \mathbb{Z}_p$. It then sets the keys as:

$$\text{PK} = (\mathbb{G}, p, g, h, u, v, w, e(g,g)^\alpha), \quad \text{MSK} = (\text{PK}, \alpha).$$

Again, we will view the attribute universe as consisting of elements in $\mathbb{Z}_p$.

Extract(MSK, S). The extract algorithm takes as input the master secret key MSK and an attribute set $S = \{A_1, A_2, \ldots, A_k\} \subseteq \mathbb{Z}_p$. The algorithm chooses random values $r, r_1, r_2, \ldots, r_k \in \mathbb{Z}_p$. It then computes $K_0 := g^\alpha w^r, K_1 := g^r$, and for $i = 1$ to k, it computes

$$K_{i,2} := g^{r_i} \quad K_{i,3} := \left(u^{A_i} h\right)^{r_i} v^{-r}.$$

The private key is $\text{SK} := (S, K_0, K_1, \{K_{i,2}, K_{i,3}\}_{i \in [1,k]})$.

Offline.Encrypt(PK). The offline encryption algorithm takes in the public parameters only. Here we describe the basic system which assumes a maximum bound of P rows in any LSSS access structure used in a ciphertext. We describe more advanced variations in Section 4.1. The algorithm first picks a random $s \in \mathbb{Z}_p$ and computes

$$\text{key} := e(g,g)^{\alpha s} \quad C_0 := g^s.$$

Next, for $j = 1$ to P, it chooses random $\lambda'_j, x_j, t_j \in \mathbb{Z}_p$ and computes

$$C_{j,1} := w^{\lambda'_j} v^{t_j} \quad C_{j,2} := (u^{x_j} h)^{-t_j} \quad C_{j,3} := g^{t_j}.$$

One can view this as encrypting for a random attribute x_j with a random "share" λ'_j of s, where this will be corrected in the online phase. We remark that the work done in the offline phase is roughly equivalent to the work of the regular encryption algorithm in [19, Section 4].

Intermediate ciphertext is $\text{IT} := (\text{key}, s, C_0, \{\lambda'_j, t_j, x_j, C_{j,1}, C_{j,2}, C_{j,3}\}_{j \in [1,P]})$.

Online.Encrypt$(\text{PK}, \text{IT}, (M, \rho))$. The online encryption KEM algorithm takes as input the public parameters, an intermediate ciphertext IT, and an LSSS access structure (M, ρ), where M is an $\ell \times n$ matrix and $\ell \leq P$. It picks random $y_2, \ldots, y_n \in \mathbb{Z}_p$, sets the vector $\boldsymbol{y} = (s, y_2, \ldots, y_n)^T$ (where T denotes the transpose of the matrix) and computes a vector of shares of s as $(\lambda_1, \ldots, \lambda_\ell)^T = M\boldsymbol{y}$.

For $j = 1$ to ℓ, it computes

$$C_{j,4} := \lambda_j - \lambda'_j \quad C_{j,5} := t_j \cdot (\rho(j) - x_j).$$

Intuitively, this will correct to the proper attributes and shares of s. It sets the ciphertext as:

$$\text{CT} := ((M, \rho), C_0, \{C_{j,1}, C_{j,2}, C_{j,3}, C_{j,4}, C_{j,5}\}_{j \in [1,k]}).$$

The encapsulated key is key. The dominant cost is one multiplication in $\mathbb{Z}_p$ per row of M.

Decrypt(SK, CT). The decryption algorithm in the KEM setting recovers the encapsulated key. It takes as input a ciphertext CT $= ((M, \rho), C_0, \{C_{j,1}, C_{j,2}, C_{j,3}, C_{j,4}, C_{j,5}\}_{j \in [1,k]})$ for access structure (M, ρ) and a private key SK$=(S, \{K_{i,0}, K_{i,1}, K_{i,2}\}_{i \in [1,\ell]})$ for access structure (M, ρ). If S does not satisfy this access structure, then the algorithm issues an error message. Otherwise, it sets $I := \{i : \rho(i) \in S\}$ and computes constants $w_i \in \mathbb{Z}_p$ such that $\sum_{i \in I} w_i \cdot M_i = (1, 0, \ldots, 0)$, where M_i is the i-th row of the matrix M. Then it then recovers the encapsulated key by calculating key $:= e(g, g)^{\alpha s} =$

$$\frac{e(C_0, K_0)}{e(w^{\sum_{i \in I} C_{i,4} w_i}, K_1) \cdot \prod_{i \in I} (e(C_{i,1}, K_1)} \cdot \frac{1}{e(C_{i,2} \cdot u^{C_{i,5}}, K_{j,2}) \cdot e(C_{i,3}, K_{j,3}))^{w_i}} \quad (2)$$

where j is the index of the attribute $\rho(i)$ in S (it depends on i). We note that this decryption algorithm adds one pairing operation and $|I|+1$ exponentiations over [19, Appendix C]. Alternatively, one could re-arrange the equation for no additional pairings at the cost of $2|I|$ exponentiations.

In the full version [13], we show correctness and prove the below theorem.

Theorem 2. *The above online/offline CP-AB-KEM scheme is selectively CPA-secure with respect to Definition 2 assuming that the scheme of Rouselakis and Waters [19, Section 4] is a selectively CPA-secure CP-ABE system.*

4.1 Pooling Attributes for an Unbounded Ciphertext-Policy System

In the previous section, we presented an online/offline system that imposed a bound of P rows on any LSSS access matrix associated with any ciphertext. As introduced in Section 3.2, we now show how to remove this bound by creating a "pool" from which to draw ready-made ciphertext components. As before, the intermediate ciphertext is comprised of two logical types of objects: a main module and an attribute module. During the offline phase(s), an arbitrary number of main and attribute modules are independently created. During the online phase for LSSS access structure (M, ρ), one main module and ℓ attribute modules will be consumed, where M is an $\ell \times n$ matrix. Any attribute module can be attached to any main module.

Specifically, during Offline.Encrypt, a main module is computed as follows. It picks a random $s \in \mathbb{Z}_p$ and sets $\text{IT}_{main} := (\text{key}, C_0)$, where these values are computed as

$$\text{key} := e(g, g)^{\alpha s} \quad C_0 := g^s.$$

During Offline.Encrypt, an attribute module is computed as follows. It picks a random $\lambda, x, t \in \mathbb{Z}_p$ and sets $\text{IT}_{att} := (\lambda, x, t, C_1, C_2, C_3)$, where these values are computed as

$$C_1 := w^\lambda v^t \quad C_2 := (u^x h)^t \quad C_3 := g^t.$$

During Online.Encrypt for an LSSS access structure (M, ρ), where M is an $\ell \times n$ matrix, the algorithm selects any one main module $\text{IT}_{main} := (\text{key}, C_0)$ and any ℓ attribute modules $\text{IT}_{att,j} := (\lambda_j, x_j, t_j, C_{j,1}, C_{j,2}, C_{j,3})$ available in the pool. It picks random $y_2, \ldots, y_n \in \mathbb{Z}_p$, sets the vector $\boldsymbol{y} = (s, y_2, \ldots, y_n)^T$ (where T denotes the transpose of the matrix) and computes a vector of shares of s as $(\lambda_1, \ldots, \lambda_\ell)^T = M\boldsymbol{y}$.

Finally, it computes CT as $((M, \rho), C_0, \{C_{j,1}, C_{j,2}, C_{j,3}, C_{j,4}, C_{j,5}\}_{j \in [1,\ell]})$, where

$$C_{j,4} := \lambda_j - \lambda'_j \quad C_{j,5} := t_j \cdot (\rho(j) - x_j).$$

The encapsulated key is key. The dominant cost in the online encryption algorithm is one modular multiplication per row in M. The security discussion at the end of Section 3.2 applies here as well.

5   Online/Offline ABE Key Generation

Private key generation in ABE systems requires the master secret key MSK. This key is so valuable that any organization granting keys might do well to store it on only a small number of well-guarded servers. At the same time, this could create a bottleneck in systems with many users, especially when private keys are reissued each time period for revocation purposes. In this section, we discuss how the key generation operation in the KP-ABE system of Section 3 and the CP-ABE system of Section 4 can operate in an online/offline fashion as well. Thus, the bulk of the key generation work can be performed by servers that are truly *offline* (or otherwise well secured). These pre-computations can be passed to the online servers, where incoming requests can be processed quickly.

In the KP-ABE setting, a private key embeds an LSSS access structure, whereas in the CP-ABE setting, the private key embeds a set of attributes. We will borrow ideas from the prior two sections to deal with these objects, where again we can employ both the "correct and connect" and "pooling" concepts.

To capture online/offline key generation, one needs to replace the Extract algorithm with an offline algorithm that takes in the MK and produces a intermediate private key (or pool of private key parts) and an online algorithm that takes in this intermediate key (or pool) together with an access structure and then produces the private key. The security experiment is essentially unchanged except that the Create oracle (called in Phases 1 and 2) now calls Offline.Extract and Online.Extract in sequence to create a private key.

5.1 Online/Offline Key Generation for KP-ABE Keys

The Setup and encryption algorithms remain the same as Section 3. We present a pooling solution, and because the structure of the private keys change, so must the decryption algorithm.

Offline.Extract(MSK). There are no "main" key modules. A "row" module is computed by selecting random $\lambda', x, t \in \mathbb{Z}_p$ and outputting $I_{row} := (\lambda', x, t, K_0, K_1, K_2)$ where $K_0 := g^{\lambda'} w^t$, $K_1 := (u^x h)^{-t}$ and $K_2 := g^t$.

Online.Extract(pool, (M, ρ)). Let M be an $\ell \times n$ matrix. The algorithm initially chooses random values $y_2, \ldots, y_n \in \mathbb{Z}_p$. It then computes ℓ shares of the master secret key as $(\lambda_1, \lambda_2, \ldots, \lambda_\ell) := M \cdot (\alpha, y_2, \ldots, y_n)$. Next select any ℓ row modules from the pool. For $i = 1$ to ℓ, set $K_{i,3} := \lambda_i - \lambda_i'$ and $K_{i,4} := t_i \cdot (\rho(i) - x_i)$. The private key is SK $:= ((M, \rho), \{K_{i,0}, K_{i,1}, K_{i,2}, K_{i,3}, K_{i,4}\}_{i \in [1,\ell]})$. The dominant cost is one multiplication per row of M.

Decrypt(SK, CT). Using the prior steps and notation, it recovers the encapsulated key $:= \prod_{i \in I} \left(e(C_0, K_{i,0} \cdot g^{K_{i,3}}) \cdot e(C_{j,1}, K_{i,1} \cdot u^{K_{i,4}}) \cdot e(C_{j,2} \cdot u^{C_{j,3}}, K_{i,2}) \right)^{w_i} = e(g, g)^{\alpha s}$. This adds $2|I|$ exponentiations over the construction in Section 3.

5.2 Online/Offline Key Generation for CP-ABE Keys

The CP-ABE system in Section 4 can be extended in a similar manner. In that system, there will be a "main" key module which contains K_0, K_1 and $K_v := v^{-r}$. The attribute modules are identical to those of Section 3.2 and the keys are assembled as in the online phase of 3.2. The decryption equation is then key $:= e(C_0, K_0)/D$, where $D = e(w^{\sum_{i \in I} C_{i,4} w_i}, K_1) \cdot \prod_{i \in I} (e(C_{i,1}, K_1) \cdot e(C_{i,2} \cdot u^{C_{i,5}}, K_{j,2} \cdot u^{K_{j,4}}) \cdot e(C_{i,3}, K_{j,3}))^{w_i}$, resulting in $e(g, g)^{\alpha s}$.

6 Performance Analysis

We provide estimates on the performance of the proposed schemes in Figures 1 and 2. These numbers are extrapolated from operation times on a 256-bit Bareto-Naehrig curve using version 0.3.1 of the RELIC library [3]. Times are measured in milliseconds (averaged over 10,000 iterations) and were computed on an Intel Core i7 processor with 16GB RAM [2]. We ignore small numbers of operations which will be negligible by comparison, such as arithmetic in $\mathbb{Z}_p$.

A natural question to ask is: how much pre-processing can I do for an ABE encryption (similarly, key generation) before I know the message I want to encrypt or the access structure that I want to encrypt under? It may come as a surprise that the results are so drastic. Indeed, our estimates show that the answer to this question is: you can do *almost all* of the encryption work, before you know any of the specifics of what/to whom you are encrypting.

Indeed, our *worst*-case for encryption was key-policy ABE in pooling mode, and even then over 99% of the work could be done offline. Similarly, the worst-case for key generation was ciphertext-policy ABE in pooling mode, and even

Encryption Algorithm	Bilinear Operations	Est. Time $P = 10$	Est. Time $P = 100$
KP-ABE from [19, App. C]	$1\mathbb{E}_T + (3P + 2)\mathbb{E}_1 + 2P\mathbb{M}_1$	.133	1.134
KP-Offline Sec. 3	$1\mathbb{E}_T + (3P + 2)\mathbb{E}_1 + 2P\mathbb{M}_1$	.133	1.134
KP-Online Sec. 3	0	< .001	< .001
KP-Pool-Offline Sec. 3.2	$1\mathbb{E}_T + (3P + 2)\mathbb{E}_1 + P\mathbb{M}_1$	.133	1.132
KP-Pool-Online Sec. 3.2	$P\mathbb{M}_1$	< .001	.001
CP-ABE from [19]	$1\mathbb{E}_T + (5P + 1)\mathbb{E}_1 + 2P\mathbb{M}_1$	.203	1.870
CP-Offline Sec. 4	$1\mathbb{E}_T + (5P + 1)\mathbb{E}_1 + 2P\mathbb{M}_1$	.203	1.870
CP-Online Sec. 4	0	< .001	< .001
CP-Pool-Offline Sec. 4.1	$1\mathbb{E}_T + (5P + 1)\mathbb{E}_1 + 2P\mathbb{M}_1$	.203	1.870
CP-Pool-Online Sec. 4.1	0	< .001	.001

Fig. 1. Performance estimates for regular and online/offline encryption algorithms. We mapped these algorithms into the asymmetric bilinear setting, placing the ciphertexts in $\mathbb{G}_1$ and keys in $\mathbb{G}_2$. Let $\mathbb{E}_i$ (resp., $\mathbb{M}_i$) denote an exponentiation (reps., multiplication) in the group $\mathbb{G}_i$. The bilinear operations are the dominate cost, so we ignore minor factors such as arithmetic in $\mathbb{Z}_p$. The variable P represents the size of the attribute list (in KP-ABE) or the complexity of the access policy (in CP-ABE). The times are in seconds. It is helpful to compare the cost of the original scheme (with a citation) to the cost of the online phase of the given algorithms. In three of the four schemes presented, all bilinear group operations for encryption can be shifted to the offline phase.

then over 99% of the work could be done offline. It is also worth noting that the total computation required between the offline and online phases is nearly identical to the work required by the original scheme. Thus, the total work remains the same, but the vast majority of it can be shifted in time to a moment when the device is least busy or has access to a power source.

We remark that the operation counts given here for the schemes in [19] differ slightly from the summary given in that work. The counts from [19] were obtained from the Charm [1] benchmarking utility, which may have performed various optimizations, whereas ours are a strict count of operations from the algorithms as presented in the paper [19]. We do not expect these differences to have any significant impact on the estimates in Figures 1 and 2.

7   Conclusions

We are exploring methods to make attribute-based encryption (ABE) more efficient for deployment. To this end, we investigated how devices might quickly encrypt ABE messages or generate user keys, even for complex policies.

We developed new "connect and correct" techniques for ABE that split the computation for encryption and key generation into two phases: a preparation phase that does the vast majority of the work to encrypt a message or create a secret key *before* it knows the message or the attribute list/access control policy that will be used (or even the size of the list or policy). A second phase can then

Key Generation Algorithm	Bilinear Operations	Est. Time $P = 10$	Est. Time $P = 100$
KP-ABE from [19, App. C]	$5P\mathbb{E}_2 + 2PM_2$	.370	3.703
KP-Pool-Offline Sec. 5.1	$5P\mathbb{E}_2 + 2PM_2$	.370	3.703
KP-Pool-Online Sec. 5.1	0	$< .001$	$< .001$
CP-ABE from [19]	$(3P + 4)\mathbb{E}_2 + (2P + 1)M_2$	.252	2.253
CP-Pool-Offline Sec. 5.2	$(3P + 4)\mathbb{E}_2 + (P + 1)M_2$	.251	2.251
CP-Pool-Online Sec. 5.2	PM_2	$< .001$	.003

Fig. 2. Performance estimates for regular and online/offline key generation algorithms. We mapped these algorithms into the asymmetric bilinear setting, placing the ciphertexts in $\mathbb{G}_1$ and keys in $\mathbb{G}_2$. Let $\mathbb{E}_i$ (resp., M_i) denote an exponentiation (reps., multiplication) in the group $\mathbb{G}_i$. The bilinear operations are the dominate cost, so we ignore minor factors such as arithmetic in $\mathbb{Z}_p$. The variable P represents the size of the attribute list (in CP-ABE) or the complexity of the access policy (in KP-ABE). The times are in seconds. It is helpful to compare the cost of the original scheme (with a citation) to the cost of the online phase. In both schemes, our estimates show that over 99% of the work to generate a key can be shifted to the offline phase.

rapidly assemble an ABE ciphertext or key when the specifics become known. This concept is sometimes called "online/offline" encryption. We provided efficient constructions for both key-policy and ciphertext-policy ABE systems.

We provided performance estimates that showed over 99% of the computational work could be moved to offline phase in many scenarios. We expect that this technology could reduce battery consumption on mobile devices and help reduce the bottleneck on a master authority server tasked with generating user keys. Overall, it helps reduce the cost of bringing ABE into practice.

Acknowledgments. The authors thank Joseph Ayo Akinyele and Matthew Green for advice on performance numbers and other helpful comments. Susan Hohenberger was supported in part by NSF CNS-1154035 and CNS-1228443; the Defense Advanced Research Projects Agency (DARPA) and the Air Force Research Laboratory under contract FA8750-11-2-0211, DARPA N11AP20006, the Office of Naval Research under contract N00014-11-1-0470, and a Microsoft Faculty Fellowship. The views expressed are those of the authors and do not reflect the official policy or position of the Department of Defense or the U.S. Government.

References

1. Akinyele, J.A., Garman, C., Miers, I., Pagano, M.W., Rushanan, M., Green, M., Rubin, A.D.: Charm: a framework for rapidly prototyping cryptosystems. Journal of Cryptographic Engineering 3(2), 111–128 (2013)
2. Akinyele, J.A., Green, M.: Personal communication (2013)
3. Aranha, D.F., Gouvêa, C.P.L.: RELIC is an Efficient LIbrary for Cryptography, http://code.google.com/p/relic-toolkit/
4. Bethencourt, J., Sahai, A., Waters, B.: Ciphertext-policy attribute-based encryption. In: IEEE Symposium on Security and Privacy, pp. 321–334 (2007)

5. Boneh, D., Boyen, X.: Efficient selective-ID secure identity-based encryption without random oracles. In: Cachin, C., Camenisch, J.L. (eds.) EUROCRYPT 2004. LNCS, vol. 3027, pp. 223–238. Springer, Heidelberg (2004)
6. Boneh, D., Waters, B.: Conjunctive, subset, and range queries on encrypted data. In: Vadhan, S.P. (ed.) TCC 2007. LNCS, vol. 4392, pp. 535–554. Springer, Heidelberg (2007)
7. Canetti, R., Halevi, S., Katz, J.: Chosen-ciphertext security from identity-based encryption. In: Cachin, C., Camenisch, J.L. (eds.) EUROCRYPT 2004. LNCS, vol. 3027, pp. 207–222. Springer, Heidelberg (2004)
8. Chow, S.S.M., Liu, J.K., Zhou, J.: Identity-based online/offline key encapsulation and encryption. In: ASIACCS, pp. 52–60 (2011)
9. Even, S., Goldreich, O., Micali, S.: On-line/off-line digital signatures. J. Cryptology 9(1), 35–67 (1996)
10. Goyal, V., Pandey, O., Sahai, A., Waters, B.: Attribute-based encryption for fine-grained access control of encrypted data. In: ACM Conference on Computer and Communications Security, pp. 89–98 (2006)
11. Green, M., Hohenberger, S., Waters, B.: Outsourcing the decryption of ABE ciphertexts. In: USENIX Security Symposium (2011)
12. Guo, F., Mu, Y., Chen, Z.: Identity-based online/Offline encryption. In: Tsudik, G. (ed.) FC 2008. LNCS, vol. 5143, pp. 247–261. Springer, Heidelberg (2008)
13. Hohenberger, S., Waters, B.: Online/offline attribute-based encryption, The full version is available from the IACR ePrint Archive, Report 2014/021 (2014)
14. Lewko, A., Waters, B.: Unbounded HIBE and attribute-based encryption. In: Paterson, K.G. (ed.) EUROCRYPT 2011. LNCS, vol. 6632, pp. 547–567. Springer, Heidelberg (2011)
15. Lewko, A., Waters, B.: New proof methods for attribute-based encryption: Achieving full security through selective techniques. In: Safavi-Naini, R., Canetti, R. (eds.) CRYPTO 2012. LNCS, vol. 7417, pp. 180–198. Springer, Heidelberg (2012)
16. Liu, J.K., Zhou, J.: An efficient identity-based online/Offline encryption scheme. In: Abdalla, M., Pointcheval, D., Fouque, P.-A., Vergnaud, D. (eds.) ACNS 2009. LNCS, vol. 5536, pp. 156–167. Springer, Heidelberg (2009)
17. Liu, Z., Xu, L., Chen, Z., Mu, Y., Guo, F.: Hierarchical identity-based online/offline encryption. In: ICYCS, pp. 2115–2119 (2008)
18. Pirretti, M., Traynor, P., McDaniel, P., Waters, B.: Secure attribute-based systems. In: ACM Conference on Computer and Communications Security, pp. 99–112 (2006)
19. Rouselakis, Y., Waters, B.: Practical constructions and new proof methods for large universe attribute-based encryption. In: ACM Conference on Computer and Communications Security, pp. 463–474 (2013)
20. Sahai, A., Waters, B.: Fuzzy identity-based encryption. In: Cramer, R. (ed.) EUROCRYPT 2005. LNCS, vol. 3494, pp. 457–473. Springer, Heidelberg (2005)
21. Selvi, S.S.D., Vivek, S.S., Rangan, C.P.: Identity based online/Offline encryption and signcryption schemes revisited. In: Joye, M., Mukhopadhyay, D., Tunstall, M. (eds.) InfoSecHiComNet 2011. LNCS, vol. 7011, pp. 111–127. Springer, Heidelberg (2011)
22. Shamir, A., Tauman, Y.: Improved online/Offline signature schemes. In: Kilian, J. (ed.) CRYPTO 2001. LNCS, vol. 2139, pp. 355–367. Springer, Heidelberg (2001)
23. Traynor, P., Butler, K.R.B., Enck, W., McDaniel, P.: Realizing massive-scale conditional access systems through attribute-based cryptosystems. In: NDSS (2008)
24. Waters, B.: Ciphertext-policy attribute-based encryption: An expressive, efficient, and provably secure realization. In: Catalano, D., Fazio, N., Gennaro, R., Nicolosi, A. (eds.) PKC 2011. LNCS, vol. 6571, pp. 53–70. Springer, Heidelberg (2011)

Scale-Invariant Fully Homomorphic Encryption over the Integers

Jean-Sébastien Coron[1], Tancrède Lepoint[1,2,3], and Mehdi Tibouchi[4]

[1] University of Luxembourg, Luxembourg
jean-sebastien.coron@uni.lu
[2] École Normale Supérieure, France
[3] CryptoExperts, France
tancrede.lepoint@cryptoexperts.com
[4] NTT Secure Platform Laboratories, Japan
tibouchi.mehdi@lab.ntt.co.jp

Abstract. At Crypto 2012, Brakerski constructed a scale-invariant fully homomorphic encryption scheme based on the LWE problem, in which the same modulus is used throughout the evaluation process, instead of a ladder of moduli when doing "modulus switching". In this paper we describe a variant of the van Dijk et al. FHE scheme over the integers with the same scale-invariant property. Our scheme has a single secret modulus whose size is linear in the multiplicative depth of the circuit to be homomorphically evaluated, instead of exponential; we therefore construct a leveled fully homomorphic encryption scheme. This scheme can be transformed into a pure fully homomorphic encryption scheme using bootstrapping, and its security is still based on the Approximate-GCD problem.

We also describe an implementation of the homomorphic evaluation of the full AES encryption circuit, and obtain significantly improved performance compared to previous implementations: about 23 seconds (resp. 3 minutes) per AES block at the 72-bit (resp. 80-bit) security level on a mid-range workstation.

Finally, we prove the equivalence between the (error-free) decisional Approximate-GCD problem introduced by Cheon et al. (Eurocrypt 2013) and the classical computational Approximate-GCD problem. This equivalence allows to get rid of the additional noise in all the integer-based FHE schemes described so far, and therefore to simplify their security proof.

1 Introduction

Fully Homomorphic Encryption. In 2009, Gentry constructed the first fully homomorphic encryption scheme (FHE), i.e. a scheme allowing a worker to evaluate any circuit on plaintext values while manipulating only ciphertexts. The first generation of FHE schemes [Gen09, DGHV10, SV10, GH11, BV11a, BV11b] and [CMNT11, CNT12, CCK+13] followed Gentry's blueprint to achieve a fully homomorphic scheme.

H. Krawczyk (Ed.): PKC 2014, LNCS 8383, pp. 311–328, 2014.

The first step of Gentry's blueprint is to construct a somewhat homomorphic encryption scheme (SWHE) capable of evaluating "low degree" polynomials homomorphically. Inherent to this construction is the property that ciphertexts are "noisy", and noises grow slightly with homomorphic additions and substantially with homomorphic multiplications. Thus ciphertexts need to be refreshed to maintain a low noise level and allow subsequent homomorphic operations. To obtain a FHE scheme, Gentry's key-idea, referred to as *bootstrapping*, states that a SWHE capable of evaluating its own decryption procedure (and an additional multiplication) can be transformed into a FHE scheme. Bootstrapping consists in evaluating the decryption circuit of the SWHE scheme using the decryption key bits in encrypted form, thus resulting in a different encryption of the same plaintext but with reduced noise. In practice, the scheme parameters are generally determined so that the refreshed ciphertexts can handle one additional homomorphic multiplication [GH11, CMNT11, CNT12, CCK+13]. Unfortunately, the downside of these settings is that one needs to call the (very costly) bootstrapping procedure after each homomorphic multiplication.

Modulus Switching and Scale Invariance. To avoid bootstrapping a new noise management technique, called *modulus switching*, was introduced by Brakerski, Gentry and Vaikuntanathan [BGV12]. The authors obtained a *leveled* FHE scheme: i.e. a scheme in which the noise grows *linearly* with the multiplicative depth instead of exponentially as in somewhat homomorphic encryption. Therefore any circuit with polynomial depth can be evaluated. The technique consists in scaling down the noise by converting a ciphertext modulo q into a ciphertext modulo a smaller q'; the noise being reduced by roughly a factor q/q'. By carefully calibrating the ladder of moduli, the noise growth can then be made linear with the number of homomorphic multiplications. The technique was also adapted to the DGHV fully homomorphic encryption scheme over the integers [DGHV10] in [CNT12]. Unfortunately for a circuit with L layers of multiplication, the technique requires to store the equivalent of L public-keys, yielding a huge storage requirement.

At Crypto 2012, Brakerski introduced a new tensor product technique for LWE-based leveled FHE [Bra12] so that the *same* modulus is used throughout the evaluation process instead of a layer of moduli; the noise growth is still linear in the number of homomorphic multiplications. This was achieved by considering ciphertexts such that $\langle c, s \rangle = \lfloor q/2 \rfloor \cdot m + e \bmod q$, instead of $\langle c, s \rangle = m + 2e \bmod q$, as in Regev's initial scheme [Reg05].

Implementations of FHE Schemes. Independently at Crypto 2012, Gentry et al. benchmarked a LWE-based scheme by homomorphically evaluating an AES circuit [GHS12b], yielding to the first "real-world" circuit homomorphically evaluated by a FHE scheme. This implementation used the modulus switching technique of [BGV12] and additionally a batching technique [SV11, BGV12, GHS12a] that allows one to encrypt vectors of plaintexts in a single ciphertext, and to perform any permutation on the underlying plaintext vector while manipulating only the ciphertext. They obtained a timing of about 5 minutes *per AES block* homomorphically encrypted. Similar results were later obtained for the integer-based DGHV scheme [DGHV10], extending the batching technique and homomorphically evaluating AES on a desktop computer in about 12 minutes per block for 72 bits of security [CCK+13, CLT13].

Our Contributions. In this paper, we describe a variant of the DGHV scheme over the integers with the same scale-invariant property as in [Bra12]; i.e. our scheme does not use modulus switching and the noise grows linearly with the multiplicative depth. We obtain a DGHV variant with a single secret modulus p whose size is linear in the multiplicative depth (instead of exponential). Our technique is as follows.

In the original DGHV scheme, a ciphertext c of the bit message $m \in \{0, 1\}$ has the form

$$c = m + 2r + q \cdot p \,,$$

where p is the secret key, q is a large random integer, and r is a small random integer (noise). The bit message is recovered by computing $m = (c \bmod p) \bmod 2$. Adding and multiplying ciphertexts over $\mathbb{Z}$ respectively adds and multiplies the plaintexts modulo 2 while keeping them hidden. Unfortunately, the noise grows exponentially with the number of homomorphic multiplications: if two ciphertexts c_1, c_2 have ρ-bit noise, the noise of $c_3 = c_1 \cdot c_2$ has $\approx 2\rho$ bits. Therefore to evaluate a circuit with L sequential layers of multiplications without bootstrapping, the bit-size η of the modulus p must satisfy $\eta > 2^L \rho$.

In our new scheme, similar to [Bra12], instead of encrypting the bit $m \in \{0, 1\}$ in the LSB of $[c \bmod p]$, we encrypt it in the MSB of $[c \bmod p]$; additionally we work modulo p^2 instead of modulo p. More precisely, the message m is now encrypted as

$$c = r + (m + 2r^*) \cdot \frac{p-1}{2} + q \cdot p^2 \,, \tag{1}$$

where the ciphertext now contains two noises r and r^*. We decrypt c by computing $m = (2c \bmod p) \bmod 2$. Clearly adding two ciphertexts over $\mathbb{Z}$ still adds the underlying bit messages m modulo 2. However, multiplication of two ciphertexts moves the bit message m from the MSB of $[c \bmod p]$ to the MSB of $[c \bmod p^2]$. Namely, a ciphertext c obtained as the multiplication of ciphertexts c_1 and c_2 for the respective bit messages m_1 and m_2 will have the form

$$c = 2 \cdot c_1 \cdot c_2 = r + (m_1 \cdot m_2) \cdot \frac{p^2 - 1}{2} + q \cdot p^2 \,, \tag{2}$$

where $r > p$ but still $r \ll p^2$. We then describe a procedure Convert that allows to publicly convert the result of a multiplication (i.e. a ciphertext as in Equation (2)) into a ciphertext reusable in subsequent homomorphic operations (i.e. a ciphertext as in Equation (1)), either keeping the same secret p (which requires, as usual, a circular security assumption) or using a different fresh p at each level (which requires a larger secret key). The bit length of the noise in the new ciphertext grows only by a constant additive factor with respect to the noise in c_1 and c_2 (see Figure 1 for an illustration). Therefore, our scheme

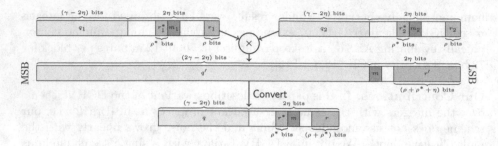

Fig. 1. Conversion of a ciphertext after a homomorphic multiplication

is a variant of the DGHV scheme that is a leveled fully homomorphic encryption scheme. It can be turned into a pure FHE scheme using bootstrapping (cf. [DGHV10, CMNT11, CNT12, CCK+13]). We also show that our scheme is semantically secure, under the Approximate-GCD assumption.

We also adapt our scale-invariant technique to the batch setting in [CCK+13] and homomorphically evaluate an AES encryption as in [GHS12b, CCK+13]. Our scheme offers competitive performances as it can evaluate the full AES circuit in about 23 seconds (resp. 3 minutes) per AES block at the 72-bit (resp. 80-bit) security level on a mid-range workstation, that is one order of magnitude faster than [CCK+13].

Finally, we prove the equivalence between the (error-free) computational Approximate-GCD problem [DGHV10] and the (error-free) decisional Approximate-GCD problem introduced in [CCK+13, KLYC13]. From this equivalence, the additional noise added during encryption to drawn the noises coming from the public key elements is no longer required. This yields automatic improvements in the parameters of all the fully homomorphic encryption schemes over the integers.

2   The Somewhat Homomorphic DGHV Scheme

In this section we first recall the somewhat homomorphic encryption scheme over the integers of van Dijk, Gentry, Halevi and Vaikuntanathan (DGHV) in [DGHV10]. We denote by λ the security parameter, τ the number of elements in the public key, γ their bit-length, η the bit-length of the secret key p and ρ (resp. ρ') the bit-length of the noise in the public key (resp. in a fresh ciphertext).

For a real number x, we denote by $\lceil x \rceil$, $\lfloor x \rfloor$ and $\lceil x \rfloor$ the upper, lower or nearest integer part of x. For integers z, p we denote the reduction of z modulo p by $(z \bmod p)$ or $[z]_p$ with $-p/2 < [z]_p \leqslant p/2$. For a specific η-bit odd integer p, we use the following distribution over γ-bit integers:

$$\mathcal{D}_{\gamma,\rho}(p) = \left\{ \begin{array}{c} \text{Choose } q \leftarrow \mathbb{Z} \cap [0, 2^\gamma/p), \ r \leftarrow \mathbb{Z} \cap (-2^\rho, 2^\rho) : \\ \text{Output } x = q \cdot p + r \end{array} \right\}.$$

DGHV. KeyGen(1^λ). Generate an η-bit random prime integer p. For $0 \leqslant i \leqslant \tau$, sample $x_i \leftarrow \mathcal{D}_{\gamma,\rho}(p)$. Relabel the x_i's so that x_0 is the largest. Restart unless x_0 is odd and $[x_0]_p$ is even. Let $\mathsf{pk} = (x_0, x_1, \ldots x_\tau)$ and $\mathsf{sk} = p$.

DGHV. Encrypt($\mathsf{pk}, m \in \{0,1\}$). Choose a random subset $S \subseteq \{1, 2, \ldots, \tau\}$ and a random integer r in $(-2^{\rho'}, 2^{\rho'})$, and output the ciphertext:

$$c = \left[m + 2r + 2 \sum_{i \in S} x_i \right]_{x_0} . \tag{3}$$

DGHV. Evaluate($\mathsf{pk}, C, c_1, \ldots, c_t$). Given the circuit C with t input bits and t ciphertexts c_i, apply the addition and multiplication gates of C to the ciphertexts, performing all the additions and multiplications over the integers, and return the resulting integer.

DGHV. Decrypt(sk, c). Output $m \leftarrow (c \bmod p) \bmod 2$.

This completes the description of the scheme. The scheme is clearly somewhat homomorphic, i.e. a limited number of homomorphic operations can be performed on ciphertexts. More precisely given two ciphertexts $c = q \cdot p + 2r + m$ and $c' = q' \cdot p + 2r' + m'$ where r and r' are ρ'-bit integers, the ciphertext $c + c'$ is an encryption of $m + m' \bmod 2$ with a $(\rho' + 1)$-bit noise and the ciphertext $c \cdot c'$ is an encryption of $m \cdot m'$ with noise bit-length $\simeq 2\rho'$. Therefore the scheme allows roughly η/ρ' successive multiplications on ciphertexts (since the noise must remain smaller than p for correct decryption).

As shown in [DGHV10] the scheme is semantically secure under the Approximate-GCD assumption.

Definition 1 (Approximate GCD). *The (ρ, η, γ)-Approximate-GCD problem consists, given a random η-bit odd integer p and given polynomially many samples from $\mathcal{D}_{\gamma,\rho}(p)$, in outputting p.*

3   Scale-Invariant DGHV Scheme

In this section we describe our variant of the DGHV scheme with the scale-invariant property. We first explain the two main ideas of our scheme, namely 1) moving the plaintext bit from the LSB to the MSB of $[c \bmod p]$ and working modulo p^2, and 2) converting the result of a ciphertext multiplication back to a ciphertext usable in subsequent homomorphic operations. We then provide the full description of our scheme.

3.1   Ciphertexts and Homomorphic Operations

As explained in introduction, instead of encrypting the plaintext $m \in \{0,1\}$ in the LSB of $[c \bmod p]$, m is now encrypted in the MSB of $[c \bmod p]$ as

$$c = r + (m + 2r^*) \cdot \frac{p-1}{2} + q \cdot p^2 , \tag{1}$$

where the ciphertext has now two noises r and r^* of respective bit-length ρ and ρ^*. We call such ciphertext a *Type-I ciphertext* and we say that c has noise length (ρ, ρ^*). To decrypt c, one computes $(2c \bmod p) \bmod 2 = m$.

Homomorphic additions are performed as additions over $\mathbb{Z}$: namely given two Type-I ciphertexts c_1 and c_2 of noise (ρ, ρ^*):

$$c_1 = r_1 + (m_1 + 2r_1^*) \cdot (p-1)/2 + q_1 \cdot p^2$$
$$c_2 = r_2 + (m_2 + 2r_2^*) \cdot (p-1)/2 + q_2 \cdot p^2$$

we get

$$c_1 + c_2 = r_3 + (m_1 + m_2 + 2r_3^*) \cdot \frac{p-1}{2} + q_3 \cdot p^2 \ ,$$

for some integers r_3, r_3^* and q_3, with $\log_2 |r_3| \leqslant \rho + 1$ and $\log_2 |r_3^*| \leqslant \rho^* + 1$.

Next, to homomorphically multiply the ciphertexts c_1 and c_2, one computes $c_3 = 2 \cdot c_1 \cdot c_2$ over $\mathbb{Z}$. This gives

$$c_3 = 2 \cdot c_1 \cdot c_2 = 2r_1r_2 + \big(r_1(m_2 + 2r_2^*) + r_2(m_1 + 2r_1^*)\big) \cdot (p-1) +$$
$$(m_1 + 2r_1^*) \cdot (m_2 + 2r_2^*) \cdot \frac{(p-1)^2}{2} + q_3' \cdot p^2$$
$$= r_3' + (m_1 + 2r_1^*) \cdot (m_2 + 2r_2^*) \cdot \frac{(p-1)^2}{2} + q_3' \cdot p^2$$

for some integers q_3' and r_3', with $\log_2 |r_3'| \leqslant \eta + \rho + \rho^* + 3$, where η is the bit-size of p. We use $\eta \gg \rho, \rho^*$. Then, there exist integers r_3 and q_3 such that

$$c_3 = r_3 + m_3 \cdot \frac{p^2 - 1}{2} + q_3 \cdot p^2 \ , \tag{2}$$

where $m_3 = m_1 \cdot m_2$. We call an integer c verifying Equation (2) a *Type-II ciphertext*. The bit-length of noise r_3 satisfies $\log_2 |r_3| \leqslant \eta + \rho + \rho^* + 4$, assuming $\rho^* < \rho$. We refer to Figure 1 for a graphical representation of the homomorphic multiplication.

3.2   Conversion from Type-II Ciphertext to Type-I Ciphertext

We show that we can efficiently convert a Type-II ciphertext back to a Type-I ciphertext, using only the public-key. Our procedure Convert uses essentially the same technique as the modulus switching technique for DGHV in [CNT12]. Namely modulus switching in [CNT12] enables to convert a classical DGHV ciphertext modulo a prime p into a new ciphertext modulo a prime p', with noise scaled by a factor p'/p. Similarly, our Convert procedure converts a Type-II ciphertext modulo p^2 back to a ciphertext where the noise is modulo p (therefore the noise is scaled by a factor $p/p^2 = 1/p$), but still somehow encrypted modulo p^2.

More precisely, we start from a Type-II ciphertext:

$$c = r + \frac{p^2 - 1}{2} \cdot m + q \cdot p^2 \tag{4}$$

where $|r| \leqslant 2^{\rho'}$. Let κ be such that $|c| < 2^{\kappa}$. Let z be a vector of Θ rational numbers in $[0, 2^{\eta})$ with κ bits of precision after the binary point, and let s be a vector of Θ bits such that

$$\frac{2^{\eta}}{p^2} = \langle s, z \rangle + \varepsilon \mod 2^{\eta}, \tag{5}$$

where $|\varepsilon| \leqslant 2^{-\kappa}$. Here Θ is a parameter to be chosen later for security. We use the same BitDecomp and PowersofTwo procedures as in [BGV12].

- BitDecomp$_\eta(v)$: For $v \in \mathbb{Z}^n$, let $v_i \in \{0,1\}^n$ be such that $v \mod 2^\eta = \sum_{i=0}^{\eta-1} v_i \cdot 2^i$. Output the vector

$$(v_0, \ldots, v_{\eta-1}) \in \{0,1\}^{n \cdot \eta} .$$

- PowersofTwo$_\eta(w)$: For $w \in \mathbb{Z}^n$, output the vector

$$(w, 2 \cdot w, \ldots, 2^{\eta-1} \cdot w) \in \mathbb{Z}^{n \cdot \eta} .$$

Given the vector s from (5), we let $s' = $ PowersofTwo$_\eta(s)$, and let

$$\sigma = q \cdot p^2 + r + \left\lfloor s' \cdot \frac{p}{2^{\eta+1}} \right\rceil \tag{6}$$

be an "encryption" of the vector s', where $q \leftarrow (\mathbb{Z} \cap [0, 2^{\gamma}/p^2))^{\eta \cdot \Theta}$ and $r \leftarrow (\mathbb{Z} \cap (-2^{\rho}, 2^{\rho}))^{\eta \cdot \Theta}$. We can now define the Convert algorithm:

Convert(z, σ, c). First compute $c = (\lfloor c \cdot z_i \rceil \mod 2^{\eta})_{1 \leqslant i \leqslant \Theta}$ and its decomposition $c' = $ BitDecomp$_\eta(c)$. Finally, output

$$c' \leftarrow 2 \langle \sigma, c' \rangle .$$

The following Lemma shows that our procedure Convert enables one to transform a Type-II ciphertext back to a Type-I ciphertext. We provide the proof in the full version of the paper [CLT14].

Lemma 1. *Let ρ' be such that $\rho' \geqslant \eta + \rho + \log_2(\eta\Theta)$. The procedure Convert above converts a Type-II ciphertext with noise size ρ' into a Type-I ciphertext with noise $(\rho' - \eta + 5, \log_2 \Theta)$.*

Assume that initially the two ciphertexts c_1, c_2 are Type-I ciphertexts with noise $(\rho_1, \log_2 \Theta)$. After computing $c_3 = 2 \cdot c_1 \cdot c_2$ which has noise size at most $\rho' = \eta + \rho_1 + \log_2 \Theta + 4$ (see previous section) one can convert c_3 back into a Type-I ciphertext with noise (ρ_3, ρ_3^*) with $\rho_3 = \rho_1 + \log_2 \Theta + 9$ and $\rho_3^* = \log_2 \Theta$, from Lemma 1. Therefore the noise length in bits has only grown by an additive factor $\log_2 \Theta + 9$. Therefore the ciphertext noise grows only linearly with the number of homomorphic multiplications.

3.3 Description of the Public-Key Leveled Fully Homomorphic Scheme

We are now ready to describe our scale-invariant version of the DGHV encryption scheme. For a specific η-bit odd integer p and an integer q_0 in $[0, 2^\gamma/p^2)$, we define the set:

$$\mathcal{D}_{p,q_0}^\rho = \{q \cdot p^2 + r : q \in \mathbb{Z} \cap [0, q_0), r \in \mathbb{Z} \cap (-2^\rho, 2^\rho)\} \ .$$

SIDGHV. KeyGen(1^λ). Generate an odd η-bit integer p and a γ-bit integer $x_0 = q_0 \cdot p^2 + r_0$ with $r_0 \leftarrow (-2^\rho, 2^\rho) \cap \mathbb{Z}$ and $q_0 \leftarrow [0, 2^\gamma/p^2) \cap \mathbb{Z}$. Let $x_i \leftarrow \mathcal{D}_{p,q_0}^\rho$ for $1 \leqslant i \leqslant \tau$. Let also $y' \leftarrow \mathcal{D}_{p,q_0}^\rho$ and $y = y' + (p-1)/2$.

Let $\boldsymbol{z}$ be a vector of Θ numbers with $\kappa = 2\gamma + 2$ bits of precision after the binary point, and let $\boldsymbol{s}$ be a vector of Θ bits such that

$$\frac{2^\eta}{p^2} = \langle \boldsymbol{s}, \boldsymbol{z} \rangle + \varepsilon \bmod 2^\eta,$$

with $|\varepsilon| \leqslant 2^{-\kappa}$. Now, define

$$\boldsymbol{\sigma} = \boldsymbol{q} \cdot p^2 + \boldsymbol{r} + \left\lfloor \mathsf{PowersofTwo}_\eta(\boldsymbol{s}) \cdot \frac{p}{2^{\eta+1}} \right\rceil,$$

where the components of $\boldsymbol{q}$ (resp. $\boldsymbol{r}$) are randomly chosen from $[0, q_0) \cap \mathbb{Z}$ (resp. $(-2^\rho, 2^\rho) \cap \mathbb{Z}$).

The secret-key is $\mathsf{sk} = \{p\}$ and the public-key is $\mathsf{pk} = \{x_0, x_1, \ldots, x_\tau, y, \boldsymbol{\sigma}, \boldsymbol{z}\}$.

SIDGHV. Encrypt($\mathsf{pk}, m \in \{0,1\}$). Choose a random subset $S \subset \{1, \ldots, \tau\}$ and output

$$c \leftarrow \left[m \cdot y + \sum_{i \in S} x_i\right]_{x_0}.$$

SIDGHV. Add(pk, c_1, c_2). Output $c \leftarrow c_1 + c_2 \bmod x_0$.

SIDGHV. Convert(pk, c). Output $c' \leftarrow 2 \cdot \langle \boldsymbol{\sigma}, \mathsf{BitDecomp}_\eta(\boldsymbol{c}) \rangle$ where $\boldsymbol{c} = \big(\lfloor c \cdot z_i \rceil \bmod 2^\eta\big)_{1 \leqslant i \leqslant \Theta}$.

SIDGHV. Mult(pk, c_1, c_2). Output $c' \leftarrow \mathsf{SIDGHV}.\,\mathsf{Convert}(\mathsf{pk}, 2 \cdot c_1 \cdot c_2) \bmod x_0$.

SIDGHV. Decrypt(sk, c). Output $m \leftarrow ((2c) \bmod p) \bmod 2$.

Remark 1. This describes a *leveled* fully homomorphic encryption scheme, because the noise growth is only linear in the number of levels. The scheme can be bootstrapped to obtain a (pure) fully homomorphic encryption scheme, as in [DGHV10, CCK+13],

3.4   Constraints on the Parameters

The parameters of the scheme must meet the following constraints (where λ is the security parameter):

- $\rho = \Omega(\lambda)$ to avoid brute force attack on the noise [CN12, CNT12],
- $\eta \geqslant \rho + \mathcal{O}(L \log \lambda)$ where L is the multiplicative depth of the circuit to be evaluated,
- $\gamma = \omega(\eta^2 \cdot \log \lambda)$ in order to thwart lattice-based attacks (see [DGHV10] and [CMNT11, CH12]),
- $\Theta^2 = \gamma \cdot \omega(\log \lambda)$ to avoid lattice attacks on the subset sum (see [CMNT11]),

- $\tau \geqslant \gamma + 2\lambda$ in order to apply the Leftover Hash Lemma (see Section 3.5).

To satisfy the above constraints one can take $\rho = 2\lambda$, $\eta = \tilde{\mathcal{O}}(L + \lambda)$, $\gamma = \tilde{\mathcal{O}}(L^2\lambda + \lambda^2)$, $\Theta = \tilde{\mathcal{O}}(L\lambda)$ and $\tau = \gamma + 2\lambda$.

3.5   Semantic Security

We show that the semantic security of our scheme can be based on the following variant of the decisional problem introduced in [KLYC13], called the Decisional-Approximate-GCD problem. Roughly speaking, it should be hard to distinguish integers from $\mathcal{D}^\rho_{p,q_0}$ from completely uniform integers modulo x_0, where:

$$\mathcal{D}^\rho_{p,q_0} = \{q \cdot p^2 + r : q \in \mathbb{Z} \cap [0, q_0), r \in \mathbb{Z} \cap (-2^\rho, 2^\rho)\}.$$

Definition 2 ((ρ, η, γ)-Decisional-Approximate-GCD). *Let p be a random odd integer of η bits, q_0 an integer uniformly distributed in $[0, 2^\gamma/p^2)$, r_0 an integer uniformly distributed in $(-2^\rho, 2^\rho)$. Given $x_0 = q_0 \cdot p^2 + r_0$, polynomially many samples from $\mathcal{D}^\rho_{p,q_0}$ and $y \leftarrow \mathcal{D}^\rho_{p,q_0} + (p-1)/2$, determine $b \in \{0, 1\}$ from $c = x + b \cdot r \bmod x_0$ where $x \leftarrow \mathcal{D}^\rho_{p,q_0}$ and $r \leftarrow [0, x_0) \cap \mathbb{Z}$.*

The following theorem shows that our scheme is semantically secure under the Decisional-Approximate-GCD assumption; below we only consider a subset of our scheme without the procedure Convert, i.e. without the public parameters z and σ. To prove the semantic security of the full scheme it suffices to include z and σ in the above decisional assumption.[1]

---

[1] Usually in FHE we first show the semantic security of a restricted scheme, and then a 'circular security' assumption is used to get the semantic security of the entire FHE; that is we assume that the encryption scheme remains secure even when the adversary is given encryptions of the individual bits of the private-key.

  Here we first prove that the scheme is secure without the terms z and σ. If the scheme is 'circular secure' (secure even with encryptions of the invariant switching, i.e. z and σ) then it remains semantically secure. This circular security assumption can be avoided by using the classical modulus switching technique [CNT12] instead of our scale-invariance technique.

Theorem 1. *The above scale-invariant DGHV scheme without the parameters z, σ is semantically secure under the (ρ, η, γ)-Decisional-Approximate-GCD assumption.*

To prove the theorem, we use a preliminary Lemma from [KLYC13] stating that the distribution of the public-key elements is indistinguishable from random elements in $[0, x_0)$ if the Decisional-Approximate-GCD problem is hard; the proof follows from a standard hybrid argument.

Lemma 2. *For the parameters (ρ, η, γ), let $\mathsf{pk} = (x_0, \{x_i\}_i, y)$ and $\mathsf{sk} = p$ be chosen as in the KeyGen procedure. Define $\mathsf{pk}' = (x_0, \{x_i'\}_i, y)$ for x_i' uniformly generated in $[0, x_0)$. Then pk and pk' are indistinguishable under the Decisional-Approximate-GCD assumption.*

Proof (of Theorem 1). Under the attack scenario the attacker first receives the public key, and an encryption of a random bit $b \in \{0, 1\}$. The attacker outputs a guess b' and succeeds if $b' = b$. We use a sequence of games and denote by S_i the event that the attacker succeeds in **Game**$_i$.

Game$_0$: This is the attack scenario. We simulate the challenger by running KeyGen to obtain pk and sk.

Game$_1$: We replace the x_i's in the public key by elements uniformly drawn in $[0, x_0)$. By Lemma 2, we have

$$|\Pr[S_1] - \Pr[S_0]| \leqslant \tau \cdot \varepsilon_{\mathrm{dagcd}} .$$

Game$_2$: By the Leftover Hash Lemma (Lemma 5 in Appendix A), $\sum_{i \in S} x_i \bmod x_0$ is ε-statistically indistinguishable from uniform modulo x_0, with $\varepsilon = 2^{(\gamma - \tau)/2}$. Therefore we can replace the challenge ciphertext by a uniform integer modulo x_0; this no longer gives any information on b and therefore $\Pr[S_2] = 1/2$. Moreover we have $|\Pr[S_2] - \Pr[S_1]| \leqslant \varepsilon$. This gap can be made negligible by satisfying the constraints on the parameters from Section 3.4, which concludes the proof. $\qquad\square$

Remark 2. We show in Section 6 that the (Error-Free) Decisional-Approximate-GCD problem is equivalent to the computational (Error-Free) Approximate-GCD problem. Thus our scheme is automatically based on the *computational* Approximate-GCD problem as in previous works on the DGHV schemes [DGHV10, CMNT11, CNT12].

4   Generalization to Batch Scale-Invariant DGHV Scheme

We now describe a generalization of the previous scheme to the batch setting (as in RLWE-based schemes [BV11a, BV11b] and integer schemes [CCK+13]). The goal is to pack ℓ plaintext bits $m_0, \ldots, m_{\ell-1}$ into a single ciphertext. Homomorphic addition and multiplication will then apply in parallel and component-wise on the m_i's.

Our batch generalization is similar to [CCK+13]. A ciphertext encrypting a vector $m = (m_0, \dots, m_{\ell-1})$ has the form:

$$c = \mathsf{CRT}_{q_0, p_0^2, \dots, p_{\ell-1}^2} \left(q, \dots, r_i + (2r_i^* + m_i) \cdot \frac{p_i - 1}{2}, \dots \right) \qquad (7)$$

for a tuple of $\ell + 1$ coprime integers $q_0, p_0, \dots, p_{\ell-1}$, where we denote by $\mathsf{CRT}_{b_i}(a_i)$ the unique integer u such that $0 \leqslant u < \prod_i b_i$ and $u \bmod b_i = a_i$ for all i. We call such ciphertext a *batch Type-I ciphertext*. Modulo each of the p_j's the ciphertext c behaves as in the SIDGHV scheme in Section 3. Accordingly, the addition of two ciphertexts yields a new ciphertext that decrypts to the componentwise sum modulo 2 of the original plaintexts.

To homomorphically multiply two ciphertexts c_1 and c_2, as previously one computes $c_3 = 2 \cdot c_1 \cdot c_2$ in $\mathbb{Z}$. As previously there exists small integers $r_{3,j}$ such that

$$c_3 \equiv r_{3,j} + m_j \cdot \frac{p_j^2 - 1}{2} \pmod{p_j} \quad \text{for } j = 0, \dots, \ell - 1, \qquad (8)$$

where each m_j is the product of the corresponding plain text components of c_1 and c_2. We call c_3 a *batch Type-II ciphertext*. Modulo each of the p_j's, the ciphertext c_3 behaves as a Type-II ciphertext given by Equation (2); therefore the message bit m_j is the MSB of $[c \bmod p_j^2]$ for all j. As in Section 3, there exists an efficient conversion procedure Convert to convert any Type-II ciphertext to a new Type-I ciphertext. As shown below the procedure Convert is actually the same as in Section 3, with adapted public parameters.

Namely let z be a vector of Θ rational numbers in $[0, 2^\eta)$ with κ bits of precision after the binary point (where $|c| < 2^\kappa$), and let (s_j) be a set of ℓ vectors of Θ bits such that, for all $j = 0, \dots, \ell - 1$,

$$\frac{2^\eta}{p_j^2} = \langle s_j, z \rangle + \varepsilon_j \mod 2^\eta$$

where $|\varepsilon_j| \leqslant 2^{-\kappa}$. Let $s_j' = \mathsf{PowersofTwo}_\eta(s_j) \in \mathbb{Z}^{\eta\Theta}$. Define $\sigma = (\sigma_1, \dots, \sigma_{\eta\Theta})$ so that, for all $1 \leqslant i \leqslant \eta\Theta$:

$$\sigma_i = \mathsf{CRT}_{q_0, p_0^2, \dots, p_{\ell-1}^2} \left(q_i, r_{0,i} + \left\lfloor s_{0,i}' \cdot \frac{p_0}{2^{\eta+1}} \right\rceil, \dots, r_{\ell-1,i} + \left\lfloor s_{\ell-1,i}' \cdot \frac{p_{\ell-1}}{2^{\eta+1}} \right\rceil \right)$$

is an encryption of $(s_{j,i}')_{1 \leqslant j \leqslant \ell}$. For Convert we use the same algorithm as in Section 3:

Convert(z, σ, c). First compute $c = (\lfloor c \cdot z_i \rceil \bmod 2^\eta)_{1 \leqslant i \leqslant \Theta}$ and then its decomposition $c' = \mathsf{BitDecomp}_\eta(c)$. Finally, output

$$c' \leftarrow 2\langle \sigma, c' \rangle \bmod x_0 .$$

The proof of the following lemma follows directly from the proof of Lemma 1 applied modulo each of the p_j's.

Lemma 3. *The procedure* Convert *above converts a Type-II ciphertext with noise size ρ' into a Type-I ciphertext with noise $(\rho' - \eta + 5, \log_2 \Theta)$, for $\rho' - \eta \geqslant \rho + \log_2(\eta\Theta)$.*

In the full version of this paper [CLT14] we provide a full description of the resulting batch leveled fully homomorphic scheme. We also show that the batch scheme is semantically secure under a variant of the previous Decisional-Approximate-GCD assumption with error-free x_0.

5 Practical Implementation

In this section, we provide concrete parameters and timings for a homomorphic evaluation of AES with our batch scale-invariant DGHV scheme. For homomorphic AES evaluations we compare our timings with the RLWE-based leveled-FHE scheme in [GHS12b] and with the batch (bootstrapping-based) DGHV scheme in [CCK+13, CLT13]. We use the following existing optimizations:

1. Subset-sum: as in [CMNT11] we use β-bit integers b_i instead of bits in the subset sum, to reduce the value of τ. Namely the condition becomes $\beta \cdot \tau \geqslant \gamma + 2\lambda$.

2. Public-key compression: the technique in [CNT12, CLT13] enables to compress the ciphertexts in the public-key from γ to roughly $\ell \cdot \eta$ bits.

3. Ciphertext expand [CNT12]: the technique consists in generating the z_i's with a special structure instead of pseudo-random. Let δ be a parameter to be specified later. One generates a random z with $\kappa + \delta \cdot \Theta \cdot \eta$ bits of precision after the binary point, and one defines the z_i's for $\ell + 1 \leqslant i \leqslant \Theta$ as

$$z_i = \left[z \cdot 2^{i \cdot \delta \cdot \eta} \right]_{2^\eta},$$

keeping only κ bits of precision after the binary point for each z_i as previously. We fix $z_1, \ldots, z_\ell$ so that the previous equalities hold. Then the ciphertext expansion can be computed as follows, for all $\ell + 1 \leqslant i \leqslant \Theta$:

$$c_i = \lfloor c \cdot z_i \rceil \bmod 2^\eta = \lfloor c \cdot z \cdot 2^{i \cdot \delta \cdot \eta} \rceil \bmod 2^\eta .$$

Therefore computing all the z_i's (except the first ℓ) is now essentially a single multiplication $c \cdot z$. A lattice attack against this optimization is described in [CNT12]; the authors show that the attack is thwarted by selecting δ such that $\delta \cdot \Theta \cdot \eta \geqslant 3\gamma$.

5.1 Optimization of Scalar Product

We describe an additional optimization for computing the scalar product $c' = 2\langle \sigma, c' \rangle$ computed in Convert, similar to the ciphertext expand optimization above. The vectors σ and c' have $\eta\Theta$ elements. We first divide the vectors σ and c' into subvectors of Θ elements, and we compute the scalar products of the subvectors separately. In the following for simplicity we keep the same notations and now assume that $\boldsymbol{\sigma}$ and $\boldsymbol{c'}$ have Θ elements each.

We generate the vector $\boldsymbol{\sigma} \in \mathbb{Z}^\Theta$ such that:

$$\sigma_i = \lfloor \sigma \cdot 2^{i \cdot \delta \cdot \eta} \rceil + v_i$$

for small public corrections $|v_i| \leqslant 2^{\eta \cdot \ell}$ for all $1 \leqslant i \leqslant \Theta$, where the large public random σ has $\delta \eta \Theta$ bits of precision after the binary point, and $\gamma + \delta \eta \Theta$ bits in total. Then

$$c' = 2\langle \boldsymbol{\sigma}, \boldsymbol{c'} \rangle = 2 \sum_{i=1}^{n} \lfloor \sigma \cdot 2^{i \cdot \delta \cdot \eta} \rceil \cdot c_i' + 2\langle \boldsymbol{v}, \boldsymbol{c'} \rangle = 2 \sum_{i=1}^{n} \left(\sigma \cdot 2^{i\delta\eta} + u_i \right) c_i' + 2\langle \boldsymbol{v}, \boldsymbol{c'} \rangle$$

$$= 2\sigma \cdot \left(\sum_{i=1}^{n} c_i' \cdot 2^{i\delta\eta} \right) + 2\langle \boldsymbol{v}, \boldsymbol{c'} \rangle + u = \left\lfloor 2\sigma \cdot \left(\sum_{i=1}^{n} c_i' \cdot 2^{i\delta\eta} \right) \right\rceil + 2\langle \boldsymbol{v}, \boldsymbol{c'} \rangle + u' \,,$$

where $|u_i| \leqslant 1/2$, $|u| \leqslant \Theta$, and $u' \in \mathbb{Z}$ is such that $|u'| \leqslant \Theta + 1$. Then the scalar product becomes essentially one multiplication and another scalar product but with much smaller entries v_i's instead of σ_i's.

Therefore with vectors $\boldsymbol{\sigma}$ and $\boldsymbol{c'}$ with $\eta \Theta$ elements each instead of Θ, the scalar product $2\langle \boldsymbol{\sigma}, \boldsymbol{c'} \rangle$ becomes essentially η multiplications and another scalar product but with much smaller entries v_i's instead of σ_i's. Note that the size of c' is now $\gamma + \Theta\delta\eta$ bits instead of γ; therefore one must increase κ by twice the same additive factor (to support multiplications of two such converted ciphertexts).

Finally we use the following straightforward optimization: instead of using BitDecomp and PowersofTwo with bits, we use words of size ω bits instead. This decreases the size of the vector $\boldsymbol{\sigma}$ by a factor ω, at the cost of increasing the resulting noise by roughly ω bits. In particular the scalar product $2\langle \boldsymbol{\sigma}, \boldsymbol{c'} \rangle$ then requires essentially $\lceil \eta/\omega \rceil$ multiplications and another scalar product but with smaller entries v_i's instead of σ_i's. In our code we used $\omega = 64$.

5.2 Concrete Parameters and AES Evaluation

In Table 1 we derive concrete parameters as in [CNT12, CCK+13], taking into account the known attacks on the Approximate-GCD problem (see [DGHV10] and [CMNT11, CNT12, CN12, CH12]).

AES evaluation has become a standard evaluation circuit for fully homomorphic encryption [GHS12b, CCK+13]. The main difference between [GHS12b] and [CCK+13] (apart from the underlying FHE scheme) is that bootstrapping was used in the later while in the former the parameters could be made large enough so that no bootstrapping was required to evaluate the full-fledged AES circuit (thanks to the linear growth of the noise). In our scheme we also chose large enough parameters so that the entire AES evaluation could be performed without bootstrapping.

In practice we have evaluated the AES circuit using the state-wise bitslicing variant described in [CLT13] and we obtained the results in Table 1. In this variant, the state is represented as an array of 128 ciphertexts, each ciphertext

Table 1. Benchmarking of a C++ implementation of our scale-invariant batch DGHV scheme with a compressed public key on an Intel Xeon E5-2690 at 2.9 GHz on the state-wise AES implementation, using GMP [Gt13]

Instance	λ	ℓ	ρ	η	$\gamma \times 10^{-6}$	τ, Θ	pk size	KeyGen	Encrypt	Decrypt	Mult	Convert
Toy	42	9	42	971	0.27	135	3.2 MB	0.5s	0.0s	0.0s	0.0s	0.1s
Small	52	35	52	976	1.1	525	45 MB	11s	0.2s	0.0s	0.0s	0.3s
Medium	62	140	62	981	4.2	2100	704 MB	5min	0.2s	0.0s	0.0s	2.8s
Large	72	569	72	986	15.8	8535	11 GB	2h 50min	45s	3.3s	0.1s	33s
Extra	80	1875	86	993	35.9	28125	100 GB	213h	5min	24s	0.3s	277s

Instance	λ	$\ell = \#$ of enc. in parallel	AddRoundKey	SubBytes	ShiftRows	MixColumns	Total Time	Time/AES block
Toy	42	9	0.0s	1.5s	0.0s	0.0s	15.1s	**1.7s**
Small	52	35	0.1s	9.9s	0.0s	0.0s	1min 40s	**2.9s**
Medium	62	140	0.3s	80.5s	0.0s	0.1s	13min 29s	**5.8s**
Large	72	569	2.1s	21min	0.0s	0.6s	3h 35min	**23s**
Extra	80	1875	6.9s	10h 9min	0.1s	1.6s	102h	**195s**

representing one bit of the state of ℓ different AES blocks encrypted in parallel. In [CCK+13, CLT13], the authors obtained a time per AES block of 12 min 46 s on a 4-core machine at 3.4 GHz whereas we obtained 23 s on a 16-core machine at 2.9 GHz for the same security level (72 bits of security); which is *one order of magnitude faster*. For 80 bits of security, timings are competitive with [GHS12b] (3 min vs. 5 min).

6   Equivalence between the (Error-Free) Decisional and Computational Approximate-GCD Problems

In this section, we show the equivalence between the (error-free) decisional and computational Approximate-GCD problems. As a consequence, it follows directly that the additional noises in the fully homomorphic encryption schemes over the integers [DGHV10, CMNT11, CNT12, CLT13] can be removed (as in [CCK+13, Section 3]), simplifying both the schemes and the security proofs. In the following for simplicity we only consider integers $r \in [0, 2^\rho)$ instead of $(-2^\rho, 2^\rho)$. One can always go from one distribution to another by an appropriate centering. Therefore, for a η-bit integer p and $q_0 \in [0, 2^\gamma/p)$, we consider the following distribution over γ-bit integers:

$$\mathcal{D}_\rho(p, q_0) = \{ \text{Choose } q \leftarrow [0, q_0), r \leftarrow \mathbb{Z} \cap [0, 2^\rho) : \text{Output } y = q \cdot p + r \}.$$

Let us recall the definition of the computational and decisional Error-Free Approximate-GCD problems.

Definition 3 (Error-Free (Computational) Approximate-GCD). *The* (ρ, η, γ)*-error-free Approximate-GCD problem is: For a random η-bit prime p, given a γ-bit 2^{λ^2}-rough integer $x_0 = q_0 \cdot p$ where q_0 is a random integer in $[0, 2^\gamma/p)$, and polynomially many samples from $\mathcal{D}_\rho(p, q_0)$, output p.*

Algorithm 1. Learn-LSB(z, pk)

Input: $z = qp + r \in [0, 2^\gamma)$ with $|r| \leqslant 2^\rho$, and $x_0 = q_0 \cdot p$.

Output: The least significant bit of q

  Generate $x_1, \ldots, x_\tau \leftarrow \mathcal{D}_\rho(p, q_0)$

  for $j = 1$ **to** $\mathsf{poly}(\lambda/\epsilon)$ **do**

    Choose randomly and uniformly a noise $r_j \leftarrow [0, 2^{\rho'})$, a bit $\delta \leftarrow \{0, 1\}$ and a random subset $S_j \subset \{1, \ldots, \tau\}$

    Set $y_j = z + \delta + 2r_j + 2\sum_{i \in S_j} x_i \bmod x_0$

    Call $\mathcal{A}$ to get a prediction of $(r \bmod 2) \oplus \delta$: $a_j \leftarrow \mathcal{A}(y_j)$

    Set $b_j \leftarrow a_j \oplus \mathsf{parity}(z) \oplus \delta$

  end for

  Output the majority vote among the b_j's

Definition 4 (Error-Free Decisional Approximate-GCD). *The (ρ, η, γ)-error-free Decisional-Approximate-GCD problem is: For a random η-bit prime p, given a γ-bit 2^{λ^2}-rough integer $x_0 = q_0 \cdot p$ and polynomially many samples from $\mathcal{D}_\rho(p, q_0)$, determine $b \in \{0, 1\}$ from $z = x + r \cdot b \bmod x_0$ where $x \leftarrow \mathcal{D}_\rho(p, q_0)$ and $r \leftarrow \mathbb{Z} \cap [0, x_0)$.*

We also consider the following decisional problem.

Definition 5 (Error-Free LSB Approximate-GCD Problem). *The (ρ, η, γ)-error-free LSB Approximate-GCD problem is: For a random η-bit prime p, given a γ-bit 2^{λ^2}-rough integer $x_0 = q_0 \cdot p$ and polynomially many samples from $\mathcal{D}_\rho(p, q_0)$, determine $b \in \{0, 1\}$ from $z = q \cdot p + 2r + b \cdot c$ where $q \leftarrow [0, q_0)$, $r \leftarrow \mathbb{Z} \cap [0, 2^{\rho-1})$ and $c \leftarrow \{0, 1\}$.*

One can show that the problems from Definitions 3 and 5 are equivalent. Indeed, we can construct a high-accuracy LSB predictor subroutine (cf. Algorithm 1 below) using an adversary $\mathcal{A}$ having a non-negligible advantage ϵ against the (ρ', η, γ)-Error-Free LSB Approximate-GCD problem (with $\rho' > \log_2(\tau + 1) + \rho + \lambda)^2$, and by using it in Step 2 of the security proof of [DGHV10], we automatically get the equivalence.

Let us show that Definitions 4 and 5 are equivalent. We consider the sequence of distributions for $\rho \leqslant i \leqslant \eta + \lambda$:

$$\mathcal{D}'_\rho(p, q_0, i) = \left\{ \begin{array}{l} \text{Choose } q \leftarrow [0, q_0), r \leftarrow \mathbb{Z} \cap [0, 2^i) : \\ \text{Output } y = q \cdot p + 2^{\lambda + \eta - i} \cdot r \bmod x_0 \end{array} \right\}.$$

Note that in the distribution $\mathcal{D}'_\rho(p, q_0, i)$ above the size of the random r is i-bit instead of ρ bit. For $i = \rho$, the distribution of y is the same as the distribution $\mathcal{D}_\rho(p, q_0)$, up to a factor $2^{\lambda + \eta - \rho}$ modulo x_0. One can show that for $i = \eta + \lambda$, the distribution $\mathcal{D}'_\rho(p, q_0, i)$ is $2^{-\lambda}$-statistically close to uniform modulo x_0. Therefore by a standard hybrid argument, if a distinguisher solves the

---

[2] The additional noise is use to drawn the noise due to the public key elements and z.

Error-Free Decisional-Approximate-GCD problem with some non-negligible advantage, then he must be able to distinguish between two successive distributions $\mathcal{D}'_\rho(p, q_0, i)$ and $\mathcal{D}'_\rho(p, q_0, i + 1)$ for some i.

Let us consider the challenge from the Error-Free LSB Approximate-GCD problem:

$$z = q \cdot p + 2r + b \cdot c$$

where $r \leftarrow \mathbb{Z} \cap [0, 2^{\rho-1})$ and $c \leftarrow \{0, 1\}$. We let:

$$y = 2^{\lambda+\eta-i-1} \cdot (2^\rho \cdot u + z) \bmod x_0$$

where $u \leftarrow \mathbb{Z} \cap [0, 2^{i+1-\rho})$. This gives:

$$y = q' \cdot p + 2^{\lambda+\eta-i-1} \cdot (2^\rho \cdot u + 2r + b \cdot c) \bmod x_0$$
$$= q' \cdot p + 2^{\lambda+\eta-i-1} \cdot (2r' + b \cdot c)$$

for some $q' \in \mathbb{Z}$, where $r' \leftarrow \mathbb{Z} \cap [0, 2^i)$.

If $b = 0$ then we get $y = q' \cdot p + 2^{\lambda+\eta-i} \cdot r'$ which corresponds to the distribution $\mathcal{D}'_\rho(p, q_0, i)$. If $b = 1$ then we get $y = q' \cdot p + 2^{\lambda+\eta-i-1} \cdot r''$ where $r'' \leftarrow \mathbb{Z} \cap [0, 2^{i+1})$, which corresponds to the distribution $\mathcal{D}'_\rho(p, q_0, i + 1)$. Therefore we can use the previous distinguisher to solve the Error-Free LSB Approximate-GCD problem.

References

[BGV12]   Brakerski, Z., Gentry, C., Vaikuntanathan, V.: (Leveled) fully homomorphic encryption without bootstrapping. In: Goldwasser, S. (ed.) ITCS 2012, pp. 309–325. ACM (2012)

[Bra12]   Brakerski, Z.: Fully homomorphic encryption without modulus switching from classical GapSVP. In: Safavi-Naini, R., Canetti, R. (eds.) CRYPTO 2012. LNCS, vol. 7417, pp. 868–886. Springer, Heidelberg (2012)

[BV11a]   Brakerski, Z., Vaikuntanathan, V.: Efficient fully homomorphic encryption from (standard) LWE. In: FOCS 2011, pp. 97–106. IEEE Computer Society (2011)

[BV11b]   Brakerski, Z., Vaikuntanathan, V.: Fully homomorphic encryption from Ring-LWE and security for key dependent messages. In: Rogaway, P. (ed.) CRYPTO 2011. LNCS, vol. 6841, pp. 505–524. Springer, Heidelberg (2011)

[CCK+13]   Cheon, J.H., Coron, J.-S., Kim, J., Lee, M.S., Lepoint, T., Tibouchi, M., Yun, A.: Batch fully homomorphic encryption over the integers. In: Johansson, T., Nguyen, P.Q. (eds.) EUROCRYPT 2013. LNCS, vol. 7881, pp. 315–335. Springer, Heidelberg (2013)

[CH12]   Cohn, H., Heninger, N.: Approximate common divisors via lattices. In: ANTS X (2012)

[CLT13]   Coron, J.-S., Lepoint, T., Tibouchi, M.: Batch fully homomorphic encryption over the integers. Cryptology ePrint Archive, Report 2013/036 (2013), http://eprint.iacr.org/

[CLT14]   Coron, J.-S., Lepoint, T., Tibouchi, M.: Scale-invariant fully homomorphic encryption over the integers. Full version of this paper. Cryptology ePrint Archive, Report 2014/032 (2014), http://eprint.iacr.org/

[CMNT11]   Coron, J.-S., Mandal, A., Naccache, D., Tibouchi, M.: Fully homomorphic
           encryption over the integers with shorter public keys. In: Rogaway, P. (ed.)
           CRYPTO 2011. LNCS, vol. 6841, pp. 487–504. Springer, Heidelberg (2011)
[CN12]   Chen, Y., Nguyen, P.Q.: Faster algorithms for approximate common di-
           visors: Breaking fully-homomorphic-encryption challenges over the inte-
           gers. In: Pointcheval, D., Johansson, T. (eds.) EUROCRYPT 2012. LNCS,
           vol. 7237, pp. 502–519. Springer, Heidelberg (2012)
[CNT12]   Coron, J.-S., Naccache, D., Tibouchi, M.: Public key compression and
           modulus switching for fully homomorphic encryption over the integers. In:
           Pointcheval, D., Johansson, T. (eds.) EUROCRYPT 2012. LNCS, vol. 7237,
           pp. 446–464. Springer, Heidelberg (2012)
[DGHV10]   van Dijk, M., Gentry, C., Halevi, S., Vaikuntanathan, V.: Fully homomor-
           phic encryption over the integers. In: Gilbert, H. (ed.) EUROCRYPT 2010.
           LNCS, vol. 6110, pp. 24–43. Springer, Heidelberg (2010)
[Gen09]   Gentry, C.: Fully homomorphic encryption using ideal lattices. In: Mitzen-
           macher, M. (ed.) STOC, pp. 169–178. ACM (2009)
[GH11]   Gentry, C., Halevi, S.: Implementing Gentry's fully-homomorphic encryp-
           tion scheme. In: Paterson, K.G. (ed.) EUROCRYPT 2011. LNCS, vol. 6632,
           pp. 129–148. Springer, Heidelberg (2011)
[GHS12a]   Gentry, C., Halevi, S., Smart, N.P.: Fully homomorphic encryption with
           polylog overhead. In: Pointcheval, D., Johansson, T. (eds.) EUROCRYPT
           2012. LNCS, vol. 7237, pp. 465–482. Springer, Heidelberg (2012)
[GHS12b]   Gentry, C., Halevi, S., Smart, N.P.: Homomorphic evaluation of the AES
           circuit. In: Safavi-Naini, R., Canetti, R. (eds.) CRYPTO 2012. LNCS,
           vol. 7417, pp. 850–867. Springer, Heidelberg (2012)
[Gt13]   Torbjörn Granlund and the GMP development team. GNU MP: The GNU
           Multiple Precision Arithmetic Library, 5.1.3 edition (2013),
           http://gmplib.org/
[HILL99]   Håstad, J., Impagliazzo, R., Levin, L.A., Luby, M.: A pseudorandom gen-
           erator from any one-way function. SIAM Journal on Computing 28, 12–24
           (1999)
[KLYC13]   Kim, J., Lee, M.S., Yun, A., Cheon, J.H.: CRT-based fully homomorphic
           encryption over the integers. Cryptology ePrint Archive, Report 2013/057
           (2013), http://eprint.iacr.org/
[Reg05]   Regev, O.: On lattices, learning with errors, random linear codes, and cryp-
           tography. In: Gabow, H.N., Fagin, R. (eds.) STOC 2005, pp. 84–93. ACM
           (2005)
[SV10]   Smart, N.P., Vercauteren, F.: Fully homomorphic encryption with rela-
           tively small key and ciphertext sizes. In: Nguyen, P.Q., Pointcheval, D.
           (eds.) PKC 2010. LNCS, vol. 6056, pp. 420–443. Springer, Heidelberg (2010)
[SV11]   Smart, N.P., Vercauteren, F.: Fully homomorphic SIMD operations. IACR
           Cryptology ePrint Archive, 2011:133 (2011)

A   Leftover Hash Lemma

We recall the classical Leftover Hash Lemma (LHL), following [DGHV10]. A family $\mathcal{H}$ of hash functions from X to Y, both finite sets, is said to be pairwise-independent if for all distinct $x, x' \in X$, $\Pr_{h \leftarrow H}[h(x) = h(x')] = 1/|Y|$. A distribution D is ε-uniform if its statistical distance from the uniform distribution is at most ε, where the statistical distance $\Delta(D_1, D_2)$ between two distributions D_1, D_2 over a finite domain X is given by $\Delta(D_1, D_2) = \frac{1}{2} \sum_{x \in X} |D_1(x) - D_2(x)|$.

Lemma 4 (Leftover Hash Lemma [HILL99]). *Let $\mathcal{H}$ be a family of pairwise hash functions from X to Y. Suppose that $h \leftarrow \mathcal{H}$ and $x \leftarrow X$ are chosen uniformly and independently. Then, $(h, h(x))$ is $\frac{1}{2}\sqrt{|Y|/|X|}$-uniform over $\mathcal{H} \times X$.*

From the LHL one can deduce the following Lemma for finite sums modulo an integer M, as proved in [DGHV10]:

Lemma 5. *Set $x_1, \ldots, x_m \leftarrow \mathbb{Z}_M$ uniformly and independently, set $s_1, \ldots, s_m \leftarrow \{0, 1\}$, and set $y = \sum_{i=1}^{m} s_i \cdot x_i \bmod M$. Then $(x_1, \ldots, x_m, y)$ is $1/2\sqrt{M/2^m}$-uniform over $\mathbb{Z}_M^{m+1}$.*

Proof. We consider the following hash function family $\mathcal{H}$ from $\{0, 1\}^m$ to $\mathbb{Z}_M$. Each member $h \in \mathcal{H}$ is parameterized by the elements $(x_1, \ldots, x_m) \in \mathbb{Z}_M^m$. Given $s \in \{0, 1\}^m$, we define $h(s) = \sum_{i=1}^{m} s_i \cdot x_i \in \mathbb{Z}_M$. The hash function family is clearly pairwise independent. Therefore by Lemma 4, $(h, h(x))$ is $1/2\sqrt{M/2^m}$-uniform over $\mathbb{Z}_M^{m+1}$. $\qquad\square$

Enhanced Chosen-Ciphertext Security and Applications

Dana Dachman-Soled[1], Georg Fuchsbauer[2], Payman Mohassel[3],
and Adam O'Neill[4]

[1] University of Maryland
danadach@ece.umd.edu
[2] Institute of Science and Technology Austria
georg.fuchsbauer@ist.ac.at
[3] University of Calgary
pmohasse@cpsc.ucalgary.ca
[4] Georgetown University
adam@cs.georgetown.edu

Abstract. We introduce and study a new notion of *enhanced chosen-ciphertext security* (ECCA) for public-key encryption. Loosely speaking, in the ECCA security experiment, the decryption oracle provided to the adversary is augmented to return not only the output of the decryption algorithm on a queried ciphertext but also of a *randomness-recovery* algorithm associated to the scheme. Our results mainly concern the case where the randomness-recovery algorithm is efficient.

We provide constructions of ECCA-secure encryption from adaptive trapdoor functions as defined by Kiltz *et al.* (EUROCRYPT 2010), resulting in ECCA encryption from standard number-theoretic assumptions. We then give two applications of ECCA-secure encryption: (1) We use it as a unifying concept in showing equivalence of adaptive trapdoor functions and tag-based adaptive trapdoor functions, resolving an open question of Kiltz *et al.* (2) We show that ECCA-secure encryption can be used to securely realize an approach to public-key encryption with non-interactive opening (PKENO) originally suggested by Damgård and Thorbek (EUROCRYPT 2007), resulting in new and practical PKENO schemes quite different from those in prior work.

Our results demonstrate that ECCA security is of both practical and theoretical interest.

1 Introduction

This paper introduces and studies a new notion of security for public-key encryption (PKE) we call *enhanced* chosen-ciphertext security (ECCA). Besides being interesting in its own right, we find that ECCA security plays a fundamental role in contexts where randomness-recovering encryption (as discussed informally in e.g. [29]) is important, such as adaptive trapdoor functions [25] and PKE with non-interactive opening [15]. We also believe ECCA will find further applications in the future. Below we describe our results concerning ECCA in more detail; for a pictorial summary, see Figure 1.

H. Krawczyk (Ed.): PKC 2014, LNCS 8383, pp. 329–344, 2014.

1.1   ECCA Security Definition and Variants

Recall that in the standard formulation of CCA security [30], the adversary, given a public key pk, must guess which of the two possible messages its challenge ciphertext c encrypts, while being allowed to query a decryption oracle on any ciphertext c' different from c. Very informally, our "enhancement" is that the decryption oracle, when queried on a ciphertext c', returns not only the output of the decryption algorithm of the scheme run on c', but also of an associated *randomness-recovery* algorithm. This randomness-recovery algorithm, given sk and an honestly generated encryption c of m with coins r, is guaranteed to output some coins r' such that the encryption of m with coins r' is also c. (However, like the decryption algorithm — which is only guaranteed to output the right message on honestly generated ciphertexts — its behavior on other, maliciously generated ciphertexts depends on its specification.)

Note that in general we do not require that $r = r'$ above, but in the special case that this holds we say that the scheme is *uniquely* randomness-recovering. Looking ahead, our constructions of ECCA-secure PKE will be uniquely RR, but for some applications this is not strictly necessary as long as the scheme has perfect correctness (i.e., zero decryption error).

Our study of ECCA security is largely motivated by the related concept of randomness-recovering (RR) encryption, in which case the randomness-recovery algorithm is efficient. Indeed, we show that not every CCA-secure RR encryption scheme is ECCA-secure (cf. Proposition 1). This means that in applications of RR encryption that require ECCA security, it may not be sufficient to use a scheme proven CCA-secure.

1.2   Constructions of ECCA-Secure PKE

ECCA-Secure PKE from Adaptive TDFs. The first standard-model construction of CCA-secure randomness-recovering PKE was achieved by Peikert and Waters [29], based on their new concept of "lossy" trapdoor functions (TDFs). A line of subsequent work [31,25] focused on achieving CCA-secure PKE from progressively weaker assumptions on TDFs.[1] This leads one to wonder whether these assumptions suffice for ECCA-secure RR PKE as well. Ideally, one would achieve ECCA-secure, uniquely RR PKE — the strongest form of randomness-recovery — based on adaptive TDFs, the weakest of these assumptions. (Intuitively, adaptivity is a form of CCA security for TDFs, asking that the TDF remain one-way even when the adversary may query an inversion oracle on points other than its challenge.) This is exactly what our results obtain.

Challenges and Techniques. Our construction is technically novel, as the construction of CCA-secure encryption from adaptive TDFs in the earlier work

---

[1] Wee [32] showed that a weaker notion of adaptivity for *trapdoor relations* suffices; however, as this is not an assumption on trapdoor *functions* it does not seem to yield RR encryption and won't be useful for our results.

of [25] seems to be neither RR nor ECCA-secure (we achieve both, and more-over *unique* randomness recovery). Indeed, in the construction of [25] a general transform of [27] is used to convert a one-bit CCA-secure PKE from ATDFs to a multi-bit CCA-secure one. However, this transform does not seem to preserve either randomness-recovery nor ECCA-security of the one-bit scheme. Further-more, the one-bit scheme of [25] — which works by re-sampling a domain point x until the hardcore bit of x equals the message — is not uniquely RR, since de-cryption does not recover the "thrown away" x's. (Note that the "naïve" one-bit scheme from ATDFs that simply XOR's the message bit with a hardcore bit of the ATDF is trivially malleable by flipping the last bit of a ciphertext and thus is *not* CCA-secure.)

We solve these problems via a novel application of *detectable CCA (DCCA) security*, introduced recently by Hohenberger *et al.* [24]. Informally, DCCA is de-fined relative to a "detecting" function $\mathcal{F}$ (which must satisfy some definitions) that determines whether two ciphertexts are related; in the DCCA experiment, the adversary is not allowed to ask for decryptions of ciphertexts related to the challenge ciphertext according to $\mathcal{F}$. The work of [24] gives a transform from any DCCA-secure PKE to a CCA-secure encryption one. In particular, bit-by-bit encryption using a 1-bit CCA-secure encryption scheme is DCCA-secure, thus encompassing the earlier work of [27]. Our novelty is that we construct a DCCA-secure scheme from ATDFs also using bit-by-bit encryption, but where the underlying one-bit encryption scheme is *not* CCA-secure — namely, we use the "naïve" one-bit scheme described above. We show this one-bit scheme is uniquely RR and moreover satisfies a notion of DCCA with analogous "en-hanced" security (where the decryption oracle also returns coins).

More Efficient Schemes. We note that the above is a feasibility result in terms of minimal assumptions. We also show more efficient constructions of ECCA-secure encryption from *tag-based* ATDFs as defined in [25] and from ATDFs having a large number of simultaneous hardcore bits (using the KEM/DEM paradigm). See Section 4.2 and the full version [14].

1.3   Applications to Adaptive Trapdoor Functions

Going the other direction, we next give applications of ECCA-security to the theory of adaptive TDFs. Namely, we show (1) adaptive TDFs are in fact *equiva-lent* to *uniquely* randomness-recovering ECCA-secure PKE. This helps us better understand the power and complexity of ATDFs. We furthermore show (2) "tag-based" ATDFs as defined in [25] are likewise equivalent to uniquely randomness-recovering ECCA-secure PKE. A corollary of (1) and (2) is that tag-based and non-tag-based ATDFs are themselves equivalent, which resolves a foundational question left open by [25]. We note that it is in fact much easier to construct uniquely RR ECCA-secure PKE from tag-based ATDFs than from non-tag-based ATDFs. (The rough intuition is that in the tag-based case, a signature scheme can be used to "glue together" many one-bit encryptions via a com-mon tag, namely a single verification key.) Indeed, the apparent extra power of tag-based ATDFs makes it surprising that they turn out to be equivalent to (non-tag-based) ATDFs. We note that unlike the TDF case, the equivalence of tag-based and standard PKE is much easier to prove [26].

1.4   Applications to PKE with Non-interactive Opening

PKENO. Public-key encryption with non-interactive opening (PKENO), introduced by Damgård an Thorbeck [16] and studied in detail by [15,19,20], allows a receiver to non-interactively prove to anyone that a ciphertext c decrypts to a message m. As discussed in the above-mentioned work, PKENO has applications to multiparty computation (*e.g.*, auctions and elections), secure message transmission, group signatures, and more. But despite numerous applications, such schemes have been difficult to realize. Secure constructions of PKENO currently exist from identity-based encryption [15] and robust non-interactive threshold encryption [20], which are somewhat heavy-weight primitives.

Resurrecting a Simple Approach. We show that ECCA-secure encryption can be used to securely realize (for the first time) a simple approach to PKENO originally suggested by [16]. The basic idea is to use a randomness-recovering PKE and have the receiver provide the recovered coins as the proof. However, several issues need to be addressed for this approach to work. One problem already discussed in [20, Sect. 4.1] is that there must be a way for the receiver to prove the claimed behavior of the decryption algorithm on ciphertexts that are not an output of the encryption algorithm, and for which necessarily no underlying coins exist. (Note that such ciphertexts may or may not decrypt to $\perp$ in general.) More fundamentally, we observe that the encryption scheme *must be ECCA secure* (which was not even defined in prior work); standard chosen-ciphertext security is not enough, because here the adversary in the corresponding PKENO security game has the ability to see random coins underlying ciphertexts of its choosing. We now describe our results in more detail.

PKENO-Compatible ECCA Encryption. First, we formalize a notion of *PKENO-compatible* ECCA-secure encryption, for which we can overcome the above problems and safely use the underlying message and randomness as the non-interactive opening of a ciphertext. There are two requirements for such a scheme: (1) It has a "partial-randomness" recovery algorithm that, informally, recovers enough coins to uniquely identify the underlying message. (Here "full" randomness-recovery is not needed, and would not permit constructions where the ciphertext contains randomized parts that are verifiable without coins, like a one-time signature or zero-knowledge proof.) This should also be true for ciphertexts *outside* the range of the encryption algorithm but which do not decrypt to $\perp$.[2]

---

[2] For example, consider a scheme that always outputs ciphertexts whose last bit is "0," but whose decryption algorithm ignores this last bit. Then clearly we can still recover the randomness underlying ciphertexts ending in "1" despite the fact that such ciphertexts are outside the range of the encryption algorithm.

(2) The scheme has *ciphertext verifiability*, meaning one can check without the secret key (but possibly with the help of the recovered partial coins) whether the decryption of a ciphertext is ⊥. We define ECCA security of such schemes with respect to the partial-randomness recovery algorithm.

We also define an analogous notion of PKENO-compatible ECCA-secure *tag-based* PKE. We show that one can efficiently transform such a scheme into a (non-tag-based) PKENO-compatible ECCA-secure PKE scheme using either of the two "BCHK transforms" [9]. (Recall that [9] give a "basic" transform using one-time signatures and a "more efficient" transform based on symmetric-key primitives.)

Constructing PKENO. We show a generic way to achieve PKENO-compatibility from any ECCA-secure RR PKE by adding a non-interactive zero-knowledge (NIZK) proof of "well-formedness" to a ciphertext, namely that there exist some underlying message and random coins. (The idea of adding such a proof to achieve PKENO comes from [16,20], although not in connection with ECCA.) For this approach to work, the PKE scheme does not need to be uniquely RR, but it needs perfect correctness. Moreover, we show the NIZK needs to be simulation-sound.

While this construction is generic, it is also inefficient. Towards more efficient schemes, we show our construction of ECCA-secure *tag-based* PKE from tag-based ATDFs can be made PKENO-compatible if its starting tag-based ATDF has "range verifiability", meaning that anyone can verify preimage existence of a range point. We propose two efficient such tag-based ATDFs. The first instantiates a general tag-based ATDF construction from [25] using a lossy and all-but-one TDF as defined in [29]. Specifically, we use the lossy and all-but-one TDFs of Freeman *et al.* [18] based on the decision-linear (DLIN) assumption. We show that in this case preimage existence is a "Groth-Sahai" statement [22], for which we know efficient NIZK constructions in bilinear groups.[3] Interestingly, we show simulation-soundness is not needed in this case, illustrating another efficiency benefit over the generic approach. The second is a tag-based ATDF from [25] based on the "instance-independent" RSA assumption, which we observe intrinsically has range verifiability because it is a *permutation*. The resulting PKENO scheme based on II-RSA is quite practical.

1.5   Related Work

ECCA is similar in spirit to *coin-revealing selective opening attack* (SOA-C) [10,17,3,8]. In the latter setting, there are say n ciphertexts encrypting related (but unknown) messages under independent random coins, and the adversary requests the plaintexts and random coins corresponding to some subset of them, the question is whether the "unopened" ciphertexts remain secure. However, it

---

[3] Technically, when the NIZK is added, the tag-based ATDF is not a trapdoor function anymore but is already a tag-based PKE scheme (because the NIZK part is randomized), but we gloss over this technicality in our informal exposition.

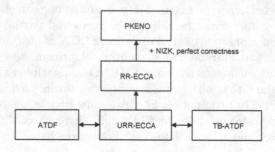

Fig. 1. Relations between various primitives studied in this paper. "(U)RR-ECCA" is (uniquely) randomness-recovering enhanced-chosen-ciphertext secure PKE, "(TB-)ATDF" is (tag-based) adaptive trapdoor function, and "PKENO" is public-key encryption with non-interactive opening.

seems to us that SOA-C is neither implied by, nor implies, ECCA. It is an interesting question whether ECCA has any applications in the domain of SOA-C.

An analogue of ECCA (in the case of inefficient randomness-recovery) has been previously defined for *commitment schemes* by Canetti *et al.* [12], which they call CCA-secure commitments. These are commitment schemes that remain secure when the adversary has access to an *unbounded decommitment oracle* that it can call on commitments other than the challenge. They are interested in such schemes that are interactive but in the plain model, meaning there are no public keys. Thus, our setting seems incomparable (as we disallow interaction but allow public keys). However, we view their work as supporting the claim that ECCA is a natural notion of security to consider for encryption.

Other variants of CCA-security for encryption considered before include *replayable* CCA security [11], *constrained* CCA security [23], and *detectable* CCA security [24]. Notably, these are all *relaxations* of CCA security, whereas we consider a strengthening. Another strengthening of CCA security previously considered is *plaintext awareness* [7,2,5].

2   Preliminaries

2.1   Notation and Conventions

If A is an algorithm then $y \leftarrow A(x_1, \ldots, x_n; r)$ means we run A on inputs $x_1, \ldots, x_n$ and coins r and denote the output by y. By $y \leftarrow_\$ A(x_1, \ldots, x_n)$ we denote the operation of picking r at random and letting $y \leftarrow A(x_1, \ldots, x_n; r)$. Unless otherwise indicated, an algorithm may be randomized. The security parameter is denoted $k \in \mathbb{N}$. We say that an algorithm is efficient if it is probabilistic polynomial time in the security parameter. All algorithms we consider are efficient unless indicated otherwise.

2.2 Public-Key Encryption

A *public-key encryption scheme* [21] with message space *MsgSp* is a triple of algorithms PKE = (Kg, Enc, Dec). The key-generation algorithm Kg returns a public key *pk* and matching secret key *sk*. The encryption algorithm Enc takes *pk* and a plaintext *m* to return a ciphertext. The deterministic decryption algorithm Dec takes *sk* and a ciphertext *c* to return a plaintext.

Correctness. An issue that will be more important than usual in our context is *correctness*, which refers to how likely it is that an encrypted message decrypts to some other message. By default we require *perfect correctness*: for all $k \in \mathbb{N}$ and $m \in MsgSp(1^k)$,

$$\Pr[\mathsf{Dec}(sk, \mathsf{Enc}(pk, m)) = m \,:\, (pk, sk) \leftarrow_\$ \mathsf{Kg}(1^k)] = 1 .$$

If instead we allow this probability to be $1 - \nu(k)$ we say that that PKE has *decryption error* $\nu(\cdot)$.

Tag-Based. PKE is *tag-based* [26] with tag space *TagSp* if Enc and Dec take an additional input $t \in TagSp(1^k)$ called the *tag*. Again, by default we require *perfect correctness*: for all $k \in \mathbb{N}$, $m \in MsgSp(1^k)$, and $t \in TagSp(1^k)$, $\Pr[\mathsf{Dec}(sk, t, \mathsf{Enc}(pk, t, m)) = m \,:\, (pk, sk) \leftarrow_\$ \mathsf{Kg}(1^k)] = 1$. Decryption error is defined analogously.

Other Standard Primitives. We recall the definitions of other standard primitives such as (injective) trapdoor functions in the full version [14].

3   Enhanced Chosen-Ciphertext Security

Randomness Recovery. We start with a definition of *randomness recovery* for public-key encryption. For any public-key encryption scheme PKE = (Kg, Enc, Dec) we specify an additional *randomness-recovery* algorithm Rec that takes a secret key *sk* and ciphertext *c* to return coins *r*. To our knowledge, this notion has been discussed informally in the literature (*e.g.* in [29]) but our formalization is novel. Suppose Enc draws its coins from *Coins*. We require that for all messages $m \in MsgSp(1^k)$,

$$\Pr[\mathsf{Enc}(pk, m; r') \neq c \,:\, (pk, sk) \leftarrow_\$ \mathsf{Kg} \,;\, r \leftarrow_\$ Coins(1^k) \,;$$

$$c \leftarrow \mathsf{Enc}(pk, m; r) \,;\, r' \leftarrow \mathsf{Rec}(sk, c)]$$

is negligible. Note that we do *not* necessarily require $r = r'$; that is, the randomness recovery algorithm need not return the *same* coins used for encryption; indeed, it may not be possible, information theoretically, to determine *r* from *sk* and *c*. We also do not require Rec to be efficient in general. But in the special case that Rec is polynomial-time we say that PKE is *randomness recovering* (RR). Moreover, if the forgoing condition on Rec holds for $r' = r$ we say that

PKE is *uniquely* randomness recovering.[4] In the definition that follows these are important special cases, but they are not assumed by the definition.

In the tag-based case, Rec also takes a *tag* as input and we require that for all $m \in MsgSp(1^k)$ and $t \in TagSp(1^k)$, the following is negligible:

$\Pr[\mathsf{Enc}(pk, t, m; r') \neq c \ : \ (pk, sk) \leftarrow\!\!\$\, \mathsf{Kg} \ ; \ r \leftarrow\!\!\$\, Coins(1^k) \ ; \ c \leftarrow \mathsf{Enc}(pk, t, m; r) \ ; \ r' \leftarrow \mathsf{Rec}(sk, t, c)]$ is negligible. Randomness-recovery and unique RR are defined analogously.

ECCA Definition. We are now ready to state our new definition. Let $\mathsf{PKE} = (\mathsf{Kg}, \mathsf{Enc}, \mathsf{Dec})$ be a public-key encryption scheme. We associate to PKE and an adversary $A = (A_1, A_2)$ an *enhanced chosen-ciphertext attack* experiment:

$$
\begin{array}{ll}
\textbf{Experiment } \mathbf{Exp}^{\text{ind-ecca}}_{\mathsf{PKE},A}(k) & \textbf{Oracle } \mathsf{Dec}^*(sk, c) \\
\quad b \leftarrow\!\!\$\, \{0, 1\} \ ; \ (pk, sk) \leftarrow\!\!\$\, \mathsf{Kg}(1^k) & \quad m \leftarrow \mathsf{Dec}(sk, c) \\
\quad (m_0, m_1, St) \leftarrow\!\!\$\, A_1^{\mathsf{Dec}^*(sk, \cdot)}(pk) & \quad r' \leftarrow \mathsf{Rec}(sk, c) \\
\quad c^* \leftarrow\!\!\$\, \mathsf{Enc}(pk, m_b) & \quad \text{Return } (m, r') \\
\quad d \leftarrow\!\!\$\, A_2^{\mathsf{Dec}^*(sk, \cdot)}(pk, c^*, St) & \\
\quad \text{If } d = b \text{ then return } 1 \text{ else return } 0 &
\end{array}
$$

Above we require that the output of A_1 satisfies $|m_0| = |m_1|$ and that A_2 does not query c^* to its oracle. Define the *ind-ecca advantage* of A against PKE as

$$\mathbf{Adv}^{\text{ind-ecca}}_{\mathsf{PKE},A}(k) = 2 \cdot \Pr\left[\mathbf{Exp}^{\text{ind-ecca}}_{\mathsf{PKE},A}(k) \text{ outputs } 1\right] - 1 .$$

We say that PKE is *enhanced chosen-ciphertext secure* (ECCA-secure) if $\mathbf{Adv}^{\text{ind-ecca}}_{\mathsf{PKE},A}(\cdot)$ is negligible for every efficient A.

Note that when PKE is randomness recovering, the ECCA experiment is efficient. In general, however, one can still ask whether a scheme meets the notion of ECCA even when it is not RR. In this case, it may still be possible to simulate the ECCA experiment efficiently since in the proof of security we are additionally given the code of the adversary A (and so, for example, the randomness for encryption might be efficiently extractable from the code of A using non-black-box techniques). We leave exploration of ECCA security relative to an inefficient Rec algorithm for future work.

(Not) Allowing Decryption Error. Unless otherwise specified, we will always require that an ECCA-secure PKE scheme has *perfect correctness*. Indeed, in the full version [14] we show how to construct an ECCA-secure, randomness-recovering PKE scheme given any CCA-secure one if we allow *negligible decryption error* — however, an ECCA-secure scheme with negligible decryption error will not be sufficient in the applications we consider.[5] This observation and example are due to [1].

---

[4] Looking ahead, it turns out that in some applications of ECCA, non-unique randomness recovery is OK as long as the scheme has perfect correctness.

[5] The resulting ECCA-secure scheme does not have *unique* randomness recovery, though. In the case of unique randomness recovery, schemes with negligible decryption error may still have some applications, but for simplicity we do not discuss it in the paper.

CCA Does Not Imply ECCA. A next natural question to ask is whether, assuming perfect correctness, ECCA security is a stronger requirement than CCA security. We answer this question affirmatively by showing that, given a perfectly correct, CCA-secure randomness-recovering PKE scheme, we can construct another RR PKE scheme that is still CCA-secure but is *not* ECCA-secure. This motivates the construction of specialized ECCA-secure schemes in Section 4.

Consider a RR CCA-secure scheme PKE = (Kg, Enc, Dec). We transform PKE to a new scheme PKE* = (Kg*, Enc*, Dec*) which is still CCA-secure but is *not* ECCA-secure. The idea is to embed a "test" ciphertext in the public key of the new scheme, such that its decryption algorithm returns the secret key if given as input some randomness consistent with this test ciphertext. Formally, PKE* is constructed as follows (where we implicitly assume the public key is contained in the secret key):

Alg Kg*(1^k)	**Alg Enc*$((pk, c^*), m)$**	**Alg Dec*$(sk, c \| b)$**
$(pk, sk) \leftarrow_\$ \mathsf{Kg}(1^k)$	$c \leftarrow_\$ \mathsf{Enc}(pk, m)$	If $b = 1$ and $\mathsf{Enc}(pk, 0; c) = c^*$
$r \leftarrow_\$ \{0, 1\}^k$	Return $c \| 0$	then return sk
$c^* \leftarrow \mathsf{Enc}(pk, 0; r)$		Return $\mathsf{Dec}(sk, c)$
Return $((pk, c^*), sk)$		

Note that using the extra "flag bit" appended to ciphertexts ensures that PKE* maintains perfect correctness. We prove the following proposition in the full version [14].

Proposition 1. *Assuming* PKE *is CCA-secure and has perfect correctness,* PKE* *is CCA-secure but is not ECCA-secure.*

Tag-Based Definition. Let TB-PKE = (Kg, Enc, Dec) be a tag-based public-key encryption scheme with tag space *TagSp*. We associate to TB-PKE and an adversary $A = (A_1, A_2, A_3)$ a *tag-based enhanced chosen-ciphertext attack* experiment,

Experiment $\mathbf{Exp}^{\text{ind-tb-ecca}}_{\text{TB-PKE}, A}(k)$
$\quad b \leftarrow_\$ \{0, 1\}$; $(pk, sk) \leftarrow_\$ \mathsf{Kg}(1^k)$
$\quad t \leftarrow_\$ A_1(1^k)$
$\quad (m_0, m_1, St) \leftarrow_\$ A_2^{\mathsf{Dec}^*(sk, \cdot, \cdot)}(pk, t)$
$\quad c \leftarrow_\$ \mathsf{Enc}(pk, t, m_b)$
$\quad d \leftarrow_\$ A_3^{\mathsf{Dec}^*(sk, \cdot, \cdot)}(pk, t, c, St)$
$\quad$ If $d = b$ then return 1 else return 0

Oracle $\mathsf{Dec}^*(sk, t, c)$
$\quad m \leftarrow \mathsf{Dec}(sk, t, c)$
$\quad r' \leftarrow \mathsf{Rec}(sk, t, c)$
$\quad$ Return (m, r')

Above we require that the output of A_2 satisfies $|m_0| = |m_1|$ and that A_3 does not make a query of the form $\mathsf{Dec}^*(sk, t, \cdot)$ to its oracle. Define the *ind-tb-ecca advantage* of A against PKE as

$$\mathbf{Adv}^{\text{ind-tb-ecca}}_{\text{PKE}, A}(k) = 2 \cdot \Pr\left[\mathbf{Exp}^{\text{ind-tb-ecca}}_{\text{PKE}, A}(k) \text{ outputs } 1 \right] - 1.$$

We say that TB-PKE is *tag-based enhanced chosen-ciphertext secure* (TB-ECCA-secure) if $\mathbf{Adv}^{\text{ind-tb-ecca}}_{\text{PKE}, A}(\cdot)$ is negligible for every efficient A.

4   Constructions of ECCA-Secure PKE

We give several constructions of ECCA secure encryption, which are based on notions of adaptivity for trapdoor functions introduced in [25] (see the full version [14]).

4.1   ECCA Security from Adaptive Trapdoor Functions

Here we construct ECCA-secure public-key encryption from adaptive TDFs. We note that our construction applies to general ATDFs; in the case of ATDFs with a linear number of hardcore bits we obtain a much more efficient construction; see the full version [14] for details.

Overview and Intuition. As in [25] (which constructs CCA-secure PKE from ATDFs), our approach involves first constructing a one-bit encryption scheme and then transforming it into a multi-bit scheme. In doing so we heavily use the recent approach of Hohenberger *et al.* [24] and their notion of *detectable* CCA security (DCCA); this should be contrasted with [25] who rely on [27] instead. Let us explain why.

Both [24] and [27] provide a way to "tie together" many one-bit ciphertexts via "inner" and "outer" encryption layers but differ in which layer contains the one-bit ciphertexts. In [27], the inner layer is a multi-bit q-bounded non-malleable encryption scheme while the outer layer is the concatenation of one-bit ciphertexts. This means that without a randomness-recovering inner layer, [27] does *not* preserve randomness-recovery of the outer one-bit scheme. Such an inner layer seems hard to construct, as known approaches to non-malleability [28,13] crucially use randomness in an un-invertible way in their encryption algorithms (e.g., to generate a signature key-pair or a zero-knowledge proof).

On the other hand, in Hohenberger *et al.* [24] it is the inner layer that is the concatenation of one-bit ciphertexts, which obviates the problem since this inner layer is also used to encrypt randomness for use by the outer layer and thus the latter does *not* need to be randomness-recovering for the overall scheme to be so. Surprisingly, we also show that when this inner layer is RR then in all hybrid games used for the security proof the simulator is even able to the return randomness corresponding to valid ciphertexts, and thus the overall scheme also has ECCA security.

Enhanced DCCA Security. The notion of *detectable chosen-ciphertext* (DCCA) security was recently introduced by [24]. We define here the notion of *enhanced* DCCA (EDCCA) security, which parallels the notion of enhanced CCA security. In our definition, we require that the DCCA scheme be both enhanced and RR, because our application of DCCA requires both properties.

A *detectable encryption scheme* consists of a public-key encryption scheme (Kg, Enc, Dec) and a detecting function $\mathcal{F}: (pk, c', c) \mapsto b \in \{0, 1\}$ mapping a public key and two ciphertexts to a bit. The detecting function must satisfy *unpredictability*, which informally means that given the description of $\mathcal{F}$ and a public key pk, it should be hard to find a ciphertext c' that is related to a "challenge" ciphertext c, in that $\mathcal{F}(pk, c', c) = 1$, *before being given c*. See [24] for the formal definition.

Definition. We define *enhanced detectable chosen ciphertext security* for a RR scheme $\mathsf{PKE} = (\mathsf{Kg}, \mathsf{Enc}, \mathsf{Dec}, \mathsf{Rec})$ and an unpredictable detecting function $\mathcal{F}$ similarly to ECCA in Section 3, except that the decryption oracle for A_2 returns $\perp$ whenever it is queried on a ciphertext c such that $\mathcal{F}(pk, c^*, c) = 1$, where c^* is the challenge ciphertext. (see [14]).

EDCCA Security from ATDFs. Let $\mathsf{TDF} = (\mathsf{Tdg}, \mathsf{Eval}, \mathsf{Inv})$ be a trapdoor function with hardcore bit hc. We define the following multi-bit PKE scheme $\mathsf{EDCCA[TDF]} = (\mathsf{Kg_D}, \mathsf{Enc_D}, \mathsf{Dec_D})$ with message space $\{0,1\}^\ell$:

Alg $\mathsf{Kg_D}(1^k)$	**Alg** $\mathsf{Enc_D}(ek, m = m_1, \ldots, m_\ell)$	**Alg** $\mathsf{Dec}(td, C)$
(ek, td)	$x_1 \leftarrow_\$ \{0,1\}^k; \ldots; x_\ell \leftarrow_\$ \{0,1\}^k$	Parse $C = (y_1, \beta_1, \ldots, y_\ell, \beta_\ell)$
$\leftarrow_\$ \mathsf{Tdg}(1^k)$	Return $C = (\mathsf{Eval}(ek, x_1),$	For $1 \le i \le \ell$
Return (ek, td)	$\mathsf{hc}(x_1) \oplus m_1, \ldots,$	$m_i = \mathsf{hc}(\mathsf{Inv}(td, y_i)) \oplus \beta_i$
	$\mathsf{Eval}(ek, x_\ell), \mathsf{hc}(x_\ell) \oplus m_\ell)$	Return $m_1, \ldots, m_\ell$

In [14] we show that if TDF is adaptive one-way then this scheme is ED-CCA with respect to the detection function $\mathcal{F}_\mathsf{D}$, which on input pk, $C^* = (y_1^*, \beta_1^*, \ldots, y_\ell^*, \beta_\ell^*)$ and $C = (y_1, \beta_1, \ldots, y_\ell, \beta_\ell)$ outputs 1 iff for some $i, j \in [\ell]$: $y_i^* = y_j$.

Scheme $\mathsf{EDCCA[TDF]}$ is perfectly correct and *uniquely* RR, which will be crucial for our application to ATDFs in Section 5. We also wish to stress that it gives a novel example of a DCCA secure scheme; our scheme is *not* the concatenation of ciphertexts for a 1-bit CCA-secure scheme. Indeed, a ciphertext of the form $(\mathsf{Eval}(ek, x), \mathsf{hc}(x) \oplus m)$ is trivially malleable by flipping the second component.

From EDCCA to ECCA Security. We next show that the construction of a CCA-secure scheme from a DCCA-secure one in [24] allows us to go from ED-CCA to ECCA. That is, we show that the construction preserves "enhanced" security; it also preserves (unique) RR. Specifically, we instantiate the construction of [24] with the following components:

Π_D, the above RR EDCCA scheme $\mathsf{EDCCA[TDF]}$;

Π_CPA, a CPA-secure scheme with perfect correctness (which can also be instantiated with $\mathsf{EDCCA[TDF]}$); and

Π_1b, a perfectly correct 1-bounded CCA-secure[6] (which can be constructed from a multi-bit CPA scheme via the construction from [13]).

Note that all these components can be constructed in a black-box manner from ATDFs. In the full version [14] we prove that the following is a multi bit encryption scheme with message space $\{0,1\}^\ell$ that is uniquely RR, ECCA-secure and perfectly correct.

---

[6] 1-bounded CCA security means that the adversary may make only a single decryption query.

Alg $Kg_{ECCA}(1^\lambda)$	**Alg** $Enc_{ECCA}(pk, m)$	**Alg** $Dec_{ECCA}(sk, C)$
$(pk_{in}, sk_{in}) \leftarrow_\$ Kg_D(1^\lambda)$	$(r_A, r_B) \leftarrow_\$ \{0,1\}^\lambda$	$C_{in} \leftarrow_\$ Dec_{1b}(sk_A, C_A)$
$(pk_A, sk_A) \leftarrow_\$ Kg_{1b}(1^\lambda)$	$C_{in} \leftarrow_\$ Enc_D(pk_{in},$	$(r_A, r_B, m) \leftarrow Dec_D(sk_{in}, C_{in})$
$(pk_B, sk_B) \leftarrow_\$ Kg_{CPA}(1^\lambda)$	$\qquad (r_A, r_B, m))$	$r_{in} \leftarrow Rec_D(sk_{in}, C_{in})$
$pk \leftarrow (pk_{in}, pk_A, pk_B)$	$C_A \leftarrow Enc_{1b}(pk_A, C_{in}; r_A)$	If $C_A = Enc_{1b}(pk_A, C_{in}; r_A)$
$sk \leftarrow (sk_{in}, sk_A, sk_B)$	$C_B \leftarrow Enc_{CPA}(pk_B, C_{in}; r_B)$	$\land C_B = Enc_{CPA}(pk_B, C_{in}; r_B)$
Return (pk, sk)	Return $C = (C_A, C_B)$	$\quad$ return (r_A, r_B, m, r_{in})
		Else return $\bot$

4.2 ECCA Security from Tag-Based ATDFs

We give more efficient constructions of ECCA-secure public-key encryption from *tag-based* adaptive trapdoor functions, introduced by Kiltz *et al.* [25]. Due to space constraints, these constructions are deferred to [14].

5 Application to Adaptive Trapdoor Functions

We use ECCA-security as a unifying concept to show that the notions of adaptive TDFs and tag-based adaptive ATDFs introduced by Kiltz *et al.* [25] are *equivalent* (via fully black-box reductions), resolving a foundational open question raised in [25]. To do so, we show that both primitives are implied by *uniquely* randomness-recovering ECCA-secure PKE. Combined with Section 4, this shows that in fact uniquely RR PKE, adaptive TDFs, and tag-based ATDFs are all equivalent. Due to space constraints, these implications are deferred to the full version [14].

6 Application to PKE with Non-interactive Opening

In this section, we show that ECCA-secure encryption is a natural building block for *public key encryption with non-interactive opening* (PKENO) [16,15,19,20]. PKENO allows the receiver to non-interactively prove that a given ciphertext decrypts to a claimed message. Our constructions yield new and practical PKENO schemes.

PKENO extends a public-key encryption scheme $PKE = (Kg, Enc, Dec)$ by the following algorithms: Prove takes a secret key sk and a ciphertext c, and outputs a proof π. Ver takes a public key pk, a ciphertext c, a plaintext m and a proof π, and outputs 0 or 1. We require *proof correctness*: for all ciphertexts (i.e. strings) c, $\Pr[Ver(pk, c, Dec(sk, c), Prove(sk, c)) \neq 1 : (pk, sk) \leftarrow_\$ Kg(1^k)]$ is negligible.

Security. In [15,19] security of PKENO is defiend by *indistinguishability under chosen-ciphertext and -proof attacks* (IND-CCPA) and *proof soundness*. The former guarantees that a ciphertext hides the plaintext even when the adversary sees decryptions of and proofs for other ciphertexts; the latter formalizes that no adversary should be able to produce a proof for a message and ciphertext that is not the encryption of that message.

Experiment $\text{Exp}_{\text{PKENO},A}^{\text{ind-ccpa}}(k)$	Experiment $\text{Exp}_{\text{PKENO},A}^{\text{proof-snd}}(k)$
$b \leftarrow_{\$} \{0,1\}$; $(pk, sk) \leftarrow_{\$} \text{Kg}(1^k)$	$(pk, sk) \leftarrow_{\$} \text{Kg}(1^k)$
$(m_0, m_1, St) \leftarrow_{\$} A_1^{\text{Dec}(sk,\cdot),\text{Prove}(sk,\cdot)}(pk)$	$(m', \pi', c') \leftarrow_{\$} A(pk, sk)$
$c \leftarrow_{\$} \text{Enc}(pk, m_b)$	$m \leftarrow \text{Dec}(sk, c')$
$d \leftarrow_{\$} A_2^{\text{Dec}(sk,\cdot),\text{Prove}(sk,\cdot)}(pk, c, St)$	If $\text{Ver}(pk, c', m', \pi') = 1$ and $m \neq m'$
If $d = b$ then return 1 else return 0	then return 1 ; else return 0

Fig. 2. Security experiments for PKENO

Formally, to a scheme $\text{PKENO} = (\text{Kg}, \text{Enc}, \text{Dec}, \text{Prove}, \text{Ver})$, and an adversary $A = (A_1, A_2)$ we associate the *chosen-ciphertext and -proof attack* experiment given in Figure 2. We require that the output of A_1 satisfies $|m_0| = |m_1|$ and that A_2 does not query c to any of its oracles. We say that PKENO is *chosen-ciphertext and -proof-attack secure* (CCPA-secure) if $2 \cdot \Pr\left[\text{Exp}_{\text{PKENO},A}^{\text{ind-ccpa}}(k) \text{ outputs } 1\right] - 1$ is negligible for every efficient A. We associate to a scheme PKENO and an adversary $A = (A_1, A_2)$ a *proof-soundness* experiment, given in Figure 2, and say that PKENO is *proof-sound* if $\Pr\left[\text{Exp}_{\text{PKENO},A}^{\text{proof-snd}}(k) \text{ outputs } 1\right]$ is negligible for every efficient A.

We note that in contrast to [15,19] our definition of proof soundness also considers adversarially produced ciphertexts, which need not even be a valid output of the encryption algorithm. Note that it is already required by proof correctness that the PKENO correctly proves decryption of such ciphertexts (which may or may not decrypt to $\bot$), so constructions should achieve this stronger notion of proof soundness anyway.

Strong Proof Soundness. An even stronger notion of proof soundness is defined in [20], which also handles maliciously chosen receiver public keys. In the full version [14] we define notions of strong proof soundness and discuss how our constructions can be adapted to meet them.

6.1   PKENO-Compatible ECCA-Secure PKE

A natural approach to building PKENO suggested by [16] is to use a randomness-recovering encryption scheme and have the receiver provide the recovered coins as the proof. A moment's reflection reveals that for this approach to work, the encryption scheme must be ECCA secure in order to protect against chosen-proof attacks. In addition, as discussed in [16,15,20], we also need a way for the receiver to prove correct decryption of ciphertexts that are not in the range of the encryption algorithm, in which case such coins may not be defined. In this section we define a notion of *PKENO-compatible ECCA-secure encryption* for which we can do this. Below we discuss the properties such a scheme must have, but due to space constraints, we defer the details to the full version [14].

Partial-Randomness Recovery. It turns out that for such schemes we do not always achieve, nor need, the notion of full RR, so we define a natural generalization we call *partial-randomness recovery*, which loosely says that enough of the random coins are recovered to uniquely identify the underlying message. However, in order to deal with the case that ciphertexts outside the range of the encryption algorithm may not decrypt to $\perp$, we also *strengthen* what we get from RR encryption in some respect.

Ciphertext Verifiability. This notion intuitively means a verifier can check (with the help of some partial random coins) whether the decryption algorithm returns $\perp$ on a given ciphertext.

PKENO-Compatibility. We say PKE is a *PKENO-compatible ECCA-secure PKE scheme* if it satisfies ECCA-security, partial-randomness recovery and ciphertext verifiability. In the full version of the paper [14] we show that a PKENO-compatible ECCA-secure PKE scheme indeed gives us PKENO by using the idea of [16] described above. We also show an analogous theorem in the case of tag-based PKE.

6.2 PKENO-Compatible PKE Using NIZK

PKENO-compatibility can be obtained generically from any ECCA-secure RR PKE by adding a non-interactive zero-knowledge proof (NIZK) of ciphertext "well-formedness." The approach of using a NIZK originates from [15,20], although not with respect to ECCA-secure encryption. We note that we do not require the starting ECCA-secure encryption scheme to be *uniquely* RR (although our constructions in Section 4 achieve this), but it should have perfect correctness. Moreover, the NIZK needs to be simulation-sound, for reasons analogous to the proof of full anonymity of the group signature construction in [4]. See [14] for the details.

6.3 Efficient PKENO-Compatible Tag-Based PKE

Our construction using NIZKs, while it applies to *any* ECCA-secure RR PKE scheme, is not very efficient unless we rely on the random-oracle model [6] for the NIZK. We show more efficient constructions by following the tag-based approach; namely, we show that our construction from tag-based ATDFs in Section 4.2 can be made PKENO-compatible by using special tag-based ATDFs (from which we can then obtain non-tag-based PKENO-compatible PKE). The idea is to use tag-based ATDF for which we have "range verifiability," meaning that anyone can verify preimage existence. In our first construction, we achieve this property by adding an efficient NIZK proof due to Groth and Sahai [22]. In our second construction, we use a tag-based ATDF that has this property because it is a permutation. Details of these constructions are again deferred to [14].

Acknowledgements. We gratefully acknowledge Mihir Bellare, whose comments improved our results and presentation. The second author was supported by EPSRC grant EP/H043454/1 and the European Research Council, ERC Starting Grant (259668-PSPC). The fourth author was supported by NSF grants CNS-1012910 and CNS-0546614.

References

1. Bellare, M.: Private communication (2012)
2. Bellare, M., Desai, A., Pointcheval, D., Rogaway, P.: Relations among notions of security for public-key encryption schemes. In: Krawczyk, H. (ed.) CRYPTO 1998. LNCS, vol. 1462, pp. 26–45. Springer, Heidelberg (1998)
3. Bellare, M., Hofheinz, D., Yilek, S.: Possibility and impossibility results for encryption and commitment secure under selective opening. In: Joux, A. (ed.) EUROCRYPT 2009. LNCS, vol. 5479, pp. 1–35. Springer, Heidelberg (2009)
4. Bellare, M., Micciancio, D., Warinschi, B.: Foundations of group signatures: Formal definitions, simplified requirements, and a construction based on general assumptions. In: Biham, E. (ed.) EUROCRYPT 2003. LNCS, vol. 2656, pp. 614–629. Springer, Heidelberg (2003)
5. Bellare, M., Palacio, A.: Towards plaintext-aware public-key encryption without random oracles. In: Lee, P.J. (ed.) ASIACRYPT 2004. LNCS, vol. 3329, pp. 48–62. Springer, Heidelberg (2004)
6. Bellare, M., Rogaway, P.: Random oracles are practical: A paradigm for designing efficient protocols. In: Ashby, V. (ed.) ACM CCS 1993, pp. 62–73. ACM Press (November 1993)
7. Bellare, M., Rogaway, P.: Optimal asymmetric encryption. In: De Santis, A. (ed.) EUROCRYPT 1994. LNCS, vol. 950, pp. 92–111. Springer, Heidelberg (1995)
8. Bellare, M., Yilek, S.: Encryption schemes secure under selective opening attack. Cryptology ePrint Archive, Report 2009/101 (2009), http://eprint.iacr.org/
9. Boneh, D., Canetti, R., Halevi, S., Katz, J.: Chosen-ciphertext security from identity-based encryption. SIAM Journal on Computing 36(5), 1301–1328 (2007)
10. Canetti, R., Feige, U., Goldreich, O., Naor, M.: Adaptively secure multi-party computation. In: 28th ACM STOC, pp. 639–648. ACM Press (May 1996)
11. Canetti, R., Krawczyk, H., Nielsen, J.B.: Relaxing chosen-ciphertext security. In: Boneh, D. (ed.) CRYPTO 2003. LNCS, vol. 2729, pp. 565–582. Springer, Heidelberg (2003)
12. Canetti, R., Lin, H., Pass, R.: Adaptive hardness and composable security in the plain model from standard assumptions. In: 51st FOCS, pp. 541–550. IEEE Computer Society Press (October 2010)
13. Choi, S.G., Dachman-Soled, D., Malkin, T., Wee, H.: Black-box construction of a non-malleable encryption scheme from any semantically secure one. In: Canetti, R. (ed.) TCC 2008. LNCS, vol. 4948, pp. 427–444. Springer, Heidelberg (2008)
14. Dachman-Soled, D., Fuchsbauer, G., Mohassel, P., O'Neill, A.: Enhanced chosen-ciphertext security and applications. Cryptology ePrint Archive, Report 2012/543 (2012)
15. Damgård, I., Hofheinz, D., Kiltz, E., Thorbek, R.: Public-key encryption with non-interactive opening. In: Malkin, T. (ed.) CT-RSA 2008. LNCS, vol. 4964, pp. 239–255. Springer, Heidelberg (2008)
16. Damgård, I.B., Thorbek, R.: Non-interactive proofs for integer multiplication. In: Naor, M. (ed.) EUROCRYPT 2007. LNCS, vol. 4515, pp. 412–429. Springer, Heidelberg (2007)
17. Dwork, C., Naor, M., Reingold, O., Stockmeyer, L.J.: Magic functions. Journal of the ACM 50(6), 852–921 (2003)
18. Freeman, D.M., Goldreich, O., Kiltz, E., Rosen, A., Segev, G.: More constructions of lossy and correlation-secure trapdoor functions. In: Nguyen, P.Q., Pointcheval, D. (eds.) PKC 2010. LNCS, vol. 6056, pp. 279–295. Springer, Heidelberg (2010)

19. Galindo, D.: Breaking and repairing damgård *et al.* public key encryption scheme with non-interactive opening. In: Fischlin, M. (ed.) CT-RSA 2009. LNCS, vol. 5473, pp. 389–398. Springer, Heidelberg (2009)
20. Galindo, D., Libert, B., Fischlin, M., Fuchsbauer, G., Lehmann, A., Manulis, M., Schröder, D.: Public-key encryption with non-interactive opening: New constructions and stronger definitions. In: Bernstein, D.J., Lange, T. (eds.) AFRICACRYPT 2010. LNCS, vol. 6055, pp. 333–350. Springer, Heidelberg (2010)
21. Goldwasser, S., Micali, S.: Probabilistic encryption. Journal of Computer and System Sciences 28(2), 270–299 (1984)
22. Groth, J., Sahai, A.: Efficient non-interactive proof systems for bilinear groups. In: Smart, N.P. (ed.) EUROCRYPT 2008. LNCS, vol. 4965, pp. 415–432. Springer, Heidelberg (2008)
23. Hofheinz, D., Kiltz, E.: Secure hybrid encryption from weakened key encapsulation. In: Menezes, A. (ed.) CRYPTO 2007. LNCS, vol. 4622, pp. 553–571. Springer, Heidelberg (2007)
24. Hohenberger, S., Lewko, A., Waters, B.: Detecting dangerous queries: A new approach for chosen ciphertext security. In: Pointcheval, D., Johansson, T. (eds.) EUROCRYPT 2012. LNCS, vol. 7237, pp. 663–681. Springer, Heidelberg (2012)
25. Kiltz, E., Mohassel, P., O'Neill, A.: Adaptive trapdoor functions and chosen-ciphertext security. In: Gilbert, H. (ed.) EUROCRYPT 2010. LNCS, vol. 6110, pp. 673–692. Springer, Heidelberg (2010)
26. MacKenzie, P.D., Reiter, M.K., Yang, K.: Alternatives to non-malleability: Definitions, constructions, and applications (extended abstract). In: Naor, M. (ed.) TCC 2004. LNCS, vol. 2951, pp. 171–190. Springer, Heidelberg (2004)
27. Myers, S., Shelat, A.: Bit encryption is complete. In: 50th FOCS, pp. 607–616. IEEE Computer Society Press (October 2009)
28. Pass, R., Shelat, A., Vaikuntanathan, V.: Construction of a non-malleable encryption scheme from any semantically secure one. In: Dwork, C. (ed.) CRYPTO 2006. LNCS, vol. 4117, pp. 271–289. Springer, Heidelberg (2006)
29. Peikert, C., Waters, B.: Lossy trapdoor functions and their applications. In: Ladner, R.E., Dwork, C. (eds.) 40th ACM STOC, pp. 187–196. ACM Press (May 2008)
30. Rackoff, C., Simon, D.R.: Non-interactive zero-knowledge proof of knowledge and chosen ciphertext attack. In: Feigenbaum, J. (ed.) CRYPTO 1991. LNCS, vol. 576, pp. 433–444. Springer, Heidelberg (1992)
31. Rosen, A., Segev, G.: Chosen-ciphertext security via correlated products. In: Reingold, O. (ed.) TCC 2009. LNCS, vol. 5444, pp. 419–436. Springer, Heidelberg (2009)
32. Wee, H.: Efficient chosen-ciphertext security via extractable hash proofs. In: Rabin, T. (ed.) CRYPTO 2010. LNCS, vol. 6223, pp. 314–332. Springer, Heidelberg (2010)

Lattice-Based Group Signature Scheme with Verifier-Local Revocation

Adeline Langlois[1], San Ling[2], Khoa Nguyen[2], and Huaxiong Wang[2]

[1] École Normale Supérieure de Lyon,
LIP (U. Lyon, CNRS, ENSL, INRIA, UCBL),
46 Allée d'Italie, 69364 Lyon Cedex 07, France
adeline.langlois@ens-lyon.fr
[2] Division of Mathematical Sciences,
School of Physical and Mathematical Sciences,
Nanyang Technological University, Singapore
{lingsan,khoantt,hxwang}@ntu.edu.sg

Abstract. Support of membership revocation is a desirable functionality for any group signature scheme. Among the known revocation approaches, verifier-local revocation (VLR) seems to be the most flexible one, because it only requires the verifiers to possess some up-to-date revocation information, but not the signers. All of the contemporary VLR group signatures operate in the bilinear map setting, and all of them will be insecure once quantum computers become a reality. In this work, we introduce the first lattice-based VLR group signature, and thus, the first such scheme that is believed to be quantum-resistant. In comparison with existing lattice-based group signatures, our scheme has several noticeable advantages: support of membership revocation, logarithmic-size signatures, and weaker security assumption. In the random oracle model, our scheme is proved to be secure based on the hardness of the $SIVP_{\widetilde{O}(n^{1.5})}$ problem in general lattices - an assumption that is as weak as those of state-of-the-art lattice-based standard signatures. Moreover, our construction works without relying on encryption schemes, which is an intriguing feature for group signatures.

Keywords: group signature, verifier-local revocation, lattice-based cryptography.

1 Introduction

Group Signatures. Group signatures have been an important research topic in public-key cryptography since their introduction by Chaum and van Heyst [15]. In these schemes, all the potential signers form a group, where each signer can anonymously issue a signature on behalf of the whole group (anonymity). On the other hand, in cases of disputes, there is a tracing mechanism which can link a given signature to the identity of the misbehaving member (traceability). These two attractive features allow group signatures to find applications in various real-life scenarios, such as anonymous online communications, digital right

H. Krawczyk (Ed.): PKC 2014, LNCS 8383, pp. 345–361, 2014.

management, e-commerce systems, and much more. Over the last two decades, many group signature schemes with different security models, different levels of efficiency and functionality have been proposed ([16,4,5,8,9,6,20,25], ...).

One desirable functionality of group signatures is the support for membership revocation. For example, misbehaving members who issue signatures for documents, which they are not allowed to sign, should be revoked from the group. In these cases, if a group signature scheme does not support revocation, then the whole system has to be re-initialized, which is obviously an unsuitable solution in practice. Currently there are two main revocation approaches for group signatures. The first approach requires all the unrevoked members to update their signing keys after each revocation ([4,12,8,11],...). At the same time, all the signature verifiers need to download the up-to-date group public key. As a consequence, it is sometimes inconvenient to practically implement such schemes. The second approach, that is group signatures with verifier-local revocation (VLR), only requires the verifiers to possess some up-to-date revocation information, but not the signers. Since in most of real-life scenarios, the number of signature verifiers is much smaller than the number of signers, this revocation approach is more flexible and more practical. Moreover, it is akin to that of the traditional Public Key Infrastructures, where the verifiers use the latest Certificate Revocation List to check the public key of the signer. The notion of VLR group signatures was considered by Brickell [10] and Kiayias et al. [22], then formalized by Boneh and Shacham [9], further investigated and extended by Nakanishi and Funabiki [33,34], Libert and Vergnaud [26], and Bichsel et al. [7]. It is worth mentioning that all the existing VLR group signatures scheme operate in the bilinear map setting. Furthermore, all these schemes will be insecure once quantum computers become a reality [39]. Thus, constructing a VLR group signature schemes which is secure against quantum computers, or even outside of the bilinear map setting, is a challenging open question.

Lattice-Based Group Signatures. Lattice-based cryptography is currently considered as the most promising candidate for post-quantum cryptography. As opposed to classical cryptography (i.e., based on the hardness of factoring or discrete log problems), lattice-based cryptography is widely believed to be resistant against quantum computers, moreover, it enjoys provable security under *worst-case* hardness assumptions ([1,37,18,31]). Designing secure and efficient lattice-based cryptographic constructions (and group signatures, in particular) becomes an intriguing challenge for the research community looking forward to the future. To the best of our knowledge, three lattice-based group signature schemes have been proposed, but none of them supports membership revocation. The first one was introduced by Gordon et al. [19] in 2010. While their scheme is of great theoretical interest, its signatures have size $\mathcal{O}(N)$, where N is the number of group users. In terms of efficiency, this is a noticeable disadvantage if the group is large, e.g., group of all employees of a big company. Camenisch et al. [13] later proposed lattice-based anonymous attribute tokens system, a primitive that can be considered as a generalization of group signature. However, in their construction, the signatures size is still linear in N. Recently, Laguillaumie et al. [23] designed a scheme featuring signature size $\widetilde{\mathcal{O}}(\log N)$, which is the first lattice-based group signature that overcomes the linear-size barrier. We remark that all the above mentioned schemes follow the traditional sign-and-encrypt-and-prove paradigm: to enable the tracing mechanism, these schemes require the signer to encrypt some private information via certain type of encryption based on the Learning With Errors (LWE) problem, and then generate a sophisticated proof to prove particularly that the ciphertext is well-formed. Relying on encryption to construct group signatures may imply two troublesome issues: firstly, it makes the construction less efficient; secondly, since the whole system is secure only if the underlying encryption scheme is secure, it usually leads to a relatively strong security assumption. In particular, the recent scheme by Laguillaumie et al. [23] is only provably secure if there is no quantum algorithm to approximate the Shortest Independent Vectors Problem (SIVP_γ) on lattices of dimension n to within certain $\gamma = \widetilde{\mathcal{O}}(n^{8.5})$. This yields several interesting open questions in this direction: Is it possible to construct a scheme that supports membership revocation? Can lattice-based group signature schemes be free of LWE-based encryptions? How to design a more efficient scheme based on weaker security assumption?

Our Contributions. In the present work, we reply to all the above open questions positively. In particular, we introduce the first group signature with verifier-local revocation from lattice assumptions, and thus, the first such scheme that is believed to be quantum-resistant. In comparison with known lattice-based group signatures, while the schemes from [19], [13] and [23] follow the CPA-*anonymity* and CCA-*anonymity* notions from [8,5], our construction satisfies the (weaker) notion of *selfless-anonymity* for VLR group signatures from [9]. Nevertheless, our scheme has several remarkable advantages over the contemporary counterparts:

1. Functionality: Our scheme is the first lattice-based group signature that supports membership revocation. As discussed above, this is a desirable functionality for any group signature scheme.
2. Simplicity: Our scheme is conceptually very simple. The signature is basically an all-in-one proof of knowledge, made non-interactive using Fiat-Shamir paradigm [17]. Moreover, the scheme departs from the traditional paradigm, and is free of LWE-based encryptions.
3. Efficiency: For a security parameter n and for a group of N members, the group public key and the signature have bit-sizes $\widetilde{\mathcal{O}}(n^2) \cdot \log N$ and $\widetilde{\mathcal{O}}(n) \cdot \log N$, respectively. This result is comparable to that of [23], and is a noticeable improvement over those of [19] and [13].
4. Security assumption: Our scheme is proved to be secure (in the random oracle model) based on the worst-case hardness of approximating the Shortest Independent Vectors Problem, for general lattices of dimension n, to within a factor $\gamma = \widetilde{\mathcal{O}}(n^{1.5})$. Surprisingly, this security assumption is as weak as those of state-of-the-art lattice-based *standard* signatures, such as [18], [14], and [29]. This is a non-trivial feature, as group signatures are more elaborate primitive than standard signatures, one would expect to rely on a stronger security assumption.

Overview of Our Techniques. The main building block of our VLR group signature scheme is an interactive protocol allowing a prover to convince the verifier that he is a certified group member (i.e., he possesses a valid secret signing key), and that he has not been revoked (i.e., his "revocation token" is not in the verifier's blacklist). The protocol is repeated many times to make the soundness error negligibly small, and then is converted to a signature scheme via Fiat-Shamir heuristic. Roughly speaking, in the random oracle model, the traceability and anonymity of the resulting group signature are based on the facts that the underlying protocol is a proof of knowledge, and it can be simulated.

We consider a group of $N = 2^\ell$ users, where each user is identified by a string $d \in \{0,1\}^\ell$ denoting the binary representation of his index in the group. Let n, m, β, and $q \geq 2$ be integers (to be determined later). Our scheme operates within the structure of a *Bonsai tree* of hard random lattices [14], i.e., a matrix $\mathbf{A} = [\mathbf{A}_0 | \mathbf{A}_1^0 | \mathbf{A}_1^1 | \ldots | \mathbf{A}_\ell^0 | \mathbf{A}_\ell^1] \in \mathbb{Z}_q^{n \times (2\ell+1)m}$, and a vector $\mathbf{u} \in \mathbb{Z}_q^n$. Initially, the group user with identity $d = d[1] \ldots d[\ell] \in \{0,1\}^\ell$ is issued a Bonsai signature of his identity, that is a small vector $\mathbf{z} \in \mathbb{Z}^{(\ell+1)m}$, such that $\|\mathbf{z}\|_\infty \leq \beta$ and $\mathbf{A}_d \cdot \mathbf{z} = \mathbf{u} \bmod q$, where $\mathbf{A}_d = [\mathbf{A}_0 | \mathbf{A}_1^{d[1]} | \ldots | \mathbf{A}_\ell^{d[\ell]}]$ - a subtree defined by d. In other words, vector $\mathbf{z}$ is a solution to the Inhomogeneous Small Integer Solution (ISIS) instance $(\mathbf{A}_d, \mathbf{u})$. To prove that he is a certified group member without leaking $\mathbf{z}$, the user can perform a proof of knowledge (e.g., [32,28,27]) to convince the verifier that he knows such a vector $\mathbf{z}$ in zero-knowledge.

At this stage, one can obtain a secure identity-based identification scheme (as shown in [38]), but it is insufficient for our purposes: to achieve anonymity, the group user also has to *hide* his identity d, and hence the matrix $\mathbf{A}_d$ should not be explicitly given. This raises an interesting question: If the verifier does not know $\mathbf{A}_d$, how could he be convinced that $\mathbf{A}_d \cdot \mathbf{z} = \mathbf{u} \bmod q$? To address this issue, we introduce the following extension: we add ℓ suitable *zero-blocks* of size m to vector $\mathbf{z}$ to obtain an extended vector $\mathbf{x} = (\mathbf{x}_0 \| \mathbf{x}_1^0 \| \mathbf{x}_1^1 \| \ldots \| \mathbf{x}_\ell^0 \| \mathbf{x}_\ell^1) \in \mathbb{Z}^{(2\ell+1)m}$, where the added zero-blocks are $\mathbf{x}_1^{1-d[1]}, \ldots, \mathbf{x}_\ell^{1-d[\ell]}$. We then have $\|\mathbf{x}\|_\infty \leq \beta$, and $\mathbf{A} \cdot \mathbf{x} = \mathbf{u} \bmod q$. Namely $\mathbf{x}$ is a solution to the ISIS instance given by the *whole* Bonsai tree, with an additional condition: for each $i = 1, \ldots, \ell$, one of the two blocks $\mathbf{x}_i^0, \mathbf{x}_i^1$ must be zero, where the arrangement of the zero-blocks is determined by d. To prove in zero-knowledge the possession of such a vector $\mathbf{x}$, we adapt the 'Stern Extension' proof system from [27], where the user identity d is hidden by a *"one-time pad"* technique. This technique is as follows. In each round of the protocol, the user samples a fresh uniformly random $e \in \{0,1\}^\ell$ and permutes the blocks of $\mathbf{x}$ to obtain the permuted vector $\mathbf{v}$, whose zero-blocks are arranged according to $d \oplus e$ (where $\oplus$ denotes the bit XOR operation). Depending on the verifier's challenge, the user later will either reveal e, or reveal $d \oplus e$ and show that $\mathbf{v}$ has the correct shape determined by $d \oplus e$. Since $d \oplus e$ is uniformly random over $\{0,1\}^\ell$, the user identity d is completely hidden. As a result, the user can anonymously prove his group membership.

We now briefly review our revocation mechanism. For each group user's secret key $\mathbf{x}$, consider the first block $\mathbf{x}_0$ that corresponds to the "root" $\mathbf{A}_0$ of the Bonsai tree, and let his revocation token be $\mathbf{A}_0 \cdot \mathbf{x}_0 \bmod q \in \mathbb{Z}_q^n$. We choose suitable parameters, and sample $\mathbf{x}_0$ from a proper distribution, so that the token is statistically close to uniform over $\mathbb{Z}_q^n$. At a high level, our revocation mechanism works as follows. The user is asked to sample a uniformly random vector $\mathbf{r}_0 \in \mathbb{Z}_q^m$, and to compute a commitment $\mathbf{c}_0$ using a (lattice-based) statistically hiding and computationally binding string commitment scheme COM, for which the value $\mathbf{A}_0 \cdot \mathbf{r}_0 \bmod q$ is part of the committed string. Depending on the verifier's challenge, the user will either reveal $\mathbf{r}_0$ or reveal $\mathbf{x}_0 + \mathbf{r}_0$. In the former case, the verifier can check for honest computation of $\mathbf{c}_0$, while in the latter case, he can perform the revocation check using a list of tokens of revoked users $RL = \{\{\mathbf{u}_i\}_i\} \subset \mathbb{Z}_q^n$, as follows: For all $\mathbf{u}_i \in RL$, check that $\mathbf{c}_0 \neq \mathsf{COM}(\mathbf{A}_0 \cdot (\mathbf{x}_0 + \mathbf{r}_0) - \mathbf{u}_i \bmod q)$. Assuming that the user has been revoked, i.e., there exists i such that $\mathbf{A}_0 \cdot \mathbf{x}_0 \bmod q = \mathbf{u}_i$. If he follows the protocol, then $\mathsf{COM}(\mathbf{A}_0 \cdot (\mathbf{x}_0 + \mathbf{r}_0) - \mathbf{u}_i \bmod q) = \mathsf{COM}(\mathbf{A}_0 \cdot \mathbf{r}_0 \bmod q) = \mathbf{c}_0$, and thus, he gets rejected. If there is a false acceptance, then we can use it to break the computational binding property of COM. On the other hand, the probability of false rejection is negligibly small, since COM is statistically regular.

Putting everything together, we obtain a lattice-based VLR group signature that has several nice features, as mentioned earlier. In the process, we exploit the rich structure of the Bonsai tree [14], and the versatility of the "Stern Extension" proof system [27]. We also employ a special *"one-time pad"* technique, and a novel revocation mechanism.

2 Preliminaries

NOTATIONS. Vectors are denoted in bold lower-case letters and matrices in bold upper-case letters. We assume that all vectors are column vectors. The concatenation of vectors $\mathbf{x} \in \mathbb{R}^m$ and $\mathbf{y} \in \mathbb{R}^k$ is denoted by $(\mathbf{x}\|\mathbf{y})$. We denote the column concatenation of matrices $\mathbf{A} \in \mathbb{R}^{n \times m}$ and $\mathbf{B} \in \mathbb{R}^{n \times k}$ by $[\mathbf{A}|\mathbf{B}]$. Let $\mathbf{x} = (x_i)_{1 \leq i \leq n}$, we denote by $\mathsf{Parse}(\mathbf{x}, i_1, i_2)$ the vector $(x_i)_{i_1 \leq i \leq i_2}$ for $i_1, i_2 \in [n]$.

If S is a finite set, $y \xleftarrow{\$} \mathsf{S}$ means that y is chosen uniformly at random from S. If D_1 and D_2 are two distributions over the same countable support S, then their statistical distance is defined as $\Delta(D_1, D_2) = \frac{1}{2} \sum_{x \in S} |D_1(x) - D_2(x)|$. Two distributions are statistically close if their statistical distance is negligible.

2.1 VLR Group Signature

The presentation in this section follows [9]. A VLR group signature consists of 3 following algorithms:

- KeyGen(n, N): On input a security parameter n and the number of group users N, this PPT algorithm outputs a group public key gpk, a vector of user secret keys gsk $= (\mathsf{gsk}[0], \mathsf{gsk}[1], \ldots, \mathsf{gsk}[N-1])$, and a vector of user revocation tokens grt $= (\mathsf{grt}[0], \mathsf{grt}[1], \ldots, \mathsf{grt}[N-1])$.
- Sign$(\mathsf{gpk}, \mathsf{gsk}[d], M)$: On input gpk, a user secret key gsk$[d]$, and a message $M \in \{0, 1\}^*$, this PPT algorithm outputs a signature Σ.

- Verify(gpk, RL, Σ, M): On input gpk, a set of revocation tokens $RL \subseteq \{\text{grt}[0], \text{grt}[1], \ldots, \text{grt}[N-1]\}$, a signature Σ, and the message M, this algorithm outputs either Valid or Invalid. The output Valid indicates that Σ is a valid signature on message M under gpk, and the signer has not been revoked.

Remark 1. Any VLR group signature has an *implicit tracing algorithm* using grt as the tracing key. The tracing algorithm works as follows: on input a valid signature Σ on a message M, it reveals the signer of Σ by running Verify(gpk, $RL = \text{grt}[d]$, Σ, M), for $d = 0, 1, \ldots$, and outputting the first index $d^* \in \{0, 1, \ldots, N-1\}$ for which the verification algorithm returns Invalid. The tracing algorithm fails if and only if the given signature is properly verified for all d.

A secure VLR group signature scheme must satisfy the following 3 requirements:

1. **Correctness:** For all (gpk, gsk, grt) outputted by KeyGen, $M \in \{0,1\}^*$, and $d \in \{0, 1, \ldots, N-1\}$:

$$\text{Verify}(\text{gpk}, RL, \text{Sign}(\text{gpk}, \text{gsk}[d], M), M) = \text{Valid} \Leftrightarrow \text{grt}[d] \notin RL.$$

2. **Selfless-anonymity:** In the following selfless-anonymity game, the adversary's goal is to determine which of the two adaptively chosen keys generated a signature. He is not given access to either key.
3. **Traceability:** The adversary's goal in the traceability game is to forge a signature that cannot be traced to one of the users in his coalition using the implicit tracing algorithm above.

The formal definitions of the selfless-anonymity and traceability games can be found at [9, Sec. 2] and in the full version of the present paper [24].

2.2 Some Cryptographic Tools from Lattices

Lattices. Let n, m, and $q \geq 2$ be integers. For matrix $\mathbf{A} \in \mathbb{Z}_q^{n \times m}$, define the m-dimensional lattice: $\Lambda^\perp(\mathbf{A}) = \{\mathbf{x} \in \mathbb{Z}^m : \mathbf{A} \cdot \mathbf{x} = \mathbf{0} \bmod q\} \subseteq \mathbb{Z}^m$. For any $\mathbf{u}$ in the image of $\mathbf{A}$, define the coset $\Lambda_{\mathbf{u}}^\perp(\mathbf{A}) = \{\mathbf{x} \in \mathbb{Z}^m : \mathbf{A} \cdot \mathbf{x} = \mathbf{u} \bmod q\}$. We recall the homogeneous and inhomogeneous Small Integer Solution problems (SIS and ISIS).

Definition 1. *The* $\text{SIS}_{n,m,q,\beta}^p$ *and* $\text{ISIS}_{n,m,q,\beta}^p$ *problem in the* ℓ_p *norm with parameters* (n, m, q, β) *are as follows: Given a uniformly random matrix* $\mathbf{A} \in \mathbb{Z}_q^{n \times m}$, *and a uniformly random vector* $\mathbf{u} \in \mathbb{Z}_q^n$,

- $\text{SIS}_{n,m,q,\beta}^p$ *asks to find a non-zero vector* $\mathbf{x} \in \Lambda^\perp(\mathbf{A})$ *such that* $\|\mathbf{x}\|_p \leq \beta$.
- $\text{ISIS}_{n,m,q,\beta}^p$ *asks to find a vector* $\mathbf{x} \in \Lambda_{\mathbf{u}}^\perp(\mathbf{A})$ *such that* $\|\mathbf{x}\|_p \leq \beta$.

The hardness of the SIS and ISIS problems is given by a worst-case to average-case reduction from standard lattice problems, such as the Shortest Independent Vectors Problem (SIVP).

Theorem 1 ([18]). *For any m, $\beta = \text{poly}(n)$, and for any $q \geq \beta \cdot \omega(\sqrt{n \log n})$, solving a random instance of the $\text{SIS}^2_{n,m,q,\beta}$ or $\text{ISIS}^2_{n,m,q,\beta}$ problem with non-negligible probability is at least as hard as approximating the SIVP^2_γ problem on any lattice of dimension n to within certain $\gamma = \beta \cdot \widetilde{O}(\sqrt{n})$ factors.*

It then follows from the relationship between the ℓ_2 and ℓ_∞ norms that the $\text{SIS}^\infty_{n,m,q,\beta}$ and $\text{ISIS}^\infty_{n,m,q,\beta}$ problems are at least as hard as SIVP^2_γ (in the ℓ_2 norm) for some $\gamma = \beta \cdot \widetilde{O}(n)$.

Gaussians over Lattices. For any positive real σ, the n-dimensional Gaussian function is defined as: $\forall \mathbf{x} \in \mathbb{R}^n$, $\rho_\sigma(\mathbf{x}) = \exp(-\pi \|\mathbf{x}\|^2 / \sigma^2)$. For any n-dimensional lattice Λ, define the discrete Gaussian distribution over Λ as: $\forall \mathbf{x} \in \Lambda$, $D_{\Lambda,\sigma}(\mathbf{x}) = \frac{\rho_\sigma(\mathbf{x})}{\rho_\sigma(\Lambda)}$. In the following lemma, we review several well-known facts about discrete Gaussian distribution:

Lemma 1 ([18][36]). *Let n and $q \geq 2$ be integers. Let $m \geq 2n \log q$, and $\sigma \geq \omega(\sqrt{\log m})$.*

1. *For all but a $2q^{-n}$ fraction of all $\mathbf{A} \in \mathbb{Z}_q^{n \times m}$, for $\mathbf{x} \hookleftarrow D_{\mathbb{Z}^m,\sigma}$, the distribution of $\mathbf{u} = \mathbf{A} \cdot \mathbf{x} \bmod q$ is statistically close to uniform over $\mathbb{Z}_q^n$. Moreover, the conditional distribution of $\mathbf{x}$ given $\mathbf{u}$ is $D_{\Lambda_{\mathbf{u}}^\perp(\mathbf{A}),\sigma}$.*
2. *For $\beta = \lceil \sigma \cdot \log m \rceil$, and $\mathbf{x} \hookleftarrow D_{\mathbb{Z}^m,\sigma}$, $\Pr\big[\|\mathbf{x}\|_\infty > \beta\big]$ is negligible.*
3. *The min-entropy of $D_{\mathbb{Z}^m,\sigma}$ is at least $m - 1$.*

We now recall results about two fundamental tools: the trapdoor generation and the preimage sampling algorithms. The following algorithms are improvements of those in the literature [2,18,35,3].

Theorem 2 ([30]). *Given integers $n \geq 1$, $q \geq 2$, and $m \geq 2n \log q$. There is a PPT algorithm $\mathsf{GenTrap}(n, m, q)$ that outputs a matrix $\mathbf{A} \in \mathbb{Z}_q^{n \times m}$ and a trapdoor $\mathbf{R_A}$, such that the distribution of $\mathbf{A}$ is $\text{negl}(n)$-far from uniform. Moreover, for any vector $\mathbf{u}$ in the image of $\mathbf{A}$ and $\sigma = \omega(\sqrt{n \log q \log n})$, there is a PPT algorithm $\mathsf{SampleD}(\mathbf{R_A}, \mathbf{A}, \mathbf{u}, \sigma)$ that outputs $\mathbf{x} \in \mathbb{Z}^m$ sampled from the distribution $D_{\mathbb{Z}^m,\sigma}$, conditioned on the event that $\mathbf{A} \cdot \mathbf{x} = \mathbf{u} \bmod q$.*

The KTX String Commitment Scheme. Kawachi et al. [21] gave a string commitment scheme $\text{COM} : \{0,1\}^* \times \{0,1\}^{\overline{m}/2} \to \mathbb{Z}_q^n$, such that:

- If $\overline{m} > 2n(1 + \delta) \log q$ for $\delta > 0$ constant, COM is statistically hiding.
- If the $\text{SIS}^\infty_{n,\overline{m},q,1}$ problem is hard, then COM is computationally binding.

In this paper, we extensively use the KTX commitment scheme. For simplicity, we omit the randomness of the commitment. Also, we choose $\overline{m}$ sufficiently large, e.g., $\overline{m} = 4n \log q$, to make COM statistically hiding.

3 Preparations

In this section, we will describe the parameters and some specific constructions that will be used in our VLR group signature scheme.

3.1 Parameters

Our group signature scheme involves 2 main parameters: a security parameter n and a desired number of group users $N = 2^\ell \in \mathsf{poly}(n)$. Given n, we fix the other scheme parameters as in Table 1.

Table 1. Parameters of our VLR group signature scheme. The sequence $\beta_1, \beta_2, \ldots, \beta_p$ satisfies $\sum_{j=1}^{p} \beta_j = \beta$, and every integer in the interval $[-\beta, \beta]$ can be efficiently expressed as a subset sum of elements in the set $\{\pm\beta_1, \pm\beta_2, \ldots, \pm\beta_p\}$.

Parameter	Value or Asymptotic bound
Modulus q	$\omega(n^2 \log n)$
Dimension m	$\geq 2n \log q$
Gaussian parameter σ	$\omega(\sqrt{n \log q} \log n)$
Integer norm bound β	$\lceil \sigma \cdot \log m \rceil$
Number of 'decompositions' p	$\lfloor \log \beta \rfloor + 1$
Sequence of integers $\beta_1, \beta_2, \beta_3, \ldots, \beta_p$	$\beta_1 = \lceil \beta/2 \rceil; \beta_2 = \lceil (\beta - \beta_1)/2 \rceil$ $\beta_3 = \lceil (\beta - \beta_1 - \beta_2)/2 \rceil; \ldots; \beta_p = 1$
Number of protocol repetitions t	$\omega(\log n)$

3.2 Some Specific Sets

We now define some specific sets of vectors and permutations that will be extensively used throughout this work. First, we denote by B_{3m} the set of all vectors in $\{-1, 0, 1\}^{3m}$ having exactly m coordinates -1; m coordinates 0; and m coordinates 1. Given a binary string $d = d[1] \ldots d[\ell] \in \{0, 1\}^\ell$, we define two sets:

- $\mathsf{Secret}_\beta(d)$: The set of all $\mathbf{x} = \left(\mathbf{x}_0 \| \mathbf{x}_1^0 \| \mathbf{x}_1^1 \| \ldots \| \mathbf{x}_\ell^0 \| \mathbf{x}_\ell^1\right) \in \mathbb{Z}^{(2\ell+1)m}$ consisting of $2\ell + 1$ *blocks* of size m, such that $\|\mathbf{x}\|_\infty \leq \beta$, and the following ℓ blocks are *zero-blocks* $\mathbf{0}^m$: $\mathbf{x}_1^{1-d[1]}, \ldots, \mathbf{x}_\ell^{1-d[\ell]}$.
- $\mathsf{SecretExt}(d)$: The set of all vectors $\mathbf{x} = \left(\mathbf{x}_0 \| \mathbf{x}_1^0 \| \mathbf{x}_1^1 \| \ldots \| \mathbf{x}_\ell^0 \| \mathbf{x}_\ell^1\right) \in \{-1, 0, 1\}^{(2\ell+1)3m}$ consisting of $2\ell + 1$ *blocks* of size $3m$, such that the $\ell + 1$ blocks $\mathbf{x}_0, \mathbf{x}_1^{d[1]}, \ldots, \mathbf{x}_\ell^{d[\ell]}$ are elements of B_{3m}, and the remaining ℓ blocks $\mathbf{x}_1^{1-d[1]}, \ldots, \mathbf{x}_\ell^{1-d[\ell]}$ are *zero-blocks* $\mathbf{0}^{3m}$.

Given a vector $\mathbf{x} = \left(\mathbf{x}_0 \| \mathbf{x}_1^0 \| \mathbf{x}_1^1 \| \ldots \| \mathbf{x}_\ell^0 \| \mathbf{x}_\ell^1\right) \in \mathbb{Z}^{(2\ell+1)3m}$ consisting of $2\ell + 1$ blocks of size $3m$, we define two sets of permutations of $\mathbf{x}$:

- The set $\mathcal{S}$ of all permutations that keep the arrangement of the blocks: If $\pi \in \mathcal{S}$, then $\pi(\mathbf{x}) = \left(\tau_0(\mathbf{x}_0) \| \tau_1^0(\mathbf{x}_1^0) \| \tau_1^1(\mathbf{x}_1^1) \| \ldots \| \tau_\ell^0(\mathbf{x}_\ell^0) \| \tau_\ell^1(\mathbf{x}_\ell^1)\right)$, where $\tau_0, \tau_1^0, \tau_1^1, \ldots, \tau_\ell^0, \tau_\ell^1$ are certain permutations of $3m$ elements.
- The set $\mathcal{T} = \{T_e \mid e \in \{0, 1\}^\ell\}$, where for $e = e[1] \ldots e[\ell]$, $T_e \in \mathcal{T}$ rearranges the blocks as: $T_e(\mathbf{x}) = \left(\mathbf{x}_0 \| \mathbf{x}_1^{e[1]} \| \mathbf{x}_1^{1-e[1]} \| \ldots \| \mathbf{x}_\ell^{e[\ell]} \| \mathbf{x}_\ell^{1-e[\ell]}\right)$.

In particular, given $d, e \in \{0,1\}^\ell$, $\pi \in \mathcal{S}$, and $\mathbf{x} \in \mathbb{Z}^{(2\ell+1)3m}$, it can be checked that:

$$\mathbf{x} \in \mathsf{SecretExt}(d) \Leftrightarrow \pi(\mathbf{x}) \in \mathsf{SecretExt}(d) \Leftrightarrow T_e \circ \pi(\mathbf{x}) \in \mathsf{SecretExt}(d \oplus e). \quad (1)$$

3.3 The Decomposition - Extension Technique

Ling et al. [27] proposed a Stern-type zero-knowledge proof of knowledge for the $\mathsf{ISIS}^\infty_{n,m,q,\beta}$ problem, which relies on a Decomposition-Extension framework. Adapting their technique, we construct the following procedures:

Elementary Decomposition. On input a vector $\mathbf{v} = (v_1, v_2, \ldots, v_m) \in \mathbb{Z}^m$ such that $\|\mathbf{v}\|_\infty \leq \beta$, the procedure EleDec outputs $p = \lfloor \log \beta \rfloor + 1$ vectors $\widetilde{\mathbf{w}}_1, \ldots, \widetilde{\mathbf{w}}_p \in \{-1, 0, 1\}^m$, such that $\sum_{j=1}^{p} \beta_j \cdot \widetilde{\mathbf{w}}_j = \mathbf{v}$. This procedure works as follows:

1. For each $i \in [m]$, express v_i as $v_i = \beta_1 \cdot v_{i,1} + \beta_2 \cdot v_{i,2} + \ldots + \beta_p \cdot v_{i,p}$, where $\forall j \in [p] : v_{i,j} \in \{-1, 0, 1\}$. It was noted in [27] that for $\beta_1, \beta_2, \ldots, \beta_p$ given in Table 1, this step can easily be done.
2. For each $j \in [p]$, let $\widetilde{\mathbf{w}}_j := (v_{1,j}, v_{2,j}, \ldots, v_{m,j}) \in \{-1, 0, 1\}^m$. Output $\widetilde{\mathbf{w}}_1, \ldots, \widetilde{\mathbf{w}}_p$.

Elementary Extension. On input a vector $\widetilde{\mathbf{w}} \in \{-1, 0, 1\}^m$, EleExt extends $\widetilde{\mathbf{w}}$ to a vector $\mathbf{w} \in \mathsf{B}_{3m}$. This procedure works as follows:

1. Let $\lambda^{(-1)}$, $\lambda^{(0)}$ and $\lambda^{(1)}$ be the numbers of coordinates of $\widetilde{\mathbf{w}}$ that equal to -1, 0, and 1 respectively.
2. Pick a random vector $\widehat{\mathbf{w}} \in \{-1, 0, 1\}^{2m}$ that has exactly $(m - \lambda^{(-1)})$ coordinates -1, $(m - \lambda^{(0)})$ coordinates 0, and $(m - \lambda^{(1)})$ coordinates 1. Output $\mathbf{w} = (\widetilde{\mathbf{w}} \| \widehat{\mathbf{w}}) \in \mathsf{B}_{3m}$.

Witness Decomposition and Extensions. On input $\mathbf{x} \in \mathsf{Secret}_\beta(d)$ for some $d = d[1] \ldots d[\ell] \in \{0,1\}^\ell$, the procedure $\mathsf{WitnessDE}$ outputs p vectors $\mathbf{z}_1, \ldots \mathbf{z}_p \in \mathsf{SecretExt}(d)$. This procedure works as follows:

1. Write $\mathbf{x}$ as the concatenation of $2\ell + 1$ blocks of size m, namely: $\mathbf{x} = (\mathbf{x}_0 \| \mathbf{x}_1^0 \| \mathbf{x}_1^1 \| \ldots \| \mathbf{x}_\ell^0 \| \mathbf{x}_\ell^1)$.
2. Run EleDec on each of the $\ell + 1$ blocks $\mathbf{x}_0, \mathbf{x}_1^{d[1]}, \ldots, \mathbf{x}_\ell^{d[\ell]}$ to obtained $(\ell + 1)p$ decomposed vectors. Then run EleExt on each of the decomposed vectors to obtain $(\ell + 1)p$ vectors in B_{3m}, denoted respectively by $\{\mathbf{w}_{0,j}\}_{j=1}^p, \{\mathbf{w}_{1,j}^{d[1]}\}_{j=1}^p, \ldots, \{\mathbf{w}_{\ell,j}^{d[\ell]}\}_{j=1}^p$.
3. Create ℓp *zero-vectors* of dimension $3m$, and denote them by: $\{\mathbf{w}_{1,j}^{1-d[1]}\}_{j=1}^p, \ldots, \{\mathbf{w}_{\ell,j}^{1-d[\ell]}\}_{j=1}^p$.
4. For each $j \in [p]$, let $\mathbf{z}_j = (\mathbf{w}_{0,j} \| \mathbf{w}_{1,j}^0 \| \mathbf{w}_{1,j}^1 \| \ldots \| \mathbf{w}_{\ell,j}^0 \| \mathbf{w}_{\ell,j}^1)$. Output $\mathbf{z}_1, \ldots, \mathbf{z}_p \in \mathsf{SecretExt}(d)$.

Matrix Extension. On input $\mathbf{A} \in \mathbb{Z}_q^{n \times (2\ell+1)m}$, the following procedure $\mathsf{MatrixExt}$ outputs $\mathbf{A}^* \in \mathbb{Z}_q^{n \times (2\ell+1)3m}$:

1. Write $\mathbf{A}$ as the concatenation of $2\ell + 1$ component-matrices in $\mathbb{Z}_q^{n \times m}$.
2. Append $2m$ *zero-columns* to each of the component-matrices, then output the extended matrix $\mathbf{A}^*$.

In particular, let $\{\mathbf{z}_j\}_{j=1}^p \leftarrow \mathsf{WitnessDE}(\mathbf{x})$ and $\mathbf{A}^* \leftarrow \mathsf{MatrixExt}(\mathbf{A})$ then we have $\mathbf{A} \cdot \mathbf{x} = \mathbf{A}^* \cdot (\sum_{j=1}^p \beta_j \cdot \mathbf{z}_j)$. We illustrate our technique in Figure 1.

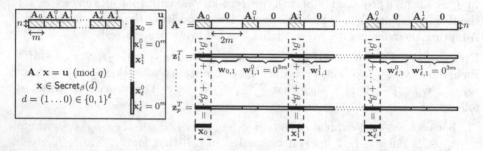

Fig. 1. An illustration of our Decomposition-Extension technique, where the first bit of d is 1 and its last bit is 0. We denote by ▬▬▬ an element of B_{3m}. After performing Decomposition-Extension, one has that $\mathbf{z}_j \in \mathsf{SecretExt}(d)$ for all $j \in [p]$, and $\mathbf{A}^* \cdot (\sum_{j=1}^p \beta_j \cdot \mathbf{z}_j) = \mathbf{A} \cdot \mathbf{x} = \mathbf{u} \bmod q$.

Therefore, in the protocol in Section 4, to prove that $\mathbf{x} \in \mathsf{Secret}_\beta(d)$ for some $d \in \{0,1\}^\ell$, and $\mathbf{A} \cdot \mathbf{x} = \mathbf{u} \bmod q$, one can instead prove that:

$$\begin{cases} \mathbf{A}^* \cdot (\sum_{j=1}^p \beta_j \cdot \mathbf{z}_j) = \mathbf{u} \bmod q, \\ \forall j \in [p], \pi \in \mathcal{S}, e \in \{0,1\}^\ell : T_e \circ \pi(\mathbf{z}_j) \in \mathsf{SecretExt}(d \oplus e), \end{cases}$$

where the second relation follows from the fact that $\mathbf{z}_j \in \mathsf{SecretExt}(d)$ for all $j \in [p]$, and from (1).

4   The Underlying Interactive Protocol

We recall that the main building block of our VLR group signature scheme is an interactive protocol that allows the prover to convince the verifier that he is a certified group member (i.e., he has a valid secret key), and that he has not been revoked (i.e., his revocation token is not in the verifier's list RL). In Section 5, the protocol is repeated $t = \omega(\log n)$ times to make the soundness error negligibly small, and then is transform to a signature scheme via Fiat-Shamir heuristic. The interactive protocol is summarized as follows:

- The public parameters are $\mathbf{A} = [\mathbf{A}_0 | \mathbf{A}_1^0 | \mathbf{A}_1^1 | \dots | \mathbf{A}_\ell^0 | \mathbf{A}_\ell^1] \in \mathbb{Z}_q^{n \times (2\ell+1)m}$ and $\mathbf{u} \in \mathbb{Z}_q^n$.

- The prover's witness is a $\mathbf{x} = (\mathbf{x}_0 \| \mathbf{x}_1^0 \| \mathbf{x}_1^1 \| \dots \| \mathbf{x}_\ell^0 \| \mathbf{x}_\ell^1) \in \mathsf{Secret}_\beta(d)$ for some $d \in \{0,1\}^\ell$. The verifier's additional input is a set $RL = \{\{\mathbf{u}_i\}_i\} \subset \mathbb{Z}_q^n$, whose cardinality is at most $N - 1$.
- The prover's goal is to convince the verifier in that:
  1. $\mathbf{A} \cdot \mathbf{x} = \mathbf{u} \bmod q$ and $\mathbf{x} \in \mathsf{Secret}_\beta(d)$, while keeping d secret.
  2. $\mathbf{A}_0 \cdot \mathbf{x}_0 \bmod q \notin RL$.

4.1   Description of the Protocol

Let COM be the KTX commitment scheme [21]. Let $\mathbf{A}^* \leftarrow \mathsf{MatrixExt}(\mathbf{A})$. Prior to the interaction, the prover applies the Decomposition-Extension technique on his witness: Let $\mathbf{z}_1, \dots, \mathbf{z}_p \leftarrow \mathsf{WitnessDE}(\mathbf{x})$. The protocol follows Stern's approach for three-pass zero-knowledge identification schemes [40], for which we employ an additional commitment $\mathbf{c}_0$ to enable the revocation mechanism. The details are as follows:

1. **Commitment:** The prover samples a string $e \xleftarrow{\$} \{0,1\}^\ell$, p permutations $\pi_1, \dots, \pi_p \xleftarrow{\$} \mathcal{S}$, and p vectors $\mathbf{r}_1, \dots, \mathbf{r}_p \xleftarrow{\$} \mathbb{Z}_q^{(2\ell+1)\cdot 3m}$. For each $j \in [p]$, let $\mathbf{r}_{j,0} = \mathsf{Parse}(\mathbf{r}_j, 1, m)$. Then it sends the commitment $\mathrm{CMT} = (\mathbf{c}_0, \mathbf{c}_1, \mathbf{c}_2, \mathbf{c}_3) \in (\mathbb{Z}_q^n)^4$ to the verifier, where

$$\begin{cases} \mathbf{c}_0 = \mathsf{COM}(e, \{\pi_j\}_{j=1}^p, \ \mathbf{A}_0 \cdot \big(\sum_{j=1}^p \beta_j \cdot \mathbf{r}_{j,0}\big) \bmod q), \\ \mathbf{c}_1 = \mathsf{COM}(e, \{\pi_j\}_{j=1}^p, \ \mathbf{A}^* \cdot \big(\sum_{j=1}^p \beta_j \cdot \mathbf{r}_j\big) \bmod q), \\ \mathbf{c}_2 = \mathsf{COM}(\{T_e \circ \pi_j(\mathbf{r}_j)\}_{j=1}^p), \\ \mathbf{c}_3 = \mathsf{COM}(\{T_e \circ \pi_j(\mathbf{z}_j + \mathbf{r}_j)\}_{j=1}^p). \end{cases} \tag{2}$$

2. **Challenge:** The verifier sends $Ch \xleftarrow{\$} \{1,2,3\}$ to the prover.
3. **Response:** Depending on the challenge, the prover computes the response RSP differently:
   - Case $Ch = 1$: $\forall j \in [p]$, let $\mathbf{v}_j = T_e \circ \pi_j(\mathbf{z}_j)$, $\mathbf{w}_j = T_e \circ \pi_j(\mathbf{r}_j)$, $d_1 = d \oplus e$, and set:
   $$\mathrm{RSP} = (d_1, \{\mathbf{v}_j\}_{j=1}^p, \{\mathbf{w}_j\}_{j=1}^p). \tag{3}$$
   - Case $Ch = 2$: $\forall j \in [p]$, let $\phi_j = \pi_j$, $\mathbf{s}_j = \mathbf{z}_j + \mathbf{r}_j$, $d_2 = e$, and set:
   $$\mathrm{RSP} = (d_2, \{\phi_j\}_{j=1}^p, \{\mathbf{s}_j\}_{j=1}^p). \tag{4}$$
   - Case $Ch = 3$: $\forall j \in [p]$, let $\psi_j = \pi_j$, $\mathbf{h}_j = \mathbf{r}_j$, $d_3 = e$, and set:
   $$\mathrm{RSP} = (d_3, \{\psi_j\}_{j=1}^p, \{\mathbf{h}_j\}_{j=1}^p). \tag{5}$$

Verification: Receiving RSP, the verifier proceeds as follows:

- Case $Ch = 1$: Parse RSP as in (3). Check that $\forall j \in [p] : \mathbf{v}_j \in \mathsf{SecretExt}(d_1)$, and that:
$$\mathbf{c}_2 = \mathsf{COM}(\{\mathbf{w}_j\}_{j=1}^p) \text{ and } \mathbf{c}_3 = \mathsf{COM}(\{\mathbf{v}_j + \mathbf{w}_j\}_{j=1}^p).$$

- Case $Ch = 2$: Parse RSP as in (4). $\forall j \in [p]$, let $\mathbf{s}_{j,0} = \mathsf{Parse}(\mathbf{s}_j, 1, m)$. Check that:

$$\begin{cases} \forall \mathbf{u}_i \in RL : \mathbf{c}_0 \neq \mathsf{COM}\big(d_2, \{\phi_j\}_{j=1}^p, \mathbf{A}_0 \cdot \big(\sum_{j=1}^p \beta_j \cdot \mathbf{s}_{j,0}\big) - \mathbf{u}_i \bmod q\big) \\ \mathbf{c}_1 = \mathsf{COM}\big(d_2, \{\phi_j\}_{j=1}^p, \mathbf{A}^* \cdot \big(\sum_{j=1}^p \beta_j \cdot \mathbf{s}_j\big) - \mathbf{u} \bmod q\big); \\ \mathbf{c}_3 = \mathsf{COM}\big(\{\mathbf{T}_{d_2} \circ \phi_j(\mathbf{s}_j)\}_{j=1}^p\big). \end{cases}$$

- Case $Ch = 3$: Parse RSP as in (5). $\forall j \in [p]$, let $\mathbf{h}_{j,0} = \mathsf{Parse}(\mathbf{h}_j, 1, m)$. Check that:

$$\begin{cases} \mathbf{c}_0 = \mathsf{COM}\big(d_3, \{\psi_j\}_{j=1}^p, \mathbf{A}_0 \cdot \big(\sum_{j=1}^p \beta_j \cdot \mathbf{h}_{j,0}\big) \bmod q\big) \\ \mathbf{c}_1 = \mathsf{COM}\big(d_3, \{\psi_j\}_{j=1}^p, \mathbf{A}^* \cdot \big(\sum_{j=1}^p \beta_j \cdot \mathbf{h}_j\big) \bmod q\big); \\ \mathbf{c}_2 = \mathsf{COM}\big(\{\mathbf{T}_{d_3} \circ \psi_j(\mathbf{h}_j)\}_{j=1}^p\big). \end{cases}$$

The verifier outputs Valid if and only if all the conditions hold. Otherwise, he outputs Invalid.

4.2 Witness Extraction

The following lemma says that in our protocol, one can extract a satisfying witness under specific conditions. The proof of the lemma is given in the full version [24, Appendix A].

Lemma 2. *Assume that for a given commitment* CMT, *there exist* 3 *valid responses* $\mathsf{RSP}^{(1)}$, $\mathsf{RSP}^{(2)}$, *and* $\mathsf{RSP}^{(3)}$ *corresponding to all* 3 *possible values of the challenge* Ch. *If* COM *is a computationally binding commitment scheme, then one can efficiently extract a vector* $\mathbf{y}$ *such that* $\mathbf{y} = \big(\mathbf{y}_0\|\mathbf{y}_1^0\|\mathbf{y}_1^1\|\cdots\|\mathbf{y}_\ell^0\|\mathbf{y}_\ell^1\big) \in \mathbb{Z}^{(2\ell+1)m}$ *satisfying* $\mathbf{A} \cdot \mathbf{y} = \mathbf{u} \bmod q$, $\mathbf{y} \in \mathsf{Secret}_\beta(d)$ *for some* $d \in \{0,1\}^\ell$, *and* $\mathbf{A}_0 \cdot \mathbf{y}_0 \bmod q \notin RL$.

5   The VLR Group Signature Scheme

In this Section we will describe and analyze our lattice-based VLR group signature scheme. The scheme uses the protocol in Section 4 as its building block.

5.1   Description of the Scheme

Keys Generation. The algorithm $\mathsf{KeyGen}(n, N)$, works as follows:

1. Run $\mathsf{GenTrap}(n, m, q)$ to get $\mathbf{A}_0 \in \mathbb{Z}_q^{n \times m}$ and trapdoor $\mathbf{R}$.

2. Sample $\mathbf{u} \xleftarrow{\$} \mathbb{Z}_q^n$, and $\mathbf{A}_i^b \xleftarrow{\$} \mathbb{Z}_q^{n \times m}$ for all $b \in \{0, 1\}$ and $i \in [\ell]$. Then define the matrix $\mathbf{A} = [\mathbf{A}_0|\mathbf{A}_1^0|\mathbf{A}_1^1|\ldots|\mathbf{A}_\ell^0|\mathbf{A}_\ell^1] \in \mathbb{Z}_q^{n \times (2\ell+1)m}$.

3. For group user with index $d \in \{0, 1, \ldots, N-1\}$, let $d[1] \ldots d[\ell] \in \{0, 1\}^\ell$ denote the binary representation of d, and do the following:

(a) Sample vectors $\mathbf{x}_1^{d[1]}, \ldots, \mathbf{x}_\ell^{d[\ell]} \leftarrow D_{\mathbb{Z}^m, \sigma}$. Compute $\mathbf{z} = \sum_{i=1}^\ell \mathbf{A}_i^{d[i]} \cdot$
$\mathbf{x}_i^{d[i]} \bmod q$, and sample $\mathbf{x}_0 \in \mathbb{Z}^m$ with $\mathbf{x}_0 \leftarrow \mathsf{SampleD}(\mathbf{R}, \mathbf{A}_0, \mathbf{u} - \mathbf{z}, \sigma)$. Let $\mathbf{x}_1^{1-d[1]}, \ldots, \mathbf{x}_\ell^{1-d[\ell]}$ be zero-vectors $\mathbf{0}^m$, and define $\mathbf{x}^{(d)} = (\mathbf{x}_0 \| \mathbf{x}_1^0 \| \mathbf{x}_1^1 \| \cdots \| \mathbf{x}_\ell^0 \| \mathbf{x}_\ell^1) \in \mathbb{Z}^{(2\ell+1)m}$. If $\|\mathbf{x}^{(d)}\|_\infty \le \beta$ then go to step (3b); else, repeat step (3a).

(b) Let the user secret key be $\mathsf{gsk}[d] = \mathbf{x}^{(d)}$, and the revocation token be $\mathsf{grt}[d] = \mathbf{A}_0 \cdot \mathbf{x}_0 \in \mathbb{Z}_q^n$.

4. The algorithm outputs $(\mathsf{gpk}, \mathsf{gsk}, \mathsf{grt})$, where $\mathsf{gpk} = (\mathbf{A}, \mathbf{u}); \mathsf{gsk} = (\mathsf{gsk}[0], \mathsf{gsk}[1], \ldots, \mathsf{gsk}[N-1]); \mathsf{grt} = (\mathsf{grt}[0], \mathsf{grt}[1], \ldots, \mathsf{grt}[N-1])$.

Remark 2. We have some observations on the behaviour of the above key generation algorithm:

- By Theorem 2, the distribution of $\mathbf{A}_0$ generated by $\mathsf{GenTrap}(n, m, q)$ is statistically close to uniform over $\mathbb{Z}_q^{n \times m}$. Thus, the distribution of gpk output by $\mathsf{KeyGen}(n, N)$ is statistically close to uniform over $\mathbb{Z}_q^{n \times (2\ell+1)m} \times \mathbb{Z}_q^n$. We note that the pair $(\mathbf{A}, \mathbf{u})$ resembles the Bonsai tree structure [14], where $\mathbf{A}_0$ is the "root" of the tree.
- In Step (3a), each coordinate of vector $\mathbf{x}^{(d)}$ is either 0 or distributed according to the distribution $D_{\mathbb{Z}, \sigma}$ (see Theorem 2 regarding the output distribution of algorithm $\mathsf{SampleD}$). By setting $\beta = \lceil \sigma \cdot \log m \rceil$, we ensure that $\|\mathbf{x}^{(d)}\|_\infty \le \beta$ with overwhelming probability (see Lemma 1). Thus, the event that Step (3a) needs to be repeated only occurs with negligible probability.
- The secret key $\mathbf{x}^{(d)}$ of group user with index d satisfies $\mathbf{A} \cdot \mathbf{x}^{(d)} = \mathbf{u} \bmod q$, and $\mathbf{x}^{(d)} \in \mathsf{Secret}_\beta(d)$.
- By Lemma 1, the distribution of each user revocation token $\mathsf{grt}[d]$ is statistically close to uniform over $\mathbb{Z}_q^n$. The trivial requirement is that the revocation tokens of two different group users must be different. In the very rare event of conflict (i.e., there exist $d_1, d_2 \in \{0, \ldots, N-1\}$ such that $d_2 > d_1$ and $\mathsf{grt}[d_1] = \mathsf{grt}[d_2]$), the algorithm simply re-samples the key and token for user with index d_2.

Signing Algorithm. Let $\mathcal{H} : \{0, 1\}^* \to \{1, 2, 3\}^t$ be a hash function, modelled as a random oracle. Given $\mathsf{gpk} = (\mathbf{A}, \mathbf{u})$, to sign a message $M \in \{0, 1\}^*$ using the secret key $\mathsf{gsk}[d] = \mathbf{x} \in \mathsf{Secret}_\beta(d)$, the user runs the randomized algorithm $\mathsf{Sign}(\mathsf{gpk}, \mathsf{gsk}[d], M)$, which is as follow:

1. Generate a proof that the user is a certified group members and that he has not been revoked. This is done by repeating $t = \omega(\log n)$ times the basic protocol from Section 4 with public parameter $(\mathbf{A}, \mathbf{u})$ and prover's witness $\mathbf{x}$, and then making it non-interactive with the Fiat-Shamir heuristic as a triple $(\{\mathrm{CMT}^{(k)}\}_{k=1}^t, \mathrm{CH}, \{\mathrm{RSP}^{(k)}\}_{k=1}^t)$, where $\mathrm{CH} = (\{Ch^{(k)}\}_{k=1}^t) = \mathcal{H}(M, \{\mathrm{CMT}^{(k)}\}_{k=1}^t) \in \{1, 2, 3\}^t$.
2. Output the group signature:

$$\Sigma = (M, \{\mathrm{CMT}^{(k)}\}_{k=1}^t, \{Ch^{(k)}\}_{k=1}^t, \{\mathrm{RSP}^{(k)}\}_{k=1}^t). \tag{6}$$

Verification Algorithm. On input $\mathsf{gpk} = (\mathbf{A}, \mathbf{u})$, a set of tokens $RL = \{\{\mathbf{u}_i\}_i\} \subset \mathbb{Z}_q^n$ whose cardinality is at most $N - 1$, a message $M \in \{0,1\}^*$, and a purported group signature Σ on M, the verifier runs the deterministic algorithm $\mathsf{Verify}(\mathsf{gpk}, RL, \Sigma, M)$, which performs the following steps:

1. Parse the signature Σ as in (6).
2. Check if $(Ch^{(1)}, \ldots, Ch^{(t)}) = \mathcal{H}(M, \mathrm{CMT}^{(1)}, \ldots, \mathrm{CMT}^{(t)})$.
3. For $k = 1$ to t, run the verification of the protocol from Section 4 to check the validity of $\mathrm{RSP}^{(k)}$ with respect to $\mathrm{CMT}^{(k)}$ and $Ch^{(k)}$. If any of the conditions does not hold, then output Invalid and terminate.
4. Output Valid.

5.2 Analysis of the Scheme

We now will analyze the efficiency and security properties of the VLR group signature described in Section 5.1.

Efficiency. The parameters in Table 1 are set so that all of the algorithms in Section 5.1 can be implemented in polynomial time. Asymptotically, the group public key has bit-size $\ell \cdot \widetilde{\mathcal{O}}(n^2) = \log N \cdot \widetilde{\mathcal{O}}(n^2)$, while the group signatures have bit-size $\ell \cdot \widetilde{\mathcal{O}}(n) = \log N \cdot \widetilde{\mathcal{O}}(n)$. The revocation check, i.e., the check against $\mathbf{c}_0^{(k)}$ in the case $Ch^{(k)} = 2$, runs in linear time in the number of revoked users, as it seems unavoidable for secure VLR group signature schemes.

Security. The correctness, selfless-anonymity, and traceability of our VLR group signature scheme are stated in theorems 3, 4 and 5, respectively. The proofs of these theorems are provided in the full version of the paper [24].

Theorem 3. *The VLR group signature scheme is correct with overwhelming probability.*

In the random oracle model, our scheme is selfless-anonymous.

Theorem 4. *If COM is a statistically hiding string commitment scheme, then the VLR group signature scheme in Section 5.1 is selfless-anonymous in the random oracle model.*

Finally, in the random oracle model, our VLR group signature scheme is traceable if the $\mathsf{SIS}_{n,(\ell+1)\cdot m,q,2\beta}^\infty$ problem is hard.

Theorem 5. *If there is a traceability adversary $\mathcal{A}$ with success probability ϵ and running time T, then there is an algorithm $\mathcal{F}$ that solves the $\mathsf{SIS}_{n,(\ell+1)\cdot m,q,2\beta}^\infty$ problem with success probability $\epsilon' > \left(1 - (7/9)^t\right) \cdot \frac{1}{2N}$, and running time $T' = 32 \cdot T \cdot q_{\mathcal{H}}/(\epsilon - 3^{-t}) + \mathsf{poly}(n, N)$, where $q_{\mathcal{H}}$ is the number of queries to the random oracle $\mathcal{H} : \{0,1\}^* \to \{1,2,3\}^t$.*

The results of Theorem 1 and Theorem 5 imply that the traceability of our scheme in the random oracle model can be based on the worst-case hardness of the SIVP_γ^2 problem, with $\gamma = 2\beta \cdot \widetilde{\mathcal{O}}(n) = \widetilde{\mathcal{O}}(n^{1.5})$.

Acknowledgements. The authors would like to thank D. Stehlé, B. Libert, R. Bhattacharyya, J. Chen, and the anonymous reviewers for their helpful comments. The research is supported in part by the Singapore Ministry of Education under Research Grant MOE2013-T2-1-041. Adeline Langlois is supported in part by ERC Starting Grant ERC-2013-StG-335086-LATTAC.

References

1. Ajtai, M.: Generating Hard Instances of Lattice Problems (Extended Abstract). In: STOC, pp. 99–108. ACM (1996)
2. Ajtai, M.: Generating Hard Instances of the Short Basis Problem. In: Wiedermann, J., Van Emde Boas, P., Nielsen, M. (eds.) ICALP 1999. LNCS, vol. 1644, pp. 1–9. Springer, Heidelberg (1999)
3. Alwen, J., Peikert, C.: Generating Shorter Bases for Hard Random Lattices. Theory Comput. Syst. 48(3), 535–553 (2011)
4. Ateniese, G., Camenisch, J., Joye, M., Tsudik, G.: A Practical and Provably Secure Coalition-Resistant Group Signature Scheme. In: Bellare, M. (ed.) CRYPTO 2000. LNCS, vol. 1880, pp. 255–270. Springer, Heidelberg (2000)
5. Bellare, M., Micciancio, D., Warinschi, B.: Foundations of Group Signatures: Formal Definitions, Simplified Requirements, and a Construction Based on General Assumptions. In: Biham, E. (ed.) EUROCRYPT 2003. LNCS, vol. 2656, pp. 614–629. Springer, Heidelberg (2003)
6. Bellare, M., Shi, H., Zhang, C.: Foundations of Group Signatures: The Case of Dynamic Groups. In: Menezes, A. (ed.) CT-RSA 2005. LNCS, vol. 3376, pp. 136–153. Springer, Heidelberg (2005)
7. Bichsel, P., Camenisch, J., Neven, G., Smart, N.P., Warinschi, B.: Get Shorty via Group Signatures without Encryption. In: Garay, J.A., De Prisco, R. (eds.) SCN 2010. LNCS, vol. 6280, pp. 381–398. Springer, Heidelberg (2010)
8. Boneh, D., Boyen, X., Shacham, H.: Short Group Signatures. In: Franklin, M. (ed.) CRYPTO 2004. LNCS, vol. 3152, pp. 41–55. Springer, Heidelberg (2004)
9. Boneh, D., Shacham, H.: Group Signatures with Verifier-local Revocation. In: ACM-CCS, pp. 168–177. ACM (2004)
10. Brickell, E.: An Efficient Protocol for Anonymously Providing Assurance of the Container of the Private Key. Submitted to the Trusted Comp. Group (April 2003)
11. Camenisch, J., Groth, J.: Group Signatures: Better Efficiency and New Theoretical Aspects. In: Blundo, C., Cimato, S. (eds.) SCN 2004. LNCS, vol. 3352, pp. 120–133. Springer, Heidelberg (2005)
12. Camenisch, J., Lysyanskaya, A.: Dynamic Accumulators and Application to Efficient Revocation of Anonymous Credentials. In: Yung, M. (ed.) CRYPTO 2002. LNCS, vol. 2442, pp. 61–76. Springer, Heidelberg (2002)
13. Camenisch, J., Neven, G., Rückert, M.: Fully Anonymous Attribute Tokens from Lattices. In: Visconti, I., De Prisco, R. (eds.) SCN 2012. LNCS, vol. 7485, pp. 57–75. Springer, Heidelberg (2012)

14. Cash, D., Hofheinz, D., Kiltz, E., Peikert, C.: Bonsai Trees, or How to Delegate a Lattice Basis. In: Gilbert, H. (ed.) EUROCRYPT 2010. LNCS, vol. 6110, pp. 523–552. Springer, Heidelberg (2010)
15. Chaum, D., van Heyst, E.: Group Signatures. In: Davies, D.W. (ed.) EUROCRYPT 1991. LNCS, vol. 547, pp. 257–265. Springer, Heidelberg (1991)
16. Chen, L., Pedersen, T.P.: New Group Signature Schemes (Extended Abstract). In: De Santis, A. (ed.) EUROCRYPT 1994. LNCS, vol. 950, pp. 171–181. Springer, Heidelberg (1995)
17. Fiat, A., Shamir, A.: How to Prove Yourself: Practical Solutions to Identification and Signature Problems. In: Odlyzko, A.M. (ed.) CRYPTO 1986. LNCS, vol. 263, pp. 186–194. Springer, Heidelberg (1987)
18. Gentry, C., Peikert, C., Vaikuntanathan, V.: Trapdoors for Hard Lattices and New Cryptographic Constructions. In: STOC, pp. 197–206. ACM (2008)
19. Gordon, S.D., Katz, J., Vaikuntanathan, V.: A Group Signature Scheme from Lattice Assumptions. In: Abe, M. (ed.) ASIACRYPT 2010. LNCS, vol. 6477, pp. 395–412. Springer, Heidelberg (2010)
20. Groth, J.: Fully Anonymous Group Signatures Without Random Oracles. In: Kurosawa, K. (ed.) ASIACRYPT 2007. LNCS, vol. 4833, pp. 164–180. Springer, Heidelberg (2007)
21. Kawachi, A., Tanaka, K., Xagawa, K.: Concurrently Secure Identification Schemes Based on the Worst-Case Hardness of Lattice Problems. In: Pieprzyk, J. (ed.) ASIACRYPT 2008. LNCS, vol. 5350, pp. 372–389. Springer, Heidelberg (2008)
22. Kiayias, A., Tsiounis, Y., Yung, M.: Traceable Signatures. In: Cachin, C., Camenisch, J.L. (eds.) EUROCRYPT 2004. LNCS, vol. 3027, pp. 571–589. Springer, Heidelberg (2004)
23. Laguillaumie, F., Langlois, A., Libert, B., Stehlé, D.: Lattice-Based Group Signatures with Logarithmic Signature Size. In: Sako, K., Sarkar, P. (eds.) ASIACRYPT 2013, Part II. LNCS, vol. 8270, pp. 41–61. Springer, Heidelberg (2013)
24. Langlois, A., Ling, S., Nguyen, K., Wang, H.: Lattice-based Group Signature Scheme with Verifier-local Revocation. Cryptology ePrint Archive, Report 2014/033 (2014), http://eprint.iacr.org/2014/033
25. Libert, B., Peters, T., Yung, M.: Group Signatures with Almost-for-Free Revocation. In: Safavi-Naini, R., Canetti, R. (eds.) CRYPTO 2012. LNCS, vol. 7417, pp. 571–589. Springer, Heidelberg (2012)
26. Libert, B., Vergnaud, D.: Group Signatures with Verifier-Local Revocation and Backward Unlinkability in the Standard Model. In: Garay, J.A., Miyaji, A., Otsuka, A. (eds.) CANS 2009. LNCS, vol. 5888, pp. 498–517. Springer, Heidelberg (2009)
27. Ling, S., Nguyen, K., Stehlé, D., Wang, H.: Improved Zero-Knowledge Proofs of Knowledge for the ISIS Problem, and Applications. In: Kurosawa, K., Hanaoka, G. (eds.) PKC 2013. LNCS, vol. 7778, pp. 107–124. Springer, Heidelberg (2013)
28. Lyubashevsky, V.: Lattice-Based Identification Schemes Secure Under Active Attacks. In: Cramer, R. (ed.) PKC 2008. LNCS, vol. 4939, pp. 162–179. Springer, Heidelberg (2008)
29. Lyubashevsky, V.: Lattice Signatures without Trapdoors. In: Pointcheval, D., Johansson, T. (eds.) EUROCRYPT 2012. LNCS, vol. 7237, pp. 738–755. Springer, Heidelberg (2012)
30. Micciancio, D., Peikert, C.: Trapdoors for Lattices: Simpler, Tighter, Faster, Smaller. In: Pointcheval, D., Johansson, T. (eds.) EUROCRYPT 2012. LNCS, vol. 7237, pp. 700–718. Springer, Heidelberg (2012)
31. Micciancio, D., Regev, O.: Lattice-based Cryptography. In: Post-Quantum Cryptography, pp. 147–191. Springer (2009)

32. Micciancio, D., Vadhan, S.P.: Statistical Zero-Knowledge Proofs with Efficient Provers: Lattice Problems and More. In: Boneh, D. (ed.) CRYPTO 2003. LNCS, vol. 2729, pp. 282–298. Springer, Heidelberg (2003)
33. Nakanishi, T., Funabiki, N.: Verifier-Local Revocation Group Signature Schemes with Backward Unlinkability from Bilinear Maps. In: Roy, B. (ed.) ASIACRYPT 2005. LNCS, vol. 3788, pp. 533–548. Springer, Heidelberg (2005)
34. Nakanishi, T., Funabiki, N.: A Short Verifier-Local Revocation Group Signature Scheme with Backward Unlinkability. In: Yoshiura, H., Sakurai, K., Rannenberg, K., Murayama, Y., Kawamura, S.-I. (eds.) IWSEC 2006. LNCS, vol. 4266, pp. 17–32. Springer, Heidelberg (2006)
35. Peikert, C.: An Efficient and Parallel Gaussian Sampler for Lattices. In: Rabin, T. (ed.) CRYPTO 2010. LNCS, vol. 6223, pp. 80–97. Springer, Heidelberg (2010)
36. Peikert, C., Rosen, A.: Efficient Collision-Resistant Hashing from Worst-Case Assumptions on Cyclic Lattices. In: Halevi, S., Rabin, T. (eds.) TCC 2006. LNCS, vol. 3876, pp. 145–166. Springer, Heidelberg (2006)
37. Regev, O.: On Lattices, Learning with Errors, Random Linear Codes, and Cryptography. In: STOC, pp. 84–93. ACM (2005)
38. Rückert, M.: Adaptively Secure Identity-Based Identification from Lattices without Random Oracles. In: Garay, J.A., De Prisco, R. (eds.) SCN 2010. LNCS, vol. 6280, pp. 345–362. Springer, Heidelberg (2010)
39. Shor, P.W.: Polynomial-Time Algorithms for Prime Factorization and Discrete Logarithms on a Quantum Computer. SIAM Journal on Computing 26(5), 1484–1509 (1997)
40. Stern, J.: A New Paradigm for Public Key Identification. IEEE Transactions on Information Theory 42(6), 1757–1768 (1996)

Leakage-Resilient Signatures
with Graceful Degradation

Jesper Buus Nielsen[1], Daniele Venturi[2,*], and Angela Zottarel[1]

[1] Aarhus University
[2] Sapienza University of Rome

Abstract. We investigate new models and constructions which allow leakage-resilient signatures secure against existential forgeries, where the signature is much shorter than the leakage bound. Current models of leakage-resilient signatures against existential forgeries demand that the adversary cannot produce a new valid message/signature pair (m, σ) even after receiving some λ bits of leakage on the signing key. If $|\sigma| \leq \lambda$, then the adversary can just choose to leak a valid signature σ, and hence signatures must be larger than the allowed leakage, which is impractical as the goal often is to have large signing keys to allow a lot of leakage.

We propose a new notion of leakage-resilient signatures against existential forgeries where we demand that the adversary cannot produce $n = \lfloor \lambda/|\sigma| \rfloor + 1$ distinct valid message/signature pairs $(m_1, \sigma_1), \ldots, (m_n, \sigma_n)$ after receiving λ bits of leakage. If $\lambda = 0$, this is the usual notion of existential unforgeability. If $1 < \lambda < |\sigma|$, this is essentially the usual notion of existential unforgeability in the presence of leakage. In addition, for $\lambda \geq |\sigma|$ our new notion still guarantees the best possible, namely that the adversary cannot produce more forgeries than he could have leaked, hence graceful degradation.

Besides the game-based notion hinted above, we also consider a variant which is more simulation-based, in that it asks that from the leakage a simulator can "extract" a set of $n - 1$ messages (to be thought of as the messages corresponding to the leaked signatures), and no adversary can produce forgeries not in this small set. The game-based notion is easier to prove for a concrete instantiation of a signature scheme. The simulation-based notion is easier to use, when leakage-resilient signatures are used as components in larger protocols.

We prove that the two notion are equivalent and present a generic construction of signature schemes meeting our new notion and a concrete instantiation under fairly standard assumptions. We further give an application, to leakage-resilient identification.

1 Introduction

The problem of message authentication is one of the most basic in cryptography. Alice wants to transmit a message m to Bob via an insecure channel, with the

---

* Part of the work done while at Aarhus University supported by the DFF Starting Grant 10-081612.

H. Krawczyk (Ed.): PKC 2014, LNCS 8383, pp. 362–379, 2014.

guarantee that the message will reach the destination without any modification by a third party on the communication channel. In a world where public-key cryptography exists the latter can be achieved via a *digital signature*: Before sending m, Alice computes a signature σ (via her signing key sk) of the message, and transmits (m, σ) over the channel. The idea is that Bob can later verify the signature using Alice's verification key vk, and thus establish whether the received message is consistent with the original.

Traditionally, security of signatures schemes (and other primitives) is modeled in a black-box fashion where an adversary can only access the algorithms underlying the scheme as a black-box. For instance, in the case of a signature scheme, we require that no computationally bounded adversary is able to forge a signature of a message (with respect to some verification key vk) even given black-box access to an oracle returning signatures of arbitrarily chosen messages (computed via the signing key corresponding to vk).[1] However, as pointed out by recent research, the model above might be too restrictive, in that in practice there are several ways by which an adversary can learn partial information (a.k.a. leakage) on the secrets used within a cryptographic primitive, and thus easily step out of the security model. This includes so-called side-channel attacks, based on timings [27], power analysis [28] and electromagnetic radiation [35].

A large body of work has extended standard cryptographic definitions such that they can capture different flavours of security against leakage, both in the game-based setting (e.g. [13,33,1,30,24,14,8,10,11,6]) and in the simulation-based setting [17,21,4,31]. In the case of a signature scheme, a simple extension of the black-box setting requires that no computationally bounded adversary is able to forge a signature of a message (with respect to some verification key vk) even given black-box access to an oracle returning signatures on arbitrarily chosen messages (computed via the signing key corresponding to vk) and to a leakage oracle returning bounded (but otherwise arbitrary) information on the signing key sk. This is often referred to as the *bounded* leakage model, and on this we focus our work. See Section 1.2 for a discussion on other models.

The modeling above requires two *necessary* limitations. The first limitation is that the total amount of leakage must be smaller than the length of the signing key, as otherwise the entire key can be learned by the adversary, leaving no hope for security. The second limitation is that a signature has to be longer than the leakage bound, as otherwise a leakage query can just leak a forgery which is a valid attack against the security definition. A similar issue was already observed by Alwen, Dodis and Wichs [1], in their work on leakage-resilient public-key cryptography in the so-called bounded retrieval model. In this setting, the secret key is made intentionally large (say, 100 gigabytes) such that it may be infeasible/impractical for the attacker to download "too much" data (say, more than 1 gigabytes). Still, the length of the public key and the computational overhead are essentially independent from the size of the secret key. For the very same reason pointed out above, no signature scheme can be proven existentially unforgeable

---

[1] The restriction is of course that the forgery should not correspond to one of the messages asked to the oracle.

in the bounded retrieval model, as the leakage could simply consist of a forgery. To tackle this issue the authors in [1] considered a weaker notion, which they name *entropic unforgeability*, where, after the leakage phase, the adversary is required to forge the signature of a message sampled from a (potentially adversarially chosen) distribution of high enough min-entropy (given the entire view of the adversary). [1] then shows that entropic unforgeability can be achieved in the random oracle model [3], by applying the Fiat-Shamir transform [16] to a certain class of interactive protocols.

In this work we propose more granular ways to model (bounded) leakage resilience for signature schemes where the length of the signature is smaller than the length of the secret key. In a nutshell, our simplest notion says that an adversary leaking λ bits will always be able to produce $\lfloor \lambda/|\sigma| \rfloor$ forgeries, but not more than that. At first glance it may seem that our notion gives a weaker guarantee. However, the number of forgeries the adversary is required to produce strictly depends on the actual leakage, so if an adversary asks for no leakage (i.e. we are in the black-box model), our notion is equivalent to standard existential unforgeability, as now $\lfloor \lambda/|\sigma| \rfloor = 0$. On the other hand, when leakage does happen, our definition offers a graceful degradation of security and, as we argue in more details below, still allows for interesting, non-trivial, applications.

1.1   Our Contribution

We investigate new models and constructions which allow leakage-resilient signatures secure against existential forgeries, where the signature is much shorter than the leakage bound. Our main contributions are discussed in detail below.

One-more unforgeability. As a first contribution, we state a variant of leakage resilience for signature schemes where the length of the secret key is much larger than the length of a signature.[2] We name our notion *one-more unforgeability*, since it has a similar flavour to the unforgeability notion for blind signatures [34]. The attacker (given the verification key vk) can access a signing oracle and a leakage oracle; at the end he has to output n forgeries $(m_1, \sigma_1), \ldots, (m_n, \sigma_n)$ and wins the game if and only if all the forgeries are valid, the messages are pairwise distinct, and n is strictly larger than the number of forgeries one could have leaked via leakage queries. See Section 3 for a precise definition.

We also formulate a seemingly stronger variant, which we name *constrained-one-more* unforgeability. Here we introduce a simulator S which first looks at the state of the adversary A after the leakage phase ended and then defines a set of messages Q^* of size strictly smaller than n, as defined above. A signature scheme is secure in this setting if, for all A, there exists such a simulator for which A is not able to forge a message which is not contained in Q^* (and was not already asked to the signing oracle). This captures the intuition that the forgeries are

---

[2] Note that this in general encompasses schemes with short signatures, and not necessarily signature schemes in the bounded retrieval model.

already fixed after the leakage is ended, and the adversary is "constrained" in the sense that those are the only messages for which he can forge.[3]

We show that one-more unforgeability and constrained-one-more unforgeability are equivalent. The tricky direction is to show that the former implies the latter. The intuition is using an adversary breaking constrained-one-more unforgeability and rewinding him to obtain a sufficiently large set of forgeries: if at each rewinding we use a strictly larger set Q^* (including all previous forgeries output by the adversary), after n steps we end-up with n forgeries which allow to break one-more unforgeability. The actual analysis is more involved, as we need to take care of the fact that we are rewinding the adversary at the point where he is already committed to the leakage.

A construction. As a second contribution we present a scheme achieving one-more-unforgeability, based on a perfectly hiding (homomorphic) commitment scheme and a non-interactive zero knowledge argument of knowledge system.

The secret key consists of the coefficients δ_i of a d-degree polynomial $\delta(\cdot)$ over a finite field, together with the openings r_i for the commitments com_i to δ_i. The verification key consists of the set of all com_i together with a common reference string for the argument system. To sign a message m, we compute $\delta(m)$ and we produce a zero-knowledge argument of knowledge that the evaluation of the polynomial was performed correctly using the coefficients whose commitments are in the verification key. The signature consists of such an argument.

We prove that the scheme is one-more unforgeable whenever the commitment is perfectly hiding (and computationally binding), as long as the leakage is smaller than $(1/2 - o(1)) \cdot |sk|$. We also show a particular instantiation, using standard building blocks such as Pedersen commitments [32] and Groth-Sahai proofs [19,20]. Security follows from the DLIN assumption [5]. We remark that for our concrete instantiation it is indeed the case that the length of a signature is essentially independent of the length of the secret key.

Application to identification protocols. Besides being a notion of theoretical interest, we also show that one-more unforgeability can be applied in the context of identification protocols. We focus on the public-key setting, where a prover P wants to be identified from a verifier V holding P's public key.

Following [1], we define security in the presence of leakage by considering an adversary having black-box access to the prover and to a leakage oracle

---

[3] We note that constrained-one-more unforgeability is strictly stronger than entropic unforgeability [1]. If a scheme is constrained-one-more unforgeable, then after the leakage is done, a poly-sized set of messages Q^* is defined and the adversary cannot forge for a message outside Q^*, whereas a high entropy message will hit inside Q^* with negligible probability. On the other hand consider a signature scheme where a signature is given as $\sigma = \Pi^{-1}(m)$ for a one-way trapdoor permutation Π hard to invert on high-entropy m. Such a scheme is entropic secure in the presence of $\lambda = 0$ bits of leakage, by definition, but is clearly not constrained-one-more unforgeable in the presence of $\lambda = 0$ bits of leakage, as the adversary can always sample one more random message/signature pair as $m = \Pi(\sigma)$ for random σ.

(depending on the prover's secret key) in a first phase. In a second phase the adversary is given one chance to convince the verifier. The above notion is reminiscent of so-called *active* security [23,25].

We show that the classical protocol for public-key identification, where the verifier challenges the prover with a random message and the prover has to respond with a signature on that message, achieves the above notion of active security[4] with leakage, provided that the underlying signature scheme is constrained-one-more unforgeable.

1.2   Other Related Work

In this work (similarly to [1,10,15]) we focus on bounded leakage resilience, i.e., we assume that there is an a-priori upper bound on the length of the maximum tolerated leakage. Furthermore, we consider a setting where the leakage can only depend on the signing key and not on the full state of the signer (including, e.g., the signer's random coins). A strictly stronger notion of *fully* leakage-resilient signatures (where the leakage is bounded but can depend on the entire state of the signer) was considered in [24,6].

In the continual leakage setting [7,9,29,6], there is no *a priori* bound on the length of the leakage. This requires an efficient procedure to update the secret key (while leaving the public key unchanged), and to assume that the leakage is bounded only between two updates (and during the update process itself).

An independent line of research (see, e.g. [22,26]) aims at constructing signature schemes (in the black-box model) which are as short as possible. Even though this is not our purpose, we believe that our notions could have interesting implications in this setting, when studying leakage resilience of such schemes.

2   Preliminaries

2.1   Notation

For $a, b \in \mathbb{R}$, we let $[a, b] = \{x \in \mathbb{R} ; a \leq x \leq b\}$; for $a \in \mathbb{N}$ we let $[a] = \{1, 2, \ldots, a\}$. If x is a string, we denote its length by $|x|$; if $\mathcal{X}$ is a set, $|\mathcal{X}|$ represents the number of elements in $\mathcal{X}$. When x is chosen randomly in $\mathcal{X}$, we write $x \leftarrow \mathcal{X}$. When A is an algorithm, we write $y \leftarrow A(x)$ to denote a run of A on input x and output y; if A is randomized, then y is a random variable and $A(x; r)$ denotes a run of A on input x and randomness r. An algorithm A is *probabilistic polynomial-time* (PPT) if A is randomized and for any input $x, r \in \{0, 1\}^*$ the computation of $A(x; r)$ terminates in at most $poly(|x|)$ steps.

Throughout the paper we let κ denote the security parameter. We say that a function $\nu : \mathbb{N} \to \mathbb{R}$ is negligible in the security parameter κ if $\nu(\kappa) = \kappa^{-\omega(1)}$. For two ensembles $\mathcal{X} = \{X_\kappa\}_{\kappa \in \mathbb{N}}$ and $\mathcal{Y} = \{Y_\kappa\}_{\kappa \in \mathbb{N}}$, we write $\mathcal{X} \equiv \mathcal{Y}$ if they

---

[4] In fact, as argued in [2], without leakage the signature based protocol is even secure against man-in-the-middle attacks. It is not hard to see, however, that our result does not extend to man-in-the-middle security.

are identically distributed and $\mathcal{X} \approx_s \mathcal{Y}$ to denote that the statistical distance between the two distributions is negligible in the security parameter. We say that $\mathcal{X}$ and $\mathcal{Y}$ are computationally indistinguishable if for all PPT distinguishers D it holds that $|\mathbb{P}[\mathsf{D}(1^\kappa, X) = 1] - \mathbb{P}[\mathsf{D}(1^\kappa, Y) = 1]|$ is negligible in κ.

The min-entropy of a random variable X over a set $\mathcal{X}$ is defined as $\mathbb{H}_\infty(X) := -\log\max_x \mathbb{P}[X = x]$ and represents the best chance of guessing X by an unbounded adversary. Average min-entropy captures how hard it is to guess X on average, given some side information Z (possibly related to X):

$$\widetilde{\mathbb{H}}_\infty(X|Z) = -\log \mathbb{E}_z \left[\max_x \mathbb{P}[X = x|Z = z] \right].$$

The min-entropy of a distribution conditioned to some side information cannot decrease more than the bit-length of the side information itself:

Lemma 1 ([12]). *For all random variables $X \in \mathcal{X}$ and $\Lambda \in \{0,1\}^\lambda$ we have that $\widetilde{\mathbb{H}}_\infty(X|\Lambda) \geq \mathbb{H}_\infty(X) - \lambda$.*

We let $\mathcal{O}^\ell(s)$ be an oracle parametrized by a value s, which takes as input efficiently computable functions $f : \{0,1\}^* \to \{0,1\}^*$ and outputs $f(s)$, returning a total of at most ℓ bits.

2.2   Commitment Schemes

A (non-interactive) commitment scheme $\mathcal{COM}$ is a tuple of algorithms (Setup, Commit), defined as follows: (1) Algorithm Setup takes as input the security parameter and outputs a public key pk; (2) Algorithm Commit takes as input a message $m \in \mathcal{M}$, randomness $r \in \mathcal{R}$, the public key pk and outputs a value $com \in \mathcal{C}$. To open a commitment com we output (m, r); an opening is valid if and only if $com = \mathsf{Commit}(m; r)$.

A commitment scheme has two properties, known as binding and hiding. In Section 4 we need a scheme with the following flavour.

Computationally Binding : For any PPT adversary A, the following is negligible:

$$\mathbb{P}\left[\mathsf{Commit}(m_0; r_0) = \mathsf{Commit}(m_1; r_1) : \begin{array}{l} pk \leftarrow \mathsf{Setup}(1^\kappa); \\ ((m_0, r_0), (m_1, r_1)) \leftarrow \mathsf{A}(pk) \end{array} \right].$$

Statistically Hiding : For all messages $m_0, m_1 \in \mathcal{M}$, we have that

$$\{pk, \mathsf{Commit}(pk, m_0)\}_{\kappa \in \mathbb{N}} \approx_s \{pk, \mathsf{Commit}(pk, m_1)\}_{\kappa \in \mathbb{N}},$$

where the two ensembles are considered as random variables over the choice of the randomness to generate $pk \leftarrow \mathsf{Setup}(1^\kappa)$ and to compute the commitment. If the two ensembles are identically distributed, we say that the commitment is *perfectly* hiding.

Whenever $\mathcal{M}$ and $\mathcal{R}$ are a finite field $\mathbb{F}$, we say that $\mathcal{COM}$ is *linearly homomorphic* in the following sense: Given commitments com and com' and a field element $c \in \mathbb{F}$, one can compute commitments com^* and com'' such that being able to open com and com' to m and m' (respectively) allows to open com^* to $m + m'$ and com'' to $c \cdot m$. We will write the mapping $(com, com') \mapsto com^*$ as $com \cdot com'$ and the mapping $(c, com) \mapsto com''$ as com^c. Similarly, for the opening information we will write the mappings as $com^* = \mathsf{Commit}(pk, m + m'; r + r')$ and $com'' = \mathsf{Commit}(pk, c \cdot m; c \cdot r)$. The above can be generalized to abstract operations over $\mathcal{M}$, $\mathcal{R}$ and $\mathcal{C}$, but for simplicity, and to be consistent with the concrete instantiation given in Section 4.2, we stick to this formulation here.

2.3 Non-interactive Zero-Knowledge Arguments of Knowledge

For a relation $\mathfrak{R} \subseteq \{0,1\}^* \times \{0,1\}^*$, the language associated with $\mathfrak{R}$ is $\mathfrak{L}_{\mathfrak{R}} = \{x : \exists w \text{ s.t. } (x, w) \in \mathfrak{R}\}$. A non-interactive argument system $\mathcal{NIZK}$ for a relation $\mathfrak{R}$ is a tuple of algorithms $(\mathsf{Init}, \mathsf{Prove}, \mathsf{Ver})$, defined as follows: (1) Algorithm Init takes as input the security parameter and outputs a common reference string $\mathsf{crs} \leftarrow \mathsf{Init}(1^\kappa)$; (2) Algorithm Prove takes as input a pair (x, w) such that $(x, w) \in \mathfrak{R}$ and outputs an argument π; (3) Algorithm Ver takes as input a pair (x, π) and outputs a judgement in $\{0, 1\}$.

We require the following properties for $\mathcal{NIZK}$ [36,10].

Completeness: For every $(x, w) \in \mathfrak{R}$ we have that

$$\Pr[\mathsf{Ver}(\mathsf{crs}, (x, \pi)) = 1 : \mathsf{crs} \leftarrow \mathsf{Init}(1^\kappa); \pi \leftarrow \mathsf{Prove}(\mathsf{crs}, (x, w))] \geq 1 - negl(\kappa).$$

Multi-theorem zero-knowledge: There exists a PPT simulator $\mathsf{Sim} = (\mathsf{Sim}_1, \mathsf{Sim}_2)$ such that, for all PPT adversaries A, the ensembles $\{\mathsf{Real}(\kappa)\}_{\kappa \in \mathbb{N}}$ and $\{\mathsf{Simu}(\kappa)\}_{\kappa \in \mathbb{N}}$ are computationally close, where

$$\mathsf{Real}(\kappa) := \left\{ \mathsf{crs} \leftarrow \mathsf{Init}(1^\kappa); out \leftarrow \mathsf{A}^{\mathsf{Prove}(\mathsf{crs}, \cdot)}(\mathsf{crs}) \right\}$$

$$\mathsf{Simu}(\kappa) := \left\{ (\mathsf{crs}, tk) \leftarrow \mathsf{Sim}_1(1^\kappa); out' \leftarrow \mathsf{A}^{\widetilde{\mathsf{Sim}_2}(tk, \cdot)}(\mathsf{crs}) \right\}$$

and $\widetilde{\mathsf{Sim}_2}(tk, (x, w))$ outputs $\mathsf{Sim}_2(tk, x)$ if $(x, w) \in \mathfrak{R}$, and $\bot$ otherwise.

Simulation extractability: There exists a PPT algorithm $\mathsf{Xtr} = (\mathsf{Xtr}_1, \mathsf{Xtr}_2)$ such that, for all PPT adversaries A, we have that

$$\mathbb{P}\left[\begin{array}{c} (\mathsf{crs}, tk, xk) \leftarrow \mathsf{Xtr}_1(1^k); (x, \pi) \leftarrow \mathsf{A}^{\mathsf{Sim}_2(tk, \cdot)}(\mathsf{crs}); \\ w \leftarrow \mathsf{Xtr}_2(xk, (x, \pi)); (x, w) \notin \mathfrak{R} \wedge (x, \pi) \notin \mathcal{Q} \wedge \mathsf{Ver}(\mathsf{crs}, (x, \pi)) = 1 \end{array} \right]$$

is negligible, where the list $\mathcal{Q}$ contains the successful pairs (x_i, π_i) that A has queried to Sim_2. We say that $\mathcal{NIZK}$ is *true* simulation-extractable if oracle $\mathsf{Sim}_2(tk, x)$ is replaced by $\widetilde{\mathsf{Sim}_2}(tk, (x, w))$ that outputs the same as $\mathsf{Sim}_2(tk, x)$ if and only if $(x, w) \in \mathfrak{R}$ (and outputs $\bot$ otherwise).

3   One-More Unforgeability

A signature scheme is a triple of algorithms $SS = (\mathsf{KGen}, \mathsf{Sign}, \mathsf{Verify})$ defined as follows: (1) The key generation algorithm takes as input the security parameter κ and outputs a verification key/signing key pair $(vk, sk) \leftarrow \mathsf{KGen}(1^\kappa)$; (2) The signing algorithm takes as input a message $m \in \mathcal{M}$ and the signing key sk and outputs a signature $\sigma \leftarrow \mathsf{Sign}(sk, m)$; (3) The verification algorithm takes as input the verification key vk and a pair (m, σ) and outputs $\mathsf{Verify}(vk, (m, \sigma)) \in \{0, 1\}$. We denote by $|\sigma|$ the size of a signature output via $\mathsf{Sign}(sk, \cdot)$.

Given a signature scheme SS, consider the following experiment $\mathsf{Exp}_{SS,A}^{one-more}(\kappa, \ell, \gamma)$ running with a PPT adversary A and parametrized by the security parameter $\kappa \in \mathbb{N}$, the leakage bound $\ell \in \mathbb{N}$ and the slack parameter $\gamma \in (0, 1]$:

1. Compute $(vk, sk) \leftarrow \mathsf{KGen}(1^\kappa)$ and give vk to A.
2. The adversary A can adaptively access oracles $\mathsf{Sign}(sk, \cdot)$ and $\mathcal{O}^\ell(sk, \cdot)$, where $\mathcal{O}^\ell(sk, f)$ returns $f(sk)$. We let $\Lambda \in \{0, 1\}^\lambda$ be the total information returned by $\mathcal{O}^\ell$ (with $\lambda \le \ell$), and we write $\mathcal{Q}$ for the set of messages A forwarded to the signing oracle.
3. A outputs n pairs $(m_1, \sigma_1), \ldots, (m_n, \sigma_n)$.
4. The experiment outputs 1 iff if the following conditions are satisfied:
    (a) $\mathsf{Verify}(vk, (m_i, \sigma_i)) = 1$ and $m_i \notin \mathcal{Q}$, for all $i \in [n]$.
    (b) The messages $m_1, \ldots, m_n$ are pairwise distinct.
    (c) $n \ge \lfloor \lambda/(\gamma|\sigma|) \rfloor + 1$.

Definition 1 (One-more unforgeability). *We say that $SS = (\mathsf{KGen}, \mathsf{Sign}, \mathsf{Verify})$ is $(\ell, \gamma, \varepsilon)$-one-more unforgeable if for every PPT adversary A we have that $\mathbb{P}[\mathsf{Exp}_{SS,A}^{one-more}(\kappa, \ell, \gamma) = 1] \le \varepsilon$. Whenever ε is negligible in the security parameter, we simply say that SS is (ℓ, γ)-one-more unforgeable.*

Remark 1 (on γ). The parameter γ specifies how close to optimal security SS is. In particular, in case $\gamma = 1$ one-more unforgeability requires that A cannot forge even a single signature more than what it could have leaked via leakage queries. As γ decreases, so does the strength of the signature scheme (the extreme case being $\gamma = |\mathcal{M}|^{-1}$, where we have no security).

Note that the number of signatures the adversary has to forge depends on the length of the leakage he asks to see. In particular (ℓ, γ)-one-more unforgeability implies standard unforgeability for any adversary asking no leakage ($\lambda = 0$).

Finally, we remark that for any $\gamma \in (0, 1]$ we have that (ℓ, γ)-one-more unforgeability implies (ℓ', γ)-one-more unforgeability for all $\ell' \le \ell$.

3.1   An Alternative Definition

Definition 1 may seem a weak security guarantee for a signature scheme, as an adversary is able to forge a certain number of signatures. If the messages to forge could be chosen at will at any time, this would be a rather useless security guarantee. Here, we state a seemingly stronger flavour of one-more unforgeability where a simulator can look at the state of the adversary after he is done with leakage queries and output a set $\mathcal{Q}^* \subset \mathcal{M}$, of size less than n, thought of as the messages corresponding to the forgeries leaked so far; now the adversary is successful if he can produce a forgery for a message of his choice not contained in $\mathcal{Q}^*$ (and not already asked to the signing oracle). In a certain sense, we get a notion that is similar to the standard unforgeability notion, with the twist that the adversary can ask a few extra signing queries (via leakage queries, though).

Given a signature scheme $\mathcal{SS}$, consider the experiment $\mathsf{Exp}_{\mathcal{SS},\mathsf{A},\mathsf{S}}^{\mathrm{poly-sim-one-more}}(\kappa, \ell, \gamma)$ below, running with a PPT adversary $\mathsf{A} = (\mathsf{A}_1, \mathsf{A}_2)$ and a PPT simulator S and parametrized by the security parameter $\kappa \in \mathbb{N}$, the leakage bound $\ell \in \mathbb{N}$ and the slack parameter $\gamma \in (0, 1]$:

1. Compute $(vk, sk) \leftarrow \mathsf{KGen}(1^\kappa)$ and give vk to A.
2. The adversary A_1 can adaptively access oracles $\mathsf{Sign}(sk, \cdot)$ and $\mathcal{O}^\ell(sk, \cdot)$, where $\mathcal{O}^\ell(sk, f)$ returns $f(sk)$. We let $\Lambda \in \{0,1\}^\lambda$ be the total information returned by $\mathcal{O}^\ell$ (with $\lambda \leq \ell$), and we write $\mathcal{Q}$ for the set of messages A_1 forwarded to the signing oracle.
3. Let st be the state of A_1 at the end of step 2 above, i.e., all his inputs, all his random choices, and all replies from the oracles. The simulator is given st and outputs $\mathcal{Q}^* \leftarrow \mathsf{S}(1^\kappa, vk, st)$ such that $\mathcal{Q}^* \subset \mathcal{M}$ and $|\mathcal{Q}^*| \leq \lfloor \lambda/(\gamma|\sigma|) \rfloor$.
4. A_2 is given $\mathcal{Q}^*$ and st and outputs a forgery (m^*, σ^*).
5. The experiment outputs 1 iff $\mathsf{Verify}(vk, (m^*, \sigma^*)) = 1$ and $m^* \notin \mathcal{Q} \cup \mathcal{Q}^*$.

Definition 2 (Poly-constrained one-more unforgeability). *We say that* $\mathcal{SS} = (\mathsf{KGen}, \mathsf{Sign}, \mathsf{Verify})$ *is* $(\ell, \gamma, \varepsilon)$*-poly-constrained one-more unforgeable if for every PPT adversary* A *there exists a PPT simulator* S *such that*

$$\mathbb{P}[\mathsf{Exp}_{\mathcal{SS},\mathsf{A},\mathsf{S}}^{\mathrm{poly-sim-one-more}}(\kappa, \ell, \gamma) = 1] \leq \varepsilon.$$

Whenever ε *is negligible in the security parameter, we simply say that* $\mathcal{SS}$ *is* (ℓ, γ)*-poly-constrained one-more unforgeable.*

3.2   Yet another Alternative Definition

Definition 2 requires that $\mathcal{Q}^*$ can be computed in poly-time, effectively requiring that the adversary *knows* the small set of forgeries he leaked. In most applications we are aware of, it seems, however, enough that such a small set *exists*. And, there seems to be a difference between these notions. Consider an adversary who leaks a few values of the form $v_i = H(m_i) \oplus \sigma_i$, where H is a hash function, for random messages m_i (with $i \in [n]$) and σ_i a signature on m_i. Given any m_i as input it can compute a "forgery" $\sigma_i = v_i \oplus H(m_i)$, but until it is given m_i it does not know the set of messages it can forge signatures on, at least it would be hard to compute this set efficiently in a black-box manner. We formulate a security notion which still considers leakage of a few such "unknown" σ_i as benign.

We simply restate Definition 2, but we now allow S unbounded computing time. We can massage this relaxed definition a bit to get a simpler, equivalent definition. Consider the following generic simulator $\mathsf{S}_{\min}(1^\kappa, vk, st)$: it iterates over all $Q^* \subset \mathcal{M}$ with $|Q^*| \leq \lfloor \lambda/(\gamma|\sigma|) \rfloor$ and computes the probability p_{Q^*} that $A_2(Q^*, st)$ outputs (m^*, σ^*) such that $\mathsf{Verify}(vk, (m^*, \sigma^*)) = 1$ and $m^* \notin Q \cup Q^*$. It then outputs the Q^* minimizing p_{Q^*}. It is clear that if for some adversary A there exists an unbounded simulator S fulfilling Definition 2 for A, then also S_{min} will fulfil Definition 2 for A. Hence we can equivalently hardwire S_{min} into the definition. If we at the same time use that the expected value of a random value over $\{0, 1\}$ is equal to the probability that it is 1, we get the below more compact definition. Consider the following experiment $\mathsf{Exp}_{SS,A}^{sim-one-more}(\kappa, \ell, \gamma)$:

1. Compute $(vk, sk) \leftarrow \mathsf{KGen}(1^\kappa)$ and give vk to A_1.
2. The adversary A_1 can adaptively access oracles $\mathsf{Sign}(sk, \cdot)$ and $\mathcal{O}^\ell(sk, \cdot)$, where $\mathcal{O}^\ell(sk, f)$ returns $f(sk)$. We let $\Lambda \in \{0, 1\}^\lambda$ be the total information returned by $\mathcal{O}^\ell$ (with $\lambda \leq \ell$), and we write Q for the set of messages A_1 forwarded to the signing oracle.
3. Let st be the state of A_1 at the end of step 2 above.
4. Output

$$\min_{\substack{Q^* \subset \mathcal{M}: \\ |Q^*| \leq \lfloor \lambda/(\gamma|\sigma|) \rfloor}} (\mathbb{P}[(m^*, \sigma^*) \leftarrow A_2(Q^*, st) : \mathsf{Verify}(vk, (m^*, \sigma^*)) \wedge m^* \notin Q \cup Q^*]).$$

Definition 3 (Constrained one-more unforgeability). *We say that $SS =$ $(\mathsf{KGen}, \mathsf{Sign}, \mathsf{Verify})$ is $(\ell, \gamma, \varepsilon)$-constrained one-more unforgeable if it holds that $\mathbb{E}[\mathsf{Exp}_{SS,A}^{sim-one-more}(\kappa, \ell, \gamma)] \leq \varepsilon$ for every PPT adversary A, where the expected value is over the random choices used to generate (vk, sk) and the random choices of A_1. Whenever ε is negligible in the security parameter, we simply say that SS is (ℓ, γ)-constrained one-more unforgeable.*

3.3   Equivalence of Two Definitions

We argue below that one more unforgeability and constrained-one-more unforgeability are equivalent. It is clear that security under Definition 2 implies security under Definition 3. We conjecture that Definition 3 is strictly weaker than Definition 2.

Theorem 1. *Definition 1 and Definition 3 are equivalent up to a constant factor 4 in security.*

Proof. For space reasons, we prove only that Definition 1 implies Definition 3; the proof of the other direction can be found in the full version. We give a proof by contradiction. Assume there exists a polynomial ε and PPT adversary $A' = (A_1', A_2')$ such that $\mathbb{E}[\mathsf{Exp}_{SS,A'}^{sim-one-more}(\kappa, \ell, \gamma)] > \varepsilon$ for infinitely many values of κ.

Since $0 \leq \mathbb{E}[\mathsf{Exp}_{SS,A'}^{sim-one-more}(\kappa, \ell, \gamma)] \leq 1$ this implies that $\mathbb{P}[\mathsf{Exp}_{SS,A'}^{sim-one-more}(\kappa, \ell, \gamma) \geq \varepsilon/2] \geq \varepsilon/2$ for infinitely many values of κ. Let E be the event that $\mathbb{P}[\mathsf{Exp}_{SS,A'}^{sim-one-more}(\kappa, \ell, \gamma) \geq \varepsilon/2]$.

We now describe A, running in experiment $\mathsf{Exp}_{SS,A}^{one-more}(\kappa, \ell, \gamma)$. When reading the description keep in mind that it is defined to work when E occurs.

1. Receive the verification key vk and initialize $\mathcal{Q}^* = \emptyset$.
2. Run $\mathsf{A}'_1(1^\kappa, vk)$ and simulate leakage queries and signature queries using oracles $\mathcal{O}^\ell(sk, \cdot)$ and $\mathsf{Sign}(sk, \cdot)$. Let $\Lambda \in \{0,1\}^\lambda$ be the overall information retrieved by A'_1.
3. Define $n := \lfloor \lambda/(\gamma|\sigma|) \rfloor + 1$. Repeat the following steps, for $i = 1, \ldots, n$:
    (a) Run $8(\log_2(n) + \kappa)/\varepsilon$ copies of $\mathsf{A}'_2(1^\kappa, st, \mathcal{Q}^*)$ in parallel. If any of the copies outputs (m_i^*, σ_i^*) such that $\mathsf{Verify}(vk, (m^*, \sigma^*)) = 1$ and $m^* \notin \mathcal{Q} \cup \mathcal{Q}^*$, then go to the next step, otherwise give up and terminate.
    (b) Set $\mathcal{Q}^* := \mathcal{Q}^* \cup \{m_i^*\}$ for one of the forgeries from above.
4. Output $(m_1^*, \sigma_1^*), \ldots, (m_n^*, \sigma_n^*)$.

Assume that E occurs. Then the probability that any copy $\mathsf{A}'_2(1^\kappa, st, \mathcal{Q}^*)$ in Step 1 outputs (m_i^*, σ_i^*) such that $\mathsf{Verify}(vk, (m^*, \sigma^*)) = 1$ and $m^* \notin \mathcal{Q} \cup \mathcal{Q}^*$ is $\geq \varepsilon/2$. Hence one of the copies will output such (m_i^*, σ_i^*), except with probability $2^{-\log_2(n)-\kappa}$, by construction. Thus, by a union bound, the probability that A gives up in any of the iterations is at most $n \cdot 2^{-\log_2(n)-\kappa} = 2^{-\kappa}$.

Clearly, when A does not give up in any of the iterations, we have that $\mathsf{Exp}_{\mathcal{SS},\mathsf{A}}^{\mathrm{one-more}}(\kappa, \ell, \gamma) = 1$. Hence $\mathbb{P}[\mathsf{Exp}_{\mathcal{SS},\mathsf{A}}^{\mathrm{one-more}}(\kappa, \ell, \gamma) = 1] \geq \mathbb{P}[E](1 - 2^{-\kappa}) = \varepsilon(1 - 2^{-\kappa})/2 > \varepsilon/4$ for infinitely many values of κ. This concludes the proof as A is PPT.

4   Construction

We give a construction of a one-more unforgeable signature scheme (cf. Definition 1) based on the following building blocks:

- A non-interactive zero knowledge argument of knowledge system $\mathcal{NIZK} = (\mathsf{Init}, \mathsf{Prove}, \mathsf{Ver})$.
- A perfectly hiding and computationally binding, linearly homomorphic[5] commitment scheme $\mathcal{COM} = (\mathsf{Setup}, \mathsf{Commit})$, with message and randomness space equal to a finite field $\mathbb{F}$.

Our scheme $\mathcal{SS} = (\mathsf{KGen}, \mathsf{Sign}, \mathsf{Verify})$ has message space equal to $\mathbb{F}$ and is described below:

Key Generation. Run $pk \leftarrow \mathsf{Setup}(1^\kappa)$ and $\mathsf{crs} \leftarrow \mathsf{Init}(1^\kappa)$. For some parameter $d \in \mathbb{N}$, sample $\delta_0, \ldots, \delta_d$ and $r_0, \ldots, r_d$ uniformly from $\mathbb{F}$, and compute commitments $com_i = \mathsf{Commit}(pk, \delta_i; r_i)$ for $i = 0, \ldots, d$. Let $\boldsymbol{\delta} = (\delta_0, \ldots, \delta_d)$ and $\mathbf{r} = (r_0, \ldots, r_d)$; output $sk = (\boldsymbol{\delta}, \mathbf{r})$ and $vk = (\mathsf{crs}, pk, \{com_i\}_{i=0}^d)$.
Signature. To sign a message $m \in \mathbb{F}$, let $\delta(X)$ be the degree d polynomial having δ_i's as coefficients, i.e. $\delta(X) = \sum_{i=0}^d \delta_i \cdot X^i$. Consider the following polynomial-time relation:

$$\mathfrak{R} := \{(pk, com^*); (\tilde{m}, \tilde{r}) : com^* = \mathsf{Commit}(pk, \tilde{m}; \tilde{r})\} .$$

---

[5] For notational convenience, we assume that the product of commitments give commitments to the sum of messages using the sum of the randomness as randomness, *à la* Pedersen [32].

Compute $\tilde{m} = \delta(m)$ and $\tilde{r} = \sum_{i=0}^{d} r_i \cdot m^i$. Note that both values $\tilde{m}$, $\tilde{r}$ can be computed efficiently as a function of the signing key $(\boldsymbol{\delta}, \mathbf{r})$ and the message to be signed. Using crs as common reference string, generate a NIZK argument π that $(pk, \prod_{i=0}^{d} (com_i)^{m^i}) \in \mathfrak{L}_{\mathfrak{R}}$, the language generated by the above relation $\mathfrak{R}$. Output $\sigma = \pi$.

Verification. Given a pair (m, σ), parse σ as $\sigma = \pi$ and compute $com^* = \prod_{i=0}^{d} (com_i)^{m^i}$. Output the same as $\mathsf{Ver}(\mathsf{crs}, \pi, (pk, com^*))$.

Let us first argue that the signature scheme satisfies the correctness property. This follows from the fact that $\mathcal{COM}$ is linearly homomorphic (cf. Section 2.2):

$$com^* = \prod_{i=0}^{d} (com_i)^{m^i} = \prod_{i=0}^{d} \mathsf{Commit}(\delta_i \cdot m^i; r_i \cdot m^i) = \mathsf{Commit}\Big(\underbrace{\sum_{i=0}^{d} \delta_i \cdot m^i}_{\tilde{m}}; \underbrace{\sum_{i=0}^{d} r_i \cdot m^i}_{\tilde{r}}\Big).$$

We prove the following result:

Theorem 2. *Assume that $\mathcal{COM}$ is perfectly hiding and computationally binding, and that $\mathcal{NIZK}$ is a NIZK argument of knowledge system for relation $\mathfrak{R}$. Then the scheme $\mathcal{SS}$ described above is (ℓ, γ)-one-more unforgeable, as long as*

$$\ell = d \log |\mathbb{F}| \quad \text{and} \quad \gamma = \frac{\log |\mathbb{F}|}{|\sigma|}.$$

4.1   Proof of Theorem 2

To prove the theorem we will rely on the following property of any perfectly hiding commitment scheme $\mathcal{COM} = (\mathsf{Setup}, \mathsf{Commit})$. Define the following experiment $\mathsf{Exp}_{\mathcal{COM}, \mathsf{A}}^{\mathsf{guess}}(\kappa, \ell, d)$, featuring an unbounded adversary A:

1. Run $pk \leftarrow \mathsf{Setup}(1^\kappa)$ and sample $x_1, \ldots, x_d \in \mathcal{M}$ uniformly at random. Compute $com_i = \mathsf{Commit}(pk, x_i; r_i)$ and give $(\{com_i\}_{i=1}^{d}, pk)$ to A. Store $s = (\{x_i\}_{i=1}^{d}, \{r_i\}_{i=1}^{d})$.
2. The adversary can access adaptively oracle $\mathcal{O}^\ell(s, \cdot)$. Let $\Lambda \in \{0,1\}^\lambda$ be the overall information retrieved by A (with $\lambda \leq \ell$).
3. The adversary can open a subset of size t of $(x_1, \ldots, x_d)$: Given a set of indexes $(i_1, \ldots, i_t)$ such that each $i_j \in [d]$, the values $(\{x_{i_j}\}_{j=1}^{t}, \{r_{i_j}\}_{j=1}^{t})$ are forwarded to A.
4. The experiment returns 1 if A outputs the remaining values x_i, for all $i \in [d] \setminus \{i_1, \ldots, i_t\}$.

Lemma 2. *Let $\mathcal{COM} = (\mathsf{Setup}, \mathsf{Commit})$ be a perfectly hiding commitment scheme with message space $\mathcal{M}$. Then for every computationally unbounded adversary A we have that*

$$\mathbb{P}\Big[\mathsf{Exp}_{\mathcal{COM}, \mathsf{A}}^{\mathsf{guess}}(\kappa, \ell, d) = 1\Big] \leq \frac{2^\lambda}{|\mathcal{M}|^{d-t}}.$$

The proof of Lemma 2 appears in the full version of this paper.

We now prove Theorem 2. Let A be a PPT machine running in experiment $\mathsf{Exp}_{\mathcal{SS},A}^{\mathrm{one-more}}(\kappa, \ell, \gamma)$. We recall how the experiment is held for our scheme $\mathcal{SS}$.

1. The signing key $sk = (\boldsymbol{\delta}, \mathbf{r})$ and the verification key $vk = (pk, \{com_i\}_{i=0}^d)$ are computed. In particular, $pk \leftarrow \mathsf{Setup}(1^\kappa)$ and $\mathsf{crs} \leftarrow \mathsf{Init}(1^\kappa)$. Here, $\boldsymbol{\delta} = (\delta_0, \ldots, \delta_d) \leftarrow \mathbb{F}^{d+1}$, $com_i = \mathsf{Commit}(\delta_i; r_i)$ and $\mathbf{r} = (r_0, \ldots, r_d) \leftarrow \mathbb{F}^{d+1}$.

2. The adversary A is given vk and can access oracles $\mathsf{Sign}(sk, \cdot)$ and $\mathcal{O}^\ell(sk, \cdot)$.
   - The signing oracle $\mathsf{Sign}(sk, m)$ computes $\tilde{m} = \sum_{i=0}^d \delta_i \cdot m^i$ and $\tilde{r} = \sum_{i=0}^d r_i \cdot m^i$, together with an argument π that $(pk, com^*) \in \mathcal{L}_{\mathfrak{R}}$ for $com^* = \mathsf{Commit}(\tilde{m}; \tilde{r})$; hence, it returns $\sigma = \pi$.
   - The leakage oracle $\mathcal{O}^\ell(sk, f)$ returns $f(sk)$.

3. A outputs n pairs $(m_1, \pi_1), \ldots, (m_n, \pi_n)$.

4. The experiment outputs 1 iff the following conditions are satisfied:
   (a) $\mathsf{Verify}(vk, (m_i, \sigma_i)) = 1$ and $m_i \notin \mathcal{Q}$, for all $i \in [n]$.
   (b) The messages $m_1, \ldots, m_n$ are pairwise distinct.
   (c) $n \geq \lfloor \lambda/(\gamma|\sigma|) \rfloor + 1$.

The proof proceeds by a series of games.

Game$_0$. This is the real experiment, as described above.

Game$_1$. This game is identical to Game$_0$, but we replace the Init algorithm with $(\mathsf{crs}, tk) \leftarrow \mathsf{Sim}_1(1^\kappa)$. Moreover, each time a signing query for message m is asked, we simulate the argument by running $\pi \leftarrow \mathsf{Sim}_2(tk, (pk, com^*))$. Everything else remains the same.

By a standard argument, the multi-theorem zero-knowledge property of the argument system implies that $\mathbb{P}[\text{A wins Game}_0]$ is negligibly close to $\mathbb{P}[\text{A wins Game}_1]$.

Game$_2$. This game is identical to Game$_1$, but the common reference string is sampled as $(\mathsf{crs}, tk, xk) \leftarrow \mathsf{Xtr}_1(1^\kappa)$ and before outputting 1 we check that all arguments contained in A's forgeries can be extracted via $\mathsf{Xtr}_2(xk, \cdot)$.

By a standard argument, (true) simulation extractability of $\mathcal{NIZK}$ implies that $\mathbb{P}[\text{A wins Game}_1]$ is negligibly close to $\mathbb{P}[\text{A wins Game}_2]$.

Now, we show that $\mathbb{P}[\text{A wins Game}_2]$ is negligible which proves the theorem. Define the following event Bad in Game$_2$: The event occurs whenever for at least one of the forgeries (m_j, σ_j) returned by A it holds that $\tilde{m}'_j \neq \sum_{i=0}^d \delta_i \cdot m_j^i$ for $(\tilde{m}'_j, \tilde{r}'_j) \leftarrow \mathsf{Xtr}_2(xk, \pi_j)$. In other words, there exists a valid pair (m_j, σ_j) for which the extracted value $\tilde{m}'_j$ is not the evaluation of m_j through the polynomial $\delta(X)$ having $\boldsymbol{\delta}$ as coefficients. We write

$$\mathbb{P}[\text{A wins Game}_2] \leq \mathbb{P}[\text{A wins Game}_2 \wedge Bad] + \mathbb{P}[\text{A wins Game}_2 \wedge \overline{Bad}]$$
$$\leq negl(\kappa),$$

where the last inequality comes from the two claims below.

Claim. $\mathbb{P}[\text{A wins Game}_2 \wedge \overline{Bad}] \leq 2^\lambda/|\mathbb{F}|^n$.

Proof. By contradiction, assume that $\mathbb{P}\left[\mathsf{A} \text{ wins } \mathsf{Game}_2 \wedge \overline{Bad}\right] > 2^\lambda/|\mathbb{F}|^n$. We build a PPT reduction B (running A) which wins the game of experiment $\mathsf{Exp}_{\mathcal{COM},\mathsf{B}}^{\mathsf{guess}}(\kappa, \ell, d+1)$ with at least the same advantage.

1. Given $\{com_i = \mathsf{Commit}(\delta_i; r_i)\}_{i=0}^{d}$ as input, implicitly define $sk := (\boldsymbol{\delta}, \mathbf{r})$, where

$$\boldsymbol{\delta} = (\delta_0, \delta_1, \ldots, \delta_d) \qquad \mathbf{r} = (r_0, r_1, \ldots, r_d).$$

   Run $(\mathsf{crs}, tk, xk) \leftarrow \mathsf{Xtr}_1(1^\kappa)$ and give $vk := (\mathsf{crs}, pk, \{com_i\}_{i=0}^{d})$ to A.
2. Whenever A asks a leakage query f to $\mathcal{O}^\ell((\boldsymbol{\delta}, \mathbf{r}), \cdot)$, forward the same query to $\mathcal{O}^\ell(s, \cdot)$ (where $s = (\boldsymbol{\delta}, \mathbf{r})$). Give to A the same value returned by $\mathcal{O}^\ell(s)$.
3. Whenever A asks a signing query m to $\mathsf{Sign}(sk, \cdot)$, answer as follows. Simulate an argument $\pi \leftarrow \mathsf{Sim}(tk, (pk, com^*))$ where $com^* = \prod_{i=0}^{d}(com_i)^{m^i}$. Give $\sigma = \pi$ to A.
4. Let $(m_1, \sigma_1), \ldots, (m_n, \sigma_n)$ be the forgeries output by A. Ask to open the last $t := d + 1 - n$ values, i.e. $(\{\delta_i\}_{i=n}^{d}, \{r_i\}_{i=n}^{d})$. Set $\tilde{\delta}_i = \delta_i$ for each $i = n, \ldots, d$.
5. For each of the values $\sigma_i = \pi_i$ returned by A compute $(\tilde{m}'_i, \tilde{r}'_i) \leftarrow \mathsf{Xtr}_2(xk, \pi_i)$. Solve the following linear system:

$$\begin{pmatrix} 1 & m_1 & \ldots & m_1^{n-1} \\ & & \ddots & \\ 1 & m_n & \ldots & m_n^{n-1} \end{pmatrix} \cdot \begin{pmatrix} \delta_0 \\ \vdots \\ \delta_{n-1} \end{pmatrix} = \begin{pmatrix} y_0 \\ \vdots \\ y_{n-1} \end{pmatrix}, \tag{1}$$

   where each of the values y_i is computed from known values as $y_i = \tilde{m}'_i - \sum_{j=n}^{d} \tilde{\delta}_j \cdot m_i^j$.
6. Output $(\delta_1, \ldots, \delta_n)$.

Note that B perfectly simulates the environment for A in Game_2. The choice of the parameters $\gamma = \log|\mathbb{F}|/|\sigma|$ and $\ell = d\log|\mathbb{F}|$ (as in the theorem statement), ensures that $1 \leq n \leq d + 1$. In particular, the total number of field elements known by B is at most $\frac{\lambda}{\log|\mathbb{F}|} + \left(d - \left\lfloor\frac{\lambda}{\gamma|\sigma|}\right\rfloor\right) < d + 1$, and thus there is some entropy left in the commitments.

Moreover, as the values $(m_1, \ldots, m_n)$ are pairwise distinct, the matrix of Eq. (1) has full rank and the linear system always admits a solution. Since the event Bad does not happen, we have that $\tilde{m}'_i = \tilde{m}_i = \delta(m_i)$ (for all $i \in [n]$), and thus the solution $(\delta_1, \ldots, \delta_n)$ corresponds to the same elements in the vector $\boldsymbol{\delta}$. The above contradicts Lemma 2, as

$$\mathbb{P}\left[\mathsf{Exp}_{\mathcal{COM},\mathsf{B}}^{\mathsf{guess}}(\kappa, \ell, d+1) = 1\right] \geq \mathbb{P}\left[\mathsf{A} \text{ wins } \mathsf{Game}_2 \wedge \overline{Bad}\right] > \frac{2^\lambda}{|\mathbb{F}|^n}.$$

Claim. $\mathbb{P}\left[\mathsf{A} \text{ wins } \mathsf{Game}_2 \wedge Bad\right] \leq negl(\kappa)$.

Proof. Assume that $\mathbb{P}\left[\mathsf{A} \text{ wins } \mathsf{Game}_2 \wedge Bad\right] > 1/poly(\kappa)$ for infinitely many κ. We build an attacker C breaking the binding property of the commitment scheme $\mathcal{COM}$ with non-negligible advantage. A description of C follows:

1. Receive the public parameter pk for $\mathcal{COM}$. Choose $\delta_0, \ldots, \delta_d \leftarrow \mathbb{F}$ and compute commitments $com_i = \mathsf{Commit}(pk, \delta_i; r_i)$ for randomly chosen r_0, $\ldots, r_d \leftarrow \mathbb{F}$. Generate $(\mathsf{crs}, tk, xk) \leftarrow \mathsf{Xtr}_1(1^\kappa)$.
2. Run A with input $vk := (\mathsf{crs}, pk, \{com_i\}_{i=0}^d)$ and answer signing/leakage queries from A as it would be done in Game_2.
3. When A outputs $(m_1, \pi_1), \ldots, (m_n, \pi_n)$, extract the witness $(\tilde{m}_i', \tilde{r}_i')$ from each argument of knowledge π_i, for $i \in [n]$.
4. If there exists an index $j \in [n]$ such that $\tilde{m}_j' \neq \delta(m_j)$, compute $com_j^* = \prod_{i=0}^d (com_i)^{m_j^i}$, $\tilde{m}_j = \sum_{i=0}^d \delta_i \cdot m_j^i$ and $\tilde{r}_j = \sum_{i=0}^d r_i \cdot m_j^i$ and output $(com_j^*, (\tilde{m}_j, \tilde{r}_j), (\tilde{m}_j', \tilde{r}_j'))$; otherwise abort and output $\perp$.

Notice that if Game_2 outputs 1 and event Bad occurs, then C outputs a valid pair breaking the binding property of $\mathcal{COM}$ with non-negligible probability (a contradiction). This is because both $(\tilde{m}_j, \tilde{r}_j)$ and $(\tilde{m}_j', \tilde{r}_j')$ are valid openings for com_j^* and moreover Bad implies that $(\tilde{m}_j, \tilde{r}_j) \neq (\tilde{m}_j', \tilde{r}_j')$.

4.2 A Concrete Instantiation

In this section we show how to instantiate our signature scheme, reducing security to the DLIN assumption [5]. For each of the building blocks we present an instantiation and concrete parameters.

In the following let $\mathbb{G}$ be a cyclic group of order a prime number q. Before introducing our concrete construction, let us recall the DLIN assumption:

Definition 4. *The* DLIN *assumption states that for any PPT algorithm* A *it holds that*

$$\left| \mathbb{P}\left[\mathsf{A}(\mathbb{G}, (g, g_1, g_2, g_1^a, g_2^b, g^c)) = 1 \right] - \mathbb{P}\left[\mathsf{A}(\mathbb{G}, (g, g_1, g_2, g_1^a, g_2^b, g^{a+b})) = 1 \right] \right| \leq negl(\kappa),$$

where $g, g_1, g_2 \leftarrow \mathbb{G}$ *and* $a, b, c \leftarrow \mathbb{F}_q$.

$\mathcal{COM}$: We use Pedersen commitments. The setup algorithm Setup outputs public parameters $pk = (h_1, h_2)$, where h_1 is a generator for $\mathbb{G}$ and $h_2 = h_1^a$ for a random $a \in \mathbb{F}_q$. The commitment to an element $m \in \mathbb{F}_q$ using randomness $r \leftarrow \mathbb{F}_q$ is computed as $com = \mathsf{Commit}(pk, m; r) := h_1^m \cdot h_2^r$. Whenever we want to open the commitment, we reveal (m, r).

Note that Pedersen commitment is linearly homomorphic: given $com_1 = \mathsf{Commit}(m_1; r_1)$ and $com_2 = \mathsf{Commit}(m_2; r_2)$ it holds that

$$com_1 \cdot com_2 = h_1^{m_1+m_2} \cdot h_2^{r_1+r_2} = \mathsf{Commit}(m_1 + m_2; r_1 + r_2).$$

Moreover, for all constants $c \in \mathbb{F}_q$ we have that $com^c = h_1^{c \cdot m} \cdot h_2^{c \cdot r} = \mathsf{Commit}(c \cdot m; c \cdot r)$.

$\mathcal{NIZK}$: Recall that our relation is as follows:

$$\mathfrak{R} = \{(pk, com^*); (\tilde{m}, \tilde{r}) : com^* = \mathsf{Commit}(pk, \tilde{m}; \tilde{r})\}.$$

When using Pedersen commitment, we get

$$com^* = \prod_{i=0}^{d}(com_i)^{m^i} = \prod_{i=0}^{d}\left(h_1^{\delta_i+ar_i}\right)^{m^i} = h_1^{\sum_{i=0}^{d}\delta_i m^i + ar_i m^i} = h_1^{\tilde{m}+a\cdot\tilde{r}}.$$

Thus, we can reduce the proof of knowledge of an opening for com^* to the proof of knowledge of a discrete logarithm. Groth [18] gives a simulation-extractable NIZK for proving knowledge of discrete logarithms of a group element. We remark that the length of a proof is constant, and in particular independent of the degree d of the polynomial.

Alternatively, as true simulation-extractability is sufficient for our construction, one could instantiate the NIZK using the transformation of [10], which requires a standard (non-simulation-extractable) NIZK and a labeled CCA-secure encryption scheme.

5   Application to Leaky Identification

We show how to apply one-more unforgeability to the context of (leaky) identification protocols. In a public key identification scheme a prover with public key vk attempts to prove its identity to a verifier holding vk. More formally, an identification scheme $\mathcal{ID} = (\mathsf{PGen}, \mathsf{KGen}, \mathsf{P}, \mathsf{V})$ consists of four PPT algorithms described as follows: (1) The parameters generation algorithm takes as input the security parameter and outputs public parameters $\mathsf{params} \leftarrow \mathsf{PGen}(1^\kappa)$, shared by all users.[6] (2) The key generation algorithm takes as input the security parameter and outputs a verification key/secret key pair $(vk, sk) \leftarrow \mathsf{KGen}(1^\kappa)$. (3) P and V are probabilistic Turing machines interacting in a protocol $(\mathsf{P}(sk) \rightleftarrows \mathsf{V})(vk)$; at the end of the execution V outputs a judgment $d \in \{0,1\}$, where $d = 1$ means that the identification was successful.

Following [1], we define a leaky variant of the standard notion of active security (dubbed active ℓ-security under pre-impersonation attacks with leakage), where an adversary, in a first stage, is given black-box access to the honest prover, and in a second stage is given one shot to convince the verifier. In the leaky case, during the first phase, the adversary can also access adaptively a leakage oracle $\mathcal{O}^\ell(sk)$.

We then show that the below standard way (see [2]) of constructing an identification scheme $\mathcal{ID}$ from a signature scheme $\mathcal{SS} = (\mathsf{KGen}', \mathsf{Sign}, \mathsf{Verify})$, achieves active ℓ-security under pre-impersonation attacks with leakage provided that $\mathcal{SS}$ is one-more unforgeable.

- *Parameters generation.* Algorithm PGen samples the public parameters params for the signature schemes (if any).
- *Key Generation.* Algorithm KGen runs the key generation algorithm of the signature scheme, obtaining $(vk, sk) \leftarrow \mathsf{KGen}'(1^\kappa)$.
- *Identification protocol.* The interaction is as follows: (a) The verifier sends a random $m^* \leftarrow \mathcal{M}$ to the prover; (b) The prover replies with $\sigma^* \leftarrow \mathsf{Sign}(sk, m^*)$; (c) The verifier outputs $\mathsf{Verify}(vk, (m^*, \sigma^*))$.

---

[6] In what follows all algorithms take as input params, but we omit to explicitly write this for ease of notation.

Theorem 3. *Assume that SS is (ℓ, γ)-constrained-one-more unforgeable. Then ID from above is actively ℓ-secure under pre-impersonation attacks with leakage.*

For space reasons, a formal definition and a proof of the above theorem are deferred to the full version of this paper.

References

1. Alwen, J., Dodis, Y., Wichs, D.: Leakage-resilient public-key cryptography in the bounded-retrieval model. In: Halevi, S. (ed.) CRYPTO 2009. LNCS, vol. 5677, pp. 36–54. Springer, Heidelberg (2009)
2. Bellare, M., Fischlin, M., Goldwasser, S., Micali, S.: Identification protocols secure against reset attacks. In: Pfitzmann, B. (ed.) EUROCRYPT 2001. LNCS, vol. 2045, pp. 495–511. Springer, Heidelberg (2001)
3. Bellare, M., Rogaway, P.: Random oracles are practical: A paradigm for designing efficient protocols. In: ACM Conference on Computer and Communications Security, pp. 62–73 (1993)
4. Bitansky, N., Canetti, R., Halevi, S.: Leakage-tolerant interactive protocols. In: Cramer, R. (ed.) TCC 2012. LNCS, vol. 7194, pp. 266–284. Springer, Heidelberg (2012)
5. Boneh, D., Boyen, X., Shacham, H.: Short Group Signatures. In: Franklin, M. (ed.) CRYPTO 2004. LNCS, vol. 3152, pp. 41–55. Springer, Heidelberg (2004)
6. Boyle, E., Segev, G., Wichs, D.: Fully leakage-resilient signatures. In: Paterson, K.G. (ed.) EUROCRYPT 2011. LNCS, vol. 6632, pp. 89–108. Springer, Heidelberg (2011)
7. Brakerski, Z., Kalai, Y.T., Katz, J., Vaikuntanathan, V.: Overcoming the hole in the bucket: Public-key cryptography resilient to continual memory leakage. In: FOCS, pp. 501–510 (2010)
8. Davì, F., Dziembowski, S., Venturi, D.: Leakage-resilient storage. In: Garay, J.A., De Prisco, R. (eds.) SCN 2010. LNCS, vol. 6280, pp. 121–137. Springer, Heidelberg (2010)
9. Dodis, Y., Haralambiev, K., López-Alt, A., Wichs, D.: Cryptography against continuous memory attacks. In: FOCS, pp. 511–520 (2010)
10. Dodis, Y., Haralambiev, K., López-Alt, A., Wichs, D.: Efficient public-key cryptography in the presence of key leakage. In: Abe, M. (ed.) ASIACRYPT 2010. LNCS, vol. 6477, pp. 613–631. Springer, Heidelberg (2010)
11. Dodis, Y., Lewko, A.B., Waters, B., Wichs, D.: Storing secrets on continually leaky devices. In: FOCS, pp. 688–697 (2011)
12. Dodis, Y., Ostrovsky, R., Reyzin, L., Smith, A.: Fuzzy extractors: How to generate strong keys from biometrics and other noisy data. SIAM J. Comput. 38(1), 97–139 (2008)
13. Dziembowski, S., Pietrzak, K.: Leakage-resilient cryptography. In: FOCS, pp. 293–302 (2008)
14. Faust, S., Kiltz, E., Pietrzak, K., Rothblum, G.N.: Leakage-resilient signatures. In: Micciancio, D. (ed.) TCC 2010. LNCS, vol. 5978, pp. 343–360. Springer, Heidelberg (2010)
15. Faust, S., Kohlweiss, M., Marson, G.A., Venturi, D.: On the non-malleability of the Fiat-Shamir transform. In: Galbraith, S., Nandi, M. (eds.) INDOCRYPT 2012. LNCS, vol. 7668, pp. 60–79. Springer, Heidelberg (2012)
16. Fiat, A., Shamir, A.: How to prove yourself: Practical solutions to identification and signature problems. In: Odlyzko, A.M. (ed.) CRYPTO 1986. LNCS, vol. 263, pp. 186–194. Springer, Heidelberg (1987)

17. Garg, S., Jain, A., Sahai, A.: Leakage-resilient zero knowledge. In: Rogaway, P. (ed.) CRYPTO 2011. LNCS, vol. 6841, pp. 297–315. Springer, Heidelberg (2011)
18. Groth, J.: Simulation-sound NIZK proofs for a practical language and constant size group signatures. In: Lai, X., Chen, K. (eds.) ASIACRYPT 2006. LNCS, vol. 4284, pp. 444–459. Springer, Heidelberg (2006)
19. Groth, J., Ostrovsky, R., Sahai, A.: Non-interactive zaps and new techniques for NIZK. In: Dwork, C. (ed.) CRYPTO 2006. LNCS, vol. 4117, pp. 97–111. Springer, Heidelberg (2006)
20. Groth, J., Ostrovsky, R., Sahai, A.: New techniques for noninteractive zero-knowledge. J. ACM 59(3), 11 (2012)
21. Halevi, S., Lin, H.: After-the-fact leakage in public-key encryption. In: Ishai, Y. (ed.) TCC 2011. LNCS, vol. 6597, pp. 107–124. Springer, Heidelberg (2011)
22. Hofheinz, D., Jager, T., Kiltz, E.: Short signatures from weaker assumptions. In: Lee, D.H., Wang, X. (eds.) ASIACRYPT 2011. LNCS, vol. 7073, pp. 647–666. Springer, Heidelberg (2011)
23. Juels, A., Weis, S.A.: Authenticating pervasive devices with human protocols. In: Shoup, V. (ed.) CRYPTO 2005. LNCS, vol. 3621, pp. 293–308. Springer, Heidelberg (2005)
24. Katz, J., Vaikuntanathan, V.: Signature schemes with bounded leakage resilience. In: Matsui, M. (ed.) ASIACRYPT 2009. LNCS, vol. 5912, pp. 703–720. Springer, Heidelberg (2009)
25. Kiltz, E., Pietrzak, K., Cash, D., Jain, A., Venturi, D.: Efficient authentication from hard learning problems. In: Paterson, K.G. (ed.) EUROCRYPT 2011. LNCS, vol. 6632, pp. 7–26. Springer, Heidelberg (2011)
26. Kiltz, E., Pietrzak, K., Szegedy, M.: Digital signatures with minimal overhead from indifferentiable random invertible functions. In: Canetti, R., Garay, J.A. (eds.) CRYPTO 2013, Part I. LNCS, vol. 8042, pp. 571–588. Springer, Heidelberg (2013)
27. Kocher, P.C.: Timing attacks on implementations of diffie-hellman, RSA, DSS, and other systems. In: Koblitz, N. (ed.) CRYPTO 1996. LNCS, vol. 1109, pp. 104–113. Springer, Heidelberg (1996)
28. Kocher, P.C., Jaffe, J., Jun, B.: Differential power analysis. In: Wiener, M. (ed.) CRYPTO 1999. LNCS, vol. 1666, pp. 388–397. Springer, Heidelberg (1999)
29. Malkin, T., Teranishi, I., Vahlis, Y., Yung, M.: Signatures resilient to continual leakage on memory and computation. In: Ishai, Y. (ed.) TCC 2011. LNCS, vol. 6597, pp. 89–106. Springer, Heidelberg (2011)
30. Naor, M., Segev, G.: Public-key cryptosystems resilient to key leakage. IACR Cryptology ePrint Archive, 105 (2009)
31. Nielsen, J.B., Venturi, D., Zottarel, A.: On the connection between leakage tolerance and adaptive security. In: Kurosawa, K., Hanaoka, G. (eds.) PKC 2013. LNCS, vol. 7778, pp. 497–515. Springer, Heidelberg (2013)
32. Pedersen, T.P.: Non-interactive and information-theoretic secure verifiable secret sharing. In: Feigenbaum, J. (ed.) CRYPTO 1991. LNCS, vol. 576, pp. 129–140. Springer, Heidelberg (1992)
33. Pietrzak, K.: A leakage-resilient mode of operation. In: Joux, A. (ed.) EUROCRYPT 2009. LNCS, vol. 5479, pp. 462–482. Springer, Heidelberg (2009)
34. Pointcheval, D., Stern, J.: Security arguments for digital signatures and blind signatures. J. Cryptology 13(3), 361–396 (2000)
35. Quisquater, J.-J., Samyde, D.: ElectroMagnetic analysis (EMA): Measures and counter-measures for smart cards. In: Attali, S., Jensen, T. (eds.) E-smart 2001. LNCS, vol. 2140, pp. 200–210. Springer, Heidelberg (2001)
36. De Santis, A., Di Crescenzo, G., Ostrovsky, R., Persiano, G., Sahai, A.: Robust non-interactive zero knowledge. In: Kilian, J. (ed.) CRYPTO 2001. LNCS, vol. 2139, pp. 566–598. Springer, Heidelberg (2001)

On the Lossiness of the Rabin Trapdoor Function

Yannick Seurin

ANSSI, Paris, France
yannick.seurin@m4x.org

Abstract. Lossy trapdoor functions, introduced by Peikert and Waters (STOC '08), are functions that can be generated in two indistinguishable ways: either the function is injective, and there is a trapdoor to invert it, or the function is lossy, meaning that the size of its range is strictly smaller than the size of its domain. Kakvi and Kiltz (EUROCRYPT 2012) proved that the Full Domain Hash signature scheme based on a lossy trapdoor function has a *tight* security reduction from the lossiness of the trapdoor function. Since Kiltz, O'Neill, and Smith (CRYPTO 2010) showed that the RSA trapdoor function is lossy under the Φ-Hiding assumption of Cachin, Micali, and Stadler (EUROCRYPT '99), this implies that the RSA Full Domain Hash signature scheme has a *tight* security reduction from the Φ-Hiding assumption (for public exponents $e < N^{1/4}$). In this work, we consider the Rabin trapdoor function, *i.e.* modular squaring over $\mathbb{Z}_N^*$. We show that when adequately restricting its domain (either to the set $\mathbb{QR}_N$ of quadratic residues, or to $(\mathbb{J}_N)^+$, the set of positive integers $1 \leq x \leq (N-1)/2$ with Jacobi symbol $+1$) the Rabin trapdoor function is lossy, the injective mode corresponding to Blum integers $N = pq$ with $p, q \equiv 3 \bmod 4$, and the lossy mode corresponding to what we call pseudo-Blum integers $N = pq$ with $p, q \equiv 1 \bmod 4$. This lossiness result holds under a natural extension of the Φ-Hiding assumption to the case $e = 2$ that we call the 2-$\Phi/4$-Hiding assumption. We then use this result to prove that deterministic variants of Rabin-Williams Full Domain Hash signatures have a tight reduction from the 2-$\Phi/4$-Hiding assumption. We also show that these schemes are unlikely to have a tight reduction from the factorization problem by extending a previous "meta-reduction" result by Coron (EUROCRYPT 2002), later corrected by Kakvi and Kiltz (EUROCRYPT 2012). These two results therefore answer one of the main questions left open by Bernstein (EUROCRYPT 2008) in his work on Rabin-Williams signatures.

1 Introduction

1.1 Background

Lossy Trapdoor Functions. Lossy Trapdoor Functions (LTF) were introduced by Peikert and Waters [28] and have since then found a wide range of applications in cryptography such as deterministic public-key encryption [8], hedged public-key encryption [2], and security against selective opening attacks [3, 14]

H. Krawczyk (Ed.): PKC 2014, LNCS 8383, pp. 380–398, 2014.

to name a few. Informally, an LTF consists of two families of functions: functions in the first family are injective (and efficiently invertible using some trapdoor), while functions in the second family are non-injective and hence lose information on their input. The key requirement for an LTF is that functions sampled from the first and the second family be computationally indistinguishable. Many constructions of LTF are known from various hardness assumptions such as DDH, LWE, etc. [28]. In particular, Kiltz, O'Neill, and Smith showed [24] that the RSA trapdoor function $f : x \mapsto x^e \bmod N$, where $N = pq$ is an RSA modulus, is lossy under the $\varPhi$-Hiding assumption, introduced by Cachin, Micali, and Stadler [9]. When e is coprime with $\phi(N)$ ($\phi(\cdot)$ is Euler's totient function), f is injective on the domain $\mathbb{Z}_N^*$, while when e divides $\phi(N)$ (but e^2 does not), f is e-to-1 on $\mathbb{Z}_N^*$. The $\varPhi$-Hiding assumption states that given (N, e) where $e < N^{1/4}$, it is hard to tell whether $\gcd(e, \phi(N)) = 1$ or $e|\phi(N)$, which corresponds to respectively the injective and lossy modes of the RSA function.

Full Domain Hash Signatures. Full Domain Hash (FDH) signatures [4] are a class of signature schemes which can be based on any trapdoor function f: the signature of a message m is computed as $\sigma = f^{-1}(H(m))$, where H is some hash function (the secret signature key is the trapdoor enabling to invert f). For a long time, the only known security result for FDH signatures, due to Coron [11] (improving on a previous result [4]), had been a *non-tight* reduction from the problem of inverting the trapdoor function, losing a factor q_s (the maximal number of signature queries made by the forger). Recently, Kakvi and Kiltz [22] showed that the FDH signature scheme, when based on a trapdoor function which is lossy, has a *tight* reduction from the problem of distinguishing the injective from the lossy mode of the LTF. In particular, this applies to RSA-FDH signatures with public exponents $e < N^{1/4}$, which hence have a tight security reduction from the $\varPhi$-Hiding problem.[1] Moreover, in the same paper, Kakvi and Kiltz corrected a previous "meta-reduction" result due to Coron [12] stating that the security reduction of [11] losing a factor q_s is essentially optimal. More precisely, they showed that when the trapdoor function is *certified* (meaning that there is an efficient algorithm distinguishing injective from non-injective members of the function family), any security reduction from inverting the trapdoor function to breaking FDH signatures must lose a factor q_s (unless inverting the trapdoor function is easy). This applies in particular to RSA-FDH signatures with public exponents $e > N^{1/4}$ since RSA is certified for these parameters [23].

1.2   Contributions of This Work

Lossiness of the Rabin Trapdoor Function. We show that the Rabin trapdoor function, *i.e.* modular squaring, is lossy (with exactly one or two bits of lossiness) when adequately restricting its domain. Since any quadratic residue

---

[1] Tight security reductions are important for adequately setting security parameters, see the discussion of this point in [22].

modulo an RSA modulus $N = pq$ has exactly four square roots, it is not immediately obvious how to render this function injective. It is well known that when N is a so-called Blum integer, $i.e.$ $p, q \equiv 3 \bmod 4$, any quadratic residue has a unique square root which is also a quadratic residue, named its *principal* square root. Hence, in this case, modular squaring defines a permutation over the set of quadratic residues $\mathbb{QR}_N$. One potential problem with this definition of the injective mode is that the domain of the permutation is (presumably) not efficiently recognizable (this is exactly the Quadratic Residuosity assumption). A different way to restrict the domain of modular squaring is to consider the set $(\mathbb{J}_N)^+$ of integers $1 \le x \le (N-1)/2$ with Jacobi symbol $+1$ (which is efficiently recognizable). We show that when restricting its domain to either $\mathbb{QR}_N$ or $(\mathbb{J}_N)^+$ to make it injective, modular squaring becomes an LTF. The lossy mode corresponds to integers $N = pq$ such that $p, q \equiv 1 \bmod 4$, that we call pseudo-Blum integers. It can be shown that in that case, modular squaring becomes 4-to-1 over $\mathbb{QR}_N$ and 2-to-1 over $(\mathbb{J}_N)^+$. Indistinguishability of the injective and lossy modes is then exactly the problem of distinguishing Blum from pseudo-Blum integers, which is equivalent to tell whether 2 divides $\phi(N)/4$ or not. This can be seen as the extension of the traditional Φ-Hiding assumption to exponent $e = 2$, so that we call this problem the 2-Φ/4-Hiding problem. Details can be found in Sections 2 and 3.

Application to Rabin-Williams Signatures. We apply our finding to the security of deterministic Rabin-Williams Full Domain Hash signatures. The Rabin signature scheme [29] is one of the oldest provably secure digital signature scheme. Its security relies on the difficulty of computing modular square roots, which is equivalent to factoring integers. Given an RSA modulus $N = pq$, the general principle of Rabin signatures is to first map the message $m \in \{0,1\}^*$ to a quadratic residue h modulo N using some hash function H, and then return a square root s of h. Since only 1/4 of integers in $\mathbb{Z}_N^*$ are quadratic residues, directly using $h = H(m) \bmod N$ will fail for roughly 3 out of 4 messages. This can be coped with using a randomized padding. The simplest one, Probabilistic Full Domain Hash with ℓ-bit salts (ℓ-PFDH) [12], computes $h = H(r, m)$ for random ℓ-bit salts r, until h is a quadratic residue (r is then included in the signature for verification). A way to avoid this probabilistic method is to use a tweak, as proposed by Williams [31].[2] For any RSA modulus N, one can find four values $\alpha_1, \alpha_2, \alpha_3, \alpha_4 \in \mathbb{Z}_N^*$ such that for any $h \in \mathbb{Z}_N^*$, there is a unique $i \in [1; 4]$ such that $\alpha_i^{-1} h \bmod N$ is a quadratic residue.[3] When $p \equiv 3 \bmod 8$ and $q \equiv 7 \bmod 8$, one can use the set of values $\{1, -1, 2, -2\}$. This way, the signature becomes a so-called tweaked square root (α, s), where s is a square root of

---

[2] Williams' paper [31] was primarily concerned with public key encryption. The idea of using a tweak for deterministic signing is implicit in the ISO/IEC 9796 standard published in 1991, and was later made more explicit in a paper by Kurosawa and Ogata [25].

[3] The sufficient condition for this is that the pairs of Legendre symbols $\left(\left(\frac{\alpha_i}{p} \right), \left(\frac{\alpha_i}{q} \right) \right)$ take each of the four values $(1,1)$, $(-1,1)$, $(1,-1)$ and $(-1,-1)$ for exactly one α_i.

$\alpha^{-1}H(m)$ mod N for the correct value $\alpha \in \{1, -1, 2, -2\}$, and the verification algorithm now checks whether $\alpha s^2 = H(m)$ mod N. This enables to define FDH Rabin-Williams signatures.

Since any quadratic residue modulo an RSA modulus N has four square roots, one must also specify which (tweaked) square root of the hash to use as the signature. There are basically two ways to proceed. The first one is simply to pick a square root at random. However, when no randomization (or randomization with only a small number of bits) is used in the input to the hash function, one must be careful not to output two non-trivially distinct square roots if the same message is signed twice, since this would reveal the factorization of the modulus N. In consequence, the signature algorithm must either be stateful and store all signatures previously output (which is cumbersome), or generate the bits for deciding which root to use pseudo-randomly.[4] However, in constrained environments, implementors might be reluctant to pay the additional cost of a pseudorandom function (moreover, how exactly this derandomization is done is not always precisely discussed, and may have security implications as explained in [26]).

The second option is to define some deterministic rule telling which square root to use as the signature. The most popular way to do so is to use for N a Blum integer and to use the principal square root. A variant is to use what we call the absolute principal square root, *i.e.* $|s \bmod N|$, where s is the principal square root represented by an integer in $[-(N-1)/2; (N-1)/2]$. This turns out to also be the unique square root in $(\mathbb{J}_N)^+$. We will call these ways to choose a square root Principal Rabin-Williams (PRW) and Absolute Principal Rabin-Williams (APRW) respectively.[5] When no randomization in the input to the hash function is used, the signature algorithm then becomes entirely deterministic (without having to appeal to an auxiliary pseudorandom function), which is attractive from an implementation point of view.

Bernstein [7] proposed an extensive study of possible variants of Rabin-Williams signature schemes depending on the length of the salt and the square root selection method. In particular, for FDH signatures, he showed a tight security reduction from the factoring assumption for the probabilistic square root selection method (Fixed Unstructured). On the other hand, for PRW and APRW, only a loose reduction from factoring is known using methods of Coron [11, 7]. Our main result is a tight security reduction from the 2-Φ/4-Hiding problem for the PRW and APRW schemes, building on the results of [22]. Details can be found in Section 4.

Extending the Coron-Kakvi-Kiltz Meta-reduction Result. Recall that Coron's meta-reduction result [12] as corrected by Kakvi and Kiltz [22] states that when the trapdoor function is *certified*, any security reduction from

---

[4] This method was called Fixed Unstructured Rabin-Williams in [7], and Probabilistic Rabin-Williams (PRW) in [26].

[5] PRW was called Fixed Principal in [7] and Deterministic Rabin-Williams (DRW) in [26], while APRW was called Fixed |Principal| in [7].

inverting the trapdoor function to breaking FDH signatures must lose a factor q_s. Since this only applies for certified trapdoor functions, this leaves open the question of whether there might exist a tight reduction from inverting the trapdoor function to breaking FDH signatures when the trapdoor function is not certified. In particular, the question whether there exists a tight security reduction from factoring (or equivalently, computing modular square roots) for the PRW and APRW schemes was left as an open problem in [7]. However, we observe that the meta-reduction result still holds (namely, any security reduction from inverting the trapdoor function to breaking FDH signatures must lose a factor q_s) when the underlying trapdoor function is *gap one-way*, meaning that inverting the injective mode of the function is hard even with the help of an oracle distinguishing injective from non-injective modes of the trapdoor function. This implies in particular that if factoring with the help of an oracle solving the 2-$\Phi/4$-Hiding problem is hard, the PRW and APRW signature schemes cannot have a tight security reduction from the factorization problem. This essentially answers the open question of [7] regarding the security reductions for these schemes. Details can be found in Section 5.

1.3   Related and Future Work

Two constructions of lossy trapdoor functions based on modular squaring were previously proposed, however they are slightly more complicated than the basic Rabin trapdoor function. Mol and Yilek [27] gave a construction whose security relies on an assumption close in spirit (though more involved) to the 2-$\Phi/4$-Hiding assumption. Freeman *et al.* [16] gave a construction relying on the Quadratic Residuosity problem.

The cryptographic applications of the set $(\mathbb{J}_N)^+$ when N is a Blum integer were previously considered by Goldwasser *et al.* [19], Fischlin and Schnorr [15], and Hofheinz and Kiltz [21] (in this last paper, it was denoted $\mathbb{QR}_N^+$ and named *group of signed quadratic residues*). In particular, it was showed in [21] that under the factoring assumption, the Strong Diffie-Hellman problem [1] is hard in this group.

The Coron-Kakvi-Kiltz meta-reduction result [12, 22] was extended by Hofheinz *et al.* [20] to the case where the signature scheme is re-randomizable (rather than with unique signatures).

Kiltz *et al.* [24] showed that lossiness of RSA implies that the RSA-OAEP encryption scheme [5] meets indistinguishability under chosen-plaintext attacks in the standard model (under appropriate assumptions on the hash functions used to instantiate OAEP). An interesting question is whether lossiness of the Rabin trapdoor function can be used to argue about the security of Rabin-OAEP encryption as was done in [24] for RSA. Though from a theoretical point of view the results of [24] apply to OAEP used with any LTF, they provide some meaningful security insurance only when the amount of lossiness is sufficiently high. This requires more careful investigation in the case of Rabin-OAEP. As a first step in this direction, we note that if "multi-primes" pseudo-Blum integers $N = p_1 \cdots p_m$, with $p_1, \ldots, p_m \equiv 1 \bmod 4$ are indistinguishable from 2-primes pseudo-Blum integers, lossiness of the Rabin trapdoor function with domain $(\mathbb{J}_N)^+$ can be amplified from 1 bit to $m-1$ bits. Similar arguments were used for RSA in [24].

2 Preliminaries

2.1 General Notation

The set of integers i such that $a \leq i \leq b$ will be denoted $[a;b]$. The security parameter will be denoted k. A function f of the security parameter is said *negligible* if for any $c > 0$, $f(k) \leq 1/k^c$ for sufficiently large k. When S is a non-empty finite set, we write $s \leftarrow_\$ S$ to mean that a value is sampled uniformly at random from S and assigned to s. By $z \leftarrow \mathcal{A}^{\mathcal{O}_1, \mathcal{O}_2, \cdots}(x, y, \ldots)$ we denote the operation of running the (possibly probabilistic) algorithm $\mathcal{A}$ on inputs $x, y, \ldots$ with access to oracles $\mathcal{O}_1, \mathcal{O}_2, \ldots$ (possibly none), and letting z be the output.

2.2 Basic Definitions

Given an (odd for most of what follows) integer N, the multiplicative group of integers modulo N is denoted $\mathbb{Z}_N^*$. This group has order $\phi(N)$ where $\phi(\cdot)$ is the Euler function. We denote $\mathbb{J}_N$ the subgroup of $\mathbb{Z}_N^*$ of all elements $x \in \mathbb{Z}_N^*$ with Jacobi symbol $\left(\frac{x}{N}\right) = 1$. This subgroup has index 2 and order $\phi(N)/2$ in $\mathbb{Z}_N^*$. Moreover it is efficiently recognizable even without the factorization of N since the Jacobi symbol is efficiently computable given only N. We also denote $\bar{\mathbb{J}}_N$ the coset of elements $x \in \mathbb{Z}_N^*$ such that $\left(\frac{x}{N}\right) = -1$. Finally, we denote $\mathbb{QR}_N$ the subgroup of quadratic residues of $\mathbb{Z}_N^*$. This subgroup is widely believed not to be efficiently recognizable when N is composite and its factorization is unknown: this is the Quadratic Residuosity assumption.

We will represent elements of $\mathbb{Z}_N$ as signed integers in $[-(N-1)/2, (N-1)/2]$. Given an integer x, we denote $|x \bmod N|$ the absolute value of $x \bmod N$. For any subset $S \subset \mathbb{Z}_N$, we denote $S^+ = S \cap [1; (N-1)/2]$ and $S^- = S \cap [-(N-1)/2; -1]$. Note that $(\mathbb{J}_N)^+$, $(\mathbb{J}_N)^-$, $(\bar{\mathbb{J}}_N)^+$ and $(\bar{\mathbb{J}}_N)^-$ form a partition of $\mathbb{Z}_N^*$.

We call an integer $N = pq$ which is the product of two distinct odd primes a *Blum integer* when $p, q \equiv 3 \bmod 4$, and a *pseudo-Blum integer* when $p, q \equiv 1 \bmod 4$, and we denote

$\mathsf{Bl}(k) = \{(N, p, q) : N = pq,\ p \neq q \text{ are } \lfloor k/2 \rfloor\text{-bit primes with } p, q \equiv 3 \bmod 4\}$

$\widetilde{\mathsf{Bl}}(k) = \{(N, p, q) : N = pq,\ p \neq q \text{ are } \lfloor k/2 \rfloor\text{-bit primes with } p, q \equiv 1 \bmod 4\}$.

We call a Blum integer $N = pq$ such that moreover $p \equiv 3 \bmod 8$ and $q \equiv 7 \bmod 8$ a *Williams integer*, and a pseudo-Blum integer such that $p \equiv 5 \bmod 8$ and $q \equiv 1 \bmod 8$ a *pseudo-Williams* integer. We denote

$$\mathsf{Wi}(k) = \{(N, p, q) \in \mathsf{Bl}(k) : p \equiv 3 \bmod 8, q \equiv 7 \bmod 8\}$$

$$\widetilde{\mathsf{Wi}}(k) = \{(N, p, q) \in \widetilde{\mathsf{Bl}}(k) : p \equiv 5 \bmod 8, q \equiv 1 \bmod 8\} \ .$$

Note that:

- when N is a Blum integer, $-1 \in \mathbb{J}_N \setminus \mathbb{QR}_N$;
- when N is a pseudo-Blum integer, $-1 \in \mathbb{QR}_N$;
- when N is a Williams or a pseudo-Williams integer, $2 \in \overline{\mathbb{J}}_N$.

A quadratic residue modulo an RSA modulus $N = pq$ has four square roots, two of which are in $(\mathbb{Z}_N^*)^+$ and two of which are in $(\mathbb{Z}_N^*)^-$. The two square roots in $(\mathbb{Z}_N^*)^+$ will be called the *absolute* square roots in what follows. The following lemma will be important when proving lossiness of the Rabin trapdoor function.

Lemma 1. *Let $N = pq$ be a RSA modulus with $N \equiv 1 \bmod 4$. Let $x \in \mathbb{QR}_N$, and let s_1 and s_2 be the two absolute square roots of x (the two other square roots being $-s_1$ and $-s_2$). Then:*

- *if N is a Blum integer, exactly one s_i is in $(\mathbb{J}_N)^+$ and the other is in $(\overline{\mathbb{J}}_N)^+$; moreover if $s_i \in (\mathbb{J}_N)^+$ then either $s_i \in \mathbb{QR}_N$ or $-s_i \in \mathbb{QR}_N$;*
- *if N is a pseudo-Blum integer, then $s_1, s_2, -s_1, -s_2$ are either all in $\mathbb{QR}_N$, or all in $\mathbb{J}_N \setminus \mathbb{QR}_N$, or all in $\overline{\mathbb{J}}_N$.*

Proof. Consider $x \in \mathbb{QR}_N$. Denote $x_p = x \bmod p$ and $x_q = x \bmod q$. Let also $\pm r_p$ and $\pm r_q$ denote the two square roots of respectively x_p (mod p) and x_q (mod q). The four square roots of x modulo N are obtained by combining $\pm r_p$ and $\pm r_q$ by the Chinese Remainder Theorem, *i.e.* there are to integers c_p and c_q such that the four square roots of x are $\pm(pc_p r_q \pm qc_q r_p) \bmod N$. Assume that one of the two absolute square roots is $s_1 = (pc_p r_q + qc_q r_p) \bmod N$ (the reasoning is similar if it is $-(pc_p r_q + qc_q r_p) \bmod N$). Then the other absolute square root satisfies $s_2 = \alpha(pc_p r_q - qc_q r_p) \bmod N$, with $\alpha = \pm 1$ so that:

$$\left(\frac{s_2}{p}\right) = \left(\frac{\alpha}{p}\right)\left(\frac{-1}{p}\right)\left(\frac{s_1}{p}\right) \quad \text{and} \quad \left(\frac{s_2}{q}\right) = \left(\frac{\alpha}{q}\right)\left(\frac{s_1}{q}\right).$$

Consequently:

- when N is a Blum integer, s_1 and s_2 have opposite Jacobi symbols; moreover, assuming $s_1 \in (\mathbb{J}_N)^+$ then since -1 is a non-quadratic residue, either $s_1 \in \mathbb{QR}_N$ or $-s_1 \in \mathbb{QR}_N$;
- when N is a pseudo-Blum integer, we see that

$$\left(\frac{s_1}{p}\right) = \left(\frac{-s_1}{p}\right) = \left(\frac{s_2}{p}\right) = \left(\frac{-s_2}{p}\right)$$

$$\text{and} \quad \left(\frac{s_1}{q}\right) = \left(\frac{-s_1}{q}\right) = \left(\frac{s_2}{q}\right) = \left(\frac{-s_2}{q}\right),$$

from which the claim on the localization of the four square roots follows.

This concludes the proof. □

Hence when N is a Blum integer, the two absolute square roots can easily be distinguished through their Jacobi symbol. In the following, given a Blum integer N and $x \in \mathbb{QR}_N$, we will call the unique square root of x which is in $\mathbb{QR}_N$ the *principal* square root of x, and denote it $\mathtt{psr}(x)$. We will also call the unique square root of x which is in $(\mathbb{J}_N)^+$ the *absolute principal* square root of x, and will denote it $|\mathtt{psr}|(x)$. The notation is chosen so that $|\mathtt{psr}|(x) = |\mathtt{psr}(x) \bmod N|$.

Tweaked Square Roots. Let N be a Williams integer. Then for any $x \in \mathbb{Z}_N^*$ there is a unique $\alpha \in \{1, -1, 2, -2\}$ such that $\alpha^{-1}x \bmod N$ is a quadratic residue.[6] The four pairs $(\alpha, s_i)_{i=1,\ldots,4}$ where $(s_i)_{i=1,\ldots,4}$ are the four square roots of $\alpha^{-1}x \bmod N$ are named the *tweaked square roots* of x, and α is named the *tweak*. Hence, (α, s) with $\alpha \in \{1, -1, 2, -2\}$ is a tweaked square root of $x \in \mathbb{Z}_N^*$ iff $\alpha s^2 = x \bmod N$. By extension, the principal tweaked square root of x is the unique tweaked square root (α, s) such that $s \in \mathbb{QR}_N$, and the absolute principal tweaked square root is the unique tweaked square root (α, s) such that $s \in (\mathbb{J}_N)^+$. Overloading the notation, they will be denoted respectively $\mathtt{psr}(x)$ and $|\mathtt{psr}|(x)$.

2.3 Trapdoor Functions

We recall some formal definitions associated with trapdoor functions (we follow closely the ones of [22]). We also introduce the concept of *gap one-way trapdoor function*, which is informally a trapdoor function which is hard to invert even when given access to an oracle which tells whether a member of the family is injective or lossy.

Definition 1 (Trapdoor Function). *A trapdoor function (TDF) is a tuple of polynomial-time algorithms* $\mathtt{TDF} = (\mathtt{InjGen}, \mathtt{Eval}, \mathtt{Invert})$ *with the following properties:*

- $\mathtt{InjGen}(1^k)$: *a probabilistic algorithm which on input the security parameter* 1^k, *outputs a public description* $\mathtt{pub}$ *(with implicitly understood domain* $\mathcal{D}_{\mathtt{pub}}$*) and a trapdoor* $\mathtt{td}$;
- $\mathtt{Eval}(\mathtt{pub}, x)$: *a deterministic algorithm which on input* $\mathtt{pub}$ *and a point* $x \in \mathcal{D}_{\mathtt{pub}}$, *outputs a point* $y \in \{0,1\}^*$; *we denote* $f_{\mathtt{pub}} : x \mapsto \mathtt{Eval}(\mathtt{pub}, x)$;
- $\mathtt{Invert}(\mathtt{td}, y)$: *a deterministic algorithm which on input* $\mathtt{td}$ *and a point* $y \in \{0,1\}^*$, *outputs a point* $x \in \mathcal{D}_{\mathtt{pub}}$ *when* $y \in f_{\mathtt{pub}}(\mathcal{D}_{\mathtt{pub}})$ *(and* $\bot$ *otherwise).*

We require that for any k *and any* $(\mathtt{pub}, \mathtt{td})$ *possibly output by* $\mathtt{InjGen}(1^k)$, *the function* $f_{\mathtt{pub}} : x \mapsto \mathtt{Eval}(\mathtt{pub}, x)$ *be injective, and* $y \mapsto \mathtt{Invert}(\mathtt{td}, y)$ *be its inverse* $f_{\mathtt{pub}}^{-1}$. *We also require that* $\mathcal{D}_{\mathtt{pub}}$ *and* $f_{\mathtt{pub}}(\mathcal{D}_{\mathtt{pub}})$ *be efficiently samplable.*

Definition 2 (One-Way TDF). *A trapdoor function* $\mathtt{TDF} = (\mathtt{InjGen}, \mathtt{Eval}, \mathtt{Invert})$ *is said to be* (t, ε)-*one-way if for any adversary* $\mathcal{A}$ *running in time at most* t, *one has:*

$$\Pr\left[\mathtt{pub} \leftarrow \mathtt{InjGen}(1^k), x \leftarrow_\$ \mathcal{D}_{\mathtt{pub}}, x' \leftarrow \mathcal{A}(\mathtt{pub}, \mathtt{Eval}(\mathtt{pub}, x)) : x' = x\right] \leq \varepsilon .$$

---

[6] This follows easily from the fact that the pairs of Legendre symbols $\left(\left(\frac{\alpha}{p}\right), \left(\frac{\alpha}{q}\right)\right)$ for $\alpha = 1, -1, 2,$ and -2 are respectively $(1, 1)$, $(-1, -1)$, $(-1, 1)$ and $(1, -1)$.

Definition 3 (Certified TDF). *A trapdoor function* TDF = (InjGen, Eval, Invert) *is said to be* certified *if there exists a deterministic polynomial-time algorithm* Certify *which, on input an arbitrary string* pub *(not necessarily generated by* InjGen*) returns 1 iff the function* $x \mapsto$ Eval(pub, x) *is injective over* $\mathcal{D}_{\text{pub}}$.

Definition 4 (Lossy TDF). *A lossy trapdoor function (LTF) with absolute lossiness* ℓ *is a tuple of algorithms* LTF = (InjGen, LossyGen, Eval, Invert) *such that* (InjGen, Eval, Invert) *is a TDF as per Definition 1, and moreover* LossyGen *is a probabilistic algorithm which on input* 1^k, *outputs a public description* pub$'$ *such that the range of the function* $f_{\text{pub}'} : x \mapsto$ Eval(pub$'$, x) *over* $\mathcal{D}_{\text{pub}'}$ *satisfies:*

$$\frac{|\mathcal{D}_{\text{pub}'}|}{|f_{\text{pub}'}(\mathcal{D}_{\text{pub}'})|} \geq \ell \ .$$

We say that LTF *is* (t, ε)*-secure if for any adversary* $\mathcal{A}$ *running in time at most* t*, the following advantage is less than* ε:

$$\big| \Pr[(\text{pub}, \text{td}) \leftarrow \text{InjGen}(1^k) : 1 \leftarrow \mathcal{A}(\text{pub})]$$
$$- \Pr[\text{pub}' \leftarrow \text{LossyGen}(1^k) : 1 \leftarrow \mathcal{A}(\text{pub}')]\big| \ .$$

We say that LTF *is a regular* (ℓ, t, ε)*-lossy trapdoor function if* LTF *is* (t, ε)*-secure and all functions generated by* LossyGen *are* ℓ*-to-1 on* $\mathcal{D}_{\text{pub}'}$.

Remark 1. One can easily show that if TDF is a regular (ℓ, t, ε)-lossy TDF, then it is (t', ε')-one way with $t' \simeq t$ and $\varepsilon' \leq \varepsilon + 1/\ell$. Note in particular that asymptotically, if $\ell = \mathcal{O}(1)$ is constant (as is the case for the trapdoor functions considered in this paper), this only implies that TDF is weakly one-way [18].

Definition 5 (Gap One-Way TDF). *A trapdoor function* TDF = (InjGen, Eval, Invert) *is said* (t, ε, n)*-gap one-way if for any adversary* $\mathcal{A}$ *running in time at most* t *and making at most* n *queries to a* Certify($\cdot$) *oracle which on input a string* pub, *returns 1 iff the function* $x \mapsto$ Eval(pub, x) *is injective over* $\mathcal{D}_{\text{pub}}$, *one has:*

$$\Pr\big[\text{pub} \leftarrow \text{InjGen}(1^k), x \leftarrow_{\$} \mathcal{D}_{\text{pub}},$$
$$x' \leftarrow \mathcal{A}^{\text{Certify}(\cdot)}(\text{pub}, \text{Eval}(\text{pub}, x)) : x' = x\big] \leq \varepsilon \ .$$

Informally, for a lossy TDF, being gap one-way means that inverting the injective mode of the function cannot be black-box reduced to the lossiness of the TDF. Note that for a certified TDF, being gap one-way is equivalent to being one-way since the Certify oracle can be efficiently implemented.

2.4   Signature Schemes

A signature scheme Σ is a tuple of algorithms (Σ.KeyGen, Σ.Sig, Σ.Ver) where Σ.KeyGen(1^k) outputs a pair of public/secret key (pk, sk), Σ.Sig(sk, m), on input a secret key sk and a message $m \in \{0, 1\}^*$, outputs a signature σ, and

Σ.Ver(pk, m, σ), on input a public key pk, a message m, and a purported signature σ, either outputs 1 (accepts) or 0 (rejects). A signature scheme is said to have *unique signatures* if for all k, for any public key pk possibly output by KeyGen(1^k), and any message $m \in \{0,1\}^*$, there is exactly one string σ such that Ver(pk, m, σ) accepts. The usual security definition for a signature scheme is existential unforgeability under chosen-message attacks (EUF-CMA security). We recall this definition in the full version of the paper [30].

FDH Signatures Based on an Arbitrary TDF. Let TDF = (InjGen, Eval, Invert) be a trapdoor function. The Full Domain Hash signature scheme TDF-FDH is defined as follows: the key generation algorithm KeyGen(1^k) runs InjGen(1^k) to obtain (pub, td), selects a random hash function $\boldsymbol{H} : \{0,1\}^* \rightarrow f_{\mathrm{pub}}(\mathcal{D}_{\mathrm{pub}})$, and sets pk = (pub, $\boldsymbol{H}$) and sk = td. The signature algorithm, on input td and m, computes $h = \boldsymbol{H}(m)$ and returns $\sigma = \mathrm{Invert}(\mathrm{td}, h)$. The verification algorithm, on input pub, m and σ, checks that Eval(pub, σ) = $\boldsymbol{H}(m)$. This scheme can be shown EUF-CMA secure in the Random Oracle Model under the assumption that TDF is (strongly) one-way [4, 11], but the reduction loses a factor q_s, where q_s is the maximal number of signature queries of the adversary, and this loss cannot be avoided assuming that TDF is certified [12, 22].

3 The 2-Φ/4-Hiding Assumption and Lossiness of the Rabin Trapdoor Function

3.1 Definition

We introduce the 2-Φ/4-Hiding assumption, an extension of the traditional Φ-Hiding assumption to the case $e = 2$. The Φ-Hiding assumption, introduced by Cachin *et al.* in [9], roughly states that given an RSA modulus $N = pq$ and a random prime $3 \le e < N^{1/4}$, it is hard to distinguish whether e divides $\phi(N)$ or not (when $e \ge N^{1/4}$ and $e|\phi(N)$, N can be factored using Coppersmith's method for finding small roots of univariate modular equations [10, 9]). Kiltz *et al.* [24] were the first to observe that the Φ-Hiding assumption can be interpreted in terms of lossiness of the RSA trapdoor permutation.

The original definition of the Φ-Hiding assumption was formulated for primes e randomly drawn in $[3; N^{1/4}[$. Since in practice RSA is often used with a fixed, small prime e (*e.g.* $e = 3$ or $e = 2^{16} + 1$), Kakvi and Kiltz [22] introduced the Fixed-Prime Φ-Hiding assumption, which states, for a fixed prime e, that it is hard, given an RSA modulus $N = pq$, to distinguish whether e divides $\phi(N)$ or not (the exact statement of the assumption is slightly different for $e = 3$ and $e > 3$ in order to avoid trivial distinguishers). The 2-Φ/4-Hiding assumption is the extension of the Fixed-Prime Φ-Hiding assumption to the case $e = 2$. Since for an RSA modulus N (more generally for any number which has at least two distinct prime factors) one always has that 4 divides $\phi(N)$, the problem will be to distinguish whether 2 divides $\phi(N)/4$ or not. Moreover, when $N \equiv 3 \bmod 4$, one can check that 2 always divides $\phi(N)/4$, so that the instances will be restricted to RSA moduli such that $N \equiv 1 \bmod 4$. As a matter of fact, distinguishing whether 2 divides $\phi(N)/4$ or not when $N \equiv 1 \bmod 4$ turns out to be equivalent to distinguishing Blum integers from pseudo-Blum integers. Indeed, if N is a Blum integer, then $p = 4p' + 3$ and $q = 4q' + 3$, so that $\phi(N) = 4(2p' + 1)(2q' + 1)$ and $2 \nmid (\phi(N)/4)$. On the other hand, if N is a pseudo-Blum integer, then $p = 4p' + 1$ and $q = 4q' + 1$, so that $\phi(N) = 16p'q'$ and $2 | (\phi(N)/4)$. We now precisely formalize the assumption.

Definition 6 (2-Φ/4-Hiding Assumption). *We say that the 2-Φ/4-Hiding problem is (t, ε)-hard if for any algorithm $\mathcal{A}$ running in time at most t, the following advantage is less than ε:*

$$\mathrm{Adv}^{2-\Phi/4}(\mathcal{A}) \overset{\mathrm{def}}{=} \Big| \Pr[(N, p, q) \leftarrow_{\$} \mathsf{Bl}(k) : 1 \leftarrow \mathcal{A}(N)] -$$

$$\Pr[(N, p, q) \leftarrow \widetilde{\mathsf{Bl}}(k) : 1 \leftarrow \mathcal{A}(N)] \Big| .$$

A variant of this problem is obtained by switching from Blum integers to Williams integers, *i.e.* replacing $\mathsf{Bl}(k)$ and $\widetilde{\mathsf{Bl}}(k)$ in the above definition by respectively $\mathsf{Wi}(k)$ and $\widetilde{\mathsf{Wi}}(k)$. Clearly, the hardness of this variant is polynomially related to the hardness of the original problem, under the plausible assumption that roughly half of Blum, resp. pseudo-Blum integers are Williams, resp. pseudo-Williams integers.

3.2   Lossiness of the Rabin and Rabin-Williams Trapdoor Functions

We now show that the 2-Φ/4-Hiding assumption implies that squaring is a lossy trapdoor function over the domains $\mathbb{QR}_N$ or $(\mathbb{J}_N)^+$, for $N \equiv 1 \bmod 4$, with respectively two bits or one bit of lossiness. The injective mode corresponds to N being a Blum integer, and the lossy mode corresponds to N being a pseudo-Blum integer.

The Rabin LTFs. We first define two related LTFs, that we name respectively the Principal Rabin LTF PR-LTF and the Absolute Principal Rabin LTF APR-LTF as follows:

- on input 1^k, PR-LTF.InjGen and APR-LTF.InjGen both draw $(N, p, q) \leftarrow_{\$}$ $\mathsf{Bl}(k)$, and output $\mathtt{pub} = N$ and $\mathtt{td} = (p, q)$;
- on input 1^k, PR-LTF.LossyGen and APR-LTF.LossyGen both draw $(N, p, q) \leftarrow_{\$}$ $\widetilde{\mathsf{Bl}}(k)$, and output $\mathtt{pub}' = N$;
- the domain is $\mathcal{D}_N = \mathbb{QR}_N$ for PR-LTF, and $\mathcal{D}_N = (\mathbb{J}_N)^+$ for APR-LTF; the evaluation algorithms PR-LTF.Eval(N, x) and APR-LTF.Eval(N, x) both output $f_N(x) = x^2 \bmod N$; in both cases $f_N(\mathcal{D}_N) = \mathbb{QR}_N$ in injective mode;
- the inversion algorithm PR-LTF.Invert$((p, q), y)$ outputs the principal square root $\mathtt{psr}(y)$, while APR-LTF.Invert$((p, q), y)$ outputs the absolute principal square root $|\mathtt{psr}|(y)$ (for N a Blum integer and $y \in \mathbb{QR}_N$).

Theorem 1. *Assuming the 2-Φ/4-Hiding problem is (t, ε)-hard, the Principal Rabin trapdoor function* PR-LTF *is a regular $(4, t, \varepsilon)$-LTF, while the Absolute Principal Rabin trapdoor function* APR-LTF *is a regular $(2, t, \varepsilon)$-LTF.*

Proof. Indistinguishability of the injective and lossy modes is exactly the 2-Φ/4-Hiding problem. It follows from Lemma 1 that when N is a Blum integer, any $y \in \mathbb{QR}_N$ has exactly one pre-image in $\mathbb{QR}_N$ or $(\mathbb{J}_N)^+$, while when N is pseudo-Blum integer, any y in the range $f_N(\mathbb{QR}_N)$ has exactly 4 pre-images in $\mathbb{QR}_N$, and any y in the range $f_N((\mathbb{J}_N)^+)$ has exactly 2 pre-images in $(\mathbb{J}_N)^+$. $\square$

The Rabin-Williams LTFs. The PR-LTF and APR-LTF LTFs can be straightforwardly extended to what we call the Principal Rabin-Williams LTF PRW-LTF and Absolute Principal Rabin-Williams LTF APRW-LTF as follows:

– on input 1^k, PRW-LTF.InjGen and APRW-LTF.InjGen both draw a random Williams integer $(N, p, q) \leftarrow_\$ \text{Wi}(k)$, and output $\text{pub} = N$ and $\text{td} = (p, q)$;
– on input 1^k, PRW-LTF.LossyGen and APRW-LTF.LossyGen both draw a random pseudo-Williams integer $(N, p, q) \leftarrow_\$ \widetilde{\text{Wi}}(k)$ and output $\text{pub}' = N$;
– the domain of PRW-LTF is $\mathcal{D}_N = \{1, -1, 2, -2\} \times \mathbb{QR}_N$, while the domain of APRW-LTF is $\mathcal{D}_N = \{1, -1, 2, -2\} \times (\mathbb{J}_N)^+$; the evaluation algorithms PRW-LTF.Eval$(N, (\alpha, x))$ and APRW-LTF.Eval$(N, (\alpha, x))$ compute the function $f_N(\alpha, x) = \alpha x^2 \bmod N$; in both cases $f_N(\mathcal{D}_N) = \mathbb{Z}_N^*$ in injective mode;
– algorithm PRW-LTF.Invert$((p, q), y)$ computes the principal tweaked square root $\text{psr}(y)$, while APRW-LTF.Invert$((p, q), y)$ computes the absolute principal tweaked square root $|\text{psr}|(y)$ (for N a Williams integer and $y \in \mathbb{Z}_N^*$).

Theorem 2. *Under the assumption that Williams and pseudo-Williams integers are (t, ε)-indistinguishable, the Principal Rabin-Williams trapdoor function* PRW-LTF *is a regular $(4, t, \varepsilon)$-LTF, while the Absolute Principal Rabin-Williams trapdoor function* APRW-LTF *is a regular $(2, t, \varepsilon)$-LTF.*

Proof. Indistinguishability of the injective and lossy modes is exactly indistinguishability of Williams and pseudo-Williams integers, which follows from the 2-Φ/4-Hiding assumption and the additional (reasonable) assumption that roughly half of Blum, resp. pseudo-Blum integers, are Williams, resp. pseudo-Williams integers. Injectivity of f_N for both PRW-LTF and APRW-LTF follows directly from Lemma 1 and the discussion about tweaked square roots in Section 2. Assume now that N is a pseudo-Williams integer, and let $y \in f_N(\mathcal{D}_N)$ with $\mathcal{D}_N = \{1, -1, 2, -2\} \times \mathbb{QR}_N$. We show that y has exactly 4 pre-images in $\mathcal{D}_N$, which will establish that PRW-LTF is 4-to-1 on $\mathcal{D}_N$. Let $(\alpha, x) \in \mathcal{D}_N$ be such that $\alpha x^2 = y \bmod N$. Then by Lemma 1, y has at least 4 pre-images in $\mathcal{D}_N$, all with the same tweak α. Assume that y has an extra pre-image $(\alpha', x') \in \mathcal{D}_N$ with $\alpha' \neq \alpha$. Note that when $N = pq$ is a pseudo-Williams integer (*i.e.* $p \equiv 5 \bmod 8$ and $q \equiv 1 \bmod 8$), the pairs of Legendre symbols $\left(\left(\frac{\alpha}{p}\right), \left(\frac{\alpha}{q}\right)\right)$ for $\alpha = 1, -1, 2,$ and -2 are respectively $(1, 1)$, $(1, 1)$, $(-1, 1)$ and $(-1, 1)$. Hence it must be that $\alpha' = -\alpha$, so that $x^2 = -(x')^2 \bmod N$. Let a be any square root of -1 modulo

N. Since $a^2 = -1 \bmod N$, we observe (denoting $p = 8p' + 5$ and $q = 8q' + 1$) that:

$$\left(\frac{a}{p}\right) \equiv a^{\frac{p-1}{2}} \equiv a^{\frac{8p'+4}{2}} \equiv (-1)^{2p'+1} \equiv -1 \bmod p$$

$$\left(\frac{a}{q}\right) \equiv a^{\frac{q-1}{2}} \equiv a^{\frac{8q'}{2}} \equiv (-1)^{2q'} \equiv 1 \bmod q \ ,$$

so that $a \in \bar{\mathbb{J}}_N$. Hence, we have that $x^2 = (ax')^2 \bmod N$, with $x, x' \in \mathbb{QR}_N$. Yet by Lemma 1, one should have $ax' \in \mathbb{QR}_N$ as well, which is impossible since $a \in \bar{\mathbb{J}}_N$. Hence y has exactly 4 pre-images in $\mathcal{D}_N$.

The proof that APRW-LTF is 2-to-1 on $\mathcal{D}_N = \{1, -1, 2, -2\} \times (\mathbb{J}_N)^+$ is very similar. See the full version of the paper [30]. $\qquad\square$

4   Application to Rabin-Williams Signatures

There are two very close ways to define deterministic Rabin-Williams FDH signatures, called principal and |principal| in the terminology of Bernstein [7]. We will use the name *Absolute Principal* Rabin-Williams signatures for the latter in this paper. Before defining precisely these schemes, we stress that the exact definition of the verification algorithm is important, especially with respect to how a forgery is defined (since a forgery is exactly a string which is accepted by the verification algorithm). Hence, to be more precise, we will define in total four "real" signature schemes: Principal Rabin-Williams (PRW), Absolute Principal Rabin-Williams (APRW), as well as two slightly different variants that we call PRW* and APRW*, which differ from respectively PRW and APRW only in their verification algorithm. We will also define a "theoretical" scheme PRW** where the verification algorithm is inefficient (this will be necessary to establish a clean security reduction). For the five schemes, the signing algorithm first hashes the message $h = \boldsymbol{H}(m)$; then, for the PRW, PRW*, and PRW** schemes, the signing algorithm returns the principal tweaked square root of h, whereas for the APRW and APRW* schemes, the signing algorithm returns the absolute principal tweaked square root of h. In all the following, we assume that if h is not coprime with N, the signing algorithm outputs some fixed signature, *e.g.* $(1, 1)$. Since this happens only with negligible probability when $\boldsymbol{H}$ is modeled as a random oracle, this does not affect the security analysis.

We now proceed to the formal definition. First, all the schemes share exactly the same key generation algorithm:

- (A)PRW(*,**).KeyGen(1^k): on input the security parameter 1^k, draw uniformly at random $(N, p, q) \leftarrow_{\$} \text{Wi}(k)$. Select a hash function $\boldsymbol{H} : \{0,1\}^* \to \mathbb{Z}_N$. The public key is $\text{pk} = (N, \boldsymbol{H})$ and the secret key is $\text{sk} = (p, q)$.

Note that the hash function will usually be selected once for each security parameter k and common to all public keys, but this affects the security proof only up to negligible terms, see Bernstein [7].

The signing algorithm for PRW, PRW*, and PRW** on one hand, and for APRW and APRW* on the other hand, are the same, and are defined as follows:

- PRW(*,**).Sig(sk, m): To sign a message m, compute $h = \boldsymbol{H}(m)$, and output the principal tweaked square root $\sigma = (\alpha, s) = \mathtt{psr}(h)$.
- APRW(*).Sig(sk, m): To sign a message m, compute $h = \boldsymbol{H}(m)$, and output the absolute principal tweaked square root $\sigma = (\alpha, s) = |\mathtt{psr}|(h)$.

The verification algorithms for the five schemes are very close, and differ only with respect to an additional check on the Jacobi symbol of the signature made for PRW* and APRW*, and on the quadratic residuosity of the signature for PRW**. They are defined as follows:

- (A)PRW(*,**).Ver(pk, m, σ): To check a purported signature $\sigma = (\alpha, s)$ on message m, first ensure that $s \in S$, and then check that $\alpha s^2 = \boldsymbol{H}(m) \bmod N$. Accept if this holds, and reject otherwise;

where the set S is defined as:

- $S = \mathbb{Z}_N^*$ for PRW, $S = \mathbb{J}_N$ for PRW*, and $S = \mathbb{QR}_N$ for PRW**;
- $S = (\mathbb{Z}_N^*)^+$ for APRW and $S = (\mathbb{J}_N)^+$ for APRW*.

Note that the verification algorithm is (presumably) inefficient for PRW** since it needs to decide whether the signature is indeed the principal square root, *i.e.* a quadratic residue.

The following claims are straightforward:

- in PRW, each message has exactly four valid signatures: $(\alpha, s_1) = |\mathtt{psr}|(\boldsymbol{H}(m))$, $(\alpha, -s_1)$, and (α, s_2), $(\alpha, -s_2)$ with $s_2 \in (\overline{\mathbb{J}}_N)^+$;
- in PRW*, each message has exactly two valid signatures: $(\alpha, s) = |\mathtt{psr}|(\boldsymbol{H}(m))$ and $(\alpha, -s)$;
- in PRW**, each message has a unique valid signature: $(\alpha, s) = \mathtt{psr}(\boldsymbol{H}(m))$;
- in APRW, each message has exactly two valid signatures: $|\mathtt{psr}|(\boldsymbol{H}(m))$ and (α, s_2) with $s_2 \in (\overline{\mathbb{J}}_N)^+$;
- in APRW*, each message has a unique valid signature: $|\mathtt{psr}|(\boldsymbol{H}(m))$.

We now relate the security of PRW, PRW*, and PRW** on one hand, and APRW and APRW* on the other hand.

Lemma 2. *The security of PRW, PRW* and PRW** on one hand, and APRW and APRW* on the other hand, is related as depicted in Figure 1, where an arrow labeled $(t, f(\varepsilon))$ from scheme A to scheme B means that if scheme A is $(t, \varepsilon, q_h, q_s)$-EUF-CMA secure in the ROM, then scheme B is $(t', f(\varepsilon), q_h, q_s)$-EUF-CMA secure for $t' \simeq t$.*

Proof. See the full version of the paper [30]. □

Hence, one can see that PRW and PRW* on one hand, and APRW and APRW* on the other hand, have the same security up to a factor 2. In other words, omitting the additional check on the Jacobi symbol has negligible impact on security. Since computing a Jacobi symbol might be costly (in particular, it is more expensive than modular squaring), we see that PRW and APRW are superior in terms of security/efficiency trade-off.

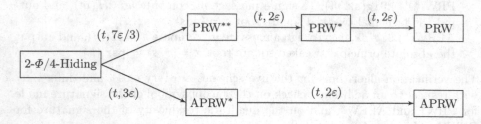

Fig. 1. Set of reductions proved in Lemma 2. An arrow labeled $(t, f(\varepsilon))$ from scheme A to scheme B means that if scheme A is $(t, \varepsilon, q_h, q_s)$-EUF-CMA secure in the ROM, then scheme B is $(t', f(\varepsilon), q_h, q_s)$-EUF-CMA secure for $t' \simeq t$. The reduction from 2-Φ/4-Hiding to breaking PRW** and APRW* is Theorem 4.

In the following, we give a tight reduction for PRW** and APRW* from the 2-Φ/4-Hiding assumption, which extends to PRW and APRW by Lemma 2. It is easy to see that the PRW**, resp. APRW* signature scheme is exactly the instantiation of the generic TDF-FDH scheme recalled in Section 2.4 with PRW-LTF, resp. APRW-LTF. In order to conclude about the security of these schemes, we appeal to the main result of [22]. This theorem was originally stated for trapdoor *permutations*, but it can be straightforwardly extended to trapdoor functions such that $\mathcal{D}_{\mathrm{pub}}$ and $f_{\mathrm{pub}}(\mathcal{D}_{\mathrm{pub}})$ are efficiently samplable.

Theorem 3 ([22]). *Assume* LTF *is a regular* (ℓ, t', ε')-LTF *for* $\ell \geq 2$. *Then for any* (q_h, q_s), *the TDF-FDH signature scheme instantiated with* LTF *is* $(t, \varepsilon, q_h, q_s)$-EUF-CMA *secure in the ROM, where*

$$\varepsilon = \left(\frac{2\ell - 1}{\ell - 1}\right)\varepsilon' \quad and \quad t = t' - q_h T_{\mathtt{Eval}} ,$$

where $T_{\mathtt{Eval}}$ *is the time to run algorithm* Eval *of* LTF.

Theorem 4. *Assuming the* 2-Φ/4-Hiding *problem is* (t', ε')-*hard, then for any* (q_h, q_s), *the* PRW** *signature scheme is* $(t, \varepsilon, q_h, q_s)$-EUF-CMA *secure, where* $\varepsilon = 7\varepsilon'/3$ *and* $t = t' - \mathcal{O}(q_h k^3)$, *and the* APRW* *signature scheme is* $(t, \varepsilon, q_h, q_s)$-*EUF-CMA secure, where* $\varepsilon = 3\varepsilon'$ *and* $t = t' - \mathcal{O}(q_h k^3)$.

Proof. This follows directly from Theorems 2 and 3 (noting that $\mathbb{QR}_N$ and $(\mathbb{J}_N)^+$ are efficiently samplable). Combined with Lemma 2, this yields tight security reductions for PRW and APRW (see Figure 1 for a clear picture).   □

Remark 2. The global security reduction from the 2-Φ/4-Hiding assumption to breaking the signature scheme is slightly looser for PRW (factor 28/3) than for APRW (factor 6 = 18/3). We also remark that a PRW signature oracle is (potentially) slightly more powerful than an APRW signature oracle because it reveals some non-trivial information regarding the quadratic residuosity of the square roots of the hash of the message (whereas this information, which is unnecessary for verifying signatures, is "canceled" in an APRW signature oracle). Since APRW signatures are not more costly than PRW signatures (and even slightly more communication efficient), these two observations make a case in favor of APRW signatures.

As explained in [22], these results can be extended to PSS-R [6], allowing a smaller overhead of the randomized signature under the 2-Φ/4-Hiding assumption. It seems also likely (though we have not checked the details) that the same techniques can be used to prove a tight security reduction from the 2-Φ/4-Hiding assumption for Rabin-Williams Partial Domain Hash signatures [13, 17].

5   Extending the Coron-Kakvi-Kiltz Meta-reduction Result

In this section, we complete the picture of the security of FDH signatures by extending Coron's meta-reduction result [11] as corrected by Kakvi and Kiltz [22]. In a nutshell, this result says that if a trapdoor function TDF is certified, then any reduction from inverting the trapdoor function to breaking the EUF-CMA security of the TDF-FDH signature scheme must lose a factor q_s (the maximal number of signature queries made by the forger) in its time-to-success ratio. The theorem below extends this to trapdoor functions which are not necessarily certified, assuming that TDF is gap one-way. The proof is straightforwardly adapted from the one of [11, 22]: when simulating the forger, the meta-reduction checks as a preliminary step that the public key received from the reduction contains a parameter pub which defines an injective function. When TDF is certified, this can be done efficiently by the meta-reduction itself. In the variant below, the meta-reduction uses a Certify oracle for this step, hence breaking the gap one-wayness (rather than classical one-wayness) of the trapdoor function.

Theorem 5. *Let* TDF *be a trapdoor function. Let* $t_R, \varepsilon_R, n, \varepsilon_F, q_h, q_s$ *be functions of the security parameter with* $q_h > q_s$. *Assume there exists a reduction* $\mathcal{R}$ *which* $(t_R, \varepsilon_R, n, \varepsilon_F, q_h, q_s)$-reduces *breaking the one-wayness of* TDF *to breaking EUF-CMA security of the TDF-FDH signature scheme. Then there exists a meta-reduction* $\mathcal{M}$ *which* (t_M, ε_M, n)-breaks *the gap one-wayness of* TDF, *where:*

$$t_M \leq (n+1)t_R$$

$$\varepsilon_M \geq \varepsilon_R - \varepsilon_F \cdot \frac{n \cdot \exp(-1)}{q_s} \left(1 - \frac{q_s}{q_h}\right)^{-1}.$$

Proof. A precise definition of a (black-box) reduction and a sketch of the proof are provided in the full version of the paper [30].   □

Remark 3. Theorem 5 above can be straightforwardly extended to any non-interactive computational problem which is hard relative to a Certify oracle (instead of the one-wayness of the underlying trapdoor function).

Consequences for RSA and Rabin-Williams FDH Signatures. We know by Theorem 8 of [22] that RSA-FDH with public exponents $e < N^{1/4}$ has a tight security reduction from the Φ-Hiding assumption. By Theorem 7 of [22] we also know that RSA-FDH with public exponents $e > N^{1/4}$ cannot have a tight security reduction from the problem of inverting RSA —nor any non-interactive hard problem— since RSA is certified for this class of exponents [23]. Theorem 5 above implies that it is unlikely as well that RSA-FDH with $e < N^{1/4}$ can have a tight security reduction from inverting RSA: unless inverting RSA with the help of an oracle solving the Φ-Hiding problem is easy, any reduction from inverting RSA to breaking the EUF-CMA security of RSA-FDH with $e < N^{1/4}$ must lose a factor q_s.

This extends to Rabin-Williams FDH signatures as follows: unless computing modular square roots (or equivalently factoring) with the help of an oracle solving the 2-Φ/4-Hiding problem is easy, any reduction from factoring to breaking the EUF-CMA security of the PRW and APRW schemes must lose a factor q_s.

References

[1] Abdalla, M., Bellare, M., Rogaway, P.: The Oracle Diffie-Hellman Assumptions and an Analysis of DHIES. In: Naccache, D. (ed.) CT-RSA 2001. LNCS, vol. 2020, pp. 143–158. Springer, Heidelberg (2001)

[2] Bellare, M., Brakerski, Z., Naor, M., Ristenpart, T., Segev, G., Shacham, H., Yilek, S.: Hedged Public-Key Encryption: How to Protect against Bad Randomness. In: Matsui, M. (ed.) ASIACRYPT 2009. LNCS, vol. 5912, pp. 232–249. Springer, Heidelberg (2009)

[3] Bellare, M., Hofheinz, D., Yilek, S.: Possibility and Impossibility Results for Encryption and Commitment Secure under Selective Opening. In: Joux, A. (ed.) EUROCRYPT 2009. LNCS, vol. 5479, pp. 1–35. Springer, Heidelberg (2009)

[4] Bellare, M., Rogaway, P.: Random Oracles are Practical: A Paradigm for Designing Efficient Protocols. In: ACM Conference on Computer and Communications Security, pp. 62–73 (1993)

[5] Bellare, M., Rogaway, P.: Optimal Asymmetric Encryption. In: De Santis, A. (ed.) EUROCRYPT 1994. LNCS, vol. 950, pp. 92–111. Springer, Heidelberg (1995)

[6] Bellare, M., Rogaway, P.: The Exact Security of Digital Signatures - How to Sign with RSA and Rabin. In: Maurer, U.M. (ed.) EUROCRYPT 1996. LNCS, vol. 1070, pp. 399–416. Springer, Heidelberg (1996)

[7] Bernstein, D.J.: Proving Tight Security for Rabin-Williams Signatures. In: Smart, N.P. (ed.) EUROCRYPT 2008. LNCS, vol. 4965, pp. 70–87. Springer, Heidelberg (2008)

[8] Boldyreva, A., Fehr, S., O'Neill, A.: On Notions of Security for Deterministic Encryption, and Efficient Constructions without Random Oracles. In: Wagner, D. (ed.) CRYPTO 2008. LNCS, vol. 5157, pp. 335–359. Springer, Heidelberg (2008)

[9] Cachin, C., Micali, S., Stadler, M.: Computationally Private Information Retrieval with Polylogarithmic Communication. In: Stern, J. (ed.) EUROCRYPT 1999. LNCS, vol. 1592, pp. 402–414. Springer, Heidelberg (1999)

[10] Coppersmith, D.: Finding a Small Root of a Univariate Modular Equation. In: Maurer, U.M. (ed.) EUROCRYPT 1996. LNCS, vol. 1070, pp. 155–165. Springer, Heidelberg (1996)

[11] Coron, J.-S.: On the Exact Security of Full Domain Hash. In: Bellare, M. (ed.) CRYPTO 2000. LNCS, vol. 1880, pp. 229–235. Springer, Heidelberg (2000)

[12] Coron, J.-S.: Optimal Security Proofs for PSS and Other Signature Schemes. In: Knudsen, L.R. (ed.) EUROCRYPT 2002. LNCS, vol. 2332, pp. 272–287. Springer, Heidelberg (2002)

[13] Coron, J.-S.: Security Proof for Partial-Domain Hash Signature Schemes. In: Yung, M. (ed.) CRYPTO 2002. LNCS, vol. 2442, pp. 613–626. Springer, Heidelberg (2002)

[14] Fehr, S., Hofheinz, D., Kiltz, E., Wee, H.: Encryption Schemes Secure against Chosen-Ciphertext Selective Opening Attacks. In: Gilbert, H. (ed.) EUROCRYPT 2010. LNCS, vol. 6110, pp. 381–402. Springer, Heidelberg (2010)

[15] Fischlin, R., Schnorr, C.-P.: Stronger Security Proofs for RSA and Rabin Bits. Journal of Cryptology 13(2), 221–244 (2000)

[16] Freeman, D.M., Goldreich, O., Kiltz, E., Rosen, A., Segev, G.: More Constructions of Lossy and Correlation-Secure Trapdoor Functions. In: Nguyen, P.Q., Pointcheval, D. (eds.) PKC 2010. LNCS, vol. 6056, pp. 279–295. Springer, Heidelberg (2010)

[17] Gentry, C.: How to Compress Rabin Ciphertexts and Signatures (and More). In: Franklin, M. (ed.) CRYPTO 2004. LNCS, vol. 3152, pp. 179–200. Springer, Heidelberg (2004)

[18] Goldreich, O.: Foundations of Cryptography - vol. 1, Basic Tools. Cambridge University Press (2001)

[19] Goldwasser, S., Micali, S., Rivest, R.L.: A Digital Signature Scheme Secure Against Adaptive Chosen-Message Attacks. SIAM J. Comput. 17(2), 281–308 (1988)

[20] Hofheinz, D., Jager, T., Knapp, E.: Waters Signatures with Optimal Security Reduction. In: Fischlin, M., Buchmann, J., Manulis, M. (eds.) PKC 2012. LNCS, vol. 7293, pp. 66–83. Springer, Heidelberg (2012)

[21] Hofheinz, D., Kiltz, E.: The Group of Signed Quadratic Residues and Applications. In: Halevi, S. (ed.) CRYPTO 2009. LNCS, vol. 5677, pp. 637–653. Springer, Heidelberg (2009)

[22] Kakvi, S.A., Kiltz, E.: Optimal Security Proofs for Full Domain Hash, Revisited. In: Pointcheval, D., Johansson, T. (eds.) EUROCRYPT 2012. LNCS, vol. 7237, pp. 537–553. Springer, Heidelberg (2012)

[23] Kakvi, S.A., Kiltz, E., May, A.: Certifying RSA. In: Wang, X., Sako, K. (eds.) ASIACRYPT 2012. LNCS, vol. 7658, pp. 404–414. Springer, Heidelberg (2012)

[24] Kiltz, E., O'Neill, A., Smith, A.: Instantiability of RSA-OAEP under Chosen-Plaintext Attack. In: Rabin, T. (ed.) CRYPTO 2010. LNCS, vol. 6223, pp. 295–313. Springer, Heidelberg (2010)

[25] Kurosawa, K., Ogata, W.: Efficient Rabin-type Digital Signature Scheme. Des. Codes Cryptography 16(1), 53–64 (1999)

[26] Leurent, G., Nguyen, P.Q.: How Risky Is the Random-Oracle Model? In: Halevi, S. (ed.) CRYPTO 2009. LNCS, vol. 5677, pp. 445–464. Springer, Heidelberg (2009)

[27] Mol, P., Yilek, S.: Chosen-Ciphertext Security from Slightly Lossy Trapdoor Functions. In: Nguyen, P.Q., Pointcheval, D. (eds.) PKC 2010. LNCS, vol. 6056, pp. 296–311. Springer, Heidelberg (2010)

[28] Peikert, C., Waters, B.: Lossy trapdoor functions and their applications. In: Dwork, C. (ed.) Symposium on Theory of Computing, STOC 2008, pp. 187–196. ACM (2008)

[29] Rabin, M.O.: Digitalized signatures and public-key functions as intractable as factorization. Technical Report 212. MIT Laboratory for Computer Science (1979)

[30] Seurin, Y.: On the Lossiness of the Rabin Trapdoor Function. Full version of this paper, http://eprint.iacr.org/2013/256

[31] Williams, H.C.: A modification of the RSA public-key encryption procedure. IEEE Transactions on Information Theory 26(6), 726–729 (1980)

Solving Random Subset Sum Problem by l_p-norm SVP Oracle[*]

Gengran Hu, Yanbin Pan, and Feng Zhang

Key Laboratory of Mathematics Mechanization, NCMIS,
Academy of Mathematics and Systems Science, Chinese Academy of Sciences
Beijing 100190, China
hudiran10@mails.ucas.ac.cn, {panyanbin,zhangfeng}@amss.ac.cn

Abstract. It is well known that almost all random subset sum instances with density less than 0.6463... can be solved with an l_2-norm SVP oracle by Lagarias and Odlyzko. Later, Coster *et al.* improved the bound to 0.9408... by using a different lattice. In this paper, we generalize this classical result to l_p-norm. More precisely, we show that for $p \in \mathbb{Z}^+$, an l_p-norm SVP oracle can be used to solve almost all random subset sum instances with density bounded by δ_p, where $\delta_1 = 0.5761$ and $\delta_p = 1/(\frac{1}{2^p} \log_2(2^{p+1} - 2) + \log_2(1 + \frac{1}{(2^p-1)(1-(\frac{1}{2^{p+1}-2})^{(2^p-1)})}))$ for $p \geq 3$(asymptotically, $\delta_p \approx 2^p/(p+2)$). Since δ_p goes increasingly to infinity when p tends to infinity, it can be concluded that an l_p-norm SVP oracle with bigger p can solve more subset sum instances. An interesting phenomenon is that an l_p-norm SVP oracle with $p \geq 3$ can help solve almost all random subset sum instances with density one, which are thought to be the most difficult instances.

Keywords: SVP, random subset sum problems, lattice, l_p-norm.

1 Introduction

Lattices are discrete subgroup in $\mathbb{R}^n$ and have many important applications in both cryptanalysis and cryptographic constructions. Many lattice-based cryptographic primitives have been presented, such as the public-key cryptosystems [1,2,21,9,11], the digital signature scheme NTRUSign [12] and the fully homomorphic encryption [8]. Usually, the securities of these schemes can be based on the hardness of some lattice problems, like SVP (the shortest vector problem). SVP refers to finding a shortest non-zero vector in a given lattice and is one of the most famous computational problems of lattice. Many famous algorithms are proposed to solve SVP, including the famous LLL algorithm [14]. These algorithms can also be used to attack knapsack-based public-key cryptosystems (See [15] for more details).

---

[*] This work was supported in part by the NNSF of China (No.11071285, No.11201458, and No.61121062), in part by 973 Project (No. 2011CB302401) and in part by the National Center for Mathematics and Interdisciplinary Sciences, CAS.

H. Krawczyk (Ed.): PKC 2014, LNCS 8383, pp. 399–410, 2014.

The knapsack problem, or the subset sum problem (SSP), is a well-known NP-hard problem. It asks to choose some elements in a given set such that the sum of these elements is exactly equal to a given number. When all of the elements of the set are uniformly random over some set, it comes to the random subset sum problem (RSSP), which is also a significant computational problem.

The hardness of RSSP is still not clear. However, it seems that there is a very close relationship between the hardness of RSSP and its density. When the density is large enough, it can be solved via dynamic programming. When the density is small enough, it can be solved by LLL algorithm [15]. In [13], Impagliazzo and Naor showed that the hardest instances of RSSP lie in those with density equal to 1.

Some relations between SVP and RSSP have been exploited. In 1985, Lagarias and Odlyzko [15] showed that the l_2-norm SVP oracle can be used to solve almost all random subset sum instances with density bounded by 0.6463 when the size of the subset sum instance is large enough. Later, Coster *et al.* [5] improved this bound to 0.9408. However, it is a long standing open problem to solve the RSSP instances with density 1 using the lattice l_2-norm SVP oracle.

In this work, we give a very interesting result that any l_p-norm SVP oracle $(p > 2)$ can help to solve the RSSP with density 1 efficiently. More precisely, if $p \in \mathbb{Z}^+$, an l_p-norm SVP oracle can be used to solve almost all random subset sum instances with density bounded by $\delta_p = 1/(\frac{1}{2^p} \log_2(2^{p+1} - 2) + \log_2(1 + \frac{1}{(2^p-1)(1-(\frac{1}{2^{p+1}-2})^{(2^p-1)})})))$. It is easy to see that δ_p goes increasingly to infinity as p tends to infinity, which implies that an l_p-norm SVP oracle with bigger p can solve more subset sum instances. Especially, an l_∞-norm SVP oracle can solve all the subset sum instances, which coincides with the deterministic reduction from subset sum problem to l_∞-norm SVP. It seems that the hardness of l_p-norm SVP increases as p gets bigger. However, in practice, the existing SVP algorithms are mostly in l_2-norm, even the l_p-norm SVP algorithm in [6] uses the MV algorithm(an l_2-norm SVP algorithm in [18]) as a starting point.

In fact, it is well known that the l_∞-norm SVP is NP-hard under deterministic reduction, whereas SVP for other norms are proved to be NP-hard under only probabilistic reductions (see [3,17,19]). In addition, Regev and Rosen [22] proved for any $\epsilon > 0$, l_2-norm $SVP_{1+\epsilon}$ can be probabilistically reduced to l_p-norm SVP for all $1 \le p \le \infty$ which showed that the l_2-norm $SVP_{1+\epsilon}$ is easiest. Unfortunately, reduction from exact l_2-norm SVP to l_p-norm SVP has still not been found.

We would like to point out that if RSSP can be proved to be NP-hard, then by our result, we can prove l_p-norm SVP $(p > 2, p \in \mathbb{Z}^+)$ is NP-hard under probabilistic reduction. Such a reduction will be more simple and clear, compared to the previous reductions.

Moreover, as a byproduct, we give an upper bound of the number of the integer points in an l_p ball, which is shown to be very nice for $p \ge 3$.

Roadmap. The remainder of the paper is organized as follows. In Section 2, we give some preliminaries needed. In Section 3, we describe our probabilistic reduction from random subset sum problem to l_p-norm SVP in details. Finally, we give a short conclusion in Section 4.

2   Preliminaries

We denote by $\mathbb{Z}$ the integer ring. We use bold letters to denote vectors. If $\mathbf{v} \in \mathbb{R}^n$ is a vector, then we denote by v_i the i-th entry of $\mathbf{v}$. Let $\|\mathbf{v}\|_p$ be the l_p norm of $\mathbf{v}$, that is, $\|\mathbf{v}\|_p = (\sum_{i=1}^{n} |v_i|^p)^{1/p}$.

2.1   Lattice

Given a matrix $B = (b_{ij}) \in \mathbb{R}^{m \times n}$ with rank n, the lattice $\mathcal{L}(B)$ spanned by the columns of B is

$$\mathcal{L}(B) = \{Bx = \sum_{i=1}^{n} x_i b_i | x_i \in \mathbb{Z}\},$$

where b_i is the i-th column of B. We call m the dimension of $\mathcal{L}(B)$ and n its rank.

Definition 1 (l_p-norm SVP). *Given a lattice basis B, the l_p-norm SVP asks to find a nonzero vector in $\mathcal{L}(B)$ with the smallest l_p-norm.*

2.2   Random Subset Sum Problem

Given $\mathbf{a} = (a_1, a_2, \ldots, a_n)$ distributed uniformly in $[1, A]^n$ and $s = \sum_{i=1}^{n} e_i a_i$ where $\mathbf{e} = (e_1, e_2, \ldots, e_n) \in \{0,1\}^n$, RSSP refers to finding some $\mathbf{c} = (c_1, c_2, \ldots, c_n) \in \{0,1\}^n$ such that $s = \sum_{i=1}^{n} c_i a_i$ without knowing $\mathbf{e}$. Notice that the solution $\mathbf{c}$ may not be the original $\mathbf{e}$.

The density of these a_i's is defined by

$$d = \frac{n}{\log_2(A)}.$$

It was shown by Lagarias and Odlyzko [15] that almost all the subset sum problem with density less than $0.6463\ldots$ would be solved in polynomial time with a single call to an oracle that can find the shortest vector in a special lattice. Later, Coster *et al.* [5] improved the bound to $0.9408\ldots$ by finding a shortest nonzero vector with an l_2-norm SVP oracle in the following lattice spanned by the columns of

$$\begin{pmatrix} 1 & 0 & \cdots & 0 & \frac{1}{2} \\ 0 & 1 & \cdots & 0 & \frac{1}{2} \\ \vdots & \vdots & & \vdots & \vdots \\ 0 & 0 & \cdots & 1 & \frac{1}{2} \\ Na_1 & Na_2 & \cdots & Na_n & Ns \end{pmatrix},$$

where N is a big enough integer.

2.3   Estimation of the Combinatorial Number

By Stirling's Formula, we have the following estimation for the combinatorial number,

$$\binom{\alpha n}{\beta n} = \tilde{O}(2^{\alpha H(\beta/\alpha)n}),$$

where

$$H(x) = -x \log_2 x - (1-x) \log_2(1-x) \text{ and } \tilde{O}(f(n)) = O(f(n) * poly(\log(f(n)))).$$

3   Solving Random Subset Sum Problem by l_p-norm SVP Oracle

3.1   The Upper Bound of the Number of Integer Points in an l_p-Ball

We first give some results about the number of the integer points in an l_p-ball, that is, $\#\{\mathbf{x} \in \mathbb{Z}^{n+1} | \|\mathbf{x}\|_p \leq \frac{1}{2}(n+1)^{\frac{1}{p}}\}$.

Theorem 1. *For all $n \geq 1$,*

- *If $p = 1$ and n large enough,*

$$\#\{\mathbf{x} \in \mathbb{Z}^n | \|\mathbf{x}\|_1 \leq \frac{1}{2}n\} \leq 2^{c_1 n},$$

  where $c_1 = 1.7357$.
- *If $p = 2$,*

$$\#\{\mathbf{x} \in \mathbb{Z}^n | \|\mathbf{x}\|_2 \leq \frac{1}{2}\sqrt{n}\} \leq 2^{c_2 n},$$

  where $c_2 = 1.0628$.
- *If $p \geq 3$ and $p \in \mathbb{Z}^+$,*

$$\#\{\mathbf{x} \in \mathbb{Z}^n | \|\mathbf{x}\|_p \leq \frac{1}{2}n^{\frac{1}{p}}\} \leq 2^{c_p n},$$

  where $c_p \approx \frac{1}{2^p} \log_2(2^{p+1} - 2) + \log_2(1 + \frac{1}{2^p-1})$.

Proof. We will prove the theorem in three cases.

- $p = 1$:
  For simplicity, we assume n is even (the case when n is odd is similar). Let $R(m,n) \triangleq \#\{\mathbf{x} \in \mathbb{Z}^n, \mathbf{x} \text{ has } m \text{ nonzero entries} \mid \|\mathbf{x}\|_1 \leq \frac{1}{2}n\}$, then

$$\#\{\mathbf{x} \in \mathbb{Z}^n | \|\mathbf{x}\|_1 \leq \frac{1}{2}n\} = \sum_{m=0}^{n/2} R(m,n).$$

It is easy to know that $R(m,n) = 2^m \binom{n}{m} \sum_{j=m}^{n/2} \binom{j-1}{m-1} = 2^m \binom{n}{m} \binom{n/2}{m}$. Assume $R(m_n, n) = \max_m R(m, n)$, then $\#\{\mathbf{x} \in \mathbb{Z}^n | \|\mathbf{x}\|_1 \leq \frac{1}{2}n\} \leq \frac{1}{2}n(R(m_n, n))$. Noticing that

$$R(m+1, n)/R(m, n) = \frac{2^{m+1}\binom{n}{m+1}\binom{n/2}{m+1}}{2^m \binom{n}{m}\binom{n/2}{m}}$$

$$= \frac{(n-m)(n-2m)}{(m+1)^2}$$

is decreasing with respect to m, we have

$$\begin{cases} R(m_n, n)/R(m_n - 1, n) \geq 1, \\ R(m_n + 1, n)/R(m_n, n) \leq 1, \end{cases}$$

which implies that

$$\begin{cases} m_n \leq 0.381966n + 0.658359, \\ m_n \geq 0.381966n - 0.828427, \end{cases}$$

since $m_n \leq n/2$. We obtain $m_n \approx 0.381966n$. Thus, we have the bound

$$\#\{\mathbf{x} \in \mathbb{Z}^n | \|\mathbf{x}\|_1 \leq \frac{1}{2}n\} \leq \frac{1}{2}n2^{0.381966n}\binom{0.5n-1}{0.381966n-1}\binom{n}{0.381966n}.$$

Using the estimation $\binom{\alpha n}{\beta n} = \tilde{O}(2^{\alpha H(\beta/\alpha)n})$, finally we have for n large enough

$$\#\{\mathbf{x} \in \mathbb{Z}^n | \|\mathbf{x}\|_1 \leq \frac{1}{2}n\} = \tilde{O}(2^{0.381966n+0.39422n+0.9594187n}) = \tilde{O}(2^{1.7356047n}) \leq 2^{1.7357n}.$$

– If $p = 2$:
It has been proven in Section 3 in [5].
– If $p \geq 3$ and $p \in \mathbb{Z}^+$:
Let $\theta(z) = 1 + 2\sum_{i=1}^{\infty} z^{i^p}$ and $r_n(k)$ be the number of integer solutions to

$$\sum_{i=1}^{n} |x_i|^p = k.$$

Then

$$(\theta(z))^n = \sum_{k=0}^{\infty} r_n(k)z^k.$$

For all $x > 0$, we have

$$\#\{\mathbf{x} \in \mathbb{Z}^n \,|\, \|\mathbf{x}\|_p \leq \frac{1}{2}n^{\frac{1}{p}}\} = \#\{\mathbf{x} \in \mathbb{Z}^n \,|\, \|\mathbf{x}\|_p^p \leq \frac{1}{2^p}n\}$$

$$= \sum_{k \leq \frac{1}{2^p}n} r_n(k)$$

$$\leq \sum_{k \leq \frac{1}{2^p}n} r_n(k)e^{\frac{1}{2^p}nx}e^{-kx}$$

$$\leq \sum_{k=0}^{\infty} r_n(k)e^{\frac{1}{2^p}nx}e^{-kx}$$

$$= e^{\frac{1}{2^p}nx}\sum_{k=0}^{\infty} r_n(k)e^{-kx}$$

$$= e^{\frac{1}{2^p}nx}(\theta(e^{-x}))^n.$$

Let

$$f_p(x) = \frac{1}{2^p}x + \ln\theta(e^{-x}).$$

We have

$$\#\{\mathbf{x} \in \mathbb{Z}^n \,|\, \|\mathbf{x}\|_p \leq \frac{1}{2}n^{\frac{1}{p}}\} \leq e^{f_p(x)n} = 2^{(\log_2 e)f_p(x)n}$$

holds for all $x > 0$.

So we only need to compute $\min\limits_{x>0} f_p(x)$. It is difficult to give the exact value of $\min\limits_{x>0} f_p(x)$. Next we give an upper bound for $\min\limits_{x>0} f_p(x)$.

Noticing that

$$f_p(x) = \frac{1}{2^p}x + \ln\theta(e^{-x}) = \frac{1}{2^p}x + \ln(1 + 2e^{-1^p x} + 2e^{-2^p x} + 2e^{-3^p x} + \cdots + 2e^{-k^p x} + \cdots),$$

we define

$$l_p(x) \triangleq \frac{1}{2^p}x + \ln(1 + 2e^{-x})$$

and

$$u_p(x) \triangleq \frac{1}{2^p}x + \ln(1 + 2e^{-x} + 2e^{-2^p x} + 2e^{-(2^p + 2^p - 1)x} + \cdots + 2e^{-((k-1)2^p - (k-2))x} + \cdots)$$

$$= \frac{1}{2^p}x + \ln(1 + \frac{2e^{-x}}{1 - e^{-(2^p-1)x}}).$$

When $p \geq 1$, the difference sequence $(2^p - 1^p, 3^p - 2^p, 4^p - 3^p, \cdots)$ is not decreasing, then for $k \geq 2$,

$$2e^{-k^p x} = 2e^{-x(1 + (2^p - 1^p) + (3^p - 2^p) + \cdots + (k^p - (k-1)^p))}$$

$$\leq 2e^{-x(1 + (2^p - 1^p) + (2^p - 1) + \cdots + (2^p - 1))}$$

$$= 2e^{-((k-1)2^p - (k-2))x}$$

So we have
$$l_p(x) \leq f_p(x) \leq u_p(x)$$
holds for all $x > 0$, which implies
$$\min_{x>0} l_p(x) \leq \min_{x>0} f_p(x) \leq \min_{x>0} u_p(x).$$

Because $l_p(x)$ takes the minimum
$$l_p(x_0(p)) = \frac{1}{2^p} \ln(2^{p+1} - 2) + \ln(1 + \frac{1}{2^p - 1})$$
at
$$x_0(p) = \ln(2^{p+1} - 2)$$
and
$$u_p(x_0(p)) = \frac{1}{2^p} \ln(2^{p+1} - 2) + \ln(1 + \frac{1}{(2^p - 1)(1 - (\frac{1}{2^{p+1}-2})^{(2^p-1)})}),$$

we have an interval estimate $[l_p(x_0(p)), \quad u_p(x_0(p))]$ for $\min_{x>0} f_p(x)$ since
$$l_p(x_0(p)) = \min_{x>0} l_p(x) \leq \min_{x>0} f_p(x) \leq \min_{x>0} u_p(x) \leq u_p(x_0(p)).$$

Taking $c_p = \log_2 e \cdot u_p(x_0(p))$, the result for $p \geq 3$ follows.

We would like to point out that $2^{c_p n}$ is a very nice estimation of the number of integer points in the l_p ball $\{\mathbf{x} \in \mathbb{Z}^n | \|\mathbf{x}\|_p \leq \frac{1}{2} n^{\frac{1}{p}}\}$ for $p \geq 3$. In fact, we can easily have an asymptotic rough lower bound for the number of integer points by just considering those vectors in the ball with exactly $\frac{1}{2^p} n$ entries in $\{-1, 1\}$ and other entries equal to 0. The total number of such vectors is $2^{\frac{1}{2^p} n} \cdot \binom{n}{\frac{1}{2^p} n}$, which is approximately equal to $2^{(H(\frac{1}{2^p}) + \frac{1}{2^p})n}$. Hence for $p \in \mathbb{Z}^+$ and n large enough, we have
$$\#\{\mathbf{x} \in \mathbb{Z}^n | \|\mathbf{x}\|_p \leq \frac{1}{2} n^{\frac{1}{p}}\} \geq 2^{k_p n},$$
where $k_p = \frac{p+1}{2^p} - (1 - \frac{1}{2^p}) \log_2(1 - \frac{1}{2^p})$. Interestingly, we find that k_p is exactly the total lower bound $\log_2 e \cdot l_p(x_0(p))$ obtained above.

The table below gives the values of $l_p(x_0(p))(= \ln 2 \cdot k_p)$ and $u_p(x_0(p))$ for p from three to ten.

p	3	4	5	6	7	8	9	10
l_p	0.4634	0.2771	0.1607	0.0913	0.0511	0.2827	0.0155	0.0084
u_p	0.4634	0.2771	0.1607	0.0913	0.0511	0.2827	0.0155	0.0084

It can be seen that $u_p(x_0(p))$ is a very good estimation of $\min_{x>0} f_p(x)$, since for $p \geq 3$, $l_p(x_0(p))$ and $u_p(x_0(p))$ are nearly the same. Similarly, $2^{c_p n}$ is a very nice estimation of the number of integer points in the l_p ball for $p \geq 3$, since the upper bound and the lower bound are also nearly the same. In fact, the asymptotic forms for $l_p(x_0(p))$ and $u_p(x_0(p))$ are the same:
$$l_p(x_0(p)) \approx \ln 2 \cdot \frac{p+2}{2^p}, u_p(x_0(p)) \approx \ln 2 \cdot \frac{p+2}{2^p}.$$

3.2   Solving Random Subset Sum Problem by l_p-norm SVP Oracle

To solve the subset sum problem defined by $a_i (1 \le i \le n)$ and s, we consider the lattice $\mathcal{L}(B)$ generated by the columns of B where

$$
B = \begin{pmatrix}
1 & 0 & \cdots & 0 & \frac{1}{2} \\
0 & 1 & \cdots & 0 & \frac{1}{2} \\
\vdots & \vdots & & \vdots & \vdots \\
0 & 0 & \cdots & 1 & \frac{1}{2} \\
0 & 0 & \cdots & 0 & \frac{1}{2} \\
Na_1 & Na_2 & \cdots & Na_n & Ns
\end{pmatrix},
$$

and $N > \frac{1}{2}(n+1)^{\frac{1}{p}}$ is an positive integer. Notice that our lattice is a little different from Coster $et\ al.$'s, which leads a more simple reduction. The additional row in the lattice basis matrix can bound the last integer coefficient more tightly(see section 3 of [5] for more details).

Any $\mathbf{x} = (x_1, x_2 \ldots x_n, x_{n+1}, x_{n+2})^T \in \mathcal{L}(B)$ can be written as

$$
\begin{cases}
x_i = w_i + \frac{1}{2}w & (i = 1, 2 \ldots n) \\
x_{n+1} = \frac{1}{2}w \\
x_{n+2} = N(\sum_{i=1}^{n} w_i a_i + ws)
\end{cases}
\tag{1}
$$

with all the w_i's and w in $\mathbb{Z}$.

For any solution $\mathbf{e}$ of the subset problem, taking $w_i = e_i$, $w = -1$, we get $\mathcal{L}(B)$ contains a corresponding lattice vector $\mathbf{e}' = (e_1' \ldots e_n', -\frac{1}{2}, 0)$ with $e_i' = e_i - \frac{1}{2} \in \{-\frac{1}{2}, \frac{1}{2}\}$. Obviously, $\|\mathbf{e}'\|_p = \frac{1}{2}(n+1)^{\frac{1}{p}}$.

On the other hand, it is easy to know that any $\mathbf{y} = (y_1, y_2 \ldots y_n, y_{n+1}, y_{n+2})^T \in \mathcal{L}(B)$ of the form

$$
\begin{cases}
y_i \in \{-\frac{1}{2}w, \frac{1}{2}w\} & (i = 1, 2 \ldots n) \\
y_{n+1} = -\frac{1}{2}w \\
y_{n+2} = 0
\end{cases}
$$

where $w \in \mathbb{Z} \setminus \{0\}$ yields an solution $(y_1 - \frac{1}{2}, y_2 - \frac{1}{2}, \cdots, y_n - \frac{1}{2})$ of the RSSP. Thus, we define the solution set of the subset sum instance

$$
S_n = \{ \ w(y_1, y_2 \ldots y_n, -\frac{1}{2}, 0)^T \ \mid \ |y_i| = \frac{1}{2}, \ w \in \mathbb{Z} \setminus \{0\} \ \}.
$$

Then $\pm \mathbf{e}' \in S_n$.

By querying the l_p-norm SVP oracle with $\mathcal{L}(B)$, we get a non-zero shortest vector $\mathbf{x}$. If $\mathbf{x} \in S_n$, then we can recover one solution of the RSSP. So the failure possibility is at most

$$
P = \Pr(\exists \mathbf{x} \in \mathcal{L}(B) \quad s.t. \quad 0 < \|\mathbf{x}\|_p \le \|\mathbf{e}'\|_p \ , \mathbf{x} \notin S_n).
$$

For $\mathbf{x} \in \mathcal{L}(B)$ with $\|\mathbf{x}\|_p \le \|\mathbf{e}'\|_p = \frac{1}{2}(n+1)^{\frac{1}{p}}, \mathbf{x} \notin S_n$, we have $x_{n+2} = 0$ since $N > \frac{1}{2}(n+1)^{\frac{1}{p}}$, which implies

$$\sum_{i=1}^{n} w_i a_i + w s = 0. \tag{2}$$

If w is odd, then $\mathbf{x} \notin \mathbb{Z}^{n+2}$ and $|x_i| \ge \frac{1}{2}$ for $i = 1, 2 \ldots n+1$ by (1). Noticing that $\|\mathbf{x}\|_p \le \frac{1}{2}(n+1)^{\frac{1}{p}}$, we must have $|x_i| = \frac{1}{2}$ and $w = \pm 1$, which means $\mathbf{x} \in S_n$ in this case.

Thus w is even and $\mathbf{x} \in \mathbb{Z}^{n+2}$. Using $x_i = w_i + \frac{1}{2}w$ and $x_{n+1} = \frac{1}{2}w$, together with (2), we have

$$\sum_{i=1}^{n} x_i a_i + 2 x_{n+1} s - x_{n+1} \sum_{i=1}^{n} a_i = 0.$$

As a result, the above probability P can be bounded as

$$P = \Pr(\exists \mathbf{x} \in \mathcal{L}(B) \quad \text{s.t.} \quad 0 < \|\mathbf{x}\|_p \le \frac{1}{2}(n+1)^{\frac{1}{p}}, \quad \mathbf{x} \notin S_n)$$

$$\le \Pr(\exists \mathbf{x} \in \mathbb{Z}^{n+1} \quad \text{s.t.} \quad 0 < \|\mathbf{x}\|_p \le \frac{1}{2}(n+1)^{\frac{1}{p}},$$

$$\sum_{i=1}^{n} x_i a_i + 2 x_{n+1} s - x_{n+1} \sum_{i=1}^{n} a_i = 0, (\mathbf{x}^T, 0)^T \notin S_n)$$

$$\le \Pr(\sum_{i=1}^{n} x_i a_i + 2 x_{n+1} s - x_{n+1} \sum_{i=1}^{n} a_i = 0 : 0 < \|\mathbf{x}\|_p \le \frac{1}{2}(n+1)^{\frac{1}{p}}, (\mathbf{x}^T, 0)^T \notin S_n)$$

$$\cdot \#\{\mathbf{x} \in \mathbb{Z}^{n+1} \quad | \quad \|\mathbf{x}\|_p \le \frac{1}{2}(n+1)^{\frac{1}{p}}\}.$$

For any solution $\mathbf{e}$, we have $s = \sum_{i=1}^{n} e_i a_i$. Taking $z_i = x_i + 2 x_{n+1} e_i - x_{n+1}$, we get

$$\sum_{i=1}^{n} x_i a_i + 2 x_{n+1} s - x_{n+1} \sum_{i=1}^{n} a_i = 0 \iff \sum_{i=1}^{n} z_i a_i = 0.$$

So we have

$$P \le \Pr(\sum_{i=1}^{n} z_i a_i = 0, \quad (\mathbf{x}^T, 0)^T \notin S_n) \cdot \#\{\mathbf{x} \in \mathbb{Z}^{n+1} \quad | \quad \|\mathbf{x}\|_p \le \frac{1}{2}(n+1)^{\frac{1}{p}}\}.$$

We next show that there exists a j s.t. $z_j \ne 0$. For contradiction, if all $z_j = 0$, then $x_j = (1 - 2e_j)x_{n+1}$. Hence $|x_j| = |x_{n+1}|$ since $e_j \in \{0, 1\}$. By $0 < \|\mathbf{x}\|_p \le \frac{1}{2}(n+1)^{\frac{1}{p}}$, we know that $0 < x_j < \frac{1}{2}$, which contradicts that x_j's are integer. So there exists a j s.t. $z_j \ne 0$. Let $z' = -\sum_{i \ne j} z_i a_i / z_j$, then

$$\Pr(\sum_{i=1}^{n} z_i a_i = 0, (\mathbf{x}^T, 0)^T \notin S_n) = \Pr(\sum_{i=1}^{n} z_i a_i = 0, z_j \neq 0)$$

$$= \Pr(a_j = z')$$

$$= \sum_{k=1}^{A} \Pr(a_j = z' | z' = k) \cdot \Pr(z' = k)$$

$$= \sum_{k=1}^{A} \Pr(a_j = k) \cdot \Pr(z' = k)$$

$$= \frac{1}{A} \sum_{k=1}^{A} \Pr(z' = k)$$

$$\leq \frac{1}{A}.$$

Now we obtain

$$P \leq \frac{1}{A} \cdot \#\{\mathbf{x} \in \mathbb{Z}^{n+1} | \|\mathbf{x}\|_p \leq \frac{1}{2}(n+1)^{\frac{1}{p}}\}. \tag{3}$$

By Theorem 1, we can bound P as

$$P \leq \frac{2^{c_p(n+1)}}{A} = \frac{2^{c_p(n+1)}}{2^{(n/d)}}$$

When $d < 1/c_p \triangleq \delta_p$, P is exponentially small on n, meaning almost all random subset sum instances with density less than δ_p can be solved by l_p-norm SVP oracle. Hence we get the following theorem.

Theorem 2. *For $p \in \mathbb{Z}^+$ and large enough n, let A be a positive integer, $a_i(1 \leq i \leq n)$ be independently uniformly random integers between 1 and A, $e = (e_1, e_2, \cdots, e_n)$ be arbitrary non-zero vector in $\{0,1\}^n$, and $s = \sum_{i=1}^{n} a_i e_i$. If the density*

$$d = \frac{n}{\log_2 A} < \delta_p = \begin{cases} 0.5761, p = 1 \\ 0.9408, p = 2 \\ 1/(\frac{1}{2^p}\log_2(2^{p+1} - 2) + \log_2(1 + \frac{1}{(2^p-1)(1-(\frac{1}{2^{p+1}-2})^{(2^p-1))}})))), p \geq 3 \end{cases} \tag{4}$$

then with probability exponentially close to 1, the subset sum problem defined by $a_i(1 \leq i \leq n)$ and s can be solved in polynomial time with a single call to an l_p-norm SVP oracle.

The table below gives the values of δ_p for p from one to ten.

p	1	2	3	4	5	6	7	8	9	10
δ_p	0.5761	0.9408	1.4957	2.5013	4.3127	7.5907	13.564	24.521	44.750	82.302

We also plot the ten $\log_2 \delta_p$'s values in the following picture.

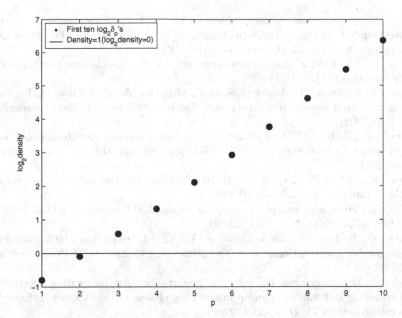

Roughly speaking, the asymptotic form for δ_p is $2^p/(p+2)$. It's easy to see that the upper bound δ_p will go increasingly to infinity when p tends to infinity, which implies that an l_p-norm SVP oracle with larger p will help to solve more random subset sum problems. Another interesting phenomenon is that we can solve the RSSP with density one with the l_p-norm SVP oracle with $p \geq 3$ but we can not solve them with l_2-norm SVP oracle by now. It seems that the hardness of l_p-norm SVP is not decreasing as p gets larger.

4   Conclusion

In this paper, we generalize the classical probabilistic reduction from random subset sum problem to l_2-norm SVP to the case for l_p-norm. For any $p \in \mathbb{Z}^+$, we can use an l_p-norm SVP oracle to solve almost all random subset sum problem with density bounded by δ_p. Since δ_p increases as p gets bigger, an l_p-norm SVP oracle with larger p will help to solve more random subset sum problems. Moreover, an l_p-norm SVP oracle with $p \geq 3$ can help solve almost all random subset sum instances with density one, which are thought to be the most difficult instances.

Acknowledgement. We thank the anonymous referees for putting forward their excellent suggestions on how to improve the presentation of this paper.

References

1. Ajtai, M.: Gennerating hard instances of lattice problems. In: STOC 1996, pp. 99–108. ACM Press, New York (1996)
2. Ajtai, M., Dwork, C.: A public-key cryptosystem with worst-case/average-case equivalence. In: STOC 1997, pp. 284–293. ACM Press, New York (1997)

3. Ajtai, M.: The shortest vector problem in L2 is NP-hard for randomized reductions(extended abstract). In: 30th Annual ACM Symposium on Theory of Computing, pp. 266–275. ACM Press, New York (1998)

4. Babai, L.: On Lovasz' lattice reduction and the nearest lattice point problem. Combinatorica 6(1), 1–13 (1986)

5. Coster, M.J., Joux, A., Lamacchia, B.A., Odlyzko, A.M., Schnorr, C.P., Stern, J.: An improved low-density subset sum algorithm. Computational Complexity 2, 111–128 (1992)

6. Dadush, D., Peikert, C., Vempala, S.: Enumerative lattice algorithms in any norm via M-ellipsoid coverings. In: FOCS 2011, pp. 580–589. IEEE Computer Society Press (2011)

7. Frieze, A.M.: On the Lagarias-Odlyzko algorithm for the subset sum problem. SIAM J. Comput. 18, 550–558 (1989)

8. Gentry, C.: Fully homomorphic encryption using ideal lattices. In: STOC 2009, pp. 169–178. ACM Press, New York (2009)

9. Gentry, C., Peikert, C., Vaikuntanathan, V.: Trapdoors for hard lattices and new cryptographic constructions. In: STOC 2008, pp. 197–206. ACM Press, New York (2008)

10. Goldreich, D., Micciancio, D., Safra, S., Seifert, J.P.: Approximating shortest lattice vectors is not harder than approximating closest lattice vectors. Information Processing Letters 71(2), 55–61 (1999)

11. Hoffstein, J., Pipher, J., Silverman, J.H.: NTRU: A Ring-Based Public Key Cryptosystem. In: Buhler, J.P. (ed.) ANTS 1998. LNCS, vol. 1423, pp. 267–288. Springer, Heidelberg (1998)

12. Hoffstein, J., Howgrave-Graham, N., Pipher, J., Silverman, J.H., Whyte, W.: NTRUSIGN: Digital Signatures Using the NTRU Lattice. In: Joye, M. (ed.) CT-RSA 2003. LNCS, vol. 2612, pp. 122–140. Springer, Heidelberg (2003)

13. Impagliazzo, R., Naor, M.: Efficient Cryptographic Schemes Provably as Secure as Subset Sum. Journal of Cryptology 9, 199–216 (1996)

14. Lenstra, A.K., Lenstra Jr., H.W., Lovasz, L.: Factoring polynomials with rational coefficients. Mathematische Annalen 261, 513–534 (1982)

15. Lagarias, J.C., Odlyzko, A.M.: Solving low-density subset sum problems. J. Assoc. Comp. Mach. 32(1), 229–246 (1985)

16. Lyubashevsky, V., Micciancio, D., Peikert, C., Rosen, A.: SWIFFT: A modest proposal for FFT hashing. In: Nyberg, K. (ed.) FSE 2008. LNCS, vol. 5086, pp. 54–72. Springer, Heidelberg (2008)

17. Micciancio, D., Goldwasser, S.: Complexity of Lattice Problems: A Cryptography Perspective. Kluwer Academic Publishes (2002)

18. Micciancio, D., Voulgaris, P.: A deterministic single exponential time algorithm for most lattice problems based on Voronoi cell computations. In: STOC 2010, pp. 351–358. ACM Press, New York (2010)

19. Micciancio, D.: Inapproximability of the Shortest Vector Problem: Toward a Deterministic Reduction. Theory of Computing 8(1), 487–512 (2012)

20. Regev, O.: Lattices in computer science. Lecture notes of a course given in Tel Aviv University (2004)

21. Regev, O.: On lattices, learning with errors, random linear codes, and cryptography. In: STOC 2005, pp. 84–93. ACM Press, New York (2005)

22. Regev, O., Rosen, R.: Lattice problems and norm embeddings. In: STOC 2006, pp. 447–456. ACM Press, New York (2006)

Parallel Gauss Sieve Algorithm: Solving the SVP Challenge over a 128-Dimensional Ideal Lattice[*]

Tsukasa Ishiguro[1], Shinsaku Kiyomoto[1],
Yutaka Miyake[1], and Tsuyoshi Takagi[2]

[1] KDDI R&D Laboratories Inc., 2-1-15 Ohara, Fujimino, Saitama 356-8502, Japan
{tsukasa,kiyomoto,miyake}@kddilabs.jp
[2] Institute of Mathematics for Industry, Kyushu University, 744, Motooka, Nishi-ku,
Fukuoka 819-0395, Japan
takagi@imi.kyushu-u.ac.jp

Abstract. In this paper, we report that we have solved the SVP Challenge over a 128-dimensional lattice in Ideal Lattice Challenge from TU Darmstadt, which is currently the highest dimension in the challenge that has ever been solved. The security of lattice-based cryptography is based on the hardness of solving the shortest vector problem (SVP) in lattices. In 2010, Micciancio and Voulgaris proposed a Gauss Sieve algorithm for heuristically solving the SVP using a list L of Gauss-reduced vectors. Milde and Schneider proposed a parallel implementation method for the Gauss Sieve algorithm. However, the efficiency of the more than 10 threads in their implementation decreased due to the large number of non-Gauss-reduced vectors appearing in the distributed list of each thread. In this paper, we propose a more practical parallelized Gauss Sieve algorithm. Our algorithm deploys an additional Gauss-reduced list V of sample vectors assigned to each thread, and all vectors in list L remain Gauss-reduced by mutually reducing them using all sample vectors in V. Therefore, our algorithm allows the Gauss Sieve algorithm to run for large dimensions with a small communication overhead. Finally, we succeeded in solving the SVP Challenge over a 128-dimensional ideal lattice generated by the cyclotomic polynomial $x^{128} + 1$ using about 30,000 CPU hours.

Keywords: shortest vector problem, lattice-based cryptography, ideal lattice, Gauss Sieve algorithm, parallel algorithm.

1 Introduction

Lattice-based cryptography has been considered a powerful primitive for constructing useful cryptographic protocols. The security of lattice-based cryptography is based on the hardness of solving the shortest vector problem (SVP), which involves searching for the shortest nonzero vectors in lattices. Ajtai proved that the worst case complexity of solving the SVP is NP-hard under randomized

---

[*] The full-version of this paper is appeared in [13].

H. Krawczyk (Ed.): PKC 2014, LNCS 8383, pp. 411–428, 2014.

reductions [1]. The α-SVP [17] is an approximation problem of the SVP, which searches for elements with the size of the shortest vector multiplied by a small approximation factor α. Many cryptographic primitives have been built on lattices due to their security against quantum computers and their novel functionalities: Ajtai-Dwork scheme [2], NTRU [10], fully-homomorphic cryptosystems [8], and multi-linear maps [7].

There are several approaches for solving the SVP and the α-SVP. The fastest deterministic algorithm is the Voronoi cell algorithm [18], which runs in exponential time $2^{O(n)}$ and space $2^{O(n)}$ for n-dimensional lattices. The sieving algorithms, which are explained in the next subsection, are probabilistic algorithms that require exponential time $2^{O(n)}$ and space $2^{O(n)}$ [3,21,5]. The enumeration algorithms are exhaustive search algorithms that need time $2^{O(n^2)}$ or $2^{O(n \log n)}$, but only the polynomial size of space [29,30,6], and they are suitable for parallelization using multicore CPUs and GPUs. Moreover, the lattice basis reduction such as LLL or BKZ is a polynomial-time approximation algorithm [16,28]. Generally, enumeration algorithms are also used in lattice basis reduction algorithms as a subroutine for solving the α-SVP. On the other hand, sieving algorithms are used only for solving the SVP.

1.1   Sieving Algorithms and Ideal Lattices

In 2001 Ajtai *et al.* proposed the first sieve algorithm for solving the SVP [3]. There are many variants of the sieving algorithm [21,5] that try to improve the computational costs of the algorithm. In 2009 Micciancio and Voulgaris proposed a practical sieving algorithm, called the Gauss Sieve algorithm [19]. The Gauss Sieve algorithm consists of a list L of vectors in the lattice and a reduction algorithm that outputs a shorter vector from two input vectors. List L manages the vectors reduced by the reduction algorithm. The number of vectors in L increases but the norm of several vectors L is shrunk by the reduction algorithm, and eventually the shortest nonzero vector can be found in list L.

The theoretical upper boundary of the computation time of the Gauss Sieve algorithm is not yet proved; however, the Gauss Sieve algorithm is faster than any other sieve algorithm in practice, because it deploys a list L of pair-wise Gauss-reduced vectors that can gradually reduce the norm of vectors in the list. The time complexity of the Gauss sieve is estimated to be asymptotically $2^{0.52n}$ for n-dimensional lattices [19]. In 2011 Milde and Schneider considered a parallelization variant of the Gauss Sieve algorithm. From the experiment by Milde and Schneider, once the number of threads increases to more than ten, the speed-up factor does not exceed around five. Therefore, it is difficult to apply to large-scale parallel computation.

In order to realize efficient construction of lattice-based cryptography, ideal lattices are often used. Using ideal lattices, many cryptographic primitives work faster and require less storage [10,7]. One of the open problems is whether the computational problems related to the ideal lattices are easier to solve compared with those of random lattices [23]. First, Micciancio and Voulgaris mentioned the possibility of speeding up the sieving algorithm for ideal lattices [19]. In ideal lattices, several vectors of similar norms have a rotation structure, and thus it is possible to compute the set of vectors in the reduction algorithm derived from the sieve algorithm without a large overhead. Schneider proposed the Ideal Gauss Sieve algorithm, which uses the rotation structure of the *Anti-cyclic lattice* generated by the polynomial $x^n + 1$ where n is a power of two [26]. Then, their proposed algorithm enables the Gauss Sieve algorithm to run about 25 times faster on 60-dimensional ideal lattices.

1.2 Our Contribution

We propose a parallelized Gauss Sieve algorithm using an additional list V generated by the multisampling technique of vectors in the lattice. Our algorithm mutually reduces the vectors in both L and V, so that all vectors in both lists V and L remain pair-wisely Gauss-reduced. Using this technique, the reduction algorithm can be easily parallelized. Additionally, even if the number of threads increases, our algorithm keeps the vector set pairwise-reduced and efficiency is maintained. Therefore, our algorithm enables the Gauss Sieve algorithm to run without excessive overhead even in a large-scale parallel computation.

With the result of our proposed algorithm, we succeeded in solving the SVP Challenge over a 128-dimensional ideal lattice generated by the cyclotomic polynomial $x^{128} + 1$ using about 30,000 CPU hours. In our experiment, we used 84 instances and each instance runs 32 threads, namely the number of threads is 2,688 in total. The communication overhead among threads was less than ten percents of the total running time.

2 Definitions and Problems

In this section, we provide a short overview of the definition of the SVP on the lattice. We then explain the definitions of Gauss-reduced and pairwise-reduced for a set of vectors on the lattice used for the Gauss Sieve algorithm.

Let $B = \{\mathbf{b}_1, \ldots, \mathbf{b}_n\}$ be a set of n linearly independent vectors in $\mathbb{R}^m$. The lattice generated by B is the set $\mathcal{L}(B) = \mathcal{L}(\mathbf{b}_1, \ldots, \mathbf{b}_n) = \{\sum_{1 \leq i \leq n} x_i \mathbf{b}_i, x_i \in \mathbb{Z}\}$ of all integer linear combinations of the vectors in B. The set $\bar{B}$ is called *basis* of the lattice $\mathcal{L}(B)$. In the following, we denote by $\mathcal{L}(\mathbf{B})$ the lattice of basis B as the matrix representation $\mathbf{B} = (\mathbf{b}_1, \ldots, \mathbf{b}_n) \in \mathbb{R}^{m \times n}$. If $n = m$, the lattice $\mathcal{L}(\mathbf{B})$ is called full-rank. In this paper, for the sake of simplicity, we will consider only full-rank lattices and assume that all the basis vectors $\mathbf{b}_i (i = 1, 2, ..., n)$ have only integer entries.

The Euclidean norm of vector $\mathbf{v} = (v_0, \ldots, v_{n-1}) \in \mathcal{L}(\mathbf{B})$ is denoted by $\|\mathbf{v}\| - \sum_{0 \leq i < n} v_i^2$. The norm of the shortest nonzero vectors in $\mathcal{L}(\mathbf{B})$ is denoted by $\lambda_1(\mathcal{L}(\mathbf{B}))$. The inner product of two vectors $\mathbf{a} = (a_0, \ldots, a_{n-1}), \mathbf{b} = (b_0, \ldots, b_{n-1}) \in \mathcal{L}(\mathbf{B})$ is defined by $\langle \mathbf{a} \cdot \mathbf{b} \rangle = \sum_{0 \leq i < n} a_i b_i$. For $x \in \mathbb{R}$, $\lfloor x \rceil$ denotes the nearest integer to x, namely $\lfloor x + 1/2 \rfloor$.

We define the shortest vector problem (SVP) on a lattice as follow.

Definition 1 (Shortest vector problem on a lattice). *Given a lattice* $\mathcal{L}(\mathbf{B})$, *find a shortest nonzero vector of the length* $\lambda_1(\mathcal{L}(\mathbf{B}))$ *in* $\mathcal{L}(\mathbf{B})$.

From the Gaussian heuristic, the length of a shortest vector in lattice $\mathcal{L}(\mathbf{B})$ is estimated to be $\lambda_1(\mathcal{L}(\mathbf{B})) = (1/\sqrt{\pi})\Gamma(\frac{n}{2} + 1)^{\frac{1}{n}} \cdot \det(\mathcal{L}(\mathbf{B}))^{\frac{1}{n}}$, where $\Gamma(x)$ is the gamma-function and $\det(\mathbf{B})$ is the determinant of matrix $\mathbf{B}$.

Let $g(x) \in \mathbb{Z}[x]$ be a monic polynomial of degree n, and let I be an ideal of ring $\mathbb{Z}[x]/(g(x))$. All elements of ideal I are represented by polynomials $\mathbf{v}(x) = \sum_{0 \le i < n} v_i x^i$ in $\mathbb{Z}[x]/(g(x))$. We identify $\mathbf{v}(x)$ with vectors $\mathbf{v} = (v_0, \dots, v_{n-1}) \in \mathbb{Z}^n$. The ideal I is an additive subgroup of $\mathbb{Z}[x]/(g(x))$, and the set $\{\mathbf{v} = (v_0, \dots, v_{n-1}) \in \mathbb{Z}^n | \mathbf{v}(x) = \sum_{0 \le i < n} v_i x^i \in I\}$ becomes a lattice. This is called the ideal lattice generated by $\mathbf{v}(x)$, and its basis B consists of the rotation vectors $x^i \mathbf{v}(x) \in \mathbb{Z}[x]/(g(x))$ for $i = 0, 1, \dots, n-1$. The cyclotomic polynomials, such as $g(x) = x^n + 1$ for $n = 2^h$ with some positive integer h, are often used for generating the ideal lattice in cryptography.

2.1 Gauss-Reduced and Pairwise-Reduced

We define Gauss-reduced and pairwise-reduced for a set of vectors on lattice $\mathcal{L}(\mathbf{B})$. We then explain an algorithm for determining and reducing two given vectors of lattice $\mathcal{L}(\mathbf{B})$.

First, the definition of Gauss-reduced is as follows.

Definition 2 (Gauss-reduced). *If two different vectors* $\mathbf{a}, \mathbf{b} \in \mathcal{L}(\mathbf{B})$ *satisfy* $\|\mathbf{a} \pm \mathbf{b}\| \ge \max(\|\mathbf{a}\|, \|\mathbf{b}\|)$, *then* $\mathbf{a}, \mathbf{b}$ *are called Gauss-reduced.*

Micciancio and Voulgaris explained about the way to convert two vectors $\mathbf{a}, \mathbf{b}$ in $\mathcal{L}(\mathbf{B})$ to be Gauss-reduced. The conversion algorithm uses the Reduce algorithm (Alg.1), which outputs vectors $\mathbf{a}'$ for two vectors $\mathbf{a}, \mathbf{b}$ in $\mathcal{L}(\mathbf{B})$. The reduced vector $\mathbf{a}'$ is a linear combination of $\mathbf{a}$ and $\mathbf{b}$, which has a shorter norm than $\max(\mathbf{a}, \mathbf{b})$, or otherwise $\mathbf{a}' = \mathbf{a}$. From this, we can determine whether two vectors $\mathbf{a}, \mathbf{b}$ in $\mathcal{L}(\mathbf{B})$ are Gauss-reduced. Indeed, we can easily prove the following lemma.

Lemma 1. *Let* $\mathbf{a}, \mathbf{b}$ *be two vectors in* $\mathcal{L}(\mathbf{B})$. *We set* $\mathbf{a}' = Reduce(\mathbf{a}, \mathbf{b})$ *and* $\mathbf{b}' = Reduce(\mathbf{b}, \mathbf{a})$. *If both* $\mathbf{a} = \mathbf{a}'$ *and* $\mathbf{b} = \mathbf{b}'$ *hold, then* $\mathbf{a}, \mathbf{b}$ *are Gauss-reduced.*

If two vectors $\mathbf{a}, \mathbf{b}$ are not Gauss-reduced, then $\mathbf{a} \ne \mathbf{a}'$ or $\mathbf{b} \ne \mathbf{b}'$ holds by Lemma 1. Recall that the reduced vector $\mathbf{a}' \leftarrow Reduce(\mathbf{a}, \mathbf{b})$ has the property $\|\mathbf{a}'\| \le \|\mathbf{a}\|$. After performing both $Reduce(\mathbf{a}, \mathbf{b})$ and $Reduce(\mathbf{b}, \mathbf{a})$, we know that the resulting vectors $(\mathbf{a}', \mathbf{b}')$ are either Gauss-reduced or $\mathbf{a}'$ (or $\mathbf{b}'$) is strictly shorter than $\mathbf{a}$ (or $\mathbf{b}$), respectively. If we repeatedly run the Reduce algorithm for $\mathbf{a} = \mathbf{a}'$ and $\mathbf{b} = \mathbf{b}'$, then we expect the resulting vectors $(\mathbf{a}', \mathbf{b}')$ to become Gauss-reduced. From our experiments in the 100-dimensional lattices, we can obtain the Gauss-reduced vectors after at most 10 iterations in most cases.

If $\mathbf{a}, \mathbf{b}$ are linearly dependent, the output of $Reduce(\mathbf{a}, \mathbf{b})$ is always the zero vector, $i.e.$, $\|\mathbf{a}'\| = 0$, which is called a "collision". The collision is used as the condition for terminating the Gauss Sieve algorithm.

Algorithm 1. Reduce [19]

Require: Vectors p_1, p_2 in lattice $\mathcal{L}(\mathbf{B})$

Ensure: Vector p_1 in lattice $\mathcal{L}(\mathbf{B})$ s.t. $|\frac{\langle p_1, p_2 \rangle}{\langle p_2, p_2 \rangle}| \le \frac{1}{2}$

1: **if** $|2 \cdot \langle p_1 \cdot p_2 \rangle| > \langle p_2 \cdot p_2 \rangle$ **then**

2:     $p_1 \leftarrow p_1 - \left\lfloor \frac{\langle p_1, p_2 \rangle}{\langle p_2, p_2 \rangle} \right\rceil \cdot p_2$ /* Make p_1 closest to p_2 in $p_1 + p_2 \mathbb{Z}$ */

3: **return** p_1

Definition 3 (Pairwise-reduced). *Let A be a set of d vectors in $\mathcal{L}(\mathbf{B})$. If every pair of two vectors $(\mathbf{a}_i, \mathbf{a}_j)$ in A for $i, j = 1, \ldots, d, i \neq j$ is Gauss-reduced, then the A is called pairwise-reduced.*

In general, if we append a vector $\mathbf{b} \in \mathcal{L}(\mathbf{B})$ to a pairwise-reduced set A, then $A \cup \{\mathbf{b}\}$ is not always pairwise-reduced. If every pair of two vectors $(\mathbf{a}_i, \mathbf{b})$ for $\mathbf{a}_1, \ldots, \mathbf{a}_d \in A$ is Gauss-reduced, then the union $A \cup \{\mathbf{b}\}$ becomes pairwise-reduced from the definition. Obviously we can prove the following lemma that shows that the union of two pairwise-reduced sets of vectors becomes pairwise-reduced by checking whether the all pairs of two vectors from A and B are Gauss-reduced.

Lemma 2 (Combining Lemma). *Let $A = \{\mathbf{a}_1, \ldots, \mathbf{a}_r\}$ and $B = \{\mathbf{b}_1, \ldots, \mathbf{b}_m\}$ be sets of vectors in $\mathcal{L}(\mathbf{B})$. Assume that both A and B are pairwise-reduced. If every pair of two vectors $(\mathbf{a}_i, \mathbf{b}_j)$ in A, B for $1 \le i \le r, 1 \le j \le m$ is Gauss-reduced, then the union $A \cup B$ is pairwise-reduced.*

This lemma is used for constructing our proposed parallel algorithm for the Gauss Sieve algorithm.

3   Gauss Sieve Algorithm

In this section, we briefly explain the Gauss Sieve algorithm [19] and the Ideal Gauss Sieve algorithm [26].

3.1   Gauss Sieve [19]

The Gauss Sieve (GS) algorithm was proposed by Micciancio and Voulgaris in 2009 [19] and it was implemented as **gsieve** library by Voulgaris [32]. We prepare two auxiliary lists L and S, where L and S are defined by a set of vectors and a stack of vectors, respectively. L and S are initially assigned as empty. In the beginning of the GS algorithm, a new vector $\mathbf{v}$ is randomly sampled using Klein's randomized rounding algorithm [15].

The GS algorithm runs a subroutine, Gauss Reduce, which updates $\mathbf{v}, L, S$ by the steps in the following two parts. The first part runs the Reduce algorithm using a list L for updating $\mathbf{v}' = \text{Reduce}(\mathbf{v}, \ell_i)$ for all vectors $\ell_i \in L$. Once the $\mathbf{v}'$ is not equal to $\mathbf{v}$, this vector $\mathbf{v}'$ is moved to stack S. The reason is that if $\mathbf{v}$ is reduced using $\ell_i \in L$, then $\mathbf{v}'$ and $\ell_j, (i > j)$ are not always Gauss-reduced.

If the **v** is not changed by Reduce(**v**, ℓ_i) for all $\ell_i \in L$, the steps in the second part are performed. The second part runs the Reduce algorithm using a list L that makes the list pairwise-reduced. If $\ell_i' \neq \ell_i$ holds for $\ell_i' = \text{Reduce}(\ell_i, \mathbf{v})$, then the vector ℓ_i' is moved to stack S and deleted from L. By the above steps, all pairs (**v**, ℓ_i) are always Gauss-reduced, where $\ell_i \in L$. Therefore, $L \cup v$ becomes pairwise-reduced by Lemma 2. Then L is updated by $L \cup \mathbf{v}$ and the iteration is continued . If the stack is not empty, **v** is popped from the stack S, otherwise, **v** is newly sampled . The termination condition of the GS algorithm is determined by the number of collisions of the zero vector ($\|\mathbf{a}'\| = 0$) that appears in L.

The theoretical upper bound of the complexity of the GS algorithm is not yet proved; however, in practice, the GS algorithm is faster than any other sieving algorithms. According to Micciancio and Voulgaris [19], the complexity of the GS algorithm is asymptotically estimated as time $2^{0.52n}$ and space $2^{0.2n}$. Moreover, Micciancio and Voulgaris showed some experiments that the GS algorithm outputs a shortest vector in some lattices of up to 60 dimensions, but it is not theoretically proved that the GS algorithm always outputs a shortest vector [19].

3.2   Ideal Gauss Sieve Algorithm [26]

Schneider proposed an Ideal Gauss Sieve algorithm [26] that uses the structure of an ideal lattice to improve the processing speed of the Gauss Sieve algorithm. If n is a power of two, an ideal lattice generated by the cyclotomic polynomial $g(x) = x^n + 1$ is called an *Anti-cyclic lattice*. In this type, the rotation of vector **v** is $\text{rot}(\mathbf{v}) = (-v_{n-1}, v_0, \ldots, v_{n-2})$. The rotation of the *Anti-cyclic lattice* can generate new vectors that have a similar norm virtually for free. Therefore, we can implement the Gauss Sieve algorithm using the list L with the rotated vectors $\text{rot}^i(\mathbf{v})$ for $i = 1, 2, \ldots, n-1$ in addition to **v** with a small overhead. The algorithm enables the Gauss Sieve algorithm to run about 25 times faster on 60-dimensional ideal lattices [26].

4   Proposed Parallel Gauss Sieve Algorithm

In this section, we propose the parallelized algorithm derived from the Gauss Sieve algorithm. We design our algorithm so that the list L remains pairwise-reduced as with the Gauss Sieve algorithm, even though this algorithm works in parallel.

4.1   Overview

Let t be the number of threads used in our algorithm. Our algorithm prepares the auxiliary list V of r vectors in $\mathcal{L}(\mathbf{B})$, where each thread treats at most $s = \lfloor r/t \rfloor$ sample vectors for the list V. We also use the same list L and stack S in the Gauss Sieve algorithm, and the vectors in list L remain pairwise-reduced during our algorithm by control with list V. Each thread has list V, list L, and stack S, where we write $V = \{\mathbf{v}_1, \ldots, \mathbf{v}_r\}$ and $L = \{\ell_1, \ldots, \ell_m\}$. After each

Algorithm 2. Proposed Parallel Gauss Sieve

Require: Lattice basis $\mathbf{B}$, the number of sample vectors $r \in \mathbb{N}$, $\alpha, \beta \in \mathbb{R}$
Ensure: A shortest vector $\mathbf{v}$ in $\mathcal{L}(\mathbf{B})$
1: $L \leftarrow \{\}, V \leftarrow \{\}, S \leftarrow \{\}, K \leftarrow 0$
    /* **Multisampling of vectors** (Steps from 2 to 9)*/
2: **while** $K < \alpha |L| + \beta$ **do**
3:      **if** $|S| \neq 0$ **then**
4:          $t \leftarrow \min(r, |S|)$
5:          **for** $j = 1, \ldots, t$ **do**
6:              Pop from Stack S to $\mathbf{v}_j$
7:      **if** $|S| < r$ **then**
8:          **for** $j = |S| + 1, \ldots, r$ **do**
9:              Generate a new vector $\mathbf{v}_j$ using Klein's randomized rounding algorithm [15]
10:     $V \leftarrow \{\mathbf{v}_1, ..., \mathbf{v}_r\}, V' \leftarrow \{\}, V'' \leftarrow \{\}, L' \leftarrow \{\}$
11:     $L = \{\ell_1, ..., \ell_m\}$
    /***Reduction sample vectors using list vectors** (Steps from 12 to 22)*/
12:     **for** $i = 1, \ldots, r$ **do**
13:         $\mathbf{w}_i \leftarrow \mathbf{v}_i$
14:         **for** $j = 1, \ldots, m$ **do**
15:             $\mathbf{w}_i \leftarrow \text{Reduce}(\mathbf{w}_i, \ell_j)$ /* This step can be ran in parallel */
16:         **if** $\|\mathbf{w}_i\| = 0$ **then**
17:             $K \leftarrow K + 1$
18:         **else if** $\mathbf{w}_i \neq \mathbf{v}_i$ **then**
19:             $S \leftarrow S \cup \{\mathbf{w}_i\}$
20:         **else**
21:             $V' \leftarrow V' \cup \{\mathbf{w}_i\}$
22:     $V' = \{\mathbf{v}_1, ..., \mathbf{v}_{r'}\}$
    /***Reduction sample vectors using sample vectors** (Steps from 23 to 34)
    */
23:     **for** $i = 1, \ldots, r'$ **do**
24:         $\mathbf{w}_i \leftarrow \mathbf{v}_i$
25:         **for** $j = 1, \ldots, r'$ **do**
26:             **if** $i \neq j$ **then**
27:                 $\mathbf{w}_i \leftarrow \text{Reduce}(\mathbf{w}_i, \mathbf{v}_j)$ /* This step can be ran in parallel */
28:         **if** $\|\mathbf{w}_i\| = 0$ **then**
29:             $K \leftarrow K + 1$
30:         **else if** $\mathbf{w}_i \neq \mathbf{v}_i$ **then**
31:             $S \leftarrow S \cup \{\mathbf{w}_i\}$
32:         **else**
33:             $V'' \leftarrow V'' \cup \{\mathbf{w}_i\}$
34:     $V'' = \{\mathbf{v}_1, ..., \mathbf{v}_{r''}\}$
    /* **Reduction list vectors using sample vectors** (Steps from 35 to 45)*/
35:     **for** $i = 1, \ldots, m$ **do**
36:         $\mathbf{w}_i \leftarrow \ell_i$
37:         **for** $j = 1, \ldots, r''$ **do**
38:             $\mathbf{w}_i \leftarrow \text{Reduce}(\mathbf{w}_i, \mathbf{v}_j)$ /* This step can be ran in parallel */
39:         **if** $\|\mathbf{w}_i\| = 0$ **then**
40:             $K \leftarrow K + 1$
41:         **else if** $\mathbf{w}_i \neq \ell_i$ **then**
42:             $S \leftarrow S \cup \{\mathbf{w}_i\}$
43:         **else**
44:             $L' \leftarrow L' \cup \{\mathbf{w}_i\}$
45:     $L' = \{\ell_1, ..., \ell_{m'}\}$
46:     $L \leftarrow L' \cup V''$
47: **return** a shortest vector in L

iteration of the loop in our algorithm, we pop vectors from the stack S to list V. If the size of V is smaller than r, we generate new sample vectors by the multisampling techniques. We explain how to construct the proposed threads in the following. There are three different reduction steps in our algorithm, namely **Reduction sample vectors using list vectors**, **Reduction sample vectors using sample vectors**, and **Reduction list vectors using sample vectors**. Our algorithm requires to use Alg.1 at most $\max(rm, r^2)$ times in each step, in other words, at most $\max(\lfloor rm/t \rfloor, \lfloor r^2/t \rfloor)$ times in each thread.

In the **Reduction sample vectors using list vectors**, let $s = \lfloor r/t \rfloor$ be the number of sample vectors treated by a thread, where r is the size of list V. Each thread has the distributed list $V_i = \{\mathbf{v}_{(i-1)s+1}, \dots, \mathbf{v}_{is}\}$ and list L, where $V = \cup_i V_i$ and $i = 1, 2, \dots, t$. Each thread i independently deals with list L and the sample vectors V_i, and runs $\mathbf{v}'_k = \text{Reduce}(\mathbf{v}_k, \boldsymbol{\ell}_j)$, where $\mathbf{v}_k \in V_i, \boldsymbol{\ell}_j \in L$, identical to a Gauss Sieve algorithm. If $\mathbf{v}'_k \neq \mathbf{v}_k$ holds, then the thread i moves the reduced vector $\mathbf{v}'_k$ into the stack S, otherwise, the thread i moves this vector $\mathbf{v}'_k$ into new list V'. At the end of this part, any vector $\mathbf{v}$ in list V' satisfies $\mathbf{v} = \text{Reduce}(\mathbf{v}, \boldsymbol{\ell})$ for all vectors $\boldsymbol{\ell}$ in list L.

In the **Reduction sample vectors using sample vectors**, each thread has list V', which consists of r' vectors on a lattice. Let $s' = \lfloor r'/t \rfloor$ be the number of sample vectors treated by a thread. Each thread i deals with only a sample list V' and runs $\mathbf{v}'_k = \text{Reduce}(\mathbf{v}_k, \mathbf{v}_j)$, where $\mathbf{v}_k \in \{\mathbf{v}_{(i-1)s'+1}, \dots, \mathbf{v}_{is'}\}, \mathbf{v}_j \in V'$ with $k \neq j$. If $\mathbf{v}'_k \neq \mathbf{v}_k$ holds, then the thread i moves the reduced vectors $\mathbf{v}'_k$ into the stack S, otherwise, the thread i moves the vectors $\mathbf{v}'_k$ into new list V''. At the end of this part, list V'' becomes pairwise-reduced and we have the relationship $V'' \subset V' \subset V$.

In the **Reduction list vectors using sample vectors**, let $\bar{s} = \lfloor m/t \rfloor$ be the number of list vectors treated by a thread, where m is the size of list L. Each thread has list $L_i = \{\boldsymbol{\ell}_{(i-1)\bar{s}+1}, \dots, \boldsymbol{\ell}_{i\bar{s}}\}$ and V'', where $L = \cup_i L_i$, and $i = 1, 2, \dots, t$. From our assumption, L is pairwise-reduced before processing this part. Each thread i deals with a distributed list L_i and a list V'' and runs $\boldsymbol{\ell}'_k = \text{Reduce}(\boldsymbol{\ell}_k, \mathbf{v}_j)$, where $\boldsymbol{\ell}_k \in L_i, \mathbf{v}_j \in V''$. If $\boldsymbol{\ell}'_k \neq \boldsymbol{\ell}_k$ holds, then the thread i moves the reduced vector $\boldsymbol{\ell}'_k$ into the stack S, otherwise, the thread i moves the vectors $\boldsymbol{\ell}_k$ into new list L'. At the end of this part, any vector $\boldsymbol{\ell}_k$ in the new list L' satisfies $\boldsymbol{\ell}_k = \text{Reduce}(\boldsymbol{\ell}_k, \mathbf{v}_j)$ for all vectors $\mathbf{v}_j$ in list V''. Here both L' and V'' are pairwise-reduced due to relationship $L' \subset L$ and $V'' \subset V'$, respectively.

After the above three reduction steps, our algorithm merges list L' and list V'' to create the new list $L = L' \cup V''$. Note that $\boldsymbol{\ell} = \text{Reduce}(\boldsymbol{\ell}, \mathbf{v})$ and $\mathbf{v} = \text{Reduce}(\mathbf{v}, \boldsymbol{\ell})$ hold for any vector $\boldsymbol{\ell} \in L'$ and $\mathbf{v} \in V''$. Therefore, any pair of two vectors $(\boldsymbol{\ell}, \mathbf{v})$ in L', V'' is Gauss-reduced by Lemma 1, and thus the union $L = L' \cup V''$ becomes pairwise-reduced by Lemma 2.

We show the algorithm derived from the proposed parallelized Gauss Sieve Algorithm in Alg.2. The inputs of this algorithm are a lattice on basis $\mathbf{B}$, the number of samplings $r \in \mathbb{N}$, and termination conditions α, β. Here r is determined by the experimental scale, for example, the number of CPU cores or the available memory (we discuss the most suitable value based on an experiment described in section 5). In the following, we explain the details of the proposed algorithm.

4.2   Multisampling of Vectors (Steps from 3 to 9 in Alg.2)

We sample r vectors in lattice $\mathcal{L}(\mathbf{B})$ and construct a list $V = (\mathbf{v}_1, \ldots, \mathbf{v}_r)$ at the beginning of the iteration from step 3 to step 9 in Alg.2. Sample vector $\mathbf{v}_i$ is samples in two ways, (*i.e.*, popping from stack S or newly generating just as in the case the Gauss Sieve algorithm). If $|S| \geq r$, all vectors $\mathbf{v}_i$ are popped from the stack S, where $1 \leq i \leq r$. If $0 < |S| < r$, we pop $|S|$ vectors from the stack S and generate $(r - |S|)$ vectors using Klein's sampling algorithm. If S is empty, all vectors $\mathbf{v}_i$ are newly generated using Klein's sampling algorithm.

4.3   Reduction of Sample Vectors Using List Vectors (Steps from 12 to 22 in Alg.2)

In this part, by reducing the sample vectors in V using all vectors in list L we will construct the list V', which consists of vectors $\mathbf{v}_i \in V$ that satisfy $Reduce(\mathbf{v}_i, \ell_j) = \mathbf{v}_i$ for all $\ell_j \in L$. Here denote $V = \{\mathbf{v}_1, \ldots, \mathbf{v}_r\}$ and $L = \{\ell_1, \ldots, \ell_m\}$. At the beginning of this part, we assign $\mathbf{w}_i \leftarrow \mathbf{v}_i$ at step 13 in Alg.2. For $i = 1, 2, ..., r$, this part runs $Reduce(\mathbf{w}_i, \ell_j)$ from $j = 1$ to m for the fixed first input $\mathbf{w}_i$ and updates $\mathbf{w}_i$ using its output repeatedly. After running $Reduce(\mathbf{w}_i, \ell_j)$ for $\ell_j \in L$, if $\mathbf{w}_i$ is changed (*i.e.*, $\mathbf{w}_i \neq Reduce(\mathbf{w}_i, \ell_j)$ for some ℓ_j), this vector $\mathbf{w}_i$ is moved to stack S, otherwise, $\mathbf{w}_i(= \mathbf{v}_i)$ is moved to the distributed list V'. This part runs the Reduce algorithm in the following order.

$$
\begin{array}{lll}
\mathbf{w}_1 \leftarrow Reduce(\mathbf{w}_1, \ell_1) & \mathbf{w}_i \leftarrow Reduce(\mathbf{w}_i, \ell_1) & \\
\vdots & \vdots & \mathbf{w}_r \leftarrow Reduce(\mathbf{w}_r, \ell_1) \\
\mathbf{w}_1 \leftarrow Reduce(\mathbf{w}_1, \ell_m) & \mathbf{w}_i \leftarrow Reduce(\mathbf{w}_i, \ell_m) & \vdots \\
\vdots & \vdots & \mathbf{w}_r \leftarrow Reduce(\mathbf{w}_r, \ell_m)
\end{array}
$$

At the end of this part, we re-index the vectors in V' from 1 to r' in no particular order, and rename the vectors in list V' from $\{\mathbf{w}_1, ..., \mathbf{w}_{r'}\}$ to $\{\mathbf{v}_1, ..., \mathbf{v}_{r'}\}$ at step 22 in Alg.2. Recall that any vector $\mathbf{v}_i$ in list V' satisfies $\mathbf{v}_i = Reduce(\mathbf{v}_i, \ell_j)$ for all vectors ℓ_j in list L. We have the relationship $V' \subseteq V$ and $|V'| = r' \leq r$.

This part can simply be parallelized without heavy overhead. Let t be the number of threads and s be the number of sample vectors treated by a thread, where $s = \lfloor r/t \rfloor$. While a thread $i(1 \leq i \leq t)$ computes $Reduce(\mathbf{w}_i, \ell_1)$ to $Reduce(\mathbf{w}_i, \ell_m)$, another thread $j(j \neq i)$ can compute $Reduce(\mathbf{w}_j, \ell_1)$ to $Reduce(\mathbf{w}_j, \ell_m)$, because the vectors ℓ_{l_0} in list L are not changed in this part. Therefore, the inner loop (from step 14 to step 21) can be fully parallelized and the degree of parallelization is at most r, if we set $s = 1$. If $s > 1$, the thread i has $V_i = \{\mathbf{v}_{(i-1)s+1}, \ldots, \mathbf{v}_{is}\}$ and list L, where $V = \cup_i V_i$. And then the thread i runs $Reduce(\mathbf{w}_{(i-1)s+1}, \ell_1)$ to $Reduce(\mathbf{w}_{is}, \ell_m)$ sequentially in the following order.

$$\boxed{\text{Thread 1}}$$

$\mathbf{w}_1 \leftarrow Reduce(\mathbf{w}_1, \boldsymbol{\ell}_1)$
$\vdots$
$\mathbf{w}_1 \leftarrow Reduce(\mathbf{w}_1, \boldsymbol{\ell}_m)$
$\vdots$
$\mathbf{w}'_s \leftarrow Reduce(\mathbf{w}_s, \boldsymbol{\ell}_1)$
$\vdots$
$\mathbf{w}'_s \leftarrow Reduce(\mathbf{w}_s, \boldsymbol{\ell}_m)$

$\cdots$

$$\boxed{\text{Thread } t}$$

$\mathbf{w}_{s(t-1)+1} \leftarrow Reduce(\mathbf{w}_{s(t-1)+1}, \boldsymbol{\ell}_1)$
$\vdots$
$\mathbf{w}_{s(t-1)+1} \leftarrow Reduce(\mathbf{w}_{s(t-1)+1}, \boldsymbol{\ell}_m)$
$\vdots$
$\mathbf{w}_{st} \leftarrow Reduce(\mathbf{w}_{st}, \boldsymbol{\ell}_1)$
$\vdots$
$\mathbf{w}_{st} \leftarrow Reduce(\mathbf{w}_{st}, \boldsymbol{\ell}_m)$

4.4 Reduction of Sample Vectors Using Sample Vectors (Steps from 23 to 34 in Alg.2)

In this part we try to convert the list $V' = \{\mathbf{v}_1, \ldots, \mathbf{v}_{r'}\}$ to be a pairwise-reduced list V''. We reduce sample vectors $\mathbf{v}_i \in V'$ using all vectors in $V' \setminus \{\mathbf{v}_i\}$ and construct list V'', which consists of vectors $\mathbf{v}_i$ that satisfy $Reduce(\mathbf{v}_i, \mathbf{v}_j) = \mathbf{v}_i$ for all $\mathbf{v}_j \in V''$ with $i \neq j$. At the beginning of this part, we assign $\mathbf{w}_i \leftarrow \mathbf{v}_i$ at step 24 in Alg.2. For $i = 1, 2, ..., r'$, this part runs $Reduce(\mathbf{w}_i, \mathbf{v}_j)$ from $j = 1$ to m without $j = i$ for the fixed first input $\mathbf{w}_i$ and updates $\mathbf{w}_i$ using its output repeatedly. During all reductions, just after $\mathbf{w}_i$ is reduced even once, this vector $\mathbf{w}_i$ is moved to stack S as in the first reduction part. If $\mathbf{w}_i$ is not reduced ($\mathbf{w}_i = Reduce(\mathbf{w}_i, \mathbf{v}_j)$), this vector $\mathbf{w}_i(= \mathbf{v}_i)$ is moved to list V''.

At the end of this part, we re-index the vectors in V'' from 1 to r'' in no particular order, and rename the vectors in list V'' from $\{\mathbf{w}_1, ..., \mathbf{w}_{r''}\}$ to $\{\mathbf{v}_1, ..., \mathbf{v}_{r''}\}$ at step 34 in Alg.2. Recall that list V'' becomes pairwise-reduced because $Reduce(\mathbf{v}_i, \mathbf{v}_j) = \mathbf{v}_i$ holds for all vectors $\mathbf{v}_i, \mathbf{v}_j \in V''$ with $i \neq j$. We then have relationship $V'' \subseteq V' \subseteq V$ and $|V''| = r'' \leq r' \leq r$.

This part also can be parallelized in a similar way as the first part. Let t be the number of threads and s' be the number of sample vectors treated by a thread, where $s' = \lfloor r'/t \rfloor$. Each thread i deals with only a sample list V' and runs $\mathbf{w}_k \leftarrow Reduce(\mathbf{w}_k, \mathbf{v}_j)$, where $(i-1)s' + 1 \leq k \leq is', \mathbf{v}_j \in V'$ with $k \neq j$. When thread i computes $\mathbf{w}_i \leftarrow Reduce(\mathbf{w}_i, \mathbf{v}_j)$, another thread h can compute $\mathbf{w}_h \leftarrow Reduce(\mathbf{w}_h, \mathbf{v}_j)$ for all $\mathbf{v}_j \in V'$.

4.5 Reduction of List Vectors Using Sample Vectors (Steps from 35 to 45 in Alg.2)

In this part, by reducing the vectors $\boldsymbol{\ell}_i$ in L using all sample vectors in $V'' = \{\mathbf{v}_1, \ldots, \mathbf{v}_{r''}\}$, we will construct the list L', which consists of vectors $\boldsymbol{\ell}_i \in L$ that satisfy $Reduce(\boldsymbol{\ell}_i, \mathbf{v}_j) = \boldsymbol{\ell}_i$ for all $\mathbf{v}_j \in V''$. At the beginning of this part, we assign $\mathbf{w}_i \leftarrow \boldsymbol{\ell}_i$ at step 36 in Alg.2. For $i = 1, 2, ..., m$, this part runs $Reduce(\mathbf{w}_i, \mathbf{v}_j)$ from $j = 1$ to r'' for the fixed first input $\mathbf{w}_i$ and updates $\mathbf{w}_i$ using its output repeatedly. During all reduction steps, if $\mathbf{w}_i$ is changed (i.e., $\mathbf{w}_i \neq Reduce(\mathbf{w}_i, \mathbf{v}_i)$ for some $\mathbf{v}_i$), this vector $\mathbf{w}_i$ is moved to stack S, otherwise, this vector $\mathbf{w}_i(= \boldsymbol{\ell}_i)$ is moved to the distributed list L'.

At the end of this part, we re-index the vectors in L' from 1 to m' in no particular order, and rename the vectors in list L' from $\{\mathbf{w}_1, ..., \mathbf{w}_{m'}\}$ to $\{\boldsymbol{\ell}_1, ..., \boldsymbol{\ell}_{m'}\}$ at Step 45 in Alg.2. Recall that any vector $\boldsymbol{\ell}_i$ in list L' satisfies $\mathrm{Reduce}(\boldsymbol{\ell}_i, \mathbf{v}_j) = \boldsymbol{\ell}_i$ for all vectors $\mathbf{v}_j$ in list V''. We then have relationships $L' \subseteq L$ and $|L'| = m' \leq m$. After this part, our algorithm merges list L' and list V'' to become the new list $L = L' \cup V''$ at Step 46 in Alg.2.

This step can be simply parallelized without heavy overhead in a similar way as the first part, and the degree of parallelization is at most r''. Each thread of index i updates $\bar{s}$ vectors in list L_i (*i.e.*, $L_i = \{\boldsymbol{\ell}_{(i-1)\bar{s}+1}, \ldots, \boldsymbol{\ell}_{i\bar{s}}\}$), where $\bar{s} = \lfloor m/r'' \rfloor$).

4.6 Properties of the Proposed Algorithm

In our algorithm, list L remains pairwise-reduced at any iteration for the following reasons. After the three reduction steps, our algorithm merges list L' and list V'' to become the new list $L = L' \cup V''$. Note that $\boldsymbol{\ell} = \mathrm{Reduce}(\boldsymbol{\ell}, \mathbf{v})$ and $\mathbf{v} = \mathrm{Reduce}(\mathbf{v}, \boldsymbol{\ell})$ hold for any vector $\boldsymbol{\ell}$ in L' and $\mathbf{v} \in V''$ by the first and third reduction parts. And then, V'' is pair-wise reduced by the second part. Therefore, any pair of two vectors $(\boldsymbol{\ell}, \mathbf{v})$ in L', V'' is Gauss-reduced by Lemma 1, and thus the union $L = L' \cup V''$ becomes pairwise-reduced by Lemma 2.

Our algorithm is a natural extension of the Gauss Sieve algorithm. If only one vector is sampled (*i.e.*, $r = 1$), all the pairs of $(\boldsymbol{\ell}_j, \mathbf{v}_1)$ and $(\mathbf{v}_1, \boldsymbol{\ell}_j)$ are Gauss-reduced by the first and third reduction part, where $\boldsymbol{\ell}_j \in L$. There is nothing to do in the second reduction part. Therefore, this algorithm is equal to the Gauss Sieve algorithm when $r = 1$.

5 Implementation and Experimental Results

In this section, we explain the parallel implementation of the proposed parallel Gauss Sieve algorithm on a multicore CPU, and we also present some algorithmic improvement in our experiment.

5.1 Implementation Using Amazon EC2

We use the instance cc1.8xlarge in AmazonEC2 [4]. Our implementation is based on the **gsieve** library, published by Voulgaris [32] and written in C++. We assume the following properties from our preliminary experiment:

- *all absolute values of entries of vectors are less than 2^{16}*
- *the computational cost of the inner product is dominant (step 1 in Alg.1)*

We optimize the code for the inner product (step 1 in Alg.1) using the SIMD operation. Intel Xeon E5-2670 and g++4.1.2 support SSE4.2, and we can use a 128-bit SSE register. Using the SSE, we can treat eight elements in one SSE operation in parallel. This technique enables our program to run about four times faster.

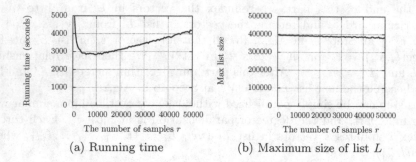

(a) Running time   (b) Maximum size of list L

Fig. 1. Results for solving the SVP Challenge of a 80-dimensional lattice. Fig (a) shows the running time using one instance (32 threads). Fig (b) shows the maximum size of list L. The horizontal axis indicates the number of sample vector r.

5.2 Space Complexity

In this section, we discuss the space complexity with a large number of sample vectors r and a fixed number of threads t. The space complexity of our algorithm is dominated by the size of lists L, V, and stack S. We evaluate the size of a list by the number of vectors in the list. In our experiment of solving the SVP Challenge of 80 dimensions [27], the sizes of list L between Gauss Sieve algorithm ($r = 1$) and our algorithm ($r > 1$) are similar within several percent. Indeed, Figure 1(b) shows the maximum size of list L for $r = 1, 2, \ldots, 5000$ and fixed $t = 32$ using one instance, and there is no increase of the maximum size of list L from 400,000 even if r increases.

Next, in our algorithm, the maximum size of list V is at most r because V is selected by r random vectors on a lattice at the beginning of iteration (from step 12) and then the size of V shrinks by each iteration from step 12 to step 46. If we choose a suitable value of r which minimizes the total running time of our proposed algorithm, then r is much smaller than the maximum size of list L. Indeed, Figure 1(a) shows that the running time for solving the SVP Challenge of 80 dimensions becomes relatively fast when the number of sample vectors r is in the range of about 4,000 to 10,000.

Finally, in our experiment, the size of stack S in our proposed algorithm does not increase that of the original Gauss Sieve algorithm. As a result, the space complexity of our algorithm with a large r is not greater than that of the Gauss Sieve algorithm of $2^{0.2n}$.

5.3 Communication Complexity

In this section, we discuss the communication complexity between threads in our proposed parallel algorithm. We evaluate the communication comlexity in terms of the size of the lists communicated among the threads.

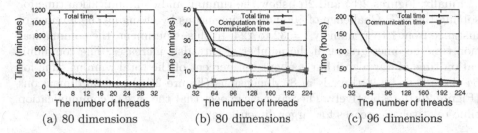

(a) 80 dimensions   (b) 80 dimensions   (c) 96 dimensions

Fig. 2. Results for solving the SVP Challenge on lattices of 80 and 90 dimensions. Fig (a) shows the running time of solving the SVP Challenge of 80 dimensions for $t = 1, 2, \ldots, 32$. Fig (b) shows the running and communication time of solving the SVP Challenge of 80 dimensions for $t = 32, 64, \ldots, 224$. Fig (c) shows the running and communication time of solving the SVP Challenge of 96 dimensions for $t = 32, 64, \ldots, 224$.

At first, we estimate the communication complexity of our algorithm. The dominant part of the communication complexity of our algorithm is the timing of broadcasting the whole list L in the beginning of iterations (from step 12) because the size of the list V is much smaller than that of the list L for large dimensions n. In the previous section, we estimated that the space complexity of our algorithm was $2^{0.2n}$, which was the maximum size of list L. In the following, we estimate the number of broadcasting the list L among threads in our algorithm. A main thread broadcasts the whole list L to t threads in each iteration (from step 12 to step 46 in Alg.2), and thus the communication complexity of our algorithm becomes $t2^{0.2n}$ per one iteration. Therefore, the total communication complexity of broadcasting the list L is $t\gamma 2^{0.2n}$, where γ is the number of iterations (from step 12 to step 46 in Alg.2). Here, the number of iterations γ can be estimated as $2^{0.29n}$ in the case of $r = 1$ and $t = 1$ [18]. On the other hand, in our experiment of the proposed algorithm in from 60 to 80 dimensions, γ was estimated as $2^{0.25n}$ for $r = 8192$ and $t = 32$. Note that the number of iterations γ is independent of t and, γ remains the same for a fixed number of sampling r. If r is bigger than 8192 with fixed t, then we have more samples r in the beginning of the iteration (from step 12 to step 46 in Alg.2) and γ is not greater than $2^{0.25n}$. Therefore, the communication complexity of our algorithm is at most $2^{0.45n}$ which is smaller than the computation time of each thread, i.e., $2^{0.52n}$.

Next, we describe some experiments on both the running and communication time for solving the SVP Challenge [27] of 80 and 96 dimensions for changing the number of threads t. Figure 2 shows the running and communication time of our algorithm for solving the SVP Challenge of 80 and 96 dimensions by changing the number of threads for $t = 1, \ldots, 224$. Figure 2(a) shows the total time for solving the SVP Challenge of 80 dimensions for $t = 1, \ldots, 32$ using one instance that has 32 threads. Note that there is no communication cost among 32 threads in one instance because they share one common memory in the instance. The total time becomes $1/t$ by using t threads for $t \leq 16$.

Finally, Figures 2(b) and 2(c) show the running and communication time for solving the SVP Challenge of 80 and 96 dimensions by changing the number of instance from 1 to 7, namely $t = 32$ to 224. In this experiment, the communication time becomes greater if the number of threads t increases. The communication time of our algorithm is about ten percent of the total running time for 64 threads and 128 threads in 80 dimensions (Figure 2(b)) and 96 dimensions (Figure 2(c)), respectively. Therefore, we expect that the rate of communication time relatively decreases for larger dimensions n.

5.4   Sampling Short Vectors and Shrinking Ratio

If we are able to sample shorter vectors at step 9 in Alg.2, then the running time of the proposed Gauss Sieve algorithm can be improved. However, it takes longer time to sample such shorter vectors on a lattice in general. Therefore, we try to adjust the parameter which determines the tradeoff between the length of the norm of sample vectors and the running time of our algorithm.

In the **gsieve** library [32], Klein's randomized rounding algorithm [15] is implemented. The details of the algorithm are explained by Gentry *et al.* [9]. In the following we adjust the parameter of the core subroutine in the **gsieve** library, namely the *SampleD* algorithm described in [9]. For the two inputs (u, c), *SampleD* chooses an integer x from the range $[c - u \cdot d, c + u \cdot d]$, where $d = \log n$ in the **gsieve** library. We determine a more suitable value of d instead of $d = \log n$ used in the **gsieve** library. The *SampleD* outputs x with probability $\rho_{u,c}(x - c)$, otherwise repeats choosing x, where $\rho_{u,c}(x)$ denoted a Gaussian function on $\mathbb{R}$ that is defined by $\rho_{u,c}(x) = \exp(-\pi|x - c|^2/u^2)$ for any $x \in \mathbb{R}$. If the *SampleD* algorithm outputs a smaller integer, Klein's sampling algorithm outputs a shorter vector. However, the computational time of the *SampleD* algorithm increases as the length of the output vector decreases.

In our experiment, we found the parameter $d = \log n/70$ which is most suitable for speeding up our proposed parallel Gauss sieve algorithm. In this case, the average value of the norms of all the sample vectors using the parameter $d = \log n/70$ becomes 3.7 times shorter than that using the parameter $d = \log n$ in the **gsieve** library. This technique enables our proposed algorithm to run about two times faster.

Next, we estimate how the norm of sample vectors becomes smaller in the final list L in our proposed algorithm. Our proposed algorithm terminates and outputs a shorter vector from the final list L at step 47 in Alg.2. Here denote by GH the Gaussian heuristic bound $(1/\sqrt{\pi})\Gamma(\frac{n}{2} + 1)^{\frac{1}{n}} \cdot \det(\mathcal{L}(\mathbf{B}))^{\frac{1}{n}}$ for a lattice $\mathcal{L}(\mathbf{B})$ of dimensions n, which is heuristically estimated as the length $\lambda_1(\mathcal{L}(\mathbf{B}))$ of a shortest vector in $\mathcal{L}(\mathbf{B})$. In our experiment, we used a lattice $\mathcal{L}(\mathbf{B})$ of 80 dimensions whose GH is equal to 2179. The average value of the norm of all the sample vectors is 1.66 GH and that of vectors in the final list L is 1.24 GH. The norm of the shortest vector in the final list L at the termination of our proposed algorithm achieves 1.04 GH. More details are described in [13].

5.5   Improvement of the Ideal Gauss Sieve

In [26], there are three types of ideal lattices generated by specific polynomials (including two cyclotomic polynomials), which are suitable for the rotate operation $\mathbf{rot}(\mathbf{v})$ of a vector $\mathbf{v}$. We define a new type of an ideal lattice, which is called a *Trinomial lattice*.

A *Trinomial lattice* is generated by the trinomials in the cyclotomic polynomials. Note that the *Trinomial lattice* is not used in cryptography, but we use this type for the speeding up for solving the SVP Challenge in Ideal lattice Challenge [22]. There are two conditions for a *Trinomial lattice*, as follows:

- *Condition 1* : If $n/2$ is a power of three, where n is an even dimension of a lattice, an *Trinomial lattice* is generated by the cyclotomic polynomial $g(x) = x^n + x^{n/2} + 1$. In this condition, the rotation of vector $\mathbf{v}$ is $\mathbf{rot}(\mathbf{v}) = (-v_{n-1}, v_0, \ldots, v_{\frac{n}{2}-2}, v_{\frac{n}{2}-1} - v_{n-1}, v_{\frac{n}{2}}, \ldots, v_{n-2})$.
- *Condition 2* : If the dimension n is the product of both a power of two and a power of three, an *Trinomial lattice* is generated by the cyclotomic polynomial $g(x) = x^n - x^{n/2} + 1$. In this condition, the rotation of vector $\mathbf{v}$ is $\mathbf{rot}(\mathbf{v}) = (-v_{n-1}, v_0, \ldots, v_{\frac{n}{2}-2}, v_{\frac{n}{2}-1} + v_{n-1}, v_{\frac{n}{2}}, \ldots, v_{n-2})$.

The rotate operation $\mathbf{rot}(\mathbf{v})$ using the *Trinomial lattice* requires no greater computational cost than that using the *Anti-cyclic lattice*.

In a *Trinomial lattice*, repeating the rotate operation increases the norm gradually. Therefore, the total running time of our algorithm increases with too large a number of rotate operations. Then, we derived the most suitable number of rotate operations from the experiment to solve the SVP Challenge of 72 dimensions with each number of rotations. In our experiment, it was found that the most suitable number was 6, and this technique enables our parallel Gauss Sieve algorithm to run about 5.5 times faster. More details are described in [13].

5.6   Solving the SVP Challenge

We have solved several problems in the Ideal Lattice Challenge [22]. The problem setting in these challenges has been published in [23]. We pre-computed the BKZ-reduced basis with a block size of 30 using NTL library [31]. Because this precomputation requires much less time than the Gauss Sieve algorithm, we do not include the timing in the following. In our experiment, we used the instance cc1.8xlarge in AmazonEC2. We fix the number of threads at 32 per an instance.

In the Ideal Lattice Challenge [22], we solved the SVP Challenges of 80, 96 and 128 dimensions. In this challenge, a basis of n-dimensional ideal lattice is generated from one of cyclotomic polynomials of degree n. In our experiment we chose the 80-dimensional lattice generated by cyclotomic polynomial given as a filename "ideallatticedim80index220seed0.txt". The basis of 96-dimensional lattice was selected to be a *Trinomial lattice* generated by $g(x) = x^{96} - x^{48} + 1$ given as filename "ideallatticedim96index288seed0.txt", and that of 128-dimensional SVP Challenge was selected to be an *Anti-cyclic lattice* generated by cyclotomic polynomial $g(x) = x^{128} + 1$ given as filename "ideallatticedim128index256seed0.txt".

Table 1. Results of the Ideal Lattice Challenge [22]. SVP Challenges of 96 and 128 dimensions in the Ideal Lattice Challenge are generated by cyclotomic polynomials $x^{96} - x^{48} + 1$ and $x^{128} + 1$, respectively.

dimension	instance hours	# thread t	# sample vectors r	type
80	0.9	32	8,192	*Ideal lattice*
96	8	32	8,192	*Trinomial lattice*
128	29,994	2,688	688,128	*Anti-cyclic lattice*

In our experiment of the 80-dimensional ideal lattice, our parallel algorithm required about one CPU hour using 32 threads and 8,192 sample vectors, which are the same time cost compared with our experiment for a random lattice in the SVP Challenge [27]. Additionally, in our experiment of the 96-dimensional ideal lattice, our parallel algorithm required about 8 CPU hours using 32 threads and 8,192 sample vectors. We also solved the SVP Challenge of 96 dimensions using four instances of 128 threads and 32,768 sample vectors. As a result, our parallel algorithm required about 200 CPU hours. The proposed techniques for *Trinomial lattice* (Section 5.5) enable us to speedup about 25 times faster than the random lattice of the same dimension.

In our experiment of the 128-dimensional ideal lattice, our parallel algorithm require 29,994 CPU hours using 84 instances, where we can set that the number of total threads and sample vectors are $t = 2,688$ and $r = 688,128$, respectively. The Euclidean norm of the output vector is 2,959 which is 1.03 times larger than the Gaussian heuristic bound of this ideal lattice, namely this vector is a solution of SVP Challenge. In the experiment, the communication overhead among threads for solving the SVP Challenge of 128 dimensions was less than ten percents for the total running time of our proposed parallel Gauss Sieve algorithm. More details are described in [13].

6   Conclusion

In this paper, we proposed a parallel Gauss Sieve algorithm, which is an extension of Gauss Sieve algorithm suitable for parallel computation of a large number of threads. We implemented the proposed parallel Gauss Sieve algorithm by the SIMD operation in AmazonEC2 which supports hyper-threading technology. Our experiment deploys 32 threads per instance cc1.8xlarge of 16 CPU cores. We tried to solve the SVP Challenge in the Ideal Lattice Challenge from TU Darmstadt (http://www.latticechallenge.org/).

Then we successfully solved the SVP Challenge of 128 dimensions on the ideal lattice generated by the cyclotomic polynomial $x^{128} + 1$, where this type of ideal lattice is often used for efficient implementation of lattice-based cryptography. Our experiment required 29,994 CPU hours by executing 2,688 threads over 84 instances in total. In the experiment, the communication overhead among threads is less than ten percents of the total running time. To the best of our knowledge, this is currently the highest dimensions of solving the SVP Challenge over ideal lattices.

References

1. Ajtai, M.: The Shortest Vector Problem in L^2 is NP-hard for Randomized Reductions (Extended Abstract). In: Proceedings of the 30th Annual ACM Symposium on Theory of Computing, STOC 1998, pp. 10–19. ACM (1998)
2. Ajtai, M., Dwork, C.: A Public-key Cryptosystem with Worst-case/average-case Equivalence. In: Proceedings of the 29th Annual ACM Symposium on Theory of Computing, STOC 1997, pp. 284–293. ACM (1997)
3. Ajtai, M., Kumar, R., Sivakumar, D.: A Sieve Algorithm for the Shortest Lattice Vector Problem. In: Proceedings of the 33th Annual ACM Symposium on Theory of Computing, STOC 2001, pp. 601–610. ACM (2001)
4. Amazon. Amazon Elastic Compute Cloud, http://aws.amazon.com/jp/ec2/
5. Arvind, V., Joglekar, P.S.: Some Sieving Algorithms for Lattice Problems. In: Proceedings of the IARCS Annual Conference on Foundations of Software Technology and Theoretical Computer Science, FSTTCS 2008. LIPIcs, vol. 2, pp. 25–36. Schloss Dagstuhl–Leibniz-Zentrum fuer Informatik (2008)
6. Gama, N., Nguyen, P., Regev, O.: Lattice Enumeration Using Extreme Pruning. In: Gilbert, H. (ed.) EUROCRYPT 2010. LNCS, vol. 6110, pp. 257–278. Springer, Heidelberg (2010)
7. Garg, S., Gentry, C., Halevi, S.: Candidate Multilinear Maps from Ideal Lattices. Cryptology ePrint Archive. Report 2012/610 (2012)
8. Gentry, C.: Fully Homomorphic Encryption Using Ideal Lattices. In: Proceedings of the 41st Annual ACM Symposium on Theory of Computing, STOC 2009, pp. 169–178. ACM (2009)
9. Gentry, C., Peikert, C., Vaikuntanathan, V.: Trapdoors for Hard Lattices and New Cryptographic Constructions. In: Proceedings of the 40th Annual ACM Symposium on Theory of Computing, STOC 2008, pp. 197–206. ACM (2008)
10. Hoffstein, J., Pipher, J., Silverman, J.: NTRU: A Ring-based Public Key Cryptosystem. In: Buhler, J.P. (ed.) ANTS 1998. LNCS, vol. 1423, pp. 267–288. Springer, Heidelberg (1998)
11. Hanrot, G., Stehlé, D.: Improved Analysis of Kannan's Shortest Lattice Vector Algorithm. In: Menezes, A. (ed.) CRYPTO 2007. LNCS, vol. 4622, pp. 170–186. Springer, Heidelberg (2007)
12. Hanrot, G., Pujol, X., Stehlé, D.: Algorithms for the Shortest and Closest Lattice Vector Problems. In: Chee, Y.M., Guo, Z., Ling, S., Shao, F., Tang, Y., Wang, H., Xing, C. (eds.) IWCC 2011. LNCS, vol. 6639, pp. 159–190. Springer, Heidelberg (2011)
13. Ishiguro, T., Kiyomoto, S., Miyake, Y., Takagi, T.: Parallel Gauss Sieve Algorithm: Solving the SVP Challenge over a 128-Dimensional Ideal Lattice. Cryptology ePrint Archive. Report 2013/388 (2013)
14. Kannan, R.: Improved Algorithms for Integer Programming and Related Lattice Problems. In: Proceedings of the 15th ACM Symposium on Theory of Computing, STOC 1983, pp. 193–206. ACM (1983)
15. Klein, P.: Finding the Closest Lattice Vector When it's Unusually Close. In: Proceedings of the 11th Annual ACM-SIAM Symposium on Discrete Algorithms, SODA 2000, pp. 937–941. ACM (2000)
16. Lenstra, A., Lenstra, H., Lovász, L.: Factoring Polynomials with Rational Coefficients. Journal of Mathematische Annalen 261(4), 515–534 (1982)
17. Micciancio, D.: The Shortest Vector in a Lattice is Hard to Approximate to within Some Constant. In: Proceedings of the 39th Annual Symposium on Foundations of Computer Science, FOCS 1998, pp. 92–98. IEEE Computer Society (1998)

18. Micciancio, D., Voulgaris, P.: A Deterministic Single Exponential Time Algorithm for Most Lattice Problems Based on Voronoi Cell Computations. In: Proceedings of the 42nd ACM Symposium on Theory of Computing, STOC 2010, pp. 351–358. ACM (2010)
19. Micciancio, D., Voulgaris, P.: Faster Exponential Time Algorithms for the Shortest Vector Problem. In: Proceedings of the 21st Annual ACM-SIAM Symposium on Discrete Algorithms, SODA 2010, vol. 65, pp. 1468–1480. SIAM (2010)
20. Milde, B., Schneider, M.: A Parallel Implementation of GaussSieve for the Shortest Vector Problem in Lattices. In: Malyshkin, V. (ed.) PaCT 2011. LNCS, vol. 6873, pp. 452–458. Springer, Heidelberg (2011)
21. Nguyen, P.Q., Vidick, T.: Sieve Algorithms for the Shortest Vector Problem Are Practical. Journal of Mathematical Cryptology 2, 181–207 (2008)
22. Plantard, T., Schneider, M.: Ideal Lattice Challenge, http://www.latticechallenge.org/ideallattice-challenge/
23. Plantard, T., Schneider, M.: Creating a Challenge for Ideal Lattices. Cryptology ePrint Archive. Report 2013/039 (2013)
24. Pujol, X., Stehle, D.: Solving the Shortest Lattice Vector Problem in Time $2^{2.465n}$. Cryptology ePrint Archive. Report 2009/605 (2009)
25. Schneider, M.: Analysis of Gauss-Sieve for Solving the Shortest Vector Problem in Lattices. In: Katoh, N., Kumar, A. (eds.) WALCOM 2011. LNCS, vol. 6552, pp. 89–97. Springer, Heidelberg (2011)
26. Schneider, M.: Computing Shortest Lattice Vectors on Special Hardware. PhD thesis, Technische Universität Darmstadt (2011)
27. Schneider, M., Gama, N.: SVP Challenge, http://www.latticechallenge.org/svp-challenge/
28. Schnorr, C.-P.: A Hierarchy of Polynomial Time Lattice Basis Reduction Algorithms. Journal of Theoretical Computer Science 53(2-3), 201–224 (1987)
29. Schnorr, C.-P.: Lattice Basis Reduction: Improved Practical Algorithms and Solving Subset Sum Problems. Journal of Mathematical Programming, 181–191 (1993)
30. Schnorr, C.-P., Hörner, H.H.: Attacking the Chor-Rivest Cryptosystem by Improved Lattice Reduction. In: Guillou, L.C., Quisquater, J.-J. (eds.) EUROCRYPT 1995. LNCS, vol. 921, pp. 1–12. Springer, Heidelberg (1995)
31. Shoup, V.: Number Theory Library (NTL) for C++. Available at Shoup's homepage, http://shoup.net/ntl
32. Voulgaris, P.: Gauss Sieve beta 0.1 (2010) Available at Voulgaris' homepage at the University of California, San Diego http://cseweb.ucsd.edu/~pvoulgar/impl.html

Lazy Modulus Switching for the BKW Algorithm on LWE

Martin R. Albrecht[1], Jean-Charles Faugère[3,2,4], Robert Fitzpatrick[5], and Ludovic Perret[2,3,4]

[1] Technical University of Denmark, Denmark
[2] Sorbonne Universités, UPMC Univ Paris 06, POLSYS,
UMR 7606, LIP6, F-75005, Paris, France
[3] INRIA, Paris-Rocquencourt Center, POLSYS Project
[4] CNRS, UMR 7606, LIP6, F-75005, Paris, France
[5] Information Security Group
Royal Holloway, University of London
Egham, Surrey TW20 0EX, United Kingdom
maroa@dtu.dk, jean-charles.faugere@inria.fr,
robert.fitzpatrick.2010@live.rhul.ac.uk, ludovic.perret@lip6.fr

Abstract. Some recent constructions based on LWE do not sample the secret uniformly at random but rather from some distribution which produces small entries. The most prominent of these is the binary-LWE problem where the secret vector is sampled from $\{0,1\}^*$ or $\{-1,0,1\}^*$. We present a variant of the BKW algorithm for binary-LWE and other small secret variants and show that this variant reduces the complexity for solving binary-LWE. We also give estimates for the cost of solving binary-LWE instances in this setting and demonstrate the advantage of this BKW variant over standard BKW and lattice reduction techniques applied to the SIS problem. Our variant can be seen as a combination of the BKW algorithm with a lazy variant of modulus switching which might be of independent interest.

1 Introduction

Learning With Errors (LWE) [20] has received widespread attention from the cryptographic community since its introduction. LWE-based cryptography is mainly motivated by its great flexibility for instantiating cryptographic solution as well as a deep worst-case/average-case connections [20]: solving LWE on the average is not easier than solving worst-case instances of several famous lattice approximation problems.

The motivation behind this work comes from the observation that some recent constructions based on LWE do not sample the secret uniformly at random but rather from some distribution which produces small entries (e.g. [5,1,13,12,19]). From a theoretical point of view, this is motivated by the observation that every LWE instance can be transformed into an instance where the secret follows the same distribution as the noise [5].[1] However, many constructions use secrets

---

[1] Also in [15] for the LPN case.

H. Krawczyk (Ed.): PKC 2014, LNCS 8383, pp. 429–445, 2014.
© International Association for Cryptologic Research 2014

which are considerably smaller. For example, binary-LWE samples the secret from $\{0,1\}^*$ [8] or $\{-1,0,1\}^*$ [12]. The presence of such small secrets provokes the question of what implications such choices have on the security of LWE. Is solving LWE with, say, binary secrets easier than standard LWE? From a theoretical point of view, [8] proves that their binary-LWE is as secure as LWE. In this paper, we try to address the question from an algorithmic point of view; i.e. what is the actual impact of small secrets on concrete parameters.

1.1 Algorithms for Solving LWE

Three families of algorithms for solving LWE are known in the literature. The most prominent approach is to reduce LWE to a problem that can be solved via lattice reduction, for example, by reducing it to the Short Integer Solution (SIS) problem. Indeed, most parameter choices in the literature are based on the hardness of lattice reduction such as [16,10,17]. These estimates for a given set of parameters n (number of components of the secret), q (size of the modulus) and σ (standard deviation of the noise) are usually produced by extrapolating running times from small instances.

A second approach is due to Arora and Ge who reduce LWE to solving a system of non-linear equations [6]. This algorithm allow us to solve LWE in sub-exponential time as soon as the Gaussian distribution is sufficiently narrow, i.e. $\alpha \cdot q < \sqrt{n}$. Recall that the security reduction [20] for LWE requires to consider discrete Gaussian with standard deviation $\alpha \cdot q$ strictly bigger than $\sqrt{n}$. However, from a practical point of view, the constants involved in this algorithm are so large that it is much more costly than other approaches for the parameters typically considered in cryptographic applications [2].

The third family of algorithms are combinatorial algorithms which can all be seen as variants of the BKW algorithm. The BKW algorithm was proposed by Blum, Kalai and Wasserman [7] as a method for solving the Learning Parity with Noise problem, with sub-exponential complexity, requiring $2^{O(n/\log n)}$ samples, space and time. The algorithm can be adapted for tackling LWE with complexity $2^{O(n)}$ when the modulus is taken to be polynomial in n [20]. BKW proceeds by splitting the n components of LWE samples into a groups of b components each. For each of the a groups of components the algorithm then searches for collisions in these b components to eliminate them. The overall complexity of the algorithm is $\approx (a^2 n) \cdot \frac{q^b}{2}$ operations, and $a \cdot \frac{q^b}{2}$ memory, where a and b depend on the n, q and α.

The behaviour of the algorithm is relatively well understood and it was shown to outperform lattice reduction estimates when reducing LWE to SIS (when q is small), thus it provides a solid basis for analysing the concrete hardness of LWE instances [3].

1.2 Organisation of the Paper and Main Results

While none of the algorithms above take advantage of the presence of small secrets, we may combine them with *modulus switching*. Recall that modulus switching was initially introduced to improve the performance of homomorphic encryption schemes [9] and was recently used to reduce the hardness of LWE with polynomially sized moduli to GAPSVP [8]. Modulus switching is essentially the same as computing with a lower precision similar to performing floating point computations with a low fixed precision. Namely, let $(\mathbf{a}, c = \langle \mathbf{a}, \mathbf{s} \rangle + e) \in \mathbb{Z}_q^n \times \mathbb{Z}_q$ be LWE sample where $\mathbf{s} \in \mathbb{Z}_q^n$ is the secret vector, and $e \in \mathbb{Z}_q$ is an error. Let also some $p < q$ and consider $(\lfloor p/q \cdot \mathbf{a} \rceil, \lfloor p/q \cdot c \rceil)$ with

$$\left\lfloor \frac{p}{q} \cdot c \right\rceil = \left\lfloor \frac{p}{q} (\langle \mathbf{a}, \mathbf{s} \rangle + q \cdot u + e) \right\rceil , \text{ for some } u \in \mathbb{Z}$$

$$\left\lfloor \frac{p}{q} \cdot c \right\rceil = \left\lfloor \left\langle \frac{p}{q} \cdot \mathbf{a}, \mathbf{s} \right\rangle_p + \frac{p}{q} \cdot e \right\rceil = \left\lfloor \left\langle \left\lfloor \frac{p}{q} \cdot \mathbf{a} \right\rceil, \mathbf{s} \right\rangle_p + \left\langle \frac{p}{q} \cdot \mathbf{a} - \left\lfloor \frac{p}{q} \cdot \mathbf{a} \right\rceil, \mathbf{s} \right\rangle_p + \frac{p}{q} \cdot e \right\rceil$$

$$= \left\langle \left\lfloor \frac{p}{q} \cdot \mathbf{a} \right\rceil, \mathbf{s} \right\rangle_p + \left\langle \frac{p}{q} \cdot \mathbf{a} - \left\lfloor \frac{p}{q} \cdot \mathbf{a} \right\rceil, \mathbf{s} \right\rangle_p + \frac{p}{q} \cdot e + e', \text{ where } e' \in [-0.5, 0.5]$$

$$= \left\langle \left\lfloor \frac{p}{q} \cdot \mathbf{a} \right\rceil, \mathbf{s} \right\rangle_p + e'' + \frac{p}{q} \cdot e + e'. \tag{1}$$

where $\langle \mathbf{x}, \mathbf{y} \rangle_p$ denotes the modulo p inner product of $\mathbf{x}$ and $\mathbf{y}$.

Since $p/q \cdot \mathbf{a} - \lfloor p/q \cdot \mathbf{a} \rceil$ takes values $\in [-0.5, 0.5]$ we have that e'' is small if $\mathbf{s}$ is small. We may hence compute with the smaller 'precision' p at the cost of a slight increase of the noise rate by a 'rounding error' e''.

Modulus switching allows to map a LWE instance $\mod q$ to a scaled instance of LWE $\mod p$. Thus, modulus switching can be used in the solving of small secret instances of LWE, a folklore approach which has not been explicitly studied in the literature. Namely, if we pick p such that e'' is not much larger than $p/q \cdot e$ then, for example, the running time of the BKW algorithm improves from $(a^2 n) \cdot \frac{q^b}{2}$ to $(a^2 n) \cdot \frac{p^b}{2}$. Since typically $b \approx n/\log n$ this may translate to substantial improvements. Indeed, we can pick p such that $|\langle p/q \cdot \mathbf{a} - \lfloor p/q \cdot \mathbf{a} \rceil, \mathbf{s} \rangle| \approx p/q \cdot |e|$. This implies $\sigma_s \cdot \sqrt{\frac{n}{12}} \approx p/q \cdot \sigma$, or $p \approx \min \{ q, \frac{\sigma_s}{\sigma} \cdot \sqrt{\frac{n}{12}} \cdot q \}$, where σ_s is the standard deviation of elements in the secret $\mathbf{s}$.

In this paper, we refine this approach and present a variant of the BKW algorithm which fuses modulus switching and BKW-style reduction. In particular, this work has two main contributions. Firstly, in Section 2 we present a modulus switching strategy for the BKW algorithm in which switching is delayed until necessary. In a nutshell, recall that the BKW algorithm performs additions of elements which collide in certain components. Our variant will search for such collisions in 'low precision' $\mathbb{Z}_p$ but will perform arithmetic in 'high precision' $\mathbb{Z}_q$. We call *rounding error* the inner product of the sub-vector of 'low bits' of $\mathbf{a}$ with the secret $\mathbf{s}$. Our strategy permits to decrease rounding errors and allows to reduce p by a factor of $\sqrt{a}$.

Secondly, this perspective enables us to choose reductors in the BKW algorithm which minimise the rounding errors further (Section 3). Namely, we favour components a with small distance $|\lfloor p/q \cdot a \rceil - p/q \cdot a|$ in already reduced components, called 'child components' in this work. Our strategy ensures that the probability of finding such elements is highest for those components which are considered first by the BKW algorithm, i.e. those components which contribute most to the noise. We note that the first contribution relies on standard independence assumptions only, while the second contribution relies on stronger assumptions, which however seem to hold in practice.

We then discuss the complexity of our variants in Section 4. For typical choices of parameters – i.e. $q \approx n^c$ for some small constant $c \geq 1$, $a = \log_2 n$ and $b = n/\log_2 n$ – the complexity of BKW as analysed in [3] is $\mathcal{O}\left(2^{cn} \cdot n \log_2^2 n\right)$. For small secrets, a naive modulus switching technique allows reducing this complexity to $\mathcal{O}\left(2^{n\left(c + \frac{\log_2 d}{\log_2 n}\right)} \cdot n \log_2^2 n\right)$ where $0 < d \leq 1$ is a small constant. If the secret distribution does not depend on n and if an unbounded number of LWE samples is available our improved version of BKW allows to get a complexity of:

$$\mathcal{O}\left(2^{n\left(c + \frac{\log_2 d - \frac{1}{2}\log_2 \log_2 n}{\log_2 n}\right)} \cdot n \log_2^2 n\right).$$

We then study the behaviour of this algorithm by applying it to various instances of LWE with binary secrets. In Section 5, we compare the results with plain BKW and BKZ under modulus switching and a simple meet-in-the-middle approach or generalised birthday attack. We show that our lazy-modulus-switching variant of the BKW algorithm provides better results than applying plain BKW after modulus reduction. We also demonstrate that under the parameters considered here this algorithm also – as n increases – outperforms the most optimistic estimates for BKZ when we apply BKZ to the same task as that to which we apply BKW: finding short vectors in the (scaled-)dual lattice – we obtain this perspective by viewing the rounding error as an increase in the noise rate while still finding short vectors in the (scaled)-dual p-ary lattice determined by our modulus-reduced LWE samples. Indeed, our results indicate that our algorithm outperforms BKZ 2.0 when both are used to find a short vector in the (scaled)-dual lattice in dimension as low as ≈ 256 when considering LWE parameters from [20] with binary secret. However, we stress again that we always assume an unbounded number of samples to be available for solving.

1.3   Notations

To fix the notations, we reproduce below the definition of LWE.

Definition 1 (LWE [20]). *Let n, q be positive integers, χ be a probability distribution on $\mathbb{Z}_q$ and $\mathbf{s}$ be a secret vector in $\mathbb{Z}_q^n$. We denote by $L_{\mathbf{s},\chi}$ the probability distribution on $\mathbb{Z}_q^n \times \mathbb{Z}_q$ obtained by choosing $\mathbf{a} \in \mathbb{Z}_q^n$ uniformly at random, choosing $e \in \mathbb{Z}_q$ according to χ, and returning $(\mathbf{a}, c) = (\mathbf{a}, \langle \mathbf{a}, \mathbf{s} \rangle + e) \in \mathbb{Z}_q^n \times \mathbb{Z}_q$. We define Decision-LWE as the problem of deciding whether pairs $(\mathbf{a}, c) \in \mathbb{Z}_q^n \times \mathbb{Z}_q$ are sampled according to $L_{\mathbf{s},\chi}$ or the uniform distribution on $\mathbb{Z}_q^n \times \mathbb{Z}_q$. Search-LWE is the problem of recovering $\mathbf{s}$ from $(\mathbf{a}, c) = (\mathbf{a}, \langle \mathbf{a}, \mathbf{s} \rangle + e) \in \mathbb{Z}_q^n \times \mathbb{Z}_q$ sampled according to $L_{\mathbf{s},\chi}$.*

The noise follows some distribution χ which is classically chosen to be a discrete Gaussian distribution over $\mathbb{Z}$ with mean 0 and standard deviation

$\sigma = s/\sqrt{2\pi} = \alpha q/\sqrt{2\pi}$, reduced modulo q. In the following, we always start counting at zero. We denote vectors as well as matrices in bold, vectors in lower case, and matrices in upper case. Given a vector $\mathbf{a}$, we denote by $\mathbf{a}_{(i)}$ the i-th entry in $\mathbf{a}$, i.e. a scalar, and by $\mathbf{A}_{(i,j)}$ the entry at index i, j. For vectors $\mathbf{a}$ we denote by $\mathbf{a}_{(a,b)}$ the vector $(\mathbf{a}_{(a)}, \ldots, \mathbf{a}_{(b-1)})$. When given a list of vectors, we index its elements by subscript, e.g. $\mathbf{a}_0, \mathbf{a}_1, \mathbf{a}_2$, to denote the first three vectors of the list. This means that $\mathbf{a}_{i,(j)}$ is the j-th component of the vector $\mathbf{a}_i$. When we write $(\mathbf{a}_i, c_i)$ we always mean the output of an oracle which should be clear from the context. In particular, $(\mathbf{a}_i, c_i)$ does not necessarily refer to samples following the initial distribution. We write $\tilde{\mathbf{a}}$ instead of $\mathbf{a}$ to indicate $\mathbf{a}$ has some short elements. We represent elements in $\mathbb{Z}_q$ as integers in $[-\frac{q}{2}, \ldots, \frac{q}{2}]$, similarly for $\mathbb{Z}_p$. We write $\chi_{\alpha,q}$ for the distribution obtained by considering a discrete Gaussian distribution over $\mathbb{Z}$ with standard deviation $\alpha q/\sqrt{2\pi}$, mean 0, considered modulo q.

2   A Modified BKW Algorithm: Lazy Modulus Switching

Following [3], we consider BKW – applied to Decision-LWE – as consisting of two stages: *sample reduction* and *hypothesis testing*. In this work, we only modify the first stage.

2.1   The Basic Idea

We briefly recall the principle of classical BKW. Assume we are given samples of the form $(\mathbf{a}, c)$ following either $L_{\mathbf{s},\chi}$ or $\mathcal{U}(\mathbb{Z}_q^n) \times \mathcal{U}(\mathbb{Z}_q)$. Our goal is to distinguish between the two cases. BKW proceeds by producing samples $(\mathbf{a}^*, c^*)$ with $\mathbf{a}^*$ being all zero such that statistical tests can be applied to c^* to decide whether they follow $\mathcal{U}(\mathbb{Z}_q)$ or some distribution related to $L_{\mathbf{s},\chi}$. This is achieved by grouping the n components of all vectors into a groups of b components each (assuming a and b divide n for simplicity). If two vectors collide on all b entries in one group, the first is subtracted from the second, producing a vector with at least b all zero entries. These vectors are then again combined to produce more all zero entries and so forth until all a groups are eliminated to zero. However, as we add up vectors the noise increases. Overall, after ℓ addition levels the noise has standard deviation $\sqrt{2^\ell}\alpha q$. Our algorithm, too, will be parametrized by a positive integer $b \leq n$ (the window width), and $a := \lceil n/b \rceil$ (the addition depth).

Recall that the complexity of BKW algorithm is essentially q^b. However, b only depends on the ratio $\alpha q/\sqrt{2\pi}q = \alpha\sqrt{2\pi}$ and thus not on q. Hence, it is clear that applying modulus reduction before running the BKW algorithm may greatly improve its running time: b is preserved whilst q is reduced to p. However, instead of applying modulus reduction in 'one shot' prior to executing BKW, we propose switching to a lower precision only when needed. For this, we actually never switch the modulus but simply consider elements in $\mathbb{Z}_q$ 'through the perspective' of $\mathbb{Z}_p$. We then essentially only consider the top-most $\log_2 p$ bits of $\mathbb{Z}_q$.

Under this perspective, given samples of the form $(\mathbf{a}, c)$ we aim to produce $(\tilde{\mathbf{a}}, \tilde{c} = \langle \tilde{\mathbf{a}}, \mathbf{s} \rangle + \tilde{e})$, where $\tilde{\mathbf{a}}$ is short enough, i.e.

$$|\langle \tilde{\mathbf{a}}, \mathbf{s} \rangle| \approx \sqrt{2^a} \alpha q. \tag{2}$$

Although other choices are possible, this choice means balancing the noise $\tilde{e}$ after a levels of addition and the contribution of $|\langle \tilde{\mathbf{a}}, \mathbf{s} \rangle|$ such that neither dominates. We call the term $\langle \tilde{\mathbf{a}}, \mathbf{s} \rangle$ the *rounding error*. So, condition (2) is such that after a levels of additions performed by the BKW algorithm the escalated initial noise and the noise coming from rounding errors have the same size.

2.2   Sample Reduction for Short Secrets

Let $(\mathbf{a}_0, c_0), \ldots, (\mathbf{a}_{m-1}, c_{m-1})$ be samples which follow $L_{\mathbf{s}, \chi}$ or $\mathcal{U}(\mathbb{Z}_q^n) \times \mathcal{U}(\mathbb{Z}_q)$. We now explain how to produce samples $(\tilde{\mathbf{a}}_i, \tilde{c}_i)_{i \geq 0}$ that satisfy condition (2). For simplicity, we assume from now on that $p = 2^\kappa$. [2]

The main idea of the algorithm is to search for collisions among the first b components of samples $(\mathbf{a}_i, c_i)$ by only considering their top $\log_2 p$ bits. If such a collision is found, we proceed as in the normal BKW algorithm, i.e. we subtract the colliding samples to clear the first b components. In our case, we clear the topmost $\log_2 p$ bits of the first b components. Hence, instead of managing elimination tables for every bit of all components, we only manage elimination tables for the most significant κ bits. Put differently, all arithmetic is performed in $\mathbb{Z}_q$ but collisions are searched for in $\mathbb{Z}_p$ after rescaling or modulus switching.

As in [3], we realise the first stage of the BKW algorithm as a (recursively constructed) series of oracles $B_{\mathbf{s}, \chi}(b, \ell, p)$. In our case, we have $0 \leq \ell < a$, where $B_{\mathbf{s}, \chi}(b, a-1, p)$ produces the final output and $B_{\mathbf{s}, \chi}(b, -1, p)$ calls the LWE oracle. We will make use of a set of tables T^ℓ (maintained across oracle calls) to store (randomly-chosen) vectors that will be used to reduce samples arising from our oracles. However, compared to [3] our oracles $B_{\mathbf{s}, \chi}(b, \ell, p)$ take an additional parameter p which specifies the precision which we consider. Hence, if $p = q$ then we recover the algorithm from [3] where we perform no modulus reduction at all. In particular, $B_{\mathbf{s}, \chi}(b, \ell, p)$ proceeds as follows:

1. For $\ell = -1$, we can obtain samples from $B_{\mathbf{s}, \chi}(b, -1, p)$ by simply calling the LWE oracle $L_{\mathbf{s}, \chi}$ and returning the output.
2. For $\ell = 0$, we repeatedly query the oracle $B_{\mathbf{s}, \chi}(b, 0, p)$ to obtain (at most) $(p^b - 1)/2$ samples $(\mathbf{a}, c)$ with distinct non-zero vectors $\lfloor p/q \cdot \mathbf{a}_{(0,b)} \rceil$. We use these samples to populate the table T^0, indexed by $\lfloor p/q \cdot \mathbf{a}_{(0,b)} \rceil$. We store $(\mathbf{a}, c)$ in the table. During this course of this population, whenever we obtain a sample $(\mathbf{a}', c')$ from $B_{\mathbf{s}, \chi}(b, -1, p)$, if $\lfloor p/q \cdot \mathbf{a}'_{(0,b)} \rceil$ (resp. the negation) match $\lfloor p/q \cdot \mathbf{a}_{(0,b)} \rceil$ such that the pair $(\mathbf{a}, c)$ is already in T^1, we return $(\mathbf{a}' \pm \mathbf{a}, c' \pm c)$, as a sample from $B_{\mathbf{s}, \chi}(b, 0, p)$. Note that, if $\lfloor p/q \cdot \mathbf{a}_{(0,b)} \rceil$

---

[2] While we do not have to restrict our attention to p of the form 2^κ, we choose it for ease of exposition and implementation.

is zero, we return $(\mathbf{a}', c')$ as a sample from $B_{\mathbf{s},\chi}(b, 0, p)$. Further calls to the oracle $B_{\mathbf{s},\chi}(b, 0, p)$ proceed in a similar manner, but using (and potentially adding entries to) the same table T^0.

3. For $0 < \ell < a$, we proceed as above: we make use of the table T^ℓ (constructed by calling $B_{\mathbf{s},\chi}(b, \ell - 1, p)$ up to $(p^b - 1)/2$ times) to reduce any output sample from $B_{\mathbf{s},\chi}(b, \ell - 1, p)$ with $\lfloor p/q \cdot \mathbf{a}_{(b\cdot\ell, b\cdot\ell+b)} \rceil$ by an element with a matching such vector, to generate a sample returned by $B_{\mathbf{s},\chi}(b, \ell, p)$.

Pseudo-code for the modified oracle $B_{\mathbf{s},\chi}(b, \ell, p)$, for $0 \leq \ell < a$, is given in the full version of this work.

2.3   Picking p

Yet, we still have to establish the size of p to satisfy Condition 2. We note that in our approach we do not actually multiply by p/q. Let σ_r be the standard deviation of uniformly random elements in $\mathbb{Z}_{\lfloor q/p \rceil}$. Performing one-shot modulus switching in this setting would mean splitting $\mathbf{a}$ into two vectors, $\mathbf{a}'$ with the 'high order' bits and $\mathbf{a}''$ with 'low order' bits. The components of the latter would contribute to the final noise as the rounding error, the components of the former would be eliminated by BKW. The standard deviation of the components of $\mathbf{a}''$ is σ_r. For each component of $\mathbf{a}_{(i)}$ one-shot modulus switching would add a noise with standard deviation $\sigma_r \sigma_s$. Hence, after applying BKW to these pre-processed samples, the standard deviation of the noise contributed by modulus-switching in the final output would be

$$\sqrt{n \cdot 2^a \cdot \sigma_r^2 \sigma_s^2} = \sqrt{a\, b \cdot 2^a \cdot \sigma_r^2 \sigma_s^2}. \tag{3}$$

However, as the following lemma establishes, we may consider smaller p because the final noise contributed by modulus switching in our algorithm is smaller than in (3). This is because if $(\tilde{\mathbf{a}}_i, \tilde{c}_i)$ are final output samples then the entries $\tilde{\mathbf{a}}_{i,(b\cdot a - 1)}$ will be significantly smaller than $\tilde{\mathbf{a}}_{i,(0)}$.

Yet, to formalise this, we need to make a (standard) simplifying assumption, namely that the outputs of the BKW algorithm (at every stage) are independent. That is, we make the assumption that, during the course of the algorithm described, all components of each sample from $B_{\mathbf{s},\chi}(b, \ell, p)$ are independent from every other sample. We emphasize that similar assumptions are standard in treatments of combinatorial algorithms for LPN/LWE (cf. [3,11]).

Assumption 1. *We assume that all outputs of $B_{\mathbf{s},\chi}(b, \ell, p)$ are independent.*

Assumption 1 allows to establish the following lemma:

Lemma 1. *Let $n \geq 1$ be the dimension of the* LWE *secret vector, q be a modulus, $b \in \mathbb{Z}$ with $1 < b < n$. Let also σ_r be the standard deviation of uniformly random elements in $\mathbb{Z}_{\lfloor q/p \rceil}$. Under Assumption 1, the components of $\tilde{\mathbf{a}} = \mathbf{a} - \mathbf{a}'$ returned by $B_{\mathbf{s},\chi}(b, \ell, p)$ satisfy:*

$$\mathrm{Var}(\tilde{\mathbf{a}}_{(i)}) = 2^{\ell - \lfloor i/b \rfloor} \sigma_r^2, \text{ for } 0 \leq \lfloor i/b \rfloor \leq \ell$$

and $\mathrm{Var}(\mathcal{U}(\mathbb{Z}_q))$ *for* $\lfloor i/b \rfloor > \ell$.

Proof. The proof is omitted here but available in the full version of this work.

Using Lemma 1 we may adapt our choice of p, because the noise contributed by modulus switching for a given p is smaller:

Corollary 1. *Let $n \geq 1$ be the dimension of the LWE secret vector, q be a modulus, $b \in \mathbb{Z}$ with $1 \leq b \leq n$. Let σ_r be the standard deviation of uniformly random elements in $\mathbb{Z}\lfloor q/p \rceil$ and σ_s be the standard deviation of the distribution from which the secret $\mathbf{s}$ is sampled. Let $(\tilde{a}, \tilde{c})$ be an output of $B_{\mathbf{s},\chi}(b, a-1, p)$. Under Assumption 1, the noise added by lazy modulus switching in the final output of $B_{\mathbf{s},\chi}(b, a-1, p)$, that is $|\langle \tilde{a}, \mathbf{s} \rangle|$, has standard deviation*

$$\sqrt{b \cdot \left(\sum_{i=0}^{a-1} 2^{a-i-1} \right) \cdot \sigma_r^2 \sigma_s^2} = \sqrt{b \cdot (2^a - 1) \cdot \sigma_r^2 \sigma_s^2}.$$

Proof. The proof is omitted here but available in the full version of this work.

Now, compare Corollary 1 with the standard deviation in (3). We see that the standard deviation obtained using our lazy modulus switching is divided by a factor $\sqrt{a}$ w.r.t. to a naive use of modulus-switching, i.e. as in (3). As a consequence, we may reduce p by a factor $\sqrt{a}$.

3 Improved Algorithm: Stunting Growth by Unnatural Selection

Based on the strategy in the previous section, we now introduce a pre-processing step which allows us to further reduce the magnitude of the noise present in the outputs of $B_{\mathbf{s},\chi}(b, a-1, p)$ by reducing rounding errors further. For this, it will be useful to establish notation to refer to various components of $\mathbf{a}_i$ in relation to $B_{\mathbf{s},\chi}(b, \ell, p)$.

Children: are all those components with index $j < b \cdot \ell$, i.e. those components that were reduced by some $B_{\mathbf{s},\chi}(b, k, p)$ with $k < \ell$: *they grow up so quickly.*

Parents: are those components of $\mathbf{a}_i$ with index $b \cdot \ell \leq j < b \cdot \ell + b$, i.e. those components among which collisions are searched for in $B_{\mathbf{s},\chi}(b, \ell, p)$: *collisions among parents produce children.*

Strangers: with respect to $B_{\mathbf{s},\chi}(b, \ell, p)$ are all other components $j \geq b \cdot \ell + b$: *they are indifferent towards each other.*

3.1 The Basic Idea

For the general idea and intuition, assume $b = 1$ and that $\tilde{a}_i$ are outputs of $B_{\mathbf{s},\chi}(b, 0, p)$ and we hence have $\mathrm{Var}(\tilde{a}_{i,(0)}) = \sigma_r^2$. Now, some of these $\tilde{a}_i$ will be stored in Table T^1 by $B_{\mathbf{s},\chi}(b, 1, p)$ based on the value in the parent component $\tilde{a}_{i,(1)}$. All future outputs of $B_{\mathbf{s},\chi}(b, 1, p)$ which collide with $\tilde{a}_i$ in the parent component at index 1 will have $\tilde{a}_i$ added/subtracted to it, we are hence adding a value with $\mathrm{Var}(\tilde{a}_{i,(0)}) = \sigma_r^2$ in index 0.

Now, however, if the $\tilde{\mathbf{a}}_{i,(0)}$ happened to be unusually short, all $B_{\mathbf{s},\chi}(b,\ell,p)$ for $\ell > 0$ would output vectors with a shorter $\tilde{\mathbf{a}}_{i,(0)}$ added/subtracted in, i.e. would also have unusually small child components (although to a lesser degree). That is, improving the outputs of $B_{\mathbf{s},\chi}(b,1,p)$ – i.e. decreasing the magnitude of the $\tilde{\mathbf{a}}_{i,(0)}$ stored in T^1 – has a knock-on effect on all later outputs. More generally, improving the outputs of $B_{\mathbf{s},\chi}(b,\ell,p)$ will improve the outputs of $B_{\mathbf{s},\chi}(b,k,p)$ for $k > \ell$.

On the other hand, improving the outputs of $B_{\mathbf{s},\chi}(b,\ell,p)$ where ℓ is small, is easier than for larger values of ℓ. In the algorithm as described so far, when we obtain a collision between a member of T^ℓ and an output $(\mathbf{a}_i,c_i)$ of $B_{\mathbf{s},\chi}(b,\ell - 1,p)$, we reduce $(\mathbf{a}_i,c_i)$ using the colliding member of T^ℓ, retaining this member in the table. Alternatively we can reduce $(\mathbf{a}_i,c_i)$ using the *in-situ* table entry, replace the table entry with (the now reduced) $(\mathbf{a}_i,c_i)$ and return the former table entry as the output of $B_{\mathbf{s},\chi}(b,\ell,p)$. If we selectively employ this alternative strategy using the relative magnitudes of the child components of $(\mathbf{a}_i,c_i)$ and the table entry as a criterion, we can improve the 'quality' of our tables as part of a pre-processing phase.

That is, in $B_{\mathbf{s},\chi}(b,\ell,p)$ for each collision in a parent component we may inspect the child components for their size and keep that in T^ℓ where the child components are smallest. Phrased in the language of 'children' and 'parents': we do not let 'nature', i.e. randomness, run its course but intervene and select children based on their size. As the number of child components is $b \cdot \ell$ it becomes more difficult as ℓ increases to find vectors where all child components are short.

3.2   Algorithms

This leads to a modified algorithm $B_{small,\mathbf{s},\chi}(b,\ell,p)$ given in Algorithm 1 which acts as a pre-processing phase.

1 **begin**
2     $T^\ell \leftarrow$ table with p^b rows maintained across all runs of $B_{small,\mathbf{s},\chi}(b,\ell,p)$;
3   Find $(\mathbf{a}',c') \leftarrow T_{\mathbf{z}}^\ell$ that collides with a fresh sample $(\mathbf{a},c)$ from $B_{\mathbf{s},\chi}(b,\ell - 1,p)$;
4   **if** $\sum_{i=0}^{b \cdot \ell - 1} |\mathbf{a}'_{(i)}| > \sum_{i=0}^{b \cdot \ell - 1} |\mathbf{a}_{(i)}|$ **then**
5        $T_{\mathbf{z}}^\ell \leftarrow (\mathbf{a},c)$;
6   **return** $(\mathbf{a} - \mathbf{a}', c - c')$;

Algorithm 1. $B_{small,\mathbf{s},\chi}(b,\ell,p)$ for $0 \le \ell < a$

3.3   Picking p

It remains to be established what the effect of such a strategy is, i.e. how fast children grow up or how fast rounding errors accumulate. In particular, given n vectors $\mathbf{x}_i$ sampled from some distribution $\mathcal{D}$ where each component has standard deviation σ, i.e. $\mathrm{Var}(\mathbf{x}_{i,(j)}) = \sigma^2$ we are interested in the standard deviation σ_n of each component for $\mathbf{x}^* = \min_{abs}(\mathbf{x}_0, \ldots, \mathbf{x}_{n-1})$ where $\min_{abs}$ picks that vector where $\sum_{j=0}^{b \cdot \ell - 1} |\mathbf{x}_{(j)}|$ is minimal. At this point we know no closed algebraic expression for σ_n. However, we found (as detailed in the full version of this work) that σ_n can be estimated as follows:

Assumption 2. *Let the vectors $\mathbf{x}_0, \ldots, \mathbf{x}_{n-1} \in \mathbb{Z}_q^\tau$ be sampled from some distribution $\mathcal{D}$ such that $\sigma^2 = \mathrm{Var}(\mathbf{x}_{i,(j)})$ where $\mathcal{D}$ is any distribution on (sub-)vectors observable in our algorithm. Let $\mathbf{x}^* = \min_{abs}(\mathbf{x}_0, \ldots, \mathbf{x}_{n-1})$ where $\min_{abs}$ picks that vector $\mathbf{x}^*$ with $\sum_{j=0}^{b \cdot \ell - 1} |\mathbf{x}_{(j)}^*|$ minimal. The stddev $\sigma_n = \sqrt{\mathrm{Var}(\mathbf{x}_{(0)}^*)} = \cdots = \sqrt{\mathrm{Var}(\mathbf{x}_{(\tau-1)}^*)}$ of components in $\mathbf{x}^*$ satisfies*

$$\sigma/\sigma_n \geq c_\tau \sqrt[3]{n} + (1 - c_\tau)$$

with c_τ as in Table 1 for $\tau \leq 10$ and

$$c_\tau = 0.20151418166952917\sqrt{\tau} + 0.32362108131969386 \approx \frac{1}{5}\sqrt{\tau} + \frac{1}{3}$$

otherwise.

Table 1. c_τ for small values of τ

τ	1	2	3	4	5
c_τ	0.405799353869	0.692447899282	0.789885269135	0.844195936036	0.854967912468
τ	6	7	8	9	10
c_τ	0.895446987232	0.91570933651	0.956763578012	0.943424544282	0.998715322134

With Assumption 2 we can now estimate the size of the entries of the variance matrix associated with our elimination tables. That is, a matrix $\mathbf{M}$ where the entry $\mathbf{M}_{(i,j)}$ holds the variance of entries $(b \cdot j, \ldots, b \cdot j + b - 1)$ in T^i. We give an algorithm for constructing $\mathbf{M}$ in Algorithm 2 which repeatedly applies Assumptions 1 and 2. We discuss this algorithm in detail and back up the expectation that it gives a reasonable approximation of the variances in T^ℓ with empirical evidence the full version of this work.

Using the matrix $\mathbf{M}$ computed by Algorithm 2, we can estimate the variances of components of $\tilde{\mathbf{a}}_i$ as output by $B_{\mathbf{s},\chi}(b, a-1, p)$. This result follows immediately from Assumption 2.

Lemma 2. *Let $n \geq 1$, q be a modulus, $b \in \mathbb{Z}$ with $1 \leq b \leq n$ and σ_r be the standard deviation of $\mathcal{U}(\mathbb{Z}_{\lfloor q/p \rfloor})$. Define $a := \lceil n/b \rceil$ and pick some $p < q$ and let $\mathbf{M}$ be the output of Algorithm 2 under these parameters. Let $(\tilde{\mathbf{a}}_i, c_i)$ be samples returned by $B_{\mathbf{s},\chi}(b, a - 1, p)$. Finally, define $\mathbf{v}$ as the a−vector of variances of the components of $\tilde{\mathbf{a}}$ where $\mathbf{v}_{(k)}$ holds the variance of the components $\tilde{\mathbf{a}}_{(b \cdot k)}$ to $\tilde{\mathbf{a}}_{(b \cdot k + b - 1)}$. Under Assumption 2, the components of $\mathbf{v}$ satisfy:*

$$\mathbf{v}_{(i)} = \sigma_r^2 + \sum_{j=i+1}^{a} \mathbf{M}_{(j,i)}.$$

```
 1  begin
 2  │   T ← 2 · p^b/2; // fudge factor: 2
 3  │   n ← (m*)/((a+1)·T) + 1;
 4  │   Var_red = Var(U(Z_⌊q/p⌉)) = σ_r^2; // the var. of fresh red. elements
 5  │   M is an a × a matrix;
 6  │   for 0 ≤ r < a do
 7  │   │   for 0 ≤ c < a do
 8  │   │   └   M_(r,c) ← Var(U(Z_q)); // el. on and above main diag. not red.
 9  │   for 1 ≤ t < a do
    │   │   // row t = sum of prev. rows + 1 fresh el. for each index
10  │   │   for 0 ≤ i < t do
11  │   │   └   M_(t,i) ← Var_red + Σ_{j=i+1}^{t-1} M_(j,i);
12  │   │   τ ← b · ℓ;
13  │   │   for 0 ≤ i < t do
14  │   │   └   M_(t,i) ← M_(t,i) / (c_τ ⁿ√(n+1)-c_τ)^2;
```

Algorithm 2. Constructing M

This now allows us to given an expression for the noise distribution output by $B_{\mathbf{s},\chi}(b, a-1, p)$.

Lemma 3. *Let $n \geq 1$ be the dimension of the LWE secret vector, q be a modulus, $b \in \mathbb{Z}$ with $1 \leq b \leq n$. Define $a := \lceil n/b \rceil$ and pick some $p < q$ and let $\mathbf{v}$ be as in Lemma 2. Let $(\tilde{\mathbf{a}}_i, \tilde{c}_i)$ be outputs of $B_{\mathbf{s},\chi}(b, a-1, p)$. We assume that Assumptions 1 and 2 hold. Then as a increases the distribution of $\tilde{c}_i$ approaches a discrete Gaussian distribution modulo q with standard deviation*

$$\sigma_{total} := \sqrt{2^a \sigma + b\,\sigma_r^2 \sigma_s^2 \sum_{i=0}^{a-1} \mathbf{v}_{(i)}} \leq \sqrt{2^a \sigma + (2^a - 1) \cdot b \cdot \sigma_r^2 \sigma_s^2}.$$

Proof. The standard deviation follows from Assumption 1 and Lemma 2. Since the distribution is formed by adding up 2^a vectors it approaches a discrete Gaussian distribution when considered over $\mathbb{Z}$ as a increases by the Central Limit Theorem.   □

Assumption 3. *We assume that Lemma 3 holds for $128 \leq n$, i.e. the values of n considered in this work.*

4 Complexity

Finally, we analyse the complexity of the presented algorithms. To do so, we assume that Assumptions 1, 2, and 3 hold. Lemma 3 allows us to estimate the numbers of samples needed to distinguish the outputs of $B_{\mathbf{s},\chi}(b, a-1, p)$ if $B_{\mathbf{s},\chi}(b, -1, p)$ returns LWE samples from uniform. For this, we rely on standard estimates [16] for the number of samples required to distinguish. This estimate provides a good approximation for the advantage obtainable in distinguishing between $\mathcal{U}(\mathbb{Z}_q)$ and a discrete Gaussian reduced mod q with standard deviation σ_{total}. In particular, we compute the advantage as

$$\text{Adv} = \exp\left(-\pi \left(\frac{\sigma_{total} \cdot \sqrt{2\pi}}{q}\right)^2\right).$$

We can now state the overall complexity of running the algorithm in Theorem 1. Remark that the proof of next two results are omitted; they follow by an easy adaptation of the proof of Lemma 2 in [3].

Theorem 1. *Let $n \geq 1$ be the dimension of the LWE secret vector, q be a modulus, $b \in \mathbb{Z}$ with $1 \leq b \leq n$ and σ_s the standard deviation of the secret vector components. Let also σ_r be the variance of random elements in $\mathbb{Z}_{\lfloor q/p_{small}\rceil}$. Define $a := \lceil n/b \rceil$ and pick a pair (p_{small}, m^*) such that $b\sigma_r^2\sigma_s^2 \sum_{i=0}^{a-1} \mathbf{v}_{(i)} \leq 2^a\sigma$, where $\mathbf{v}_{(i)}$ is defined as in Lemma 3. Then $B_{s,\chi}(b, a-1, p)$ will return $(\tilde{\mathbf{a}}_0, \tilde{c}_0), \ldots, (\tilde{\mathbf{a}}_{m-1}, \tilde{c}_{m-1})$ where $\tilde{c}_i$ has standard deviation $\leq \sqrt{2^{a+1}} \cdot \sigma$. Furthermore, this costs*

$$\frac{p_{small}^b}{2} \cdot \left(\frac{a(a-1)}{2} \cdot (n+1)\right) + (m+m^*)\,n\,a$$

additions in $\mathbb{Z}_q$ and $a \cdot \left(\frac{p_{small}^b}{2}\right) + m + m^*$ calls to $L_{s,\chi}$.

The memory requirement for storing each table is established in Corollary 2 below.

Corollary 2. *The memory required to store the table T^i is upper-bounded by*

$$\frac{p_{small}^b}{2} \cdot a \cdot (n+1)$$

elements in $\mathbb{Z}_q$, each of which requires $\lceil \log_2(q) \rceil$ bits of storage.

To clarify the impact of Theorem 1, we consider $m^* = 0$ – i.e. the case discussed in Section 2 – on classical parameters of LWE.

Corollary 3. *Let $q \approx n^c$, for some constant $c > 0$, and $\alpha = n^{1/2-c}$ such that $\sigma \approx \alpha q \approx \sqrt{n}$. Furthermore, let $a = \log_2 n$ and $b = n/\log_2 n$ be the usual choices of parameters for BKW. Assume σ_s does not depend on n. Then, solving Decision-LWE costs at most*

$$\mathcal{O}\left(2^{n\left(c + \frac{\log_2 d - \frac{1}{2}\log_2 \log_2 n}{\log_2 n}\right)} \cdot n \log_2^2 n\right)$$

operations in $\mathbb{Z}_q$. We also need to store $\mathcal{O}\left(2^{n\left(c + \frac{\log_2 d - \frac{1}{2}\log_2 \log_2 n}{\log_2 n}\right)} \cdot n \log_2 n\right)$ elements in $\mathbb{Z}_q$.

Proof. The proof is omitted here but available in the full version of this work.

5   Parameters

To understand the behaviour of our more careful modulus switching technique for concrete parameters, we compare it with one-shot modulus switching. Specifically, we consider the "plain" BKW algorithm [7] as analysed in [3]. Furthermore, to make this work somewhat self-contained we also compare with the BKZ (2.0) algorithm when applied to SIS instances derived from LWE samples and with a simple meet-in-the-middle (MITM) approach or generalised birthday attack.

INSTANCES. We choose $n \in [128, 256, 512, 1024, 2048]$ and – using [4] – pick $q \approx n^2$ and $\sigma = \frac{q}{\sqrt{2\pi n \log_2^2 n}}$ as in Regev's original encryption scheme [20]. We then consider binary-LWE as defined in [12]: $s \leftarrow_\$ \mathcal{U}(\{-1, 0, 1\}^n)$ (we consider the case $s \leftarrow_\$ \mathcal{U}(\mathbb{Z}_2^n)$ as in [8] in the full version of this work). However, we assume an unbounded number of samples being available to the attacker to establish the performance of the algorithms discussed here under optimal conditions.

BKW. For complexity estimates of the plain BKW algorithm we rely on [3]. There the BKW algorithm takes a parameter t which controls the addition depth $a := t \log_2 n$. Here we first pick $t = 2(\log_2 q - \log_2 \sigma)/\log_2 n$ which ensures that the standard deviation of the noise after a levels of additions grows only as large as the modulus. We then slowly increase t in steps of 0.1 until the performance of the algorithm is not estimated to improve any further because too many samples are needed to perform the distinguishing step. Following [3], we translate operations in $\mathbb{Z}_q$ into "bit operations" by multiplying by $\log_2 q$.

BKZ. To estimate the cost of the BKZ (2.0) algorithm we follow [18,16]. In [18], the authors briefly examine an approach for solving LWE by distinguishing between valid matrix-LWE samples of the form $(\mathbf{A}, \mathbf{c}) = (\mathbf{A}, \mathbf{As} + \mathbf{e})$ and samples drawn from the uniform distribution over $\mathbb{Z}_q^n \times \mathbb{Z}_q$. Given a matrix of samples $\mathbf{A}$, one way of constructing such a distinguisher is to find a short vector $\mathbf{u}$ such that $\mathbf{uA} = \mathbf{0} \bmod q$. If $\mathbf{c}$ belongs to the uniform distribution over $\mathbb{Z}_q^n$, then $\langle \mathbf{u}, \mathbf{c} \rangle$ belongs to the uniform distribution on $\mathbb{Z}_q$. On the other hand, if $\mathbf{c} = \mathbf{As} + \mathbf{e}$, then $\langle \mathbf{u}, \mathbf{c} \rangle = \langle \mathbf{u}, \mathbf{As} + \mathbf{e} \rangle = \langle \mathbf{u}, \mathbf{e} \rangle$, where samples of the form $\langle \mathbf{u}, \mathbf{e}_i \rangle$ are governed by another discrete, wrapped Gaussian distribution. Following the work of Micciancio and Regev [18], the authors of [16] give estimates for the complexity of distinguishing between LWE samples and uniform samples by estimating the cost of the BKZ algorithm in finding a short enough vector. In particular, given n, q, σ and a target distinguishing advantage ϵ we set $s = \sigma \cdot \sqrt{2\pi}$ and compute $\beta = q/s \cdot \sqrt{\log(1/\epsilon)/\pi}$. From this β we then compute the required root Hermite factor $\delta_0 = 2^{\log_2^2(\beta)/(4n \log_2 q)}$.

Given δ_0 we then approximate the running time of BKZ 2.0 in seconds using two different strategies. Both strategies treat δ_0 as the dominant influence in determining the running time. The first strategy denoted "BKZ" follows [16] and defines $\log_2 T_{sec} = 1.8/\log_2 \delta_0 - 110$. The second strategy denoted "BKZ2" follows [3] who interpolated data points from [17] as $\log_2 T_{sec} = 0.009/\log_2^2 \delta_0 - 27$.

We translate the running time in seconds figure into bit operations by assuming $2.3 \cdot 10^9$ bit operations per second on a 2.3 GHz CPU, which is pessimistic. Furthermore, for BKZ choosing advantage $\epsilon \ll 1$ and running the algorithms about $1/\epsilon$ times is usually more efficient than choosing $\epsilon \approx 1$ directly, i.e. we generate a new lattice of optimal sub-dimension each time using fresh LWE samples.

MITM. One can also solve small secret LWE with a meet-in-the-middle attack that requires $\approx \mathfrak{c}^{n/2}$ time and space where $\mathfrak{c}$ is the cardinality of the set from which each component of the secret is sampled (so $\mathfrak{c} = 2$ or $\mathfrak{c} = 3$ for binary-LWE depending on the definition used): compute and store a sorted list of all $\mathbf{A s}'$ where $\mathbf{s}' = (\mathbf{s}_{(0)}, \ldots, \mathbf{s}_{(n/2)-1}, 0, 0, \ldots, 0)$ for all possible $\mathfrak{c}^{n/2}$ choices for $\mathbf{s}'$. Then compute $\mathbf{c} - \mathbf{A s}''$ where we have $\mathbf{s}'' = (0, 0, \ldots, 0, \mathbf{s}_{(n/2)}, \ldots, \mathbf{s}_{n-1})$ and check for a vector that is close to this value in the list.

In Table 2 we give the number of bit operations ("$\log \mathbb{Z}_2$"), calls to the LWE oracle ("$\log L_{\mathbf{s}, \chi}$") and memory requirement ("$\log \mathrm{mem}$") for BKW without any modulus reduction to establish the baseline. All costs are given for the high advantage case, i.e. if $\epsilon \ll 1$ we multiply the cost by $1/\epsilon$.

Table 3 gives the running times after modulus reduction with $p = q\sqrt{n/12}\sigma_s/\sigma$. In particular, Table 3 lists the expected running time (number of oracle calls and where applicable memory requirements) of running BKW and BKZ after applying modulus reduction.

Finally, Table 4 gives the expected costs for solving these LWE instances using the techniques described in this work. We list two variants: one with and one without "unnatural selection". This is because these techniques rely on more assumptions than the rest of this work which means we have greater confidence in the predictions avoiding such assumptions.

Table 2. Cost for solving Decision-LWE with advantage ≈ 1 for BKW, BKZ and MITM where q and σ are chosen as in [20] and $\mathbf{s} \leftarrow_\$ \mathcal{U}(\{-1, 0, 1\}^n)$

	MITM		BKZ [16]			BKZ 2.0 [17]				BKW [3]		
n	$\log \mathbb{Z}_2$	$\log \mathrm{mem}$	$\log \epsilon$	$\log L_{\mathbf{s},\chi}$	$\log \mathbb{Z}_2$	$\log \epsilon$	$\log L_{\mathbf{s},\chi}$	$\log \mathbb{Z}_2$	t	$\log L_{\mathbf{s},\chi}$	$\log \mathbb{Z}_2$	$\log \mathrm{mem}$
128	105.2	101.4	-18	26.5	65.4	-14	22.5	65.7	3.18	83.9	97.6	90.0
256	206.9	202.9	-29	38.5	179.5	-35	44.5	178.5	3.13	167.2	182.1	174.2
512	409.9	405.8	-48	58.5	390.9	-94	104.5	522.8	3.00	344.7	361.0	352.8
1024	815.8	811.5	-82	93.5	785.0	-265	276.5	1606.2	2.99	688.0	705.5	697.0
2048	1627.5	1623.0	-141	153.6	1523.6	-773	785.4	5100.0	3.00	1369.8	1388.7	1379.9

Table 3. Cost for solving Decision-LWE with advantage ≈ 1 for BKW and BKZ variants where q, σ are chosen as in [20] and $\mathbf{s} \leftarrow_\$ \mathcal{U}(\{-1, 0, 1\}^n)$ after one-shot modulus reduction with $p = q\sqrt{n/12}\sigma_s/\sigma$

	BKZ [16]			BKZ 2.0 [17]			BKW [3]			
n	$\log \epsilon$	$\log L_{\mathbf{s},\chi}$	$\log \mathbb{Z}_2$	$\log \epsilon$	$\log L_{\mathbf{s},\chi}$	$\log \mathbb{Z}_2$	t	$\log L_{\mathbf{s},\chi}$	$\log \mathbb{Z}_2$	$\log \mathrm{mem}$
128	-21	29.3	70.2	-16	24.4	69.8	2.85	76.8	90.2	82.4
256	-31	40.3	175.3	-37	46.3	172.8	2.85	150.4	165.6	153.7
512	-50	60.3	365.0	-90	100.2	467.0	2.76	293.8	309.6	301.9
1024	-81	92.3	710.1	-236	247.2	1339.1	2.78	570.3	587.4	579.4
2048	-134	146.3	1342.3	-647	659.2	4006.5	2.71	1149.0	1167.3	1159.1

Table 4. Cost for solving Decision-LWE with advantage ≈ 1 with the algorithms discussed in this work when $\mathbf{s} \leftarrow_\$ \mathcal{U}(\{-1,0,1\}^n)$

| | this work (w/o unnatural selection) | | | | | | this work | | | | |
n	t	$\log p$	$\log m^*$	$\log L_{\mathbf{s},\chi}$	$\log \mathbb{Z}_2$	$\log$ mem	t	$\log p$	$\log m^*$	$\log L_{\mathbf{s},\chi}$	$\log \mathbb{Z}_2$	$\log$ mem
128	2.98	10	0	64.7	78.2	70.8	2.98	6	61	61.0	75.2	46.3
256	2.83	11	0	127.8	142.7	134.9	2.83	5	118	118.0	133.5	67.1
512	2.70	11	0	235.1	251.2	243.1	2.70	8	225	225.0	241.8	180.0
1024	2.59	12	0	477.4	494.8	486.5	2.59	10	467	467.0	485.0	407.5
2048	2.50	12	0	971.4	990.7	907.9	2.50	12	961	961.0	980.2	907.9

DISCUSSION. The results in this section indicate that the variants of the BKW algorithms discussed in this work compare favourably for the paramters considered. The results in this table also indicate that the unnatural selection strategy has little impact on the overall time complexity. However, it allows to reduce the data complexity, in some cases, considerably. In particular, e.g. considering line 1 of Table 4, we note that applying this technique can make the difference between a feasible ($\approx 80 \cdot 1024^4$ bytes) and infeasible ($\approx 1260 \cdot 1024^6$ bytes) attack for a well-equipped attacker [14]. Finally, we note that our results indicate that lattice reduction benefits from modulus reduction. However, this seems somewhat implausible judging from the used algorithms. This might indicate that the lattice reduction estimates from the literature above might need to be revised.

6   Conclusion and Future Work

We investigated applying modulus switching to exploit the presence of a small secret in LWE instances and demonstrated that it can make a significant impact on the complexity of solving such instances. We also adapted the BKW algorithm to perform modulus-switching 'on-the-fly', showing that this approach is superior to performing 'one-shot' modulus reduction on LWE samples prior to solving. Our first variant improves the target modulus by a factor of $\sqrt{\log_2 n}$ in typical scenarios; our second variant mainly improves the memory requirements of the algorithm, one of the key limiting aspects of the BKW algorithm. Our algorithms, however, rely on various assumptions which, though appearing sound, are unproven. Our estimates should thus be considered heuristic, as are performance estimates for all currently-known algorithms for solving LWE. Verifying these assumptions is hence a promising direction for future research. Furthermore, one of the main remaining obstacles for applying the BKW algorithm to cryptographic constructions based on LWE is that it requires an unbounded number of samples to proceed. Lifting this requirement, if only heuristically, is hence a pressing research question.

Acknowledgement. We thank Steven Galbraith for helpful comments on an earlier draft of this work. We also thank anonymous referees for detailed comments which greatly improved this work. Jean-Charles Faugère, and Ludovic Perret have been partially supported supported by the Computer Algebra and Cryptography (CAC) project (ANR-09-JCJCJ-0064-01) and the HPAC grant (ANR ANR-11-BS02-013) of the French National Research Agency.

References

1. Akavia, A., Goldwasser, S., Vaikuntanathan, V.: Simultaneous hardcore bits and cryptography against memory attacks. In: Reingold, O. (ed.) TCC 2009. LNCS, vol. 5444, pp. 474–495. Springer, Heidelberg (2009)
2. Albrecht, M., Cid, C., Faugère, J.-C., Fitzpatrick, R., Perret, L.: On the complexity of the arora-ge algorithm against lwe. In: SCC 2012: Proceedings of the 3rd International Conference on Symbolic Computation and Cryptography, Castro-Urdiales, pp. 93–99 (July 2012)
3. Albrecht, M.R., Cid, C., Faugère, J.-C., Fitzpatrick, R., Perret, L.: On the complexity of the BKW algorithm on LWE. Designs, Codes and Cryptography, 1–30 (2013)
4. Albrecht, M.R., Fitzpatrick, R., Cabracas, D., Gpfert, F., Schneider, M.: A generator for LWE and Ring-LWE instances (2013),
http://www.iacr.org/news/files/2013-04-29lwe-generator.pdf
5. Applebaum, B., Cash, D., Peikert, C., Sahai, A.: Fast cryptographic primitives and circular-secure encryption based on hard learning problems. In: Halevi, S. (ed.) CRYPTO 2009. LNCS, vol. 5677, pp. 595–618. Springer, Heidelberg (2009)
6. Arora, S., Ge, R.: New algorithms for learning in presence of errors. In: Aceto, L., Henzinger, M., Sgall, J. (eds.) ICALP 2011, Part I. LNCS, vol. 6755, pp. 403–415. Springer, Heidelberg (2011)
7. Blum, A., Kalai, A., Wasserman, H.: Noise-tolerant learning, the parity problem, and the statistical query model. J. ACM 50(4), 506–519 (2003)
8. Brakerski, Z., Langlois, A., Peikert, C., Regev, O., Stehlé, D.: Classical hardness of Learning with Errors. In: STOC 2013, pp. 575–584. ACM, New York (2013)
9. Brakerski, Z., Vaikuntanathan, V.: Efficient fully homomorphic encryption from (standard) LWE. In: Ostrovsky, R. (ed.) IEEE 52nd Annual Symposium on Foundations of Computer Science, FOCS 2011, pp. 97–106. IEEE (2011)
10. Chen, Y., Nguyen, P.Q.: BKZ 2.0: better lattice security estimates. In: Lee, D.H., Wang, X. (eds.) ASIACRYPT 2011. LNCS, vol. 7073, pp. 1–20. Springer, Heidelberg (2011)
11. Levieil, É., Fouque, P.-A.: An improved LPN algorithm. In: De Prisco, R., Yung, M. (eds.) SCN 2006. LNCS, vol. 4116, pp. 348–359. Springer, Heidelberg (2006)
12. Gentry, C., Halevi, S., Smart, N.P.: Homomorphic evaluation of the AES circuit. In: Safavi-Naini, R., Canetti, R. (eds.) CRYPTO 2012. LNCS, vol. 7417, pp. 850–867. Springer, Heidelberg (2012)
13. Goldwasser, S., Kalai, Y.T., Peikert, C., Vaikuntanathan, V.: Robustness of the Learning with Errors assumption. In: ICS, pp. 230–240. Tsinghua University Press (2010)
14. Hill, K.: Blueprints of NSA's ridiculously expensive data center in Utah suggest it holds less info than thought (2013),
http://www.forbes.com/sites/kashmirhill/2013/07/24/
blueprints-of-nsa-data-center-in-utah-suggest-its-
storage-capacity-is-less-impressive-than-thought/
15. Kirchner, P.: Improved generalized birthday attack. Cryptology ePrint Archive, Report 2011/377 (2011), http://eprint.iacr.org/
16. Lindner, R., Peikert, C.: Better key sizes (and attacks) for LWE-based encryption. IACR Cryptology ePrint Archive, 2010:592 (2010)

17. Liu, M., Nguyen, P.Q.: Solving BDD by enumeration: An update. In: Dawson, E. (ed.) CT-RSA 2013. LNCS, vol. 7779, pp. 293–309. Springer, Heidelberg (2013)
18. Micciancio, D., Regev, O.: Lattice-based cryptography. In: Bernstein, D.J., Buchmann, J., Dahmen, E. (eds.) Post-Quantum Cryptography, pp. 147–191. Springer, Heidelberg (2009)
19. Pietrzak, K.: Subspace LWE. In: Cramer, R. (ed.) TCC 2012. LNCS, vol. 7194, pp. 548–563. Springer, Heidelberg (2012)
20. Regev, O.: On lattices, learning with errors, random linear codes, and cryptography. J. ACM 56(6) (2009)

Practical Cryptanalysis of a Public-Key Encryption Scheme Based on New Multivariate Quadratic Assumptions

Martin R. Albrecht[1], Jean-Charles Faugère[3,2,4], Robert Fitzpatrick[5], Ludovic Perret[2,3,4], Yosuke Todo[6], and Keita Xagawa[6]

[1] Technical University of Denmark, Denmark
[2] Sorbonne Universités, UPMC Univ Paris 06, POLSYS,
UMR 7606, LIP6, F-75005, Paris, France
[3] INRIA, Paris-Rocquencourt Center, POLSYS Project
[4] CNRS, UMR 7606, LIP6, F-75005, Paris, France
[5] Information Security Group
Royal Holloway, University of London
Egham, Surrey TW20 0EX, United Kingdom
[6] NTT Secure Platform Laboratories
maroa@dtu.dk, jean-charles.faugere@inria.fr,
robert.fitzpatrick.2010@live.rhul.ac.uk, ludovic.perret@lip6.fr,
{todo.yosuke,xagawa.keita}@lab.ntt.co.jp

Abstract. In this paper, we investigate the security of a public-key encryption scheme introduced by Huang, Liu and Yang (HLY) at PKC'12. This new scheme can be provably reduced to the hardness of solving a set of quadratic equations whose coefficients of highest degree are chosen according to a discrete Gaussian distributions. The other terms being chosen uniformly at random. Such a problem is a variant of the classical problem of solving a system of non-linear equations (PoSSo), which is known to be hard for random systems. The main hypothesis of Huang, Liu and Yang is that their variant is not easier than solving PoSSo for random instances. In this paper, we disprove this hypothesis. To this end, we exploit the fact that the new problem proposed by Huang, Liu and Yang reduces to an easy instance of the Learning With Errors (LWE) problem. The main contribution of this paper is to show that security and efficiency are essentially incompatible for the HLY proposal. That is, one cannot find parameters which yield a secure and a practical scheme. For instance, we estimate that a public-key of at least 1.03 GB is required to achieve 80-bit security against the simplest of our attacks. As a proof of concept, we present 3 practical attacks against all the parameters proposed by Huang, Liu and Yang. With the most efficient attack, we have been able to recover the private-key in roughly 5 minutes for the first challenge (i.e. Case 1) proposed by HLY and less than 30 minutes for the second challenge (i.e. Case 2).

1 Introduction

At PKC 2012 Huang, Liu and Yang (HLY) proposed a new public-key encryption scheme [17]. It follows a line of research, called Multivariate Quadratic ($\mathcal{MQ}$)

H. Krawczyk (Ed.): PKC 2014, LNCS 8383, pp. 446–464, 2014.
© International Association for Cryptologic Research 2014

cryptography, to construct public-key encryption schemes from the known hard problem of solving systems of polynomial equations. This line of research dates back to the mid eighties with the design of C* [24], later followed by many other proposals. While this family of designs is commonly considered to be an interesting alternative to constructions based on number-theoretic problems (in the post-quantum setting), it suffers from a lack of clear security reductions to well-understood problems, leading to a series of attacks.

In contrast, [17] is part of a recent trend in $\mathcal{MQ}$ cryptography of designing cryptosystems whose security can be provably reduced to the the hardness of solving a system of non-linear equations (other examples include [3,8]). The key innovation of Huang-Liu-Yang [17] is a $\mathcal{MQ}$ scheme in which the public key is noise-free and non-linear but ciphertexts are noisy and linear. Hence, the scheme proposed by Huang, Liu, and Yang can be viewed as a hybrid between the Learning with Errors (LWE) problem [27] and $\mathcal{MQ}$ cryptosystems. The semantic security of the scheme [17] can be provably reduced to the difficulty of solving a system of non-linear equations which is somewhat structured as the coefficients of the non-linear parts of the polynomials are chosen according to a discrete Gaussian. The main assumption of [17] is that this new problem is not easier than the problem of solving a random system of quadratics equations.

1.1 Organisation of the Paper and Overview of the Results

After this introduction, the paper is organized as follows. We first provide a brief introduction to lattices and algorithms for solving LWE in Section 2. In particular, we briefly recall in Section 2.2 Micciancio and Regev's [26,21] distinguishing approach and Kannan's embedding technique [18] for solving LWE. We then describe the HLY proposal in Section 3. The new hard problem introduced by Huang, Liu and Yang is as follows:

Definition 1 (MQ$(n, m, \Phi_\zeta, H_\beta)$). *Let n be positive integer, $m = cn$ for some $c \geq 1$, q be a polynomially bounded prime, a constant $\beta, 0 < \beta < q/2$ and $\mathbf{s}$ be a secret vector in $H_\beta := [-\beta, \ldots, \beta]^n \subseteq \mathbb{Z}_q^n$. We denote by $\mathbb{Z}_q^{\Phi_\zeta}[x_1, \ldots, x_n]$ the distribution on quadratic polynomials of $\mathbb{Z}_q[x_1, \ldots, x_n]$ obtained by sampling the monomials of degree 2 according to a discrete Gaussian distribution Φ_ζ of standard deviation $\zeta \in O(1)$ and centred on zero and by sampling the others coefficients (linear, and constant parts) uniformly at random. $MQ_{s,\Phi}^{(n)}$ is the probability distribution on the $\mathbb{Z}_q[x_1, \ldots, x_n]^m \times \mathbb{Z}_q^m$ obtained by sampling $\mathbf{p} = (p_1, \ldots, p_m)$ from $\mathbb{Z}_q^{\Phi_\zeta}[\mathbf{x}]^m$, and returning $(\mathbf{p}, \mathbf{c}) = (\mathbf{p}, \mathbf{p}(\mathbf{s})) \in \mathbb{Z}_q[x_1, \ldots, x_n]^m \times \mathbb{Z}_q^m$. $MQ(n, m, \Phi_\zeta, H_\beta)$ is the problem of finding $\mathbf{s} \in H_\beta^n$ given a pair $(\mathbf{p}, \mathbf{p}(\mathbf{s})) \leftarrow_\$ MQ_{s,\Phi}^{(n)}$.*

The main assumption from [17] is that MQ$(n, m, \Phi_\zeta, H_\beta)$ is not easier than the problem of solving a random system of quadratic equations (Assumption 1). Remark that the latter problem is notoriously known as a hard problem from a theoretical [14] and practical point of view [5,6,7]. In this paper, we show that MQ$(n, m, \Phi_\zeta, H_\beta)$ is in fact related to a much easier problem. The starting point of our analysis is to simply remark

(Fact 1) that $MQ(n, m\Phi_\zeta, H_\beta)$ resembles to a LWE problem with a discrete Gaussian with variance $\gamma^2 = O(n^2\beta^2\zeta^2)$ (centred at zero).

We use this fact, together with the Micciancio-Regev distinguisher and the lattice-reduction complexity model of Lindner and Peikert to derive a new necessary conditions on the security of the HLY scheme (Section 4). In particular, such scheme has at most τ-bit security – with regard to constructing a distinguisher of advantage d – if $(n, \beta, c, k, \tau, d)$ verifies

$$\exp\left(-\tfrac{\pi^2}{12\beta^2} \cdot (c\,k)^{-2} \cdot n^{-4} \cdot 2^{\frac{3.6cn}{\tau+78.9}}\right) = d.$$

For example, with $\beta = c = 2$, $k = 12$, $d = 0.5$, setting $n = 1140$ satisfies this condition for $\tau = 80$. With $n = 1140$, however, the public-key is of size ≈ 1.03 GB.

It appears then that all parameters suggested in [17] (reproduced Table 1) are too small to verify our new security condition. Indeed, we have been able to mount several practical attacks: distinguishing attack with Micciancio-Regev, and a key-recovery attack with the embedding technique, and an improved key-recovery attack exploiting the presence of a small secret (Section 5). We successfully run the two first attacks in roughly one day for the first challenge (i.e. Case 1)) and in roughly three days for the second challenge (i.e. Case 2) proposed by the authors [17]. The last practical attack is attack even more efficient. For the first challenge, we recovered the secret-key in less than 5 minutes and less than 30 minutes for the second challenge. The experimental results are detailed in Section 6.

2 Preliminaries

Notation. In the following we always start counting at zero, denote vectors and matrices in bold, vectors in lower case, and matrices in upper case. Given a vector $\mathbf{a}$, we denote by $\mathbf{a}_{(i)}$ the i-th entry in $\mathbf{a}$, and by $\mathbf{A}_{(i,j)}$ the entry at index (i, j). When given a list of vectors, we index its elements by subscript, e.g. $\mathbf{a}_0, \mathbf{a}_1, \mathbf{a}_2$, to denote the first three vectors of the list. Let q be a prime. We represent elements in $\mathbb{Z}_q$ as integers in $[-\tfrac{q}{2}, \dots, \tfrac{q}{2}]$. We work in the Euclidean norm throughout. We denote by $\overline{\mathbb{Z}_q}$ the algebraic closure of $\mathbb{Z}_q$.

2.1 Background on Lattices

A lattice Λ in $\mathbb{R}^m$ is a discrete additive subgroup. For a general introduction, the reader is referred to [25]. We view a lattice as being generated by a (non-unique) basis $\mathbf{B} = \{\mathbf{b}_0, \dots, \mathbf{b}_{n-1}\} \subset \mathbb{Z}^m$ of linearly-independent integer vectors. We assume that the vectors $\mathbf{b}_0, \dots, \mathbf{b}_{n-1}$ form the rows of the $n \times m$ matrix $\mathbf{B}$. That is: $\Lambda = \mathcal{L}(\mathbf{B}) = \mathbb{Z}^n \cdot \mathbf{B} = \left\{\sum_{i=0}^{n-1} x_i \cdot \mathbf{b}_i \mid x_0, \dots, x_{n-1} \in \mathbb{Z}\right\}$. In this work, we are concerned only with q-ary lattices which are those such that $q\mathbb{Z}^m \subseteq \Lambda \subseteq \mathbb{Z}^m$. We also restrict our attention to *full-rank* lattices i.e. those in which $\dim(\text{span}(\Lambda)) = m$. The determinant or volume $\text{vol}(\Lambda)$ of a (full-rank) lattice Λ is the determinant of any given basis of Λ, hence $\text{vol}(\Lambda) = \det(\mathbf{B})$.

The *dual* of a lattice Λ, denoted by Λ^*, is the lattice consisting of the set of all vectors $\mathbf{z} \in \mathbb{R}^m$ such that $\langle \mathbf{y}, \mathbf{z} \rangle \in \mathbb{Z}$ for all vectors $\mathbf{y} \in \Lambda$. Given a lattice Λ, we denote by $\lambda_i(\Lambda)$ the i-th minimum of Λ defined as $\lambda_i(\Lambda) := \inf \left\{ r \mid \dim(\mathrm{span}(\Lambda \cap \bar{\mathcal{B}}_m(\mathbf{0}, r))) \geq i \right\}$, where $\bar{\mathcal{B}}_m(\mathbf{0}, r)$ denotes the closed, zero-centered m-dimensional (Euclidean) ball of radius r. We define the minimum distance from a given point $\mathbf{t} \in \mathbb{R}^m$ to the lattice by $\mathrm{dist}(\Lambda, \mathbf{t}) = \min \{ \|\mathbf{t} - \mathbf{x}\|_2 \mid \mathbf{x} \in \Lambda \}$.

Minkowski's second theorem gives us a bound on the geometric mean of the successive minima. Given an m-dimensional lattice Λ and any $1 \leq k \leq m$ we have $\left(\prod_{i=1}^{k} \lambda_i(\Lambda) \right)^{1/k} \leq \sqrt{\gamma_m} \cdot \mathrm{vol}(\Lambda)^{1/m}$, where γ_m denotes Hermite's constant of dimension m. However, determining the exact value of γ_m is a long-standing open problem in the geometry of numbers, with the exact values being known for only $1 \leq m \leq 8$ and $m = 24$. Heuristically speaking, given a *random* lattice Λ of dimension m and a Euclidean ball $\bar{\mathcal{B}}_m(\mathbf{x}, r)$. We expect that the number of lattice points which lie in $\Lambda \cap \bar{\mathcal{B}}_m(\mathbf{x}, r)$ to be approximately equal to $\frac{\mathrm{vol}(\bar{\mathcal{B}}_m(\mathbf{x}, r))}{\mathrm{vol}(\Lambda)}$.

The lattices we consider here are not random, rather they are 'Ajtai' lattices, possessing reductions from worst-case Approx-SVP to average-case Hermite-SVP. For more details on the nature of random lattices, the reader is referred to [16]. However, it is generally assumed in the literature, as in this work, that the Gaussian heuristic holds reasonably well for Ajtai lattices. If this approximate equality was to hold for any such ball, then by considering the unit ball in $\bar{\mathcal{B}}_m(\mathbf{0}, 1) \subset \mathbb{R}^m$, we would have $|\Lambda \cap \bar{\mathcal{B}}_m(\mathbf{0}, 1)| \approx \frac{\pi^{m/2}}{\Gamma(1+m/2) \cdot \mathrm{vol}(\Lambda)}$, where Γ denotes the standard gamma function $\Gamma(z) = \int_0^\infty x^{z-1} e^{-x} dx$, $z \in \mathbb{C}$.

Hence we would expect that

$$\lambda_1(\Lambda) \approx \left(\frac{\mathrm{vol}(\Lambda)}{\mathrm{vol}(\bar{\mathcal{B}}_m(\mathbf{0}, 1))} \right)^{1/m} = \frac{\mathrm{vol}(\Lambda)^{1/m} \cdot \Gamma(1+m/2)^{1/m}}{\sqrt{\pi}} \approx \mathrm{vol}(\Lambda)^{1/m} \cdot \sqrt{\frac{m}{2\pi e}}$$

For random lattices, it is known that, with overwhelming probability, the above holds (for all successive minima) [1]. This provides the motivation for the Hermite-SVP problem, which we define below. More generally, we list below the four main lattice problems of relevance to this work.

First, the *approximate Shortest Vector problem* (γ-SVP) is as follows: Given a lattice $\Lambda = \mathcal{L}(\mathbf{B})$, find a vector $\mathbf{v} \in \Lambda$ such that $0 < \|\mathbf{v}\| \leq \gamma \cdot \lambda_1(\Lambda)$. In the same vain, the *approximate Hermite Shortest Vector problem* (γ-HSVP) is: Given a lattice $\Lambda = \mathcal{L}(\mathbf{B})$, find a vector $\mathbf{v} \in \Lambda$ such that $0 < \|\mathbf{v}\| \leq \gamma \cdot \det(\Lambda)^{\frac{1}{m}}$. Any algorithm which solves γ-SVP also solves Hermite-SVP with factor $\gamma \sqrt{\gamma_n}$. Note also that (γ-SVP) ($\gamma \geq 1$) is NP-Hard under randomized reduction for any $\gamma < 2^{(\log n)^{1/2-\epsilon}}$, where $\epsilon > 0$ is an arbitrarily small constant [19].

We also consider the *bounded distance decoding problem* (BDD$_\eta$): Given a lattice Λ and a vector $\mathbf{t}$ such that $\mathrm{dist}(\mathbf{t}, \Lambda) < \eta \cdot \lambda_1(\Lambda)$, find the lattice vector $\mathbf{y}$ which is closest to $\mathbf{t}$. We note that, when considering BDD$_\eta$ from a complexity theory approach, arbitrary values for η can be considered while in practical settings, the problem is often defined with the restriction that $\eta \leq \frac{1}{2}$. The case of solving BDD$_{\eta > \frac{1}{2}}$ corresponds to list-decoding in coding parlance. BDD$_\eta$ is known to be NP-hard for any constant factor $\eta > \frac{1}{\sqrt{2}}$ [22]. Finally:

Finally, the GapSVP (promise) problem (GapSVP$_\gamma$) is: Given a lattice Λ, a radius $r > 0$ and approximation factor $\gamma > 1$, is $\lambda_1(\Lambda) \leq r$? If so return YES, else if $\lambda_1(\Lambda) > \gamma r$ return NO, and otherwise return YES or NO. Note that GapSVP$_\gamma$ is NP-Hard for any constant γ[19].

Lattice Reduction. The predominant approaches for solving the Learning with Errors (LWE) problem [27] rely on reducing a lattice basis (determined by a subset of the LWE samples) to obtain either a single short vector in the (scaled) dual lattice [26] or a 'good' (relatively orthogonal) basis of the primal lattice [21], as measured by the norms of the Gram-Schmidt vectors of such a basis. In the first case, since we do not know $\lambda_1(\Lambda)$ *a priori*, it is customary to measure the 'strength' of a basis reduction algorithm by the γ-HSVP factor it can attain. In the latter case, similar notions are used, with the added heuristic that the norms of the Gram-Schmidt vectors of a reduced-basis decrease geometrically.

We briefly recall some notions of lattice basis reduction (from a Hermite-SVP perspective). While finding the shortest vector in low-dimensional lattices is relatively easy, only approximation algorithms can be realistically run in higher dimensions. With respect to the Hermite-SVP problem, we aim to find a vector $\mathbf{v}$ in the lattice such that $\gamma = \|\mathbf{v}\|/\text{vol}(\Lambda)^{\frac{1}{m}}$ is small. The famed LLL algorithm [20] discloses lattice vectors with Hermite factor $\leq (4/3)^{(m-1)/4}$ while the more powerful Block Korkine-Zolotarev (BKZ) algorithm, parameterised by a block-size β, discloses lattice vectors with Hermite factor $\leq \sqrt{\gamma_\beta}^{1+(m-1)/(\beta-1)}$ [13].

In practice, however, both LLL and BKZ perform much better than their worst-case provable bounds and both are commonly characterised by a 'root Hermite-factor' δ_0 such that $\delta_0^m \approx \|\mathbf{v}\|/\text{vol}(\Lambda)^{\frac{1}{m}}$. Given a fixed algorithm, the value of δ_0 appears to rapidly converge to a fixed value as the lattice dimension increases. In [13], the authors report the results of extensive experiments, partly aimed at determining root Hermite factors for LLL and BKZ with selected block-sizes. The results of [13] indicate that, in practise, LLL achieves a $\delta_0 \approx 1.0219$ while BKZ-20 and BKZ-28 achieve $\delta_0 \approx 1.0128$ and $\delta_0 \approx 1.0109$, respectively, conjecturing that the current limits of 'practical' lattice reduction appear to be a root Hermite factor of ≈ 1.01, with $\delta_0 = 1.005$ being far beyond reach (in high dimension). However, estimation of the running time of BKZ in high dimension with a large block-size is difficult, with the asymptotic running time being doubly-exponential in the block-size. To attempt a conservative prediction of the running time of BKZ with large block-size, the authors of [21] assume that δ_0 is the dominant influence on the running-time of BKZ in high dimension and proposed a simple extrapolation of running times as a function of δ_0 leading to the model

$$\log_2 T_{\text{sec}} = 1.8/\log_2 \delta_0 - 110. \tag{1}$$

We can translate this figure into bit operations by assuming $2.3 \cdot 10^9$ bit operations per second on a 2.3 GHz CPU.

However, the accuracy and hence utility of such models is debatable, with such models giving infeasibly low complexity estimates for the application of LLL.

2.2 Learning with Errors (LWE)

We briefly review the results on LWE required in our cryptanalysis. The central idea of our attack is to observe that the security of HLY scheme actually relies on weak instances of LWE. After providing the definition of LWE, we recall a modulus-switching result from [9] which we exploit to improve our basic attack. Finally, we briefly review some known techniques for solving LWE. In this work, we consider the short dual-lattice vector distinguishing attack [26] to distinguish LWE instances arising in our attack of HLY scheme. The LWE problem is as follows:

Definition 2 (LWE [27]). *Let n, q be a positive integers, χ be a probability distribution on $\mathbb{Z}_q$ and s be a secret vector in $\mathbb{Z}_q^n$. We denote by $L_{s,\chi}^{(n)}$ the probability distribution on $\mathbb{Z}_q^n \times \mathbb{Z}_q$ obtained by choosing $\mathbf{a} \in \mathbb{Z}_q^n$ uniformly at random, choosing $e \in \mathbb{Z}_q$ according to χ, and returning $(\mathbf{a}, c) = (\mathbf{a}, \langle \mathbf{a}, \mathbf{s} \rangle + e) \in \mathbb{Z}_q^n \times \mathbb{Z}_q$. We shall call* Decision-LWE *the problem of deciding whether pairs $(\mathbf{a}, c) \in \mathbb{Z}_q^n \times \mathbb{Z}_q$ are sampled according to $L_{s,\chi}^{(n)}$ or the uniform distribution on $\mathbb{Z}_q^n \times \mathbb{Z}_q$.*

The noise follows some distribution χ which is classically chosen to be a discrete Gaussian distribution over $\mathbb{Z}$ with mean 0, reduced modulo q. This distribution (over $\mathbb{Z}$) is obtained by rounding the (continuous) Gaussian distribution $\mathcal{N}(\mu, \sigma^2)$ with mean μ and standard deviation $\sigma = s/\sqrt{2\pi} = \alpha q/\sqrt{2\pi}$, i.e. we consider $\lceil \mathcal{N}(\mu, \sigma^2) \rfloor$. The modulus q is typically taken to be polynomial in n. It was shown [27,9] that if $\alpha q > 2\sqrt{n}$, then (worst-case) $\mathrm{GapSVP}_{\tilde{O}(n/\alpha)}$ reduces to (average-case) LWE.

Remark 1 (Modulus reduction). Modulus switching was introduced to improve the performance of homomorphic encryption schemes [10] and was recently used to reduce the hardness of LWE with polynomially sized moduli to GAPSVP [9]. It also possible to use such technique for attacking schemes. As soon as the secret s follows a distribution with small standard deviation σ_s, then we can perform modulus reduction. That is, given $p \ll q$ we can consider a new LWE sample $(\lfloor p/q \cdot \mathbf{a}_i \rfloor, \lfloor p/q \cdot c_i \rfloor)$ in place of the initial LWE $(\mathbf{a}_i, c_i)$ at the cost of a slight increase in the noise level. We do not consider this approach further in this work as it only provides a moderate improvement over the results presented in Section 6.

Solving LWE with Lattice Reduction. For solving LWE, several approaches exist in the literature. Asymptotically, combinatorial approaches are superior [2] while in practise lattice-based approaches are often more efficient. The most straight-forward approach [26] is to apply lattice basis reduction to the (scaled) dual lattice determined by the LWE samples. This allows to obtain a short vector in this lattice and leads to a distinguisher of valid LWE samples and uniformly random samples. Note that thanks to the classical decision to search equivalence for LWE [27] any distinguisher can be actually used to recover the secret key. This multiplies the cost of the distinguisher by a polynomial factor q (more precisely, by the size of the secret space).

Given a set of m LWE samples $(\mathbf{a}_i, c_i)$, we denote by $\mathbf{A} \in \mathbb{Z}_q^{n \times m}$ the matrix whose columns are the $\mathbf{a}_i^T$'s. We then consider the following q-ary lattice

$$\Lambda_q(\mathbf{A}) := \{ \mathbf{z} \in \mathbb{Z}^m \mid \exists \mathbf{s} \in \mathbb{Z}^n \text{ such that } \mathbf{s}\mathbf{A} \equiv \mathbf{z} \bmod q \}$$

and a corresponding (scaled) dual lattice

$$\Lambda_q^\perp(\mathbf{A}) := \{ \mathbf{y} \in \mathbb{Z}^m \mid \mathbf{A}\mathbf{y}^T \equiv \mathbf{0} \bmod q \}.$$

In [26], the authors briefly examine an approach for solving LWE by distinguishing between valid matrix-LWE samples of the form $(\mathbf{A}, \mathbf{c}) = (\mathbf{A}, \mathbf{s}\mathbf{A} + \mathbf{e})$ and samples drawn from the uniform distribution over $\mathbb{Z}_q^{n \times m} \times \mathbb{Z}_q^m$. Given a matrix of samples $\mathbf{A}$, one way of constructing such a distinguisher is to find a short vector $\mathbf{u}$ in the (scaled) dual lattice $\Lambda_q^\perp(\mathbf{A})$, the vector $\mathbf{u}$ is such that $\mathbf{A}\mathbf{u}^T = \mathbf{0} \bmod q$. If $\mathbf{c}$ belongs to the uniform distribution over $\mathbb{Z}_q^m$, then $\langle \mathbf{u}, \mathbf{c} \rangle$ belongs to the uniform distribution on $\mathbb{Z}_q$. On the other hand, if $\mathbf{c} = \mathbf{s}\mathbf{A} + \mathbf{e}$, then $\langle \mathbf{u}, \mathbf{c} \rangle = \langle \mathbf{u}, \mathbf{s}\mathbf{A} + \mathbf{e} \rangle = \langle \mathbf{u}, \mathbf{e} \rangle$. Each sample of the form $\langle \mathbf{u}, \mathbf{e}_i \rangle$ are governed by another discrete, wrapped Gaussian distribution. Following the work of Micciancio and Regev [26], the authors of [21] investigates the algorithmic hardness of Decision-LWE by estimating the cost of the BKZ algorithm in finding a short enough vector, using the model mentioned above (Section 2.1).

In particular, given $m, n, q, \sigma = \alpha q$, we set $s = \sigma \sqrt{2\pi}$. Then, given a vector $\mathbf{v}$ in the dual lattice, a good approximation for the distinguishing advantage obtained through this approach is

$$\epsilon \approx \exp\left(-\pi \cdot (\|\mathbf{v}\| \cdot s/q)^2\right). \tag{2}$$

Thus, given a target distinguishing advantage ϵ, we can compute the required norm of a vector in the (scaled) dual lattice to be: $v = (q/s) \cdot \sqrt{-\log(\epsilon)/\pi}$. We also let

$$\lambda_1(\Lambda_q(\mathbf{A})) = \min\left\{ q, q^{n/m} \cdot \sqrt{m/(2\pi \cdot e)} \right\}$$

be the length of the shortest vector according to the Gaussian heuristic. Once again, we note that while the q-ary lattices derived from LWE instances are not random in a strict sense and thus we cannot *a priori* expect the Gaussian heuristic to be verified, in practice the heuristic holds extremely well. Hence, as do other works, we assume this also in our case.

To estimate the root Hermite factor δ_0 we need to achieve, we rely on the heuristic – but experimentally sound – model in which we expect the norm of the shortest vectors found to be approximately $q^{n/m} \delta_0^m$. Then, the optimal sub-lattice dimension for the attack is $m_{\text{opt}} = \sqrt{n \log(q)/\log(\delta_0)}$. Assuming that we have enough LWE samples to construct a lattice of the optimal dimension, we then require the application of a basis-reduction algorithm with root-factor given by $\delta_0 = 2^{\frac{\log^2 v}{4n \log q}}$.

An alternative method for solving LWE (and for BDD in general) using lattice reduction is to employ Kannan's embedding method. Here, we take a lattice $\Lambda = \mathcal{L}(\mathbf{B}) \subset \mathbb{R}^m$ and a point $\mathbf{t} \in \mathbb{R}^m$ which is close to a lattice point $\mathbf{y}$ with $\|\mathbf{y} - \mathbf{t}\| < \lambda_1(\Lambda)/2$. We then construct

$$\mathbf{B}' = \begin{pmatrix} \mathbf{B} & \mathbf{0} \\ \mathbf{t} & \|\mathbf{y} - \mathbf{t}\| \end{pmatrix}.$$

It can be shown [23] that if $\sqrt{2} \cdot \|\mathbf{y} - \mathbf{t}\| < \lambda_1(\Lambda)$ then $[\mathbf{t} \mid \|\mathbf{y} - \mathbf{t}\|]$ is a shortest (non-zero) vector in $\mathcal{L}(\mathbf{B}')$. This leads to an instance of unique-SVP - an instance of SVP in which we are given the additional guarantee that there is a certain 'gap' between $\lambda_1(\mathcal{L}(\mathbf{B}'))$ and $\lambda_2(\mathcal{L}(\mathbf{B}'))$. Note that, in practise, one would choose the embedding factor to be smaller than $\|\mathbf{y} - \mathbf{t}\|$ to (probabilistically) maximise this gap. In this work, we employ both large and small embedding factors, 'small' meaning an embedding factor of 1. In the latter case (see section 5.1) we make the simplifying assumption that the second minimum of the embedding lattice is approximately equal to the first minimum of the original lattice, to gain an estimation of the gap. However, compared to alternative approaches for solving LWE, the efficacy of the embedding approach is poorly understood at present with no good models (to the best of our knowledge) to predict when the approach will succeed. It is known, however, that the presence of a λ_2/λ_1 gap makes finding the shortest vector somewhat easier, with an exponential gap clearly allowing disclosure of a shortest non-zero vector by application of LLL. With smaller gaps, the success of the approach is known to be probabilistic [13].

3   A New Multivariate Quadratic Assumption and LWE with Small Secrets

in this section we describe the public-key encryption scheme proposed by Huang, Liu and Yang (HLY) [17] at PKC'12 as well as the new hard problem underlying their scheme. We will revisit the fact that the hardness of this new problem is related to the difficulty of solving a LWE-style problem for a very small secret. In [17] the authors introduced a variant of the classical Polynomial System Solving Problem (PoSSo).

Definition 3. *Let $f_0, \ldots, f_{m-1} \in \mathbb{Z}_q[x_0, \ldots, x_{n-1}]$ be non-linear polynomials. PoSSo is the problem of finding – if any – $\mathbf{s} \in \overline{\mathbb{Z}}_q^n$ such that $f_0(\mathbf{s}) = 0, \ldots, f_{m-1}(\mathbf{s}) = 0$.*

It is well known [14] that this problem is NP-hard. Note that PoSSo remains NP-hard [14] even if we suppose that the input polynomials are quadratics. In this case, PoSSo is also called MQ. Huang, Liu and Yang proposed a variant of MQ where the monomials of highest degree (i.e. 2) in the system have their coefficients chosen according to a discrete Gaussian distribution of standard deviation $\zeta \in O(1)$ and centered on zero. Following [17], we denote this distribution by Φ_ζ.[1] The remaining coefficients (linear, and constant parts) are chosen uniformly at random. We denote this distribution on $\mathbb{Z}_q[x_1, \ldots, x_n]$ by $\mathbb{Z}_q^{\Phi_\zeta}[\mathbf{x}]$. The problem introduced by Huang, Liu and Yang will be the main concern of this work:

Definition 4 ($\mathrm{MQ}(n, m, \Phi_\zeta, H_\beta)$). *Let n be positive integer, $m \in O(n)$, q be a polynomially bounded prime, a constant β, $0 < \beta < q/2$ and $\mathbf{e}$ be a secret vector in $H_\beta :=$ $[-\beta, \ldots, \beta]^n \subset \mathbb{Z}_q^n$. We denote by $\mathrm{MQ}_{s,\Phi}^{(n)}$ the probability distribution on $\mathbb{Z}_q[x_1, \ldots, x_n]^m \times \mathbb{Z}_q^m$ obtained by sampling $\mathbf{p} = (p_1, \ldots, p_m)$ from $\mathbb{Z}_q^{\Phi_\zeta}[\mathbf{x}]^m$, and returning $(\mathbf{p}, \mathbf{c}) = (\mathbf{p}, \mathbf{p}(\mathbf{s}))$ $\in \mathbb{Z}_q[x_1, \ldots, x_n]^m \times \mathbb{Z}_q^m$.*

---

[1] The parameter ζ is called α in [17] but this notation clashes with the standard notation for LWE.

$MQ(n, m, \Phi_\zeta, H_\beta)$ is the problem of finding $\mathbf{s} \in H_\beta^n$ given a pair $(\mathbf{p}, \mathbf{p}(\mathbf{s})) \leftarrow_\$ MQ_{\mathbf{s},\Phi}^{(n)}$.

The decision problem associated to $MQ(n, m, \Phi_\zeta, H_\beta)$ is the task of distinguishing $MQ_{\mathbf{s},\Phi}^{(n)}$ from the uniform distribution on $\mathbb{Z}_q[x_1, \ldots, x_n]^m \times \mathbb{Z}_q^m$.

As mentioned in [17], $MQ(n, m, \Phi_\zeta, H_\beta)$ is rather close to LWE:

Fact 1. Each $(\mathbf{p}, \mathbf{p}(\mathbf{s})) \leftarrow_\$ MQ_{\mathbf{s},\Phi}^{(n)}$ can be mapped to a LWE instance. To do so, we just consider the matrix $A_\mathbf{p} \in \mathbb{Z}_q^{n \times m}$ corresponding to the linear part of $\mathbf{p}$. We then remark that each component of $\mathbf{p}(\mathbf{s}) - \mathbf{s} \cdot A_\mathbf{p} - \mathbf{p}(\mathbf{0})$ is the sum of $\frac{n(n+1)}{2}$ discrete Gaussians each having variance $\left(\frac{(2\beta+1)^2-1}{12}\right) \cdot \zeta^2$. From now, we assume that this sum is a discrete Gaussian of variance $\gamma^2 = \frac{n(n+1)}{2} \cdot \left(\frac{(2\beta+1)^2-1}{12}\right) \cdot \zeta^2$ (centered at zero).

It is proven in [17] that $MQ(n, m, \Phi_\zeta, H_\beta)$ has decision to search equivalence. Such equivalence makes the problem appealing to design an encryption scheme. The public-key of the scheme proposed in [17] is a pair of the form $(\mathbf{p}, \mathbf{p}(\mathbf{s})) = (\mathbf{p}, \mathbf{c}) \in \mathbb{Z}_q^{\Phi_\zeta}[\mathbf{x}]^m \times \mathbb{Z}_q^m$. To encrypt a bit b, we choose $\mathbf{r} \in H_{n^\lambda} := [-n^\lambda, \ldots, n^\lambda]^m \subset \mathbb{Z}_q^m$ with λ being a new parameter. We then compute : $c = (A_\mathbf{p} \cdot \mathbf{r}^T, \langle \mathbf{r}, \mathbf{c} - p(\mathbf{0}) \rangle + b \cdot \lfloor q/2 \rceil)$. Thus, each encryption of zero produces a LWE sample whose error has variance: $m \cdot n^{2\lambda} \cdot \gamma^2$. As a consequence, we expect the noise to have size $\sqrt{\frac{2}{\pi}} \cdot \sqrt{m} \cdot n^\lambda \cdot \gamma$. Note that [17] also proposed a Key Encapsulation Mechanism (KEM) scheme, based on the same new hard problem, but which we do not discuss here.

Regarding the security, [17] showed that breaking the semantic security of the encryption scheme is equivalent to solving $MQ(n, m, \Phi_\zeta, H_\beta)$. More precisely:

Theorem 2 ([17]). Let $\mathcal{A}$ be an adversary breaking the semantic security of the scheme working in time T with advantage ϵ. Then, there exists a probabilistic algorithm $\mathcal{B}$ solving $MQ(n, m, \Phi_\zeta, H_\beta)$ in time at most $T \cdot \frac{128}{\epsilon^2} \cdot (2\beta + 1) \cdot (n^2 \log q)^2$ with success probability at least $\epsilon/(4q)$.

A similar result holds for the KEM scheme, i.e. breaking the semantic security of the KEM scheme allows to solve $MQ(n, m, \Phi_\zeta, H_\beta)$.

Such reduction is then used to establish concrete parameters for the proposed encryption scheme. The basic hypothesis for setting the parameter is to assume that solving $\mathbf{p} - \mathbf{p}(\mathbf{s}) = \mathbf{0}$, for $(\mathbf{p}, \mathbf{p}(\mathbf{s})) \leftarrow_\$ MQ_{\mathbf{s},\Phi}^{(n)}$, is essentially not easier than solving a random system of equations [17].

Assumption 1 (HLY Hardness Hypothesis). Solving $MQ(n, m, \Phi_\zeta, H_\beta)$ is as hard as solving a random system of m quadratic equations in n variables modulo q with a pre-assigned solution in H_β^n.

Remark 2. The fact that the secret is in H_β^n implies that one can always add n equations of degree $2\beta + 1$ of the form $\prod_{j \in H_\beta}(x_i - j)$. Clearly, the evaluation of such equations on any $\mathbf{s} \in H_\beta^n$ will be zero.

Arguably, this connection between the semantic security and hardness of PoSSo is the main difference between the HLY scheme and the classical encryption scheme based on LWE. Indeed, the HLY scheme is very similar to a textbook LWE encryption scheme equipped with a Gaussian of standard deviation $\sqrt{m} \cdot n^\lambda \cdot \gamma$ with a very small secret. A noteworthy difference lies in the fact that we also consider small (i.e. of norm bounded by n^λ) linear combinations of public samples. In the classical LWE encryption scheme due to Regev [27], we consider only linear combinations with coefficients in $\{-1, 0, 1\}$ of the public samples.

Assumption 1 allows to estimate the cost of the best attack against $MQ(n, m, \Phi_\zeta, H_\beta)$. A well-established approach to solve PoSSo is to compute a Gröbner basis [11]. The cost of solving a (zero-dimensional, i.e. finite number of solutions) system of m non-linear equations in n variables with the F_5 algorithm [5,12] is $O\left(\binom{n+D_{reg}}{D_{reg}}^\omega\right)$, where D_{reg} is the maximum degree reached during the Gröbner basis computation, and ω is the matrix multiplication exponent (or the linear-algebra constant) as defined in [31, Chapter 12]. We recall that $\omega \in [2, 2.3727]$).

In general, it is a hard problem to predict *a priori* the degree of regularity of a given system of equations. However, Assumption 1 implies that the system of non-linear equations involved is no easier to solve than semi-regular equations [5,6,7]. Precisely, D_{reg} is bounded from below by the index of the first non-positive coefficient of: $\sum_{k\geq 0} c_k z^k = (1-z^2)^m (1-z^{(2\beta+1)})^n / (1-z)^n$. This is the degree of regularity of a system of m equations of degree 2 plus n equations of degree $2\beta + 1$ in n variables.[2] From now on, we will denote by $T_{ref}(m, n, q)$ the cost of solving such system with F_5 algorithm, and by ϵ_{ref} the success probability. Usually, a Gröbner basis computation always succeeds, but one can relax this condition by randomly fixing variables. Precisely, a success probability ϵ_{ref} allows to fix $r_{ref} = \lceil \log_{2\beta+1}(1/\epsilon_{ref}) \rceil$ variables for systems sampled according to $MQ_{s,\Phi}^{(n)}$.

It is worth mentioning and commending that [17] propose concrete parameters for their scheme (reproduced in Table 1). The parameters are chosen as follows. Assume there exist an adversary $\mathcal{A}$ breaking the semantic security of the HLY encryption in time $T_{dist} = 2^\ell$ with advantage $\epsilon_{dist} = 2^{-s}$. According to Theorem 2, we can construct an algorithm $\mathcal{B}$ solving $MQ(n, m, \Phi_\zeta, H_\beta)$ in time $T_{search}(T_{dist}, \epsilon_{dist}, n, q)$ with success probability $\epsilon_{search}(\epsilon_{dist}, q)$. From Assumption 1, the best algorithm for solving $MQ(n, m, \Phi_\zeta, H_\beta)$ works in time $T_{ref}(m, n - r_{ref}, q)$ with a success probability ϵ_{ref}. The parameters m, n, q are chosen such that

$$T_{search}(T_{dist}, \epsilon_{dist}, n, q) < T_{ref}(m, n, q) \text{ and } \epsilon_{search}(\epsilon_{dist}, q) < \epsilon_{ref}.$$

Under the HLY hypothesis (Assumption 1), this means that no adversary can break the semantic security of the scheme in time less than 2^ℓ with success probability better than 2^{-s}.

4 Analysis of the Parameters

In this part, we show that security and efficiency are essentially incompatible for HLY. To do so, we derive a set of conditions on the parameters that would thwart the simplest

---

[2] Note that this quantity can be explicitly computed for any value of n, m and β.

known attack against LWE-style systems such as those discussed above. That is, we want to find parameters such that both computing a Gröbner basis and lattice attacks (in particular the non-optimal Micciancio-Regev approach) are exponentially hard in the security parameter τ. Below, we recall the constraints on the parameters from [17]:

1. $k \cdot \zeta \cdot n^{2+\lambda} \cdot m \cdot \beta^2 \leq q/4$ (to allow for correct decryption)
2. $m \cdot \log(2n^\lambda + 1) \geq (n + 1) \log q + 2k$ (to make sure the subset sum problem is hard)
3. n, m, q, ζ, β (to satisfy the condition in the MQ assumption such that $MQ(n, m, q, \Psi_\zeta, H_\beta)$ is hard to solve).

For the number of equations, we may restrict $m = c \cdot n$ where c is a constant (we remark that the challenges proposed in [17] have $c = 2$). In this case, we can assume that MQ is hard (that is, the cost of computing a Gröbner basis is exponential in the number of variables [5,6,7]. From Condition 2, we then get $m \cdot \log(2n^\lambda + 1) \geq (n + 1) \log q + 2k \geq n \log q$ and

$$c \cdot \log(2n^\lambda + 1) \geq \log q$$

by replacing m with cn. This means that $2n^\lambda$ should be roughly (or at least) $q^{1/c}$. Hence, the first condition yields:

$$k \cdot \zeta \cdot n^{2+\lambda} \cdot m \cdot \beta^2 \leq q/4$$
$$k \cdot \zeta \cdot n^{2+\lambda} \cdot c \cdot n \cdot \beta^2 \leq 2^{(c-2)} n^{c\lambda}$$
$$\zeta \cdot n^2 \cdot \beta^2 \leq (ck)^{-1} 2^{(c-2)} n^{(c-1)\lambda - 1}$$

as a bound on the noise in each of the m samples. As explained in Section 2.2, (heuristically) lattice reduction will produce vectors of length

$$v = q^{n/m} \cdot \delta_0^m = q^{1/c} \cdot \delta_0^{cn} \leq 2n^\lambda \cdot \delta_0^{cn}.$$

By combining this with the above, we get a distinguishing advantage (as defined in (2)) of

$$\exp\left(-\frac{\pi s^2 v^2}{q^2}\right) = \exp\left(-\frac{\pi s^2 4n^{2\lambda} \delta_0^{2cn}}{q^2}\right) = \exp\left(-\frac{2\pi^2 \sigma^2 4n^{2\lambda} \delta_0^{2cn}}{q^2}\right)$$
$$= \exp\left(-\frac{2\pi^2 \sigma^2 4n^{2\lambda} \delta_0^{2cn}}{4^c n^{2c\lambda}}\right) = \exp\left(-(4^{(1-c+\frac{1}{2})} \pi^2 \sigma^2 n^{2\lambda(1-c)} \delta_0^{2cn})\right).$$

Now, we can write:

$$\sigma^2 = \zeta^2 \cdot \frac{n(n+1)}{2} \cdot \left(\frac{(2\beta+1)^2 - 1}{12}\right) = \left(\zeta^{\frac{1}{2}} \cdot n \cdot \beta\right) \cdot \left(\zeta^{\frac{3}{2}} \cdot \frac{n+1}{2} \cdot \frac{\beta+1}{3}\right)$$
$$= \left(\zeta^{\frac{1}{2}} \cdot n \cdot \beta\right) \cdot \left(\frac{1}{6} \cdot \zeta^{\frac{3}{2}} \cdot (n+1) \cdot (\beta+1)\right) \approx \frac{1}{6} \cdot \zeta \cdot \left(\zeta \cdot n^2 \cdot \beta^2\right).$$

This gives:

$$\zeta \lessapprox \frac{(ck)^{-1} 2^{(c-2)} n^{(c-1)\lambda - 1}}{n^2 \cdot \beta^2}.$$

Thus:

$$\sigma^2 \lessapprox \frac{1}{6} \cdot n^2 \cdot \beta^2 \cdot \left(\frac{(ck)^{-2} 2^{2(c-2)} n^{2(c-1)\lambda - 2}}{n^4 \cdot \beta^4}\right) = \frac{(ck)^{-2} 2^{2(c-2)} n^{2(c-1)\lambda - 4}}{6\beta^2}.$$

Hence we can lower-bound the distinguishing advantage by:

$$\exp\left(-(4^{\frac{3}{2}-c}\pi^2\sigma^2 n^{2\lambda(1-c)}\delta_0^{2cn})\right) = \exp\left(-\frac{\pi^2}{12\beta^2}\cdot(ck)^{-2}n^{-4}\cdot\delta_0^{2cn}\right)$$

We now introduce a parameter τ, representing the bit-complexity of solving such instances using the model of Lindner and Peikert. We then replace δ_0 by $2^{(1.8/(\tau+78.9))}$ (employing (1) to deliver an estimate of the number of bit operations required to obtain such a root Hermite factor) and require that the advantage is constant in terms of τ. In other words

$$\exp\left(-\frac{\pi^2}{12\beta^2}\cdot(ck)^{-2}\cdot n^{-4}\cdot 2^{3.6cn/(\tau+78.9)}\right) = d. \tag{3}$$

For example, for $\tau = 80$, with $\beta = 2$, $c = 2$, $k = 12$ and $d = 0.5$, setting $n = 1140$ satisfies this condition. For $\tau = 128$, the same parameters require $n = 1530$. We note, however, that setting $n = 1140$ already results in a public key of considerable size (optimistically setting $\zeta = 10$):

$$\frac{m\cdot\binom{n+2}{2}\cdot\log_2(2\pi\zeta)}{8\cdot 1024^3} \approx 1.03\text{ GB}, \tag{4}$$

while setting $n = 1530$ results in a public-key of size 2.49 GB.

Furthermore, we stress that these parameters do not take potential other attack vectors into account and should be viewed as a somewhat loose *upper-bound* on the complexity of solving such instances. In particular, this discussion does not reflect the possibility of exploiting the small secret for example through modulus reduction (Remark 1) and the approach discussed next.

5 Improved Embedding Attack

We present an improved version of the embedding attack described in Section 2.2. To do so, we exploit the fact that the secret key **s** is *extremely short*. Recall that the coefficients of the secret lie in a small subset $H = [-\beta,\beta] \subset \mathbb{Z}_q$. Typically, Huang, Liu and Yang suggested to take $\beta = 2$ (Table 1).

Let $(\mathbf{p},\mathbf{p}(\mathbf{s})) = (\mathbf{p},\mathbf{c}) \leftarrow_\$ \text{MQ}^{(n)}_{\mathbf{s},\Phi}$ be a public-key of HLY scheme. Let $A_\mathbf{p} \in \mathbb{Z}_q^{n\times m}$ be the matrix corresponding to the linear part of **p**. According to Fact 1, we can write:

$$\mathbf{c} \equiv \mathbf{s}\cdot A_\mathbf{p} + \mathbf{e} + \mathbf{p}(\mathbf{0}) \bmod q,$$

where $\mathbf{e} \equiv \mathbf{p}(\mathbf{s}) - \mathbf{s}\cdot A_\mathbf{p} - \mathbf{p}(\mathbf{0}) \bmod q$. Notice that each coefficient of **e** is the sum of $n(n + 1)/2$ discrete Gaussians. From now on, we let $\mathbf{y} \equiv \mathbf{c} - \mathbf{p}(\mathbf{0}) \equiv \mathbf{s}\cdot A_\mathbf{p} + \mathbf{e} \bmod q$ to ignore the constant part.

The basic idea is to consider the lattice defined by the following basis **B**:

$$\mathbf{B} = \begin{pmatrix} q\mathbf{1}_m & \mathbf{0} & \mathbf{0} \\ A_\mathbf{p} & \mathbf{I}_n & \mathbf{0} \\ -\mathbf{y} & \mathbf{0} & 1 \end{pmatrix}.$$

Since $\mathbf{y} \equiv \mathbf{s}A_\mathbf{p} + \mathbf{e}$ (mod q), there exists $\mathbf{k} \in \mathbb{Z}^m$ satisfying $\mathbf{y} = \mathbf{s} \cdot A_\mathbf{p} + \mathbf{e} + q\mathbf{k} \in \mathbb{Z}^m$. Notice that the lattice $\mathcal{L}(\mathbf{B})$ contains a short vector $\mathbf{w} = [-\mathbf{e} \mid \mathbf{s} \mid 1] \in \mathbb{Z}^{m+n+1}$, since $[\mathbf{k} \mid \mathbf{s} \mid 1] \cdot \mathbf{B} = [q\mathbf{k} + \mathbf{s}A_\mathbf{p} - \mathbf{y} \mid \mathbf{s} \mid 1] = \mathbf{w}$. Applying the reduction algorithm to the lattice $\mathcal{L}(\mathbf{B})$ is less efficient than the basic embedding attack. The dimension $m + n + 1$ is larger than $m + 1$ and the short vector $\mathbf{w} = [-\mathbf{e} \mid \mathbf{s} \mid 1] \in \mathbb{Z}^{m+n+1}$ contains $\mathbf{e}$ entirely.

However, we can consider *a truncated lattice* defined by an $(m' + n + 1)$-dimension right-bottom submatrix $\mathbf{B}'$ of $\mathbf{B}$. By this truncation, we have the following relations:

$$[\mathbf{k}' \mid \mathbf{s} \mid 1] \cdot \begin{pmatrix} q\mathbf{I}_{m'} & \mathbf{0} & 0 \\ A'_\mathbf{p} & \mathbf{I}_n & 0 \\ -\mathbf{y}' & \mathbf{0} & 1 \end{pmatrix} = [-\mathbf{e}' \mid \mathbf{s} \mid 1] \in \mathbb{Z}^{m'+n+1}.$$

We note that $\mathbf{w}' = [-\mathbf{e}' \mid \mathbf{s} \mid 1]$ should be shorter than the previous $\mathbf{w}$. Hence, we could expect a 'less powerful' basis reduction algorithm to be required for recovery of $\pm\mathbf{w}'$ as compared to one required for recovery of the previous $\mathbf{w}$. We finally note that, if $m' < m - n$, then the dimension is smaller than that of the lattice in the direct approach.

5.1 Estimation of the Expected Gap

For an N dimensional lattice Λ, we define $\sigma(\Lambda) \approx \sqrt{N/2\pi e} \cdot \mathrm{vol}(\Lambda)^{1/N}$ to be the expected first minimum $\lambda_1(\Lambda)$ according to the Gaussian heuristic. We have

$$\sigma(\mathcal{L}(\mathbf{B}')) \approx \sqrt{(n + m' + 1)/2\pi e} \cdot q^{m'/(n+m'+1)}.$$

Next, we estimate $\|\mathbf{w}'\| = \sqrt{\|\mathbf{s}\|^2 + \|\mathbf{e}'\|^2 + 1}$. Since $\mathbf{s}$ is chosen from $\{-\beta, \dots, \beta\}$ uniformly at random, the expected value of $\|\mathbf{s}\|^2$ is $n \cdot \frac{1}{2\beta+1} \sum_{i=-\beta}^{\beta} i^2 = n\beta(\beta + 1)/3$. As mentioned above, each coefficient of $\mathbf{e}'$ follows a discrete Gaussian of standard deviation γ. Hence, $E[\|\mathbf{e}'\|]$ can be estimated as $\sqrt{m'} \cdot \gamma$. Summarizing the above, we obtain (using $\beta = 2$):

$$E[\|\mathbf{w}'\|] \approx \sqrt{m'\gamma^2 + 2n + 1} \approx \sqrt{m' \cdot \zeta^2 \cdot n \cdot (n + 1) + 2n}.$$

Hence, the expected gap is expected to be

$$\frac{\sigma(\mathcal{L}(\mathbf{B}'))}{\|\mathbf{w}'\|} \approx \sqrt{\frac{n+m'+1}{2\pi e n(m'\zeta^2(n+1)+2)}} \cdot q^{m'/(n+m'+1)}. \tag{5}$$

We finally note that, when comparing the efficacy of embedding attacks, the expected gaps should be compared with those of lattices of *the same dimension*. If the dimensions differ, we derive less information regarding the success of the lattice-reduction algorithm in finding the shortest vector.

6   Practical Attacks against HLY Challenges

From the discussion in Section 4, we expect that all parameters suggested in [17] should be weak against a lattice-reduction attack. To mount such attacks practically we make

Table 1. Suggested parameters in [17]

Case	n	m	ζ	β	q	Hardness (T,μ)
1	200	400	10	2	$1803131754697263278851 9 \approx 2^{73.93}$	$(2^{156}, 2^{-100})$
2	256	512	10	2	$5232440279576267872487 3 \approx 2^{75.47}$	$(2^{205}, 2^{-104})$

use of the fact that we can view the hard problem from [17] as an LWE instance and then solve these instances using lattice reduction. In particular, we consider all the parameter sets proposed in [17] (Table 1).

The column "Hardness" (T,μ) is a strict lower bound [17] on the complexity of solving $MQ(n, m, \Phi_\zeta, H_\beta)$ under Assumption 1. The parameters of Case (1) are chosen such that no adversary running in time less than 2^{82} can break the semantic security of the HLY bit-encryption scheme with advantage better than 2^{-11}. For the KEM, Case (1) provides a security of $(2^{85}, 2^{-10})$ (which denotes (time, advantage). Case (2) was expected to provide a security level of $(2^{130}, 2^{-11})$ for the bit encryption scheme (and a security level of $(2^{130}, 2^{-10})$ for the KEM scheme).

Case (1)

Distinguishing. We have $m = 400$ equations in $n = 200$ unknowns. Coefficients for quadratic terms are chosen from a discrete Gaussian with standard deviation $\zeta = 10$ and the secret is in $[-\beta, \ldots, \beta]$ for $\beta = 2$. If we ignore all quadratic terms and only consider the linear part, we have an LWE-style instance with $m = 400, n = 200, q \approx 2^{73.93}$ and standard deviation $\gamma = \sqrt{\frac{200 \cdot 201}{2} \cdot 10^2 \cdot \left(\frac{5^2-1}{12}\right)^2} \approx 2^{11.47}$. In this instance, the optimal sub-lattice dimension for applying LLL is $\sqrt{n \log(q)/\log(1.0219)} \approx 688$. However, applying LLL in dimension 400 is expected to return a vector of norm $v = q^{n/m} \cdot \delta_0^m \approx 2^{49.47}$ which is more than sufficient to distinguish between such LWE samples and random with advantage $\epsilon = \exp\left(-\frac{\pi s^2 v^2}{q^2}\right) \approx 0.9999$. We ran the LLL algorithm as implemented in fpLLL [29] on lattice instances as in Case (1), i.e., with $m = 400, n = 200, q = 1803131754697263278851 9$. More precisely, we ran LLL (using Sage's default parameters [30]) on the 400×400 dual lattice. The shortest vector recovered by LLL had norm $2^{49.76}$ while we predicted a norm of $2^{49.47}$. The entire computation took 26 hours on a single core.

Modulus Reduction. A slightly more efficient variant is to perform modulus reduction before performing LLL in order to keep coefficients small. We may apply modulus reduction technique (Remark 1) with the above parameters and pick $p \approx 2^{65.00}$ and $\gamma \approx 2^{3.59}$. Applying LLL in dimension 400 is expected to return a vector of norm $v = 2^{45.00}$ which translates into a distinguishing advantage of $\epsilon \approx 1$.

Embedding. We may also consider the embedding attack as described in Section 2.2. We apply LLL to the 401×401 extended primal lattice and using a (conservative) embedding factor $\lceil \sqrt{m} \cdot \sigma \rceil$. The λ_2/λ_1 gap in this case is approximately

$$\frac{\mathrm{vol}(\mathcal{L}(\mathbf{B}))^{1/m} \cdot \Gamma(1+m/2)^{1/m}}{\sqrt{2\pi m}\sigma} \approx \frac{q^{\frac{m-n}{m}}\sqrt{\frac{m}{2\pi e}}}{\sqrt{2m}\sigma} \approx 2^{22.94}.$$

The attack recovered the 'noise' from the public key, allowing the private key (or an equivalent) to be recovered by simple linear algebra. We note that this attack obviates the need for a separate search-to-distinguishing phase, as required in the dual-lattice method, the attack taking again ~26 hours using a single core.

Improved Embedding. We set $m' = 66 \approx 200/3$. Our attack can recover the secret key $\mathbf{s}$ from every vector $\mathbf{y} = \mathbf{c} - \mathbf{p}(\mathbf{0})$. The running times vary from 268.69 to 295.34 seconds and the average (on 10 instances) of them is 278.16 seconds. We notice that the expected gap (5) is $\approx 2^{6.267}$. This attack was mounted on a Core i7 PC using the NTL library [28] with GMP [15]. In each case, we ran the BKZ algorithm (G_BKZ_FP with $\delta = 0.99$, block size = 30, and prune = 10) on 267-dimensional lattices constructed from the public-keys. We computed m' by incrementing m' from 1 until we success to recover in a test case.

Case (2)

Distinguishing. We have $m = 512$ equations in $n = 256$ unknowns modulo $q \approx 2^{75.47}$. Coefficients for quadratic terms are chosen from a discrete Gaussian with standard deviation $\zeta = 10$ and the secret is in $[-2, \ldots, 2]$ for $\beta = 2$. This gives a standard deviation $\gamma = \sqrt{\frac{256 \cdot 257}{2} \cdot 10^2 \cdot \left(\frac{5^2-1}{12}\right)^2} \approx 2^{11.82}$. Applying LLL in dimension 512 is expected to return a vector of norm $v = q^{n/m} \cdot \delta_0^m \approx 2^{53.74}$ which is more than sufficient to distinguish between such LWE samples and random with advantage $\epsilon = \exp\left(-\frac{\pi s^2 v^2}{q^2}\right) \approx 1$.

Modulus Reduction. Using modulus reduction, we pick $p \approx 2^{66.36}$ and $\gamma \approx 2^{3.76}$. Applying LLL in dimension 512 is expected to return a vector of norm $v = 2^{16.00}$ which translates into a distinguishing advantage of $\epsilon \approx 1$.

Improved Embedding. We set $m' = 90$ as a slightly larger integer than a third of n. Our attack successfully recovers the secret keys from all ten public-keys. The running times vary from 898.14 to 1119.53 seconds and the average of them is 964.83 seconds (≈ 16 minutes). We note that the expected gap is $\approx 2^{7.176}$.

Beyond the Challenges. To examine how the improved embedding attack scales, we consider larger parameters than those provided by the two challenges of Huang, Liu and Yang. In order to extend these challenges, we fix $\zeta = 10, \beta = 2, m = 2n, k = 12$, and $\lambda = 5$ and calculate q. From the correctness condition in [17] (see also Section 4), we should set $q \geq \mathrm{NextPrime}(4k\zeta\beta^2 mn^{2+\lambda}) = \mathrm{NextPrime}(3840n^8)$. From the provable security side, in order to employ the leftover hash lemma, Huang et al. [17] require q to satisfy $m \cdot \log(2n^\lambda + 1) \geq (n+1)\log q + 2k$. We here take q as small as possible, that is, we take $q = \text{NextPrime}(3840n^8)$, which always satisfies the correctness constraint and the security constraint.

Employing a single core of an i7 machine (3.4GHz), we ran the LLL algorithm on lattices constructed from the public keys with the parameter n increasing from 100 with intervals of 25. We computed m' on each n by incrementing m' from 30 at an interval of 10 until we were able to successfully recover a shortest vector in such a test case. The implementation of LLL in the NTL library consists of a number of variants of LLL capable of handling differing precision levels. Additionally, to enhance numerical stability, Givens orthogonalization can be used in place of Gram-Schmidt orthogonalization, the use of Given orthogonalization being denoted by a G_ prefix. The variants which concern us are: G_LLL_FP - LLL with Givens orthogonalization + double precision; G_LLL_QP - LLL with Givens orthogonalization + quadratic precision and G_LLL_RR - LLL with Givens orthogonalization and arbitrary precision - we used a precision of 150 bits.

Table 2 summarises the results of experiments using G_LLL_FP, G_LLL_QP, and G_LLL_RR (with precision 150), respectively. Due to precision limitations, G_LLL_FP fails at $n = 300$ while G_LLL_QP stops at $n = 450$. We also ran G_LLL_RR with default precision 150. Due to time constraints, we only ran this algorithm for parameters up to and including $n = 325$.

We can approximate the charts of the logarithm of T_{FP}, T_{QP}, and T_{RR}, which are the running times (in seconds) for these algorithms; $\log_2(T_{FP}) = 6.9675 \log(n) - 27.238$, $\log_2(T_{QP}) = 7.3037 \log(n) - 27.208$, and $\log_2(T_{RR}) = 6.4345 \log(n) - 18.502$, By using $T_{cycle} = T \cdot 3.4 \cdot 10^9$, we obtain bit-operation complexity estimation formulae $\log_2(T_{FP,cycle}) = 6.9675 \log(n) + 4.425$, $\log_2(T_{QP,cycle}) = 7.3037 \log(n) + 4.459$, and $\log_2(T_{RR,cycle}) = 6.4345 \log(n) + 13.161$.

Our experiment shows that G_LLL_QP can find the secret keys up to $n = 425$ in approximately 2 days. Although we could run G_LLL_RR on $n \geq 425$ to avoid the

Table 2. Experimental results using G_LLL_FP, G_LLL_QP, and G_LLL_RR with precision 150

n	q	G_LLL_FP		G_LLL_QP		G_LLL_RR *	
		m'	T_{FP} (sec.)	m'	T_{QP} (sec.)	m'	T_{RR} (sec.)
100	$\approx 2^{65.058}$	30	$31 \approx 2^{4.954}$	30	$115 \approx 2^{6.845}$	30	$2412 \approx 2^{11.237}$
125	$\approx 2^{67.533}$	40	$82 \approx 2^{6.358}$	40	$294 \approx 2^{8.200}$	40	$5960 \approx 2^{12.541}$
150	$\approx 2^{69.737}$	50	$177 \approx 2^{7.468}$	50	$626 \approx 2^{9.290}$	50	$11974 \approx 2^{13.548}$
175	$\approx 2^{71.517}$	70	$466 \approx 2^{8.864}$	70	$1411 \approx 2^{10.463}$	70	$27190 \approx 2^{14.731}$
200	$\approx 2^{73.057}$	80	$810 \approx 2^{9.662}$	80	$2441 \approx 2^{11.253}$	80	$50976 \approx 2^{15.638}$
225	$\approx 2^{74.417}$	100	$1456 \approx 2^{10.508}$	100	$4513 \approx 2^{12.140}$	100	$86427 \approx 2^{16.399}$
250	$\approx 2^{75.633}$	120	$2487 \approx 2^{11.280}$	120	$7587 \approx 2^{12.889}$	120	$135423 \approx 2^{17.047}$
275	$\approx 2^{76.733}$	140	$3784 \approx 2^{11.886}$	130	$11720 \approx 2^{13.517}$	140	$203450 \approx 2^{17.634}$
300	$\approx 2^{77.737}$	—	fail	160	$19285 \approx 2^{14.235}$	160	$292092 \approx 2^{18.156}$
325	$\approx 2^{78.661}$			200	$32016 \approx 2^{14.967}$	190	$439574 \approx 2^{18.746}$
350	$\approx 2^{79.516}$			230	$44158 \approx 2^{15.430}$		
375	$\approx 2^{80.313}$			280	$82369 \approx 2^{16.330}$		
400	$\approx 2^{81.057}$			330	$119767 \approx 2^{16.870}$		
425	$\approx 2^{81.757}$			400	$175007 \approx 2^{17.417}$		
450	$\approx 2^{82.417}$			—	fail		

precision problems with G_LLL_QP beyond this point, we only ran it up to $n = 325$ due to time constraints. If we ran G_LLL_RR on $n = 450$, our model indicates that around $2^{20.808}$ seconds ≈ 21 days would be required. However, we expect that LLL will be insufficient to recover the private key (with probability ~ 1) in this manner for values of n greater than ~ 500. For such values of n, lattice reduction algorithms achieving lower root Hermite factors will be required [3]. We expect this to be the case due to observations made in [13] and [4] that we can expect to solve unique-SVP instances with a certain probability p whenever we have

$$\lambda_2(\mathcal{L})/\lambda_1(\mathcal{L}) \geq \tau_p \cdot \delta_0^{\dim(\mathcal{L})}$$

for some $\tau_p \in (0, 1]$. The values of τ_p derived experimentally in [13] ranged from 0.18 to 0.45, though with unspecified p. In [4], values of $\tau_{0.1}$ were derived experimentally for LWE instances, with values between 0.385 and 0.400 being obtained. Though there are 'structural' differences in the lattices employed in this work and [13],[4], we expect the model above to also hold reasonably well.

In any case, our experimental results suggest that the security bounds derived in Section 4 are already very pessimistic; even bigger keys than (4), for example, should be considered to thwart the improved embedding attack.

Acknowledgement. Jean-Charles Faugère and Ludovic Perret have been partially supported supported by the Computer Algebra and Cryptography (CAC) project (ANR-09-JCJCJ-0064-01) and the HPAC grant (ANR ANR-11-BS02-013) of the French National Research Agency.

References

1. Ajtai, M.: Generating hard instances of lattice problems (extended abstract). In: STOC, pp. 99–108 (1996)
2. Albrecht, M.R., Cid, C., Faugère, J.-C., Fitzpatrick, R., Perret, L.: On the complexity of the BKW algorithm on LWE. Cryptology ePrint Archive, Report 2012/636 (2012), http://eprint.iacr.org/; Des. Codes Cryptogr. (2013)
3. Albrecht, M.R., Farshim, P., Faugère, J.-C., Perret, L.: Polly Cracker, revisited. In: Lee, D.H., Wang, X. (eds.) ASIACRYPT 2011. LNCS, vol. 7073, pp. 179–196. Springer, Heidelberg (2011), http://eprint.iacr.org/
4. Albrecht, M.R., Fitzpatrick, R., Gopfert, F.: On the efficacy of solving lwe by reduction to unique-svp. Cryptology ePrint Archive, Report 2013/602 (2013), http://eprint.iacr.org/
5. Bardet, M.: Étude des systèmes algébriques surdéterminés. Applications aux codes correcteurs et à la cryptographie. PhD thesis, Université Paris VI (2004)
6. Bardet, M., Faugère, J.-C., Salvy, B.: Complexity of Gröbner basis computation for semi-regular overdetermined sequences over F_2 with solutions in F_2. Technical Report 5049, INRIA (December 2003), http://www.inria.fr/rrrt/rr-5049.html

---

[3] However, further improved embedding attacks may enable larger values of n to be attacked using only LLL, but we do not deal with this here.

7. Bardet, M., Faugère, J.-C., Salvy, B.: On the complexity of Gröbner basis computation of semi-regular overdetermined algebraic equations. In: Proc. International Conference on Polynomial System Solving (ICPSS), pp. 71–75 (2004)

8. Berbain, C., Gilbert, H., Patarin, J.: QUAD: A multivariate stream cipher with provable security. J. Symb. Comput. 44(12), 1703–1723 (2009)

9. Brakerski, Z., Langlois, A., Peikert, C., Regev, O., Stehlé, D.: Classical hardness of Learning with Errors. To appear STOC 2013 (2013)

10. Brakerski, Z., Vaikuntanathan, V.: Efficient fully homomorphic encryption from (standard) LWE. In: Ostrovsky, R. (ed.) IEEE 52nd Annual Symposium on Foundations of Computer Science, FOCS 2011, pp. 97–106. IEEE (2011)

11. Buchberger, B.: Ein Algorithmus zum Auffinden der Basiselemente des Restklassenringes nach einem nulldimensionalen Polynomideal. PhD thesis, University of Innsbruck (1965)

12. Faugère, J.-C.: A new efficient algorithm for computing Gröbner bases without reduction to zero (F5). In: Proceedings of the 2002 International Symposium on Symbolic and Algebraic Computation, pp. 75–83. ACM, New York (2002)

13. Gama, N., Nguyen, P.Q.: Predicting lattice reduction. In: Smart, N.P. (ed.) EUROCRYPT 2008. LNCS, vol. 4965, pp. 31–51. Springer, Heidelberg (2008)

14. Garey, M.R., Johnson, D.S.: Computers and Intractability: A Guide to the Theory of NP-Completeness. W. H. Freeman (1979)

15. G.: GMP: The GNU multiple precision arithmetic library, http://gmplib.org/

16. Goldstein, D., Mayer, A.: On the equidistribution of hecke points (2003)

17. Huang, Y.-J., Liu, F.-H., Yang, B.-Y.: Public-key cryptography from new multivariate quadratic assumptions. In: Fischlin, M., Buchmann, J., Manulis, M. (eds.) PKC 2012. LNCS, vol. 7293, pp. 190–205. Springer, Heidelberg (2012)

18. Kannan, R.: Minkowski's convex body theorem and integer programming. Mathematics of Operations Research 12(3), 415–440 (1987)

19. Khot, S.: Hardness of approximating the shortest vector problem in lattices. J. ACM 52(5), 789–808 (2005)

20. Lovász, L., Lenstra Jr., H.W., Lenstra, A.K.: Factoring polynomials with rational coefficients. Mathematische Annalen 261, 515–534 (1982)

21. Lindner, R., Peikert, C.: Better key sizes (and attacks) for lwe-based encryption. IACR Cryptology ePrint Archive, 592 (2010)

22. Liu, Y.-K., Lyubashevsky, V., Micciancio, D.: On Bounded Distance Decoding for General Lattices. In: Díaz, J., Jansen, K., Rolim, J.D.P., Zwick, U. (eds.) APPROX 2006 and RANDOM 2006. LNCS, vol. 4110, pp. 450–461. Springer, Heidelberg (2006)

23. Lyubashevsky, V., Micciancio, D.: On bounded distance decoding, unique shortest vectors, and the minimum distance problem. In: Halevi, S. (ed.) CRYPTO 2009. LNCS, vol. 5677, pp. 577–594. Springer, Heidelberg (2009)

24. Matsumoto, T., Imai, H.: Public quadratic polynomial-tuples for efficient signature-verification and message-encryption. In: Günther, C.G. (ed.) EUROCRYPT 1988. LNCS, vol. 330, pp. 419–453. Springer, Heidelberg (1988)

25. Micciancio, D., Goldwasser, S.: Complexity of Lattice Problems: a cryptographic perspective. The Kluwer International Series in Engineering and Computer Science, vol. 671. Kluwer Academic Publishers, Boston (2002)

26. Micciancio, D., Regev, O.: Lattice-based cryptography. In: Bernstein, D.J., Buchmann, J., Dahmen, E. (eds.) Post-Quantum Cryptography, pp. 147–191. Springer, Heidelberg (2009)

27. Regev, O.: On lattices, learning with errors, random linear codes, and cryptography. J. ACM 56(6) (2009)
28. Shoup, V.: NTL: A library for doing number theory, http://shoup.net/ntl/
29. Stéhle, D., et al.: fpLLL 4.0.4. fpLLL Development Team (2013), http://perso.ens-lyon.fr/damien.stehle/fplll/
30. Stein, W.A., et al.: Sage Mathematics Software (Version 5.2). The Sage Development Team (2012), http://www.sagemath.org
31. von Zur Gathen, J., Gerhard, J.: Modern computer algebra, 2nd edn. Cambridge University Press (2003)

Related Randomness Attacks
for Public Key Encryption

Kenneth G. Paterson, Jacob C.N. Schuldt, and Dale L. Sibborn*

Information Security Group, Royal Holloway, University of London
{kenny.paterson,jacob.schuldt,dale.sibborn.2011}@rhul.ac.uk

Abstract. Several recent and high-profile incidents give cause to believe that randomness failures of various kinds are endemic in deployed cryptographic systems. In the face of this, it behoves cryptographic researchers to develop methods to immunise – to the extent that it is possible – cryptographic schemes against such failures. This paper considers the practically-motivated situation where an adversary is able to force a public key encryption scheme to reuse random values, and functions of those values, in encryption computations involving adversarially chosen public keys and messages. It presents a security model appropriate to this situation, along with variants of this model. It also provides necessary conditions on the set of functions used in order to attain this security notation, and demonstrates that these conditions are also sufficient in the Random Oracle Model. Further standard model constructions achieving weaker security notions are also given, with these constructions having interesting connections to other primitives including: pseudo-random functions that are secure in the related key attack setting; Correlated Input Secure hash functions; and public key encryption schemes that are secure in the auxiliary input setting (this being a special type of leakage resilience).

1 Introduction

Modern cryptographic primitives are heavy consumers of randomness. Unfortunately, random number generators (RNGs) used to provide this randomness often fail in practice [16,18,20,21,13,1,15,26]. This is due to issues including poor algorithmic design, software bugs, insufficient or poor estimation of system entropy, and the handling of randomness across virtual machine resets [27]. The results of randomness failures can be catastrophic and newsworthy in practice – DSA, ECDSA and Schnorr private signing keys can be exposed [9,27]; plaintext recovery for low entropy plaintext becomes possible in the the public key encryption setting; key generation processes can be severely weakened [13,24,22,10]; ephemeral Diffie-Hellman keys can become predictable leading to compromise of session keys [18]; and electronic wallet security can be compromised [11].

Evidently, randomness failures are a major problem in practice. The cryptography research community has begun to address this problem only relatively

---

* All authors were supported by EPSRC Leadership Fellowship EP/H005455/1.

H. Krawczyk (Ed.): PKC 2014, LNCS 8383, pp. 465–482, 2014.

recently [28,29,23,2,33,27]. Accepting that randomness failures are endemic and unlikely to be eliminated in totality, a basic approach is to try to *hedge* against randomness failures, that is, to design cryptographic primitives that still offer a degree of security in the face of randomness failures. For signatures, there is a folklore de-randomisation technique which neatly sidesteps security issues arising from randomness failures: simply augment the signature scheme's private key with a key for a pseudo-random function (PRF), and derive any randomness needed during signing by applying this PRF to the message to be signed; meanwhile verification proceeds as normal. In the symmetric encryption setting, previous work has considered nonce-based encryption [28], misuse-resistant authenticated encryption (which concerns residual security when nonces are repeated) [29], and encryption in a chosen-randomness setting (wherein the adversary is given control over the randomness used for encryption) [23]. Ristenpart and Yilek [27] studied the use of "hedging" as a general technique for protecting against broad classes of randomness failures in already-deployed systems, and implemented and benchmarked this technique in OpenSSL. Hedging in the sense of [27] involves replacing the random value r required in some cryptographic scheme with a hash of r together with other contextual information, such as a message, algorithm or unique operation identifier, etc. Their results, while applying to a variety of different randomness failure types (see in particular [27, Figure 3]), all have their security analyses restricted to the ROM. Work in the public key encryption setting can be summarised as follows:

- Bellare *et al.* [2] considered security under *chosen distribution attack*, wherein the joint distribution of message and randomness is specified by the adversary, subject to containing a reasonable amount of min entropy. The PKE scheme designer's challenge is to find a way of "extracting" this entropy in a secure way. Bellare *et al.* gave several designs for PKE schemes achieving this notion in the Random Oracle Model (ROM) and in the standard model. This is a powerful and general approach, but does have its limitations: under extreme failure conditions, the joint message-randomness distribution may simply *fail* to contain sufficient entropy, at which point all security guarantees may be lost; moreover, for technical reasons, the model in [2] requires the target public key to be hidden from the adversary until all encryption queries have been made. This is impractical in real world applications.
- Yilek [33], inspired by virtual machine reset attacks in [27], considered the scenario where the adversary does not know the randomness (in contrast to the chosen-randomness setting of [23]), but can instead force the reuse of random values that are otherwise well-distributed. This is referred to in [33] as the *Reset Attack* (RA) setting. To fully reflect the reality of randomness failures in this setting, Yilek provides the adversary with the ability to encrypt chosen messages under adversarially generated public keys using the unknown but repeated random values. This makes his model very powerful, to the extent that certain trivial attacks must be excluded by assuming the adversary is *equality-pattern respecting*. In [33], Yilek also gave a general construction in which the random coins of the encryption algorithm are used

as a key to a PRF, the input to the PRF is the public key concatenated with the message to be encrypted, and the output of the PRF is then used as the 'randomness' for the encryption algorithm. This is sufficient to achieve security in his RA setting. Note that the RA security model is incomparable with the CDA model of [2].

1.1 Motivation

Inspired by the challenge of preserving security under randomness failures, we initiate the study of security for PKE in what we call the *Related Randomness Attack* (RRA) setting. Our RRA setting builds on the RA setting from [33] and brings the theory of hedging PKE against randomness failures closer to practice. As we shall see, it also has interesting connections with related key attacks for PRFs and PKE, as developed in [5,3,4,6,32], and leakage resilient cryptography (and in particular, the techniques developed in [14] to provide security for PKE in the auxiliary input setting).

In our RRA setting, the adversary can now not only force the reuse of existing random values as in the RA setting, but can also force the use of *functions of* those random values. This power is analogous to the power granted to the adversary in the Related Key Attack (RKA) setting, wherein an adversary is able to tamper with private (or secret) keys used during cryptographic operations. The RA setting arises as the special case of our RRA setting where only the identity function is allowed. The extra adversarial power in the RRA setting allows the modelling of reset attacks in which the adversary does not have an exact reset capability, but where the randomness used after a reset is in some way related to that used on previous resets. Such behaviours were observed in the experimental work in [27]. Furthermore, our RRA setting allows modelling of situations where the randomness used in a scheme comes from a PRNG which is not regularly refreshed with new entropy, but which steps forward under some deterministic state evolution function Next and output function Out; here the appropriate functions in our RRA setting would be the compositions $\text{Out}(\text{Next}^i(\cdot))$.

More generally, RRA security has a strong theoretical motivation as being a stepping stone towards giving the adversary enhanced control over the inputs to cryptographic algorithms – messages (in the standard PKE setting), keys (in the RKA setting), and now randomness (in our new RRA setting). It is an interesting direction for future research to develop this theme further, by examining security in a combined RKA/RRA setting, where the adversary would be able to simultaneously tamper with *all* the inputs to a PKE scheme.

1.2 Our Contributions

RRA security model. In this paper, we provide a strong model and security definition for PKE in the RRA setting, which we name RRA-ATK security (where ATK = CPA or CCA) . Our model is inspired by that of Yilek for the RA setting: via access to an **Enc** oracle, we allow the adversary to get arbitrary messages encrypted under arbitrary public keys, using functions ϕ of an initial set of well-distributed but unknown random values. The public keys can even be maliciously generated, and the adversary can of course know all the corresponding private keys. The adversary is tasked with winning an indistinguishability-style game, via an **LR** oracle which gives access to encryptions of left or right messages with respect to an honestly generated target public key pk^*, but again where the adversary can force the use of functions ϕ of the initial random values. When the functions ϕ are limited to coming from some set Φ, we speak of a Φ-restricted adversary.

Because the adversary may know all but one of the private keys, it can check that its challenger is behaving correctly with respect to its encryption queries. This also rules out the possibility of achieving RRA-ATK security for any randomness recovering PKE scheme, like RSA-OAEP [7] and PKE schemes based on the Fujisaki-Okamoto transformation [17]. Moreover, the encryption queries concern public keys that are outside the control of the challenger. This increases the technical challenge of achieving security in the RRA setting. This facet of the RRA setting bears comparison with the RKA setting for PKE [4,6,32]. In the RKA setting, the tampering via related key functions only affects the PKE scheme's private key, and so only comes into play when simulating *decryption* queries. By contrast, it is *encryption* queries that require special treatment in our RRA setting.

Given the power of the adversary in the RRA setting, we have to exclude certain sets of adversarial queries to prevent the adversary from trivially breaking security. For example, as in the RKA setting, constant functions ϕ must be disallowed for security to be achievable. See Section 2 for further discussion.

ROM construction. We are able to show that, in the ROM, these necessary conditions on the function set Φ are actually also sufficient. More specifically, we show how to transform any IND-ATK secure PKE scheme PKE into a new PKE scheme Hash-PKE that is RRA-ATK secure, simply by hashing the random input together with the public key and message during encryption. In fact, this is just an application of the hedging approach from [27], and an instance of the randomized-encrypt-with-hash (REwH) scheme from [2]. Our result then shows that this approach also provides security in our new RRA setting.

Standard model constructions. Having dealt with the ROM, we then turn our attention to constructions in the standard model. Reinforcing the connections to RKA security, we are able to show that any Φ-restricted RKA-PRF can be used to build a RRA-ATK secure PKE scheme for Φ-restricted adversaries, thus transferring security from the RKA setting (for PRFs) to the RRA setting for PKE. But the limited range of RKA-PRFs currently available in the literature [25,3] essentially restricts the obtained RRA-ATK secure PKE scheme to a class of functions Φ consisting of *linear* or *group-induced* functions. To achieve an RRA-ATK secure PKE scheme for richer classes of functions, we must seek alternative methods of construction.

Unfortunately, we have not been able to achieve our full RRA-ATK security notion for more interesting function classes using other constructions. So we must resort to exploring alternative versions of this notion in order to make progress. We relax RRA-ATK security along two independent dimensions: the degree of control that the adversary enjoys over the public keys under which it can force encryptions for related random values, and the degree of adaptivity it has in the selection of functions $\phi \in \Phi$:

- We first consider the situation where the public keys are all honestly generated at the start of the security game, and the public keys and all but one of the private keys are then given to the adversary — the honest-key, related randomness attack (HK-RRA) setting. This is a reasonable relaxation in that, in practice, all the public keys that the adversary might be able to induce a user to encrypt under would be properly generated by users and then certified by a CA ahead of time. In this setting, we provide a generic construction for a scheme achieving HK-RRA-ATK security based on combining any IND-ATK secure PKE scheme with a Correlated-Input Secure (CIS) hash function [19]. Currently known instantiations of CIS hash functions allow us to obtain selective, HK-RRA-ATK security for Φ-restricted adversaries where Φ is a large class of polynomial functions (as opposed to the linear functions we can achieve using our RKA-PRF-based construction). Here, selectivity refers to the adversary committing at the start of the game to the set of functions it will use.
- We then consider the situation where there is no restriction on public keys, but the adversary is committed up-front to a vector of functions $\phi = (\phi_1, \ldots, \phi_q)$ that it will use in its attack, and where security is in the end quantified over all choices of ϕ from some set Φ. This quantification is subtly different from allowing the adversary a fully adaptive choice of functions $\phi \in \Phi$ (for a detailed discussion, see Section 2). In this situation, we refer to the function-vector, related randomness attack (FV-RRA) model. Here, we are able to give a direct construction for a PKE scheme that is FV-RRA-ATK secure solely under the DDH assumption, assuming the component functions ϕ_i of ϕ are simultaneously hard to invert on a random input. Our scheme is inspired by a PKE scheme of Boneh et al. [12] that is secure in the so-called *auxiliary input setting*, wherein the adversary is given a hard-to-invert function of the secret key as part of its input. By swapping the roles of secret key and randomness in the Boneh et al. scheme, we are able to obtain security in a setting where a hard-to-invert function of the encryption randomness is leaked to the adversary. This leakage is then sufficient to allow us to simulate the encryptions for adversarially chosen public keys. For technical reasons, to obtain a construction, we must also limit our adversary to using the identity function when accessing its **LR** oracle.

To summarise, in the standard model, we can achieve our full security notion, RRA-ATK security, but only for a limited class of functions Φ (inherited from known results on RKA-PRFs), while we can achieve alternative security notions for richer classes Φ.

1.3   Future Directions

In this paper, we concentrate on PKE, but RRA security notions can be developed for other primitives. As previously noted, the case of signatures is quite simple, provided one is prepared to extend a scheme's private key. We would expect symmetric key encryption and key exchange primitives to be more complex. Also as noted above, our RRA setting is related to the RKA setting, and it is an open problem to develop these connections further, possibly by considering a combined RKA/RRA setting.

2   Related Randomness Security for PKE

We now formalise our notions of related randomness security for PKE. We give a detailed treatment of our strongest notion, before sketching restricted versions. The description of our security notions will utilise code-based games and the associated language (see [8]).

Our strongest security notion, RRA-CCA security, is defined via the game in Figure 1. Here, a challenge key pair (pk^*, sk^*) for a PKE scheme PKE = (PKE.K, PKE.E, PKE.D) with randomness space Rnd is honestly generated, and the adversary is considered successful if it wins an indistinguishability game with respect to messages encrypted under pk^*. Extending the standard PKE setting, the adversary is able to control which one of polynomially many random values $r_i \in$ Rnd is used in responding to each encryption query for pk^*; furthermore, the adversary is able to obtain the encryption of messages of its choice under (possibly maliciously generated) arbitrary public keys. Extending the model of Yilek [33], our adversary not only specifies which one of the random values r_i is to be used in each query, but also specifies, for each query he makes, a function ϕ on Rnd; the value $\phi(r_i)$ is used for encryption in place of r_i. In the CCA setting, the adversary also has access to a regular decryption oracle for private key sk^*. Note that if the adversary uses *only* the identity function, then we recover the Resettability Attack (RA) model of Yilek [33].

It is not difficult to see that, as in the RA setting, an adversary may trivially win this game if no restrictions are placed on oracle queries.[1] We will shortly introduce an *equality-pattern respecting* definition for adversaries, designed to prevent trivial wins of this kind. This extends the related RA definition from [33]. However, restrictions on the functions ϕ will also be required. To illustrate the issue, consider as an extreme case the constant function ϕ_C (with $\phi_C(r) = C$ for all $r \in$ Rnd). Suppose the adversary submits **LR** query (m_0, m_1, j, ϕ_C) for any $m_0 \neq m_1$ and any $j \in \mathbb{N}$; the adversary receives a ciphertext c^* and then

---

[1] For example, if an adversary requests the encryption of m under the target public key using coins $\phi(r_i)$, PKE.E$(pk^*, m; \phi(r_i))$, and submits **LR** query (m, m', i, ϕ), then the adversary guesses b is 0 if the two ciphertexts match, otherwise he guesses b is 1. This adversary wins the game with probability 1. As in the RA setting, such wins are unavoidable in our setting since encryption essentially becomes deterministic when the same random coins and functions ϕ are used.

proc. Initialise(λ):	proc. LR(m_0, m_1, i, ϕ):	proc. Enc(pk, m, i, ϕ):
$b \leftarrow_\$ \{0,1\}$;	If CoinTab[i] $= \perp$	If CoinTab[i] $= \perp$
$(pk^*, sk^*) \leftarrow_\$ \text{PKE.K}(1^\lambda)$;	CoinTab[i] $\leftarrow_\$$ Rnd	CoinTab[i] $\leftarrow_\$$ Rnd
CoinTab $\leftarrow \emptyset$;	$r_i \leftarrow$ CoinTab[i]	$r_i \leftarrow$ CoinTab[i]
$\mathcal{S} \leftarrow \emptyset$; Return pk^*	$c \leftarrow \text{PKE.E}(pk^*, m_b; \phi(r_i))$	$c \leftarrow \text{PKE.E}(pk, m; \phi(r_i))$
	$\mathcal{S} \leftarrow \mathcal{S} \cup \{c\}$	Return c
proc. Dec(c):	Return c	
If $c \in \mathcal{S}$, then return $\perp$		**proc. Finalise**(b'):
Else return PKE.D(sk^*, c)		If $b = b'$, return 1

Fig. 1. Game RRA-ATK. (Note that if ATK = CPA, then the adversary's access to **proc. Dec** is removed.)

computes $c_0 = \text{PKE.E}(pk^*, m_0; C)$; the adversary outputs guess $b' = 0$ if and only if $c^* = c_0$. It is easy to see that this adversary wins the RRA-ATK game with probability 1. This example is analogous to one in the related key attack setting for PRFs in [5]. Hence, we will need to restrict the class of functions which the adversary is allowed to access in its queries to come from some set Φ, in which case we speak of Φ-restricted adversaries. We have already seen that constant functions must be excluded from Φ if we are to have any hope of achieving our related randomness security notion.

Thus we have two sets of constraints that we need to consider to prevent trivial wins: those on messages and randomness indices (analogous to the RA setting from [33]) and those on functions ϕ (analogous to the RKA setting for PRFs from [5]). Let us deal with the first set of constraints first and define what it means for an adversary to be equality-pattern respecting. The following definition is adapted from [33] for our purposes.

Definition 1. *Let $\mathcal{A}$ be a Φ-restricted adversary in Game RRA-ATK that queries r different randomness indices to its **LR** and **Enc** oracles and makes $q_{i,\phi}$ queries to its **LR** oracle with index i and function $\phi \in \Phi$. Let $E_{i,\phi}$ be the set of all messages m such that $\mathcal{A}$ makes **Enc** query (pk^*, m, i, ϕ). Let $(m_0^{i,\phi,1}, m_1^{i,\phi,1}), \ldots,$ $(m_0^{i,\phi,q_{i,\phi}}, m_1^{i,\phi,q_{i,\phi}})$ be $\mathcal{A}$'s **LR** queries for index $i \in [r]$ and $\phi \in \Phi$. Suppose that for all pairs $(i, \phi) \in [r] \times \Phi$ and for all $j \neq k \in [q_{i,\phi}]$, we have:*

$$m_0^{i,\phi,j} = m_0^{i,\phi,k} \text{ iff } m_1^{i,\phi,j} = m_1^{i,\phi,k}$$

and that, for all pairs $(i, \phi) \in [r] \times \Phi$, and for all $j \in [q_{i,\phi}]$, we have:

$$m_0^{i,\phi,j} \notin E_{i,\phi} \wedge m_1^{i,\phi,j} \notin E_{i,\phi}.$$

Then we say that $\mathcal{A}$ is equality-pattern respecting.

Notice that if the adversary is restricted to using only the identity function, then this definition reduces to the equality-pattern respecting definition for the RA setting, cf. [33, Appendix A].

Definition 2. *We define the advantage of an equality-pattern respecting, RRA-ATK adversary $\mathcal{A}$ against a PKE scheme* PKE *to be:*

$$\mathbf{Adv}_{\mathrm{PKE},\mathcal{A}}^{\mathrm{rra\text{-}atk}}(\lambda) := 2 \cdot \mathbb{P}[\mathrm{RRA\text{-}ATK}_{\mathrm{PKE}}^{\mathcal{A}}(\lambda) \Rightarrow 1] - 1.$$

A PKE scheme PKE *is said to be Φ-RRA-ATK secure if the advantage of any Φ-restricted, equality-pattern respecting, RRA-ATK adversary against* PKE *that runs in polynomial time is negligible in the security parameter λ.*

2.1   Alternative Security Notions

The above definition for Φ-RRA-ATK security is very powerful: it allows an adversary to submit *any* public key to its encryption oracle and allows the adversary to *adaptively* choose the functions ϕ, the only restriction being that they lie in Φ. In Section 2.2 we will exhibit conditions that are both necessary and sufficient for achieving security in this sense in the ROM (given a starting PKE scheme that satisfies the usual definition of IND-ATK security). In the standard model, we will give a construction that relies on RKA-PRFs. Since constructions for these are currently very limited in terms of the function classes they can handle, we will now consider alternative versions of the Φ-RRA-ATK notion.

The first alternative notion we consider is called *Honest Key Related Randomness* (HK-RRA) security. The security game has two parameters, λ and ℓ. Informally, the game itself generates a polynomial number ℓ of key pairs and returns the public keys to the adversary. The adversary then chooses which public key he wishes to be the target key, and is given the private keys corresponding to all the non-target public keys. Meanwhile, the adversary's queries to its **Enc** oracle are restricted to using the public keys generated by the game. Suitable Φ-HK-RRA-ATK security notions follow by analogy with our earlier definitions.

One may consider notions intermediate between Φ-RRA-ATK security and Φ-HK-RRA-ATK security. For example, a registered key notion could be defined, in which the adversary chooses and registers key pairs (pk, sk), with registration involving a test for validity by some procedure, and all queries involve only registered public keys. One may also consider weaker variants of these notions in which the adversary's choice of functions ϕ is non-adaptive (or *selective*). That is, the adversary must submit a set of functions $\{\phi\} \subset \Phi$ of polynomial size to the game before he is allowed to see the target public key (or set of public keys, if playing in the Honest Key setting). In this setting, we refer to Φ-sHK-RRA-ATK security.

The final alternative notion we consider is called *Function-Vector Related Randomness* (FV-RRA) security, and is based on the game in Figure 2. Here, the adversary is parameterised by a vector of functions $\boldsymbol{\phi} = (\phi_1, \ldots, \phi_q)$, and is limited to using only these functions in its oracle queries. Additionally, we restrict the adversary by demanding that the **LR** queries use only the identity function. However, once again, the adversary has complete freedom over public keys submitted to its encryption oracle. Furthermore, security will be quantified over *all* choices of vector from a particular class. (Specifically, in our construction

proc. Initialise(λ):	proc. $\mathbf{LR}(m_0, m_1, i)$:	proc. $\mathbf{Enc}(pk, m, i, j)$:
$b \leftarrow_\$ \{0,1\}$;	If CoinTab$[i] = \perp$,	If CoinTab$[i] = \perp$,
$(pk^*, sk^*) \leftarrow_\$ \text{PKE.K}(1^\lambda)$;	CoinTab$[i] \leftarrow_\$$ Rnd	CoinTab$[i] \leftarrow_\$$ Rnd
CoinTab $\leftarrow \emptyset$; $\mathcal{S} \leftarrow \emptyset$;	$r_i \leftarrow$ CoinTab$[i]$	$r_i \leftarrow$ CoinTab$[i]$
return pk^*	$c \leftarrow \text{PKE.E}(pk^*, m_b; r_i)$	$c \leftarrow \text{PKE.E}(pk, m; \phi_j(r_i))$
	$\mathcal{S} \leftarrow \mathcal{S} \cup \{c\}$	return c
	return c	
proc. $\mathbf{Dec}(c)$:		proc. $\mathbf{Finalise}(b')$:
If $c \in \mathcal{S}$, then return $\perp$		If $b = b'$, return 1
Else return PKE.D(sk^*, c)		

Fig. 2. Game ϕ-FV-RRA-ATK, where $\phi = (\phi_1, \ldots, \phi_q)$. (As usual, if ATK = CPA, then the adversary's access to **proc. Dec** is removed.)

in Section 5, we will demand that security holds over all vectors ϕ that are simultaneously hard to invert on a common random input r.) This quantification actually makes our notion rather strong.

Definition 3. *Let $\phi = (\phi_1, \ldots, \phi_q)$ be a vector of $q := q(\lambda)$ functions. We define the advantage of an equality-pattern respecting, ϕ-FV-RRA-ATK adversary $\mathcal{A}$ against a PKE scheme PKE to be:*

$$\mathbf{Adv}_{\text{PKE}, \mathcal{A}}^{\phi\text{-fv-rra-atk}}(\lambda) := 2 \cdot \mathbb{P}[\phi\text{-FV-RRA-ATK}_{\text{PKE}}^{\mathcal{A}}(\lambda) \Rightarrow 1] - 1.$$

If $\boldsymbol{\Phi}$ is a set of vectors of functions, then a PKE scheme PKE is said to be $\boldsymbol{\Phi}$-FV-RRA-ATK secure if, for all $\phi \in \boldsymbol{\Phi}$, the advantage of any equality-pattern respecting, ϕ-FV-RRA-ATK adversary against PKE that runs in polynomial time is negligible in the security parameter λ.

Comparison of security notions. The first alternative security notion, HK-RRA-ATK security, is easily seen to be a strictly weaker notion than full RRA-ATK security[2]. Likewise, the selective models are easily seen to be weaker then their adaptive counterparts. However, the relation between full RRA-ATK security and FV-RRA-ATK security is not immediately obvious. Aside from the restriction on **LR**-queries in FV-RRA-ATK security, there is a subtle distinction between requiring security for all vectors ϕ of functions from a particular set Φ and requiring security for a fully adaptive choice of functions $\phi \in \Phi$. In particular, the former notion will allow a security reduction to consider multiple runs of an adversary with different random coins for a fixed choice of function vector ϕ, whereas the latter notion will leave open the possibility that an adversary will chose a different sequence of functions ϕ in each run. Also note that FV-RRA-ATK security guarantees that there is no choice of ϕ for which the

---

[2] A separation can be established by considering a scheme where public keys generated by the key generation algorithm always have a certain bit set to 0, and where the encryption algorithm, given a public key with this bit set to 1 (i.e. a maliciously generated public key), will expose the randomness used for the encryption.

considered scheme is weak, even if this choice might be computationally hard for an adaptive adversary to find. Furthermore, the relation between the notions might also be influenced by the considered class of functions Φ. It remains future work to fully explore and categorise the possible notions of RRA security.

It is not hard to see that our RRA security notions are incomparable with the CDA security notions of [2]. In the RA setting, Yilek defines only an equivalent of our full RRA-ATK notion; it is clear that RRA-ATK security is stronger than his RA-ATK security whenever the function set Φ contains the identity function. The same would carry over to relaxed versions of RA-ATK security.

2.2   Function Restrictions

Above, we briefly alluded to the fact that the class of functions Φ used by our RRA adversaries must be restricted in various ways. The example given showed that constant functions must always be excluded. Here, we exhibit much stronger necessary conditions on Φ that must be satisfied, namely output-unpredictability and collision-resistance. These notions are closely related to notions with the same names arising in the setting of related key security for PRFs that was considered in [5]. Here, however, we are concerned with functions acting on the randomness used in PKE schemes rather than on PRF keys.

Definition 4 (Output-unpredictability for Φ). *Let Φ be a set of functions from* Rnd *to* Rnd. *Let α and β be positive integers. Then the (α, β)-output-unpredictability of Φ is defined to be:*

$$\mathrm{InSec}_{\Phi}^{\mathrm{up}}(\alpha, \beta) = \max_{P \subseteq \Phi, X \subseteq \mathcal{R}, |P| \leq \alpha, |X| \leq \beta} \left\{ \mathbb{P}\left[r \leftarrow_{\$} \mathrm{Rnd} : \{\phi(r) : \phi \in P\} \cap X \neq \emptyset\right] \right\}.$$

Definition 5 (Collision-resistance for Φ). *Let Φ be a set of functions from* Rnd *to* Rnd. *Let α be a positive integer. Then the α-collision-resistance of Φ is defined to be:*

$$\mathrm{InSec}_{\Phi}^{\mathrm{cr}}(\alpha) = \max_{P \subseteq \Phi, |P| \leq \alpha} \left\{ \mathbb{P}\left[r \leftarrow_{\$} \mathrm{Rnd} : |\{\phi(r) : \phi \in P\}| < |P|\right] \right\}.$$

Regarding these two definitions, we have the two following results.

Theorem 1 (Necessity of output-unpredictability). *Let Φ be a class of functions from* Rnd *to* Rnd. *Suppose there are natural numbers $\alpha = \mathrm{poly}_1(\lambda)$ and $\beta = \mathrm{poly}_2(\lambda)$ such that $\mathrm{InSec}_{\Phi}^{\mathrm{up}}(\alpha, \beta) = p$, where $p := p(\lambda)$ is non-negligible. Then no PKE scheme can be RRA-ATK secure with respect to the class of functions Φ.*

Theorem 2 (Necessity of collision-resistance). *Let Φ be a class of functions from* Rnd *to* Rnd. *Suppose there is a natural number $\alpha = \mathrm{poly}_1(\lambda)$ such that $\mathrm{InSec}_{\Phi}^{\mathrm{cr}}(\alpha) = p$, where $p := p(\lambda)$ is non-negligible. Then no PKE scheme can be RRA-ATK secure with respect to the class of functions Φ.*

Alg. PRF-PKE.K(1^λ):	Alg. PRF-PKE.E(pk, m):	Alg. PRF-PKE.D(sk, c):
$(pk, sk) \leftarrow_\$ \text{PKE.K}(1^\lambda)$	$r \leftarrow_\$ \text{Rnd}$	$m \leftarrow \text{PKE.D}(sk, c)$
	$r' \leftarrow F_r(pk\|\|m)$	return m
	$c \leftarrow \text{PKE.E}(pk, m; r')$	
	return c	

Fig. 3. Scheme PRF-PKE built from a standard PKE scheme, PKE and a PRF, F

We note that many classes of functions that arise from practical attacks satisfy these conditions. For example, the class of functions that flip bits at certain positions, or the class of functions that fix the value of certain bits, are both output-unpredictable and collision-resistant (provided at least a polynomial number of bits are not fixed, in the latter case).

In the RO model, these conditions are sufficient to achieve security in our strongest randomness attacks. More specifically, we can transform any IND-ATK secure scheme into a RRA-ATK secure scheme, simply by hashing string representations of the public key, the message, and appropriate randomness, and then using the output as randomness for the standard encryption scheme. This is an instance of the randomized-encrypt-with-hash (REwH) scheme from [2]. If the class of functions Φ is sufficiently collision-resistant and output-unpredictable, then this scheme is RRA-ATK-secure. We defer the details to the full version.

3 Related Randomness Security from RKA-PRFs

Since the RA setting of [33] is a special case of our RRA setting, an obvious way to try to achieve RRA security is to extend the main construction from [33]. That construction combines a PRF with an IND-ATK secure PKE scheme. Specifically, the randomness r is used as a key to the PRF, and the input to the PRF is the "context" $pk\|\|m$; the output from the PRF is then used as the actual randomness for encryption. This construction extends directly to our setting, and security is guaranteed against Φ-restricted adversaries in our strongest RRA-ATK models, under the assumption that the PRF is Φ-RKA-secure (i.e. secure against related key attacks for the *same* class of functions Φ). Thus the construction transfers RKA security for PRFs to RRA-ATK security for PKE. Figure 3 formalises the construction, and Theorem 3 our security result.

Theorem 3. *Suppose A is a Φ-restricted, equality-pattern respecting adversary in the* RRA-ATK *game against the scheme* PRF-PKE *defined in Figure 3. Suppose A makes q_{LR} LR queries, q_s Enc queries, and uses q_r randomness indices. Then there exists a Φ-restricted RKA-PRF adversary B and an IND-ATK adversary C such that*

$$\mathbf{Adv}^{\text{rra-atk}}_{\text{PRF-PKE},A}(\lambda) \leq q_{LR} \cdot q_r \cdot \mathbf{Adv}^{\text{ind-atk}}_{\text{PKE},C}(\lambda) + 2q_r \cdot \mathbf{Adv}^{\text{rka-prf}}_{F,B}(\lambda).$$

Adversaries B and C run in approximately the same time as A. Adversary C makes 1 LR query and the same number of Dec queries as A. Adversary B makes at most $q_{LR} + s$ queries to its oracle.

Notice that our RO scheme (mentioned in Section 2) may be interpreted as an instantiation of our scheme in Figure 3, since a random oracle can be viewed as an (unkeyed) RKA-PRF.

The previous theorem is seductively simple, but currently of limited application because the set of known RKA-secure PRFs is rather sparse. RKA-PRFs were first formalised in 2003 by Bellare and Kohno [5], and some initial (though not fully satisfactory) constructions were given in [5] and [25]. Setting these aside, the only known constructions are due to Bellare and Cash [3]. They gave a first construction for an RKA-PRF (based on the Naor-Reingold PRF) which is provably secure under the DDH assumption for related key functions Φ corresponding to component-wise multiplication on the key-space $(\mathbb{Z}_p^*)^{n+1}$. They also provided a second construction achieving a similar result under the DLIN assumption. A third construction for related key functions Φ corresponding to component-wise *addition* on the key-space $(\mathbb{Z}_p)^n$ was recently withdrawn by the authors of [3].

The limited nature of existing RKA-PRF families forces us to find alternative approaches to achieving security in the RRA setting. The application for RKA-PRFs implied by Theorem 3 also provides yet more motivation for the fundamental problem of constructing RKA-PRFs for richer classes of related key function.

4   Related Randomness PKE from CIS Hash Functions

To address some of the limitations encountered in the previous approach, we show how a PKE scheme secure in the RRA setting can be constructed using correlated-input secure (CIS) hash functions as introduced in [19]. While the currently known instantiations of CIS hash functions only allow us to obtain selective HK-RRA-ATK security, we are able to obtain security for a large class of polynomial functions, as opposed to linear functions to which the previous construction is currently restricted.

In its strongest form, a CIS hash function h (with key k) will yield output $h_k(x)$ which is pseudorandom, even when given the hash value of multiple correlated input values $(h_k(\phi_1(x)), \ldots, h_k(\phi_q(x)))$, where the correlation functions $\phi_1, \ldots, \phi_q$ are maliciously chosen. This type of CIS hash function is closely related to RKA-secure PRFs. In fact, the authors of [19] show that given a CIS hash function h, an RKA-secure *weak* PRF F can be obtained simply by exchanging the role of the key and the input of h:

$$F_K(x) := h_x(K).$$

Recall that weak PRF security does not allow an adversary to choose the function inputs, but instead, the inputs are chosen uniformly at random in the security game.

Alg. CI-Hash-PKE.K(1^λ):	Alg. CI-Hash-PKE.E($\hat{pk}, m$):	Alg. CI-Hash-PKE.D($\hat{sk}, c$):
$(pk, sk) \leftarrow_\$ \text{PKE.K}(1^\lambda)$	$(pk\|k) \leftarrow \hat{pk}$	$m \leftarrow \text{PKE.D}(\hat{sk}, c)$
$k \leftarrow_\$ \text{CI-HASH.K}(1^\lambda)$	$r \leftarrow_\$ \text{Rnd}$	return m
$(\hat{pk}, \hat{sk}) \leftarrow (pk\|k, sk)$	$r' \leftarrow h_k(r)$	
	$r'' \leftarrow F_{r'}(\hat{pk}\|m)$	
	$c \leftarrow \text{PKE.E}(pk, m; r'')$	
	return c	

Fig. 4. Scheme CI-Hash-PKE built from PKE scheme PKE, PRF F, and hash function family $\mathcal{H}$

The authors of [19] furthermore give a concrete construction of a CIS hash function secure for a class of correlation functions consisting of uniform-output[3] polynomials of bounded degree, albeit in a restricted security model where the adversary's function queries are non-adaptive. This then yields a non-adaptive, RKA-secure weak PRF.

Unfortunately, such a PRF this is not sufficient for our purposes. Surprisingly, however, by making a relatively simple modification to the above construction of PRFs from CIS hash functions, it is possible to obtain a primitive similar to an RKA-secure (standard) PRF. More specifically, consider a CIS hash function h and a standard PRF f. We introduce a public parameter c of F which will correspond to the key for h, and then, instead of using the output of h directly, we use h to derive a key for f. More specifically, we define

$$F_{c,K}(x) := f_{h_c(K)}(x).$$

Whilst not strictly an RKA-secure PRF due to the presence of the public parameter c, this primitive allows adaptively chosen inputs x, while remaining secure under related key attacks. This 'partial' RKA-secure PRF will allow us to obtain HK-RRA-ATK secure encryption schemes for the function families of the underlying CIS hash function h. However, to achieve this, we need to extend the definitions and theorems of [19] to the multi-key setting (reflecting the fact that in the HK-RRA setting, our adversary can interact with multiple public keys). The extensions of the security definitions are relatively straightforward, and we defer definitions of a *multi-key selective correlated-input pseudorandom* (MK-SCI-PR) secure family of hash functions to the full version.

Based on an ordinary PKE scheme PKE, a PRF F, and a family of hash functions $\mathcal{H}$, we construct a PKE scheme CI-Hash-PKE as shown in Figure 4. The following theorem establishes the selective ℓ-HK-RRA-ATK security of this scheme based on the IND-ATK security of PKE, the multi-key selective CIS security of $\mathcal{H}$, and the (regular) pseudorandomness of F.

Theorem 4. *Suppose $\mathcal{A}$ is a Φ-restricted, equality pattern respecting adversary in the selective ℓ-HK-RRA-ATK game against the scheme CI-Hash-PKE in*

---

[3] A polynomial is said to be a uniform-output polynomial if its output range is equal to its domain i.e. evaluating the polynomial on all values in the domain will again yield the elements of the domain.

*Figure 4. Suppose $\mathcal{A}$ makes q_{LR} **LR** queries, uses q_r randomness indices, and uses q_ϕ functions in its oracle queries. Then there exists a Φ-restricted, multi-key, selective correlated-input hash adversary $\mathcal{B}$, a PRF adversary $\mathcal{C}$ and an IND-ATK adversary $\mathcal{D}$ such that*

$$\mathbf{Adv}^{\ell\text{-shk-rra-atk}}_{\text{CI-Hash-PKE},\mathcal{A}}(\lambda) \leq 2q_\phi \cdot q_r \cdot \mathbf{Adv}^{\ell\text{-mk-sci-pr}}_{\mathcal{H},\mathcal{B}}(\lambda) + 2q_\phi \cdot q_r \cdot \mathbf{Adv}^{\text{prf}}_{F,\mathcal{C}}(\lambda)$$

$$+\ell \cdot q_{LR} \cdot q_r \cdot \mathbf{Adv}^{\text{ind-atk}}_{\text{PKE},\mathcal{D}}(\lambda) + \frac{\ell^2 \cdot q_r}{|\text{HashKeySpace}|}.$$

*Adversaries $\mathcal{B}$, $\mathcal{C}$ and $\mathcal{D}$ run in approximately the same time as $\mathcal{A}$. Adversary $\mathcal{C}$ makes at most q_{LR} queries, and $\mathcal{D}$ makes 1 **LR** query and as many **Dec** queries as $\mathcal{A}$.*

It remains to show that we can instantiate a hash function satisfying the multi-key correlated-input security notion. We achieve this by extending the security results for the CIS hash function defined in [19]. Concretely, the CIS hash function from [19] is defined as follows:

$\texttt{GenFun}(1^\lambda)$: Pick a group $\mathbb{G}$ of prime order p, and set the keyspace to $\mathcal{K} = \mathbb{G} \times \mathbb{Z}_p$, the domain to $\mathcal{D} = \mathbb{Z}_p$, and the range to $\mathcal{R} = \mathbb{G}$. Return $(\mathcal{K}, \mathcal{D}, \mathcal{R}, h)$ where h is a description of the function defined below.

$h_k(x)$: For $k \in \mathcal{K}$ and $x \in \mathcal{D}$, parse k as $(g, a) \in \mathbb{G} \times \mathbb{Z}_p$ and return

$$h_k(x) = g^{\frac{1}{x+a}},$$

where $1/(m + a)$ is computed modulo p

Based on the decisional q-Diffie Hellman Inversion (q-DDHI) assumption in $\mathbb{G}$, and extending the results of [19], we are able to show that the above hash function achieves multi-key correlated-input pseudorandomness for a class of functions consisting of uniform-output polynomials of bounded degree.

Theorem 5. *Assume the decisional q-DDHI assumption holds in $\mathbb{G}$, and let Φ be a class of uniform-output polynomials over $\mathbb{Z}_p$. Then there exists no polynomial time Φ-restricted adversary $\mathcal{A}$ with non-negligible advantage in the (Φ, ℓ)-MK-SCI-PR security game when interacting with $\mathcal{H}$ defined as above, provided that $\ell \cdot d \leq q + 1$, where d is an upper bound on the sum of the degrees of the polynomials submitted by $\mathcal{A}$. More precisely, if $\ell \cdot d \leq q + 1$, then for any polynomial time Φ-restricted $\mathcal{A}$, there exists a polynomial time algorithm $\mathcal{B}$ such that*

$$\mathbf{Adv}^{\ell\text{-mk-sci-pr}}_{\mathcal{H},\mathcal{A}}(\lambda) \leq 2n\ell \cdot \mathbf{Adv}^{q\text{-ddhi}}_{\mathbb{G},\mathcal{B}}(\lambda)$$

where n is the number of polynomials submitted by $\mathcal{A}$.

Note 1. Our 'partial' RKA-secure PRF is only secure when an adversary's function queries are non-adaptive, which is why we are only able to prove selective HK-RRA-ATK security. If we had a result similar to Theorem 5 for adaptive function queries, then we would immediately obtain a PKE scheme that is (adaptively) HK-RRA-ATK secure.

Note 2. The above construction is only shown to achieve HK-RRA-ATK security, as opposed to RRA-ATK security. The technical reason for this is that public keys include a hash key, and the CIS hash function is only assumed to be secure for honestly generated keys. An alternative solution would be to introduce a *common reference string* (CRS) containing a single hash key, and let all users make use of this. While this requires a trusted third party to initially set up the CRS, it would be possible to show RRA-ATK security of the above construction in a security model appropriately extended to model the presence of a CRS.

Likewise, if we had a multi-key CIS hash function that remained secure for maliciously chosen keys, then we would be able to obtain full RRA-ATK security for the above construction. Unfortunately, we are currently unaware of how to obtain such CIS hash functions.

5   Function-Vector Related Randomness Security

Our previous standard model constructions concerned functions ϕ that are linear (scheme PRF-PKE analysed in Theorem 3 combined with known RKA-PRF families), or of bounded degree and having unpredictable outputs (scheme CI-Hash-PKE analysed in Theorem 5). We now turn our attention to alternative classes of functions. Specifically, we will propose a construction for a PKE scheme that is Φ-FV-RRA-ATK secure for the set Φ of vectors of functions that are hard to invert, in a sense that we make precise next.

Definition 6. *Let $\phi = (\phi_1, \ldots, \phi_q)$ denote a vector of functions on a set Rnd_λ, where $q := q(\lambda)$ is polynomial in the security parameter λ. Let $\delta(\lambda)$ be a function. We say that ϕ is $\delta(\lambda)$-hard-to-invert if, for all polynomial time algorithms $\mathcal{A}$ and all sufficiently large λ, we have:*

$$\mathbb{P}[r \leftarrow \mathcal{A}(\phi_1(r), \ldots, \phi_q(r)) : r \leftarrow_\$ \mathrm{Rnd}_\lambda] \leq \delta(\lambda).$$

We say that a set of vectors of functions Φ is δ-hard-to-invert if each vector $\phi \in \Phi$ is δ-hard-to-invert (note that the vectors in such a set Φ need not all be of the same dimension, but we assume they each have dimension that is polynomial in λ).

We will now construct a PKE scheme that offers Φ-FV-RRA-CPA security, where Φ is the set of *all* sufficiently hard-to-invert vectors of functions on the scheme's randomness space Rnd. As noted in Section 2, security in this setting is quantified over *all* vectors in Φ, and the adversary is allowed to work with any set of public keys (even maliciously generated) in its attack. This makes our result relatively strong.

With these definitions in hand, Figure 5 defines our PKE scheme mBHHO which offers security in the FV-RRA-CPA setting. This scheme is obtained by modifying a PKE scheme of Boneh *et al.* [12] (the BHHO scheme) which Dodis *et al.* [14] showed to be secure in the auxiliary input setting. To arrive at our modified scheme mBHHO, we swap the roles of secret key and randomness in the original

Alg. mBHHO.K(1^λ):	Alg. mBHHO.E(pk, m):	Alg. mBHHO.D($sk, (c_1, c_2)$):
$g_1, \ldots, g_\lambda \leftarrow_\$ \mathbb{G}$	$r \leftarrow_\$ \{0, 1\}^\lambda$	$(K, r') \leftarrow f(c_1^x)$
$x \leftarrow_\$ \mathbb{Z}_p$	$c_1 = \prod_{i=1}^\lambda g_i^{r_i}$	$m \leftarrow \text{DEM.D}(K, c_2)$
$pk = (g_1, \ldots, g_\lambda, g_1^x \ldots, g_\lambda^x)$	$(K, r') \leftarrow f(\prod_{i=1}^\lambda (g_i^x)^{r_i})$	
$sk = x$	$r'' \leftarrow F_{r'}(pk \| m)$	
	$c_2 = \text{DEM.E}(K, m; r'')$	
	$c = (c_1, c_2)$	

Fig. 5. Modified BHHO scheme mBHHO, constructed using a PRF, F, a KDF, f, and a DEM DEM

BHHO scheme. This then enables us to provide the values $\phi_i(r)$ as auxiliary inputs without undermining the usual IND-CPA security of the scheme; in turn, these values enables our security reduction to properly handle **Enc** queries involving any function ϕ_i. The following theorem gives our formal result concerning the security of this scheme.

Theorem 6. *Let Φ be the set of δ-hard-to-invert vectors of functions on $\{0, 1\}^\lambda$. The PKE scheme mBHHO in Figure 5 is Φ-FV-RRA-CPA secure. More precisely, consider any polynomial-size vector of functions $\phi \in \Phi$ and any equality-pattern respecting, ϕ-FV-RRA-CPA adversary $\mathcal{A}$ against mBHHO. Suppose $\mathcal{A}$ makes q_{LR} LR queries and uses q_r randomness indices. Then there exists a DDH adversary $\mathcal{B}$, a KDF adversary $\mathcal{D}$, a PRF adversary $\mathcal{E}$, and an IND-CPA adversary $\mathcal{F}$, all running in polynomial time, such that:*

$$\mathbf{Adv}_{\text{mBHHO}, \mathcal{A}}^{\phi\text{-fv-rra-cpa}}(\lambda) < 2\lambda q_r \cdot \mathbf{Adv}_{\mathbb{G}, \mathcal{B}}^{\text{ddh}}(\lambda) + 2q_r \cdot \mathbf{Adv}_{f, \mathcal{D}}^{\text{kdf}}(\lambda)$$
$$+ 2q_r \cdot \mathbf{Adv}_{F, \mathcal{E}}^{\text{prf}}(\lambda) + q_r \cdot \mathbf{Adv}_{\text{DEM}, \mathcal{F}}^{\text{ind-cpa}}(\lambda)$$
$$+ q_r p^2 \sqrt[3]{512\lambda\delta}.$$

In particular, when δ is sufficiently small the advantage of $\mathcal{A}$ is negligible in the security parameter λ.

The class of related randomness functions which our scheme mBHHO can tolerate is quite different from those in our previous constructions: linear and bounded-degree polynomials are certainly not hard-to-invert in general. Our proof of Theorem 6 actually shows that even if $\phi(r)$ were to completely leak to the adversary (instead of merely being indirectly accessible via **Enc** queries), the scheme mBHHO would still be secure. This would not be the case if the analogous $\phi(r)$ values were to leak in our earlier schemes PRF-PKE and CI-Hash-PKE, since the adversary could actually reconstruct r from this leakage for the relevant ϕ functions and win the security game. Furthermore, the functions are not required to be collision-resistant or output-unpredictable. These restrictions are only strictly required of the functions queried to the **LR** oracle. However, since an an adversary is restricted to using only the identity function (which *is* collision-resistant and output-unpredictable) in its **LR** queries, the functions in Φ do not need to satisfy these conditions.

References

1. Becherer, A., Stamos, A., Wilcox, N.: Cloud computing security: Raining on the trendy new parade. In: BlackHat, USA (2009)
2. Bellare, M., Brakerski, Z., Naor, M., Ristenpart, T., Segev, G., Shacham, H., Yilek, S.: Hedged public-key encryption: How to protect against bad randomness. In: Matsui, M. (ed.) ASIACRYPT 2009. LNCS, vol. 5912, pp. 232–249. Springer, Heidelberg (2009)
3. Bellare, M., Cash, D.: Pseudorandom functions and permutations provably secure against related-key attacks. In: Rabin, T. (ed.) CRYPTO 2010. LNCS, vol. 6223, pp. 666–684. Springer, Heidelberg (2010)
4. Bellare, M., Cash, D., Miller, R.: Cryptography secure against related-key attacks and tampering. In: Lee, D.H., Wang, X. (eds.) ASIACRYPT 2011. LNCS, vol. 7073, pp. 486–503. Springer, Heidelberg (2011)
5. Bellare, M., Kohno, T.: A theoretical treatment of related-key attacks: RKA-PRPs, RKA-PRFs, and applications. In: Biham, E. (ed.) EUROCRYPT 2003. LNCS, vol. 2656, pp. 491–506. Springer, Heidelberg (2003)
6. Bellare, M., Paterson, K.G., Thomson, S.: RKA security beyond the linear barrier: IBE, encryption and signatures. In: Wang, X., Sako, K. (eds.) ASIACRYPT 2012. LNCS, vol. 7658, pp. 331–348. Springer, Heidelberg (2012)
7. Bellare, M., Rogaway, P.: Optimal asymmetric encryption. In: De Santis, A. (ed.) EUROCRYPT 1994. LNCS, vol. 950, pp. 92–111. Springer, Heidelberg (1995)
8. Bellare, M., Rogaway, P.: The security of triple encryption and a framework for code-based game-playing proofs. In: Vaudenay (ed.) [31], pp. 409–426
9. Bendel, M.: Hackers describe PS3 security as epic fail, gain unrestricted access (2011), http://www.exophase.com/20540/hackers-describe-ps3-security-as-epic-fail-gain-unrestricted-access/
10. Bernstein, D.J., Chang, Y.-A., Cheng, C.-M., Chou, L.-P., Heninger, N., Lange, T., van Someren, N.: Factoring RSA keys from certified smart cards: Coppersmith in the wild. Cryptology ePrint Archive, Report 2013/599 (2013), http://eprint.iacr.org/
11. Bitcoin.org. Android security vulnerability (2013), http://bitcoin.org/en/alert/2013-08-11-android
12. Boneh, D., Halevi, S., Hamburg, M., Ostrovsky, R.: Circular-secure encryption from decision diffie-hellman. In: Wagner, D. (ed.) CRYPTO 2008. LNCS, vol. 5157, pp. 108–125. Springer, Heidelberg (2008)
13. Debian: Debian Security Advisory DSA-1571-1: OpenSSL – predictable random number generator (2008), http://www.debian.org/security/2008/dsa-1571
14. Dodis, Y., Goldwasser, S., Tauman Kalai, Y., Peikert, C., Vaikuntanathan, V.: Public-key encryption schemes with auxiliary inputs. In: Micciancio, D. (ed.) TCC 2010. LNCS, vol. 5978, pp. 361–381. Springer, Heidelberg (2010)
15. Dodis, Y., Pointcheval, D., Ruhault, S., Vergnaud, D., Wichs, D.: Security analysis of pseudo-random number generators with input: /dev/random is not robust. IACR Cryptology ePrint Archive, 338 (2013)
16. Dorrendorf, L., Gutterman, Z., Pinkas, B.: Cryptanalysis of the random number generator of the Windows operating system. ACM Trans. Inf. Syst. Secur. 13(1) (2009)
17. Fujisaki, E., Okamoto, T.: Secure integration of asymmetric and symmetric encryption schemes. In: Wiener, M. (ed.) CRYPTO 1999. LNCS, vol. 1666, pp. 537–554. Springer, Heidelberg (1999)

18. Goldberg, I., Wagner, D.: Randomness and the Netscape browser (1996), http://www.drdobbs.com/windows/184409807
19. Goyal, V., O'Neill, A., Rao, V.: Correlated-input secure hash functions. In: Ishai, Y. (ed.) TCC 2011. LNCS, vol. 6597, pp. 182–200. Springer, Heidelberg (2011)
20. Gutterman, Z., Malkhi, D.: Hold your sessions: An attack on java session-id generation. In: Menezes, A. (ed.) CT-RSA 2005. LNCS, vol. 3376, pp. 44–57. Springer, Heidelberg (2005)
21. Gutterman, Z., Pinkas, B., Reinman, T.: Analysis of the linux random number generator. In: IEEE Symposium on Security and Privacy, pp. 371–385. IEEE Computer Society (2006)
22. Heninger, N., Durumeric, Z., Wustrow, E., Alex Halderman, J.: Mining your Ps and Qs: Detection of widespread weak keys in network devices. In: Proceedings of the 21st USENIX Security Symposium (August 2012)
23. Kamara, S., Katz, J.: How to encrypt with a malicious random number generator. In: Nyberg, K. (ed.) FSE 2008. LNCS, vol. 5086, pp. 303–315. Springer, Heidelberg (2008)
24. Lenstra, A.K., Hughes, J.P., Augier, M., Bos, J.W., Kleinjung, T., Wachter, C.: Public keys. In: Safavi-Naini, R., Canetti, R. (eds.) CRYPTO 2012. LNCS, vol. 7417, pp. 626–642. Springer, Heidelberg (2012)
25. Lucks, S.: Ciphers secure against related-key attacks. In: Roy, Meier (eds.) [30], pp. 359–370
26. Michaelis, K., Meyer, C., Schwenk, J.: Randomly failed! the state of randomness in current java implementations. In: Dawson, E. (ed.) CT-RSA 2013. LNCS, vol. 7779, pp. 129–144. Springer, Heidelberg (2013)
27. Ristenpart, T., Yilek, S.: When good randomness goes bad: Virtual machine reset vulnerabilities and hedging deployed cryptography. In: NDSS. The Internet Society (2010)
28. Rogaway, P.: Nonce-based symmetric encryption. In: Roy, Meier (eds.) [30], pp. 348–359
29. Rogaway, P., Shrimpton, T.: A provable-security treatment of the key-wrap problem. In: Vaudenay (ed.) [31], pp. 373–390
30. Roy, B., Meier, W. (eds.): FSE 2004. LNCS, vol. 3017. Springer, Heidelberg (2004)
31. Vaudenay, S. (ed.): EUROCRYPT 2006. LNCS, vol. 4004. Springer, Heidelberg (2006)
32. Wee, H.: Public key encryption against related key attacks. In: Fischlin, M., Buchmann, J., Manulis, M. (eds.) PKC 2012. LNCS, vol. 7293, pp. 262–279. Springer, Heidelberg (2012)
33. Yilek, S.: Resettable public-key encryption: How to encrypt on a virtual machine. In: Pieprzyk, J. (ed.) CT-RSA 2010. LNCS, vol. 5985, pp. 41–56. Springer, Heidelberg (2010)

Encryption Schemes Secure under Related-Key and Key-Dependent Message Attacks

Florian Böhl[1,*], Gareth T. Davies[2,**], and Dennis Hofheinz[1,***]

[1] Karlsruhe Institute of Technology (KIT)
[2] University of Bristol

Abstract. We construct secret-key encryption (SKE) schemes that are secure against related-key attacks *and* in the presence of key-dependent messages (RKA-KDM secure). We emphasize that RKA-KDM security is not merely the conjunction of individual security properties, but covers attacks in which ciphertexts of key-dependent messages under related keys are available. Besides being interesting in their own right, RKA-KDM secure schemes allow to garble circuits with XORs very efficiently (Applebaum, TCC 2013). Until now, the only known RKA-KDM secure SKE scheme (due to Applebaum) is based on the LPN assumption. Our schemes are based on various other computational assumptions, namely DDH, LWE, QR, and DCR.

We abstract from Applebaum's construction and proof, and formalize three generic technical properties that imply RKA-KDM security: one property is IND-CPA security, and the other two are the existence of suitable oracles that produce ciphertexts under related keys, resp. of key-dependent messages. We then give simple SKE schemes that achieve these properties. Our constructions are variants of known KDM-secure public-key encryption schemes. To additionally achieve RKA security, we isolate suitable homomorphic properties of the underlying schemes in order to simulate ciphertexts under related keys in the security proof. RKA-KDM security for our schemes holds w.r.t. affine functions (over the respective mathematical domain).

From a conceptual point of view, our work provides a generic and extensible way to construct encryption schemes with multiple special security properties.

Keywords: related key attacks, key-dependent message security, garbled circuits.

1 Introduction

Motivation and Overview. The standard notion of security for secret-key encryption (SKE) is indistinguishability of ciphertexts (short: IND-CPA or IND-CCA, depending on whether passive or active attacks are considered).

* Supported by MWK grant "MoSeS".
** Work partially conducted while visiting KIT.
*** Supported by DFG grant GZ HO 4534/2-1.

H. Krawczyk (Ed.): PKC 2014, LNCS 8383, pp. 483–500, 2014.

However, in certain applications, ciphertext indistinguishability is not sufficient. For instance, in harddisk encryption, encryptions of the secret key itself naturally occur (see [25]). Security in the presence of such key-dependent messages (KDM security [23]) is not implied by IND-CPA or IND-CCA security [23, 1]. There are numerous other specialized notions of encryption scheme security, such as security under related-key attacks (RKAs [7]), leakage-resilience [35, 29], security under bad randomness [10], security under selective openings [11], and others.

In this paper, we consider two such specialized notions of security for SKE schemes in a combined fashion. In particular, we will derive SKE schemes that are secure in the presence of key-dependent messages encrypted under related keys. This notion, dubbed RKA-KDM security and already considered by Applebaum [3] (as RK-KDM security), combines the notions of KDM and RKA security, but is more than just their conjunction. RKA-KDM secure SKE schemes are of course suitable for all applications in which RKA or KDM security is required. In fact, there are even applications that explicitly require the combined RKA-KDM notion: Applebaum [3] uses RKA-KDM secure SKE schemes in a garbled circuit construction in which XOR gates can be garbled for free (in the sense that XOR gates require no explicit encryption whatsoever). Besides, "aggregating" security properties as in RKA-KDM security may eventually lead to more "ideal" and universally useful security notions and encryption schemes.

RKA and KDM Security. To give more details, we first recall the definitions of IND-CPA, RKA, and KDM security. In a nutshell, an SKE scheme has indistinguishable ciphertexts (or, is IND-CPA secure [30][1]), if no efficient adversary $\mathcal{A}$ can tell apart whether it is interacting with an oracle Real, or with an oracle Fake. Here, upon input M, oracle Real returns an encryption $\mathsf{E}_k(M)$ of M, while Fake returns an encryption $\mathsf{E}_k(0^{|M|})$ of a zero-string of the same length. (In other words, $\mathcal{A}$ is asked to tell authentic encryptions from encryptions of meaningless messages of the same length.)

For security under key-dependent messages (KDM security [23]), we require the same, except that messages are now functions in the secret key. That is, upon input a function ψ, Real returns $\mathsf{E}_k(\psi(k))$, and Fake returns $\mathsf{E}_k(0^{|\psi(k)|})$. Depending on the class of allowed functions Ψ, there are many constructions of KDM-secure encryption schemes from various computational assumptions, e.g. [23, 31, 33, 25, 5, 28, 6, 26, 27, 34, 8, 12, 4, 32]. However, most of these works follow the design principle of Boneh et al. [25] (henceforth BHHO). Namely, it should be publicly possible (or at least given some "harmless" extra information) to construct key-dependent encryptions from regular ones. Intuitively, if this is the case, then clearly the presence of key-dependent encryptions is no more harmful than the presence of "regular", key-independent encryptions.

For security under related-key attacks (RKA security [9]), we again require the same as for IND-CPA security, except that an adversary $\mathcal{A}$ now specifies a function φ on secret keys alongside each message M to be encrypted.

---

[1] In the following, for ease of exposition, we describe a modified but equivalent version of IND-CPA security.

Real then returns an encryption $E_{\varphi(k)}(M)$ of M under the related key $\varphi(k)$, and Fake returns $E_{\varphi(k)}(0^{|M|})$. RKA security draws its motivation primarily from the wide range of *attacks* that are known in this setting, e.g. [16, 17, 18, 19, 21, 20, 22]. There are also a number of constructions of RKA secure schemes, e.g. [7, 13, 36, 3]. As with KDM security, the main idea is to generate encryptions under related keys from "regular" encryptions.

RKA-KDM Security. It is of course easy to combine RKA and KDM security into a combined notion, which we call RKA-KDM security here. Concretely, RKA-KDM security is defined like IND-CPA security above, only that an adversary supplies functions φ and ψ along with the message M to be encrypted. Then, Real returns $E_{\varphi(k)}(\psi(k))$, and Fake returns $E_{\varphi(k)}(0^{|\psi(k)|})$. This notion has already been defined by Applebaum [3] (dubbed RK-KDM security there), who used RKA-KDM secure schemes to garble circuits with XOR gates in a very elegant and efficient way. As a proof of concept, Applebaum also constructed an RKA-KDM secure encryption scheme, starting from the KDM-secure scheme of Applebaum et al. [5] based on the LPN assumption. (Along the way, he also shows that RKA-KDM security is strictly stronger than the conjunction of RKA and KDM security.) Currently, no further RKA-KDM secure schemes are known.

Our Contribution. In this work, we provide a generic framework to construct RKA-KDM secure encryption schemes, and we instantiate this framework under several computational assumptions. In particular, we provide RKA-KDM secure schemes from the decisional Diffie-Hellman (DDH), learning with errors (LWE), quadratic residuosity and decisional Diffie-Hellman (QR+DDH) [2], and decisional composite residuosity (DCR) assumptions. Our constructions support affine KDM and RKA functions in the "natural domain" of the respective secret keys. Furthermore, with the exception of the DCR-based scheme, all of our schemes can be directly used in the application of Applebaum [3]. Additionally, they fit the construction of Bellare et al. [14], and thus can be extended from projection-KDM security to bounded-KDM security while maintaining the same level of RKA security.

Our Approach. Based on an informal remark of Applebaum [3, Remark 3.6 in full version], we first reduce RKA-KDM security to three technical properties of the scheme in question:
(a) IND-CPA security in the usual sense,
(b) the existence of an oracle (that itself has access to an $E_k(\cdot)$ oracle) that generates ciphertexts $E_{\varphi(k)}(M)$ under related keys, and
(c) the existence of an oracle (with access to $E_k(\cdot)$) that generates ciphertexts $E_k(\psi(k))$ of key-dependent messages.
Intuitively, property (b) allows to reduce any RKA-KDM attack to a KDM attack, which in turn can be reduced (using (c)) to an IND-CPA attack. We

---

[2] Similar to Hofheinz [32], we have to use the DDH assumption in the group of quadratic residues modulo N.

note that it seems possible to add further oracles (e.g., for encryption queries with leakage) to achieve even stronger combined security notions from individual and isolated technical properties.

We then proceed to construct several RKA-KDM secure encryption schemes. Our constructions are slight variations of the known KDM-secure schemes from [25, 5, 6, 26, 34]. For these schemes, properties (a) and (c) already follow (with slight modifications) from the KDM security proofs of the underlying schemes. Showing property (b) then boils down to showing suitable homomorphic properties of the encryption, resp. decryption algorithm.

Example: Our DDH-Based Scheme. To give a taste of the proof, we outline our DDH-based scheme (which is based upon the DDH-based public-key encryption scheme from [25]). In this scheme, a ciphertext is of the form

$$C = (g_1^{r_1}, \ldots, g_\lambda^{r_\lambda}, g^M \cdot g_0),$$

where λ is the security parameter, g and the g_i are uniformly random generators of the underlying cyclic group, the r_i are uniformly random exponents, and $g_0 = \prod_{i \in [\lambda]} (g_i^{r_i})^{-k_i}$ for the secret key $k = (k_1, \ldots, k_\lambda) \in \{0,1\}^\lambda$. (In the original public-key encryption scheme from [25], all r_i are identical.)

We show property (b) for functions of the form $\varphi_\Delta : \{0,1\}^\lambda \to \{0,1\}^\lambda$ with $\varphi_\Delta(k) = k \oplus \Delta$ for some $\Delta \in \{0,1\}^\lambda$. (This will be sufficient for the application in [3].) To show (b), we only need to show that any given ciphertext $C = \mathsf{E}_k(M)$ as above can be transformed into a ciphertext $C' = \mathsf{E}_{\varphi_\Delta(k)}(M)$. For simplicity, assume that $\Delta = (1, 0, \ldots, 0)$. In this case, it is easy to see that

$$C' = (1/g_1^{r_1}, g_2^{r_2}, \ldots, g_\lambda^{r_\lambda}, (g^M \cdot g_0) \cdot g_1^{r_1})$$

is a perfectly distributed encryption of M under key $k' = k \oplus \Delta$ (with randomness $r_1' = -r_1$ and $r_i' = r_i$ for $i > 1$). This shows property (b) – the other properties follow as in [25].[3]

Our other constructions proceed similarly, starting from the schemes of Applebaum et al. [5], Brakerski and Goldwasser [26], and Malkin et al. [34]. The latter is only contained in our full version [24].

2   Preliminaries

Notation. For $n \in \mathbb{N}$, let $[n] := \{1, \ldots, n\}$. Throughout the paper, $\lambda \in \mathbb{N}$ denotes the security parameter. For a finite set $\mathcal{S}$, we denote by $s \leftarrow \mathcal{S}$ the process of sampling s uniformly from $\mathcal{S}$. For a distribution X, we denote by $x \leftarrow X$ the process of sampling x from X. For a probabilistic algorithm A, we denote with $y := A(x; r)$ the process of running A on input x and with

---

[3] We note that our technical change to the scheme from [25] – namely, using *different* r_i – can be proven to be not crucial to its security (see Theorem 7). Instead, choosing different r_i simplifies expressing the scheme in our framework, and in particular separating the KDM, RKA, and IND-CPA properties.

randomness r, and assigning y the result. We let $\mathcal{R}_A$ denote the randomness space of A; we require $\mathcal{R}_A$ to be of the form $\mathcal{R}_A = \{0,1\}^\ell$. We write $y \leftarrow A(x)$ for $y \leftarrow A(x;r)$ with uniformly chosen $r \in \mathcal{R}_A$. If A's running time is polynomial in λ, then A is called probabilistic polynomial-time (PPT). For a real number x, let the floor function $\lfloor x \rfloor$ denote the largest integer not greater than x. For a vector $\mathbf{v}$, $\mathbf{v}_i$ denotes the ith element of $\mathbf{v}$.

Two sequences of random variables $X = (X_\lambda)_{\lambda \in \mathbb{N}}$ and $Y = (Y_\lambda)_{\lambda \in \mathbb{N}}$ are *computationally indistinguishable* (denoted $X \overset{c}{\approx} Y$) iff for any PPT algorithm D, the probability $\mathbf{Pr}\left[D(1^\lambda, X_\lambda) = 1\right] - \mathbf{Pr}\left[D(1^\lambda, Y_\lambda)\right]$ is negligible in λ. $X = (X_\lambda)_{\lambda \in \mathbb{N}}$ and $Y = (Y_\lambda)_{\lambda \in \mathbb{N}}$ are *statistically indistinguishable* (denoted $X \overset{s}{\approx} Y$) iff the same holds for any algorithm D with unbounded runtime.

SKE Schemes. A secret-key encryption (SKE) scheme consists of four PPT algorithms $(\mathsf{Pg}, \mathsf{Kg}, \mathsf{E}, \mathsf{D})$. Parameter generation $\mathsf{Pg}(1^\lambda)$ outputs public parameters π for the scheme. Key generation $\mathsf{Kg}(\pi)$ outputs a (secret) key k. Encryption $\mathsf{E}_k(M)$ takes a key k and a message M, and outputs a ciphertext C. Decryption $\mathsf{Dec}_k(C)$ takes a key k and a ciphertext C, and outputs a message M or $\bot$ if decryption fails. For correctness, we stipulate $\mathsf{D}_k(C) = M$ for all M, all $k \leftarrow \mathsf{Kg}(\mathsf{Pg}(1^\lambda))$, and all $C \leftarrow \mathsf{E}_k(M)$.

Definition 1 (RKA-KDM[Φ, Ψ] Security.). *Let $\Sigma = (\mathsf{Pg}, \mathsf{Kg}, \mathsf{E}, \mathsf{D})$ be a symmetric encryption scheme, $\pi \leftarrow \mathsf{Pg}(1^\lambda)$ be public parameters and $b \leftarrow \{0,1\}$ be a bit chosen by the challenger. A key $k \leftarrow \mathsf{Kg}(\pi)$ is randomly chosen. Adversary $\mathcal{A}$ makes encryption queries by submitting $(\varphi \in \Phi, \psi \in \Psi)$ and receives a response from one of the following oracles, depending on the bit b.*

- *If $b = 1$, oracle Real_k takes as input (φ, ψ) and returns $C \leftarrow \mathsf{E}_{\varphi(k)}(\psi(k))$.*
- *If $b = 0$, oracle Fake_k takes as input (φ, ψ) and returns $C \leftarrow \mathsf{E}_{\varphi(k)}(0^{|\psi(k)|})$.*

Scheme Σ is RKA-KDM *secure w.r.t. Φ and Ψ if for all PPT adversaries $\mathcal{A}$*

$$\left| \Pr[\mathcal{A}^{\mathsf{Real}(\varphi,\psi)}(\pi) = 1] - \Pr[\mathcal{A}^{\mathsf{Fake}(\varphi,\psi)}(\pi) = 1] \right|$$

is a negligible function in λ.

Throughout this paper each class of KDM functions Ψ implicitly contains constant functions $\psi_M(k) := M$ for all messages $M \in \mathcal{M}$ where $\mathcal{M}$ is the message space of the encryption scheme at hand.

Further Security Definitions. The standard definition of *RKA security* follows from restricting the KDM function class Ψ to constant functions, and the definition of *KDM security* follows from restricting the RKA function class Φ to the identity function. *IND-CPA security* follows from applying both of these restrictions at once.

2.1   A Generic Approach

In this section we prove that an SKE scheme Σ is RKA-KDM$[\Phi, \Psi]$ secure if
- Σ is IND-CPA secure,
- there is a so called RKA$[\Phi]$ oracle (defined below) for Σ that takes as input $\mathsf{E}_k(M)$ and RKA function $\varphi \in \Phi$, and returns something that is indistinguishable from $\mathsf{E}_{\varphi(k)}(M)$ without knowledge of the key k,
- there is a so called KDM$[\Psi]$ oracle (defined below) for Σ that takes as input $\mathsf{E}_k(M)$ and KDM function $\psi \in \Psi$, and returns something that is indistinguishable from $\mathsf{E}_k(\psi(k))$ without knowledge of the key k (M is the constant part of ψ here).

Definition 2 (RKA$[\Phi]$ oracle). *Let $\Sigma = (\mathsf{Pg}, \mathsf{Kg}, \mathsf{E}, \mathsf{D})$ be a secret key encryption scheme with message space $\mathcal{M}$. We say that a function $\mathcal{F}_{\mathsf{RKA}[\Phi]}(\varphi, C)$ is an RKA$[\Phi]$ oracle for Σ iff for all PPT adversaries $\mathcal{A}$ that make queries (φ, M) for $\varphi \in \Phi$ and $M \in \mathcal{M}$*

$$\left| \Pr\left[\mathcal{A}^{\mathcal{F}_{\mathsf{RKA}[\Phi]}(\varphi, \mathsf{E}_k(\cdot))}(\pi, k) = 1 : \pi \leftarrow \mathsf{Pg}(1^\lambda), k \leftarrow \mathsf{Kg}(\pi) \right] \right.$$

$$\left. - \Pr\left[\mathcal{A}^{\mathsf{E}_{\varphi(k)}(\cdot)}(\pi, k) = 1 : \pi \leftarrow \mathsf{Pg}(1^\lambda), k \leftarrow \mathsf{Kg}(\pi) \right] \right|$$

is a negligible function in λ. Here, $\mathcal{A}^{\mathcal{F}_{\mathsf{RKA}[\Phi]}(\varphi, \mathsf{E}_k(\cdot))}$ denote the interaction of $\mathcal{A}$ with an oracle that, upon input M, outputs $\mathcal{F}_{\mathsf{RKA}[\Phi]}(\varphi, \mathsf{E}_k(M))$.

Definition 3 (KDM$[\Psi]$ oracle). *Let $\Sigma = (\mathsf{Pg}, \mathsf{Kg}, \mathsf{E}, \mathsf{D})$ be a secret key encryption scheme with message space $\mathcal{M}$. We say that a function $\mathcal{F}_{\mathsf{KDM}[\Psi]}(\psi, C)$ is a KDM$[\Psi]$ oracle for Σ iff for all PPT adversaries $\mathcal{A}$ that make queries ψ for $\psi \in \Psi$ (where M denotes the constant part of ψ, i.e., $\psi(0)$)*

$$\left| \Pr\left[\mathcal{A}^{\mathcal{F}_{\mathsf{KDM}[\Psi]}(\psi, \mathsf{E}_k(M))}(\pi, k) = 1 : \pi \leftarrow \mathsf{Pg}(1^\lambda), k \leftarrow \mathsf{Kg}(\pi) \right] \right.$$

$$\left. - \Pr\left[\mathcal{A}^{\mathsf{E}_k(\psi(k))}(\pi, k) = 1 : \pi \leftarrow \mathsf{Pg}(1^\lambda), k \leftarrow \mathsf{Kg}(\pi) \right] \right|$$

is a negligible function in λ.

Note that for constant functions $\psi \in \Psi$ a sufficient behaviour of $\mathcal{F}_{\mathsf{KDM}[\Psi]}$ is to output the ciphertext it received without changes. All KDM$[\Psi]$ oracles presented in this paper implicitly adopt this behaviour.

Theorem 4. *Let Σ be an SKE scheme that is IND-CPA secure, $\mathcal{F}_{\mathsf{RKA}[\Phi]}$ be an RKA$[\Phi]$ oracle for Σ and $\mathcal{F}_{\mathsf{KDM}[\Psi]}$ be a KDM$[\Psi]$ oracle for Σ. Then Σ is RKA-KDM$[\Phi, \Psi]$ secure.*

Proof. We prove the theorem by a sequence of games.

Game 0. In Game 0 $\mathcal{A}$ plays the original RKA-KDM$[\Phi, \Psi]$ experiment (see Theorem 1).

Game 1. In Game 1, instead of computing $E_{\varphi(k)}(\psi(k))$ the experiment computes $C_{KDM} \leftarrow E_k(\psi(k))$ and outputs $\mathcal{F}_{RKA[\Phi]}(\varphi, C_{KDM})$ to the adversary. This game is indistinguishable from Game 0 due to the indistinguishability of $\mathcal{F}_{RKA[\Phi]}$ (see Theorem 2).

Game 2. In Game 2, instead of computing $E_k(\psi(k))$, the experiment computes $C_{CPA} \leftarrow E_k(M)$ where M is the constant part of ψ and sets $C_{KDM} := \mathcal{F}_{KDM[\Psi]}(\psi, C_{CPA})$. Given a distinguisher $\mathcal{D}$ between this game and Game 1, we can construct an adversary $\mathcal{S}$, henceforth called simulator, on the indistinguishability of $\mathcal{F}_{KDM[\Psi]}$. First, the simulator forwards the public parameters π to $\mathcal{D}$ and picks a bit $b \leftarrow \{0,1\}$. For $b = 1$ and each query (φ, ψ) from $\mathcal{D}$, the simulator queries its oracle for ψ and either gets a response $\mathcal{F}_{KDM[\Psi]}(\psi_M, C_{CPA})$ or $E_k(\psi_M(k))$ (see Theorem 3). It then applies $\mathcal{F}_{RKA[\Phi]}$ with φ to the response and sends the result to $\mathcal{D}$. The responses to the queries of the simulator are that of Game 2 if itself gets responses of type $\mathcal{F}_{KDM[\Psi]}(\psi_M, C_{CPA})$ and that of Game 1 for responses of type $E_k(\psi_M(k))$. Analogously for $b = 0$, where the simulator queries $0^{|\psi(k)|}$ instead of ψ. The advantage of $\mathcal{S}$ is that of $\mathcal{D}$ and must be negligible due to the indistinguishability $\mathcal{F}_{KDM[\Psi]}$.

Game 3. In Game 3 we replace $C_{CPA} \leftarrow E_k(M)$ by $C_{CPA} \leftarrow E_k(0^{|M|})$. Analogously to the indistinguishability of Game 1 and Game 2, we can easily transform a distinguisher between this game and the previous game into an IND-CPA adversary for Σ.

We observe that the advantage of any PPT adversary in Game 3 is 0 since the behaviour of the oracle given to the adversary is is independent of the bit b picked by the experiment. This concludes our proof since Game 3 and Game 0 are indistinguishable.

3   RKA-KDM-Secure Encryption Schemes

3.1   Boneh et al. [25]

The PKE scheme of Boneh et al. [25] was the first construction provably KDM secure under standard assumptions. In this section we detail a SKE analogue of the 'basic' version of their scheme. We construct an RKA[Φ] oracle and a KDM[Ψ] oracle for the scheme. The class of RKA functions Φ allows for XOR operations on the key while the class of KDM functions Ψ brings circular KDM security, i.e., encryptions of the secret key are possible (as in the original paper). The security of the scheme is based on the DDH assumption.

DDH Assumption. The *decisional Diffie-Hellman (DDH) assumption* over a group $\mathbb{G}$ (that may depend on the security parameter λ) stipulates that

$$(g, g^x, g^y, g^{xy}) \overset{c}{\approx} (g, g^x, g^y, g^z),$$

where $g \leftarrow \mathbb{G}$ and $x, y, z \leftarrow [\|\mathbb{G}\|]$ are uniformly distributed.

For the sake of readability we introduce the scheme Σ'_{BHHO} with message space $\{0,1\}$. Canonical concatenation at the end will yield the scheme Σ_{BHHO} with message space $\{0,1\}^\lambda$.

The SKE Scheme Σ'_{BHHO}. Let $\mathbb{G}$ be a group of prime order p and g be a generator of $\mathbb{G}$. The scheme Σ'_{BHHO} for $M \in \{0,1\}$ is defined as follows:

- $\mathsf{Pg}(1^\lambda)$ picks generators $g_1, \ldots, g_\lambda \leftarrow \mathbb{G}\backslash\{1\}$ and returns $\pi := (\mathbb{G}, g, g_1, \ldots, g_\lambda)$.
- $\mathsf{Kg}(\pi)$ returns a random bitstring $k \leftarrow \{0,1\}^\lambda$.
- $\mathsf{E}_k(M)$ picks $r_1, \ldots, r_\lambda \leftarrow \mathbb{Z}_p$. Sets $g_0 := \prod_{i \in [\lambda]} (g_i^{r_i})^{-k_i}$ and returns

$$C := (g_1^{r_1}, \ldots, g_\lambda^{r_\lambda}, g^M \cdot g_0) \in \mathbb{G}^{\lambda+1}.$$

- $\mathsf{D}_k(C)$ parses C as $(x_1, \ldots, x_\lambda, y)$. Computes $\tilde{M} := y \cdot \prod_{i \in [\lambda]} x_i^{k_i}$. Returns 0 if $\tilde{M} = 1$, returns 1 if $\tilde{M} = g$, otherwise returns $\bot$.

The RKA[Φ] Oracle. For the concrete class of RKA functions

$$\Phi := \{\varphi_\Delta : \{0,1\}^\lambda \to \{0,1\}^\lambda, k \mapsto k \oplus \Delta : \Delta \in \{0,1\}^\lambda\}$$

we find an RKA[Φ] oracle $\mathcal{F}_{\mathsf{RKA}[\Phi]}$ for Σ'_{BHHO} as follows: Given a ciphertext $C = (x_1, \ldots, x_\lambda, y)$ and a function φ_Δ it outputs

$$C' := (x_1', \ldots, x_\lambda', y') := (x_1^{(-1)^{\Delta_1}}, \ldots, x_\lambda^{(-1)^{\Delta_\lambda}}, y \cdot \prod_{i \in [\lambda]} x_i^{\Delta_i})$$

To understand this better we assume that C is an honestly generated ciphertext (as it will be in the indistinguishability experiment for $\mathcal{F}_{\mathsf{RKA}[\Phi]}$). Then we have $y = g^M \cdot \prod_{i \in [\lambda]} x_i^{-k_i}$. We observe

$$y' = g^M \cdot \prod_{i \in [\lambda]} x_i^{-k_i} \cdot \prod_{i \in [\lambda]} x_i^{\Delta_i} = g^M \cdot \prod_{i \in [\lambda]} x_i'^{(-1)^{\Delta_i}(-k_i + \Delta_i)} \stackrel{(*)}{=} g^M \cdot \prod_{i \in [\lambda]} x_i'^{-(k_i \oplus \Delta_i)}$$

and $(*)$ since

$$(-1)^{\Delta_i}(-k_i + \Delta_i) = \left\{ \begin{array}{c} -k_i \text{ if } \Delta_i = 0 \\ -(1 - k_i) \text{ if } \Delta_i = 1 \end{array} \right\} = -(k_i \oplus \Delta_i)$$

Therefore C' decrypts to M under key $k \oplus \Delta$.

Lemma 5. $\mathcal{F}_{\mathsf{RKA}[\Phi]}$ *is an* RKA[Φ] *oracle in the sense of Theorem 2.*

Proof. It is easy to see that the distributions of $\mathcal{F}_{\mathsf{RKA}[\Phi]}(\varphi_\Delta, \mathsf{E}_k(M))$ and $\mathsf{E}_{k \oplus \Delta}(M)$ are perfectly indistinguishable (even for someone knowing k and Δ): The x_i' just look like $r_i' = (-1)^{\Delta_i} r_i$ was used as randomness for the ith component (which yields the same distribution) and we have $y' = g^M \cdot \prod_{i \in [\lambda]} (x_i')^{-(k_i \oplus \Delta_i)}$.

The KDM[Ψ'] Oracle. For the class of KDM functions

$$\Psi' := \{\psi_{i,b} : \{0,1\}^\lambda \to \{0,1\}, k \mapsto k_i \oplus b : i \in [\lambda], b \in \{0,1\}\}$$

we find the following KDM[Ψ'] oracle $\mathcal{F}_{\mathsf{KDM}[\Psi']}$ for Σ'_{BHHO}: Given a function $\psi_{i,b}$ and an honestly generated ciphertext of b (the constant part of $\psi_{i,b}$ is b) denoted $C = (x_1, \ldots, x_\lambda, y)$ it outputs

$$C' := (x'_1, \ldots, x'_\lambda, y') := (x_1, \ldots, x_{i-1}, x_i \cdot g^{(-1)^b}, x_{i+1}, \ldots, x_\lambda, y)$$

We check that this ciphertext decrypts to $k_i \oplus b$:

$$y \cdot \prod_{j \in [\lambda]} x'_j{}^{k_j} \overset{(*)}{=} y \cdot \left(\prod_{j \in [\lambda]} x_j{}^{k_j} \right) \cdot g^{(-1)^b \cdot k_i} = g^b \cdot \left(\prod_{j \in [\lambda]} x_j{}^{-k_j} \cdot x_j{}^{k_j} \right) \cdot g^{(-1)^b \cdot k_i} = g^{k_i \oplus b}$$

(*) since $x'_i = x_i \cdot g^{(-1)^b}$ and $x'_j = x_j$ for $j \in [\lambda] \setminus \{i\}$.

Lemma 6. $\mathcal{F}_{\mathsf{KDM}[\Psi']}$ *is a* KDM[Ψ'] *oracle in the sense of Theorem 3.*

Proof. We show that the distributions of $\mathcal{F}_{\mathsf{KDM}[\Psi']}(\psi_{i,b}, \mathsf{E}_k(b))$ and $\mathsf{E}_k(\psi_{i,b}(k))$ are perfectly indistinguishable. First, we observe that $x_i = g_i^{r_i}$ and $g = g_i^\alpha$ for $\alpha := \log_{g_i}(g)$, i.e., $x'_i = g^{r_i + (-1)^b \cdot \alpha}$. Furthermore we have $y = g^b \cdot \prod_{j \in [\lambda]} x_j^{-k_j} = g^b \cdot \prod_{j \in [\lambda]} x_j^{-k_j} g^{-(-1)^b \cdot k_i} g^{(-1)^b \cdot k_i} = g^{b + (-1)^b} \cdot \prod_{j \in [\lambda]} x'_j{}^{-k_j}$. Hence the output of the oracle looks like a normal encryption of $k_i \oplus b$ where $r_i + (-1)^b \cdot \alpha$ was used as randomness in the ith component.

Lemma 7. *The SKE scheme* Σ'_{BHHO} *is IND-CPA secure if DDH is hard over the underlying group* $\mathbb{G}$.

Proof. Intuitively, we first use the hardness of DDH over $\mathbb{G}$ to collapse the randomness used by the encryption oracle to one random exponent per ciphertext, so instead of $r_1, \ldots, r_\lambda$ all generators are taken to the same random exponent r. This modified scheme is the 'basic' version of [25] with a smaller message space. We can then simply reduce security to the IND-CPA security of Boneh et al's scheme.

More concretely, we prove the lemma with the following sequence of games.

Game 0. In Game 0 $\mathcal{A}$ plays the original IND-CPA experiment.

Game 1 to Game $\lambda - 1$ form a hybrid argument to collapse the randomness used by the encryption oracle. In hybrid i ($i \in [\lambda - 1]$) we pick the same randomness for the first $i + 1$ components of the ciphertext. I.e., the format of a ciphertext output by the encryption oracle in game i is

$$\left(g_1^r, \ldots, g_{i+1}^r, g_{i+2}^{r_{i+2}}, \ldots, g_\lambda^{r_\lambda}, g^M \cdot \left(\prod_{i \in [i+1]} g_i^{-rk_i} \right) \left(\prod_{i \in [\lambda] \setminus [i+1]} g_i^{-r_i k_i} \right) \right)$$

Analysis. Each of the game hops above is indistinguishable due to the hardness of DDH over $\mathbb{G}$. The simulation for a hop from Game $i-1$ to Game i ($i \in [\lambda-1]$) works as follows: The simulator $\mathcal{S}$ gets a DDH challenge $(g, X := g^x, Y := g^y, Z := g^{xy/z})$. For $j \in [\lambda] \setminus \{i+1\}$ it picks $\alpha_j \leftarrow \mathbb{Z}_p$, sets $g_j := g^{\alpha_j}$ and $g_{i+1} := X$. Subsequently it picks a key $k \leftarrow \{0,1\}^\lambda$ and sends the public parameters $\pi := (\mathbb{G}, g, g_1, \ldots, g_\lambda)$ to $\mathcal{A}$. If $\mathcal{A}$ requests an encryption of message M, $\mathcal{S}$ picks randomness $r, r_{i+2}, \ldots, r_\lambda, a, b \leftarrow \mathbb{Z}_p$ and sets $\hat{Y} := g^a \cdot Y^b$ and $\hat{Z} := X^a \cdot Z^b$ to re-randomize the DDH challenge. Finally, $\mathcal{S}$ sends

$$\left(\hat{Y}^{r\alpha_1}, \ldots, \hat{Y}^{r\alpha_i}, \hat{Z}^r, g_{i+2}^{r_{i+2}}, \ldots, g^M \cdot g_0 \right)$$

to the adversary where g_0 is computed as usual ($\mathcal{S}$ knows k). If $Z = g^z$, the output of $\mathcal{S}$ looks like that of game $i-1$, otherwise (for $Z = g^{xy}$) it looks like that of game i. Any PPT distinguisher between those games with non-negligible advantage can thus be used to break DDH.

Finally, only one fresh random exponent is used for each ciphertext in game $\lambda - 1$. The output now looks like that of the BHHO (public key) cryptosystem with message space $\{g^0, g^1\}$.

In **Game** λ, we replace the message with 0. The indistinguishability of game $\lambda - 1$ and game λ can be reduced to the IND-CPA security of Boneh et al's original scheme in a straightforward way (using the generators from the public key as public parameters). Hence IND-CPA security of Σ'_{BHHO} follows.

The Full Scheme Σ_{BHHO}. Finally, we assemble the SKE scheme Σ_{BHHO} from λ instances of Σ'_{BHHO} that use the same public parameters π and the same key k. A ciphertext under Σ_{BHHO} is a matrix from $\mathbb{G}^{\lambda \times (\lambda+1)}$ where each row is an instance of Σ'_{BHHO} (using π and key k). To encrypt a message $M \in \{0,1\}^\lambda$ under key k we encrypt M_i in row i (while picking fresh randomness r_i, $i \in [\lambda]$ for each row). Decryption also works row-wise.

For the $\mathsf{RKA}[\Phi]$ oracle we apply $\mathcal{F}_{\mathsf{RKA}[\Phi]}$ to each row. The class of KDM functions Ψ' changes to

$$\Psi := \{ \psi_{\mathbf{i}, \Delta} : \{0,1\}^\lambda \to \{0,1\}^\lambda, k \mapsto (k_{\mathbf{i}_1} \oplus \Delta_1, \ldots, k_{\mathbf{i}_\lambda} \oplus \Delta_\lambda) : \mathbf{i} \in [\lambda]^\lambda, \Delta \in \{0,1\}^\lambda \}$$

I.e., each bit of the message can be an arbitrarily picked key bit. For the $\mathsf{KDM}[\Psi]$ oracle provided with function $\psi_{\mathbf{i}}$, we apply $\mathcal{F}_{\mathsf{KDM}[\Psi']}$ with function $\psi_{\mathbf{i}_j} \in \Psi'$ to the jth row of the ciphertext where Ψ' is the class of KDM functions for Σ'_{BHHO}. Since the oracles work row-wise it is easy to check that the indistinguishability results from Theorem 5 and Theorem 5 carry over to Σ_{BHHO}. Analogously for the IND-CPA security of Σ_{BHHO}. Finally, by Theorem 4, we get

Theorem 8. *The SKE scheme Σ_{BHHO} is $\mathsf{RKA\text{-}KDM}[\Phi, \Psi]$ secure (for Φ and Ψ as defined above in this section) if DDH is hard over the underlying group $\mathbb{G}$.*

3.2   Applebaum et al. [5]

In this section, we present a secret-key version of the PKE scheme of Applebaum et al. [5] and prove it RKA-KDM secure. For compatibility with Applebaum's application, however, we slightly change the space of secret keys from $\mathbb{Z}_p^m$ to $\{0,1\}^m$. Our RKA and KDM oracles allow encryptions under keys $k \oplus \Delta$ (for arbitrary $\Delta \in \{0,1\}^m$) of arbitrary components of the secret key. Security is based on the LWE assumption.

For ease of exposition, we do not detail the choices of the following parameters – these can occur as in [5] (with adaptations as in [2] due to the different choice of secret key). Let q be a polynomial in the security parameter λ, and let $m > n$ be integers (that may also depend on λ). By χ, we denote a (discretized Gaussian) error distribution with suitable parameters over $\mathbb{Z}_q$.

LWE Assumption. Let $s \in \mathbb{Z}_q^n$ be uniformly chosen. Let $\mathsf{LWE_s}$ be the oracle that (on trivial input) returns $(\mathbf{a}, \langle \mathbf{a}; \mathbf{s} \rangle + x) \in \mathbb{Z}_q^n \times \mathbb{Z}_q$ for freshly chosen $\mathbf{a} \leftarrow \mathbb{Z}_q^n$ and $x \leftarrow \chi$. Let RND be the oracle that returns a freshly and independently chosen $(\mathbf{a}, \mathbf{b}) \leftarrow \mathbb{Z}_q^n \times \mathbb{Z}_q$. The LWE assumption states that oracle access to $\mathsf{LWE_s}$ is computationally indistinguishable from oracle access to RND.

Applebaum et al. [5] show that the LWE assumption over $\mathbb{Z}_q = \mathbb{Z}_{p^2}$ and with $\mathbf{s} \leftarrow \mathbb{Z}_p^n$ is equivalent to the LWE assumption as above (for $q = p$). Furthermore, Akavia et al. [2] show that the LWE assumption with $\mathbf{s} \leftarrow \{0,1\}^n$ is implied by the LWE assumption as above (for different parameters of n, m). In the following, we will consider $q = p^2$ and $\mathbf{s} \in \{0,1\}^n$. Furthermore, for $x \in \mathbb{R}$, we write $\lceil x \rfloor_p := \lceil x + 1/2 \rceil \bmod p$ for the nearest integer to x modulo p.

The SKE Scheme Σ'_{ACPS}. The scheme Σ'_{ACPS} (with $M \in \mathbb{Z}_p$) is defined as follows:

- $\mathsf{Pg}(1^\lambda)$ returns the empty bitstring.
- $\mathsf{Kg}(\pi)$ returns a random bitstring $k := \mathbf{s} \leftarrow \{0,1\}^m$.
- $\mathsf{E}_k(M)$ picks $\mathbf{A} \leftarrow \mathbb{Z}_q^{n \times m}$ and $\mathbf{r}, \mathbf{x} \leftarrow \chi^m$, and returns

$$C := (\mathbf{A} \cdot \mathbf{r}, -(\mathbf{s}^T \cdot \mathbf{A} + \mathbf{x}^T) \cdot \mathbf{r} + p \cdot M) = (\mathbf{A} \cdot \mathbf{r}, -\mathbf{s}^T \cdot \mathbf{A} \cdot \mathbf{r} - \langle \mathbf{x}; \mathbf{r} \rangle + p \cdot M) \in \mathbb{Z}_q^m \times \mathbb{Z}_q$$

- $\mathsf{D}_k(C)$ parses $C =: (\mathbf{y}, z)$ and computes and returns $M := \lceil (\langle \mathbf{s}; \mathbf{y} \rangle + z)/p \rfloor_p$.

Compared to the PKE scheme of [5], we choose $\mathbf{s}$ slightly differently, and also choose different $\mathbf{A}, \mathbf{x}$ upon each encryption. We note that correctness holds only with overwhelming probability over the choice of $\mathbf{r}$ and $\mathbf{x}$. In particular, $|\langle \mathbf{x}; \mathbf{r} \rangle| < p/2$ with overwhelming probability.

The RKA[Φ] Oracle. For the concrete class of RKA functions

$$\Phi := \{\varphi_\Delta : \{0,1\}^m \to \{0,1\}^m, k \mapsto k \oplus \Delta : \Delta \in \{0,1\}^m\},$$

we find an RKA[Φ] oracle $\mathcal{F}_{\mathsf{RKA}[\Phi]}$ for Σ'_{ACPS} as follows: Given a ciphertext $C = (\mathbf{y}, z)$ and a function φ_Δ, it outputs

$$C' := (\mathbf{y}', z') \quad \text{with} \quad \mathbf{y}'_i = (-1)^{\Delta_i} \mathbf{y}_i \quad \text{and} \quad z' = z + \sum_{i \in [m]} \Delta_i \mathbf{y}_i$$

As with the BHHO scheme, a quick calculation shows that C' is a perfectly distributed ciphertext of M under $k \oplus \Delta$. Thus:

Lemma 9. $\mathcal{F}_{\mathsf{RKA}[\Phi]}$ is an RKA[Φ] oracle in the sense of Theorem 2.

The KDM[Ψ'] Oracle. For the class of KDM functions

$$\Psi' := \{\psi_{i,b} : \{0,1\}^\lambda \to \{0,1\}, k \mapsto k_i \oplus b : i \in [\lambda], b \in \{0,1\}\}$$

and following [5], we find the following KDM[Ψ'] oracle $\mathcal{F}_{\mathsf{KDM}[\Psi']}$ for Σ'_{ACPS}: Given a function $\psi_{i,b}$ and an honestly generated ciphertext $C = (\mathbf{y}, z)$ of $M = b$, it outputs

$$C' := \left(\mathbf{y} + \left((-1)^b p\right) \mathbf{e}_i, z\right) \qquad \text{for the } i\text{-th unit vector } \mathbf{e}_i.$$

We check that this ciphertext decrypts to $k_i \oplus b$:

$$\mathsf{D}_k(C') = \left\lceil \left(\langle \mathbf{s}; \mathbf{y} + \left((-1)^b p\right) \mathbf{e}_i \rangle + z\right) / p \right\rfloor_p = \left\lceil \left(\langle \mathbf{s}; \mathbf{y} \rangle + \left((-1)^b p\right) \mathbf{s}_i + z\right) / p \right\rfloor_p$$

$$= \left\lceil \left(\mathbf{s}^T \mathbf{Ar} + \left((-1)^b p\right) \mathbf{s}_i + z\right) / p \right\rfloor_p = \left\lceil \left(\left((-1)^b p\right) \mathbf{s}_i - \langle \mathbf{x}; \mathbf{r} \rangle + pb\right) / p \right\rfloor_p, = \mathbf{s}_i \oplus b.$$

In fact, it is easy to see that ciphertexts C' as produced by $\mathcal{F}_{\mathsf{KDM}[\Psi']}$ are perfectly distributed ciphertexts of $\mathbf{s}_i \oplus b$. We get:

Lemma 10. $\mathcal{F}_{\mathsf{KDM}[\Psi']}$ *is a* KDM[Ψ'] *oracle in the sense of Theorem 3.*

Lemma 11. *The SKE scheme Σ'_{ACPS} is* IND-CPA *secure if the LWE assumption holds for the respective parameters.*

A sketch of the proof is contained in the full version of this paper [24].

The Full Scheme Σ_{ACPS}. As in the BHHO setting, we can construct the full scheme Σ_{ACPS} with message space $\mathbb{Z}_p^m$ from m instances of Σ'_{ACPS} that use the same public parameters and key in a straightforward manner.

Likewise, by transferring Theorem 9, Theorem 10 and Theorem 11 from Σ'_{ACPS} to Σ_{ACPS} and by Theorem 4, we get

Theorem 12. *The SKE scheme Σ_{ACPS} is* RKA-KDM[Φ, Ψ] *secure (for Φ as defined above in this section and Ψ from the full BHHO scheme) if the LWE assumption holds for the respective parameters.*

3.3   Brakerski-Goldwasser [26]

In this section we consider the encryption scheme of Brakerski and Goldwasser [26], modified to the symmetric setting. The KDM security of the original (public-key) scheme relies on the hardness of deciding quadratic residuosity in the group $\mathbb{Z}_N^*$, for Blum integer $N = p \cdot q$. To construct our SKE scheme Σ_{BG} resilient against related key attacks, we additionally have to stipulate that DDH is hard over the subgroup of quadratic residues QR_N. We achieve security against the same class of KDM functions as for Σ_{BHHO} from Section 3.1.

QR Assumption. Let N be a Blum integer of bitlength λ. With $\mathbb{Z}_N^*[+1]$ we denote the set of elements in $\mathbb{Z}_N^*$ with Jacobi symbol $+1$ and with $\mathsf{QR}_N := \{x^2 \bmod N : x \in \mathbb{Z}_N^*\}$ the set of Quadratic Residues modulo N. Then we say that the Quadratic Residuosity (QR) assumption holds in $\mathbb{Z}_N^*$ if

$$|\Pr[\mathcal{A}(N, x) = 1 : x \leftarrow \mathbb{Z}_N^*[+1]] - \Pr[\mathcal{A}(N, x) = 1 : x \leftarrow \mathsf{QR}_N]|$$

is negligible for all PPT adversaries $\mathcal{A}$.

The SKE Scheme Σ'_{BG}. We define the scheme for messages $M \in \{0, 1\}$.

- $\mathsf{Pg}(1^\lambda)$ picks a random Blum integer N of length $\ell(\lambda)$.[4] Then samples quadratic residues $g_1, \ldots, g_\lambda \leftarrow \mathsf{QR}_N$ and returns $\pi := (N, g_1, \ldots, g_\lambda)$.
- $\mathsf{Kg}(\pi)$ returns a random bitstring $k \leftarrow \{0, 1\}^\lambda$.
- $\mathsf{E}_k(M)$ picks $r_1, \ldots, r_\lambda \leftarrow [N^2]$, computes $g_0 := \prod_{i \in [\lambda]} (g_i^{r_i})^{-k_i}$ and outputs

$$C := (g_1^{r_1}, \ldots, g_\lambda^{r_\lambda}, (-1)^M \cdot g_0) \in \mathbb{Z}_N^{\lambda+1}$$

- $\mathsf{D}_k(C)$ parses C as $(x_1, \ldots, x_\lambda, y)$. Computes $\tilde{M} := y \cdot \prod_{i \in [\lambda]} x_i^{k_i}$. Returns 0 if $\tilde{M} = 1$, returns 1 if $\tilde{M} = -1$, otherwise returns $\perp$.

The RKA[Φ] Oracle. The RKA[Φ] oracle $\mathcal{F}_{\mathsf{RKA}[\Phi]}$ for Σ'_{BG} works exactly like the RKA[Φ] for Σ'_{BHHO} from Section 3.1, i.e., Φ allows for transformations of the secret key under XOR. Analogously to Theorem 5 we have

Lemma 13. $\mathcal{F}_{\mathsf{RKA}[\Phi]}$ *is an* RKA[Φ] *oracle for* Σ'_{BG} *in the sense of Theorem 2.*

The KDM[Ψ'] Oracle. Analogously to Σ'_{BHHO} we define

$$\Psi' := \{\psi_{i,b} : \{0, 1\}^\lambda \to \{0, 1\}, k \mapsto k_i \oplus b : i \in [\lambda], b \in \{0, 1\}\}$$

Given a function $\psi_{i,b}$ and a ciphertext $C = (x_1, \ldots, x_\lambda, y)$, the KDM[$\Psi'$] oracle $\mathcal{F}_{\mathsf{KDM}[\Psi']}$ for Σ'_{BG} simply returns

$$C' := (x'_1, \ldots, x'_\lambda, y') := (x_1, \ldots, x_{i-1}, (-1) \cdot x_i, x_{i+1}, \ldots, x_\lambda, y)$$

We check that this decrypts to $k_i \oplus b$ if $\mathcal{F}_{\mathsf{KDM}[\Psi']}$ is given an honestly generated ciphertext of b (the constant part of $\psi_{i,b}$), i.e., $y = (-1)^b \cdot \prod_{j \in [\lambda]} x_j^{-k_j}$:

$$\mathsf{D}_k(C') = y' \cdot \prod_{j \in [\lambda]} x'^{k_j}_j \overset{(*)}{=} y \cdot (-1)^{k_i} \cdot \prod_{j \in [\lambda]} x_j^{k_j} = (-1)^{b+k_i} \cdot \prod_{j \in [\lambda]} x_j^{-k_j} \cdot x_j^{k_j} = (-1)^{k_i \oplus b}$$

$(*)$ since $x'_i = (-1) \cdot x_i$ and $x'_j = x_j$ for $j \in [\lambda] \setminus \{i\}$.

Lemma 14. $\mathcal{F}_{\mathsf{KDM}[\Psi']}$ *is a* KDM[Ψ'] *oracle for* Σ'_{BG} *in the sense of Theorem 3 if QR is hard in the underlying group* $\mathbb{Z}_N^*$.

Proof. To show the indistinguishability of $\mathcal{F}_{\mathsf{KDM}[\Psi']}$'s output we use the interactive vector game (IV) from [26], Section 5. In the interactive λ-vector game the experiment picks a Blum integer N, a quadratic residues $g_1, \ldots, g_\lambda \leftarrow \mathsf{QR}_N$ and a bit $b \leftarrow \{0, 1\}$ and sends $N, g_1, \ldots, g_\lambda$ to a PPT adversary $\mathcal{A}$ that has to guess b. It then provides $\mathcal{A}$ with an oracle that, given a query $\mathbf{a} \in \{0, 1\}^\lambda$, returns

---

[4] We use $\ell(\lambda)$ here since the IND-CPA security of Brakerski and Goldwasser's original scheme requires that N is substantially shorter than the number of components/key length λ, e.g., $\ell(\lambda) = \lambda/2$. We refer to [26], Theorem 6.1 for details.

$((-1)^{\mathbf{a}_1} g_1^r, \ldots, (-1)^{\mathbf{a}_\lambda} g_\lambda^r)$ if $b = 0$ and $(g_1^r, \ldots, g_\lambda^r)$ if $b = 1$ for fresh randomness r. [26] show that $\mathcal{A}$'s advantage is negligible if the QR assumption holds in $\mathbb{Z}_N^*$.

Let $\mathcal{D}$ be a PPT algorithm to distinguish $\mathcal{F}_{\mathsf{KDM}[\Psi']}(\psi, \mathsf{E}_k(M))$ from $\mathsf{E}_k(\psi(k))$ in the sense of Theorem 3. We construct an adversary $\mathcal{S}$ on the interactive 1-vector game that utilizes $\mathcal{D}$: First, $\mathcal{S}$ sets π to the parameters $(N, g_1, \ldots, g_\lambda)$ received from the interactive λ-vector game, samples a key $k \leftarrow \{0,1\}^\lambda$ and then sends π and k to $\mathcal{D}$. For each query $\psi_{i,b}$ received from $\mathcal{D}$, $\mathcal{S}$ picks randomness $r_1, \ldots, r_{i-1}, r_{i+1}, \ldots, r_\lambda \leftarrow [N^2]$ and queries the interactive λ-vector game with vector $\mathbf{a} \in \{0,1\}^\lambda$ where $\mathbf{a}_i := 1$ and $\mathbf{a}_j := 0$ for $j \neq i$. $\mathcal{S}$ gets a response $(x_1, \ldots, x_\lambda)$ and sets $x_i' := x_i$ and $x_j' := x_j^{r_j}$ for $j \neq r$. It then sends $(x_1', \ldots, x_\lambda', (-1)^b \cdot \prod_{j \in [\lambda]} x_j'^{-k_j})$ to $\mathcal{D}$. It is easy to check that this equals $\mathcal{F}_{\mathsf{KDM}[\Psi']}(\psi_{i,b}, \mathsf{E}_k(b; \hat{r}))$ if the bit picked by the λ-vector game is 0, or $\mathsf{E}_k(\psi(k); \hat{r})$ otherwise (where randomness $\hat{r} := (rr_1, \ldots, r_{i-1}, r, r_{i+1}, \ldots, rr_\lambda)$).

The advantage of $\mathcal{S}$ is the advantage of $\mathcal{D}$ at the same asymptotic time complexity. Thus, if QR holds in $\mathbb{Z}_N^*$, no such adversary $\mathcal{D}$ with non-negligible advantage can exist.

Lemma 15. *The SKE scheme Σ_{BG}' is IND-CPA secure if QR is hard over the group $\mathbb{Z}_N^*$ and DDH is hard over the subgroup of quadratic residues QR_N.*

Proof. This proof is completely analogous to the IND-CPA proof for Σ_{BHHO}' (see Theorem 7). We first collapse the randomness to one random exponent per ciphertext. For this we rely on the hardness of DDH over QR_N. Subsequently we utilize the IND-CPA security of Brakerski and Goldwasser's original scheme to conclude the proof.

The Full Scheme Σ_{BG}. Analogously to the setting for BHHO (Section 3.1), we can canonically construct the full scheme Σ_{BG} for message space $\{0,1\}^\lambda$ from λ instances of Σ_{BG}' using the same public parameters and the same key. The class of RKA functions remains the same, while the class of KDM functions automatically extends from Ψ' to

$$\Psi := \{\psi_{\mathbf{i},M} : \{0,1\}^\lambda \to \{0,1\}^\lambda, k \mapsto (k_{\mathbf{i}_1} \oplus \Delta_1, \ldots, k_{\mathbf{i}_\lambda} \oplus \Delta_\lambda) : \mathbf{i} \in [\lambda]^\lambda, \Delta \in \{0,1\}^\lambda\}$$

Since we can canonically transfer Theorem 13, Theorem 14 and Theorem 15 from Σ_{BG}' to Σ_{BG} we get the final result of this section by Theorem 4.

Theorem 16. *The SKE scheme Σ_{BG} is $\mathsf{RKA\text{-}KDM}[\Phi, \Psi]$ secure (for Φ and Ψ as defined above in this section) if QR is hard in the underlying group $\mathbb{Z}_N^*$ and DDH is hard over the subgroup of quadratic residues QR_N.*

3.4   Bellare et al. [14]

Since Applebaum's work on KDM amplification [4], it is known that projection-KDM security implies bounded-KDM security. Projection-KDM security allows for KDM functions where each output bit depends only on one input bit (key bit). Bounded-KDM security means that the class of KDM functions is the set of all functions that can be represented by a circuit of bounded size L. We refer to this function class as $\Psi_{bnd(L)}$ from now on. To our knowledge, currently the most efficient way to construct a bounded-KDM secure scheme from a projection-KDM secure one is the approach of Bellare, Hoang, and Rogaway [14] (henceforth BHR). In this section we observe that their construction also maintains RKA security in our sense. Thus, we can plug all of our projection-KDM secure schemes (i.e., Σ_{BG}, Σ_{ACPS} and Σ_{BHHO}) into their framework to get RKA-bounded-KDM secure schemes. Obviously, this result holds for any projection-KDM secure scheme that is RKA secure (with a suitable oracle in our sense).

(Projective) Garbling Schemes. What follows is a quick introduction to garbling schemes established by [14]. A *garbling scheme* is a tuple of algorithms $(GC_{garble}, GC_{encode}, GC_{decode}, GC_{eval})$.[5] The algorithm GC_{garble} is probabilistic while the remaining algorithms are deterministic. Given an encoding of the security parameter and a function f, $GC_{garble}(1^\lambda, f)$ outputs the description of a garbled circuit (F, e, d). Here, F is a function mapping garbled inputs to garbled outputs. E.g., F could be a circuit in terms of gates and wires together with a garbled table for each gate. The outputs e and d contain information to encode and decode the input and output of F respectively. We say that a garbling scheme is *correct* if $GC_{decode}(d, GC_{eval}(F, GC_{encode}(M, e))) = f(M)$ for all functions f (from a certain class), inputs $M \in \{0,1\}^\lambda$ and descriptions $(F, e, d) \leftarrow GC_{garble}(1^\lambda, f)$ of garbled circuits for f.

For our application we need so-called *projective* garbling schemes. Basically, a garbling scheme is *projective* if for all $\mathbf{x} := GC_{encode}(e, M)$ and $\mathbf{x}' := GC_{encode}(e, M')$, we have $|\mathbf{x}_i| = |\mathbf{x}'_i|$ for $i \in [\lambda]$ and $\mathbf{x}_i = \mathbf{x}'_i$ for $i \in [\lambda]$ with $M_i = M'_i$ (see [15] for a rigorous definition). One well-known way to construct a projective garbling scheme is to assign a pair of keys to each wire corresponding to low and high voltage (0/1) respectively. Then e is a tuple of pairs of keys and $GC_{encode}(M, e)$ picks the keys from e corresponding to the bits of M.

Furthermore, we say that a garbling scheme is *privacy preserving* if for any two (adversarially chosen) functions f_0, f_1 with the same circuit size and inputs x_0, x_1 of same length with $f_0(x_0) = f_1(x_1)$, no adversary can distinguish $(F_0, GC_{encode}(e_0, x_0), d_0)$ from $(F_1, GC_{encode}(e_1, x_1), d_1)$ (where (F_b, e_b, d_b) $\leftarrow GC_{garble}(1^\lambda, f_b), b \in \{0,1\}$). We refer to [15] for a more detailed definition.

The Construction of BHR. The construction creates a symmetric KDM$[\Psi_{bnd(L)}]$-secure encryption scheme $\Sigma_{BHR} = (Pg, Kg, E, D)$ from any projection-KDM-secure encryption scheme $\Sigma' = (Pg', Kg', E', D')$ and any privacy preserving projective garbling scheme $(GC_{garble}, GC_{encode}, GC_{decode}, GC_{eval})$ as follows.

---

[5] For simplicity we omit the additional evaluation function from [14] and restrict to inputs of length λ here.

- $\mathsf{Pg}(1^\lambda)$ returns $\mathsf{Pg}'(1^\lambda)$.
- $\mathsf{Kg}(\pi)$ returns $\mathsf{Kg}'(\pi)$.
- $\mathsf{E}_k(M)$ first generates a garbled circuit for the identity function ID_λ on bit-strings of length λ: $(F, e, d) \leftarrow \mathsf{GC}_{\mathsf{garble}}(1^\lambda, \mathsf{ID}_\lambda)$. It then encodes the message $\mathbf{x} := \mathsf{GC}_{\mathsf{encode}}(e, M)$ (w.l.o.g. $\mathbf{x} \in \{0,1\}^{\lambda \times \lambda}$). Finally, it outputs the ciphertext $C := (F, d, \mathsf{E}'_k(\mathbf{x}_i))$.
- $\mathsf{D}_k((F, d, (\mathbf{c}_i)_{i \in [\lambda]}))$ first decrypts the keys for the input wires $\mathbf{x}_i := \mathsf{D}'_k(\mathbf{c}_i)$ and then evaluates the circuit to compute and output the message $M := \mathsf{GC}_{\mathsf{decode}}(d, \mathsf{GC}_{\mathsf{eval}}(F, \mathbf{x}))$.

An RKA[Φ] oracle for Σ_{BHR}. Given an RKA[Φ] oracle $\mathcal{F}'_{\mathsf{RKA}[\Phi]}$ for Σ', we can construct an RKA[Φ] oracle $\mathcal{F}_{\mathsf{RKA}[\Phi]}$ for Σ_{BHR} (note that we maintain the class of RKA functions). Let $C = (F, d, (\mathbf{c}_i)_{i \in [\lambda]})$ be an honestly generated ciphertext and $\varphi \in \Phi$ be an RKA function. We define $\mathcal{F}_{\mathsf{RKA}[\Phi]}(C) := (F, d, (\mathcal{F}'_{\mathsf{RKA}[\Phi]}(\mathbf{c}_i))_{i \in [\lambda]})$. A straightforward hybrid argument over the $\mathbf{c}_i$, based on the indistinguishability of $\mathcal{F}'_{\mathsf{RKA}[\Phi]}$, shows the indistinguishability of $\mathcal{F}_{\mathsf{RKA}[\Phi]}(C)$.

Theorem 17. *Let Σ' be a RKA-KDM[Φ, Ψ]-secure SKE scheme with an indistinguishable RKA[Φ] oracle $\mathcal{F}_{\mathsf{RKA}[\Phi]}$. If Ψ covers projections, then Σ_{BHR} is an RKA-KDM[$\Phi, \Psi_{\mathsf{bnd}(L)}$]-secure SKE for any arbitrary but fixed bound L.*

Proof. We only sketch the proof here, which is straightforward and based on a short sequence of games. Our first game is the original RKA-KDM[Φ, Ψ] experiment (see Theorem 1). In the next game, we no longer use the secret key itself to answer the RKA part of queries. More concretely, for a given RKA-KDM query (φ, ψ), we compute $C \leftarrow \mathsf{E}_k(\psi(k))$ and output $\mathcal{F}_{\mathsf{RKA}[\Phi]}(\varphi, C)$ instead of directly returning $\mathsf{E}_{\varphi(k)}(\psi(k))$. The indistinguishability of this game hop follows directly from the indistinguishability of RKA[Φ]. Finally, we can simply follow the strategy from [15], Theorem 15, to compute C. This strategy requires that the garbling scheme used to construct Σ_{BHR} is privacy preserving and projective.

Acknowledgements. The authors would like to thank Martijn Stam for useful discussions and Rafael Dowsley for kindling our interest in the topic. Furthermore, we would like to thank Viet Tung Hoang for pointing out a more efficient and less complicated way to achieve bounded-KDM security (based on [14]) than the one we first decided on (based on [6]).

References

[1] Adão, P., Bana, G., Herzog, J.C., Scedrov, A.: Soundness of Formal Encryption in the Presence of Key-Cycles. In: de Capitani di Vimercati, S., Syverson, P.F., Gollmann, D. (eds.) ESORICS 2005. LNCS, vol. 3679, pp. 374–396. Springer, Heidelberg (2005)

[2] Akavia, A., Goldwasser, S., Vaikuntanathan, V.: Simultaneous Hardcore Bits and Cryptography against Memory Attacks. In: Reingold, O. (ed.) TCC 2009. LNCS, vol. 5444, pp. 474–495. Springer, Heidelberg (2009)

[3] Applebaum, B.: Garbling XOR gates "For free" in the standard model. In: Sahai, A. (ed.) TCC 2013. LNCS, vol. 7785, pp. 162–181. Springer, Heidelberg (2013)

[4] Applebaum, B.: Key-Dependent Message Security: Generic Amplification and Completeness. In: Paterson, K.G. (ed.) EUROCRYPT 2011. LNCS, vol. 6632, pp. 527–546. Springer, Heidelberg (2011)

[5] Applebaum, B., Cash, D., Peikert, C., Sahai, A.: Fast Cryptographic Primitives and Circular-Secure Encryption based on Hard Learning Problems. In: Halevi, S. (ed.) CRYPTO 2009. LNCS, vol. 5677, pp. 595–618. Springer, Heidelberg (2009)

[6] Barak, B., Haitner, I., Hofheinz, D., Ishai, Y.: Bounded Key-Dependent Message Security. In: Gilbert, H. (ed.) EUROCRYPT 2010. LNCS, vol. 6110, pp. 423–444. Springer, Heidelberg (2010)

[7] Bellare, M., Cash, D.: Pseudorandom Functions and Permutations Provably Secure against Related-Key Attacks. In: Rabin, T. (ed.) CRYPTO 2010. LNCS, vol. 6223, pp. 666–684. Springer, Heidelberg (2010)

[8] Bellare, M., Keelveedhi, S.: Authenticated and Misuse-Resistant Encryption of Key-Dependent Data. In: Rogaway, P. (ed.) CRYPTO 2011. LNCS, vol. 6841, pp. 610–629. Springer, Heidelberg (2011)

[9] Bellare, M., Kohno, T.: A Theoretical Treatment of Related-Key Attacks: RKA-PRPs, RKA-PRFs, and Applications. In: Biham, E. (ed.) EUROCRYPT 2003. LNCS, vol. 2656, pp. 491–506. Springer, Heidelberg (2003)

[10] Bellare, M., Brakerski, Z., Naor, M., Ristenpart, T., Segev, G., Shacham, H., Yilek, S.: Hedged Public-Key Encryption: How to Protect against Bad Randomness. In: Matsui, M. (ed.) ASIACRYPT 2009. LNCS, vol. 5912, pp. 232–249. Springer, Heidelberg (2009)

[11] Bellare, M., Hofheinz, D., Yilek, S.: Possibility and Impossibility Results for Encryption and Commitment Secure under Selective Opening. In: Joux, A. (ed.) EUROCRYPT 2009. LNCS, vol. 5479, pp. 1–35. Springer, Heidelberg (2009)

[12] Bellare, M., Cash, D., Keelveedhi, S.: Ciphers that Securely Encipher their own Keys. In: ACM Conference on Computer and Communications Security, pp. 423–432 (2011)

[13] Bellare, M., Cash, D., Miller, R.: Cryptography Secure against Related-Key Attacks and Tampering. In: Lee, D.H., Wang, X. (eds.) ASIACRYPT 2011. LNCS, vol. 7073, pp. 486–503. Springer, Heidelberg (2011)

[14] Bellare, M., Hoang, V.T., Rogaway, P.: Foundations of garbled circuits. In: Proceedings of the 2012 ACM Conference on Computer and Communications Security, pp. 784–796. ACM (2012)

[15] Bellare, M., Hoang, V.T., Rogaway, P.: Foundations of garbled circuits. Cryptology ePrint Archive, Report 2012/265 (2012), http://eprint.iacr.org/

[16] Biham, E.: New types of Cryptoanalytic Attacks using Related Keys. In: Helleseth, T. (ed.) EUROCRYPT 1993. LNCS, vol. 765, pp. 398–409. Springer, Heidelberg (1994)

[17] Biham, E., Dunkelman, O., Keller, N.: A Related-Key Rectangle Attack on the Full KASUMI. In: Roy, B. (ed.) ASIACRYPT 2005. LNCS, vol. 3788, pp. 443–461. Springer, Heidelberg (2005)

[18] Biham, E., Dunkelman, O., Keller, N.: Related-Key Impossible Differential Attacks on 8-Round AES-192. In: Pointcheval, D. (ed.) CT-RSA 2006. LNCS, vol. 3860, pp. 21–33. Springer, Heidelberg (2006)

[19] Biham, E., Dunkelman, O., Keller, N.: A Simple Related-Key Attack on the Full SHACAL-1. In: Abe, M. (ed.) CT-RSA 2007. LNCS, vol. 4377, pp. 20–30. Springer, Heidelberg (2006)

[20] Biryukov, A., Khovratovich, D.: Related-Key Cryptanalysis of the Full AES-192 and AES-256. In: Matsui, M. (ed.) ASIACRYPT 2009. LNCS, vol. 5912, pp. 1–18. Springer, Heidelberg (2009)

[21] Biryukov, A., Khovratovich, D., Nikolić, I.: Distinguisher and Related-Key Attack on the Full AES-256. In: Halevi, S. (ed.) CRYPTO 2009. LNCS, vol. 5677, pp. 231–249. Springer, Heidelberg (2009)

[22] Biryukov, A., Dunkelman, O., Keller, N., Khovratovich, D., Shamir, A.: Key Recovery Attacks of Practical Complexity on AES-256 Variants with up to 10 Rounds. In: Gilbert, H. (ed.) EUROCRYPT 2010. LNCS, vol. 6110, pp. 299–319. Springer, Heidelberg (2010)

[23] Black, J., Rogaway, P., Shrimpton, T.: Encryption-Scheme Security in the Presence of Key-Dependent Messages. In: Nyberg, K., Heys, H.M. (eds.) SAC 2002. LNCS, vol. 2595, pp. 62–75. Springer, Heidelberg (2003)

[24] Böhl, F., Davies, G.T., Hofheinz, D.: Encryption schemes secure under related-key and key-dependent message attacks. IACR Cryptology ePrint Archive 653 (2013)

[25] Boneh, D., Halevi, S., Hamburg, M., Ostrovsky, R.: Circular-secure encryption from Decision Diffie-Hellman. In: Wagner, D. (ed.) CRYPTO 2008. LNCS, vol. 5157, pp. 108–125. Springer, Heidelberg (2008)

[26] Brakerski, Z., Goldwasser, S.: Circular and Leakage Resilient Public-Key Encryption under Subgroup Indistinguishability - (or: Quadratic Residuosity strikes back). In: Rabin, T. (ed.) CRYPTO 2010. LNCS, vol. 6223, pp. 1–20. Springer, Heidelberg (2010)

[27] Brakerski, Z., Goldwasser, S., Kalai, Y.T.: Black-Box Circular-Secure Encryption beyond Affine Functions. In: Ishai, Y. (ed.) TCC 2011. LNCS, vol. 6597, pp. 201–218. Springer, Heidelberg (2011)

[28] Camenisch, J., Chandran, N., Shoup, V.: A Public Key Encryption Scheme Secure against Key Dependent Chosen Plaintext and Adaptive Chosen ciphertext Attacks. In: Joux, A. (ed.) EUROCRYPT 2009. LNCS, vol. 5479, pp. 351–368. Springer, Heidelberg (2009)

[29] Dziembowski, S., Pietrzak, K.: Leakage-Resilient Cryptography. In: FOCS, pp. 293–302 (2008)

[30] Goldwasser, S., Micali, S.: Probabilistic Encryption. J. Comput. Syst. Sci. 28(2), 270–299 (1984)

[31] Halevi, S., Krawczyk, H.: Security under Key-Dependent Inputs. In: ACM Conference on Computer and Communications Security, pp. 466–475 (2007)

[32] Hofheinz, D.: Circular Chosen-Ciphertext Security with Compact Ciphertexts. In: Johansson, T., Nguyen, P.Q. (eds.) EUROCRYPT 2013. LNCS, vol. 7881, pp. 520–536. Springer, Heidelberg (2013)

[33] Hofheinz, D., Unruh, D.: Towards Key-Dependent Message Security in the Standard Model. In: Smart, N.P. (ed.) EUROCRYPT 2008. LNCS, vol. 4965, pp. 108–126. Springer, Heidelberg (2008)

[34] Malkin, T., Teranishi, I., Yung, M.: Efficient Circuit-Size Independent Public Key Encryption with KDM Security. In: Paterson, K.G. (ed.) EUROCRYPT 2011. LNCS, vol. 6632, pp. 507–526. Springer, Heidelberg (2011)

[35] Micali, S., Reyzin, L.: Physically Observable Cryptography. In: Naor, M. (ed.) TCC 2004. LNCS, vol. 2951, pp. 278–296. Springer, Heidelberg (2004)

[36] Wee, H.: Public Key Encryption against Related Key Attacks. In: Fischlin, M., Buchmann, J., Manulis, M. (eds.) PKC 2012. LNCS, vol. 7293, pp. 262–279. Springer, Heidelberg (2012)

Functional Signatures and Pseudorandom Functions

Elette Boyle[1,*], Shafi Goldwasser[2,3,**,***], and Ioana Ivan[2]

[1] Technion – Israel Institute of Technology
eboyle@alum.mit.edu
[2] MIT CSAIL
shafi@theory.csail.mit.edu, ioanai@mit.edu
[3] Weizmann Institute of Science

Abstract. We introduce two new cryptographic primitives: *functional digital signatures* and *functional pseudorandom functions*.

In a functional signature scheme, in addition to a master signing key that can be used to sign any message, there are *signing keys for a function* f, which allow one to sign any message in the range of f. As a special case, this implies the ability to generate keys for predicates P, which allow one to sign any message m for which $P(m) = 1$.

We show applications of functional signatures to constructing succinct non-interactive arguments and delegation schemes. We give several general constructions for this primitive based on different computational hardness assumptions, and describe the trade-offs between them in terms of the assumptions they require and the size of the signatures.

In a functional pseudorandom function, in addition to a master secret key that can be used to evaluate the pseudorandom function F on any point in the domain, there are additional *secret keys for a function* f, which allow one to evaluate F on any y for which there exists an x such that $f(x) = y$. As a special case, this implies *pseudorandom functions with selective access*, where one can delegate the ability to evaluate the pseudorandom function on inputs y for which a predicate $P(y) = 1$ holds. We define and provide a sample construction of a functional pseudorandom function family for prefix-fixing functions. This construction yields, in particular, *punctured pseudorandom functions*, which have proven an invaluable tool in recent advances in obfuscation (Sahai and Waters ePrint 2013).

* The research of the first author has received funding from the European Union's Tenth Framework Programme (FP10/ 2010-2016) under grant agreement no. 259426 ERC-CaC. This work was primarily completed while the first author was a student at MIT.
** This work was supported in part by Trustworthy Computing: NSF CCF-1018064.
*** This material is based on research sponsored by the Air Force Research Laboratory under agreement number FA8750-11-2-0225. The U.S. Government is authorized to reproduce and distribute reprints for Governmental purposes notwithstanding any copyright notation thereon. The views and conclusions contained herein are those of the authors and should not be interpreted as necessarily representing the official policies or endorsements, either expressed or implied, of the Air Force Research Laboratory or the U.S. Government.

H. Krawczyk (Ed.): PKC 2014, LNCS 8383, pp. 501–519, 2014.
© International Association for Cryptologic Research 2014

1   Introduction

We introduce new cryptographic primitives with a variety of accompanying constructions: *functional digital signatures (FDS)*, *functional pseudorandom functions (F-PRF)*, and *psuedorandom functions with selective access (PRF-SA)*.[1]

Functional Signatures

In digital signature schemes, as defined by Diffie and Hellman [11], a signature on a message provides information which enables the receiver to verify that the message has been created by a proclaimed sender. The sender has a secret *signing key*, used in the signing process, and there is a corresponding verification key, which is public and can be used by anyone to verify that a signature is valid. Following Goldwasser, Micali and Rackoff [20], the standard security requirement for signature schemes is unforgeability against chosen-message attack: an adversary that runs in probabilistic polynomial time and is allowed to request signatures for a polynomial number of messages of his choice, cannot produce a signature of any new message with non-negligible probability.

In this work, we extend the classical digital signature notion to what we call *functional signatures*. In a functional signature scheme, in addition to a *master signing key* that can be used to sign any message, there are secondary *signing keys for functions* f (called sk_f), which allow one to sign any message in the range of f. These additional keys are derived from the master signing key. The notion of security we require such a signature scheme to satisfy is that any probabilistic polynomial time (PPT) adversary, who can request signing keys for functions $f_1 \ldots f_l$ of his choice, and signatures for messages $m_1, \ldots m_q$ of his choice, can only produce a signature of a message m with non-negligible probability, if m is equal to one of the queried messages $m_1, \ldots m_q$, or if m is in the range of one of the queried functions $f_1 \ldots f_l$.

An immediate application of a functional signature scheme is the ability to delegate the signing process from a master authority to another party. Suppose someone wants to allow their assistant to sign on their behalf only those messages with a certain tag, such as "signed by the assistant". Let P be a predicate that outputs 1 on messages with the proper tag, and 0 on all other messages. In order to delegate the signing of this restricted set of messages, one would give the assistant a signing key for the following function:

$$f(m) := \begin{cases} m \text{ if } P(m) = 1 \\ \bot \text{ otherwise} \end{cases}.$$

---

[1] We note that independently the notion of pseudorandom functions with selective access was studied by Boneh-Waters under the name of *constrained pseudorandom functions* [9] and by Kiayias, Papadopoulos, Triandopoulos and Zacharias under the name *delegatable pseudorandom functions* [23]. Subsequent to our posting of an earlier manuscript of this work, [4] and [2] have additionally posted similar results on functional signatures.

P could also be a predicate that checks if the message does not contain a given phrase, if it is related to a certain subject, or if it satisfies a more complex policy.

Another application of functional signatures is to certify that only allowable computations were performed on data. For example, imagine the setting of a digital camera that produces signed photos (i.e the original photos produced by the camera can be certified). In this case, one may want to allow photo-processing software to perform minor touch-ups of the photos, such as changing the color scale or removing red-eyes, but not allow more significant changes such as merging two photos or cropping a picture. Functional signatures can naturally address this problem by providing the photo processing software with keys which enable it to sign only the allowable modifications of an original photograph. Generalizing, we think of a client and a server (e.g. photo-processing software), where the client provides the server with data (e.g. signed original photos, text documents, medical data) which he wants to be processed in a restricted fashion. A functional signature of the processed data provides proof of allowable processing.

Functional signatures can also be used to construct a delegation scheme. In this setting, there is a client who wants to allow a more powerful server to compute a function f on inputs chosen by the client, and wants to be able to verify that the result returned by the server is correct. The verification process should be more efficient than for the client to compute f himself. The client can give the server a key for the function $f'(x) = (f(x)|x)$. To prove that $y = f(x)$, the prover gives the client a signature of $y|x$, which he could only have obtained if $y|x$ is in the range of f'; that is, if $y = f(x)$.

A desirable property of a functional signature scheme is *function privacy*: the signature should reveal neither the function f corresponding to the key used in the signing process, nor the message m that f was applied to. In the example with the signed photos, one might not wish to reveal the original image, just that the final photographs were obtained by running one of the allowed functions on some image taken with the camera.

An additional desirable property is *succinctness*: the size of the signature should only depend on the size of the output $f(m)$ and the security parameter (or just the security parameter), rather than the size of the circuit for computing f.

Functional Pseudorandomness

Pseudorandom functions (PRFs), introduced by Goldreich, Goldwasser, and Micali [14], are a family of indexed functions $F = \{F_s\}$ such that: (1) given the index s, F_s can be efficiently evaluated on all inputs, and (2) no probabilistic polynomial-time algorithm *without* s can distinguish evaluations $F_s(x_i)$ for inputs x_i of its choice from random values. Pseudorandom functions are useful for numerous symmetric-key cryptographic applications, including generating pass words, identify-friend-or-foe systems, and symmetric-key encryption schemes secure against chosen-ciphertext attacks.

In this work, we extend pseudorandom functions to a primitive which we call *functional pseudorandom functions (F-PRF)*. The idea is that in addition to a master secret key (that can be used to evaluate the pseudorandom function F_s

on any point in the domain), there are additional *secret keys sk_f per function f*, which allow one to evaluate F_s on any y for which there exists x such that $f(x) = y$ (i.e $y \in Range(f)$). An immediate application of such a construct is to specify succinctly the randomness to be used by parties in a randomized distributed protocol with potentially faulty players, so as to force honest behavior. A centralized authority holds an index s of a pseudorandom function F_s. One may think of this authority as providing a service which dispenses pseudorandomness (alternatively, the secret s can be shared among players in an MPC). The authority provides each party id with a secret key s_{id} which enables party id to (1) evaluate $F_s(y)$ whenever $y = "id\|h"$, where h corresponds to say the public history of communication, and (2) use $F_s(y)$ as her next sequence of coins in the protocol. To prove that the appropriate randomness was used, id can utilize NIZK proofs. An interesting open question is how to achieve a *verifiable* F-PRF, where there is additional information vk_s that can be used to verify that a given pair $(x, F_s(x))$ is valid, without assuming the existence of an honestly generated common reference string, as in the NIZK setting. Note that in this example the function $f(x) = y$ is simply the function which appends the string prefix id to x. We note that there are many other ways to force the use of proper randomness in MPC protocols by dishonest parties, starting with the classical paradigm [19,15] where parties interact to execute a "coin flip in the well" protocol forcing players to use the results of these coins, but we find the use of F-PRF appealing in its simplicity, lack of interaction and potential efficiency.

The notion of functional pseudorandom functions has many variations. One natural variant that immediately follows is *PRFs with selective access*, in which secondary keys sk_P can be produced per predicate P to enable computing $F_s(x)$ on inputs x for which $P(x) = 1$. This is a special case of F-PRF, as we can take the secret key for predicate P to be sk_f where $f(x) = x$ if $P(x) = 1$ and $\perp$ otherwise. The special case of *punctured PRFs*, in which secondary keys allow computing $F_s(x)$ on all inputs except one, is similarly implied and has recently been shown to have important applications (e.g., [29,22]). Another variant is *hierarchical PRFs*, with an additional property that parties with functional keys sk_f may also generate subordinate keys sk_g for functions g of the form $g = f \circ f'$ (i.e., first evaluate f', then evaluate f). Note that the range of such composition g is necessarily contained within the range of f.

1.1 Our Results on Functional Signatures and Their Applications

We provide a construction of functional signatures achieving function privacy and succinctness, assuming the existence of succinct non-interactive arguments of knowledge (SNARKS) and (standard) non-interactive zero-knowledge arguments of knowledge (NIZKAoKs) for NP languages.

As a building block, we first give a construction of a functional signature scheme that is not succinct or function private, based on a much weaker assumption: the existence of one-way functions.

Theorem 1 (Informal). *Based on any one-way function, there exists a functional signature scheme that supports signing keys for any function f computable by a polynomial-sized circuit. This scheme satisfies the unforgeability requirement for functional signatures, but not function privacy or succinctness.*

Overview of the Construction: The master signing and verification keys for the functional signature scheme will correspond to a key pair, $(\mathsf{msk}, \mathsf{mvk})$, in an underlying (standard) signature scheme. To generate a signing key for a function f, we sample a fresh signing and verification key pair $(\mathsf{sk}', \mathsf{vk}')$ in the underlying signature scheme, and sign the concatenation $f|\mathsf{vk}'$ using msk. The signing key for f consists of this signature together with sk'. Given this signing key, a user can sign any message $m^* = f(m)$ by signing m using sk', and outputting this signature, together with the signature of $f|\mathsf{vk}'$ given as part of sk_f.

We then now show how to use SNARKs, together with this initial construction, to construct a *succinct, function-private* functional signature scheme.

A SNARK system for an NP language L with corresponding relation R is an extractable proof system where the size of a proof is sublinear in the size of the witness corresponding to an instance. SNARKs have been constructed under various non-falsifiable [26] assumptions. Bitansky et al. [6] construct zero-knowledge SNARKs where the length of the proof and the verifier's running time are bounded by a polynomial in the security parameter, and the *logarithm* of running time of the corresponding relation $R(x, w)$, assuming the existence of collision-resistant hash functions and a knowledge-of-exponent assumption.[2] (More details are given in the full version).

Theorem 2 (Informal). *Assuming the existence of SNARK and NIZKAoK for NP, and a functional signature scheme that is not necessarily function-private or succinct, there exists a succinct, function-private functional signature scheme that supports signing keys for the class of polynomial-sized circuits.*

Overview of the Construction: In the setup algorithm for our functional signature scheme, we sample a key pair $(\mathsf{msk}, \mathsf{mvk})$ for the underlying (non-succinct, non-function-pivate) functional signature scheme FS1, and a common reference string crs for the SNARK system. We use msk as the new master singing key and $(\mathsf{mvk}, \mathsf{crs})$ as the new master verification key. The sk_f key generation algorithm is the same as in the underlying functional signature scheme FS1. To sign a message m^* using a resulting key sk_f, we generate a zero-knowledge SNARK for the following statement: $\exists \sigma$ such that σ is a valid signature of m^* under mvk in the functional signature scheme FS1. To verify the signature, we run the verification algorithm for the SNARK argument system.

Resorting to non-falsifiable assumptions, albeit strong, seems necessary to obtain succinctness for functional signatures. We show that, given a functional signature scheme with short signatures, we can construct a SNARG system.

---

[2] In [5], Bitansky et al. also show that any SNARK + NIZKAoK directly yield zero-knowledge (ZK)-SNARK with analogous parameters.

Theorem 3 (Informal). *If there exists a functional signature scheme supporting keys for all polynomial-sized circuits f, with short signatures (i.e., of size $poly(k) \cdot (|f(m)| + |m|)^{o(1)}$ for security parameter k), then there exists a SNARG scheme with preprocessing for any language $L \in NP$ with proof size $poly(k) \cdot (|w| + |x|)^{o(1)}$, where w is the witness and x is the instance.*

The main idea in the SNARG construction is for the verifier (CRS generator) to give out a single signing key sk_f for a function whose range consists of exactly those strings that are in the language L. Then, with sk_f, the prover will be able to sign only those messages x that are in L, and thus can use this (short) signature as his proof.

Gentry and Wichs showed in [13] that SNARG schemes with proof size $poly(k) \cdot (|w| + |x|)^{o(1)}$ cannot be obtained using black-box reductions to falsifiable assumptions. We can thus conclude that in order to obtain a functional signature scheme with signature size $poly(k) \cdot (|f(m)| + |m|)^{o(1)}$ we must either rely on non-falsifiable assumptions (as in our SNARK construction) or make use of non black-box techniques.

Finally, we can construct a scheme which satisfies unforgeability and functional privacy but not succinctness, based on the weaker assumption of non-interactive zero-knowledge arguments of knowledge (NIZKAoK) for NP.

Theorem 4 (Informal). *Assuming the existence of non-interactive zero-knowledge arguments of knowledge (NIZKAoK) for NP, there exists a functional signature scheme that supports signing keys for any function f computable by a polynomial-sized circuit. This scheme satisfies function privacy, but not succinctness: the size of the signature is dependent on the size of f and m.*

Overview of the Construction: The construction is analogous to the SNARK-based construction above, with the SNARK replaced with NIZKAoK. Namely, a signature will be a NIZK Argument of Knowledge for the following statement: $\exists \sigma$ such that σ is a valid signature of m^* under mvk, in an underlying non-succinct, non-function-private functional signature scheme, as before (recall such a scheme exists based on OWF). The signature size is now polynomial in the size of σ, which, if $m^* = f(m)$, and sigma was generated using sk_f, is itself polynomial in the security parameter, $|m|$, and $|f|$.

Relation to Delegation: Functional signatures are highly related to delegation schemes. A delegation scheme allows a client to outsource evaluation of a function f to a server, allowing the client to verify the correctness of the computation more efficiently than evaluating f himself. We show that given *any* functional signature scheme supporting a class of functions $\mathcal{F}$, we can obtain a delegation scheme in the preprocessing model for functions in $\mathcal{F}$, with related parameters.

Theorem 5 (Informal). *If there exists a functional signature scheme for function class $\mathcal{F}$, with signature size $s(k)$, and verification time $t(k)$, then there exists a one-round delegation scheme for functions in $\mathcal{F}$, with server message size $s(k)$ and client verification time $t(k)$.*

Overview of the Construction: The client gives the server a key $\mathsf{sk}_{f'}$ for the function $f'(x) = (f(x)|x)$. To prove that $y = f(x)$, the prover gives the client a signature of $y|x$, which he could only have obtained if $y|x$ is in the range of f'; that is, if $y = f(x)$. The length of a proof is equal to the length of a signature in the functional signature scheme, $s(k)$, and the verification time for the delegation scheme is equal to the verification time of the functional signature scheme.

1.2   Summary of Our Results on Functional Pseudorandom Functions and Selective Pseudorandom Functions

We present formal definitions and constructions of functional pseudorandom functions (F-PRF) and pseudorandom functions with selective access (PRF-SA). In particular, we present a construction based on one-way functions of an F-PRF supporting the class of *prefix-fixing functions*. Our construction is based on the Goldreich-Goldwasser-Micali (GGM) tree-based PRF construction [GGM86].

Theorem 6 (Informal). *Assuming the existence of OWF, there exists an F-PRF supporting keys for the class of prefix-matching functions:* $\mathcal{F}_{\mathsf{pre}} = \{f_z | z \in \{0,1\}^m, m \leq n\}$, *where* $f_z(x) = x$ *if* z *is a prefix of* x, *and* $\perp$ *otherwise. The pseudorandomness property holds against a selective adversary, who declares the functions he will query before seeing the public parameters.*

We remark that one can directly obtain a *fully* secure F-PRF for $\mathcal{F}_{\mathsf{pre}}$, in which security holds against an adversary who adaptively requests key queries, from our selectively secure construction, with a loss of 2^{-n} in security for each functional secret key sk_{f_z} queried by the adversary, via standard complexity leveraging. For appropriate choices of the input length n, security of the underlying OWF, and number of key queries, this still provides desirable security.

Overview of the Construction. We show that the original Goldreich-Goldwasser-Micali (GGM) tree-based PRF construction [14] provides the desired functionality, where the functional key sk_f corresponding to a prefix-fixing function $f_z(x) = z_1 z_2 \cdots z_i x_{i+1} \cdots x_n$ will be given by the partial evaluation of the PRF down the tree, at the node corresponding to prefix $z_1 z_2 \cdots z_i$.

This partial evaluation clearly enables a user to compute all possible continuations in the evaluation tree, corresponding to the output of the PRF on any input possessing prefix z. Intuitively, security holds since the other partial evaluations at this level i in the tree still appear random given the evaluation sk_f (indeed, this corresponds to a truncated i-bit input GGM construction).

Punctured pseudorandom functions. Punctured pseudorandom functions [29] are a special case of functional PRFs, where one can generate keys for the function family $\mathcal{F} = \{f_x(y) = y \text{ if } y \neq x, \text{ and } \perp \text{ otherwise}\}$. Namely, a key for function f_x allows one to compute the pseudorandom function on any input except for x. Punctured PRFs have recently proven useful as one of the main techniques used in proving the security of various cryptographic primitives based on the existence of indistinguishability obfuscation. Some examples include a construction of public-key encryption from symmetric-key encryption and the construction of deniable encryption given by Sahai and Waters in [29], as well as an instantiation of random oracles with a concrete hash function for full-domain hash applications by Hohenberger et al. in [22].

We note that the existence of a functional PRF for the prefix-fixing function family gives a construction of punctured PRFs. A key that allows one to compute the PRF on all inputs except $x = x_1 \ldots x_n$ consists of n functional keys for the prefix-fixing function family for prefixes: $\bar{x}_1, x_1\bar{x}_2, x_1x_2\bar{x}_3, \ldots, x_1x_2 \cdots x_{n-1}\bar{x}_n$.

Corollary 1 (Informal). *Assuming the existence of OWF, there exists a (selectively secure) punctured PRF for any desired poly-size input length.*

Our construction has the additional beneficial property of *hierarchical key generation*: i.e., a party with a functional key sk_{f_z} for a prefix z may generate valid "subordinate" functional keys $\mathsf{sk}_{f_{z'}}$ for any prefix $z' = z|*$. That is, we prove the following additional statement.

Corollary 2 (Informal). *Assuming the existence of OWF, there exists a (selectively secure)* hierarchical *functional PRF for the class of functions* F_{pre}.

1.3   Other Related Work

Functional Encryption. This work is inspired by recent results on the problem of functional encryption, introduced by Sahai and Waters [28], and formalized by Boneh et al. [8]. In the past few years there has been significant progress on constructing functional encryption schemes for general classes of functions (e.g., [21,17,18]). In this setting, a party with access to a master secret key can generate secret keys sk_f for functions f, which allow a third party with sk_f and an encryption of a message m to learn $f(m)$, but nothing else about m. In [17], Goldwasser et al. construct a functional encryption scheme supporting general functions, and secure according to a simulation-based definition, as long as a single key is given out. In [1], Agrawal et al. show that constructing functional encryption schemes achieving this notion of security in the presence of an unbounded number of secret keys is impossible for general functions. In contrast, no such impossibility results are known in the setting of functional signatures.

Connections to Obfuscation. The goal of program obfuscation is to construct a compiler O that takes as input a program P and outputs a program $O(P)$ that preserves the functionality of P, but hides all other information about the original program. Following [3], this is often formalized by requiring that the single-bit output of an efficient adversary given access to an obfuscation of P can be simulated given only black-box access to P. However, Barak et al. [3] show that this definition is unachievable for general functions. Furthermore, in [16], Goldwasser and Kalai give evidence that several natural cryptographic algorithms, including the signing algorithm of any unforgeable signature scheme, are not obfuscatable with respect to this strong definition.

Consider the function Sign ∘ f, where Sign is the signing algorithm of an unforgeable signature scheme, f is an arbitrary function and ∘ denotes function composition. Based on the results in [16] we would expect this function not to be obfuscatable according to the black-box simulation definition. A meaningful relaxation of the definition is that, while having access to an obfuscation of this function might not hide all information about the signing algorithm, it does not completely reveal the secret key, and does not allow one to sign messages that are not in the range of f. In our function signature scheme, the signing key corresponding to a function f achieves exactly this definition of security, and we can think of it as an obfuscation of Sign ∘ f according to this relaxed definition. Indeed it has recently come to our attention that Barak in an unpublished manuscript has considered *delegatable signatures*, a highly related concept.

Homomorphic Signatures. In a homomorphic signature scheme, a third party is able to perform computations over *already-signed* data, and obtain a new signature that authenticates the resulting message with respect to this computation. In [12], Gennaro and Wichs construct homomorphic (privately verifiable) message authentication codes. For homomorphic signature schemes with public verification, the most general construction of Boneh and Freeman [7] only allows the evaluation of multivariate polynomials on signed data. Constructing homomorphic signature schemes for general functions remains an open problem.

Signatures of correct computation. Papamanthou, Shi and Tamassia consider a notion of functional signatures under the name "signatures of correct computation" [27]. They give constructions for schemes that support operations over multivariate polynomials, such as polynomial evaluation and differentiation. Their schemes are secure in the random oracle model and allow efficient updates to the signing keys: the keys can be updated in time proportional to the number of updated coefficients. In contrast, our constructions that support signing keys for general functions, in the plain model, assuming the existence of succinct non-interactive arguments of knowledge.

Independent work. Finally, as mentioned earlier, related notions to functional PRFs appear in the concurrent and independent works [9,23]. Based on the Multilinear Decisional Diffie-Hellman assumption (a recently coined assumption related to existence of secure multilinear maps), [9] show that PRFs with Selective Access can be constructed for all predicates describable as polynomial-sized circuits. We remark that this is not equivalent to functional PRFs for polynomial-sized circuits, which additionally captures NP relations (i.e., the predicate $y \in Range(f)$ may not be efficiently testable directly). Subsequent to our posting of an earlier manuscript of this work, [4] and [2] have additionally posted similar results on functional signatures.

1.4 Overview of the Paper

In Section 2, we give a formal definition of functional signature schemes, and present three constructions satisfying the definition. In Section 3, we show how to construct delegation schemes and succinct non-interactive arguments (SNARGs) from functional signatures schemes. In Section 4, we give a formal definition of functional pseudorandom functions and pseudorandom functions with selective access, and present a sample construction for the prefix-fixing function family. In Section 5, we discuss open problems. Due to space constraints, we defer the preliminaries and proofs of theorem statements to the full version of the paper [10].

2   Functional Signatures: Definition and Constructions

We now give a formal definition of a functional signature scheme, specifying the desired unforgeability, function-privacy, and succinctness properties.

Definition 1. *A functional signature scheme for a message space $\mathcal{M}$, and function family $\mathcal{F} = \{f : \mathcal{D}_f \to \mathcal{M}\}$ consists of algorithms (FS.Setup, FS.KeyGen, FS.Sign, FS.Verify):*

- *FS.Setup$(1^k) \to (\mathsf{msk}, \mathsf{mvk})$: the setup algorithm takes as input the security parameter and outputs the master signing key and master verification key.*
- *FS.KeyGen$(\mathsf{msk}, f) \to \mathsf{sk}_f$: the key generation algorithm takes as input the master signing key and a function $f \in \mathcal{F}$ (represented as a circuit), and outputs a signing key for f.*
- *FS.Sign$(f, \mathsf{sk}_f, m) \to (f(m), \sigma)$: the signing algorithm takes as input the signing key for a function $f \in \mathcal{F}$ and an input $m \in \mathcal{D}_f$, and outputs $f(m)$ and a signature of $f(m)$.*
- *FS.Verify$(\mathsf{mvk}, m^*, \sigma) \to \{0, 1\}$: the verification algorithm takes as input the master verification key mvk, a message m and a signature σ, and outputs 1 if the signature is valid.*

We require the following conditions to hold:

Correctness
$\forall f \in \mathcal{F}, \forall m \in \mathcal{D}_f, (\mathsf{msk}, \mathsf{mvk}) \leftarrow \mathsf{FS.Setup}(1^k), \mathsf{sk}_f \leftarrow \mathsf{FS.KeyGen}(\mathsf{msk}, f),$
$(m^*, \sigma) \leftarrow \mathsf{FS.Sign}(f, \mathsf{sk}_f, m),$ *it holds that* $\mathsf{FS.Verify}(\mathsf{mvk}, m^*, \sigma) = 1.$

Unforgeability
The scheme is unforgeable if the advantage of any PPT algorithm A in the following game is negligible:

- *The challenger generates $(\mathsf{msk}, \mathsf{mvk}) \leftarrow \mathsf{FS.Setup}(1^k)$, and gives mvk to A.*
- *The adversary is allowed to query a key generation oracle $\mathsf{O_{key}}$, and a signing oracle $\mathsf{O_{sign}}$, that share a dictionary indexed by tuples $(f, i) \in \mathcal{F} \times \mathbb{N}$, whose entries are signing keys: $\mathsf{sk}_f^i \leftarrow \mathsf{FS.KeyGen}(\mathsf{msk}, f)$. This dictionary keeps track of the keys that have been previously generated during the unforgeability game. The oracles are defined as follows :*
    - *$\mathsf{O_{key}}(f, i)$:*

* if there exists an entry for the key (f, i) in the dictionary, then output the corresponding value, sk_f^i.
* otherwise, sample a fresh key $\mathsf{sk}_f^i \leftarrow \mathsf{FS.KeyGen}(\mathsf{msk}, f)$, add an entry $(f, i) \rightarrow \mathsf{sk}_f^i$ to the dictionary, and output sk_f^i

- $O_{\mathsf{sign}}(f, i, m)$:
  * if there exists an entry for the key (f, i) in the dictionary, then generate a signature on $f(m)$ using this key: $\sigma \leftarrow \mathsf{FS.Sign}(f, \mathsf{sk}_f^i, m)$.
  * otherwise, sample a fresh key $\mathsf{sk}_f^i \leftarrow \mathsf{FS.KeyGen}(\mathsf{msk}, f)$, add an entry $(f, i) \rightarrow \mathsf{sk}_f^i$ to the dictionary, and generate a signature on $f(m)$ using this key: $\sigma \leftarrow \mathsf{FS.Sign}(f, \mathsf{sk}_f^i, m)$.

- *The adversary wins if it can produce* (m^*, σ) *such that*
  - $\mathsf{FS.Verify}(\mathsf{mvk}, m^*, \sigma) = 1$.
  - *there does not exist* m *such that* $m^* = f(m)$ *for any* f *which was sent as a query to the* O_{key} *oracle.*
  - *there does not exist a* (f, m) *pair such that* (f, m) *was a query to the* O_{sign} *oracle and* $m^* = f(m)$.

Function Privacy

Intuitively, we require the distribution of signatures on a message m' *generated via different keys* sk_f *to be computationally indistinguishable,* even given the secret keys and master signing key. *Namely, the advantage of any PPT adversary in the following game is negligible:*

- *The challenger honestly generates a key pair* $(\mathsf{mvk}, \mathsf{msk}) \leftarrow \mathsf{FS.Setup}(1^k)$ *and gives both values to the adversary.*
- *The adversary chooses a function* f_0 *and receives an (honestly generated) secret key* $\mathsf{sk}_{f_0} \leftarrow \mathsf{FS.KeyGen}(\mathsf{msk}, f_0)$.
- *The adversary chooses a second function* f_1 *for which* $|f_0| = |f_1|$ *(where padding can be used if there is a known upper bound) and receives an (honestly generated) secret key* $\mathsf{sk}_{f_1} \leftarrow \mathsf{FS.KeyGen}(\mathsf{msk}, f_1)$.
- *The adversary chooses a pair of values* m_0, m_1 *for which* $|m_0| = |m_1|$ *and* $f_0(m_0) = f_1(m_1)$.
- *The challenger selects a random bit* $b \leftarrow \{0, 1\}$ *and generates a signature on the image message* $m' = f_0(m_0) = f_1(m_1)$ *using secret key* sk_{f_b}, *and gives the resulting signature* $\sigma \leftarrow \mathsf{FS.Sign}(\mathsf{sk}_{f_b}, m_b)$ *to the adversary.*
- *The adversary outputs a bit* b', *and wins the game if* $b' = b$.

Succinctness

There exists a polynomial $s(\cdot)$ *such that for every* $k \in \mathbb{N}, f \in \mathcal{F}, m \in \mathcal{D}_f$, *it holds with probability 1 over* $(\mathsf{msk}, \mathsf{mvk}) \leftarrow \mathsf{FS.Setup}(1^k)$, $\mathsf{sk}_f \leftarrow \mathsf{FS.KeyGen}(\mathsf{msk}, f)$, $(f(m), \sigma) \leftarrow \mathsf{FS.Sign}(f, \mathsf{sk}_f, m)$ *that the resulting signature on* $f(m)$ *has size* $|\sigma| \le s(k, |f(m)|)$. *In particular, the signature size is independent of the size* $|m|$ *of the input to the function, and of the size* $|f|$ *of a description of the function* f.

Constructions. In the full version of the paper, we give three constructions of functional signature schemes, and describe the trade-offs between them in terms of the assumptions they require and the function privacy and succinctness properties of the functional signature scheme.

Theorem 7. *The following three implications hold:*

1. *Assuming the existence of one-way functions, there exists a functional signature scheme for the class $\mathcal{F}$ of polynomial-size circuits that satisfies the unforgeability requirement described above.*
2. *Assuming the existence of Non-Interactive Zero Knowledge Arguments of Knowledge for* NP *and one-way functions, there exists a function-private (but not necessarily succinct) functional signature scheme for the class $\mathcal{F}$ of polynomial-size circuits.*
3. *Assuming the existence of an unforgeable (but not necessarily succinct or function-private) functional signature scheme supporting the class of functions $\mathcal{F}$, and an adaptive zero-knowledge Succinct Non-Interactive Argument of Knowledge (SNARK) system for* NP, *there exists succinct, function-private functional signatures for $\mathcal{F}$.*

As a corollary, it follows that succinct, function-private functional signatures for the class of polynomial-size circuits can be based on SNARKs for NP and OWFs.

3 Applications of Functional Signatures

In this section we discuss applications of functional signatures to other cryptographic problems, such as constructing delegation schemes and succinct non-interactive arguments (SNARGs).

3.1 SNARGs from Functional Signatures

Recall that in a SNARG system for a language L, there is a verifier V, and a prover P who wishes to convince the verifier that an input x is in L. To achieve succinctness, proofs produced by the prover must be sublinear in the size of the input plus the size of the witness.

We show how to use a functional signature scheme supporting keys for functions f describable as polynomial-size circuits, and which has short signatures (i.e of size $r(k) \cdot (|f(m)| + |m|)^{o(1)}$ for a polynomial $r(\cdot)$) to construct a SNARG scheme with preprocessing for any language $L \in NP$ with proof size bounded by $r(k) \cdot (|w| + |x|)^{o(1)}$, where w is the witness and x is the instance. We note that this is the proof size used in the lower bound of [13].

Let L be an NP-complete language, and R the corresponding relation. The main idea in the construction is for the verifier (or CRS setup) to give out a single signing key for a function whose range consists of exactly those strings that are in L. Note that this can be efficiently described by use of the relation R (where the function also takes as input a witness). Then, with sk_f for this appropriate function f, the prover will be able to sign *only* those messages that are in the language L, and hence can use a signature on x as a convincing argument that $x \in L$. The resulting argument is succinct and publicly verifiable.

More explicitly, let $\mathsf{FS} = (\mathsf{FS.Setup}, \mathsf{FS.KeyGen}, \mathsf{FS.Sign}, \mathsf{FS.Verify})$ be a succinct functional signature scheme (as in Definition 1) supporting the class $\mathcal{F}$ of polynomial-size circuits. We construct the desired SNARG system $\Pi = (\Pi.\mathsf{Gen}, \Pi.\mathsf{Prove}, \Pi.\mathsf{Verify})$ for NP language L with relation R, as follows:

- $\Pi.\mathsf{Gen}(1^k)$:
    - run the functional signature scheme setup: $(\mathsf{mvk}, \mathsf{msk}) \leftarrow \mathsf{FS.Setup}(1^k)$.
    - generate a signing key $\mathsf{sk}_f \leftarrow \mathsf{FS.KeyGen}(\mathsf{msk}, f)$ for the function $f(x|w) := x$ if $R(x, w) = 1, \bot$ otherwise, and output $\mathsf{crs} = (\mathsf{mvk}, \mathsf{sk}_f)$.
- $\Pi.\mathsf{Prove}(x, w, \mathsf{crs})$: output $\mathsf{FS.Sign}(f, \mathsf{sk}_f, x|w)$.
- $\Pi.\mathsf{Verify}(\mathsf{crs}, x, \pi)$: output $\mathsf{FS.Verify}(\mathsf{mvk}, x, \pi)$.

Theorem 8. *If* FS *is a functional signature scheme supporting the class $\mathcal{F}$ of polynomial-sized circuits, then* Π *is a succinct non-interactive argument (SNARG) for NP language L.*

We defer the proof of Theorem 8 to the full version.

Remark 1 (Functional PRFs as Functional MACs). Note that functional pseudorandom functions directly imply a notion of *functional message authentication codes (MACs)*, where the master PRF seed s serves as the (shared) master secret MAC key, and a functional PRF subkey sk_f enables one to both MAC and verify messages $f(m)$. Using the transformation above with such a functional MAC in the place of functional signatures yields a *privately verifiable* SNARG system.

Remark 2 (Lower bound of [13]). Gentry and Wichs showed in [13] that SNARG schemes for NP, with proof size $r(k) \cdot (|x| + |w|)^{o(1)}$ for polynomial $r(\cdot)$ cannot be obtained using black-box reductions to falsifiable assumptions [26]. Therefore, combined with Theorem 8, it follows that in order to obtain a functional signature scheme with signature size $r(k) \cdot (|f(m)| + |m|)^{o(1)}$ we must either rely on non-falsifiable assumptions (as in our SNARK-based construction) or make use of non black-box techniques.

In the full version of this paper, we demonstrate a similar implication of functional signatures on the existence of efficient delegation schemes.

4 Functional Pseudorandom Functions

In a standard pseudorandom function family, the ability to evaluate the chosen function is all-or-nothing: a party who holds the secret seed s can compute $F_s(x)$ on all inputs x, whereas a party without knowledge of s cannot distinguish evaluations $F_s(x)$ on requested inputs x from random. We propose the notion of a *functional pseudorandom function (F-PRF)* family, which partly fills this gap between evaluation powers. The idea is that, in addition to a master secret key that can be used to evaluate the pseudorandom function F on any point in the domain, there are additional *secret keys per function f*, which allow one to evaluate F on y for any y for which there exists an x such that $f(x) = y$ (i.e., y is in the range of f).

Definition 2 (Functional PRF). *We say that a PRF family $\{F_s : D \to R\}_{s \in S}$ is a* functional pseudorandom function (F-PRF) *with respect to a class of functions $\mathcal{F} = \{f : A_f \to D\}$ if there exist additional algorithms*

KeyGen(s, f) : *On input a seed $s \in S$ and function description $f \in \mathcal{F}$, the algorithm* KeyGen *outputs a key* sk_f.
Eval(sk_f, f, x) : *On input key* sk_f, *function $f \in \mathcal{F}$, and input $x \in A_f$, then* Eval *outputs the PRF evaluation $F_s(f(x))$.*

which satisfy the following properties:

- **Correctness:** *For every $f \in \mathcal{F}$, $\forall x \in A_f$, it holds that $\forall s \leftarrow S$, $\forall \text{sk}_f \leftarrow$* KeyGen$(s, f)$, Eval$(\text{sk}_f, f, x) = F_s(f(x))$.
- **Pseudorandomness:** *Given a set of keys $\text{sk}_{f_1} \ldots \text{sk}_{f_\ell}$ for functions $f_1 \ldots f_\ell$, the evaluation of $F_s(y)$ should remain pseudorandom on all inputs y that are not in the range of any of the functions $f_1 \ldots f_\ell$. That is, for any PPT adversary $\mathcal{A}$, the advantage of $\mathcal{A}$ in distinguishing between the following two experiments is negligible (for any polynomial $\ell = \ell(k)$):*

Experiment Rand	**Experiment PRand**
Key query Phase	*Key query Phase*
$(\text{pp}, s) \leftarrow \text{Gen}(1^k)$	$(\text{pp}, s) \leftarrow \text{Gen}(1^k)$
$f_1 \leftarrow \mathcal{A}(\text{pp})$	$f_1 \leftarrow \mathcal{A}(\text{pp})$
$\text{sk}_{f_1} \leftarrow \text{KeyGen}(s, f_1)$	$\text{sk}_{f_1} \leftarrow \text{KeyGen}(s, f_1)$
$\vdots$	$\vdots$
$f_\ell \leftarrow \mathcal{A}(\text{pp}, f_1, \text{sk}_{f_1}, \ldots, f_{l-1}, \text{sk}_{f_{l-1}})$	$f_\ell \leftarrow \mathcal{A}(\text{pp}, f_1, \text{sk}_{f_1}, \ldots, f_{l-1}, \text{sk}_{f_{l-1}})$
$\text{sk}_{f_\ell} \leftarrow \text{KeyGen}(s, f_\ell)$	$\text{sk}_{f_\ell} \leftarrow \text{KeyGen}(s, f_\ell)$
Challenge Phase	*Challenge Phase*
$H \leftarrow \mathbb{F}_{D \to R}$ a random function	
$b \leftarrow \mathcal{A}^{\mathcal{O}_{s,H}^{\{f_i\}}(\cdot)}(f_1, \text{sk}_{f_1}, \ldots, f_\ell, \text{sk}_{f_\ell})$	$b \leftarrow \mathcal{A}^{F_s(\cdot)}(f_1, \text{sk}_{f_1}, \ldots, f_\ell, \text{sk}_{f_\ell})$

where $\mathcal{O}_{s,H}^{\{f_i\}}(y) := \begin{cases} F_s(y) & \text{if } \exists i \in [l] \text{ and } x \text{ s.t. } f_i(x) = y \\ H(y) & \text{otherwise} \end{cases}$.

Note that, as defined, the oracle $\mathcal{O}_{s,H}^{\{f_i\}}(y)$ need not be efficiently computable. This inefficiency stems both from sampling a truly random function H, and from testing whether the adversary's evaluation queries y are contained within the range of one of his previously queried functions f_i. However, within particular applications, the system can be set up so that this oracle is efficiently simulatable: For example, evaluations of a truly random function can be simulated by choosing each queried evaluation one at a time; Further, the range of the relevant functions f_i may be efficiently testable given trapdoor information (e.g., determining the range of $f : r \mapsto \mathsf{Enc}(\mathsf{pk}, 0; r)$ for a public-key encryption scheme is infeasible given only pk but efficiently testable given the secret key).

We also consider a weaker security definition, where the adversary has to reveal which functions he will request keys for before seeing the public parameters or any of the keys. Namely, the key query phase takes place as follows:

Selective Key query Phase

$(\mathsf{pp}, s) \leftarrow \mathsf{Gen}(1^k)$

$(f_1, \ldots, f_\ell) \leftarrow \mathcal{A}(\mathsf{pp})$

For $i \in [\ell]$, $\mathsf{sk}_{f_i} \leftarrow \mathsf{KeyGen}(s, f_i)$

We refer to this as a *selectively secure F-PRF*.

A special case of functional PRFs arises when access control is to be determined by predicates. (Indeed, fitting within the F-PRF framework, one can emulate predicate policies by considering the corresponding functions $f_P(x) = x$ if $P(x) = 1$ and $= \perp$ if $P(x) = 0$). We refer to this as *PRFs with selective access*.

Finally, we consider *hierarchical* F-PRFs, where a party holding key sk_f for function $f : B \to D$ can generate subsidiary keys $\mathsf{sk}_{f \circ g}$ for functions $g : A \to B$.

We present formal definitions of these notions in the full version of this paper.

4.1   Construction Based on OWF

We now construct a functional pseudorandom function family $F_s : \{0,1\}^n \to \{0,1\}^n$ supporting the class of prefix-fixing functions, building upon the Goldreich-Goldwasser-Micali (GGM) tree-based PRF construction [14]. More precisely, our construction supports the function class

$$\mathcal{F}_{\mathsf{pre}} = \left\{ f_z(x) : \{0,1\}^n \to \{0,1\}^n \mid z \in \{0,1\}^m \text{ for } m \leq n \right\},$$

$$\text{where } f_z(x) := \begin{cases} x & \text{if } (x_1 = z_1) \wedge \cdots \wedge (x_m = z_m) \\ \perp & \text{otherwise} \end{cases}.$$

Recall that the GGM construction makes use of a length-doubling pseudorandom generator $G : \{0,1\}^k \to \{0,1\}^{2k}$ (which can be constructed from any one-way function). Denoting the two halves of the output of G as $G(y) = G_0(y)G_1(y)$, the PRF with seed s is defined as $F_s(y) = G_{y_k}(\cdots G_{y_2}(G_{y_1}(s)))$.

We show that we can obtain a functional PRF for $\mathcal{F}_{\mathsf{pre}}$ by adding the following two algorithms on top of the GGM PRF construction. Intuitively, in these algorithms the functional secret key sk_{f_z} corresponding to a queried function $f_z \in \mathcal{F}_{\mathsf{pre}}$ will be the partial evaluation of the GGM prefix corresponding to prefix z: i.e., the label of the node corresponding to node z in the GGM evaluation tree. Given this partial evaluation, a party will be able to compute the completion for any input x which has z as a prefix. However, as we will argue, the evaluation on all other inputs will remain pseudorandom.

$\mathsf{KeyGen}(s, f_z)$: output $G_{z_m}(\cdots G_{z_2}(G_{z_1}(s)))$, where $m = |z|$

$\mathsf{Eval}(\mathsf{sk}_{f_z}, y)$: output $\begin{cases} G_{y_n}(\cdots G_{y_{m+2}}(G_{y_{m+1}}(\mathsf{sk}_{f_z}))) & \text{if } y_1 = z_1 \wedge \cdots \wedge y_m = z_m \\ \bot & \text{otherwise} \end{cases}$

Theorem 9. *Based on the existence of one-way functions, the GGM pseudorandom function family together with algorithms* KeyGen *and* Eval *defined as above, yields a selectively secure functional PRF for the class of functions* $\mathcal{F}_{\mathsf{pre}}$.

We remark that one can directly obtain a *fully* secure F-PRF for $\mathcal{F}_{\mathsf{pre}}$ (as in Definition 2) from our selectively secure construction, with a loss of 2^{-n} in security for each secret key sk_{f_z} queried by the adversary. This is achieved simply by guessing the adversary's query $f_z \in \mathcal{F}_{\mathsf{pre}}$. For appropriate choices of input size n and security parameter k, this can still provide useful security.

As an immediate corollary of Theorem 9, we obtain a (selectively secure) *PRF with selective access* for the class of equivalent prefix-matching predicates $\mathcal{P}_{\mathsf{pre}} = \{P_z : \{0,1\}^n \to \{0,1\} | z \in \{0,1\}^m \text{ for } m \leq n\}$, where $P_z(x) := 1$ if $(x_1 = z_1) \wedge \cdots \wedge (x_m = z_m)$ and 0 otherwise.

Our F-PRF construction has the additional benefit of being *hierarchical*. Given a secret key sk_{f_z} for a prefix $z \in \{0,1\}^m$, a party can generate subordinate secret keys $\mathsf{sk}_{f_{z'}}$ for any $z' \in \{0,1\}^{m'}$, $m' > m$ that aligns with z on its first m bits. This secondary key generation process is accomplished simply by applying the PRGs to sk_{f_z}, traversing the GGM tree according to the additional bits of z'.

Punctured Pseudorandom Functions. Punctured PRFs, formalized by [29], are a special case of functional PRFs where one can generate keys for the function family $\mathcal{F} = \{f_x(y) = y \text{ if } y \neq x, \text{ and } \bot \text{ otherwise}\}$. Such PRFs have recently been shown to have important applications, including use as a primary technique in proving security of various cryptographic primitives based on the existence of indistinguishability obfuscation (see, e.g., [29,22]).

The existence of a functional PRF for the prefix-fixing function family gives a construction of punctured PRFs. Namely, a punctured key sk_x allowing one to compute the PRF on all inputs except $x = x_1 \ldots x_n$ consists of n functional keys for the prefix-fixing function family for prefixes:

$$(\bar{x}_1), (x_1 \bar{x}_2), (x_1 x_2 \bar{x}_3), \ldots, (x_1 x_2 \ldots x_{n-1} \bar{x}_n).$$

Our GGM-based construction in the previous section thus directly yields a selectively secure punctured PRF based on OWFs.

Corollary 3 (Selectively-Secure Punctured PRFs). *Assuming the existence of OWF, there exists a selectively secure punctured PRF for any desired poly-size input length.*

We remark that full security can be achieved with a security loss of 2^{-n} (as the reduction needs only to guess which of the 2^n query sets will be made by the adversary, corresponding to the 2^n possible point puncturings).

5 Open Problems

The size of the signatures in our SNARK-based functional signature scheme is dependent only on the security parameter (as one would desire), but the construction is based on non-falsifiable assumptions. In Section 3, we show that, for any sufficiently expressive functional signature scheme (supporting a function class $\mathcal{F}$ that contains any NP-complete relation), a functional signature for $y = f(x)$ cannot be sublinear in the size of y or x, unless the construction is either proven secure under a non-falsifiable assumption or makes use of non-black-box techniques. However, no lower bound exists that relates the size of the signature to the description of f (which may have short inputs/outputs x, y but a large description). Constructing functional signatures with short (sublinear in the size of the functions supported) signatures and verification time under falsifiable assumptions remains an open problem.

An interesting problem left open by this work is to construct a functional PRF that is also *verifiable*. A verifiable PRF, introduced by Micali, Rabin and Vadhan in [25] has the property that, in addition to the secret seed s of the PRF, there is a corresponding public key pk_s and a way to generate a proof π_x given the secret seed, such that given pk_s, x, y and π_x, one can check that y is indeed the consistent output of the PRF on x. (The challenge arises in guaranteeing soundness even though the public key is produced by the potentially malicious party. This, for example, rules out direct application of non-interactive zero-knowledge proofs, which require an honestly generated common reference string.) The public parameters and proofs π_x should not allow an adversary to distinguish the outputs of the PRF from random on any point x' for which the adversary has not received a proof. A construction of standard verifiable PRFs was given by Lysyanskaya based on the many-DH assumption in bilinear groups in [24].

One may extend the notion of verifiable PRFs to the setting of functional PRFs by enabling a user with functional key sk_f to also generate verifiable proofs π_x of correctness for evaluations of the PRF on inputs x for which his key allows. We note that such a verifiable functional pseudorandom function family supporting keys for a function class $\mathcal{F}$, implies a functional signature scheme that supports signing keys for the same function class, so the lower bound mentioned for functional signatures applies also to the proofs output in the verifiable functional PRF context.

References

1. Agrawal, S., Gorbunov, S., Vaikuntanathan, V., Wee, H.: Functional encryption: New perspectives and lower bounds. In: Canetti, R., Garay, J.A. (eds.) CRYPTO 2013, Part II. LNCS, vol. 8043, pp. 500–518. Springer, Heidelberg (2013)

2. Backes, M., Meiser, S., Schröder, D.: Delegatable functional signatures. Cryptology ePrint Archive, Report 2013/408 (2013)
3. Barak, B., Goldreich, O., Impagliazzo, R., Rudich, S., Sahai, A., Vadhan, S.P., Yang, K.: On the (im)possibility of obfuscating programs. In: Kilian, J. (ed.) CRYPTO 2001. LNCS, vol. 2139, pp. 1–18. Springer, Heidelberg (2001)
4. Bellare, M., Fuchsbauer, G.: Policy-based signatures. Cryptology ePrint Archive, Report 2013/413 (2013)
5. Bitansky, N., Canetti, R., Chiesa, A., Tromer, E.: From extractable collision resistance to succinct non-interactive arguments of knowledge, and back again. In: ITCS, pp. 326–349 (2012)
6. Bitansky, N., Canetti, R., Chiesa, A., Tromer, E.: Recursive composition and bootstrapping for snarks and proof-carrying data. In: STOC, pp. 111–120 (2013)
7. Boneh, D., Freeman, D.M.: Homomorphic signatures for polynomial functions. In: Paterson, K.G. (ed.) EUROCRYPT 2011. LNCS, vol. 6632, pp. 149–168. Springer, Heidelberg (2011)
8. Boneh, D., Sahai, A., Waters, B.: Functional encryption: Definitions and challenges. In: Ishai, Y. (ed.) TCC 2011. LNCS, vol. 6597, pp. 253–273. Springer, Heidelberg (2011)
9. Boneh, D., Waters, B.: Constrained pseudorandom functions and their applications. Cryptology ePrint Archive, Report 2013/352 (2013)
10. Boyle, E., Goldwasser, S., Ivan, I.: Functional signatures and pseudorandom functions. Cryptology ePrint Archive, Report 2013/401 (2013)
11. Diffie, W., Hellman, M.E.: New directions in cryptography. IEEE Transactions on Information Theory 22(6), 644–654 (1976)
12. Gennaro, R., Wichs, D.: Fully homomorphic message authenticators. IACR Cryptology ePrint Archive, 2012:290 (2012)
13. Gentry, C., Wichs, D.: Separating succinct non-interactive arguments from all falsifiable assumptions. In: STOC, pp. 99–108 (2011)
14. Goldreich, O., Goldwasser, S., Micali, S.: How to construct random functions. J. ACM 33(4), 792–807 (1986)
15. Goldreich, O., Micali, S., Wigderson, A.: How to prove all np-statements in zero-knowledge, and a methodology of cryptographic protocol design. In: Odlyzko, A.M. (ed.) CRYPTO 1986. LNCS, vol. 263, pp. 171–185. Springer, Heidelberg (1987)
16. Goldwasser, S., Kalai, Y.T.: On the impossibility of obfuscation with auxiliary input. In: FOCS, pp. 553–562 (2005)
17. Goldwasser, S., Kalai, Y.T., Popa, R.A., Vaikuntanathan, V., Zeldovich, N.: Succinct functional encryption and applications: Reusable garbled circuits and beyond. IACR Cryptology ePrint Archive, 2012:733 (2012)
18. Goldwasser, S., Kalai, Y.T., Popa, R.A., Vaikuntanathan, V., Zeldovich, N.: How to run turing machines on encrypted data. In: Canetti, R., Garay, J.A. (eds.) CRYPTO 2013, Part II. LNCS, vol. 8043, pp. 536–553. Springer, Heidelberg (2013)
19. Goldwasser, S., Micali, S.: Probabilistic encryption and how to play mental poker keeping secret all partial information. In: STOC, pp. 365–377 (1982)
20. Goldwasser, S., Micali, S., Rivest, R.L.: A digital signature scheme secure against adaptive chosen-message attacks. SIAM J. Comput. 17(2), 281–308 (1988)
21. Gorbunov, S., Vaikuntanathan, V., Wee, H.: Functional encryption with bounded collusions via multi-party computation. In: Safavi-Naini, R., Canetti, R. (eds.) CRYPTO 2012. LNCS, vol. 7417, pp. 162–179. Springer, Heidelberg (2012)
22. Hohenberger, S., Sahai, A., Waters, B.: Replacing a random oracle: Full domain hash from indistinguishability obfuscation. Cryptology ePrint Archive, Report 2013/509 (2013)

23. Kiayias, A., Papadopoulos, S., Triandopoulos, N., Zacharias, T.: Delegatable pseudorandom functions and applications. Cryptology ePrint Archive, Report 2013/379 (2013)
24. Lysyanskaya, A.: Unique signatures and verifiable random functions from the dh-ddh separation. In: Yung, M. (ed.) CRYPTO 2002. LNCS, vol. 2442, pp. 597–612. Springer, Heidelberg (2002)
25. Micali, S., Rabin, M.O., Vadhan, S.P.: Verifiable random functions. In: FOCS, pp. 120–130 (1999)
26. Naor, M.: On cryptographic assumptions and challenges. In: Boneh, D. (ed.) CRYPTO 2003. LNCS, vol. 2729, pp. 96–109. Springer, Heidelberg (2003)
27. Papamanthou, C., Shi, E., Tamassia, R.: Signatures of correct computation. In: Sahai, A. (ed.) TCC 2013. LNCS, vol. 7785, pp. 222–242. Springer, Heidelberg (2013)
28. Sahai, A., Waters, B.: Fuzzy identity-based encryption. In: Cramer, R. (ed.) EUROCRYPT 2005. LNCS, vol. 3494, pp. 457–473. Springer, Heidelberg (2005)
29. Sahai, A., Waters, B.: How to use indistinguishability obfuscation: Deniable encryption, and more. Cryptology ePrint Archive, Report 2013/454 (2013)

Policy-Based Signatures

Mihir Bellare[1] and Georg Fuchsbauer[2]

[1] Department of Computer Science and Engineering,
University of California San Diego, USA
[2] Institute of Science and Technology Austria

Abstract. We introduce policy-based signatures (PBS), where a signer can only sign messages conforming to some authority-specified policy. The main requirements are unforgeability and privacy, the latter meaning that signatures not reveal the policy. PBS offers value along two fronts: (1) On the practical side, they allow a corporation to control what messages its employees can sign under the corporate key. (2) On the theoretical side, they unify existing work, capturing other forms of signatures as special cases or allowing them to be easily built. Our work focuses on definitions of PBS, proofs that this challenging primitive is realizable for arbitrary policies, efficient constructions for specific policies, and a few representative applications.

1 Introduction

PBS. In a standard digital signature scheme [25,29], a signer who has established a public verification key vk and a matching secret signing key sk can sign any message that it wants. We introduce policy-based signatures (PBS), where a signer's secret key sk_p is associated to a policy $p \in \{0,1\}^*$ that allows the signer to produce a valid signature σ of a message m only if the message satisfies the policy, meaning (p, m) belongs to a *policy language* $L \subseteq \{0,1\}^* \times \{0,1\}^*$ associated to the scheme.

This cannot be achieved if the signer creates her keys in a standalone way. In our model, a signer is issued a signing key sk_p for a particular policy p by an authority, as a function of a master secret key msk held by the authority. Verification that σ is a valid signature of m is then done with respect to the authority's public parameters pp.

Within this framework, we consider a number of security goals. The most basic are unforgeability and privacy. Unforgeability says that producing a valid signature for message m is infeasible unless one has a secret key sk_p for some policy p such that $(p, m) \in L$. (You can only sign messages that you are allowed to sign.) Privacy requires that signatures not reveal the policy under which they were created. We will propose and explore different formalizations of these goals.

A trivial way to achieving PBS is via certificates. In more detail, to issue a secret key sk_p for policy p, the authority generates a fresh key pair (sk, pk) for an ordinary signature scheme, creates a certificate $cert$ consisting of a signature of (p, pk) under the authority's signing key msk, and returns $sk_p = (sk, pk, p, cert)$

H. Krawczyk (Ed.): PKC 2014, LNCS 8383, pp. 520–537, 2014.

to the signer. The latter's signature on m is now an ordinary signature of m under sk together with $(pk, p, cert)$, and verification is possible given the public verifying key pp of the authority. However, while this will provide unforgeability, it does not provide privacy, because the policy must be revealed in the signature to allow for verification. Similarly, privacy in the absence of unforgeability is also trivial. The combination of the two requirements, however, results in a non-trivial goal.

PBS may be viewed as an authentication analogue of functional encryption [15]. We can view the latter as allowing decryption to be policy-restricted rather than total, an authority issuing decryption keys in a way that enforces the policy. Correspondingly, in PBS the signing capability is policy-restricted, an authority issuing signing keys in a way that enforces the policy.

WHY PBS? Given that there already exist many forms of signatures, one might ask why another. PBS offers value along two fronts, practical and theoretical. On the practical side, the setup of PBS is natural in a corporate or other hierarchical environment. For example, a corporation may want to allow employees to sign under the company public key pp, but may want to restrict the signing capability of different employees based on their positions and privileges. However, the company policies underlying the restrictions need to be kept private. On the theoretical side, PBS decreases rather than increases complexity in the area because it serves as an umbrella notion unifying existing notions by capturing some as special cases and allowing others to be derived in simple and natural ways. In particular, this is true for a significant body of work on signatures that have privacy features, including group signatures [22,10], proxy signatures [35], ring signatures [38,14], mesh signatures [17], anonymous proxy signatures [28], attribute-based signatures [34] and anonymous credentials [19,6].

POLICY LANGUAGES. We wish to allow policies as expressive and general as possible. We accordingly allow the policy language to be any language in **P**, which captures most typical applications, where one can test in polynomial time whether a given policy allows a given message. At first this may seem as general as one can get, but we go further, allowing the policy language to be any language in **NP**. This means that the policies that can be expressed and enforced are restricted neither in form nor type, the only condition being that, given a witness, one can test in polynomial time whether a policy allows a given message. We will see applications where it is important that policy languages can be in **NP** rather than merely in **P**.

DEFINITIONS AND RELATIONS. We first provide an unforgeability definition and an indistinguishability based privacy definition. Unforgeability says that an adversary cannot create a valid signature of a message m without having a key for some policy p such that $(p, m) \in L$, even when it can obtain keys for other policies, and signatures for other messages under the target policy. Indistinguishability says that the verifier cannot tell under which of two keys a signature was created assuming both policies associated to the keys permit the corresponding message. Our definition also implies that the verifier cannot decide whether two signatures were created using the same key.

However, indistinguishability may not always provide privacy. For example, if for each message m there is only one policy p_m such that $(p_m, m) \in L$ then even a scheme where a signature of m reveals p_m satisfies indistinguishability. We provide a stronger, simulatability-based privacy notion that says that real signatures look like ones a simulator could generate without knowledge of the policy or any key. This strong notion of privacy is not subject to the above-discussed weaknesses of indistinguishability. The situation parallels that for functional encryption (FE), where an indistinguishability-based requirement was shown to not always suffice [15,37] and stronger simulatability requirements have been defined and considered [15,37,11,23,2,5,36]. However, for FE, impossibility results show that the strongest and most desirable simulation-based definitions are not achievable [15,11,23,2,36]. In contrast, for PBS we show that our simulatability notion is achievable in the standard model under standard assumptions.

We also strengthen unforgeability to provide an extractability notion for PBS. We show that simulatability implies indistinguishability, and simulatability+extractability implies unforgeability. Simulatability+extractability emerges as a powerful security notion that enables a wide range of applications.

CONSTRUCTIONS. PBS for arbitrary **NP** policy languages achieving simulatability+extractability is an ambitious target. The first question that emerges is whether this can be achieved, even in principle, let alone efficiently. We answer in the affirmative via two generic constructions based on standard primitives. The first uses ordinary signatures, IND-CPA encryption and standard non-interactive zero-knowledge (NIZK) proofs. The second uses only ordinary signatures and simulation(-sound) extractable NIZK proofs [30].

While our generic constructions prove the theoretical feasibility of PBS, their use of general NIZKs makes them inefficient. We ask whether more efficient solutions may be given without resorting to the random-oracle model [12]. Combining Groth-Sahai proofs [31] and structure-preserving signatures [1], we design efficient PBS schemes for policy languages expressible via equations over a bilinear group. This construction requires a twist over usual applications of Groth-Sahai proofs; namely, in order to hide the policy, we swap the roles of constants and variables. This provides a tool that, like structure-preserving signatures, is useful in cryptographic applications where policies may be about group elements.

APPLICATIONS AND IMPLICATIONS. We illustrate applicability by showing how to derive a variety of other primitives from PBS in simple and natural ways. This shows how PBS can function as a unifying framework for signatures and beyond. In Section 5 we show that PBS implies group signatures meeting the strong CCA version of the definition of [10]. In the full version [7] we also show that PBS implies attribute-based signatures [34] and signatures of knowledge [21]. These applications are illustrative rather than exhaustive, many more being possible.

Our generic constructions discussed above show which primitives are sufficient to build PBS. A natural question is which primitives are necessary, namely, which fundamental primitives are implied by PBS? In [7], we address this and show that PBS implies seemingly unrelated primitives like IND-CPA encryption and simulation-extractable NIZK proofs [30]. By [39] this means PBS implies IND-CCA encryption. In particular, this means the assumptions we make for our generic constructions are not only sufficient but necessary.

DELEGATABLE PBS. In Section 6 we extend the PBS framework to allow delegation. This means that an entity receiving from the authority a key sk_{p_1} for a policy p_1 can then issue to another entity a key $sk_{p_1\|p_2}$ that allows the signing of messages m which satisfy both policies p_1 and p_2. The holder of $sk_{p_1\|p_2}$ can further delegate a key $sk_{p_1\|p_2\|p_3}$, and so on. This is useful in a hierarchical setting, where a company president can delegate to vice presidents, who can then delegate to managers, and so on. We provide definitions which extend and strengthen those for the basic PBS setting; in particular, privacy must hold even when the adversary chooses the user keys. We then show how to achieve delegatable PBS for policy chains of arbitrary polynomial length. For simplicity, we base our construction, achieving sim+ext security, on append-only signatures [33], which can however be easily constructed from ordinary signatures.

DISCUSSION. In the world of digital signatures, extensions of functionality typically involve some form of delegation of signing rights: group signatures allow members to sign on behalf of a whole group, in attribute-based signatures (ABS) and types of anonymous credentials, keys are also issued by an authority, and (anonymous) proxy signatures model delegation and re-delegation explicitly. For most of these primitives, anonymity or privacy notions have been considered. A group signature, for example, should not reveal which group member produced a signature on behalf of the group (while an authority can trace group signatures to their signer). In ABS, users hold keys corresponding to their attributes and can sign messages with respect to a policy, which is a predicate over attributes. Users should only be able make signatures for policies satisfied by their attributes. Privacy for ABS means that a signature should reveal nothing about the attributes of the key under which it was produced, other than the fact that it satisfies the policy.

In the models of primitives such as ABS or mesh signatures, the policy itself is always public, as is the warrant specifying the policy in (even anonymous) proxy signatures. With PBS, we ask whether this is a natural limitation of privacy notions, and whether it is inherently unavoidable that objects like the policy (which specify *why* the message could be signed) need to be public.

Consider the example of a company implementing a scheme where each employee gets a signing key and there is one public key which is used by outsiders to verify signatures in the name of the company. A group-signature scheme would allow every employee holding a key to sign on behalf of the company, but there is no fine-grained control over who is allowed to sign which documents. This can be achieved using attribute-based signatures, where each user is assigned attributes, and a message is signed with respect to a policy like (*CEO* or (*board member and general manager*)). However, it is questionable whether a verifier needs to know the company-internal policy used to sign a specific message, and there is no apparent reason he should know; all he needs to be assured of is that the message was signed by someone entitled to, but not who this person is, what she is entitled to sign, nor whether two messages were signed by the same person. This is what PBS provides.

Another issue is that when using ABS we have to assume that the verifier can tell which messages can be signed under which policies. An attribute-based signature which is valid under the policy (*CEO* or *intern*) tells a verifier that it could have been produced by an intern, but it does not provide any guarantees as to whether an intern would have been entitled to sign the message. We ask whether it is possible to avoid having these types of public policies at all. PBS answers this in the affirmative.

RELATED WORK. The use of NIZKs for signatures begins with [8], who built an ordinary signature scheme from a NIZK, a pseudorandom function (PRF) and a commitment scheme. Encryption and ordinary signatures were combined with NIZKs to create group signatures in [10]. Our first generic construction builds on these ideas. Our second generic construction, inspired by [26,9], exploits the power of simulation-extractable NIZKs to give a conceptually simpler scheme that, in addition to the NIZK, uses only an ordinary signature scheme.

In independent and concurrent work, Boyle, Goldwasser and Ivan (BGI) [18] introduce functional signatures, where an authority can provide a key for a function f that allows the signing of any message in the range of f. This can be captured as a special case of PBS in which the policy is f and the policy language is the set of all (f, m) such that m is in the range of f, a witness for membership being a pre-image of m under f. BGI define unforgeability and an indistinguishability-based privacy requirement, but not the stronger simulatability or extractability conditions that we define and achieve. BGI have a succinctness condition which we do not have.

A related primitive is malleable signatures, introduced by Chase, Kohlweiss, Lysyanskaya and Meiklejohn [20]. They are defined with respect to a set of functions $\mathcal{F}$, so that given a signature of m, anyone can derive a signature of $f(m)$ for $f \in \mathcal{F}$. Concurrently to our work, Backes, Meiser and Schröder [3] introduced delegatable functional signatures, but in their model delegatees have public keys and signatures are verified under the authority's and the delegatee's keys. Privacy means that signatures from delegatees are indistinguishable from signatures from the authority.

Three recent works independently and concurrently introduce PRFs where one may issue a key to evaluate the PRF on a subset of the points of the domain [16,18,32]. These can be viewed as PRF analogues of policy-based signatures in which a policy corresponds to a set of inputs and a key allows computation of the PRF on the inputs in the set. Boneh and Waters [16] also provide a policy-based key-distribution scheme.

In their treatment of policy-based cryptography, Bagga and Molva [4] mention both policy-based encryption and policy-based signatures. However they do not consider privacy, without which, as noted above, the problem is easy. Moreover, they have no formal definitions of security requirements or proofs that their bilinear-map-based schemes achieve any well-defined security goal.

2   Preliminaries

NOTATIONS AND CONVENTIONS. If S is a finite set then $|S|$ denotes its size and $s \leftarrow_\$ S$ denotes picking an element uniformly from S and assigning it to s. For $i \in \mathbb{N}$ we let $[i] = \{1, \ldots, i\}$. We denote by $\lambda \in \mathbb{N}$ the security parameter and by 1^λ its unary representation. Algorithms are randomized unless otherwise indicated and "PT" stands for "polynomial-time". By $y \leftarrow A(x_1, \ldots; R)$, we denote the operation of running algorithm A on inputs $x_1, \ldots$ and coins R and letting y denote the output. By $y \leftarrow_\$ A(x_1, \ldots)$, we denote letting $y \leftarrow A(x_1, \ldots; R)$ with R chosen at random. We denote by $[A(x_1, \ldots)]$ the set of points that have positive probability of being output by A on inputs $x_1, \ldots$.

A map $\mathsf{R}: \{0,1\}^* \times \{0,1\}^* \to \{0,1\}^*$ is said to be an **NP**-relation if it is computable in time polynomial in the length of its first input. For $x \in \{0,1\}^*$ we let $\mathsf{WS}_\mathsf{R}(x) = \{w : \mathsf{R}(x, w) = 1\}$ be the *witness set* of x. We let $\mathcal{L}(\mathsf{R}) = \{x : \mathsf{WS}_\mathsf{R}(x) \neq \emptyset\}$ be the *language* associated to R. The fact that R is an **NP**-relation means that $\mathcal{L}(\mathsf{R}) \in \mathbf{NP}$.

GAME-PLAYING FRAMEWORK. For our security definitions and proofs we use the code-based game-playing framework of [13]. A game **Exp** (Figure 1, for example) consists of a finite number of procedures. We execute a game with an adversary $\mathcal{A}$ and security parameter $\lambda \in \mathbb{N}$ as follows. The adversary gets 1^λ as input. It can then query game procedures. Its first query must be to INITIALIZE with argument 1^λ, and its last to FINALIZE, and these must be the only queries to these oracles. The output of the execution, denoted $\mathbf{Exp}_\mathcal{A}(\lambda)$ is the output of FINALIZE. The running time of the adversary $\mathcal{A}$ is a function of λ in which oracle calls are assumed to take unit time.

3   Policy-Based Signatures

POLICY LANGUAGES. A *policy checker* is an **NP**-relation PC: $\{0,1\}^* \times \{0,1\}^* \to \{0,1\}$. The first input is a pair (p, m) representing a policy $p \in \{0,1\}^*$ and a message $m \in \{0,1\}^*$, while the second input is a witness $w \in \{0,1\}^*$. The associated language $\mathcal{L}(\mathsf{PC}) = \{(p, m) : \mathsf{WS}_\mathsf{PC}((p, m)) \neq \emptyset\}$ is called the *policy language* associated to PC. That $(p, m) \in \mathcal{L}(\mathsf{PC})$ means that signing m is permitted under policy p. We say that (p, m, w) is PC-valid if $\mathsf{PC}((p, m), w) = 1$.

PBS SCHEMES. A *policy-based signature scheme* $\mathcal{PBS} = (\mathsf{Setup}, \mathsf{KeyGen}, \mathsf{Sign}, \mathsf{Verify})$ is a 4-tuple of PT algorithms:

1. Setup: On input the unary-encoded security parameter 1^λ, setup algorithm Setup returns public parameters pp and a master secret key msk.
2. KeyGen: On input msk and p, where $p \in \{0,1\}^*$ is a policy, key-generation algorithm KeyGen outputs a signing key sk for p.
3. Sign: On input sk, m and w, where $m \in \{0,1\}^*$ is a message and $w \in \{0,1\}^*$ is a witness, signing algorithm Sign outputs a signature σ.
4. Verify: On input pp, m and σ, verification algorithm Verify outputs a bit.

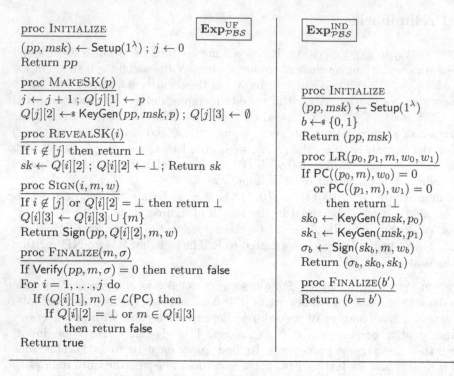

Fig. 1. Games defining unforgeability and indistinguishability for PBS

We say that the scheme is *correct* relative to policy checker PC if for all $\lambda \in \mathbb{N}$, all PC-valid (p, m, w), all $(pp, msk) \in [\mathsf{Setup}(1^\lambda)]$ and all $\sigma \in [\mathsf{Sign}(\mathsf{KeyGen}(msk, p), m, w)]$ we have $\mathsf{Verify}(pp, m, \sigma) = 1$.

UNFORGEABILITY. Our basic unforgeability requirement is that it be hard to create a valid signature of m without holding a key for some policy p such that $(p, m) \in \mathcal{L}(\mathsf{PC})$. The formalization is based on game $\mathbf{Exp}_{\mathcal{PBS}}^{\mathrm{UF}}$ in Figure 1. For $\lambda \in \mathbb{N}$ we let $\mathbf{Adv}_{\mathcal{PBS},\mathcal{A}}^{\mathrm{UF}}(\lambda) = \Pr[\mathbf{Exp}_{\mathcal{PBS},\mathcal{A}}^{\mathrm{UF}} \Rightarrow \mathsf{true}]$. We say that $\mathcal{PBS}$ is *unforgeable*, or UF-*secure*, if $\mathbf{Adv}_{\mathcal{PBS},\mathcal{A}}^{\mathrm{UF}}(\cdot)$ is negligible for every PT $\mathcal{A}$. Via a MAKESK query, the adversary can have the game create a key for a policy p. Then, via SIGN, it can obtain a signature under this key for any message of its choice. (This models a chosen-message attack.) It may also, via its REVEALSK oracle, obtain the key itself. (This models corruption of users or the formation of collusions of users who pool their keys.) These queries naturally give the adversary the capability of creating signatures for certain messages, namely messages m such that for some p with $(p, m) \in \mathcal{L}(\mathsf{PC})$, it either obtained a key for p or obtained a signature for m. Unforgeability asks that it cannot sign any other messages. Note that we did not explicitly specify how Sign behaves when run on a key for p, and m, w with $\mathsf{PC}((p, m), w) = 0$. However, if it outputs a valid signature, this can be used to break UF-security.

INDISTINGUISHABILITY. Privacy for policy-based signatures requires that a signature not reveal the policy associated to the key and neither the witness that was used to create the signature. A first idea would be the following formalization: an adversary outputs a message m, two policies p_0, p_1, and two witnesses w_0, w_1, such that (p_0, m, w_0) and (p_1, m, w_1) are PC-valid. For either p_0 or p_1 the experiment computes a secret key and uses it to produce a signature on m, from which the adversary has to determine which policy was used. It turns out that this notion is too weak, as it does not guarantee that two signatures produced under the same secret key do not link, as seen as follows. Consider a scheme satisfying the security notion just sketched and modify it by attaching to each secret key a random string during key generation and alter Sign to append to the signature the random string contained in the secret key. Clearly, two signatures under the same key are linkable, but yet the scheme satisfies the definition. We therefore give the adversary both secret keys in addition to the signature.

Let $\mathbf{Exp}_{\mathcal{PBS}, \mathcal{A}}^{\mathrm{IND}}$ be the game defined in Figure 1. We say that $\mathcal{PBS}$ has *indistinguishability* if for all PT adversaries $\mathcal{A}$ we have that $\mathbf{Adv}_{\mathcal{PBS}, \mathcal{A}}^{\mathrm{IND}}(\lambda) = \Pr[\mathbf{Exp}_{\mathcal{PBS}, \mathcal{A}}^{\mathrm{IND}}(\lambda) \Rightarrow \text{true}] - \frac{1}{2}$ is negligible in λ. We assume that either all policy descriptions p are of equal length, or that $\mathcal{A}$ outputs p_0 and p_1 with $|p_0| = |p_1|$.

Unlinkability could be formalized via a game where an adversary is given two signatures and must decide whether they were created using the same key. Indistinguishability implies unlinkability, as an adversary against the latter could be used to build another one against indistinguishability, who can simulate the unlinkability game by using the received signing keys to produce signatures.

DISCUSSION. The unforgeability and indistinguishability notions we have defined above are basic, intuitive, and suffice for many applications. However, they have some weaknesses, and some applications call for stronger requirements.

First, we claim that indistinguishability does not always provide the privacy we may expect. To see this, consider a policy checker PC such that for every message m there is only one p with $(p, m) \in \mathcal{L}(\mathsf{PC})$. (See our construction of group signatures in Section 5 for an example of such a PC.) Now consider a scheme which satisfies indistinguishability, and modify it so that the key contains the policy and the signing algorithm appends the policy to the signature. This scheme clearly does not hide the policy, yet still satisfies indistinguishability. Indeed, in $\mathbf{Exp}_{\mathcal{PBS}}^{\mathrm{IND}}$, in order to satisfy $\mathsf{PC}((p_0, m), w_0) = 1 = \mathsf{PC}((p_1, m), w_1)$, the adversary must return $p_0 = p_1$. If the signatures in the original scheme have not revealed the bit b then attaching the same policy to both will not do so either. The notion of simulatability we provide below will fill the gap. It asks that there is a simulator which can create simulated signatures without having access to any signing key or witness, and that these signatures are indistinguishable from real signatures.

With regard to unforgeability, one issue is that in general it cannot be efficiently verified whether an adversary has won the game, as this involves checking whether $(p, m) \in \mathcal{L}(\mathsf{PC})$ for all p queried to MAKESK and m from the adversary's final output, and membership in $\mathcal{L}(\mathsf{R})$ may not be efficiently decidable. (This is the case for $\mathcal{L}(\mathsf{R})$ defined in (4) in Section 5.) Although not a problem

$\mathbf{Exp}^{\mathrm{SIM}}_{\mathcal{PBS}}$	$\mathbf{Exp}^{\mathrm{EXT}}_{\mathcal{PBS}}$

proc INITIALIZE
$b \leftarrow\!\!\$ \{0,1\}$; $j \leftarrow 0$
$(pp_0, msk_0, tr) \leftarrow\!\!\$ \mathsf{SimSetup}(1^\lambda)$
$(pp_1, msk_1) \leftarrow\!\!\$ \mathsf{Setup}(1^\lambda)$
Return (pp_b, msk_b)
 	
proc KEY(p)
$j \leftarrow j+1$; $sk_0 \leftarrow\!\!\$ \mathsf{SKeyGen}(tr, p)$
$sk_1 \leftarrow\!\!\$ \mathsf{KeyGen}(msk_1, p)$
$Q[j][1] \leftarrow p$; $Q[j][2] \leftarrow sk_1$
Return sk_b
 	
proc SIGNATURE(i, m, w)
If $i \notin [j]$ then return $\perp$
If $\mathsf{PC}((Q[i][1], m), w) = 1$
    then $\sigma_0 \leftarrow\!\!\$ \mathsf{SimSign}(tr, m)$
Else $\sigma_0 \leftarrow \perp$
$\sigma_1 \leftarrow\!\!\$ \mathsf{Sign}(Q[i][2], m, w)$; Return σ_b
 	
proc FINALIZE(b')
Return $(b = b')$
	proc INITIALIZE
	$(pp, msk, tr) \leftarrow\!\!\$ \mathsf{SimSetup}(1^\lambda)$
	$Q_K \leftarrow \emptyset$; $Q_S \leftarrow \emptyset$; Return pp
	
	proc SKEYGEN(p)
	$sk \leftarrow\!\!\$ \mathsf{SKeyGen}(tr, p)$
	$Q_K \leftarrow Q_K \cup \{p\}$; Return sk
	
	proc SIMSIGN(m)
	$\sigma \leftarrow\!\!\$ \mathsf{SimSign}(tr, m)$
	$Q_S \leftarrow Q_S \cup \{(m, \sigma)\}$; Return σ
	
	proc FINALIZE(m, σ)
	If $\mathsf{Verify}(pp, m, \sigma) = 0$
	    then return false
	If $(m, \sigma) \in Q_S$ then return false
	$(p, w) \leftarrow \mathsf{Extr}(tr, m, \sigma)$
	If $p \notin Q_K$ or $\mathsf{PC}((p, m), w) = 0$
	    then return true
	Return false

Fig. 2. Games defining simulatability and extractability for PBS

in itself, it can become one, for example when using the notion in a proof by game hopping, as a distinguisher between two games must efficiently determine whether an adversary has won the game. (See [7] for such a proof.) The extractability notion we will provide below will fill this gap as well as be more useful in applications. It requires that from a valid signature, using a trapdoor one can extract a policy and a valid witness. To satisfy this notion, a signature must contain information on the policy and can thus not hide its length. For simplicity, we assume from now on that all policies are of the same length.

SIMULATABILITY. We formalize *simulatability* by requiring that there exist the following algorithms: SimSetup, which outputs parameters and a master key that are indistinguishable from those output by Setup, as well as a trapdoor; SKeyGen, which outputs keys indistinguishable from those output by KeyGen; and SimSign, which on input the trapdoor and a message (but no signing key nor witness) produces signatures that are indistinguishable from regular signatures.

Let $\mathbf{Exp}^{\mathrm{SIM}}_{\mathcal{PBS}}$ be the game defined in Figure 2. We require that for every PT adversary $\mathcal{A}$ we have $\mathbf{Adv}^{\mathrm{SIM}}_{\mathcal{PBS}, \mathcal{A}}(\lambda) = \Pr[\mathbf{Exp}^{\mathrm{SIM}}_{\mathcal{PBS}, \mathcal{A}}(\lambda) \Rightarrow \mathsf{true}] - \frac{1}{2}$ is negligible in λ. Note that in all our constructions, tr contains msk and SKeyGen is defined as KeyGen. We included SKeyGen to make the definition more general.

EXTRACTABILITY. We define our notion in the spirit of *"sim-ext"* security for signatures of knowledge [21]. Let $\mathbf{Adv}^{\mathrm{EXT}}_{\mathcal{PBS}, \mathcal{A}}(\lambda) = \Pr[\mathbf{Exp}^{\mathrm{EXT}}_{\mathcal{PBS}, \mathcal{A}}(\lambda) \Rightarrow \mathsf{true}]$ with

$\mathbf{Exp}_{\mathcal{PBS}}^{\mathrm{EXT}}$ defined in Figure 2. We say that $\mathcal{PBS}$ has *extractability* if there exists an algorithm Extr which taking a trapdoor, a message and a signature outputs a pair $(p, w) \in \{0,1\}^*$, such that $\mathbf{Adv}_{\mathcal{PBS},\mathcal{A}}^{\mathrm{EXT}}(\cdot)$ is negligible for every PT $\mathcal{A}$.

Although the definition might not seem completely intuitive at first, it implies that, as long as the adversary outputs a valid message/signature pair and does not simply copy a SimSign query/response pair, the only signed messages it can output are those that satisfy the policy of one of the queried keys: assume $\mathcal{A}$ outputs (m^*, σ^*) such that $(*)$ for all $p \in Q_K$: $(p, m^*) \notin \mathcal{L}(\mathsf{PC})$. Then let $(p^*, w^*) \leftarrow \mathsf{Extr}(tr, m, \sigma)$. If $\mathsf{PC}((p^*, m^*), w^*) = 0$, the adversary wins $\mathbf{Exp}_{\mathcal{PBS}}^{\mathrm{EXT}}$. On the other hand, if $\mathsf{PC}((p^*, m^*), w^*) = 1$ then $(p^*, m^*) \in \mathcal{L}(\mathsf{PC})$, thus by $(*)$ we have $p^* \notin Q_K$ and it wins too. Note that this notion corresponds to *strong unforgeability* for signature schemes.

SIM-EXT SECURITY IMPLIES IND AND UF. In [7] we show that our two latter security notions are indeed strengthenings of the former two:

Theorem 1. *Any policy-based signature scheme which satisfies simulatability satisfies indistinguishability. Any PBS scheme which satisfies simulatability and extractability satisfies unforgeability.*

4   Constructions of Policy-Based Signature Schemes

We first show that PBS satisfying SIM+EXT can be achieved for any language in **NP**. Then we develop more efficient schemes for specific policy languages.

4.1   Generic Constructions

We now show how to construct policy-based signatures satisfying simulatability and extractability (and, by Theorem 1, IND and UF) for any **NP**-relation PC. In [7] we show that the assumptions we make are not only sufficient but necessary.

An first approach could be the following, similar to the generic construction of group signatures in [10]: The issuer creates a signature key pair (mvk, msk) and publishes mvk as pp. When a user is issued a key for a policy p, the issuer creates a key pair (vk_U, sk_U), signs $p\|vk_U$ and sends this certificate to the user together with (p, vk_U, sk_U). To sign a message m, the user first signs it under sk_U, thereby establishing a chain $mvk \rightarrow vk_U \rightarrow m$ via the certificate and the signature. The actual signature is a (zero-knowledge) proof of knowledge of such a chain and the fact that the message satisfies the policy signed in the certificate.

While this approach yields a scheme satisfying IND and UF, it would fail to achieve extractability. We thus choose a different approach: The user's key is simply a signature from the issuer on the policy. Now to sign a message, the user first picks a key pair (ovk, osk) for a strongly unforgeable one-time signature scheme[1] and makes a zero-knowledge proof π that he knows either (I) an issuer

---

[1] In such a scheme it must be infeasible for an adversary, after receiving a verification key ovk and after obtaining a signature σ on one message m of his choice, to output a signature σ^* on a message m^*, such that $(m, \sigma) \neq (m^*, \sigma^*)$.

$\underline{\mathsf{Setup}(1^\lambda)}$

  $crs \leftarrow_{\$} \mathsf{Setup}_{\mathrm{nizk}}(1^\lambda)$
  $(pk, dk) \leftarrow_{\$} \mathsf{KeyGen}_{\mathrm{pke}}(1^\lambda)$
  $(mvk, msk) \leftarrow_{\$} \mathsf{KeyGen}_{\mathrm{sig}}(1^\lambda)$
  Return $pp \leftarrow (crs, pk, mvk)$ and msk

$\underline{\mathsf{KeyGen}(msk, p)}$

  $s \leftarrow_{\$} \mathsf{Sign}_{\mathrm{sig}}(msk, 1\|p)$
  Return $sk_p \leftarrow (pp, p, s)$

$\underline{\mathsf{Sign}(sk_p, m, w)}$

  Parse $((crs, pk, mvk), p, s) \leftarrow sk_p$
  If $\mathsf{PC}((p, m), w) = 0$ then return $\perp$
  $(ovk, osk) \leftarrow_{\$} \mathsf{KeyGen}_{\mathrm{ots}}(1^\lambda)$
  $\rho_p, \rho_s, \rho_w \leftarrow_{\$} \{0,1\}^\lambda;\ C_p \leftarrow \mathsf{Enc}(pk, p; \rho_p)$
  $C_s \leftarrow \mathsf{Enc}(pk, s; \rho_s);\ C_w \leftarrow \mathsf{Enc}(pk, w; \rho_w)$
  $\pi \leftarrow_{\$} \mathsf{Prove}(crs, (pk, mvk, C_p, C_s, C_w,$
                  $ovk, m), (p, s, w, \rho_p, \rho_s, \rho_w))$
  $\tau \leftarrow_{\$} \mathsf{Sign}_{\mathrm{ots}}(osk, (m, C_p, C_s, C_w, \pi))$
  Return $\sigma \leftarrow (ovk, C_p, C_s, C_w, \pi, \tau)$

$\underline{\mathsf{Verify}(pp, m, \sigma)}$

  Parse $(crs, pk, mvk) \leftarrow pp$
  Parse $(ovk, C_p, C_s, C_w, \pi, \tau) \leftarrow \sigma$
  Return 1 iff
    $\mathsf{Verify}_{\mathrm{nizk}}(crs, (pk, mvk, C_p, C_s, C_w,$
                  $ovk, m), \pi) = 1$ and
    $\mathsf{Verify}_{\mathrm{ots}}(ovk, (m, C_p, C_s, C_w, \pi), \tau) = 1$

$\underline{\mathsf{SimSetup}(1^\lambda)}$

  $crs \leftarrow_{\$} \mathsf{Setup}_{\mathrm{nizk}}(1^\lambda)$
  $(pk, dk) \leftarrow_{\$} \mathsf{KeyGen}_{\mathrm{pke}}(1^\lambda)$
  $(mvk, msk) \leftarrow_{\$} \mathsf{KeyGen}_{\mathrm{sig}}(1^\lambda)$
  Return $pp \leftarrow (crs, pk, mvk),\ msk$
     and $tr \leftarrow (msk, dk)$

$\underline{\mathsf{SKeyGen}((msk, dk), p)}$

  $s \leftarrow_{\$} \mathsf{Sign}_{\mathrm{sig}}(msk, 1\|p)$
  Return $sk_p \leftarrow (pp, p, s)$

$\underline{\mathsf{SimSign}((msk, dk), m)}$

  $(ovk, osk) \leftarrow_{\$} \mathsf{KeyGen}_{\mathrm{ots}}(1^\lambda)$
  $s \leftarrow_{\$} \mathsf{Sign}_{\mathrm{sig}}(msk, 0\|ovk)$
  $\rho_p, \rho_s, \rho_w \leftarrow_{\$} \{0,1\}^\lambda$
  $C_p \leftarrow \mathsf{Enc}(pk, 0; \rho_p)$
  $C_s \leftarrow \mathsf{Enc}(pk, s; \rho_s)$
  $C_w \leftarrow \mathsf{Enc}(pk, 0; \rho_w)$
  $\pi \leftarrow_{\$} \mathsf{Prove}(crs, (pk, mvk, C_p, C_s,$
                  $C_w, ovk, m), (0, s, 0, \rho_p, \rho_s, \rho_w))$
  $\tau \leftarrow_{\$} \mathsf{Sign}_{\mathrm{ots}}(osk, (m, C_p, C_s, C_w, \pi))$
  Return $\sigma \leftarrow (ovk, C_p, C_s, C_w, \pi, \tau)$

$\underline{\mathsf{Extr}((msk, dk), m, \sigma)}$

  Parse $(ovk, C_p, C_s, C_w, \pi, \tau) \leftarrow \sigma$
  $p \leftarrow \mathsf{Dec}(dk, C_p)\ ;\ w \leftarrow \mathsf{Dec}(dk, C_w)$
  Return (p, w)

Fig. 3. Generic construction of PBS

signature on a policy p such that $(p, m) \in \mathcal{L}(\mathsf{PC})$ or (II) an issuer signature on ovk. Finally, he adds a signature under ovk of both the message and the proof. As we will see, this construction satisfies both SIM (where the simulator can make a signature on ovk and use clause (II) for the proof) and EXT (as π is a proof of knowledge).

We formalize the above: Let $\mathcal{S}ig = (\mathsf{KeyGen}_{\mathrm{sig}}, \mathsf{Sign}_{\mathrm{sig}}, \mathsf{Verify}_{\mathrm{sig}})$ be a signature scheme which is unforgeable under chosen-message attacks (UF-CMA), $\mathcal{O}t\mathcal{S}ig = (\mathsf{KeyGen}_{\mathrm{ots}}, \mathsf{Sign}_{\mathrm{ots}}, \mathsf{Verify}_{\mathrm{ots}})$ a strongly unforgeable one-time signature scheme and let $\mathcal{PKE} = (\mathsf{KeyGen}_{\mathrm{pke}}, \mathsf{Enc}, \mathsf{Dec})$ be an IND-CPA-secure public-key encryption scheme. For a policy checker PC we define the following **NP**-relation:

$$((pk, mvk, C_p, C_s, C_w, ovk, m), (p, s, w, \rho_p, \rho_s, \rho_w)) \in R_{\mathrm{NP}}$$
$$\iff C_p = \mathsf{Enc}(pk, p; \rho_p) \wedge C_s = \mathsf{Enc}(pk, s; \rho_s) \wedge C_w = \mathsf{Enc}(pk, w; \rho_w)$$
$$\wedge \left[(\mathsf{Verify}_{\mathrm{sig}}(mvk, 1\|p, s) = 1 \wedge \mathsf{PC}((p, m), w) = 1) \right. \tag{1}$$
$$\left. \vee\ \mathsf{Verify}_{\mathrm{sig}}(mvk, 0\|ovk, s) = 1 \right]$$

Setup(1^λ)

$crs \leftarrow_\$ \mathsf{Setup}_{\mathrm{nizk}}(1^\lambda)$
$(mvk, msk) \leftarrow_\$ \mathsf{KeyGen}_{\mathrm{sig}}(1^\lambda)$
Return $pp \leftarrow (crs, mvk), msk$

KeyGen(msk, p)

$c \leftarrow_\$ \mathsf{Sign}_{\mathrm{sig}}(msk, p)$
Return $sk \leftarrow (pp, p, c)$

Sign($sk = ((crs, mvk), p, c), m, w$)

$\sigma \leftarrow_\$ \mathsf{Prove}(crs, (mvk, m), (p, c, w))$
Return σ

Verify($pp = (crs, mvk), m, \sigma$)

Return $\mathsf{Verify}_{\mathrm{nizk}}(crs, (mvk, m), \sigma)$

SimSetup(1^λ)

$(crs, tr) \leftarrow_\$ \mathsf{SimSetup}_{\mathrm{nizk}}(1^\lambda)$
$(mvk, msk) \leftarrow_\$ \mathsf{KeyGen}_{\mathrm{sig}}(1^\lambda)$.
Return $pp \leftarrow (crs, mvk), msk,$
$\quad\quad tr_{\mathrm{pbs}} \leftarrow (pp, msk, tr)$

SKeyGen($(pp, msk, tr), p$)

$c \leftarrow_\$ \mathsf{Sign}_{\mathrm{sig}}(msk, p)$; Return $sk \leftarrow (pp, p, c)$

SimSign($((crs, mvk), msk, tr), m$)

Return $\sigma \leftarrow_\$ \mathsf{SimProve}(crs, tr, (mvk, m))$

Extr($((crs, mvk), msk, tr), m, \sigma$)

$(p, c, w) \leftarrow \mathsf{Extr}_{\mathrm{nizk}}(tr, (mvk, m), \sigma)$
Return (p, w)

Fig. 4. PBS based on SE-NIZKs

Let $\mathcal{NIZK} = (\mathsf{Setup}_{\mathrm{nizk}}, \mathsf{Prove}, \mathsf{Verify}_{\mathrm{nizk}})$ be a non-interactive zero-knowledge (NIZK) proof system for $\mathcal{L}(R_{\mathrm{NP}})$. Our construction $\mathcal{PBS}$ for a policy checker PC is detailed in Figure 3, and in [7] we prove the following:

Theorem 2. *If $\mathcal{PKE}$ satisfies IND-CPA, $\mathcal{S}ig$ is UF-CMA , $\mathcal{O}t\mathcal{S}ig$ is a strongly unforgeable one-time signature scheme and $\mathcal{NIZK}$ is a NIZK proof system for $\mathcal{L}(R_{\mathrm{NP}})$ then $\mathcal{PBS}$, defined in Figure 3, satisfies simulatability and extractability.*

We now present a much simpler construction of PBS by relying on a more advanced cryptographic primitive: simulation-extractable (SE) NIZK proofs [30] (see [7] for the definition). Let $\mathcal{S}ig = (\mathsf{KeyGen}_{\mathrm{sig}}, \mathsf{Sign}_{\mathrm{sig}}, \mathsf{Verify}_{\mathrm{sig}})$ be a signature scheme and for a policy checker PC let $\mathcal{NIZK} = (\mathsf{Setup}_{\mathrm{nizk}}, \mathsf{Prove}, \mathsf{Verify}_{\mathrm{nizk}}, \mathsf{SimSetup}_{\mathrm{nizk}}, \mathsf{SimProve}, \mathsf{Extr}_{\mathrm{nizk}})$ be a SE-NIZK for the following **NP**-relation, whose statements are of the form $X = (vk, m)$ with witnesses $W = (p, c, w)$ and

$$((vk, m), (p, c, w)) \in R_{\mathrm{NP}} \iff \mathsf{Verify}_{\mathrm{sig}}(vk, p, c) = 1 \wedge ((p, m), w) \in \mathrm{PC}$$

Then the scheme in Figure 4 is a PBS for PC which satisfies SIM+EXT. In [7] we prove this for a more general scheme allowing delegation.

4.2 Efficient Construction via Groth-Sahai Proofs

Our efficient construction of PBS will be defined over a *bilinear group*. This is a tuple $(p, \mathbb{G}, \mathbb{H}, \mathbb{T}, G, H)$, where $\mathbb{G}, \mathbb{H}$ and $\mathbb{T}$ are groups of prime order p, generated by G and H, respectively, and $e: \mathbb{G} \times \mathbb{H} \to \mathbb{T}$ is a bilinear map such that $e(G, H)$ generates $\mathbb{T}$. We denote the group operation multiplicatively and let $1_{\mathbb{G}}$, $1_{\mathbb{H}}$ and $1_{\mathbb{T}}$ denote the neutral elements of $\mathbb{G}, \mathbb{H}$ and $\mathbb{T}$. Groth-Sahai proofs [31] let us prove that there exists a set of elements $(\boldsymbol{X}, \boldsymbol{Y}) = (X_1, \ldots, X_n, Y_1, \ldots, Y_\ell) \in \mathbb{G}^n \times \mathbb{H}^\ell$ which satisfy equations $\mathsf{E}(\underline{\boldsymbol{X}}, \underline{\boldsymbol{Y}})$ of the form

$$\prod_{i=1}^{k} e(P_i, Q_i) \prod_{j=1}^{\ell} e(A_j, \underline{Y_j}) \prod_{i=1}^{n} e(\underline{X_i}, B_i) \prod_{i=1}^{n}\prod_{j=1}^{\ell} e(\underline{X_i}, \underline{Y_j})^{\gamma_{ij}} = 1_{\mathbb{T}} \qquad (2)$$

Such an equation E is called a *pairing-product equation*[2] (PPE) and is uniquely defined by its constants P, Q, A, B and $\Gamma := (\gamma_{ij})_{i \in [n], j \in [\ell]}$. These equations have already found many uses in cryptography, of which the following two are relevant here: they can define the verification predicate of a digital signature (see [1]), or witness the fact that a ciphertext encrypts a certain value (see [7]). Our aim is to construct policy-based signatures where policies define (sets of) PPEs, which must be satisfied by the message and the witness.

Groth and Sahai define a setup algorithm which on input a bilinear group outputs a common reference string *crs* and an extraction key *xk*. On input *crs*, an equation E and a satisfying witness $(\boldsymbol{X}, \boldsymbol{Y})$, algorithm $\mathsf{Prove}_{\mathsf{gs}}$ outputs a proof π. Proofs are verified by $\mathsf{Verify}_{\mathsf{gs}}(crs, \mathsf{E}(\underline{\cdot}, \underline{\cdot}), \pi)$. Under the SXDH assumption (see [31]), proofs are *witness-indistinguishable* [27], that is, proofs for an equation using different witnesses are computationally indistinguishable. Moreover, they are *extractable* and thus proofs of knowledge [24]: From every valid proof π, $\mathsf{Extr}_{\mathsf{gs}}(xk, \mathsf{E}(\underline{\cdot}, \underline{\cdot}), \pi)$ extracts a witness $(\boldsymbol{X}, \boldsymbol{Y})$ such that $\mathsf{E}(\boldsymbol{X}, \boldsymbol{Y}) = 1$.

In our Groth-Sahai-based construction of PBS, messages and witnesses will be group elements and a policy defines a set of equations as in (2) that have to be satisfied. The policy checker is thus defined as follows: the policy p defines a set of equations $(\mathsf{E}_1, \ldots, \mathsf{E}_n)$ and $\mathsf{PC}((p, m), w) = 1$ iff $\mathsf{E}_i(m, w) = 1$ for all $i \in [n]$, where $m \in \mathbb{G}^{n_m} \times \mathbb{H}^{\ell_m}$ and $w \in \mathbb{G}^{n_w} \times \mathbb{H}^{\ell_w}$.

GS proofs only allow us to extract group elements; however, an equation—and thus a policy—is defined by a set of group elements and exponents γ_{ij}. In order to hide a policy, we need to swap the roles of constants and variables in an equation, as this will enable us to hide the policy defined by the constants. We first transform equations as in (2) into a set of equivalent equations without exponents. To do so, we introduce auxiliary variables $\widehat{Y}_{ij}$, add $i \cdot j$ new equations and define the set $\mathsf{E}^{(\text{no-exp})}$ as follows:

$$\prod e(P_i, Q_i) \prod e(A_j, \underline{Y_j}) \prod e(\underline{X_i}, B_i) \prod \prod e(\underline{X_i}, \widehat{Y}_{ij}) = 1_{\mathbb{T}}$$
$$\wedge \bigwedge_{i,j} e(G, \underline{\widehat{Y}_{ij}}) = e(G^{\gamma_{ij}}, \underline{Y_j}) \quad (3)$$

A witness $(\boldsymbol{X}, \boldsymbol{Y})$ satisfies E in (2) iff $(\boldsymbol{X}, \boldsymbol{Y}, (\widehat{Y}_{ij} := Y_j^{\gamma_{ij}})_{i,j})$ satisfies the set of equations $\mathsf{E}^{(\text{no-exp})}$ in (3). Now we can show that a (clear) message $(\boldsymbol{M}, \boldsymbol{N})$ satisfies a "hidden" policy defined by equation E, witnessed by elements $(\boldsymbol{V}, \boldsymbol{W})$, since we can express policies as sets of group elements.

Our second building block are structure-preserving signatures [1], which were designed to be combined with GS proofs: their keys, messages and signatures consist of elements from $\mathbb{G}$ and $\mathbb{H}$ and signatures are verified by evaluating PPEs. GS proofs let us prove knowledge of keys, messages, and/or signatures which satisfy verification, without revealing anything beyond this fact.

Our construction now follows the blueprint of the generic scheme in Figure 3. The setup creates a CRS for GS proofs and a key pair (mvk, msk) for a structure-

---

[2] This is a *simulatable* pairing-product equation, that is, one for which Groth-Sahai proofs can be made zero-knowledge.

preserving scheme Sig_{sp}. (Note that here we need not encrypt any witnesses like in the generic construction, since GS proofs are extractable.) We transform every PPE E contained in a policy to a set of equations $E^{(no-exp)}$ without exponents. The policies can thus be expressed as sets of group elements describing the equations $E^{(no-exp)}$, which can be signed by Sig_{sp}.

A signing key is a signature on the policy under msk and signing is done by choosing a one-time signature key pair (ovk, osk), proving a statement analogous to (1) and signing the proof and the message with osk. A further technical obstacle is that we need to express the disjunction in the statement to be proven as (a conjunction of) sets of PPEs. We achieve this by following Groth's approach in [30]. The details of the construction can be found in [7].

A SIMPLE USE CASE. Messages that are elements of bilinear groups and policies demanding that they satisfy PPEs will prove useful to construct other cryptographic schemes like group signatures. Yet, our pairing-based construction might seem too abstract for deploying PBS to manage signing rights in a company—one of the motivations given in the introduction.

However, consider the following simple example: A company issues keys to their employees which should allow them to sign only messages $h\|m$ that start with a particular *header* h. (E.g. h could be "Contract with company X", so employees are limited to signing contracts with X.) This can be implemented by mapping messages $h\|m$ to $(F(h), F(m))$ via a collision-resistant hash function $F: \{0,1\}^* \to \mathbb{G}$. (E.g. first hash to $\mathbb{Z}_p$ via some f and then set $F(x) = G^{f(x)}$.) The policy p^* requiring messages to start with h^* can then be expressed as $PC((p^*, h\|m)) = 1 \Leftrightarrow e(F(h^*), H)\, e(F(h), H^{-1}) = 1$.

Another option would be to additionally demand that an employee hold a credential (verified via PPEs), which she must use as a witness when signing.

5   Applications and Implications

Here we illustrate how PBS can provide a unifying framework for work on advanced forms of signatures and beyond, capturing some primitives as special cases and allowing others to be derived in simple and natural ways. Here we show how PBS allows one to easily obtain group signatures [10]. In [7] we show that they imply signatures of knowledge [21] and attribute-based signatures [34]. These applications are illustrative rather than exhaustive.

Section 4.1 shows which primitives are sufficient for policy-based signatures. We now ask the converse question, namely which primitives are necessary, that is, which fundamental cryptographic primitives are implied by PBS? In [7] we show that PBSs imply simulation-extractable NIZKs and IND-CPA encryption. By a result [39] they thus imply IND-CCA public-key encryption. The sufficient assumptions we make in our constructions of Section 4.1 are thus also necessary.

CCA-SECURE GROUP SIGNATURES FROM PBS. Group signatures [22] let members sign anonymously on behalf of a group. To deter misuse, the group manager holds a secret key which can *open* signatures, that is, reveal the member that made the signature. As defined in [10], a group-signature scheme $\mathcal{GS}$ is a 4-tuple of PT algorithms. On input 1^λ and the group size 1^n, key generation algorithm GKg returns the group public key gpk, the manager's secret key $gmsk$ and a vector of member secret keys $\mathbf{gsk}$. On input $\mathbf{gsk}[i]$ and a message $m \in \{0,1\}^*$, signing algorithm GSig returns a group signature γ by member i on m. On input gpk, m and γ, verification algorithm GVf outputs a bit. On input $gmsk, m$ and γ, the opening algorithm Open returns an identity $i \in [n]$ or $\perp$.

Full anonymity requires that an adversary cannot decide which of two group members of its choice produced a group signature, even when given an oracle that opens any other signature. Traceability means that an adversary, which is allowed to corrupt users, cannot produce a group signature which opens to a user that was not corrupted. (We give a formal definition in [7].)

We now construct group signatures from CCA-secure public-key encryption and PBS. Since the former can be constructed from PBS (as we show in [7]), this means that PBS implies group signatures. The main idea is to define a group signature as a ciphertext plus a PBS. When making a group signature on a message m, a member is required to encrypt her identity as c and then sign (c, m). This is enforced by issuing to the member a PBS key whose policy ensures that c must be an encryption of the member's identity. Let $\mathcal{PKE} =$ (KeyGen$_{\text{pke}}$, Enc, Dec) be a public-key encryption scheme satisfying IND-CCA and let $\mathcal{PBS} =$ (Setup, KeyGen$_{\text{pbs}}$, Sign, Verify) be a PBS for the following **NP**-relation:

$$PC((((ek, i), (c, m)), r) \iff c = \text{Enc}(ek, i; r) . \tag{4}$$

(See [7] for an encryption scheme such that (4) lies in the language of our efficient PBS from Section 4.2.) In [7] we sow that the following group-signature scheme satisfies full anonymity and traceability as formalized by [10].

GKg$(1^\lambda, 1^n)$
> $(pp, msk) \leftarrow_\$ \text{Setup}(1^\lambda)$
> $(ek, dk) \leftarrow_\$ \text{KeyGen}_{\text{pke}}(1^\lambda)$
> For $i = 1, \ldots, n$ do
>> $sk_i \leftarrow_\$ \text{KeyGen}_{\text{pbs}}(msk, (ek, i))$
>> $\mathbf{gsk}[i] \leftarrow (pp, ek, i, sk_i)$
> Return $(gpk \leftarrow (pp, ek), gmsk \leftarrow dk, \mathbf{gsk})$

GVf$((pp, ek), m, (c, \sigma))$
> Return Verify$(pp, (c, m), \sigma)$

GSig$((pp, ek, i, sk_i), m)$
> $r \leftarrow_\$ \{0, 1\}^\lambda$
> $c \leftarrow \text{Enc}(ek, i; r)$
> $\sigma \leftarrow_\$ \text{Sign}(sk_i, (c, m), r)$
> Return (c, σ)

Open$(gmsk, m, (c, \sigma))$
> If Verify$(pp, (c, m), \sigma) = 0$
> Then return $\perp$
> Return Dec$(gmsk, c)$

6 Delegatable Policy-Based Signatures

In an organization, policies may be hierarchical, reflecting the organization structure. Thus, a president may declare a high-level policy to vice presidents and issue keys to them. Each of the vice presidents augments the policy with their own sub-policies for managers below them, and so on. To support this, we extend PBS to allow delegation. We define and achieve *delegatable* policy-based signatures, where a user holding a key for some policy can delegate her key to another user and possibly restrict the associated policy. We formalize this by associating keys to *vectors* of policies and require that keys can (only) sign messages which are allowed under *all* policies associated to the key. In order to restrict the policy at delegation, users can add policies to the associated vector.

Consider the following simple use case: A company issues a key to a manager Alice which enables her to sign contracts with companies X, Y and Z. Now Bob is negotiating a contract with Z on behalf of Alice, so she gives Bob a key that only lets him sign contracts with Z.

In [7] we provide a syntax and definitions of UF and IND, as well as SIM and EXT, which are straightforward generalizations of those for PBS. However, we strengthen IND by letting the adversary (who obtains msk) construct the keys under one of which the experiment makes a signature. This ensures that when Alice delegates different keys to Bob and Carol, she will not be able to tell by whom a message was signed. Analogously, we let the adversary choose the key in SIM.

With regard to a construction, we note that in the PBS schemes in Figures 3 and 4, a signing key sk_p is simply a signature from the authority on the associated policy p. We add delegation to PBS by replacing the signature with an *append-only signature* [33]. These signatures allow anyone holding a signature on a message p to create a signature on $p\|p'$ for any p'. One can thus append a new part to a signed message, but this is the only transformation allowed. Append-only signatures can be constructed from any signature scheme. Holding a key, which is a signature on a vector of policies p, a user can delegate the key after (possibly) appending a new policy.

Due to space constraints, the definitions as well as the constructions are deferred to the full version [7].

Acknowledgments. Mihir Bellare was supported in part by NSF grants CNS-1228890, CNS-1116800, CNS-0904380 and CCF-0915675. Georg Fuchsbauer was supported by the European Research Council, ERC Starting Grant (259668-PSPC); part of his work was done while at Bristol University, supported by EPSRC grant EP/H043454/1.

References

1. Abe, M., Fuchsbauer, G., Groth, J., Haralambiev, K., Ohkubo, M.: Structure-preserving signatures and commitments to group elements. In: Rabin, T. (ed.) CRYPTO 2010. LNCS, vol. 6223, pp. 209–236. Springer, Heidelberg (2010)
2. Agrawal, S., Gorbunov, S., Vaikuntanathan, V., Wee, H.: Functional encryption: New perspectives and lower bounds. In: Canetti, R., Garay, J.A. (eds.) CRYPTO 2013, Part II. LNCS, vol. 8043, pp. 500–518. Springer, Heidelberg (2013)
3. Backes, M., Meiser, S., Schröder, D.: Delegatable functional signatures. Cryptology ePrint Archive, Report 2013/408 (2013)
4. Bagga, W., Molva, R.: Policy-based cryptography and applications. In: S. Patrick, A., Yung, M. (eds.) FC 2005. LNCS, vol. 3570, pp. 72–87. Springer, Heidelberg (2005)

5. Barbosa, M., Farshim, P.: On the semantic security of functional encryption schemes. In: Kurosawa, K., Hanaoka, G. (eds.) PKC 2013. LNCS, vol. 7778, pp. 143–161. Springer, Heidelberg (2013)

6. Belenkiy, M., Chase, M., Kohlweiss, M., Lysyanskaya, A.: P-signatures and noninteractive anonymous credentials. In: Canetti, R. (ed.) TCC 2008. LNCS, vol. 4948, pp. 356–374. Springer, Heidelberg (2008)

7. Bellare, M., Fuchsbauer, G.: Policy-based signatures. Cryptology ePrint Archive, Report 2013/413 (2013)

8. Bellare, M., Goldwasser, S.: New paradigms for digital signatures and message authentication based on non-interactive zero knowledge proofs. In: Brassard, G. (ed.) CRYPTO 1989. LNCS, vol. 435, pp. 194–211. Springer, Heidelberg (1990)

9. Bellare, M., Meiklejohn, S., Thomson, S.: Key-versatile signatures and applications: RKA, KDM and Joint Enc/Sig. Cryptology ePrint Archive, Report 2013/326 (2013)

10. Bellare, M., Micciancio, D., Warinschi, B.: Foundations of group signatures: Formal definitions, simplified requirements, and a construction based on general assumptions. In: Biham, E. (ed.) EUROCRYPT 2003. LNCS, vol. 2656, pp. 614–629. Springer, Heidelberg (2003)

11. Bellare, M., O'Neill, A.: Semantically-secure functional encryption: Possibility results, impossibility results and the quest for a general definition. In: Abdalla, M., Nita-Rotaru, C., Dahab, R. (eds.) CANS 2013. LNCS, vol. 8257, pp. 218–234. Springer, Heidelberg (2013)

12. Bellare, M., Rogaway, P.: Random oracles are practical: A paradigm for designing efficient protocols. In: Ashby, V. (ed.) ACM CCS 1993, pp. 62–73. ACM Press (November 1993)

13. Bellare, M., Rogaway, P.: The security of triple encryption and a framework for code-based game-playing proofs. In: Vaudenay, S. (ed.) EUROCRYPT 2006. LNCS, vol. 4004, pp. 409–426. Springer, Heidelberg (2006)

14. Bender, A., Katz, J., Morselli, R.: Ring signatures: Stronger definitions, and constructions without random oracles. In: Halevi, S., Rabin, T. (eds.) TCC 2006. LNCS, vol. 3876, pp. 60–79. Springer, Heidelberg (2006)

15. Boneh, D., Sahai, A., Waters, B.: Functional encryption: Definitions and challenges. In: Ishai, Y. (ed.) TCC 2011. LNCS, vol. 6597, pp. 253–273. Springer, Heidelberg (2011)

16. Boneh, D., Waters, B.: Constrained pseudorandom functions and their applications. Cryptology ePrint Archive, Report 2013/352 (2013)

17. Boyen, X.: Mesh signatures. In: Naor, M. (ed.) EUROCRYPT 2007. LNCS, vol. 4515, pp. 210–227. Springer, Heidelberg (2007)

18. Boyle, E., Goldwasser, S., Ivan, I.: Functional signatures and pseudorandom functions. Cryptology ePrint Archive, Report 2013/401 (2013)

19. Camenisch, J., Lysyanskaya, A.: An efficient system for non-transferable anonymous credentials with optional anonymity revocation. In: Pfitzmann, B. (ed.) EUROCRYPT 2001. LNCS, vol. 2045, pp. 93–118. Springer, Heidelberg (2001)

20. Chase, M., Kohlweiss, M., Lysyanskaya, A., Meiklejohn, S.: Malleable signatures: Complex unary transformations and delegatable anonymous credentials. Cryptology ePrint Archive, Report 2013/179 (2013)

21. Chase, M., Lysyanskaya, A.: On signatures of knowledge. In: Dwork, C. (ed.) CRYPTO 2006. LNCS, vol. 4117, pp. 78–96. Springer, Heidelberg (2006)

22. Chaum, D., van Heyst, E.: Group signatures. In: Davies, D.W. (ed.) EUROCRYPT 1991. LNCS, vol. 547, pp. 257–265. Springer, Heidelberg (1991)

23. De Caro, A., Iovino, V., Jain, A., O'Neill, A., Paneth, O., Persiano, G.: On the achievability of simulation-based security for functional encryption. In: Canetti, R., Garay, J.A. (eds.) CRYPTO 2013, Part II. LNCS, vol. 8043, pp. 519–535. Springer, Heidelberg (2013)

24. De Santis, A., Micali, S., Persiano, G.: Noninteractive zero-knowledge proof systems. In: Pomerance, C. (ed.) CRYPTO 1987. LNCS, vol. 293, pp. 52–72. Springer, Heidelberg (1988)

25. Diffie, W., Hellman, M.E.: New directions in cryptography. IEEE Transactions on Information Theory 22(6), 644–654 (1976)

26. Dodis, Y., Haralambiev, K., López-Alt, A., Wichs, D.: Efficient public-key cryptography in the presence of key leakage. In: Abe, M. (ed.) ASIACRYPT 2010. LNCS, vol. 6477, pp. 613–631. Springer, Heidelberg (2010)

27. Feige, U., Shamir, A.: Witness indistinguishable and witness hiding protocols. In: 22nd ACM STOC, pp. 416–426. ACM Press (May 1990)

28. Fuchsbauer, G., Pointcheval, D.: Anonymous proxy signatures. In: Ostrovsky, R., De Prisco, R., Visconti, I. (eds.) SCN 2008. LNCS, vol. 5229, pp. 201–217. Springer, Heidelberg (2008)

29. Goldwasser, S., Micali, S., Rivest, R.L.: A digital signature scheme secure against adaptive chosen-message attacks. SIAM Journal on Computing 17(2), 281–308 (1988)

30. Groth, J.: Simulation-sound NIZK proofs for a practical language and constant size group signatures. In: Lai, X., Chen, K. (eds.) ASIACRYPT 2006. LNCS, vol. 4284, pp. 444–459. Springer, Heidelberg (2006)

31. Groth, J., Sahai, A.: Efficient non-interactive proof systems for bilinear groups. In: Smart, N.P. (ed.) EUROCRYPT 2008. LNCS, vol. 4965, pp. 415–432. Springer, Heidelberg (2008)

32. Kiayias, A., Papadopoulos, S., Triandopoulos, N., Zacharias, T.: Delegatable pseudorandom functions and applications. Cryptology ePrint Archive, Report 2013/379 (2013)

33. Kiltz, E., Mityagin, A., Panjwani, S., Raghavan, B.: Append-only signatures. In: Caires, L., Italiano, G.F., Monteiro, L., Palamidessi, C., Yung, M. (eds.) ICALP 2005. LNCS, vol. 3580, pp. 434–445. Springer, Heidelberg (2005)

34. Maji, H.K., Prabhakaran, M., Rosulek, M.: Attribute-based signatures. In: Kiayias, A. (ed.) CT-RSA 2011. LNCS, vol. 6558, pp. 376–392. Springer, Heidelberg (2011)

35. Mambo, M., Usuda, K., Okamoto, E.: Proxy signatures for delegating signing operation. In: ACM CCS 1996, pp. 48–57. ACM Press (March 1996)

36. Matt, C., Maurer, U.: A constructive approach to functional encryption. Cryptology ePrint Archive, Report 2013/559 (2013)

37. O'Neill, A.: Definitional issues in functional encryption. Cryptology ePrint Archive, Report 2010/556 (2010)

38. Rivest, R.L., Shamir, A., Tauman, Y.: How to leak a secret. In: Boyd, C. (ed.) ASIACRYPT 2001. LNCS, vol. 2248, pp. 552–565. Springer, Heidelberg (2001)

39. Sahai, A.: Non-malleable non-interactive zero knowledge and adaptive chosen-ciphertext security. In: 40th FOCS, pp. 543–553. IEEE Computer Society Press (October 1999)

Generalizing Homomorphic MACs
for Arithmetic Circuits

Dario Catalano[1], Dario Fiore[2], Rosario Gennaro[3], and Luca Nizzardo[4],[*]

[1] Università di Catania, Italy
catalano@dmi.unict.it
[2] IMDEA Software Institute, Spain
dario.fiore@imdea.org
[3] City College of New York, USA
rosario@cs.ccny.cuny.edu
[4] Università degli Studi di Milano-Bicocca, Italy
l.nizzardo@campus.unimib.it

Abstract. Homomorphic MACs, introduced by Gennaro and Wichs in 2013, allow anyone to validate computations on authenticated data without knowledge of the secret key. Moreover, the secret-key owner can verify the validity of the computation without needing to know the original (authenticated) inputs. Beyond security, homomorphic MACs are required to produce short tags (succinctness) and to support composability (i.e., outputs of authenticated computations should be re-usable as inputs for new computations).

At Eurocrypt 2013, Catalano and Fiore proposed two realizations of homomorphic MACs that support a restricted class of computations (arithmetic circuits of polynomial degree), are practically efficient, but fail to achieve both succinctness and composability at the same time.

In this paper, we generalize the work of Catalano and Fiore in several ways. First, we abstract away their results using the notion of encodings with limited malleability, thus yielding new schemes based on different algebraic settings. Next, we generalize their constructions to work with graded encodings, and more abstractly with k-linear groups. The main advantage of this latter approach is that it allows for homomorphic MACs which are (somewhat) composable while retaining succinctness. Interestingly, our construction uses graded encodings in a generic way. Thus, all its limitations (limited composability and non-constant size of the tags) solely depend on the fact that currently known multilinear maps share similar constraints. This means, for instance, that our scheme would support arbitrary circuits (polynomial depth) if we had compact multilinear maps with an exponential number of levels.

1 Introduction

Following the recent development of cloud computing, it is becoming popular for users to delegate the storage of their data to remote service providers. On

---

[*] Work done while visiting CUNY.

H. Krawczyk (Ed.): PKC 2014, LNCS 8383, pp. 538–555, 2014.

one hand, this paradigm presents several benefits. For instance, users can access the data from different devices and different places. Moreover, even devices with limited storage capacity (e.g., smartphones) can have access to large amounts of data. On the other hand, outsourcing data to remote (possibly untrusted) providers exposes the users to severe risks of privacy and integrity. While the community has devoted a lot of effort to finding ways to solve the privacy issue (notably the ground-breaking work on fully-homomorphic encryption [29]), the problem of integrity has received less attention. In particular, in this work we consider the following problem. Imagine that Alice wants to outsource a large amount of data to the cloud so that she can later (reliably) delegate the cloud to perform computation on such data. By "reliably" here we mean that the cloud should perform the computation and also be able to convince Alice that the computation was carried out correctly. What makes this task non trivial is that Alice does not keep a local copy of her data (i.e., the input of the computation) and that the communication complexity of the protocol should not depend on the size of the input. The latter restriction, for instance, rules out trivial solutions in which Alice can send signed data to the cloud and then ask the same (signed) data back in order to rerun the computation locally.

To solve this problem Gennaro and Wichs [28] put forward the notion of *homomorphic message authenticators* (homomorphic MACs, for short). Informally, a homomorphic MAC allows anyone, *without* knowledge of the secret key, to validate computations on authenticated data, and allows the secret-key owner to verify the results of these computations *without* knowing the original authenticated inputs. Slightly more in detail, a homomorphic MAC scheme enables a user to use his secret key to generate a tag σ that authenticates a message m. Later, given tags $\sigma_1, \ldots, \sigma_n$ for messages $m_1, \ldots, m_n$, *anyone* can run a program $\mathcal{P}$ over $\sigma_1, \ldots, \sigma_n$ to generate a short tag that authenticates (the output of) $\mathcal{P}(m_1, \ldots, m_n)$. To properly formalize the idea of authenticating a program's output, Gennaro and Wichs introduced the notion of *labeled* data and programs. The label of some message m is simply some string τ, which is used as auxiliary information to authenticate m. Intuitively, one can think of labels as names (or indexing) of the data. For instance, if a company outsources a database with information on its employees, the label "$(salary, i)$" might be used to indicate the salary value in the record corresponding to employee i. A *labeled program* $\mathcal{P}$ generalizes labeling to computations as follows. $\mathcal{P}$ is defined by a circuit f and a set of labels $(\tau_1 \ldots, \tau_n)$, one for each of the circuit's input wires. Intuitively, labeled programs provide a way to specify on which inputs the circuit has to be evaluated, without having to specify the exact values for such inputs. Basically, input labels can be seen as variable names in programming languages. In this sense, given a labeled program $\mathcal{P} = (f, \tau_1, \ldots, \tau_n)$ and a set of tags $\sigma_1, \ldots, \sigma_n$—each authenticating m_i under label τ_i—anybody can run the (homomorphic) evaluation algorithm $\sigma \leftarrow \mathsf{Eval}(\mathcal{P}, \sigma_1, \ldots, \sigma_n)$ to obtain a tag σ that authenticates $m = \mathcal{P}(m_1, \ldots, m_n)$ as the output of $\mathcal{P}$ run on inputs labeled by $\tau_1, \ldots, \tau_n$ respectively.

Homomorphic MACs are required to satisfy three main properties. (1) They must be *secure*, i.e., an adversary that can (adaptively) see the tags corresponding to polynomially many messages of his own choice, should not be able to produce valid tags for messages that are not produced as the output of $\mathcal{P}$. (2) A homomorphic MAC should be *succinct*, in the sense that the authenticity of $\mathcal{P}$'s output should be certifiable using much less communication than what required to send the original inputs. (3) Finally, a homomorphic MAC should be *composable*, in the sense that tags authenticating previous computations should be usable as inputs to further authenticate new computations, i.e., computations executed on the results of other computations.

In terms of realizations, Gennaro and Wichs [28] proposed a *fully* homomorphic MAC scheme that achieves all the above three properties for arbitrary programs. On the negative side, their construction is unfortunately rather inefficient as it relies on the full power of fully homomorphic encryption. Moreover, it guarantees security only with respect to adversaries that are allowed to ask a constant number of verification queries. In recent work [16], Catalano and Fiore proposed a realization of homomorphic MACs that, while less general than [28], is more interesting from a practical point of view: it is more efficient, it guarantees security for an unbounded number of verification queries, and it can be based on minimal assumptions (OWFs). On the negative side, this efficiency gain comes at the cost of a somewhat reduced flexibility. More precisely, in [16] two solutions are proposed. The first one achieves full composability but guarantees succinctness only for circuits of low degree. The second construction, instead, achieves succinctness but does not guarantee fully-fledged composability[1].

Our Contribution. In this paper, we generalize the work of Catalano and Fiore, by proposing new constructions and extensions for their paradigm. In particular, our contribution is threefold.

First, we devise a general methodology to construct succinct homomorphic MACs using the notion of *encodings with limited malleability* first introduced in [8]. Very informally, these are encodings that are additively homomorphic and, at the same time, believed *not* to be multiplicative homomorphic. A bit more precisely, for the case of deterministic encodings, we require that given the econding of the ℓ powers of a random x, it must be computationally hard to come up with the encoding of $1/x$. We show that by encoding x as g^x, then the original scheme in [16] can be seen as an instance of our abstraction.

By replacing g^x in [16] with $\mathsf{Enc}(x)$, and presenting encodings based on different intractability assumptions, we then obtain new homomorphic MAC schemes, relying on such assumptions. In particular, we discuss encoding instantiations based on partially-homomorphic encryption schemes, such as Paillier [36], Boneh-Goh-Nissim [13] and Brakerski-Vaikuntanathan [15]. We remark that all such schemes, constitute examples of *randomized* encodings. In order for our proofs to go through, however, we need to be able to check when two encodings

---

[1] This second scheme guarantees what the authors call *local composability*. In a nutshell, local composability allows to arbitrarily compose programs only when all the compositions are performed by the same entity.

encode the same element. To accommodate this, our security assumption must be strengthened to assume that computing an encoding of $1/x$ remains hard *even if* these encryption schemes are *not* semantically secure[2].

The final resulting assumption (which we call ℓ-inversion resistance in the paper) is quite strong and somewhat non-standard: it is "non-constant" as it depends on the parameter ℓ, and also requires, in the security simulation, the hypothetical existence of a "distinguisher" that breaks the semantic security of the underlying encryption schemes. Yet assumptions of this type have been regularly used for many protocols in this area (e.g. [8,26], cf. Footnote 2), and an intriguing open problem is to figure out how necessary they are.

For the same reason as in [16], though, the use of encodings for obtaining compact tags undermines the composability property. Our second contribution is a solution to this issue, which is obtained by further generalizing the idea of encodings with limited malleability. In particular, we build on so-called *graded encodings*, a notion recently proposed by Garg, Gentry and Halevi [24], that also provides an "approximate" realization of (leveled) multilinear groups. Basically, graded encodings are encodings that are additively homomorphic in the usual sense and multiplicatively homomorphic in a limited sense.[3] Our second construction uses graded encodings to obtain a homomorphic MAC scheme that achieves both composability and succinctness at the same time. In particular, if we instantiate our MAC by using the GGH graded encoding, we then obtain a scheme that allows for the following process: (1) one can generate constant-size tags, each authenticating the results of a computation $y_i = f_i(m_1, \ldots, m_n)$ for $i = 1$ to t, where each f_i is an arithmetic circuit of degree at most $D = \mathsf{poly}(\lambda)$; (2) one can compose the above computations f_i by using a "composition circuit" ϕ of degree at most k. Namely, one can finally authenticate $y = \phi(y_1, \ldots, y_t) = f^*(m_1, \ldots, m_n)$, where $f^* = \phi(f_1, \ldots, f_t)$. Here k is the degree of the multilinear groups. The size of the produced tags is linear in the degree of the composition circuit ϕ. Compared to the scheme of Catalano and Fiore, ours supports the same class of computations (i.e., arithmetic circuits of polynomial degree) but enjoys a higher degree of composability, and preserves succinctness as long as the composition circuit is low-degree.

Finally, we observe that our second scheme discussed above is *generically* built from multilinear maps. In particular, all its limitations (bounded circuits and size of the tags) are inherited from the current realizations of multilinear maps (e.g., GGH encodings): we support circuits of polynomial degree because the maps

---

[2] There is no contradiction here, as we are requiring the adversary to *compute* something ($\mathsf{Enc}(1/x)$) even if it is easy to decide if a given value t is an encoding of 0 or not. A similar situation arises in the SNARK protocols of [8,26], when implemented with a randomized encoding – however in their case the assumptions made on the encoding are knowledge, non-falsifiable, ones (i.e. it is hard to compute $t = enc(x)$ with x satisfying certain constraints, without knowing x). Our assumption is falsifiable and conceptually simpler, though we do not know of any reduction from one to the other.

[3] Roughly speaking, the multiplicative homomorphism is limited in the sense that the result of a multiplication lies into a different encoding set.

have polynomially-many levels, and our tags have size linear in the degree of the composition circuit because the maps are not compact. This means that our scheme would support arbitrary circuits (polynomial depth) if we had compact multilinear maps with an exponential number of levels. Furthermore, our generic construction is proven secure against adversaries making an unbounded number of verification queries, in contrast to the fully-homomorphic MAC of Gennaro-Wichs, that can support only a constant number of verification queries. Therefore, although such powerful algebraic tools are not known, our result has the potential of yielding a fully-fledged homomorphic MAC.

Related Work. The problem of realizing homomorphic (mostly linear) authenticators either in the symmetric setting (MACs) or in the asymmetric one (signatures) has been the subject of several recent papers, starting with the seminal work of Johnson et al. [33]. The subject became popular more recently, due to an important application of homomorphic signatures to linear network coding. Efficient schemes of this primitive have been proposed both in the random oracle [10,27,12,17] and in the standard model [1,2,18,19,23,3]. Realizations for more complex functionalities (i.e., beyond linear) have been proposed only very recently [11,28,16,4]. In addition to the works of Gennaro-Wichs [28] and Catalano-Fiore [28] that we already discussed in the previous section, it is worth mentioning two more works that are closely related to ours. Boneh and Freeman defined the notion of (fully) homomorphic signatures and showed a realization for bounded (constant) degree polynomials, from ideal lattices [11]. Compared to our work (and more in general to homomorphic MACs) this solution has the obvious advantage of allowing for public verifiability. On the negative side, however, it is not truly practical and the bound on the degree of the supported polynomials is more stringent than in our case (as they can support only polynomials of constant degree). Very recently, Backes, Fiore and Reischuk [4] put forward the notion of homomorphic MACs with efficient verification, which extends homomorphic MACs by requiring the verification algorithm to run more efficiently than the time necessary to compute the program $\mathcal{P}$ against which it verifies (precisely, they require amortized constant time). In [4], they propose a construction of this primitive based on the decision linear assumption and show applications to verifiable delegation of computation on outsourced data.

Other Related Work. Homomorphic signatures could be realized by using *Succinct Non-interactive Arguments of Knowledge* (SNARKs) [6]. Informally, a SNARK allows to construct a succinct argument that can be used to prove knowledge of the witness of a given any NP statement. SNARKs enjoy the nice property that the size of the proof is independent of the size of both statement and witness. A drawback of SNARKs is that they are not very efficient in practice and require either the random oracle model [35] or non-standard, non-falsifiable assumptions [30]. Moreover, the composability of homomorphic signatures obtained via SNARKs seems to be very limited [39,7].

Homomorphic authenticators are also related to memory delegation [20] and verifiable computation [34,35,31,25,5,37,22]. We refer to [28] for a detailed discussion about similarities with these primitives.

2   Background and Definitions

In our work we use the notion of arithmetic circuits and related definitions. For lack of space, we refer the interested reader to [38] for a nice survey on this subject.

2.1   Homomorphic Message Authenticators

Labeled Programs. First, let us recall the notion of labeled programs introduced by Gennaro and Wichs in [28]. A labeled program $\mathcal{P}$ is defined by a tuple $(f, \tau_1, \ldots, \tau_n)$ where $f : \mathbb{F}^n \to \mathbb{F}$ is a circuit, and the binary strings $\tau_1, \ldots, \tau_n \in \{0,1\}^*$ are the *labels* of the input nodes of f. Given some labeled programs $\mathcal{P}_1, \ldots, \mathcal{P}_t$ and a function $g : \mathbb{F}^t \to \mathbb{F}$, the *composed program* $\mathcal{P}^* = g(\mathcal{P}_1, \ldots, \mathcal{P}_t)$ is the circuit which evaluates a circuit g on the outputs of $\mathcal{P}_1, \ldots, \mathcal{P}_t$ respectively. The labeled inputs of $\mathcal{P}^*$ are all distinct labeled inputs of $\mathcal{P}_1, \ldots, \mathcal{P}_t$, i.e., all inputs with the same label are put together in a single input of the new program. We denote with $\mathcal{I}_\tau = (g_{id}, \tau)$ the *identity program* with label τ where g_{id} is the canonical identity function and $\tau \in \{0,1\}^*$ is some input label. Notice that any program $\mathcal{P} = (f, \tau_1, \ldots, \tau_n)$ can be expressed as the composition of n identity programs $\mathcal{P} = f(\mathcal{I}_{\tau_1}, \ldots, \mathcal{I}_{\tau_n})$.

Homomorphic Authenticator Scheme. A homomorphic message authenticator scheme HomMAC consists of the following four algorithms:

KeyGen(1^λ): on input the security parameter λ, the key generation algorithm outputs a secret key sk and a public evaluation key ek.

Auth(sk, τ, m): given the secret key sk, an input-label τ and a message $m \in \mathcal{M}$, it outputs a tag σ.

Ver(sk, m, $\mathcal{P}$, σ): given the secret key sk, a message $m \in \mathcal{M}$, a program $\mathcal{P} = (f, \tau_1, \ldots, \tau_n)$ and a tag σ, the verification algorithm outputs 0 (reject) or 1 (accept).

Eval(ek, f, $\boldsymbol{\sigma}$): given the evaluation key ek, a circuit $f : \mathcal{M}^n \to \mathcal{M}$ and a vector of tags $\boldsymbol{\sigma} = (\sigma_1, \ldots, \sigma_n)$, the evaluation algorithm outputs a new tag σ.

AUTHENTICATION CORRECTNESS. Intuitively, a homomorphic MAC satisfies this property if any tag σ generated by the algorithm Auth(sk, τ, m) authenticates with respect to the identity program $\mathcal{I}_\tau$. Formally, we require that for any message $m \in \mathcal{M}$, all keys (sk, ek) $\xleftarrow{\$}$ KeyGen(1^λ), any label $\tau \in \{0,1\}^*$, and any tag $\sigma \xleftarrow{\$}$ Auth(sk, τ, m), it holds: $\Pr[\text{Ver}(\text{sk}, m, \mathcal{I}_\tau, \sigma) = 1] = 1$.

EVALUATION CORRECTNESS. Informally, this property states that if the evaluation algorithm is given a vector of tags $\boldsymbol{\sigma} = (\sigma_1, \ldots, \sigma_n)$ such that each σ_i authenticates some message m_i as the output of a labeled program $\mathcal{P}_i$, then the tag σ produced by Eval must authenticate $f(m_1, \ldots, m_n)$ as the output of the composed program $f(\mathcal{P}_1, \ldots, \mathcal{P}_n)$.

More formally, let us fix a pair of keys (sk, ek) $\xleftarrow{\$}$ KeyGen(1^λ), a function $g : \mathcal{M}^t \to \mathcal{M}$ and any set of message/program/tag triples $\{(m_i, \mathcal{P}_i, \sigma_i)\}_{i=1}^t$ such that Ver(sk, m_i, $\mathcal{P}_i$, σ_i) = 1. If $m^* = g(m_1, \ldots, m_t)$, $\mathcal{P}^* = g(\mathcal{P}_1, \ldots, \mathcal{P}_t)$, and $\sigma^* = \text{Eval}(\text{ek}, g, (\sigma_1, \ldots, \sigma_t))$, then it must hold: Ver(sk, m^*, $\mathcal{P}^*$, σ^*) = 1.

SUCCINCTNESS. The size of a tag is bounded by some fixed polynomial in the security parameter, that is independent of the number of inputs taken by the evaluated circuit.

SECURITY. Here we recall the security definition of homomorphic MACs proposed by Catalano and Fiore [16] (which slightly weakens the one of Gennaro and Wichs [28]). A homomorphic MAC scheme HomMAC is secure if for any PPT adversary $\mathcal{A}$ we have $\Pr[\text{HomUF}-\text{CMA}_{\mathcal{A},\text{HomMAC}}(\lambda) = 1] \leq \epsilon(\lambda)$ where $\epsilon(\lambda)$ is a negligible function, and $\text{HomUF}-\text{CMA}_{\mathcal{A},\text{HomMAC}}(\lambda)$ is the experiment below.

Setup. The challenger generates $(\text{sk}, \text{ek}) \xleftarrow{\$} \text{KeyGen}(1^\lambda)$ and gives ek to $\mathcal{A}$. Also a list $T = \emptyset$ is initialized.

Authentication queries. The adversary can adaptively ask for tags on label-message pairs of its choice. Given a query (τ, m), if $(\tau, m) \in T$ (i.e., the query was previously made), then the challenger replies with the same tag generated before. If T already contains a pair $(\tau, m') \in T$ with $m' \neq m$ (i.e., the label τ was already queried with a different message), then the challenger ignores the query. Otherwise, if $(\tau, m) \notin T$, the challenger computes $\sigma \xleftarrow{\$}$ $\text{Auth}(\text{sk}, \tau, m)$, returns σ to $\mathcal{A}$ and updates the list $T = T \cup (\tau, m)$.

Verification queries. The adversary is also given access to a verification oracle. $\mathcal{A}$ can submit a query $(m, \mathcal{P}, \sigma)$ and the challenger replies with the output of $\text{Ver}(\text{sk}, m, \mathcal{P}, \sigma)$.

Forgery. When the adversary stops running, the experiment outputs 1 if one of the verification queries made by $\mathcal{A}$, say $(m^*, \mathcal{P}^*, \sigma^*)$, is a forgery.

The description of the experiment is thus concluded by defining what is a forgery. To this end, we first recall the notion of a *well-defined* program with respect to a list T. Informally, there are two ways for a program $\mathcal{P}^* = (f^*, \tau_1^*, \ldots, \tau_n^*)$ to be well-defined. Either all the τ_i^*'s are in T or, if there are some labels τ_i^* that are not in T, then the inputs associated with such labels are "ignored" by f^* when computing the output. In other words, inputs corresponding to labels not in T do not affect the behavior of f^* in any way.

More formally, a labeled program $\mathcal{P}^* = (f^*, \tau_1^*, \ldots, \tau_n^*)$ is *well defined with respect to* T if either one of the following two cases occurs:

1. there exists $i \in \{1, \ldots, n\}$ such that $(\tau_i^*, \cdot) \notin T$ (i.e., $\mathcal{A}$ never asked an authentication query with label τ_i^*), and $f^*(\{m_j\}_{(\tau_j, m_j) \in T} \cup \{\tilde{m}_j\}_{(\tau_j, \cdot) \notin T})$ outputs the same value for all possible choices of $\tilde{m}_j \in \mathcal{M}$;
2. T contains tuples $(\tau_1^*, m_1), \ldots, (\tau_n^*, m_n)$, for some messages $m_1, \ldots, m_n$.

In the experiment HomUF−CMA, a tuple $(m^*, \mathcal{P}^*, \sigma^*)$ is a forgery if and only if $\text{Ver}(\text{sk}, m^*, \mathcal{P}^*, \sigma^*) = 1$ and one of the following conditions holds:

− *Type 1 Forgery:* $\mathcal{P}^*$ is not well-defined w.r.t. T.
− *Type 2 Forgery:* $\mathcal{P}^*$ is well defined w.r.t. T and $m^* \neq f^*(\{m_j\}_{(\tau_j, m_j) \in T})$, i.e., m^* is not the correct output of the labeled program $\mathcal{P}^*$ when executed on previously authenticated messages $(m_1, \ldots, m_n)$.

As already noted in [16], the experiment HomUF−CMA requires the challenger to recognize whether a program submitted by the adversary in a verification query is well-defined or not, but the latter check might not be doable in polynomial time, at least for certain classes of computations. Catalano and Fiore observe that this is not a problem for the class of arithmetic circuits of polynomial degree and over an exponentially large finite field. Here we give a simple proposition (for lack of space its proof appears in the full version) to show that testing whether a program is well-defined can be done even for arithmetic circuits of degree d, over a finite field of order p such that $d/p < 1/2$.[4]

Proposition 1. *Let $\lambda, n \in \mathbb{N}$ and let $\mathcal{F}$ be the class of arithmetic circuits $f : \mathbb{F}^n \to \mathbb{F}$ over a finite field $\mathbb{F}$ of order p and such that the degree of f is at most d, for $\frac{d}{p} < \frac{1}{2}$. Then, there exists a probabilistic algorithm that for any given $f \in \mathcal{F}$, decides if there exists $y \in \mathbb{F}$ such that $f(\boldsymbol{u}) = y, \forall \boldsymbol{u} \in \mathbb{F}^n$ (i.e., if f is constant) and is correct with probability at least $1 - 2^{-\lambda}$.*

Furthermore, for the same class of computations, we show that Type-1 forgeries essentially "collapse" into Type-2 forgeries. Namely, we show that any adversary winning in the experiment by producing a Type-1 forgery can be converted into another adversary that wins by producing a Type-2 forgery. This is formalized in the following proposition whose proof is deferred to the full version:

Proposition 2. *Let $\lambda \in \mathbb{N}$ be the security parameter, and let $\mathcal{F}$ be the class of arithmetic circuits $f : \mathbb{F}^n \to \mathbb{F}$ over a finite field $\mathbb{F}$ of order p and such that the degree of f is at most d, for $\frac{d}{p} < \frac{1}{2}$. Let $\mathcal{E}_b$ be the event that the adversary wins in experiment HomUF−CMA by producing a Type-b forgery (for $b = 1, 2$). Then, if for any adversary $\mathcal{B}$ we have that $\Pr[\mathsf{HomUF-CMA}_{\mathcal{B},\mathsf{HomMAC}}(\lambda) = 1 \wedge \mathcal{E}_2] \leq \epsilon$, then for any adversary $\mathcal{A}$ producing a Type-1 forgery it holds $\Pr[\mathsf{HomUF-CMA}_{\mathcal{A},\mathsf{HomMAC}}(\lambda) = 1 \wedge \mathcal{E}_1] \leq Q(\epsilon + 2^{-\lambda})$.*

3   Compact Homomorphic MACs Based on Encodings with Limited Malleability

In this section we describe a generalization of the scheme of Catalano and Fiore [16] which uses a more general encoding to compress the tags. First we define the encoding that we are going to use to compress the tags. We then show the compact scheme and prove its security. Finally we show that the scheme from [16] can be seen as an instance of this generalization, and we also present a different implementation based on partially-homomorphic encryption.

Limited Malleability Encoding. An encoding $\mathcal{E}$ consists of three algorithms (EncGen, Enc, Test) defined as follows:

---

[4] For simplicity, we show this for $1/2$. The same argument can be extended to $d/p < 1/c$ for some constant c.

EncGen(1^λ). Given the security parameter λ, it outputs a pair of public/secret keys pk, dk, the message space $\mathbb{Z}_p$ where p is a prime of at least λ-bits, and an encoding space T. We denote with $+, \cdot$ the usual additions/multiplications over $\mathbb{Z}_p$, while T is assumed to be an abelian group under operation $\times$.

Enc(pk, m). A possibly randomized algorithm which takes as input $m \in \mathbb{Z}_p$ and returns a value $t \in T$.

Test(dk, m, t) A deterministic algorithm which on input $m \in \mathbb{Z}_p$ and $t \in T$ outputs 1 if $t \in$ Enc(pk, m), and 0 otherwise.

ON THE TESTING ALGORITHM. We note that if the encoding algorithm is deterministic, the testing procedure can be easily carried out by re-encoding m and checking that is equal to t. Also, note that in this case there is no need of a secret key to test. This is the case for the discrete-log based encoding in [16]. For more general encodings where the encoding algorithm might be randomized, a secret decoding key dk might be needed to "decode" t and check that is equal to m.

Definition 1. *We say that an encoding is* additively homomorphic *if for all* $m, m' \in \mathbb{Z}_p$, *and for all* $h \in$ Enc(pk, m) *and* $h' \in$ Enc(pk, m') *we have that* $h \times h' \in$ Enc($pk, m + m'$).

LIMITED MALLEABILITY. We now define our security assumption for the encodings $\mathcal{E}$ that we use in our scheme. Basically, we ask that given $t_i =$ Enc(pk, x^i) for $i = 0, \ldots, \ell$ it must be hard to compute $t =$ Enc($pk, 1/x$), even in the presence of an oracle which decides if an element of T is an encoding of 0 or not. More formally, define the oracle $O(\mathsf{dk}, \tau)$ which answers "yes" if $\tau \in$ Enc(pk, 0) and "no" otherwise. Then for any PPT (adversary) $\mathcal{A}$, consider the following experiment **E-INV**$_\mathcal{A}(\lambda, \ell)$:

1. (pk, dk, p, T) $\leftarrow$ EncGen(1^λ);
2. $x \leftarrow \mathbb{Z}_p^*$;
3. $h_i \leftarrow$ Enc(pk, x^i) for $i = 1, \ldots, \ell$;
4. $t \leftarrow \mathcal{A}^{O(\mathsf{dk}, \cdot)}(\mathsf{pk}, p, T, h_0, \ldots, h_\ell)$

We define $\mathcal{A}$'s advantage in winning the **E-INV**$_\mathcal{A}(\lambda, \ell)$ game as $\mathbf{Adv}_\mathcal{A}^{\mathcal{E}-INV}(\lambda, \ell)$ $= \Pr[t \in$ Enc($pk, 1/x$)].

Definition 2. *We say that* $\mathcal{E}$ *is* ℓ-inversion-resistant *if for every PPT* $\mathcal{A}$ *we have that* $\mathbf{Adv}_\mathcal{A}^{\mathcal{E}-INV}(\lambda, \ell)$ *is negligible in* λ.

The assumption states that *computing* Enc(pk, $1/x$) must be difficult *even if* we were able to efficiently *decide* if a string is the encoding of $1/x$ (because of homomorphic properties of $\mathcal{E}$ deciding if τ is an encoding of 0 is equivalent to deciding if τ is an encoding of an arbitrary element of $\mathbb{Z}_p$).

We remark that we do *not* require the existence of the oracle to implement the encoding and our scheme. It is just needed by the simulation (therefore making our assumption stronger than just computing Enc(pk, $1/x$)).

The Scheme. We now describe a homomorphic MAC scheme that works for arithmetic circuits of polynomial degree D (but does not support composition).

The authentication tags produced by our construction have size which is independent of the size/depth of the circuit. The description of our scheme follows.

KeyGen($1^\lambda, D$). Let λ be the security parameter, and D be a parameter of size poly(λ). The key generation works as follows. Run EncGen(1^λ) to generate pk, dk, p, T. We assume that our circuits work over $\mathbb{Z}_p$. Next, select $x \xleftarrow{\$} \mathbb{Z}_p$, a seed K of a pseudorandom function $F_K : \{0,1\}^* \to \mathbb{Z}_p$, and compute $h_i = $ Enc(pk, x^i), for $i = 0$ to $D - 1$. Output sk $= (K, \mathsf{dk}, x)$, ek $= (h_0, \ldots, h_{D-1})$.

Auth(sk, τ, m). To authenticate a message $m \in \mathbb{Z}_p$ with label $\tau \in \{0,1\}^\lambda$, compute $r_\tau = F_K(\tau)$, set $y_0 = m$, $y_1 = (r_\tau - m)/x \bmod p$, and output $\sigma = (y_0, y_1) \in \mathbb{Z}_p^2$. The authentication tags produced by Auth are interpreted as degree-1 polynomials $y(X) = y_0 + y_1 X$ over the ring $\mathbb{Z}_p[X]$.

Eval(ek, $f, \boldsymbol{\sigma}$). The first step of this algorithm is the same as the Eval algorithm of the homomorphic MACs construction based on OWFs proposed in [16]. The input is the evaluation key ek, an arithmetic circuit $f : \mathbb{Z}_p^n \to \mathbb{Z}_p$, and a vector $\boldsymbol{\sigma}$ of tags $(\sigma_1, \ldots, \sigma_n)$ where each σ_i is a polynomial $y^{(i)}(X) \in \mathbb{Z}_p[X]$. The first step is to compute the polynomial $y(X)$ obtained by (homomorphically) evaluating the circuit f over the polynomial ring $\mathbb{Z}_p[X]$, i.e., $y(X) \leftarrow f(y^{(1)}(X), \ldots, y^{(n)}(X))$. Namely, additions and multiplications over $\mathbb{Z}_p$ are replaced by additions and multiplications of polynomials over $\mathbb{Z}_p[X]$. Let $y_0, \ldots, y_d$ be the coefficients of the polynomial $y(X)$ (note that $d \leq D$). If $d = 1$ then the algorithm returns $\sigma = (y_0, y_1)$, otherwise it computes $\Lambda = \Pi_{i=0}^{d-1} h_i^{y_{i+1}}$ (where this product is computed in the group T defined by the encoding) and returns $\sigma = \Lambda$.

Ver(sk, $m, \mathcal{P}, \sigma$). Let $\mathcal{P} = (f, \tau_1, \ldots, \tau_n)$ be a labeled program, $m \in \mathbb{Z}_p$ and σ be a tag of either the form $(y_0, y_1) \in \mathbb{Z}_p^2$, or $\Lambda \in T$.
First, compute $\rho = f(r_{\tau_1}, \ldots, r_{\tau_n})$ where $r_{\tau_i} \leftarrow F_K(\tau_i)$. Next, according to the form of σ perform the following checks:

1. If $\sigma = (y_0, y_1)$, then output 1 only if $\rho = y_0 + y_1 \cdot x \,\wedge\, y_0 = m$.
2. If $\sigma = \Lambda$, then let $t = \Lambda^x$ and output Test(dk, $\rho - m, t$)

It is not difficult to check that the scheme is correct by the construction of the polynomials $y(X)$ and the correctness of the encoding $\mathcal{E}$. The following theorem proves the security of our construction. For lack of space, the proof of Theorem 1 as well as a full proof of correctness appear in the full version.

Theorem 1. *If $\mathcal{E}$ is $(D-1)$-inversion resistant, and F is a pseudorandom function, then the scheme described in Section 3 is a secure homomorphic MAC.*

Possible Instantiations

DISCRETE-LOG BASED ENCODING. We first show that the protocol of Catalano and Fiore [16] fits into the abstraction we just described. In their case the encoding algorithms are as follows:

– EncGen(1^λ) chooses a prime p of size at least λ, and a cyclic group T of order p, and a generator g for it. pk $=$ dk $= (p, T, g)$. Note that the decoding key is not secret.

- $\mathsf{Enc}(\mathsf{pk}, m) = g^m$. Note that the encoding scheme is deterministic.
- $\mathsf{Test}(\mathsf{dk}, m, t)$ checks if $t = g^m$

The assumption that this encoding is ℓ-inversion resistant is equivalent to the ℓ-Diffie-Hellman inversion assumption [14]: given $g, g^x, g^{x^2}, \ldots, g^{x^\ell}$ it is hard to compute $g^{1/x}$. Note that the oracle which test if t is an encoding of 0 is trivially implemented by checking if $t = 1$, since the encoding is deterministic.

PARTIALLY HOMOMORPHIC ENCRYPTION SCHEMES. Any encryption scheme which is additively homomorphic over a prime field but is believed to be multiplicative homomorphic only up to a *constant* degree, constitutes a suitable candidate to be an ℓ-inversion resistant encoding. Let (KG, Enc, Dec) be such an encryption scheme, then:

- $\mathsf{EncGen}(1^\lambda)$ runs $KG(1^\lambda)$ to choose a public/secret key pair $(\mathsf{pk}, \mathsf{sk})$. It sets pk to be the encoding public key and $\mathsf{dk} = \mathsf{sk}$ its secret decoding key.
- $\mathsf{Enc}(\mathsf{pk}, m) = Enc(\mathsf{pk}, m)$. Note that in this case the encoding scheme is randomized.
- $\mathsf{Test}(\mathsf{dk}, m, t)$ checks if $Dec(\mathsf{sk}, t) = m$

Examples of encryption schemes with such a partial homomorphic property include the "basic" version of the Brakerski and Vaikuntanathan FHE [15], Boneh, Goh and Nissim [13], and Paillier [36] schemes. [5] Note that to use these schemes in our protocol we need to require them to be ℓ-inversion resistant as defined earlier. This is a strong notion of security: we require them to be one-way in a strong sense (given encryptions of ℓ successive powers of x, it is impossible to come up with an encryption of $1/x$) *even in the presence of an oracle that breaks the semantic security of the scheme.*

4   A Compact Scheme with k-degree Composition

In this section we propose a homomorphic MAC based on multilinear groups. Compared to [16], the main advantage of this scheme is that it provides a way to both compress the tags and enable their (later) composition. Before describing the scheme, we first recall the definition of graded encoding and its abstraction of leveled multilinear maps.

Leveled Multilinear Maps and Graded Encodings. Informally speaking, a k-graded encoding system for a ring R includes a system of sets $\{S_i^{(\alpha)} \subset \{0, 1\}^* : i \in [0, k], \alpha \in R\}$ such that for every fixed $i \in [0, k]$ the sets $\{S_i^{(\alpha)} : \alpha \in R\}$ are disjoint. The set $S_i^{(\alpha)}$ essentially contains the level-i encodings of $\alpha \in R$.

---

[5] Although Paillier and BGN schemes operate over the ring Z_N where N is the product of two large primes, note that the zero-divisors are only a negligible fraction of $\mathbb{Z}_N$. Moreover, it is hard to find such divisors if we assume that factoring N is hard. Therefore, it is not hard to see that with minor modifications the proof of Theorem 1 can be changed to accomodate this. More details appear in the full version.

As a first requirement, the system needs an algorithm to obtain an encoding $a_i \in S_i^{(\alpha)}$ of some ring element α (notice that such encoding can be randomized). Additionally, the encoding system is homomorphic in a graded sense. Namely, let us abuse notation and assume that every set $S_i^{(\alpha)}$ is a ring where $+, \cdot$ are the usual addition/multiplication operations. Then, for any $a_i \in S_i^{(\alpha)}$ and $b_i \in S_i^{(\beta)}$ we have $a_i + b_j \in S_i^{(\alpha+\beta)}$. Furthermore, for $a_i \in S_i^{(\alpha)}$ and $b_j \in S_j^{(\beta)}$ we have $a_i \cdot b_j \in S_{i+j}^{(\alpha \cdot \beta)}$, if $i + j \le k$. Finally, the encoding system has an algorithm to test if a given a is an encoding of 0 at level i, i.e., $a \in S_i^{(0)}$.

Garg, Gentry and Halevi [24] recently proposed a candidate construction of a randomized graded encoding system, which has some additional algorithms to deal with the fact that the encoding is randomized. Another candidate was also proposed by Coron, Lepoint and Tibouchi [21]. We refer to these works for a precise definition of graded encodings. Here we note that graded encodings define an "approximate" version of a multilinear group family. For ease of exposition, we proceed our description of graded encodings by using the more abstract and simpler multilinear groups. Although graded encodings slightly depart from this abstraction (mainly because of the randomized "noisy" procedures), they can be adapted to work in place of multilinear groups.

In generic multilinear groups we assume the existence of an algorithm $\mathcal{G}(1^\lambda, k)$ that, on input the security parameter and an integer k indicating the number of levels (i.e., the number of allowed pairing operations), generates the description pp of leveled multilinear groups $(\mathbb{G}_1, \ldots, \mathbb{G}_k)$, each of large prime order $p > 2^\lambda$. We let g_i be a canonical generator of $\mathbb{G}_i$ and we assume that pp includes $g_1 \in \mathbb{G}_1$. The groups are such that there exists a set of bilinear maps $\{e_{i,j} : \mathbb{G}_i \times \mathbb{G}_j \to \mathbb{G}_{i+j}\}_{i,j \ge 1, i+j \le k}$ such that $\forall a, b \in \mathbb{Z}_p$: $e_{i,j}(g_i^a, g_j^b) = g_{i+j}^{ab}$. When it is obvious from the context the indices i, j are dropped from $e_{i,j}$.

LIMITED MALLEABILITY. To prove the security of our scheme we assume that the encoding system is homomorphic *only* in a graded sense. Namely, given the level-1 encodings of the ℓ powers of $w \in R$, it must be hard to compute a level-k encoding of $w^{\ell k+1}$. Framed in the context of multilinear groups, this assumption can be seen as an extension of the computational Bilinear Diffie-Hellman Inversion assumption (first defined by Boneh, Boyen and Goh [9]) to the multilinear setting. Its hardness in the generic multilinear group follows by the same argument as in the "master theorem" of [9], i.e., by the linear independence of the polynomial $x^{\ell k+1}$ w.r.t. the polynomials $x, x^2, \ldots, x^{\ell k}$. It is worth noting that a similar assumption, in the multilinear groups setting, has been recently used by Hohenberger, Sahai and Waters [32].

Definition 3 ((ℓ, k)-Multilinear Diffie-Hellman Inversion). *Let* pp *be the description of a set of multilinear groups and* $g_1 \in \mathbb{G}_1$ *be a random generator. Let* $w \xleftarrow{\$} \mathbb{Z}_p$ *be chosen at random. We define the advantage of an adversary* $\mathcal{A}$ *in solving the* (ℓ, k)*-MDHI problem as* $\mathbf{Adv}_{\mathcal{A}}^{MDHI}(\lambda) = \Pr[\mathcal{A}(g_1, g_1^w, \ldots, g_1^{w^\ell}) = g_k^{w^{k\ell+1}}]$, *and we say that the* (ℓ, k)*-MDHI assumption holds for* $\mathcal{G}$ *if for every PPT* $\mathcal{A}$ *and for* $\ell = \mathsf{poly}(\lambda)$, $\mathbf{Adv}_{\mathcal{A}}^{MDHI}(\lambda)$ *is negligible in* λ.

The Scheme. Our homomorphic MAC based on k-linear groups allows for the following process: (1) one can generate constant-size tags, each authenticating the results of a computation $v_i = f_i(m_1, \ldots, m_n)$ for $i = 1$ to t, where each f_i is an arithmetic circuit of degree at most $D = \mathsf{poly}(\lambda)$; (2) one can compose the above computations f_i by using a "composition circuit" ϕ of degree at most k. Namely, one can finally authenticate $v = \phi(v_1, \ldots, v_t) = f^*(m_1, \ldots, m_n)$, where $f^* = \phi(f_1, \ldots, f_t)$.

Before describing our scheme in full detail, we first provide an intuitive description. The basic idea of our construction is to first generate the authentication tags as in [16] – i.e., as polynomials $y(X)$ – and to publish in the evaluation key level-1 encodings of the D powers of the secret value x, i.e., $h_i = g_1^{x^i}, i = 1, \ldots, D$. To authenticate a computation $v_i = f_i(m_1, \ldots, m_n)$, one first computes the polynomial $y^{(i)}(X) \leftarrow f_i(y_1(X), \ldots, y_n(X)) \in \mathbb{Z}_p[X]$, and then generates its "compressed" representation by computing the level-1 encoding $\Lambda_i = g_1^{y^{(i)}(x) - y^{(i)}(0)} = \prod_{j=1}^{d} (g_1^{x^j})^{y_j^{(i)}}$. To further authenticate the composed computation $\phi(v_1, \ldots, v_t)$ (with ϕ of degree k), the idea is to compute the k-level encoding $\Lambda = (g_k^{a^{k-1}})^{y(x) - y(0)}$, where $y(X) \in \mathbb{Z}_p[X]$ is the polynomial obtained from $\phi(y^{(1)}(X), \ldots, y^{(t)}(X))$. Precisely, Λ is computed by homomorphically evaluating ϕ over the level-1 encodings $\{\Lambda_i\}_i$: additions in ϕ are replaced by the group operation and multiplications are replaced by the pairing. In our scheme we also publish encodings $\{\eta_i = g_1^{ax^i} = h_i^a\}_{i=0}^{d}$ where $a \in \mathbb{Z}_p$ is randomly chosen, and we include in every tag another element $\Gamma = \Lambda^a$ computed by using the values $\{\eta_i\}_i$. Very roughly, these additional encodings are introduced to enable one to "move up" an encoding Λ_j from $\mathbb{G}_j$ to $\mathbb{G}_{j+1}$ without publishing the generator $g_1 \in \mathbb{G}_1$, i.e., one computes $\Lambda_{j+1} = e_{j,1}(\Lambda_j, g_1^a)$.

A full description of our scheme follows.

$\mathsf{KeyGen}(1^\lambda, D, k)$. Let λ be the security parameter, and D, k be two parameters of size $\mathsf{poly}(\lambda)$. The key generation works as follows.

Run $\mathcal{G}(1^\lambda, k)$ to generate the description of k-linear groups $\mathbb{G}_1, \ldots, \mathbb{G}_k$ of order p where p is a prime number of at least λ bits. Let $g_1 \xleftarrow{\$} \mathbb{G}_1$ be a random generator, and choose random values $a, x \xleftarrow{\$} \mathbb{Z}_p$, and a seed K of a pseudorandom function $F_K : \{0, 1\}^* \to \mathbb{Z}_p$. Next, for $i = 1$ to D, compute $h_i = g_1^{x^i}, \eta_i = h_i^a$ and $A_1 = g_1^a$. Also, we let $g_i \in \mathbb{G}_i$ be the canonical generator of $\mathbb{G}_i$ which is obtained by repeatedly applying the graded map to g_1, i.e., let $g_2 = e(g_1, g_1)$ and $g_i = e(g_{i-1}, g_1)$. Similarly, we define A_i from A_1 and we observe that $A_i = g_i^{a^i}$. Finally, compute $\sigma_U = (1, (r_U - 1)/x)$ for a random $r_U \xleftarrow{\$} \mathbb{Z}_p$. σ_U is essentially a tag for the value 1 under a fixed canonical label (cf. the authentication algorithm).

Output $\mathsf{sk} = (K, g_1, x, a), \mathsf{ek} = (A_1, h_1, \eta_1, \ldots, h_D, \eta_D, \sigma_U)$ and let the message space $\mathcal{M}$ be $\mathbb{Z}_p$.

$\mathsf{Auth}(\mathsf{sk}, \tau, m)$. To authenticate a message $m \in \mathbb{Z}_p$ with label $\tau \in \{0, 1\}^\lambda$, compute $r_\tau = F_K(\tau)$, set $y_0 = m$, $y_1 = (r_\tau - m)/x \bmod p$, and output $\sigma = (y_0, y_1) \in \mathbb{Z}_p^2$. The authentication tags produced by Auth are interpreted as degree-1 polynomials $y(X) = y_0 + y_1 X$ over the ring $\mathbb{Z}_p[X]$.

$\mathsf{Eval}_1(\mathsf{ek}, f, \boldsymbol{\sigma})$. This algorithm is the same as the Eval algorithm of the homomorphic MACs construction based on OWFs proposed in [16]: The input is the evaluation key ek, an arithmetic circuit $f : \mathbb{Z}_p^n \to \mathbb{Z}_p$, and a vector $\boldsymbol{\sigma}$ of tags $(\sigma_1, \ldots, \sigma_n)$ where each σ_i is a polynomial $y^{(i)}(X) \in \mathbb{Z}_p[X]$. The authentication tag σ computed by Eval_1 is the polynomial $y(X)$ obtained by (homomorphically) evaluating the circuit f over the polynomial ring $\mathbb{Z}_p[X]$, i.e., $y(X) \leftarrow f(y^{(1)}(X), \ldots, y^{(n)}(X))$. Namely, additions/multiplications over $\mathbb{Z}_p$ are replaced by additions/multiplications of polynomials over $\mathbb{Z}_p[X]$.

$\mathsf{Compress}(\mathsf{ek}, \sigma)$. This algorithm takes as input an authentication tag σ of the form $y(X) \in \mathbb{Z}_p[X]$ of degree d (i.e., $y(X)$ consists of $d+1$ coefficients $(y_0, \ldots, y_d)$), and "compresses" the polynomial into a shorter value of constant size. The resulting tag is a triple $(y_0, \Lambda_1, \Gamma_1) \in \mathbb{Z}_p \times \mathbb{G}_1 \times \mathbb{G}_1$ where Λ_1 and Γ_1 are computed as follows: $\Lambda_1 = \prod_{i=1}^{d} h_i^{y_i}$, $\Gamma_1 = \prod_{i=1}^{d} \eta_i^{y_i}$.

$\mathsf{Eval}_2(\mathsf{ek}, \phi, \boldsymbol{\sigma})$. This algorithm allows to further apply homomorphic operations on tags that were obtained using Eval_1 and later compressed using $\mathsf{Compress}$. Eval_2 takes as input the evaluation key ek, an arithmetic circuit $\phi : \mathbb{Z}_p^n \to \mathbb{Z}_p$ of degree at most k and a vector $\boldsymbol{\sigma}$ of tags $(\sigma_1, \ldots, \sigma_n)$ such that each σ_i is a triple $(y_0^{(i)}, \Lambda_1^{(i)}, \Gamma_1^{(i)}) \in \mathbb{Z}_p \times \mathbb{G}_1 \times \mathbb{G}_1$. Without loss of generality, we assume that in the circuit ϕ addition gates take inputs of the same degree i.[6]

Eval$_2$ evaluates the circuit ϕ over the tags by replacing additions and multiplications as follows:

- $\mathsf{Add}(\mathsf{ek}, \sigma_1, \sigma_2)$. On input two tags $\sigma_1 = (y_0^{(1)}, \Lambda_i^{(1)}, \Gamma_i^{(1)})$ and $\sigma_2 = (y_0^{(2)}, \Lambda_i^{(2)}, \Gamma_i^{(2)})$, it computes a tag $\sigma = (y_0, \Lambda_i, \Gamma_i)$ as follows: $y_0 = y_0^{(1)} + y_0^{(2)}$, $\Lambda_i = \Lambda_i^{(1)} \cdot \Lambda_i^{(2)}$, $\Gamma_i = \Gamma_i^{(1)} \cdot \Gamma_i^{(2)}$.

- $\mathsf{ConstMult}(\mathsf{ek}, \sigma_1, c)$. On input a tag $\sigma_1 = (y_0^{(1)}, \Lambda_i^{(1)}, \Gamma_i^{(1)})$ and a constant $c \in \mathbb{Z}_p$, it computes the tag $\sigma = (y_0, \Lambda_i, \Gamma_i)$: $y_0 = c \cdot y_0^{(1)}$, $\Lambda_i = (\Lambda_i^{(1)})^c$, $\Gamma_i = (\Gamma_i^{(1)})^c$.

- $\mathsf{Mult}(\mathsf{ek}, \sigma_1, \sigma_2)$. This takes as input two tags $\sigma_1 = (y_0^{(1)}, \Lambda_i^{(1)}, \Gamma_i^{(1)})$ and $\sigma_2 = (y_0^{(2)}, \Lambda_j^{(2)}, \Gamma_j^{(2)})$ and outputs a tag $\sigma = (y_0, \Lambda_d, \Gamma_d)$ where $d = i+j$. σ is computed as follows:

$$y_0 = y_0^{(1)} \cdot y_0^{(2)}$$
$$\Lambda_d = e(\Lambda_i^{(1)}, \Gamma_j^{(2)}) \cdot e(\Lambda_i^{(1)}, A_j)^{y_0^{(2)}} \cdot e(A_i, \Lambda_j^{(2)})^{y_0^{(1)}}$$
$$\Gamma_d = e(\Gamma_i^{(1)}, \Gamma_j^{(2)}) \cdot e(\Gamma_i^{(1)}, A_j)^{y_0^{(2)}} \cdot e(A_i, \Gamma_j^{(2)})^{y_0^{(1)}}$$

$\mathsf{Ver}(\mathsf{sk}, m, \mathcal{P}, \sigma)$. Let $\mathcal{P} = (f, \tau_1, \ldots, \tau_n)$ be a labeled program, $m \in \mathbb{Z}_p$ and σ be a tag of either the form $(y_0, y_1) \in \mathbb{Z}_p^2$, or $(y_0, \Lambda_i, \Gamma_i) \in \mathbb{Z}_p \times \mathbb{G}_i^2$. First, compute $\rho = f(r_{\tau_1}, \ldots, r_{\tau_n})$ where $r_{\tau_i} \leftarrow F_K(\tau_i)$. Next, according to the form of σ perform the following checks:

1. If $\sigma = (y_0, y_1) \in \mathbb{Z}_p^2$, then output 1 only if $\rho = y_0 + y_1 \cdot x \ \wedge \ y_0 = m$.

---

[6] Note that any circuit can be changed to meet this assumption: simply add multiplications by a special variable with value 1. This change does not increase the circuit's degree, and its homomorphic evaluation can be performed by using the tag σ_U.

2. If $\sigma = (y_0, \Lambda_i, \Gamma_i) \in \mathbb{Z}_p \times \mathbb{G}_1^2$, then output 1 only if $y_0 = m$ $\wedge$ $(g_i^{a^{i-1}})^{\rho - m} = \Lambda_i$ $\wedge$ $\Lambda_i^a = \Gamma_i$.

For lack of space, the correctness of the scheme is shown in the full version.

In the following theorem we prove the security of the scheme for the class of arithmetic circuits of (total) degree Δ such that $\Delta < p$, and in particular when $0 < \Delta/p < 1$ is the inverse of a small constant (e.g., $1/2$). For lack of space, the proof of the theorem appears in the full version.

Theorem 2. *If F is a PRF and the computational (D, k)-MDHI assumption holds for $\mathcal{G}$, then the homomorphic MAC scheme described in Section 4 is secure.*

Possible Candidates. Here we discuss the possible instantiations of our scheme. A brief summary is also provided in Table 1.

GGH GRADED ENCODINGS. A first instantiation is obtained by using the recent proposal of multilinear maps [24,21]. Since these realizations allow for a number of levels k which is polynomial in the security parameter, we obtain a homomorphic MAC that supports circuits of bounded polynomial degree and that, in particular, allows for degree-k composition. Also, due to the properties of the current multilinear maps realizations, the size of the final authentication tags (i.e., as generated by Eval_2) is $O(d)$ where $d \leq k$ is the degree of the composition circuit ϕ. This limitation stems from the fact that in all current realizations the size of an encoding at level d is $O(d)$. Hence, we obtain the following corollary.

Corollary 1. *Assume that F is a PRF, $\mathcal{G}$ is an instantiation of multilinear maps as in [24,21], and the computational (D, k)-MDHI assumption holds for $\mathcal{G}$ with $D, k = \mathsf{poly}(\lambda)$. Then the scheme of Section 4 is a secure homomorphic MAC with authentication tags of size $O(k)$ and that supports computations expressed by arithmetic circuits of degree at most D and composition circuits of degree at most k.*

SUPPORTING CIRCUITS OF POLYNOMIAL DEPTH VIA COMPACT MULTILINEAR MAPS. We note that the succinctness and the expressiveness (i.e., the class of circuits that are supported) of our construction crucially depend on the properties of the graded encoding. In particular, it is interesting to note that, in principle, we could support almost arbitrary circuits (i.e., of polynomial depth) and achieve full succinctness if the scheme is implemented with multilinear maps that allow for an exponential number of levels and that are compact. In this case, it is not even necessary to distinguish between Eval_1 and Eval_2: we can "merge" the algorithms Auth and $\mathsf{Compress}$ in order to create tags that are directly level-1 encodings, and then use Eval_2 to perform all the homomorphic operations. Although multilinear groups with such properties are not known, our result has the potential of yielding a fully-fledged homomorphic MAC. Indeed, our construction uses multilinear maps in a generic way, and its security holds against adversaries making an unbounded number of verification queries, in contrast to the fully-homomorphic MAC of Gennaro-Wichs, that can support only a constant number of verification queries.

Table 1. Summary of homomorphic MACs instantiations with message space $\mathbb{Z}_p$. The last column indicates whether unbounded verification queries are supported or not.

Scheme	Tag Size	Composability	Supported Computations	Assumption	Verif. Queries
CF13-1 [16]	$O(d)$	✓	degree-d circuits	OWF	✓
CF13-2 [16]	$O(1)$	×	degree-D circuits	D-DHI	✓
GW13 [28]	$O(\lambda)$	✓	Arbitrary circuits	FHE	×
This work with graded encodings [24,21]	$O(k)$	degree-k circuits	degree-$(D+k)$ circuits	(D,k)-MDHI	✓
This work with ideal k-linear maps	$O(1)$	✓	degree-k circuits $\forall k : k/p < 1/2$	$(1,k)$-MDHI	✓

Corollary 2. *Assume that F is a PRF, $\mathcal{G}$ is an (ideal) instantiation of compact multilinear maps, and the computational $(1, k)$-MDHI assumption holds for $\mathcal{G}$ for any $k < p/2 \approx 2^{\lambda-1}$. Then the scheme of Section 4 is a secure homomorphic MAC with authentication tags of size $O(1)$ and that supports computations expressed by arithmetic circuits of degree at most k.*

Acknowledgements. The research of Dario Fiore is partially supported by the European Commission's Seventh Framework Programme Marie Curie Cofund Action AMAROUT II (grant no. 291803). The research of Rosario Gennaro was sponsored by the U.S. Army Research Laboratory and the U.K. Ministry of Defense and was accomplished under Agreement Number W911NF-06-3-0001. The views and conclusions contained in this document are those of the author(s) and should not be interpreted as representing the official policies, either expressed or implied, of the U.S. Army Research Laboratory, the U.S. Government, the U.K. Ministry of Defence or the U.K. Government. The U.S. and U.K. Governments are authorized to reproduce and distribute reprints for Government purposes notwithstanding any copyright notation hereon.

References

1. Agrawal, S., Boneh, D.: Homomorphic MACs: MAC-based integrity for network coding. In: Abdalla, M., Pointcheval, D., Fouque, P.-A., Vergnaud, D. (eds.) ACNS 2009. LNCS, vol. 5536, pp. 292–305. Springer, Heidelberg (2009)
2. Attrapadung, N., Libert, B.: Homomorphic network coding signatures in the standard model. In: Catalano, D., Fazio, N., Gennaro, R., Nicolosi, A. (eds.) PKC 2011. LNCS, vol. 6571, pp. 17–34. Springer, Heidelberg (2011)
3. Attrapadung, N., Libert, B., Peters, T.: Efficient completely context-hiding quotable and linearly homomorphic signatures. In: Kurosawa, K., Hanaoka, G. (eds.) PKC 2013. LNCS, vol. 7778, pp. 386–404. Springer, Heidelberg (2013)
4. Backes, M., Fiore, D., Reischuk, R.M.: Verifiable delegation of computation on outsourced data. In: 2013 ACM Conference on Computer and Communication Security. ACM Press (November 2013)

5. Benabbas, S., Gennaro, R., Vahlis, Y.: Verifiable delegation of computation over large datasets. In: Rogaway, P. (ed.) CRYPTO 2011. LNCS, vol. 6841, pp. 111–131. Springer, Heidelberg (2011)
6. Bitansky, N., Canetti, R., Chiesa, A., Tromer, E.: From extractable collision resistance to succinct non-interactive arguments of knowledge, and back again. In: ITCS 2012: Proceedings of the 3rd Symposium on Innovations in Theoretical Computer Science (2012)
7. Bitansky, N., Canetti, R., Chiesa, A., Tromer, E.: Recursive composition and bootstrapping for snarks and proof-carrying data. In: STOC (2013)
8. Bitansky, N., Chiesa, A., Ishai, Y., Paneth, O., Ostrovsky, R.: Succinct noninteractive arguments via linear interactive proofs. In: Sahai, A. (ed.) TCC 2013. LNCS, vol. 7785, pp. 315–333. Springer, Heidelberg (2013)
9. Boneh, D., Boyen, X., Goh, E.-J.: Hierarchical identity based encryption with constant size ciphertext. In: Cramer, R. (ed.) EUROCRYPT 2005. LNCS, vol. 3494, pp. 440–456. Springer, Heidelberg (2005)
10. Boneh, D., Freeman, D., Katz, J., Waters, B.: Signing a linear subspace: Signature schemes for network coding. In: Jarecki, S., Tsudik, G. (eds.) PKC 2009. LNCS, vol. 5443, pp. 68–87. Springer, Heidelberg (2009)
11. Boneh, D., Freeman, D.M.: Homomorphic signatures for polynomial functions. In: Paterson, K.G. (ed.) EUROCRYPT 2011. LNCS, vol. 6632, pp. 149–168. Springer, Heidelberg (2011)
12. Boneh, D., Freeman, D.M.: Linearly homomorphic signatures over binary fields and new tools for lattice-based signatures. In: Catalano, D., Fazio, N., Gennaro, R., Nicolosi, A. (eds.) PKC 2011. LNCS, vol. 6571, pp. 1–16. Springer, Heidelberg (2011)
13. Boneh, D., Goh, E.-J., Nissim, K.: Evaluating 2-DNF formulas on ciphertexts. In: Kilian, J. (ed.) TCC 2005. LNCS, vol. 3378, pp. 325–341. Springer, Heidelberg (2005)
14. Boyen, X.: The uber-assumption family. In: Galbraith, S.D., Paterson, K.G. (eds.) Pairing 2008. LNCS, vol. 5209, pp. 39–56. Springer, Heidelberg (2008)
15. Brakerski, Z., Vaikuntanathan, V.: Efficient fully homomorphic encryption from (standard) LWE. In: Ostrovsky, R. (ed.) 52nd FOCS, pp. 97–106. IEEE Computer Society Press (October 2011)
16. Catalano, D., Fiore, D.: Practical homomorphic mACs for arithmetic circuits. In: Johansson, T., Nguyen, P.Q. (eds.) EUROCRYPT 2013. LNCS, vol. 7881, pp. 336–352. Springer, Heidelberg (2013)
17. Catalano, D., Fiore, D., Gennaro, R., Vamvourellis, K.: Algebraic (Trapdoor) one-way functions and their applications. In: Sahai, A. (ed.) TCC 2013. LNCS, vol. 7785, pp. 680–699. Springer, Heidelberg (2013)
18. Catalano, D., Fiore, D., Warinschi, B.: Adaptive pseudo-free groups and applications. In: Paterson, K.G. (ed.) EUROCRYPT 2011. LNCS, vol. 6632, pp. 207–223. Springer, Heidelberg (2011)
19. Catalano, D., Fiore, D., Warinschi, B.: Efficient network coding signatures in the standard model. In: Fischlin, M., Buchmann, J., Manulis, M. (eds.) PKC 2012. LNCS, vol. 7293, pp. 680–696. Springer, Heidelberg (2012)
20. Chung, K.-M., Kalai, Y.T., Liu, F.-H., Raz, R.: Memory delegation. In: Rogaway, P. (ed.) CRYPTO 2011. LNCS, vol. 6841, pp. 151–168. Springer, Heidelberg (2011)
21. Coron, J.-S., Lepoint, T., Tibouchi, M.: Practical multilinear maps over the integers. In: Canetti, R., Garay, J.A. (eds.) CRYPTO 2013, Part I. LNCS, vol. 8042, pp. 476–493. Springer, Heidelberg (2013)

22. Fiore, D., Gennaro, R.: Publicly verifiable delegation of large polynomials and matrix computations, with applications. In: 2012 ACM Conference on Computer and Communication Security. ACM Press (October 2012)

23. Freeman, D.M.: Improved security for linearly homomorphic signatures: A generic framework. In: Fischlin, M., Buchmann, J., Manulis, M. (eds.) PKC 2012. LNCS, vol. 7293, pp. 697–714. Springer, Heidelberg (2012)

24. Garg, S., Gentry, C., Halevi, S.: Candidate multilinear maps from ideal lattices. In: Johansson, T., Nguyen, P.Q. (eds.) EUROCRYPT 2013. LNCS, vol. 7881, pp. 1–17. Springer, Heidelberg (2013)

25. Gennaro, R., Gentry, C., Parno, B.: Non-interactive verifiable computing: Outsourcing computation to untrusted workers. In: Rabin, T. (ed.) CRYPTO 2010. LNCS, vol. 6223, pp. 465–482. Springer, Heidelberg (2010)

26. Gennaro, R., Gentry, C., Parno, B., Raykova, M.: Quadratic span programs and succinct NIZKs without PCPs. In: Johansson, T., Nguyen, P.Q. (eds.) EUROCRYPT 2013. LNCS, vol. 7881, pp. 626–645. Springer, Heidelberg (2013)

27. Gennaro, R., Katz, J., Krawczyk, H., Rabin, T.: Secure network coding over the integers. In: Nguyen, P.Q., Pointcheval, D. (eds.) PKC 2010. LNCS, vol. 6056, pp. 142–160. Springer, Heidelberg (2010)

28. Gennaro, R., Wichs, D.: Fully homomorphic message authenticators. In: Sako, K., Sarkar, P. (eds.) ASIACRYPT 2013, Part II. LNCS, vol. 8270, pp. 301–320. Springer, Heidelberg (2013)

29. Gentry, C.: Fully homomorphic encryption using ideal lattices. In: Mitzenmacher, M. (ed.) 41st ACM STOC, pp. 169–178. ACM Press (May/June 2009)

30. Gentry, C., Wichs, D.: Separating succinct non-interactive arguments from all falsifiable assumptions. In: Fortnow, L., Vadhan, S.P. (eds.) 43rd ACM STOC, pp. 99–108. ACM Press (June 2011)

31. Goldwasser, S., Kalai, Y.T., Rothblum, G.N.: Delegating computation: interactive proofs for muggles. In: Ladner, R.E., Dwork, C. (eds.) 40th ACM STOC, pp. 113–122. ACM Press (May 2008)

32. Hohenberger, S., Sahai, A., Waters, B.: Full domain hash from (Leveled) multilinear maps and identity-based aggregate signatures. In: Canetti, R., Garay, J.A. (eds.) CRYPTO 2013, Part I. LNCS, vol. 8042, pp. 494–512. Springer, Heidelberg (2013)

33. Johnson, R., Molnar, D., Song, D., Wagner, D.: Homomorphic signature schemes. In: Preneel, B. (ed.) CT-RSA 2002. LNCS, vol. 2271, pp. 244–262. Springer, Heidelberg (2002)

34. Kilian, J.: A note on efficient zero-knowledge proofs and arguments. In: 24th ACM STOC, pp. 723–732. ACM Press (May 1992)

35. Micali, S.: Cs proofs. In: 35th FOCS (November 1994)

36. Hawkes, P.: XOR and non-XOR differential probabilities. In: Stern, J. (ed.) EUROCRYPT 1999. LNCS, vol. 1592, pp. 272–285. Springer, Heidelberg (1999)

37. Parno, B., Raykova, M., Vaikuntanathan, V.: How to delegate and verify in public: Verifiable computation from attribute-based encryption. In: Cramer, R. (ed.) TCC 2012. LNCS, vol. 7194, pp. 422–439. Springer, Heidelberg (2012)

38. Shpilka, A., Yehudayoff, A.: Arithmetic circuits: A survey of recent results and open questions. Foundations and Trends in Theoretical Computer Science 5(3-4), 207–388 (2010)

39. Valiant, P.: Incrementally verifiable computation or proofs of knowledge imply time/space efficiency. In: Canetti, R. (ed.) TCC 2008. LNCS, vol. 4948, pp. 1–18. Springer, Heidelberg (2008)

General Impossibility of Group Homomorphic Encryption in the Quantum World

Frederik Armknecht[1], Tommaso Gagliardoni[2,*],
Stefan Katzenbeisser[2], and Andreas Peter[3,**]

[1] Universität Mannheim, Germany
armknecht@uni-mannheim.de
[2] Technische Universität Darmstadt and CASED, Germany
tommaso.gagliardoni@cased.de
katzenbeisser@seceng.informatik.tu-darmstadt.de
[3] University of Twente, The Netherlands
a.peter@utwente.nl

Abstract. Group homomorphic encryption represents one of the most important building blocks in modern cryptography. It forms the basis of widely-used, more sophisticated primitives, such as CCA2-secure encryption or secure multiparty computation. Unfortunately, recent advances in quantum computation show that many of the existing schemes completely break down once quantum computers reach maturity (mainly due to Shor's algorithm). This leads to the challenge of constructing quantum-resistant group homomorphic cryptosystems.

In this work, we prove the *general* impossibility of (abelian) group homomorphic encryption in the presence of quantum adversaries, when assuming the IND-CPA security notion as the minimal security requirement. To this end, we prove a new result on the probability of sampling generating sets of finite (sub-)groups if sampling is done with respect to an arbitrary, unknown distribution. Finally, we provide a sufficient condition on homomorphic encryption schemes for our quantum attack to work and discuss its satisfiability in non-group homomorphic cases. The impact of our results on recent fully homomorphic encryption schemes poses itself as an open question.

Keywords: Public-Key Cryptography, Homomorphic Encryption, Semantic Security, Quantum Algorithms, Sampling Group Generators.

1 Introduction

Since the introduction of public-key cryptography by Diffie and Hellman [13] in 1976, researchers strived to construct encryption schemes that are *group homomorphic*. This property can be characterized by requiring the encryption scheme

* Supported by the German Federal Ministry of Education and Research (BMBF) within the EC-SPRIDE project.
** Supported by the THeCS project as part of the Dutch national program COMMIT.

H. Krawczyk (Ed.): PKC 2014, LNCS 8383, pp. 556–573, 2014.

to have a homomorphic decryption procedure, while the plaintext and cipher-text spaces form groups. Ever since, the topic of homomorphic encryption is of central importance in cryptography. The recent advances in fully homomorphic encryption (FHE) [7,16,17] constitute just one example of this trend. In practice, *group* homomorphic encryption schemes lie at the heart of several important applications, such as electronic voting [9], private information retrieval [24], or multiparty computation [8] to name just a few. Moreover, the group homomorphic property comes quite naturally, as witnessed by a number of encryption schemes, for example RSA [29], ElGamal [14], Goldwasser-Micali [20], where the homomorphic property was not a design goal, but rather arose "by chance".

So far, these cryptosystems were all analyzed in the classical model of computation. However, it is reasonable to assume that the *quantum* model of computation will become more realistic in the future. Unfortunately, in this model all aforementioned cryptosystems are insecure due to Shor's algorithm [30], which allows to efficiently solve the discrete logarithm problem and to factor large integers. That is, until today nobody has been able to come up with a group homomorphic encryption scheme that can withstand quantum attackers.

It seems that such a scheme would require other design approaches. For instance, when considering ElGamal-like encryption schemes, simply replacing the underlying computational hardness assumption by a supposedly quantum-resistant one, say code-based, is not enough [3]. In fact although there is a substantial number of classical cryptographic primitives that can be proven secure against quantum attackers, e.g. [22], we still know little about what classical primitives can be realized in the quantum world and what not. Indeed this applies to the case of group homomorphic encryption schemes as well: so far it was even undecided whether *group homomorphic encryption can exist at all in the quantum world*. In other words, does the absence of a quantum secure group homomorphic encryption scheme so far imply that the right approach has not been found yet (but may be in the future) or are there universal reasons that prevent the existence of such schemes?

1.1 Our Contributions

Basic Impossibility Result. The central contribution of this work is to give a *negative* answer to the above question:

> *It is impossible to construct secure group homomorphic encryption in the quantum world, if the plaintext and ciphertext spaces form abelian groups.*

More precisely, we prove that any such scheme[1] cannot meet the minimal security notion of IND-CPA security in the presence of quantum adversaries. Observe that this result not only re-confirms the insecurity of *existing* schemes, but shows that *all* group homomorphic encryption schemes (including all yet to come schemes) are inevitably insecure in the quantum world.

---

[1] Although we postulate that our result is extendible to arbitrary solvable groups, we focus on the abelian case, since it is the most important one for reasons of practicability in real-world applications.

Quantum Attack. In order to prove this impossibility, we start by exhibiting the fact that the IND-CPA security of any group homomorphic encryption scheme can be reduced to an abstract *Subgroup Membership Problem* (SMP), introduced by Cramer and Shoup [10], which is much easier to analyze. Roughly speaking, this problem states that given a group G with subgroup H and a randomly sampled (according to some arbitrary distribution $\mathcal{D}$) element $g \in G$, decide whether $g \in H$ or not. This reduction to the SMP tells us that in order to break the IND-CPA security of a given group homomorphic encryption scheme in the quantum world, it is sufficient to give a quantum algorithm that breaks the SMP. Now, the basic idea for breaking the SMP for groups (G, H) is to use Watrous' variant [31] of the famous group order-finding quantum algorithm, which will effectively decide membership.

Sampling Generators in Finite Groups. Unfortunately, this algorithm only works when given a set of generators of H which we commonly do not have. Hence we restrict to the generic case that an attacker has only access to an efficient *sampling algorithm* for H that samples according to some distribution $\mathcal{D}$. We distinguish between the following two cases:

- **Uniform Distribution.** If $\mathcal{D}$ is uniform, Erdös and Rényi [15] show that sampling polynomially many times from H will give a generating set with high probability—a result that has been improved by Pak and Bratus [27]: If $k = \lceil \log_2(|H|) \rceil$, then $k+4$ samples are enough to get a set of generators with probability $\geq 3/4$. After obtaining a generating set for H, we use Watrous' quantum algorithm to decide membership in H, and hence efficiently break the SMP for (G, H).
- **Arbitrary/Unknown Distribution.** In general, the distribution $\mathcal{D}$ does not have to be uniform, but can be arbitrary, or completely unknown. Interestingly, we prove that, even then, breaking the SMP is possible with (almost) linearly many samples only. Observe that as we do not make any restrictions on the sampling algorithm, we cannot exclude seemingly exotic cases where regions of H are hardly (or never) reached by the sampling algorithm. Thus, the best we can aim for is to find a generating set for a subgroup H^* of H such that the probability that a random sample (with respect to $\mathcal{D}$) does fall into H^* is above an arbitrarily chosen threshold δ. We call such subgroups to be δ-*covering*. It turns out that having a generating set for such a subgroup is enough to break the SMP for (G, H). The main challenge, however, is to find a generating set for a δ-covering subgroup. To this end, we prove a new result on the probability of sampling generating sets of finite (sub-)groups with unknown sampling distribution. More precisely, we show that for any chosen probability threshold δ^*, there exists a value N, which grows at most logarithmically in k and does not depend on $\mathcal{D}$, such that $N \cdot k + 1$ samples yield a generating set for a δ-covering subgroup with probability at least δ^*. This result represents one of the main technical contribution of our work. We believe that it is also applicable in other research areas, e.g., computational group theory, and hence might be of independent interest.

Possible Extensions to Fully Homomorphic Encryption Schemes. Finally, we provide a general sufficient condition on a homomorphic encryption scheme for our quantum attack to work and discuss the applicability in FHE schemes. The decision of whether our attack breaks any of the existing FHE schemes [7,16,17] proves itself to be a highly non-trivial task and lies outside the scope of this paper. We leave it as interesting future work.

1.2 Related Work

There are many papers dealing with the construction of IND-CPA secure group homomorphic encryption schemes [26,18,12,3,28]. Some of these works attempted to build such schemes using post-quantum primitives [1], which did not succeed (for a good reason as our results show). Also, for a restricted class of group homomorphic schemes, [3] shows the impossibility of using linear codes as the ciphertext group. Furthermore, we mention the impossibility (even in the classical world) of *algebraically homomorphic* encryption schemes [6], which are deterministic encryption schemes and thus do not fall into the class IND-CPA secure cryptosystems.

In the quantum world, there is an even more efficient algorithm for breaking such algebraically homomorphic schemes [11]. In this vein, there are many variants of Shor's algorithm [30] that are being used to solve different computational problems [25,31], leading to the breakdown of certain cryptosystems. On the other hand, there are several papers dealing with the analysis of classical primitives in the presence of quantum adversaries [21,22]. However, none of these works show a general impossibility of group homomorphic cryptosystems.

With respect to the sampling from finite groups, there are many papers that are concerned with the improvement of probability bounds on finding generating sets when sampling uniformly at random [15,5,27]. Similar strong results for the arbitrary sampling from finite groups are not known.

Finally, we mention the recent advances in fully homomorphic encryption (FHE) [7,16,17]. These schemes are not classified as being group homomorphic, as they follow a different design approach. Rather than having a group homomorphic decryption algorithm, the decryption is only guaranteed to run correctly for polynomially many evaluations of the group operation. Interestingly enough, our results show that since current FHE schemes are based on post-quantum hardness assumptions, they had to follow a different approach than the group homomorphic one.

1.3 Outline

We recall standard notation in Section 2 and show some basic observations on group homomorphic encryption and the Subgroup Membership Problem (SMP) in Section 3. Section 4 covers the main Theorem, showing the impossibility of group homomorphic encryption in the quantum world, thereby giving our new insights in the sampling of group generators. We discuss non-group homomorphic encryption, such as somewhat and (leveled) fully homomorphic encryption in Section 5.

2   Notation

Throughout the paper, we use some standard notation that we briefly want to recall. We write $x \longleftarrow X$ if X is a random variable or distribution and x is to be chosen randomly from X according to its distribution. In the case where X is solely a set, $x \xleftarrow{U} X$ denotes that x is chosen uniformly at random from X. If we sample an element x from X by using a specific distribution $\mathcal{D}$, we write $x \xleftarrow{\mathcal{D}} X$ (or $x \longleftarrow X$ when there is no doubt about the distribution $\mathcal{D}$). For a distribution $\mathcal{D}$ on X, the term $\mathcal{D}(x)$ for $x \in X$ expresses the probability with which x is sampled according to $\mathcal{D}$, i.e., the probability mass function at $x \in X$.

For an algorithm $\mathcal{A}$ we write $x \longleftarrow \mathcal{A}(y)$ if $\mathcal{A}$ outputs x on fixed input y according to $\mathcal{A}$'s distribution. Sometimes, we need to specify the randomness of a probabilistic algorithm $\mathcal{A}$ explicitly. To this end, we interpret $\mathcal{A}$ in the usual way as a deterministic algorithm $\mathcal{A}(y; r)$, which has access to values $r \longleftarrow$ Rnd that are randomly chosen from some randomness space Rnd. Moreover, two distribution ensembles $X = \{X_\lambda\}_{\lambda \in \mathbb{N}}$ and $Y = \{Y_\lambda\}_{\lambda \in \mathbb{N}}$ taking values in a finite set S_λ (indexed by a parameter λ) are said to be *computationally indistinguishable*, if for all probabilistic polynomial time (PPT) algorithms $\mathcal{A}$ there exists a negligible function `negl` such that

$$\mathrm{Adv}_{\mathcal{A}}^{X,Y}(\lambda) := \left| \Pr_{x \longleftarrow X_\lambda}[\mathcal{A}(x) = 1] - \Pr_{y \longleftarrow Y_\lambda}[\mathcal{A}(y) = 1] \right| \leq \mathtt{negl}(\lambda).$$

We denote this by $X \stackrel{c}{=} Y$.

For a group G, we denote the neutral element by 1, and denote the binary operation on G by ".", i.e., G is written in *multiplicative notation*. We recall that a subgroup H of a group G is said to be *normal* if $z \cdot h \cdot z^{-1} \in H$ for all $z \in G, h \in H$. In particular, this means that if G is an abelian group, then every subgroup H is normal.

In general, we will consider sequences of abelian groups $(G_\lambda)_\lambda$ indexed by a parameter λ, where any element of every G_λ admits a representation of size at most polynomial in λ. We might assume, without loss of generality, that the choice of this polynomial is the identity, and in particular that every G_λ has order upper bounded by 2^λ. We will just write G instead of G_λ for any fixed choice of λ.

By a *description* of a finite group G we mean an efficient (i.e., PPT in λ) sampling algorithm (where sampling is denoted by $x \longleftarrow G$), the neutral element 1, an efficient algorithm for performing the group operation on G, and one for the inversion of group elements. Notice that the output distribution of the sampling algorithm does not have to be necessarily uniform. We abuse notation and write G both for the description and for the group itself. Furthermore, for elements $x_1, \ldots, x_k \in G$, we write $\langle x_1, \ldots, x_k \rangle$ for the subgroup generated by $x_1, \ldots, x_k$.

3   Group Homomorphic Encryption

We recall the notion of public-key *group homomorphic* encryption, which roughly can be described as usual public-key encryption where the decryption algorithm is a group homomorphism.

Definition 1 (Group Homomorphic Encryption [3,23]). *A public key encryption scheme* $\mathcal{E} = (\mathsf{KeyGen}, \mathsf{Enc}, \mathsf{Dec})$ *is called* group homomorphic, *if for every output* $(\mathsf{pk}, \mathsf{sk})$ *of* $\mathsf{KeyGen}(\lambda)$, *the plaintext space* $\mathcal{P}$ *and the ciphertext space* $\widehat{\mathcal{C}}$ *are non-trivial groups such that*

- *the set of all encryptions* $\mathcal{C} := \{\mathsf{Enc}_{\mathsf{pk}}(m; r) \mid m \in \mathcal{P}, r \in \mathsf{Rnd}\}$ *is a non-trivial subgroup of* $\widehat{\mathcal{C}}$
- *the decryption* $\mathsf{Dec}_{\mathsf{sk}}$ *is a group homomorphism on* $\mathcal{C}$, *i.e.*

$$\mathsf{Dec}_{\mathsf{sk}}(c \cdot c') = \mathsf{Dec}_{\mathsf{sk}}(c) \cdot \mathsf{Dec}_{\mathsf{sk}}(c'), \text{ for all } c, c' \in \mathcal{C}.^2$$

Notice that the scheme does *not* include a membership testing algorithm (i.e., an algorithm to test whether a group element is a valid encryption or not). The standard security notion for such homomorphic encryption schemes is that of *indistinguishability under chosen-plaintext attack*, denoted by IND-CPA [3]. Informally, this notion states whenever an adversary picks two plaintext messages of his choosing and gets to see an encryption of either of them, it should be computationally infeasible for him to decide which of the two messages was encrypted. Formally, for a given security parameter λ, group homomorphic encryption scheme $\mathcal{E} = (\mathsf{KeyGen}, \mathsf{Enc}, \mathsf{Dec})$, and PPT adversary $\mathcal{A}$, we consider the experiment $\mathbf{Exp}_{\mathcal{A},\mathsf{KeyGen}}^{\text{ind-cpa}}(\lambda)$, where $\mathcal{A}$ chooses two different plaintexts m_0, m_1 and is then provided an encryption $\mathsf{Enc}_{\mathsf{pk}}(m_b)$ for a randomly chosen bit b and a public key pk output by $\mathsf{KeyGen}(\lambda)$. The experiment succeeds (outputs 1) if b is guessed correctly. We say that $\mathcal{E}$ is IND-CPA *secure* if the advantage

$$\left| \Pr\left[\mathbf{Exp}_{\mathcal{A},\mathsf{KeyGen}}^{\text{ind-cpa}}(\lambda) = 1 \right] - \frac{1}{2} \right| \text{ is negligible for all PPT adversaries } \mathcal{A}.$$

Moreover, we recall a fact showing the strong group-theoretic structure of the set of encryptions of $1 \in \mathcal{P}$ for *any* group-homomorphic encryption scheme. For this, we introduce the *set of all encryptions of* $m \in \mathcal{P}$

$$\mathcal{C}_m := \{c \in \mathcal{C} \mid \mathsf{Dec}_{\mathsf{sk}}(c) = m\}.$$

Fact 1 (Basic Properties [3]). *Let* $\mathcal{E} = (\mathsf{KeyGen}, \mathsf{Enc}, \mathsf{Dec})$ *be an arbitrary group homomorphic encryption scheme. It holds that*

---

^{2} Note that the decryption might output an error $\perp$ on inputs in $\widehat{\mathcal{C}} \setminus \mathcal{C}$. Therefore, requiring it to be homomorphic on $\mathcal{C}$ is as general as possible since we do not give any restriction on its behaviour outside of $\mathcal{C}$.

1. $\mathcal{C}_m = \mathsf{Enc}_{\mathsf{pk}}(m; r) \cdot \mathcal{C}_1$ for all $m \in \mathcal{P}$ and all $r \in \mathsf{Rnd}$, and
2. $\mathcal{C}_1$ is a proper normal subgroup of $\mathcal{C}$ such that $|\mathcal{C}_1| = |\mathcal{C}_m|$ for all $m \in \mathcal{P}$.

It follows that the set $\{\mathsf{Enc}_{\mathsf{pk}}(m; r) \mid m \in \mathcal{P}\}$ for a fixed r is a system of representatives of $\mathcal{C}/\mathcal{C}_1$.

With this notation, the IND-CPA security of $\mathcal{E}$ is equivalent to saying that the distribution on $\mathcal{C}_{m_0}$ (induced by the encryption algorithm $\mathsf{Enc}_{\mathsf{pk}}(m)$) is computationally indistinguishable from the distribution on $\mathcal{C}_{m_1}$ for any two messages m_0 and m_1 [19, Ch. 5.2], i.e., $\mathcal{C}_{m_0} \stackrel{c}{=} \mathcal{C}_{m_1}$.

Necessary Security Condition. We briefly recall the *Subgroup Membership Problem* (SMP) which was introduced by Cramer and Shoup in [10].

Definition 2 (Subgroup Membership Problem). *Let* Gen *be a PPT algorithm that takes a security parameter* λ *as input and outputs descriptions* (G, H) *where* H *is a non-trivial, proper subgroup of a finite group* G. *Additionally, we assume here that there is an algorithm that allows for the efficient sampling from* $G \setminus H$. *We consider the following experiment for a given algorithm* Gen, *algorithm* $\mathcal{A}$ *and parameter* λ:

Experiment $\mathbf{Exp}_{\mathcal{A},\mathsf{Gen}}^{\mathrm{smp}}(\lambda)$:

1. $(G, H) \longleftarrow \mathsf{Gen}(\lambda)$
2. *Choose* $b \xleftarrow{U} \{0, 1\}$. *If* $b = 1$: $z \longleftarrow G \setminus H$. *Otherwise:* $z \longleftarrow H$.
3. $d \longleftarrow \mathcal{A}(G, H, z)$ *where* $d \in \{0, 1\}$
4. *The output of the experiment is defined to be 1 if* $d = b$ *and 0 otherwise.*

We say that the SMP is hard for (G, H) *(or relative to* Gen*) if the advantage*

$$\left| \Pr\left[\mathbf{Exp}_{\mathcal{A},\mathsf{Gen}}^{\mathrm{smp}}(\lambda) = 1 \right] - \frac{1}{2} \right| \text{ is negligible for all PPT algorithms } \mathcal{A}.$$

We stress the fact that the efficient sampling from $G \setminus H$ does not have to be uniform. Let $\mathcal{E} = (\mathsf{KeyGen}, \mathsf{Enc}, \mathsf{Dec})$ be a group homomorphic encryption scheme with the group $\mathcal{C}$ of all encryptions and the subgroup $\mathcal{C}_1$ of all encryptions of the neutral element 1. In fact, the hardness of SMP for $(\mathcal{C}, \mathcal{C}_1)$ (i.e., relative to KeyGen) is a necessary condition for $\mathcal{E}$ to be IND-CPA secure. Recall that the sampling algorithms for the groups $\mathcal{C}$ and $\mathcal{C}_1$ are the ones inherited from the encryption algorithm of $\mathcal{E}$. In particular, sampling an element c from $\mathcal{C} \setminus \mathcal{C}_1$ is done by choosing a random message $m \in \mathcal{P}$ with $m \neq 1$ and then computing c as $\mathsf{Enc}_{\mathsf{pk}}(m; r)$ for $r \longleftarrow \mathsf{Rnd}$. We have the following immediate result:

Theorem 1 (Necessary Condition on IND-CPA Security). *For a group homomorphic encryption scheme* $\mathcal{E} = (\mathsf{KeyGen}, \mathsf{Enc}, \mathsf{Dec})$ *we have:*

$$\mathcal{E} \text{ is IND-CPA secure} \implies \text{SMP is hard (relative to } \mathsf{KeyGen}).$$

The above holds regardless of the type of adversary (i.e., classical vs quantum) taken into account. A straightforward proof of this Theorem can be found in the appendix of the full version of this paper [2]. Since it is a popular belief (and for reasons of completeness), we want to point out that the converse of the Theorem does *not* hold in general. This can be seen by considering a somewhat pathological example, which we also present in the appendix of [2]. Note that the converse of Theorem 1 *does*, however, hold for so-called *shift-type homomorphic encryption schemes* [4], which describe a certain subclass of group homomorphic encryption schemes that actually encompasses all existing instances. Furthermore, it also holds for bit encryption schemes, since there are only two messages, 0 and 1.

4   General Impossibility in the Quantum World

Let Gen be a PPT algorithm that takes a security parameter λ as input and outputs descriptions (G, H) where H is a non-trivial, proper subgroup of a finite group G with an additional algorithm for the efficient sampling from $G \setminus H$ (cf. Section 3). Now, assume that for any such algorithm Gen, we can construct a quantum algorithm $\mathcal{A}_Q$ that breaks the hardness of SMP relative to Gen. In particular, for a given group homomorphic encryption scheme $\mathcal{E} = (\text{KeyGen}, \text{Enc}, \text{Dec})$ this means that we have a quantum algorithm $\mathcal{A}_Q$ that breaks the hardness of SMP relative to KeyGen. However, by Theorem 1, this implies that we can construct an algorithm that breaks the IND-CPA security of $\mathcal{E}$. Since we had no restriction on the encryption scheme $\mathcal{E}$, this would imply that *any* group homomorphic encryption scheme $\mathcal{E}$ is insecure in terms of IND-CPA in the quantum world. This is the result we want to prove in this section, at least for the abelian case, i.e., when G is an abelian group. Therefore, let Gen be as above but with G being abelian.

It is well-known that a modification of the famous order-finding quantum algorithm [31] can efficiently find the order of an abelian group, given that we have its description by a set of generators.

Theorem 2 (Quantum Order-Finding Algorithm with Generators [31]). *Let G be a finite abelian group with $k = \lceil \log_2(|G|) \rceil$. Then, there exists a quantum algorithm which, given a generating set of G and an error probability ε as an input, outputs the order of G with probability at least $1 - \varepsilon$ in time $o(\text{poly}(k + \log_2(1/\varepsilon)))$.*

This Theorem already is sufficient to break the hardness of SMP (relative to Gen), *if* the description of H contains a set of generators, as the next Theorem shows.

Theorem 3 (Quantum Attack on SMP with Generators). *Let (G, H) be the output of Gen(λ), for some security parameter λ, such that H contains a set of generators $g_1, \ldots, g_r$. Since Gen is a PPT algorithm, this implies that $k = k(\lambda) = \lceil \log_2(|H|) \rceil$ is a polynomial in λ. There exists a quantum algorithm which, given $g_1, \ldots, g_r$ (i.e., the description of H), breaks the hardness of SMP with probability at least $(1 - \varepsilon)^2$ in time $o(\text{poly}(k + \log_2(1/\varepsilon)))$.*

Proof. Let z denote the challenge in the SMP game (Def. 2), i.e., $z \in G \setminus H$ if $b = 1$, and $z \in H$ otherwise. Since H contains a set of generators $g_1, \ldots, g_r$, we can run the quantum algorithm in Theorem 2 twice: the first time on the generating set and the second time on the generating set plus the element z. Provided that both runs succeed, we have that $z \in H$ (i.e., $b = 0$) if and only if the two subgroup orders, obtained from the two algorithm runs, are the same. But both runs succeed with probability $(1 - \varepsilon)^2$. This proves the Theorem.   □

Recall that the original definition of SMP gives no set of generators for H a priori, since the description of a group only contains standard algorithms for the group operations and a sampling algorithm (cf. Section 2). However, we show that the previous Theorem extends to this case, i.e., when only having a sampling algorithm. For the sake of readability, we will first treat the case of sampling *uniformly at random* from H (Section 4.1), and will then show the general case with arbitrary (possibly unknown) sampling from H (Section 4.2).

4.1   Breaking SMP with Uniform Sampling

It is well-known that if we have a sampling algorithm for H that samples *uniformly at random*, we can obtain a set of generators by sampling polynomially (in the base-2 logarithm of the order of H) many times from H. If $k = \lceil \log_2(|H|) \rceil$, Pak and Bratus [27] show that $k + 4$ samples are sufficient to generate the whole group with probability $> 3/4$. This result is an improvement over a result by Erdös and Rényi [15]. We recall it in the following Theorem:

Theorem 4 (Probability of Finding a Generating Set with Uniform Sampling [27]). *Let H be a finite abelian group of order n where $k = \lceil \log_2(n) \rceil$. Then:*

$$\Pr_{x_1, \ldots, x_{k+4} \xleftarrow{U} H} [\langle x_1, \ldots, x_{k+4} \rangle = H] > \frac{3}{4}.$$

As an immediate corollary of this Theorem and Theorem 3 we have the main result of this section.

Theorem 5 (Quantum Attack on SMP with Uniform Sampling). *Let (G, H) be the output of $\mathsf{Gen}(\lambda)$ with $k = \lceil \log_2(|H|) \rceil$, for some security parameter λ, such that the sampling algorithm in the description of H samples* uniformly at random *from H. Then, there exists a quantum algorithm which breaks the hardness of SMP with probability at least $\frac{3}{4}(1 - \varepsilon)^2$ in time $o(\mathsf{poly}(k + \log_2(1/\varepsilon)))$, and by sampling only $k + 4$ times from H.*

We remark that the constant $\frac{3}{4}$ can be greatly improved by increasing the number of samples we take from H, approximating 1 very quickly. In general, by performing $k + l$ random sampling, the success probability approximates 1 exponentially fast in l.

4.2   Breaking SMP with Arbitrary/Unknown Sampling

In this section, we show an extension of Theorem 5 to the general case, where the description of H only contains a sampling algorithm with *unknown/arbitrary distribution* $\mathcal{D}$. Since we do not make any restrictions on the sampling algorithm, we cannot exclude seemingly exotic cases where parts of H are hardly (or not at all) reached by the sampling algorithm. Consider the following example:

Example 1. Let $\lambda \geq 1$ be the security parameter. We define a family of groups by $G_\lambda := GF(2)^\lambda$ together with sampling distributions $\mathcal{D}_\lambda$ on G_λ as through the probability mass function

$$\mathcal{D}_\lambda(v_1, \ldots, v_\lambda) := \begin{cases} \frac{1}{2^{\lambda-1}} - \frac{1}{2^{\lambda \cdot (\lambda-1)}} & , \text{if } v_1 = 0 \\ \frac{1}{2^{\lambda \cdot (\lambda-1)}} & , \text{otherwise.} \end{cases} \tag{1}$$

Here, $(v_1, \ldots, v_\lambda)$ denotes an arbitrary element from $GF(2)^\lambda$. Observe that the probability of sampling one vector $(v_1, \ldots, v_\lambda)$ with $v_1 = 1$ is $2^{-\lambda}$. However, at least one such sample is necessary for a generating set of the whole group. This shows that the probability of sampling a generating set for the whole group is negligible in λ.

As the examples illustrates, the best we can aim for (in general) is to find a generating set for a subgroup of H such that the probability that a random sample (with respect to $\mathcal{D}$) does fall into this group is sufficiently large. This motivates the following definition:

Definition 3 (Covering Subgroup). *Let a finite group H be given, together with a sampling distribution $\mathcal{D}$. For a value $0 \leq \delta \leq 1$, we say that a subgroup $H^* \leq H$ is a δ-covering subgroup of H with respect to $\mathcal{D}$ if*

$$\Pr_{x \xleftarrow{\mathcal{D}} H} [x \in H^*] \geq \delta. \tag{2}$$

Example 2. Observe that the whole group H is trivially a δ-covering subgroup. A less trivial example is the following. We order the elements $h \in H$ in descending order according to their probabilities of being sampled, that is $h_1, h_2, \ldots$ with $\mathcal{D}(h_i) \geq \mathcal{D}(h_{i+1})$ for all i. Now, let b denote the smallest index such that $\sum_{i=1}^{b} \mathcal{D}(h_i) \geq \delta$. Then $\langle h_1, \ldots, h_b \rangle$ is for sure a δ-covering subgroup.

Obviously, it follows directly from Theorem 3 that given generators of a δ-covering subgroup, there exists a quantum attack on SMP with success probability at least $\delta \cdot (1 - \varepsilon)^2$ in time $o(\text{poly}(k + \log_2(1/\varepsilon)))$. Thus in the remainder of this section, we consider the task of finding, with probability $\geq \sigma$, a generating set for a δ-covering subgroup (for fixed, but arbitrary values δ, σ) if only a sampling algorithm Sample is given which samples according to an arbitrary (possibly unknown) distribution $\mathcal{D}$. To this end, we prove the following new result on the probability of finding a δ-covering subgroup (with generators) of a finite group with arbitrary/unknown sampling distribution and a given value δ.

Algorithm 1. Sample generating set of a δ-covering subgroup

Given: A group H with sampling algorithm Sample, an integer $k = \lceil \log_2 |H| \rceil$, a membership testing procedure that efficiently tests for any subset $S \subseteq H$ and any $x \in H$ whether $x \in \langle S \rangle$, two real values $0 \le \delta, \sigma \le 1$.
Output: A set S of elements that generate a δ-covering subgroup of H with probability at least σ.

1:
2: $x \leftarrow$ Sample, $S \leftarrow \{x\}$ {Initial candidate for a generating set}
3: $N := \left\lceil \frac{\log(1-\sigma) - \log(k)}{\log(\delta)} \right\rceil$ {Number of samples per round}
4:
5: **for** $j = 1, \ldots, k$ **do**
6:     $x_i \leftarrow$ Sample, $i = 1, \ldots, N$ {Sample N elements from H}
7:     **if** $x_i \in \langle S \rangle$ for all $i = 1, \ldots, N$ **then**
8:        Abort **for**-loop   {Abort as all samples are already in $\langle S \rangle$}
9:     **else**
10:       $S \leftarrow S \cup \{x_1, \ldots, x_N\}$ {Extend candidate generating set}
11:    **end if**
12: **end for**
13:
14: **return** S

Theorem 6 (Sampling a Generating Set for a δ-covering Subgroup).
Let H be a finite group, together with a sampling algorithm Sample that samples according to a (possibly unknown) distribution $\mathcal{D}$, and let $k = \lceil \log_2(|H|) \rceil$. Moreover, fix two values $0 \le \delta, \sigma \le 1$ and set $N := \left\lceil \frac{\log(1-\sigma) - \log(k)}{\log(\delta)} \right\rceil$.

Let $x_1, \ldots, x_{N \cdot k+1} \in H$ be $N \cdot k + 1$ samples from H by invoking the sampling algorithm, i.e., $x_i \leftarrow$ Sample for $i = 1, \ldots, N \cdot k + 1$. Then with probability at least σ, the group $H^* := \langle x_1, \ldots, x_{N \cdot k+1} \rangle$ is a δ-covering subgroup of H.

Observe that like in the case of uniform sampling, a polynomial number of samples (almost linear in k) is sufficient. Interestingly, this number of samples is independent of the distribution.

For the sake of readability, we prove Theorem 6 in two steps. In the first step, we present an algorithm (Algorithm 1) that makes *at most* $N \cdot k + 1$ samples and outputs a set $S \subseteq H$. We prove that S is a generating set for a δ-covering subgroup with probability at least σ. The algorithm relies on the assumption of the existence of an efficient membership testing procedure. But in the second step we present a modification of the algorithm, Algorithm 2, that works *without* the membership testing procedure and has at least the same success probability. In fact, Algorithm 2 makes *exactly* $N \cdot k + 1$ samples, hence proving Theorem 6.

We start with Algorithm 1 and prove the following result:

Theorem 7 (Correctness of Algorithm 1). *With a probability of at least σ, the output S of Alg. 1 is a generating set for a δ-covering subgroup.*

Algorithm 2. Sample generating set of a δ-covering subgroup

Given: A group H with sampling algorithm Sample, an integer $k = \lceil \log_2 |H| \rceil$, and two real values $0 \leq \delta, \sigma \leq 1$

Output: A set S of elements that generate a δ-covering subgroup of H with probability $\geq \sigma$

1:
2: $x \leftarrow$ Sample, $S \leftarrow \{x\}$ {Initial candidate for a generating set}
3: $N := \left\lceil \frac{\log(1-\sigma) - \log(k)}{\log(\delta)} \right\rceil$ {Number of samples per round}
4:
5: **for** $j = 1, \ldots, k$ **do**
6:     $x_i \leftarrow$ Sample, $i = 1, \ldots, N$ {Sample N elements from H}
7:     $S \leftarrow S \cup \{x_1, \ldots, x_N\}$ {Extend candidate generating set}
8: **end for**
9:
10: **return** S

Proof. Let S denote the output of Alg. 1 and $H^* := \langle S \rangle$. There are two possibilities: (i) the algorithm aborted the **for**-loop for some value $j < k$ or (ii) the algorithm executed all k **for**-loops.

First, we consider case (i). At the same time, assume that H^* is *not* a δ-covering subgroup, that is

$$\delta^* := \Pr\left[x \in H^* | x \xleftarrow{\mathcal{D}} H \right] < \delta$$

(this would be a failure of the algorithm). As the algorithm aborted the **for**-loops for some value $j < k$ by assumption, this can only happen if $x_i \in \langle S \rangle =: H^*$ for all N samples made in round j although $\delta^* < \delta$. As the samples are made independently, the probability of this error event happening at a certain round is $(\delta^*)^N < \delta^N$; since there are at most $k - 1$ independent rounds in case (i), the probability that an error occurs in any of them is at most $k \cdot \delta^N < 1 - \sigma$ by definition of N. Hence, the probability that no error happens and the output is correct, i.e., is a generating set of a δ-covering subgroup, is at least $1 - (1-\sigma) = \sigma$. This concludes the first case.

Now, we consider case (ii), i.e., the algorithm has executed all k **for**-loops. For simplicity, we index the sets S according to the round number. More precisely, let S_0 denote the initial candidate for the generating set (line 2). Moreover, let S_ℓ denote the set S at the end of the while loop (after being extended - see line 10) and we define $H_\ell := \langle S_\ell \rangle$ for $\ell \geq 0$. Observe that $H_\ell \subseteq H$ for all ℓ by construction. The output of the algorithm is $S = S_k$. We make use of the following inequalities that we prove afterwards:

$$\text{ord}(H_\ell) \geq 2^\ell \quad, \forall \ell \geq 0. \tag{3}$$

A consequence of (3) is that $\text{ord}(H_k) \geq 2^k \geq \text{ord}(H)$ which implies that $H_k = H$. Hence, $H^* = H_k = H$ is the whole group and trivially a δ-covering group for any value $0 \leq \delta \leq 1$.

It remains to prove the inequalities in (3), i.e., $\text{ord}(H_\ell) \geq 2^\ell$ for all $0 \leq \ell \leq k$. Observe that H_ℓ is a proper subgroup of $H_{\ell+1}$ for every $\ell < k$. Thus, the number $\frac{|H_{\ell+1}|}{|H_\ell|}$ (which is an integer, by Lagrange's Theorem), must be strictly greater than 1. Hence $|H_{\ell+1}| \geq 2 |H_\ell|$, and this proves (3) since $|H_0| = 1$.   □

Observe that Alg. 1 runs at most k for-loops and uses the membership test procedure only for deciding if the algorithm can be stopped earlier. Hence, we consider a variant, namely Alg. 2, which simply drops this test and always runs all k loops. That is, the only difference between Algorithms 1 and 2, respectively, is that the latter may run longer (but still at most k loops) and outputs a superset S' of the output S of Alg. 1. Of course, if S is a generating set for a δ-covering subgroup, then this is certainly true for S' as well. This shows that Alg. 2 "inherits" the success probability of Alg. 1:

Corollary 1. *[Correctness of Algorithm 2] With a probability of at least σ, the output S of Algorithm 2 is a generating set for a δ-covering subgroup.*

Observe that Alg. 2 simply outputs $N \cdot k + 1$ samples. Hence, the proof of Theorem 6 is a direct consequence of Corollary 1. The remainder of this section is straightforward. Given a generating set S of a δ-covering subgroup, we can apply Theorem 3 in order to break the SMP for (G, H).

Theorem 8 (Quantum Attack on SMP with Arbitrary Sampling). *Let (G, H) be the output of $\mathsf{Gen}(\lambda)$ with $k = \lceil \log_2(|H|) \rceil$, for some security parameter λ. We denote the distribution of the sampling algorithm contained in the description of H by $\mathcal{D}$. Let $0 \leq \varepsilon^* \leq 1$ be an arbitrary fixed positive value. Then, there exists a value $N = N(k, \varepsilon^*)$ (which only grows at most logarithmically in k) and a quantum algorithm which breaks the hardness of SMP with probability at least $(1 - \varepsilon^*)(1 - \varepsilon)^2$ in time $o(\mathsf{poly}(k + \log_2(1/\varepsilon)))$, and by sampling only $N \cdot k + 1$ times from H (where ε is the error probability of Theorem 2).*

In particular, we can construct a quantum algorithm that breaks SMP with probability at least $\frac{3}{4}(1 - \varepsilon)^2$ in time $o(\mathsf{poly}(k + \log_2(1/\varepsilon)))$ while only sampling $7k \cdot (2 + \lceil \log(k) \rceil) + 1$ times from H.

Proof. In principle, the attacker $\mathcal{A}$ is the same as described in Theorems 3 and 5, the only difference being the approach for finding an appropriate generating set. Given the value ε^*, the attacker chooses two positive values δ, σ such that $\delta \cdot \sigma \geq (1 - \varepsilon^*)$, for example $\delta = \sigma = \sqrt{1 - \varepsilon^*}$. Then, the attacker makes $N \cdot k + 1$ samples as explained in Theorem 6. Let H^* denote the subgroup of H that is generated by these $N \cdot k + 1$ samples. Due to Corollary 1, we know that H^* is a δ-covering subgroup of H with probability σ. From this point on, the attack continues as specified in Theorem 3, while using the $N \cdot k + 1$ samples as generators, i.e., we let z denote the challenge in the SMP game (Def. 2), so $z \in G \backslash H$ if $b = 1$, and $z \in H$ otherwise. If $b = 1$ (which happens with probability $\frac{1}{2}$), we know that $z \notin H^*$ and the attacker $\mathcal{A}$ will recognize this with probability $\geq (1 - \varepsilon)^2$ (as in the proof of Theorem 3). If $b = 0$ (which also happens with probability $\frac{1}{2}$), several sub-cases do exist (depending on whether H^* is δ-covering and whether $z \in H^*$). In case that both properties are true (which happens with probability $\geq \sigma \cdot \delta$), the attacker recognizes that $z \in H^*$ again with probability $\geq (1 - \varepsilon)^2$. As the success probabilities in the other sub-cases are at least zero, it follows that

$$\Pr\left[\mathbf{Exp}_{\mathcal{A},\mathsf{Gen}}^{\mathsf{smp}}(\lambda) = 1\right] \geq \frac{(1 - \varepsilon)^2 + \delta\sigma(1 - \varepsilon)^2}{2} \geq \delta\sigma(1 - \varepsilon)^2 \geq (1 - \varepsilon^*)(1 - \varepsilon)^2$$

which concludes the proof of the first part of the Theorem. For the second part, we see that when choosing $\varepsilon^* = \frac{1}{4}$ and $\delta = \sigma = \frac{1}{2}\sqrt{3}$, the above attacker $\mathcal{A}$ has a success probability of at least $\frac{3}{4}(1 - \varepsilon)^2$ by sampling only $N \cdot k + 1$ times from H where $N = \left\lceil \frac{\log(1-\sigma)-\log(k)}{\log(\delta)} \right\rceil \leq 7 \left(\lceil\log(k)\rceil + 2\right)$. □

Finally, Theorems 8 and 1 together immediately imply our main result: the general impossibility of group homomorphic encryption in the quantum world, if the plaintext and ciphertext groups are abelian.

Theorem 9 (Impossibility of Group Homomorphic Encryption in the Quantum World). *Let $\mathcal{E} = (\mathsf{KeyGen}, \mathsf{Enc}, \mathsf{Dec})$ be an* IND-CPA *secure group homomorphic encryption scheme with abelian plaintext and ciphertext groups. Then, there exists a quantum PPT algorithm that breaks the security of $\mathcal{E}$ with non-negligible probability.*

5 Discussion

In this section, we provide an informal discussion about the applicability of our quantum attack to non-group homomorphic encryption schemes and elaborate on fully homomorphic encryption (FHE). In abstract terms, existing FHE schemes are standard public-key encryption schemes $\mathcal{E} = (\mathsf{KeyGen}, \mathsf{Enc}, \mathsf{Dec})$ with the following extras [16]:

- the plaintext space $\mathcal{P}$ and ciphertext space $\widehat{\mathcal{C}}$ are rings,
- there is an algorithm Eval that takes as input a public key pk, a circuit C, a tuple $(c_1, \ldots, c_t)$ of ciphertexts (one for every input node of C), and outputs another ciphertext c, and
- for all outputs $(\mathsf{pk}, \mathsf{sk})$ by $\mathsf{KeyGen}(\lambda)$, all polynomials $p(\lambda)$ in λ, all $t \leq \mathsf{poly}(\lambda)$, all plaintexts $m_1, \ldots, m_t \in \mathcal{P}$ corresponding to fresh encryptions $c_i \longleftarrow \mathsf{Enc}_{\mathsf{pk}}(m_i)$, $i = 1 \ldots t$, and all t-input circuits C of depth $\leq p(\lambda)$, we have the following *correctness* condition:

$$\mathsf{Dec}_{\mathsf{sk}}(\mathsf{Eval}_{\mathsf{pk}}(C, c_1, \ldots, c_t)) = C(m_1, \ldots, m_t). \tag{4}$$

Homomorphic encryption schemes for which the polynomial depth $p(\lambda)$ of the circuits C is bounded a priori (i.e., fixed in the public key pk) are called *leveled* FHE. For very small polynomials $p(\lambda)$, we say that the scheme is *somewhat homomorphic*. At a first glance, there a two main differences to the notion of *group* homomorphic encryption (see Fig. 1 for a pictorial explanation):

1. The set of all (fresh) encryptions $\mathcal{C} = \{\mathsf{Enc}_{\mathsf{pk}}(m; r) \mid m \in \mathcal{P}, r \in \mathsf{Rnd}\}$ is only a *subset* (and not necessarily a subgroup) of the ring $\widehat{\mathcal{C}}$.

2. The decryption is not necessarily a group homomorphism as it is only guaranteed to run correctly with circuits that are polynomially bounded in depth; this polynomial bound can be dynamically chosen in the "pure" FHE case, while it is fixed in the public key for leveled FHE and somewhat homomorphic schemes. But if the decryption is group homomorphic, it particularly must run correctly (at least theoretically) on all unbounded circuits consisting only of group-operation gates.

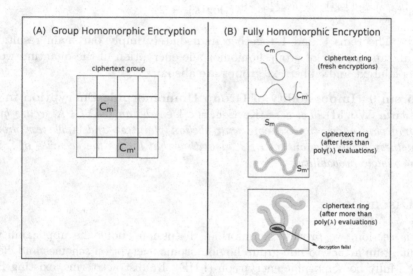

Fig. 1. Differences between group homomorphic encryption and FHE: (A) shows that each $\mathcal{C}_m$ is a coset of $\mathcal{C}_1$ in $\mathcal{C}$ (Fact 1), while the decryption is a group homomorphism; (B) shows first that $\mathcal{C}_m$ and $\mathcal{C}_{m'}$ are subsets and not necessarily cosets in $\mathcal{C}$, second that the decryption runs correctly on $\mathsf{poly}(\lambda)$ evaluations of ciphertexts, and third that the decryption might fail if exponentially many evaluations have been performed, meaning that the decryption is not necessarily group homomorphic

If the decryption is not a group homomorphism, the set of fresh encryptions of the neutral element in $\mathcal{P}$ is not necessarily a group, but only a subset of $\widehat{\mathcal{C}}$. However, the quantum order-finding algorithm of Theorem 2 only works on (solvable) *groups*. This immediately gives us the first important observation:

Observation 1. *Our quantum attack from Section 4 on group homomorphic encryption schemes is not immediately applicable to more general homomorphic encryption schemes, such as somewhat and (leveled) FHE schemes.*

A sufficient condition that we need a homomorphic scheme to have for our quantum attack to work is the following:

Sufficient Condition (Quantum Attack). For any output $(\mathsf{pk}, \mathsf{sk})$ by $\mathsf{KeyGen}(\lambda)$, there exist two plaintexts $m, m' \in \mathcal{P}$ and a subgroup G of $\widehat{\mathcal{C}}$ such that

1. there exists an efficient PPT algorithm which outputs a generating set for G of size at most $\mathsf{poly}(\lambda)$,
2. the probability $\Pr\limits_{c \leftarrow \mathsf{Enc_{pk}}(m)} [c \in G]$ is non-negligible in λ, and
3. the probability $\Pr\limits_{c' \leftarrow \mathsf{Enc_{pk}}(m')} [c' \notin G]$ is non-negligible in λ.

In the setting of group homomorphic encryption schemes, the plaintext m would be the neutral element 1, while $m' \neq 1$ can be any other plaintext. The group G satisfying the above conditions would be a δ-covering subgroup of the group $\mathcal{C}_1$ of all (fresh) encryptions of 1, for a sufficiently small δ. For more general homomorphic encryption schemes, such as somewhat or (leveled) FHE schemes, the situation looks more like in Fig. 2.

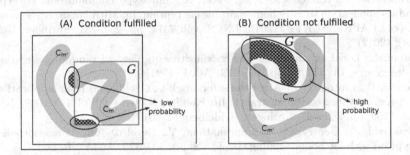

Fig. 2. Our condition in the FHE case: (A) shows pictorially when the condition is fulfilled; (B) shows the case when item 3 of the condition is not met and G intersects with a large part of encryptions of m'

The important observation here is, that as long as only polynomially many evaluations of the ciphertexts have been performed, the decryption still runs correctly (cf. correctness condition in Equation (4)). But for any scheme to be IND-CPA secure, the set of encryptions of a given message m must be exponentially large, so in particular, a group G that fulfills condition 2 is required to be exponentially large. Hence, the decryption is not guaranteed to run correctly on G and might fail. More precisely, condition 3 for our attack to work will most likely be unsatisfied. However, proving or disproving that any of the existing somewhat or (leveled) FHE schemes satisfies our sufficient condition is a highly non-trivial task (due to the very general and abstract nature of the requirement) and lies outside the scope of this work. We leave it as interesting future work. Interestingly enough, since most of the existing FHE schemes base their security on supposedly quantum-resistant hardness assumptions (such as LWE), spotting a scheme that is susceptible to our quantum attack will effectively break the underlying hardness assumption and thereby disprove its quantum-resistance.

Acknowledgements. We would like to thank Richard Lindner and Pooya Farshim for helpful discussions. We are also grateful for the constructive comments by the anonymous reviewers.

References

1. Armknecht, F., Augot, D., Perret, L., Sadeghi, A.R.: On constructing homomorphic encryption schemes from coding theory. In: Chen, L. (ed.) IMACC 2011. LNCS, vol. 7089, pp. 23–40. Springer, Heidelberg (2011)
2. Armknecht, F., Gagliardoni, T., Katzenbeisser, S., Peter, A.: General impossibility of group homomorphic encryption in the quantum world. Cryptology ePrint Archive, Report 2014/029 (2014), http://eprint.iacr.org/
3. Armknecht, F., Katzenbeisser, S., Peter, A.: Group homomorphic encryption: characterizations, impossibility results, and applications. Designs, Codes and Cryptography, 1–24, 10.1007/s10623-011-9601-2
4. Armknecht, F., Katzenbeisser, S., Peter, A.: Shift-type homomorphic encryption and its application to fully homomorphic encryption. In: Mitrokotsa, A., Vaudenay, S. (eds.) AFRICACRYPT 2012. LNCS, vol. 7374, pp. 234–251. Springer, Heidelberg (2012)
5. Babai, L.: Local expansion of vertex-transitive graphs and random generation in finite groups. In: STOC, pp. 164–174. ACM (1991)
6. Boneh, D., Lipton, R.J.: Algorithms for black-box fields and their application to cryptography (extended abstract). In: Koblitz, N. (ed.) CRYPTO 1996. LNCS, vol. 1109, pp. 283–297. Springer, Heidelberg (1996)
7. Brakerski, Z., Gentry, C., Vaikuntanathan, V.: (leveled) fully homomorphic encryption without bootstrapping. In: ITCS. pp. 309–325. ACM (2012)
8. Cramer, R., Damgård, I., Nielsen, J.B.: Multiparty computation from threshold homomorphic encryption. In: Pfitzmann, B. (ed.) EUROCRYPT 2001. LNCS, vol. 2045, pp. 280–299. Springer, Heidelberg (2001)
9. Cramer, R., Gennaro, R., Schoenmakers, B.: A secure and optimally efficient multi-authority election scheme. In: Fumy, W. (ed.) EUROCRYPT 1997. LNCS, vol. 1233, pp. 103–118. Springer, Heidelberg (1997)
10. Cramer, R., Shoup, V.: Universal hash proofs and a paradigm for adaptive chosen ciphertext secure public-key encryption. In: Knudsen, L.R. (ed.) EUROCRYPT 2002. LNCS, vol. 2332, pp. 45–64. Springer, Heidelberg (2002)
11. van Dam, W., Hallgren, S., Ip, L.: Quantum algorithms for some hidden shift problems. SIAM J. Comput. 36(3), 763–778 (2006)
12. Damgård, I., Geisler, M., Krøigaard, M.: Homomorphic encryption and secure comparison. IJACT 1(1), 22–31 (2008)
13. Diffie, W., Hellman, M.E.: New directions in cryptography. IEEE Transactions on Information Theory 22(6), 644–654 (1976)
14. El Gamal, T.: A public key cryptosystem and a signature scheme based on discrete logarithms. In: Blakely, G.R., Chaum, D. (eds.) CRYPTO 1984. LNCS, vol. 196, pp. 10–18. Springer, Heidelberg (1985)
15. Erdös, P., Rényi, A.: Probabilistic methods in group theory. J. Analyse Math. 14, 127–138 (1965)
16. Gentry, C.: Fully homomorphic encryption using ideal lattices. In: STOC. pp. 169–178. ACM (2009)

17. Gentry, C., Halevi, S., Smart, N.P.: Homomorphic evaluation of the aes circuit. In: Safavi-Naini, R., Canetti, R. (eds.) CRYPTO 2012. LNCS, vol. 7417, pp. 850–867. Springer, Heidelberg (2012)
18. Gjøsteen, K.: Homomorphic cryptosystems based on subgroup membership problems. In: Dawson, E., Vaudenay, S. (eds.) Mycrypt 2005. LNCS, vol. 3715, pp. 314–327. Springer, Heidelberg (2005)
19. Goldreich, O.: The Foundations of Cryptography, vol. 2, Basic Applications. Cambridge University Press (2004)
20. Goldwasser, S., Micali, S.: Probabilistic encryption. J. Comput. Syst. Sci. 28(2), 270–299 (1984)
21. Hallgren, S., Kolla, A., Sen, P., Zhang, S.: Making classical honest verifier zero knowledge protocols secure against quantum attacks. In: Aceto, L., Damgård, I., Goldberg, L.A., Halldórsson, M.M., Ingólfsdóttir, A., Walukiewicz, I. (eds.) ICALP 2008, Part II. LNCS, vol. 5126, pp. 592–603. Springer, Heidelberg (2008)
22. Hallgren, S., Smith, A., Song, F.: Classical cryptographic protocols in a quantum world. In: Rogaway, P. (ed.) CRYPTO 2011. LNCS, vol. 6841, pp. 411–428. Springer, Heidelberg (2011)
23. Hemenway, B., Ostrovsky, R.: On homomorphic encryption and chosen-ciphertext security. In: Fischlin, M., Buchmann, J., Manulis, M. (eds.) PKC 2012. LNCS, vol. 7293, pp. 52–65. Springer, Heidelberg (2012)
24. Kushilevitz, E., Ostrovsky, R.: Replication is not needed: Single database, computationally-private information retrieval. In: FOCS. pp. 364–373 (1997)
25. Mosca, M.: Quantum computing, cryptography and compilers. In: ISMVL. pp. 154–156. IEEE (2012)
26. Paillier, P.: Public-key cryptosystems based on composite degree residuosity classes. In: Stern, J. (ed.) EUROCRYPT 1999. LNCS, vol. 1592, pp. 223–238. Springer, Heidelberg (1999)
27. Pak, I., Bratus, S.: On sampling generating sets of finite groups and product replacement algorithm (extended abstract). In: ISSAC, pp. 91–96. ACM (1999)
28. Peter, A., Kronberg, M., Trei, W., Katzenbeisser, S.: Additively homomorphic encryption with a double decryption mechanism, revisited. In: Gollmann, D., Freiling, F.C. (eds.) ISC 2012. LNCS, vol. 7483, pp. 242–257. Springer, Heidelberg (2012)
29. Rivest, R.L., Shamir, A., Adleman, L.M.: A method for obtaining digital signatures and public-key cryptosystems. Commun. ACM 21(2), 120–126 (1978)
30. Shor, P.W.: Algorithms for quantum computation: Discrete logarithms and factoring. In: FOCS, pp. 124–134. IEEE Computer Society (1994)
31. Watrous, J.: Quantum algorithms for solvable groups. In: STOC, pp. 60–67. ACM (2001)

On Minimal Assumptions for Sender-Deniable Public Key Encryption

Dana Dachman-Soled

University of Maryland
danadach@ece.umd.edu

Abstract. The primitive of deniable encryption was introduced by Canetti et al. (CRYPTO, 1997). Deniable encryption is an encryption scheme with the added feature that after transmitting a message m, both sender and receiver may produce random coins showing that the transmitted ciphertext was an encryption of any message m' in the message space. Deniable encryption is a key tool for constructing incoercible protocols, since it allows a party to send one message and later provide apparent evidence to a coercer that a different message was sent. In addition, deniable encryption may be used to obtain *adaptively*-secure multiparty computation (MPC) protocols and is secure under *selective-opening* attacks. Different flavors such as sender-deniable and receiver-deniable encryption, where only the sender or receiver produce fake random coins, have been considered.

Recently, over 15 years after the primitive was first introduced, Sahai and Waters (IACR Cryptology ePrint Archive, 2013), gave the first construction of sender-deniable encryption schemes with super-polynomial security, where an adversary has negligible advantage in distinguishing real and fake openings. Their construction is based on the construction of an indistinguishability obfuscator for general programs recently introduced in a breakthrough result of Garg et al. (FOCS, 2013). Although feasibility has now been demonstrated, the question of determining the *minimal* assumptions necessary for sender-deniable encryption with super-polynomial security remains open.

The primitive of simulatable public key encryption (PKE), introduced by Damgård and Nielsen (CRYPTO, 2000), is a public key encryption scheme with additional properties that allow oblivious sampling of public keys and ciphertexts. It is one of the low-level primitives used to construct adaptively-secure MPC protocols and was used by O'Neill et al. in their construction of bi-deniable encryption in the multi-distributional model (CRYPTO, 2011). Moreover, the original construction of sender-deniable encryption with polynomial security given by Canetti et al. can be instantiated with simulatable PKE. Thus, a natural question to ask is whether it is possible to construct sender-deniable encryption with *super-polynomial security* from simulatable PKE.

In this work, we investigate the possibility of constructing sender-deniable public key encryption from simulatable PKE in a black-box manner. We show that there is no black-box construction of sender-deniable public key encryption with super-polynomial security from simulatable PKE. This indicates that improving on the original construction of Canetti et al. requires the use of non-black-box techniques, stronger assumptions, or interaction, thus giving some evidence that strong assumptions such as those used by Sahai and Waters are necessary.

Keywords: sender-deniable encryption, simulatable PKE, black-box separation.

H. Krawczyk (Ed.): PKC 2014, LNCS 8383, pp. 574–591, 2014.

1   Introduction

Deniable encryption was first introduced by Canetti et al. [3]. In its strongest form, called bi-deniable encryption, this primitive allows a sender and receiver to communicate via a public key encryption scheme (sending some message m) and then later allows both parties to produce apparent evidence (i.e. secret key and random coins) that the ciphertext sent/received was actually an encryption of any message m' in the message space. Deniable encryption is useful for designing protocols that resist coercion (c.f. [5]) as well as for designing *adaptively*-secure protocols. Moreover, deniable encryption is is secure under *selective-opening* attacks. As a concrete example, consider a voting scheme where parties encrypt their votes using the voting authority's public key and send the ciphertext to the voting authority over a public channel. The voting authority is then trusted to decrypt and tally the votes[1]. In the voting scheme described, voters can carry away a *receipt*, the ciphertext sent to the authority along with the random coins used to encrypt, which can later be used to prove to a third party that a particular vote was cast. Although obtaining a receipt may seem desirable, it also means that voters or the voting authority can later be coerced by some third party to reveal the vote cast by a particular ciphertext. Thus, such a voting scheme is highly susceptible to coercion. However, using a bi-deniable encryption scheme instead of a regular public key encryption scheme allows both the voters and the authority to claim that a specific ciphertext corresponds to a vote for a particular candidate regardless of the actual effective vote. One may also consider weaker versions of bi-deniable encryption such as sender-deniable encryption and receiver-deniable encryption, where only the sender (resp. receiver) can produce fake coins.

Constructing deniable encryption schemes seems difficult due to two conflicting goals: Parties must be able to communicate effectively with each other, but if coerced, both parties must be able to produce seemingly correctly distributed randomness and/or secret keys consistent with *any* message m in the message space. Now it seems that surely deniability must interfere with effective communication since the receiver cannot tell which message m was the intended message and the sender cannot be assured that his intended message m was received. Indeed, it was shown by [2] that (non-interactive) receiver-deniable encryption (with negligible distinguishing advantage), and thus (non-interactive) bi-deniable encryption is impossible to achieve.

The case of *sender*-deniable encryption, however, is more optimistic. Indeed, very recently, Sahai and Waters [27], gave the first construction of sender-deniable encryption schemes with super-polynomial security, where an adversary has negligible advantage in distinguishing real and fake openings. Their construction is based on the construction of an indistinguishability obfuscator for general programs recently introduced in a breakthrough result of Garg et al. [12], and thus inherits the same non-standard hardness assumptions.

Prior to the result of [27], there were known constructions of deniable encryption (c.f. [3]) with *non-negligible* distinguishing advantage, where an adversary may distinguish real and fake openings of ciphertexts with probability $1/\text{poly}$ for some polynomial.

---

[1] Alternatively, the voting authority may be required to give a zero-knowledge proof that the final tally is consistent with the transmitted ciphertexts.

We say that such schemes have *polynomial security*. As discussed in more detail below, the construction of [3] can be based on the existence of *simulatable* public key encryption, which can in turn be based on standard assumptions such as DDH and RSA.

This leaves open the following important question:

> What are the minimal assumptions required for sender-deniable public-key encryption with super-polynomial security?

Relationship to Adaptive Security and Simulatable Public Key Encryption

There is a strong link between deniable encryption and another primitive known as *non-committing encryption* [4]. The main difference between the two is that a Non-Committing Encryption scheme consists of two sets of Key Generation and Encryption algorithms—one for honest players and one for the simulator. Moreover, only honest parties need to communicate effectively, while only the simulator needs to equivocate ciphertexts. Both deniable encryption and non-committing encryption can be used to achieve *adaptively* secure multiparty computation and both are secure under *selective opening* attacks. One of the standard low-level assumptions used to construct non-committing encryption is a primitive known as *simulatable public key encryption (PKE)* introduced by Damgård and Nielsen[9][2]. Loosely speaking, a simulatable public key encryption scheme is an encryption scheme with special algorithms for obliviously sampling public keys and random ciphertexts without learning the corresponding secret keys and plaintexts; in addition, both of these oblivious sampling algorithms should be efficiently invertible. Simulatable public key encryption schemes can be based on the assumptions of DDH and RSA[3].

Simulatable public key encryption has been a useful tool for constructing variants of deniable encryption. O'Neill et al. showed how to use simulatable PKE to construct bi-deniable encryption in the multi-distributional model [24]. Moreover, it is not hard to see that the original construction of sender-deniable public key encryption given by [3] can be instantiated with simulatable PKE instead of trapdoor permutations, although in their paper they do not explicitly use simulatable PKE.

Thus, a natural and imperative direction to explore is whether it is possible to construct sender-deniable encryption with super-polynomial security from simulatable PKE.

Our Results

We consider the possibility of constructing non-interactive sender-deniable encryption, known as *sender-deniable public key encryption*, with super-polynomial security in a *black-box manner* from simulatable PKE. We provide a negative answer to the above question by showing the following:

Theorem 1 (Main Theorem, Informal). *There is no (fully) black-box reduction of sender-deniable public key encryption with super-polynomial security to simulatable PKE.*

---

[2] In fact, an even weaker primitive called *trapdoor-simulatable PKE* [6] is sufficient for non-committing encryption.

[3] Trapdoor-simulatable PKE can be constructed from these assumptions as well as hardness of factoring.

In particular, we show that every black-box construction of a sender-deniable public key encryption scheme from simulatable PKE which makes $m = m(n)$ queries to the simulatable PKE scheme cannot achieve security better than $O(m^4(n))$. Our results indicate that improving upon the original scheme of [3] requires the use of non-black-box techniques, stronger underlying assumptions or interaction thus giving some evidence that strong assumptions such as those used by Sahai and Waters [27] are necessary.

Black-Box Separations

Impagliazzo and Rudich [19] were the first to develop a technique to rule out the existence of an important class of reductions between primitives known as black-box reductions. Indeed, most known reductions between cryptographic primitives are black-box (see the works of [28,16,26,17,15,20,18,23,22] for a small sampling). Intuitively, black-box reductions are reductions where the primitive is treated as an oracle or a "black-box". There are actually several flavors of black-box reductions (fully black-box, semi black-box and weakly black-box [25]). In our work, we only deal with fully black-box reductions, and so we will focus on this notion here. Informally, a fully black-box reduction from a primitive Q to a primitive P is a pair of *oracle* PPT Turing machines (G, S) such that the following two properties hold:

Correctness: For every implementation f of primitive P, $g = G^f$ implements Q.

Security: For every implementation f of primitive P, and every adversary A, if A breaks G^f (as an implementation of Q) then $S^{A,f}$ breaks f. (Thus, if f is "secure", then so is G^f.)

We remark that an *implementation* of a primitive is any specific scheme that meets the requirements of that primitive (e.g., an implementation of a public-key encryption scheme provides samplability of key pairs, encryption with the public-key, and decryption with the private key). Correctness thus states that when G is given oracle access to any valid implementation of P, the result is a valid implementation of Q. Furthermore, security states that any adversary breaking G^f yields an adversary breaking f. The reduction here is *fully* black-box in the sense that the adversary S breaking f uses A in a black-box manner.

Our Techniques

Following the paradigm introduced by [19], we define an oracle O and consider constructions of simulatable PKE and sender-deniable public key encryption relative to this oracle. The oracle O that we use is similar to the by now standard oracle first introduced by [13]. This oracle implements an ideal trapdoor function with the important property that it is difficult to obliviously sample from the range of the function. Namely, it is hard to find an image in the range of the function without first sampling the corresponding preimage.

Relative to the oracle O, we show the following:

- There exists a simulatable PKE scheme, $\mathcal{E}_{\mathsf{Sim}}$ secure against all (computationally unbounded) adversaries $\mathcal{A}$ making at most polynomial number of queries.

- For every implementation $\mathcal{E}$ of a sender-deniable public key encryption scheme relative to O, there exists an adversary $\mathcal{A}$ making at most polynomial number of queries such that $\mathcal{A}$ breaks $\mathcal{E}$.

The above is sufficient to imply that there is no fully black-box construction of sender-deniable public key encryption from simulatable PKE.

Now, recall that a sender-deniable public key encryption scheme is a public key encryption scheme with an additional algorithm, Fake, which takes an honestly generated sender's view View_{S_0} encrypting a bit b and returns a fake view, $\mathsf{View}_{S_1} = \mathsf{Fake}(\mathsf{View}_{S_0})$, encrypting the bit $1 - b$. A simple but key observation is the following: If the distributions over the corresponding views, View_{S_0} and View_{S_1} are indistinguishable, then one should be able to now compute $\mathsf{View}_{S_2} = \mathsf{Fake}(\mathsf{View}_{S_1})$ obtaining a fake view encrypting the bit b and such that the distributions over the views, View_{S_1} and View_{S_2} are again indistinguishable. We note that somewhat similar arguments were used in [2]. In general, in any sender-deniable public key encryption scheme with negligible distinguishing advantage, one must be able to run Fake iteratively on the output of the previous Fake invocation for any (unbounded) polynomial number of times. Otherwise, if there is a fixed polynomial upper bound $p(n)$ on the number of times that Fake can be applied to a fresh ciphertext (before failure), then we can distinguish View_{S_0} from $\mathsf{View}_{S_{p(n)}} = \bot = \mathsf{Fake}^{p(n)}(\mathsf{View}_{S_0})$ (where by $\mathsf{Fake}^{p(n)}$ we denote the composition of Fake, $p(n)$ times). So by a hybrid argument there must be some i such that $\mathsf{Fake}^i(\mathsf{View}_{S_0})$, $\mathsf{Fake}^{i+1}(\mathsf{View}_{S_0})$ can be distinguished with probability $1/p(n)$. Finally, this means that real and fake openings View_{S_0} and View_{S_1} can be distinguished, contradicting the security of the sender-deniable public key encryption scheme[4]. Thus, in order to prove the lower bound it is sufficient to show that relative to our oracle, Fake can be repeatedly applied only a fixed polynomial number of times before failure.

To gain some intuition for why this is the case, it is instructive to recall the construction of [3][5]. Let $\{F_{pk}\}$ be a family of trapdoor functions with pseudorandom range such that given the secret key sk of F_{pk}, one can distinguish between elements y in the range of F_{pk} and random elements, but given only pk, random elements in the range of F_{pk} are indistinguishable from random strings. In [3], the secret key of the sender-deniable public key encryption scheme is the secret key sk of the trapdoor function F. The public key pk is the public key of F. Each ciphertext consists of m number of strings $s_1, \ldots, s_m$. To encrypt a 1, choose an a set of indeces $I \subseteq [m]$ of odd cardinality; otherwise choose a set $I \subseteq [m]$ of even cardinality. Compute m strings in the following way: For the i-th string, if $i \in I$, choose a random x_i and compute $y_i = f(x_i)$. If $i \notin I$, choose y_i to be a random string. The sender sends these m strings to the receiver. The receiver then checks which of the m strings $y_1, \ldots, y_m$ are valid images. If an odd number of strings are valid, output 1. Otherwise, output 0. It is not hard to see that the Fake algorithm works by having the sender claim that a pseudorandom string is really random (but note that the sender cannot claim the reverse).

Clearly, the Fake algorithm described above can be run iteratively at most m times for a given ciphertext, since the sender claims to have made one less query each time Fake is run and there are at most m queries total. Unfortunately, our analysis is more

---

[4] Simply run Fake iteratively i number of times on View_{S_0} and then use the distinguisher above.
[5] We simplify their construction here somewhat.

complicated since we must also consider candidate schemes where the Fake algorithm might *add* queries to the outputted view. It may seem at first glance that it is impossible for Fake to add new queries to the sender's view that were not in the original view since it would seem to require inverting a random image y without access to the corresponding secret key. However, this is not necessarily the case (see the full version [7] for a toy example where this occurs).

Thus, we must show that even for candidate schemes whose Fake algorithms may both remove and add queries, Fake can be repeatedly applied only a fixed polynomial number of times before failure. Intuitively, the reason we can handle such schemes is that it is infeasible to add an unbounded number of new queries to the fake view, since many queries must be removed from the previous view for each new query that is added. In order to show that this intuition indeed holds, we leverage the fact that in our oracle, with overwhelming probability, random strings are not valid images of the trapdoor function. Much of the technical part of the proof is in showing that the above intuition holds for *all* possible constructions of sender-deniable public key encryption schemes relative to our oracle.

Technical Overview of Proof. The high-level approach of the proof will be to consider the distribution $\mathcal{D}_{\mathsf{Fake}}^{10m^2(n)}$, where $m(n)$ is the maximum number of queries made by sender and receiver, and a draw from $\mathcal{D}_{\mathsf{Fake}}^{10m^2(n)}$ is obtained in the following way:

- Draw an oracle O and original views, Views_0, View_R, for sender and receiver from the correct distributions.
- For $1 \le i \le 10m^2(n)$, set $\mathsf{Views}_i = \mathsf{Fake}^\mathsf{O}(\mathsf{Views}_{i-1})$.
- Output $\mathsf{O}, \mathsf{View}_\mathsf{R}, \mathsf{Views}_0, \ldots, \mathsf{Views}_{10m^2(n)}$

In our analysis, we will look at the properties of sequences of fake openings Views_0, $\ldots, \mathsf{Views}_{10m^2(n)}$ drawn from this distribution. Note that for any sender-deniable public key encryption scheme it should (at the very least) be the case that w.v.h.p. for every consecutive $i, i + 1$, Views_i and Views_{i+1} are valid encryptions of bits b_i and $b_{i+1} = 1 - b_i$, respectively. Furthermore, we show that if a public key encryption scheme has the deniability property then with high probability a sequence drawn from $\mathcal{D}_{\mathsf{Fake}}^{10m^2(n)}$ will have several additional properties. However, we will also argue that it is impossible for a sequence of fake openings of length $10m^2(n)$ to satisfy all of the required properties simultaneously. Thus, a sequence drawn from $\mathcal{D}_{\mathsf{Fake}}^{10m^2(n)}$ will with high probability not satisfy at least one of the required properties. This leads to contradiction and so we conclude that the encryption scheme is not sender-deniable.

In what follows, we give a slightly innacurate but intuitive overview of what these properties are and the techniques we use to prove that with high probability a sequence of fake openings will possess these properties.

First, note that a fake opening is simply a view Views_i of the sender which consists of a transcript, W (i.e. a public key, PK, and ciphertext c), and a set of queries $Q(\mathsf{S}_i)$ made by the sender. We also consider the set $Q(E)_i$ which, intuitively, is a set of queries that includes all queries the honest sender (with view Views_i) believes may have been made by both him and the receiver. The set of queries in $Q(E)_i$ can be found by running an algorithm that is very similar to the Eve algorithm of [1], which finds intersection queries based only on the transcript (and does not depend on the sender's view, as in our case). During the execution of the Eve algorithm, Eve finds pairs (pk^*, y^*) such that it is likely the sender queried $F(pk^*, x) = y^*$ for some x. If Eve identifies a such a pair (pk^*, y^*) and, indeed, a corresponding $F(pk^*, x^*) = y^*$ is found in Views_{S_i}, then the query is "added" and placed in Q_i^{made}. If Eve identifies a such a pair (pk^*, y^*), however, and no corresponding $F(pk^*, x^*) = y^*$ is found in Views_{S_i}, then the query is "removed" and placed in Q_i^{skipped}.

Now for each fake opening Views_{S_i} we consider two types of queries "A" type queries and "B" type queries. Intuitively, "A" type queries are those queries that were originally in Views_{S_0} and have either not been removed in some Q_j^{skipped} set (for $j \leq i$), or were removed and then added again in some Q_k^{made} set (for $j < k \leq i$). "B" type queries are new queries that do not appear in the original view Views_{S_0}, were added in some Q_j^{made} set (for $j \leq i$) and have not been subsequently removed in a Q_k^{skipped} set (for $j < k \leq i$). Thus, each view Views_{S_i} is associated with a set, A^i, of "A" type queries and a set, B^i, of "B" type queries.

We will show that with high probability a draw of fake openings $\text{Views}_{S_0}, \ldots,$ $\text{Views}_{S_{10m^2(n)}}$ and corresponding sequence $(A^0, B^0), \ldots, (A^{10m^2(n)}, B^{10m^2(n)})$ must satisfy the following properties:

- $(\text{Views}_{S_0}, \text{Views}_{S_1}, \ldots, \text{Views}_{S_{10m^2(n)}})$ are valid openings.
- $A^i \subseteq A^{i-1}$ for $1 \leq i \leq 10m^2(n)$
- $(A^{i-1}, B^{i-1}) \neq (A^i, B^i)$ for $1 \leq i \leq 10m^2(n)$
- If the same set A^* appears consecutively β times within the sequence above, and all corresponding consecutive B sets are different, then $\beta \leq 10m(n)$.

Much of the technical portion of this work is dedicated to showing that these properties hold (see Claim 2, Lemma 4 and Lemma 5). Then, we will show that it is, in fact, impossible to realize all of the above properties simultaneously (see the end of Section 5).

Related Work

In their seminal paper, Canetti et al. [3] introduce the primitive of deniable encryption and present constructions. However, for the strongest form of deniable encryption which assumes that the same key generation and encryption algorithms are always used, [3] achieve only sender-deniable and receiver-deniable schemes with polynomial security. [3] also rule out the existence of a specific type of sender-deniable encryption scheme with negligible distinguishing advantage (or super-polynomial security) called *separable* schemes (which, roughly speaking, are a generalization of the scheme of [3]). Our impossibility result is incomparable to theirs since ours rules out a larger class of reductions (black-box reductions), but only rules out reductions to the specific primitive of simulatable PKE.

O'Neill et al. [24] recently constructed a bi-deniable encryption scheme in the multi-distributional model, in which the parties run alternative key-generation and encryption algorithms for equivocable communication, but claim under coercion to have run the prescribed algorithms. This weaker model was also initially considered by [3]. Although useful in some settings, the multi-distributional model does not achieve the strongest form of deniability which we consider in this work. We note that it is essential for our impossibility result that the *same* encryption algorithm is run for both real and equivocable communication, which is why our result does not contradict the work of [24].

Recently, Dürmuth and Freeman announced a fully-deniable (receiver/sender)-deniable interactive cryptosystem with negligible security [10]. However their result was later showed to be incorrect by Peikert and Waters (see [11] for details). The protocol constructed by [10] was both interactive and utilized the fact that for the trapdoor function used, a random element in the range could be sampled obliviously. We note that in our analysis it is essential both that the schemes we consider are non-interactive and that the trapdoor function implemented by our oracle does not allow oblivious sampling of the range. Thus, an interesting open question is whether removing these two restrictions can help achieve fully-deniable encryption schemes.

Subsequently, [2] showed, using an information-theoretic argument, that (non-interactive) receiver-deniable encryption with negligible distinguishing advantage do not exist, unconditionally. We note, however, that the work of [2] does not address the case of sender-deniable encryption and it does not seem that their techniques may be applied to our case.

Recently, Sahai and Waters [27] showed how to construct sender-deniable encryption from indistinguishability ofuscation. In a breakthrough result, a candidate construction of an indistinguishability obfuscator for general programs was put forward by Garg et al. [12]. In their followup paper, [27] show that indistinguishability obfuscation can be used to achieve sender-deniable encryption[6] We note that the candidate construction of [12] is based on newly introduced hardness assumptions such as "multilinear jigsaw puzzles". Thus, the construction of [27] also requires these non-standard assumptions.

Organization

In Section 2 we formally define sender-deniable public key encryption and simulatable PKE as well as the notion of a black-box construction of sender-deniable public key encryption from simulatable PKE. In Section 3 we define our oracle and in Section 4 we define some additional useful notations, algorithms and corresponding properties which will be used in the main result. Finally, in Section 5 we prove our main theorem, with some technical parts deferred to the Appendix.

2 Definitions

Definition 1 (Sender-Deniable Public Key Encryption). *A sender-deniable (bit) public key encryption scheme is a tuple of algorithms* (Gen, Enc, Dec, Fake) *defined as follows:*

- *The key-generation, encryption and decryption algorithms* Gen, Enc, Dec *are defined as usual for public-key encryption.*

---

[6] Simply called "deniable encryption" in their work.

- *The* sender faking algorithm $\mathsf{Fake}(\mathrm{PK}, r_S, b)$, *given a public key* PK, *original coins* r_S *and bit b of* Enc, *outputs faked random coins* r_S^* *for* Enc *and the bit* $1 - b$.

We require the following properties:

Correctness. $(\mathsf{Gen}, \mathsf{Enc}, \mathsf{Dec})$ *forms a correct public-key encryption scheme*[7].
Deniability. For $b \in \{0, 1\}$, we require that the following two probability ensembles are computationally indistinguishable:
- $\{(\mathrm{PK}, c, r_S) | \mathrm{PK} \leftarrow \mathsf{Gen}(1^n; r_G), c \leftarrow \mathsf{Enc}(\mathrm{PK}, b; r_S)\}_n$
- $\{(\mathrm{PK}, c, r_S^*) | \mathrm{PK} \leftarrow \mathsf{Gen}(1^n; r_G), c \leftarrow \mathsf{Enc}(\mathrm{PK}, 1-b; r_S), r_s^* \leftarrow \mathsf{Fake}(\mathrm{PK}, r_S, b)\}_n$

It follows from the definition that a sender-deniable public key encryption scheme is also semantically secure.

Remark 1. In this work, we also consider constructions of deniable public key encryption schemes that do not achieve negligible distinguishing advantage. We say that a deniable encryption scheme has security $p(n)$ for some polynomial $p(\cdot)$ if correctness holds and every probabilistic polynomial time adversary $\mathcal{A}$ distinguishes the following two probability ensembles with advantage at most $1/p(n)$:

- $\{(\mathrm{PK}, c, r_S) | \mathrm{PK} \leftarrow \mathsf{Gen}(1^n; r_G), c \leftarrow \mathsf{Enc}(\mathrm{PK}, b; r_S)\}_n$
- $\{(\mathrm{PK}, c, r_S^*) | \mathrm{PK} \leftarrow \mathsf{Gen}(1^n; r_G), c \leftarrow \mathsf{Enc}(\mathrm{PK}, 1 - b; r_S), r_s^* \leftarrow \mathsf{Fake}(\mathrm{PK}, r_S, b)\}_n$.

We note that in this case semantic security does not follow from deniability and is an additional requirement.

Definition 2 (Simulatable PKE). *A ℓ-bit simulatable encryption scheme consists of an encryption scheme* $(\mathsf{Gen}, \mathsf{Enc}, \mathsf{Dec})$ *augmented with* $(\mathsf{oGen}, \mathsf{oRndEnc}, \mathsf{rGen}, \mathsf{rRndEnc})$. *Here,* oGen *and* oRndEnc *are the oblivious sampling algorithms for public keys and ciphertexts, and* rGen *and* rRndEnc *are the respective inverting algorithms,* rGen *(resp.* rRndEnc) *takes* r_G *(resp.* (PK, r_E, m)) *as the trapdoor information. We require that, for all messages $m \in \{0, 1\}^\ell$, the following distributions are computationally indistinguishable:*

$$\{\mathsf{rGen}(r_G), \mathsf{rRndEnc}(\mathrm{PK}, r_E, m), \mathrm{PK}, c \mid (\mathrm{PK}, \mathrm{SK}) = \mathsf{Gen}(1^k; r_G), c = \mathsf{Enc}_{\mathrm{PK}}(m; r_E)\}$$
$$\text{and } \{\hat{r}_G, \hat{r}_E, \hat{\mathrm{PK}}, \hat{c} \mid (\hat{\mathrm{PK}}, \bot) = \mathsf{oGen}(1^k; \hat{r}_G), \hat{c} = \mathsf{oRndEnc}_{\hat{\mathrm{PK}}}(1^k; \hat{r}_E)\}$$

It follows from the definition that a simulatable encryption scheme is also semantically secure.

Definition 3 (Sender-Deniable Public Key Encryption from Simulatable PKE). *For oracle algorithms* $(\mathsf{Gen}, \mathsf{Enc}, \mathsf{Dec}, \mathsf{Fake})$ *we call* $\mathcal{E} = (\mathsf{Gen}, \mathsf{Enc}, \mathsf{Dec}, \mathsf{Fake})$ *a black-box construction of sender-deniable public key encryption based on simulatable PKE if the following properties hold:*

- **Implementation:** *The algorithms* $(\mathsf{Gen}, \mathsf{Enc}, \mathsf{Dec}, \mathsf{Fake})$ *get oracle access to simulatable PKE scheme $\mathcal{E}_{\mathsf{Sim}}$ and $\mathcal{E}$ is an implementation of sender-deniable public key encryption.*

---

[7] Note that *perfect* correctness is not possible.

- **Security:** *There is a polynomial-time oracle algorithm S with the following property. For any simulatable PKE $\mathcal{E}_{\mathsf{Sim}} = (\mathsf{Gen}, \mathsf{Enc}, \mathsf{Dec}, \mathsf{oGen}, \mathsf{oRndEnc}, \mathsf{rGen}, \mathsf{rRndEnc})$, given as oracle, if $\mathcal{A}$ breaks the security of $\mathcal{E}$ then $S^{\mathcal{E}_{\mathsf{Sim}},\mathcal{A}}$ breaks the security of $\mathcal{E}_{\mathsf{Sim}}$.*

3 Oracle

The oracle O consists of three functions G, F, F^{-1} defined below for every security parameter n.

- $G : \{0,1\}^n \to \{0,1\}^{3n}$ is an injective function taking inputs sk of length n bits to outputs pk of length $3n$ bits.
- $F : \{0,1\}^{4n} \to \{0,1\}^{12n}$ is an injective function taking inputs pk, x of length $4n$ bits to outputs y of length $12n$ bits.
- $F^{-1} : \{0,1\}^{13n} \to \{0,1\}^n$ takes inputs of the form sk, y where $sk \in \{0,1\}^n$ and $y \in \{0,1\}^{12n}$. F^{-1} returns $x \in \{0,1\}^n$ if $G(sk) = pk$ and $F(pk, x) = y$ and $\perp$ otherwise.

Note that the oracle above behaves like a trapdoor function, where G is the key generation functionality, F evaluates the trapdoor function and F^{-1} is the inversion function. Additionally, note that we may easily construct a simulatable PKE scheme relative to this oracle.

We denote by Υ the uniform distribution over all possible oracles O.

Lemma 1. *There is a construction of a simulatable PKE scheme $\mathcal{E}_{\mathsf{Sim}}$ relative to oracle O, such that for every unbounded adversary $\mathcal{A}$, making a polynomial number of queries to O:*

$$\Pr_{\mathsf{O} \sim \Upsilon}[\mathcal{A}^{\mathsf{O}} \text{ breaks } \mathcal{E}_{\mathsf{Sim}}^{\mathsf{O}}] \leq \mathrm{neg}(n).$$

The proof of the Lemma above is by now standard (c.f. [13,14]) and so we omit it.

4 Preliminaries

In this section we introduce some useful notation, algorithms and properties of sender-deniable public key encryption schemes.

Given a deniable public key encryption scheme $\mathcal{E} = (\mathsf{Gen}, \mathsf{Enc}, \mathsf{Dec}, \mathsf{Fake})$, we will consider the natural two-message protocol $\langle \mathsf{S}, \mathsf{R} \rangle$ between a *Receiver*, R (who sends a public key in the first message) and a *Sender*, S (who sends a ciphertext in the second message).

The view of the Receiver (resp. Sender) consists of the transcript W, random tape, r_R (resp. r_S) and queries made to the oracle along with the responses. The view of the Receiver, denoted by $\mathsf{View}_R = (\mathsf{View}_G, \mathsf{View}_D)$, consists of two parts where View_G includes queries and responses made during Gen and View_D includes queries and responses made during Dec. The view of the Sender, denoted by View_S includes queries and responses made during Enc. We denote the queries to O in View_R by $Q(\mathsf{R}) = Q(G) \cup Q(D)$. We denote the queries to O in View_S by $Q(\mathsf{S})$.

We assume without loss of generality that:

- No queries to F^{-1} are made during Gen. This is WLOG since with overwhelming probability either the corresponding query to F was already made, or F^{-1} returns $\perp$.
- Each party queries $G(sk) = pk$ before querying $F^{-1}(sk, y)$.
- Either Fake returns a valid opening or returns $\perp$ and $\mathsf{Fake}(\perp) = \perp$.

Additionally, relative to our oracle O, we assume WLOG that Fake takes $\mathsf{View_S}$ and returns another $\mathsf{View_S}$ with the *same* public key and ciphertext but *different* randomness and input bit (i.e. $\mathsf{View}_{S_{i+1}} = \mathsf{Fake}^O(\mathsf{View}_{S_i})$). By $\mathsf{Fake}^{O,i}$ we denote composing Fake with itself i times.

4.1 Useful Distributions

Distribution $\mathcal{D}$: $\mathcal{D}$ is a distribution over tuples $(\mathsf{View_S}, \mathsf{View_R})$ resulting from an execution of $\langle S, R \rangle$. A draw from $\mathcal{D}$ is obtained as follows:

- Draw $O \sim \Upsilon$, $b \leftarrow \{0,1\}$, $r_R, r_S \leftarrow \{0,1\}^{p(n)}$, for some polynomial $p(\cdot)$ and execute $\langle S, R \rangle$ with O, r_R, r_S and input bit b.
- Output: The views $(\mathsf{View_S}, \mathsf{View_R})$ resulting from the execution of $\langle S, R \rangle$ above.

Distribution $\mathcal{D}^i$: $\mathcal{D}^i$ is a distribution over tuples $(\mathsf{View}_{S_i}, \mathsf{View_R})$ as before, but here we begin to use the Fake algorithm. A draw from $\mathcal{D}^i$ is obtained as follows:

- Draw $O \sim \Upsilon$, $b \leftarrow \{0,1\}$, $r_R, r_S \leftarrow \{0,1\}^{p(n)}$. and execute $\langle S, R \rangle$ with O, r_R, r_S and input bit b.
- Let $\mathsf{View}_{S_0} = \mathsf{View_S}$, $\mathsf{View_R}$ containing PK, c, b, r_S be the resulting views from the execution of $\langle S, R \rangle$. Compute $\mathsf{View}_{S_i} = \mathsf{Fake}^{O,i}(\mathsf{View_S})$.
- Output: O and the views $(\mathsf{View}_{S_i}, \mathsf{View_R})$.

For every fixed polynomial $p(\cdot)$, we additionally define the following distribution:

Distribution $\mathcal{D}_{\mathsf{Fake}}^{p(n)}$: $\mathcal{D}_{\mathsf{Fake}}^{p(n)}$ is a distribution over tuples $(O, \mathsf{View_S}, \mathsf{View}_{S_1}, \ldots, \mathsf{View}_{S_{p(n)}})$. A draw from $\mathcal{D}_{\mathsf{Fake}}^{p(n)}$ is obtained as follows:

- Draw $O \sim \Upsilon$, $b \leftarrow \{0,1\}$, $r_R, r_S \leftarrow \{0,1\}^{p(n)}$. and execute $\langle S, R \rangle$ with O, r_R, r_S and input bit b.
- Let $\mathsf{View}_{S_0} = \mathsf{View_S}$, $\mathsf{View_R}$ containing PK, c, b, r_S be the resulting views from the execution of $\langle S, R \rangle$.
- Output: $(O, \mathsf{View_R}, \mathsf{View}_{S_0} = \mathsf{View_S}, \mathsf{View}_{S_1} = \mathsf{Fake}^O(\mathsf{View_S}), \mathsf{View}_{S_2} = \mathsf{Fake}^O(\mathsf{View}_{S_1}), \ldots, \mathsf{View}_{S_{p(n)}} = \mathsf{Fake}^O(\mathsf{View}_{S_{p(n)-1}}))$.

4.2 Algorithms for Finding Likely Queries

As in [19,1,8,13,21], we will be concerned with finding *intersection queries*, or common information about the oracle shared by S and R. We note that in our setting there are two ways to get an intersection query:

- One party makes a query of the form $G(sk) = pk$, $F(pk, x) = y$, or $F^{-1}(sk, y)$ and the other party makes the same query.
- One of the parties queries both $G(sk)$, $F^{-1}(sk, y) = x$ and the other party queries $F(pk, x) = y$.

We now (informally) define the Eve algorithm: For a more formal specification, see the full version [7]. Eve runs the following algorithm, using threshold $\varepsilon = \varepsilon_1 = 1/m^{16}$ during the first pass (before S sends its message) and using threshold $\varepsilon = \varepsilon_2 = 1/m^6$ during the second pass (after S sends its message).

(0) *Eve queries F on all possible inputs up to length $4\hat{n} = 4\log(10m^{34})$ and adds all queries and responses to E.*

(1) *As long as there exists a query q of the form $G(sk)$, $F(pk, x)$, or $F^{-1}(sk, y)$ that was previously made by S or R with probability at least ε (conditioned on Eve's current knowledge, E), then ask q from the oracle and add q paired with its answer to E.*

(2) *As long as there exists a pair (pk^*, y^*) such that $G(sk) = pk^* \in Q(E)$, $F(pk^*, x) = y^* \notin Q(E)$ and with probability at least ε, R made a query of the form $F(pk^*, x) = y^*$ for some x (conditioned on Eve's current knowledge, E), then query the oracle on $F^{-1}(sk, y^*)$. If $F^{-1}(sk, y^*)$ returns some value x, then add $F(pk^*, x) = y^*$ to E. If $F^{-1}(sk, y^*)$ returns $\bot$ then add $F^{-1}(sk, y^*) = \bot$ to E.*

(3) *As long as there exists a pair (pk^*, y^*) such that $F(pk^*, x) = y^* \notin Q(E)$ and with probability at least ε, S made a query of the form $F(pk^*, x) = y^*$ for some x (conditioned on Eve's current knowledge, E), then if $F(pk^*, x) = y^* \in Q(S)$, add q paired with its answer to E and add (pk^*, y^*) to Q^{made}. Otherwise, add (pk^*, y^*) to $Q^{skipped}$.*

We denote by $Q(E)_G$ the Eve queries made after the first message is sent from R to S and denote by $Q(E)_S$ the Eve queries made after the second message is sent from S to R. Thus $Q(E) = Q(E)_G \cup Q(E)_S$.

The following Lemma appeared in [8], but there was proven with respect to a random oracle.

Lemma 2. *Let $\langle S, R \rangle$ be a protocol as specified above in which the Sender and Receiver ask at most $2m$ queries each from the oracle O. Then there is a universal constant c such that on input parameter ε:*

- (cm/ε)-**Efficiency:** *Eve is deterministic and, over the randomness of the oracle and S and R's private randomness, the expected number of Eve queries from the oracle O is at most cm/ε_1.*
- $(c\sqrt{m\varepsilon})$-**Security:** *Let W be the transcript of messages sent between R and S so far, and let E be the additional information that Eve has learned till the end of the i'th round. We denote by $Q(E)$ the oracle query/answer pairs that Eve has asked. Let $\mathcal{D}(W, E)$ be the joint distribution over the views (Views, ViewR) of S and R only conditioned on (W, E). By $\mathcal{D}_R(\cdot, \cdot)$ and $\mathcal{D}_S(\cdot, \cdot)$ we refer to the projections of $\mathcal{D}(W, E)$ over its first or second components.*
  With probability at least $1 - c\sqrt{m\varepsilon}$ over the randomness of S, R, and the random oracle O the following holds at all moments during the protocol when Eve is

done with her learning phase in that round: There are independent *distributions* $S(W, E), \mathcal{R}(W, E)$ *such that:*

1. *The statistical distance between* $S(W, E) \times \mathcal{R}(W, E)$ *and* $\mathcal{D}(W, E)$ *is at most* $\Delta(S(W, E) \times \mathcal{R}(W, E), \mathcal{D}(W, E)) \leq c\sqrt{m\varepsilon}$.
2. *For every oracle query* $q \notin Q(E)$ *it holds that* $\Pr_{(\text{Views} \sim S(W,E), \text{View}_R \sim \mathcal{R}(W,E))}$ $[q \in Q(S) \cup Q(R)] \leq \varepsilon$.

- **Robustness.** *The learning algorithm is robust to the input parameter* ε *in the following sense. If the parameter* ε *changes in the interval* $\varepsilon \in [\varepsilon_1, \varepsilon_2]$ *arbitrarily during the learner's execution (even inside a learning phase of a specific round), it still preserves* $O(cm/\varepsilon_1)$-*efficiency and* $(c\sqrt{m\varepsilon_2})$-*security.*

See the full version [7] for the proof of Lemma 2 which is based on the proofs found in [1,8,21].

Remark 2. Note that the Eve algorithm as described above requires knowledge of Views but not of View$_R$. Thus, Eve can only be simulated by a party who has knowledge of Views. This is a key difference between our results and the results of [13]. Note that we can actually implement oblivious transfer relative to our oracle, since although it is hard to sample valid public keys without knowing the corresponding secret key, a party can call $F(pk, \cdot)$ with any string pk and receive a value y indistinguishable from a "valid" image. In contrast, [13] show that oblivious transfer does not exist relative to their oracle. The fact that only S can simulate Eve but not R is the reason that our results do not contradict those of [13].

Remark 3. Note that since the expected number of Eve queries is at most cm/ε, we may consider a modified algorithm Eve' which simulates Eve but aborts if Eve makes more than cm/ε^2 number of queries. By Markov's inequality, this occurs with probability at most $O(\varepsilon)$ and so executions of Eve and Eve' are identical with probability $1 - O(\varepsilon)$. Thus, all properties stated above for Eve hold also for Eve'. In the following, we assume that we run Eve', making at most $N = O(m^{33}) = \text{poly}(n)$ number of queries, to generate the sets $E, Q(E)$. We additionally assume that $N \leq 2^{\hat{n}}/1600m^2$.

4.3 Properties of Fake Openings

Definition 4 (Iterative Indistinguishability). *Let* $\mathcal{E} = (\text{Gen}, \text{Enc}, \text{Dec}, \text{Fake})$ *be an implementation of a sender-deniable public key encryption scheme relative to oracle* O. *We say that* $\mathcal{E}$ *is iteratively indistinguishable up to* $p(n)$, *where* $p(\cdot)$ *is some polynomial, if for every* i *where* $1 \leq i \leq p(n)$, *and every adversary* $\mathcal{A}$ *making at most a polynomial number of oracle queries we have:*

$$\Pr_{\text{Views} \sim \mathcal{D}_S}[\mathcal{A}^O(\text{Views}) \text{ outputs } 1] - \Pr_{\text{Views}_i \sim \mathcal{D}_S^i}[\mathcal{A}^O(\text{Views}_i) \text{ outputs } 1] \leq i/80p(n).$$

In what follows, we split the queries found in a given view Views$_i$ into two types: "A" type queries and "B" type queries. Informally, "A" type queries are queries that were also made in the original Views$_0$ = Views. "B" type queries are new queries that were added which do not appear in Views$_0$. Details follow.

For a given draw $(O, \text{View}_R, \text{Views}_{S_0}, \text{Views}_{S_1}, \ldots, \text{Views}_{S_{p(n)}}) \sim \mathcal{D}_{\text{Fake}}^{p(n)}$, we consider a run of the Eve' algorithm with $(O, \text{View}_R, \text{Views}_{S_0})$ yielding sets $Q(E), Q^{\text{made}}, Q^{\text{skipped}}$ and a run of the Eve' algorithm with $(O, \text{View}_R, \text{Views}_{S_i})$ for each $1 \leq i \leq p(n)$ yielding sets $Q(E)_i, Q_i^{\text{made}}, Q_i^{\text{skipped}}$.

We define the sets A^0, B^0 corresponding to $(\text{View}_R, \text{Views}_{S_0})$ as follows: $A^0 = Q(S_0), B^0 = \emptyset$. For $i \geq 1$, we define the sets A^i, B^i corresponding to $(\text{View}_R, \text{Views}_{S_i})$ as follows [8]:

$$A^i = \left(A^{i-1} \setminus Q_i^{\text{skipped}}\right) \cup \left(Q_i^{\text{made}} \cap Q(S_0)\right), \quad B^i = \left(B^{i-1} \setminus Q_i^{\text{skipped}}\right) \cup \left(Q_i^{\text{made}} \setminus Q(S_0)\right).$$

Note that every draw $(O, \text{View}_R, \text{Views}_{S_0}, \text{Views}_{S_1}, \ldots, \text{Views}_{S_{p(n)}}) \sim \mathcal{D}_{\text{Fake}}^{p(n)}$, is associated with a unique sequence $(A^0, B^0), (A^1, B^1), \ldots, (A^{p(n)}, B^{p(n)})$.

Definition 5 (Well-formed Sequences). *Let $\mathcal{E} = (\text{Gen}, \text{Enc}, \text{Dec}, \text{Fake})$ be an implementation of a sender-deniable public key encryption scheme relative to oracle O. We say that an opening $(O, \text{View}_R, \text{Views}_{S_0}, \text{Views}_{S_1}, \ldots, \text{Views}_{S_{p(n)}}) \sim \mathcal{D}_{\text{Fake}}^{p(n)}$ is well-formed if it has the following properties:*

(1) $(\text{Views}_{S_0}, \text{Views}_{S_1}, \ldots, \text{Views}_{S_{p(n)}})$ *are valid openings.*

(2) $\left(Q(G) \cap \bigcup_{i=1}^{p(n)} Q(S_i)\right) \setminus Q(E)_G = \emptyset$.

(3) $A^i \subseteq A^{i-1}$ *for* $1 \leq i \leq p(n)$.

(4) *For every query of the form* $F(pk, x) = y$ *that appears in* $Q(E)_i$ *for some* $1 \leq i \leq p(n)$, *the pair* (pk, y) *does not appear in* Q_j^{skipped} *for all* $1 \leq j \leq i$.

Claim 2. *Let $\mathcal{E} = (\text{Gen}, \text{Enc}, \text{Dec}, \text{Fake})$ be an implementation of a sender-deniable public key encryption scheme relative to oracle O and let $m = m(n)$ be the maximum number of queries made by $(\text{Gen}, \text{Enc}, \text{Dec}, \text{Fake})$. If $\mathcal{E}$ is iteratively indistinguishable up to $10m^2(n)$ then $(O, \text{View}_R, \text{Views}_{S_0}, \text{Views}_{S_1}, \ldots, \text{Views}_{S_{10m^2(n)}}) \sim \mathcal{D}_{\text{Fake}}^{10m^2(n)}$ is well-formed with probability $9/10$.*

We defer the proof to the full version [7].

5   Analysis

In this section, we prove our main theorem:

Theorem 3 (Main Theorem, Formal). *Let $\mathcal{E} = (\text{Gen}, \text{Enc}, \text{Dec}, \text{Fake})$ be a black-box construction of sender-deniable public key encryption from simulatable PKE and let $m = m(n)$ be the maximum number of queries made by $(\text{Gen}, \text{Enc}, \text{Dec}, \text{Fake})$. Then $\mathcal{E}$ has security at most $O(m^4)$.*

We first present the following Lemma, which will be our main technical Lemma:

---

[8] By the notation below, we mean to remove from A^{i-1} all queries of the form $F(pk, x) = y$ such that the pair $(pk, y) \in Q^{\text{skipped}}$. The same holds for the following definitions.

Lemma 3. *Let $\mathcal{E} = (\text{Gen}, \text{Enc}, \text{Dec}, \text{Fake})$ be an implementation of a sender-deniable public key encryption scheme relative to oracle O and let $m = m(n)$ be the maximum number of queries made by $(\text{Gen}, \text{Enc}, \text{Dec}, \text{Fake})$. Then $\mathcal{E}$ is not iteratively indistinguishable up to $10m^2 = 10m^2(n)$.*

We present the following corollary and use it to prove our main theorem:

Corollary 1. *Let $\mathcal{E} = (\text{Gen}, \text{Enc}, \text{Dec}, \text{Fake})$ be an implementation of a sender-deniable public key encryption scheme relative to oracle O and let $m = m(n)$ be the maximum number of queries made by $(\text{Gen}, \text{Enc}, \text{Dec}, \text{Fake})$. Then there exists an adversary $\mathcal{A}$ making a polynomial number of oracle queries such that*

$$\Pr_{\text{Views} \sim \mathcal{D}}[\mathcal{A}^O(\text{Views}) \text{ outputs } 1] - \Pr_{\text{Views}_1 \sim \mathcal{D}^1}[\mathcal{A}^O(\text{Views}_1) \text{ outputs } 1] \geq 1/8000m^4.$$

Lemma 1 and Corollary 1 imply our main theorem:

Proof (Proof of Main Theorem using Lemma 1 and Corollary 1.). Assume towards contradiction that there is some fully black-box reduction $(\mathcal{E}, S)$ of sender-deniable public key encryption with distinguishing advantage $o(1/m^4)$ to simulatable PKE, where S is a probabilitic polynomial time reduction. Then, since there exists a construction of simulatable PKE relative to oracle O, we have that $\mathcal{E}$ is also a sender-deniable public key encryption scheme relative to O. Now, Corollary 1 implies that with probability at least $1/16000m^4(n)$ over $O \sim \Upsilon$, there exists an adversary $\mathcal{A}$ making at most a polynomial number of oracle queries such that $\mathcal{A}$ distinguishes with probability at least $1/16000m^4(n)$. Thus, with probability at least $1/16000m^4(n)$ over $O \sim \Upsilon$, $\mathcal{A}$ breaks $\mathcal{E}$. However, since S makes at most a polynomial number of calls to $\mathcal{A}$, $S^{\mathcal{A}}$ also makes at most polynomial number of queries and so Lemma 1 implies that with probability $1 - \text{neg}(n)$ over $O \sim \Upsilon$, $S^{\mathcal{A}}$ does not break $\mathcal{E}_{\text{Sim}}$. Thus, there must exist some fixed O such that $\mathcal{A}$ breaks $\mathcal{E}$ with distinguishing advantage $\Omega(1/m^4)$, but $S^{O,\mathcal{A}}$ does not break $\mathcal{E}_{\text{Sim}}$, which means that the reduction $(\mathcal{E}, S)$ fails and so we arrive at contradiction.

We now turn to proving Lemma 3. We define two events and prove they occur with small probability.

Event E_{rSets}: E_{rSets} is the event that a draw $(O, \text{Views}_{S_0}, \text{Views}_{S_1}, \dots, \text{Views}_{S_{10m^2(n)}}) \sim \mathcal{D}_{\text{Fake}}^{10m^2(n)}$ has the property that $(A^i, B^i) = (A^{i+1}, B^{i+1})$ for some $0 \leq i \leq 10m^2(n) - 1$.

Event E_{rA}: E_{rA} is the event that a draw $(O, \text{Views}_{S_0}, \text{Views}_{S_1}, \dots, \text{Views}_{S_{10m^2(n)}}) \sim \mathcal{D}_{\text{Fake}}^{10m^2(n)}$ has the property that for some A^* there are $\beta > 10m(n)$ number of consecutive pairs of the form $(A^*, B^j), \dots, (A^*, B^{j+\beta-1})$ such that $B^{j+i} \neq B^{j+i+1}$ for $0 \leq i \leq \beta - 2$.

Lemma 4. *Let $\mathcal{E} = (\text{Gen}, \text{Enc}, \text{Dec}, \text{Fake})$ be an implementation of a sender-deniable public key encryption scheme relative to O and let $m = m(n)$ be the maximum number of queries made by $(\text{Gen}, \text{Enc}, \text{Dec}, \text{Fake})$. Let $\mathcal{E}$ be iteratively indistinguishable up to $10m^2(n)$. The probability that upon a draw $(O, \text{Views}_{S_0}, \text{Views}_{S_1}, \dots, \text{Views}_{S_{10m^2(n)}}) \sim \mathcal{D}_{\text{Fake}}^{10m^2(n)}$ Event E_{rSets} occurs is at most $1/2$.*

Next, we give some intuition for the proof of Lemma 4.

Proof Intuition for Lemma 4. We show that if for two consecutive views Views_{S_i}, $\text{Views}_{S_{i+1}}$, we have that $(A^i, B^i) = (A^{i+1}, B^{i+1})$, then the set of "intersection queries" $Q(E)$ found by the Eve' algorithm when it is run on Views_{S_i} and $\text{Views}_{S_{i+1}}$ are the same.

Now, intuitively, Lemma 2 tells us that conditioned on the transcript W and intersection queries $Q(E)$, the views of S and R are independent. Since both the transcript (which cannot be changed by the Fake algorithm) and the intersection queries $Q(E)$ are the same for the i-th and $i + 1$-th opening, this means that the views of the receiver conditioned on Views_{S_i} and $\text{Views}_{S_{i+1}}$ should be distributed nearly identically. But note that Views_{S_i} is supposed to be an encryption of a bit b, while Views_{S_i} is supposed to be an encryption of the bit $1 - b$. Thus, by the correctness of the encryption scheme, the views of the receiver should be statistically far when conditioning on Views_{S_i} and $\text{Views}_{S_{i+1}}$. This leads to a contradiction.

Lemma 5. *Let $\mathcal{E} = (\text{Gen}, \text{Enc}, \text{Dec}, \text{Fake})$ be an implementation of a sender-deniable public key encryption scheme relative to O and let $m = m(n)$ be the maximum number of queries made by $(\text{Gen}, \text{Enc}, \text{Dec}, \text{Fake})$. Let $\mathcal{E}$ be iteratively indistinguishable up to $10m^2(n)$. The probability that upon a draw $(O, \text{Views}_{S_0}, \text{Views}_{S_1}, \ldots, \text{Views}_{S_{10m^2(n)}}) \sim \mathcal{D}^{10m^2(n)}_{\text{Fake}}$ Event E_{rA} occurs is at most $1/5$.*

Next, we give some intuition for the proof of Lemma 5.

Proof Intuition for Lemma 5. We show that given Views_{S_0}, View_R, oracle O, the set $A^* \subseteq Q(S_0)$ plus some additional small amount of information we can reconstruct the entire sequence $(A^*, B^j), \ldots, (A^*, B^{j+\beta-1})$. The following is an imprecise description of the reconstruction algorithm:

1. Execute the two-message protocol $\langle S, R \rangle$ with Receiver's view View_R and Sender's view Views_{S_0}.
2. Use the transcript W generated above and begin running the Eve' algorithm to reconstruct set $B^{j+\beta-1}$. The only additional information necessary to reconstruct $B^{j+\beta-1}$ is upon encountering a pair (pk, y) whether to return $F^{-1}(sk, y) = x$ and add the query to $B^{j+\beta-1}$ or whether to add this query to $Q^{\text{skipped}}_{j+\beta-1}$.
3. Continue to construct sets $B^{j+\beta-2}$ through B^j in the same way as above.

The additional information needed to reconstruct $(A^*, B^j), \ldots, (A^*, B^{j+\beta-1})$ can be encoded by a list of α elements. More specifically, when encountering the pair (pk, y) as the ℓ-th query in the run of the Eve' algorithm reconstructing the set B^{j+i}, the algorithm checks whether the index ℓ appears on the list. If it does, the reconstruction algorithm adds $F^{-1}(sk, y) = x$ to B^{j+i}. Otherwise, it adds (pk, y) to Q^{skipped}_{j+i}.

Now, since the Eve' algorithm is efficient and makes N queries (where $N \leq 2^{\hat{n}}/1600m^2$) to reconstruct each B set, we only need $\log N$ bits to encode each of the α elements of the list above. Thus, we need "additional information" of length at most $\alpha \cdot \log N$.

We use properties (2) and (4) of well-formed sequences (see Definition 5) to show that for almost all sequences, when a pair (pk, y) is encountered when running the Eve' algorithm to reconstruct set B^{j+i}, if the corresponding query ($F^{-1}(sk, y)$ or $F(pk, x) = y$) has already been made by the reconstruction algorithm, then (pk, y)

is always added to B^{j+i}. Thus, we do not need to include such pairs in the list at all. This implies that since $B^{j+i} \neq B^{j+i+1}$ for all i, we must have $\alpha \geq \beta$. Moreover, the above implies that at the point when a pair (pk, y) is encountered as the ℓ-th Eve' query and the index ℓ appears on the list then it must be that the corresponding query $F(pk, x) = y$ has not yet been made by the reconstruction algorithm.

This means that at the point where we encounter each of these α queries on the list, the probability that an oracle O chosen *conditioned on the view of the reconstruction algorithm thus far* has the string y in its image is at most $1/2^{\hat{n}}$. Thus, the probability that an O chosen conditioned only on View_S, View_R has each of the α-many encountered strings $y_1, \ldots, y_\alpha$ in its image is at most $(1/2^{\hat{n}})^\alpha$.

Finally, taking a union bound over all sets $A^* \subseteq Q(S)$ and all sequences S we show that the probability that an oracle O chosen conditioned only on View_{S_0}, View_R is consistent with *any* well-formed sequence corresponding to some set $A^* \subseteq Q(S_0)$ and some and sequence S of length $\alpha \geq \beta$ is small.

We complete the proof of Lemma 3 using the above lemmas. We defer the proofs of Lemmas 4 and 5 to the full version [7].

Proof (Proof of Lemma 3 using Lemmas 4 and 5). Assume towards contradiction that there is some implementation of a sender-deniable public key encryption scheme, $\mathcal{E} = $ (Gen, Enc, Dec), relative to oracle O that is iteratively indistinguishable up to $10m^2 = 10m^2(n)$. By Claim 2, we may assume that, with probability at least $9/10$, a draw $(\text{O}, \text{View}_R, \text{View}_{S_0}, \text{View}_{S_1}, \ldots, \text{View}_{S_{10m^2(n)}}) \sim \mathcal{D}_{\text{Fake}}^{10m^2(n)}$ is well-formed. In particular, this implies that with probability at least $9/10$ over draws, Property (1) and (3) hold so we have that with probability $9/10$ the openings $(\text{View}_{S_1}, \ldots, \text{View}_{S_{10m^2(n)}})$ are all valid and $A^{i+1} \subseteq A^i$ for every $0 \leq i \leq 10m^2(n) - 1$. This implies that with probability $9/10$ over draws there must be some set A^* that appears at least $10m = 10m(n)$ times. Moreover, since Lemma 4 guarantees that event $E_{r\text{Sets}}$ occurs with probability at most $1/2$, we have that with probability at least $9/10 - 1/2 = 2/5$, there is some set A^* that appears at least $10m$ times consecutively and for this A^*, for all $0 \leq i \leq 10m - 2$, $B^{j+i} \neq B^{j+i+1}$. Now, by definition of Event E_{rA}, this means that with probability at least $2/5$ over draws $(\text{O}, \text{View}_R, \text{View}_{S_0}, \text{View}_{S_1}, \ldots, \text{View}_{S_{10m^2(n)}}) \sim \mathcal{D}_{\text{Fake}}^{10m^2(n)}$, we have that Event E_{rA} occurs. But by Lemma 5 we have that event E_{rA} occurs with probability at most $1/5$. Thus, we have arrived at contradiction and so the Lemma is proved.

References

1. Barak, B., Mahmoody-Ghidary, M.: Merkle puzzles are optimal — an $O(n^2)$-query attack on any key exchange from a random oracle. In: Halevi, S. (ed.) CRYPTO 2009. LNCS, vol. 5677, pp. 374–390. Springer, Heidelberg (2009)
2. Bendlin, R., Nielsen, J.B., Nordholt, P.S., Orlandi, C.: Lower and upper bounds for deniable public-key encryption. In: Lee, D.H., Wang, X. (eds.) ASIACRYPT 2011. LNCS, vol. 7073, pp. 125–142. Springer, Heidelberg (2011)
3. Canetti, R., Dwork, C., Naor, M., Ostrovsky, R.: Deniable encryption. In: Kaliski Jr., B.S. (ed.) CRYPTO 1997. LNCS, vol. 1294, pp. 90–104. Springer, Heidelberg (1997)
4. Canetti, R., Feige, U., Goldreich, O., Naor, M.: Adaptively secure multi-party computation. In: STOC, pp. 639–648 (1996)
5. Canetti, R., Gennaro, R.: Incoercible multiparty computation (extended abstract). In: FOCS, pp. 504–513 (1996)

6. Choi, S.G., Dachman-Soled, D., Malkin, T., Wee, H.: Improved non-committing encryption with applications to adaptively secure protocols. In: Matsui, M. (ed.) ASIACRYPT 2009. LNCS, vol. 5912, pp. 287–302. Springer, Heidelberg (2009)
7. Dachman-Soled, D.: On the impossibility of sender-deniable public key encryption. IACR Cryptology ePrint Archive, 2012:727 (2012)
8. Dachman-Soled, D., Lindell, Y., Mahmoody, M., Malkin, T.: On the black-box complexity of optimally-fair coin tossing. In: Ishai, Y. (ed.) TCC 2011. LNCS, vol. 6597, pp. 450–467. Springer, Heidelberg (2011)
9. Damgård, I.B., Nielsen, J.B.: Improved non-committing encryption schemes based on a general complexity assumption. In: Bellare, M. (ed.) CRYPTO 2000. LNCS, vol. 1880, pp. 432–450. Springer, Heidelberg (2000)
10. Dürmuth, M., Freeman, D.M.: Deniable encryption with negligible detection probability: An interactive construction. In: Paterson, K.G. (ed.) EUROCRYPT 2011. LNCS, vol. 6632, pp. 610–626. Springer, Heidelberg (2011)
11. Dürmuth, M., Freeman, D.M.: Deniable encryption with negligible detection probability: An interactive construction. IACR Cryptology ePrint Archive, 2011:66 (2011)
12. Garg, S., Gentry, C., Halevi, S., Raykova, M., Sahai, A., Waters, B.: Candidate indistinguishability obfuscation and functional encryption for all circuits. In: FOCS, pp. 40–49 (2013)
13. Gertner, Y., Kannan, S., Malkin, T., Reingold, O., Viswanathan, M.: The relationship between public key encryption and oblivious transfer. In: FOCS, pp. 325–335 (2000)
14. Gertner, Y., Malkin, T., Myers, S.: Towards a separation of semantic and CCA security for public key encryption. In: Vadhan, S.P. (ed.) TCC 2007. LNCS, vol. 4392, pp. 434–455. Springer, Heidelberg (2007)
15. Goldreich, O., Goldwasser, S., Micali, S.: How to construct random functions. J. ACM 33(4), 792–807 (1986)
16. Goldwasser, S., Micali, S.: Probabilistic encryption. J. Comput. Syst. Sci. 28(2), 270–299 (1984)
17. Håstad, J., Impagliazzo, R., Levin, L.A., Luby, M.: A pseudorandom generator from any one-way function. SIAM J. Comput. 28(4), 1364–1396 (1999)
18. Impagliazzo, R., Luby, M.: One-way functions are essential for complexity based cryptography (extended abstract). In: FOCS, pp. 230–235 (1989)
19. Impagliazzo, R., Rudich, S.: Limits on the provable consequences of one-way permutations. In: STOC, pp. 44–61 (1989)
20. Luby, M., Rackoff, C.: How to construct pseudorandom permutations from pseudorandom functions. SIAM J. Comput. 17(2), 373–386 (1988)
21. Maji, H.: On Computational Intractability Assumptions in Cryptography. PhD thesis, University of Illinois at Urbana-Champaign, Champaign, Illinois (2011)
22. Naor, M.: Bit commitment using pseudorandomness. J. Cryptology 4(2), 151–158 (1991)
23. Naor, M., Yung, M.: Universal one-way hash functions and their cryptographic applications. In: STOC, pp. 33–43 (1989)
24. O'Neill, A., Peikert, C., Waters, B.: Bi-deniable public-key encryption. In: Rogaway, P. (ed.) CRYPTO 2011. LNCS, vol. 6841, pp. 525–542. Springer, Heidelberg (2011)
25. Reingold, O., Trevisan, L., Vadhan, S.P.: Notions of reducibility between cryptographic primitives In: Naor, M. (ed.) TCC 2004. LNCS, vol. 2951, pp. 1–20. Springer, Heidelberg (2004)
26. Rompel, J.: One-way functions are necessary and sufficient for secure signatures. In: STOC, pp. 387–394 (1990)
27. Sahai, A., Waters, B.: How to use indistinguishability obfuscation: Deniable encryption, and more. IACR Cryptology ePrint Archive, 2013:454 (2013)
28. Yao, A.C.-C.: Theory and applications of trapdoor functions. In: FOCS, pp. 80–91 (1982)

Traceable Group Encryption

Benoît Libert[1], Moti Yung[2], Marc Joye[1], and Thomas Peters[3],*

[1] Technicolor
[2] Google Inc. and Columbia University
[3] Université Catholique de Louvain

Abstract. Group encryption (GE) is the encryption analogue of group signatures. It allows a sender to verifiably encrypt a message for some certified but anonymous member of a group. The sender is further able to convince a verifier that the ciphertext is a well-formed encryption under some group member's public key. As in group signatures, an opening authority is empowered with the capability of identifying the receiver if the need arises. One application of such a scheme is secure repository at an unknown but authorized cloud server, where the archive is made accessible by a judge order in the case of misbehavior, like a server hosting illegal transaction records (this is done in order to balance individual rights and society's safety). In this work we describe Traceable GE system, a group encryption with refined tracing capabilities akin to those of the primitive of "traceable signatures" (thus, balancing better privacy vs. safety). Our primitive enjoys the properties of group encryption, and, in addition, it allows the opening authority to reveal a user-specific trapdoor which makes it possible to publicly trace all the ciphertexts encrypted for that user without harming the anonymity of other ciphertexts. In addition, group members are able to non-interactively prove that specific ciphertexts are intended for them or not. This work provides rigorous definitions, concrete constructions in the standard model, and security proofs.

Keywords: Group encryption, traceability, anonymity, provable security, standard model.

1 Introduction

Group signatures [10] are a fundamental privacy primitive allowing members of a group to sign messages on behalf of the group while hiding their identity. To deter abuses, an authority is capable of identifying the author of any valid signature using privileged information. Group encryption (GE) is a primitive suggested by Kiayias, Tsiounis and Yung [19], which is the encryption analogue of group signatures [10]. Namely, it allows the sender of a ciphertext to hide the identity of the receiver within a population of certified users —under the control of a group manager (GM)— while providing universally verifiable guarantees that this receiver belongs to the group. If necessary, an opening authority (OA)

---

* This author was supported by the CAMUS Walloon Region Project.

H. Krawczyk (Ed.): PKC 2014, LNCS 8383, pp. 592–610, 2014.

is empowered with a key allowing it to "open" a ciphertext and pin down the receiver's identity in the same way as group signatures can be opened. Moreover, the system should support a mechanism allowing the sender to convince any verifier that (1) the ciphertext is well-formed and intended for some registered group member who will be able to decrypt; (2) the opening authority can identify the receiver if the need arises; (3) the plaintext satisfies certain properties such as being a witness for some public relation.

As a natural use case, group encryption allows a firewall to block all encrypted emails attempting to enter a network unless they are generated for some certified organization member and they carry a proof of malware-freeness. The GE primitive was also motivated by privacy applications such as anonymous trusted third parties (TTP) or oblivious retriever storage. In optimistic protocols, it allows verifiably encrypting messages to *anonymous* trusted third parties which remain offline most of their lifetime and only wake up when there is a problem to sort out. Group encryption provides a convenient way to hide the identity of users' preferred trusted third party, which can be a privacy-sensitive piece information by itself as it can betray, e.g., the participant's citizenship.

Group encryption also finds applications in cloud storage systems. When encrypting datasets on a remote storage server, the sender can convince this server that the data is intended for some legitimate certified user without disclosing the latter's identity.

As exemplified in [19], group encryption also allows constructing hierarchical group signatures [27], where signers can flexibly specify how a set of trustees should operate to open their signatures.

Here we suggest a primitive extending the group encryption primitive and describe a refined traceability mechanism analogous to the way traceable signatures [18] extend group signatures. Specifically, when a given group member is suspected of conducting illegal activities, the opening authority is able to release a trapdoor allowing anyone to publicly trace ciphertexts encrypted for this member *without affecting the anonymity of other users*. As in the case of traceable signatures, the tracing trapdoor can be distributed to several tracing agents who can proceed in parallel when it comes to search for a given group member's ciphertexts. In contrast, in ordinary GE schemes, this task requires the OA to sequentially operate on all ciphertexts.

RELATED WORK. Kiayias, Tsiounis and Yung (KTY) [19] formalized the notion of group encryption and provided a modular design using zero-knowledge proofs, digital signatures, anonymous CCA-secure public-key encryption and commitment schemes. They also gave an efficient instantiation using Paillier's cryptosystem [25] and Camenisch-Lysyanskaya signatures [8]. While efficient, their scheme uses interactive proof systems. It can be made non-interactive using the Fiat-Shamir paradigm [13] at the cost of relying on the random oracle model [4], which is understood to only provide heuristic arguments in terms of security.

Qin et al. [26] considered a sort of group encryption mechanism with non-interactive proofs and short ciphertexts. However, they appeal to random oracles and interactive assumptions in their security analysis. A non-interactive realization in the standard model was put forth by Cathalo, Libert and Yung [9]. More recently, El Aimani and Joye [12] considered more efficient interactive and non-interactive constructions using various optimizations.

As a matter of fact, none of the above solutions makes it possible to trace specific users' ciphertexts and only those ones. If messages encrypted for a specific misbehaving user have to be identified within a collection of, say $n = 100000$ ciphertexts, the opening authority has to open all of these in order to find those it is looking for. This is clearly harmful to the privacy of honest users who lose their anonymity just because they belong to the same group as a rogue user. In [18], Kiayias, Tsiounis and Yung suggested a technique to address this concern in the context of group signatures. To our knowledge, no real encryption analogue of their primitive has been studied so far.

The closest work addressing the problem at hand is that of Izabachène, Pointcheval and Vergnaud [17] who focus on eliminating subliminal channels by means of randomizable encryption. However, their mediated traceable anonymous encryption primitive does not provide all the functionalities we are aiming at. First, their scheme only provides message confidentiality and anonymity against *passive* adversaries, who have no access to decryption oracles at any time. Second, while their constructions enable individual user traceability, they do not provide a mechanism allowing the authority to identify the receiver of a ciphertext in $O(1)$ time. If their scheme is set up for groups of up to n users, their opening algorithm requires $O(n)$ operations in the worst case. Finally, the schemes of [17] provide no method allowing users to claim or disclaim ciphertexts they are the recipients of or not without disclosing their private keys.

OUR CONTRIBUTION. This paper suggests a primitive called *traceable group encryption* (TGE) as the direct encryption analogue of traceable signatures, as suggested by Kiayias, Tsiounis and Yung [18]. Beyond the usual functionalities of group encryption, a TGE system allows the opening authority to reveal trapdoors associated with specific group members. These trapdoors enable the recognition of ciphertexts intended for these group members and leak no information about the identity of other ciphertexts' recipients. For example, when an employee leaves a company, the firewall can use a tracing trapdoor to sieve out all incoming ciphertexts encrypted for that former employee without learning anything else. As in the traceable signature scenario [18], this implicit tracing process can be run in parallel by clerks equipped with a copy of the tracing trapdoor.

In addition, similarly to the claiming mechanism of traceable signatures [18], TGE schemes support a procedure whereby group members are able to claim and prove that they are the legitimate receiver of some initially anonymous ciphertexts. Moreover, we further consider the dual problem of allowing group members to disclaim ciphertexts that are *not* encrypted under their public keys (this feature was not part of the original traceable signature model but it can be added on top of it in a modular way). Of course, our security notions explicitly require that group members be unable to falsely claim or disclaim ciphertexts.

The above claiming and disclaiming capabilities can serve in certain applications like cloud storage. While storage servers may require anonymous data retrievers to hold a certificate from some authority, the disclaiming procedure allows group members to convince investigators that they are not the intended recipient of some suspicious ciphertext without revealing their private key.

The first contribution of this paper is to define the primitive and to further provide stringent security definitions for traceable group encryption systems: like its group encryption counterpart [19], our model considers powerful adversaries who have oracle access to the private key functionalities of all users and authorities. As a second contribution, we provide a concrete construction and prove its security in the standard model under non-interactive assumptions. Our system is not just a proof of concept. At the 128-bit security level, ciphertexts and proofs fit within 2.18 and 9.38 kB, respectively. The efficiency is thus competitive with that of state-of-the-art group signatures [15] or traceable signatures [22] relying on non-interactive assumptions in the standard model.

2   Background

In the paper, when S is a set, $x \xleftarrow{R} S$ denotes the action of choosing x at random in S. By $a \in \mathsf{poly}(\lambda)$, we mean that a is a polynomial in λ while $b \in \mathsf{negl}(\lambda)$ says that b is a negligible function of λ. When a and b are two binary strings, $a\|b$ stands for their concatenation. For equal-dimension vectors $\vec{A}$ and $\vec{B}$ containing group elements, $\vec{A} \odot \vec{B}$ stands for their component-wise product.

2.1   Complexity Assumptions

We use groups $(\mathbb{G}, \mathbb{G}_T)$ of prime order p with an efficiently computable map $e : \mathbb{G} \times \mathbb{G} \to \mathbb{G}_T$ such that $e(g^a, h^b) = e(g, h)^{ab}$ for any $(g, h) \in \mathbb{G} \times \mathbb{G}, a, b \in \mathbb{Z}$ and $e(g, h) \neq 1_{\mathbb{G}_T}$ whenever $g, h \neq 1_{\mathbb{G}}$. In this setting, we consider several problems.

Definition 1 ([6]). *The* Decision Linear Problem *(DLIN) in* $\mathbb{G}$, *is to distinguish the distribution of* $D_1 = \{(g, g^a, g^b, g^{ac}, g^{bd}, g^{c+d}) \mid a, b, c, d \xleftarrow{R} \mathbb{Z}_p\}$ *from the distribution* $D_2 = \{(g, g^a, g^b, g^{ac}, g^{bd}, g^z) \mid a, b, c, d, z \xleftarrow{R} \mathbb{Z}_p\}$.

We also rely on a problem whose generic hardness of which was proved in [1].

Definition 2 ([1]). *In a group* $\mathbb{G}$ *of prime order* p, *the* q-Simultaneous Flexible Pairing Problem *(q-SFP) is, given* $(g_z, h_z, g_r, h_r, a, \tilde{a}, b, \tilde{b}) \in \mathbb{G}^8$ *as well as* q *tuples* $(z_j, r_j, s_j, t_j, u_j, v_j, w_j) \in \mathbb{G}^7$ *such that*

$$e(a, \tilde{a}) = e(g_z, z_j) \cdot e(g_r, r_j) \cdot e(s_j, t_j) \quad and \quad e(b, \tilde{b}) = e(h_z, z_j) \cdot e(h_r, u_j) \cdot e(v_j, w_j),$$

to find a new tuple $(z^\star, r^\star, s^\star, t^\star, u^\star, v^\star, w^\star) \in \mathbb{G}^7$ *satisfying the above equations and such that* $z^\star \notin \{1_{\mathbb{G}}, z_1, \ldots, z_q\}$.

Definition 3 ([7]). *The* Decision 3-party Diffie-Hellman Problem *(D3DH) in* $\mathbb{G}$, *is to distinguish the distributions* $(g, g^a, g^b, g^c, g^{abc})$ *and* (g, g^a, g^b, g^c, g^z), *where* $a, b, c, z \xleftarrow{R} \mathbb{Z}_p$.

2.2   Groth-Sahai Proof Systems

In symmetric pairing configurations, the Groth-Sahai (GS) proof systems [16] use a common reference string (CRS) consisting of three vectors $\vec{g_1}, \vec{g_2}, \vec{g_3} \in \mathbb{G}^3$, where $\vec{g_1} = (g_1, 1, g)$, $\vec{g_2} = (1, g_2, g)$ for some $g_1, g_2 \in \mathbb{G}$. To commit to a group element $X \in \mathbb{G}$, the prover computes $\vec{C} = (1, 1, X) \odot \vec{g_1}^r \odot \vec{g_2}^s \odot \vec{g_3}^t$ with $r, s, t \xleftarrow{R} \mathbb{Z}_p$. When the proof system is configured to provide perfectly sound proofs, $\vec{g_3}$ is set as $\vec{g_3} = \vec{g_1}^{\xi_1} \odot \vec{g_2}^{\xi_2}$ with $\xi_1, \xi_2 \xleftarrow{R} \mathbb{Z}_p$. In this case, commitments $\vec{C} = (g_1^{r+\xi_1 t}, g_2^{s+\xi_2 t}, X \cdot g^{r+s+t(\xi_1+\xi_2)})$ can be interpreted as Boneh-Boyen-Shacham (BBS) ciphertexts as X can be recovered by running the BBS decryption algorithm using the private key $(\alpha_1, \alpha_2) = (\log_g(g_1), \log_g(g_2))$. When the CRS is set up to give perfectly witness indistinguishable (WI) proofs, $\vec{g_1}, \vec{g_2}$ and $\vec{g_3}$ are linearly independent vectors, so that $\vec{C}$ is a perfectly hiding commitment to $X \in \mathbb{G}$: a typical choice is $\vec{g_3} = \vec{g_1}^{\xi_1} \odot \vec{g_2}^{\xi_2} \odot (1, 1, g)^{-1}$. Under the DLIN assumption, the two distributions of CRS are computationally indistinguishable.

To commit to an exponent $x \in \mathbb{Z}_p$, the prover computes $\vec{C} = \vec{\varphi}^x \odot \vec{g_1}^r \odot \vec{g_2}^s$, with $r, s \xleftarrow{R} \mathbb{Z}_p$, using a CRS containing $\vec{\varphi}, \vec{g_1}, \vec{g_2}$. In the perfect soundness setting $\vec{\varphi}, \vec{g_1}, \vec{g_2}$ are linearly independent (typically $\vec{\varphi} = \vec{g_3} \odot (1, 1, g)$ where $\vec{g_3} = \vec{g_1}^{\xi_1} \odot \vec{g_2}^{\xi_2}$) whereas, in the perfect WI setting, choosing $\vec{\varphi} = \vec{g_1}^{\xi_1} \odot \vec{g_2}^{\xi_2}$ yields perfectly hiding commitments since $\vec{C}$ is statistically independent of x.

Efficient NIWI proofs are available for pairing-product relations, which are equations of the form $\prod_{i=1}^{n} e(\mathcal{A}_i, \mathcal{X}_i) \cdot \prod_{i=1}^{n} \cdot \prod_{j=1}^{n} e(\mathcal{X}_i, \mathcal{X}_j)^{a_{ij}} = t_T$, for variables $\mathcal{X}_1, \ldots, \mathcal{X}_n \in \mathbb{G}$ and constants $t_T \in \mathbb{G}_T$, $\mathcal{A}_1, \ldots, \mathcal{A}_n \in \mathbb{G}$, $a_{ij} \in \mathbb{Z}_p$, for $i, j \in \{1, \ldots, n\}$. Efficient proofs also exist for multi-exponentiation equations like $\prod_{i=1}^{m} \mathcal{A}_i^{y_i} \cdot \prod_{j=1}^{m} \mathcal{X}_j^{b_j} \cdot \prod_{i=1}^{m} \cdot \prod_{j=1}^{n} \mathcal{X}_j^{y_i \gamma_{ij}} = T$, for variables $\mathcal{X}_1, \ldots, \mathcal{X}_n \in \mathbb{G}$, $y_1, \ldots, y_m \in \mathbb{Z}_p$ and constants $T, \mathcal{A}_1, \ldots, \mathcal{A}_m \in \mathbb{G}$, $b_1, \ldots, b_n \in \mathbb{Z}_p$ and $\gamma_{ij} \in \mathbb{Z}_p$, for $i \in \{1, \ldots, m\}, j \in \{1, \ldots, n\}$.

Multi-exponentiation equations always admit non-interactive zero-knowledge (NIZK) proofs at no additional cost. On a perfectly witness indistinguishable CRS, a trapdoor (like the hidden exponents $(\xi_1, \xi_2) \in \mathbb{Z}_p^2$ when $\vec{g_3} = \vec{g_1}^{\xi_1} \odot \vec{g_2}^{\xi_2} \odot (1, 1, g)^{-1})$ allows simulating proofs without knowing the witnesses and simulated proofs are perfectly indistinguishable from real proofs. As for pairing-product equations, zero-knowledge proofs are often possible – this is usually the case when the right-hand side member t_T is a product of pairings involving known group elements – but the number of group elements per proof may not be constant anymore. Here, when using such NIZK simulators, we just introduce a constant number of extra group elements in the proofs.

2.3   Chameleon Hash Functions

A chameleon hash function [21] is a tuple $\mathsf{CMH} = (\mathsf{CMKg}, \mathsf{CMhash}, \mathsf{CMswitch})$ that contains an algorithm CMKg that, given a security parameter λ, outputs a key pair $(hk, tk) \leftarrow \mathcal{G}(\lambda)$. The hashing algorithm outputs $y = \mathsf{CMhash}(hk, m, r)$ given the public key hk, a message m and random coins $r \in \mathcal{R}_{hash}$. On input of messages m, m', random coins $r \in \mathcal{R}_{hash}$ and the trapdoor key tk, the switching algorithm $r' \leftarrow \mathsf{CMswitch}(tk, m, r, m')$ computes $r' \in \mathcal{R}_{hash}$ such that $\mathsf{CMhash}(hk, m, r) = \mathsf{CMhash}(hk, m', r')$. The collision-resistance property mandates that it be infeasible to come up with pairs $(m', r') \neq (m, r)$ such that $\mathsf{CMhash}(hk, m, r) = \mathsf{CMhash}(hk, m', r')$ without knowing the trapdoor key tk. Uniformity guarantees that the distribution of hash values is independent of the message m: for all hk, and all m, m', the distributions $\{r \leftarrow \mathcal{R}_{hash} : \mathsf{CMHash}(hk, m, r)\}$ and $\{r \leftarrow \mathcal{R}_{hash} : \mathsf{CMHash}(hk, m', r)\}$ are identical.

3 Traceable Group Encryption

3.1 Syntax

Traceable group encryption (TGE) schemes involve a sender, a verifier, a group manager (GM) that manages the group of receivers and an opening authority (OA) that is able to uncover the identity of ciphertext receivers.

A group encryption system is formally specified by the description of a relation $\mathcal{R}$ and a collection $\mathsf{TGE} = (\mathsf{SETUP}, \mathsf{JOIN}, \langle \mathcal{G}_r, \mathcal{R}, \mathsf{sample}_{\mathcal{R}} \rangle, \mathsf{ENC}, \mathsf{DEC}, \langle \mathcal{P}, \mathcal{V} \rangle,$ $\mathsf{OPEN}, \mathsf{REVEAL}, \mathsf{TRACE}, \mathsf{CLAIM/DISCLAIM}, \mathsf{CLAIM\text{-}VERIFY}, \mathsf{DISCLAIM\text{-}}$ $\mathsf{VERIFY})$ of algorithms or protocols. Among these, SETUP is a set of initialization procedures that all take (explicitly or implicitly) a security parameter λ as input. They can be split into one that generates a set of public parameters param (a common reference string), one for the GM and another one for the OA. We call them $\mathsf{SETUP_{init}}(\lambda)$, $\mathsf{SETUP_{GM}}(\mathsf{param})$ and $\mathsf{SETUP_{OA}}(\mathsf{param})$, respectively. The latter two procedures are used to produce key pairs $(\mathsf{pk_{GM}}, \mathsf{sk_{GM}})$, $(\mathsf{pk_{OA}}, \mathsf{sk_{OA}})$ for the GM and the OA. In the following, param is incorporated in the inputs of all algorithms although we sometimes omit to explicitly write it.

$\mathsf{JOIN} = (\mathsf{J_{user}}, \mathsf{J_{GM}})$ is an interactive protocol between the GM and the prospective user. As in [9], we will aim for two-message protocols: the first message is the user's public key pk sent by $\mathsf{J_{user}}$ to $\mathsf{J_{GM}}$ and the latter's response is a certificate $\mathsf{cert_{pk}}$ for pk vouching for the user's group membership. The user is not required to prove knowledge of his private key sk. Valid public keys are assumed to be publicly recognizable, so that proofs of validity are not necessary either. After the execution of JOIN, the GM stores the public key pk and its certificate $\mathsf{cert_{pk}}$ in a public directory $\mathsf{database}$.

Algorithm sample allows sampling pairs $(x, w) \in \mathcal{R}$ (comprised of a public value x and a witness w) using public / secret parameters $(\mathsf{pk_{\mathcal{R}}}, \mathsf{sk_{\mathcal{R}}})$ produced by $\mathcal{G}_r$ for $\mathcal{R}$. Depending on the relation, $\mathsf{sk_{\mathcal{R}}}$ may be the empty string, as in the scheme we describe. The testing procedure $\mathcal{R}(x, w)$ returns 1 iff $(x, w) \in \mathcal{R}$. To encrypt a witness w such that $(x, w) \in \mathcal{R}$ for some public x, the sender picks the pair $(\mathsf{pk}, \mathsf{cert_{pk}})$ from $\mathsf{database}$ and runs the encryption algorithm. The latter takes as input w, a label L, the receiver's pair $(\mathsf{pk}, \mathsf{cert_{pk}})$ as well as public keys $\mathsf{pk_{GM}}$ and $\mathsf{pk_{OA}}$. Its output is a ciphertext $\psi \leftarrow \mathsf{ENC}(\mathsf{pk_{GM}}, \mathsf{pk_{OA}}, \mathsf{pk}, \mathsf{cert_{pk}}, w, L)$. On input of the same elements, the certificate $\mathsf{cert_{pk}}$, the ciphertext ψ and the random encryption coins $coins_{\psi}$, the non-interactive algorithm $\mathcal{P}$ generates a proof π_{ψ} that there exists a certified receiver whose public key was registered in $\mathsf{database}$ and that is able to decrypt ψ and obtain a witness w such that

$(x, w) \in \mathcal{R}$. The verification algorithm $\mathcal{V}$ takes as input ψ, $\mathsf{pk}_{\mathsf{GM}}$, $\mathsf{pk}_{\mathsf{OA}}$, π_ψ and the description of $\mathcal{R}$ and outputs 0 or 1. Given ψ, L and the receiver's private key sk, the output of DEC is either a witness w such that $(x, w) \in \mathcal{R}$ or $\bot$.

The next three algorithms provide explicit and implicit tracing capabilities. First, OPEN takes as input a ciphertext/label pair (ψ, L) and the OA's secret key $\mathsf{sk}_{\mathsf{OA}}$ and returns a receiver's identity i. Algorithm REVEAL takes as input the joining transcript $\mathsf{transcript}_i$ of user i and allows the OA to extract a tracing trapdoor trace_i using its private key $\mathsf{sk}_{\mathsf{OA}}$. This tracing trapdoor can be subsequently used to determine whether or not a given ciphertext-label pair (ψ, L) is a valid encryption under the public key pk_i of user i: namely, algorithm TRACE takes in public keys $\mathsf{pk}_{\mathsf{GM}}$ and $\mathsf{pk}_{\mathsf{OA}}$ as well as a pair (ψ, L) and the tracing trapdoor trace_i associated with user i. It returns 1 if and only if (ψ, L) is believed to be a valid encryption intended for user i.

Finally, algorithms (CLAIM/DISCLAIM, CLAIM-VERIFY, DISCLAIM-VERIFY) implement a functionality that allows user to convincingly claim or disclaim being the legitimate recipient of a given anonymous ciphertext. Concretely, CLAIM/DISCLAIM takes as input all public keys $(\mathsf{pk}_{\mathsf{GM}}, \mathsf{pk}_{\mathsf{OA}}, \mathsf{pk})$, a ciphertext-label pair (ψ, L) and a private key sk. It reveals a publicly verifiable piece of evidence τ that (ψ, L) is or is not a valid encryption under the public key pk. Algorithms CLAIM-VERIFY and DISCLAIM-VERIFY are then used to verify the assertion established by τ. They take as input all public keys, a pair (ψ, L) and a claim/disclaimer τ and output 1 or 0.

3.2 Security Definitions

Beyond the standard correctness requirement, our security model involves four properties called message privacy, anonymity, soundness and claiming soundness. In the definitions hereunder, we use the notation $\langle \mathsf{output}_A | \mathsf{output}_B \rangle \leftarrow \langle A(\mathsf{input}_A), B(\mathsf{input}_B) \rangle (\mathsf{common\text{-}input})$ to denote the execution of a protocol between A and B obtaining their own outputs from their respective inputs.

CORRECTNESS. The following experiment should return 1 w.h.p.

Experiment $\mathbf{Expt}^{\mathrm{correctness}}(\lambda)$
  $\mathsf{param} \leftarrow \mathsf{SETUP}_{\mathsf{init}}(\lambda)$; $(\mathsf{pk}_\mathcal{R}, \mathsf{sk}_\mathcal{R}) \leftarrow \mathcal{G}_r(\lambda)$; $(x, w) \leftarrow \mathsf{sample}_\mathcal{R}(\mathsf{pk}_\mathcal{R}, \mathsf{sk}_\mathcal{R})$;
  $(\mathsf{pk}_{\mathsf{GM}}, \mathsf{sk}_{\mathsf{GM}}) \leftarrow \mathsf{SETUP}_{\mathsf{GM}}(\mathsf{param})$; $(\mathsf{pk}_{\mathsf{OA}}, \mathsf{sk}_{\mathsf{OA}}) \leftarrow \mathsf{SETUP}_{\mathsf{OA}}(\mathsf{param})$;
  $\langle \mathsf{pk}_i, \mathsf{sk}_i, \mathsf{cert}_{\mathsf{pk}_i} | \mathsf{pk}_i, \mathsf{cert}_{\mathsf{pk}_i} \rangle \leftarrow \langle \mathsf{J}_{\mathsf{user}}, \mathsf{J}_{\mathsf{GM}}(\mathsf{sk}_{\mathsf{GM}}) \rangle (\mathsf{pk}_{\mathsf{GM}})$;
  $\psi \leftarrow \mathsf{ENC}(\mathsf{pk}_{\mathsf{GM}}, \mathsf{pk}_{\mathsf{OA}}, \mathsf{pk}_i, \mathsf{cert}_{\mathsf{pk}_i}, w, L)$;
  $\pi_\psi \leftarrow \mathcal{P}(\mathsf{pk}_{\mathsf{GM}}, \mathsf{pk}_{\mathsf{OA}}, \mathsf{pk}_i, \mathsf{cert}_{\mathsf{pk}_i}, x, w, L, \psi, coins_\psi)$;
  If $\big((w \neq \mathsf{DEC}(\mathsf{sk}_i, \psi, L)) \vee (i \neq \mathsf{OPEN}(\mathsf{sk}_{\mathsf{OA}}, \psi, L))$
      $\vee (\mathcal{V}(\psi, L, \pi_\psi, \mathsf{pk}_{\mathsf{GM}}, \mathsf{pk}_{\mathsf{OA}}) = 0)\big)$ return 0 else return 1.

MESSAGE PRIVACY. This property is defined by an experiment where the adversary has access to oracles that may be stateless or maintain a state across queries:

- DEC(sk): is an oracle for the user decryption function. When it is restricted not to decrypt a ciphertext-label pair (ψ, L), we denote it by $\mathsf{DEC}^{\neg\langle\psi,L\rangle}$.
- $\mathsf{CH}^b_{\mathsf{ror}}(\lambda, \mathsf{pk}, w, L)$: is a real-or-random challenge oracle that is only queried once. It returns $(\psi, coins_\psi)$ such that $\psi \leftarrow \mathsf{ENC}(\mathsf{pk}_{\mathsf{GM}}, \mathsf{pk}_{\mathsf{OA}}, \mathsf{pk}, \mathsf{cert}_{\mathsf{pk}}, w, L)$ if $b = 1$ whereas, if $b = 0$, $\psi \leftarrow \mathsf{ENC}(\mathsf{pk}_{\mathsf{GM}}, \mathsf{pk}_{\mathsf{OA}}, \mathsf{pk}, \mathsf{cert}_{\mathsf{pk}}, w', L)$ encrypts a random plaintext uniformly chosen in the space of plaintexts of length $O(\lambda)$. In either case, $coins_\psi$ are the random coins used to generate ψ.
- $\mathsf{PROVE}^b_{\mathcal{P},\mathcal{P}'}(\mathsf{pk}_{\mathsf{GM}}, \mathsf{pk}_{\mathsf{OA}}, \mathsf{pk}, \mathsf{cert}_{\mathsf{pk}}, \mathsf{pk}_\mathcal{R}, x, w, \psi, L, coins_\psi)$: is a stateful oracle that the adversary can query on multiple occasions. If $b = 1$, it runs the real prover $\mathcal{P}$ on the inputs to produce an actual proof π_ψ. If $b = 0$, the oracle runs a simulator $\mathcal{P}'$ that uses the same inputs as $\mathcal{P}$ except w and $coins_\psi$ and generates a simulated proof.
- CLAIM/DISCLAIM($\mathsf{pk}_{\mathsf{GM}}, \mathsf{pk}_{\mathsf{OA}}, \psi, L, \mathsf{sk}$): is a stateful oracle that generates claims or disclaimer proofs for arbitrary ciphertexts. Specifically, the oracle first uses the private key sk to determine whether (ψ, L) is a valid ciphertext-label pair w.r.t. the public key pk. If so, the oracle uses sk to compute and return a non-interactive claim τ for ψ. Otherwise, the oracle generates a disclaimer proof τ showing that (ψ, L) is not a valid encryption under pk. In either case, (ψ, L) is stored in a list claims, which is initially empty.

These oracles are used in an experiment where the adversary controls the GM, the OA and all members but the honest receiver. The adversary $\mathcal{A}$ is the dishonest GM that certifies the honest receiver in an execution of JOIN. It has oracle access to the decryption function DEC of that receiver. At the challenge phase, it probes the challenge oracle for a label and a pair $(x, w) \in \mathcal{R}$ of her choice. After the challenge phase, $\mathcal{A}$ can also invoke the PROVE oracle on multiple occasions and eventually aims to guess the bit b chosen by the challenger.

As pointed out in [19], designing an efficient simulator $\mathcal{P}'$ (for executing $\mathsf{PROVE}^b_{\mathcal{P},\mathcal{P}'}(.)$ when $b = 0$) is part of the security proof and might require a simulated common reference string.

Definition 4. *A TGE scheme satisfies message security if, for any PPT adversary $\mathcal{A}$, the experiment below returns 1 with probability at most $1/2 + \mathsf{negl}(\lambda)$.*

Experiment $\mathbf{Expt}^{\mathsf{sec}}_{\mathcal{A}}(\lambda)$
  $\mathsf{param} \leftarrow \mathsf{SETUP}_{\mathsf{init}}(\lambda);$ $(\mathsf{aux}, \mathsf{pk}_{\mathsf{GM}}, \mathsf{pk}_{\mathsf{OA}}) \leftarrow \mathcal{A}(\mathsf{param});$
  $\langle \mathsf{pk}, \mathsf{sk}, \mathsf{cert}_{\mathsf{pk}} | \mathsf{aux} \rangle \leftarrow \langle \mathsf{J}_{\mathsf{user}}, \mathcal{A}(\mathsf{aux}) \rangle(\mathsf{pk}_{\mathsf{GM}});$
  $(\mathsf{aux}, x, w, L, \mathsf{pk}_\mathcal{R}) \leftarrow \mathcal{A}^{\mathsf{DEC}(\mathsf{sk},.),\ \mathsf{CLAIM/DISCLAIM}(\mathsf{pk}_{\mathsf{GM}},\mathsf{pk}_{\mathsf{OA}},\cdots,\mathsf{sk})}(\mathsf{aux});$
  If $(x, w) \notin \mathcal{R}$ return 0; $b \xleftarrow{R} \{0,1\};$ $(\psi, coins_\psi) \leftarrow \mathsf{CH}^b_{\mathsf{ror}}(\lambda, \mathsf{pk}, w, L);$
  $b' \leftarrow \mathcal{A}^{\mathsf{PROVE}^b_{\mathcal{P},\mathcal{P}'}(\mathsf{pk}_{\mathsf{GM}},\mathsf{pk}_{\mathsf{OA}},\mathsf{pk},\mathsf{cert}_{\mathsf{pk}},\mathsf{pk}_\mathcal{R},x,w,\psi,L,coins_\psi),\mathsf{DEC}^{\neg\langle\psi,L\rangle}(\mathsf{sk},.),}$

$\qquad\qquad\qquad\qquad\qquad {}^{\mathsf{CLAIM/DISCLAIM}(\mathsf{pk}_{\mathsf{GM}},\mathsf{pk}_{\mathsf{OA}},\cdots,\mathsf{sk})}(\mathsf{aux}, \psi);$

  If $b = b'$ return 1 else return 0.

ANONYMITY. In anonymity attacks, the adversary controls the entire system except the opening authority. One way to jeopardize the anonymity property is to mount a chosen-ciphertext attack on the encryption scheme used by the OA. A difference with the usual group encryption scenario is that we must pay attention to the information revealed by the traceability components of ciphertexts. Throughout the game, the adversary can act as a dishonest group manager and register honest users in the system. In the challenge phase, the adversary A chooses a pair $(x, w) \in \mathcal{R}$ and the public keys $\mathsf{pk}_0, \mathsf{pk}_1$ of two honest users. In return, it receives an encryption of w under the public key pk_b for some $b \in \{0, 1\}$ chosen by the challenger. It has access to the following oracles:

- USER($\mathsf{pk}_{\mathsf{GM}}$): is a stateful oracle simulating executions of $\mathsf{J}_{\mathsf{user}}$ on behalf of new honest users who are requested to join the group. It uses an initially empty list keys. At its i-th invocation, the output $(i, \mathsf{pk}_i, \mathsf{sk}_i, \mathsf{cert}_{\mathsf{pk}_i})$ of $\mathsf{J}_{\mathsf{user}}$ is stored in keys if the adversary, which emulates the GM, provides a valid certificate $\mathsf{cert}_{\mathsf{pk}_i}$. If the JOIN protocol does not successfully terminate, the oracle stores $(i, \perp)$ in keys.
- CORR(.): is a stateful oracle that allows the adversary to corrupt honest group members. When invoked on input of an index i, the oracle first checks if the list keys contains an entry of the form $(i, \mathsf{pk}_i, \mathsf{sk}_i, \mathsf{cert}_{\mathsf{pk}_i})$. If so, it returns sk_i and adds i to the set Corr, which is initially empty.
- DEC(., .): is a stateless decryption oracle that provides a decryption capability for each secret key. It takes as input an index i and a ciphertext-label pair (ψ, L). It first checks if the list keys contains an entry of the form $(i, \mathsf{pk}_i, \mathsf{sk}_i, \mathsf{cert}_{\mathsf{pk}_i})$. If no such entry exists, it returns $\perp$. Otherwise, it uses sk_i to run DEC on the input (ψ, L) and returns the result. When this oracle is restricted not to decrypt a ciphertext-label pair (ψ, L) for some user index $i \in \{i_0, i_1\}$, we denote it by $\mathsf{DEC}^{\neg \{i_0, i_1\} \times \langle \psi, L \rangle}$.
- OPEN($\mathsf{sk}_{\mathsf{OA}}$, .): is a stateless oracle that runs the opening algorithm on behalf of the OA. On input of a TGE ciphertext, it returns the receiver's identity i.
- REVEAL($\mathsf{sk}_{\mathsf{OA}}$, .): is an oracle that takes as input a user index i and simulates the REVEAL algorithm on behalf of the OA. If no user was assigned the index i in keys, it returns $\perp$. Otherwise, it recovers the transcript $\mathsf{transcript}_i$ of user i in database and uses $\mathsf{sk}_{\mathsf{OA}}$ to extract and return the i-th group member's tracing trapdoor trace_i. It also adds i to the set Revs.
- $\mathsf{CH}_{\mathsf{anon}}^b(\mathsf{pk}_{\mathsf{GM}}, \mathsf{pk}_{\mathsf{OA}}, \mathsf{pk}_0, \mathsf{pk}_1, w, L)$: is a challenge oracle that can only be queried once. It returns a pair $(\psi, \mathit{coins}_\psi)$ consisting of a ciphertext $\psi \leftarrow \mathsf{ENC}(\mathsf{pk}_{\mathsf{GM}}, \mathsf{pk}_{\mathsf{OA}}, \mathsf{pk}_b, \mathsf{cert}_{\mathsf{pk}_b}, w, L)$ and the coin tosses used to generate ψ.
- $\mathcal{P}(\mathsf{pk}_{\mathsf{GM}}, \mathsf{pk}_{\mathsf{OA}}, \mathsf{pk}_b, \mathsf{cert}_{\mathsf{pk}_b}, \mathsf{pk}_{\mathcal{R}}, x, w, \psi, L, \mathit{coins}_\psi)$: is a stateful oracle which can be queried several times after the challenge phase. It runs the real prover $\mathcal{P}$ on the inputs to produce an actual proof π_ψ using the random coins coins_ψ involved in the generation of the challenge. It returns the resulting proof π_ψ.
- CLAIM/DISCLAIM($\mathsf{pk}_{\mathsf{GM}}, \mathsf{pk}_{\mathsf{OA}}, \psi, L, i$): is a stateful oracle. It takes as input an index i and a ciphertext/label pair. It first checks whether keys contains a tuple $\mathsf{transcript}_i = (i, \mathsf{pk}_i, \mathsf{sk}_i, \mathsf{cert}_{\mathsf{pk}_i})$. If not, it returns $\perp$. Otherwise, it uses the private key sk_i to determine whether (ψ, L) is a valid ciphertext-label pair w.r.t. the public key pk_i. If yes, the oracle uses sk_i to generate a non-interactive claim τ for (ψ, L). Otherwise, the oracle generate a disclaimer τ guaranteeing that (ψ, L) is not a valid encryption under pk_i. In either case, (i, ψ, L) is stored in a list claims, which is initially empty.

Definition 5. *A TGE scheme satisfies anonymity if, for any PPT adversary $\mathcal{A}$, the experiment below returns 1 with a probability not exceeding $1/2 + \mathsf{negl}(\lambda)$.*

Experiment $\mathbf{Expt}_{\mathcal{A}}^{\mathrm{anon}}(\lambda)$
   $\mathsf{param} \leftarrow \mathsf{SETUP}_{\mathsf{init}}(\lambda); \ (\mathsf{pk}_{\mathsf{OA}}, \mathsf{sk}_{\mathsf{OA}}) \leftarrow \mathsf{SETUP}_{\mathsf{OA}}(\mathsf{param});$
   $(\mathsf{aux}, \mathsf{pk}_{\mathsf{GM}}) \leftarrow \mathcal{A}(\mathsf{param}, \mathsf{pk}_{\mathsf{OA}});$
   $(i_0, i_1, \mathsf{aux}, x, w, L, \mathsf{pk}_{\mathcal{R}}) \leftarrow \mathcal{A}^{\mathsf{USER}(\mathsf{pk}_{\mathsf{GM}}), \ \mathsf{OPEN}(\mathsf{sk}_{\mathsf{OA}}, \cdot),}$
$\qquad\qquad\qquad\quad {}^{\mathsf{REVEAL}(\mathsf{sk}_{\mathsf{OA}}, \cdot), \ \mathsf{DEC}(\cdot, \cdot), \ \mathsf{CLAIM/DISCLAIM}(\mathsf{pk}_{\mathsf{GM}}, \mathsf{pk}_{\mathsf{OA}}, \cdot, \cdot, \cdot), \ \mathsf{CORR}(\cdot)}(\mathsf{aux});$
   If $(i_0, \mathsf{pk}_0, \mathsf{sk}_0, \mathsf{cert}_{\mathsf{pk}_0}) \notin \mathsf{keys} \ \vee \ (i_1, \mathsf{pk}_1, \mathsf{sk}_1, \mathsf{cert}_{\mathsf{pk}_1}) \notin \mathsf{keys} \ return \ 0;$
   If $(x, w) \notin \mathcal{R} \ return \ 0; \quad b \xleftarrow{R} \{0, 1\};$
   $(\psi, coins_{\psi}) \leftarrow \mathsf{CH}^b_{\mathrm{anon}}(\mathsf{pk}_{\mathsf{GM}}, \mathsf{pk}_{\mathsf{OA}}, \mathsf{pk}_0, \mathsf{pk}_1, w, L);$
   $b' \leftarrow \mathcal{A}^{\mathsf{USER}(\mathsf{pk}_{\mathsf{GM}}), \ \mathcal{P}(\mathsf{pk}_{\mathsf{GM}}, \mathsf{pk}_{\mathsf{OA}}, \mathsf{pk}_b, \mathsf{cert}_{\mathsf{pk}_b}, x, w, \psi, L, coins_{\psi}), \ \mathsf{OPEN}^{\neg\langle \psi, L \rangle}(\mathsf{sk}_{\mathsf{OA}}, \cdot), \ \mathsf{CORR}(\cdot)}$
$\qquad {}^{\mathsf{REVEAL}^{\neg\{i_0, i_1\}}(\mathsf{sk}_{\mathsf{OA}}, \cdot), \ \mathsf{DEC}^{\neg\{i_0, i_1\} \times \langle \psi, L \rangle}(\cdot, \cdot), \ \mathsf{CLAIM/DISCLAIM}(\mathsf{pk}_{\mathsf{GM}}, \mathsf{pk}_{\mathsf{OA}}, \cdot, \cdot, \cdot)}(\mathsf{aux}, \psi);$
   If $((i_0, \psi, L) \in \mathsf{claims}) \ \vee \ ((i_1, \psi, L) \in \mathsf{claims}) \ return \ 0;$
   If $(i_0 \in \mathsf{Revs} \cup \mathsf{Corr}) \ \vee \ (i_1 \in \mathsf{Revs} \cup \mathsf{Corr}) \ return \ 0;$
   If $b = b' \ return \ 1 \ else \ return \ 0.$

As shown in [19], TGE schemes satisfying the above notion necessarily subsume a key-private (a.k.a. receiver anonymous) [3] cryptosystem.

SOUNDNESS. In a soundness attack, the adversary creates the group of receivers by interacting with the honest GM. Its goal is to create a ciphertext ψ and a convincing proof that ψ is valid w.r.t. a relation $\mathcal{R}$ of its choice but either (1) the opening fails to identify a certified group member as the legitimate recipient of ψ; (2) the implicit tracing mechanism TRACE does not point to the group member pinned down by OPEN; (3) the ciphertext C is not in the language $\mathcal{L}^{x, L, \mathsf{pk}_{\mathcal{R}}, \mathsf{pk}_{\mathsf{GM}}, \mathsf{pk}_{\mathsf{OA}}, \mathsf{pk}_i} = \{\mathsf{ENC}(\mathsf{pk}_{\mathsf{GM}}, \mathsf{pk}_{\mathsf{OA}}, \mathsf{pk}_i, \mathsf{cert}_{\mathsf{pk}_i}, w, L) \mid (x, w) \in \mathcal{R}; \ (\mathsf{pk}_i, \mathsf{cert}_{\mathsf{pk}_i}) \in \mathsf{valid}\}$, where valid is the set of properly certified keys. This notion is formalized by a game where the adversary is given access to a user registration oracle $\mathsf{REG}(\mathsf{sk}_{\mathsf{GM}}, \cdot)$ that emulates J_{GM}. This oracle maintains a repository database where registered public keys and their certificates are stored.

Definition 6. *A TGE scheme is sound if, for any PPT adversary $\mathcal{A}$, the experiment below returns 1 with negligible probability.*

Experiment $\mathbf{Expt}_{\mathcal{A}}^{\mathrm{soundness}}(\lambda)$
   $\mathsf{param} \leftarrow \mathsf{SETUP}_{\mathsf{init}}(\lambda); \ (\mathsf{pk}_{\mathsf{OA}}, \mathsf{sk}_{\mathsf{OA}}) \leftarrow \mathsf{SETUP}_{\mathsf{OA}}(\mathsf{param});$
   $(\mathsf{pk}_{\mathsf{GM}}, \mathsf{sk}_{\mathsf{GM}}) \leftarrow \mathsf{SETUP}_{\mathsf{GM}}(\mathsf{param});$
   $(\mathsf{pk}_{\mathcal{R}}, x, \psi, \pi_{\psi}, L, \mathsf{aux}) \leftarrow \mathcal{A}^{\mathsf{REG}(\mathsf{sk}_{\mathsf{GM}}, \cdot)}(\mathsf{param}, \mathsf{pk}_{\mathsf{GM}}, \mathsf{pk}_{\mathsf{OA}}, \mathsf{sk}_{\mathsf{OA}});$
   If $\mathcal{V}(\psi, L, \pi_{\psi}, \mathsf{pk}_{\mathsf{GM}}, \mathsf{pk}_{\mathsf{OA}}) = 0 \ return \ 0;$
   $i \leftarrow \mathsf{OPEN}(\mathsf{sk}_{\mathsf{OA}}, \psi, L);$
   If $((i = \perp) \vee (\psi \notin \mathcal{L}^{x, L, \mathsf{pk}_{\mathcal{R}}, \mathsf{pk}_{\mathsf{GM}}, \mathsf{pk}_{\mathsf{OA}}, \mathsf{pk}_i})) \ then \ return \ 1;$
   $\mathsf{trace}_i \leftarrow \mathsf{REVEAL}(\mathsf{transcript}_i, \mathsf{sk}_{\mathsf{OA}});$
   If $(i \neq \mathsf{TRACE}(\mathsf{pk}_{\mathsf{GM}}, \mathsf{pk}_{\mathsf{OA}}, \psi, \mathsf{trace}_i)) \ then \ return \ 1;$
   $Return \ 0.$

The above properties are similar to those for group encryption. We need to introduce the new notion of *claiming soundness* (which is not part of the group encryption model [19]) that formalizes the soundness of the claiming process.

CLAIMING SOUNDNESS. The last security notion considers an adversary attacking the soundness of the claiming algorithm by either claiming other users' ciphertexts as its own or disclaiming ciphertexts that are actually encrypted under its public key. Moreover, the verifier of a claim/disclaimer should be convinced of the group member's intentionality to claim or repudiate ciphertexts. We require that only users be able to claim/disclaim ciphertexts encrypted under their key or not: even the sender (who knows the encryption coins) should not do this.

In the model, the adversary controls the GM and the OA. It has access to oracles $\mathsf{USER}(\mathsf{pk_{GM}})$, $\mathsf{CORR}(.)$, $\mathsf{DEC}(.,.)$ and $\mathsf{CLAIM/DISCLAIM}(\mathsf{pk_{GM}}, \mathsf{pk_{OA}}, \psi, L, i)$, which are identical to those of the anonymity property.

The adversary's goal is to create a public repository database satisfying the integrity check, a ciphertext ψ and a statement statement consisting of a claim/disclaimer τ and a public key pk but either: (1) the implicit tracing mechanism TRACE does not point to the group member i pinned down by OPEN; (2) statement $= (\tau, \mathsf{pk})$ is a valid claim although $\mathsf{pk} \neq \mathsf{pk}_i$, where pk_i is associated with user i in database; (3) statement $= (\tau, \mathsf{pk})$ is a valid disclaimer whereas $\mathsf{pk} = \mathsf{pk}_i$ coincides with the public key associated with user i in database; (4) statement $= (\tau, \mathsf{pk}_j)$ is a valid claim/disclaimer for the public key pk_j of some uncorrupted user $j \in \mathsf{database} \backslash \mathsf{Corr}$ in the database and the pair (τ, pk_j) was not produced by the CLAIM/DISCLAIM oracle.

Definition 7. *A TGE scheme provides claiming-soundness if, for any PPT adversary $\mathcal{A}$, the experiment below returns 1 with negligible probability.*

Experiment $\mathbf{Expt}_{\mathcal{A}}^{\text{claiming-soundness}}(\lambda)$

param $\leftarrow \mathsf{SETUP_{init}}(\lambda)$; $(\mathsf{pk_{GM}}, \mathsf{aux}_0) \leftarrow \mathcal{A}(\mathsf{param})$;
$(\mathsf{pk_{OA}}, \mathsf{sk_{OA}}) \leftarrow \mathsf{SETUP_{OA}}(\mathsf{param})$;
$(\mathsf{pk}_{\mathcal{R}}^\star, x^\star, \psi^\star, L^\star, \pi_\psi^\star, \mathsf{statement}^\star, \mathsf{database}^\star, \mathsf{aux}) \leftarrow \mathcal{A}^{\mathsf{USER}(\mathsf{pk_{GM}}), \mathsf{CORR}(.),}$
$\qquad\qquad {}^{\mathsf{DEC}(.,.), \ \mathsf{CLAIM/DISCLAIM}(\mathsf{pk_{GM}},\mathsf{pk_{OA}},.,.,.)}(\mathsf{param}, \mathsf{pk_{OA}}, \mathsf{sk_{OA}}, \mathsf{aux}_0)$;
If DATABASE-CHECK(param, database) $= 0$ *return* 0;
If $\mathcal{V}(\psi^\star, L^\star, \pi_\psi^\star, \mathsf{pk_{GM}}, \mathsf{pk_{OA}}) = 0$ *return* 0;
$i \leftarrow \mathsf{OPEN}(\mathsf{sk_{OA}}, \psi^\star, L^\star)$; $\mathsf{trace}_i \leftarrow \mathsf{REVEAL}(\mathsf{transcript}_i, \mathsf{sk_{OA}})$;
If $(i \neq \mathsf{TRACE}(\mathsf{pk_{GM}}, \mathsf{pk_{OA}}, \psi^\star, \mathsf{trace}_i))$ *then return* 1;
If $\big(\mathsf{statement}^\star = (\tau^\star, \mathsf{pk}^\star) \ s.t. \ (\mathsf{pk}^\star \neq \mathsf{pk}_i)$
$\qquad \wedge \mathsf{CLAIM\text{-}VERIFY}(\mathsf{pk_{GM}}, \mathsf{pk_{OA}}, \psi^\star, L^\star, \mathsf{pk}^\star, \tau^\star) = 1\big)$ *then return* 1;
If $\big(\mathsf{statement}^\star = (\tau^\star, \mathsf{pk}^\star) \ s.t. \ (\mathsf{pk}^\star = \mathsf{pk}_i)$
$\qquad \wedge \mathsf{DISCLAIM\text{-}VERIFY}(\mathsf{pk_{GM}}, \mathsf{pk_{OA}}, \psi^\star, L^\star, \mathsf{pk}^\star, \tau^\star) = 1\big)$ *then return* 1;
If $\big(\mathsf{statement}^\star = (\tau^\star, \mathsf{pk}_j) \ s.t. \ (j, \mathsf{pk}_j, \mathsf{cert}_j, .) \in \mathsf{database} \ \wedge \ (j \notin \mathsf{Corr})$
$\qquad \wedge (\psi^\star, L^\star, \mathsf{pk}_j) \notin Q_c \ \wedge \ (\mathsf{CLAIM\text{-}VERIFY}(\mathsf{pk_{GM}}, \mathsf{pk_{OA}}, \psi^\star, L^\star, \mathsf{pk}_j, \tau^\star) = 1$
$\qquad \vee \mathsf{DISCLAIM\text{-}VERIFY}(\mathsf{pk_{GM}}, \mathsf{pk_{OA}}, \psi^\star, L^\star, \mathsf{pk}_j, \tau^\star) = 1)\big)$ *then return* 1;
Return 0.

In the above notations, Q_c is the set of CLAIM/DISCLAIM queries made by $\mathcal{A}$.

We note that there is no need for a REVEAL oracle in the definition. Indeed, since $\mathcal{A}$ knows $\mathsf{sk}_{\mathsf{OA}}$, it can obtain tracing trapdoors by itself, by decrypting the verifiable encryptions sent by honest users when the USER oracle is invoked.

4   A Non-interactive Traceable Group Encryption Scheme

We use the Libert-Yung (LY) scheme [23], which is a publicly verifiable variant of Cramer-Shoup [11]. We take advantage of the observation that, if certain public key components are shared by all users as common public parameters, the scheme can simultaneously provide receiver anonymity *and* publicly verifiable ciphertexts. In other words, anyone can publicly verify that a ciphertext is valid without knowing who the receiver is. When proofs are generated for the ciphertext, this saves the prover from having to provide evidence that the ciphertext is valid and thus yields shorter proofs.

The message is encrypted under the receiver's public key using the LY scheme. At the same time, the two last components of the receiver's public key is encrypted under the public key of the opening authority using Kiltz's encryption scheme [20]. We use this scheme because it is the most efficient DLIN-based CCA2-secure cryptosystem where the validity of ciphertexts is publicly verifiable and we do not need it to hide the public key under which it is generated.

When new users join the group, the GM provides them with a membership certificate made of a structure-preserving signature [14,1,2] on their public key which comprises group elements (X_1, X_2). We chose to work with the scheme of Abe, Haralambiev and Ohkubo (AHO) [1,2] because it allows working exclusively with linear pairing-product equations and thus obtain a better efficiency.

The implicit tracing mechanism must allow the OA to disclose user-specific tracing trapdoors. To this end, we include in each membership certificate a pair $(\Gamma_1, \Gamma_2) = (g^{\gamma_1}, g^{\gamma_2}) \in \mathbb{G}^2$, where $(\gamma_1, \gamma_2) \in \mathbb{Z}_p^2$ are part of the user's private key. When users join the group, they are thus requested to produce a pair $(\Gamma_1, \Gamma_2) = (g^{\gamma_1}, g^{\gamma_2})$ for which $g^{\gamma_1 \gamma_2}$ will serve as a tracing trapdoor for them. Since $g^{\gamma_1 \gamma_2}$ cannot be publicly revealed, we appeal to a verifiable encryption mechanism as was suggested in [5] in a related context: namely, the prospective user provides the GM with an encryption Φ_{venc} of $g^{\gamma_1 \gamma_2}$ under the OA's public key and generates a non-interactive proof that the encrypted value is indeed an element $g^{\gamma_1 \gamma_2}$ such that $(g, g^{\gamma_1}, g^{\gamma_2}, g^{\gamma_1 \gamma_2})$ is a Diffie-Hellman tuple. The REVEAL algorithm thus uses the OA's private key to decrypt Φ_{venc} so as to expose $g^{\gamma_1 \gamma_2}$. Armed with the information $\mathsf{trace}_i = g^{\gamma_1 \gamma_2}$, a tracing agent can test whether a ciphertext ψ is prepared for user i as follows. We require each ciphertext ψ to contain elements of the form $(T_1, T_2, T_3) = (g^\delta, \Gamma_1^{\delta/\varrho}, \Gamma_2^\varrho)$, where $\delta, \varrho \in_R \mathbb{Z}_p$ are chosen by the sender. Since $(\Gamma_1, \Gamma_2) = (g^{\gamma_1}, g^{\gamma_2})$, the TRACE algorithm concludes that user i is indeed the receiver if $e(T_1, g^{\gamma_1 \gamma_2}) = e(T_2, T_3)$. At the same time, we can show that recognizing ciphertexts encrypted for user i without trace_i is as hard as solving the D3DH problem.

For technical reasons, we need to introduce an extra traceability component $T_4 = (\Lambda_0^{\mathsf{VK}} \cdot \Lambda_1)^\delta$, where $\Lambda_0, \Lambda_1 \in \mathbb{G}$ are part of common public parameters and

VK is the verification key of a one-time signature. The reason is that, in order to prove anonymity in our model, we need to bind (T_1, T_2, T_3) to the one-time verification key VK in a non-malleable way. Otherwise, an anonymity adversary could break the anonymity by having access to a CLAIM/DISCLAIM oracle.

In order to prove or disprove that he is the intended recipient of a given pair (ψ, L), a user i can use the traceability components $(T_1, T_2, T_3) = (g^\delta, \Gamma_1^{\delta/\varrho}, \Gamma_2^\varrho)$ of ψ and his private key $\gamma_1 = \log_g(\Gamma_1)$ to compute $\Gamma_1^\delta = T_1^{\gamma_1}$ (although he does not know δ), which allows anyone to realize that $(g, T_1, \Gamma_1, \Gamma_1^\delta)$ forms a Diffie-Hellman tuple and that $e(\Gamma_1^\delta, \Gamma_2) = e(T_2, T_3)$. This is sufficient for proving that (ψ, L) was created for the public key $\mathsf{pk} = (X_1, X_2, \Gamma_1, \Gamma_2)$. In order to make sure that only the user will be able to compute non-interactive claims, we also require him to provide a non-interactive proof of knowledge of $\Gamma_{-1} = g^{1/\gamma_1}$ satisfying $e(\Gamma_1^\delta, \Gamma_{-1}) = e(T_1, g)$. Moreover, the claim is non-malleably bound to (ψ, L, pk) – where pk is the claimer's public key —by generating the non-interactive Groth-Sahai proof for a CRS $(\vec{g_1}, \vec{g_2}, \vec{h}_v)$ that depends on the ciphertext which is being claimed and the receiver's public key (the idea of data-dependent CRS is borrowed from [24]): this prevents malicious users from convincingly claiming other users' ciphertexts. To eliminate an annoying case in the proof of anonymity, we chose to derive the vector $\vec{h}_v$ from a bit string obtained by applying a chameleon hash function [21] (rather than a an ordinary hash function) to (ψ, L, pk).

We build a non-interactive group encryption scheme for the Diffie-Hellman relation $\mathcal{R} = \{(X, Y), W\}$ where $e(g, W) = e(X, Y)$, for which the keys are $\mathsf{pk}_\mathcal{R} = \{\mathbb{G}, \mathbb{G}_T, g\}$ and $\mathsf{sk}_\mathcal{R} = \varepsilon$.

$\mathsf{SETUP}_{\mathsf{init}}(\lambda)$: Let $\ell \in \mathsf{poly}(\lambda)$ be a polynomial, where $\lambda \in \mathbb{N}$ is the security parameter.

1. Choose bilinear groups $(\mathbb{G}, \mathbb{G}_T)$ of prime order $p > 2^\lambda$ with $g, g_1, g_2,$ $\Lambda_0, \Lambda_1 \xleftarrow{R} \mathbb{G}$. Construct a perfectly sound Groth-Sahai CRS $\mathbf{g} = (\vec{g_1}, \vec{g_2}, \vec{g_3})$ using $\vec{g_1} = (g_1, 1, g)$, $\vec{g_2} = (1, g_2, g)$ and $\vec{g_3} = \vec{g_1}^{\,\xi_1} \odot \vec{g_2}^{\,\xi_2}$ with $\xi_1, \xi_2 \xleftarrow{R} \mathbb{Z}_p$.
2. For $i = 0$ to ℓ choose $\zeta_{i,1}, \zeta_{i,2} \xleftarrow{R} \mathbb{Z}_p$ and set $\vec{h}_i = \vec{g_1}^{\,\zeta_{i,1}} \odot \vec{g_2}^{\,\zeta_{i,2}}$ so as to obtain vectors $\{\vec{h}_i\}_{i=0}^\ell$.
3. Choose $\eta_1, \eta_2 \xleftarrow{R} \mathbb{Z}_p$ and compute $\vec{f} = \vec{g_1}^{\,\eta_1} \odot \vec{g_2}^{\,\eta_2} = (f_{3,1}, f_{3,2}, f_{3,3})$ so as to form another CRS $\mathbf{f} = (\vec{g_1}, \vec{g_2}, \vec{f})$.
4. Select a strongly unforgeable one time signature $\Sigma = (\mathcal{G}, \mathcal{S}, \mathcal{V})$ and a chameleon hash function $\mathcal{CMH} = (\mathsf{CMKg}, \mathsf{CMhash}, \mathsf{CMswitch})$ with a key pair $(hk, tk) \leftarrow \mathcal{G}(\lambda)$. Public parameters are

$$\mathsf{param} = \{\lambda, \mathbb{G}, \mathbb{G}_T, g, \vec{g_1}, \vec{g_2}, \vec{g_3}, \vec{f}, \{\vec{h}_i\}_{i=0}^\ell, \Lambda_0, \Lambda_1, \Sigma, \mathcal{CMH}, hk\}.$$

$\mathsf{SETUP}_{\mathsf{GM}}(\mathsf{param})$: This algorithm runs the setup algorithm of the structure-preserving signature of Abe $et\ al.$ [1] for messages of length $n = 4$. The secret key is $\mathsf{sk}_{\mathsf{GM}} = (\alpha_a, \alpha_b, \gamma_z, \delta_z, \{\gamma_i, \delta_i\}_{i=1}^4)$ while the public key consists of $\mathsf{pk}_{\mathsf{GM}} = (G_r, H_u, G_z, H_z, \{G_i, H_i\}_{i=1}^4, \Omega_a, \Omega_b) \in \mathbb{G}^8 \times \mathbb{G}_T^2$.

$\mathsf{SETUP}_{\mathsf{OA}}(\mathsf{param})$: generates $\mathsf{pk}_{\mathsf{OA}} = (Y_1, Y_2, Y_3, Y_4) = (g^{y_1}, g^{y_2}, g^{y_3}, g^{y_4})$, as a public key for Kiltz's encryption scheme [20], and the corresponding private key as $\mathsf{sk}_{\mathsf{OA}} = (y_1, y_2, y_3, y_4)$.

JOIN : The prospective user $\mathcal{U}_i$ and the GM run the following protocol.

1. $\mathcal{U}_i$ picks $x_1, x_2, z, \gamma_1, \gamma_2 \overset{R}{\leftarrow} \mathbb{Z}_p$ and computes $\mathsf{pk} = (X_1, X_2, \Gamma_1, \Gamma_2)$, where

$$X_1 = g_1^{x_1} \cdot g^z, \qquad X_2 = g_2^{x_2} \cdot g^z, \qquad \Gamma_1 = g^{\gamma_1}, \qquad \Gamma_2 = g^{\gamma_2} .$$

The private key is defined to be $\mathsf{sk} = (x_1, x_2, z, \gamma_1, \gamma_2)$. Here, (X_1, X_2) form a public key for the LY encryption scheme recalled in [23] whereas (Γ_1, Γ_2) will provide user traceability.

2. $\mathcal{U}_i$ defines $\Gamma_0 = g^{\gamma_1 \gamma_2}$ and generates a verifiable encryption of Γ_0 under $\mathsf{pk}_{\mathsf{OA}}$. To this end, he chooses $w_1, w_2 \overset{R}{\leftarrow} \mathbb{Z}_p$ and computes $\Phi_{venc} = (\Phi_0, \Phi_1, \Phi_2) = (\Gamma_0 \cdot g^{w_1 + w_2}, Y_1^{w_1}, Y_2^{w_2})$. Then, $\mathcal{U}_i$ generates a NIZK proof π_{venc} that Φ_{venc} encrypts Γ_0 such that $e(\Gamma_0, g) = e(\Gamma_1, \Gamma_2)$. Namely, $\mathcal{U}_i$ uses the CRS $\mathbf{f} = (\vec{g_1}, \vec{g_2}, \vec{f})$ to generate GS commitments $\vec{C}_{W_1}, \vec{C}_{W_2}$ to the group elements $W_1 = g^{w_1}$ and $W_2 = g^{w_2}$, respectively, and non-interactively prove that $e(\Phi_0, g) = e(\Gamma_1, \Gamma_2) \cdot e(g, W_1) \cdot e(g, W_2)$ and

$$e(\Phi_1, g) = e(Y_1, W_1) \qquad\qquad e(\Phi_2, g) = e(Y_2, W_2) .$$

These are linear pairing product equations. However, since their proofs must be NIZK proofs, they cost 21 group elements to prove altogether We denote by π_{venc} the resulting NIZK proof. The prospective user $\mathcal{U}_i$ then sends to the group manager a certification request consisting of $\left(\mathsf{pk} = (X_1, X_2, \Gamma_1, \Gamma_2), \Phi_{venc}, \vec{C}_{W_1}, \vec{C}_{W_2}, \pi_{venc}\right)$.

3. If database already contains a record $\mathsf{transcript}_j$ for which the certified public key $\mathsf{pk}_j = (X_{j,1}, X_{j,2}, \Gamma_{j,1}, \Gamma_{j,2})$ is such that $(X_1, X_2) = (X_{j,1}, X_{j,2})$ or $e(\Gamma_{j,1}, \Gamma_{j,2}) = e(\Gamma_1, \Gamma_2)$, the GM returns $\perp$. Otherwise, the GM generates a certificate $\mathsf{cert}_{\mathsf{pk}} = (Z, R, S, T, U, V, W) \in \mathbb{G}^7$ for pk, which consists of an AHO signature on the tuple $(X_1, X_2, \Gamma_1, \Gamma_2)$. Then, it stores the entire interaction transcript

$$\mathsf{transcript}_i = \left(\mathsf{pk} = (X_1, X_2, \Gamma_1, \Gamma_2), (\Phi_{venc}, \vec{C}_{W_1}, \vec{C}_{W_2}, \pi_{venc}), \mathsf{cert}_{\mathsf{pk}}\right)$$

in database. We also define the DATABASE-CHECK algorithm in such a way that it returns 0 (meaning that database is not well-formed) if database contains two distinct records $\mathsf{transcript}_i$ and $\mathsf{transcript}_j$ for which the corresponding public keys $\mathsf{pk}_i = (X_{i,1}, X_{i,2}, \Gamma_{i,1}, \Gamma_{i,2})$ and $\mathsf{pk}_j = (X_{j,1}, X_{j,2}, \Gamma_{j,1}, \Gamma_{j,2})$ are such that $(X_{i,1}, X_{i,2}) = (X_{j,1}, X_{j,2})$ or $e(\Gamma_{i,1}, \Gamma_{i,2}) = e(\Gamma_{j,1}, \Gamma_{j,2})$. Otherwise, it returns 1.

ENC($\mathsf{pk}_{\mathsf{GM}}, \mathsf{pk}_{\mathsf{OA}}, \mathsf{pk}, \mathsf{cert}_{\mathsf{pk}}, M, L$) : To encrypt $M \in \mathbb{G}$ s.t. $((A, B), M) \in \mathcal{R}_{dh}$ (for public $A, B \in \mathbb{G}$), parse $\mathsf{pk}_{\mathsf{GM}}, \mathsf{pk}_{\mathsf{OA}}$ and pk as $(X_1, X_2, \Gamma_1, \Gamma_2) \in \mathbb{G}^4$.

1. Generate a one-time signature key pair $(\mathsf{SK}, \mathsf{VK}) \leftarrow \mathcal{G}(\lambda)$.

2. Generate traceability components $(T_1, T_2, T_3, T_4) \in \mathbb{G}^4$ by choosing $\delta, \varrho \overset{R}{\leftarrow} \mathbb{Z}_p$ and computing $T_1 = g^\delta$, $T_2 = \Gamma_1^{\delta/\varrho}$, $T_3 = \Gamma_2^\varrho$ and $T_4 = (\Lambda_0^{\mathsf{VK}} \cdot \Lambda_1)^\delta$.

3. Compute a LY encryption of M under the label L. Namely,

   (a) Choose $\theta_1, \theta_2 \overset{R}{\leftarrow} \mathbb{Z}_p$ and compute $C_0 = M \cdot X_1^{\theta_1} \cdot X_2^{\theta_2}$, $C_1 = g_1^{\theta_1}$, $C_2 = g_2^{\theta_2}$ and $C_3 = g^{\theta_1 + \theta_2}$.

(b) Construct a vector $\vec{g}_{\mathsf{VK}} = \vec{g_3} \cdot (1, 1, g)^{\mathsf{VK}}$ and use $\mathbf{g}_{\mathsf{VK}} = (\vec{g_1}, \vec{g_2}, \vec{g}_{\mathsf{VK}})$ as a Groth-Sahai CRS to generate a NIZK proof that $(g, g_1, g_2, C_1, C_2, C_3)$ form a linear tuple. More precisely, generate commitments $\vec{C}_{\theta_1}, \vec{C}_{\theta_2}$ to $\theta_1, \theta_2 \in \mathbb{Z}_p$ (namely, compute $\vec{C}_{\theta_i} = \vec{g}_{\mathsf{VK}}^{\theta_i} \cdot \vec{g_1}^{r_i} \cdot \vec{g_2}^{s_i}$ with $r_i, s_i \xleftarrow{R} \mathbb{Z}_p$ for each $i \in \{1, 2\}$) and a proof π_{LIN} that they satisfy

$$C_1 = g_1^{\theta_1}, \qquad C_2 = g_2^{\theta_2}, \qquad C_3 = g^{\theta_1 + \theta_2} . \qquad (1)$$

The whole proof for (1) consists of $\vec{C}_{\theta_1}, \vec{C}_{\theta_2}$ and π_{LIN} is obtained as

$$\pi_{\mathsf{LIN}} = (\pi_1, \pi_2, \pi_3, \pi_4, \pi_5, \pi_6) = \left(g_1^{r_1}, g_1^{s_1}, g_2^{r_2}, g_2^{s_2}, g^{r_1 + r_2}, g^{s_1 + s_2} \right) .$$

(c) Define the partial LY ciphertext $\psi_{\mathsf{LY}} = (C_0, C_1, C_2, C_3, \vec{C}_{\theta_1}, \vec{C}_{\theta_2}, \pi_{\mathsf{LIN}})$.

4. For $i = 1, 2$, choose $z_{i,1}, z_{i,2} \xleftarrow{R} \mathbb{Z}_p$ and encrypt Γ_i under $\mathsf{pk}_{\mathsf{OA}}$ using Kiltz's cryptosystem using the same one-time verification key VK as in step 1. Let $\{\psi_{\mathsf{K}_i}\}_{i=1,2}$ be the ciphertexts.

5. Set the TGE ciphertext ψ as $\psi = \mathsf{VK} \| (T_1, T_2, T_3, T_4) \| \psi_{\mathsf{LY}} \| \psi_{\mathsf{K}_1} \| \psi_{\mathsf{K}_2} \| \sigma$ where $\sigma = \mathcal{S}(\mathsf{SK}, ((T_1, T_2, T_3, T_4) \| \psi_{\mathsf{LY}} \| \psi_{\mathsf{K}_1} \| \psi_{\mathsf{K}_2} \| L))$.

Return (ψ, L) and $coins_\psi$ consist of $\delta, \varrho, \{(z_{i,1}, z_{i,2})\}_{i=1}^2$ and (θ_1, θ_2). If the one-time signature of [14] is used, the pair (VK, σ) takes 5 group elements, so that ψ comprises 35 elements of $\mathbb{G}$.

$\mathcal{P}(\mathsf{pk}_{\mathsf{GM}}, \mathsf{pk}_{\mathsf{OA}}, \mathsf{pk}, \mathsf{cert}_{\mathsf{pk}}, (X, Y), M, \psi, L, coins_\psi)$: Parse $\mathsf{pk}_{\mathsf{GM}}, \mathsf{pk}_{\mathsf{OA}}, \mathsf{pk}$ and ψ as above. Using the vectors $\mathbf{f} = (\vec{g_1}, \vec{g_2}, \vec{f})$ as a Groth-Sahai CRS, generate a non-interactive proof for ψ.

1. Parse $\mathsf{cert}_{\mathsf{pk}}$ as $(Z, R, S, T, U, V, W) \in \mathbb{G}^7$ and re-randomize it to obtain $(Z', R', S', T', U', V') \leftarrow \mathsf{ReRand}(\mathsf{pk}_{\mathsf{GM}}, (Z, R, S, T, U, V, W))$ (as explained in [1]). Generate GS commitments $\vec{C}_{Z'}, \vec{C}_{R'}, \vec{C}_{U'}$ to Z', R' and U'. Then, set $com_{\mathsf{cert}_{\mathsf{pk}}} = (\vec{C}_{Z'}, \vec{C}_{R'}, \vec{C}_{U'}, S', T', V', W') \in \mathbb{G}^{13}$.

2. Generate Groth-Sahai commitments to the components of the public key $\mathsf{pk} = (X_1, X_2, \Gamma_1, \Gamma_2)$ and obtain the set $com_{\mathsf{pk}} = \{\vec{C}_{X_i}, \vec{C}_{\Gamma_i}\}_{i=1,2}$, which consists of 12 group elements.

3. Generate a proof $\pi_{\mathsf{cert}_{\mathsf{pk}}}$ that $com_{\mathsf{cert}_{\mathsf{pk}}}$ is a commitment to a valid certificate for the public key contained in com_{pk}. The proof $\pi_{\mathsf{cert}_{\mathsf{pk}}}$ is a NIWI that (Z', R', S', T', U', V') is a valid AHO signature on pk.

4. Generate a NIZK proof π_T that $(T_1, T_2, T_3) = (g^\delta, \Gamma_1^{\delta/\varrho}, \Gamma_2^\varrho)$ for some $\delta, \varrho \in \mathbb{Z}_p$. To this end, generate a commitment $\vec{C}_\Upsilon$ to the group element $\Upsilon = g^{\delta/\varrho}$ and generate a NIZK proof that

$$e(\Upsilon, T_3) = e(T_1, \Gamma_2), \qquad e(T_2, g) = e(\Gamma_1, \Upsilon) .$$

5. For $i = 1, 2$, generate NIZK proofs $\pi_{eq\text{-}key,i}$ that $\vec{C}_{\Gamma_i}$ and ψ_{K_i} are encryptions of the same Γ_i. If $\psi_{\mathsf{K}_i} = (V_{i,0}, V_{i,1}, V_{i,2}, V_{i,3}, V_{i,4})$ is a Kiltz encryption comprising $(V_{i,0}, V_{i,1}, V_{i,2}) = (\Gamma_i \cdot g^{z_{i,1} + z_{i,2}}, Y_1^{z_{i,1}}, Y_2^{z_{i,2}})$ and $\vec{C}_{\Gamma_i}$ is parsed as $(c_{\Gamma_{i1}}, c_{\Gamma_{i2}}, c_{\Gamma_{i3}}) = (g_1^{\rho_{i1}} \cdot f_{3,1}^{\rho_{i3}}, g_2^{\rho_{i2}} \cdot f_{3,2}^{\rho_{i3}}, \Gamma_i \cdot g^{\rho_{i1} + \rho_{i2}} \cdot f_{3,3}^{\rho_{i3}})$, where $z_{i,1}, z_{i,2} \in coins_\psi$, $\rho_{i1}, \rho_{i2}, \rho_{i3} \in \mathbb{Z}_p$ and $\vec{f} = (f_{3,1}, f_{3,2}, f_{3,3})$, this

amounts to prove knowledge of values $z_{i,1}, z_{i,2}, \rho_{i1}, \rho_{i2}, \rho_{i3} \in \mathbb{Z}_p$ such that $\left(\frac{V_{i,1}}{c_{\Gamma_{i1}}}, \frac{V_{i,2}}{c_{\Gamma_{i2}}}, \frac{V_{i,0}}{c_{\Gamma_{i3}}} \right)$ is of the form

$$\left(Y_1^{z_{i,1}} \cdot g_1^{-\rho_{i1}} \cdot f_{3,1}^{-\rho_{i3}}, Y_2^{z_{i,2}} \cdot g_2^{-\rho_{i2}} \cdot f_{3,2}^{-\rho_{i3}}, g^{z_{i,1}+z_{i,2}-\rho_{i1}-\rho_{i2}} \cdot f_{3,3}^{-\rho_{i3}} \right) .$$

6. Generate a NIZK proof $\pi_{\mathcal{R}}$ that ψ_{LY} encrypts a group element $M \in \mathbb{G}$ such that $((A, B), M) \in \mathcal{R}$. To this end, generate a commitment $com_M = (c_{M,1}, c_{M,2}, c_{M,3}) = (g_1^{\rho_1} \cdot f_{3,1}^{\rho_3}, g_2^{\rho_2} \cdot f_{3,2}^{\rho_3}, M \cdot g^{\rho_1+\rho_2} \cdot f_{3,3}^{\rho_3})$ and prove that the underlying M is the same as the one for which $C_0 = M \cdot X_1^{\theta_1} \cdot X_2^{\theta_2}$ in ψ_{LY}. In other words, prove knowledge of $\theta_1, \theta_2, \rho_1, \rho_2, \rho_3$ such that $\left(C_1, C_2, \frac{C_1}{c_{M,1}}, \frac{C_2}{c_{M,2}}, \frac{C_0}{c_{M,3}} \right)$ equals

$$\left(g_1^{\theta}, g_2^{\theta}, g_1^{\theta_1-\rho_1} \cdot f_{3,1}^{-\rho_3}, g_2^{\theta_2-\rho_2} \cdot f_{3,2}^{-\rho_3}, g^{-\rho_1-\rho_2} \cdot f_{3,3}^{-\rho_3} \cdot X_1^{\theta_1} \cdot X_2^{\theta_2} \right) .$$

The entire proof $\pi_\psi = com_{\mathsf{cert_{pk}}} \| com_{\mathsf{pk}} \| \pi_{\mathsf{cert_{pk}}} \| \pi_T \| \pi_{eq\text{-}key,1} \| \pi_{eq\text{-}key,2} \| \pi_{\mathcal{R}}$ takes 150 elements.

$\mathcal{V}(\mathsf{param}, \psi, L, \pi_\psi, \mathsf{pk_{GM}}, \mathsf{pk_{OA}})$: Parse $\mathsf{pk_{GM}}$, $\mathsf{pk_{OA}}$, pk, ψ and π_ψ as above. Return 1 if and only if the conditions below are all satisfied.

1. $\mathcal{V}(\mathsf{VK}, \sigma, ((T_1, T_2, T_3, T_4) \| \psi_{\mathsf{LY}} \| \psi_{\mathsf{K}_1} \| \psi_{\mathsf{K}_2} \| L)) = 1$.
2. $e(T_1, \Lambda_0^{\mathsf{VK}} \cdot \Lambda_1) = e(g, T_4)$ and ψ_{LY} is a valid LY ciphertext.
3. All proofs verify and if $\{\psi_{\mathsf{K}_i}\}_{i=1}^{2}$ are valid Kiltz encryptions w.r.t. VK.

$\mathsf{DEC}(\mathsf{sk}, \psi, L)$: Parse ψ as $\mathsf{VK} \| (T_1, T_2, T_3, T_4) \| \psi_{\mathsf{LY}} \| \psi_{\mathsf{K}_1} \| \psi_{\mathsf{K}_2} \| \sigma$. Return $\bot$ in the event that either: (i) $\mathcal{V}(\mathsf{VK}, \sigma, ((T_1, T_2, T_3, T_4) \| \psi_{\mathsf{LY}} \| \psi_{\mathsf{K}_1} \| \psi_{\mathsf{K}_2} \| L)) = 0$; (ii) $e(T_1, \Lambda_0^{\mathsf{VK}} \cdot \Lambda_1) \neq e(g, T_4)$ or ψ_{LY} and $\{\psi_{\mathsf{K}_i}\}_{i=1,2}$ are not all valid ciphertexts. Otherwise, use sk to decrypt (ψ_{LY}, L).

$\mathsf{REVEAL}(\mathsf{transcript}_i, \mathsf{sk_{OA}})$: Parse $\mathsf{transcript}_i$ as

$$\left((X_{i,1}, X_{i,2}, \Gamma_{i,1}, \Gamma_{i,2}), (\Phi_{venc,i}, \vec{C}_{W_{i,1}}, \vec{C}_{W_{i,2}}, \pi_{venc,i}), \mathsf{cert}_{\mathsf{pk},i} \right) .$$

Parse $\Phi_{venc,i}$ as a BBS ciphertext $(\Phi_{i,0}, \Phi_{i,1}, \Phi_{i,2}) \in \mathbb{G}^3$ and verify that $(\vec{C}_{W_{i,1}}, \vec{C}_{W_{i,2}}, \pi_{venc,i})$ form a valid proof fo. If not, return $\bot$. Otherwise, use $\mathsf{sk_{OA}} = (y_1, y_2, y_3, y_4)$ to compute $\Gamma_{i,0} = \Phi_{i,0} \cdot \Phi_{i,1}^{-1/y_1} \cdot \Phi_{i,2}^{-1/y_2}$. Return the resulting plaintext $\mathsf{trace}_i = \Gamma_{i,0} \in \mathbb{G}$ which can serve as a tracing trapdoor for user i as it is necessarily of the form $\Gamma_{i,0} = \Gamma_{i,2}^{\log_g(\Gamma_{i,1})}$.

$\mathsf{TRACE}(\mathsf{pk_{GM}}, \mathsf{pk_{OA}}, \psi, \mathsf{trace}_i)$: Given $\psi = \mathsf{VK} \| (T_1, T_2, T_3, T_4) \| \psi_{\mathsf{LY}} \| \psi_{\mathsf{K}_1} \| \psi_{\mathsf{K}_2} \| \sigma$ and the tracing trapdoor trace_i as a group element $\Gamma_{i,0} \in \mathbb{G}$. If the equality $e(T_1, \Gamma_{i,0}) = e(T_2, T_3)$ holds, it returns 1. Otherwise, it outputs 0.

$\mathsf{OPEN}(\mathsf{sk_{OA}}, \psi, L)$: Parse ψ as $\mathsf{VK} \| (T_1, T_2, T_3, T_4) \| \psi_{\mathsf{LY}} \| \psi_{\mathsf{K}_1} \| \psi_{\mathsf{K}_2} \| \sigma$. Return $\bot$ if $\{\psi_{\mathsf{K}_i}\}_{i=1}^{2}$ are not both valid ciphertexts w.r.t. VK or if σ is an invalid one time signature for VK. Otherwise, decrypt $\{\psi_{\mathsf{K}_i}\}_{i=1,2}$ to obtain $\Gamma_1, \Gamma_2 \in \mathbb{G}$ and look up $\mathsf{database}$ in order to find a record $\mathsf{transcript}_i$ containing a key $\mathsf{pk}_i = (X_{i,1}, X_{i,2}, \Gamma_{i,1}, \Gamma_{i,2})$ such that $(\Gamma_{i,1}, \Gamma_{i,2}) = (\Gamma_1, \Gamma_2)$ (note that, unless $\mathsf{database}$ is ill-formed, such a record is unique if it exists). If such a record is found, output the matching i. Otherwise, output $\bot$.

CLAIM/DISCLAIM($\mathsf{pk_{GM}}, \mathsf{pk_{OA}}, \psi, L, \mathsf{sk}$) : Given $\mathsf{sk} = (x_1, x_2, z, \gamma_1, \gamma_2)$, parse ψ as $\mathsf{VK} \| (T_1, T_2, T_3, T_4) \| \psi_{\mathsf{LY}} \| \psi_{\mathsf{K}_1} \| \psi_{\mathsf{K}_2} \| \sigma$. To generate a claim/disclaimer τ for the ciphertext ψ, first verify that $e(T_1, \Lambda_0^{\mathsf{VK}} \cdot \Lambda_1) = e(g, T_4)$ and that σ is a valid one-time signature. If these conditions, do not hold, return $\perp$. Otherwise, compute $T_{\delta,1} = T_1^{\gamma_1} = \Gamma_1^{\delta}$, where $\delta = \log_g(T_1)$. Then, compute a collision-resistant hash $\mathsf{v} = \mathsf{CMhash}(hk, (\psi, L, \mathsf{pk}), s_{hash}) \in \{0,1\}^{\ell}$, where $s_{hash} \xleftarrow{R} \mathcal{R}_{hash}$. Then, parse v as $\mathsf{v}[1] \dots \mathsf{v}[\ell] \in \{0,1\}^{\ell}$ and assemble the vector $\vec{h}_{\mathsf{v}} = \vec{h}_0 \odot \bigodot_{i=1}^{\ell} \vec{h}_i^{\mathsf{v}[i]}$. Using $(\vec{g_1}, \vec{g_2}, \vec{h}_{\mathsf{v}})$ as a Groth-Sahai CRS, generate a commitment $\vec{C}_{\Gamma_{-1}}$ to $\Gamma_{-1} = g^{1/\gamma_1}$ and a NIZK proof that Γ_{-1} satisfies $e(T_{\delta,1}, \Gamma_{-1}) = e(T_1, g)$. To this end, generate a commitment $\vec{C}_{\mathcal{X}_{\tau}}$ to the auxiliary variable $\mathcal{X}_{\tau} = g$ and non-interactive proofs $\pi_{\tau,1}, \pi_{\tau,2}$ for the equations

$$e(T_{\delta,1}, \Gamma_{-1}) = e(T_1, \mathcal{X}_{\tau}), \qquad e(g, \mathcal{X}_{\tau}) = e(g, g) . \qquad (2)$$

The claim/disclaimer is $\tau = (T_{\delta,1}, \vec{C}_{\Gamma_{-1}}, \vec{C}_{\mathcal{X}_{\tau}}, \pi_{\tau,1}, \pi_{\tau,2}, s_{hash}) \in \mathbb{G}^{14}$.

CLAIM-VERIFY($\mathsf{pk_{GM}}, \mathsf{pk_{OA}}, \psi, L, \mathsf{pk}, \tau$): Given $\mathsf{pk} = (X_1, X_2, \Gamma_1, \Gamma_2)$ and the ciphertext $\psi = \mathsf{VK} \| (T_1, T_2, T_3, T_4) \| \psi_{\mathsf{LY}} \| \psi_{\mathsf{K}_1} \| \psi_{\mathsf{K}_2} \| \sigma$, parse τ as above. Return 1 if and only if $e(T_{\delta,1}, \Gamma_2) = e(T_2, T_3)$ and $e(T_1, \Gamma_1) = e(g, T_{\delta,1})$ and $\pi_{\tau,1}, \pi_{\tau,2}$ are valid proofs for (2) w.r.t. the Groth-Sahai CRS $(\vec{g_1}, \vec{g_2}, \vec{h}_{\mathsf{v}})$, where $\vec{h}_{\mathsf{v}} = \vec{h}_0 \odot \bigodot_{i=1}^{\ell} \vec{h}_i^{\mathsf{v}[i]}$ and $\mathsf{v} = \mathsf{CMhash}(hk, (\psi, L, \mathsf{pk}), s_{hash}) \in \{0,1\}^{\ell}$.

DISCLAIM-VERIFY($\mathsf{pk_{GM}}, \mathsf{pk_{OA}}, \psi, L, \mathsf{pk}, \tau$) : Parse pk, ψ and τ as previously. Return 1 if and only if $e(T_{\delta,1}, \Gamma_2) \neq e(T_2, T_3)$, $e(T_1, \Gamma_1) = e(g, T_{\delta,1})$ and $\pi_{\tau,1}, \pi_{\tau,2}$ are valid proofs for (2) and the Groth-Sahai CRS $(\vec{g_1}, \vec{g_2}, \vec{h}_{\mathsf{v}})$, where $\vec{h}_{\mathsf{v}} = \vec{h}_0 \odot \bigodot_{i=1}^{\ell} \vec{h}_i^{\mathsf{v}[i]}$ and $\mathsf{v} = \mathsf{CMhash}(hk, (\psi, L, \mathsf{pk}), s_{hash}) \in \{0,1\}^{\ell}$.

The length of ciphertexts is about 2.18 kB using symmetric pairings with a 512-bit representation for each group element (at the 128-bit security level). Our proofs only require 9.38 kB (against roughly 32 kB for the same security in [9]). More detailed comparisons with [19,9] are given in the full version of the paper.

The correctness of the scheme stems from that of Groth-Sahai proofs. From a security point of view, we prove the security properties under the q-SFP, D3DH and DLIN assumptions and also require the one-time signatures to be strongly unforgeable. All proofs are given in the full version of the paper.

References

1. Abe, M., Haralambiev, K., Ohkubo, M.: Signing on elements in bilinear groups for modular protocol design. Cryptology ePrint Archive: Report 2010/133 (2010)
2. Abe, M., Fuchsbauer, G., Groth, J., Haralambiev, K., Ohkubo, M.: Structure-preserving signatures and commitments to group elements. In: Rabin, T. (ed.) CRYPTO 2010. LNCS, vol. 6223, pp. 209–236. Springer, Heidelberg (2010)
3. Bellare, M., Boldyreva, A., Desai, A., Pointcheval, D.: Key-privacy in public-key encryption. In: Boyd, C. (ed.) ASIACRYPT 2001. LNCS, vol. 2248, pp. 566–582. Springer, Heidelberg (2001)

4. Bellare, M., Rogaway, P.: Random oracles are practical: A paradigm for designing efficient protocols. In: ACM CCS 1993 (1993)
5. Benjumea, V., Choi, S.G., Lopez, J., Yung, M.: Fair traceable multi-group signatures. In: Tsudik, G. (ed.) FC 2008. LNCS, vol. 5143, pp. 231–246. Springer, Heidelberg (2008)
6. Boneh, D., Boyen, X., Shacham, H.: Short group signatures. In: Franklin, M. (ed.) CRYPTO 2004. LNCS, vol. 3152, pp. 41–55. Springer, Heidelberg (2004)
7. Boneh, D., Franklin, M.: Identity based encryption from the Weil pairing. SIAM J. of Computing 32(3), 586–615 (2003), Kilian, J. (ed.) CRYPTO 2001. LNCS, vol. 2139, pp. 213–615. Springer, Heidelberg (2001)
8. Camenisch, J.L., Lysyanskaya, A.: A signature scheme with efficient protocols. In: Cimato, S., Galdi, C., Persiano, G. (eds.) SCN 2002. LNCS, vol. 2576, pp. 268–289. Springer, Heidelberg (2003)
9. Cathalo, J., Libert, B., Yung, M.: Group encryption: Non-interactive realization in the standard model. In: Matsui, M. (ed.) ASIACRYPT 2009. LNCS, vol. 5912, pp. 179–196. Springer, Heidelberg (2009)
10. Chaum, D., van Heyst, E.: Group signatures. In: Davies, D.W. (ed.) EUROCRYPT 1991. LNCS, vol. 547, pp. 257–265. Springer, Heidelberg (1991)
11. Cramer, R., Shoup, V.: A practical public key cryptosystem provably secure against adaptive chosen ciphertext attack. In: Krawczyk, H. (ed.) CRYPTO 1998. LNCS, vol. 1462, pp. 13–25. Springer, Heidelberg (1998)
12. El Aimani, L., Joye, M.: Toward practical group encryption. In: Jacobson, M., Locasto, M., Mohassel, P., Safavi-Naini, R. (eds.) ACNS 2013. LNCS, vol. 7954, pp. 237–252. Springer, Heidelberg (2013)
13. Fiat, A., Shamir, A.: How to prove yourself: Practical solutions to identification and signature problems. In: Odlyzko, A.M. (ed.) CRYPTO 1986. LNCS, vol. 263, pp. 186–194. Springer, Heidelberg (1987)
14. Groth, J.: Simulation-sound NIZK proofs for a practical language and constant size group signatures. In: Lai, X., Chen, K. (eds.) ASIACRYPT 2006. LNCS, vol. 4284, pp. 444–459. Springer, Heidelberg (2006)
15. Groth, J.: Fully anonymous group signatures without random oracles. In: Kurosawa, K. (ed.) ASIACRYPT 2007. LNCS, vol. 4833, pp. 164–180. Springer, Heidelberg (2007)
16. Groth, J., Sahai, A.: Efficient non-interactive proof systems for bilinear groups. In: Smart, N.P. (ed.) EUROCRYPT 2008. LNCS, vol. 4965, pp. 415–432. Springer, Heidelberg (2008)
17. Izabachène, M., Pointcheval, D., Vergnaud, D.: Mediated traceable anonymous encryption. In: Abdalla, M., Barreto, P.S.L.M. (eds.) LATINCRYPT 2010. LNCS, vol. 6212, pp. 40–60. Springer, Heidelberg (2010)
18. Kiayias, A., Tsiounis, Y., Yung, M.: Traceable signatures. In: Cachin, C., Camenisch, J.L. (eds.) EUROCRYPT 2004. LNCS, vol. 3027, pp. 571–589. Springer, Heidelberg (2004)
19. Kiayias, A., Tsiounis, Y., Yung, M.: Group encryption. In: Kurosawa, K. (ed.) ASIACRYPT 2007. LNCS, vol. 4833, pp. 181–199. Springer, Heidelberg (2007)
20. Kiltz, E.: Chosen-ciphertext security from tag-based encryption. In: Halovi, S., Rabin, T. (eds.) TCC 2006. LNCS, vol. 3876, pp. 581–600. Springer, Heidelberg (2006)
21. Krawczyk, H., Rabin, T.: Chameleon signatures. In: NDSS 2000 (2000)
22. Libert, B., Yung, M.: Efficient Traceable Signatures in the Standard Model. In: Shacham, H., Waters, B. (eds.) Pairing 2009. LNCS, vol. 5671, pp. 187–205. Springer, Heidelberg (2009)

23. Libert, B., Yung, M.: Non-interactive CCA-secure threshold cryptosystems with adaptive security: New framework and constructions. In: Cramer, R. (ed.) TCC 2012. LNCS, vol. 7194, pp. 75–93. Springer, Heidelberg (2012)
24. Malkin, T., Teranishi, I., Vahlis, Y., Yung, M.: Signatures resilient to continual leakage on memory and computation. In: Ishai, Y. (ed.) TCC 2011. LNCS, vol. 6597, pp. 89–106. Springer, Heidelberg (2011)
25. Paillier, P.: Public-key cryptosystems based on composite degree residuosity classes. In: Stern, J. (ed.) EUROCRYPT 1999. LNCS, vol. 1592, pp. 223–238. Springer, Heidelberg (1999)
26. Qin, B., Wu, Q., Susilo, W., Mu, Y.: Publicly verifiable privacy-preserving group decryption. In: Yung, M., Liu, P., Lin, D. (eds.) Inscrypt 2008. LNCS, vol. 5487, pp. 72–83. Springer, Heidelberg (2009)
27. Trolin, M., Wikström, D.: Hierarchical group signatures. In: Caires, L., Italiano, G.F., Monteiro, L., Palamidessi, C., Yung, M. (eds.) ICALP 2005. LNCS, vol. 3580, pp. 446–458. Springer, Heidelberg (2005)

Practical Covert Authentication

Stanislaw Jarecki

University of California Irvine
stasio@ics.uci.edu

Abstract. Von Ahn, Hopper, and Langford [vAHL05] introduced the
notion of two-party *steganographic* a.k.a. *covert* computation, which as-
sures that neither party can distinguish its counterparty from a random
noise generator, except for what is revealed by the final output of the
securely computed function. The flagship motivation for covert computation is *covert authentication*, where two parties want to authenticate
each other, e.g. as some credential holders, but a party who lacks the
credentials is not only unable to pass the authentication protocol, but
cannot even distinguish a protocol instance from random noise.

Previous work on covert computation [vAHL05,CGOS07] showed
general-purpose protocols whose efficiency is linear in the size of the circuit representation of the computed function. Here we show the first practical (assuming a large-enough random steganographic channel) covert
protocol for the specific task of two-party mutual authentication, secure under the strong RSA, DQR, and DDH assumptions. The protocol
takes 5 rounds (3 in ROM), $O(1)$ modular exponentiations, and supports
revocation and identity escrow. The main technical contribution which
enables it is a compiler from a special honest-verifier zero-knowledge
proof to a *covert conditional key encapsulation mechanism* for the same
language.

1 Introduction

Steganography addresses a security/privacy property which is not usually considered in cryptography, which is how to make the very fact of secure protocol
execution hidden from the adversary. Such hiding of a protocol instance is in
principle possible if the public channels connecting the communicating parties
are *steganographic* in the sense that they have some intrinsic entropy. A protocol
is steganographic, or *covert*, if its messages can be efficiently injected into such
channels in a way that the resulting communication cannot be distinguished from
the (assumed) a priori random behavior of these channels. A simple example of
a steganographic channel is a *random channel*, which can be implemented e.g.
using protocol nonces, random padding bits, lower bits of time stamps, and various other standard communication mechanisms which exhibit inherent entropy.
Assuming such random channels between two parties $A \to B$ and $B \to A$, party
A would encode its protocol messages as bitstrings which are indistinguishable
from random, inject its out-going messages into the $A \to B$ channel, and interpret the messages on the $B \to A$ channel as B's responses in the protocol.

H. Krawczyk (Ed.): PKC 2014, LNCS 8383, pp. 611–629, 2014.

A and B must synchronize the timing of using these channels, so they know which bits to interpret as protocol messages, but this can be public information: The covertness of the protocol implies that the messages which A and B exchange cannot be distinguished from the a priori behavior of these channels.

Covert computation was formalized for two parties in [vAHL05] and in the multi-party setting in [CGOS07] as a protocol that lets the participants securely compute the desired functionality on their inputs, with the additional property that no party can distinguish the other participants from "random beacons" which send random bitstrings of fixed length instead of proscribed protocol messages, except for what is revealed by the final output of the computed function. Both [vAHL05] and [CGOS07] show protocols for covert computation of any functionality which tolerate malicious adversaries, resp. in the two-party and the multi-party setting, but the costs of these protocols are linear in the size of the circuit representation of the computed function. Moreover, these protocols are not constant-round, and the subsequent work of [GJ10] showed that this is a fundamental limitation on maliciously-secure covert computation in the standard model, i.e. without access to trusted parameters or public keys. Still, this begs the question whether useful two-party (or multi-party) tasks can be accomplished covertly in a more practical way, with constant-round protocols and constant number of public-key operations, in applications where common trusted parameters and/or public keys are naturally available.

Indeed, the flagship motivation for covert computation, including [vAHL05] and [CGOS07], was *covert authentication*, where two parties want to authenticate each other, e.g. as holders of mutually accepted certificates, but a party who lacks proper certificate is not only unable to pass in the authentication protocol, but cannot even distinguish an instance of such protocol from a random beacon. In this work we show the first practical covert Mutual Authentication (MA) protocol for the setting where mutually accepted certificates are defined as group membership certificates issued by the same group manager. A very similar mutual authentication setting was considered by "Secret Handshakes" a.k.a. *Private Mutual Authentication*, see e.g. [JL09], but the goal of *private* authentication is to protect the privacy of all authentication protocol inputs, including the group public key assumed by each party in the protocol, while *covert* authentication goes a step further, and aims to hide the very fact that the authentication protocol takes place.

Our covert MA protocol relies on a covert *Conditional Key Encapsulation Mechanism* (CKEM), a covert variant of Conditional Oblivious Transfer [COR99] and a variant of the *ZKSend* gadget used in [CGOS07]. A covert CKEM is a steganographic form of a zero-knowledge proof: It establishes a shared key between the prover and the verifier if and only if it is run on a true statement. Unlike a zero-knowledge proof which involves an explicit verification which distinguishes the prover from a random beacon, a CKEM instance could appear indistinguishable from a random noise to either participant. We show an efficient compiler which converts a special Σ-protocol, i.e. a public-coin HVZK proof of knowledge with certain (commonly satisfied) additional properties, into a covert

CKEM for the same language. A key property of this compiler is that it constructs a CKEM with a proof-of-knowledge property, which ensures extraction of a witness for a verifier's statement given a prover who distinguishes the verifier from a random beacon. Witness-extraction makes covert CKEM's more useful as protocol building blocks, as we exemplify in our covert MA construction below.

Our covert MA scheme requires a group signature scheme which works by committing to a group membership certificate and then proving in ZK that the committed certificate is valid under the group public key. If the commitment is covert and the ZK proof is replaced with a covert CKEM for the same language, the result is a covert MA scheme. Crucially, if the CKEM enables extraction of a witness given an adversary who breaks protocol covertness, then a security reduction can extract a new membership certificate (and thus break the unforgeability of the underlying group signature scheme) given an adversary who distinguishes an MA counterparty from a random beacon.

Note that covert CKEM's without the proof-of-knowledge property, for relations involving discrete logarithm equalities, can be implemented using a Smooth Projective Hash Function (SPHF) [CS01], if the verifier sends to the prover the projection key, which is usually a tuple of random group elements, and so it can be encoded as a random bitstring. What makes our covert CKEM construction interesting is its proof-of-knowledge property, which is achieved as follows: On statement x, the prover covertly commits to its first message a as C, sends response z to the verifier's challenge c, and then the two parties run an SPHF on the statement that the prover's presumed first message a, which can be computed from (x, c, z), is indeed committed in C. Simulation follows from the covertness of the commitment, and extraction follows by the standard rewinding technique from the binding property of the commitment. The "special" property of the Σ-protocol required by our CKEM construction is that a can be efficiently computed given (x, c, z), and that z is an integer tuple distributed statistically close to uniform over some integer ranges (and thus can be encoded as a random bitstring), which is commonly the case in Σ-protocols for various arithmetic relations on discrete logarithm and representations.

Organization. Section 2 introduces basic concepts and tools related to covert computation. In Section 3 we define a covert CKEM and a covert MA scheme. In Section 4 we construct a covert CKEM for any language which admits a special Σ-protocol. In Section 5 we construct a covert MA scheme from (an interactive version of) a group signature and a covert CKEM for a related language. In Section 5.1 we instantiate this construction with the group signature of [ACJT00].

2   Preliminaries

Covertness. The paradigm of covert computation used in [vAHL05,CGOS07], as well as in the work on steganographic key exchange of [vAH04], assumes that the participants in a covert protocol are connected by a channel with sufficient entropy, henceforth called a *steganographic* channel, and that the participants communicate by using a steganographic algorithm, e.g. [HLvA02], to embed protocol messages into this steganographic channel. As was shown by Ahn et al. [vAHL05], if a protocol is covert for a *random channel*, i.e. if its messages are indistinguishable from random bitstrings of some fixed length, then applying a steganographic encoding to each protocol message makes the protocol covert for the corresponding steganographic channel. Consequently we can limit our goal to creating protocols whose messages are indistinguishable from random bitstrings. Moreover, many steganographic channels are already uniform over fixed-length bitstrings, e.g. a channel provided by random nonces in TCP/IP control packets, in which case the steganographic encoding consists of simple splitting of protocol messages into segments of length dictated by this channel. We use the following notation to capture indistinguishability of a protocol participant from a random beacon, i.e. a source that broadcasts random bitstrings of fixed length. Let A be an interactive algorithm which engages in a fixed number k of protocol rounds in each protocol instance, and where for each $i = 1, .., k$, A's i-th message is a bitstring of length $u_i(\tau)$, where u_i is a polynomial and τ is a security parameter. Let $u = (u_1, ..., u_k)$. We denote by $A^{\$(u)}$ an interactive protocol which takes k rounds s.t. its i-th outgoing message is a random bitstring of length $u_i(\tau)$.

Covert Encodings. Our goal is to create efficient protocols whose messages are indistinguishable from random bitstrings of fixed length. We will accomplish this by designing protocols which communicate values which are indistinguishable from either random group elements or random integers on integer intervals, and then encoding these as fixed-length bitstrings using randomized encodings. Let $|R|$ denote the bit-length of R, and let $[R]$ and $\pm[R]$ denote sets $\{0, \ldots, R-1\}$ and $\{-R+1, \ldots, R-1\}$, respectively. Encoding $\mathsf{EC}_{[R]}$ maps $v \in [R]$ to an $(|R| + \tau)$-bit string by outputting $\bar{v} = v + Rk$ (over integers) for random k in $\{0, \ldots, \lfloor 2^{|R|+\tau}/R \rfloor\}$. Decoding $\mathsf{DC}_{|R|}(\bar{v})$ outputs $v = \bar{v} \bmod R$. Encoding $\mathsf{EC}_{\pm[R]}$ maps $v \in \pm[R]$ to an $(|2R-1|+\tau)$-bit string by outputting $\mathsf{EC}_{[2R-1]}(v+(R-1))$, while $\mathsf{DC}_{\pm[R]}$ reverses this process. Finally, if $I = I_1 \times \ldots \times I_t$ is a cross-product of integer intervals then EC_I maps I into bitstrings of length $|I_1|+\ldots+|I_t|+t\cdot\tau$ by outputting $\bar{v} = (\mathsf{EC}_{I_1}(v_1), \ldots, \mathsf{EC}_{I_t}(v_t))$ on input $v = (v_1, \ldots, v_t)$, while DC_I reverses this process. All these encodings are covert on their respective message spaces in the following sense: $(\mathsf{EC}_S, \mathsf{DC}_S)$ is a *covert encoding* on space S if the distribution $\{\mathsf{EC}_S(v)\}_{v \leftarrow S}$ is statistically close to uniform over $\{0,1\}^t$ for some t.

3   Covert KEM and Authentication Definitions

Covert Conditional KEM. Conditional OT (COT) for an NP relation $\mathcal{R}$ (and an associated language $\mathcal{L}^{\mathcal{R}}$), introduced by Di Crescenzo et al. [COR99], is a pair of algorithms for sender S and receiver R, where S runs on a message m and a statement x and R runs on a witness w, s.t. the receiver learns m if $(x, w) \in \mathcal{R}$, while the sender learns nothing from the protocol. COT sender's *privacy* requires that the receiver learns nothing about *both m and x* unless $(x, w) \in \mathcal{R}$ [COR99,Cre00]. Since COT can be thought of as an interactive encryption, we introduce a KEM-like version of this notion, a *Conditional Key Encapsulation*

Mechanism (CKEM). We define CKEM in a *public parameter model*, as a tuple (PG, S, R) where S and R are interactive algorithms running on respective inputs (π, x_S) and (π, x_R, w), for $\pi \leftarrow$ PG(1^τ). Both S and R output τ-bit keys, respectively K and K', s.t. key K generated by S is a random bitstring, while K' output by R is equal to K if $((\pi, x_S), w) \in \mathcal{R}$ (and $x_R = x_S$), and independent from K if $((\pi, x_S), w) \notin \mathcal{R}$. Note that CKEM implies COT if S encrypts its message m under key K. Jarecki and Liu [JL09] introduced *strong* sender security for COT, where an efficient extractor can extract w s.t. $(x_S, w) \in \mathcal{R}$ from an adversary which breaks sender's security. We adapt this notion because witness-extraction makes CKEM into a more useful protocol building block. Indeed, our mutual authentication scheme of Section 5 relies on strong sender covertness of CKEM to enable the reduction to extract a valid certificate (and thus forge a certificate) from an adversary who breaks authentication security/privacy.

Definition 1 (Receiver Covertness). *A CKEM* (PG, S, R) *for relation $\mathcal{R}$ (and language $\mathcal{L}^\mathcal{R}$) is* receiver covert *if for some polynomial sequence $u = (u_1, u_2, ...)$, for any efficient algorithm $\mathcal{A}$, the difference between the probability of $\mathcal{A}$ outputting 1 in the following two experiments is a negligible function of τ. Both experiments run* PG(1^τ) *to choose parameter π, and $\mathcal{A}(\pi)$ chooses (x, w), and then in the first experiment $\mathcal{A}$ interacts with* R(π, x, w)*, while in the second experiment $\mathcal{A}$ interacts with* R$^{\$(u)}$*.*

Definition 2 (Strong Sender Covertness). *A CKEM* (PG, S, R) *for relation $\mathcal{R}$ (and language $\mathcal{L}^\mathcal{R}$) is* strong sender covert *if there is a polynomial sequence u, an efficient algorithm* Ext*, and a polynomial p s.t. for any efficient algorithm $\mathcal{A}$ there exists a negligible function δ, s.t. for any τ, any π output by* PG(1^τ)*, and any x of size polynomial in τ, it holds that* Ext *on input (π, x) and an oracle access to $\mathcal{A}$ outputs w s.t. $((x, \pi), w) \in \mathcal{R}$ with probability at least $p(\epsilon_{\mathcal{A}, \pi, x, u} - \delta(\tau))$, where $\epsilon_{\mathcal{A}, \pi, x, u}$ is defined as the difference between the probability that $\mathcal{A}$ outputs 1 in the following two games: In the "real" game, $\mathcal{A}$ interacts with* S(π, x) *and then receives key K output by this S instance, while in the "random" game, $\mathcal{A}$ interacts with* S$^{\$(u)}$ *and then receives K generated as a random τ-bit string.*

Note on Computational Restrictions. We define CKEM covertness only for computationally bounded adversaries because our CKEM construction in Section 4 depends on these bounds in both directions. Receiver's covertness is computational because it encrypts the first Σ-protocol message using a commitment which is only computationally hiding/covert, while sender's covertness relies on collision-resistance of a hash function. (Additionally, the 2-round version of this CKEM, which works in the Random Oracle Model (ROM) for hash functions, requires a polynomial bound on the number of adversary's hash function queries.)

CKEM vs. Zero-Knowledge Proofs. One can view CKEM as an encryption counterpart to a Zero-Knowledge Proof, with S playing the role of the Verifier and R that of a Prover, except that in CKEM, the point is not for S to learn anything about statement x, but for R to receive S's key only if R has w s.t. $(x, w) \in \mathcal{R}$. In particular, one can view CKEM receiver privacy as a form of zero-knowledge and CKEM strong sender security as a form of strong soundness, i.e. a proof of knowledge. Indeed, both strong sender covertness and strong soundness of an interactive proof require that if some algorithm $\mathcal{A}$ "ϵ-succeeds" on statement x, then an efficient extractor can use $\mathcal{A}$ to extract w s.t. $(x, w) \in \mathcal{R}$. In an interactive proof $\mathcal{A}$'s success is defined as convincing a verifier that $x \in \mathcal{L}^{\mathcal{R}}$, while CKEM covertness defines $\mathcal{A}$'s success as distinguishing an interaction with $\mathsf{S}(\pi, x)$ followed by the key K output by this instance of S, from an interaction with a random beacon followed by a random τ-bit string.

CKEM vs. SPHF. CKEM's can be seen as a generalization of Smooth Projective Hash Functions [CS01] to interactive protocols. An SPHF gives rise to a one-round CKEM by sending the projection key and treating the hash value as the key K. Such CKEM is covert if the projection key can be covertly encoded, but it is not *strongly* covert because it does not assure witness extraction.

CKEM vs. Covert 2PC. Our CKEM construction of Section 4 satisfies the above game-based CKEM definition, but it is not a covert secure computation of a CKEM functionality [vAHL05,CGOS07]. In particular, it enables extraction of the witness w input by R but not the statement x input by S.

Covert Mutual Authentication. Consider a group manager GM who issues certificates to group members and publishes revocation tokens for the users whose membership it wants to revoke. An (implicit) *Mutual Authentication* (MA) scheme, with verifier-local revocation, is a tuple of algorithms (KGen, CG, Auth) which work as follows. KGen on security parameter τ outputs a master secret key msk and a public key mpk. To issue a membership certificate to user P_i, GM gives her a *certificate* generated as $(\mathsf{sk}_i, \mathsf{rt}_i) \leftarrow \mathsf{CG}(\mathsf{msk})$. To revoke membership, GM adds rt_i to an initially empty revocation list CRL, which should then be propagated to all current group members. If two players P_i and P_j want to authenticate to each other, each player follows the interactive algorithm Auth, where P_i runs on private inputs $(\mathsf{mpk}, (\mathsf{sk}_i, \mathsf{rt}_i), \mathsf{CRL})$ while P_j runs on $(\mathsf{mpk}', (\mathsf{sk}_j, \mathsf{rt}_j), \mathsf{CRL}')$. Each participant's local outputs is a τ-bit session key, respectively K and K'. If both parties follows the protocol then $K = K'$ if (1) $\mathsf{mpk} = \mathsf{mpk}'$, (2) both $(\mathsf{sk}_i, \mathsf{rt}_i)$ and $(\mathsf{sk}_j, \mathsf{rt}_j)$ are valid certificates under mpk, (3) neither certificate is revoked in the CRL of the other player, i.e. $\mathsf{rt}_i \notin \mathsf{CRL}'$ and $\mathsf{rt}_j \notin \mathsf{CRL}$.

Intuitively, we call an MA scheme *covert* if no one except a valid group member can distinguish an interaction in the authentication scheme with a member of the same group from an interaction with a random beacon. Formally, we define MA covertness via the following game between an adversary $\mathcal{A}$ and a game G. Let k be the number of message rounds in protocol Auth, and let $u = (u_1, u_2, ..., u_k)$ be some sequence of polynomials. The MA security experiment, denoted $G_{\mathcal{A}}(1^\tau, b)$, is defined by an interaction between game G and an attacker $\mathcal{A}$ which proceeds as follows:

Init. G on input $(1^\tau, b)$ for bit b sets $(\mathsf{msk}, \mathsf{mpk}) \leftarrow \mathsf{KGen}(1^\tau)$, $\mathsf{CRL} \leftarrow \emptyset$, and generates $(\mathsf{sk}_i, \mathsf{rt}_i) \leftarrow \mathsf{CG}(\mathsf{msk})$ for $i = 1, \ldots, N(\tau)$ for a fixed polynomial N.
Corruptions. $\mathcal{A}$, on input $(1^\tau, \mathsf{mpk})$, specifies a subset CorSet of corrupt players, and for each $i \in \mathsf{CorSet}$, $\mathcal{A}$ receives $(\mathsf{sk}_i, \mathsf{rt}_i)$, and rt_i is added to CRL.

Queries. $\mathcal{A}$ can (concurrently) make any number of Exec queries and a single Test query, to which G responds as follows:

Exec(i, CRL*): Execute Auth(mpk, (sk_i, rt_i), CRL*), interacting with $\mathcal{A}$.

Test(i): If $i \notin$ CorSet, respond as follows:

   If $b = 1$, execute Auth(mpk, (sk_i, rt_i), CRL), interacting with $\mathcal{A}$, and send the local output K of this Auth instance to $\mathcal{A}$;

   If $b = 0$, execute Auth$^{\$(u)}$, and send a random τ-bit string K' to $\mathcal{A}$.

Guess. If $\mathcal{A}$ halts and outputs a bit, G halts and outputs the same bit.

Definition 3 (MA Covertness). *We call an MA scheme* (KGen, CG, Auth) *covert if for some polynomial sequence* u *function* $\epsilon_{\mathcal{A}}(\tau) = |\Pr[G_{\mathcal{A}}(1^\tau, 0) = 1] - \Pr[G_{\mathcal{A}}(1^\tau, 1) = 1]|$ *is negligible for any efficient algorithm* $\mathcal{A}$.

Revocation and Escrow. The MA definition implies that $\mathcal{A}$ can corrupt or participate in Auth instances with any party, but this will not help $\mathcal{A}$ in distinguishing an Auth instance ran by a *non-corrupted* party from a random beacon. This can hold only if the honest party executes on a revocation list containing revocation tokens of all corrupted players. (Otherwise the adversary could run an Auth instance on a certificate of a corrupted player.) Note that we allow $\mathcal{A}$ to interact with Auth instances executing on wrong revocation lists, to model the fact that honest parties can execute on outdated or otherwise incorrect revocation lists. While such instances can be recognizable to $\mathcal{A}$, they should not endanger covertness of instances which use the correct revocation list. One limitation of our "verifier-local" revocation model, which we adopt from the work on group signatures by Boneh and Shacham [BS04], is the lack of "perfect-forward covertness", i.e. an adversary who learns some party's certificate can break the covertness of all past protocol instances executed by this party. We model this in the security experiment by requiring that the tested player is not on the revocation list. However, this revocation model naturally supports *identity escrow*, because GM can use revocation tokens to link protocol transcripts to users.

Authentication Security. MA covertness implies standard authentication security because an attacker without a valid certificate cannot distinguish the key output by a group member from a random string. However, our MA notion is quite far from a full-fledged Authenticated Key Exchange (AKE) [BCK98,CK01]. First of all, an adversary gets to see a session key only on a single tested session, so there are no guarantees of independence between keys created by different instances, and no guarantees of security against the man-in-the-middle attacks. In other limitations, we offer only static security, because all corruptions must precede protocol instance executions, and we offer limited security against malicious insiders, because we never expose the session keys on Exec(i, CRL*) instances.

4   Covert Conditional KEM Construction

We show a general compiler which uses a covert commitment with associated SPHF to convert a special Σ-protocol for a given language, a form of three-round public-coin Honest-Verifier Zero-Knowledge (HVZK) proof of knowledge, into a covert CKEM for the same language. When the covert commitment is instantiated as we explain below, the CKEM construction relies on the DDH assumption on a prime-order subgroup of a prime residue group Z_p^*, and its cost is that of the underlying Σ-protocol plus 2 exponentiations in Z_p^* for the sender and 3 for the receiver, assuming that the encoding of bitstrings output by the CKEM into the underlying steganographic channel is not computationally intensive, e.g. because the underlying steganographic channel is a random channel. Below we first introduce our tools, the special Σ-protocol and the covert commitment with associated SPHF, and then we show the covert CKEM construction.

Special Σ-Protocol. The notion of Σ-*protocol* was used by Damgard (see e.g. [Dam10]) to describe common features of HVZK proof systems which extend Schnorr's proof of knowledge of the discrete logarithm to various arithmetic relations on discrete logarithms and representations. Let algorithm triple (P_1, P_2, V) define a 3-round public-coin proof system for relation $\mathcal{R}$, where P_1 on input $(x, w) \in \mathcal{R}$ and internal randomness r outputs the prover's first message a, P_2 on input (x, w, r) and a τ-bit challenge c outputs the prover's second message z, and V on input (x, a, c, z) outputs the verifier's accept/reject decision bit. We say that (P_1, P_2, V) is a *Special Σ-Protocol* for $\mathcal{R}$ if it satisfies the following additional properties: (1) ("special soundness") There exists an efficient extractor which outputs w s.t. $(x, w) \in \mathcal{R}$ given any two accepting transcripts that share the same prover's first message a but differ on the challenge c, i.e. given (x, a, c, z, c', z') s.t. $V(x, a, c, z) = V(x, a, c', z') = 1$ and $c' \neq c$; (2) The prover's second message z is a sequence of integers distributed statistically close to uniform over some integer ranges, i.e. for any $(x, w) \in \mathcal{R}$ and $c \in \{0, 1\}^\tau$, the distribution of z's output by $P_2(x, w, r, c)$ on random r is statistically close to uniform over $\boldsymbol{I} = I_1 \times \ldots \times I_t$ for some integer ranges $I_1, \ldots, I_t$; (3) ("special simulation") There exists an efficiently computable function f_V s.t. $V(x, a, c, z) = 1$ iff $a = f_V(x, c, z)$, $c \in \{0, 1\}^\tau$, and $z \in \boldsymbol{I'}$ for some cross-product of ranges $\boldsymbol{I'}$. These properties are satisfied by Σ-protocols for many relations on discrete logarithms and representations (see e.g. [CM99] for examples). Such Σ-protocols are usually given for prime order groups, but they extend to the QR_n subgroup of Z_n^* for a safe RSA modulus n, such as the Σ-protocol for ACJT group signature[ACJT00] possession (see Appendix A) used in the instantiation of our covert MA construction in Section 5.1.

Covert Commitment with Associated SPHF. We call a tuple of efficient algorithms (PG, Com, Hash, PHash) a *perfectly binding covert commitment with associated smooth projective hash function (SPHF)* if the following requirements are satisfied. (1) First, pair (PG, Com) is a *covert commitment* defined as follows: There is a polynomial $l(\cdot)$ s.t. for any efficient algorithm $\mathcal{A}$, quantity $|p_0 - p_1|$ is a negligible function of τ, where p_β is defined as the probability that $b = 1$ in the following experiment: Generate $\pi \leftarrow PG(1^\tau)$, pick $\mathcal{A}$'s randomness r, and generate $m \leftarrow \mathcal{A}(\pi; r)$. If $\beta = 1$ generate $C \leftarrow Com(\pi, m)$, otherwise $C \leftarrow \{0, 1\}^{l(\tau)}$. Finally, let $b \leftarrow \mathcal{A}(\pi, C; r)$. Note that commitment covertness implies the standard notion of hiding for a commitment scheme. (2) Secondly, this commitment must be *perfectly binding*, i.e. for any τ, any $\pi \leftarrow PG(1^\tau)$, any m, m', r, r', if $\mathsf{Com}((\pi, m); r) = \mathsf{Com}((\pi, m'); r')$ then $m = m'$. (3) Thirdly, $(\mathsf{Hash}, \mathsf{PHash})$ is an SPHF system for the language of correct commitments, i.e. $\mathsf{Hash}(\pi, C, m)$ outputs hash value h and projection key pk s.t. (3a) the SPHF is correct in the sense that $\mathsf{PHash}(\pi, pk, m, r) = h$ if $C = \mathsf{Com}((\pi, m); r)$ for some r, and (3b) the SPHF is *covert* in the sense that for any τ, any $\pi \leftarrow \mathsf{PG}(1^\tau)$, any C, m s.t. $C \neq \mathsf{Com}((\pi, m); r)$ for all r, the pair (h, pk) output by $\mathsf{Hash}(\pi, C, m)$ is statistically close to a random bitstring of some length $u(\tau)$. Note that SPHF covertness implies the standard notion of SPHF smoothness, because if m is not committed in C then the hash value h is statistically independent of the projection key pk.

We construct such commitment using ElGamal encryption in a prime residue group: Let $\mathsf{PG}(1^\tau)$ output $\pi = (p, q, k, g, \mathcal{H})$ where p, q are primes s.t. $p = qk + 1$ and $\gcd(q, k) = 1$, g is a generator of subgroup G of order q in Z_p^*, and $\mathcal{H}$ is a universal hash from Z_p^* to $\{0, 1\}^\tau$ s.t. for any distribution D over Z_p^* which has at least $|p|$ bits of entropy, $\{\mathcal{H}(x)\}_{x \leftarrow D}$ is statistically close to $\{0, 1\}^\tau$. Algorithm $\mathsf{Com}(\pi, m)$ for m in message space $\mathbb{Z}_q$ picks $(t, z_1, z_2) \leftarrow \mathbb{Z}_q \times Z_p^* \times Z_p^*$, and outputs $C = (\mathsf{EC}_{[p]}(e), \mathsf{EC}_{[p]}(f))$, where $e = g^t \cdot z_1^q \bmod p$ and $f = g^{t^2 + m} \cdot z_2^q \bmod p$. Under the DDH assumption on subgroup G of Z_p^* this commitment is covert, because then pair (g^t, g^{t^2}) is indistinguishable from two random G elements, which makes pair (e, f) indistinguishable from two random Z_p^* elements. Algorithm $\mathsf{Hash}(\pi, C, m)$ decodes e and f from C, picks $\alpha, \beta \leftarrow \mathbb{Z}_q$ and $z_3 \leftarrow Z_p^*$, and outputs (h, pk) where $h = \mathcal{H}(e^{k^2 \cdot \alpha} \cdot (fg^{-m})^{k^2 \cdot \beta})$ and $pk = \mathsf{EC}_{[p]}(g^{k \cdot \alpha} \cdot e^{k \cdot \beta} \cdot z_3^q)$. Algorithm $\mathsf{PHash}(\pi, pk, m, r)$ for $r = (t, z_1, z_2)$ decodes $v \leftarrow \mathsf{DC}_{[p]}(pk)$ and outputs $h = \mathcal{H}(v^{kt})$. Note that for both parties $h = \mathcal{H}(w)$ for $w = g^{tk^2 \alpha + t^2 k^2 \beta}$ because $(z_i^q)^k = z_i^{p-1} = 1$. On the other hand, if C is not a commitment to m then (h, pk) output by $\mathsf{Hash}(\pi, C, m)$ are distributed as $(\mathcal{H}(w), \mathsf{EC}_{[p]}(x))$ for $w = g^{k^2 \cdot (t\alpha + t^2 \beta + \delta_m \beta)}$ and $x = g^{k \cdot (\alpha + t\beta)} z_3^q$ for $\delta_m \neq 0 \bmod q$. Since (α, β, z_3) is random in $\mathbb{Z}_q \times \mathbb{Z}_q \times Z_p^*$, pair (w, x) is uniform in $G \times Z_p^*$, and therefore $(\mathcal{H}(w), \mathsf{EC}_{[p]}(x))$ is statistically close to uniform in $\{0, 1\}^\tau \times \{0, 1\}^{|p| + \tau}$.

Covert CKEM Construction. Let (P_1, P_2, V) be a special Σ-protocol for relation $\mathcal{R}$, with the associated integer ranges I, let $(\mathsf{PG}, \mathsf{Com}, \mathsf{Hash}, \mathsf{PHash})$ be a perfectly binding covert commitment with associated SPHF, and let H be a collision-resistant hash onto the message space of the commitment. Fig. 1 shows algorithms S and R for a covert CKEM $(\mathsf{PG}, \mathsf{S}, \mathsf{R})$ for relation $\mathcal{R}$. Note that the security argument for this construction uses rewinding, which degrades exact security. Using the 2-round ROM version of this construction (see below), τ should be at least 160, and H should hash onto at least 480-bit strings. If the covert commitment is implemented using group Z_p^* as shown above, this means that the order q of the subgroup G of Z_p^* must satisfy $|q| \geq 480$.

Theorem 1. *Tuple* $(\mathsf{PG}, \mathsf{S}, \mathsf{R})$ *where* S, R *are specified in Fig. 1 is a receiver covert and strong sender covert CKEM for relation* $\mathcal{R}$ *if* $(\mathsf{PG}, \mathsf{Com}, \mathsf{Hash}, \mathsf{PHash})$ *is a perfectly binding covert commitment with associated SPHF,* (P_1, P_2, V) *is a special Σ-protocol for* $\mathcal{R}$, *and* H *is a collision resistant hash function.*

On R's inputs (π, x, w) and S's inputs (π, x) for π generated by $\mathsf{PG}(1^\tau)$.

R: Pick random (r, r'), compute Σ-protocol first message $a \leftarrow P_1(x, w, r)$, compute its hash $C \leftarrow \mathsf{Com}((\pi, H(a)); r')$, and send C to S.

S: Pick challenge $c \leftarrow \{0, 1\}^\tau$ and send c to R.

R: Compute Σ-protocol response as $z \leftarrow P_2(x, w, r, c)$, send $\bar{z} \leftarrow \mathsf{EC}_I(z)$ to S.

S: Decode $z \leftarrow \mathsf{DC}_I(\bar{z})$, use Σ-protocol verification to compute $a \leftarrow f_V(x, c, z)$, compute $(h, pk) \leftarrow \mathsf{Hash}(\pi, C, H(a))$, send pk to R and output key $K = h$.

R: On sender's message pk, output key $K' = \mathsf{PHash}(\pi, pk, H(a), r')$.

Fig. 1. A Covert CKEM for relation $\mathcal{R}$

Proof Sketch. To argue receiver covertness note that in the real execution the adversary sees $(C, \bar{z})$ generated as in Fig. 1, and this pair is indistinguishable from two random bitstrings of appropriate size: First, by covertness of the commitment scheme, commitment C can be replaced by a random bitstring incurring at most negligible change in the adversary's behavior. Secondly, since z is statistically close to random in I by the properties of the Σ-protocol, and EC_I is covert on I, it follows that $\bar{z}$ is statistically close to a random bitstring. For strong sender covertness, take any τ, any π output by $\mathsf{PG}(1^\tau)$, any x polynomial in τ, and an efficient algorithm $\mathcal{A}$. Let $\epsilon_{\mathcal{A}, \pi, x, u} = |p_0 - p_1|$ where p_0 is the probability that $\mathcal{A}(\pi, x)$ outputs 1 in an interaction where it gets $(pk, K) = (pk, h)$ computed by $\mathsf{S}(\pi, x)$, and p_1 is the probability that $\mathcal{A}(\pi, x)$ outputs 1 given a random $u(\tau)$-bit string where u is given by the covertness property of the SPHF for the commitment scheme (see property 3b in the definition above). First consider executions where $\mathcal{A}$ sends $(C, \bar{z})$ to S s.t. C is not a commitment to $H(a)$ for $a = f_V(x, c, \mathsf{DC}_I(\bar{z}))$. By the covertness of the SPHF for the commitment scheme, in such executions pair (pk, h) is statistically indistinguishable random $u(\tau)$-bit string. Let $\epsilon_{\mathsf{sphf}}(\tau)$ be the upper-bound on the (negligible) amount such executions can contribute to $\mathcal{A}$'s distinguishing advantage $\epsilon_{\mathcal{A}, \pi, x, u}$. We conclude that with probability at least $\epsilon' = \epsilon_{\mathcal{A}, \pi, x, u} - \epsilon_{\mathsf{sphf}}(\tau)$, a random interaction with $\mathcal{A}(\pi, x)$ outputs $(C, c, \bar{z})$ s.t. C is a commitment to $H(a)$ for $a = f_V(x, c, \mathsf{DC}_I(\bar{z}))$. Running such interaction twice with $\mathcal{A}$'s initial randomness fixed until $\mathcal{A}$ outputs C creates a "fork" with two transcripts $(C, c, \bar{z})$ and $(C, c', \bar{z'})$ s.t. with probability at least $\epsilon'' = (\epsilon')^2/2$ (if $\epsilon' \geq 2 \cdot 2^{-\tau}$) we have that $c \neq c'$ and both transcripts are successful in the sense that C is a commitment to $H(a)$ for $a = f_V(x, c, z)$ and C is a commitment to $H(a')$ for $a' = f_V(x, c', z')$, for $(z, z') = \mathsf{DC}_I(\bar{z}, \bar{z'})$. $H(a) = H(a')$ by perfect binding of Com. Let $\epsilon_{\mathsf{crh}}(\tau)$ be the (negligible) upper-bound on the probability that this forked execution, running $\mathcal{A}(\pi, x)$ twice, produces a collision in H. Therefore with probability at least $\epsilon'' - \epsilon_{\mathsf{crh}}(\tau)$ we have that $a = a'$, in which case the extractor implied by the special soundness of the Σ-protocol outputs w s.t. $(x, w) \in \mathcal{R}$ when executed on input (x, a, c, z, c', z'), which implies strong sender covertness for $\delta(\tau) = 2^{-\tau+2} + 2\epsilon_{\mathsf{sphf}}(\tau) + 4\sqrt{\epsilon_{\mathsf{crh}}(\tau)}$ and $p(\epsilon) = \epsilon^2/16$.

2-round Covert CKEM in ROM. The same construction becomes a 2-round CKEM in the Random Oracle Model (ROM), if c is computed as $c = H'(x, C)$ for a hash function H' onto $\{0, 1\}^\tau$ modeled as a random oracle. If $\mathcal{A}(\pi, x)$ can make at most $q_H(\tau)$ hash queries then using the version of the forking lemma in [BN06] we get a (forking) algorithm which on input (π, x) runs two executions of $\mathcal{A}(\pi, x)$ and creates the same two transcripts as above with probability $\epsilon'' = (\epsilon')^2/(2q_H(\tau))$ given $\epsilon' \geq 2 \cdot q_H(\tau)/2^\tau$, which implies sender covertness for $\delta(\tau) = q_H(\tau) \cdot 2^{-\tau+2} + 2\epsilon_{\mathsf{sphf}}(\tau) + 4\sqrt{q_H(\tau)\epsilon_{\mathsf{crh}}(\tau)}$ and $p(\epsilon) = \epsilon^2/(16q_H(\tau))$.

5 Covert Mutual Authentication Scheme

We construct a covert Mutual Authentication (MA) from an Identity Escrow (IE) scheme [KP98] where a group member commits to its certificate and then proves in zero-knowledge that the committed value is a valid certificate under the group public key. We turn such IE scheme into a covert MA scheme by replacing the zero-knowledge proof with a covert CKEM for the same relation. For revocation we require that each commitment can be linked to a committed certificate given the revocation token corresponding to this certificate, and to assure covertness we need this certificate commitment to be covert until the revocation token is made public. Identity Escrow [KP98] is an interactive form of a group signature [CvH91], and many group signatures can be converted to an IE scheme which fits the above structure. Below we formalize the properties our MA scheme construction requires of an IE scheme, and we show how to build a covert MA protocol from such IE scheme and a covert CKEM for committed certificate validity. In Section 5.1 we show how to instantiate this construction by modifying the Ateniese-Camenisch-Joye-Tsudik (ACJT) group signature [ACJT00] into an IE scheme that satisfies the properties required by this construction.

Compatible Identity Escrow Scheme. An IE scheme is a tuple of algorithms (KG, CG, Ver, IECom, TraceCom), where $\mathsf{KG}(1^\tau)$ outputs a group secret key gsk and a public key gpk, $\mathsf{CG}(\mathsf{gsk})$ generates a certificate $(\mathsf{sk}, \mathsf{rt})$, where sk is a user secret and rt a revocation token, s.t. $\mathsf{Ver}(\mathsf{gpk}, (\mathsf{sk}, \mathsf{rt})) = 1$, $\mathsf{IECom}(\mathsf{gpk}, (\mathsf{sk}, \mathsf{rt}))$ generates a commitment C to $(\mathsf{sk}, \mathsf{rt})$, and $\mathsf{TraceCom}(\mathsf{gpk}, C, \mathsf{rt}) = 1$ if $C \leftarrow \mathsf{IECom}(\mathsf{gpk}, (\mathsf{sk}, \mathsf{rt}))$. We call an IE scheme *covert-MA-compatible* if it satisfies the following four properties. (1) First, (KG, Ver) must form an *unforgeable certificate scheme*, i.e. for any efficient algorithm $\mathcal{A}$, the probability that $\mathcal{A}(\mathsf{gpk})$, on access to an oracle $\mathsf{CG}(\mathsf{gsk})$, generates $(\mathsf{sk}^*, \mathsf{rt}^*)$ s.t. $\mathsf{Ver}(\mathsf{gpk}, (\mathsf{sk}^*, \mathsf{rt}^*)) = 1$ and $\mathsf{rt}^* \neq \mathsf{rt}_i$ for all $(\mathsf{sk}_i, \mathsf{rt}_i)$ pairs $\mathcal{A}$ receives from $\mathsf{CG}(\mathsf{gsk})$, is negligible, for $(\mathsf{gsk}, \mathsf{gpk})$ randomly generated by $\mathsf{KG}(1^\tau)$. (2) Second, the scheme must be *traceable*, i.e. for any τ, any $(\mathsf{gsk}, \mathsf{gpk})$ output by $\mathsf{KG}(1^\tau)$, and any C and rt, it holds that $\mathsf{TraceCom}(\mathsf{gpk}, C, \mathsf{rt}) = 1$ if and only if $C = \mathsf{IECom}((\mathsf{gpk}, (\mathsf{sk}, \mathsf{rt})); r)$ for some sk, r. (3) We define a *committed certificate validity* relation $\mathcal{R}^{IE}$ as the set $((\mathsf{gpk}, C), (\mathsf{sk}, \mathsf{rt}, r))$ s.t. $C = \mathsf{IECom}((\mathsf{gpk}, (\mathsf{sk}, \mathsf{rt})); r)$ and $\mathsf{Ver}(\mathsf{gpk}, (\mathsf{sk}, \mathsf{rt})) = 1$. The third property of an IE scheme is that $\mathcal{R}^{IE}$ admits a *special Σ-protocol*, so that it can be converted into a covert CKEM by the construction in Fig. 1.

(4) The last property is the covertness of the commitment IECom. Note that traceability implies that IECom cannot be semantically secure because the rt part of the committed plaintext can be efficiently linked to the commitment. However, the commitment must hide the committed certificate (sk, rt) as long as the revocation token rt is not made public, and we need this commitment to be covert and not just plaintext-hiding. Thus, we require the IE scheme to be *revocably covert* in the sense that there exists some function l polynomial in τ s.t. for any efficient algorithm $\mathcal{A}$, quantity $|p_0 - p_1|$ is a negligible function of τ, where p_β is defined as the probability that $b = 1$ in the following experiment: Generate $(\mathsf{gsk}, \mathsf{gpk}) \leftarrow \mathsf{KG}(1^\tau)$ and $(\mathsf{sk}_t, \mathsf{rt}_t) \leftarrow \mathsf{CG}(\mathsf{gsk})$, and then let $\mathcal{A}(\mathsf{gpk})$ repeatedly query the $\mathsf{CG}(\mathsf{gsk})$ oracle which generates $(\mathsf{sk}, \mathsf{rt})$ and gives it to $\mathcal{A}$, and an oracle which returns $C \leftarrow \mathsf{IECom}(\mathsf{gpk}, (\mathsf{sk}_t, \mathsf{rt}_t))$ for $\beta = 1$, or $C \leftarrow \{0,1\}^{l(\tau)}$ for $\beta = 0$. $\mathcal{A}$ outputs bit b, its guess of bit β, after polynomially many queries of both types.

Covert MA Scheme Construction. Fig. 2 constructs a covert MA scheme given a covert-MA-compatible IE scheme $(\mathsf{KG}, \mathsf{CG}, \mathsf{Ver}, \mathsf{IECom}, \mathsf{TraceCom})$ and a receiver covert and strong sender covert CKEM $(\mathsf{PG}, \mathsf{S}, \mathsf{R})$ for the associated committed certificate validity relation $\mathcal{R}^{IE}$. In the figure, u_S stands for the polynomial sequence implied by CKEM strong sender covertness.

<u>KGen</u>(1^τ): Set $(\mathsf{gsk}, \mathsf{gpk}) \leftarrow \mathsf{KG}(1^\tau)$, $\pi \leftarrow \mathsf{PG}(1^\tau)$, $\mathsf{mpk} = (\mathsf{gpk}, \pi)$, and $\mathsf{msk} = \mathsf{gsk}$.

<u>CG</u>(gsk): Generate $(\mathsf{sk}, \mathsf{rt})$ following the $\mathsf{CG}(\mathsf{gsk})$ algorithm of the IE scheme.

<u>Auth</u> protocol for $P_i((\mathsf{gpk}, \pi), (\mathsf{sk}_i, \mathsf{rt}_i), \mathsf{CRL}_i)$ and $P_j((\mathsf{gpk}, \pi), (\mathsf{sk}_j, \mathsf{rt}_j), \mathsf{CRL}_j)$:

1. P_i sets $C_i \leftarrow \mathsf{IECom}((\mathsf{gpk}, (\mathsf{sk}_i, \mathsf{rt}_i)); r_i)$ for random r_i and sends C_i to P_j.
   P_j sets $C_j \leftarrow \mathsf{IECom}((\mathsf{gpk}, (\mathsf{sk}_j, \mathsf{rt}_j)); r_j)$ for random r_j and sends C_j to P_i.

   P_i sets $\mathsf{F}_i \leftarrow 1$ if $\mathsf{TraceCom}(\mathsf{gpk}, C_j, \mathsf{rt}) = 1$ for any $\mathsf{rt} \in \mathsf{CRL}_i \cup \{\mathsf{rt}_i\}$,
       and $\mathsf{F}_i \leftarrow 0$ otherwise.
   P_j sets $\mathsf{F}_j \leftarrow 1$ if $\mathsf{TraceCom}(\mathsf{gpk}, C_i, \mathsf{rt}) = 1$ for any $\mathsf{rt} \in \mathsf{CRL}_j \cup \{\mathsf{rt}_j\}$,
       and $\mathsf{F}_j \leftarrow 0$ otherwise.

2. P_i runs protocol R on $(\pi, (\mathsf{gpk}, C_i), (\mathsf{sk}_i, \mathsf{rt}_i, r_i))$, interacting with P_j who runs protocol S on $(\pi, (\mathsf{gpk}, C_i))$ if $\mathsf{F}_j = 0$, or runs $\mathsf{S}^{\$(u_\mathsf{S})}$ if $\mathsf{F}_j = 1$.
   P_i sets $K_{i,\mathsf{R}}$ as its local output in R.
   P_j sets $K_{j,\mathsf{S}}$ as its local output in S if $\mathsf{F}_j = 0$, otherwise $K_{j,\mathsf{S}} \leftarrow \{0,1\}^\tau$.

3. P_j runs protocol R on $(\pi, (\mathsf{gpk}, C_j), (\mathsf{sk}_j, \mathsf{rt}_j, r_j))$, interacting with P_i who runs protocol S on $(\pi, (\mathsf{gpk}, C_j))$ if $\mathsf{F}_i = 0$, or runs $\mathsf{S}^{\$(u_\mathsf{S})}$ if $\mathsf{F}_i = 1$.
   P_j sets $K_{j,\mathsf{R}}$ as its local output in R.
   P_i sets $K_{i,\mathsf{S}}$ as its local output in S if $\mathsf{F}_i = 0$, otherwise $K_{i,\mathsf{S}} \leftarrow \{0,1\}^\tau$.

P_i's local output is $K_i = K_{i,\mathsf{R}} \oplus K_{i,\mathsf{S}}$ and P_j's local output is $K_j = K_{j,\mathsf{R}} \oplus K_{j,\mathsf{S}}$.

Fig. 2. A Covert Mutual Authentication Scheme $(\mathsf{KGen}, \mathsf{CG}, \mathsf{Auth})$

Theorem 2. (KGen, CG, Auth) *in Fig. 2 is a* Covert Mutual Authentication Scheme *if* (KG, CG, Ver, IECom, TraceCom) *is a covert-MA-compatible IE scheme and* (PG, S, R) *is a receiver covert and strong sender covert CKEM for* $\mathcal{R}^{IE}$.

Proof Sketch. By the symmetry of the Auth protocol we can assume that in all the Auth protocol instances adversary invokes its counterparty plays the role of P_i in Fig. 2. Let $l(\cdot)$ be the length polynomial implied by revocable covertness of the IE scheme, and let u_R and u_S be the polynomial sequences implied by the receiver and sender covertness of the CKEM. The polynomial sequence u which defines the random beacon $\text{Auth}^{\$(u)}$ is composed of $l(\cdot)$ followed by the elements of u_R and then the elements of u_S, because P_i first sends C_i, then performs R, and then S (or $S^{\$(u)}$). Let $\mathcal{A}$ be an efficient algorithm with the distinguishing advantage $\epsilon_{\mathcal{A}}$ in the MA covertness experiment (see Definition 3). For any $i \in \{0, \ldots, N(\tau)\}$, consider a game $G(1^\tau, b, i^*)$ which follows $G(1^\tau, b)$ but fixes the index i used by $\mathcal{A}$ in the Test query by halting and outputting 1 if $\mathcal{A}$ calls the Test(i) query for $i \neq i^*$. There must exist an index i^* s.t. $\mathcal{A}$'s advantage in distinguishing between $G_1 = G(1^\tau, 1, i^*)$ and $G_0 = G(1^\tau, 0, i^*)$ is at least $\epsilon_{\mathcal{A}}/N(\tau)$. By a series of modifications starting from game G_1 we show that $\mathcal{A}$'s distinguishing advantage between G_1 and G_0 must be negligible, implying that $\epsilon_{\mathcal{A}}$ is negligible. In the following we will only consider Exec(i, CRL^*) queries for i s.t. $\text{rt}_i \notin \text{CRL}$, because $\mathcal{A}$ can execute the game response on such queries for $i \in \text{CRL}$ using the $(\text{sk}_i, \text{rt}_i)$ certificate $\mathcal{A}$ received by corrupting P_i.

A hybrid argument shows that G_1 is indistinguishable from G_2 where all Auth instances followed by P_i on Exec(i, CRL^*) queries are modified by replacing $R(\pi, (\text{gpk}, C_i), (\text{sk}_i, \text{rt}_i, r_i))$ with $R^{\$(u_R)}$ in step (2) of Auth. Let $G_1(t)$ be a hybrid between G_1 and G_2 which responds to the first t of Exec queries as in G_2, and to the remaining ones as in G_1. $\mathcal{A}$'s advantage in distinguishing $G_1(t - 1)$ and $G_1(t)$ must be negligible for each t by CKEM receiver covertness. A reduction which shows it runs on input π, generates (gsk, gpk), interacts with either $R(\pi, (\text{gpk}, C_i), (\text{sk}_i, \text{rt}_i, r_i))$ or $R^{\$(u_R)}$ on $\mathcal{A}$'s t-th query Exec(i, CRL^*), and simulates the rest of $\mathcal{A}$'s view in either game.

Let $\text{CorSet}^+ = \text{CorSet} \cup \{i^*\}$ and $\text{CRL}^+ = \text{CRL} \cup \{\text{rt}_{i^*}\}$. By another hybrid we modify G_2 into G_3 by replacing the C_i values generated in the Auth instances by each P_i for $i \notin \text{CorSet}^+$, with random strings of length $l(\tau)$. This hybrid goes over the players rather than over the Exec sessions. Let $G_2(t)$ be a game which follows G_2 in servicing each Exec(i, CRL^*) query for $i > t$, but on queries Exec(i, CRL^*) for $i \leq t$ and $i \notin \text{CorSet}^+$ it replaces C_i generated as $C_i \leftarrow \text{IECom}(\text{gpk}, (\text{sk}_i, \text{rt}_i))$ with a random $l(\tau)$-bit string. Note that the subsequent steps of P_t in the Auth instances triggered by Exec queries in G_2 do not depend on either C_t or $(\text{sk}_t, \text{rt}_t, r_t)$, which allows us to reduce $\mathcal{A}$'s advantage in distinguishing $G_2(t - 1)$ and $G_2(t)$ to an attack on the revocable covertness of the IE scheme. The challenger generates $(\text{gsk}, \text{gpk}) \leftarrow \text{KG}(1^\tau)$ and $(\text{sk}_t, \text{rt}_t) \leftarrow \text{CG}(\text{gsk})$, the reduction on input gpk receives certificates $(\text{sk}_i, \text{rt}_i)$ for all $i \neq t$ from the CG(gsk) oracle, receives either a sequence of C_t's computed as $C_t \leftarrow \text{IECom}(\text{gpk}, (\text{sk}_t, \text{rt}_t))$ or as a sequence of random bitstrings, and simulates everything else $\mathcal{A}$ sees in either game.

Note that G_3 responds to each $\mathsf{Exec}(i, \mathsf{CRL}^*)$ query for $i \notin \mathsf{CorSet}^+$ by picking C_i as a random string in step (1), running $\mathsf{R}^{\$(u_R)}$ in step (2), and running $\mathsf{S}(\pi, (\mathsf{gpk}, C_j))$ for C_j supplied by $\mathcal{A}$ in step (3). Therefore G_3 can be simulated given π, gpk, and the certificates $(\mathsf{rt}_i, \mathsf{sk}_i)$ for $i \in \mathsf{CorSet}^+$. Let G_4 be G_3 with P_{i^*}'s code in the Auth instance triggered by the $\mathsf{Test}(i^*)$ query modified by replacing the $\mathsf{S}(\pi, (\mathsf{gpk}, C_j))$ protocol P_{i^*} follows if $\mathsf{F}_{i^*} = 0$ with a random beacon $\mathsf{S}^{\$(u_S)}$ and a random key $K_{i^*, \mathsf{S}}$. If we assume that $\mathcal{A}$'s advantage in distinguishing between G_3 and G_4 is non-negligible, then by the strong sender covertness of CKEM it follows that there is an efficient extractor which, on input $(\mathsf{gpk}, \pi, \{\mathsf{sk}_i, \mathsf{rt}_i\}_{i \in \mathsf{CorSet}^+})$, extracts with non-negligible probability a witness $(\mathsf{sk}, \mathsf{rt}, r)$ s.t. $((\mathsf{gpk}, C_j), (\mathsf{sk}, \mathsf{rt}, r)) \in \mathcal{R}^{IE}$, i.e. $C_j = \mathsf{IECom}((\mathsf{gpk}, (\mathsf{sk}, \mathsf{rt})); r)$ and $\mathsf{Ver}(\mathsf{gpk}, (\mathsf{sk}, \mathsf{rt})) = 1$. Since the difference in this modification appears only for $\mathsf{F}_{i^*} = 0$ (otherwise P_{i^*} executes $\mathsf{S}^{\$(u_S)}$ in either case), we can consider only sessions where $\mathsf{TraceCom}(\mathsf{gpk}, C_j, \mathsf{rt}_i) = 0$ for all $\mathsf{rt}_i \in \mathsf{CRL}^+$. By the traceability property this implies that the extracted witness $(\mathsf{sk}, \mathsf{rt}, r)$ must satisfy $\mathsf{rt} \notin \mathsf{CRL}^+$. Therefore a reduction which simulates $\mathcal{A}$'s view on input gpk, and on $(\mathsf{sk}_i, \mathsf{rt}_i)$ pairs for $i \in \mathsf{CorSet}^+$, can with non-negligible probability compute $(\mathsf{sk}, \mathsf{rt})$ s.t. $\mathsf{Ver}(\mathsf{gpk}, (\mathsf{sk}, \mathsf{rt})) = 1$ and $\mathsf{rt} \neq \mathsf{rt}_i$ for all $i \in \mathsf{CorSet}^+$, which breaks the unforgeability of the $(\mathsf{KG}, \mathsf{Ver})$ certificate scheme.

Note that in G_4 key $K_{i^*, \mathsf{S}}$, computed in the $\mathsf{Test}(i^*)$ query, masks key $K_{i^*, \mathsf{R}}$, so now the latter key becomes irrelevant to $\mathcal{A}$'s view and K_{i^*} can be picked at random. This allows us to modify G_4 into G_5, by replacing $\mathsf{R}(\pi, (\mathsf{gpk}, C_{i^*}), (\mathsf{sk}_{i^*}, \mathsf{rt}_{i^*}, r_{i^*}))$ in the Auth instance triggered by the $\mathsf{Test}(i^*)$ query with $\mathsf{R}^{\$(u_R)}$. By CKEM receiver covertness we get that $G_4 \approx G_5$, via a reduction similar to the one which shows that $G_1(t-1) \approx G_1(t)$. We then modify G_5 into G_6, by replacing C_{i^*} in all Auth instances (in both $\mathsf{Test}(i^*)$ and $\mathsf{Exec}(i^*, \mathsf{CRL}^*)$) with a random $l(\tau)$-bit string. By revocable covertness of the IE scheme we get that $G_5 \approx G_6$, via a reduction similar to the one which shows that $G_2(t-1) \approx G_2(t)$. Note that in G_6 player P_{i^*} responds to the $\mathsf{Test}(i^*)$ query as $\mathsf{Auth}^{\$(u)}$ and outputs a random τ-bit string as key K_{i^*}, but also each P_i for $i \notin \mathsf{CorSet}$ responds to every $\mathsf{Exec}(i, \mathsf{CRL}^*)$ query by sending a random string instead of C_i in step (1) and following $\mathsf{R}^{\$(u_R)}$ instead of R in step (2). However, we can roll back those changes in responses to $\mathsf{Exec}(i, \mathsf{CRL}^*)$ queries. Using a similar argument as above for arguing indistinguishability of G_2 and G_3, we first change P_i's responses in $\mathsf{Exec}(i, \mathsf{CRL}^*)$ queries by replacing random C_i's back with $C_i \leftarrow \mathsf{IECom}(\mathsf{gpk}, (\mathsf{sk}_i, \mathsf{rt}_i))$. Then, using a similar argument as above for arguing indistinguishability of G_1 and G_2 we change P_i's responses to $\mathsf{Exec}(i, \mathsf{CRL}^*)$ queries by replacing $\mathsf{R}^{\$(u_R)}$ back with $\mathsf{R}(\pi, (\mathsf{gpk}, C_i), (\mathsf{sk}_i, \mathsf{rt}_i, r_i))$. After these modifications the game is identical to G_0, which completes the proof.

5.1   Covert MA Instantiation from ACJT Group Signature

RSA Setting. We first introduce the cryptographic setting required by the ACJT group signature scheme and by the covert encodings we will apply to it. The *safe* RSA setting modulus of length $l_n = 2l + 2$, for l polynomial in security parameter τ, is a product $n = pq$ of two primes p, q s.t. $p = 2p' + 1$

and $q = 2q' + 1$ where p', q' are also primes and $|p'| = |q'| = l$. The subgroup of quadratic residues in Z_n^*, denoted QR_n, is a cyclic group of order $n' = p'q'$. Let g be a generator of QR_n. Note that $-1 \notin \mathsf{QR}_n$ but $J_n(-1)$, the Jacobi symbol of $-1 \bmod n$, is equal to 1. We use $\pm\mathsf{QR}_n$ to denote the set of elements whose Jacobi symbol is 1. ($\pm\mathsf{QR}_n$ contains x and $-x$ for $x \in \mathsf{QR}_n$.) We use the following assumptions on safe RSA moduli, where negl stands for a negligible function:

Definition 4 (Strong RSA Assumption). *For all efficient algorithms $\mathcal{A}$ there is a negligible function negl s.t. if n is a random safe RSA modulus of length l_n, and z is a random element in Z_n^*, the probability that $\mathcal{A}(n, z)$ outputs (x, e) s.t. $e \neq 1$ and $x^e = z \bmod n$, is upper-bounded by $\mathsf{negl}(l_n)$. (Note that since QR_n makes 1/4-th of $Z_n^*\ast$, same assumption holds if z is sampled from QR_n.)*

Definition 5 (Decisional Quadratic Residuosity (DQR) Assumption). *For all efficient algorithms $\mathcal{A}$ there is a negligible function negl s.t. if n is a random safe RSA modulus of length l_n, the distinguishability advantage $|\epsilon_0 - \epsilon_1|$, where $\epsilon_0 = \Pr[1 \leftarrow \mathcal{A}(n, a)]$ for $a \in \mathsf{QR}_n$ and $\epsilon_1 = \Pr[1 \leftarrow \mathcal{A}(n, a)]$ for $a \pm \mathsf{QR}_n$, is upper-bounded by $\mathsf{negl}(l_n)$.*

Definition 6 (Decisional Diffie-Hellman (DDH) Assumption on QR_n). *For all efficient algorithms $\mathcal{A}$ there is a negligible function negl s.t. if n is a random safe RSA modulus of length l_n, and $\hat{g}$ is a random generator of QR_n, the distinguishability advantage $|\epsilon_0 - \epsilon_1|$, where $\epsilon_0 = \Pr[1 \leftarrow \mathcal{A}(\hat{g}, \hat{g}^a, \hat{g}^b, \hat{g}^c)]$ for $a, b, c \leftarrow Z_{n'}$ and $\epsilon_1 = \Pr[1 \leftarrow \mathcal{A}(n, \hat{g}, \hat{g}^a, \hat{g}^b, \hat{g}^{ab})]$ for $a, b \leftarrow Z_{n'}$, is upper-bounded by $\mathsf{negl}(l_n)$.*

Covert Encoding for QR_n. The ACJT group signature works in the QR_n subgroup of Z_n^*, but a protocol whose messages are elements of QR_n would not be covert because one can distinguish QR_n from Z_n^* by computing a Jacobi symbol mod n. We can handle it using the DQR assumption as follows. Let ν be any element in Z_n^* of order $2n'$ s.t. $J_n(\nu) = -1$. Let $\mathsf{EC}_{\pm\mathsf{QR}_n}$ be an encoding of $\pm\mathsf{QR}_n$ where $\mathsf{EC}_{\pm\mathsf{QR}_n}(v)$ picks a random bit β and returns $\mathsf{EC}_{[n]}(\nu^\beta \cdot v)$. The decoding $\mathsf{DC}_{\pm\mathsf{QR}_n}(\overline{v})$ computes $v' \leftarrow \mathsf{DC}_{[n]}(\overline{v})$ and outputs $v = v'$ if $J(v', n) = 1$ and $v = v'/\nu \bmod n$ if $J(v', n) = -1$. $\mathsf{EC}_{\pm\mathsf{QR}_n}$ is covert for message space $\pm\mathsf{QR}_n$ because $\pm\mathsf{QR}_n \times \{1, \nu\}$ is isomorphic to Z_n^* and Z_n^* is statistically indistinguishable from $[n]$. Since under the DQR assumption QR_n is indistinguishable from $\pm\mathsf{QR}_n$, the same encoding is also covert for message space QR_n, assuming DQR.

Covert-MA-Compatible IE Scheme from ACJT Group Signature. We explain how the ACJT group signature [ACJT00] can be transformed into a *covert-MA-compatible* IE scheme $(\mathsf{KG}, \mathsf{CG}, \mathsf{Ver}, \mathsf{IECom}, \mathsf{TraceCom})$ which we will call a *ACJT-IE*. This provides an installation of the covert MA construction of Fig. 2 because by the property (4) of a covert-MA-compatible IE scheme, we can construct a receiver covert and strong sender covert CKEM for the $\mathcal{R}^{IE}$ relation associated with this IE scheme using the CKEM construction in Fig. 1, and then we can use this CKEM together with the rest of the IE scheme in the covert MA construction in Fig. 2. By combining the assumptions required for the ACJT-IE scheme and for the CKEM construction (as stated in Theorem 1), we get the following corollary of Theorem 2:

Corollary 1. *The* (KGen, CG, Auth) *in Fig. 2 instantiated with the ACJT-IE scheme and the CKEM scheme of Fig.1, is a* Covert Mutual Authentication Scheme, *assuming the strong RSA and DQR assumptions on* Z_n^* *for the safe RSA modulus n, the DDH assumption on the* QR_n *subgroup of* Z_n^*, *and the DDH assumption on a prime-order subgroup of a prime residue group.*

We show the ACJT-IE scheme (KG, CG, Ver, IECom, TraceCom) and explain how it relies on the strong RSA, DDH, and DQR assumptions stated above. Algorithm KG sets the group public key as $gpk = (n, a, a_0, y, g, h)$, as in the original ACJT group signature [ACJT00], where n is a safe RSA modulus and a, a_0, y, g, h are all random generators of QR_n. The group secret key gsk is the factorization of n. CG outputs $(sk_i, rt_i) = ((A_i, e_i), x_i)$ where $x_i \leftarrow 2^{\lambda_1} \pm [2^{\lambda_2}]$, e_i is a random prime in $2^{\gamma_1} \pm [2^{\gamma_2}]$, and $A_i = (a^{x_i} a_0)^{1/e_i} \bmod n$, for parameters $\lambda_1, \lambda_2, \gamma_1, \gamma_2$ set as $\lambda_2 \approx 2l_n = 2|n|$, $\lambda_1 \approx \lambda_2 + \tau$, $\gamma_2 \approx \lambda_1 + 2$, and $\gamma_1 \approx \gamma_2 + \tau$. Algorithm Ver(gpk, $(A_i, e_i), x_i$) returns 1 if $A_i^{e_i} = a^{x_i} a_0 \bmod n$ and 0 otherwise. Commitment IECom on inputs (gpk, $((A_i, e_i), x_i)$) picks $w \leftarrow [n/4]$ and computes $T_1 \leftarrow A_i y^w$, $T_2 \leftarrow g^w$, and $T_3 \leftarrow g^{e_i} h^w$, just like in the ACJT scheme, but in addition it picks a random QR_n element T_4, computes $T_5 \leftarrow (T_4)^{x_i}$, and outputs $C = (\overline{T}_1, \ldots, \overline{T}_5)$ where $\overline{T}_i \leftarrow EC_{\pm QR_n}(T_i)$ for each i. TraceCom(gpk, C, x_i) outputs 1 iff $T_5 = (T_4)^{x_i}$ for T_4, T_5 decoded from $\overline{T}_4, \overline{T}_5$ in C.

Unforgeability of the (KG, Ver) certificate scheme is argued in [ACJT00] under the strong RSA assumption on QR_n. Traceability follows by the fact that procedure TraceCom(gpk, C, x_i) computes T_5 from T_4 in the same way as IECom on x_i. As for revocable covertness, since $\lambda_2 \geq 2|n|$ we have that for x_i uniform in $2^{\lambda_1} \pm [2^{\lambda_2}]$ value ($x_i \bmod n'$) is statistically indistinguishable from uniform over $Z_{n'}$. Therefore, for secret x_i, under DDH assumption on QR_n the 5-tuple $(T_1, \ldots, T_5)$ is indistinguishable from uniform over $(QR_n)^5$, and therefore by covertness of $EC_{\pm QR_n}$ commitment $\overline{T}$ is indistinguishable from a random bit-string. Finally, the HVZK proof system given for the ACJT group signature in [ACJT00], amended by the simple consistency check for the new (T_4, T_5) values, is a special Σ-protocol for the associated relation $\mathcal{R}^{IE}$. We include this amended proof system of [ACJT00] in Appendix A.

Efficiency of the Resulting Covert MA Scheme. The Covert MA protocol of Fig. 2 can be condensed to three rounds in ROM: Player P_i can piggyback R's message in the CKEM instance of step 2 with the commitment C_i it sends in step 1. Then player P_j can piggyback its commitment C_j with S's response in the CKEM instance of Step 2 and with R's message in the CKEM instance of step 3. Finally P_i would respond with S's response in the CKEM instance of step 3. As for the computational cost of this scheme instantiated with ACJT-IE scheme, note that ACJT-IE uses 4 multi-exp's in the certificate commitment IECom and that the Σ-protocol for the associated relation $\mathcal{R}^{IE}$ uses 5 multi-exp's for each party. Since each party plays the prover in one direction and the verifier in the other, the total comes to 14 (multi-)exp's in Z_n^*. The CKEM protocol in Fig. 1 adds 5 exp's in Z_p^* for each party (2 as the sender and 3 as the receiver). Moduli p and n can both be 2048 bits long, but exp's in Z_p^* are with much smaller exponents. Looking closer at the 14 multi-exp's in Z_n^* in the computation of T_i's, and d_i's in either step 1 for the prover or step 4 for the verifier (see the Σ-protocol in Appendix A), for $|n| = 2048$ and $\tau = 160$ this makes four 2048-bit exp's (i.e. T_1, T_2, and d_3 for both parties) and ten exp's with exponents between 4000 and 5000 bits. By comparison, the five exp's in Z_p^* have only 480-bit exponents. The total cost for each party, of these 14 exp's in Z_n^* and 5 exp's in Z_p^*, can be approximated as 30 full exp's in Z_n^* for $|n| = 2048$. However, each party additionally performs $|CRL| + 1$ exp's in Z_n^* in the TraceCom checks for each rt in CRL and for one's own rt. Since exponents x_i are roughly twice longer than $|n|$, the total cost is approximately $32 + 2|CRL|$ full exp's in Z_n^* with $|n| = 2048$ and $\tau = 160$. The bandwidth is about 29Kb in each direction. Note that these costs are almost exactly as in the underlying ACJT group signature scheme, so the practicality of our ACJT-based covert MA scheme depends on whether the two parties have access to a random steganographic channel with enough capacity to transmit 29Kb.

References

ACJT00.   Ateniese, G., Camenisch, J.L., Joye, M., Tsudik, G.: A practical and prov-
          ably secure coalition-resistant group signature scheme. In: Bellare, M. (ed.)
          CRYPTO 2000. LNCS, vol. 1880, pp. 255–270. Springer, Heidelberg (2000)
BCK98.   Bellare, M., Canetti, R., Krawczyk, H.: A modular approach to the design
          and analysis of authentication and key exchange protocols. In: STOC 1998,
          pp. 419–428 (1998)
BN06.   Bellare, M., Neven, G.: Multisignatures in the plain publickey model and a
          general forking lemma. In: Proceedings of ACM CCS (2006)
BS04.   Boneh, D., Shacham, H.: Group signatures with verifier-local revocation. In:
          ACM Conference on Computer and Communications Security, pp. 168–177
          (2004)
CGOS07.   Chandran, N., Goyal, V., Ostrovsky, R., Sahai, A.: Covert multi-party com-
          putation. In: FOCS, pp. 238–248 (2007)
CK01.   Canetti, R., Krawczyk, H.: Analysis of key-exchange protocols and their use
          for building secure channels. In: Pfitzmann, B. (ed.) EUROCRYPT 2001.
          LNCS, vol. 2045, pp. 453–474. Springer, Heidelberg (2001)
CM99.   Camenisch, J.L., Michels, M.: Proving in zero-knowledge that a number is
          the product of two safe primes. In: Stern, J. (ed.) EUROCRYPT 1999. LNCS,
          vol. 1592, pp. 107–122. Springer, Heidelberg (1999)
COR99.   Di Crescenzo, G., Ostrovsky, R., Rajagopalan, S.: Conditional oblivious
          transfer and timed-release encryption. In: Stern, J. (ed.) EUROCRYPT 1999.
          LNCS, vol. 1592, pp. 74–89. Springer, Heidelberg (1999)
Cre00.   Di Crescenzo, G.: Private selective payment protocols. In: Financial Cryp-
          tography, pp. 72–89 (2000)
CS01.   Cramer, R., Shoup, V.: Universal hash proofs and and a paradigm for adap-
          tive chosen ciphertext secure public-key encryption. Electronic Colloquium
          on Computational Complexity (ECCC) 8(072) (2001)

CvH91.   Chaum, D., van Heyst, E.: Group signatures. In: Davies, D.W. (ed.) EURO-CRYPT 1991. LNCS, vol. 547, pp. 257–265. Springer, Heidelberg (1991)

Dam10.   Ivan Damgard. On Σ-protocols (2010),
         http://www.cs.au.dk/~ivan/Sigma.pdf

GJ10.   Goyal, V., Jain, A.: On the round complexity of covert computation. In: STOC (2010)

HLvA02. Hopper, N.J., Langford, J., von Ahn, L.: Provably secure steganography. In: Yung, M. (ed.) CRYPTO 2002. LNCS, vol. 2442, pp. 77–92. Springer, Heidelberg (2002)

JL09.   Jarecki, S., Liu, X.: Private mutual authentication and conditional oblivious transfer. In: Halevi, S. (ed.) CRYPTO 2009. LNCS, vol. 5677, pp. 90–107. Springer, Heidelberg (2009)

KP98.   Kilian, J., Petrank, E.: Identity escrow. In: Krawczyk, H. (ed.) CRYPTO 1998. LNCS, vol. 1462, pp. 169–185. Springer, Heidelberg (1998)

vAH04.   von Ahn, L., Hopper, N.J.: Public-key steganography. In: Cachin, C., Camenisch, J.L. (eds.) EUROCRYPT 2004. LNCS, vol. 3027, pp. 323–341. Springer, Heidelberg (2004)

vAHL05. von Ahn, L., Hopper, N.J., Langford, J.: Covert two-party computation. In: STOC, pp. 513–522 (2005)

A   Special Σ-Protocol for the ACJT-IE Scheme

We show a proof system for the committed certificate validity relation $\mathcal{R}^{IE}$ in the ACJT-IE scheme of Section 5.1, which satisfies the properties of a *special Σ-protocol*, and hence it can be compiled into a covert CKEM for the same relation using our CKEM construction in Fig. 1. The proof system below is a simple modification of the proof system for the ACJT group signature [ACJT00] extended by a check that $T_5 = T_4^{x_i}$. Relation $\mathcal{R}^{IE}$ for the ACJT-IE scheme consists of pairs $(\hat{x}, \hat{w}) = (((n, a, a_0, y, g, h), (\overline{T}_1, \ldots, \overline{T}_5)), ((A_i, e_i), x_i, w))$ which satisfy the following set of relations for T_i's decoded from $\overline{T}_i$'s using $\mathsf{DC}_{\pm\mathsf{QR}_n}$:

$$T_1 = A_i y^w, \; T_2 = g^w, \; T_3 = g^{e_i} h^w, \; T_5 = T_4^{x_i}, \; A_i^{e_i} = a^{x_i} a_0, \; x_i \in 2^{\lambda_1} \pm [2^{\lambda_2 + 2\tau}]$$

Below is the special Σ-protocol for this relation, which the honest prover executes on $(x_i, e_i, w) \in (\, 2^{\lambda_1} \pm [2^{\lambda_2}] \times 2^{\gamma_1} \pm [2^{\gamma_2}] \times [2^{l_n - 2}] \,)$:

1. P_1 picks $(r_1, r_2, r_3, r_4) \leftarrow \pm[2^{\gamma_2 + 2\tau}] \times \pm[2^{\lambda_2 + 2\tau}] \times \pm[2^{\gamma_1 + l_n + 2\tau}] \times \pm[2^{l_n + 2\tau}]$,
    sets $(d_1, d_2, d_3, d_4, d_5) \leftarrow (T_1^{r_1}/(a^{r_2} y^{r_3}), T_2^{r_1}/g^{r_3}, g^{r_4}, g^{r_1} h^{r_4}, T_4^{r_2})$,
    sets $r = (r_1, r_2, r_3, r_4)$, and outputs $a = (d_1, d_2, d_3, d_4, d_5)$.
2. Public coin challenge c is chosen as $c \leftarrow \{0,1\}^\tau$.
3. P_2 sets $z = (z_1, z_2, z_3, z_4)$ for $z_1 \leftarrow r_1 - c(e_i - 2^{\gamma_1})$, $z_2 \leftarrow r_2 - c(x_i - 2^{\lambda_1})$, $z_3 \leftarrow r_3 - ce_i w$, $z_4 \leftarrow r_4 - cw$ [all computed over integers]
4. V accepts if $z = (z_1, \ldots, z_4)$ lies in the cross-space $I' = (I'_1 \times I'_2 \times I'_3 \times I'_4)$, for
    $I'_1 = \pm[2^{\gamma_2 + 2\tau + 1}]$, $I'_2 = \pm[2^{\lambda_2 + 2\tau + 1}]$, $I'_3 = \pm[2^{\gamma_1 + l_n + 2\tau + 1}]$, $I'_4 = \pm[2^{l_n + 2\tau + 1}]$,
    and if $a = f_V(\hat{x}, c, z)$ where $f_V(\hat{x}, c, z)$ computes $(d_1, \ldots, d_5)$ as follows:

$$d_1 \overset{?}{=} a_0^c T_1^{z_1 - c2^{\gamma_1}}/(a^{z_2 - c2^{\lambda_1}} y^{z_3}) \qquad d_2 \overset{?}{=} T_1^{z_1 - c2^{\gamma_1}}/g^{z_3}$$

$$d_3 \overset{?}{=} T_2^c g^{z_4} \qquad d_4 \overset{?}{=} T_3^c g^{z_1 - c2^{\gamma_1}} h^{z_4} \qquad d_5 \overset{?}{=} T_5^c T_4^{z_2 - c2^{\lambda_1}}$$

By the constraints on (x_i, e_i, w) used by an honest prover, z is statistically close to uniform over $I = I_1 \times I_2 \times I_3 \times I_4$ where $I_1 = \pm[2^{\gamma_2+2\tau}]$, $I_2 = \pm[2^{\lambda_2+2\tau}]$, $I_3 = \pm[2^{\gamma_1+l_n+2\tau}]$, $I_4 = \pm[2^{l_n+2\tau}]$. The proof of knowledge property of the ACJT proof system [ACJT00] satisfies the requirement that a valid witness $\hat{w} = ((A_i, x_i), e_i, w)$ is efficiently extractable from two accepting proof transcripts (a, c, z) and (a, c', z') s.t. $c' \neq c$, and this property holds for our extension which involves the check that $T_5 = T_4^{x_i}$.

Fine-Tuning Groth-Sahai Proofs

Alex Escala[1] and Jens Groth[2,*]

[1] Scytl Secure Electronic Voting, Spain
[2] University College London, United Kingdom

Abstract. Groth-Sahai proofs are efficient non-interactive zero-knowledge proofs that have found widespread use in pairing-based cryptography. We propose efficiency improvements of Groth-Sahai proofs in the SXDH setting, which is the one that yields the most efficient non-interactive zero-knowledge proofs.

- We replace some of the commitments with ElGamal encryptions, which reduces the prover's computation and for some types of equations reduces the proof size.
- Groth-Sahai proofs are zero-knowledge when no public elements are paired to each other. We observe that they are also zero-knowledge when base elements for the groups are paired to public constants.
- The prover's computation can be reduced by letting her pick her own common reference string. By giving a proof she has picked a valid common reference string this does not compromise soundness.
- We define a type-based commit-and-prove scheme, which allows commitments to be reused in many different proofs.

Keywords: Non-interactive zero-knowledge proofs, commit-and-prove schemes, Groth-Sahai proofs, type-based commitments.

1 Introduction

Non-interactive zero-knowledge (NIZK) proofs [BFM88] can be used to demonstrate a statement is true without revealing any other information. NIZK proofs are fundamental building blocks in cryptography and are used in numerous cryptographic schemes. It is therefore important to increase their efficiency since even small improvements will lead to significant performance gains when aggregated over many applications.

NIZK proofs were invented more than two decades ago but early constructions [BFM88, FLS99, Dam92, KP98] were very inefficient. This changed when Groth, Ostrovsky and Sahai [GOS12] introduced pairing-based techniques for constructing NIZK proofs. In a series of works [BW06, Gro06, BW07, GS12] pairing-friendly NIZK proofs were developed. This line of research culminated

* The research leading to these results has received funding from the European Research Council under the European Union's Seventh Framework Programme (FP/2007-2013) / ERC Grant Agreement n. 307937 and the Engineering and Physical Sciences Research Council grants EP/G013829/1 and EP/J009520/1.

H. Krawczyk (Ed.): PKC 2014, LNCS 8383, pp. 630–649, 2014.

in Groth and Sahai [GS12] that gave efficient and practical NIZK proofs that are now widely used in pairing-based cryptography.

Groth-Sahai proofs [GS12] can be instantiated in many ways with either symmetric or asymmetric pairings and over groups that may have either composite order or prime order. The asymmetric setting with prime order groups yields the smallest group elements [GPS08]. We will therefore focus on improving Groth-Sahai proofs for prime order asymmetric bilinear groups, since the better efficiency makes it the most important setting for use in practice.

Let us give some more details of what can be done with Groth-Sahai proofs. The setting they consider is a bilinear group $(p, \hat{\mathbb{G}}, \check{\mathbb{H}}, \mathbb{T}, e, \hat{g}, \check{h})$, where $\hat{\mathbb{G}}, \check{\mathbb{H}}, \mathbb{T}$ are prime order p groups, $\hat{g}$ and $\check{h}$ are generators of $\hat{\mathbb{G}}$ and $\check{\mathbb{H}}$ respectively and $e : \hat{\mathbb{G}} \times \check{\mathbb{H}} \to \mathbb{T}$ is a non-degenerate bilinear map. The prover wants to show that there are values $\hat{x}_i \in \hat{\mathbb{G}}, \check{y}_j \in \check{\mathbb{H}}, x_i, y_j \in \mathbb{Z}_p$ simultaneously satisfying a set of equations. Groth and Sahai formulate four types of equations, which using additive notation for group operations and multiplicative notation for the bilinear map e can be written as follows.

Pairing-product equation: Public constants $\hat{a}_j \in \hat{\mathbb{G}}, \check{b}_i \in \check{\mathbb{H}}, \gamma_{ij} \in \mathbb{Z}_p, t_{\mathbb{T}} \in \mathbb{T}$.

$$\sum_i \hat{x}_i \cdot \check{b}_i + \sum_j \hat{a}_j \cdot \check{y}_j + \sum_i \sum_j \gamma_{ij} \hat{x}_i \cdot \check{y}_j = t_{\mathbb{T}}.$$

Multi-scalar multiplication equation in $\hat{\mathbb{G}}$: Public constants $\hat{a}_j \in \hat{\mathbb{G}}, b_i \in \mathbb{Z}_p, \gamma_{ij} \in \mathbb{Z}_p, \hat{t} \in \hat{\mathbb{G}}$.

$$\sum_i \hat{x}_i b_i + \sum_j \hat{a}_j y_j + \sum_i \sum_j \gamma_{ij} \hat{x}_i y_j = \hat{t}.$$

Multi-scalar multiplication equation in $\check{\mathbb{H}}$: Public constants $a_j \in \mathbb{Z}_p, \check{b}_i \in \check{\mathbb{H}}, \gamma_{ij} \in \mathbb{Z}_p, \check{t} \subset \check{\mathbb{H}}$.

$$\sum_i x_i \check{b}_i + \sum_j a_j \check{y}_j + \sum_i \sum_j \gamma_{ij} x_i \check{y}_j = \check{t}.$$

Quadratic equation in $\mathbb{Z}_p$: Public constants $a_j \in \mathbb{Z}_p, b_i \in \mathbb{Z}_p, \gamma_{ij} \in \mathbb{Z}_p, t \in \mathbb{Z}_p$.

$$\sum_i x_i b_i + \sum_j a_j y_j + \sum_i \sum_j \gamma_{ij} x_i y_j = t.$$

These four types of equations express in a direct way statements arising in pairing-based cryptography. For this reason Groth-Sahai proofs are used in numerous pairing-based protocols including group signatures [Gro07], anonymous credentials [BCKL08, DCC+09], e-cash [FPV09], etc.

Groth-Sahai proofs are witness-indistinguishable proofs that enable a prover to convince a verifier that a statement is true without revealing which witness the prover knows. For a slightly more restricted set of statements where all pairing-product equations have $t_{\mathbb{T}} = 0_{\mathbb{T}}$, Groth-Sahai proofs are actually zero-knowledge proofs that leak no information besides the truth of the statement.

There have been several papers that extend or improve the Groth-Sahai proof system in different directions. [Mei09] suggested how to create perfectly extractable commitments, something which is not given by the commitments used by Groth and Sahai. [CHP07, BFI$^+$10] reduced the computational cost of the verification of the proofs using batch techniques, at the cost of trading perfect soundness for statistical soundness. [Seo12] gave another map for verifying proofs in the symmetric setting which reduces the computational cost of the verification of the proofs. On the other hand, they prove that the map proposed by Groth and Sahai in the asymmetric setting is optimal. [GSW10] proposed another assumption on which Groth-Sahai proofs can be based. [BCKL08, BCC$^+$09] exploited rerandomization properties of Groth-Sahai proofs, which they used in anonymous credentials. [Fuc11] proposed a witness-indistinguishable commit-and-prove scheme based on Groth-Sahai proofs in the symmetric setting. [CKLM12] introduced a new notion of malleable proof systems, which can be built from Groth-Sahai proofs. While there has been significant research effort devoted to pairing-based NIZK proofs, Groth-Sahai proofs still remain the most efficient NIZK proofs that are based on standard intractability assumptions and there has not been any progress in reducing their size or the prover's computation except for special purpose statements [EHKRV13, JR13].

1.1   Our Contributions

We focus on improving efficiency and propose several ways to fine-tune Groth-Sahai zero-knowledge proofs in the asymmetric bilinear group setting.

- Groth-Sahai proofs use public constants and committed variables. We introduce two new types of values: public base elements and encrypted variables. This reduces the size of proofs for statements involving these values.
- We recast Groth-Sahai proofs as a commit-and-prove scheme. This makes it possible to reuse commitments in the proofs of different statements even when these statements depend on previous commitments and proofs.
- We show that the prover's computation can be reduced by letting her pick her own provably correct common reference string.

Encrypted Variables. The common reference string in Groth-Sahai proofs contains a public commitment key that the prover uses to commit to variables. The prover then proceeds to prove that the committed variables satisfy the equations in the statement. In our scheme we allow the prover to encrypt variables using ElGamal encryption as an alternative to the commitment scheme. ElGamal encryption reduces the prover's computation when compared to the commitment operation. Moreover, equations that use ElGamal ciphertexts instead of commitments have simpler proofs. However, using ElGamal encryption means we cannot get perfect zero-knowledge, so we rely on the Decision Diffie-Hellman (DDH) assumption to get computational zero-knowledge and we place some restrictions on the types of equations where ElGamal encryptions can be used.

Base Elements. We observe that the commitment keys can be set up to allow simulation in pairing-product equations where $t_T = \hat{a} \cdot \check{h} + \hat{g} \cdot \check{b}$ for public constants $\hat{a} \in \hat{\mathbb{G}}$ and $\check{b} \in \check{\mathbb{H}}$. This extension of Groth-Sahai proofs comes at no extra cost, so we save the costly rewriting of the equations proposed in [GS12] which was required to get zero-knowledge in those kinds of equations.

In addition, a similar observation allows us to have shorter Groth-Sahai zero-knowledge proofs for multi-scalar multiplications equations in $\hat{\mathbb{G}}$ or in $\check{\mathbb{H}}$ in which all the field elements are the constants $\hat{t} = \hat{g}$ or $\check{t} = \check{h}$.

Using Commitment Keys with Known Discrete Logarithms. In Groth-Sahai proofs, a common reference string created by a trusted entity is shared between the prover and the verifier. We show how to reduce the prover's computation by allowing her to choose her *own common reference string*, which we think of as her public key. This change reduces the cost of computing her commitments from 4 scalar multiplications to 2 scalar multiplications and it also reduces the cost of computing proofs.

To enforce soundness, the prover will give a Groth-Sahai proof to the prover, using a common reference string the verifier does trust, for the public key being correct. The cost of such proof is 12 group elements in total, which is a one-off cost as the public key can be used for many commitments and proofs.

Viewing the common reference string as the prover's public key gives us some flexibility in the setup. Instead of proving the public key correct in the common reference string model, the prover could use the multi-string model [GO07] where we only assume a majority out of n common reference strings are honest. Alternatively, the prover could give a zero-knowledge proof of knowledge to a trusted third party that the public key is correct and get a certificate on the public key.

Type-Based Commit-and-Prove Schemes. A natural generalization of zero-knowledge proofs are commit-and-prove schemes [Kil90, CLOS02], where the prover can commit to values and prove statements about the committed values. Commit-and-prove schemes provide extra flexibility and reduce communication; it is for instance possible to choose values to be committed to in an adaptive fashion that depends on previous commitments or proofs. The traditional definition of zero-knowledge proofs would require the prover to make an entirely new set of commitments for each statement to be proven.

Groth-Sahai proofs can be used to build a non-interactive commit-and-prove scheme in a natural way; Belenkiy et al. [BCKL08] for instance explicitly let the commitments be part of the statements and define witness-indistinguishable proofs for such statements. Fuchsbauer [Fuc11] defines a witness-indistinguishable Groth-Sahai based commit-and-prove scheme and uses it in the construction of delegatable anonymous credentials. Our definition of a non-interactive commit-and-prove scheme will resemble Fuchsbauer's [Fuc11]. However, we are in a different situation because we have more types of elements that we want to commit to. A group element in $\hat{\mathbb{G}}$ may for instance be committed using the perfectly binding/perfectly hiding commitment scheme or using ElGamal encryption.

To give a generally applicable definition of non-interactive commit-and-prove schemes, we propose the notion of *type-based* commitments. A type-based commitment scheme enables the prover to commit to a message m with a publicly known type t and we require that the type and message pair (t, m) belong to a message space $\mathcal{M}_{ck}$. One example of a type could for instance be $t = \text{enc}_{\hat{\mathbb{G}}}$ meaning the value m should be encrypted (as opposed to using the more expensive commitment operation) and it should be done in group $\hat{\mathbb{G}}$. This increases the flexibility of the commitment scheme, we can for instance create a type $(\text{pub}_{\hat{\mathbb{G}}}, x)$ that publicly declares the committed value x. Since the type is public this commitment is no longer hiding, however, as we shall see it simplifies our commit-and-prove scheme because we can now commit to both public constants and secret variables without having to treat them differently.

Applications. To illustrate the advantages of our fine-tuned Groth-Sahai proofs we give an example based on the weak Boneh-Boyen signature scheme [BB04], which is widely used in pairing-based protocols. The verification key is an element $\hat{v} \in \hat{\mathbb{G}}$ and a signature on a message $m \in \mathbb{Z}_p$ is a group element $\check{\sigma} \in \check{\mathbb{H}}$ such that

$$(\hat{v} + m\hat{g}) \cdot \check{\sigma} = \hat{g} \cdot \check{h}.$$

Suppose the prover has commitments to $\hat{v}$ and $\check{\sigma}$ and wants to demonstrate that they satisfy the verification equation for a (public) message m. With traditional Groth-Sahai proofs the commitments c and d to $\hat{v}$ and $\check{\sigma}$ would be treated as part of the statement and one would carefully demonstrate the existence of openings of c and d to $\hat{v}$ and $\check{\sigma}$ satisfying the pairing-product equation. With a commit-and-prove system, we can instead jump directly to demonstrating that the values inside $\hat{v}$ and $\check{\sigma}$ satisfy the verification equation without having to treat the openings of the commitments as part of the witness. This saves several group elements each time one of the commitments is used.

Next, observe that the pairing-product equation has $t_{\mathbb{T}} = \hat{g} \cdot \check{h}$. A direct application of Groth-Sahai proofs would therefore not yield a zero-knowledge proof but only give witness-indistinguishability. To get zero-knowledge we could use the workaround suggested by Groth-Sahai, which would consist of committing to a new variable $\check{y}$, prove that $\check{y} = \check{h}$ and simultaneously $(\hat{v} + m\hat{g}) \cdot \check{\sigma} - \hat{g} \cdot \check{y} = 0_{\mathbb{T}}$. This workaround would increase the cost of the proof from 8 group elements to 16 group elements, so we save 8 group elements by enabling a direct proof.

Now assume the prover has created her own common reference string pk and has already sent it together with the well-formedness proof to the verifier. The prover could now use pk to compute the zero-knowledge proof for the equation $(\hat{v} + m\hat{g}) \cdot \check{\sigma} = \hat{g}\check{h}$. By using pk, she would need to do 10 scalar multiplications in $\hat{\mathbb{G}}$ and 6 scalar multiplications in $\check{\mathbb{H}}$ to compute the proof. In contrast, if she was computing the proof using the commitment key ck, she would need to do 12 scalar multiplications in $\hat{\mathbb{G}}$ and 10 scalar multiplications in $\check{\mathbb{H}}$. As the operations in $\check{\mathbb{H}}$ are usually significantly more expensive than the operations in $\hat{\mathbb{G}}$, the prover is essentially saving 4 expensive operations of the 10 that she would need to do if she used ck. Therefore, our techniques reduce the computational cost of creating the zero-knowledge proof by roughly 40%. In addition, the computational cost of computing the commitments to $\hat{v}$ and $\check{v}$ would also be reduced by 50%.

Finally, we can obtain a saving by encrypting one of the variables instead of committing to it. If we encrypt $\hat{v}$ for instance, the ciphertext is 2 group elements just as a commitment would be, but the cost of the proof for the pairing-product equation is reduced from 8 group elements to 6 group elements. In total we have reduced the cost by 63% from 16 group elements to 6 group elements.

In the full paper [EG13] we give two concrete examples of existing schemes using Groth-Sahai proofs where our techniques can improve efficiency.

2   Commit-and-Prove Scheme Definitions

Let R_L be a polynomial time verifiable relation containing triples (ck, x, w). We will call ck the commitment key or the common reference string, x the statement and w the witness. We define the key-dependent language L_{ck} as the set of statements x for which there exists a witness w such that $(ck, x, w) \in R_L$.

We will now define a commit-and-prove scheme for a relation R_L. In the commit-and-prove scheme, we may commit to different values $w_1, \ldots, w_N$ and prove for different statements x that a subset of the committed values $w = (w_{i_1}, \ldots, w_{i_n})$ constitute a witness for $x \in L_{ck}$, i.e., $(ck, x, w) \in R_L$.

We will divide each committed value into two parts $w_i = (t_i, m_i)$. The first part t_i can be thought of as a public part that does not need to be kept secret, while the second part m_i can be thought of as a secret value that our commit-and-prove scheme should not reveal. The first part t_i will be useful later on to specify the type of value m_i is, for instance a group element or a field element, and to specify which type of commitment we should make to m_i. This is a natural and useful generalization of standard commitment schemes.

A commit-and-prove scheme $CP = (\text{Gen}, \text{Com}, \text{Prove}, \text{Verify})$ consists of four polynomial time algorithms. The algorithms Gen, Prove are probabilistic and the algorithms Com, Verify are deterministic.

$\text{Gen}(1^k)$: Generates a commitment key ck. The commitment key specifies a message space $\mathcal{M}_{ck}$, a randomness space $\mathcal{R}_{ck}$ and a commitment space $\mathcal{C}_{ck}$. Membership of either space can be decided efficiently.

$\text{Com}_{ck}(t, m; r)$: Given a commitment key ck, a message $(t, m) \in \mathcal{M}_{ck}$ and randomness r such that $(t, r) \in \mathcal{R}_{ck}$ returns a commitment c such that $(t, c) \in \mathcal{C}_{ck}$.

$\text{Prove}_{ck}(x, (t_1, m_1, r_1), \ldots, (t_n, m_n, r_n))$: Given a commitment key ck, statement x and commitment openings such that $(t_i, m_i) \in \mathcal{M}_{ck}, (t_i, r_i) \in \mathcal{R}_{ck}$ and $(ck, x, t_1, m_1, \ldots, t_n, m_n) \in R_L$ returns a proof π.

$\text{Verify}_{ck}(x, (t_1, c_1), \ldots, (t_n, c_n), \pi)$: Given a commitment key ck, a statement x, a proof π and commitments $(t_i, c_i) \in \mathcal{C}_{ck}$ returns 1 (accept) or 0 (reject).

Definition 1 (Perfect correctness). *The commit-and-prove system* CP *is (perfectly) correct if for all adversaries* $\mathcal{A}$

$$\Pr\left[\begin{array}{l} ck \leftarrow \text{Gen}(1^k) \ ; \ (x, w_1, r_1, \ldots, w_n, r_n) \leftarrow \mathcal{A}(ck) \ ; \ c_i \leftarrow \text{Com}_{ck}(w_i; r_i) \ ; \\ \pi \leftarrow \text{Prove}_{ck}(x, w_1, r_1, \ldots, w_n, r_n) : \text{Verify}_{ck}(x, (t_1, c_1), \ldots, (t_n, c_n), \pi) = 1 \end{array}\right] = 1,$$

where $\mathcal{A}$ *outputs* w_i, r_i *such that* $w_i = (t_i, m_i) \in \mathcal{M}_{ck}, (t_i, r_i) \in \mathcal{R}_{ck}$ *and* $(ck, x, w_1, \ldots, w_n) \in R_L$.

We say a commit-and-prove scheme is sound if it is impossible to prove a false statement. Strengthening the usual notion of soundness, we will associate unique values to the commitments, and these values will constitute a witness for the statement. This means that not only does a valid proof guarantee the truth of the statement, but also each commitment will always contribute a consistent witness towards establishing the truth of the statement.

Definition 2 (Perfect soundness). *The commit-and-prove system* CP *is (perfectly) sound if there exists a deterministic (unbounded) opening algorithm* Open *such that for all adversaries* $\mathcal{A}$

$$\Pr\left[\begin{matrix} ck \leftarrow \mathrm{Gen}(1^k) \ ; \ (x, t_1, c_1, \ldots, t_n, c_n, \pi) \leftarrow \mathcal{A}(ck) \ ; \ m_i \leftarrow \mathrm{Open}_{ck}(t_i, c_i) : \\ \mathrm{Verify}_{ck}(x, t_1, c_1, \ldots, t_n, c_n, \pi) = 0 \ \vee \ (ck, x, (t_1, m_1), \ldots, (t_n, m_n)) \in R_L \end{matrix}\right] = 1.$$

Extending the notion of soundness we may define a proof of knowledge as one where it is possible to efficiently extract a witness for the truth of the statement proven when given an extraction key xk. Actually, the commit-and-prove schemes we construct will not allow the extraction of all types of witnesses due to the hardness of the discrete logarithm problem. However, following Belenkiy et al. [BCKL08] we can specify a function F such that we can extract $F(ck, w)$ from a commitment. Efficient extraction of a witness corresponds to the special case where $F(ck, w) = m$, with m being the secret part of the witness $w = (t, m)$.

Definition 3 (Perfect F-extractability). *Let in the following* ExtGen *and* Ext *be two algorithms as described below.*

- ExtGen *is a probabilistic polynomial time algorithm that on* 1^k *returns* (ck, xk). *We call* ck *the commitment key and* xk *the extraction key. We require that the probability distributions of* ck *made by* ExtGen *and* Gen *are identical.*
- Ext *is a deterministic polynomial time algorithm that given an extraction key* xk *and* $(t, c) \in \mathcal{C}_{ck}$ *returns a value.*

The commit-and-prove scheme CP *with perfect soundness for opening algorithm* Open *is* F*-extractable if for all adversaries* $\mathcal{A}$

$$\Pr\left[\begin{matrix} (ck, xk) \leftarrow \mathrm{ExtGen}(1^k) \ ; \ (t, c) \leftarrow \mathcal{A}(ck, xk) : \\ (t, c) \notin \mathcal{C}_{ck} \ \vee \ \mathrm{Ext}_{xk}(t, c) = F(ck, (t, \mathrm{Open}(t, c))) \end{matrix}\right] = 1.$$

A commit-and-prove scheme is zero-knowledge if it does not leak information about the secret parts of the committed messages besides what is known from the public parts. This is defined as the ability to simulate commitments and proofs without knowing the secret parts of the messages (the types are known) if instead some secret simulation trapdoor is known.

Following [Gro06, GOS12] we define a strong notion of zero-knowledge called composable zero-knowledge. Composable zero-knowledge says the commitment key can be simulated, and if the commitment key is simulated it is not possible to distinguish real proofs from simulated proofs even if the simulation trapdoor is known.

Definition 4 (Composable zero-knowledge). *The commit-and-prove system* CP *is (computationally) composable zero-knowledge if there exist probabilistic polynomial time algorithms* SimGen, SimCom, SimProve *such that for all non-uniform polynomial time stateful interactive adversaries* $\mathcal{A}$ [1]

$$\Pr\left[ck \leftarrow \mathrm{Gen}(1^k) : \mathcal{A}(ck) = 1\right] \approx \Pr\left[(ck, tk) \leftarrow \mathrm{SimGen}(1^k) : \mathcal{A}(ck) = 1\right]$$

and

$$\Pr\left[\begin{array}{l} (ck, tk) \leftarrow \mathrm{SimGen}(1^k); (x, i_1, \ldots, i_n) \leftarrow \mathcal{A}^{\mathrm{Com}_{ck}(\cdot)}(ck, tk); \\ \pi \leftarrow \mathrm{Prove}_{ck}(x, w_{i_1}, r_{i_1}, \ldots, w_{i_n}, r_{i_n}) : \mathcal{A}(\pi) = 1 \end{array}\right]$$

$$\approx \Pr\left[\begin{array}{l} (ck, tk) \leftarrow \mathrm{SimGen}(1^k); (x, i_1, \ldots, i_n) \leftarrow \mathcal{A}^{\mathrm{SimCom}_{tk}(\cdot)}(ck, tk); \\ \pi \leftarrow \mathrm{SimProve}_{tk}(x, t_{i_1}, s_{i_1}, \ldots, t_{i_n}, s_{i_n}) : \mathcal{A}(\pi) = 1 \end{array}\right],$$

where

- *tk is a trapdoor key used to construct simulated proofs*
- $\mathrm{Com}_{ck}(\cdot)$ *on* $w_i = (t_i, m_i) \in \mathcal{M}_{ck}$ *picks uniformly random* r_i *such that* $(t_i, r_i) \in \mathcal{R}_{ck}$ *and returns* $c_i = \mathrm{Com}_{ck}(w_i; r_i)$
- $\mathrm{SimCom}_{tk}(\cdot)$ *on* $w_i = (t_i, m_i) \in \mathcal{M}_{ck}$ *runs* $(c_i, s_i) \leftarrow \mathrm{SimCom}_{tk}(t_i)$ *and returns* c_i, *where* s_i *is some auxiliary information used to construct simulated proofs*
- $\mathcal{A}$ *picks* $(x, i_1, \ldots, i_n)$ *such that* $(ck, x, w_{i_1}, \ldots, w_{i_n}) \in R_L$

3 Preliminaries

3.1 Bilinear Group

Let $\mathcal{G}$ be a probabilistic polynomial time algorithm that on input 1^k returns $(p, \hat{\mathbb{G}}, \check{\mathbb{H}}, \mathbb{T}, e, \hat{g}, \check{h})$, where $\hat{\mathbb{G}}, \check{\mathbb{H}}$ and $\mathbb{T}$ are groups of prime order p, $\hat{g}$ and $\check{h}$ generate $\hat{\mathbb{G}}$ and $\check{\mathbb{H}}$ respectively, and $e : \hat{\mathbb{G}} \times \check{\mathbb{H}} \to \mathbb{T}$ is an efficiently computable, non-degenerate bilinear map.

Notation. We will write elements $\hat{x} \in \hat{\mathbb{G}}$ with a hat and elements $\check{y} \in \check{\mathbb{H}}$ with an inverted hat to make it easy to distinguish elements from the two groups. We denote the neutral elements in the groups $\hat{\mathbb{G}}, \check{\mathbb{H}}$ and $\mathbb{T}$ with $\hat{0}, \check{0}$ and $0_{\mathbb{T}}$.

---

[1] Given two functions $f, g : \mathbb{N} \to [0, 1]$ we write $f(k) \approx g(k)$ when $|f(k) - g(k)| = O(k^{-c})$ for every positive integer c. We say that f is *negligible* when $f(k) \approx 0$ and that it is *overwhelming* when $f(k) \approx 1$.

It will be convenient to use additive notation for all three groups $\hat{\mathbb{G}}, \check{\mathbb{H}}$ and $\mathbb{T}$. This notation deviates from standard practice ($\hat{\mathbb{G}}, \check{\mathbb{H}}$ are sometimes written multiplicatively and $\mathbb{T}$ is usually written multiplicatively) but will greatly simplify our paper and make it possible to use linear algebra concepts such as vectors and matrices in a natural way. We stress that even though we are using additive notation it is hard to compute discrete logarithms in the groups.

It will also be convenient to write the pairing e with multiplicative notation. So we define

$$\hat{x} \cdot \check{y} = e(\hat{x}, \check{y}).$$

Writing the pairing multiplicatively allows us to use linear algebra notation in a natural way, we have for instance

$$\hat{x} \cdot \begin{pmatrix} \check{0} & \check{y} \\ \check{z} & \check{0} \end{pmatrix} e^\top = \begin{pmatrix} \hat{x} \cdot \check{y} \\ 0_\mathbb{T} \end{pmatrix},$$

for $\hat{x} \in \hat{\mathbb{G}}, \check{y}, \check{z} \in \check{\mathbb{H}}$ and $e = (0, 1)$. Note that as $\hat{x}a \cdot \check{y} = \hat{x} \cdot a\check{y}$ we will use the simpler notation $\hat{x}a\check{y} = \hat{x}a \cdot \check{y} = \hat{x} \cdot a\check{y}$.

3.2   SXDH Assumption

Let $(p, \hat{\mathbb{G}}, \check{\mathbb{H}}, \mathbb{T}, e, \hat{g}, \check{h})$ be a bilinear group. The Decision Diffie-Hellman (DDH) problem in $\hat{\mathbb{G}}$ is to distinguish the two distributions $(\hat{g}, \xi\hat{g}, \rho\hat{g}, \xi\rho\hat{g})$ and $(\hat{g}, \xi\hat{g}, \rho\hat{g}, \kappa\hat{g})$, where $\xi, \rho, \kappa \leftarrow \mathbb{Z}_p$. The DDH problem in $\check{\mathbb{H}}$ is defined in a similar way.

Definition 5. *The Symmetric eXternal Diffie-Hellman (SXDH) assumption holds relative to $\mathcal{G}$ if the DDH problems are computationally hard in both $\hat{\mathbb{G}}$ and $\check{\mathbb{H}}$ for $(p, \hat{\mathbb{G}}, \check{\mathbb{H}}, \mathbb{T}, e, \hat{g}, \check{h}) \leftarrow \mathcal{G}(1^k)$.*

3.3   ElGamal Encryption

The ElGamal encryption scheme [EG84] is a public key encryption scheme given by the following algorithms:

- **Setup:** on input a security parameter 1^k, output a cyclic group $\hat{\mathbb{G}}$ of prime order p, an element $\hat{g} \in \hat{\mathbb{G}}$ and an element $\xi \leftarrow \mathbb{Z}_p^*$. Then, define the public key as $pk = (\hat{\mathbb{G}}, \hat{v})$, where $\hat{v} = (\xi\hat{g}, \hat{g})^\top \in \hat{\mathbb{G}}^{2\times 1}$ and the secret decryption key as $xk = (pk, \boldsymbol{\xi})$, where $\boldsymbol{\xi} = (-\xi^{-1} \bmod p, 1)$.
- **Encrypt:** the encryption algorithm takes as input the public key pk and a message $\hat{x} \in \hat{\mathbb{G}}$, picks a random $r \leftarrow \mathbb{Z}_p$ and outputs the ciphertext $\hat{c} = e^\top \hat{x} + \hat{v}r \in \hat{\mathbb{G}}^{2\times 1}$, where $e = (0, 1)$.
- **Decrypt:** the decryption algorithm takes as input the secret key xk and a ciphertext $\hat{c} \in \hat{\mathbb{G}}^{2\times 1}$ and outputs $\hat{x} = \boldsymbol{\xi}\hat{c}$. Note $\boldsymbol{\xi}e^\top = 1$ and $\boldsymbol{\xi}\hat{v} = 0$ so simple linear algebra shows decryption is correct.

The ElGamal encryption scheme is IND-CPA secure if the DDH problem is computationally hard in $\hat{\mathbb{G}}$ [TY98]. ElGamal encryption can be defined similarly in $\check{\mathbb{H}}$ and if the SXDH assumption holds we then have IND-CPA secure encryption schemes in both $\hat{\mathbb{G}}$ and $\check{\mathbb{H}}$.

3.4   Pairing-Product Equations and Other Types of Equations

Using the linear algebra friendly additive notation for group operations and multiplicative notation for the pairing, we can express the four types of equations given in the introduction (Sec. 1) in a compact way.

Consider elements $\hat{x}_1, \ldots, \hat{x}_m \in \hat{\mathbb{G}}$ and $\check{y}_1, \ldots, \check{y}_n \in \check{\mathbb{H}}$, which may be publicly known constants (called $\hat{a}_j$ and $\check{b}_i$ in the introduction) or secret variables. Let furthermore the matrix $\Gamma = \{\gamma_{ij}\}_{i=1,j=1}^{m,n} \in \mathbb{Z}_p^{m \times n}$ and $t_\mathbb{T} \in \mathbb{T}$ be public values. We can now write the pairing product equation simply as

$$\hat{x} \Gamma \check{y} = t_\mathbb{T},$$

where $\hat{x} = (\hat{x}_1, \ldots, \hat{x}_m)$ and $\check{y} = (\check{y}_1, \ldots, \check{y}_n)^\top$.

We can in a similar fashion write multi-scalar multiplication equations in $\hat{\mathbb{G}}$, multi-scalar multiplication equations in $\check{\mathbb{H}}$, and quadratic equations in $\mathbb{Z}_p$ as

$$\hat{x} \Gamma y = \hat{t} \qquad x \Gamma \check{y} = \check{t} \qquad x \Gamma y = t$$

for suitable choices of $m, n \in \mathbb{N}, \Gamma \in \mathbb{Z}_p^{m \times n}, \hat{x} \in \hat{\mathbb{G}}^{1 \times m}, \check{y} \in \check{\mathbb{H}}^{n \times 1}, x \in \mathbb{Z}_p^{1 \times m}, y \in \mathbb{Z}_p^{n \times 1}, \hat{t} \in \hat{\mathbb{G}}, \check{t} \in \check{\mathbb{H}}$ and $t \in \mathbb{Z}_p$. The vectors $\hat{x}, \check{y}, x, y$ may contain a mix of known public values and secret variables.

Groth and Sahai [GS12] made the useful observation that by subtracting $\hat{t} \cdot 1, 1 \cdot \check{t}$ and $1 \cdot t$ on both sides of the respective equations we may without loss of generality assume $\hat{t} = \hat{0}, \check{t} = \check{0}$ and $t = 0$ in all multi-scalar multiplication equations and quadratic equations.

To get zero-knowledge proofs, we will in addition like Groth and Sahai restrict ourselves to $t_\mathbb{T} = 0_\mathbb{T}$ in all pairing product equations. Groth and Sahai [GS12] do not allow pairings of public constants in the pairing product equations in their zero-knowledge proofs, which we express by requiring the matrix Γ to contain entries $\gamma_{i,j} = 0$ whenever $\hat{x}_i$ and $\check{y}_j$ both are public values. This is because their zero-knowledge simulator breaks down when public values are paired. Groth and Sahai offers a work-around to deal with public values being paired with each other but it involves introducing additional multi-scalar multiplication equations and therefore increases the complexity of the zero-knowledge proof by many group elements. We will show that zero-knowledge simulation is possible when base elements $\hat{g}$ or $\check{h}$ are paired with each other or other public values. Since we do not need the additional multi-scalar multiplication equation used in Groth and Sahai's work-around this yields a significant efficiency gain whenever $\hat{g}$ or $\check{h}$ are paired with each other or other public values.

4   Commitment Keys and Commitments

Like in Groth-Sahai proofs, commitment keys come in two flavours: extraction keys that give perfect soundness and simulation keys that give zero-knowledge. The two types of key generation algorithms are given in Fig. 1 and by the

ExtGen(1^k)	SimGen(1^k)
$(p, \hat{\mathbb{G}}, \check{\mathbb{H}}, \mathbb{T}, e, \hat{g}, \check{h}) \leftarrow \mathcal{G}(1^k)$	$(p, \hat{\mathbb{G}}, \check{\mathbb{H}}, \mathbb{T}, e, \hat{g}, \check{h}) \leftarrow \mathcal{G}(1^k)$

$$\begin{array}{ll}
\rho \leftarrow \mathbb{Z}_p, \xi \leftarrow \mathbb{Z}_p^* & \sigma \leftarrow \mathbb{Z}_p, \psi \leftarrow \mathbb{Z}_p^* \\
\hat{v} \leftarrow (\xi\hat{g}, \hat{g})^\top & \check{v} \leftarrow (\psi\check{h}, \check{h}) \\
\hat{w} \leftarrow \rho\hat{v} & \check{w} \leftarrow \sigma\check{v} \\
\hat{u} \leftarrow \hat{w} + (\hat{0}, \hat{g})^\top & \check{u} \leftarrow \check{w} + (\check{0}, \check{h}) \\
\xi \leftarrow (-\xi^{-1} \bmod p, 1) & \psi \leftarrow (-\psi^{-1} \bmod p, 1)^\top \\
ck \leftarrow (p, \hat{\mathbb{G}}, \check{\mathbb{H}}, \mathbb{T}, e, \hat{u}, \hat{v}, \hat{w}, \check{u}, \check{v}, \check{w}) \\
xk \leftarrow (ck, \xi, \psi) \\
\text{Return } (ck, xk)
\end{array}$$

$$\begin{array}{ll}
\rho \leftarrow \mathbb{Z}_p, \xi \leftarrow \mathbb{Z}_p^* & \sigma \leftarrow \mathbb{Z}_p, \psi \leftarrow \mathbb{Z}_p^* \\
\hat{v} \leftarrow (\xi\hat{g}, \hat{g})^\top & \check{v} \leftarrow (\psi\check{h}, \check{h}) \\
\hat{w} \leftarrow \rho\hat{v} - (\hat{0}, \hat{g})^\top & \check{w} \leftarrow \sigma\check{v} - (\check{0}, \check{h}) \\
\hat{u} \leftarrow \hat{w} + (\hat{0}, \hat{g})^\top & \check{u} \leftarrow \check{w} + (\check{0}, \check{h}) \\
\\
ck \leftarrow (p, \hat{\mathbb{G}}, \check{\mathbb{H}}, \mathbb{T}, e, \hat{u}, \hat{v}, \hat{w}, \check{u}, \check{v}, \check{w}) \\
tk \leftarrow (ck, \rho, \sigma) \\
\text{Return } (ck, tk)
\end{array}$$

Fig. 1. Generator algorithms

SXDH assumption extraction keys and simulation keys are computationally indistinguishable.[2]

The column vectors $\hat{v}, \hat{w}, \hat{u} \in \hat{\mathbb{G}}^{2\times 1}$ will be used to make commitments $\hat{c}$ to group elements $\hat{x} \in \hat{\mathbb{G}}$ and scalars $x \in \mathbb{Z}_p$. Commitments to group elements and scalars are computed as

$$\hat{c} \leftarrow e^\top \hat{x} + \hat{v}r + \hat{w}s \qquad \text{and} \qquad \hat{c} \leftarrow \hat{u}x + \hat{v}r,$$

where $r, s \in \mathbb{Z}_p$. Commitments, usually denoted $\check{d}$, to group elements $\hat{y} \in \check{\mathbb{H}}$ and scalars $y \in \mathbb{Z}_p$ are made analogously using the row vectors $\check{v}, \check{w}, \check{u} \in \check{\mathbb{H}}^{1\times 2}$.

The commitment scheme is similar to [GS12], however, we will have several different types of commitments and the randomness $r, s \in \mathbb{Z}_p$ we use will depend on the type. Fig. 2 summarizes the commitment types and describes the message, randomness and commitment spaces specified by the public key ck.

The type $t = (\text{pub}_{\hat{\mathbb{G}}}, \hat{x})$ corresponds to a commitment to a public value $\hat{x}$ using randomness $r = s = 0$. It is easy for the verifier to check whether a commitment $\hat{c} = e^\top \hat{x}$ is indeed a correct commitment to a public value $\hat{x}$. Explicitly allowing public values in the commitments simplifies the description of the proofs because we can now treat all elements $\hat{x}_1, \ldots, \hat{x}_m$ in a pairing product equation as committed values regardless of whether they are public or secret. Suppose some of the elements $\hat{x} \in \hat{\mathbb{G}}^{1\times m}$ that appear in a pairing-product equation are committed as constant and others as Groth-Sahai commitments. The matrix consisting of all the commitments $\hat{C} = (\hat{c}_1 \cdots \hat{c}_m) \in \hat{\mathbb{G}}^{2\times m}$ can be written in a compact way as $\hat{C} = e^\top \hat{x} + \hat{v}r_x + \hat{w}s_x$, where for a constant $\hat{x}_i$ we just have $r_{x_i} = 0$ and $s_{x_i} = 0$.

In a standard Groth-Sahai proof, group element variables are committed as type $t = \text{com}_{\hat{\mathbb{G}}}$ using randomness $r, s \leftarrow \mathbb{Z}_p$. We will for greater efficiency also

---

[2] The commitment keys are not defined exactly as in [GS12]: by defining $\hat{v}$ as $(\xi\hat{g}, \hat{g})^\top$ instead of $(\hat{g}, \xi\hat{g})^\top$ we will be able to reduce the computational cost of the prover, as explained in Sec. 6. Besides this small difference, the keys $\hat{v}, \hat{w}, \hat{u}, \check{v}, \check{w}$ and $\check{u}$ correspond to u_1, u_2, u, v_1, v_2 and v in [GS12].

t	m	(r,s)	$\hat{c}$	t	m	(r,s)	$\check{d}$
$(\mathrm{pub}_{\hat{\mathbb{G}}}, m)$	$\hat{m} \in \hat{\mathbb{G}}$	$r = s = 0$	$\hat{c} = (\hat{0}, \hat{m})^{\top}$	$(\mathrm{pub}_{\check{\mathbb{H}}}, m)$	$\check{m} \in \check{\mathbb{H}}$	$r = s = 0$	$\check{d} = (\check{0}, \check{m})$
$\mathrm{enc}_{\hat{\mathbb{G}}}$	$\hat{m} \in \hat{\mathbb{G}}$	$r \in \mathbb{Z}_p, s = 0$	$\hat{c} \in \hat{\mathbb{G}}^{2 \times 1}$	$\mathrm{enc}_{\check{\mathbb{H}}}$	$\check{m} \in \check{\mathbb{H}}$	$r \in \mathbb{Z}_p, s = 0$	$\check{d} \in \check{\mathbb{H}}^{1 \times 2}$
$\mathrm{com}_{\hat{\mathbb{G}}}$	$\hat{m} \in \hat{\mathbb{G}}$	$r, s \in \mathbb{Z}_p$	$\hat{c} \in \hat{\mathbb{G}}^{2 \times 1}$	$\mathrm{com}_{\check{\mathbb{H}}}$	$\check{m} \in \check{\mathbb{H}}$	$r, s \in \mathbb{Z}_p$	$\check{d} \in \check{\mathbb{H}}^{1 \times 2}$
$\mathrm{base}_{\hat{\mathbb{G}}}$	$\hat{m} = \hat{g}$	$r = s = 0$	$\hat{c} = (\hat{0}, \hat{g})^{\top}$	$\mathrm{base}_{\check{\mathbb{H}}}$	$m = \check{h}$	$r = s = 0$	$\check{d} = (\check{0}, \check{h})$
$\mathrm{sca}_{\hat{\mathbb{G}}}$	$m \in \mathbb{Z}_p$	$r \in \mathbb{Z}_p, s = 0$	$\hat{c} \in \hat{\mathbb{G}}^{2 \times 1}$	$\mathrm{sca}_{\check{\mathbb{H}}}$	$m \in \mathbb{Z}_p$	$r \in \mathbb{Z}_p, s = 0$	$\check{d} \in \check{\mathbb{H}}^{1 \times 2}$
$\mathrm{unit}_{\hat{\mathbb{G}}}$	$m = 1$	$r = s = 0$	$\hat{c} = \hat{u}$	$\mathrm{unit}_{\check{\mathbb{H}}}$	$m = 1$	$r = s = 0$	$\check{d} = \check{u}$

Fig. 2. $\mathcal{M}_{ck}, \mathcal{R}_{ck}$ and $\mathcal{C}_{ck}$

allow commitments of type $t = \mathrm{enc}_{\hat{\mathbb{G}}}$ where $s = 0$. A type $t = \mathrm{enc}_{\hat{\mathbb{G}}}$ commitment to a group element $\hat{x}$ is $\hat{c} \leftarrow e^{\top}\hat{x} + \hat{v}r$, which is an ElGamal encryption of $\hat{x}$ as described in Sec. 3.3. Using encryption of variables instead of commitments reduces the computation and in some instances the size of the proofs. However, even on a simulation key the encryptions are only computationally hiding, so we must take care to ensure that it is possible to simulate proofs.

We also introduce the type $t = \mathrm{base}_{\hat{\mathbb{G}}}$ for a commitment to the base element $\hat{g}$ using $r = s = 0$. This type allows us to differentiate $\hat{g}$ from other public values, which is important because simulation becomes problematic when public values are paired with each other. However in the special case when $\hat{g}$ is paired with $\check{h}$ or public constants it is possible to simulate. In addition, one can get shorter zero-knowledge proofs for certain equations by using the special properties of commitments with types $t = \mathrm{base}_{\hat{\mathbb{G}}}$ and $t = \mathrm{base}_{\check{\mathbb{H}}}$.

Scalars have the type $t = \mathrm{sca}_{\hat{\mathbb{G}}}$ and we use the type $t = \mathrm{unit}_{\hat{\mathbb{G}}}$ for a commitment to the scalar 1 using $r = s = 0$. Please note that $t = \mathrm{unit}_{\hat{\mathbb{G}}}$ suffices to incorporate any public value $a \in \mathbb{Z}_p$ into our equations by multiplying the corresponding row in the matrix Γ with a. With these two types we can therefore commit to both variables and constants in $\mathbb{Z}_p$, which simplifies the description of the proofs.

We have now described the types of commitments in $\hat{\mathbb{G}}$ and similar types for commitments in $\check{\mathbb{H}}$ are given in Fig. 2. The commitment algorithm is described in Fig. 3.

The extraction key xk includes a vector $\boldsymbol{\xi}$ such that $\boldsymbol{\xi}\hat{v} = \boldsymbol{\xi}\hat{w} = \hat{0}$ and $\boldsymbol{\xi}e^{\top} = 1, \boldsymbol{\xi}\hat{u} = \hat{g}$. On a commitment to a group element $\hat{c} = e^{\top}\hat{x} + \hat{v}r + \hat{w}s$ or on an encryption to a group element $\hat{c} = e^{\top}\hat{x} + \hat{v}r$ we can extract $\hat{x}$ by computing $\hat{x} = \boldsymbol{\xi}\hat{c}$. On a commitment to a scalar $\hat{c} = \hat{u}x + \hat{v}r$ we extract $\hat{g}x = \boldsymbol{\xi}\hat{c}$, which uniquely determines the committed value x. The extraction algorithm is given in Fig. 4.

The simulated commitment algorithm $\mathrm{SimCom}_{tk}(t)$ commits honestly to public constants, base elements $\hat{g}, \check{h}$ and units 1, which is easy to verify using public information. For all other types it commits to 0. We refer to the full paper [EG13] for a detailed specification.

On a simulation key, the commitments of types $\mathrm{com}_{\hat{\mathbb{G}}}$ or $\mathrm{sca}_{\hat{\mathbb{G}}}$ are perfectly hiding. Commitments of types $(\mathrm{pub}_{\hat{\mathbb{G}}}, \hat{x})$ or $\mathrm{enc}_{\hat{\mathbb{G}}}$ on the other hand are perfectly binding. However, by the SXDH assumption commitments of type $\mathrm{enc}_{\hat{\mathbb{G}}}$ cannot

Input	Randomness	Output
$(\text{pub}_{\hat{\mathbb{G}}}, \hat{x}), \hat{x}$	$r \leftarrow 0, s \leftarrow 0$	$\hat{c} \leftarrow e^\top \hat{x}$
$\text{enc}_{\hat{\mathbb{G}}}, \hat{x}\ (\star)$	$r \leftarrow \mathbb{Z}_p, s \leftarrow 0$	$\hat{c} \leftarrow e^\top \hat{x} + \hat{v}r$
$\text{com}_{\hat{\mathbb{G}}}, \hat{x}$	$r \leftarrow \mathbb{Z}_p, s \leftarrow \mathbb{Z}_p$	$\hat{c} \leftarrow e^\top \hat{x} + \hat{v}r + \hat{w}s$
$\text{base}_{\hat{\mathbb{G}}}, \hat{g}\ (\star)$	$r \leftarrow 0, s \leftarrow 0$	$\hat{c} \leftarrow e^\top \hat{g}$
$\text{sca}_{\hat{\mathbb{G}}}, x$	$r \leftarrow \mathbb{Z}_p, s \leftarrow 0$	$\hat{c} \leftarrow \hat{u}x + \hat{v}r$
$\text{unit}_{\hat{\mathbb{G}}}, 1$	$r \leftarrow 0, s \leftarrow 0$	$\hat{c} \leftarrow \hat{u}$

Input	Randomness	Output
$(\text{pub}_{\check{\mathbb{H}}}, \check{y}), \check{y}$	$r \leftarrow 0, s \leftarrow 0$	$\check{d} \leftarrow \check{y}e$
$\text{enc}_{\check{\mathbb{H}}}, \check{y}\ (\star)$	$r \leftarrow \mathbb{Z}_p, s \leftarrow 0$	$\check{d} \leftarrow \check{y}e + r\check{v}$
$\text{com}_{\check{\mathbb{H}}}, \check{y}$	$r \leftarrow \mathbb{Z}_p, s \leftarrow \mathbb{Z}_p$	$\check{d} \leftarrow \check{y}e + r\check{v} + s\check{w}$
$\text{base}_{\check{\mathbb{H}}}, \check{h}\ (\star)$	$r \leftarrow 0, s \leftarrow 0$	$\check{d} \leftarrow \check{h}e$
$\text{sca}_{\check{\mathbb{H}}}, y$	$r \leftarrow \mathbb{Z}_p, s \leftarrow 0$	$\check{d} \leftarrow y\check{u} + r\check{v}$
$\text{unit}_{\check{\mathbb{H}}}, 1$	$r \leftarrow 0, s \leftarrow 0$	$\check{d} \leftarrow \check{u}$

Fig. 3. Commitment algorithm. [GS12] do not have the types marked with $(\star)$

$\text{Ext}_{xk}(t, \hat{c})$ where $\hat{c} \in \hat{\mathbb{G}}^{2 \times 1}$	$\text{Ext}_{xk}(t, \check{d})$ where $\check{d} \in \check{\mathbb{H}}^{1 \times 2}$
Return $\hat{x} \leftarrow \boldsymbol{\xi}\hat{c}$	Return $\check{y} \leftarrow \check{d}\boldsymbol{\psi}$

Fig. 4. Extraction algorithm

be distinguished from commitments to other elements. Commitments of type $(\text{pub}_{\hat{\mathbb{G}}}, \hat{x})$ are public, so we do not require any hiding property.

Commitments to $\hat{g}$ and 1 of types $\text{base}_{\hat{\mathbb{G}}}$ and $\text{unit}_{\hat{\mathbb{G}}}$ are interesting. The secret simulation key specifies ρ such that $\hat{u} = \rho\hat{v}$ and $e^\top \hat{g} = \rho\hat{v} - \hat{w}$. This means that commitments of types $\text{base}_{\hat{\mathbb{G}}}$ and $\text{unit}_{\hat{\mathbb{G}}}$ can be equivocated as either commitments to $\hat{g}$ and 1 or as commitments to $\hat{0}$ and 0. The zero-knowledge simulator will use the equivocations to simulate proofs involving the base element $\hat{g}$ or constants in $\mathbb{Z}_p$.

5 Proofs

We will first explain how the proofs work using the example of pairing product equations to give intuition. We want to prove that committed values $\hat{x}, \check{y}$ satisfy the equation

$$\hat{x}\Gamma\check{y} = 0_{\mathbb{T}}.$$

Assume that we have committed to $\hat{x}, \check{y}$ as $\hat{C} = e^\top \hat{x} + \hat{v}r_x + \hat{w}s_x$ and $\check{D} = \check{y}e + r_y\check{v} + s_y\check{w}$. We then have

$$\begin{aligned}
\hat{C}\Gamma\check{D} &= (e^\top \hat{x} + \hat{v}r_x + \hat{w}s_x)\Gamma(\check{y}e + r_y\check{v} + s_y\check{w}) \\
&= e^\top \hat{x}\Gamma\check{y}e + \hat{v}r_x\Gamma\check{D} + \hat{w}s_x\Gamma\check{D} + e^\top \hat{x}\Gamma r_y\check{v} + e^\top \hat{x}\Gamma s_y\check{w} \\
&= 0_{\mathbb{T}} + \hat{v}\check{\pi}'_{\hat{v}} + \hat{w}\check{\pi}'_{\hat{w}} + \hat{\pi}'_{\check{v}}\check{v} + \hat{\pi}'_{\check{w}}\check{w}
\end{aligned}$$

where $\check{\pi}'_{\hat{v}} = r_x\Gamma\check{D}$, $\check{\pi}'_{\hat{w}} = s_x\Gamma\check{D}$, $\hat{\pi}'_{\check{v}} = e^\top \hat{x}\Gamma r_y$, $\hat{\pi}'_{\check{w}} = e^\top \hat{x}\Gamma s_y$.

The prover randomizes $\check{\pi}'_{\hat{v}}, \check{\pi}'_{\hat{w}}, \hat{\pi}'_{\check{v}}, \hat{\pi}'_{\check{w}}$ as $\check{\pi}_{\hat{v}} = \check{\pi}'_{\hat{v}} + \alpha\check{v} + \beta\check{w}$, $\check{\pi}_{\hat{w}} = \check{\pi}'_{\hat{w}} + \gamma\check{v} + \delta\check{w}$, $\hat{\pi}_{\check{v}} = \hat{\pi}'_{\check{v}} - \hat{v}\alpha - \hat{w}\gamma$, $\hat{\pi}_{\check{w}} = \hat{\pi}'_{\check{w}} - \hat{v}\beta - \hat{w}\delta$. This gives us a randomized proof $\check{\pi}_{\hat{v}}, \check{\pi}_{\hat{w}}, \hat{\pi}_{\check{v}}, \hat{\pi}_{\check{w}}$ satisfying the verification equation

$$\hat{C}\Gamma\check{D} = \hat{v}\check{\pi}_{\hat{v}} + \hat{w}\check{\pi}_{\hat{w}} + \hat{\pi}_{\check{v}}\check{v} + \hat{\pi}_{\check{w}}\check{w}.$$

Soundness and F-extractability. An extraction key xk contains $\boldsymbol{\xi}, \boldsymbol{\psi}$ such that $\boldsymbol{\xi}\hat{v} = \boldsymbol{\xi}\hat{w} = \hat{0}$ and $\check{v}\boldsymbol{\psi} = \check{w}\boldsymbol{\psi} = \check{0}$. Multiplying the verification equation by $\boldsymbol{\xi}$ and $\boldsymbol{\psi}$ on the left and right side respectively, we get

$$\boldsymbol{\xi}\hat{C}\Gamma\check{D}\boldsymbol{\psi} = \boldsymbol{\xi}\hat{v}\check{\pi}_{\hat{v}}\boldsymbol{\psi} + \boldsymbol{\xi}\hat{w}\check{\pi}_{\hat{w}}\boldsymbol{\psi} + \boldsymbol{\xi}\hat{\pi}_{\check{v}}\check{v}\boldsymbol{\psi} + \boldsymbol{\xi}\hat{\pi}_{\check{w}}\check{w}\boldsymbol{\psi} = 0_{\mathbb{T}}.$$

Observe, $\hat{x} = \boldsymbol{\xi}\hat{C}$ are the values the extractor Ext_{xk} gets from the commitments $\hat{C}$ and $\check{y} = \check{D}\boldsymbol{\psi}$ are the values the extractor Ext_{xk} gets from the commitments $\check{D}$. The extracted values from the commitments therefore satisfy $\hat{x}\Gamma\check{y} = 0_{\mathbb{T}}$. This gives us perfect soundness and perfect F-extractability, where F on group elements in $\hat{\mathbb{G}}$ and $\check{\mathbb{H}}$ is the identity function.

Zero-Knowledge. The simulator will simulate proofs by equivocating the commitments to values $\hat{x}, \check{y}$ that satisfy the equation $\hat{x}\Gamma\check{y} = 0_{\mathbb{T}}$. On a simulation key, commitments with types $\mathrm{com}_{\hat{\mathbb{G}}}, \mathrm{com}_{\check{\mathbb{H}}}$ are perfectly hiding. The simulator can therefore use $\hat{x}_i = \hat{0}$ or $\check{y}_j = \check{0}$. Commitments with types $\mathrm{base}_{\hat{\mathbb{G}}}, \mathrm{base}_{\check{\mathbb{H}}}$ are also equivocable to $\hat{0}$ or $\check{0}$ since on a simulation key $e^\top\hat{g} = \hat{v}\rho - \hat{w}$ and $\check{h}e = \sigma\check{v} - \check{w}$. By using equivocations to $\hat{0}$ and $\check{0}$ we can now ensure that $\hat{x}_i\gamma_{i,j}\check{y}_j = 0_{\mathbb{T}}$ whenever $t_{x_i} \in \{\mathrm{base}_{\hat{\mathbb{G}}}, \mathrm{com}_{\hat{\mathbb{G}}}\}$ or $t_{y_j} \in \{\mathrm{base}_{\check{\mathbb{H}}}, \mathrm{com}_{\check{\mathbb{H}}}\}$. Commitments of type $t_{x_i} \in \{(\mathrm{pub}_{\hat{\mathbb{G}}}, \hat{x}), \mathrm{enc}_{\hat{\mathbb{G}}}\}$ and $t_{y_j} \in \{(\mathrm{pub}_{\check{\mathbb{H}}}, \check{y}), \mathrm{enc}_{\check{\mathbb{H}}}\}$ cannot be equivocated and, to get zero-knowledge, we will therefore assume $\gamma_{i,j} = 0$ whenever such types are paired (as is also the case in [GS12]).

We now have that the simulator can equivocate commitments and base elements to $\hat{0}$ and $\check{0}$ such that the resulting $\hat{x}, \check{y}$ satisfy $\hat{x}\Gamma\check{y} = 0_{\mathbb{T}}$. The randomization of the proofs ensures that they will not leak information about whether we are giving a real proof or simulating. Recall the prover randomized $\check{\pi}'_{\hat{v}}, \check{\pi}'_{\hat{w}}, \hat{\pi}'_{\check{v}}, \hat{\pi}'_{\check{w}}$ as $\check{\pi}_{\hat{v}} = \check{\pi}'_{\hat{v}} + \alpha\check{v} + \beta\check{w}$, $\check{\pi}_{\hat{w}} = \check{\pi}'_{\hat{w}} + \gamma\check{v} + \delta\check{w}$, $\hat{\pi}_{\check{v}} = \hat{\pi}'_{\check{v}} - \hat{v}\alpha - \hat{w}\gamma$, $\hat{\pi}_{\check{w}} = \hat{\pi}'_{\check{w}} - \hat{v}\beta - \hat{w}\delta$. On a simulation key this means regardless of whether we are giving a real proof or a simulated proof $\check{\pi}_{\hat{v}}, \check{\pi}_{\hat{w}}$ are uniformly random and $\hat{\pi}_{\check{v}}, \hat{\pi}_{\check{w}}$ are the unique values that make the verification equation true. Finally, the encrypted elements are computationally hidden by the SXDH assumption, so here the simulator may use encryptions of $\hat{0}$ and $\check{0}$ instead of the witness and as we shall show the proofs can be constructed on top of the ciphertexts such that they do not reveal whether the underlying plaintext are part of a real witness or are set to zero by the simulator.

Optimizations. Now let us return to the prover. Observe that r_x, s_x, r_y, s_y may have some zero elements. In particular, assume that all elements in s_x are 0. This happens if all $\hat{x}_i$ in the statement have types $\mathrm{enc}_{\hat{\mathbb{G}}}$, $(\mathrm{pub}_{\hat{\mathbb{G}}}, \hat{x}_i)$ or $\mathrm{base}_{\hat{\mathbb{G}}}$. Moreover, assume that all elements $\check{y}$ have as types either $\mathrm{com}_{\check{\mathbb{H}}}$ or $\mathrm{base}_{\check{\mathbb{H}}}$ so that a simulator uses $\check{y} = \check{0}$ in the simulated proof. This sets $\check{\pi}'_{\hat{w}} = \hat{0}$. As $\check{\pi}'_{\hat{w}}$ is the same for all witnesses, even for "simulated witnesses", we might as well set $\gamma = \delta = 0$. For such equations, we therefore save 2 group elements or 25% of the proof size compared to Groth and Sahai [GS12] where there is no $\mathrm{enc}_{\hat{\mathbb{G}}}$ or $\mathrm{enc}_{\check{\mathbb{H}}}$ types. We refer to the full paper [EG13] for a list of equation types and the corresponding proof sizes.

5.1   The Full Proof System

We divide the possible statements into 16 different types. They are summarized in Fig. 5, which provides an algorithm for checking that the statement format is correct. The relation R_L is defined in Fig. 6, which provides an algorithm to check whether a statement is true. The relation first checks that the types of the witnesses and the types of the equations match according to Fig. 5 and then whether the relevant pairing product, multi-scalar multiplication or quadratic equation is satisfied.

CheckFormat$_{ck}(T, \Gamma, \{t_{x_i}\}_{i=1}^m, \{t_{y_j}\}_{j=1}^n)$

Check $\Gamma \in \mathbb{Z}_p^{m \times n}$

Check that the equation and message types match each other according to the table below

T	$t_{x_1}, \ldots, t_{x_m}$	$t_{y_1}, \ldots, t_{y_n}$
PPE	base$_{\hat{G}}$, (pub$_{\hat{G}}$, $\hat{x}_i$), enc$_{\hat{G}}$, com$_{\hat{G}}$	base$_{\check{H}}$, (pub$_{\check{H}}$, $\check{y}_j$), enc$_{\check{H}}$, com$_{\check{H}}$
PEnc$_{\hat{G}}$	base$_{\hat{G}}$, (pub$_{\hat{G}}$, $\hat{x}_i$), enc$_{\hat{G}}$	base$_{\check{H}}$, com$_{\check{H}}$
PConst$_{\hat{G}}$	base$_{\hat{G}}$, (pub$_{\hat{G}}$, $\hat{x}_i$)	base$_{\check{H}}$, com$_{\check{H}}$
PEnc$_{\check{H}}$	base$_{\hat{G}}$, com$_{\hat{G}}$	base$_{\check{H}}$, (pub$_{\check{H}}$, $\check{y}_j$), enc$_{\check{H}}$
PConst$_{\check{H}}$	base$_{\hat{G}}$, com$_{\hat{G}}$	base$_{\check{H}}$, (pub$_{\check{H}}$, $\check{y}_j$)
ME$_{\hat{G}}$	base$_{\hat{G}}$, (pub$_{\hat{G}}$, $\hat{x}_i$), enc$_{\hat{G}}$, com$_{\hat{G}}$	unit$_{\check{H}}$, sca$_{\check{H}}$
MEnc$_{\hat{G}}$	base$_{\hat{G}}$, (pub$_{\hat{G}}$, $\hat{x}_i$), enc$_{\hat{G}}$	unit$_{\check{H}}$, sca$_{\check{H}}$
MConst$_{\hat{G}}$	base$_{\hat{G}}$, (pub$_{\hat{G}}$, $\hat{x}_i$)	unit$_{\check{H}}$, sca$_{\check{H}}$
MLin$_{\hat{G}}$	base$_{\hat{G}}$, com$_{\hat{G}}$	unit$_{\check{H}}$
ME$_{\check{H}}$	unit$_{\hat{G}}$, sca$_{\hat{G}}$	base$_{\check{H}}$, (pub$_{\check{H}}$, $\check{y}_j$), enc$_{\check{H}}$, com$_{\check{H}}$
MEnc$_{\check{H}}$	unit$_{\hat{G}}$, sca$_{\hat{G}}$	base$_{\check{H}}$, (pub$_{\check{H}}$, $\check{y}_j$), enc$_{\check{H}}$
MConst$_{\check{H}}$	unit$_{\hat{G}}$, sca$_{\hat{G}}$	base$_{\check{H}}$, (pub$_{\check{H}}$, $\check{y}_j$)
MLin$_{\check{H}}$	unit$_{\hat{G}}$	base$_{\check{H}}$, com$_{\check{H}}$
QE	unit$_{\hat{G}}$, sca$_{\hat{G}}$	unit$_{\check{H}}$, sca$_{\check{H}}$
QConst$_{\hat{G}}$	unit$_{\hat{G}}$	unit$_{\check{H}}$, sca$_{\check{H}}$
QConst$_{\check{H}}$	unit$_{\hat{G}}$, sca$_{\hat{G}}$	unit$_{\check{H}}$

If $T = \text{PPE}$ check $\Gamma_{i,j} = 0$ for all (i,j) where $t_{x_i} \in \{(\text{pub}_{\hat{G}}, \hat{x}_i), \text{enc}_{\hat{G}}\}$ and $t_{y_j} \in \{(\text{pub}_{\check{H}}, \check{y}_j), \text{enc}_{\check{H}}\}$
Accept format if all checks pass, else abort

Fig. 5. Equation - message types check

The prover and verifier are given in Fig. 7. The prover constructs a proof for the relevant type of equation assuming the input is a correctly formatted statement with valid openings of commitments to a satisfying witness. The verifier uses the matching verification equation to check validity of a proof.

Let F be given by

$$
\begin{aligned}
F(ck, t, \hat{x}) &= \hat{x} & &\text{for } t \in \{(\text{pub}_{\hat{G}}, \hat{x}), \text{enc}_{\hat{G}}, \text{com}_{\hat{G}}, \text{base}_{\hat{G}}\} \\
F(ck, t, x) &= \hat{g}x & &\text{for } t \in \{\text{sca}_{\hat{G}}, \text{unit}_{\hat{G}}\} \\
F(ck, t, \hat{y}) &= \check{y} & &\text{for } t \in \{(\text{pub}_{\check{H}}, \check{y}), \text{enc}_{\check{H}}, \text{com}_{\check{H}}, \text{base}_{\check{H}}\} \\
F(ck, t, y) &= y\check{h} & &\text{for } t \in \{\text{sca}_{\check{H}}, \text{unit}_{\check{H}}\}
\end{aligned}
$$

$$\frac{R_L(ck,(T,\Gamma),(\{(t_{x_i},x_i)\}_{i=1}^m,\{(t_{y_j},y_j)\}_{j=1}^n))}{\text{CheckFormat}_{ck}(T,\Gamma,\{t_{x_i}\}_{i=1}^m,\{t_{y_j}\}_{j=1}^n)}$$

For all i,j check $(t_{x_i},x_i) \in \mathcal{M}_{ck}$ and $(t_{y_j},y_j) \in \mathcal{M}_{ck}$

If $\boldsymbol{x} \in \hat{\mathbb{G}}^m$ and $\boldsymbol{y} \in \check{\mathbb{H}}^n$ check $\boldsymbol{x}\Gamma\boldsymbol{y} = 0_{\mathsf{T}}$

If $\boldsymbol{x} \in \hat{\mathbb{G}}^m$ and $\boldsymbol{y} \in \mathbb{Z}_p^n$ check $\boldsymbol{x}\Gamma\boldsymbol{y} = \hat{0}$

If $\boldsymbol{x} \in \mathbb{Z}_p^m$ and $\boldsymbol{y} \in \check{\mathbb{H}}^n$ check $\boldsymbol{x}\Gamma\boldsymbol{y} = \check{0}$

If $\boldsymbol{x} \in \mathbb{Z}_p^m$ and $\boldsymbol{y} \in \mathbb{Z}_p^n$ check $\boldsymbol{x}\Gamma\boldsymbol{y} = 0$

Accept if and only if all checks pass

Fig. 6. Relation that defines the key-dependent languages for our proofs

$$\text{Prove}_{ck}(T,\Gamma,\{(t_{x_i},x_i,(r_{x_i},s_{x_i}))\}_{i=1}^m,\{(t_{y_j},y_j,(r_{y_j},s_{y_j}))\}_{j=1}^n)$$

If $\boldsymbol{x} \in \hat{\mathbb{G}}^m$ define $\hat{C} = \boldsymbol{e}^\top \boldsymbol{x} + \hat{\boldsymbol{v}} \boldsymbol{r}_x + \hat{\boldsymbol{w}} \boldsymbol{s}_x$ else if $\boldsymbol{x} \in \mathbb{Z}_p^m$ define $\hat{C} = \hat{\boldsymbol{u}}\boldsymbol{x} + \hat{\boldsymbol{v}}\boldsymbol{r}_x$

If $\boldsymbol{y} \in \check{\mathbb{H}}^n$ define $\check{D} = \boldsymbol{y}\boldsymbol{e} + \boldsymbol{r}_y\check{\boldsymbol{v}} + \boldsymbol{s}_y\check{\boldsymbol{w}}$ else if $\boldsymbol{y} \in \mathbb{Z}_p^n$ define $\check{D} = \boldsymbol{y}\check{\boldsymbol{u}} + \boldsymbol{r}_y\check{\boldsymbol{v}}$

Set $\alpha = \beta = \gamma = \delta = 0$

If $T = \text{PPE}$ pick $\alpha,\beta,\gamma,\delta \leftarrow \mathbb{Z}_p$

If $T \in \{\text{PEnc}_{\hat{\mathbb{G}}},\text{ME}_{\check{\mathbb{H}}}\}$ pick $\alpha,\beta \leftarrow \mathbb{Z}_p$

If $T \in \{\text{PEnc}_{\check{\mathbb{H}}},\text{ME}_{\hat{\mathbb{G}}}\}$ pick $\alpha,\gamma \leftarrow \mathbb{Z}_p$

If $T \in \{\text{MEnc}_{\hat{\mathbb{G}}},\text{MEnc}_{\check{\mathbb{H}}},\text{QE}\}$ pick $\alpha \leftarrow \mathbb{Z}_p$

$\quad \check{\boldsymbol{\pi}}_{\hat{v}} \leftarrow \boldsymbol{r}_x\Gamma\check{D} + \alpha\check{v} + \beta\check{w} \qquad \hat{\boldsymbol{\pi}}_{\check{v}} \leftarrow (\hat{C} - \hat{\boldsymbol{v}}\boldsymbol{r}_x - \hat{\boldsymbol{w}}\boldsymbol{s}_x)\Gamma\boldsymbol{r}_y - \hat{v}\alpha - \hat{w}\gamma$

$\quad \check{\boldsymbol{\pi}}_{\hat{w}} \leftarrow \boldsymbol{s}_x\Gamma\check{D} + \gamma\check{v} + \delta\check{w} \qquad \hat{\boldsymbol{\pi}}_{\check{w}} \leftarrow (\hat{C} - \hat{\boldsymbol{v}}\boldsymbol{r}_x - \hat{\boldsymbol{w}}\boldsymbol{s}_x)\Gamma\boldsymbol{s}_y - \hat{v}\beta - \hat{w}\delta$

Return $\pi = (\check{\boldsymbol{\pi}}_{\hat{v}},\check{\boldsymbol{\pi}}_{\hat{w}},\hat{\boldsymbol{\pi}}_{\check{v}},\hat{\boldsymbol{\pi}}_{\check{w}})$

$$\text{Verify}_{ck}(T,\Gamma,\{(t_{x_i},\hat{\boldsymbol{c}}_i)\}_{i=1}^m,\{(t_{y_j},\check{\boldsymbol{d}}_j)\}_{j=1}^n,\pi)$$

$\text{CheckFormat}_{ck}(T,\Gamma,\{t_{x_i}\}_{i=1}^m,\{t_{y_j}\}_{j=1}^n)$

Check $\hat{C} = (\hat{\boldsymbol{c}}_1 \cdots \hat{\boldsymbol{c}}_m) \in \hat{\mathbb{G}}^{2\times m}$ and $\check{D} = (\check{\boldsymbol{d}}_1 \cdots \check{\boldsymbol{d}}_n)^\top \in \check{\mathbb{H}}^{n\times 2}$

Check $\pi = (\check{\boldsymbol{\pi}}_{\hat{v}},\check{\boldsymbol{\pi}}_{\hat{w}},\hat{\boldsymbol{\pi}}_{\check{v}},\hat{\boldsymbol{\pi}}_{\check{w}}) \in \check{\mathbb{H}}^{2\times 1} \times \check{\mathbb{H}}^{2\times 1} \times \hat{\mathbb{G}}^{1\times 2} \times \hat{\mathbb{G}}^{1\times 2}$

Check $\hat{C}\Gamma\check{D} = \hat{\boldsymbol{v}}\check{\boldsymbol{\pi}}_{\hat{v}} + \hat{\boldsymbol{w}}\check{\boldsymbol{\pi}}_{\hat{w}} + \hat{\boldsymbol{\pi}}_{\check{v}}\check{v} + \hat{\boldsymbol{\pi}}_{\check{w}}\check{w}$

Return 1 if all checks pass, else return 0

Fig. 7. Prover and verifier algorithms

Theorem 1. *The commit-and-prove scheme given in Figs. 1,3,4 and 7 has perfect correctness, perfect soundness and F-extractability for the function F defined above, and computational composable zero-knowledge if the SXDH assumption holds relative to $\mathcal{G}$.*

Due to lack of space, the description of the zero-knowledge simulator and the proof of the theorem is given in the full version [EG13].

6   NIZK Proofs with Prover-Chosen CRS

In Groth-Sahai proofs, the prover uses a common reference string shared between the prover and the verifier to construct NIZK proofs. We can improve efficiency by letting the prover choose her own common reference string, which we will refer to as her public key. To maintain the soundness of the NIZK proof, the prover will create its public key as a perfectly binding key and will make a NIZK proof using the shared common reference string to prove that the public key is binding. In this section we will explain how the prover creates her public key, proves its well-formedness and we explain what the efficiency improvement obtained is. In the full version of this paper [EG13] we give definitions for commit-and-prove schemes with prover-chosen CRS and we prove the security of our scheme.

6.1   Creating the Public Key

Like commitment keys, public keys can be created in two ways: they can either be perfectly binding or perfectly hiding. These two types of keys are computationally indistinguishable if the SXDH assumption holds. As we already argued, we will require the prover to create her public key in a perfectly binding way. However, the zero-knowledge simulator will create a perfectly hiding public key and simulate the NIZK proof for well-formedness.

ProverGen(ck)		SimProverGen(ck)	
$\rho_P \leftarrow \mathbb{Z}_p$	$\sigma_P \leftarrow \mathbb{Z}_p$	$\rho_P \leftarrow \mathbb{Z}_p$	$\sigma_P \leftarrow \mathbb{Z}_p$
$\hat{v}_P \leftarrow \hat{v}$	$\check{v}_P \leftarrow \check{v}$	$\hat{v}_P \leftarrow \hat{v}$	$\check{v}_P \leftarrow \check{v}$
$\hat{w}_P \leftarrow \rho_P \hat{v}_P$	$\check{w}_P \leftarrow \sigma_P \check{v}_P$	$\hat{w}_P \leftarrow \rho_P \hat{v}_P - (\hat{0}, \hat{g})^\top$	$\check{w}_P \leftarrow \sigma_P \check{v}_P - (\check{0}, \check{h})$
$\hat{u}_P \leftarrow \hat{w}_P + (\hat{0}, \hat{g})^\top$	$\check{u}_P \leftarrow \check{w}_P + (\check{0}, \check{h})$	$\hat{u}_P \leftarrow \hat{w}_P + (\hat{0}, \hat{g})^\top$	$\check{u}_P \leftarrow \check{w}_P + (\check{0}, \check{h})$
$pk \leftarrow (\hat{u}_P, \hat{v}_P, \hat{w}_P, \check{u}_P, \check{v}_P, \check{w}_P)$		$pk \leftarrow (\hat{u}_P, \hat{v}_P, \hat{w}_P, \check{u}_P, \check{v}_P, \check{w}_P)$	
$sk \leftarrow (pk, \rho_P, \sigma_P)$		$sk \leftarrow (pk, \rho_P, \sigma_P)$	
Return (pk, sk)		Return (pk, sk)	

Fig. 8. Public key generator algorithms

As shown in Fig. 8, the public key is created in a similar way to how the commitment key is created. The main difference is that the bilinear group $(p, \hat{\mathbb{G}}, \check{\mathbb{H}}, \mathbb{T}, e, \hat{g}, \check{h})$ is already fixed, and that we allow the prover to reuse the elements $\hat{v}, \check{v}$. This both reduces the size of the public key and also ensures that the prover's commitments are extractable even when using her own key.

Once the prover has created her pair of public key and secret key, she has to compute an NIZK proof to show that her pk is perfectly binding. A valid public key is defined by the existence of some ρ_P, σ_P such that $\hat{w}_P = \rho_P \hat{v}$ and $\check{w}_P = \sigma_P \check{v}$, which can be written as two equations of type MConst$_{\hat{\mathbb{G}}}$ involving public elements in $\hat{\mathbb{G}}$ and a secret ρ_P committed in $\check{\mathbb{H}}$, and two equations of type MConst$_{\check{\mathbb{H}}}$ involving public elements in $\check{\mathbb{H}}$ and a secret σ_P committed in $\hat{\mathbb{G}}$. These are simple statements that each have a proof consisting of a single group element. In the full version of this paper [EG13] we give the exact NIZK proofs that have to be computed. The total cost of communicating the public key, which is determined by the commitments to ρ_P and σ_P and the NIZK proofs is 12 group elements. Since we are using a commit-and-prove scheme we can consider this as a one-off cost for each verifier engaging with the prover after which the public key may be used for many commitments and proofs.

6.2   Computing Commitments and NIZK Proofs

Once the prover has created her public key pk and has proven its well-formedness, she can make commitments and prove statements using pk instead of ck. The commitments and proofs are created and verified in exactly the same way as described in Fig. 3 and Fig. 7, but the number of scalar multiplications needed to compute commitments and NIZK proofs can be reduced using her knowledge of the discrete logarithms in sk. We have for instance

$$\hat{c} = e^\top \hat{x} + \hat{v}r + \hat{w}_P s = e^\top \hat{x} + \hat{v}(r + \rho_P s),$$

so the prover can compute a commitment with 2 scalar multiplications instead of 4 scalar multiplications.

By using the secret key sk the prover can reduce the number of scalar multiplications by 50% for commitments to group elements and commitments to elements in $\mathbb{Z}_p$. Computing NIZK proofs is more complicated and there are many operations that cannot be avoided by using the secret key sk. However, in some cases the improvement is very noticeable as in the case of quadratic equations ($T = \text{QE}$) where the number of scalar multiplications is reduced by 50%[3]. Furthermore, in most applications found in the literature there are only a few variables in the equations, which makes our improvements more significant. The exact savings can be found in the full version of this paper [EG13].

References

[BB04]   Boneh, D., Boyen, X.: Short signatures without random oracles. In: Cachin, C., Camenisch, J.L. (eds.) EUROCRYPT 2004. LNCS, vol. 3027, pp. 56–73. Springer, Heidelberg (2004)

[BCC+09]   Belenkiy, M., Camenisch, J., Chase, M., Kohlweiss, M., Lysyanskaya, A., Shacham, H.: Randomizable proofs and delegatable anonymous credentials. In: Halevi, S. (ed.) CRYPTO 2009. LNCS, vol. 5677, pp. 108–125. Springer, Heidelberg (2009)

[BCKL08]   Belenkiy, M., Chase, M., Kohlweiss, M., Lysyanskaya, A.: P-signatures and noninteractive anonymous credentials. In: Canetti, R. (ed.) TCC 2008. LNCS, vol. 4948, pp. 356–374. Springer, Heidelberg (2008)

[BFI+10]   Blazy, O., Fuchsbauer, G., Izabachène, M., Jambert, A., Sibert, H., Vergnaud, D.: Batch Groth-Sahai. In: Zhou, J., Yung, M. (eds.) ACNS 2010. LNCS, vol. 6123, pp. 218–235. Springer, Heidelberg (2010)

---

[3] We assume that operations in $\mathbb{\check{H}}$ are more computationally expensive than operations in $\mathbb{\hat{G}}$, as usually $\mathbb{\hat{G}}$ is an elliptic curve over a prime order field and $\mathbb{\check{H}}$ is the same elliptic curve over an extension field [GPS08]. Therefore, we have tried to reduce the numbers of operations in $\mathbb{\check{H}}$ as much as possible. In addition, we have for simplicity assumed that the commitments that appear in the NIZK proof have as many randomization factors as possible conditioned to the equation type T.

[BFM88]   Blum, M., Feldman, P., Micali, S.: Non-interactive zero-knowledge and its applications. In: Proceedings of the Twentieth Annual ACM Symposium on Theory of Computing, STOC 1988, pp. 103–112. ACM, New York (1988)

[BW06]   Boyen, X., Waters, B.: Compact group signatures without random oracles. In: Vaudenay, S. (ed.) EUROCRYPT 2006. LNCS, vol. 4004, pp. 427–444. Springer, Heidelberg (2006)

[BW07]   Boyen, X., Waters, B.: Full-domain subgroup hiding and constant-size group signatures. In: Okamoto, T., Wang, X. (eds.) PKC 2007. LNCS, vol. 4450, pp. 1–15. Springer, Heidelberg (2007)

[CHP07]   Camenisch, J.L., Hohenberger, S., Pedersen, M.Ø.: Batch verification of short signatures. In: Naor, M. (ed.) EUROCRYPT 2007. LNCS, vol. 4515, pp. 246–263. Springer, Heidelberg (2007)

[CKLM12]   Chase, M., Kohlweiss, M., Lysyanskaya, A., Meiklejohn, S.: Malleable proof systems and applications. In: Pointcheval, D., Johansson, T. (eds.) EUROCRYPT 2012. LNCS, vol. 7237, pp. 281–300. Springer, Heidelberg (2012)

[CLOS02]   Canetti, R., Lindell, Y., Ostrovsky, R., Sahai, A.: Universally composable two-party and multi-party secure computation. In: 34th ACM STOC, pp. 494–503. ACM Press (2002)

[Dam92]   Damgård, I.B.: Non-interactive circuit based proofs and non-interactive perfect zero-knowledge with preprocessing. In: Rueppel, R.A. (ed.) EUROCRYPT 1992. LNCS, vol. 658, pp. 341–355. Springer, Heidelberg (1993)

[EG13]   Alex Escala and Jens Groth. Fine-Tuning Groth-Sahai Proofs. Cryptology ePrint Archive, Report 2013/662

[EG84]   El Gamal, T.: A public key cryptosystem and a signature scheme based on discrete logarithms. In: Blakely, G.R., Chaum, D. (eds.) CRYPTO 1984. LNCS, vol. 196, pp. 10–18. Springer, Heidelberg (1985)

[EHKRV13]   Escala, A., Herold, G., Kiltz, E., Ràfols, C., Villar, J.: An Algebraic Framework for Diffie-Hellman Assumptions. In: Canetti, R., Garay, J.A. (eds.) CRYPTO 2013, Part II. LNCS, vol. 8043, pp. 129–147. Springer, Heidelberg (2013)

[Fuc11]   Fuchsbauer, G.: Commuting Signatures and Verifiable Encryption. In: Paterson, K.G. (ed.) EUROCRYPT 2011. LNCS, vol. 6632, pp. 224–245. Springer, Heidelberg (2011)

[FLS99]   Feige, U., Lapidot, D., Shamir, A.: Multiple non-interactive zero knowledge proofs under general assumptions. SIAM Journal on Computing 29(1), 1–28 (1999)

[FPV09]   Fuchsbauer, G., Pointcheval, D., Vergnaud, D.: Transferable Constant-Size Fair E-Cash. In: Garay, J.A., Miyaji, A., Otsuka, A. (eds.) CANS 2009. LNCS, vol. 5888, pp. 226–247. Springer, Heidelberg (2009)

[GO07]   Groth, J., Ostrovsky, R.: Cryptography in the Multi-string Model. In: Menezes, A. (ed.) CRYPTO 2007. LNCS, vol. 4622, pp. 323–341. Springer, Heidelberg (2007)

[GOS12]   Groth, J., Ostrovsky, R., Sahai, A.: New techniques for noninteractive zero-knowledge. J. ACM 59(3), 11 (2012)

[GPS08]   Galbraith, S.D., Paterson, K.G., Smart, N.P.: Pairings for cryptographers. Discrete Applied Mathematics 156(16), 3113–3121 (2008)

[Gro06]   Groth, J.: Simulation-sound NIZK proofs for a practical language and constant size group signatures. In: Lai, X., Chen, K. (eds.) ASIACRYPT 2006. LNCS, vol. 4284, pp. 444–459. Springer, Heidelberg (2006)

[Gro07]   Groth, J.: Fully Anonymous Group Signatures Without Random Oracles. In: Kurosawa, K. (ed.) ASIACRYPT 2007. LNCS, vol. 4833, pp. 164–180. Springer, Heidelberg (2007)

[GS12]   Groth, J., Sahai, A.: Efficient non-interactive proof systems for bilinear groups. SIAM Journal on Computing 41(5), 1193–1232 (2012)

[GSW10]   Ghadafi, E., Smart, N.P., Warinschi, B.: Groth-Sahai proofs revisited. In: Nguyen, P.Q., Pointcheval, D. (eds.) PKC 2010. LNCS, vol. 6056, pp. 177–192. Springer, Heidelberg (2010)

[JR13]   Jutla, C.S., Roy, A.: Shorter Quasi-Adaptive NIZK Proofs for Linear Subspaces. In: Sako, K., Sarkar, P. (eds.) ASIACRYPT 2013, Part I. LNCS, vol. 8269, pp. 1–20. Springer, Heidelberg (2013)

[Kil90]   Kilian, J.: Uses of randomness in algorithms and protocols. MIT Press (1990)

[KP98]   Kilian, J., Petrank, E.: An efficient noninteractive zero-knowledge proof system for NP with general assumptions. Journal of Cryptology 11(1), 1–27 (1998)

[Mei09]   Meiklejohn, S.: An Extension of the Groth-Sahai Proof System. Master's thesis, Brown University, Providence, RI (2009)

[Seo12]   Seo, J.H.: On the (Im)possibility of Projecting Property in Prime-Order Setting. In: Wang, X., Sako, K. (eds.) ASIACRYPT 2012. LNCS, vol. 7658, pp. 61–79. Springer, Heidelberg (2012)

[TY98]   Tsiounis, Y., Yung, M.: On the security of ELGamal based encryption. In: Imai, H., Zheng, Y. (eds.) PKC 1998. LNCS, vol. 1431, pp. 117–134. Springer, Heidelberg (1998)

Cross-Domain Secure Computation*

Chongwon Cho[1], Sanjam Garg[2], and Rafail Ostrovsky[3]

[1] Information and Systems Science Laboratory, HRL Laboratories
[2] IBM Research T.J. Watson
[3] Computer Science Department and Mathematics Department, UCLA

Abstract. Consider the setting of two mutually distrustful parties Alice and Bob communicating over the Internet, who want to securely evaluate desired functions on their private inputs. In this setting all known protocols for securely evaluating general functions either require honest parties to trust an external party or provide only weaker notions of security. Thus, the question of minimizing or removing trusted set-up assumptions remains open. In this work, we introduce the cross-domain model (CD) for secure computation as a means to reducing the level of required trust. In this model, each domain consists of a set of mutually trusting parties along with a key-registration authority, where we would like parties from distinct domains to be able to perform multiple secure computation tasks concurrently. In this setting, we show the followings:

- **Positive Construction for 2 domains:** We give a multiparty-party protocol that concurrently and securely evaluates any function in the CD model with two domains, using only a *constant* number of rounds and relying only on *standard assumptions*.

- **Impossibility Results for 3 or more domains:** Consider a deterministic function (e.g., 1-out-of-2 bit OT) that Alice and Bob in the standalone setting cannot evaluate trivially and which allows only Bob to receive the output. In this setting if besides Alice and Bob there is a third party (such that all three are from distinct domains) then they cannot securely compute any such function in the CD model in *concurrent* setting even when their inputs are *pre-specified*.

These results extend to the setting of multiple parties as well. In particular, there exists an n-party concurrently secure protocol in the CD model of n domains if and only if there are exactly n domains in the system.

Keywords: Multi-party computation, Concurrent security.

* The significant part of this work was done while the first and second authors were Ph.D. students at UCLA. Research supported in part by NSF grants CNS-0830803; CCF-0916574; IIS-1065276; CCF-1016540; CNS-1118126; CNS-1136174; US-Israel BSF grant 2008411, OKAWA Foundation Research Award, IBM Faculty Research Award, Xerox Faculty Research Award, B. John Garrick Foundation Award, Teradata Research Award, and Lockheed-Martin Corporation Research Award. This material is also based upon work supported by the Defense Advanced Research Projects Agency through the U.S. Office of Naval Research under Contract N00014-11-1-0392. The views expressed are those of the authors and do not reflect the official policy or position of the Department of Defense or the U.S. Government.

H. Krawczyk (Ed.): PKC 2014, LNCS 8383, pp. 650–668, 2014.

1   Introduction

Consider the following scenario: Amazon and Walmart are two giant wholesale stores. Each store has a distributed set of servers to handle client requests. In order to establish best prices, Amazon and Walmart often need to collaborate on a real-time basis. In other words they need to compute functions of their confidential data which itself is distributed across the different servers. Neither do they trust each other nor are they willing to trust a third-party setup.

The well-studied notion of *secure computation* [40,18] allows them to do so, however only in the *stand-alone* setting where security holds only if a single protocol session is executed in isolation. However, the requirement of free collaborations between Amazon and Walmart in the above requires security to hold even when multiple sessions are executed concurrently as in the Internet. What if Amazon in parallel wants to collaborate with another wholesale store Costco while protecting its confidential data even if Walmart and Costco collude with each other?

Background: Concurrent Security. In the past few years a lot of effort has been made in obtaining secure computation protocols in the demanding network setting where there might be multiple concurrent protocol executions. A large number of secure protocols (in fact under an even stronger notion of security called Universal Composability (UC)) based on various trusted third-party setup assumptions [8,7,2,11,24,12,30,22,21,15] have been proposed. One of main aims to this line of work has been to reduce the level of trust that honest parties need to place in the trusted third-party setup. For example, Katz [24] considered the hardware token model. In his model, honest parties program tokens and send them to other parties. Since honest parties can program their own tokens, they only need to trust their hardware token manufacturer. Groth and Ostrovsky [22] initiated the study of constructing UC secure protocols without relying on a single trusted external entity. In other words, one of the main goals in this line of works is to achieve those notions of security in a setting which is as close to the "plain model" as possible (also see [21,15] for subsequent works).

The Dark Side of Concurrency. Unfortunately, very strong impossibility results have been proved ruling out the existence of secure protocols in the concurrent setting. UC secure protocols for most functionalities of interest have been ruled out by [8,6]. Concurrent self-composability[1] for a large class of interesting functionalities (i.e., bit transmitting functionalities) was first ruled out [31] only in a setting in which the honest parties choose their inputs *adaptively* (i.e., "on the fly"). Subsequently, a series of works [3,19,1,17] show that it is impossible to achieve concurrent self-composition even in the very natural setting of *static* (pre-specified) inputs. In summary, these results have firmly established that for obtaining the most general result some setup is needed unless we are willing to consider more constrained models. Finally even in a setting with bounded num-

---

[1] Concurrent self-composition requires that a protocol remain secure even when multiple copies of the same protocol are executed concurrently.

ber of players [23], an impossibility result has been established. However, this is for the more demanding setting in which honest parties choose their inputs adaptively.

1.1 Overview of Our Setting and Results

We introduce a new set-up model, called the Cross-Domain(CD) model. A domain consists of a set of mutually trusting parties along with a key-registration authority. We prove the following for the setting of n-domain multi-party protocols:

Positive result if $n = 2$. We give a multi-party protocol that concurrently and securely evaluates any function in the CD model of two fixed domains where each domain may contain arbitrarily many parties. Our protocol has a *constant round* complexity, a *black-box* proof of security and relies only on *standard assumptions*.

Impossibility results when $n \geq 3$. We show that there does not exist a two-party protocol such that parties from three distinct domain can concurrently and securely realizes any *complete* asymmetric (only one party gets the output) deterministic functionality[2] in the stand-alone setting [25,26,29,5,27]. Our impossibility results hold even in the *very restricted* setting of *static inputs* (inputs of honest parties are pre-specified) and *fixed roles* (i.e, the adversary can corrupt only two parties who play the same role across all executions).

This answers the motivating question we started with. We can equip Amazon and Walmart to collaborate freely but this can not be done if collaborations with Costco are also desired.

Our results directly extend to the setting of n-domain protocols. In particular an n-party protocol for concurrently and securely computing any function on the joint inputs of n parties form distinct domains exists, if and only if there are exactly n domains in the system.

Relation with Bare-Public Key (BPK) model. The CD model is a generalization of the BPK introduced by Canetti et al. [9] model that has been studied extensively in the literature. Recall that in the BPK model each party sets up its own public-key and private-key pair. On the other hand in our model each domain has a key-registration authority that roughly generates a public-key and a private-key pair which is then used by all parties of the domain. We stress that even in the BPK model prior to our work no results for the setting of secure computation were known and our results fully characterize what is possible in the BPK setting. We elaborate on the details of this relation in Section 6.

1.2 Previous Results with Weaker Notions of Security

To address the problem of concurrent security for general secure computation in the *plain model*, a few candidate definitions have been proposed,

---

[2] A functionality is *complete* if it can be used to securely realize any other functionality.

including input-indistinguishable security [33,16] and super-polynomial simulation [34,38,4,30,10]. Both of these notions, although very useful in specialized settings, *do not* suffice in general. Additionally, other models that limit the level of concurrency have also been considered [35,19] or allow simulation using additional outputs from the ideal functionality [20]. Among these models the model of m-bounded concurrency [36,35] which allows for m different protocol executions to be interleaved has received a lot of attention in the literature [36,35,31,32]. Unbounded concurrent oblivious transfer in the restricted model where all the inputs in all the executions are assumed to be independent has been constructed in [14]. Finally the only known positive results for concurrently secure composition in the plain model are for the zero-knowledge functionality [13,39,28,37,3].

1.3   Technical Overview

Impossibility Result. We start by giving the intuition behind the impossibility result for constructing a protocol that concurrently securely realizes the Oblivious Transfer(OT) functionality in the setting of three parties. The extension to general asymmetric two party functionalities follows using a Theorem from [1]. In the following, we consider the simplest setting where three domains exist and where each domain contains a single party.

Our impossibility result builds on the top of ideas developed by [1,17] for the setting of plain model. Even though their result holds for the two party setting, we recall their technique for the setting of three parties. Consider a scenario with three parties Alice, Bob and Charlie. Now, consider an adversary that corrupts Bob and Charlie who (as receivers of the OT protocol) are allowed to participate in an arbitrary polynomial number of executions of the protocol with honest Alice (who plays as the sender). In this setting, we can construct a real-world adversary acting as Bob that interacts with Alice in an execution of the protocol, referred to as the *main* execution, that cannot be simulated in the ideal world.

The key idea is that the adversary has secure computation at its disposal and it can use it to its advantage. The adversary on behalf of Charlie may interact with Alice in multiple *additional* executions of the secure computation protocol and use these executions to generate messages that it needs to send in the main execution on behalf of Bob. More specifically, the adversary securely realizes Bob by using garbled circuits such that the adversary needs to evaluate the garble circuit in order to generate the messages it sends on behalf of Bob. However, the adversary does not have the OT keys necessary for evaluation of the garbled circuit. Instead, the OT keys are given to the honest Alice from which the adversary obtains the desired OT keys by the (additional) concurrent executions of the OT protocol as Charlie. Finally, the existence of a simulator simulating such an adversary that is securely implementing Bob contradicts the stand-alone security of the OT protocol. The pictorial description of our real-world adversary is provided in Figure 1.

In the CD model, each domain containing Alice, Bob and Charlie generates a certificate associated with their public-keys. The key insight in our impossibility

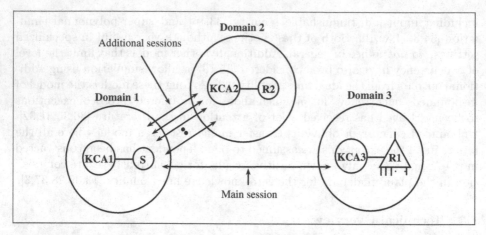

Fig. 1. Our real-world adversary $\mathcal{A}$ corrupting two receivers where R1 is Bob (replaced with the garbled circuit of its next message generator) and R2 is Charlie

result is to use the setting described above and to enable the garbled circuit securely evaluating Bob to generate Bob's public key as well. The adversary however will generate Charlie's public key and secret key by himself, which enables the adversary to interact freely on Charlie's behalf. In particular, this allows the adversary to still obtain the OT keys for the garbled circuit from Alice as in the plain model. Finally, the existence of a simulator simulating such an adversary that is securely implementing Bob (along with its key registration) contradict the stand-alone security of the OT protocol in the CD model.

Positive Result for Two Domains. The intuition behind the impossibility result above makes it abundantly clear that the adversary must be able to do secure computation with honest Alice if it wants to securely simulate Bob. However, if we restrict ourselves to the setting of two domains then the adversary essentially loses this ability, which eventually allows us to give a positive result.

Our protocol can roughly be partitioned into two phases– the preamble phase and the post-preamble phase. In the preamble phase, a party needs to demonstrate the knowledge of the secret key corresponding to its public and the certificate issued by its KCA. Subsequently in the post-preamble phase the actual secure computation happens. In the simulation for the proof of security, obtaining the knowledge of the adversary's secret key suffices for straight-line simulation.

Our protocol proceeds to the post-preamble phase only after the adversary has demonstrated knowledge of its secret key in the preamble phase. The adversary can interleave sessions arbitrarily and among these interleaved sessions consider the first session in which the protocol reaches the post-preamble phase. Let's call this session as the target session. Now note that since the target session was the first session in which the the post-preamble phase was reached, we can expect the same thing to happen with some probability on appropriate re-windings as well. We formalize this appropriately using *swapping* argument introduced in [37]. Now note that throughout this process of re-windings we never execute the post-preamble phase for any session. This allows us to avoid the technical difficulties that generally arise when constructing concurrently secure two-party computation protocols. Our protocol with this limited re-windings is able to extract the secret key of the adversary and this allows our simulator to subsequently simulate all the sessions in straight-line. For our construction and the proof we build on the techniques developed in [3,20,16].

Organization: In Section 2, we first introduce the CD model. In Section 3, we present our impossibility result for static input concurrently secure two-domain two-party computation in the CD model in a setting with at least three domains and three parties. In Section 4, we provide the formal construction of concurrently secure two-domain two-party computation protocol in the CD model (in the setting of 2 parties) and for the proof of its security, we give the construction of a black-box simulator for the protocol in Section 5. We elaborate on the details of the relation with the bare-public key model in Section 6.

2   The Cross-Domain (CD) Model

In this section we sketch the details of the CD model. In the CD model, we have multiple domains each consisting of a set of mutually trusting parties and a Key Certification Authority (KCA). Each party in a domain trusts its KCA. Intuitively, whenever a party in one domain wants to jointly compute a function with a party in another domain, each party registers its public key to its own KCA and obtains a certificate on the public key. No party communicates with the KCAs of other domains. Instead, only KCAs communicate with each other to obtain the verification information for the certificates of other parties within other KCAs. Then, every KCA delivers the obtained verification information to the parties in the own domain. The parties use the verification information of other parties received from the trusted KCA throughout the subsequent interaction. We formalize this as an interaction between multiple parties and KCA functionalities as follows. We denote a set of KCA functionalities by $\mathbf{F}_{KCA} = \{\mathbf{F}^1_{KCA}, \mathbf{F}^2_{KCA}, \ldots, \mathbf{F}^N_{KCA}\}$ where N is the number of domains.

- A party in the i-th domain registers their public key with $\mathbf{F}^i_{KCA}$. Then, functionality $\mathbf{F}^i_{KCA}$ generates a pair of signing key and verification key, signs the public key, and returns the verification key and the signature to the party. If $\mathbf{F}^i_{KCA}$ has already generated a pair of signing key and verification key for the other parties in the domain, then it will use the same signing key and verification key to certify the public key of the current requesting party.
- If an adversary corrupts a party in a domain, then we assume that all other parties in the domain are corrupted as well.[3]

We emphasize that our main aim of the above definition is to protect the privacy of inputs of parties in domains in which no corrupted party exists from

---

[3] This is because all the parties in a domain trust each other. This captures the toy scenario for Amazon and Walmart described in the introduction. Servers of Amazon and Walmart are seen as the parties in our system.

interacting with corrupted parties in the other domains. The formal definition of the CD model appears in the full version.

3   Impossibility of Concurrent Security in the CD Model

In this section, we provide strong impossibility results ruling out constructions for secure MPC protocols in the CD model. We heavily rely on the recent works of [1,17] in proving these results. In fact, we show the impossibility result in the simplest case of the CD model: We show that there does not exist a concurrently secure protocol in the CD model of two domains when three domains and three parties exist in the system. Since each party belongs to the distinct domains in the following discussion, we discuss the impossibility result simply focusing on the parties without considering the KCA functionalities.

We start by showing that string OT functionality can not be concurrently and securely realized even in the setting of *static* inputs in the bare-public key model in the setting of *three* parties even against adversaries that corrupt two parties playing the *same role*, i.e. of the sender or the receiver. Next we generalize this impossibility to essentially all functionalities of interest. Finally we extend our impossibility result to the setting of larger number of parties. In particular we show that no n-party protocol in the CD model (for a large class of functionalities, discussed later) can be concurrently secure in the setting of $n + 1$ parties. We use the notation used by [17] and some of the texts here have been taken verbatim from [17].

3.1   The Case of String OT

String OT is a two-party functionality between a sender S, with input (m_0, m_1) and a receiver R with input b which allows R to learn m_b without learning anything about m_{1-b}. At the same time the sender S learns nothing about b. More formally string OT functionality $\mathcal{F}_{OT} : (\{0,1\}^{p(k)} \times \{0,1\}^{p(k)}) \times \{0,1\} \to \{0,1\}^{p(k)}$ is defined as, $\mathcal{F}_{OT}((m_0, m_1), b) = m_b$, where $p(\cdot)$ is any polynomial and only R gets the output.

Note that string OT is a two-party functionality, however, the protocol realizing the string OT functionality can be executed among multiple parties. We consider the setting of three parties and each of the parties registers exactly one key. We show that for some polynomial $p(\cdot)$ (to be fixed later), there does not exist a protocol π that concurrently securely realizes the $\mathcal{F}_{OT}$ functionality among these three parties. More specifically we show that there exists an adversary $\mathcal{A}$ who corrupts 2 parties, registers keys on their behalf, starts a polynomial number of sessions (say $\ell(k)$) of the protocol π with the honest (with pre-specified inputs drawn from a particular distribution $\mathcal{D}$) such that no ideal-world adversary whose output is computationally indistinguishable from the output of real-world adversary $\mathcal{A}$ exists. We stress that the parties corrupted by the adversary (we construct) corrupts two parties playing the same role – either the sender S or the receiver R in all the $\ell(k)$ sessions.

Theorem 1. *(impossibility of static input concurrent-secure string OT in CD model) Let π be any protocol which implements[4] the $\mathcal{F}_{OT}$ functionality for a particular (to be determined later) polynomial p in the CD model. Then, in the setting of 3 parties (assuming one-way functions exist) there exists a polynomial ℓ and a distribution $\mathcal{D}$ over ℓ-tuple vectors of inputs and an adversarial strategy $\mathcal{A}$, that corrupts 2 parties, such that for every probabilistic polynomial-time simulation strategy $\mathcal{S}$, (see full-version for formal definition) cannot be satisfied when the inputs of the parties are drawn from $\mathcal{D}$.*

Implications for Bounded Concurrency. Observe that the attack described in the above proof (in the unboundend concurrent setting) has natural implications in the bounded setting as well. In particular, the number of sessions that our adversary executes, or the "extent" of concurrency used by the adversary in the proof above in order to arrive at a contradiction is bounded by the communication complexity of the protocol. More specifically the adversary needs to make one additional OT call for every bit that the Sender sends in the protocol.

3.2   Extending to All Asymmetric Functionalities

The goal of this section is to generalize the impossibility result for string OT provided in the previous section to all finite deterministic "non-trivial" asymmetric functionalities $\mathcal{F}$. Consider a two-party functionality $\mathcal{F}_{asym}$ between a sender S, with input x and a receiver R with input y which allows R to learn $f(x, y)$ and at the same time S should not learn anything. More formally, let $f : X \times Y \to Z$ be any finite function[5] then an asymmetric functionality $\mathcal{F}_{asym}$ is defined as, $\mathcal{F}_{asym}(x, y) = (\perp, f(x, y))$ where S gets no output and R gets $f(x, y)$. We show that there does not exist a protocol π that concurrently securely realizes any *complete* $\mathcal{F}_{asym}$ functionality as defined below.

$\mathcal{F}_{asym}$ is said to be *complete* [26][6] in the setting of stand-alone two-party computation in the presence of *malicious* adversaries iff $\forall b_0, \exists b_1, a_0, a_1$ such that

$$f(a_0, b_0) = f(a_1, b_0) \wedge f(a_0, b_1) \neq f(a_1, b_1).$$

Lemma 1 (Theorems 1 and 3, [1]). *Given any protocol ρ that concurrently securely realizes a non-trivial asymmetric functionality $\mathcal{F}$ secure under concurrent self-composition in the static-input, fixed-role setting we have that there exists a protocol Π that securely realizes the $\mathcal{F}_{OT}$ functionality secure under concurrent self-composition in the static-input, fixed-role setting.*

The proof of [1] is for the setting of plain model but extends to the setting of the CD model in a direct manner.

---

[4] We say that a protocol implements a functionality if the protocol allows two parties to evaluate the desired function. This protocol however may not be secure.

[5] Recall that a function is said to be finite if both the domain and the range are of finite size.

[6] Recall that a functionality is said to be complete if it can be used to securely realize any other functionality.

Now any hypothetical protocol for any non-trivial asymmetric functionality $\mathcal{F}$ (using Lemma 1), we will obtain a protocol for $\mathcal{F}_{OT}$, contradicting Theorem 1. This gives our impossibility result for the setting of two parties:

Theorem 2. *(impossibility of static input concurrent security for asymmetric complete functionalities) Let π be any protocol which implements any $\mathcal{F}_{asym}$ functionality that is complete in the stand-alone setting in the CD model. Then, in the setting of 3 parties (assuming one-way functions exist) there exists a polynomial ℓ and a distribution $\mathcal{D}$ over ℓ-tuple vectors of inputs and an adversarial strategy $\mathcal{A}$, that corrupts two parties, such that for every probabilistic polynomial-time simulation strategy $\mathcal{S}$, (see full-version for formal definition) cannot be satisfied when the inputs of the parties are drawn from $\mathcal{D}$.*

Extending to n-party protocols. So far we have only considered the setting of 3-parties only. We now explain how these results can be extended to the setting of $n+1$ parties executing an n party protocol. Consider an n-party functionality $f(x_1, x_2 \ldots x_n)$ with $x_1, x_2 \ldots x_n$ as input. Let S and $\overline{S}$ be disjoint partitions of the n parties such that only a subset of the parties in $\overline{S}$ get the outputs. Let g be a two-argument function obtained by viewing f as a function of $\{x_i\}_{i \in S}$ and $\{x_i\}_{i \in \overline{S}}$. For any f, if there exist such partitions S and $\overline{S}$ such that g is a complete two-party asymmetric functionality,[7] then we can use our impossibility result for concurrently securely realizing g in the CD model in the setting of 3 parties to argue that f can not be concurrently securely realized in CD model in the setting of $n+1$ parties. The proof follows in a very similar manner and we omit the details.

4   Possibility of Concurrent Security in the CD Model

In this section, we present the positive side of our result by constructing a *constant-round* concurrently secure MPC protocol in the CD model with *black-box simulation*. Our protocol, the ingredients needed and the proof build upon the construction of [16] (and its full version) and parts of the texts have been taken verbatim from there without explicitly mentioning again and again. Let $\mathcal{F}$ be a well-formed functionality where such a functionality admits a constant-round two-party computation protocol in the semi-honest setting.[8] In fact, for simplicity, we present a constant-round concurrently secure two-party computation protocol in the CD model, denoted by Π, where a party belongs to either of the two domains.

We emphasize that this two-party protocol easily extends to a concurrently secure protocol for any polynomially many parties in CD model of two fixed domains where a party is under either of two domains. Subsequently, our protocol easily extends to a concurrently secure protocol for any polynomially many parties in CD model of N fixed domains where each party belongs to one of the N domains.

---

[7] Note here this implies that at least one party in S and at least one party in $\overline{S}$ has an input.

[8] See [7] for the notion of well-formed functionality.

4.1 Building Blocks and Notations

Due to the space restrictions, see the full version for the details of the building blocks. Let $g : \{0,1\}^n \to \{0,1\}^{3n}$ be a length tripling pseudo-random generator. Let $\text{PBCOM}(\cdot)$ denote a non-interactive perfectly binding commitment scheme, and let $\langle C, R \rangle$ denote an one-slot extractable commitment scheme . Furthermore, we will denote a constant round strong WI proof system by $\langle P, V \rangle$ and a special constant-round NMWI argument of knowledge protocol by $\langle P', V' \rangle$. Finally we denote a constant-round SWI argument by $\langle P_{\text{swi}}, V_{\text{swi}} \rangle$, and a constant-round *semi-honest* two-party computation protocol by $\langle P_1^{\text{sh}}, P_2^{\text{sh}} \rangle$ which securely computes $\mathcal{F}$ as per the standard simulation-based definition of secure computation.

4.2 Construction of Our Protocol

We now provide the formal construction of concurrently secure two-party computation protocol in the CD model. Some notations and the protocol description closely resemble those of [16]. Let $\mathbf{F}_{\text{KCA}} = \{\mathbf{F}_{\text{KCA}}^1, \mathbf{F}_{\text{KCA}}^2\}$ be the key certification authority(KCA) functionality with two domains in the CD model, which is a special case of $\mathbf{F}_{\text{KCA}}$ where $N = 2$. See the formal description in full-version.

Let n be the security parameter. Let P_1 and P_2 be two parties with private inputs x_1 and x_2 respectively. Without loss of generality, let P_1 and P_2 be in the domains $\mathbf{F}_{\text{KCA}}^1$ and $\mathbf{F}_{\text{KCA}}^2$ respectively. Also, P_1 and P_2 have unique identifiers id_1 and id_2 respectively. Protocol $\Pi = \langle P_1, P_2 \rangle$ proceeds as follows. We omit session identifiers for the succinct specification.

I. Key Registration Phase

1. P_1 samples random strings sk_1^0 and sk_1^1 and sets $\text{pk}_1^0 := g(\text{sk}_1^0)$ and $\text{pk}_1^1 := g(\text{sk}_1^1)$.
2. P_1 registers both public keys pk_1^0 and pk_1^1 by sending $(register, \text{id}_1, \text{pk}_1^0)$ and $(register, \text{id}_1, \text{pk}_1^1)$ to functionality $\mathbf{F}_{\text{KCA}}^1$.[9]
3. P_1 obtains $(\sigma_{\text{pk}_1^0}, mvk_1)$ and $(\sigma_{\text{pk}_1^1}, mvk_1)$ from $\mathbf{F}_{\text{KCA}}^1$ where $\sigma_{\text{pk}_1^0}$ and $\sigma_{\text{pk}_1^1}$ are signatures on pk_1^0 and pk_1^1 respectively where mvk_1 is the respective verification key.
4. P_1 chooses a random bit $b_1 \in \{0,1\}$ and sets $\text{pk}_1 = \text{pk}_1^{b_1}$ and $\text{sk}_1 = \text{sk}_1^{b_1}$. We now denote the corresponding signature by σ_{pkpo}.
5. P_2 acts analogously, registers pk_2^0 and pk_2^1 with $\mathbf{F}_{\text{KCA}}^2$, and obtains $(\sigma_{\text{pk}_2^0}, mvk_2)$ and $(\sigma_{\text{pk}_1}, mvk_2)$. It sets $\text{pk}_2 = \text{pk}_2^{b_2}$ and $\text{sk}_2 = \text{sk}_2^{b_2}$ where b_2 is a random bit. Finally, σ_{pkpt} is the corresponding signature.

II. Trapdoor Creation Phase. Let $\mathcal{R}_1$ be a NP-relation where the NP theorem is a string mvk and the witness is a tuple $(\tilde{pk}, \tilde{sk}, \tilde{\sigma}, \tilde{c})$ such that $(mvk, \tilde{pk}, \tilde{sk}, \tilde{\sigma}, \tilde{c}) \in \mathcal{R}_1$ if and only if $\tilde{c}$ is the commitment to $\tilde{pk}||\tilde{sk}||\tilde{\sigma}$ with respect to protocol $\langle C, R \rangle$,

---

[9] The registration request is not required to be two distinct requests to the functionality. Registering pk_1^0 and pk_1^1 can be viewed as a registering one public key which is a concatenation of two public keys and the functionality simply decomposes it into two strings, signs both and returns them to the party.

$\tilde{pk} = g(sk)$, and $\mathsf{Ver}(\tilde{pk}, \tilde{\sigma}, mvk) = 1$. For convenience, we let $(mvk, t, \tilde{c}) \in \mathcal{R}_1$ if $t = \tilde{pk}||\tilde{sk}||\tilde{\sigma}$ and $(mvk, \tilde{pk}, \tilde{sk}, \tilde{\sigma}, \tilde{c}) \in \mathcal{R}_1$. In addition, let $\mathcal{R}_2$ be a NP-relation where the NP theorem is a string mvk and the witness is a tuple $(\tilde{pk}, \tilde{sk}, \tilde{\sigma})$ such that $(mvk, \tilde{pk}, \tilde{sk}, \tilde{\sigma}) \in \mathcal{R}_2$ if and only if $\tilde{pk} = g(sk)$ and $\mathsf{Ver}(\tilde{pk}, \tilde{\sigma}, mvk) = 1$. Similarly, we denote we let $(mvk, t) \in \mathcal{R}_2$ if $t = \tilde{pk}||sk||\tilde{\sigma}$ and $(mvk, \tilde{pk}, \tilde{sk}, \tilde{\sigma}) \in \mathcal{R}_2$. The trapdoor creation phase proceeds as follows.

1. $P_1 \Rightarrow P_2$: P_1 sends a request $(retrieval, \mathsf{id}_2)$ to $\mathbf{F}^1_{\mathsf{KCA}}$ and obtains mvk_2, a verification key from $\mathbf{F}^1_{\mathsf{KCA}}$. Recall that $\mathbf{F}^1_{\mathsf{KCA}}$ obtains mvk_2 by interacting with $\mathbf{F}^2_{\mathsf{KCA}}$. P_2 analogously obtains mvk_1 from $\mathbf{F}^2_{\mathsf{KCA}}$.

2. $P_1 \Rightarrow P_2$: P_1 executes $\langle C, R \rangle$ with P_2, where P_1 commits to $\mathsf{trap}_1 = \mathsf{pk}_1||\mathsf{sk}_1||\sigma_{\mathsf{pk}_1}$. We denote this execution by $\langle C, R \rangle_{1 \to 2}^{\mathsf{trap}_1}$ and the commitment by $\tilde{c}_1$. Next P_1 proves to P_2 by using strong WI proof system $\langle P, V \rangle$ with common input mvk_1, the following NP-statement: there exists $(\mathsf{pk}_1, \mathsf{sk}_1, \sigma_{\mathsf{pk}_1})$ where $(mvk_1, \mathsf{pk}_1, \mathsf{sk}_1, \sigma_{\mathsf{pk}_1}) \in \mathcal{R}_1$. If the verifier V in $\langle P, V \rangle_{1 \to 2}^{\mathsf{sk}_1}$ aborts, then P_2 aborts. We denote this execution by $\langle P, V \rangle_{1 \to 2}^{\mathsf{trap}_1}$.

3. $P_2 \Rightarrow P_1$: P_2 acts analogously in Step 2 by first committing to $\mathsf{trap}_2 = \mathsf{pk}_2||\mathsf{sk}_2||\sigma_{\mathsf{pk}_2}$ using $\langle C, R \rangle$ and then giving a proof using $\langle P, V \rangle$. We denote this execution by $\langle C, R \rangle_{2 \to 1}^{\mathsf{trap}_2}$ and $\langle P, V \rangle_{2 \to 1}^{\mathsf{trap}_2}$.

4. $P_1 \Rightarrow P_2$: P_1 commits to bit 0 as $com_1 = \mathrm{PBCOM}(0)$ and sends com_1 to P_2. Next P_1 and P_2 executes constant-round NMWI argument of knowledge $\langle P', V' \rangle$ in which P_1 and P_2 respectively play as P' and V'. The common inputs for this execution of $\langle P', V' \rangle$ are com_1 and mvk_2. In this execution, P_1 proves to P_2 that com_1 is a commitment to 0 or there exists a string t such that $(mvk_2, t) \in \mathcal{R}_2$. Honest party P_1's private input is the de-commitment information of com_1.[10] That is, by the execution of $\langle P', V' \rangle$, P_1 proves to P_2 that com_1 is a commitment to bit 0.

5. $P_2 \Rightarrow P_1$: P_2 proceeds symmetrically as does P_1 above. In summary, it generates a commitment com_2 to bit 0 and then proves the same using $\langle P', V' \rangle$.

III. Input Commitment Phase

Let $\mathsf{Enc}_{\mathsf{pk}}(\cdot)$ denote the encryption algorithm of an dense encryption scheme with pseudo-random public keys with public-keys of length ℓ.

1. $P_1 \Leftrightarrow P_2$: P_1 samples a random string $\alpha_1 \in \{0,1\}^\ell$ and sends $c'_1 = \mathrm{PBCOM}(\alpha_1)$ to P_2. Upon receiving c'_1, P_2 responds with a random string $\beta_1 \in \{0,1\}^\ell$. At this point, P_1 reveals the value α_1 to P_2 and proves the following NP-statement to P_2 by executing $\langle P_{\mathsf{swi}}, V_{\mathsf{swi}} \rangle$:
   (a) *either* there exists randomness such that c'_1 is a commitment to the string α_1,
   (b) *or* com_1 is a commitment to 1.
   Both parties set $\mathsf{pk}_c^1 = \alpha_1 \oplus \beta_1$ (public key generated using the coin flipping).

---

[10] Looking ahead the secret key corresponding to the public key pk_2 will allow the simulator to cheat in the simulation.

2. $P_2 \Leftrightarrow P_1 : P_2$ and P_1 proceed symmetrically as above to generate the public key $\mathsf{pk}_c^2 = \alpha_2 \oplus \beta_2$.

3. $P_1 \Rightarrow P_2 : P_1$ samples a random string r_1 of appropriate length which is to be used as randomness to execute semi-honest two-party computation $\langle P_1^{\mathsf{sh}}, P_2^{\mathsf{sh}} \rangle$. P_1 computes $y_1 = \mathsf{Enc}_{\mathsf{pk}_c^2}(x_1 \| r_1)$. Then, it sends y_1 to P_2.

4. $P_2 \Rightarrow P_1 : P_2$ proceeds symmetrically as does P_1 above. Let x_2 and r_2 be the input and the random string chosen by P_2 to be used in the execution of $\langle P_1^{\mathsf{sh}}, P_2^{\mathsf{sh}} \rangle$. Let $y_2 = \mathsf{Enc}_{\mathsf{pk}_c^1}(x_2 \| r_2)$ be the cipher-text generated.

IV. Secure Computation Phase. In the secure computation phase, parties P_1 and P_2 jointly evaluate the desired functionality $\mathcal{F}$ based on a constant-round semi-honest two-party computation protocol $\langle P_1^{\mathsf{sh}}, P_2^{\mathsf{sh}} \rangle$. Party P_1 plays P_1^{sh} while party P_2 plays P_2^{sh}. Note that $\langle P_1^{\mathsf{sh}}, P_2^{\mathsf{sh}} \rangle$ is secure against semi-honest adversaries. Thus, we require that the coins of participating parties are indeed uniform. Moreover, we require each party to prove the validity of every message it sends to the other party. That is, whenever a party generates and sends a message to the other party, it is required to prove by using $\langle P_{\mathsf{swi}}, V_{\mathsf{swi}} \rangle$ that the message is honestly generated with respect to its input, random coins and the instructions of $\langle P_1^{\mathsf{sh}}, P_2^{\mathsf{sh}} \rangle$. In the following, let t be the round complexity of $\langle P_1^{\mathsf{sh}}, P_2^{\mathsf{sh}} \rangle$ where each round consists of two messages: w.l.o.g. a message from P_1 followed by a message from P_2. We denote the next message generators of $\langle P_1^{\mathsf{sh}}, P_2^{\mathsf{sh}} \rangle$ simply by P_1^{sh} and P_1^{sh}. We define transcript $T_{1,i}$ (resp., $T_{2,i}$) by the set (or vector) of all the messages (belonging to $\langle P_1^{\mathsf{sh}}, P_2^{\mathsf{sh}} \rangle$) which are exchanged between P_1 and P_2 before P_1 (resp., P_2) needs to send the i-th round message of $\langle P_1^{\mathsf{sh}}, P_2^{\mathsf{sh}} \rangle$ for $i \in [t]$. In particular, P_1 obtains the i-th round message, denoted by $\beta_{1,i}$, of $\langle P_1^{\mathsf{sh}}, P_2^{\mathsf{sh}} \rangle$ as it computes $\beta_{1,i} = P_1^{\mathsf{sh}}(T_{1,i}, x_1, r_1'')$. The P_2's i-th message is symmetrically defined as $\beta_{2,i} = P_1^{\mathsf{sh}}(T_{2,i}, x_2, r_2'')$. The formal definition of the secure computation phase is provided as follows.

1. $P_1 \Rightarrow P_2 : P_1$ samples a random string r_2' of appropriate length and sends it to P_2.

2. $P_1 \Leftarrow P_2 : P_2$ similarly samples a random string r_1' of appropriate length and sends it to P_1.

3. P_1 computes $r_1'' = r_1 \oplus r_1'$ and P_2 computes $r_2'' = r_2 \oplus r_2'$. Then, r_1'' and r_2'' are the random coins to be used respectively by P_1 and P_2 in the execution of $\langle P_1^{\mathsf{sh}}, P_2^{\mathsf{sh}} \rangle$.

4. For $i \in [t]$, parties P_1 and P_2 repeats the following procedure.

   (a) $P_1 \Rightarrow P_2 : P_1$ computes $\beta_{1,i} = P_1^{\mathsf{sh}}(T_{1,i}, x_1, r_1'')$ and send it to P_2.

   (b) $P_1 \Rightarrow P_2 : P_1$ proves to P_2 by using $\langle P_{\mathsf{swi}}, V_{\mathsf{swi}} \rangle$, the NP-statement which is a disjunction of the following NP-statements:

      i. There exist values $\hat{x}_1, \hat{r}_1$ such that
         A. there exists randomness such that $y_1 - \mathsf{Enc}_{\mathsf{pk}_c^2}(x_1 \| \hat{r}_1)$
         B. and $\beta_{1,i} = P_1^{\mathsf{sh}}(T_{1,i}, \hat{x}_1, \hat{r}_1 \oplus r_1')$

      ii. com_1 is a commitment to bit 1.

   (c) $P_2 \Rightarrow P_1 : P_2$ acts symmetrically.

This completes the formal definition of protocol Π. We claim the following.

Theorem 3. *If there exist a constant-round semi-honest OT, an encryption system with dense(pseudo-random) public keys, and a family of collision-resistant hash functions, then there exists a constant-round concurrently secure two-party computation protocol for every well-formed functionality $\mathcal{F}$ in the CD model.*

5   Proof of Theorem 3 (Simulator $\mathcal{S}$)

In this section, we prove Theorem 3 by constructing an Expected Probabilistic Polynomial-Time (EPPT) simulator $\mathcal{S}$ for protocol Π. That is, the EPPT simulator $\mathcal{S}$ with a black-box access to the adversary $\mathcal{A}$ simulates the view of adversary which is computationally indistinguishable from the view of adversary interacting with a honest party in the real world execution of Π. Here we will only give a description of our simulator and refer the reader to the full version for a formal proof of indistinguishability.

Notice that the NP-statement for an instance of SWI (in Step 4b of Secure Computation Phase) is a disjunction of two NP-statements (Statement 4(b)i and Statement 4(b)ii). In the rest of the work, we refer to Statement 4(b)i as *real* theorem while we refer to Statement 4(b)ii as the *trapdoor* theorem. We call the witness corresponding to statement 4(b)i (resp. statement 4(b)ii) as *real* (resp. *trapdoor*) witness.

Notation. In the following, we denote the honest party and the adversary by H and $\mathcal{A}$ respectively. Also, let $\mathbf{F}_{\mathsf{KCA}}^{H}$ be the domain to which the honest party belong. Similarly, we use $\mathbf{F}_{\mathsf{KCA}}^{\mathcal{A}}$ to denote the domain where the adversary corrupts a party. Without loss of generality, we define our simulator in the case where the honest party (thus, the simulator in the following) sends the first message in the protocol. We omit the other case where the corrupted party sends the first message. Let $m = \mathsf{poly}(n)$ be the running time of the PPT adversary $\mathcal{A}$. And let l be the number of public keys registered by the corrupted party. The running time of $\mathcal{A}$ serves as an upper-bounds on the number of concurrent sessions and also on the number of registered public keys. In the course of simulation, simulator $\mathcal{S}$ maintains two sets denoted by $\mathtt{Database1}$ and $\mathtt{Database2}$. $\mathtt{Database1}$ contains an element of the form $(\mathsf{pk}, \mathsf{sk}, \sigma_{pk})$ for $i \in [l]$. $\mathtt{Database2}$ contains elements of the form $(\mathsf{sid}, x_i^{\mathsf{sid}}, r_i^{\mathsf{sid}})$ where $\mathsf{sid} \in [m]$ and $i \in [l]$. Initially, $\mathtt{Database1}$ and $\mathtt{Database2}$ are set to be empty. We sometimes omit the session identifier sid in order to simplify notations.

We preserve the notations for the execution of building blocks as in Section 4.2. For example, we denote by $\langle P, V \rangle_{\mathcal{S} \to \mathcal{A}}$, an instance of $\langle P, V \rangle$ where simulator $\mathcal{S}$ and corrupted party $\mathcal{A}$ play as the prover P and the verifier V respectively in the execution of the protocol $\langle P, V \rangle$. We demarcate the following two *special* messages in the protocol Π:

- **Message Σ_1^{sid}:** Σ_1^{sid} denotes the second message of $\langle C, R \rangle_{\mathcal{A} \to \mathcal{S}}^{\mathsf{trap}_{\mathcal{A}}}$ in session sid. Recall that the second message of the protocol $\langle C, R \rangle$ is a random string (challenge) from the receiver to the committer. In the execution of $\langle C, R \rangle_{\mathcal{A} \to \mathcal{S}}^{\mathsf{trap}_{\mathcal{A}}}$, this message is sent by the simulator (on behalf of H) to the adversary $\mathcal{A}$.

- **Message** Σ_2^{sid}: Σ_2^{sid} denotes the message of session sid when the simulator (on behalf of the honest party H) sends the commitment to 0 using the commitment scheme PBCOM. The simulator will behave honestly until this point and will cheat only after this point is reached.

Description of $\mathcal{S}$. We provide the simulation strategy of $\mathcal{S}$ in each phase of Π as follows.

I. SIMULATION OF KEY REGISTRATION PHASE: In the key registration phase, simulator $\mathcal{S}$ follows an honest party's strategy. That is, $\mathcal{S}$ interacting with $\mathbf{F}_{\text{KCA}}^H$ registers public keys $\mathsf{pk}_{\mathcal{S}}^0$ and $\mathsf{pk}_{\mathcal{S}}^1$ (on behalf of the honest party H) where $(\mathsf{pk}_{\mathcal{S}}^0, \mathsf{sk}_{\mathcal{S}}^0)$ and $(\mathsf{pk}_{\mathcal{S}}^1, \mathsf{sk}_{\mathcal{S}}^1)$ are obtained as in the honest setting. Finally, $\mathcal{S}$ completes the simulation of key registration phase by setting $\mathsf{pk}_{\mathcal{S}}$, $\mathsf{sk}_{\mathcal{S}}$, and $\sigma_{\mathsf{pk}_{\mathcal{S}}}$ following the honest strategy.

II. SIMULATION OF TRAPDOOR CREATION PHASE: Simulator $\mathcal{S}$ behaves according to the honest party strategy until it needs to send the Σ_2^{sid} for some session session sid $\in [m]$. At this point, $\mathcal{S}$ by interacting with $\mathbf{F}_{\text{KCA}}^H$ obtained a verification key $mvk_{\mathcal{A}}$ of $\mathbf{F}_{\text{KCA}}^{\mathcal{A}}$. To successfully simulate trapdoor creation phase, $\mathcal{S}$ wants to do the following:

1. For all sessions, $\mathcal{S}$ commits to 1 (recall that this differs from the real execution in the fact that honest party commit to 0) by executing $com_{\mathcal{S}} = \text{PBCOM}(1)$ and then sends $com_{\mathcal{S}}$ in to the adversary.
2. For all sessions, $\mathcal{S}$ proves to $\mathcal{A}$ by executing $\langle P', V' \rangle_{\mathcal{S} \rightarrow \mathcal{A}}$ using a trapdoor information $\mathsf{trap}_{\mathcal{A}}$ (stored in the database Database1) as its witness that $(mvk_{\mathcal{A}}, \mathsf{trap}_{\mathcal{A}}) \in \mathcal{R}_2$.

Thus, before sending the commitment to 1, $\mathcal{S}$ checks if Database1 contains $\mathsf{trap}_{\mathcal{A}}$ such that $(mvk_{\mathcal{A}}, \mathsf{trap}_{\mathcal{A}}) \in \mathcal{R}_2$. If so, then $\mathcal{S}$ proceeds as above. Otherwise, $\mathcal{S}$ employs a rewinding strategy to extract the trapdoor information. Note that session sid (called *target session*) is the session in which the simulator needs to send the commitment to bit 1 using the commitment scheme PBCOM without the corresponding trapdoor information in Database1. We will denote this session by sid^{target}. When this point is reached, our simulator $\mathcal{S}$ executes the following look-ahead thread strategy.[11]

1. $\mathcal{S}$ rewinds adversary $\mathcal{A}$ back to the point before $\mathcal{S}$ had sent $\Sigma_1^{\text{sid}^{target}}$ to $\mathcal{A}$.
2. In the look-ahead thread, the simulator $\mathcal{S}$ sends to $\mathcal{A}$ a fresh random challenge for the message $\Sigma_1^{\text{sid}^{target}}$ and behaves honestly subsequently. If in this look-ahead thread, the first session in which the simulator needs to send Σ_2^{sid} is not the target session (in other words sid $\neq$ sid^{target}), then $\mathcal{S}$ rewinds again and repeats this step. If the number of rewindings reaches 2^n, then $\mathcal{S}$ aborts completely and outputs Rewind Abort.

---

[11] Note that the transcript generated by the execution of look-ahead threads will not be included in the view of the main thread simulation.

3. Since $\mathcal{S}$ need to send $\Sigma_2^{\text{sid}^{target}}$ in both the main thread and the rewound thread, it must have obtained two distinct *valid* de-commitments of $\langle C, R \rangle_{\mathcal{A} \to \mathcal{S}}^{\text{trap}_{\mathcal{A}}}$ in the target session sid^{target} in both the main thread and the look-ahead threads. At this point, using two distinct valid de-commitments, $\mathcal{S}$ obtains $\text{trap}_{\mathcal{A}}$. $\mathcal{S}$ executes the rest of the main concurrent execution with the updated Database1. Notice that a single successful extraction of $\text{trap}_{\mathcal{A}}$ in one session suffices to simulate all other sessions.

III. SIMULATION OF INPUT COMMITMENT PHASE

1. The simulator behaves honestly in the generation of the public key $\text{pk}_c^{\mathcal{A}}$.
2. Now, we describe simulation strategy in generation of the public key $\text{pk}_c^{\mathcal{S}}$. $\mathcal{S}$ starts by generating a a fresh public key $\text{pk}_c^{\mathcal{S}}$ along with the secret key $\text{sk}_c^{\mathcal{S}}$. It generates the commitment $c_{\mathcal{S}}'$ as the commitment to the zero string. Then, $\mathcal{S}$ receives $\beta_{\mathcal{S}}$ from $\mathcal{A}$. Finally $\mathcal{S}$ opens $\alpha_{\mathcal{S}}$ as $\text{pk}_c^{\mathcal{S}} \oplus \beta_{\mathcal{S}}$. $\mathcal{S}$ executes $\langle P_{\text{swi}}, V_{\text{swi}} \rangle_{\mathcal{S} \to \mathcal{A}}$ where $\mathcal{S}$ uses the trapdoor witness. $\mathcal{S}$ possesses the trapdoor witness since it committed to bit 1 instead of 0 during the simulation of the trapdoor creation phase.
3. $\mathcal{S}$ generates $y_{\mathcal{S}}$ as encryption of the zero string using the public key $\text{pk}_c^{\mathcal{A}}$ and sends it to the adversary. (instead of using its actual input and random coins needed for the semi-honest two-party computation)
4. Upon the receiving $y_{\mathcal{A}}$, the simulator $\mathcal{S}$ extracts the input and randomness $x_{\mathcal{A}}^{\text{sid}}$ and $r_{\mathcal{A}}^{\text{sid}}$ of $\mathcal{A}$ using the secret key $\text{sk}_c^{\mathcal{S}}$. Now, $\mathcal{S}$ adds $(\text{sid}, x_{\mathcal{A}}^{\text{sid}}, r_{\mathcal{A}}^{\text{sid}})$ to Database2.

IV. SIMULATION OF SECURE COMPUTATION PHASE. Let S_{sh} denote the simulator for the semi-honest two-party protocol $\langle P_1^{\text{sh}}, P_2^{\text{sh}} \rangle$ used in our construction. $\mathcal{S}$ internally runs simulator S_{sh} on adversary $\mathcal{A}_{\text{sh}}$'s input $x_{\mathcal{A}} \in$ Database2. S_{sh} at some point makes a call to ideal functionality $\mathcal{F}$ in the ideal world with an input string $x_{\mathcal{A}}$. Then, $\mathcal{S}$ makes a query $(\text{sid}, x_{\mathcal{A}})$ to $\mathcal{F}$. Then, $\mathcal{S}$ forwards the output returned by $\mathcal{F}$ to S_{sh}. At some point of internal simulation of $\langle P_1^{\text{sh}}, P_2^{\text{sh}} \rangle$, S_{sh} finally halts and outputs a transcript $\beta_{S_{\text{sh}},1}, \beta_{\mathcal{A}_{\text{sh}},1}, \ldots, \beta_{S_{\text{sh}},t}, \beta_{\mathcal{A}_{\text{sh}},t}$ and associated random coin $\hat{r}_{\mathcal{A}}$. $\mathcal{S}$ proceeds with the following instructions.

1. $\mathcal{S}$ computes a random string $\tilde{r}_{\mathcal{A}}$ such that $\tilde{r}_{\mathcal{A}} = r_{\mathcal{A}} \oplus \hat{r}_{\mathcal{A}}$. Then, $\mathcal{S}$ sends $\tilde{r}_{\mathcal{A}}$ to $\mathcal{A}$.
2. For each round $j \in [t]$, $\mathcal{S}$ sends $\beta_{S_{\text{sh}},j}$ to $\mathcal{A}$. Then, $\mathcal{S}$ executes $\langle P_{\text{swi}}, V_{\text{swi}} \rangle_{\mathcal{S} \to \mathcal{A}}$ with $\mathcal{A}$ where $\mathcal{S}$ uses the trapdoor witness, decommitment information of $com_{\mathcal{S}}$ (commitment to 1 instead of 0). If $\mathcal{A}$ aborts upon $\beta_{S_{\text{sh}},j}$ for some $j \in [t]$, $\mathcal{S}$ outputs a special abort message ABORT$_1$.
3. Upon receiving $\mathcal{A}$'s next message $\beta_{\mathcal{A},j}$ in the protocol $\langle P_1^{\text{sh}}, P_2^{\text{sh}} \rangle$, $\mathcal{S}$ plays the honest verifier in an execution of $\langle P_{\text{swi}}, V_{\text{swi}} \rangle_{\mathcal{A} \to \mathcal{S}}$. For any $j \in [t]$, if the jth message $\beta_{\mathcal{A},j}$ sent by adversary $\mathcal{A}$ is not identical to $\beta_{\mathcal{A}_{\text{sh}},j}$ (obtained from the internal execution of S_{sh}) and if $\langle P_{\text{swi}}, V_{\text{swi}} \rangle_{\mathcal{A} \to \mathcal{S}}$ on $\beta_{\mathcal{A},j}$ is accepting, then $\mathcal{S}$ aborts and outputs a special abort message ABORT$_2$.

Finally, the output of simulator S contains all messages exchanged between the simulator and the adversary including the output of the adversary in the communication of all sessions.

6 Relation with the Bare-Public Key (BPK) Model

The CD model defined in this paper is a generalization of the BPK model introduced by Canetti et al. [9]. In the BPK model each party sets up its own public-key and private-key pair. It publishes its public-key in a public file while keeping the private-key secret. This phase of publishing the public-keys happens prior to any protocol executions, implicitly also placing a bound on the number of parties in the system.

The CD model is a generalization of the BPK model, where each party corresponding to the BPK model is now associated with a domain of mutually trusting entities, equipped with a key registration authority. A key registration authority in the CD model generates a common public-key for all entities in its domain and issues a private-key for each of these entities. Just as in the BPK model in which the number of parties are bounded, the CD model bounds the number of domains while putting no bound on the number of parties.

As a real-world example, consider a setting of the BPK model where one of the parties owns multiple (physically distinct) devices and would like to use each of these devices for various secure computation tasks. In the CD model, each one of these devices is seen as a separate entity and the owner who generates and distributes the keys across these devices is seen as the key registration authority.

In the BPK model, one party could coordinate between different concurrent executions that it takes part in. For example, a party could ensure that it takes part in all the protocol executions sequentially and hence avoid all the problems that arise because of concurrent executions. This coordination is certainly not desirable but might very well be acceptable in various real world applications. On the other hand in our CD model, different entities represent possibly separate devices, coordinating which is not possible. The key advantage of the CD model over the BPK model is that it makes this distinction in functionality clear.

Finally, we note that our results in the CD model, directly imply positive and negative results in the BPK model. We stress that even in the BPK model prior to our work no results for the setting of secure computation were known and our results fully characterize what is possible in this model. More formally, these results are directly implied by the following lemma.

Lemma 2. *There exists an n-party black-box concurrently secure protocol Π among n-domains in the CD-model where each party is associated with distinct domains if and only if there exists an n-party black box concurrently secure protocol Π' in the BPK model with n parties.*

Proof. We give a proof sketch here. We start by giving a protocol Π' secure in the BPK model given a protocol Π secure in the CD-model. Each party in protocol Π' that we are trying to construct executes the public setup of the key-registration authority of protocol Π and generates the private-key assuming only one entity in its domain. Subsequently to this setup phase, parties in Π' execute all concurrent execution as a party of Π using the secret key that it had generated earlier as the key-registration authority. Security of the protocol Π' follows immediately. The other direction can be argued in a similar manner.

In particular, the above lemma along with our results in the CD model implies that there exists an n-party concurrently secure protocol in the BPK model if and only if there are exactly n parties in the system.

References

1. Agrawal, S., Goyal, V., Jain, A., Prabhakaran, M., Sahai, A.: New impossibility results for concurrent composition and a non-interactive completeness theorem for secure computation. In: Safavi-Naini, R., Canetti, R. (eds.) CRYPTO 2012. LNCS, vol. 7417, pp. 443–460. Springer, Heidelberg (2012)
2. Barak, B., Canetti, R., Nielsen, J., Pass, R.: Universally composable protocols with relaxed set-up assumptions. In: FOCS, pp. 186–195 (2004)
3. Barak, B., Prabhakaran, M., Sahai, A.: Concurrent non-malleable zero knowledge. In: FOCS, pp. 345–354 (2006)
4. Barak, B., Sahai, A.: How to play almost any mental game over the net - concurrent composition via super-polynomial simulation. In: FOCS, pp. 543–552 (2005)
5. Beimel, A., Malkin, T., Micali, S.: The all-or-nothing nature of two-party secure computation. In: Wiener, M. (ed.) CRYPTO 1999. LNCS, vol. 1666, pp. 80–97. Springer, Heidelberg (1999)
6. Canetti, R., Kushilevitz, E., Lindell, Y.: On the limitations of universally composable two-party computation without set-up assumptions. J. Cryptology 19(2), 135–167 (2006)
7. Canetti, R., Lindell, Y., Ostrovsky, R., Sahai, A.: Universally composable two-party and multi-party secure computation. In: STOC, pp. 494–503 (2002)
8. Canetti, R., Fischlin, M.: Universally composable commitments. In: Kilian, J. (ed.) CRYPTO 2001. LNCS, vol. 2139, pp. 19–40. Springer, Heidelberg (2001)
9. Canetti, R., Goldreich, O., Goldwasser, S., Micali, S.: Resettable zero-knowledge (extended abstract). In: STOC, pp. 235–244 (2000)
10. Canetti, R., Lin, H., Pass, R.: Adaptive hardness and composable security in the plain model from standard assumptions. In: FOCS, pp. 541–550 (2010)
11. Canetti, R., Pass, R., Shelat, A.: Cryptography from sunspots: How to use an imperfect reference string. In: FOCS, pp. 249–259 (2007)
12. Chandran, N., Goyal, V., Sahai, A.: New constructions for uc secure computation using tamper-proof hardware. In: Smart, N.P. (ed.) EUROCRYPT 2008. LNCS, vol. 4965, pp. 545–562. Springer, Heidelberg (2008)
13. Dwork, C., Naor, M., Sahai, A.: Concurrent zero-knowledge. In: STOC, pp. 409–418 (1998)
14. Garay, J.A., MacKenzie, P.D.: Concurrent oblivious transfer. In: FOCS, pp. 314–324 (2000)
15. Garg, S., Goyal, V., Jain, A., Sahai, A.: Bringing people of different beliefs together to do uc. In: Ishai, Y. (ed.) TCC 2011. LNCS, vol. 6597, pp. 311–328. Springer, Heidelberg (2011)

16. Garg, S., Goyal, V., Jain, A., Sahai, A.: Concurrently secure computation in constant rounds. In: Pointcheval, D., Johansson, T. (eds.) EUROCRYPT 2012. LNCS, vol. 7237, pp. 99–116. Springer, Heidelberg (2012)

17. Garg, S., Kumarasubramanian, A., Ostrovsky, R., Visconti, I.: Impossibility results for static input secure computation. In: Safavi-Naini, R., Canetti, R. (eds.) CRYPTO 2012. LNCS, vol. 7417, pp. 424–442. Springer, Heidelberg (2012)

18. Goldreich, O., Micali, S., Wigderson, A.: How to play any mental game or a completeness theorem for protocols with honest majority. In: STOC, pp. 218–229 (1987)

19. Goyal, V.: Positive results for concurrently secure computation in the plain model. In. FOCS, pp. 41–50 (2012)

20. Goyal, V., Jain, A., Ostrovsky, R.: Password-authenticated session-key generation on the internet in the plain model. In: Rabin, T. (ed.) CRYPTO 2010. LNCS, vol. 6223, pp. 277–294. Springer, Heidelberg (2010)

21. Goyal, V., Katz, J.: Universally composable multi-party computation with an unreliable common reference string. In: Canetti, R. (ed.) TCC 2008. LNCS, vol. 4948, pp. 142–154. Springer, Heidelberg (2008)

22. Groth, J., Ostrovsky, R.: Cryptography in the multi-string model. In: Menezes, A. (ed.) CRYPTO 2007. LNCS, vol. 4622, pp. 323–341. Springer, Heidelberg (2007)

23. Jain, A., Ostrovsky, R., Richelson, S., Visconti, I.: Concurrent zero knowledge in the bounded player model. Cryptology ePrint Archive, Report 2012/279 (2012), http://eprint.iacr.org/

24. Katz, J.: Universally composable multi-party computation using tamper-proof hardware. In: Eurocrypt., pp. 115–128 (2007)

25. Kilian, J.: Founding cryptography on oblivious transfer. In: STOC, pp. 20–31 (1988)

26. Kilian, J.: More general completeness theorems for secure two-party computation. In: STOC, pp. 316–324 (2000)

27. Kilian, J., Kushilevitz, E., Micali, S., Ostrovsky, R.: Reducibility and completeness in private computations. SIAM J. Comput. 29(4), 1189–1208 (2000)

28. Kilian, J., Petrank, E.: Concurrent and resettable zero-knowledge in polyloalgorithm rounds. In: STOC, pp. 560–569 (2001)

29. Kushilevitz, E., Micali, S., Ostrovsky, R.: Reducibility and completeness in multi-party private computations. In: FOCS, pp. 478–489 (1994)

30. Lin, H., Pass, R., Venkitasubramaniam, M.: A unified framework for concurrent security: universal composability from stand-alone non-malleability. In: STOC, pp. 179–188 (2009)

31. Lindell, Y.: Lower bounds for concurrent self composition. In: Naor, M. (ed.) TCC 2004. LNCS, vol. 2951, pp. 203–222. Springer, Heidelberg (2004)

32. Lindell, Y.: Lower bounds and impossibility results for concurrent self composition. J. Cryptology 21(2), 200–249 (2008)

33. Micali, S., Pass, R., Rosen, A.: Input-indistinguishable computation. In: FOCS, pp. 367–378 (2006)

34. Pass, R.: Simulation in quasi-polynomial time, and its application to protocol composition. In: Biham, E. (ed.) EUROCRYPT 2003. LNCS, vol 2656, pp. 160–176. Springer, Heidelberg (2003)

35. Pass, R.: Bounded-concurrent secure multi-party computation with a dishonest majority. In: STOC, pp. 232–241 (2004)

36. Pass, R., Rosen, A.: Bounded-concurrent secure two-party computation in a constant number of rounds. In: FOCS, pp. 404–413 (2003)

37. Prabhakaran, M., Rosen, A., Sahai, A.: Concurrent zero knowledge with logarithmic round-complexity. In: FOCS, pp. 366–375 (2002)
38. Prabhakaran, M., Sahai, A.: New notions of security: achieving universal composability without trusted setup. In: STOC, pp. 242–251 (2004)
39. Richardson, R., Kilian, J.: On the concurrent composition of zero-knowledge proofs. In: Stern, J. (ed.) EUROCRYPT 1999. LNCS, vol. 1592, pp. 415–431. Springer, Heidelberg (1999)
40. Yao, A.C.C.: How to generate and exchange secrets (extended abstract). In: FOCS, pp. 162–167 (1986)

On the Security of the Pre-shared Key Ciphersuites of TLS

Yong Li[1], Sven Schäge[2,*], Zheng Yang[1], Florian Kohlar[1], and Jörg Schwenk[1]

[1] Ruhr-Universität Bochum, Germany
{yong.li,zheng.yang,florian.kohlar,joerg.schwenk}@rub.de
[2] University College London, UK
s.schage@ucl.ac.uk

Abstract. TLS is by far the most important protocol on the Internet for negotiating secure session keys and providing authentication. Only very recently, the standard ciphersuites of TLS have been shown to provide provably secure guarantees under a new notion called Authenticated and Confidential Channel Establishment (ACCE) introduced by Jager *et al.* at CRYPTO'12. In this work, we analyse the variants of TLS that make use of pre-shared keys (TLS-PSK). In various environments, TLS-PSK is an interesting alternative for remote authentication between servers and constrained clients like smart cards, for example for mobile phone authentication, EMV-based payment transactions or authentication via electronic ID cards. First, we introduce a new and strong definition of ACCE security that covers protocols with pre-shared keys. Next, we prove that all ciphersuite families of TLS-PSK meet our strong notion of ACCE security. Our results do not rely on random oracles nor on any non-standard assumption.

Keywords: TLS, TLS-PSK, ACCE, Pre-Shared Keys, Authenticated Key Exchange, Secure Channels.

1 Introduction

TLS is undeniably the most prominent key exchange protocol in use today. While the security of most web applications relies on the classical Diffie-Hellman and RSA-based ciphersuites of TLS, there also exist several important applications that make use of one of the less common ciphersuites [31,1,29]. One such application is (remote) authentication of resource-restricted clients like smart-cards. In these scenarios, computational efficiency and low power consumption often are one of the most important system features. Instead of using the public-key based ciphersuites of TLS, applications can apply a variant of TLS that assumes pre-shared symmetric keys between client and server. The corresponding ciphersuite family is termed TLS with pre-shared keys (TLS-PSK) and available in many TLS releases and libraries, for example [28,24,7].

---

* Supported by EPSRC grant number EP/J009520/1.

H. Krawczyk (Ed.): PKC 2014, LNCS 8383, pp. 669–684, 2014.

RELATED WORK: ON THE SECURITY OF TLS. Since the introduction of its predecessor SSL, the security of TLS has often been the focus of security researchers and attackers worldwide. Over the time, several attacks on TLS have been published. Most of these attacks do not directly attack the cryptographic core of TLS, but rather exploit side-channels or vulnerabilities in associated technologies, like the famous Bleichenbacher attack [6], or attacks on the domain name system or the public-key infrastructure [20,10,26]. However, despite that no serious attacks on the cryptographic core of the current TLS protocol are known, determining exactly what security guarantees TLS provides has been an elusive problem for many years. This is partly due to the fact that the popular TLS ciphersuites provably do not provide security in the sense of authenticated key exchange (AKE) protocols [3], the classical and very strong standard notion of security of key exchange protocols (which requires that the session key remains indistinguishable from random even if the adversary obtains the communication transcript of the session). Until recently only security analyses of modified versions of TLS were published [18,16,27]. At CRYPTO 2012, Jager, Kohlar, Schäge, and Schwenk (JKSS) [17] were the first to present a detailed security analysis of the *unmodified* version of one of TLS's ciphersuite families. They showed that the cryptographic core of ephemeral Diffie-Hellman with mutual authentication is a provably secure authenticated and confidential channel establishment (ACCE) protocol in the standard model. ACCE is a new security notion that is particularly well suited to capture what protocols like TLS intuitively want to achieve: the establishment of a secure channel between client and server. Among its features, it not only formalizes confidentiality and integrity of messages exchanged between client and server, but also covers replay and re-ordering attacks. Very recently, Krawczyk, Paterson, and Wee (KPW) [22] and independently Kohlar, Schäge, Schwenk (KSS) [19] presented, while relying on different cryptographic assumptions and security models[1], extensions of the JKSS result to the remaining ciphersuite families. In particular, they show that TLS-RSA and TLS-DH also constitute ACCE protocols when used for mutual authentication setting and that TLS-RSA, TLS-DH, and TLS-DHE are ACCE secure in the practically important setting of server-only authentication (for which they provide new formal security definitions).

Unfortunately, all previous results on the (ACCE) security of TLS are based on either i) new, non-standard security assumption like the PRF-ODH assumption introduced in [17] and refined in [22,19] or ii) strong idealizations such as the modeling of TLS's key derivation function as a random oracle [2] or assuming that the public-key encryption scheme in TLS-RSA is replaced with an IND-CCA secure one. Looking somewhat ahead, for the TLS-PSK ciphersuites, fortunately the situation is different, i.e. security can be based on standard assumptions only.

---

[1] The security models and complexity assumptions differ mainly with respect to the capabilities granted to the adversary when corrupting and registering new parties and the application of the random oracle model.

TLS WITH PRE-SHARED KEYS. The original specifications of the TLS protocol [11,12,13] do not explicitly include ciphersuites that support authentication and key exchange using pre-shared keys. However, since 2005 there exists an extension called "Pre-Shared Key Ciphersuites for Transport Layer Security" (TLS-PSK) which specifically describes such ciphersuites in RFC 4279 [14]. The TLS-PSK standard specifies three ciphersuites, TLS_PSK, TLS_RSA_PSK and TLS_DHE_PSK, each of which derives the master secret in a different way. In TLS_PSK, the master secret is solely based on the secret pre-shared keys. In the remaining ciphersuites the computation of the master secret is additionally dependent on freshly exchanged secrets via encrypted key transport in TLS_RSA_PSK or Diffie-Hellman key exchange in TLS_DHE_PSK. The intuition is that as long as either the pre-shared key or the freshly exchanged secret is not compromised, then the protocol produces a secure application key. All three ciphersuites assume that the client only has a pre-shared key for authentication. Although it is not as widespread as TLS with RSA key transport, several interesting and important scenarios for TLS with pre-shared keys exist where its efficiency makes TLS-PSK a much more attractive alternative than, for example, TLS with self-signed certificates.

- Since November 2010, the new electronic German ID (eID) card supports online remote authentication of the eID card holder to some online service (eService). Here TLS-PSK is applied to perform mutual authentication between the two parties [15].
- As a second example, we mention the application of TLS-PSK in the Generic Authentication Architecture, the 3GGP mobile phone standard for UMTS and LTE. According to ETSI TR 133 919 V11.0.0 (2012-11), TLS-PSK can be used to secure the communication between server and user equipment.
- An IETF draft from 2009 for EMV smart cards describes an authentication protocol based on TLS-PSK [29]. EMV chips are widely deployed and are used commonly for secure payment transactions [9].

CONTRIBUTION. In this paper, we provide a security analysis of all three TLS-PSK ciphersuites. Similar to classical TLS, it is provably impossible to show that the keys produced by TLS-PSK are indistinguishable from random. Therefore, as one of our main contributions, we introduce the first definition of ACCE security for authentication protocols with pre-shared keys. We do not propose a separate model but rather an extension of the ACCE model of JKSS to also cover authentication via pre-shared keys. Next, we introduce a strengthened variant of this definition called *asymmetric perfect forward secrecy*, that captures that protocol sessions of ACCE protocols with pre-shared keys may retain a strong level of confidentiality even if the long term secrets of the client are exposed after the protocol run. Asymmetric perfect forward secrecy is a strong security notion that can hold for protocols that do not fulfill the standard notion of perfect forward secrecy. This allows us to prove the security of such protocols in a stronger security model than was previously possible. We show that TLS_PSK is ACCE secure (without forward secrecy), TLS_RSA_PSK is ACCE secure with asymmetric perfect forward secrecy and `TLS_DHE_PSK` is secure with (classical) perfect forward secrecy. Informally, our results say that TLS-PSK guarantees confidentiality and integrity of all messages exchange between client and server, unless the adversary has learned the pre-shared key or corrupted one of the parties to learn the application/session key. In `TLS_DHE_PSK` the communication remains confidential even if the adversary corrupts the pre-shared secret later on. In contrast, in `TLS_RSA_PSK` the communication remains confidential even if the adversary manages to corrupt the pre-shared key or the server's long-term key later on, but not both of them.

DOUBLE PRFS AND FORWARD SECRECY. To prove `TLS_RSA_PSK` and `TLS_DHE_PSK`, we introduce a variant of pseudo-random functions (PRFs), called double pseudo-random function (DPRF). Roughly, a DPRF takes as input two keys only one of which is generated randomly and kept secret from the attacker (as in classical PRFs). However, when the adversary makes its queries, not only the message but also the other key can entirely be specified by the adversary. Our notion of DPRF nicely abstracts the crucial mechanism in TLS-PSK that is required to guarantee (asymmetric) perfect forward secrecy. In our security proofs, we assume that TLS's key derivation function provides a suitable DPRF in the standard model. Existing results on the security of HMAC support this assumption for TLS 1.1 when the pre-shared key has a specific bit length. Our new DPRF notion may be of independent interest beyond the scope of this work.

Note also, that for the `TLS_PSK` and `TLS_DHE_PSK` ciphersuites we neither have to rely on non-standard assumptions like the PRF-ODH assumption of JKSS to give a proof nor on idealized setup assumptions like the random oracle model. We can show that `TLS_RSA_PSK` is secure under our basic notion of ACCE security without any assumption on the public key encryption system used in TLS. This is because under the basic ACCE definition security can be derived solely from secrecy of the pre-shared keys. However, if we want to prove the ACCE security of `TLS_RSA_PSK` with asymmetric perfect forward secrecy in the *standard model* we need to assume that the public key encryption scheme is IND-CCA secure[2], similar to [22,19]. Thus, we do not consider TLS-RSA with RSA-PKCS encryption as it is currently used in practice. We remark that [22] were also able to prove security of the classical TLS ciphersuites based on RSA key transport with RSA-PKCS encryption in the random oracle model. It would be interesting to show that the results of KPW on TLS-RSA can be transferred to show that TLS-PSK with RSA-PKCS based key transport provides asymmetric perfect forward secrecy in the random oracle model.

LIMITATIONS. In our work, we give a dedicated security analysis for TLS-PSK. We believe that it is possible to give a more modularized analysis, similar to KPW [22] who analyzed the classical ciphersuites of TLS by abstracting the handshake phase into a Constrained-CCA-secure (CCCA) KEM that is combined with a secure authenticated encryption scheme. The benefit of the KPW analysis is re-usability: once the security proof is established for a generic

---

[2] KPW call this TLS-CCA.

CCCA-secure KEM, all that remains is to show that each of the ciphersuites indeed provides such a KEM.

2 Security Assumptions

To state our results, we will rely on standard security definitions for the Decisional Diffie-Hellman assumption (DDH), collision-resistant cryptographic hash functions, IND-CCA secure public key encryption schemes, (plain) pseudo-random functions (PRF), and stateful length-hiding authenticated encryption (sLHAE) schemes as recently defined in [30]. However, we will sometimes also rely on a new class of PRFs called double pseudo-random functions.

DOUBLE PSEUDO-RANDOM FUNCTIONS. Double pseudo-random functions can be thought of as a class of pseudo-random functions with two keys. Let $DPRF : \mathcal{K}_{DPRF_1} \times \mathcal{K}_{DPRF_2} \times \mathcal{M}_{DPRF} \to \mathcal{R}_{DPRF}$ denote a family of deterministic functions, where $\mathcal{K}_{DPRF_1}, \mathcal{K}_{DPRF_2}$ is the key space, $\mathcal{M}_{DPRF}$ is the domain and $\mathcal{R}_{DPRF}$ is the range of PRF.

Intuitively, security requires that the output of the DPRF is indistinguishable from random as long as one key remains hidden from the adversary even if the adversary is able to adaptively specify the second key and the input message. To formalize security we consider the following security game played between a challenger $\mathcal{C}$ and an adversary $\mathcal{A}$. Let $RF_{DPRF}(\cdot, \cdot)$ denote an oracle implemented by $\mathcal{C}$, which takes as input a key $k_j \in \mathcal{K}_{DPRF_j}$ (where j is specified by the adversary via an Init query) and message $m \in \mathcal{M}_{DPRF}$ and outputs a random value $z \in \mathcal{R}_{DPRF}$.

1. The adversary first runs $\text{Init}(j)$ with $j \in \{1, 2\}$ to specify the key $k_j \in \mathcal{K}_{DPRF_j}$ that he wants to manipulate.
2. The challenger $\mathcal{C}$ samples $\hat{b} \xleftarrow{\$} \{0, 1\}$, and sets $u = (j \mod 2) + 1$. If $\hat{b} = 0$, the challenger samples $k_u \in_R \mathcal{K}_{DPRF_u}$ and assigns $RF_{DPRF}(\cdot, \cdot)$ to either $DPRF(\cdot, k_2, \cdot)$ or $DPRF(k_1, \cdot, \cdot)$ depending on the value of u. For instance, if $u = 2$ then the random function RF_{DPRF} is assigned to $DPRF(\cdot, k_2, \cdot)$, and the $\mathcal{A}$ is allowed to specify k_1 arbitrarily in each query. If $\hat{b} = 1$, the challenger assigns RF_{DPRF} to $RF(\cdot, \cdot)$ which is a truly random function that takes as input key k_j and message m and outputs a value in the same range $\mathcal{R}_{DPRF}$ as $DPRF(\cdot, \cdot, \cdot)$.
3. The adversary may adaptively make queries $k_{j,i}, m_i$ for $1 \le i \le q$ to oracle RF_{DPRF} and receives the result of $RF_{DPRF}(k_{j,i}, m_i)$, where $k_{j,i}$ denotes the i-th key k_j chosen by $\mathcal{A}$.
4. Finally, $\mathcal{A}$ outputs its guess $\hat{b}' \in \{0, 1\}$ of $\hat{b}$. If $\hat{b} = \hat{b}'$, $\mathcal{A}$ wins.

Definition 1. *We say that* DPRF *is a* (t, ϵ)-*secure double pseudo-random function, if any adversary running in time t has at most an advantage of ϵ to distinguish the* DPRF *from a truly random function, i.e.*

$$\Pr\left[\hat{b} = \hat{b}'\right] \le 1/2 + \epsilon.$$

The number of allowed queries q is upper bounded by t.

3   A Brief Introduction to TLS-PSK

This section describes the three sets of ciphersuites specified in TLS-PSK: TLS_PSK, TLS_RSA_PSK and TLS_DHE_PSK. In each of these ciphersuites, the master secret is computed using pre-shared keys which are symmetric keys shared in advance among the communicating parties. The main differences are in the way the master secret is computed. The following description is valid for *all* TLS_PSK versions. We only describe the cryptographically relevant messages and only those that deviate from the classical TLS ciphersuites. A detailed description can be found in the full version.

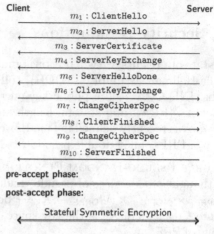

Fig. 1. Handshake in TLS-PSK

SERVERCERTIFICATE. For TLS_PSK and TLS_DHE_PSK, the message is not included. In TLS_RSA_PSK cert$_S$ contains a public key that is bound to the server's identity.

SERVERKEYEXCHANGE. Since clients and servers may have pre-shared keys with many different parties, in the ServerKeyExchange message m_4, the server provides a PSK identity hint pointing to the PSK used for authentication. However, for ephemeral Diffie-Hellman key exchange, the Diffie-Hellman (DH) key exchange parameters are also contained in the ServerKeyExchange messages including information on the DH group (e.g. a large prime number $p \in \{0,1\}^{poly(\kappa)}$, where κ is the security parameter, and a generator $\langle g \rangle$ for a prime-order q subgroup of $\mathbb{Z}_p^*$), and the DH share T_S ($T_S = g^{t_S}$, where t_S is a random value in $\mathbb{Z}_q$). (We implictly assume that the client checks whether the received parameters are valid, in particular if T_S is indeed in the group generated by g.)

CLIENTKEYEXCHANGE. Message m_6 is called ClientKeyExchange. We describe the contents of this message for the ciphersuites TLS_DHE_PSK, TLS_PSK and TLS_RSA_PSK separately:

- For TLS_PSK, the message is not included.
- For ephemeral Diffie-Hellman key exchange TLS_DHE_PSK, it contains the Diffie-Hellman share T_C of the client, i.e. $T_C = g^{t_C}$.
- For the RSA-based key exchange TLS_RSA_PSK the client selects a 46-byte random value R and sends a 2-byte version number V and the 46-byte random value R encrypted under the server's RSA public key to the server.

Also, the client sends an identifier for the pre-shared key it is going to use when communicating with the server. This information is called PSK identity.

COMPUTING THE MASTER SECRET. According to the original specification, released as RFC 4279 [14], the key derivation function of TLS, denoted here as PRF_{TLS}, is used when constructing the master secret. PRF_{TLS} takes as input a secret, a seed, and an identifying label and produces an output of arbitrary length. We first describe the generic computation of the master secret ms for all ciphersuites using pre-shared keys. Then, a detailed description of all cases (TLS_PSK, TLS_DHE_PSK, and TLS_RSA_PSK) is provided. The *master secret ms* is computed as follows:

$$ms := PRF_{TLS}(pms, label_1 || r_C || r_S) \tag{1}$$

- TLS_PSK case: For TLS_PSK, the client/server is able to compute the *master secret ms* using the pre-master secret pms, from which all further secret values are derived. If the PSK is N bytes long, the pms consists of the 2-byte representation (uint16) of the integer value N, N zero bytes, the 2-byte representation of N once again, and the PSK itself, i.e. $pms := N||0...0||N||PSK$. Since the first half of pms is constant for any PSK we get for TLS_PSK that the entire security of PRF_{TLS} only relies on the second half of pms.
- TLS_DHE_PSK case: Let Z be the value produced for DH-based ciphersuites, i.e. $Z = g^{t_s t_c} = T_C^{t_s} = T_S^{t_c}$. The pms consists of a concatenation of four values: the uint16 len_Z indicating the length of Z, Z itself, the uint16 len_{PSK} showing the length of the PSK, and the PSK itself: $pms := len_Z||Z||len_{PSK}||PSK$.
- TLS_RSA_PSK case: First, the pre-master secret concatenates the uint16 constant C = 48, the 2-byte version number V, a 46-byte random value R, the uint16 len_{PSK} containing the length of the PSK, and the PSK itself, i.e. $pms := C||V||R||len_{PSK}||PSK$.

3.1   On the Security of PRF_{TLS}

In our security proof of TLS_PSK, we assume that the pseudo-random function of TLS (PRF_{TLS}) that is used for the computation of the master-secret constitutes a secure PRF in the standard model when applied with pms as the key. However to prove (asymmetric) perfect forward secrecy in TLS_DHE_PSK and TLS_RSA_PSK, *we assume that PRF_{TLS} constitutes a secure DPRF (in the standard model)* where the key space of the DPRF consists of the key space of the pre-shared key and the key space of the freshly generated RSA or Diffie-Hellman secret. Unfortunately, existing results do not *directly* prove that PRF_{TLS} as used in TLS-PSK is a secure DPRF. Nevertheless, they might in some cases serve as a strong indicator of the security of PRF_{TLS}. We provide a more detailed analysis of the plausibility of this assumption in the full version.

4   ACCE Protocols

In this section, we present an extension of the formal security model for two party authenticated and confidential channel establishment (ACCE) protocols introduced by JKSS [17] to also cover scenarios with pre-shared, symmetric keys. Additionally, we extend the model to also address PKI-related attacks that exploit that the adversary does not have to prove knowledge of the secret key when registering a new public key [5]. (In [25] such attacks are generally called strong-key substitution attacks.) For better comparison with JKSS we will subsequently use boxes to highlight state variables that are essentially new in our model.

In this model, while emulating the real-world capabilities of an active adversary, we provide an 'execution environment' for adversaries following the tradition of the seminal work of Bellare and Rogaway [3] and its extensions [4,8,21,23,17]. Let $\mathcal{K}_0 = \{0,1\}^\kappa$ be the key space of the session key and $\mathcal{K}_1 = \{0,1\}^\kappa$ be the key space of the pre-shared keys.

Execution Environment. In the following let $\ell, d \in \mathbb{N}$ be positive integers. In the execution environment, we fix a set of ℓ honest parties $\{P_1, \ldots, P_\ell\}$. Each party is either identified by index i in the security experiment or a unique, fixed-length string id_i (which might appear in the protocol flows).

To cover authentication with symmetric keys, we extend the state of each party to also include pre-shared keys. Each party holds (symmetric) pre-shared keys with all other parties. We denote with $\mathsf{PSK}_{i,j} = \mathsf{PSK}_{j,i}$ the symmetric key shared between parties P_i and P_j. Each party P_i with $i \in \{1, \ldots, \ell\}$ also has access to a long-term public/private key pair (pk_i, sk_i). Formally, each party maintains the state variables given in Table 1.

Table 1. Internal States of Parties

Variable	Description
sk_i	stores the secret key of a public key pair (pk_i, sk_i)
$\boxed{\mathsf{PSK}_i}$	a vector which contains an entry $\mathsf{PSK}_{i,j}$ per party P_j
τ_i	denotes, that sk_i was corrupted after the τ_i-th query of $\mathcal{A}$
$\boxed{f_i}$	a vector denoting the freshness of all pre-shared keys,
	containing one entry $f_{i,j} \in \{\mathsf{exposed}, \mathsf{fresh}\}$ for each entry in PSK_i

The first two variables, sk_i and PSK_i, are used to store keys that are used in the protocol execution while the remaining variables are solely used to define security. (When defining security the latter are additionally managed and updated by the challenger.) The variables of each party P_i will be initialized according to the following rules:

- The long-term key pair (pk_i, sk_i) and pre-shared key vector PSK_i are chosen randomly from the key space. For all parties P_i, P_j with $i, j \in \{1, \ldots, \ell\}$ and with $i \neq j$, and pre-shared keys PSK_i it holds that $\mathsf{PSK}_{i,j} = \mathsf{PSK}_{j,i}$ and $\mathsf{PSK}_{i,i} := \emptyset$.
- All entries in f_i are set to fresh.
- τ_i is set to $\tau_i := \infty$, which means that all parties are initially not corrupted.

In the following, we will call party P_i uncorrupted iff $\tau_i = \infty$. Thus, we do not consider a dedicated variable that holds the corruption state of the secret key

sk_i. Each honest party P_i can sequentially and concurrently execute the protocol multiple times. This is modeled by a collection of oracles $\{\pi_i^s : i \in [\ell], s \in [d]\}$.
Oracle π_i^s behaves as party P_i carrying out a process to execute the s-th protocol instance with some partner P_j (which is determined during the protocol execution). All oracles of P_i have access to the long-term keys sk_i and PSK_i with
$j \in \{1, \ldots, \ell\}$. Moreover, we assume each oracle π_i^s maintains a list of independent internal state variables with the semantics given in Table 2. The variables Φ_i^s,

Table 2. Internal States of Oracles

Variable	Description
Φ_i^s	denotes π_i^s's execution-state in $\{\mathsf{negotiating}, \mathsf{accept}, \mathsf{reject}\}$
Pid_i^s	stores the identity of the intended communication partner
ρ_i^s	denotes the role $\rho_i^s \in \{\mathsf{Client}, \mathsf{Server}\}$
$\mathsf{K}_i^s = (k_{\mathsf{enc}}, k_{\mathsf{dec}})$	stores the application keys K_i^s
$\mathsf{St}_i^s = (u, v, st_e, st_d, C)$	stores the current states of the sLHAE scheme
T_i^s	records the transcript of messages sent and received by π_i^s
$\boxed{\mathsf{kst}_i^s}$	denotes the freshness $\mathsf{kst}_i^s \in \{\mathsf{exposed}, \mathsf{fresh}\}$ of the session key
b_i^s	stores a bit $b \in \{0, 1\}$ used to define security

$\mathsf{Pid}_i^s, \rho_i^s, \mathsf{K}_i^s, st_e, st_d$, and T_i^s are used by the oracles to execute the protocol. The
remaining variables are only used to define security. The variables of each oracle
π_i^s will be initialized by the following rules:

- The execution-state Φ_i^s is set to $\mathsf{negotiating}$.
- The variable kst_i^s is set to fresh.
- The bit b_i^s is chosen at random.
- The counters u, v are initialized to 0.
- All other variables are set to only contain the empty string $\emptyset$.

At some point, each oracle π_i^s completes the execution with a decision state
$\Phi_i^s \in \{\mathsf{accept}, \mathsf{reject}\}$. Furthermore, we will always assume (for simplicity) that
$\mathsf{K}_i^s = \emptyset$ if an oracle has not reached accept-state (yet).

Matching Conversations. To formalize the notion that two oracles engage in an
on-line communication, we define partnership via *matching conversations* as proposed by Bellare and Rogaway [3]. We use the variant by JKSS.

Definition 2. *We say that an oracle π_i^s has a* matching conversation *to oracle π_j^t,
if*

- *π_i^s has sent all protocol messages and T_j^t is a prefix of T_i^s, or*
- *π_j^t has sent all protocol messages and $\mathsf{T}_i^s = \mathsf{T}_j^t$.*

To keep our definition of ACCE protocols general we do not consider protocol-
specific definitions of partnership like for example [22] who define partnership of
TLS sessions using only the first three messages exchanged in the handshake phase.

Adversarial Model. An adversary $\mathcal{A}$ in our model is a PPT taking as input the security parameter 1^κ and the public information (e.g. generic description of above environment), which may interact with these oracles by issuing the following queries.

Send$^{\mathsf{pre}}(\pi_i^s, m)$: This query sends message m to oracle π_i^s. The oracle will respond with the next message m^* (if there is any) that should be sent according to the protocol specification and its internal states.

   After answering a Send^{pre} query, the variables $(\Phi_i^s, \mathsf{Pid}_i^s, \rho_i^s, \mathsf{K}_i^s, T_i^s)$ will be updated depending on the protocol specification. This query is essentially defined as in JKSS.

RegisterParty$(\mu, pk_\mu, [psk])$: This query allows $\mathcal{A}$ to register a new party with a new identity μ and a static public key (pk_μ) to be used for party P_μ. In response, if the same identity μ is already registered (either via a RegisterParty-query or $\mu \in [\ell]$), a failure symbol $\perp$ is returned. Otherwise, a new party P_μ is added with the static public key pk_μ. The secret key sk_μ is set to a constant. The parties registered by this query are considered corrupted and controlled by the adversary. If RegisterParty is the τ'-th query of the adversary, P_μ is initialized with $\tau_\mu = \tau'$. If the adversary also provides a pre-shared key psk, then this key will be implemented for every party P_i with $i \in [\ell]$ as key $\mathsf{PSK}_{i,\mu}$.[3] Otherwise, the simulator chooses a random key $psk \xleftarrow{\$} \{0,1\}^\kappa$ and sets $\mathsf{PSK}_{i,\mu} = \mathsf{PSK}_{\mu,i} := psk$ for all parties P_i before outputting psk. The corresponding entries $f_{i,\mu}$ in the vectors of the other parties P_i with $i \in [\ell]$ are set to exposed. Via this query we extend the ACCE model of JKSS to also model key registration.

RevealKey(π_i^s): Oracle π_i^s responds to a RevealKey-query with the contents of variable K_i^s, the application keys. At the same time the challenger sets $\mathsf{kst}_i^s = $ exposed. If at the point when $\mathcal{A}$ issues this query there exists another oracle π_j^t having matching conversation to π_i^s, then we also set $\mathsf{kst}_j^t = $ exposed for π_j^t. This query slightly deviates from JKSS.[4]

Corrupt$(P_i, [P_j])$: Depending on the second input parameter, oracle π_i^1 responds with certain long-term secrets of party P_i. This query extends the corruption capabilities of JKSS to symmetric keys.

   - If $\mathcal{A}$ queries Corrupt(P_i) or Corrupt$(P_i, \emptyset)$[5], oracle π_i^1 returns the long-term secret key sk_i of party P_i. If this query is the τ-th query issued by $\mathcal{A}$, then we say that P_i is τ-corrupted and π_i^1 sets $\tau_i := \tau$.
   - If $\mathcal{A}$ queries Corrupt(P_i, P_j), oracle π_i^1 returns the symmetric pre-shared key $\mathsf{PSK}_{i,j}$ stored in PSK_i and sets $f_{i,j} := $ exposed.
   - If $\mathcal{A}$ queries Corrupt$(P_i, \top)$, oracle π_i^1 returns the vector PSK_i and sets $f_{i,j} := $ exposed for all entries $f_{i,*} \in f_i$.

---

[3] This is just for simplicity. Modeling different pre-shared keys between the registered party and every other party is equivalent to registering multiple parties with a single shared key each.

[4] JKSS implicitly located the specification of when to set $\mathsf{kst}_j^t = $ exposed into the security definition.

[5] The party P_i is not adversarially controlled.

Encrypt($\pi_i^s, m_0, m_1, \text{len}, H$): This query takes as input two messages m_0 and m_1, length parameter len, and header data H. If $\Phi_i^s \neq$ accept then π_i^s returns $\bot$. Otherwise, it proceeds as depicted in Figure 2, depending on the random bit $b_i^s \xleftarrow{\$} \{0, 1\}$ sampled by π_i^s at the beginning of the game and the internal state variables of π_i^s. This query is essentially defined as in JKSS.

Decrypt(π_i^s, C, H): This query takes as input a ciphertext C and header data H. If π_i^s has $\Phi_i^s \neq$ 'accept' then π_i^s returns $\bot$. Otherwise, it proceeds as depicted in Figure 2. This query is essentially defined as in JKSS.

Encrypt($\pi_i^s, m_0, m_1, \text{len}, H$):	Decrypt(π_i^s, C, H):
$u := u + 1$	$v := v + 1$
$(C^{(0)}, st_e^{(0)}) \xleftarrow{\$} \mathsf{StE.Enc}(k_{enc}^\rho, \text{len}, H, m_0, st_e)$	If $b_i^s = 0$, then return $\bot$
$(C^{(1)}, st_e^{(1)}) \xleftarrow{\$} \mathsf{StE.Enc}(k_{enc}^\rho, \text{len}, H, m_1, st_e)$	$(m, st_d) = \mathsf{StE.Dec}(k_{dec}^\rho, H, C, st_d)$
If $C^{(0)} = \bot$ or $C^{(1)} = \bot$ then return $\bot$	If $v > u$ or $C \neq C_v$ or $H \neq H_v$,
$(C_u, H_u, st_e) := (C^{(b)}, H, st_e^{(b)})$	then phase $:= 1$
Return C_u	If phase $= 1$ then return m

Here $u, v, b_i^s, \rho, k_{enc}^\rho, k_{dec}^\rho, C$ denote the values stored in the internal variables of π_i^s.

Fig. 2. Encrypt and Decrypt oracles in the ACCE security experiment

Definition 3 (Correctness). *We say that an* ACCE *protocol Π is correct, if for any two oracles π_i^s, π_j^t that have matching conversations with* $\mathsf{Pid}_i^s = j$ *and* $\mathsf{Pid}_j^t = i$ *and $\Phi_i^s =$ accept and $\Phi_j^t =$ accept it always holds that $\mathsf{K}_i^s = \mathsf{K}_j^t$.*

Secure ACCE Protocols. We define security via an experiment played between a challenger $\mathcal{C}$ and an adversary $\mathcal{A}$.

SECURITY GAME. Assume there is a global variable *pinfo* which stores the role information of each party for the considered protocol Π.[6] In the game, the following steps are performed:

1. Given the security parameter κ, $\mathcal{C}$ implements the collection of oracles $\{\pi_i^s : i, j \in [\ell], s \in [d]\}$ with respect to Π and *pinfo*. In this process, $\mathcal{C}$ generates long-term keys PSK_i for all parties $i \in [\ell]$. Next it additionally generates long-term key pairs (pk_i, sk_i) for all parties $i \in [\ell]$ that require them (e.g. if the corresponding party is a server in the TLS_RSA_PSK protocol). Finally, $\mathcal{C}$ gives all identifiers $\{id_i\}$, all public keys (if any), and *pinfo* to $\mathcal{A}$.
2. Next the adversary may start issuing Send^{pre}, RevealKey, Corrupt, Encrypt, Decrypt, and RegisterParty queries.
3. At the end of the game, the adversary outputs a triple (i, s, b') and terminates.

---

[6] This information is simply used to determine which party also holds asymmetric key pairs besides the shared symmetric keys.

In the following, we provide a general security definition for ACCE protocols. It will subsequently be referred to when formalizing specific definitions for ACCE protocols that provide no forward secrecy, perfect forward secrecy or asymmetric perfect forward secrecy. We have tried to keep the details of the execution environment and the definition of security close to that of JKSS. Intuitively, our security definition mainly differs from JKSS in that it considers adversaries that also have access to the new RegisterParty query and the extended Corrupt query.

Definition 4 (ACCE Security). *We say that an adversary (t, ϵ)-breaks an ACCE protocol, if $\mathcal{A}$ runs in time t, and at least one of the following two conditions holds:*

1. *When $\mathcal{A}$ terminates, then with probability at least ϵ there exists an oracle π_i^s such that*
   - *π_i^s 'accepts' with $\mathsf{Pid}_i^s = j$ when $\mathcal{A}$ issues its τ_0-th query, and*
   - *both P_i and the intended partner P_j[7] are not corrupted throughout the security game and*
   - *π_i^s has internal state $\mathsf{kst}_i^s = \mathsf{fresh}$, and*
   - *there is no unique oracle π_j^t such that π_i^s has a matching conversation to π_j^t.*

   If an oracle π_i^s accepts in the above sense, then we say that π_i^s accepts maliciously.

2. *When $\mathcal{A}$ terminates and outputs a triple (i, s, b') such that*
   - *π_i^s 'accepts' – with a unique oracle π_j^t such that π_i^s has a matching conversation to π_j^t – when $\mathcal{A}$ issues its τ_0-th query, and*
   - *$\mathcal{A}$ did not issue a RevealKey-query to oracle π_i^s nor to π_j^t, i.e. $\mathsf{kst}_i^s = \mathsf{fresh}$, and*
   - *P_i is τ_i-corrupted and P_j is τ_j-corrupted,*

   then the probability that b' equals b_i^s is bounded by

$$|\Pr[b_i^s = b'] - 1/2| \geq \epsilon.$$

If adversary $\mathcal{A}$ outputs (i, s, b') with $b' = b_i^s$ and the above conditions are met, we say that $\mathcal{A}$ answers the encryption-challenge correctly.

We say that the ACCE protocol is (t, ϵ)-secure, if there exists no adversary that (t, ϵ)-breaks it.

Let us now define security more concretely. We consider three levels of forward secrecy. We start with a basic security definition for protocols that do not provide any form of forward secrecy.

Definition 5 (ACCE Security without Forward Secrecy). *We say that an ACCE protocol is (t, ϵ)-secure without forward secrecy (NoFS), if it is (t, ϵ)-secure with respect to Definition 4 and $\tau_i = \tau_j = \infty$.*

---

[7] The party P_j is not adversarially corrupted, i.e. $j \in [\ell]$. This means that P_j has not been registered by a RegisterParty query. Otherwise $\mathcal{A}$ may obtain all corresponding secure keys and trivially make oracle π_i^s accept.

The next definition considers PFS in the classical sense for both, client and server, as in JKSS.

Definition 6 (ACCE Security with Perfect Forward Secrecy). *We say that an ACCE protocol is (t, ϵ)-secure with perfect forward secrecy (PFS), if it is (t, ϵ)-secure with respect to Definition 4 and $\tau_i, \tau_j \geq \tau_0$.*

In the following, we provide our new definition of asymmetric perfect forward secrecy which is similar to that of classical perfect forward secrecy except that only the client is allowed to be corrupted after it has accepted.

Definition 7 (ACCE Security with Asymmetric Perfect Forward Secrecy). *We say that an ACCE protocol is (t, ϵ)-secure with asymmetric perfect forward secrecy (APFS), if it is (t, ϵ)-secure with respect to Definition 4 and it holds that $\tau_i = \infty$ and $\tau_j \geq \tau_0$ if π_i^s has internal state $\rho =$ Server or $\tau_i \geq \tau_0$ and $\tau_j = \infty$ if π_i^s has internal state $\rho =$ Client.*

5 Security Analysis of Pre-shared Key Ciphersuites for Transport Layer Security

In this section, we present our results for each of the TLS-PSK ciphersuites. Due to space restrictions, the proofs are given in the full version.

Theorem 1. *Let μ be the output length of $\mathsf{PRF_{TLS}}$ and let λ be the length of the nonces. Assume that $\mathsf{PRF_{TLS}}$ is a $(t, \epsilon_{\mathsf{PRF}})$-secure PRF when keyed with the pre-master secret $pms := N||0...0||N||\mathsf{PSK}$ or the master secret ms. Suppose the hash function H is $(t, \epsilon_{\mathsf{H}})$-secure, and the sLHAE scheme is $(t, \epsilon_{\mathsf{StE}})$-secure. Then for any adversary that $(t', \epsilon_{\mathsf{tls}})$-breaks the $\mathsf{TLS\_PSK}$ protocol in the sense of Definition 5 with $t \approx t'$ it holds that*

$$\epsilon_{\mathsf{tls}} \leq (d\ell)^2 \left(\frac{1}{2^{\lambda-1}} + 3\epsilon_{\mathsf{DPRF}} + 3\epsilon_{\mathsf{PRF}} + 2\epsilon_{\mathsf{H}} + \frac{1}{2^{\mu-1}} + 6\epsilon_{\mathsf{StE}} \right).$$

Theorem 2. *Let μ be the output length of $\mathsf{PRF_{TLS}}$ and let λ be the length of the nonces. Assume that $\mathsf{PRF_{TLS}}$ is a $(t, \epsilon_{\mathsf{DPRF}})$-secure DPRF when keyed with the pre-master secret $pms := len_Z||Z||len_{PSK}||\mathsf{PSK}$ (that consists of the pre-shared secret PSK and the Diffie-Hellman value Z). Assume that $\mathsf{PRF_{TLS}}$ is a $(t, \epsilon_{\mathsf{PRF}})$-secure PRF when keyed with the master secret ms. Suppose the hash function H is $(t, \epsilon_{\mathsf{H}})$-secure, the DDH-problem is $(t, \epsilon_{\mathsf{DDH}})$-hard in the group G used to compute Z, and the sLHAE scheme is $(t, \epsilon_{\mathsf{StE}})$-secure. Then for any adversary that $(t', \epsilon_{\mathsf{tls}})$-breaks the $\mathsf{TLS\_DHE\_PSK}$ protocol in the sense of Definition 6 with $t \approx t'$ we get*

$$\epsilon_{\mathsf{tls}} \leq (d\ell)^2 \left(\frac{1}{2^{\lambda-1}} + 3\epsilon_{\mathsf{DPRF}} + 3\epsilon_{\mathsf{PRF}} + 2\epsilon_{\mathsf{H}} + \frac{1}{2^{\mu-1}} + \epsilon_{\mathsf{DDH}} + 6\epsilon_{\mathsf{StE}} \right).$$

Theorem 3. *Let μ be the output length of $\mathsf{PRF_{TLS}}$ and let λ be the length of the nonces. Assume that $\mathsf{PRF_{TLS}}$ is a $(t, \epsilon_{\mathsf{DPRF}})$-secure DPRF when keyed with the pre-master secret $pms := C||V||R||len_{PSK}||\mathsf{PSK}$ (that consists of the pre-shared key*

PSK *and the random key* R *that is exchanged between client and server). Assume that* $\mathsf{PRF_{TLS}}$ *is a* $(t, \epsilon_{\mathsf{PRF}})$*-secure PRF when keyed with the master secret* ms*. Suppose the hash function* H *is* $(t, \epsilon_{\mathsf{H}})$*-secure, the public key encryption scheme* PKE *is* $(t, \epsilon_{\mathsf{PKE}})$*-secure (IND-CCA). Suppose that the sLHAE scheme is* $(t, \epsilon_{\mathsf{StE}})$*-secure. Then for any adversary that* $(t', \epsilon_{\mathsf{tls}})$*-breaks the* $\mathsf{TLS\_RSA\_PSK}$ *protocol (where the key transport mechanism is implemented via* PKE*) in the sense of Definition 7 with* $t \approx t'$ *it holds that*

$$\epsilon_{\mathsf{tls}} \leq (d\ell)^2 \left(\frac{1}{2^{\lambda-1}} + \epsilon_{\mathsf{PKE}} + 3\epsilon_{\mathsf{DPRF}} + 3\epsilon_{\mathsf{PRF}} + 2\epsilon_{\mathsf{H}} + \frac{1}{2^{\mu-1}} + 6\epsilon_{\mathsf{StE}} \right).$$

TECHNICAL OVERVIEW OF THE SECURITY PROOFS. At a high level, the security proofs are similar to that of JKSS. From a technical standpoint, the security proof of $\mathsf{TLS\_PSK}$ is simpler than that of the classical ciphersuites of TLS as security only relies on the secrecy of the pre-shared secrets. Roughly, in the proofs of the classical TLS ciphersuites one additionally has to establish that the key exchange mechanism produces a shared secret in the first place. To prove $\mathsf{TLS\_RSA\_PSK}$ and $\mathsf{TLS\_DHE\_PSK}$ we exploit the DPRF-security of $\mathsf{PRF_{TLS}}$. The challenge is to show that the master secret is indistinguishable from random although the adversary may reveal the pre-shared secret or a freshly generated ephemeral secret. Intuitively, if only one of these values remains unrevealed by the adversary, then at least one input key to the DPRF $\mathsf{PRF_{TLS}}$ is (indistinguishable from) random. Therefore, $\mathsf{PRF_{TLS}}$ computes a random-looking master secret which in turn can be used to derive secure application keys.

Acknowledgements. We would like to thank Kenny Paterson and the anonymous referees for their valuable comments and suggestions.

References

1. Badra, M., Urien, P.: Toward SSL integration in SIM smartcards. In: WCNC, pp. 889–893. IEEE (2004)
2. Bellare, M., Rogaway, P.: Random oracles are practical: A paradigm for designing efficient protocols. In: Denning, D.E., Pyle, R., Ganesan, R., Sandhu, R.S., Ashby, V. (eds.) ACM Conference on Computer and Communications Security, pp. 62–73. ACM (1993)
3. Bellare, M., Rogaway, P.: Entity authentication and key distribution. In: Stinson, D.R. (ed.) CRYPTO 1993. LNCS, vol. 773, pp. 232–249. Springer, Heidelberg (1994)
4. Blake-Wilson, S., Johnson, D., Menezes, A.: Key agreement protocols and their security analysis. In: Darnell, M. (ed.) Cryptography and Coding 1997. LNCS, vol. 1355, pp. 30–45. Springer, Heidelberg (1997)
5. Blake-Wilson, S., Menezes, A.: Unknown key-share attacks on the Station-to-Station (STS) protocol. In: Imai, H., Zheng, Y. (eds.) PKC 1999. LNCS, vol. 1560, pp. 154–170. Springer, Heidelberg (1999)
6. Bleichenbacher, D.: Chosen ciphertext attacks against protocols based on the RSA encryption standard PKCS #1. In: Krawczyk, H. (ed.) CRYPTO 1998. LNCS, vol. 1462, pp. 1–12. Springer, Heidelberg (1998)

7. BouncyCastle Software Developers. Bouncy Castle Crypto APIs (2013), http://www.bouncycastle.org/
8. Canetti, R., Krawczyk, H.: Analysis of key-exchange protocols and their use for building secure channels. In: Pfitzmann, B. (ed.) EUROCRYPT 2001. LNCS, vol. 2045, pp. 453–474. Springer, Heidelberg (2001)
9. Chen, C., Tang, S., Mitchell, C.J.: Building general-purpose security services on EMV payment cards. In: Keromytis, A.D., Di Pietro, R. (eds.) SecureComm 2012. LNICST, vol. 106, pp. 29–44. Springer, Heidelberg (2013)
10. Dacosta, I., Ahamad, M., Traynor, P.: Trust no one else: Detecting MITM attacks against SSL/TLS without third-parties. In: Foresti, S., Yung, M., Martinelli, F. (eds.) ESORICS 2012. LNCS, vol. 7459, pp. 199–216. Springer, Heidelberg (2012)
11. Dierks, T., Allen, C.: The TLS Protocol Version 1.0. RFC 2246 (Proposed Standard). Obsoleted by RFC 4346, updated by RFCs 3546, 5746 (January 1999)
12. Dierks, T., Rescorla, E.: The Transport Layer Security (TLS) Protocol Version 1.1. RFC 4346 (Proposed Standard). Obsoleted by RFC 5246, updated by RFCs 4366, 4680, 4681, 5746 (April 2006)
13. Dierks, T., Rescorla, E.: The Transport Layer Security (TLS) Protocol Version 1.2. RFC 5246 (Proposed Standard). Updated by RFCs 5746, 5878 (August 2008)
14. Eronen, P., Tschofenig, H.: Pre-Shared Key Ciphersuites for Transport Layer Security (TLS). RFC 4279 (Proposed Standard) (December 2005)
15. German Federal Office for Information Security (BSI). TR-03112, Das eCard-API-Framework (2005), https://www.bsi.bund.de/ContentBSI/Publikationen/TechnischeRichtlinien/tr03112/index_htm.html
16. Gajek, S., Manulis, M., Pereira, O., Sadeghi, A.-R., Schwenk, J.: Universally Composable Security Analysis of TLS. In: Baek, J., Bao, F., Chen, K., Lai, X. (eds.) ProvSec 2008. LNCS, vol. 5324, pp. 313–327. Springer, Heidelberg (2008)
17. Jager, T., Kohlar, F., Schäge, S., Schwenk, J.: On the security of TLS-DHE in the standard model. In: Safavi-Naini, R., Canetti, R. (eds.) CRYPTO 2012. LNCS, vol. 7417, pp. 273–293. Springer, Heidelberg (2012)
18. Jonsson, J., Kaliski Jr., B.S.: On the security of RSA encryption in TLS. In: Yung, M. (ed.) CRYPTO 2002. LNCS, vol. 2442, pp. 127–142. Springer, Heidelberg (2002)
19. Kohlar, F., Schäge, S., Schwenk, J.: On the security of TLS-DH and TLS-RSA in the standard model. IACR Cryptology ePrint Archive, 2013:367 (2013)
20. Kohlar, F., Schwenk, J., Jensen, M., Gajek, S.: Secure bindings of SAML assertions to TLS sessions. In: ARES, pp. 62–69. IEEE Computer Society (2010)
21. Krawczyk, H.: HMQV: A high-performance secure Diffie-Hellman protocol. In: Shoup, V. (ed.) CRYPTO 2005. LNCS, vol. 3621, pp. 546–566. Springer, Heidelberg (2005)
22. Krawczyk, H., Paterson, K.G., Wee, H.: On the security of the TLS protocol: A systematic analysis. In: Canetti, R., Garay, J.A. (eds.) CRYPTO 2013, Part I. LNCS, vol. 8042, pp. 429–448. Springer, Heidelberg (2013)
23. LaMacchia, B.A., Lauter, K., Mityagin, A.: Stronger security of authenticated key exchange. In: Susilo, W., Liu, J.K., Mu, Y. (eds.) ProvSec 2007. LNCS, vol. 4784, pp. 1–16. Springer, Heidelberg (2007)
24. Mavrogiannopoulos, N., Josefsson, S.: The GnuTLS Transport Layer Security library, http://gnutls.org (last updated March 22, 2013)
25. Menezes, A., Smart, N.P.: Security of signature schemes in a multi-user setting. Des. Codes Cryptography 33(3), 261–274 (2004)
26. Meyer, C., Schwenk, J.: Lessons learned from previous SSL/TLS attacks - a brief chronology of attacks and weaknesses. IACR Cryptology ePrint Archive, 2013:49 (2013)

27. Morrissey, P., Smart, N.P., Warinschi, B.: The TLS handshake protocol: A modular analysis. Journal of Cryptology 23(2), 187–223 (2010)

28. OpenSSL. The OpenSSL project (2013), http://www.openssl.org

29. Urien, L.C.P., Martin, P.: EMV support for TLS-PSK. draft-urien-tls-psk-emv-02 (February 2011)

30. Paterson, K.G., Ristenpart, T., Shrimpton, T.: Tag size *does* matter: Attacks and proofs for the TLS record protocol. In: Lee, D.H., Wang, X. (eds.) ASIACRYPT 2011. LNCS, vol. 7073, pp. 372–389. Springer, Heidelberg (2011)

31. Urien, P.: Introducing TLS-PSK authentication for EMV devices. In: Smari, W.W., McQuay, W.K. (eds.) CTS, pp. 371–377. IEEE (2010)

Author Index